Lecture Notes in Artificial Intelligence 2080

Subseries of Lecture Notes in Computer Science
Edited by J. G. Carbonell and J. Siekmann

Lecture Notes in Computer Science

Edited by G. Goos, J. Hartmanis and J. van Leeuwen

T0188925

Springer
Berlin
Heidelberg
New York
Barcelona
Hong Kong
London
Milan
Paris
Singapore
Tokyo

David W. Aha   Ian Watson (Eds.)

Case-Based Reasoning Research and Development

4th International Conference on Case-Based Reasoning, ICCBR 2001
Vancouver, BC, Canada, July 30 – August 2, 2001
Proceedings

 Springer

Series Editors

Jaime G. Carbonell, Carnegie Mellon University, Pittsburgh, PA, USA
Jörg Siekmann, University of Saarland, Saabrücken, Germany

Volume Editors

David W. Aha
Navy Center for Applied Research in Artificial Intelligence
Naval Research Laboratory, Code 5510
4555 Overlook Avenue, SW, Washington, DC 20375, USA
E-mail: aha@aic.nrl.navy.mil

Ian Watson
University of Auckland, Computer Science Department
Private Bag 92019, Auckland 1, New Zealand
E-mail: ian@ai-cbr.org

Cataloging-in-Publication Data applied for

Die Deutsche Bibliothek - CIP-Einheitsaufnahme

Case based reasoning research and development : proceedings / 4th
International Conference on Case Based Reasoning, ICCBR 2001, Vancouver, BC,
Canada, July 30 - August 2, 2001. David W. Aha ; Ian Watson (ed.). - Berlin ;
Heidelberg ; New York ; Barcelona ; Hong Kong ; London ; Milan ; Paris ;
Singapore ; Tokyo : Springer, 2001
    (Lecture notes in computer science ; Vol. 2080 : Lecture notes in
    artificial intelligence)
    ISBN 3-540-42358-3

CR Subject Classification (1998): I.2, J.4, J.1, F.4.1

ISBN 3-540-42358-3 Springer-Verlag Berlin Heidelberg New York

Springer-Verlag Berlin Heidelberg New York
a member of BertelsmannSpringer Science+Business Media GmbH

http://www.springer.de

© Springer-Verlag Berlin Heidelberg 2001
Printed in Germany

Typesetting: Camera-ready by author, data conversion by PTP-Berlin, Stefan Sossna
Printed on acid-free paper   SPIN: 10839273   06/3142   5 4 3 2 1 0

Preface

The 2001 International Conference on Case-Based Reasoning (ICCBR 2001, www.iccbr.org/iccbr01), the fourth in the biennial ICCBR series (1995 in Sesimbra, Portugal; 1997 in Providence, Rhode Island (USA); 1999 in Seeon, Germany), was held during 30 July – 2 August 2001 in Vancouver, Canada. ICCBR is the premier international forum for researchers and practitioners of case-based reasoning (CBR). The objectives of this meeting were to nurture significant, relevant advances made in this field (both in research and application), communicate them among all attendees, inspire future advances, and continue to support the vision that CBR is a valuable process in many research disciplines, both computational and otherwise.

ICCBR 2001 was the first ICCBR meeting held on the Pacific coast, and we used the setting of beautiful Vancouver as an opportunity to enhance participation from the Pacific Rim communities, which contributed 28% of the submissions. During this meeting, we were fortunate to host invited talks by Ralph Bergmann, Ken Forbus, Jaiwei Han, Ramon López de Mántaras, and Manuela Veloso. Their contributions ensured a stimulating meeting; we thank them all.

This conference continues the tradition that ICCBR has established of attracting high-quality research and applications papers from around the world. Among the 81 (24 application + 57 research) submissions, 23 were selected for (9 long and 14 short) oral presentation and an additional 27 for poster presentation. This volume contains the papers for all 50 presentations. Also included are papers from some of the invited speakers and an invited paper by Petra Perner on image interpretation, a topic on which we wish to encourage additional community participation.

ICCBR 2001's first day consisted of the *2001 Innovative Customer-Centered Applications Workshop* (ICCA 2001). This workshop, which was expertly co-chaired by Mehmet Göker (Americas), Hideo Shimazu (Asia & Australia), and Ralph Traphöner (Europe and Africa), focused on reports concerning mature applications and technology innovations of particular industrial interest.

The second day's events included five workshops focusing on the following research interests: Authoring Support Tools, Electronic Commerce, Creative Systems, Process-Oriented Knowledge Management, and Soft Computing. We are grateful to the Workshop Program Co-chairs, Christiane Gresse von Wangenheim and Rosina Weber, for their efforts in coordinating these workshops, along with the individual workshop chairs and participants. Materials from ICCA 2001 and the workshops were published separately and can be obtained from the ICCBR 2001 WWW site.

The Conference Chair for ICCBR 2001 was Qiang Yang of Simon Fraser University, while the Program Co-chairs were David W. Aha (U.S. Naval Research Laboratory) and Ian Watson (University of Auckland). The chairs would like to thank the program committee and the additional reviewers for their thoughtful and rigorous reviewing during the paper selection process. We also gratefully acknowledge the generous support of ICCBR 2001's sponsors, and Simon Fraser University for providing the venue. Many thanks to Penny Southby and her staff at the Simon Fraser University Conference Services for their tremendous assistance with local arrangements. Finally, thanks to Vincent Chung of the University of Auckland for his assistance with the conference WWW site.

May 2001

David W. Aha
Ian Watson

Program Chairs

David W. Aha, Naval Research Laboratory. Washington DC, USA
Ian Watson, University of Auckland, New Zealand

Conference Chair

Qiang Yang, Simon Fraser University, Vancouver, Canada

Industrial Chairs

Mehmet Göker, Kaidara International, Palo Alto, USA
Hideo Shimazu, NEC Corporation, Ikoma, Japan
Ralph Traphöener, Empolis, Kaiserslautern, Germany

Workshop Chairs

Christiane Gresse von Wangenheim, Uni. do Vale do Itajaí, Brazil
Rosina Weber, University of Wyoming, USA

Program Committee

Agnar Aamodt	Norwegian Uni. of Science and Tech.
Robert Aarts	Nokia Telecommunications, Finland
Klaus-Dieter Althoff	Fraunhofer IESE, Germany
Kevin Ashley	University of Pittsburgh, USA
Paolo Avesani	IRST Povo, Italy
Brigitte Bartsch-Spörl	BSR Consulting, Germany
Carlos Bento	University of Coimbra, Portugal
Ralph Bergmann	University of Kaiserslautern, Germany
Enrico Blanzieri	Turin University, Italy
L. Karl Branting	University of Wyoming, USA
Derek Bridge	University College, Cork, Ireland
Michael Brown	SemanticEdge, Berlin, Germany
Robin Burke	California State University, Fullerton, USA
Hans-Dieter Burkhard	Humboldt University Berlin, Germany
Bill Cheetham	General Electric Co. NY, USA
Michael Cox	Wright State University, Dayton, USA
Susan Craw	Robert Gordon University, Aberdeen, Scotland
Pádraig Cunningham	Trinity College, Dublin, Ireland
Walter Daelemans	CNTS, Belgium
Boi Faltings	EPFL Lausanne, Switzerland
Ashok Goel	Georgia Institute of Technology, USA
Andrew Golding	Lycos Inc, USA
C. Gresse von Wangenheim	Uni. do Vale do Itajaí, Brazil

Alec Holt	University of Otago, New Zealand
Igor Jurisica	Ontario Cancer Institute, Canada
Mark Keane	University College Dublin, Ireland
Janet Kolodner	Georgia Institute of Technology, USA
David Leake	Indiana University, USA
Brian Lees	University of Paisley, Scotland
Michel Manago	Kaidara International, Paris, France
Ramon López de Mántaras	IIIA-CSIC, Spain
Cindy Marling	Ohio University, USA
Bruce McLaren	OpenWebs Corp. Pennsylvania, USA
David McSherry	University of Ulster, Northern Ireland
Erica Melis	University of the Saarland, Germany
Alain Mille	Claude Bernard University, France
Héctor Muñoz-Avila	University of Maryland, USA
Petri Myllymaki	University of Helsinki, Finland
Bart Netten	TNO-TPD, The Netherlands
Petra Perner	ICVACS, Germany
Enric Plaza	IIIA-CSIC, Spain
Luigi Portinale	University of Eastern Piedmont, Italy
Lisa S. Purvis	Xerox Corporation, NY, USA
Francesco Ricci	IRST Povo, Italy
Michael M. Richter	University of Kaiserslautern, Germany
Edwina Rissland	University of Massachusetts, USA
Rainer Schmidt	University of Rostock, Germany
Barry Smyth	University College Dublin, Ireland
Einoshin Suzuki	Yokohama National University, Japan
Rosina Weber	University of Wyoming, USA
David C. Wilson	University College Dublin, Ireland

Additional Reviewers

Connor Hayes	Pietro Torasso
Markus Nick	Ivo Vollrath
Sascha Schmitt	Gabriele Zenobi
Armin Stahl	

Conference Support

ICCBR 2001 was supported by the American Association for Artificial Intelligence (AAAI), AI-CBR, ChangingWorlds, eGain, Empolis, the European Coordinating Committee for Artificial Intelligence (ECAI), Kaidara International, the INRECA Center, the Haley Enterprise, the Machine Learning Network, the Naval Research Laboratory, Simon Fraser University, Stottler Henke Associates Inc. and the University of Auckland.

Table of Contents

Invited Papers

Research Papers

Application Papers

Deployed Applications

Highlights of the European INRECA Projects

Ralph Bergmann

Department of Computer Science
University of Kaiserslautern
67653 Kaiserslautern, Germany
bergmann@informatik.uni-kl.de

Abstract. **IN**duction and **RE**asoning from **CA**ses was the title of two large
European CBR projects funded by the European Commission from 1992 –
1999. In total, the two projects (abbreviated INRECA and INRECA-II) have
obtained an overall funding of 3 MEuro, which enabled the 5 project partners to
perform 55 person years of research and development work. The projects made
several significant contributions to CBR research and helped shaping the
European CBR community. The projects initiated the rise of three SMEs that
base their main business on CBR application development, employing together
more than 100 people in 2001. This paper gives an overview of the main
research results obtained in both projects and provides links to the most
important publications of the consortium.

1. Introduction

The acronym INRECA stands for "**IN**duction and **RE**asoning from **CA**ses" and is the
name of a European consortium that jointly executed two large CBR projects named
INRECA (1992 – 1995) and INRECA-II (1996 – 1999). The projects have been
funded by the European Commission's ESPRIT program, as part of the 3rd and 4th
funding framework. The initial consortium created in 1992 consisted of the following
partners:
- AcknoSoft (now renamed to Kaidara), see: www.kaidara.com
- IMS (now renamed to IMS MAXIMS), see: www.imsmaxims.com
- TECINNO (now renamed to empolis knowledge management GmbH, which is
  part of the Bertelsmann Mohn Media Group), see: www.tecinno.com
- University of Kaiserslautern, Artificial Intelligence – Knowledge-Based Systems
  Group, see: wwwagr.informatik.uni-kl.de

The consortium's initial goal was to develop innovative technologies to help people
make smarter business decisions more quickly by using cases, and to integrate these
technologies into a single software platform that would allow the technologies to be
used more widely. The technical integration of inductive machine learning,
particularly decision tree learning and nearest-neighbor-oriented CBR, was the main
goal for the first project. Before, both techniques had been individually developed by
the project partners: AcknoSoft's tool KATE (Manago 1990) was a state-of-the-art
decision tree learning and consultation tool. The CBR system S3-CASE from
TECINNO was a follow up of PATDEX (Richter & Wess 1991) developed by the
University of Kaiserslautern.

D.W. Aha and I. Watson (Eds.): ICCBR 2001, LNAI 2080, pp. 1-15, 2001.

These goals of INRECA were achieved in late 1995: the consortium was successful both in developing and integrating technologies, and in demonstrating their usefulness for a large-scale industrial application (diagnostic of Boeing 737 engines).

In 1996, with the start of the INRECA-II project, the consortium was expanded to include DaimlerBenz (now DaimlerChrysler, see www.daimlerchrysler.com), an internationally renowned company with worldwide business activities. This partner's role in the consortium was to serve as a key user of the developed CBR and induction technology. The emphasis of the consortium's work shifted from technology to methodology. This shift was motivated by the observation that IT companies were facing a market that demands large-scale CBR projects and CBR software that fulfills quality standards. Therefore, a systematic and professional methodology for developing and maintaining CBR applications became mandatory.

In total, the two projects have obtained an overall funding of 3 MEuro, which enabled the 5 project partners to perform 55 person years of research and development work. The projects made several significant contributions to CBR research and helped shaping the European CBR community. They initiated the rise of the three SMEs which together employ more than 100 people in 2001.

This paper gives an overview of the main research results obtained in both projects. Due to the space limitations of this paper, most issues can only be touched, but links to the most important publications of the consortium are provided.

2.   Knowledge Contained in a CBR System

INRECA made several contributions to the foundations of case-based knowledge representation.

2.1   Knowledge Container

One important contribution was the knowledge container view proposed by Richter (1995). It had been developed through an analysis of the work during the INRECA project and provides a perfect framework for organizing the knowledge related to a CBR system.

In a CBR system, we have four containers in which one can store knowledge (Fig. 1): the *vocabulary* used, the *similarity measure*, the *solution transformation*, and the *case-base*. In principle, each container is able to carry all the available knowledge, but this does not mean that this is advisable. The first three containers include compiled knowledge (with "compile time" we mean the development time before actual problem solving, and "compilation" is taken in a very general sense including human coding activities), while the case-base consists of case-specific knowledge that is interpreted at run time, i.e. during actual problem solving. For compiled knowledge the maintenance task is as difficult as for knowledge-based systems in general. However, for interpreted knowledge, the maintenance task is easier because it results in updating the case-base only. In our opinion, a main attractiveness of CBR comes from the flexibility to decide pragmatically which container includes which knowledge and therefore to choose the appropriate degree of compilation. A general

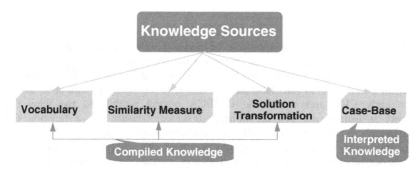

Fig. 1. The Distribution of Knowledge in a CBR System (Richter, 1995)

strategy for developing CBR systems is to compile as little knowledge as possible and as much as absolutely necessary.

2.2   Object-Oriented Case Representation and the CASUEL Language

INRECA was one of the first CBR projects that strictly bases upon object-oriented techniques for representing cases. Such representations are particularly suitable for complex domains in which cases with different structures occur. Cases are represented as collections of *objects*, each of which is described by a set of attribute-value pairs. The structure of an object is described by an *object class* that defines the set of attributes (also called slots) together with a *type* (set of possible values or sub-objects) for each attribute. Object classes are arranged in a *class hierarchy*, that is, usually an n-ary tree in which sub-classes inherit attributes as well as their definition from the parent class (predecessor). Moreover, we distinguish between *simple attributes,* which have a simple type like Integer or Symbol, and so-called *relational attributes*. Relational attributes hold complete objects of some (arbitrary) class from the class hierarchy. They represent a directed binary relation, e.g., a part-of relation, between the object that defines the relational attribute and the object to which it refers. Relational attributes are used to represent complex case structures. The ability to relate an object to another object of an arbitrary class (or an arbitrary sub-class from a specified parent class) enables the representation of cases with different structures in an appropriate way.

The object-oriented case representation has been implemented in the common case representation CASUEL (Manago et al. 1994). CASUEL is a flexible, frame-like language for storing and exchanging object-oriented vocabularies and case libraries in ASCII text files. In the early days of INRECA, the CASUEL language (together with a text editor) has been used as modeling language during the development of CBR applications. Further on, during the course of the project, graphical modeling tools have been developed that can be used without knowing the particular syntax of a modeling language. In its current version, CASUEL additionally supports a rule formalism for exchanging case completion rules and case adaptation rules, as well as mechanisms for defining similarity measures. A recent follow-up of the CASUEL language is OML, the **O**renge (**O**pen **R**etrieval **ENG**inE) **M**odeling **L**anguage (Schumacher & Traphöner 2000), which is based on XML.

2.3   Modeling Similarity Measures

In INRECA, a comprehensive approach for *modeling* similarity has been developed. The knowledge container view made clear that the similarity measure itself contains (compiled) knowledge. This is knowledge about the *utility* of an old solution re-applied in a new context (an elaboration of this is given by Bergmann et al. 2001). Unlike early CBR approaches, the INRECA project established the view that similarity is usually not just an arbitrary distance measure but a function that approximately measures utility. Hence, traditional properties that have been demanded in earlier days (such as symmetry, reflexivity, or triangle inequality) are not necessarily required any more for similarity measures (see also Jantke 1994). Connected with this observation was the need to model similarity knowledge explicitly for an application domain, as it is done with other kinds of knowledge too.

The use of an object-oriented case representation immediately asks for similarity measures that are able to cope with the representation features provided by the language. In INRECA, similarity measures for object-oriented representations are modeled by the following general scheme (Wess 1995): The goal is to determine the similarity between two objects, i.e., one object representing the case (or a part of it) and one object representing the query (or a part of it). We call this similarity *object similarity* (or *global similarity*). The object similarity is determined recursively in a bottom up fashion, i.e., for each simple attribute, a *local similarity measure* determines the similarity between the two attribute values, and for each relational slot an object similarity measure recursively compares the two related sub-objects. Then, the similarity values from the local similarity measures and the object similarity measures, respectively, are aggregated (e.g., by a weighted sum) to the object similarity between the objects being compared. This approach decomposes the similarity modeling into the modeling of:

– an individual local similarity measure for each attribute and
– an object similarity measure for each object class, defined through an aggregation function and a weight model.

This initial approach to similarity, however, did not specify how the class hierarchy influences similarity assessment. In INRECA-II we developed a framework for object similarities that allow to compare objects of different classes while considering the knowledge contained in the class hierarchy itself (Bergmann & Stahl 1998). The knowledge about similarity contained in class hierarchies is used in a similar way as the knowledge contained in symbol taxonomies (Bergmann 1998). This led to an extension of the similarity modeling approach by explicitly distinguishing between an *inter-class* and an *intra-class* similarity measure.

2.4   General Knowledge for Solution Transformation

When problems are solved by CBR, the primary kind of knowledge is contained in the specific cases which are stored in the case base. However, in many situations additional general knowledge is required to cope with the requirements of an application. In INRECA, such general knowledge is integrated into the reasoning process in a way that it complements the knowledge contained in the cases (Bergmann et al. 1996). This general knowledge itself is not sufficient to perform any kind of model-based problem solving, but it is required to interpret the available cases appropriately. General knowledge is expressed by three different kinds of rules:

- *Exclusion rules* are entered by the user during consultation and describe hard constraints (knock-out criteria) on the cases being retrieved.
- *Completion rules* are defined by the knowledge engineer during system development. They describe how to infer additional features out of known features of an old case or the current query case.
- *Adaptation rules* are also defined by the knowledge. They describe how a retrieved case can be adapted to fit the current query.

3.   Integration of Induction and CBR

One central research task, which was the motivation for the first INRECA project, was the integration of induction and CBR (Althoff et al. 1994, 1995a; Auriol et al. 1994, 1995). Initially, complementary advantages and shortcomings of both technologies were identified, so that it seemed useful to integrate both technologies in a way that the shortcomings are compensated. We identified four possible levels of integration between inductive and case-based reasoning technologies (see Fig. 2).

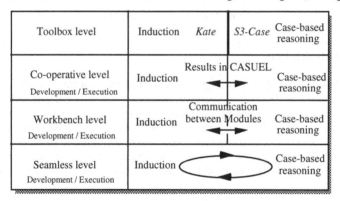

Fig. 2. Four Integration Levels between Induction and CBR

The first level consists simply of keeping both tools as stand-alone systems and letting the user choose the one s/he is interested in. In the second level of integration, called co-operative approach, the tools are kept separated but they collaborate: one tool uses the results of the other to improve or speed up its own results, or both methods are used simultaneously to reinforce the results. The third level of integration, called the workbench approach, goes a step further: the tools are separated but a "pipeline" communication is used to exchange the results of individual modules of each technique. The final level of INRECA reuses the best characteristics of each method to build a powerful integrated mechanism that avoids the weaknesses of each separate technology and preserves their advantages.

3.1 Co-operative Level

The co-operative level aims at switching between the decision tree and the case-based system when facing an unknown value in the consultation phase. Each time the decision tree consultation system cannot answer a question (the "unknown values problem", cf. Manago et al. 1993), it switches to the case-based system with the current situation as a query. The case-based system finds the most similar cases and returns the most probable diagnosis among them (Fig. 3).

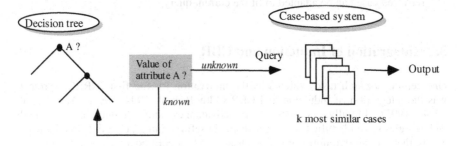

Fig. 3. The Co-operative Level

3.2 Workbench Level

The workbench level allows to toggle between the decision tree and the case-based system (see Fig. 4). Several consecutive switches between CBR and induction can happen during a single consultation. Given a (the current situation defined in the decision tree until an unknown value is encountered), the case-based system retrieves the k most similar cases. If the question concerning the value of the current attribute cannot be answered, these cases are used to determine the *most probable value* for the current attribute. Then, the decision tree can continue its diagnosis further by using this answer.

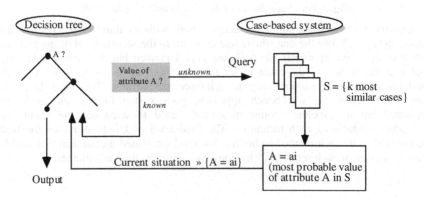

Fig. 4. The Workbench Level

Another approach that is part of the workbench-level integration is the *dynamic induction* (Auriol et al. 1994) that allows to determine the next attribute to be asked to the user dynamically during consultation time, instead of following a static decision tree that has been built in advance. The k most similar cases (to the current situation a) are retrieved during consultation and the information gain measure applied to this subset is used to determine the next question to be asked. If this question cannot be answered, the second best attribute with respect to the information gain can be asked.

3.3   Seamless Level

The most interesting part of the induction technology to be used in case-based reasoning seems to be the information gain measure (based on Shannon's entropy). Information gain is a heuristic that allows the most discriminating attributes to be selected for a given target attribute, such that the resulting tree is minimal in some sense (on average, a few questions are asked to reach a conclusion). On the other hand, the similarity measure is the basis of the case selection in a CBR system.

On the seamless level (Fig. 5), we have integrated information gain and similarity. The means to achieve this is a single tree with associated generation and retrieval algorithms that enables the combination of the information gain measure for estimating the difference between cases that belong to different classes and the similarity measure for estimating the cohesion of a set of cases that belong to the same class (Althoff et al. 1995a). This INRECA tree (an extension and modification of a k-d tree) with its associated algorithms, can be configured to be a pure decision tree or a pure indexing tree for similarity-based retrieval. The INRECA context mechanism in addition allows to do this concurrently and thereby enables the above described integration possibilities based on the seamlessly integrated system. A learning mechanism automatically extracts knowledge about the similarity of cases from a decision-tree-like INRECA tree and embeds such knowledge into the underlying similarity measure (Althoff et al.. 1994, Auriol et al. 1994, 1995). By this learning method, INRECA's k-dimensional indexing tree can gradually evolve into a decision tree. Thus, on the seamless level INRECA offers a system evolution over time from pure case-based reasoning to pure induction, based on a concept learning strategy (cf. Fig. 5).

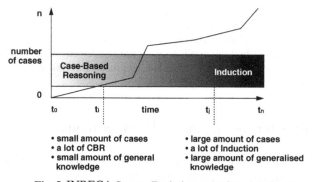

Fig. 5. INRECA System Evolution at the Seamless Level

4.   Evaluation of CBR Systems

As part of the INRECA project, a comprehensive evaluation of CBR systems has been performed. The purpose of this evaluation was manifold: The first goal was to position the initial INRECA technology with respect to existing commercial CBR tools and research prototypes and to gain insights that guide the further development towards the final INRECA software. Second, a general methodology for evaluating CBR systems was desirable as a basis for evaluating any further improvements in this area. Third, the evaluation should yield a more concrete estimation of what can be expected from case-based reasoning technology in the near and the far future.

4.1   Evaluation Criteria

The evaluation was done according to a set of systematically chosen evaluation criteria called *decision support criteria* (Althoff et al. 1995b; Althoff 1996). These criteria include:
- *technical criteria* dealing with the limitations and abilities of the systems,
- *ergonomic criteria* concerning the consultation of the execution system and application development,
- *application domain criteria* dealing with concept structure, knowledge sources, and knowledge base characteristics,
- *application task criteria* like integration of reasoning strategies, decomposition methods, and task properties.

4.2   Impact of the Evaluation

A first evaluation of industrial case-based reasoning tools (Althoff et al. 1995b) had been performed, which helped guiding future developments in the INRECA project. It also showed where the INRECA system contributes to the current state of CBR. One important issue here is the identification of four levels of integration between induction and case-based reasoning within one system architecture, especially the seamless integration of these two techniques described in the previous section.

Based on this initial evaluation, the evaluation framework was extended and used for the final evaluation of the INRECA system that was obtained at the end of the first INRECA project (Althoff 1996). We compared the INRECA CBR system with five industrial CBR tools and 20 CBR-related research prototype systems. Further, Althoff & Wilke (1997) have described the application of the framework to the validation of CBR systems. Parts of the framework have also been used for gathering information about existing CBR systems (Bartsch-Spörl et al. 1997).

5.   Methodology for Developing CBR Applications

By the end of the INRECA project in 1995, CBR technology has matured and several successful CBR applications have been built. However, companies involved in developing CBR applications were facing a market that demanded large-scale CBR projects and CBR software that fulfills quality standards. Therefore, a systematic and professional *methodology* for developing CBR applications was mandatory, as widely claimed by CBR practitioners (Kitano & Shimazu 1996; Bartsch-Spörl 1996; Curet & Jackson 1996). One core goal of the INRECA-II project, started in 1996, was to establish such a methodology for developing and maintaining CBR applications.

5.1   The INRECA Methodology in a Nutshell

The INRECA methodology (Bergmann et al. 1997, 1998b, 1999) has its origin in recent software engineering research and practices. It makes use of a software engineering paradigm that enables the reuse of software development experience by an organizational structure called *experience factory* (Basili et al. 1994). An *experience factory* is an organizational unit within a software development company or department that supports capturing and reusing software development experience and thereby supports project planning. It links with project execution so that lessons learned from previous projects can be reused. In the INRECA methodology, the experience factory provides the organizational framework for storing, accessing, and extending the guidelines for CBR application development, which are the core assets of the methodology. The guidelines themselves are documented in a process-oriented view by applying a state of the art *software process modeling* (Rombach & Verlage 1995) approach. Software process models describe the flow of activities and the exchanged results during software development.

In a nutshell, the INRECA methodology consists of collected CBR development experiences, represented as software process models and stored in the experience base of an experience factory. Hence, the basic philosophy behind the INRECA methodology is the experience-based construction of CBR applications. The approach is particularly suited because CBR application development is an activity that itself relies heavily on experience.

5.2   The INRECA Experience Base

The software processes that represent CBR development and maintenance experience can be very abstract, i.e., they can represent some very coarse development steps such as *domain model definition, similarity measure definition*, and *case acquisition*. They can also be very detailed and specific for a particular project, such as *analyzing data from Analog Device's operational amplifier product database, selecting relevant specification parameters*, and so on. The software process modeling approach allows the construction of such a hierarchically organized set of process models. Abstract processes can be described by complex methods, which are themselves a set of more detailed processes. We make use of this property to structure the experience base. The experience base is organized on three levels of abstraction: a *common generic level* at the top, a *cookbook level* in the middle, and a *specific project level* at the bottom (Bergmann et al. 1998). These levels are shown in Fig. 6.

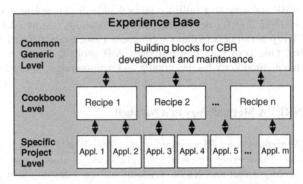

Fig. 6. Structure of the INRECA Experience Base.

Common Generic Level. At this level, processes, products, and methods are collected that are common for a very large spectrum of different CBR applications. The documented processes usually appear during the development of most CBR applications. The documented methods are very general and widely applicable, and give general guidance for how the respective processes can be enacted. The current common generic level of the INRECA methodology covers managerial, technical, and organizational aspects of development processes for analytical CBR applications. It defines processes such as: *project definition, feasibility study, management & monitoring, organizational development, training,* and *technical development,* including *knowledge acquisition and modeling, GUI development,* and *integration with existing IT environment.* Overall, 120 processes, products, and methods are defined.

Cookbook Level. At this level, processes, products, and methods are tailored for a particular class of applications (e.g., help desk, technical maintenance, product catalogue). For each application class, the cookbook level contains a so-called *recipe.* Such a recipe describes how an application of that kind should be developed and/or maintained. The cookbook-level of the INRECA methodology consists of three recipes:

- Help desk support for complex technical equipment.
- Intelligent catalog search applications.
- Technical maintenance applications.

Each recipe contains an elaborated and proven process model for application development, each of which consists of more than 100 processes, products, and methods. The recipes are particularly useful for building a new application that falls into one of the covered application classes. The recipes are the most valuable knowledge captured in the methodology. Therefore, one should first investigate the cookbook-level to identify whether a cookbook recipe can be reused directly.

Specific Project Level. The specific project level describes experience in the context of a single, particular project that has already been carried out. It contains project-specific information, such as the particular processes that were carried out, the effort that was required for these processes, the products that were produced, the methods that were used to perform the processes, and the people who were involved in executing the processes. It is a complete documentation of the project, which is more and more important today to guarantee the quality standards (e.g., ISO 9000) required by industrial clients. During the course of the INRECA project, 12 specific projects have been documented. For each of the above mentioned recipes one specific project documentation is publicly available (see Bergmann et al. 1999 and www.inreca.org).

5.3   Extended CBR Model for Help-Desk Support

One important observation we made from the development of the help-desk cookbook recipe was that the traditional 4R CBR cycle must be extended such that it comprises two linked process cycles: the *application cycle* and the *maintenance cycle* (see Fig. 7 and Göker & Roth-Berghofer 1999).

The *application cycle* takes place each time a user solves a problem with the case-based help-desk support system. During the application of the CBR system, the standard tasks *retrieve, reuse,* and *revise* must be performed. If the case solution generated during the reuse phase is not correct and cannot be repaired, a new solution has to be generated by the help-desk operator. The solution that has been retrieved by the system or created by the help-desk operator is put to use during the *recycle* task. The application cycle is performed by the end-user of the system.

Whenever a new solution is generated during system use it must be sent to the *maintenance cycle*. This cycle consists of the *retain* and *refine* tasks. While the application cycle is executed every time a help-desk operator uses the CBR system, the maintenance cycle can be executed less frequently, i.e., only when there is a need for maintaining the system or at regular intervals.

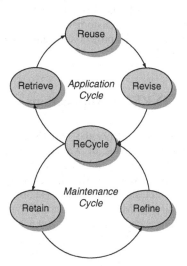

Fig. 7. Processes during the use of a case-based help-desk system

During the *retain* task, a *case author* checks the quality of the new cases that were generated by the help desk operators. S/he verifies and approves the representation and content of each case. During the *refine* phase, maintenance steps for the knowledge containers are performed by the CBR administrator. The case base, vocabulary, similarities, and adaptation knowledge have to be refined, and the potentially quality-decreasing effects of external changes in the domain, as well as the inclusion of new cases in the case base, have to be counteracted.

5.4   Impact of the Methodology

The methodology and related tools were used during the *project definition, application development,* and *system utilization* phases of new projects. The methodology had an impact on *productivity*, *quality*, *communication*, and *management decision making*. We could observe the advantages of using the methodology in each of these areas and in all three project phases, both to the customer (management and user) and to the developer (Bergmann et al. 1999).

By means of the methodology we were able to create project definitions with structured process models, task definitions, roles and responsibilities, duration, and resource allocations. The methodology enabled us to make the case-based system development process traceable both to the customers and to ourselves.

The ability to trace a structured path and the use of the software tools that were developed to support the methodology allowed us to speed up the development process significantly.

Since the processes for the acquisition, use, and maintenance of the knowledge in the case-based system are defined in the methodology, we were able to introduce new CBR systems in a much more efficient manner. The detailed definition of the duties that have to be performed and the qualification that is needed for the project group also enabled the customers to allocate the necessary resources in advance and monitor the status of the project according to the goals that had been set when the project was initiated.

6.   INRECA Applications

From 1992 – 1999 the two INRECA projects yield a large number of successful applications, most of which are in daily use at the clients' sides. A summary of applications is given by Bergmann et al. (1999); here is a list of selected applications.

- For CFM International, AcknoSoft developed a maintenance system to support troubleshooting of the CFM 56-3 aircraft engines for the BOEING 737 from case history (Manago & Auriol 1995).
- For SEPRO Robotique, AcknoSoft (supported by BSR-Consulting) built a help-desk system for supporting the robot diagnosis procedure at the after-sales service (Bartsch-Spörl 1997). This application was supported by the ESPRIT project APPLICUS[1].
- IMS developed an application for assessing wind risk factors for Irish forests at COILLTE.
- The University of Kaiserslautern conducted a feasibility study (together with DaimlerBenz) for applying INRECA technology to the task of supporting the reuse of object-oriented software (Bergmann & Eisenecker 1995).
- At ALSTOM, AcknoSoft developed an application for improving train availability to optimize operating cost.
- At Analog Devices, IMS developed an operational amplifiers product catalog application using the tools and the support provided by AcknoSoft, tec:inno, and the University of Kaiserslautern (Bergmann et al. 1999).
- At DaimlerChrysler, the main INRECA-II application called HOMER was developed by tec:inno. HOMER is an intelligent hotline support tool for CAD/CAM workstations (Göker & Roth-Berghofer 1999, Bergmann et al. 1999).

---

[1] Esprit Project 20824. Project Partners: AcknoSoft, BSR-Consulting, SEPRO Robotique.

- At IRSA (Irish Research Scientists Association), IMS developed a case-based expertise knowledge base.
- At LEGRAND, Acknosoft developed a rapid cost estimation application for plastic parts production.
- For the region Müritz (Germany), tec:inno developed a tourist information system on the Internet.
- For Odense Steel Shipyard, AcknoSoft developed a CBR application that integrates with multimedia tools for improving the performances of ship welding robots (Auriol et al. 1999).
- For Siemens, tec:inno developed the SIMATIC Knowledge Manager which provides service support for the SIMATIC industrial automation system (Lenz et al 1999, Bergmann et al. 1999).
- For the Institute of Microtechnology in Mainz (Germany), tec:inno developed the compendium "Precision from Rhineland-Palatinate", which are the Yellow Pages for high-tech manufacturing processing companies.

The above list of applications is far from being complete. Also, applications developed after the projects were finished are not included here.

Till today, the INRECA technology has been further developed by the INRECA partners. The current tools are named "empolis orenge" and "Kaidara Advisor" and are now distributed worldwide. Each of the involved companies has now expanded its business from Europe to USA and is represented with its own offices. For the University of Kaiserslautern, the results of the INRECA projects were the starting point of many further interesting research projects, funded by German Ministries and the European Commission. Today, lectures on case-based reasoning are included in the standard curriculum for computer science.

Acknowledgements. The results I had the pleasure to summarize in this paper could have only been achieved by a very tight collaboration that involved many people. The INRECA team includes: Klaus-Dieter Althoff, Eric Auriol, Gaddo Benedetti, Ralph Bergmann, Martin Bräuer, Sean Breen, Michael Carmody, Laurent Champion, Steven Clinton, Christophe Deniard, Stefan Dittrich, Derek Ennis, Nicola Faull, Sylvie Garry, Arlette Gaulène, Mehmet Göker, Harald Holz, Roy Johnston, Elena Levandowky, Bénédicte Minguy, Gholamreza Nakhaeizadeh, Pól Macanultaigh, Michel Manago, Thomas Pantleon, Carsten Priebisch, Michael M. Richter, Thomas Roth-Berghofer, Arnaud Schleich, Sascha Schmitt, Jürgen Schumacher, Reinhard Skuppin, Armin Stahl, Jutta Stehr, Emmanuelle Tartarin-Fayol, Ralph Traphöner, Stefan Wess, and Wolfgang Wilke. The INRECA team is very much indebted to the European Commission for supporting the project, to the project officers Brice Lepape and Patrick Corsi, and to the reviewers Agnar Aamodt, Patricia Arundel, Rick Magaldi, Robin Muire, and Gerhard Strube who have always pushed us in positive ways for improved results.

References

Althoff, K.-D., Wess, S., Bergmann, R., Maurer, F., Manago, M., Auriol, E., Conruyt, N., Traphöner, R., Bräuer, M. & Dittrich, S. (1994). Induction and Case-Based Reasoning for Classification Tasks. In: Bock, Lenski & Richter (Eds.) Information Systems and Data Analysis, Prospects–Foundations–Applications, Annual Conference of GfKl, Springer.

Althoff, K.-D., Wess, S. & Traphöner, R. (1995a). Inreca – A Seamless Integration of Induction and Case-Based Reasoning for Decision Support Tasks. In: Morik & Herrmann (Eds.), Proc. 8th German Workshop on Machine Learning, University of Dortmund.

Althoff, K-D, Auriol, E, Barletta, R., & Manago, M (1995b). *A Review of Industrial Case-Based Reasoning Tools.* AI Intelligence, Oxford, UK.

Althoff, K.-D. (1996). The INRECA Case Study. Habilitation Thesis. University of Kaiserslautern.

Althoff, K.-D. & Wilke, W. (1997). Potential use of case-based reasoning in experience-based construction of CBR systems. In: Bergmann, R. & Wilke, W. (Eds.) *Proceedings of the 5th German Workshop on Case-Based Reasoning (GWCBR'97),* LSA-97-01E, Centre for Learning Systems and Applications (LSA), University of Kaiserslautern, 31-38.

Auriol, E., Manago, M., Althoff, K.-D., Wess, S. & Dittrich, S. (1994). Integrating Induction and Case-Based Reasoning: Methodological Approach and First Evaluations. In: Keane, Haton & Manago (Eds.) *Advances in Case-Based Reasoning, Second European Workshop (EWCBR-94), Springer,* 145-156.

Auriol, E., Wess, S., Manago, M., Althoff, K.-D., & Traphoner, R. (1995). INRECA: A seamlessly integrated system based on inductive inference and case-based reasoning. In Aamodt, A. & Veloso, M. (Eds.) *Proceedings of the First International Conference on Case-Based Reasoning, ICCBR95,* Springer, 371-380.

Auriol, E., Crowder, R.M., MacKendrick, R., Rowe R. & Knudsen, T. (1999). Documentation: An Application for the Diagnosis of a Welding Robot at Odense Steel Shipyard. *Engineering Applications of Artificial Intelligence,* **12** (6), Elsevier.

Bartsch-Spörl, B. (1996). Towards a methodology for how to make CBR systems work in practice. In: H.-D. Burkhard & M. Lenz (Eds.), *Proceedings of the 4th German Workshop on Case-Based Reasoning,* Humboldt University Berlin, 2-9.

Bartsch-Spörl, B. (1997). How to Introduce CBR Applications in Customer Support. In Bergmann & Wilke (Eds.). *Proceedings of the 5th German CBR Workshop,* Report LSA-97-0E, University of Kaiserslautern.

Bartsch-Spörl, B., Althoff, K.-D., Meissonnier, A. (1997). Reasoning about CBR systems. In Bergmann & Wilke (Eds.). *Proceedings of the 5th German CBR Workshop,* Report LSA-97-0E, University of Kaiserslautern.

Basili, V. R., Caldiera, G. & Rombach, H. D. (1994). The experience factory. In: J. J. Marciniak (ed.), *Encyclopedia of Software Engineering,* Vol. 1, Wiley, New York.

Bergmann, R. & Eisenecker, U. (1995). Fallbasiertes Schließen zur Unterstützung der Wiederverwendung objektorientierter Software: Eine Fallstudie. In: F. Maurer & M. M. Richter (Eds.) *Proceedings der 3. Deutschen Expertensystemtagung,* Infix, 152-169.

Bergmann, R., Wilke, W., Vollrath, I. & Wess, S. (1996). Integrating general knowledge with object-oriented case representation and reasoning. In: H.-D. Burkhard & M. Lenz (Eds.) *4th German Workshop: Case-Based Reasoning,* Humboldt-University Berlin, 120-127.

Bergmann, R., Wilke, W., Althoff, K.-D., Breen, S. & Johnston, R. (1997). Ingredients for developing a case-based reasoning methodology. In: Bergmann, R. & Wilke, W. (Eds.) *Proceedings of the 5th German Workshop in Case-Based Reasoning (GWCBR'97),* University of Kaiserslautern, 49-58.

Bergmann, R. (1998). On the use of taxonomies for representing case features and local similarity measures. In Gierl & Lenz (Eds.) *6th German Workshop on CBR.*

Bergmann, R. & Stahl, S. (1998). Similarity measures for object-oriented case representations. In B. Smyth & P. Cunningham (Eds.) *Advances in Case-Based Reasoning (EWCBR'98),* Springer, 25-36.

Bergmann, R., Breen, S., Göker, M., Manago, M., & Wess, S. (1999). *Developing Industrial Case-Based Reasoning Applications: The INRECA Methodology.* Lecture Notes in Artificial Intelligence, LNAI 1612, Springer, Berlin, Heidelberg.

Bergmann, R., Breen, S., Fayol, E., Göker, M., Manago, M., Schumacher, J., Schmitt, S., Stahl, A., Wess, S. & Wilke, W. (1998b). Collecting experience on the systematic development of CBR applications using the INRECA-II Methodology. In Smyth, B. & Cunningham, P. (Eds.) *Advances in Case-Based Reasoning (EWCBR'98)*, Springer, 460-470.

Bergmann, R., Richter, M.M., Schmitt, S., Stahl, A., Vollrath, I. (2001). Utility-Oriented Matching: A New Research Direction for Case-Based Reasoning. In: Vollrath, Schmitt, & Reimer: 9th German Workshop on Case-Based Reasoning, GWCBR'01. In Schnurr, Staab, Studer, Stumme, Sure (Eds.): *Professionelles Wissensmanagement*, Shaker.

Curet, O. and Jackson, M. (1996). Towards a methodology for case-based systems. *Expert Systems'96*. Proceedings of the 16th annual workshop of the British Computer Society.

Göker, M. & Roth-Berghofer, T. (1999). The Development and Utilization of the Case-Based Help-Desk Support System HOMER. *Engineering Applications of Artificial Intelligence*, **12** (6), Elsevier.

Kitano, H. & Shimazu, H. (1996). The Experience-sharing architecture: A case-study in corporarte-wide case-based software quality control. In Leake (Ed.) *Case-Based Reasoning: Experiences, Lessons, and Future Directions*. AAAI Press.

Lenz, M., Busch, K.-H., Hübner, A., & Wess, S. (1999). SIMATIC Knowledge Manager. In Aha, Becerra-Fernandez, Maurer, Muñoz-Avila (Eds.). *Exploring Synergies of Knowledge Management and Case-Based Reasoning*. Papers from the AAAI Workshop, Technical Report WS-99-10.

Manago M. (1990). KATE: A Piece of Computer Aided Knowledge Engineering. In Gaines & Boose (Eds.) *Proc. of the 5th AAAI workshop on KA for knowledge based systems*, AAAI Press.

Manago, M., Althoff, K.-D., Auriol, E., Traphöner, R., Wess, S., Conruyt, N., Maurer, F. (1993). Induction and Reasoning from Cases. In: Richter, M. M., Wess, S., Althoff, K.-D. & Maurer, F. (Eds.) (1993). *Proc. 1st European Workshop on Case-Based Reasoning (EWCBR-93)*, University of Kaiserslautern.

Manago, M., Bergmann, R., Wess, S. & Traphöner, R. (1994). CASUEL: A common case representation language, INRECA Deliverable D1, INRECA Consortium.

Manago M. & Auriol, E. (1995). Integrating Induction and Case-Based Reasoning for Troubleshooting CFM-56 Airfract Engines. In Bartsch-Spörl, Janetzko, & Wess (Eds.). Proceedings of the 3rd German CBR Workshop, University of Kaiserslautern.

Richter, M. M. & Wess, S. (1991). Similarity, Uncertainty and Case-Based Reasoning in PATDEX. *Automated Reasoning - Essays in Honor of Woody Bledsoe*, Kluwer.

Richter, M. M. (1995). The Knowledge Contained in Similarity Measures. Invited talk at the First International Conference on CBR (ICCBR-95).
http://www.cbr-web.org/documents/Richtericcbr95remarks.html

Rombach, H. D. & Verlage, M. (1995). Directions in software process research. In: M.V. Zelkowitz (Ed.), *Advances in Computers*, Vol. 41, Academic Press, 1-61.

Schumacher, J. & Traphöner, R. (2000). Knowledge Modeling WEBSELL Deliverable 3.4, WEBSELL Consortium.

Wess, S. (1995). Fallbasiertes Problemlösen in wissensbasierten Systemen zur Entscheidungs-unterstützung und Diagnostik. PhD Thesis, DISKI 126, infix.

The Synthesis of Expressive Music: A Challenging CBR Application

Ramon López de Mántaras and Josep Lluís Arcos

IIIA, Artificial Intelligence Research Institute
CSIC, Spanish Council for Scientific Research
Campus UAB, 08193 Bellaterra, Catalonia, Spain.
{arcos, mantaras}@iiia.csic.es, http://www.iiia.csic.es

Abstract. This paper is based on an invited talk, given at ICCBR'01, about the research performed at the IIIA on the problem of synthesizing expressive music. In particular, describes several extensions and improvements of a previously reported system [5,4,6,3] capable of generating expressive music by imitating human performances. The system is based on Case-Based Reasoning (CBR) and Fuzzy techniques.

1 Introduction

One of the major difficulties in the automatic generation of music is to endow the resulting piece with the expressiveness that characterizes human performers. Following musical rules, no mater how sophisticated and complete they are, is not enough to achieve expression, and indeed computer music usually sounds monotonous and mechanical. The main problem is to grasp the performers personal touch, that is, the knowledge brought about when performing a score. A large part of this knowledge is implicit and very difficult to verbalize. For this reason, AI approaches based on declarative knowledge representations are very useful to model musical knowledge an indeed we represent such knowledge declaratively in our system, however they have serious limitations in grasping performance knowledge. An alternative approach, much closer to the observation imitation - experimentation process observed in human performers, is that of directly using the performance knowledge implicit in examples of human performers and let the system imitate these performances. To achieve this, we have developped the *SaxEx*, a case-based reasoning system capable of generating expressive performances of melodies based on examples of human performances. CBR is indeed an appropriate methodology to solve problems by means of examples of already solved similar problems.

The high difficulty of modeling the complex phenomenon of expressive music performance required the representation of highly structured complex music knowledge, as well as the use of a new knowledge intensive retrieval method. The fulfilment of these very challenging requirements allowed us to contribute to the advancement of the state of the art in CBR [2,1,6,4].

In the next section we remind the main features of the system, and we describe the fuzzy set-based extension of the reuse step. Then, we briefly mention some relevant related work and,finally, we give some conclusions.

D.W. Aha and I. Watson (Eds.): ICCBR 2001, LNAI 2080, pp. 16–26, 2001.
© Springer-Verlag Berlin Heidelberg 2001

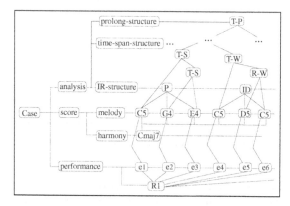

Fig. 1. Overall structure of the beginning of an 'All of me' case.

2   System Description

The problem-solving task of the system is to infer, via imitation, and using its case-based reasoning capability, a set of expressive transformations to be applied to every note of an inexpressive musical phrase given as input. To achieve this, it uses a case memory containing human performances and background musical knowledge, namely NarmourÕs theory of musical perception [17] and Lerdahl & JackendoffÕs GTTM [16]. The score, containing both melodic and harmonic information, is also given.

2.1   Modeling Musical Knowledge

Problems solved by *SaxEx*, and stored in its memory, are represented as complex structured cases embodying three different kinds of musical knowledge (see Figure 1): (1) concepts related to the score of the phrase such as notes and chords, (2) concepts related to background musical theories such as implication/realization (IR) structures and GTTM's time-span reduction nodes, and (3) concepts related to the performance of musical phrases.

A score is represented by a melody, embodying a sequence of notes, and a harmony, embodying a sequence of chords. Each note holds in turn a set of features such as its pitch (C5, G4, etc), its position with respect to the beginning of the phrase, its duration, a reference to its underlying harmony, and a reference to the next note of the phrase. Chords hold also a set of features such as name (Cmaj7, E7, etc), position, duration, and a reference to the next chord.

The musical analysis representation embodies structures of the phrase automatically inferred by *SaxEx* from the score using IR and GTTM background musical knowledge. The analysis structure of a melody is represented by a process-structure (embodying a sequence of IR basic structures), a time-span-reduction structure (embodying a tree describing metrical relations), and a prolongational-reduction structure (embodying a tree describing tensing and relaxing relations

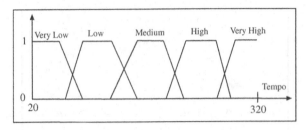

Fig. 2. Linguistic fuzzy values for rubato expressive parameter.

among notes). Moreover, a note holds the metrical-strength feature, inferred using GTTM theory, expressing the note's relative metrical importance into the phrase.

The information about the expressive performances contained in the examples of the case memory is represented by a sequence of *affective regions* and a sequence of *events*, one for each note, (extracted using the SMS sound analysis capabilities), as explained below.

Affective regions group (sub)-sequences of notes with common affective expressivity. Specifically, an affective region holds knowledge describing the following affective dimensions: *tender-aggressive*, *sad-joyful*, and *calm-restless*. These affective dimensions are described using five ordered qualitative values expressed by linguistic labels as follows: the middle label represents no predominance (for instance, neither tender nor aggressive), lower and upper labels represent, respectively predominance in one direction (for example, absolutely calm is described with the lowest label). For instance, a jazz ballad can start very tender and calm and continue very tender but more restless. Such different nuances are represented in *SaxEx* by means of different affective regions.

The expressive transformations to be decided and applied by the system affect the following expressive parameters: dynamics, rubato, vibrato, articulation, and attack. Except for the attack, the notes in the human performed musical phrases are qualified using the SMS (Spectral Modeling and Synthesis) system [18], by means of five different ordered values. For example, for dynamics the values are: very low, low, medium, high and very high and they are automatically computed relative to the average loudness of the inexpressive input phrase. The same idea is used for rubato, vibrato (very little vibrato to very high vibrato) and articulation (very legato to very staccato). In the previous system these values where mere syntactic labels but in the improved system, the meanings of these values are modeled by means of fuzzy sets such as those shown in figure 2 for Rubato. We will explain below the advantage of this extension. For the attack we have just two situations: reaching the pitch from a lower pitch or increasing the noise component of the sound.

2.2   The SaxEx CBR Task

The task of *SaxEx* is to infer a set of expressive transformations to be applied to every note of an inexpressive phrase given as input. To achieve this, *SaxEx*

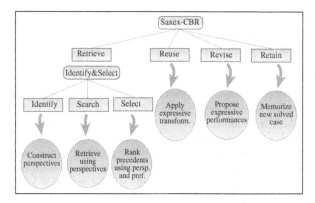

Fig. 3. Task decomposition of the *SaxEx* CBR method.

uses a CBR problem solver, a case memory of expressive performances, and background musical knowledge. Transformations concern the dynamics, rubato, vibrato, articulation, and attack of each note in the inexpressive phrase. The cases stored in the episodic memory of *SaxEx* contain knowledge about the expressive transformations performed by a human player given specific labels for affective dimensions.

For each note in the phrase, the following subtask decomposition (Figure 3) is performed by the CBR problem solving method implemented in Noos:

- *Retrieve*: The goal of the retrieve task is to choose, from the memory of cases (pieces played expressively), the set of precedent notes—the cases—most similar for every note of the problem phrase. Specifically, the following subtask decomposition is applied to each note of the problem phrase:

  - *Identify*: its goal is to build retrieval perspectives (explained in the next subsection) using the affective values specified by the user and the musical background knowledge integrated in the system (retrieval perspectives are described in Subsection 2.3). These perspectives guide the retrieval process by focusing it on the most relevant aspects of the current problem, and will be used either in the *search* or in the *select* subtasks.
  - *Search*: its goal is to search cases in the case memory using Noos retrieval methods and some previously constructed perspective(s).
  - *Select*: its goal is to rank the retrieved cases using Noos preference methods. The collection of *SaxEx* default preference methods use criteria such as similarity in duration of notes, harmonic stability, or melodic directions.

- *Reuse*: its goal is to choose, from the set of most similar notes previously retrieved, a set of expressive transformations to be applied to the current note. The default strategy of *SaxEx* is the following: the first criterion used is to adapt the transformations of the most similar note. When several notes are considered equally similar, the transformations are computed using a fuzzy combination (see section 'The use of fuzzy techniques ...'). The user can, however, select alternative criteria, not involving this fuzzy combination such as majority rule, minority rule, etc. When the retrieval task is not able to retrieve similar precedent cases for a given note, no expressive transformations are applied to that note and the situation is notified in the revision task. Nevertheless, using the current *SaxEx* case base, the retrieval perspectives allways retrieved at least one precedent in the experiments performed.

- *Revise*: its goal is to present to the user a set of alternative expressive performances for the problem phrase. Users can tune the expressive transformations applied to each note and can indicate which performances they prefer.
- *Retain*: the incorporation of the new solved problem to the memory of cases is performed automatically in *Noos* from the selection performed by the user in the *revise* task. These solved problems will be available for the reasoning process when solving future problems. Only positive feedback is given. That is, only those examples that the user judges as good expressive interpretations are actually retained.

In previous versions of *SaxEx* the CBR task was fixed. That is, the collection of retrieval perspectives, their combination, the collection of reuse criteria, and the storage of solved cases were pre-designed and the user didn't participate in the reasoning process. Moreover, the *retain* subtask was not present because it is mainly a subtask that requires an interaction with the user.

Now, in the current version of *SaxEx* we have improved the CBR method by incorporating the user in the reasoning process [4]. This new capability allows users to influence the solutions proposed by *SaxEx* in order to satisfy their interests or personal style. The user can interact with *SaxEx* in the four main CBR subtasks. This new functionality requires that the use and combination of the two basic mechanisms—perspectives and preferences— in the Retrieve and Reuse subtasks must be parameterizable and dynamically modifiable.

2.3   Retrieval Perspectives

Retrieval perspectives [2] are built by the *identify* subtask and can be used either by the *search* or the *select* subtask. Perspectives used by the *search* subtask will act as filters. Perspectives used by the *select* subtask will act only as a preference. Retrieval perspectives are built based on user requirements and background musical knowledge. Retrieval perspectives provide partial information about the relevance of a given musical aspect. After these perspectives are established, they have to be combined in a specific way according to the importance (preference) that they have.

Retrieval perspectives are of two different types: based on the affective intention that the user wants to obtain in the output expressive sound or based on musical knowledge.

1) *Affective labels* are used to determine the following declarative bias: we are interested in notes with affective labels similar to the affective labels required in the current problem by the user.

As an example, let us assume that we declare we are interested in forcing *SaxEx* to generate a calm and very tender performance of the problem phrase.

Based on this bias, *SaxEx* will build a perspective specifying as relevant to the current problem the notes from cases that belong first to "calm and very tender" affective regions (most preferred), or "calm and tender" affective regions, or "very calm and very tender" affective regions (both less preferred).

When this perspective is used in the *Search* subtask, *SaxEx* will search in the memory of cases for notes that satisfy this criterion. When this perspective is used in the *Select* subtask, *SaxEx* will rank the previously retrieved cases using this criterion.

2) *Musical knowledge* gives three sets of declarative retrieval biases: first, biases based on Narmour's implication/realization model; second, biases based on Lerdahl and Jackendoff's generative theory; and third, biases based on Jazz theory and general music knowledge.

Regarding Narmour's implication/realization model, *SaxEx* incorporates the following three perspectives:

- The *"role in IR structure"* criterion determines as relevant the role that a given note plays in an implication/realization structure. That is, the kind of IR structure it belongs to and its position (`first-note`, `inner-note`, or `last-note`). Examples of IR basic structures are the P process (a melodic pattern describing a sequence of at least three notes with similar intervals and the same ascending or descending registral direction) and the ID process (a sequence of at least three notes with the same intervals and different registral directions), among others. For instance, this retrieval perspective can specify biases such as "look for notes that are the `first-note` of a P process".
- The *"Melodic Direction"* criterion determines as relevant the kind of melodic direction in an implication/realization structure: `ascendant`, `descendant`, or `duplication`. This criterion is used for adding a preference among notes with the same IR role.
- The *"Durational Cumulation"* criterion determines as relevant the presence—in a IR structure—of a note in the last position with a duration significantly higher than the others. This characteristic emphasizes the end of a IR structure. This criterion is used—as the previous—for adding a preference among notes with the same IR role and same melodic direction.

Regarding Lerdahl and Jackendoff's GTTM theory, *SaxEx* incorporates the following three perspectives:

- The *"Metrical Strength"* criterion determines as relevant the importance of a note with respect to the metrical structure of the piece. The metrical structure assigns a weight to each note according to the beat in which it is played. That is, the metrical weight of notes played in strong beats are higher than the metrical weight of notes played in weak beats. For instance, the metrical strength bias determines as similar the notes played at the beginning of subphrases since the metrical weight is the same.
- The *"role in the Time-Span Reduction Tree"* criterion determines as relevant the structural importance of a given note according to the role that the note plays in the analysis Time-Span Reduction Tree.

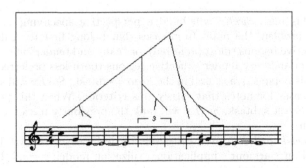

Fig. 4. Example of a Time-Span Tree for the beginning of the 'All of me' ballad.

Time-Span Reduction Trees are built bottom-up and hold two components: a segmentation into hierarchically organized rhythmic units and a binary tree that represents the relative structural importance of the notes within those units. There are two kinds of nodes in the tree: left-elaboration nodes and right-elaboration nodes.

Since the Time-Span Reduction Tree is a tree with high depth, we are only taking into account the two last levels. That is, given a note this perspective focuses on the kind of leaf the note belongs (left or right leaf) and on the kind of node the leaf belongs (left-elaboration or right-elaboration node).

For instance, in the 'All of me' ballad (see Figure 4) the first quarter note of the second bar (C) belongs to a left leaf in a right-elaboration node because the following two notes (D and C) elaborate the first note. In turn, these two notes belong to a left-elaboration (sub)node because second note (D) elaborates the third (C).

– The "*role in the Prolongational Reduction Tree*" criterion determines as relevant the structural importance of a given note according to the role that the note plays in the Prolongational Reduction Tree. Prolongational Reduction Trees are binary trees built top-down and represent the hierarchical patterns of tension and relaxation among groups of notes. There are two basic kinds of nodes in the tree (tensing nodes and relaxing nodes) with three modes of branch chaining: *strong prolongation* in which events repeat maintaining sonority (e.g., notes of the same chord); *weak prolongation* in which events repeat in an altered form (e.g., from I chord to I6 chord); and *jump* in which two completely different events are connected (e.g., from I chord to V chord).

As in the previous perspective we are only taking into account the two last levels of the tree. That is, given a note this perspective focuses on the kind of leaf the note belongs (left or right leaf), on the kind of node the leaf belongs (tensing or relaxing node), and the kind of connection of the node (strong, weak, or jump).

Finally, regarding perspectives based on jazz theory and general music knowledge, *SaxEx* incorporates the following two:

– The "*Harmonic Stability*" criterion determines as relevant the role of a given note according to the underlying harmony. Since *SaxEx* is focused on gener-

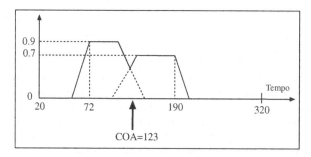

Fig. 5. Fuzzy combination and defuzzification of rubato value.

ating expressive music in the context of jazz ballads, the general harmonic theory has been specialized taking harmonic concepts from jazz theory. The Harmonic Stability criterion takes into account in the following two aspects: the position of the note within its underlying chord (e.g., first, third, seventh, ...); and the role of the note in the chord progression it belongs.
- The "*Note Duration*" criterion determines as relevant the duration of a note. That is, given a specific situation, the set of expressive transformations applied to a note will differ depending on whether the note has a long or a short duration.

2.4   The Use of Fuzzy Techniques in the Reuse Step

Having modeled the linguistic values of the expressive parameters by means of fuzzy sets, allows us to apply a fuzzy combination operator to these values of the retrieved notes in the reuse step. The following example describes this combination operation.

Let us assume that the system has retrieved two similar notes whose fuzzy values for the rubato are, respectively, 72 and 190, The system first computes the maximum degree of membership of each one of these two values with respect to the five linguistic values characterizing the *rubato* shown in figure 2. The maximum membership value of 72 corresponds to the fuzzy value *low* and is 0.90 (see figure 5) and that of 190 correponds to *medium* and is 0.70. Next, it computes a combined fuzzy membership function, based on these two values. This combination consists on the fuzzy disjunction of the fuzzy membership functions *low* and *medium* truncated, respectively, by the 0.90 and 0.70 membership degrees. That is:

$$Max(min(0.90, f_{low}), min(0.70, f_{medium}))$$

The result is shown in figure 5. Finally *defuzzifies* this result by computing the COA (Center of Area) of the combined function [15]. The defuzzification step gives the precise value for the tempo to be applied to the initially inexpressive note, in this example the obtained result is 123. An analogous process is applied to the other expressive parameters. The advantage of such fuzzy combination is that the resulting expression takes into account the contribution of all the retrieved similar notes whereas with criteria such as *minority rule, majority rule* etc. this is not the case. For example, if the system retrieves three notes from the expressive examples, and two of them had been played with low rubato and the third with medium rubato, the majority rule dictates that the inexpressive note should be played with *low rubato*. This conclusion is mapped into an a priori fixed value that is lower than the average rubato of the inexpressive input piece. It is worth noticing that each time the system concludes *low rubato* for several inexpressive notes, these note will be played with the same rubato even if the retrieved similar notes were different (*very low* would be mapped into a value much lower than the average rubato, *high* would be mapped into a value higher than the average and *very high* into a value much higher than the average and the same procedure applies to the other expressive parameters such as dynamics, vibrato and legato). With the fuzzy extension, the system is capable of increasing the variety of its performances because, after defuzzification, the final value for each expressive parameter is computed and this computation does not depend only on the linguistic value (low, etc.) of the retrieved similar notes but also on the membership degree of the actual numerical values that are used to truncate the membership functions as explained above, therefore the final value will not be the same unless, of course, the precedent retrieved notes is actually the same note.

The system is connected to the SMS (4) software for sound analysis and synthesis based on spectral modeling as pre and post processor. This allows to actually listen to the obtained results. These results clearly show that a computer system can play expressively. In our experiments, we have used Real Book jazz ballads.

3   Related Work

Previous work on the analysis and synthesis of musical expression has addressed the study of at most two expressive parameters such as rubato and vibrato [8, 11,13], rubato and dynamics [20,7] or rubato and articulation [14]. Concerning instrument modeling, the work of Dannenberg and Derenyi [9] is an important step towards high-quality synthesis of wind instrument performances. Other work such as in [10,12] has focalized on the study of how musicianÕs expressive intentions influence performers. To the best of our knowledge, the only previous works using learning techniques to generate expressive performances are those of Widmer [20], who uses explanation-based techniques to learn rules for dynamics and rubato using a MIDI keyboard, and Bressin [7], who trains an artificial neural network to simulate a human pianist also using MIDI. In our work we deal with five expressive parameters in the context of a very expressive non-MIDI instrument (tenor sax). Furthermore, ours was the first attempt to use Case-based Reasoning techniques. The use of CBR techniques was also done later by [19] but dealing only with rubato and dynamics for MIDI instruments.

4   Conclusions

We have briefly described a new improved version of our *SaxEx* system. The added interactivity improves the usability of the system and the use of fuzzy techniques in the reuse step increases the performance variety of the system. Some ideas for further work include further experimentation with a larger set of tunes as well as allowing the system to add ornamental notes and not to play some of the notes, that is moving a small step towards adding improvising capabilities to the system.

Acknowledgements. The research reported in this paper is partly supported by the **ESPRIT LTR 25500-COMRIS** *Co-Habited Mixed-Reality Information Spaces* project. We also acknowledge the support of ROLAND Electronics de España S.A. to our AI & Music project.

References

1. Josep Lluís Arcos. *The Noos representation language.* PhD thesis, Universitat Politècnica de Catalunya, 1997. online at www.iiia.csic.es/~arcos/Phd.html.
2. Josep Lluís Arcos and Ramon López de Mántaras. Perspectives: a declarative bias mechanism for case retrieval. In David Leake and Enric Plaza, editors, *Case-Based Reasoning. Research and Development*, number 1266 in Lecture Notes in Artificial Intelligence, pages 279–290. Springer-Verlag, 1997.
3. Josep Lluís Arcos and Ramon López de Mántaras. Combining fuzzy and case-based reasoning to generate human-like music performances. In B. Bouchon-Meunier, J. Gutierrez-Rios, L. Magdalena, and R.R. Yager, editors, *Technologies for Constructing Intelligent Systems*, Lecture Notes in Artificial Intelligence. Springer-Verlag, 2001. In press.
4. Josep Lluís Arcos and Ramon López de Mántaras. An interactive case-based reasoning approach for generating expressive music. *Applied Intelligence*, 14(1):115–129, 2001.
5. Josep Lluís Arcos, Ramon López de Mántaras, and Xavier Serra. Saxex : a case-based reasoning system for generating expressive musical performances. *Journal of New Music Research*, 27 (3):194–210, 1998.
6. Josep Lluís Arcos, Dolores Cañamero, and Ramon López de Mántaras. Affect-driven cbr to generate expressive music. In Karl Branting and Klaus-Dieter Althoff, editors, *Case-Based Reasoning. Research and Development. ICCBR'99*, number 1650 in Lecture Notes in Artificial Intelligence, pages 1–13. Springer-Verlag, 1999.
7. R. Bresin. Artificial neural networks based models for automatic performance of musical scores. *Journal of New Music Research*, 27 (3):239–270, 1998.
8. Manfred Clynes. Microstructural musical linguistics: composers' pulses are liked most by the best musicians. *Cognition*, 55:269–310, 1995.
9. R.B. Dannenberg and I. Derenyi. Combining instrument and performance models for high-quality music synthesis. *Journal of New Music Research*, 27 (3):211–238, 1998.
10. Giovani De Poli, Antonio Rodà, and Alvise Vidolin. Note-by-note analysis of the influence of expressive intentions and musical structure in violin performance. *Journal of New Music Research*, 27 (3):293–321, 1998.

11. P. Desain and H. Honing. Computational models of beat induction: the rule-based approach. In *Proceedings of IJCAI'95 Workshop on AI and Music*, pages 1–10, 1995.
12. A. Friberg, R. Bresin, L. Fryden, and J. Sunberg. Musical punctuation on the microlevel: automatic identification and performance of small melodic units. *Journal of New Music Research*, 27 (3):271–292, 1998.
13. H. Honing. The vibrato problem, comparing two solutions. *Computer Music Journal*, 19 (3):32–49, 1995.
14. M.L. Johnson. An expert system for the articulation of Bach fugue melodies. In D.L. Baggi, editor, *Readings in Computer-Generated Music*, pages 41–51. IEEE Computes Society Press, 1992.
15. G. Klir and B. Yuan. *Fuzzy Sets and Fuzzy Logic*. Prentice Hall, 1995.
16. Fred Lerdahl and Ray Jackendoff. An overview of hierarchical structure in music. In Stephan M. Schwanaver and David A. Levitt, editors, *Machine Models of Music*, pages 289–312. The MIT Press, 1993. Reproduced from Music Perception.
17. Eugene Narmour. *The Analysis and cognition of basic melodic structures : the implication-realization model*. University of Chicago Press, 1990.
18. Xavier Serra, Jordi Bonada, Perfecto Herrera, and Ramon Loureiro. Integrating complementary spectral methods in the design of a musical synthesizer. In *Proceedings of the ICMC'97*, pages 152–159. San Francisco: International Computer Music Asociation., 1997.
19. T. Suzuki, T. Tokunaga, and H. Tanaka. A case-based approach to the generation of musical expression. In *Proceedings of IJCAI'99*, 1999.
20. Gerhard Widmer. Learning expressive performance: The structure-level approach. *Journal of New Music Research*, 25 (2):179–205, 1996.

Why Case-Based Reasoning Is Attractive for Image Interpretation

Petra Perner

Institute of Computer Vision and Applied Computer Sciences
Arno-Nitzsche-Str. 45, 04277 Leipzig
ibaiperner@aol.com http://www.ibai-research.de

Abstract. The development of image interpretation systems is concerned with tricky problems such as a limited number of observations, environmental influence, and noise. Recent systems lack robustness, accuracy, and flexibility. The introduction of case-based reasoning (CBR) strategies can help to overcome these drawbacks. The special type of information (i.e., images) and the problems mentioned above provide special requirements for CBR strategies. In this paper we review what has been achieved so far and research topics concerned with case-based image interpretation. We introduce a new approach for an image interpretation system and review its components.

1 Introduction

Image interpretation systems are becoming increasingly popular in medical and industrial applications. The existing statistical and knowledge-based techniques lack robustness, accuracy, and flexibility. New strategies are necessary that can adapt to changing environmental conditions, user needs and process requirements. Introducing case-based reasoning (CBR) strategies into image interpretation systems can satisfy these requirements. CBR provides a flexible and powerful method for controlling the image processing process in all phases of an image interpretation system to derive information of the highest possible quality. Beyond this CBR offers different learning capabilities, for all phases of an image interpretation system, that satisfy different needs during the development process of an image interpretation system. Therefore, they are especially appropriate for image interpretation.

Although all this has been demonstrated in various applications [1]-[6][35], case-based image interpretation systems are still not well established in the computer vision community. One reason might be that CBR is not very well known within this community. Also, some relevant activities have been shied away from developing large complex systems in favor of developing special algorithms for well-constrained tasks (e.g., texture, motion, or shape recognition). In this paper, we will show that a CBR framework can be used to overcome the modeling burden usually associated with the development of image interpretation systems.

We seek to increase attention for this area and the special needs that image processing tasks require. We will review current activities on image interpretation and describe our work on a comprehensive case-based image interpretation system.

D.W. Aha and I. Watson (Eds.): ICCBR 2001, LNAI 2080, pp. 27-43, 2001.

In Section 2, we will introduce the tasks involved when interpreting an image, showing that they require knowledge sources ranging from numerical representations to sub-symbolic and symbolic representations. Different kinds of knowledge sources need different kinds of processing operators and representations, and their integration places special challenges on the system developer.

In Section 3, we will describe the special needs of an image interpretation system and how they are related to CBR topics. Then, we will describe in Section 4 the case representations possible for image information. Similarity measures strongly depend on the chosen image representation. We will overview what kinds of similarity measures are useful and what are the open research topics in Section 5. In Section 6, we will describe our approach for a comprehensive CBR system for image interpretation and what has been achieved so far. Finally, we offer conclusions based on our CBR systems working in real-world environments.

2 Tasks an Image Interpretation System Must Solve

Image interpretation is the process of mapping the numerical representation of an image into a logical representation such as suitable for scene description. An image interpretation system must be able to extract symbolic features from the pixels of an image (e.g., irregular structure inside the nodule, area of calcification, and sharp margin). This is a complex process; the image passes through several general processing steps until the final symbolic description is obtained. These include image preprocessing, image segmentation, image analysis, and image interpretation (see Figure 1). Interdisciplinary knowledge from image processing, syntactical and statistical pattern recognition, and artificial intelligence is required to build such systems. The primitive (low-level) image features will be extracted at the lowest level of an image interpretation system. Therefore, the image matrix acquired by the image acquisition component must first undergo image pre-processing to remove noise, restore distortions, undergo smoothing, and sharpen object contours. In the next step, objects of interest are distinguished from background and uninteresting objects, which are removed from the image matrix.

In the x-ray computed tomography (CT) image shown in Figure 1, the skull and the head shell is removed from the image in a preprocessing step. Afterwards, the resulting image is partitioned into objects such as brain and liquor. After having found the objects of interest in an image, we can then describe the objects using primitive image features. Depending on the particular objects and focus of interest, these features can be lines, edges, ribbon, etc. A geometric object such as a block will be described, for example, by lines and edges. The objects in the ultrasonic image shown in Figure 1 are described by regions and their spatial relation to each other. The region's features could include size, shape, or the gray level. Typically, these low-level features have to be mapped to high-level features. A symbolic feature such as *fuzzy margin* will be a function of several low-level features. Lines and edges will be grouped together by perceptual criteria such as collinearity and continuity in order to describe a block.

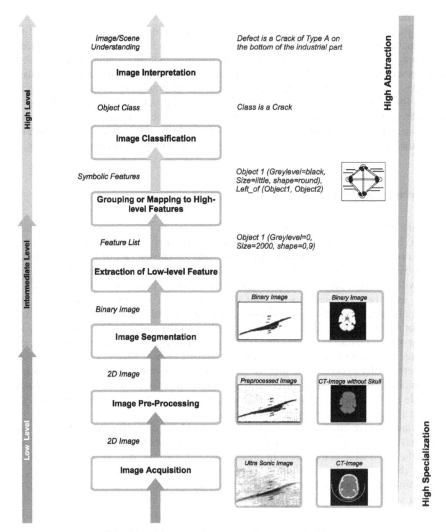

Fig. 1. Architecture of an Image Interpretation System

Image classification is usually referred to as the mapping of numeric features to predefined classes. Sometimes image interpretation requires only image classification. However, image classification is frequently only a *first* step of image interpretation. Low-level features or part of the object description are used to classify the object into different object classes in order to reduce the complexity of the search space. The image interpretation component identifies an object by finding the object that it belongs to (among the models of the object class). This is done by matching the symbolic description of the object in the scene to the model of the object stored in the knowledge base. When processing an image using an image interpretation system, an image's content is transformed into multiple representations that reflect different abstraction levels. This incrementally removes unnecessary detail from the image. The highest abstraction level will be reached after grouping the image's features. It is a product of mapping the image pixels contained in the image matrix into a logical structure. This higher level representation ensures that the image interpretation process will not be affected by noise appearing during image acquisition, and it also provides an understanding of the image's content. A bottom-up control structure is shown for the generic system in Figure 1. This control structure allows no feedback to preceding processing components if the result of the outcome of the current component is unsatisfactory. A mixture of bottom-up and top-down control would allow the outcome of a component to be refined by returning to previous component.

3 Development Concerns

Several factors influence the quality of the final result of an image interpretation system, including environmental conditions, the selected imaging device, noise, the number of observations from the task domain, and the chosen part of the task domain. These cannot often all be accounted for during system development, and many of them will only be discovered during system execution. Furthermore, the task domain cannot even be guaranteed to be limited. For example, in defect classification for industrial tasks, new defects may occur because the manufacturing tool that had been used for a long period suddenly causes scratches on the surface of the manufactured part. In optical character recognition, imaging defects (e.g., heavy print, light print, or stray marks) can occur and influence the recognition results. Rice et al. [7] attempted to systematically overview the factors that influence the result of an optical character recognition system, and how different systems respond to them. However, it is not yet possible to observe all real-world influences, nor provide a sufficiently large enough sample set for system development and testing.

A robust image interpretation system must be able to deal with such influences. It must have intelligent strategies on all levels of an image interpretation system that can adapt the processing components to these new requirements. A strategy that seems to satisfy these requirements could be case-based reasoning. CBR does not rely on a well-formulated domain theory, which is, as we have seen, often difficult to acquire.

This suggests that we must consider different aspects during system development that are frequently studied CBR issues. Because we expect users will discover new aspects of the environment and the objects during system usage, an automatic image interpretation system should be able to incrementally update the system's model, as illustrated in Figure 2. This requires knowledge maintenance and learning. The designated lifetime of a case also plays an important role. Other aspects are concerned with system competence. The range of target problems that a given system or algorithm can solve are often not quite clear to the developer of the image interpretation system. Often researchers present to the community a new algorithm that can, for example, recognize the shape of an object in a particular image and then claim that they have developed a model. Unfortunately, all too often another researcher inputs a different image to the same algorithm and finds that it fails. Did the first researcher develop a model or did they instead develop a function? Testing and evaluation of algorithms and systems is an important problem in computer vision [8], as is designing the algorithm's control structure so that it fits best to the current problem. CBR strategies can help to solve this problem in computer vision.

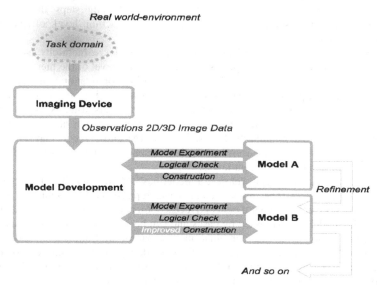

Fig. 2. Model Development Process

4 Case Representations for Images

Usually the main types of information concerned with image interpretation are image-related and non-image-related information. Image-related information can be the 1D, 2D, or 3D images of the desired application, while non-image-related information can include information about image acquisition (e.g., the type and parameters of the sensor, information about the objects, or the illumination of the scene). The type of application determines what type of information should be considered for image interpretation. For medical CT image segmentation [3], we used patient-specific parameters such as age, sex, slice thickness, and number of slices. Jarmulak [1] considered the type of sensor for a railway inspection application and his system used it to control the type of case base that the system used during reasoning.

How the 2D or 3D image matrix is represented depends on the application the developer's point of view. In principle it is possible to represent an image using one of the abstraction levels described in Section 2. An image may be described by the pixel matrix itself or by parts of this matrix (a pixel representation). It may be described by the objects contained in the image and their features (a feature-based representation). Furthermore, it can be described by a more complex model of the image scene comprising objects and their features as well as the object's spatial relationships (an attributed graph representation or semantic network).

As mentioned earlier, processing the image through multiple components and describing it by higher-level representations can reduce the number unnecessary details in its representation. This allows more noise tolerance and may speed up the retrieval process but may require additional modeling of the image content, which is difficult and time-consuming. Also, it requires processing steps that are often computationally intensive. Thus, the necessary abstraction level of the image information should be carefully chosen.

Jarmulak [1] solved this problem by using a four-level case hierarchy and different case bases for different sensor types. Stored at the lowest level of the hierarchy are the objects described by features such as their location, orientation, and type (line, parabola, or noise) parameters. The next level consists of objects of the same channel within the same subcluster. In the following level the subcluster is stored and the highest level stores the entire image scene. This representation allows cases to be matched on different granularity levels. Because the entire scene may have noise distortions and imprecise measurements, the influence of noise can be reduced by retrieving cases on these different levels.

Grimnes and Aamodt [2] developed a model-based system for the interpretation of abdominal CT images. The image's content was represented by a semantic network where concepts can be a general concept, a case, or a heuristic rule. Poorly understood parts of the model are expressed by cases and can be revised during system usage by the learning component. The combination of a partial well-understood model with cases helps to overcome the usual burden of modeling. The learning component is based on failure-driven learning and case integration. Non-image information is also stored such as sex, age, earlier diagnosis, and social condition.

In both of these systems, CBR is used only for the high-level component. We have studied different approaches for the different processing stages of an image interpretation system. For image segmentation [1], we studied a pixel-based approach and also a feature-based approach that described an image's statistical properties. Our results show that the pixel-based approach can yield better image segmentation. For the high-level approach in an ultra sonic image interpretation system, we used a graph representation [9].

Micarelli et al. [4] have also calculated image properties from images and stored them into a case base. They used the Wavelet transform because it is scale-independent, but this limits their similarity measure to consider only object rotation.

Representing images at multiple levels of abstraction presents some technical challenges. When representing an image with a high-level abstraction rather than the image matrix itself, some information will be lost. Abstraction requires deciding which details of an image are necessary. If only some objects are seen at one time, then we might think that one detail is not of interest since our decision is based on a limited number of objects. This can cause problems. Therefore, storing the images themselves is always preferable but requires high storage capacity. Also, the different representations at each abstraction level require different similarity measures.

5 Similarity Measures for Image Interpretation

Images can be rotated, translated, different in scale, or may have different contrast and energy yet still considered to be similar. In contrast, two images may be dissimilar because the object in one image is rotated by 180 degrees. The concept of *invariance* in image interpretation is closely related to that of similarity. A good similarity measure should take this into consideration.

Classical similarity measures do not consider invariance. Usually, the images or the features have to be pre-processed in order to be adapted to the scale, orientation, or shift. This process is an additional and expensive processing step that needs some a priori information, which is not always given. Matched, linear, Fourier, and Wavelet filters are especially useful for invariance under translation and rotation [4]. There has been a lot of work done to develop such filters for image interpretation. The best way to achieve scale invariance from an image is by means of invariant moments, which can also be invariant under rotation and other distortions. Some additional invariance can be obtained by normalization (to reduce the influence of energy).

Depending on the image representation (see Figure 3) we can divide similarity measures into:

1. pixel (Iconic)-matrix similarity measures;
2. similarity measures for comparing strings;
3. feature-based similarity measures (numeric, symbolic, or mixed type); and,
4. structural similarity measures.

Because a CBR image interpretation system must also account for non-image information (e.g., about the environment or the objects), similarity measures are needed that can combine non-image with image information. In [10], we described a first approach for doing this.

Systematic studies on image similarity have been conducted by Zamperoni and Starovoitov [11]. They studied how pixel-matrix similarity measures behave under different real-world influences such as translation, noise (spikes, salt and pepper noise), and different contrast. Image feature-based similarity measures have been studied from a broader perspective by Santini and Jain [12]. To our knowledge, these are the only comprehensive studies on image similarity. Otherwise, every new conference on pattern recognition contains proposals for new similarity measures for specific purposes and different kinds of image representation [13]-[23]. While there was some simultaneous research on image similarity in the CBR community (e.g., [24]), this work has also not achieved new insight. In our view, images are a special type of information source that require special similarity measures, and these measures require more rigorous analysis.

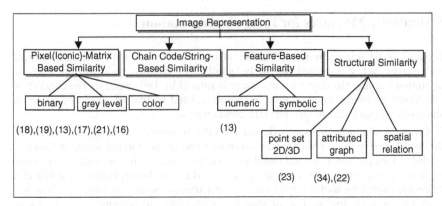

Fig. 3. Image Representation and Similarity Measures

6 A Case-Based Image Interpretation System

We proposed an architecture (Figure 5) that uses CBR on all levels of an image interpretation system in [9]. The system subdivides into a run-time part and a maintenance and learning part. During run-time, the system uses CBR strategies to reason over images while the maintenance and learning part attempt to improve system performance off-line. We are further developing this system based on an application that is called HEp-2 cell image analysis [25] (Figure 4). This kind of cell is used to identify antinuclear autoantibodies (ANA) . HEp-2 cells can recognize over 30 different nuclear and cytoplasmatic patterns, which are given by upwards of 100 different autoantibodies. This exemplifies the difficulty with this application. We have to recognize a large number of different patterns that are neither well described nor fixed in number. Furthermore, we cannot exclude the possibility of new patterns occurring.

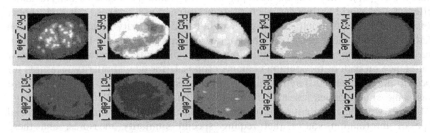

Fig. 4. Some Example Images of HEp-2 Cells

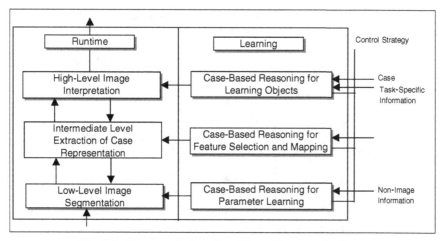

Fig. 5. Architecture of a Case-Based Image Interpretation System

6.1 Image Segmentation

Most CBR image interpretation systems (e.g., [2][6]) select among different image processing chains but they do not control the algorithm itself. This in accordance with most knowledge-based image interpretation systems described in the computer vision literature, which select a processing chain that best fits the current image analysis problem. This approach requires a large enough library of image processing procedures and special image processing knowledge.

However, modern segmentation techniques contain numerous control parameters, which can be adjusted to obtain optimal performance. Parameter selection should be done using a sufficiently large test data set that represents the entire domain well enough to support a general segmentation model. However, obtaining a suitable test set is often impossible, which means that the segmentation model does not fit the data well and must be adjusted to new data. Also, a general model does not guarantee the best segmentation for each image, but instead it guarantees an average best fit over the entire set of images. Finally, differing image quality (e.g., caused by variations in environmental conditions, image devices) requires adapting the segmentation process accordingly. This necessitates equipping the segmentation component with learning capabilities, which can incrementally acquire segmentation model knowledge.

We use a case-based approach for parameter learning, in which formerly processed cases contain their original images, their non-image information (e.g., image acquisition parameters, object characteristics), and their image segmentation parameters. Finding the best segmentation for the current image is done by retrieving similar cases from the case base. Similarity is computed using non-image and image information. The evaluation component will use the most similar case for further processing. If two or more cases have the same highest similarity score then the first of these cases is used. The image segmentation parameter associated with the selected case will then be given to the image segmentation component, which will segment the current image (see Figure 6). Images with similar image characteristics

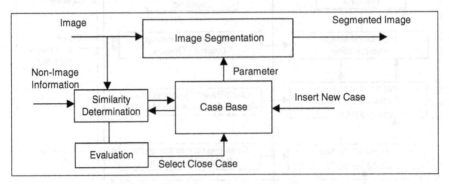

Fig. 6. Case-Based Image Segmentation Component

are assumed to yield similar good segmentation results when the same segmentation parameters were applied to these images. Superior performance for this approach has been demonstrated for CT image segmentation [3]. This approach is sufficiently flexible to be used for other applications and will therefore be used for Hep-2 cell image analysis.

6.2 Feature Selection

Feature selection is concerned with learning the most important (symbolic) features, while feature extraction is responsible for locating those features in the image and finding their values. From the preprocessed, segmented, and labeled 1-D, 2-D, or 3-D image matrix we can extract low-level or primitive image features that are corners, extended edges, textured regions, ribbons, the 2 1/2-D sketch, and semantic clusters of edges and regions. The number of primitive features that can be extracted from the image content is limited (e.g., color, gray level, spatial relations, motion). Understanding the image's content requires mapping those primitives to the desired symbolic features. In current approaches to image interpretation, performance degrades when new objects are encountered that may require the extraction of "shape primitives" not known to the system. To overcome the bottleneck of predetermined and static object features, automatic acquisition of new features using a learning approach is necessary, particularly for flexible image interpretation processes.

Therefore, we introduced for our system a library of feature extractors that can calculate all possible features. In the next step, the system selects from these features the necessary features describing the desired symbolic feature.

6.3 Signal-to-Symbol Mapping and Feature Selection

It is seldom the case that one low-level feature describes the right meaning of one quality of an object. Often a combination of a few low-level features is necessary to express a symbolic feature like *fine speckled*, which is a combination of low-level features such as number of small objects, object sizes, and their gray-level. In these situations, a mapping of (n) low-level features to the symbolic feature is needed. This problem is concerned with the selection of the right features (feature selection), their parameters, and the creation of a mapping function (classification function).

The problem here is to select this subset of features from a large/complex feature set that represent best the symbolic feature by means of classification accuracy or intra/inter class distance, see Fig. 7. To solve this problem, we use an induced decision tree [26]. This approach acts as feature filter for the image interpretation process. Once a new feature is discovered the low-level features are calculated from the image and labeled by the symbolic feature. The prototypes of the other features are taken and applied together with data from the new feature to the induction algorithm. The resulting set of rules are used as a feature selector.

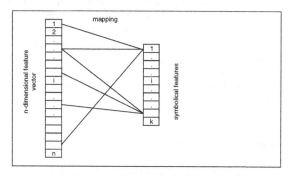

Fig. 7. Low-Level Feature Selection and Mapping to Symbolic Features

6.4 Image Interpretation

The case representation of an image's high-level information can differ among images. This ranges among semantic networks, graphs, and decision trees. Image interpretation problems always have some hidden taxonomy that, if discovered, can be used to help model the problem. An ultrasonic image showing a defect type *crack* might show a crack of a specific subclass such as *crack_under_pressure_x*. To classify this type of crack as a specific subtype might prevent the class *crack* from having large variations, which can help to improve classification results.

To discover these concepts we have found decision tree induction [26] and incremental conceptual clustering [27][36] very suitable. Based on the available cases we used C4.5 to induce a tree for indexing the case base. Our approach differs from 's [1], who also induced a tree for case indexing, in that we will incrementally update the tree structure based on newly discovered cases. Leaves in the tree where no class overlap occurs will remain as terminal leaves, while a leaf with class overlap will be pruned back until a predefined number of samples remain in the group covered by this leaf.

The query case may be clustered through the tree until it reaches a leaf node. If the leaf node is labeled with its class, then that class is assigned to the query. If it not a final node then similarity will be calculated between all cases belonging to this node. We do not divide these cases into clusters but instead incrementally update the index structure when entering a new case.

7 Maintenance & Learning

An important focus of recent CBR research is on how to develop strategies for obtaining compact, competent case-bases, as a way to improve the performance of CBR systems [28]. Although maintenance approaches have not yet been extensively studied for image interpretation systems, they will play an important. Grimnes and Aamodt [2] mention that maintaining the case base in ImageCreek is complex, and that knowledge base maintenance methods are crucial for making the architecture scale. The main problem is handling the different types of knowledge. Jarmulak [1] takes into account case addition, splits the clusters into groups of fixed size, and represents them using a prototype to speed up the matching process. Perner [3][9] takes into account case addition, learning of case classes and prototypes, and higher order constructs. We focus here on topics that, until now, have only been addressed as more specific problems.

7.1 Case Addition and Case Deletion

Case deletion in a pre-determined time window based on failure results [29] might not be appropriate for image interpretation because a failure might mean that, instead of the retrieved case being erroneous, there is some relevant knowledge that we could not describe using features. Also, cases that occur infrequently (i.e., that have not been used recently) should be recognized by the system.

The causes for case deletion or addition might differ from other CBR applications:

1. Since images may be distorted and very noisy it might not be useful to store distorted representations. Determining which representation is distorted is sometimes not easy even if you have seen only a few images, and it is usually necessary to have domain knowledge that must also be built up over time.
2. Imprecise or noisy measurements can be caused by some defects of illumination, the image acquisition device, or the object itself. If the image analysis cannot adapt to these measurements, or the reasoning process cannot handle it, then this might cause failure results. However, if this is a systematic event then it might be worthwhile to store the recent case in the case base.
3. The last fact comes from the real world environment. It is not possible to determine all real world influences a priori.

Thus, developers prefer to incorporate cases into a case base instead of forgetting them. Although case bases can grow very large, instead of forgetting cases, we would rather subdivide the case base into frequently vs. rarely used cases. This requires addressing the issue of how should the addition of cases into one of these two case bases be controlled, as well as their respective reasoning processes.

7.2 Case Acquisition Tool

A CBR system for image classification needs to have some particular features with respect to images. These features result from:
- special requirements of visual knowledge acquisition (image-language problem) and
- the need to transform an image's numerical data into a symbolic description.

The main problem with images and their translation into a language is that the knowledge about an image is usually tacit. To make this knowledge explicit is often hard. Sometimes the meaning of a word does not correspond to the correct meaning of the image. Therefore, it is necessary to support the operator in an efficient way.

Most case-based image interpretation systems do not pay attention to this problem. The only functionality these systems provide is visualization of the image or the processed image. Usually, new case knowledge is obtained via manual acquisition with the expert. This is a time-consuming and sometimes boring process for both the system developer and the expert.

A CBR system for image interpretation should have a special case acquisition tool, such as the one detailed in [30]. By using a questioning strategy and evaluating the answers given by the expert, the expert or operator is forced to specify the right knowledge for image interpretation. The questioning strategy is designed to force an expert to explain what distinguishes one object from another and to specify the right property for the object.

Recently, this problem has received attention for e-commerce applications. Automatic questioning strategies are important for acquiring customer requirements in e-commerce applications [31] because the customer acts alone on the net.

A special case acquisition tool for image segmentation was described in [3]. With the help of this tool the user can control the parameters of the image segmentation algorithm. Simultaneously, he can view the segmented image and, if he is satisfied with the segmentation quality, he can store the parameters of the image segmentation algorithm together with the case description in the case base.

7.3 Competence of Case Bases

An important problem in image interpretation concerns system competence. We follow the definition in [32] and define the competence of a system as the range of target problems the system can solve. As we have already pointed out in Section 3 it is often not clear to the computer vision community what problems the desired algorithm can solve. So we have to find a way to describe the competence of a system. This differs from what is usually understood about this problem in CBR. Competence is described based on statistical properties such as case-base size, density and distribution, or group coverage and group density. But what if some groups overlap? Smyth and McKenna [32] argue that these groups have shared competence and can be linked together in some way. However, we can also view it as having a poor description of the target problem. Based on this description we may retrieve a similar case but its solution application to the query image may be low in quality. By investigating the failure we may learn that we did not consider a property of the environment or maybe we could not specify it because it was not contained in the description of the target problem. Therefore, the system performance decreases. The measures described in [32] and [33] only view competence based on the coverage of the problem space. How do we know that cases in group 1 and group 2 belong to the same target problem group? Proximity in problem space does not imply that they belong to the same problem group; misclassifications can occur because the patterns overlap. We argue that system competence must also account for the misclassification of the target problem based on the problem description.

7.4 Control Strategies and Monitoring System Performance

An important issue in maintaining an image interpretation system involves the controlling and monitoring of system performance. The system is a complex system comprising different processing components (e.g., image analysis, feature extraction and high-level image interpretation). The quality of the results of one component strongly depends on the quality of a preceding component. Several possible strategies exist for improving system performance.

Control without Feedback (Local Optimization)

The simplest approach is to adjust the performance of each component without considering the others. Each component - segmentation, feature extraction and selection, and interpretation - acts alone. No interaction between them is allowed. Image segmentation performance may be determined by subjective evaluation of the segmentation result as done by an expert, by calculating the similarity between the original and segmented images, by interclass distances for feature extraction, or by classification error. This strategy has the advantage that the control of the system is simple. Nevertheless, it cannot optimize system performance because only local optimums can be achieved for each single component.

Control with Feedback (Global Optimization)

If after local optimization the performance of a component could not be improved or is not satisfactory, the control algorithm will lead the learning process to the preceding processing component in an attempt to further improve its performance. This process stops if the first processing component is reached and if no improvement could be established after local optimization.

The logical scheme in Table 1 shows us how control is guided. If the performance of all components is good, no action has to be taken. If the interpretation component's performance is poor, then its performance needs to be optimized. We assume that it is impossible for a preceding component to perform poorly while its successor components perform well.

Table 1. Logical Scheme of Performance Control

Segmentation (S)	Feature Extraction (FE)	Interpretation (I)	Action
Good	Good	Good	No Action
Good	Good	Poor	Optimize I
Good	Poor	Good	Impossible
Good	Poor	Poor	Optimize FE and examine effects on I
Poor	Good	Good	Impossible
Poor	Good	Poor	Impossible
Poor	Poor	Good	Impossible
Poor	Poor	Poor	Optimize S, then re-examine the performance of the other components

8 Conclusion

We surveyed special topics associated with a case-based image interpretation system. From our point of view case-based image interpretation differs in many aspects from other CBR applications that require further investigation. First, more systematic work on special image similarity measures is needed that investigates the measures under different influences that may occur in an image. Next, case representations are required for all the different abstraction levels of an image. Finally, the maintenance and learning strategies must be defined so that they can help to improve the system performance and discover the range of target problems that the system can solve.

We have recently deployed two CBR image interpretation systems. One is installed at the university hospital in Halle; it is used for image segmentation to determine the brain/liquor ratio of the head in a CT image. The second system is used to interpret ultra-sonic SAFT images. In both applications the CBR strategies we used achieved good system performance that satisfied the users and outperformed other systems. The learning and maintenance facilities installed to date have been particularly well-received.

In summary, we believe that investigations of case-based image interpretation systems can reveal special challenges to both the CBR and computer vision communities, and encourage more people to work on this topic.

Acknowledgements. We would like to thank M. Richter for helpful discussions on this topic. Special thanks to David Aha for his kind advice on this topic and for his helpful comments that significantly improved earlier versions of this paper. The implementation of the case-based image segmentation on a parallel computer has been funded by the EU project (HP-ISIS). The CBR system for Hep-2 cells is funded within in the project LernBildZell by the German Ministry of Economy .

References

1. Jarmulak, J. (1998). Case-based classification of ultrasonic B-Scans: Case-base organisation and case retrieval. In B. Smyth & P. Cunningham (Eds.) *Advances in Case-Based Reasoning* (pp. 100-111). Berlin: Springer Verlag.
2. Grimnes, M. & Aamodt, A.(1996). A two layer case-based reasoning architecture for medical image understanding, In I. Smith & B. Faltings (Eds.) *Advances in Case-Based Reasoning* (pp. 164-178). Berlin: Springer Verlag.
3. Perner, P. (1999). An architecture for a CBR image segmentation system. *Journal of Engineering Application in Artificial Intelligence, 12*(6), 749-759.
4. Micarelli, A. Neri, A., & Sansonetti, G. (2000). A case-based approach to image recognition, In E. Blanzieri & L. Portinale (Eds.) *Advances in Case-Based Reasoning* (pp. 443-454). Berlin: Springer Verlag.
5. Venkataraman, S., Krishnan, R., & Rao, K.K. (1993). A rule-rule-case based system for image analysis. In M.M. Richter, S. Wess, K.D. Althoff, & F. Maurer (Eds.) *First European Workshop on Case-Based Reasoning* (Technical Report SFB 314) (pp. 410-415). Kaiserslautern, Germany: University of Kaiserslautern.
6. Ficet-Cauchard, V., Porquet, C., & Revenu, M. (1999). CBR for the reuse of image processing knowledge: A recursive retrieval/adaption strategy. In K.-D. Althoff, R. Bergmann, & L.K. Branting (Eds.) *Case-Based Reasoning Research and Development* (pp. 438-453). Berlin: Springer.
7. Rice, S.V., Nagy, G., & Nartker, T.H. (1999). *Optical character recognition: An illustrated guide to the frontier.* London: Kluwer.
8. Klette, R., Stiehl, H.S., Viergever, M.A., & Vincken, K.L. (2000). *Performance characterization in computer vision.* London: Kluwer
9. Perner, P. (1998). Using CBR learning for the low-level and high-level unit of a image interpretation system. In S. Singh (Ed.) *Advances in Pattern Recognition* (pp. 45-54). Berlin: Springer Verlag.
10. Perner, P. (1999). An architecture for a CBR image segmentation system. In K.-D. Althoff, R. Bergmann, & L. K. Branting (Eds.) *Case-Based Reasoning Research and Development* (pp. 525-535). Berlin: Springer Verlag.
11. Zamperoni, P. & Starovoitov, V. (1995). How dissimilar are two gray-scale images? In *Proceedings of the Seventeenth DAGM Symposium* (pp.448-455). Berlin: Springer Verlag.
12. Santini, S. & Jain, R. (1999). Similarity measures *IEEE Transactions on Pattern Analysis and Machine Intelligence,. 21*(9), 871-883.
13. Horikowa, Y. (1996). Pattern recognition with invariance to similarity transformations based on third-order correlations. In *Proceedings of Internatinal Confernce on Pattern Recognition '96,* IEEE Computer Society Press (pp 200-204).
14. Leitao, F. (1999). A study of string dissimilarity measures in structural clustering. In: S. Singh (Ed.) *Advances in Pattern Recognition* (pp. 385-394). Berlin: Springer Verlag.
15. Mehrotra, G. (1993). Similar shape retrieval using a structural feature index. *Information Systems, 18* (5), 525-537.
16. Cortelazzo, C., Deretta, G., Mian, G.A., & Zamperoni, P. (1996). Normalized weighted Levensthein distance and triangle inequality in the context of similarity discrimination of bilevel images. *Pattern Recognition Letters, 17*(5), 431-437.
17. Crouzil, A., Massipo-Pail, L., & Castan, S. (1996). A new correlation criterion based on gradient fields similarity. In *Proceedings of Internatinal Confernce on Pattern Recognition '96,* IEEE Computer Society Press, (pp. 632-636).
18. Moghadda, Nastar, & Pentland (1996). A Bayesian similarity measure for direct image matching. In *Proceedings of Internatinal Confernce on Pattern Recognition '96,* IEEE Computer Society Press, (pp. 350-358).

19. Moghadda, Jebra, & Pentland (1998). Efficient MAP/ML similarity matching for visual recognition, In *Proceedings of Internatinal Confernce on Pattern Recognition'98*, IEEE Computer Society Press, (pp. 876-881).
20. Wilson, D.L., Baddely, A.J., & Owens R.A. (1997). A new metric for gray-scale image comparison, *International Journal of Computer Vision, 24*(1), 5-19.
21. Messmer, B., & Bunke, H. (2000).   Efficient subgraph isomorphism detection: A decomposition approach. *IEEE Trans. on Knowledge and Data Engineering, 12*(2), 307-323.
22. van der Heiden, A., & Vossepoel, A. A landmark-based approach of shape dissimilarity. In *Proceedings of the International Conference on Pattern Recognition'99*, IEEE Computer Society Press, (pp. 120-124).
23. Perner, P. (1998) Content-based image indexing and retrieval in a image database for technical domains, In H.H.S. Ip & A. Smuelder (Eds.) *Multimedia Information Analysis and Retrieval* (pp. 207-224). Berlin: Springer Verlag.
24. Voss, A. (Ed.) *Similarity Concepts and Retrieval Methods*. Fabel Report No. 13, GMD-1993, ISSN 0942-413.
25. Perner, P. (1998). Image analysis and classification of HEp-2 cells in fluorescent images, *Fourteenth International Conference on Pattern Recognition* (pp. 1677-1679). Brisbane Australia: IEEE Computer Society Press.
26. Perner, P., Zscherpel, U., & Jacobsen, C. (2000). Comparison between neural networks and decision trees application of machine learning in industrial radiographic testing. *Pattern Recognition Letters, 22/1*, 47-54.
27. Perner, P. (1998). Different learning strategies in a case-based reasoning system for image interpretation. In B.Smyth & P. Cunningham (Eds.) *Advances in Case-Based Reasoning* (pp. 251-261). Berlin: Springer Verlag.
28. Leake, D.B., & Wilson, D.C. (2000). Remembering why to remember: performance-guided case-base maintenance, In E. Blanzieri & L. Portinale (Eds.) *Advances in Case-Based Reasoning* (pp. 161-172). Berlin: Springer Verlag.
29. Portinale, L., Torasso, P., & Tavano, P. (1999). Speed-up, quality, and competence in multi-modal reasoning In K.-D. Althoff, R. Bergmann, & L.K. Branting (Eds.) *Case-Based Reasoning Research and Development* (pp. 303-317). Berlin: Springer.
30. Perner, P. (1994), How to use Repertory Grid for Knowledge Acquisition in Image Interpretation. HTWK Leipzig Report Nr. 2.
31. Schmitt, S., Jerusalem, D., & Nett, T. (2000) Representation and execution of questioning strategies for the acquisition of customer requirements, In M.H. Göker (Ed.) *Eighth German Workshop on Case-Based Reasoning*, p.23-37, DaimlerChrysler Research and Technology FT3/KL.
32. Smyth, B., & McKenna, E. (1998). Modeling the competence of case-bases. In B. Smyth & P. Cunningham (Eds.) *Advances in Case-Based Reasoning* (pp. 208-220). Berlin: Springer Verlag.
33. Leake, D.B., & Wilson, D.C. (2000). Remembering why to remember: performance-guided case-base maintenance. In E. Blanzieri & L. Portinale (Eds.) *Advances in Case-Based Reasoning* (pp. 161-172). Berlin: Springer Verlag.
34. Cordella, Goggia, Sansone, Tortorella, & Vento (1999). Graph matching: A fast algorithm and its evaluation. In *Proceedings of the International Conference on Pattern Recognition'99*, IEEE Computer Society Press (pp. 1582-1584).
35. Cheetham, W. & Graf, J. (1997), Case-Based Reasoning in Color Matching, In: Leake, D.B. & Plaza, E. (Eds.) *Case-Based Reasoning Research and Development*, (pp. 1-12).Berlin, Springer Verlag.
36. Bergmann, R. & Wilke, W.(1996), On the Role of Abstraction in Case Based Reasoning, In: Smith, I. & Faltings, B. (Eds.) Advances in Case-Based Reasoning, (pp. 28-43). Berlin, Springer Verlag.

Similarity Assessment for Relational CBR

Eva Armengol and Enric Plaza

IIIA - Artificial Intelligence Research Institute,
CSIC - Spanish Council for Scientific Research,
Campus UAB, 08193 Bellaterra, Catalonia (Spain).
{eva, enric}@iiia.csic.es,

Abstract. Reasoning and learning from cases are based on the concept of similarity often estimated by a distance. This paper presents LAUD, a distance measure that can be used to estimate similarity among relational cases. This measure is adequate for domains where cases are best represented by relations among entities. An experimental evaluation of the accuracy of LAUD is presented for the task of classifying marine sponges.

1 Introduction

Reasoning and learning from cases is based on the concept of similarity. Often similarity is estimated by a distance (a metric) or a pseudo-metric. This approach proceeds by a pairwise similarity comparison of a *problem* with every *precedent case* available in a case base; then one case (or k cases) with greatest (greater) similarity is (are) selected. This process is called the *retrieval* phase in Case-based Reasoning (CBR), and also plays a pivotal role in lazy learning techniques like Instance-based Learning (IBL) and k-nearest neighbor. In classification tasks, the solution class of the *problem* is inferred from the solution class of the precedent case(s) selected.

However, distance-based approaches to case retrieval are mainly used for propositional cases, i.e. cases represented as attribute-value vectors. We are interested in this paper in learning tasks where cases are best represented in a scheme that uses relations among entities. We will call this setting *relational case-based learning*. One option to achieve case-based learning in a relational setting is to adapt the process of pairwise similarity comparison by defining a distance that works upon relational instances. An example of similarity to be applied in relational cases is that used by RIBL ([7]) where the cases are represented as collections of Horn clauses (see related work on section 5).

We are interested in using cases represented in a relational way using *feature terms*[1]. Feature terms are a generalization of first order terms. In this representation entities are typed by *sorts* and relations among entities are represented by *features*. In this paper we introduce LAUD, a new distance measure that we use to estimate the similarity of relational cases represented as *feature terms*.

The structure of this paper is the following. In section 2 we introduce the feature term representation. In section 3 we introduce a new similarity for esti-

D.W. Aha and I. Watson (Eds.): ICCBR 2001, LNAI 2080, pp. 44–58, 2001.

mating the similarity of cases represented as feature terms. In section 4 we provide some results of the application of the similarity to identify marine sponges. Finally, we report some related work and the conclusions and future work.

2   Representation of the Cases

Feature Terms (also called feature structures or ψ-terms) are a generalization of first order terms. The difference between feature terms and first order terms is the following: a first order term, e.g. $f(x, y, g(x, y))$ can be formally described as a tree and a fixed tree-traversal order. In other words, parameters are identified by position. The intuition behind a feature term is that it can be described as a labelled graph i.e. parameters are identified by name. A formal definition of feature terms is the following:

Given a signature $\Sigma = \langle S, \mathcal{F}, \preceq \rangle$ (where S is a set of sort symbols that includes $\perp$; $\mathcal{F}$ is a set of feature symbols; and $\preceq$ is a decidable partial order on S such that $\perp$ is the least element) and a set ϑ of variables, we define *feature terms* as an expression of the form:

$$\psi ::= X : s[f_1 \doteq \Psi_1 \ldots f_n \doteq \Psi_n] \tag{1}$$

where X is a variable in ϑ called the *root* of the feature term, s is a sort in S, the function *root(X)* returns the sort of the root, $f_1 \ldots f_n$ are features in $\mathcal{F}$, $n \geq 0$, and each Ψ_i is a set of feature terms and variables. When $n = 0$ we are defining a variable without features. The set of variables occurring in ψ is noted as ϑ_ψ.

Sorts have an informational order relation $(\preceq)$ among them, where $\psi \preceq \psi'$ means that ψ has less information than ψ' Ñor equivalently that ψ is more general than ψ'. The minimal element $(\perp)$ is called *any* and it represents the minimum information. When a feature has unknown value it is represented as having the value *any*. All other sorts are more specific than *any*. We restrict ourselves to use sort hierarchies with single inheritance (every sort has only one most specific supersort).

Using the $\preceq$ relation, we can introduce the notion of *least upper bound (lub)* commonly used in ILP [9]. The *lub* of two sorts is the most specific sort generalizing both. As we will explain in section 2.1 the notion of *lub* will be used to define the anti-unification of two feature terms. A *path* $\pi(X, f_i)$ is defined as a sequence of features going from the variable X to the feature f_i. The *depth* of a feature f in a feature term ψ with root X is the number of features that compose the path from the root X to f, including f, with no repeated nodes. Given a particular maximum feature depth k, a *leaf feature* of a feature term is a feature f_i such that either 1) the depth of f_i is k or 2) the value of f_i is a term without features. We call *leaves(ψ, k)* the set of leaf features of a term ψ.

Let us illustrate the concepts introduced above with an example. The feature term of Figure 1 represents the description of a marine sponge. The *root* of this feature term is *s364*, the sorts are written in *italic* (for instance, *sponge, external-features, growing,* ...), some features are external-features, ecological-features, megascleres, separable, aspect, etc. Notice that the features ornamentation and

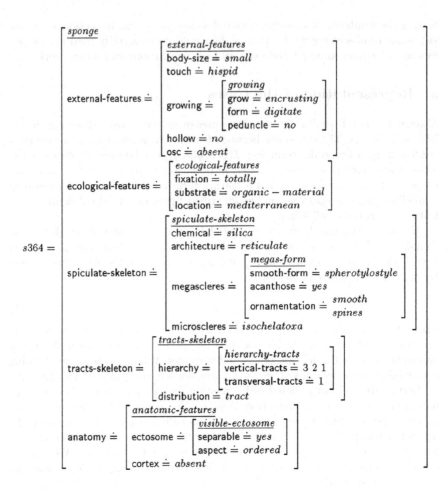

Fig. 1. Representation of a sponge using feature terms.

vertical-tracts are set-valued. The feature leaves of *s364* are the following {body-size, touch, grow, form, peduncle, hollow, osc, fixation, substrate, location, chemical, architecture, smooth-form, acanthose, ornamentation, microscleres, vertical-tracts, transversal-tracts, distribution, separable, aspect, cortex}. An example of path is $\pi(s364, \text{acanthose})$ that represents the path from the root to the leaf feature acanthose, i.e. the sequence of features (spiculate-skeleton, megascleres, acanthose).

As we have explained above, there is an order relation between sorts. Figure 2 shows the sort/subsort hierarchy for the values of the feature **megascleres**. The most general sort allowed for the values of the feature **megascleres** is *megas-form* and there are several subsorts (e.g. *triaena, style, calthrop*, etc). In turn, some of these subsorts (e.g. *triaena, style, tylote*) have subsorts. Let us suppose that

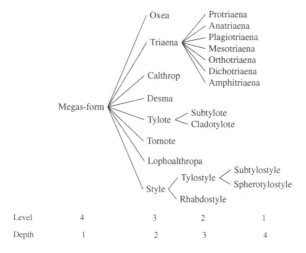

| Level | 4 | 3 | 2 | 1 |
| Depth | 1 | 2 | 3 | 4 |

Fig. 2. Part of the sort hierarchy corresponding to the values of the feature *megascleres*. It is a hierarchy of depth 4. The levels of the hierarchy will be used to determine the sort similarity.

$v_1 = protriaena$, $v_2 = anatriaena$ and $v_3 = tylostyle$. The least upper bound of v_1 and v_2, $lub(v_1, v_2)$, is *triaena* that is the most specific supersort of *protriaena* and *anatriaena* whereas the $lub(v_1, v_3)$ is *megas-form* since *protriaena* and *tylostyle* only share the fact that both are kinds of megascleres.

There are two important concepts concerning the representation using feature terms that will be used later for assessing similarity. One of them is the *subsumption* relation and the other one is the *anti-unification* operation. Both concepts are explained in the next section.

2.1 Subsumption and Anti-Unification of Feature Terms

The semantic interpretation of feature terms brings an ordering relation among feature terms that we call *subsumption*. Intuitively, a feature term ψ subsumes another feature term ψ' ($\psi \sqsubseteq \psi'$) when all information in ψ is also contained in ψ'. More formally, a feature term ψ subsumes other feature term ψ' when the following conditions are satisfied:

1. the sort of $root(\psi')$ is either the same or a subsort of $root(\psi)$,
2. if F_ψ is the set of features of ψ and $F_{\psi'}$ is the set of features of ψ' then $F_\psi \subseteq F_{\psi'}$ and
3. the values of the features in F_ψ and $F_{\psi'}$ satisfy the two conditions above.

Figure 3 shows the feature term *s-encrusting* representing sponges that have an spiculate skeleton and that grow in encrusting form. The sponge *s364* in Figure 1 is subsumed by this description (*s-encrusting* $\sqsubseteq$ *s364*) since all the

$$\text{s-encrusting} = \left[\begin{array}{l} \textit{sponge} \\[2pt] \text{external-features} \doteq \left[\begin{array}{l} \textit{external-features} \\ \text{growing} \doteq \left[\begin{array}{l} \textit{growing} \\ \text{grow} \doteq \textit{encrusting} \end{array} \right] \end{array} \right] \\[2pt] \text{spiculate-skeleton} \doteq \textit{spiculate-skeleton} \end{array} \right]$$

Fig. 3. Description of marine sponges with spiculate skeleton that grow encrusting.

information in *s-encrusting* is also contained in *s364* – although *s364* can have more (or more refined) information.

In [1] can be found a more formal explanation about the feature terms and the subsumption relation.

Feature terms form a partial ordering by means of the subsumption relation. The *anti-unification* is defined over the subsumption lattice as an upper lower bound with respect to the subsumption ($\sqsubseteq$) ordering.

Intuitively, the anti-unification (AU) of two feature terms gives what is common to both (yielding the notion of generalization) and all that is common to both (the most specific generalization). Therefore, the AU of two feature terms F_1 and F_2 produces a feature term D that contains the features that are common to both F_1 and F_2. The values of the features in D have to satisfy the following conditions:

1. If a feature f has the same value v in both examples F_1 and F_2, the value of f in D is also v.
2. In a feature f has value of sort s_1 in F_1 and value of sort s_2 in F_2, the value of f in D is the most specific sort common to s_1 and s_2, i.e. the least upper bound of s_1 and s_2 in the $\preceq$ sort order.
3. otherwise, the examples F_1 and F_2 cannot be anti-unified.

The features of feature terms can be set-valued. Let f_k be a feature that takes the set V_1 as value in F_1 and the set V_2 as value in F_2. Intuitively, the AU of V_1 and V_2 has to produce as result a set W. The cardinality of the set W is $MinCard = min(Card(V_1), Card(V_2))$ and each element in W is the AU of a value of V_1 and a value of V_2 (obtaining the most specific combination).

The elements in W are obtained as follows. First the set $C = \{(x_i, y_j) \mid x_i \in V_1 \text{ and } y_j \in V_2\}$ is obtained. Then the AU of each pair in C is computed. Finally, the set W contains the $MinCard$ most specific compatible combinations of values.

Given the feature terms $w_1 = AU(x, y)$ and $w_2 = AU(x', y')$ we say that w_1 and w_2 are *compatible* when $x \neq x'$ and $y \neq y'$. Otherwise w_1 and w_2 are *incompatible*. Intuitively, two anti-unification feature terms are compatible if they have both been obtained from the AU of different values. This means that the values of the sets to be anti-unified have been used only once.

Table 1. Example of the anti-unification of sets. $V_1 = \{anatriaena, desma\}$ and $V_2 = \{anatriaena, protriaena, calthrop\}$. Columns 1 and 2 form all the possible combinations of the values of V_1 and V_2. The third column shows the anti-unification of each possible combination of the values of V_1 and V_2.

$v \in V_1$	$u \in V_2$	$\mathrm{AU}(v, u)$
anatriaena	anatriaena	anatriaena
anatriaena	protriaena	triaena
anatriaena	calthrop	megas-form
desma	anatriaena	megas-form
desma	protriaena	megas-form
desma	clathrop	megas-form

For instance, let us suppose that we want to obtain the anti-unification of the sets $V_1 = \{anatriaena, desma\}$ and $V_2 = \{anatriaena, protriaena, calthrop\}$. The first step is to build the set C of all the possible combinations of values. In this example $C = \{$ *(anatriaena, anatriaena), (anatriaena, protriaena), (anatriaena, calthrop), (desma, anatriaena), (desma, protriaena), (desma, calthrop)*$\}$. The table 1 shows the anti-unification of each combination using the sort hierarchy in Figure 2. The anti-unification of V_1 and V_2 is a set of cardinality 2 (since $|V_1| = 2$) containing the two most specific compatible values obtained from the anti-unification. In the example, the most specific sort is *anatriaena* obtained from *AU(anatriaena, anatriaena)*. This means that all the combinations using *anatriaena* $\in V_1$ and *anatriaena* $\in V_2$ have to be eliminated because they are incompatibles with *AU(anatriaena, anatriaena)*. In this case all the remaining values have the same anti-unification (i.e. *megas-form*), thus the result is the set $W = AU(V_1, V_2) = \{anatriaena, megas\text{-}form\}$.

3   Similarity between Cases

There are three aspects that we need to define in order to perform CBR on relational cases: 1) to define a *case* from a constellation of relations, 2) to assess the similarity of values, and 3) to define a way to assess similarity between cases. These three aspects are explained in this section.

A *case* is a term defined (in feature terms) by two parameters: a *root sort* and a *depth*. That is to say, assuming a "case base" expressed as a collection of feature terms, a case is a feature term whose root node is subsumed by the *root sort* and whose depth is at most *depth*. An example of case specification is $case[\text{root-sort} \doteq sponge, \text{depth} \doteq 4]$ in the marine sponges domain (see §4).

Section 3.1 explains how to estimate the similarity between the values of a feature and section 3.2 how to estimate the similarity among cases.

3.1   Similarity between Values

For the purpose of assessing the similarity of values we distinguish between features having numerical values and features having symbolic values. For those features with numerical values we use the usual measure. For the features having simbolic values we estimate the similarity using a new distance measure called LAUD.

The similarity between cases is estimated taking into account the similarity of the features describing the cases. Let c_1 and c_2 be two cases represented as feature terms. Given a feature f taking value v_1 in c_1 and value v_2 in c_2, the similarity of the values is estimated depending of whether the values are either symbolic or numeric.

When the value of f is numerical of a range $[a, b]$ the similarity of v_1 and v_2 is computed, as usual, by means of the following expression:

$$sim(v_1, v_2) = 1 - \frac{\mid v_1 - v_2 \mid}{b - a} \tag{2}$$

When the value of f is symbolic, the similarity of two feature values v_1 and v_2 is computed using the hierarchy of the sorts S. The idea is that the similarity between two values depends on the level of the hierarchy where their *lub* is situated with respect to the whole hierarchy: the more general *lub(v_1, v_2)* the greater is the distance between v_1 and v_2.

Formally, let $S_f \in S$ be the most general sort that can take the values of a feature f. We consider S_f as the root of a subsort hierarchy, therefore the *depth* of S_f is 1. Given a subsort s of S_f (i.e. $s \preceq S_f$) we define the *level* of s as follows: $level(s) = M - depth(s)$, where M is the maximum depth of the hierarchy of root S_f.

For instance, in the part of the sort hierarchy in Figure 2 the *lub(anatriaena, orthotriaena) = triaena* is at level 3, whereas *lub(anatriaena, desma) = megasform* is at level 4. This means that *orthotriaena* is more similar to *anatriaena* than *desma*.

Thus, the similarity of two symbolic values will be estimated using the following expression:

$$sim(v_1, v_2) = \begin{cases} 1 & \text{if } v_1 = v_2 \\ 1 - \frac{1}{M}level(lub(v_1, v_2)) & \text{otherwise} \end{cases} \tag{3}$$

Proposition 1. *Let x be a feature term of sort s_1 and y a feature term of sort s_2. We consider a sort hierarchy of root S_f and maximum depth M such that $S_f \preceq s_1$ and $S_f \preceq s_2$ (i.e. s_1 and s_2 are subsorts of S_f by the $\preceq$ relation). In that situation the following measure is a distance*

$$\delta(x, y) = \begin{cases} 0 & \text{if } x = y \\ \frac{1}{M}level(lub(x, y)) & \text{otherwise} \end{cases} \tag{4}$$

Proof. A measure is a distance if the following three conditions are satisfied:

1. $0 \leq dist(x, x)$
2. $dist(x, y) = dist(y, x)$
3. $dist(x, y) \leq dist(x, z) + dist(z, y)$

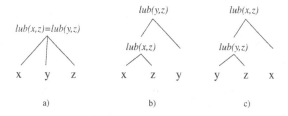

Fig. 4. Different relations that can occur between the sorts of three objects.

We will proof that the measure $\delta(x, y)$ satisfies the three conditions above.

1. $\delta(x, x) = 0$ according to the definition

2. The symmetry of $\delta(x, y)$ is proved using the symmetry of lub's
   $\delta(x, y) = \frac{1}{M} level(lub(x, y)) = \frac{1}{M} level(lub(y, x)) = \delta(y, x)$

3. To proof the triangle inequality we need to distinguish three cases, corresponding to the situations illustrated in Figure 4 (remember that S is restricted to single inheritance). Let z be a feature term of sort s_3.

   – a) $lub(x, z) = lub(z, y)$
      we can assure (Figure 4a) that also $lub(x, y) = lub(x, z)$, therefore
      $\frac{1}{M} level(lub(x, y)) = \frac{1}{M} level(lub(x, z))$, and thus
      $$\delta(x, y) = \delta(x, z) \leq \delta(x, z) + \delta(z, y)$$

   – b) $lub(x, z) \preceq lub(z, y)$
      we can assure (Figure 4b) that $lub(x, y) = lub(z, y)$ therefore
      $\frac{1}{M} level(lub(x, y)) = \frac{1}{M} level(lub(z, y))$, and thus
      $$\delta(x, y) = \delta(z, y) \leq \delta(x, z) + \delta(z, y)$$

   – c) $lub(x, z) \succeq lub(z, y)$
      we can assure (Figure 4c) that $lub(x, y) = lub(x, z)$ therefore
      $\frac{1}{M} level(lub(x, y)) = \frac{1}{M} level(lub(x, z))$, and thus
      $$\delta(x, y) = \delta(x, z) \leq \delta(x, z) + \delta(z, y)$$

Therefore $\delta(x, y)$ satisfies the three properties of distance. □

Let us now consider how to estimate the feature similarity when two cases have a set-valued feature f, i.e. when $c_i.f = V_i$ and $c_j.f = V_j$ for some sets $V_i = \{x_1 \ldots x_n\}$ and $V_j = \{y_1 \ldots y_m\}$. In this situation we compute $n \times m$ similarities between the terms in V_i and the terms in V_j, i.e for all possible pairs $P_{ij} = \{(x_h, y_k)|x_h \in V_i \wedge y_k \in V_j\}$ we compute the similarity score using the previously defined feature similarity functions. Clearly, there will be $min(n, m)$ mappings that we can establish. Moreover, since we are interested in minimizing distance, we want those pairs of P_{ij} that have lesser distances and, taken together, they have the smaller aggregate distance.

For the case when V_i and V_j are numeric we compute the similarities of all pairs in P_{ij} obtaining the set $\mathcal{S}(P_{ij})$ as follows:

$$\mathcal{S}(P_{ij}) = \{\langle(x_h, y_k), \delta(x_j, y_k)\rangle | x_h \in V_i \wedge y_k \in V_j\}$$

Let us call the set of possible pairs $S_0 = P_{ij}$. We take the pair $p_1 = (x, y) \in S_0$ with maximum similarity in $\mathcal{S}(P_{ij})$. Now, this pair and all the pairs incompatible with it have to be removed from the set S_0, i.e. we build the set $S_1 = S_0 - P_1$ where $P_1 = \{(x', y') \in S_0 | x' = x \vee y' = y\}$. Next, we take the pair p_2 from the remaining pairs in S_1 with maximum similarity in $\mathcal{S}(P_{ij})$. We proceed this way until we find all pairs $P_{min} = \{p_1 \ldots p_{min(n,m)}\}$ that together have a maximum value of similarity. Then the feature similarity is the following aggregate:

$$sim(V_1, V_2) = \frac{1}{min(n, m)} \sum_{(x_h, y_k) \in P_{min}} sim(x_h, y_k)$$

For the case when sets V_i and V_j have symbolic values the idea is also the same: finding those pairs whose similarity is higher. As we have seen, for a pair (x_j, y_k) of symbolic values the more specific their $lub(x_j, y_k)$ the higher is their similarity. Therefore we want to find the collection of pairs $\{p_1 \ldots p_{min(n,m)}\}$ whose $lubs$ are more specific. But this is precisely the definition of anti-unification shown in §2.1. Therefore the anti-unification of the values $V_i = \{x_1 \ldots x_n\}$ and $V_j = \{y_1 \ldots y_m\}$ provides the pairs that have the highest similarity.

Let $W = \{w_1 \ldots w_{min(n,m)}\}$ be the anti-unification of V_i and V_j. Each $w_l \in W$ is the result of the anti-unification of a pair (x_h, y_k) such that $x_h \in V_1$ and $y_k \in V_2$. Let us call P_W the set of those pairs:

$$P_W = \{(x_h, y_k) | x_h \in V_1 \wedge y_k \in V_2 \wedge AU(x_h, y_k) \in W\}$$

Then the aggregate similarity for sets V_1 and V_2 is as follows:

$$sim(V_1, V_2) = \frac{1}{min(n, m)} \sum_{(x_j, y_k) \in P_W} sim(x_j, y_k) \tag{5}$$

3.2 Aggregated Similarity

The similarity among cases has to be computed as an aggregation of the similarities of the feature values. In propositional cases global similarity $S(c_1, c_2)$ is usually a mean aggregation function Φ from feature-wise similarities over a fixed collection of attributes $F = (f_1, \ldots, f_m)$, i.e.

$$S(c_1, c_2) = \Phi(sim(c_1.f_1, c_2.f_1), \ldots, sim(c_1.f_m, c_2.f_m))$$

where $sim(c_1.f_j, c_2.f_j)$ is the feature similarity for the values of f_j. However, in practice cases can be incomplete, so pseudo-similaritys have to be included in that global similarity assessment, e.g. enforcing $sim(c_1.f_j, c_2.f_j) = 0$ whenever one of the two cases has a missing value in f_j.

In our experiments with relational case-based learning we have focused on exploiting the information present in the object-centered formalisms, namely *sorts* and *features*. Sorts express domain knowledge that clusters domain objects into meaningful classes; in fact, the estimation of the similarity of symbolic values using the sort hierarchy (see equation 3) captures this domain information. Information about features can be exploited because we do not (and can not) assume, as in propositional cases, that a case should have all features $F = (f_1, \ldots, f_m)$.

Using feature terms, the features with unknown value are represented by the value *any* for that features. Because *any* is the minimal element on the $\preceq$ relation, when a case has value *any* in a feature f we can think of this case as not having the feature f. For instance, the sponge *s364* in Figure 1 has two skeletons: one spiculate skeleton and one skeleton with tracts (feature **tracts-skeleton**) whereas the sponge *s252* in Figure 5 has only one spiculate skeleton and thus the feature **tracts-skeleton** does not occur in *s252*.

The similarity between two cases c_1 and c_2 is estimated taking into account both the information that they share and the information that they do not share. The *shared features* is the set of features occurring in both cases and it is obtained using the anti-unification operation (section 2.1). The *relevant features*, are those features that occurs at least in one of the two cases (notice that the relevant information also includes the shared features). The global similarity of two cases is computed by estimating the similarity of the shared features and then normalizing this result by the cardinality of the set of relevant features.

A feature term ψ can be viewed as the set $\Pi(\psi, k) = \{\pi(\psi, f_i) \mid f_i \in leaves(\psi, k)\}$, i.e. the set of paths from the root to the leaves with depth k. The anti-unification of two cases $c = AU(c_1, c_2)$ captures the common structure on these two cases. Moreover, since c is a feature term it can also be viewed as a set of paths $\Pi(c, k)$ that collects that which is common to c_1 and c_2. We assess the similarity of two cases using the feature-wise similarity measure defined in section 3.1 on the set of leaves of $c = AU(c_1, c_2)$; let $\mathcal{A}(c_1, c_2)$ denote that set of leaves. Assessing the similarity of the leaves of the paths in $\Pi(c, k)$ we are implicitly assessing the common structure of two cases represented by $\Pi(c, k)$.

Moreover, we want to take into account those features not shared by two cases. For this purpose we define the set of relevant leaves as follows $\mathcal{L}(c_1, c_2) = \{f_j \mid f_j \in leaves(c_1, k) \lor f_j \in leaves(c_2, k)\}$, i.e. the ratio $\mid \mathcal{A}(c_1, c_2) \mid / \mid \mathcal{L}(c_1, c_2) \mid$ estimates how great is the shared structure between two cases. Therefore we will use $\mathcal{L}(c_1, c_2)$ to normalize the aggregation of feature-wise similarities, as follows:

$$S(c_1, c_2) = \frac{\sum_{f_j \in \mathcal{A}(c_1, c_2)} sim(\pi(c_1, f_j), \pi(c_2, f_j))}{\mid \mathcal{L}(c_1, c_2) \mid} \qquad (6)$$

where $sim(\pi(c_1, f_j), \pi(c_2, f_j))$ is the feature-wise similarity measure applied to the values of f_j in the cases c_1 and c_2. Notice that the similarity is computed over the values in c_1 and c_2 defined by the paths found in the anti-unification.

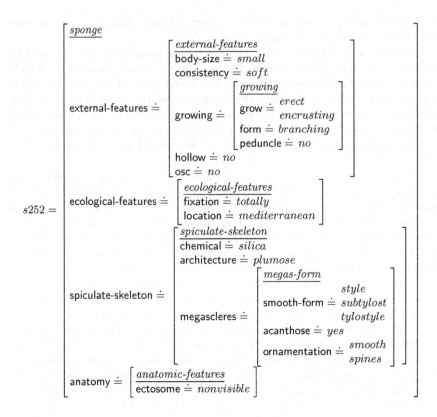

Fig. 5. Representation of a sponge using feature terms.

3.3 Example

Let us suppose that the goal is to estimate the similarity of the sponges *s364* and *s252* (Figures 1 and 5 respectively). The first step is to determine the set of leaf features of each sponge, and then the set $\mathcal{A}$ of leaf features that are common to both sponges. In our examples the set $\mathcal{A}$ is the following:

$\mathcal{A}$ = {(external-features body-size) (external-features growing grow)
    (external-features growing form) (external-features growing peduncle)
    (external-features hollow) (external-features osc)
    (ecological-features fixation) (ecological-features location)
    (spiculate-skeleton chemical) (spiculate-skeleton architecture)
    (anatomy ectosome) (spiculate-skeleton megascleres smooth-form)
    (spiculate-skeleton megascleres acanthose)
    (spiculate-skeleton megascleres ornamentation) }

The second step is to evaluate the similarity of the values that the features in $\mathcal{A}$ take in the current sponges. This similarity is the following:

- (external-features body-size). Both sponges have the same symbolic value (*small*) in this feature, therefore the similarity is 1. The following features also have similarity 1: (external-features growing peduncle), (external-features hollow), (external-features osc), (ecological-features fixation), (ecological-features location), and (spiculate-skeleton chemical).

- (external-features growing grow). The sponge *s252* has as value the set $V_1 = \{erect\ encrusting\}$ and the sponge *s364* has as value the set $V_2 = \{encrusting\}$. The similarity for this feature is estimated according to Equation 5. Therefore the first step is to determine the elements of V_1 and V_2 providing the anti-unification of both sets and then to estimate the similarity of the values belonging to this anti-unification.
  The anti-unification is $AU(V_1, V_2) = \{encrusting\}$ that has been obtained from the anti-unification of *encrusting* $\in V_1$ and *encrusting* $\in V_2$. Since both values are the same $sim(encrusting, encrusting) = 1$, and since the minimum cardinality is 1, the result following Equation 5 is 1.

- (external-features growing form). The sponge *s252* has as value $v_1 = branching$ and the sponge *s364* has as value $v_2 = digitate$. Both values are symbolic, therefore according to Equation 3 *lub(branching, digitate) = form*. Since *form* is the root of the sort hierarchy for the legal values of the feature form, the similarity on this feature is zero. The features (spiculate-skeleton architecture), and (anatomy ectosome) have also similarity zero.

- (spiculate-skeleton megascleres smooth-form). This feature takes as value the set $V_1 = \{style,\ subtylostyle,\ tylostyle\}$ in the sponge *s252* and the set $V_2 = \{spherotylostyle\}$ in the sponge *s364*. Following the Equation 5 we compute the anti-unification $AU(V_1, V_2) = tylostyle$. Since this value has been obtained from *subtylostyle* $\in V_1$ and from *spherotylostyle* $\in V_2$ following Equation 5 we have to compute

$$sim(subtylostyle, spherotylostyle) =$$
$$1 - \tfrac{1}{M} level(lub(subtylostyle, spherotylostyle)) = \tfrac{2}{4} = 0.5$$

where *lub(subtylostyle, spherotylostyle) = tylostyle*, *level(tylostyle) = 2*, and *M = 4* (see Figure 2).

Finally, the similarity of both cases is estimated as the sum of the similarities computed above normalized by the cardinality of the set of features that are in some of the both sponges.

$$S(s252, s364) = \frac{\sum_{f_j \in \mathcal{A}} sim(\pi(s252, f_j), \pi(s364, f_j))}{|\ \mathcal{L}(s252, s364)\ |} = \frac{11}{24} = 0.458$$

4   Experiments

In this section we describe some experiments that use the similarity to identify the order of marine sponges. Marine sponges are relatively little studied and

order	N	correct	incorrect	%accuracy
astrophorida	95	88	7	92.63
hadromerida	117	108	9	92.30
poecilosclerida	95	86	9	90.53
TOTAL	307	282	25	91.86

Fig. 6. Results of the application of the similarity to classify marine sponges.

most of the existing species are not yet fully described. Main problems in the identification are due to the morphological plasticity of the species, to the incomplete knowledge of many of their biological and cytological features and to the frequent description of new taxa. Moreover, there is no agreement on the species delimitation since characterization of taxa is unclear.

We used a case base containing 307 marine sponges belonging to three orders of the *demospongiae* class: *astrophorida, hadromerida* or *poecilosclerida*. The sponges are represented using feature terms as in Figures 1 and 5. Each experiment has been performed using the leave-one-out method. Thus, in one experiment we take out one sponge *sp* and then we compute the similarity of *sp* with each one of the remaining 306 sponges. Finally, *sp* is classified as belonging to the same order than the sponge estimated as more similar.

The Figure 6 shows the results of these experiments, detailing the accuracy, and the number of correct and incorrect answers for each order. Thus, there are 95 sponges in the case-base belonging to the order *astrophorida*. For 88 of these sponges the similarity finds that the most similar sponge is an *astrophorida*, i.e. they are correctly classified. Similarly, 108 of the 117 sponges of the order *hadromerida* and 86 of the 95 sponges of order *poecilosclerida* are correctly classified. Summarizing, from the 307 sponges of the case-base, 282 of them are correctly classified with respect the order where they belong. This represents an accuracy of 91.86%.

5   Related Work

Most of work in similarity assessment has been done in propositional cases but there is an active research field focusing in similarity between relational cases [5,6,4,11,3]. These approaches use the notion of "structural similarity" and use techniques of subtree-isomorphism or subgraph isomorphism to detect this similarity [6].

Two proposals for similarity measure for object-based representations are [4] and [3]. They both distinguish between inter-class and intra-class similarity. This is because they separate similarity among instances of the same class from similarity among classes for instances of different classes. However, feature terms unify this distinction using the sort hierarchy. Inter-class similarity in [3] requires the assignement of "similarity degrees" to the class hierarchy while LAUD defines a distance over the sort hierarchy. Both LAUD and [4] support set-valued attributes while [3] does not. LAUD defines precisely the idea of "shared structure" using anti-unification, while [3] requires that every instance to have all defined attributes and [4] uses a similarity measure that is expressed as a system of equations to be solved iteratively.

RIBL [7] is a first-order instance-based learner that applies IBL to an instance space composed of first-order descriptions. The similarity measures used in RIBL are applied to function-free cases. A recent improvement of RIBL [8] allows the use of lists and terms in the representation of the cases, therefore new similarity measures have to be defined in order to work with them. In particular, authors propose the use of edit distances for computing the distances between terms and lists. There are several differences between RIBL and LAUD due to the differences between Horn clauses and feature terms. First, RIBL assumes the cases and the problem are described by a fixed set of attributes, while feature terms do not make this assumption. For this reason LAUD uses anti-unification in order to determine the common features of two cases. Second, LAUD use the sort hierarchy to compute the similarity between symbolic values while RIBL just checks if two symbolic values are equal or not.

Related but different approaches are those in [11] and [2] where the cases are represented using feature terms and the similarity is estimated using the notion of "similarity term". [11] proposes to build the similarity term using the anti-unification (i.e. the most specific generalization of two cases) and then use an entropy measure [10] to assess the similarity term that is better. In [2] we consider that the "similarity term" is a feature term containing the more relevant features allowing the classification of a new case. The relevant features of the cases are determined using a heuristic.

6   Conclusions

In this paper we introduced LAUD, a new distance measure to estimate the similarity of relational cases. In particular, LAUD uses cases represented as feature terms. The representation using feature terms allows on one hand to represent partial information, i.e. the features with unknown values do not appear in the representation of the cases. This means that two cases may be described by different features. On the other hand, the values of the features are sorted and there is an informational order relation ($\preceq$) between sorts. Using the $\preceq$ relation we can define the notion of *least upper bound* and then the anti-unification of two feature terms.

The measure we propose estimates the similarity of relational cases as an aggregation of the similarities of the features that are common to both cases. These common features are obtained using the anti-unification concept. The similarity among features is estimated as usual when they take numerical values. Nevertheless, when the value of a feature is symbolic the similarity is estimated using the part of the sort hierarchy containing the legal values for that feature.

An interesting fact is that our extension of similarity assessment to relational cases is that LAUD is not much more computationally intensive than a distance-based assessment for propositional cases. First, LAUD focuses on the leaf features, which is a manageable number of elements. Second, when a leaf feature has a single value (numerical or symbolic) the computation of the distance is straightforward. Only when a leaf feature is set-valued the computation of similarity is somewhat more expensive: the anti-unification operator has to consider the combinations of pairs of values. However, this computation is not so expensive in practice and the cost is worthwhile the added power of relational cases for those CBR applications that require them.

Acknowledgements. This work has been supported by Project IBROW (IST-1999-19005). The authors thank Dr. Marta Domingo and Dr. Toni Bermudez for their assistance in collecting the case base of marine sponges.

References

[1] E. Armengol and E. Plaza. Bottom-up induction of feature terms. *Machine Learning Journal*, 41(1):259–294, 2000.

[2] E. Armengol and E. Plaza. Individual prognosis of diabetes long-term risks: A CBR approach. *Methods of Information in Medicine*, page to appear, 2001.

[3] R. Bergmann and A. Stahl. Similarity measures for object-oriented case representations. In *Proc. European Workshop on Case-Based Reasoning, EWCBR-98*, Lecture Notes in Artificial Intelligence, pages 8–13. Springer Verlag, 1998.

[4] G. Bisson. Why and how to define a similarity measure for object based representation systems, 1995.

[5] K Börner. Structural similarity as a guidance in case-based design. In *Topics in Case-Based Reasoning: EWCBR'94*, pages 197–208, 1994.

[6] H Bunke and B T Messmer. Similarity measures for structured representations. In *Topics in Case-Based Reasoning: EWCBR'94*, pages 106–118, 1994.

[7] W. Emde and D. Wettschereck. Relational instance based learning. In Lorenza Saitta, editor, *Machine Learning - Proceedings 13th International Conference on Machine Learning*, pages 122 – 130. Morgan Kaufmann Publishers, 1996.

[8] T. Horváth, S. Wrobel, and U. Bohnebeck. Relational instance-based learning with lists and terms. *Machine Learning Journal*, 43(1):53–80, 2001.

[9] Stephen Muggleton and Luc De Raedt. Inductive logic programming: Theory and methods. *Journal of Logic Programming*, 19–20:629–679, 1994.

[10] E. Plaza, R. López de Mántaras, and E. Armengol. On the importance of similitude: An entropy-based assessment. In I. Smith and B. Saltings, editors, *Advances in Case-based reasoning*, number 1168 in Lecture Notes in Artificial Intelligence, pages 324–338. Springer-Verlag, 1996.

[11] Enric Plaza. Cases as terms: A feature term approach to the structured representation of cases. In M. Veloso and A. Aamodt, editors, *Case-Based Reasoning, ICCBR-95*, number 1010 in Lecture Notes in Artificial Intelligence, pages 265–276. Springer-Verlag, 1995.

Acquiring Customer Preferences from Return-Set Selections

L. Karl Branting

LiveWire Logic, Inc.
5500 McNeely Drive, Suite 102
Raleigh, NC 27612
branting@livewirelogic.com

Abstract. This paper describes LCW, a procedure for learning customer preferences by observing customers' selections from return sets. An empirical evaluation on simulated customer behavior indicated that an uninformed hypothesis about customer weights leads to low ranking accuracy unless customers place some importance on almost all features or the total number of features is quite small. In contrast, LCW's estimate of the mean preferences of a customer population improved as the number of customers increased, even for larger numbers of features of widely differing importance. This improvement in the estimate of mean customer preferences led to improved prediction of individual customer's rankings, irrespective of the extent of variation among customers and whether a single or multiple retrievals were permitted. The experimental results suggest that the return set that optimizes benefit may be smaller for customer populations with little variation than for customer populations with wide variation.

1 Introduction

A growing proportion of sales transactions are conducted over the Internet. In business-to-customer sales, an e-commerce site must perform the *inventory selection task*, which consists of eliciting each customer's requirements, finding the item (product or service) from the business's inventory that most nearly satisfies those requirements, presenting the item to the customer, and prompting the customer to either consummate the sale or refine the requirements. An item in the inventory that satisfies the customer's requirements at least as well as any other item in the inventory is *optimal* with respect to the inventory and requirements.

Case-based reasoning (CBR) is an increasingly popular paradigm for the inventory selection task [Wil99,WLW98,SRB99]. In contrast to standard database retrieval, which is restricted to exact matches, retrieval in CBR systems can involve partial matches ordered by the degree to which each product satisfies the customer's requirements. This permits an optimal item to be presented to the customer even when nothing in the inventory completely satisfies the customer's requirements.

D.W. Aha and I. Watson (Eds.): ICCBR 2001, LNAI 2080, pp. 59–73, 2001.

While discrimination nets are sometimes used in CBR for case retrieval (e.g., [Kol84]), the most common technique in e-commerce applications of CBR is nearest-neighbor retrieval [WA95]. In this approach, inventory items are ordered by the similarity between customers' requirements and inventory items under a metric defined on a set of numeric or symbolic features that the requirements share with the inventory items.

The most common such metric is scaled Euclidean distance, e.g., for cases $c1$ and $c2$:

$$dist(c1, c2) = \sqrt{\sum_{f=1}^{n} w_f \times d(c1_f, c2_f)^2}$$

where $c1_f$ and $c2_f$ are the values of feature f for cases $c1$ and $c2$, w_f is the weight assigned to feature f, and $d(c1_f, c2_f)$ equals $c1_f - c2_f$ if feature f is numeric, 1 if f is symbolic and $c1_f = c2_f$, and 0 otherwise.

The customer is typically presented with a *return set* consisting of the rs most similar items. The customer can select any of the items in the return set or perform another retrieval with modified requirements.

Two evaluation criteria for the product selection task can be distinguished:

- **Satisfaction**, the degree to which the customer's requirements are satisfied by the best inventory item presented to the customer. Satisfaction is maximized when the return set contains an optimal item. Satisfaction is related to the recall criterion used in Information Retrieval (IR) research in that it is a function of the case quality, but (as in [BHK+97]) differs in that it assigns no penalty for unretrieved cases.
- **Cognitive load** [SCTC90] imposed on the customer to find the best inventory item that was presented. Cognitive load is a function both of the number of actions performed by the customer and the number of alternatives from which each action is selected. This criterion is related to the precision criterion used in IR research, in that low precision increases the number of alternatives from which a selection must be made.

Benefit (discussed in greater detail below) is a function of both satisfaction and cognitive load, reflecting the relative importance of both components.

In principle, there is a trade-off between satisfaction and cognitive load: satisfaction can be maximized at the expense of cognitive load by presenting the customer with all inventory items; similarly, cognitive load can be maximized at the cost of satisfaction by presenting a single choice. In practice, however, e-commerce customers tolerate only a very low cognitive load. Faced with repeated retrievals or lengthy lists of items for perusal, customers quickly abandon the site and try somewhere else [Nie00]. Thus, cognitive load must be kept low, which requires minimizing (1) the number of retrievals that the customer must perform to find an optimal item, (2) the size of each return set, and (3) the rank of the best item within each return set. Of these, the first is the most important, since each retrieval entails a network delay and an increase by the return-set size in the number of alternatives that the customer must consider.

The number of retrievals can be minimized by making the probability that an optimal item is in the initial return set as high as possible. For a given return-set size, this probability depends on how accurately the weights used in the similarity metric model the customer's preferences, i.e., the relative importance the customer attaches to the case features. If the customer's preferences can be modeled by a scaled Euclidean distance metric and the system has exact values for the feature weights, then the inventory items can be ranked perfectly. Under these circumstances, even a single-item return set can be guaranteed to contain the optimal item. In practice, however, uncertainty about feature weights means that a larger return set—and therefore larger cognitive load—is required to make it probable that an optimal item is presented.

Various approaches have been used for acquiring individual preferences. One approach is to interview the user to determine pairwise relative feature importance [KR93,Bra99]. Less intrusive approaches, such as collaborative filtering, attempt to infer preferences from *a priori* knowledge, such as group membership [GNOT92]. A third approach strives to form user models based on observations of user decisions, either in response to system suggestions ("candidate/revision" or "learn-on-failure" [BB97,Mae94]) or through passive observations [DBM+92].

This work explores the feasibility of learning customer preferences by observing customers' selections from return sets. This approach is appropriate for customer populations that share preferences to some extent. In such customer populations, two sources of uncertainty concerning an individual customer's preferences can be distinguished: uncertainty about the mean preferences of the entire customer population; and uncertainty about the individual's deviation from the population's mean on each feature. When individual variations are limited, mean customer preferences constitute a good model of most customers. Under these circumstances, a small return set is likely to contain an optimal item. The greater the variation, the larger the return set required to ensure a high-satisfaction case, and the higher the resultant cognitive load.

Mean customer preferences can be determined from a representative collection of individual customer's preferences. Individual customers' feature weights can, in turn, be estimated by observing individual return-set selections in the following manner: whenever the customer selects an item other than the item highest ranked using the current feature weights, the system adjusts the weights to make the selected item rank first. If the customer makes repeated retrievals, the weights can be repeatedly adjusted. The mean customer preferences can be estimated from the mean of the observed individual preferences.

This paper proposes a procedure for adjusting feature weights based on return-set selections and demonstrates the performance of the algorithm through experiments performed on simulated data. The experiments are intended to address the following questions:

– What is the probability of misranking an inventory item as a function of feature-weight error? Stated differently, for a given feature weight error, how large must the return set be to guarantee an acceptable probability that it will contain an optimal item?

- For a given customer variance and return-set size, how many customers must be seen to achieve an acceptable probability that the return set will contain an optimal item?
- How much difference is there in the learning rate when each customer performs only a single retrieval as opposed to repeated retrievals?
- How can the best trade-off between satisfaction and cognitive load be achieved?

In the experiments described below, several simplifying assumptions are made concerning the nature of the inventory-selection task. The inventory is assumed to consist of I items, each represented by n features with real values uniformly distributed across the interval $[0..1]$. The mean feature weights of the entire customer population are represented by an n-dimensional feature vector GW (meaning *global weights*), with all features weights normalized to the $[0..1]$ interval. The preferences of the ith customer are represented by a normalized n-dimensional feature vector, c_i. Each customer's feature weights are intended to represent the relative importance of each feature to that customer. The weights of each customers' preferences are normally distributed around the mean with some standard deviation σ[1].

The next section describes an experiment designed to gauge the importance of feature-weight accuracy. Section 3 describes LCW, a procedure for learning global weights from individual return-set selections. Section 4 then presents an experimental evaluation designed to determine the return-set size and minimum number of customers needed to achieve an acceptable probability that the return set will contain an optimal item for different values of σ.

2   The Importance of Feature-Weight Accuracy

This section investigates the degree of benefit that can be expected when a system lacks any knowledge of customers' preferences, that is, when the system does not perform any learning. An important variable in determining the importance of customer feature-weight accuracy is the actual distribution of each customer's feature weights. Intuitively, one would expect a minority of features to be of high importance, and a larger number of features to be less important (e.g., in car purchasing price may be very important, whereas seat-cover material is less important, though not inconsequential).

This distribution of feature importances, and four alternatives, can be represented by the following n-dimensional weight vectors:

1. *Two-Level.* For each feature there is 25 per cent probability that the feature weight is in the interval $[0.75..1.0]$ and a 75 per cent probability that it is in the interval $[0.0..0.25]$.

---

[1] The distribution is truncated to fit within the $[0..1]$ interval, e.g., for global weight 0.8, no values above 1.0 are permitted, to restrict values to the $[0..1]$ interval, and no values below 0.6 are permitted, so that the samples are symmetrical around the global weight.

2. *Exponential.* For $0 <= i < n$, exactly one feature has weight $\sqrt{0.75 * \frac{1}{2^i}}$.
3. *Linear.* For $0 <= i <= n - 1$, exactly one feature has weight $1 - \frac{1+i}{1+n}$.
4. *Random.* Feature weights are uniformly distributed on the $[0..1]$ interval.
5. *Equal.* All features are weighted equally.

The Two-Level distribution is intended to mimic human preferences by making a minority of features quite important and the majority of features less important, but not completely irrelevant. However, the assumption that the Two-Level distribution is the most accurate model is mere surmise that must be tested in experiments involving human subjects. It seems possible that the distribution of feature importances is context-dependent, varies among individuals, or depends on other features not yet identified. Moreover, the division of 25% more important, 75% less important, is arbitrary.

The four alternative feature weight distributions are included because of the uncertainty about the nature of human preferences. The Exponential distribution corresponds to having one very important feature, several moderately important features, and the remaining features of little importance. Linear and Random, by contrast, correspond to situations in which there is no clear division between important and unimportant features. Finally, Equal distribution corresponds to the assumption that all weights are equally important.

In each round of this experiment, an inventory of 100 items was created, together with a weight vector of one of the five distribution types, representing the actual preferences of a simulated customer, and a weight vector of random values, the *hypothesized weights*, representing an uninformed model of the customer. Finally, an additional item was created, representing the features requested by customer. This item is termed the *requirements* vector, r.

The behavior of an e-commerce site was simulated by sorting the inventory I by similarity to the requirements vector r under the hypothesized weights, HW, producing a *hypothesized ranking*. Next, the inventory item that best matched the requirements under the actual weights (i.e., the optimal item) was selected[2]. Finally, the position of the optimal item in the hypothesized ranking was determined and the cosine between the actual and hypothesized weight vectors was calculated.

One thousand rounds were performed for 2, 4, 8, 16, and 32 features for each distribution. In each trial three values were calculated:

- The mean rank of the optimal item in the hypothesized ranking.
- The mean cosine between the actual and hypothesized weight vectors.
- The minimum return-set size needed to included at least 90 per cent of the optimal cases.

Figures 1 and 2 display the mean cosine and minimum size needed to included at least 90 per cent of the optimal cases, respectively. These figures show that as the number of features increases, the cosine between the actual customer weights

---

[2] With inventory items having random, real-valued weights, there is always a unique optimal item.

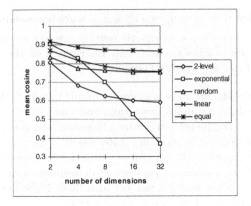

Fig. 1. The mean cosine between the actual and uninformed hypothesized weights.

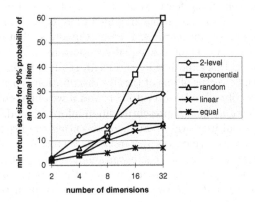

Fig. 2. The minimum return-set size needed to included at least 90 per cent of the optimal cases given uninformed weights.

and the hypothesized weights decreases and the minimum return-set size required for a 90 per cent probability of containing the optimal case increases. These changes, which correspond to decreased benefit, are more gradual for Random and Linear weight distributions than for Two-Level or Exponential. Intuitively, ranking accuracy decreases as the number of unimportant features increases[3].

These results indicate that unless customers' place some importance on almost all features or the total number of features is quite small, an uninformed

---

[3] Very similar results are obtained using equal, rather than random, hypothesized weights, except that the equal-weight hypothesis leads to the optimal item always being ranked first and a cosine of 1.0.

hypothesis about customer weights can be expected to lead to low benefit. In other words, an unacceptably large return-set size is required to guarantee a high probability that the optimal case is returned. The next section presents an algorithm for modifying an initial hypothesis based on customer observations.

3   LCW: Learning Customer Weights

The LCW (Learning Customer Weights) algorithm rests on the assumption that customer preferences can be modeled by weights normally distributed around a population-wide mean, GW. The population-wide mean is modeled by hypothesized global weights, HW, initialized to random values. HW is used as the initial hypothesis for each individual customer's weights, hc_i. These weights are adjusted based on the customer's behavior to form revised weights hc_i'. The hypothesized global weights, HW, are then revised in light of hc_i'.

LCW consists of three connected algorithms: LearnGlobalWeights, LearnCustomerWeights, and AdjustWeights. The first algorithm, LearnGlobalWeights, takes arguments inventory I and return-set size rs and revises the global hypothesis, HW, in light of the apparent preferences of each customer. When a small number of customers have been seen, HW is simply the most recent hc_i'. When enough customers have been seen, HW is assigned the value of the mean of the last 10% of customers seen[4].

```
Procedure LearnGlobalWeights(I,rs)
HW := n random values;
FOR EACH customer i DO
    hci := HW;
    hci' := LearnCustomerWeights(hci,I,rs);
    IF i - 1 (i.e., the number of customers previously seen) < 20
    THEN HW := hci'
    ELSE HW := the mean of the last 10% of the previous hc's;
```

The function LearnCustomerWeights takes hypothesized customer weights hc_i, inventory I, and return-set size rs, elicits the customer's requirements, r, ranks I by similarity to r under weight vector hc_i, and presents the closest rs for selection by the customer. When the customer selects an inventory item s in the return set other than the item that is most similar to r under weights hc_i, hc_i's weights are incrementally adjusted until s is ranked higher than any other member of the return set (or until the threshold for the maximum number of weight adjustments is exceeded). The cycle of retrieval and weight adjustment is repeated until the case ranked highest under the customer's actual weights,

---

[4] This approach speeds learning, because when few customers have been seen, each hc_i' is likely to much closer to GW than any previous customer weights and, therefore, than the mean of the previous customer weights. When many customer have been seen, however, the mean of the customers may differ from G by less than the variance between individual customers.

c_i, is ranked first under the hypothesized weights, hc_i, (corresponding to a satisfied customer making a selection) or the threshold for the maximum number of retrievals is exceeded (corresponding to a customer losing patience and terminating the sales episode). In the experiments described below, this threshold is set to either 1 or 10.

```
Function LearnCustomerWeights(hci,I,rs)
REPEAT
  HypothesizedRankings := I sorted by similarity to r under hci;
  ReturnSet := the first rs members of HypothesizedRankings;
  s := the member of ReturnSet most similar to r under ci,
        customer i's actual weight vector;
  IF s is not the first element of ReturnSet
  THEN hci := AdjustWeights(s,r,ReturnSet,hci,
                            MaximumAdjustmentLimit);
UNTIL s is the first element of ReturnSet OR
      Retrievals > MaximumRetrievalLimit.
return hci;
```

AdjustWeights iterates through each element, mri (for "misranked item"), of the return set that is incorrectly ranked higher than the customer's selection. For each such item, the weight of each feature of the hypothesized customer weights, hc_i, whose value in the requirements vector, r, is closer in value to mri than to s is decremented by the learning rate, lr. Conversely, the weight of each feature of hc_i whose value in r is closer to s than to mri is incremented.

```
Function AdjustWeights(s,r,ReturnSet,hci)
Adjustments := 0;
WHILE Adjustments < MaximumAdjustmentLimit
  SortedReturnSet := ReturnSet sorted by hci;
  MisRanked := elements of SortedReturnSet ranked above s;
  IF MisRanked = {}
  THEN return hci
  ELSE FOR EACH item mri in MisRanked
        FOR EACH feature f
          IF diff(f(mri),f(r)) < diff(f(mri),f(s))
          THEN f(hci) *= (1 + LearningRate)
          ELSE IF diff(f(mri),f(r)) > diff(f(mri),f(s))
                THEN f(hci) *= (1 - LearningRate);
return hci;
```

In the experiments below, LearningRate was 0.01 and MaximumAdjustmentLimit was 1000. Intuitively, AdjustWeights "pulls" the customer's selection s towards the customer's requirements r while "pushing" each member of MisRanked away from r [BCS97,ZY99]. Since AdjustWeights hill-climbs on a linear weight vector, it may not converge if the customer's actual preference function is not a linear function of item feature-values.

4 Experimental Evaluation

LCW induces an estimate of the mean preferences of a customer population based on estimations of each individual customer derived from that customer's behavior. Section 2 provided evidence that, absent knowledge about customers' preferences, ranking can be expected to be inaccurate if there are wide variations in feature importances unless the number of features is very low.

LCW would constitute an improvement over an uninformed weighting scheme if it satisfied the following two conditions: (1) LCW's estimate of the mean preferences of the customer population improved as the number of customers who have been seen increases, and (2) the improvement in the estimate of mean customer preferences resulted in an improvement in the accuracy of predictions of individual customers' rankings.

In the following experiment, the number of dimensions was held constant at 8, on the assumption that customers are unlikely to have the patience to enter more than 8 feature values. The inventory size was held constant at 100 items. In each round of the experiment, a new inventory was created, each item of which was an element of $[0..1]^8$, and a set of actual global weights was created, consisting of 8 values drawn from a two-level distribution. A set of 10, 20, 50, 100, or 250 customer preferences were created, each consisting of an 8-tuple of real numbers whose values were normally distributed around the global weights with $\sigma \in \{0, 0.1, 0.25, 0.5, 1\}$. Each customer was assigned a requirements vector r consisting of a random 8-tuple of real numbers. The maximum permitted retrievals was either 1 or 10, and the return-set size was $\in \{1, 2, 3, 5, 7, 10, 12, 15, 25, 50, 100\}$.

In each round, the global hypothesis, HW, was initially assigned random values, and LCW was applied to each simulated customer in turn. Fifty rounds were performed for each inventory, set of customers, σ, maximum retrievals, and return-set size.

4.1 Learning Global Weights

Figure 3 displays the mean cosine between the vectors representing the actual and hypothesized global weights as a function of the number of customers seen. Separate learning curves are shown for σ from 0 to 1.0. The learning curve is steeper for customer populations with lower σ. However, the cosine is over .90 even for the largest σ tested after 100 customers have been seen. This indicates that the first condition mentioned above—that LCW's estimate of the mean preferences of the customer population improves as the number of customers who have been seen increases—is satisfied for a wide range of σs.

4.2 Improving Ranking

Evidence that the second condition—the improvement in the estimate of mean customer preferences leads to improved accuracy in predictions of individual customers' rankings—is shown in Figure 4, which shows that the minimum return-set size needed for a 90 per cent probability that the optimal case is in the return

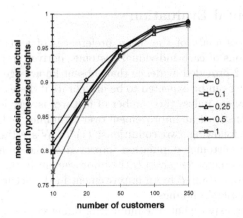

Fig. 3. The mean cosine between the actual and hypothesized global weights as a function of the number of customers seen, for σ from 0 to 1.0.

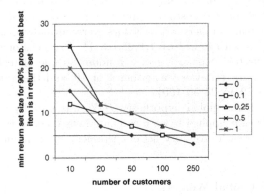

Fig. 4. The minimum return-set size needed for a 90 per cent probability that the optimal case is in the return set as a function of the number of customers, for σ from 0 to 1.0. The graph for σ of 0.5 overlaps the graph for σ of 0.25.

set decreases as the number of customers seen increases. For even the largest σ tested, 1.0, a return-set size of five is sufficient after 250 customers have been seen.

A different view of the experimental data is shown in Figure 5, which graphs the probability that the optimal item is in the return set as a function of return-set size, for customers seen of 10, 20, 50, 100, and 200 and σ of .25. The graph shows that when only 10 customers have been seen, there is a less than 90 per cent probability that the optimal case is in the return set for return-set size of less than 25. After 250 customers, however, a return-set size of 5 is sufficient.

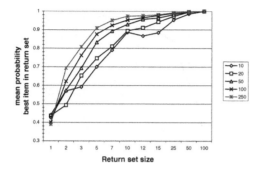

Fig. 5. The probability that the optimal item is in the return set as a function of return-set size, for 10, 20, 50, 100, and 200 customers and σ of 0.25.

4.3   Single vs. Multiple Retrievals

The experiment included two retrieval conditions. Under the first condition, each customer makes only a single retrieval. Alternatively, the customer makes repeated retrievals until the best item in the return set is ranked first up to 10 retrievals. The latter condition is intended to model relevance feedback, as in "more like this" retrievals that are permitted by some search engines. The observation above that customers seldom tolerate interactions requiring heavy cognitive load suggests that multiple retrievals, even if permitted, may be infrequent in practice.

How much opportunity for learning is lost when each customer is permitted only a single retrieval? Figure 6 compares the single versus multiple retrieval conditions by the mean probability that the optimal item is in the return set as a function of return-set size. The difference in performance under the two conditions is negligible. This reflects the fact (not shown in the graph) that the mean number of retrievals never exceeded 1.5 under any of the experimental conditions. This indicates that when a customer's estimated weights have been adjusted once, further adjustments are not likely to produce an improvement as to that customer and inventory set.

4.4   Maximizing Benefit

Choosing the optimal return-set size for a given customer population requires striking a balance between satisfaction and cognitive load. *Benefit* is intended to express the net trade-off between these two factors. The precise relative importance that should be attached to these two factors is impossible to determine *a priori*, as it depends on both the cognitive-load tolerance of the customer population and the importance that the vendor attaches to guaranteeing that an

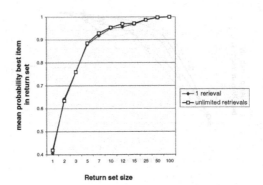

Fig. 6. The mean probability that the optimal item is in the return set as a function of return-set size, for 100 customers and σ of 0.25.

optimal case is returned. However, several heuristics for balancing satisfaction and cognitive load can be identified.

One heuristic is that an optimal case should almost always be returned. Under this heuristic, benefit is maximized by finding the smallest return set that insures a high probability of optimality. Another heuristic is that a return set of 1, which permits no learning, is about as bad as a return set consisting of all the cases, which maximizes cognitive load.

The tradeoff between satisfaction and cognitive load can be expressed in the following equation, in which k is a constant representing the relative importance of satisfaction as compared to cognitive load, rs is the return-set size, and sat represents satisfaction:

$$\text{benefit} = k \cdot rs - sat \cdot (1 - k)$$

Satisfaction, sat, can in turn be quantified by how much of an improvement the best item in the return set is over a randomly selected item. More precisely, sat can be measured by how much larger is (1) the mean distance between the requirements vector and every case in the inventory than (2) the distance between the requirements vector and the best item in the return set. Sat is normalized to the $[0..1]$ interval by dividing it by the amount by which the optimal item is an improvement over a randomly selected item (more precisely, by the mean distance between the requirement vector and every case in the inventory minus the distance between the requirements vector and the optimal item):

$$sat = \frac{MeanDistance - dist(r, best-in-return-set)}{MeanDistance - dist(r, optimal-item)}$$

If k is chosen to be .997, satisfaction is much more important than cognitive load, and the benefit is approximately the same for a return-set of size 1 as for a

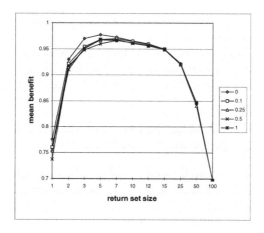

Fig. 7. Mean benefit as a function of return-set size for σ from 0 to 1.0.

return set consisting of the entire inventory. Figure 7 displays the mean benefit as a function of return-set size for $k = .997$, 100 customers, and σ from 0 to 1.0. For small return-set sizes, the benefit is greater for customer populations with lower σ. For large return-set size, however, σ has little effect on benefit. This is because when the return set is sufficiently large, the optimal case is almost always returned regardless of σ. For $\sigma = 0$, benefit is maximized by a return-set size of 5. For larger σ, benefit is maximized by a return-set of 7.

5   Conclusion

This paper has identified the task of acquiring customer preferences from return-set selections, a learning problem that can arise when case-based reasoning is applied to the inventory-selection task. The paper described LCW, a procedure for performing this task, and proposed a criterion for retrieval performance, *benefit*, which embodies both the degree to which the best item in the return set satisfies the customer's requirements and the cognitive load imposed on the customer to select that item.

   An empirical evaluation simulating the behavior of a customer population indicated that unless customers' place some importance on almost all features or the total number of features is quite small, an uninformed hypothesis about customer weights leads to low benefit. Simulation of LCW showed that, under the experimental conditions:

- LCW's estimate of the mean preferences of the customer population improves as the number of customers who have been seen increases.
- This improvement in the estimate of mean customer preferences leads to improved ranking performance for individual customers. Specifically, as the number of customers seen increases, the minimum return-set size needed to insure that an optimal item is returned decreases.

- Ranking performance when only one retrieval is permitted is almost identical to ranking performance when multiple retrievals are permitted.
- For small return-set size, benefit is higher for low σ customer populations than for high σ customer populations. The data suggest that the return set that optimizes benefit may be lower for low than for high σ customer populations.

These conclusions must be qualified by uncertainty concerning the assumptions underlying the experimental evaluation, i.e., whether:

- Customer preferences can be represented by a linear weight vector.
- For the customer population as a whole, the mean weights are distributed roughly into two levels.
- The weights of the individual customers for each feature are normally distributed around the mean value for that feature.

LCW illustrates how unobstrusive learning methods can improve the performance of web-based applications by customizing their performance to customers' behavior. Techniques for learning by observation are likely to become an increasingly important aspect of e-commerce.

References

[BB97]   K. Branting and P. Broos. Automated acquisition of user preferences. *International Journal of Human-Computer Studies*, 46:55–77, 1997.

[BCS97]   A. Bonzano, P. Cunningham, and B. Smyth. Using introspective learning to improve retrieval in CBR: A case study in air traffic control. In *Proceedings of the Second International Conference on Case-Based Reasoning*, pages 291–302, Providence, Rhode Island, July 25–27 1997. Springer.

[BHK+97]   R. Burke, K. Hammond, V. Kulyukin, S. Lytinen, N. Tomuro, and S. Schoenberg. Question answering from frequently-asked question files: Experiences with the FAQ finder system. Technical Report TR-97-05, University of Chicago, Department of Computer Science, 1997.

[Bra99]   K. Branting. Active exploration in instance-based preference modeling. In *Proceedings of the Third International Conference on Case-Based Reasoning (ICCBR-99), Lecture Notes in Artificial Intelligence 1650*, Monastery Seeon, Germany, 1999.

[DBM+92]   L. Dent, J. Boticario, J. McDermott, T. Mitchell, and D. Zabowski. A personal learning apprentice. In *Proceedings of Tenth National Conference on Artificial Intelligence*, pages 96–103, San Jose, CA, July 12–16 1992. AAAI Press/MIT Press.

[GNOT92]   D. Goldberg, D. Nichols, B. Oki, and D. Terry. Using collaborative filtering to weave an information tapestry. *Communications of the ACM*, 35(12):61–70, 1992.

[Kol84]   J. Kolodner. *Retrieval and Organizational Strategies in Conceptual Memory: a Computer Model*. Lawrence Erlbaum Associates, Hillsdale, NJ, 1984.

[KR93]   R. Keeney and H. Raiffa. *Decisions with Multiple Objectives: Preferences and Value Tradeoffs*. Cambridge University Press, second edition, 1993.

[Mae94]   P. Maes. Agents that reduce work and information overload. *Communications of the ACM*, 37(7):31–40, 1994.

[Nie00]   J. Nielson. *Designing Web Usability*. New Riders Publishing, Indianapolis, Indiana, USA, 2000.

[SCTC90]   J. Sweller, P. Chandler, P. Tierney, and M. Cooper. Cognitive load as a factor in the structuring of technical material. *Journal of Experimental Psychology: General*, pages 176–192, 1990.

[SRB99]   M. Schumacher and T. Roth-Berghofer. Architecture for integration of CBR systems with databases for e-commerce. In *Proceedings of the Seventh German Workshop on CBR (GWCBR'99)*, 1999.

[WA95]   D. Wettschereck and D. Aha. Weighting features. In *Lecture Notes in Artificial Intelligence*, pages 347–358, Sesimbra, Portugal, October 1995. Springer.

[Wil99]   W. Wilke. *Knowledge Management for Intelligent Sales Support in Electronic Commerce*. PhD thesis, University of Kaiserslautern, 1999.

[WLW98]   W. Wilke, M. Lenz, and S. Wess. Intelligent sales support with CBR. In M. Lenz, B. Bartsch-Spoerl, H.-D. Burkhard, and S. Wess, editors, *Case-Based Reasoning Technology: from Foundations to Applications. LNAI 1400*, volume 1400, pages 91–113. Springer, 1998.

[ZY99]   Z. Zhang and Q. Yang. Dynamic refinement of feture weights using quantitative introspective learning. In *International Joint Conference on Artificial Intelligence*, pages 228–233. Morgan Kaufmann, August 1999.

The Role of Information Extraction for Textual CBR*

Stefanie Brüninghaus and Kevin D. Ashley

Learning Research and Development Center,
Intelligent Systems Program, and School of Law
University of Pittsburgh
3939 O'Hara Street; Pittsburgh, PA 15260 (USA)
{steffi,ashley}@pitt.edu

Abstract. The benefits of CBR methods in domains where cases are text depend on the underlying text representation. Today, most TCBR approaches are limited to the degree that they are based on efficient, but weak IR methods. These do not allow for reasoning about the similarities between cases, which is mandatory for many CBR tasks beyond text retrieval, including adaptation or argumentation. In order to carry out more advanced CBR that compares complex cases in terms of abstract indexes, NLP methods are required to derive a better case representation. This paper discusses how state-of-the-art NLP/IE methods might be used for automatically extracting relevant factual information, preserving information captured in text structure and ascertaining negation. It also presents our ongoing research on automatically deriving abstract indexing concepts from legal case texts. We report progress toward integrating IE techniques and ML for generalizing from case texts to our CBR case representation.

1 Motivation

CBR systems are particularly promising in domains like the law, ethics, business, customer support, medicine or intelligent tutoring, where human experts accumulate experiences and reason with precedents. However, these domains are not considered "natural CBR domains" (Leake 1998, p. 5), because the cases are recorded as text, which is notoriously difficult to use. To date, reasoning with text cases either requires considerable case engineering efforts or remains restricted to basic text retrieval based on information retrieval (IR) methods. In order to overcome this case representation gap, natural language processing (NLP) techniques are necessary. For more advanced CBR, including reasoning about the similarities and differences of partially matched cases for adaptation or argumentation, meaningful features beyond single words have to be elicited from the case texts. In the past, the brittleness and inefficiency of NLP systems made them all but inapplicable for CBR. However, research on Information Extraction (IE) has made remarkable progress, yielding more efficient and robust systems.

In this paper, we discuss how a state-of-the-art IE system, AutoSlog, can be used to extract relevant information from text cases and to derive a better text representation. While IE will facilitate building TCBR systems, fact extraction alone is not sufficient. In

---

* We thank Ellen Riloff for making AutoSlog available to us. This work would not have been possible without her program AutoSlog, which inspired many of the ideas reported here.

D.W. Aha and I. Watson (Eds.): ICCBR 2001, LNAI 2080, pp. 74–89, 2001.
© Springer-Verlag Berlin Heidelberg 2001

particular for interpretive CBR or more recent research trends, like Intelligent Lessons Learned systems, the case representation has to abstract from the bare facts of the case to its relevant fact patterns or lessons. In our SMILE system, we work toward integrating IE and ML methods for automatically assigning abstract indexing concepts to text cases.

2   The Need for NLP/IE in Textual CBR

To date, most of the work in TCBR relies on available, robust and easy to use IR methods, which require minimal customization and knowledge engineering; see the collection in (Ashley & Lenz 1998). Other systems are CaseAdvisor (Racine & Yang 1997) in a tech-support application, and more recently DRAMA (Leake & Wilson 1999). DRAMA is particularly interesting because it combines CBR and IR methods for hybrid cases.

IR methods are extremely weak compared to the reasoning typically carried out in CBR, which includes the assessment of similarity among cases and the adaptation of partially matched cases. The text representation in IR is based only on the presence and absence of words; word order and text structure are not taken into account; similarity between documents is calculated based on superficial word frequency statistics. TCBR applications need to overcome these limitations, by adopting techniques for better text representation and by developing methods for mapping cases into structures that support the comparison of cases.

One way to improve upon the so-called *bag-of-words* (BOW) representation in IR is to capture word meaning. With a better text representation, a TCBR system can compare cases with similar content, but different words. The FallQ (Lenz, Hübner, & Kunze 1998) and FAQ FINDER (Burke *et al.* 1997) projects have used the lexical semantics in WordNet (Fellbaum 1998) to better represent the similarity among words. Experimental results from both projects show better case retrieval. However, WordNet was not designed to capture semantics at the text level (Fellbaum 1998, p. 7) and does not always correspond to everyday word use. We explored WordNet for our legal documents and found that this often causes undesirable inferences when one tries to find "correct" or domain-specific relations between words. In our research (Brüninghaus & Ashley 1999), we used an online domain-specific thesaurus instead, which lead to better performance for automatic indexing. We are currently working on (1) deriving a semantic representation of the language used in trade secret law cases based on a more comprehensive printed legal thesaurus (Burton 1992), and (2) integrating it with NLP tools. Recent work (Weber *et al.* 2001) has successfully used a domain ontology for TCBR.

While the most natural way to improve reasoning with text cases would be NLP, there has not been much research in TCBR that uses NLP methods to go beyond a BOW. FAQ FINDER made some use of NLP technology (Burke *et al.* 1997). A simple syntactic analysis was used both for part-of-speech tagging and for determining the type of question submitted by a user. The output of the parser was only used to further the use of WordNet and to better match documents, but not to improve text representation. Similarly, FallQ employed NLP techniques in the form of a part-of-speech tagger embedded in the stemming program to deal with the complexities of German inflection.

Two approaches have addressed the mapping of text cases into a representation that supports the comparison of cases. SPIRE aims at facilitating the task of a human indexer; Prudentia uses template mining to find basic case facts for case retrieval.

SPIRE's (Daniels & Rissland 1997) goal is to help a human locate the text passages related to CBR case features within long case texts. It combines CBR and IR methods in a two-step process. SPIRE first uses a Hypo-style CBR program to find cases to seed the IR system and select relevant new documents. In the second phase, SPIRE highlights those sections within a document to be indexed that are most likely to contain the information related to the CBR case representation. Thus, it significantly reduces the case engineering effort required to manually map text onto a symbolic representation.

Prudentia (Weber 1998) supports jurisprudential research by providing an effective case-based retrieval engine over a database of automatically indexed legal cases. The system uses a variety of pattern matching and template mining techniques to extract information from Brazilian criminal law cases. The cases are well-suited for this approach because they are comparatively short, follow strict structural rules, and use a uniform language. Compared to other legal CBR systems (Branting 1999), the case representation is relatively simple in that it includes mostly factual information like names and dates, supplemented with some more keyword-like categories. Likewise, basic pattern matching techniques have been used in FallQ (Lenz, Hübner, & Kunze 1998) to extract easily ascertainable feature/value pairs, in particular prices and technical information.

As this survey indicates, in many TCBR applications, factual information from the cases is relevant. Typically, these facts are names or locations, but may also include parametric information, like temperature or price values. For semi-structured texts, like job announcements, where a small number of standard phrases is used, pattern matching or template mining techniques (Weber 1998) are appropriate to extract this information. However, for texts without regular patterns and structure, like technical reports, these methods will not work.

Whenever the relevant information is embedded in free-form narratives, the deeper syntactic analysis of NLP/IE systems is necessary. In the past, the manual effort and large corpora of annotated training data required to set up these systems made them impractical for CBR indexing. However, IE programs have become more efficient and only require a few examples to automatically generate a problem-specific knowledge base.

To illustrate the benefits of NLP techniques for TCBR, imagine a hypothetical scenario. A well-known German carmaker has introduced a new level of service, through which customers can contact the company's hotline from their PDA without being put on hold. In response to a brief text message, the system retrieves a relevant past case. Assume a customer provides the following description: "I have a problem with my new 180. The wipe-wash system does not work, and water is oozing out at the oil dipstick." This short text includes the respective car, the reported problem and the observed symptoms. (For this example, assume the problem was caused by a rodent that chewed on the windshield washer fluid line.) A BOW representation of this case would exclude stopwords and remove suffixes, resulting in (180 dipstick new oil ooze problem system water wash wipe work). This is more like requesting a clean-up after an oil spill than the actual problem. A more meaningful representation of this example, and how NLP/IE methods can be employed to extract relevant information, is illustrated in Figure 1. The information in the target representation can be derived with techniques discussed here. This example shows three major tasks for an NLP/IE system in TCBR:

1. Extracting names and factual information,
2. Preserving information from text structure,
3. Ascertaining negation.

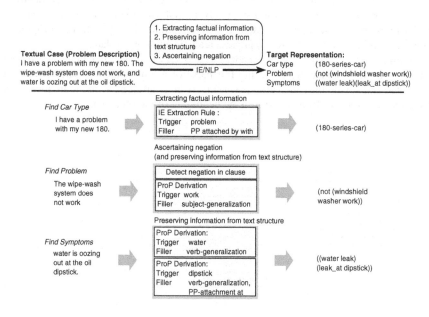

Fig. 1. Customer care example

A fourth task can be identified for domains where the case representation is based on more general facts patterns or lessons, rather than concrete facts and specific events; here, an additional abstraction step using inductive learning techniques is required to derive the case representation.

We will discuss the use of NLP/IE for the three major tasks in the next section, before investigating strategies for combining IE-based techniques and machine learning (ML) methods to induce criteria for finding more general concepts in text cases in Section 4.

3   Using AutoSlog for Case Indexing

In our research, we use a state-of-the-art NLP/IE system, AutoSlog (Riloff 1996), developed by Ellen Riloff at the University of Utah. AutoSlog employs a powerful heuristic sentence segmenter, Sundance, and a module for generating extraction rules from raw text and annotated examples. The remainder of this paper focuses on the use of AutoSlog. Presumably, our techniques are not limited to this particular program. Since most IE programs are not publicly available, however, we have not compared AutoSlog with other systems. http://www.isi.edu/~muslea/RISE/ contains pointers to more IE-related information, including software and data collections.

Before we focus on the use of IE methods for TCBR, a brief introduction to the parsing in AutoSlog is in order. IE systems typically use partial parsing to find relevant syntactic constructs, which tends to be more robust and efficient than full parsing. A conventional parser performs a complete syntactic analysis to generate a full parse tree for a sentence, while a partial parser splits the sentence into clauses and only identifies local structures that can be determined reliably. Partial parsing thus helps overcome two major problems that hampered the use of NLP techniques in the past, their brittleness and the prohibitive time required to process realistic amounts of data.

Furthermore, in domains where the language is very complex, like in the law, partial parsing can help reduce errors. In the full parse of a long sentence, early errors get promoted and spread over the entire parse. Errors in a partial parse are more local, and the parser can recover from an error in the beginning of the sentence.

Input:
"Textual Case-Based
Reasoning involves
Case-Based Reasoning
where the cases are
represented as text."

```
CLAUSE:
  NP SEGMENT (SUBJ):
    [Textual (LEX)(UNK)]
    [CASE-BASED_REASONING (LEX)(N SINGULAR(AI-TECHNOLOGY))]
  VP SEGMENT (ACTIVE_VERB):
    [involves (root: involve) (MOR)(V PRESENT)]
  NP SEGMENT (DOBJ):
    [CASE-BASED_REASONING (LEX)(N SINGULAR(AI-TECHNOLOGY))]

CLAUSE:
  [where (LEX)(C_M)]
  NP SEGMENT (SUBJ):
    [the (LEX)(ART)]
    [cases (root: case) (MOR)(N PLURAL(KNOWLEDGE-SOURCE))]
  VP SEGMENT (PASSIVE_VERB):
    [are (root: be) (LEX)(COP)]
    [represented (root: represent) (MOR)(V PAST)]
  PP SEGMENT (PREP):
    [as (LEX)(PREP)]
    NP SEGMENT:
      [text (LEX)(N SINGULAR(SIMPLE-REPRESENTATION))]
```

Fig. 2. Output of Sundance parser

Figure 2 shows the output of Sundance, the parser in AutoSlog. It breaks complex sentences into clauses, and within each of these determines the constituents, including subject, verb, direct object and prepositional phrases. Sundance also identifies established terms ("case-based_reasoning"), noun phrases ("textual case-based_reasoning"), and retrieves semantic features ("ai-technology" and "simple-representation") associated with the words in its lexicon.

3.1   Extracting Factual Information with AutoSlog

AutoSlog can help extract names and factual information related to the case representation from text. In the example in Figure 1, the first piece of information to be extracted is the kind of car; the same problem may have different answers if it occurs with an SUV or a roadster. Here, the phrase "problem with" helps identify the car. Extracting factual information in this situation is a typical IE task. Like other IE systems, AutoSlog uses a rule-like mechanism. To better illustrate how this works, we will focus on a somewhat more difficult example from a different domain. Consider a typical sentence from our TCBR application, trade secret law: "Forcier developed an ink-processing technology," which is based on the *Forcier v. Microsoft* case in Figure 6. This sentence contains important information, the subject matter of the trade secret case. A human will identify the "ink-processing technology"; a TCBR system should do the same. AutoSlog can extract the trade secret with a rule "If the verb is developed, then extract the object."

AutoSlog has extraction rules[1], which consist of a *trigger* condition and the part of the sentence to be extracted as *filler*. The trigger is a word (or a combination of words)[2], and the filler is a constituent of the sentence, like those in the parse in Figure 2. In the example rule above, the trigger is the word "developed", and the filler is the direct object of the sentence. Figure 3 shows how AutoSlog first parses the input sentence, then checks whether rules are triggered, and returns the respective filler phrases.

A simple pattern-matching rule such as "Extract the nouns following the word 'developed'" may appear to work just as well, but is not an appropriate solution. If the sentence is more complicated, for instance "Forcier developed after many years of research an ink-processing technology," AutoSlog will still return the correct filler, whereas the pattern-matching rule would fail.

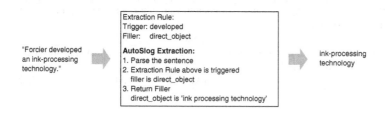

Fig. 3. Extracting information with AutoSlog

Crafting extraction rules by hand is usually a very time-consuming task, and for most applications would be prohibitively expensive. Clearly, a method for automating this process is mandatory for the practical use of an IE system. Given an example sentence and the target information, AutoSlog can reverse the extraction process and derive extraction rules automatically. It first identifies the part of the sentence that contains the target information, which will become the "then extract" filler part of the extraction rule. It then uses a set of heuristics to determine the appropriate trigger condition, preferably the verb of the sentence. Figure 4 illustrates how the extraction rule used above can be derived from the sentence "Houser developed a nut-spinner" (from *Houser v. Snap-on Tools*), where the filler was the secret invention, the "nut-spinner". For more detail on the automatic generation of extraction rules; see (Riloff 1996).

This function of AutoSlog can significantly facilitate the development of a CBR system. Even with a small number of training data, AutoSlog can produce a fairly good set of extraction rules. It should be pointed out that with real-world texts as input, the

---

[1] To prevent confusion with the terminology in Hypo (Ashley 1990), we prefer the generic phrase "extraction rule" over the Riloff's term, "caseframe".

[2] The trigger also includes the part-of-speech of the word, and in the case of verbs the form. For this discussion, we only focus on the presence of the word. We assume that part-of-speech can be ignored and that all verbs are active voice; passive voice will be indicated explicitly.

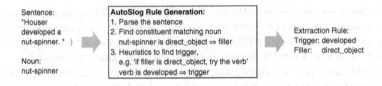

Fig. 4. Deriving an Extraction Rule from an example

rules are sometimes too general; see for instance the second and fourth example in Table 1. Statistical methods can be used to filter out those rules; see (Riloff 1996).

Table 1. Examples of extraction rules generated from squibs

Training Sentence	Product	Extraction Rule		
		Nr.	Trigger	Filler
SDRC began developing a computer program called NIESA.	computer program	(1)	developing	d_object
	NIESA	(2)	called	d_object
The plaintiff manufactures adhesive tape, including a "masking tape"	adhesive tape	(3)	manufactures	d_object
	masking tape	(4)	including	d_object

While there are other systems that can derive extraction rules from examples in a somewhat similar fashion, AutoSlog is unique in that it can generate extraction rules even if no target filler is given. If only a sentence is given as input to the rule generation module, the system parses the sentence and collects all noun phrases as candidate information to be extracted. It then generates the applicable extraction rules for every noun phrase. This function is helpful for the generation of the Propositional Patterns introduced in Section 3.2.

The extraction of factual information with AutoSlog can be useful in a wide variety of CBR applications, wherever features beyond single words from a lexicon are relevant for the case-based reasoner. In a business decision-support application, information about prices and price changes can be extracted from AP news articles. In medical applications, IE methods can be used to extract symptoms or diagnoses from clinical records (Sonderland et al. 1995). For instance, from the sentence "The patient continues to have a high, uncontrollable fever and severe chills," after (Sonderland et al. 1995), the symptom "high, uncontrollable fever" would be extracted. Another application where IE could be applied is SPIRE. One of the target features in its bankruptcy domain is the profession of the debtor. An example sentence from (Daniels 1997) is "Debtor had [...] secured employment as a receptionist-secretary," where the profession is "receptionist-secretary". From this, an extraction rule that extracts the prepositional phrase triggered by "employment as" can be derived.

AutoSlog's extraction rules can work quite well for identifying information for a CBR application even without any manual intervention; see Section 4 for a preliminary experiment. However, they are not a magical solution. The relevant information has to be embedded in a known and recognizable context. Also, AutoSlog's extraction rules tend to be overly general. They will be more accurate where the target objects play distinct roles in the domain. Parser errors, which are fairly common even with Sundance, can cause erroneous extraction rules, too. Generally, the accuracy of AutoSlog will decrease for ungrammatical or badly written text.

In Section 4, we will go beyond extracting names and show how these IE methods can be used in a novel way to make cases more useful by generalizing from individual names and entities to roles for the indexing of legal cases.

3.2 Preserving Information from Text Structure in ProPs

For CBR cases, it is usually necessary to represent what happened in a case. The text representation, whether it is used in retrieval or for automatic indexing, has to preserve the meaning captured in the word order and text structure. IR-based methods discard all syntax-related information needed to find the relevant events, whereas IE methods can be adapted to capture patterns of actions as well as negation. Typically, IE systems have been designed to extract concrete names and objects to fill slots in templates, and not to find more abstract actions or patterns. However, we think AutoSlog can be adapted for extracting not only objects but also patterns related to actions. It may be possible to accomplish this even without the need for a human to craft elaborate rules by hand.

We hope to achieve this by combining the trigger and a generalization of the filler of an extraction rule into single, more expressive features, which we call *Propositional Patterns* (ProPs). This representation is intended to capture information such as "who did what?" or "what was it done to?" ProPs are created on the fly, and only capture fairly shallow syntactic relations among words, in contrast to a representation of entire events in scripts or frames (Jurafsky & Martin 2000). The ProPs are flexible, because they focus only partial views of a sentence. Furthermore, they generalize from the particular words to more general concepts, which makes them more useful for comparing different textual cases.

In the luxury car example, the car owner's observations are summarized in the clause "Water is oozing out at the oil dipstick." In this example, it is clearly important that water, and not oil, was spotted, and where the liquid was observed. Finally, it is desirable to generalize from "ooze" to a more technical term (we assume here leak is a generalization of ooze). The resulting ProPs and the rules to derive them are shown in Figure 1. Under "Find Symptoms", the ProPs are (water leak) and (leak_at dipstick).

ProPs may be useful for a variety of TCBR applications because they are more expressive features than single words, and at the same time support generalizing from the particular wording of the case text.

Recorded lessons learned episodes, for instance, typically contain an event description and a summary of the intended lesson. A lesson could be "The incident status should be displayed by the Incident Command System." (after US Coast Guard CG-SAILS collection). From the BOW representation (command display incident status system), it is not clear what lesson can possibly be learned. Conceivably, ProPs may better capture who should make the information available as (Incident_Command_System publicize) and what measure should be taken as (publicize incident_status). (Weber *et al.* 2001) contains an example for the condition when a lesson can be reused, "A civilian airport was transformed into an intensive military operation area." For this sentence to be meaningful, it is crucial to preserve what was transformed. One way to accomplish this could be the ProP representation (civilian_airport transformed_passive) and (transformed_passive_into military_operation_area).

Another possible application for ProPs is in SIROCCO (Ashley & McLaren 2001), which reasons with engineering ethics cases. The cases are represented in terms of manually extracted Fact Primitives. The sentence "Engineer A has a degree in mechanical engineering and has performed services almost exclusively in mechanical engineering." corresponds to "Engineer A ⟨specializes_in⟩ Mechanical engineering". The related ProPs would be (engineer_a practice) and (practice_in mechanical_engineering), assuming that the domain ontology generalizes from perform services to practice. While the ProPs are not as powerful as the Fact Primitives, they capture most of the relevant information and could eliminate the need to manually encode every single document.

Whether ProPs are applicable and will improve performance depends on the type of texts; certainly not all written materials are suitable for this approach. For a system like FallQ (Lenz, Hübner, & Kunze 1998), where the queries are very short and consist mostly of product identifiers, little improvement over IR-based methods can be expected. Generally, ProPs will be more useful to the degree that the texts follow the Elements of Style (Strunk & White 1979). Also, typical NLP problems, for instance pronoun resolution, will remain an obstacle and cannot be overcome by ProPs.

3.3 Ascertaining Negation with Sundance

Apart from extracting multi-word features, NLP can also be important for dealing with negation. In the prevalent IR methods, negation is disregarded. Stopwords, including "no" and "not", are deleted, even though experimental evidence shows that small words like these can make a big difference for determining what documents are about (Riloff 1995). This may be especially true in finding more factual evidence in text documents.

Negation is considered a hard NLP problem, in part because even when evidence for negation is detected, it can be difficult to determine what is negated. Consider the sentence from our luxury car example, "The wipe-wash system does not work, and water is oozing out at the oil dipstick." In this sentence, only the functionality of the windshield washer is negated, but not the observed symptoms. Relying only on the presence of "not" is not sufficient, one has to take the scope of the clause into account.

For example, a typical sentence, which with minor variations can be found in a number of legal cases in the Case Database of our CATO program (Aleven 1997), is "The information was unique and not generally known in the industry." This sentence is evidence for CATO's CBR indexing concept F15, Unique-Product, because the information was *not* generally known. If everything in the sentence remained identical, and only the word "not" were moved in front of "unique", the sentence would not be evidence for F15, but rather for the opposite concept F20, Info-Known-to-Competitors. Simply relying on the presence of words like "not" in a sentence is insufficient for legal case texts.

We have found that negation usually covers a clause. In the example sentence above, the meaning changed when the word "not" was moved from one clause to the other. Based on this assumption, negation can be ascertained in a two-step process. First, Sundance can be used to break up a complex sentence into clauses, as in Figure 2. Second, if negation is found in any part of a clause, it can be assumed to cover all ProPs derived from that clause.

Methods for correctly representing negation are relevant for many TCBR applications. They are particularly important for the emerging area of medical CBR applications (Bellazzi *et al.* 1999), where patient records explicitly mention the absence of symptoms.

In customer service applications, it is important to correctly extract negated facts from textual descriptions of the cases. For retrieving an accurate response in the printer trouble-shooting situation discussed in (Aha, Maney, & Breslow 1998), it is crucial to know whether the user observes black streaks on the printout or not.

Likewise, finding negation can be relevant for automatically adding cases to case-based collaborative filtering applications (Burke 2000). Entree's cases are restaurant descriptions, which could be gleaned from online reviews. Negation will be needed to capture, for instance, evidence related to noise in sentences like "It is not a noisy restaurant," and "LuLus can get extremely noisy, [. . .]" (from the Pittsburgh Post-Gazette).

The fairly straight-forward method suggested here for ascertaining negation does not solve all problems related to negation, like double negation or expressions of doubt. One can easily come up with a list of exceptions for different domains. However, our goal is not to cover all possible forms of negation; instead, we try to find those cases where we can be reasonably certain and represent them correctly. It seems most useful to have a weak, but reliable method, which can be applied in all domains and expanded upon as necessary. We will assess empirically whether this approach is sufficient for our task.

4   Application: Finding Factors for CATO with SMILE

For many CBR applications, the relevant features of a case are not concrete facts, like the names, locations or numbers typically extracted by an IE system, and the CBR task is more complex than retrieving text cases. Instead, these CBR systems reason with more abstract fact patterns or relevant lessons contained in a case.

One such system is CATO (Aleven 1997), an intelligent tutoring environment for teaching skills of making arguments with cases to beginning law students. In the core of CATO is an expert model of case-based argumentation. The system has a collection of about 150 cases from the domain of trade secret misappropriation. These cases are represented in terms of 26 binary Factors, prototypical, abstract fact patterns that tend to strengthen or weaken the plaintiff's claim. For each case, we have a case summary, called a squib, and the court's full-text opinion. CATO can generate arguments comparing and contrasting cases in terms of Factors. In addition, it uses knowledge about higher-level legal knowledge to reason about abstract issues. A major obstacle for the practical use of CATO is the prohibitive cost of developing and maintaining a large casebase.

We address this problem with SMILE[3], a program to automatically index new cases. Figure 5 shows the design of SMILE. In the *Learning from Examples* phase, SMILE uses a collection of manually marked-up squibs as examples of how indexing should be done and learns classifiers, which will be used in the *Indexing New Cases* phase

---

[3] SMart Index LEarner

84   S. Brüninghaus and K.D. Ashley

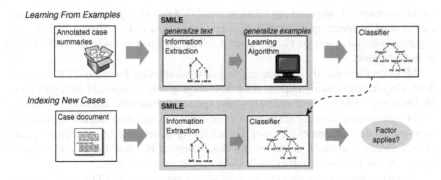

Fig. 5. Overview of SMILE

to classify new case texts under CATO's Factors. We use an inductive learning approach, because the prevalent statistical text learning algorithms, which were designed to work with massive amounts of data and rather simple concepts, are not applicable here (Brüninghaus & Ashley 1999; Brüninghaus & Ashley 1997). In a CBR context, manually annotated training data is scarce, while the indexing concepts are relatively complex. Compared to other text classification applications, CATO's Case Database of 150 documents is a very small collection, and the Factors are hard concepts to learn.

One obstacle is that a BOW representation does not allow the classifier to generalize from the examples to the abstract fact patterns related to the Factors. We therefore integrate the IE techniques in AutoSlog as a first step to generalize from the text to a more suitable example representation that captures the information relevant for finding Factors. The texts are generalized in two steps, using the techniques for better representing text cases introduced in Section 3. First, we substitute names with roles. Part of this step has been implemented, and we present a preliminary evaluation below. Second, we are planning to capture patterns of actions in ProPs and ascertain negation.

The input to SMILE are squibs, in which the sentences that provide evidence for the Factors are marked up. An example is the *Forcier* squib in Figure 6, which summarizes the facts from a real case, *Mitchell F. Forcier v. Microsoft Corporation, et. al*, 123 F.Supp2d 520. This squib reflects the relevant wording of the original court opinion.

4.1   Generalizing from Names and Objects to Roles

For comparing cases in CATO, the particular names of the parties are irrelevant features. More important is the role that a named party plays in the case. Similarly, product names and details only make similar objects appear to be different. Consider the following three sentences. They only have the word "to" in common, and there is no obvious pattern.

- Forcier disclosed information to Aha! (from Figure 6)
- Revcor gave its complete drawings to Marchal and Fulton.
- Hisel sent a letter to Chrysler explaining his idea for a glass-covered holder for license plates.

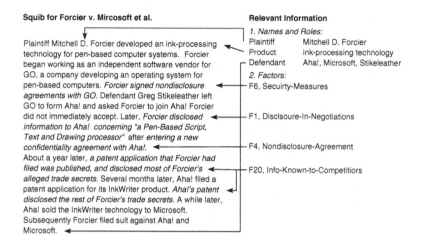

Fig. 6. Example squib for the *Forcier v. Microsoft* case

If we know more about the original cases, however, the three sentences are instances of a pattern. We can generalize them by replacing the product-related information and substituting the names by their role in the lawsuit. (I.e., Forcier, Revcor, Hisel become Plaintiff; Aha!, Marchal and Fulton, and Chrysler become Defendant.)

- Plaintiff disclosed the information to defendant.
- Plaintiff gave the information to defendants.
- Plaintiff sent a letter to defendant explaining the information.

In the modified sentences, we can find the common pattern that (1) plaintiff disseminated something, that (2) product-related information was disseminated, and that (3) the information was given to defendant. Each of these sentences is evidence for the applicability of CATO's Factor F1, Disclosure-In-Negotiations.

In SMILE, we use domain-specific heuristics implemented in Perl that exploit the typical wording and linguistic constructs like appositions to identify the plaintiff and defendant in a case; see Figure 7. This can be supplemented with AutoSlog's Extraction Rules. We have not yet conducted a formal evaluation.

We then substitute the extracted names and object references with their roles in the lawsuit, thereby generalizing from individual instances towards the goal concepts. This measure also adds information from the overall case context to the sentences.

The example sentences show that generalizing from the individual products and inventions to their more general role for the case can benefit finding Factors. Otherwise, product specific identifiers would prevent the comparison of different cases. Product-related information cannot be extracted with simple pattern matching techniques. As argued above, IE techniques will be necessary.

In a preliminary experiment, we tried to find out whether AutoSlog's extraction rules for product-related information can be derived from CATO's squibs without manual intervention and fine-tuning, like filtering out overly general rules or correcting mistakes

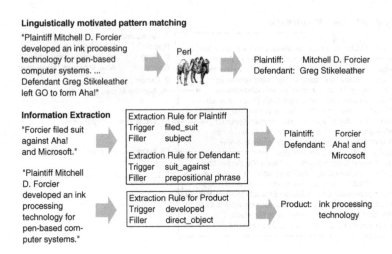

Fig. 7. Extracting the names of plaintiff and defendants and the product from the *Forcier* squib

by Sundance. For the experiment, we manually extracted product names and identifiers from CATO's squibs. We then split the collection into two subsets, and in turns derived extraction rules from one set of examples, which included the squibs and the manually extracted product information as training data. We tested these rules on the other set.

Table 1 has some examples, which suggest that some extraction rules are very accurate, while others are overly general. Extracting the direct object of the verb "including" yields many product names, but also returns a large number of references to persons. We also found some incorrect extraction rules, which were apparently the result of a parser error. One rule extracted the direct object when triggered by the word "signed". In our experiment, we therefore filtered out all extracted fillers that were automatically recognized by Sundance as persons, contract terms or dates.

In scoring the experiment, we did not consider it an error when only part of a complex noun phrase or a general term were extracted. We calculated recall as the portion of all manually marked-up names and products that were found, and precision as the portion of extracted fillers that contained the marked-up names, or other product-related information. The results, macroaveraged over each squib, were precision 66.15% ($\sigma = 0.12$) and recall 64.82% ($\sigma = 0.05$). Notice that only 75 cases, half of the collection, were used to derive the extraction rules for the test set, and that we did not do any manual fine-tuning of the extraction rules. Such adjustments are fairly common for IE systems. Increasing the number of training instances conceivably would lead to higher recall, while removing overly general or incorrect extraction rules is likely to increase precision.

4.2 Using ProPs to Classify Case Texts

Once names are substituted by roles, the next step is to ascertain negation and represent information captured in the text structure. The discussion here will focus on ProPs; for an example how negation is relevant for finding Factors, see Section 3.3.

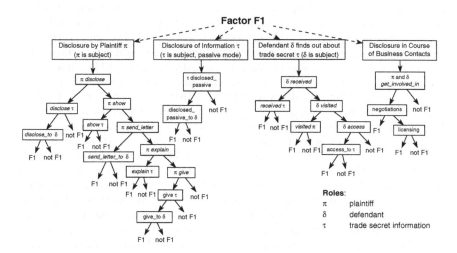

Fig. 8. Manually generated classification tree for Factor F1, Disclosure-in-Negotiations; arrow to the left indicates the feature is present, arrow to the right indicates the feature is absent.

As mentioned above, in the *Forcier* squib, the sentence "Plaintiff disclosed information to defendant . . ." contains evidence for the Factor F1, Disclosure-In-Negotiations. Another sentence from this squib is "Defendant's patent disclosed most of plaintiff's information." It shows that Factor F20, Info-Known-to-Competitors, applies, but is not related to Factor F1. The relevant difference with respect to Factor F1 between these sentences is not the word "patent," but who disclosed the information and to whom. For Factor F1 to apply, the information has to be disclosed by plaintiff to defendant. If the sentences are represented by ProPs, as (plaintiff disclosed) (disclosed information) (disclosed_to defendant) and (patent disclosed) (disclosed information), respectively, they can be readily distinguished based on who disclosed the information.

We are currently working on how to derive ProPs automatically. To give an intuition as to the goal of this research, we manually generated the type of classifier we hope to learn with SMILE. We first collected the sentences that contain evidence for Factor F1 from CATO's squibs and replaced all names by roles. Then, we abstracted from the actions, which allowed us to derive ProPs. From this representation, we generated the classification tree in Figure 8. Since this was done by hand, we focussed on the positive examples only and did not use a learning algorithm; instead, we relied on a common-sense covering strategy. The sentence "Forcier disclosed the information to Aha!", represented as (plaintiff disclosed) (disclosed information) (disclosed_to defendant), would be classified correctly as an instance of F1 through the leftmost branch in this tree. Without generalizing from the text by manually emulating the techniques introduced in Section 3, it would be impossible to derive this classification tree for F1.

5 Summary

In this paper, we discussed the limitations of IR-based TCBR approaches and how they can be addressed with a state-of-the-art NLP/IE tool, AutoSlog. Specifically, we identified three tasks where NLP/IE can improve TCBR systems. They are (1) extracting names and factual information, (2) preserving information captured in the syntax of the documents, and (3) ascertaining negation. In particular, we discussed how a new type of feature, called Propositional Patterns, can be derived from syntactic relations among words to capture information like "who did what?" These tasks were motivated with an example. We also drew examples from a variety of TCBR systems to demonstrate how these techniques can help overcome the limitations of a BOW representation.

After presenting the general techniques, we focussed on our own TCBR program SMILE for identifying CATO's Factors in legal cases. The Factors are abstract fact patterns, used to compare cases and reason about the differences between partially matched cases. We are working on integrating the three IE-based techniques above and ML methods for better generalizing from the legal case opinions. Our approach in SMILE consists of two steps. First, SMILE generalizes from the text using NLP/IE methods. We replace the names of the parties and product-related information by their role in the lawsuit, derive ProPs to preserve some of the relevant information in the text, and ascertain negation. Second, SMILE uses an ML algorithm to further generalize from examples to more abstract fact patterns in a classifier.

References

Aha, D.; Maney, T.; and Breslow, L. A. 1998. Supporting dialogue inferencing in conversational case-based reasoning. In *Proceedings of the Fourth European Workshop on Case-Based Reasoning*. Springer. LNAI 1488.

Aleven, V. 1997. *Teaching Case-Based Argumentation through a Model and Examples*. Ph.D. Dissertation, University of Pittsburgh.

Ashley, K., and Lenz, M., eds. 1998. *Textual Case-Based Reasoning, Papers from the AAAI-98 Workshop*. AAAI Press. Technical Report WS-98-12.

Ashley, K., and McLaren, B. 2001. Helping a CBR Program Know What it Knows. In *Proceedings of the Fourth International Conference on Case-Based Reasoning*. Springer.

Ashley, K. 1990. *Modeling Legal Argument, Reasoning with Cases and Hypotheticals*. MIT-Press.

Bellazzi, R.; Montani, S.; Portinale, L.; and Riva, A. 1999. Integrating Case-Based and Rule-Based Decision Making in Diabetic Patient Management. In *Proceedings of the Third International Conference on Case-Based Reasoning*. Springer. LNAI 1650.

Branting, L. 1999. *Reasoning with Rules and Precedents - A Computational Model of Legal Analysis*. Kluwer Academic Publishers.

Brüninghaus, S., and Ashley, K. 1997. Using Machine Learning for Assigning Indices to Textual Cases. In *Proceedings of the Second International Conference on Case-Based Reasoning*. Springer. LNAI 1266.

Brüninghaus, S., and Ashley, K. 1999. Bootstrapping Case Base Development with Annotated Case Summmaries. In *Proceedings of the Third International Conference on Case-Based Reasoning*. Springer. LNAI 1650.

Burke, R.; Hammond, K.; Kulyukin, V.; Lytinen, S.; Tomuro, N.; and Schonberg, S. 1997. Question-Answering from Frequently-Asked Question Files: Experiences with the FAQ-Finder System. *AI Magazine* 18(1):57–66.

Burke, R. 2000. A Case-Based Approach to Collaborative Filtering. In *Proceedings of the Fifth European Workshop on Case-Based Reasoning*. Springer. LNAI 1898.

Burton, W. 1992. *Legal Thesaurus*. Simon & Schuster Macmillan.

Daniels, J., and Rissland, E. 1997. Finding Legally Relevant Passages in Case Opinions. In *Proceedings of the Sixth International Conference on AI and Law*. ACM Press.

Daniels, J. 1997. *Retrieval of Passages for Information Reduction*. Ph.D. Dissertation, University of Massachusetts, Amherst, MA.

Fellbaum, C., ed. 1998. *WordNet: An Electronic Lexical Database*. MIT Press.

Jurafsky, D., and Martin, J. 2000. *Speech and Language Processing*. Prentice Hall.

Leake, D., and Wilson, D. 1999. Combining CBR with Interactive Knowledge Acquisition, Manipulation and Reuse. In *Proceedings of the Third International Conference on Case-Based Reasoning*. Springer. LNAI 1650.

Leake, D., ed. 1998. *Case-Based Reasoning: Experiences, Lessons & Future Directions*. MIT Press.

Lenz, M.; Hübner, A.; and Kunze, M. 1998. Textual CBR. In Lenz, M.; Bartsch, B.; Burkhard, H.-D.; and Wess, S., eds., *Case-Based Resaoning Technology*. Springer. LNAI 1400.

Racine, K., and Yang, Q. 1997. Maintaining Unstructured Case Bases. In *Proceedings of the Second International Conference on Case-Based Reasoning*. Springer. LNAI 1266.

Riloff, E. 1995. Little Words Can Make a Big Difference for Text Classification. In *Proceedings of the 18th Annual International ACM SIGIR Conference on Research and Development in Information Retrieval*. ACM Press.

Riloff, E. 1996. Automatically Generating Extraction Patterns from Untagged Text. In *Proceedings of the Thirteenth National Conference on Artificial Intelligence*. AAAI Press.

Sonderland, S.; Aronow, D.; Fisher, D.; Aseltine, J.; and Lehnert, W. 1995. Machine Learning of Text Analysis Rules for Clinical Records. Technical Report CIIR TC-39, University of Massachusetts, Amherst, MA.

Strunk, W., and White, E. 1979. *The Elements of Style*. Macmillan Publishing Co.

Weber, R.; Aha, D.; Sandhu, N.; and Munoz-Avila, H. 2001. A textual case-based reasoning framework for knowledge management applications. In *Proceedings of the Ninth German Workshop on Case-Based Reasoning*. Shaker Verlag.

Weber, R. 1998. *Intelligent Jurisprudence Research*. Ph.D. Dissertation, Federal University of Santa Catarina, Brazil.

Case-Based Reasoning in Course Timetabling: An Attribute Graph Approach

Edmund K. Burke[1], Bart MacCarthy[2], Sanja Petrovic[1], and Rong Qu[1]

[1]School of Computer Science and Information Technology, The University of Nottingham, Nottingham, NG8 1BB, U.K
{ekb, sxp, rxq}@cs.nott.ac.uk
http://www.cs.nott.ac.uk/
[2]School of Mechanical, Materials, Manufacturing Engineering and Management, The University of Nottingham, Nottingham, NG7 2RD, U.K
http://www.nottingham.ac.uk/school4m
{Bart.MacCarthy@nottingham.ac.uk}

Abstract. An earlier Case-based Reasoning (CBR) approach developed by the authors for educational course timetabling problems employed structured cases to represent the complex relationships between courses. The retrieval searches for structurally similar cases in the case base. In this paper, the approach is further developed to solve a wider range of problems. We also attempt to retrieve those cases that have common similar structures with some differences. Costs that are assigned to these differences have an input upon the similarity measure. A large number of experiments are performed consisting of different randomly produced timetabling problems and the results presented here strongly indicate that a CBR approach could provide a significant step forward in the development of automated systems to solve difficult timetabling problems. They show that using relatively little effort, we can retrieve these structurally similar cases to provide high quality timetables for new timetabling problems.

1. Introduction

1.1 CBR in Scheduling and Timetabling Problems

A timetabling problem can be thought of as a special case of the general scheduling problem. As far as the authors are aware, there are few publications in the literature on using CBR to solve such problems. In 1989, SMARTplan was proposed by Koton [1]. It used CBR to solve the airlift management problem by decomposing the problem and then combining the retrieved cases for the new problem. Hennessy utilised the theory of scheduling in a CBR system presented in 1992 to solve the autoclave management and loading problem [2]. In 1993, Bezirgan developed CBR-1 for dynamic job shop scheduling utilising rules from a pool storing different methods [3]. Miyashita and Sycara implemented the CBR system called CABIN in 1994 [4]. This system addressed the job shop scheduling problem by retrieving previous repair tactics. MacCarthy and Jou proposed general CBR frameworks for scheduling in 1995

D.W. Aha and I. Watson (Eds.): ICCBR 2001, LNAI 2080, pp. 90-104, 2001.

[5] and in 1996 they presented a survey about CBR research in scheduling [6]. In 1997, Cunningham proposed an approach to reuse portions of good schedules to solve traditional travelling salesman problems [7]. Schmidt, in 1998, stored scheduling tactics in the case base to help solving job shop scheduling problems [8].

Several types of timetabling problem are currently being studied such as course timetabling, exam timetabling, bus or rail timetabling and employee timetabling [9]. Our CBR system addresses educational course timetabling. The course timetabling problem was defined by Carter in [10]. It can be viewed as a multi-dimensional assignment problem. In a timetable, a number of courses are assigned into classrooms and a limited number of timeslots (periods of time) within a week. Students and teachers are assigned to courses.

Different timetabling problems have different constraints. This can make them very difficult to solve. A common constraint is 'no person is assigned to two or more courses simultaneously' which is known as a *hard constraint* because it should, under no circumstances, be violated. Other constraints known as *soft constraints* are desirable but it is not essential to satisfy them. Indeed, it would usually be impossible to satisfy all of them in a given problem. Examples are when two events should or should not be consecutive, or when one event should be before another.

In the early days of educational timetabling research, graph theoretic methods represented the state of the art [11]. Techniques like graph colouring were used to solve the problems. Other research using integer linear programming techniques to represent the timetabling problem was also carried out [12]. In more recent times, various meta-heuristic methods such as Tabu search [13], Simulated Annealing [14], Genetic Algorithms [15] and Memetic Algorithms [16, 17] have been employed to solve a variety of educational timetabling problems. Good results have been obtained in some specific problems by these approaches. A series of international conferences on the Practice and Theory of Automated Timetabling (PATAT) provides a forum for a wide variety of research work on timetabling and many relevant publications can be found in [18, 19, 20].

In real world applications, many timetables are produced by modifying "last year's timetable" to create a solution for the problem in hand. This is because the constraints in the new problem do not usually change significantly from the old one. Thus part of the previous timetable could be re-used and a significant amount of effort could be avoided. This observation provided some of the motivation for our research into CBR for timetabling problems.

1.2 Structured Cases in CBR

The method of using a set of feature-value pairs to represent cases is heavily used in most traditional CBR applications [21]. The nearest-neighbour method has been used extensively and the similarity is obtained by calculating a weighted sum of the individual similarity between every feature-value pair of the case from the case base and a new case. However, in some domains, objects in the problems are heavily related, such as in the timetabling problem. The constraints between the events (exams, courses, meeting, etc) represent relations between objects in the problems.

These relations affect their solutions significantly. A list of feature-value pairs is incapable of giving sufficiently important information about these relations to develop a solution. A similarity measure would be limited in reflecting the deeper similarities between the problems. Thus the retrieval process may not retrieve strongly similar cases in the case base without this important information. The adaptation based on these retrieved cases may be very difficult and may take as much effort as solving the new problem from scratch.

Structured cases have been discussed in the literature to represent problems with heavily inter-related objects, but no general theory or methodology has been identified. In most approaches, cases are represented by trees [23], graphs [24, 25] and semantic nets [24]. Many applications deal with the layout/design [26, 27] or planning problems [24, 25]. Gebhardt [28] provides more details of most existing CBR systems employing structured cases.

In [22] the authors presented an approach that employed attribute graphs to represent course timetabling problems structurally. The relations (constraints in the problems) between each pair of objects (courses in the problems) have a significant effect on the solution. The attribute graph represents a sophisticated level of knowledge about the constraints and the problem. The retrieval is also based on this information which is provided to find structurally similar cases for reuse. In this paper the proposed structured CBR approach for course timetabling problems is improved to deal with a wider range of problems than those dealt with in [22]. Section 2 describes the case base, the retrieval and adaptation processes of the proposed system. An analysis and discussions on a number of experiments carried out on the system is given in Section 3, followed by some concluding comments and directions for future work in Section 4.

2. The Structured CBR Approach

2.1 Modelling Course Timetabling Problems by Attribute Graphs

Attribute graphs were used to represent course timetabling problems structurally in [22]. Vertices represent courses and edges illustrate constraints between courses. The degree of a vertex is the number of edges adjacent to it. Fig. 1 presents a simple example of an attribute graph representing a course timetabling problem. Hard constraints and soft constraints are indicated by solid and dotted edges respectively. In the notation x:y, x is the label and y represents the value of the attribute. *Physics*, *Lab* and *MathA* are labelled by 1, indicating that they are multiple courses. Values 2, 3, 2 give the times they should be held per week respectively. Other courses labelled 0 (ordinary courses) should be held just once a week. The courses adjacent to edges labelled 7 cannot be held simultaneously. *Database* should be consecutive to *Lab* if possible (the edge between them is labelled 5) and *MathA* should not be consecutive to *MathB* if possible (the edge between them is labelled 6). The directed edge between *ComputerA* and *ComputerB* is labelled 4, denoting that *ComputerA* should be held before *ComputerB*.

Label	Attribute	Value(s)	Notes
0	Ordinary course	N/A	Takes place once a week
1	Multiple course	N (No. of times)	Takes place N times a week
2	Pre-fixed course	S (Slot No.)	Assigned to timeslot S
3	Exclusive course	S (Slot No.)	Not assigned to timeslot S

Vertex attributes of course timetabling problems

Label	Attribute	Values(s)	Notes
4	Before/after	1 or 0 (direction)	One before/after another course
5	Consecutive	N/A	Be consecutive with each other
6	Non-consecutive	N/A	Not consecutive with each other
7	Conflict	N/A	Conflict with each other

Edge attributes of course timetabling problems

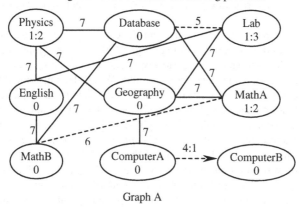

Graph A

Fig. 1. A course timetabling problem represented by an attribute graph

2.2 The Graph Isomorphism Problem and the Retrieval Algorithm

The problem of finding structurally similar cases in the case base for a new case represented by attribute graphs is a graph or sub-graph isomorphism problem. This problem is known to be NP-Complete [29]. The approach we used in [22] was based on Messmer's algorithm [30] in which all the possible (partial) permutations of the vertices representing (partial) graphs are stored in a decision tree. Those representing the same (sub-)structures are stored under the same node. In a decision tree, each node represents an attribute and has one child for each of the attribute's values [31]. Our approach adapted this algorithm to build the case base into a decision tree that contains the attribute graphs of all the previous solved cases [22]. Each pair of attributes is assigned a value (individual similarities) to indicate how similar they are. If this individual similarity exceeds a given threshold, then it reports that these vertices or edges are not similar. The retrieval starts from the root node and classifies the new case into some nodes in the tree by comparing the permutations of the courses in the new case with those stored in the decision tree. Then all the (partial) permutations under these nodes have the same (sub-)structures with similar attributes of the new cases and will be retrieved to give a solution for the new problem. A similarity measure is given by a weighted sum of the individual similarities between the pairs of the matched vertices and edges. More details can be found in [22].

2.3 Retrieval of Structurally Similar Cases

Partially Similar Cases with Differences: The previous retrieval process [22] retrieves the graphs of the cases from the case base that are graph or sub-graph isomorphic to the new case. However, cases in the case base that have common or partially similar (sub-)structures can also be reusable. In the retrieval phase developed here, not only the cases that are graph or sub-graph isomorphic to the new case are retrieved from the case base, but we also examine (partial) matches with some differences. We will describe this broader and more intelligent retrieval process in this section.

Cases in the case base need not contain all the corresponding similar edges in the new cases to be reused. For example in Fig. 2, graph B is neither graph nor sub-graph isomorphic to graph A shown in Fig. 1. However, graph B can be graph isomorphic to graph A if some vertices and edges are inserted. When dealing with difficult real world timetabling problems our approach has to be more flexible than just considering cases in the case base that are graph isomorphic to the new case. Note we can say that graph B is partially similar to graph A. In graph A, not all of its vertices and edges can match those of graph C in Fig. 2 (*Physics*, *ComputerA* and *ComputerB* cannot find a matching course in graph C). Also, not all of the vertices and edges in graph C can find a match with those in graph A (the course labelled with 1:2 with adjacent edges illustrated by light lines does not have a matching course with matching edges in graph A). These two cases have common parts that are partially similar with each other in either vertices or edges.

In the approach developed here, new cases like graphs B and C can all be seen as partially similar (but clearly have some significant differences) to graph A. The timetable associated with graph A could be reusable for the cases of graph B and C. This approach retrieves a large number of useful cases thus allowing an investigation of a much wider range of timetabling problems.

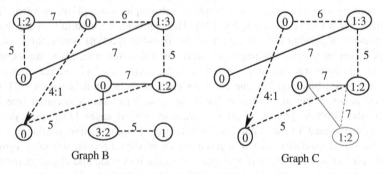

Graph B   Graph C

Fig. 2. Cases partially similar with some differences with case in Fig. 1

Similarity Measure: The similarity measure takes into account the costs assigned to the substitutions, deletions and insertions of vertices and edges labelled with particular attributes from or into the new case. Deleting vertices and edges with different attributes from the cases in the case base are assigned lower costs than those of inserting vertices and edges into them. Also inserting and deleting the edges of hard constraints is assigned a higher cost than for the soft constraints. Costs are assigned so that the operations of deletion, insertion and substitution on the attribute graphs simulate the adaptation steps (explained in the later subsection) on the timetables retrieved. Deleting, inserting and substituting the less important vertices and edges has less of an effect on adapting the timetables. Thus such cases have lower costs assigned because of the need for less adaptation. The similarity measure between new case C_2 and case C_1 in the case base is presented in formula (1).

$$S(C_1, C_2) = 1 - \frac{\sum_{i,j=0}^{n} p_{i,j} + \sum_{a=0}^{m} a_a + \sum_{d=0}^{k} d_d}{P + A + D} \tag{1}$$

The notations in formula (1) represent the following:
   n: number of matched vertices
   m, k: numbers of the vertices or edges needed to be inserted into and deleted from
      C_2 respectively
   $p_{i,j}$: cost assigned for substituting vertex or edge i in C_2 with vertex or edge j of C_1
   a_a, d_d: costs assigned for inserting and deleting a vertex or edge labelled with
      attribute into and from C_2
   P: the sum of the costs of substitution of every possible pair of vertices or edges in
      C_2 to those of C_1
   A, D: the sum of the costs of inserting and deleting all of the vertices or edges into
      and from C_2 respectively
We can see that the closer the value $S(C_1, C_2)$ is to 1, the more similar C_1 and C_2 are.

Branch and Bound in Retrieval: The retrieval needs to search through the decision tree to find all the cases in the case base that are similar to the new case. The size of the decision tree storing all the possible permutations of the previous cases may be large, resulting in extensive searching. Thus the retrieval process may be difficult and time consuming. Branch and bound [32] is employed to reduce the size of the search tree in the retrieval phase. When the permutation of the courses of the new case is input into the case base, the retrieval starts from the root node and first searches down along the branches as far as possible in the tree that stores the most similar (sub-)structures. All the possible candidate branches under one node that have a similar sub-structure and attributes with the new case are sorted by their summed costs. The branches storing the (sub-)structures whose costs exceed the given threshold are considered not to be similar to the (sub-)structures of the new cases and are all discarded. Thus the size of the search tree for retrieval can be greatly reduced because the retrieval does not need to search all the branches in the decision tree.

   Backtracking is used when the retrieval cannot find a complete match. The retrieval backtracks to the parent node and the branch that has the lowest cost among the remaining branches will be chosen. This process continues until a complete match is found. All the complete and partial matches identified during the retrieval will be collected for potential adaptation.

Usually in timetabling problems, the more conflicts a course has with the other courses, the more difficult it is to schedule it. All the courses of the new case are sorted by their difficulties (here the degrees of the vertices in the attribute graph) in decreasing order and input into the decision tree for retrieval. Thus the retrieval process can first try to find the match for the more important courses.

Reuse and Adaptation of the Solutions: Adaptation of the timetables of all the retrieved cases is performed according to the (partial) matches found. The adaptation steps for each retrieved case are:
1. According to the match found, matched courses are substituted and all the un-matched courses in the retrieved case are deleted.
2. All the courses that violate the constraints in the newly formed timetable are removed and inserted into an unscheduled list sorted by their difficulties in decreasing order. The courses in the new case that are not yet scheduled are also inserted into the sorted unscheduled list.
3. All the courses in the unscheduled list are rescheduled by the graph heuristic method described below.

Different constructive methods can be used to generate the timetables based on the partial solutions. The CBR approach presented here employs a simple graph heuristic method in the adaptation that is the same as that employed in [33] to construct a timetable based on the retrieved cases. It is briefly described below.

1. From the first one that is the most important, the courses in the unscheduled list are scheduled to the first timeslot with no violations (penalty-free);
2. The courses that cannot be assigned to a penalty-free timeslot will be scheduled to the timeslots that lead to the lowest penalty after all the others have been scheduled;
3. In the case of a tie, randomly assign the course to the first timeslot available.

The best timetable with the lowest penalty is selected as the solution of the new case.

Penalty Function: Every timetable generated for the new case is evaluated by the following formula (2):

$$Penalty = H \times 100 + U \times 100 + S \times 5 \qquad (2)$$

Here H is the number of violations of hard constraints (the clashes between courses) and U is the number of unscheduled courses. H and U are assigned a cost of 100 to ensure that an infeasible timetable has a high cost. S is the total number of the violations of the soft constraints. They are assigned lower costs (at 5) because it is desirable to avoid them but not essential when a penalty-free timetable cannot be found. In different real-world timetabling problems, soft constraints could have different weights.

3. Experiments with Different Case Bases and Course Timetabling Problems

To test the computational performance of the system on different case bases, different groups of random cases with different features have been defined systematically and stored in the case base. The determination of a number of cases needed to build a case base is not an easy task. In order to have different case bases we generated cases with a range of properties that real-world problems may have. Thus an investigation of the system on a range of possible case bases can be carried out. Also different new cases are randomly generated so that the general performance of the system can be tested on a set of different new cases that the system may meet.

Case bases with three different types of random cases were produced to solve a group of small new cases. These are 15-course simple, 15-course complex and 20-course simple cases. The complex cases have vertices whose degrees are at the lowest 1 and at the highest 4. The degrees of vertices in simple cases are at the lowest 1 and at the highest 3. The complex cases have more constraints than those simple cases and are usually more difficult to solve. The attributes are randomly selected from Tables 1 and 2. The timetables of these cases are generated by using the graph heuristic method and stored in the case base. Small new cases with 5, 10 and 15 courses, also randomly generated, are tested to give an easy evaluation on the CBR approach developed. The system is developed in C++ and the experiments are run on Pentium 450Mhz PC with 128MB of RAM under the Windows environment. A schematic diagram of the system is given in Fig. 4.

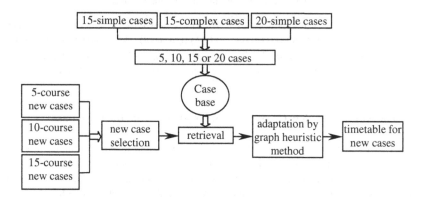

Fig. 3. Schematic diagram of the CBR system used for evaluation

3.1 Time and Memory Needed to Build the Decision Tree in the Case Base

In every case base we store 5, 10, 15 or 20 of the three types of cases. Table 1 gives the time spent and space needed to build these 12 different case bases. In the notation x/y, x gives the time in seconds and y is the number of nodes in the decision tree.

Table 1. Time spent on building the case base by 15-course simple, 15-course complex and 20-course cases

	5	10	15	20
15-simple	5.04/12689	12.58/32647	16.57/32647	24.83/52153
15-complex	8.48/23569	22.76/58475	46.88/93523	77.69/132750
20-simple	125.85/92449	273.84/141163	373.09/160887	598.36/193473

We can see that because the number of permutations grows explosively with the number of vertices in the graph, adding 20-course cases into the case base takes much more time and space than for both simple and complex 15-course cases. The time and number of nodes grows rapidly but not explosively with the number of cases in the case base. This is because many of the (partial) permutations of the cases may be stored under the node that is built for previous cases if they have the same (sub-) structures.

3.2 Time Spent in Retrieval

Table 2 gives the retrieval time for different new cases from the 12 different case bases. The values separated by '/' give the retrieval time (in seconds) in the case base with 5, 10, 15 and 20 cases respectively. We can see that the retrieval time changes in the same way as that for building the same case bases.

Table 2. Retrieval time in different case bases

	5-course new cases	10-course new cases	15-course new cases
15-simple	0.01/0.02/0.03/0.04	0.01/0.02/0.03/0.045	0.01/0.03/0.03/0.05
15-complex	0.01/0.03/0.2/0.2	0.02/0.04/0.5/0.3	0.02/0.2/0.6/0.3
20-simple	1.08/2.85/3.86/5.1	2.5/2.9/3.9/4.9	3.1/3.87/4.1/5.2

3.3 The Number of New Cases that Find Matches from the Case Base

With too few matched vertices, the retrieved cases cannot provide enough information for adaptation. Only matches that have enough courses (here more than half) in the retrieved cases are seen as helpful and retrieved for adaptation. From all the retrieved cases, a set of the most similar cases is selected as a set of candidates for the adaptation.

To test how many new cases can retrieve cases from the case base with different complexity, two groups of experiments were conducted on the case bases storing simple or complex 15-course cases. The results are given in Tables 5 and 6 respectively. The values before and after '/' give the percentages of new cases that could retrieve partial and complete matches from the case base respectively. The values in parentheses give the overall percentage, as either partial or complete matches found.

Table 3. The percentages of new cases that find case(s) from the 15-course simple case base

No. of 15- simple cases in case base	5-course new case	10-course new cases	15-course new case	Average percentages
5	100/100 (100)	100/0 (100)	30/0 (30)	76.67
10	100/100 (100)	100/0 (100)	70/0 (70)	90
15	100/100 (100)	100/0 (100)	70/0 (70)	90
20	100/100 (100)	100/45 (100)	70/0 (70)	90

Table 4. The percentages of new cases that find cases from the 15-course complex case base

No. of 15-complex cases in case base	5-course new case	10-course new cases	15-course new case	Average percentages
5	100/100(100)	100/0(100)	35/5(35)	78.3
10	100/100(100)	100/0(100)	70/5(70)	90
15	100/100(100)	100/70(100)	85/75(85)	98.33
20	100/100(100)	100/70(100)	85/80(85)	98.33

It can be seen from Table 3 that all of the 5-course and 10-course new cases can find (partial) match(s) from a case base with simple 15-course cases. No complete match can be found for new cases with 10 or more courses when the case base consists of less than 20 cases. Table 4 shows that storing complex cases in the case base enables more new cases to find matches. Higher percentages of larger new cases (10-course and 15-course new cases) retrieve cases (complete or partial matches) from the case base.

We can also see that when 10, 15 or 20 simple cases are stored in the case base, the same number of new cases (90%) can retrieve matches. Also, the same number of new cases (98.3%) can find matched cases in the case bases with 15 or 20 complex cases. This is because the attribute graphs of a certain number of cases in the case base provide a certain number of different (sub-)structures in the decision tree. Additional cases do not provide new (sub-)structures in the decision tree. Attribute graphs of complex cases can provide more (sub-)structures, thus more new cases can retrieve cases from the case base with more than 10 or 15-course complex cases.

The effect of storing larger cases with 20 courses in the case base is tested in a further experiment and the results are given in Table 5. The overall percentages of successful retrievals are higher than those with smaller simple cases but lower than those with smaller complex cases.

Table 5. The percentages of new cases that find cases from the 20-course case base

No. of 20-simple cases in case base	5-course new case	10-course new cases	15-course new case	Average percentages
5	100/100(100)	100/0(100)	85/0(85)	95
10	100/100(100)	100/0(100)	85/0(85)	95
15	100/100(100)	100/0(100)	85/0(85)	95
20	100/100(100)	100/45(100)	85/0(85)	95

Fig. 5 gives a chart of average percentages of new cases that can retrieve case(s) from the case base with different numbers of three types of cases. We can observe that storing more than 15 complex 15-course cases provides a higher percentage of success in retrieval than storing both simple 15-course and simple 20-course cases. By storing a sufficient number of complex cases, sufficient (sub-)structures can be stored in the decision tree for reuse. It is actually the number of (sub-)structures, not the number and size of the cases, that affects the percentage of successful retrievals. Thus it is not necessary to store more cases.

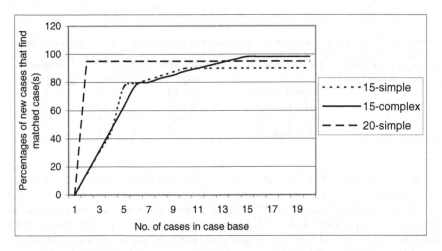

Fig. 4. Percentage of new cases that retrieve case(s) from different case bases

3.4 Adaptation of Retrieved Cases

20 different cases with 5, 10 or 15 courses are tested on the case bases with 5, 10 15 or 20 of the three types of cases respectively. So altogether 720 (=20×3×4×3) experiments were carried out. The graph heuristic method described in Section 3 is used in the adaptation to adapt all the retrieved cases and the timetable that has the lowest penalty is used as the solution for the new cases. For comparison, the same graph heuristic method is also used to generate a timetable from scratch for each new case that can retrieve cases from the case base. All the timetables generated by these methods are evaluated by using the penalty function given in (2). The number of schedule steps needed during adaptation is also taken into account in the comparison. The average penalties and schedule steps for these two methods are presented in Tables 8, 9 and 10. The y in 'x/y' gives the number of schedule steps needed to obtain a timetable that has a penalty x. Values in parentheses give the penalty and schedule steps of the timetables generated by adapting complete matches for the new cases.

Table 6. Penalties and schedule steps by graph heuristic (GH) and CBR approach with different 15-course simple case bases

No. of cases	5-course new case		10-course new cases		15-course new case	
	CBR	GH	CBR	GH	CBR	GH
5	6/7(6/8)	11/15	22.8/35.8	30.5/45.6	39.2/68	39.2/76
10	6/6(5/6)	11/15	16.5/30.2	30.5/45.6	33.2/59	36.1/59
15	6/6(5/6)	11/15	16.5/30.3	30.5/45.6	33/59.8	36.1/69
20	6/5(5/6)	11/15	17/28(23/40)	30.5/45.6	30/54.3	34/66.1

Table 7. Penalties and schedule steps by graph heuristic (GH) and CBR approach with different 15-course complex case bases

No. of cases	5-course new case		10-course new cases		15-course new case	
	CBR	GH	CBR	GH	CBR	GH
5	7/7(6/5)	11/15	19.3/30.5	30.5/45.6	30/49	15/50
10	6/6(6/5)	11/15	18.5/31.2	30.5/45.6	30/49	15/50
15	6/6(5/5)	11/15	17/31(28/39)	30.5/45.6	30/60(39/65)	39.7/69
20	6/6(5/5)	11/15	16/27(28/39)	30.5/45.6	27/61(39/68)	39.7/69

Table 8. Penalties and schedule steps by graph heuristic (GH) and CBR approach with different 20-course case bases

No. of cases	5-course new case		10-course new cases		15-course new case	
	CBR	GH	CBR	GH	CBR	GH
5	6/6.7(5/6)	11/15	16.5/28.7	30.5/45.6	37.9/55	40/66.4
10	6/6(5/5.5)	11/15	15.8/28.3	30.5/45.6	36.8/55.7	39.4/67
15	6/6.5(5/5.3)	11/15	16.4/27.3	30.5/45.6	61.7/79.3	53.4/81
20	6/6(5.3/5.4)	11/15	18/29(10/4)	30.5/45.6	62.2/76.5	46/72.4

From the results shown in Tables 8, 9 and 10 we can see that in all of the experiments solving 5-course and 10-course new cases, the timetables constructed by the graph heuristic method based on the partial solutions from the proposed CBR approach need much fewer scheduling steps and have less penalties than those constructed from scratch using the graph heuristic (GH) approach. The knowledge and experiences stored in the previously solved problems that are structurally similar to the new problems are re-used and not too much effort needs to be taken to get high quality results.

In solving the larger 15-course new cases by the case base with 5 or 10 15-course complex cases, the CBR approach finds timetables with higher penalties than those from the graph heuristic approach and takes almost the same number of schedule steps in adaptation. This is because only storing a small number of (less than 10) complex cases cannot provide enough good cases (sub-structures) and the complexity of the retrieved cases makes the adaptation difficult. Storing more complex cases provides much better results. Also, larger retrieved cases may cause more adaptation because more courses in the timetables of these cases may need more adaptation. This is why in Table 8 some of the retrieved larger cases provide high penalty timetables for the new cases.

It can also be seen that not all of the timetables adapted from the complete matching cases are better than those from the partial matching cases (although most of them are much better than those generated by the graph heuristic approach). This might be because the larger good structures of the complete matches in the timetables are more likely to be destroyed in the adaptations for the new cases.

4. Conclusions and Future Work

The CBR approach described in this paper avoids large amounts of computation and provides good results in solving timetabling problems. It shows that the retrieved cases that have similar (sub-)structures can provide high quality partial solutions for the new cases. This is because by retrieving structurally similar cases from the case base, solutions generated on similar constraints may be easily reused for the new case without significant adaptations. Timetables constructed by using the graph heuristic method on the basis of these partial solutions take less scheduling effort to get lower penalty solutions than those constructed by only using the same graph heuristic method from scratch.

The CBR system also shows that storing a certain number of cases in the case base can provide the same number of (sub-)structures as those obtained by storing more cases. We found that storing a certain number of complex cases works better than storing larger or more simple cases for providing the sub-structures for re-use. It is the number of (sub-)structures, not the number of cases in the case base that contributes to the successful retrieval of partial solutions for adaptation. It is important to build a case base with just a certain number of cases because the size of the decision tree grows rapidly when the size and the number of the cases in the case base increases.

The current approach gives promising results on solving relatively small problems. This provides a good basis for solving larger problems. Research is now being undertaken for solving larger timetabling problems based on the current system. All the cases in the current system are produced randomly to test the general performance. Tests on real-world specific timetabling problems will also be carried out. Other adaptation methods will also be studied in future work.

It is also likely that this CBR approach in timetabling can be used to solve more general problems in other domains that have inter-related objects and that can be modelled using attribute graphs.

References

1.   Koton P.: SMARTlan: A Case-Based Resource Allocation and Scheduling System. In: Proceedings: Workshop on Case-based Reasoning (DARPA). (1989) 285-289
2.   Hennessy D., Hinkle D.: Applying Case-Based Reasoning to Autoclave Loading. IEEE Expert. (1992) 7: 21-26
3.   Bezirgan A.: A Case-Based Approach to Scheduling Constraints. In: Dorn J., Froeschl K.A. (eds): Scheduling of Production Processes. Ellis Horwood Limited. (1993) 48-60
4.   Miyashita K., Sycara K.: Adaptive Case-Based Control of Scheduling Revision. In: Zweben M., Fox M.S. (eds): Intelligent Scheduling. Morgan Kaufmann. (1994) 291-308

5. MacCarthy B., Jou P.: Case-Based Reasoning in Scheduling. In: Khan M.K., Wright C.S. (eds.): Proceedings of the Symposium on Advanced Manufacturing Processes, Systems and Techniques (AMPST96). MEP Publications Ltd. (1996) 211-218
6. MacCarthy B. Jou P.: A Case-Based Expert System for Scheduling Problems with Sequence Dependent Set Up Times. In: Adey R.A., Rzevski G. (eds): Applications of Artificial Intelligence. In: Engineering X. Computational Machines Publications: Southampton. (1995) 89-96
7. Cunningham P., Smyth B.: Case-Based Reasoning in Scheduling: Reusing Solution Components. The International Journal of Production Research. (1997) **35**: 2947-2961
8. Schmidt G.: Case-Based Reasoning for Production Scheduling. International Journal of Production Economics. (1998) **56-57**: 537-546
9. Wren V.: Scheduling, Timetabling and Rostering – A Special Relationship? In: Burke E.K., Ross P. (eds.): The Practice and Theory of Automated Timetabling I. Lecture Notes in Computer Science 1153. Springer-Verlag: Berlin (1996) 46-75
10. Carter M.W., Laporte G.: Recent Developments in Practical Course Timetabling. Burke E.K., Carter M. (eds.): The Practice and Theory of Automated Timetabling II. Lecture Notes in Computer Science 1408. Springer-Verlag: Berlin (1998) 3-19
11. Werra D.: Graphs, Hypergraphs and Timetabling. Methods of Operations Research (Germany F.R.). (1985) **49**: 201–213
12. Tripathy A.: School Timetabling - A Case in Large Binary Integer Linear Programming. Management Science. (1984) **30**:1473–1489
13. Dowsland K.A.: Off-the-Peg or Made to Measure? Timetabling and Scheduling with SA and TS. In: The Practice and Theory of Automated Timetabling: Selected Papers from the 2nd International Conference. Springer-Verlag: Berlin. (Lecture Notes in Computer Science 1408). (1998) 37-52
14. Thomson J.M., Dowsland K.A.: General Cooling Schedules for a Simulate Annealing Based Timetabling System. In: Burke E.K., Ross P. (eds.): The Practice and Theory of Automated Timetabling I. Lecture Notes in Computer Science 1153. Springer-Verlag: Berlin (1996) 345-364
15. Erben W., Keppler J.: A Genetic Algorithm Solving a Weekly Course-Timeatbling Problem. In: Burke E.K., Ross P. (eds.): The Practice and Theory of Automated Timetabling I. Lecture Notes in Computer Science 1153. Springer-Verlag: Berlin (1996) 198-211
16. Burke E.K., Newell J.P., Weare R.F.: A Memetic Algorithm for University Exam Timetabling. In: Burke E.K., Ross P. (eds.): The Practice and Theory of Automated Timetabling I. Lecture Notes in Computer Science 1153. Springer-Verlag: Berlin (1996) 241-250
17. Paechter B., Cumming A., Norman M.G., Luchian H.: Extensions to a Memetic Timetabing System. In: Burke E.K., Ross P. (eds.): The Practice and Theory of Automated Timetabling I. Lecture Notes in Computer Science 1153. Springer-Verlag: Berlin (1996) 251-265
18. Burke E.K., Ross P.: The Practice and Theory of Automated Timetabling: Selected Papers from the 1st International Conference. Springer-Verlag: Berlin. (Lecture Notes in Computer Science 1153). (1996)
19. Burke E.K., Carter M.: The Practice and Theory of Automated Timetabling: Selected Papers from the 2nd International Conference. Springer-Verlag: Berlin. (Lecture Notes in Computer Science 1408). (1998)
20. Burke E.K., Wilhelm E.: Proceedings of the 3rd International Conference on Practice and Theory of Automated Timetabling. To be published by Springer-Verlag: Berlin. (2001)
21. Watson I., Marir F.: Case-Based Reasoning: a Review. The Knowledge Engineering Review. (1994) **9**: 327-354

22. Burke E.K., MacCarthy B., Petrovic S., Qu R.: Structured Cases in CBR – Re-using and Adapting Cases for Timetabling Problems. Journal of Knowledge-based System. (2000) 13(2-3): 159-165

23. Ricci F., Senter L.: Structured Cases, Trees and Efficient Retrieval. Proceedings of the Fourth European Workshop on Case-based Reasoning. Springer-Verlag: Dublin. (1998) 88-99

24. Sanders K.E., Kettler B.P., Hendler J.A.: The Case for Graph-Structured Representations. Proceedings of the Second International Conference on Case-based Reasoning. Springer-Verlag: Berlin. (1997) 245-254

25. Andersen W.A., Evett M.P., Kettler B., Hendler J.: Massively Parallel Support for Case-Based Planning. IEEE Expert. (1994) 7: 8-14

26. Börner K.: Structural Similarity as Guidance in Case-Based Design. In: Wess S., Althoff K.D., Richter M. (eds): Topics in Case-based Reasoning. Springer-Verlag: Kaiserslautern. (1993) 197-208

27. Börner K., Coulon C.H., Pippig E., Tammer E.C.: Structural Similarity and Adaptation. In: Smith I., Faltings B. (eds): Advances in Case-based Reasoning. Springer-Verlag: Switzerland. (1996) 58-75

28. Gebhardt F.: Methods and Systems for Case Retrieval Exploiting the Case Structure, FABEL-Report 39, GMD, Sankt Augustin. (1995)

29. Garey M.R., Johnson D.S.: Computers and Intractability: A Guide to the Theory of NP-Completeness. Freeman and Company: New York. (1979)

30. Messmer B.T.: Efficient Graph Matching Algorithms for Preprocessed Model Graph. PhD thesis, University of Bern. (1995)

31. Quinlan J.R.: Induction of Decision Trees. Machine Learning. Morgan Kaufmann (1986) 1: 81-106

32. Williams H.P.: Model Building in Mathematical Programming. Wiley: Chichester. (1999)

33. Burke E.K., Elliman D.G., Weare R.F.: A University Timetabling System Based on Graph Colouring and Constraint Manipulation. Journal of Research on Computing in Education. (1994) 27: 1-18

Ranking Algorithms for Costly Similarity Measures

Robin Burke

Dept. of Information Systems and Decision Sciences
California State University, Fullerton
rburke@fullerton.edu

Abstract. Case retrieval for e-commerce product recommendation is an application of CBR that demands particular attention to efficient implementation. Users expect quick response times from on-line catalogs, regardless of the underlying technology. In FindMe systems research, the cost of metric application has been a primary impediment to efficient retrieval. This paper describes several types of general and special-purpose ranking algorithms for case retrieval and evaluates their impact on retrieval efficiency with the Entree restaurant recommender.

1 Introduction

Case-based product recommendation is an important application of CBR technology for electronic commerce catalogs and on-line shopping. [1] Some of the chief problems in this application area are those of scale and efficiency. To meet the demands of Internet e-commerce and compete with alternative technologies, CBR product recommendation must be efficient without losing its accuracy. Moreover, a recommender must be able to cope with the dynamic nature of a product catalog as prices, availabilities, and contents are all subject to frequent change.

Although much case-based reasoning research has concentrated on improving the efficiency of case retrieval, many approaches do not handle case bases whose contents are dynamic. Building on the work of Shimazu et al. [10], Schumacher and Bergmann [7] have implemented e-commerce CBR retrieval on top of relational database systems, achieving impressive retrieval efficiency in a dynamic context. They work from the query to describe in SQL the region in feature space that would yield the most similar cases, using case density estimation to determine the region's desired size. This work concentrates only on retrieval, however and the retrieved results must still be ranked. Additionally, the work assumes a flat attribute-value representation.

Entree is a case-based restaurant recommendation system available on-line[1] [2,3,4]. In this and related systems, we have found that metric application itself can be chief source of inefficiency in retrieval. It is therefore important to create retrieval algorithms that minimize the number of applications of metrics. This paper introduces the problem of metric application that arises in FindMe systems, describes several possible ranking algorithms applied to the problem, and evaluates them using the Entree restaurant data.

---

[1] http://infolab.ils.nwu.edu/entree/

D.W. Aha and I. Watson (Eds.): ICCBR 2001, LNAI 2080, pp. 105-117, 2001.

2   Local and Global Similarity Measures

Entree and other FindMe systems have case representations that use single-value and set-based representations of attributes. Set-valued attributes are quite common. For example, the cuisine of a restaurant is a set-valued attribute because a restaurant may serve several different kinds of food or incorporate multiple culinary influences.

Suppose we defined A_i as a set-valued attribute of a case and a_i as the set of values associated with it. FindMe systems use the following local similarity metric for set-valued attributes:

$sim(A_i, B_i) = |\ a_i \cap b_i\ | / |\ a_i\ |$

For example, consider restaurants D, E and F, with the following values for the cuisine feature:

D: { Thai }
E: { Thai, Chinese, Vietnamese }
F: { Chinese }

This asymmetric overlap metric looks at the size of the feature set intersection relative to the size of the set in the query case. So, for example, the similarity between D and E is maximal, because E overlaps with everything found in D. The similarity between E and D is less because D only contains 1/3 of what is found in E. This metric is intentionally asymmetric, under the assumption that a user looking for Thai food would be satisfied by a restaurant that served both Thai and Chinese, but one looking for a restaurant that combined French and Japanese influences would not necessarily be happy with a restaurant that focused on one or the other.

Metrics of this type present some difficulty in case retrieval. The calculation is not efficient to perform, having complexity $|a_i| * |b_i|$. Because the metric is asymmetric, the distance between cases does not form a metric space where cases can be ordered. If we wish to cache the distance between cases, we have to store as many as c^2 values, where c is the size of the case base. Moreover, in a dynamic database, cached values would have to be recalculated frequently. The dynamics of the product database therefore rule out approaches that rely on similarity caching, such as case-retrieval nets [4] and k-d trees [5]. The alternative that we have adopted is to compute the metric at retrieval time, but design our algorithm to minimize the number of such computations.

2.1   Global Similarity Measures

FindMe systems use a global similarity metric in which local similarity measures are combined in a priority ordering. For example, restaurants are compared first with respect to cuisine and then the quality dimension is used to break ties between otherwise similar restaurants, with additional considerations applied to achieve finer-grained distinctions. This type of metric is somewhat different than the weighted combination typically found in case-based reasoning systems, but it has the important advantage that it is easy to engineer. A hierarchy of the importance of different product characteristics is simple to generate from basic domain considerations, and it is easy to envision what the consequences of any change (for example, putting price before cuisine instead of the other way around). By contrast, the setting of weights in weighted metrics has always been recognized as a difficult problem. A hierarchical metric can always be turned into a weighted combination by using weights that increase exponentially with priority.

3   Sorting Algorithms

Earlier publications on Entree [2] described a bucket sorting algorithm made possible by restricting metrics to range only over small integer values. That algorithm is also discussed below, but experience has shown that this limitation on metric formulation is too restrictive. This paper considers the general case, where the similarity function can return a real-numbered value.

The simplest solution for retrieving the best cases is to evaluate all of the metrics and sort. This Sort algorithm can be formalized as follows:

```
Sort (q, C, M)
Let q be the query case
For each case c in the case base C
      Create a vector of similarity values v_c
      For each metric m_i in the similarity function M
           v_c[i] = m_i(q, c)
Sort (C, compare)
```
where the following comparison function is used
```
compare (c1, c2)
      for i=0..|v|
           if v_c1[i] > v_c2[i] then return "c1 greater"
           if v_c2[i] > v_c1[i] then return "c2 greater"
      return "c1 = c2"
```

If an efficient sorting algorithm such as Quicksort is used, the complexity of sorting will be $O(c \log c)$, where c is the number of cases. The cost of metric application is $m*c$, if m is the number of metrics.

One feature of Entree's retrieval (as well as other e-commerce case retrieval systems) is that it aims to retrieve only a small number of responses, so that the user is not overwhelmed with alternatives. In Entree, the maximum number of restaurants retrieved is 10. When only a few of the top cases are needed, it is possible to perform a selection operation over the set of cases and return the top items.

```
Select (q, C, M)
Let q be the query case
For each case c in the case base C
      Create a vector of similarity values v_c
      For each metric m_i in the similarity function
           v_c[i] = m_i(q, c)
For i=1..k
      answer[i] = null
      For j = 1..|C|
           compare(c_j, answer[i])
           if (c_j > answer[i]) then
                answer[i] = c_j
      remove c[], answer[i]
```

using the comparison function described above.

This has efficiency O (c * k), where k is the desired number of cases returned, better than sorting for small values of k, but it is equivalent to a sort algorithm as far as metric applications are concerned: each metric must be evaluated for each case to compute the score against which to apply the maximum value test.

In practice, the whole case base would never need to be sorted or selected from. It is possible to extract a subset of the case base as the region where similar cases are to be found. This initial step can be performed with database or table lookup and can increase the efficiency of later sorting. In Entree, a simple inverted index technique was used, in which the system retrieved any case that has any possible overlap with the query case. While this technique has the advantage of not ruling out any similar cases, it was found to be excessively liberal, retrieving an average of 87% of the case base. In our later work [3], we implemented a database technique similar to Schumacher and Bergmann's [7] for retrieving this initial set.

3.1   Metric Application on Demand

Since metric computations are to be minimized, one of the major concerns regarding the Sort algorithm is that many of the metric computations are wasted. If we can determine that $c_1 > c_2$ on the basis of the first value in the value vector, then the rest of the values are not needed. It may be the case that these values are not needed to compare c_1 against any other cases. Because of the nature of the similarity measure, metric applications can be omitted without harming the quality of the sort.

This insight suggests an "on-demand" approach to metric application. Rather than computing all metric values first and sorting later, let the algorithm compute only those metric values needed to actually perform the comparisons required by the sort operation.

The Metric Application on Demand Sort (MADSort) algorithm below also uses a standard sort procedure, but it skips the initial step of pre-computing the metric values. Its comparison routine only computes a new similarity value if that value is actually needed. For example, consider a candidate set of three cases c_1, c_2, and c_3, and two metrics m_1 and m_2. When c_1 and c_2 are compared for sorting, the algorithm computes $m_1(q, c_1)$ and $m_1(q, c_2)$ and discovers that c_1 has the higher value. When c_1 is compared against c_3, the value of $m_1(q, c_1)$ does not need to be recomputed.

```
MADSort (q, C, M)
For each case c in the case base C
     Create a empty vector of similarity values v_c
Sort (C, compare_on_demand)

compare_on_demand (c1, c2)
     for i=0..|v|
          if v_c1[i] is not yet computed,
               v_c1[i] = m_i(q,c1)
          if v_c2[i] is not yet computed,
               v_c2[i] = m_i(q,c2)
          if v_c1[i] > v_c2[i] then return "c1 greater"
          if v_c2[i] > v_c1[i] then return "c2 greater"
     return "c1 = c2"
```

This algorithm's complexity depends on the "discrimination power" of the individual metrics m_i. In the worst case, $m_a = m_b$ for all c, in which case the algorithm is no different from the simple Sort. However, a similarity function with this property is useless in practice since it performs no discrimination and so the worst case does not arise.

One way to analyze the complexity is in terms of the discriminating power ρ of each metric ρ_m. One way to define the power of a metric is to consider the ability of the metric to divide the case base into equivalence classes. Assume that a metric creates equivalence classes that are equal in size across the case base. We can define ρ as follows: $\rho = 1$ implies that the metric creates an equivalence class the size of c, performing no discrimination; $\rho = 1/c$ is one that creates equivalence classes of size 1, therefore imposing a total order on the case base. So, the probability that recourse to a higher metric will be required for any two randomly chosen cases, c_1 and c_2 is dependent on the size of the equivalence classes created by the metric. Assuming equal size classes, a metric with power ρ yields classes of size $c*\rho$. c_2 will fall into the same class as c_1 according to the proportion between the size of the equivalence class after c_1 is removed ($c* \rho - 1$), and the size of the whole case base also after c_1 is removed, ($c-1$). The probability that the two are in the same class is therefore

$$\frac{c\rho - 1}{c - 1} \tag{1}$$

If c is large, this equation can be simplified to

$$\frac{c\rho - 1}{c} = \rho - \frac{1}{c} \approx \rho \tag{2}$$

The probability that we will have to apply j metrics is the product of the probabilities of needing to apply all of the metrics up to j.

$$\prod_{i=1}^{j} \rho_{i-1} \tag{3}$$

We always have to apply at least one metric, even if it is a perfect one. So, the expected number of metrics that would have to be applied to compare two randomly-chosen cases would be

$$e = 1 + \sum_{j=1}^{m-1} \prod_{i=1}^{j} \rho_{i-1} \tag{4}$$

where m is the number of metrics.

Each additional comparison adds to the expected number of metrics applied on a case. When a second comparison is made, additional metric applications will only be needed if previously-drawn distinctions are not enough. The probability of this happening is the product of the • values of the already-applied metrics. If more metrics are needed, then we can use the same considerations as in Equation 4 to calculate the expected number.

$$e' = \prod_{k=1}^{e} p_k \left(1 + \sum_{j=e+1}^{m-1} \prod_{i=1}^{j} p_{i-1} \right)$$

(5)

The total expected number of metric applications is therefore the sum of this recurrence over all comparisons performed. There is no simple closed-form solution, but the characteristics of the function are easy to evaluate numerically. An efficient sorting algorithm like Quicksort performs c log c comparisons. Each case would be compared to log c other cases. A candidate set of size 1024 would therefore entail 10 comparisons per case. If all of the metrics in the global similarity function had $\rho = 0.1$, in the 10th round of comparisons, the expected number of metrics applied to each case would be 1.55, for a total metric application count of 1593, only a quarter of the full m*c needed by the Sort algorithm. If on the other hand, the metrics are weaker with $\rho = 0.75$, for example, we would expect, by the 9th round of comparison, that all of the metrics would already be applied.

The same "on demand" technique can be applied to create a MADSelect algorithm, using the Select algorithm as above but with the on-demand comparison function. The analysis is similar except that there are k rounds of comparison, where k is the number of answers to be returned.

Since the number of metric applications is a simple statistic to collect in the operation of a retriever, this derivation also provides us a way to measure the discriminatory power of a metric or an entire similarity function. We can examine the total number of metric applications and the number of candidates retrieved and calculate a combined ρ for the whole metric. This value is the overall ρ for only the first m-1 metrics, since ρ_m does not contribute to Equation 4. We can also derive ρ for each metric in the function in isolation, simply by running the same experiment with a simplified similarity metric. This technique is applied to the Entree similarity measure in the experiments below.

3.2   Tournament Tree

Another approach to minimize the number of metric applications is to use a data structure that allows selection and comparison to be interleaved. One such data structure is the *tournament tree* [8]. A tournament tree is a binary tree where the parent of two nodes is determined by comparing the two children and copying the "winner" to the parent. Through successive comparisons, the root of the tree is the overall winner. To extract the top k elements from such a tree, the winning leaf is replaced with a null value and the log(c) competitions up to the root are recomputed.

Figure 1 shows a simple tournament tree example. Node A is the winner against both B and C, and becomes the root node. When it is removed, B is now the overall winner and is bubbled to the top. The top k elements can be found in order using only k log c comparisons, rather than the n log n required for a full sort or the k*c that would be needed in a selection algorithm.

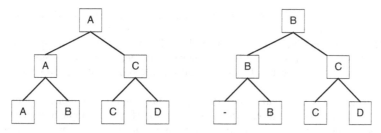

Fig. 1. Tournament tree sort

Here is a tournament tree selection algorithm that returns only the top k cases:

```
Create a vector t₀ of size c = |C| containing all
    elements of the case base
For each case
    Create a vector of similarity values v
Loop
    c = c/2
    For each c adjacent pairs c₁, cᵣ in tᵢ
        compare_on_demand (c₁, cᵣ)
        if (c₁ > cᵣ) copy c₁ to tᵢ₊₁
        else copy cᵣ to tᵢ₊₁
Until c = 1
For each case to be output
    Copy the root case c₀ to the output
    Replace c₀ in t₀ with a null value
    Recompute all the parents of c₀ in the tree
```

There are only k log c comparisons performed in this sort routine, and with on-demand metric application, the number of metric applications is e*k*log c. Table 1 shows how all the algorithms discussed so far compare with respect to metric applications.

Table 1. Expected number of metric applications

Algorithm	No. of metric applications
Sort/Select	$m \cdot c$
MADSort	$e \cdot c \cdot \log c$
MADSelect	$e \cdot k \cdot c$
Tournament tree	$e \cdot k \cdot \log c$

4   Experiments

While these theoretical results suggest the possible benefit of alternate ranking algorithms, we also performed experiments to quantify these benefits. Since our object is to minimize the number of times that metrics are applied, we use the number of metric applications performed by each algorithm as a primary evaluation metric, but run times were also examined. Five algorithms were tested: Sort, Select, MADSort, MADSelect, and Tournament Tree. Each of the 675 Chicago restaurants was used as a query against the Entree database, in a leave-one-out protocol, and the results averaged. This protocol was repeated for different result set sizes: 10, 50 and 100.

Figure 2 shows the results counting the average number of metric applications. (Select is omitted since it has the same number of metric applications as Sort.) MADSelect outperforms all the other algorithms at small retrieval sizes, but its advantage decreases with the size of the return set, equaling the Tournament Tree algorithm at set size 100.

This result is somewhat surprising given the difference in the expected number of metric applications shown in Table 1. With an average of number of retrieved cases at 585, $\log c = 9.19$: one would expect Tournament Tree to be far superior. And with $k = 10$, MADSort should have an edge that increases with k.

The explanation has to do with which cases are being compared. MADSelect operates over the cases in k passes. In the first pass, on average, half of the comparisons performed by MADSelect will be against the best candidate. Cases that are close to the best will have to be fully evaluated to determine that they are not better; and cases that are far away will be ruled out with few applications. Each successive pass follows the pattern, but the good cases will have already been fully evaluated. The Tournament Tree algorithm is not at all selective about which cases are being compared: cases are compared to their neighbors.

MADSort improves only slightly (but significantly, $p \ll 0.001$) over Sort, eliminating less than 1% of metric applications on average. Like Tournament Tree, MADSort does not concentrate its comparison effort on the best candidates, and so performs many unnecessary metric applications.

The run time results in Figure 3 show the interplay of algorithm complexity along with metric application counts. The select algorithms (Select and MADSelect) show distinct deterioration with increasing result size, while the Tournament Tree gives ground much more slowly. The simple Sort has a better run time than MADSort despite having more metric applications, probably due to lower overhead.

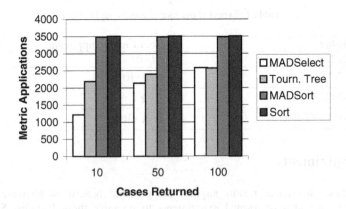

Fig. 2. Comparison of the case sorting algorithms (# of metric applications)

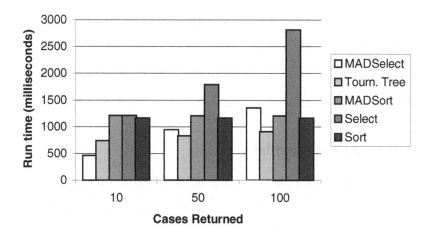

Fig. 3. Comparison of case sorting algorithms (run-time)

4.1 Calculating Discriminatory Power

As discussed above, the MADSelect experiments allow us to estimate ρ for the metrics that Entree uses. With an average number of metric applications at 1218 and the average number of restaurants sorted at 585, the ratio of applications to restaurants is just over 2. Given an expected number of 9 (log 585) comparisons per case, interpolation provides an average ρ of approximately 0.27, which seems to indicate that the metrics are, in general, fairly strong.[2] Of course, this computation assumes that the metrics are all equal in their discriminating power (which is not at all the case) and that the metrics create equivalence classes of equal size (which is also a substantial simplification). However, a rough measure of this type may be useful in comparing the quality of different global similarity measures.

To obtain a more precise picture of the power of each component of a metric, we can create a series of simplified global metrics, each containing two local metrics. Suppose we have two metrics m_a and m_b. The expected number of metric applications would be $e = 1 + a$. Our experiments yield an observed value o for the number of metric applications per case, so we can solve for ρ_a yielding $\rho_a = o - 1$.

In the case of Entree, the basic similarity algorithm combines 5 local metrics: strict cuisine similarity, approximate cuisine similarity, atmosphere, quality, and price. Table 2 shows the average ρ values for these metrics as experimentally determined.

That quality is the best discriminator is probably not surprising, since quality scales are designed to make distinctions. Cuisine is the least effective, since for most cuisines there are many restaurants. This is unfortunate since these are the first metrics applied. Atmosphere is surprisingly strong as compared with price, but the price ranges in Entree's data are fairly loose and most of the restaurants fall in the $15-30 bracket.

---

[2] Using the more complex original probability definition found in Equation 1 alters these values less than 0.1%.

Table 2. Entree metrics and their discriminatory powers

Metric	Observed ρ
Exact cuisine	0.47
Approximate cuisine	0.47
Atmosphere	0.14
Quality	0.12
Price	0.28

5   Special Case Algorithms

Earlier publications on FindMe systems, including Entree, described a different sorting procedure that takes advantage of the restricted class of metrics implemented with these systems. In particular, the similarity metrics found in FindMe systems are restricted to a small range of integer values. With such metrics, it is possible to use a binned sorting strategy such as that found in radix sort [9]. Radix sort creates a set of bins corresponding to the range of possible values and places items into each bin according to their value. The operation is repeated to achieve a multi-level or lexicographic sort on a series of values in order of priority. Because item-to-item comparisons are not used, radix sort improves on comparison-based sorting algorithms to achieve linear complexity: $O(d(n+k))$ where k is the range of values, and d is the number of keys. Here, however, the standard radix sort is not more efficient that the Tournament Tree algorithm, because it starts with the least significant comparison, working its way to the most significant. If applied directly, it would require m*c metric applications, just like the simple Sort.

The FindMe algorithm therefore uses the most significant metric first, and achieves efficiency by continuously truncating the set of candidates being sorted. The sort begins with a single bucket B_0 in which all candidates are placed. Then the most significant metric m_0 is applied and B_0 is replaced by a set of new buckets containing the contents of B_0 spread out by their value when compared using m_0. Now the contents of the top buckets are counted to find the bucket cutoff value, t

$$t \text{ s.t. } \sum_{i=0}^{t-1} |B_i| < \max \text{ and } \sum_{i=0}^{t} |B_i| > \max \tag{6}$$

In other words, we include enough buckets to be sure of having *max* cases to return. The first t buckets are used in the next round; other buckets can be discarded.

This algorithm has the effect of reducing the set of candidate cases quickly and thereby radically reduces the number of metric applications beyond what is found in the MADSelect and Tournament Tree algorithms. Figures 4 and 5 show the results of comparing this technique against these two algorithms. When the result set is small, the average number of metric applications is reduced to 68% of MADSelect (829 vs. 1218). As the number of cases increases, Bucket Sort loses some ground to the Tournament Tree, but not nearly as much as MADSelect. For run times, this effect is even more dramatic – the gap between Bucket Sort and Tournament Tree shrinks, as MADSelect falls far behind.

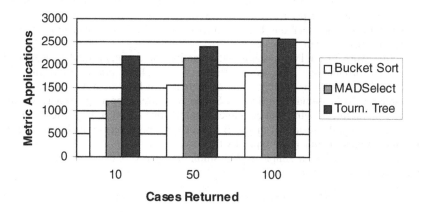

Fig. 4. Comparison of Bucket sort against MADSelect and Tournament Tree   (# of metric applications)

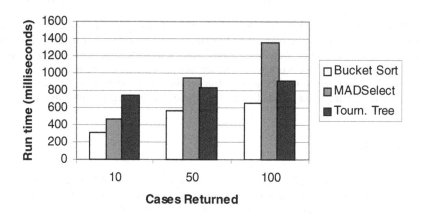

Fig. 5. Comparison of Bucket Sort against MADSelect and Tournament Tree (run time)

6   Related and Future Work

The issue of metric application cost has not surfaced as a major issue in case-based reasoning, partly because of the use of indexing methods that cache similarity information, and partly because most systems do not use the kind of prioritized similarity function described here. Bridge [11] has tackled the problem of generalizing global similarity functions and (with Ferguson) in [12] also examined prioritized combinations of similarity metrics such as those found in Entree. This research elaborates an elegant framework of partial-order-based similarity functions and rules for combining them. One of the interesting aspects of Bridge's work is the notion of generalized prioritization: a way of relaxing a strict hierarchy of metrics, maintaining priority relations between metrics that are looser than those found in Entree and discussed in this paper.

Future work in FindMe systems will examine more general (and typical) global similarity formulations such as the Bridge's generalized prioritization and linear combination. For linear combinations of metrics, we lose the advantage of a static hierarchy of local similarity influence. Suppose we are comparing two cases c and d using a hierarchical metric that combines local metrics A and B. If metric A finds c > d, we know that the results of metric B cannot have any effect on their ordering. In a linear combination, this is not typically the case.

However, consider a simple global similarity metric S that combines two local measures using weights:

$$S(c_1, c_2) = w_1 s_1(c_1, c_2) + w_2 s_2(c_1, c_2) \tag{7}$$

Suppose that $w_1 \gg w_2$, and that we are ranking two cases c and d against a query case q. If we find that c scores well with s_1 and d scores poorly, it might be mathematically impossible for d to outrank c, even if it gets the maximum score obtainable from s_2 and c gets the lowest. In this case, we can use the MAD technique to skip evaluating s_2.

This technique would only be worthwhile if the cost of applying a metric significantly exceeded the overhead of testing for the possibility of its exclusion, and if the weights in a metric were sufficiently skewed to make it possible to benefit from this optimization. Future work will examine this optimization more fully.

Finally, given the proven benefit of Bucket Sort over the other techniques, we are also interested in extending this binned technique to non-integer-valued metrics.

Conclusion

This paper has examined the problem of managing the cost of metric application in hierarchical metric combinations. Such hierarchical metrics are not as common as weighted sum similarity functions, but they have proven effective in the catalog search domains found in FindMe systems.

Several algorithms were discussed and in the general case, a selection algorithm that caches metric results demonstrated the best performance for small result set sizes, while an algorithm based on the tournament tree shows the best performance for larger result sets. For special formulations of the local similarity metrics, the previously-published bucket sort algorithm shows substantial improvement.

Finally, the analysis of the on-demand sorting algorithm allows us to examine metric performance in terms of discriminatory power, examining both overall performance of a global similarity measure and the capabilities of its individual local metrics. This capability can assist knowledge engineers in the creation of effective metrics for case-based retrieval systems.

Acknowledgments. Entree was developed at the University of Chicago in collaboration with Kristian Hammond, with the support of the Office of Naval Research under grant F49620-88-D-0058. Many others contributed to the FindMe effort at the University of Chicago, including Terrence Asselin, Kai Martin, Kass Schmitt, Robb Thomas, and Ben Young. I would also like to acknowledge David Aha and four anonymous ICCBR reviewers for their assistance in improving this paper.

References

[1] Vollrath, I., Wilke, W., Bergmann R.: Intelligent Electronic Catalogs for Sales Support -- Introducing Case-Based Reasoning Techniques to On-Line Product Selection Applications. In Roy, R., Furuhashi, T., Chawddhry, P.K. (Eds.): *Advances in Soft Computing - Engineering Design and Manufacturing*. Springer. London, 1999.

[2] Burke, R., Hammond, K., and Young, B.: The FindMe Approach to Assisted Browsing. *IEEE Expert*, 12(4), 32-40, 1997.

[3] Burke, R.: The Wasabi Personal Shopper: A Case-Based Recommender System. In *Proceedings of the 11th National Conference on Innovative Applications of Artificial Intelligence*, 844-849. AAAI, 1999.

[4] Burke, R.: Knowledge-based Recommender Systems. In A. Kent (ed.), *Encyclopedia of Library and Information Systems*. Vol. 69, Supplement 32. Marcel Dekker, New York, 2000.

[5] Lenz, M., Burkhard H. D.: Case Retrieval Nets: Basic Ideas and Extensions. In Görz G, Hölldobler, S. (Eds): *KI-96: Advances in Artificial Intelligence*. Springer Press, 1996.

[6] Wess, S., Althoff, K.-D., Derwand, G.: Using kd-trees to improve the retrieval step in case-based reasoning. In Wess, S., Althoff, K.-D., Richter, M.M. (Eds): *Topics in Case-Based Reasoning*, , 167-81, Springer-Verlag, Berlin, 1994.

[7] Schumacher, J. and Bergmann, R.: An Efficient Approach to Similarity-Based Retrieval on Top of Relational Databases. In E. Blanzieri & L. Portinale (Eds): *Advances in Case-Based Reasoning: Proceedings of the European Workshop on Case-Based Reasoning, EWCBR00*, 273-284. Springer-Verlag, Berlin, 2000.

[8] Horowitz, E., Sahni, S.: *Fundamentals of Data Structures*. Computer Science Press, Rockville, MD, 1981.

[9] Cormen, T., Lieserson, C., Rivest, R.: *Introduction to Algorithms*. MIT Press, Cambridge, MA, 1990.

[10] Shimazu, H., Kitano, H., Shibata, A.: Retrieving Cases from Relational Data-Bases: Another Stride Towards Corporate-Wide Case-Base Systems. In *Proceedings of the 1993 International Joint Conference on Artificial Intelligence*, 909-914. IJCAI, 1993.

[11] Bridge, D.: Defining and Combining Symmetric and Asymmetric Similarity Measures. In Smyth, B., Cunningham, P. (Eds.): *Advances in Case-Based Reasoning: Proceedings of the European Workshop in Case-Based Reasoning, EWCBR98*, 52-63. Springer, Berlin, 1998.

[12] Ferguson, A., Bridge, D.: Partial Orders and Indifference Relations: Being Purposefully Vague in Case-Based Retrieval. In Blanzieri, E., Portinale, L. (Eds.): *Advances in Case-Based Reasoning: Proceedings of the European Workshop on Case-Based Reasoning, EWCBR00*, 74-85. Springer, Berlin, 2000.

A Fuzzy-Rough Approach for Case Base Maintenance

Guoqing Cao, Simon Shiu, and Xizhao Wang

Department of Computing, Hong Kong Polytechnic University
Hung Hom, Kowloon, Hong Kong
{csgqcao, csckshiu, csxzwang}@comp.polyu.edu.hk

Abstract. This paper proposes a fuzzy-rough method of maintaining Case-Based Reasoning (CBR) systems. The methodology is mainly based on the idea that a large case library can be transformed to a small case library together with a group of adaptation rules, which take the form of fuzzy rules generated by the rough set technique. In paper [1], we have proposed a methodology for case base maintenance which used a fuzzy decision tree induction to discover the adaptation rules; in this paper, we focus on using a heuristic algorithm, i.e., a fuzzy-rough algorithm [2] in the process of simplifying fuzzy rules. This heuristic, regarded as a new fuzzy learning algorithm, has many significant advantages, such as rapid speed of training and matching, generating a family of fuzzy rules which is approximately simplest. By applying such a fuzzy-rough learning algorithm to the adaptation mining phase, the complexity of case base maintenance is reduced, and the adaptation knowledge is more compact and effective. The effectiveness of the method is demonstrated experimentally using two sets of testing data, and we also compare the maintenance results of using fuzzy ID3, in [1], and the fuzzy-rough approach, as in this paper.

1 Introduction

At present, large-scale CBR systems are becoming more popular, with case-library sizes ranging from thousands [3][4] to millions of cases [5]. Large case library sizes raise problems of case retrieval efficiency, and many CBR researchers pay more attention to the problem of Case Base Maintenance (CBM). According to Leake and Wilson [6] "case base maintenance is the process of refining a CBR system's case base to improve the system's performance". That is, "case base maintenance implements policies for revising the organization or contents (representation, domain content, accounting information, or implementation) of the case base, in order to facilitate future reasoning for a particular set of performance objectives".

How should we maintain large case-based reasoning systems? In the past, researchers have done much work in this area. Smyth and Keane [7] suggested a competence-preserving deletion approach. They put forward the concept of competence (or coverage), being the range of target problems that a given system can solve and also a fundamental evaluation criterion of CBR system performance. Smyth and McKenna [8] also presented a new model of case competence, and demonstrated a way in which the proposed model of competence can be used to assist case authors.

D.W. Aha and I. Watson (Eds.): ICCBR 2001, LNAI 2080, pp. 118-130, 2001.

Anand et al. [9] proposed to use data mining techniques for mining adaptation knowledge, and maintaining CBR systems.

Recently, Richter proposed the notion of knowledge containers [10][11], and it quickly became the standard paradigm for representation of the structural elements in CBR systems. Simon et al. established a methodology that could be used to transfer case knowledge to adaptation knowledge [1]. The methodology integrated identifying salient features, distinguishing different concepts, learning adaptation knowledge, computing case competence, and selecting representative cases together into a framework of CBM. Fuzzy set theory, as proposed by L.A. Zadeh [12], and rough set theory, allow the utilization of uncertain knowledge by means of fuzzy linguistic terms and their membership functions, which reflects human's understanding of the problem [13]. The rough set theory proposed by Z. Pawlak [14] enables us to find relationships between data without any additional information such as prior probability, only requiring knowledge representation as a set of if-then rules [13]. In this paper, we propose a new method of adaptation knowledge discovery, integrating rough set theory and fuzzy set theory to transfer the case knowledge to adaptation knowledge. This fuzzy-rough approach has many significant advantages, such as rapid speed of training and matching, generating a family of fuzzy rules which is approximately simplest. By applying such a fuzzy-rough learning algorithm to the phase of mining adaptation rules, the cost and complexity of case base maintenance is reduced, and the more important virtue is that the adaptation knowledge is more compact, effective and easily used.

2 Methodology for CBM Using Fuzzy-Rough Approach

In this paper, we use the framework of case base maintenance in [1] to carry out our CBM process. The details of maintaining a case-base from scratch, as proposed in [1], consists of four phases: firstly, an approach to learning feature weight automatically is used to evaluate the importance of different features in a given case base; secondly, clustering of cases will be carried out to identify different concepts in the case base using the acquired feature knowledge; thirdly, adaptation rules will be mined for each concept using fuzzy decision trees, but in this paper, we apply a fuzzy-rough approach to mine adaptation rules for each concept; finally, a selection strategy based on the concepts of ε-coverage and ε-reachability is used to select representative cases.

In the following sub-section, we briefly introduce phases 1, 2 and 4 of the methodology proposed in [1], and introduce our approach to step 3 in detail.

2.1 Phase One - Learning Feature Weights

In this section, a feature evaluation function is defined. The smaller the evaluation value, the better the corresponding features. Thus we would like to find the weights such that the evaluation function attains its minimum. The task of minimization of the evaluation function with respect to weights is performed using a gradient descent technique. We formulate this optimization problem as follows:

For a given collection of feature weights $w_j \left(w_j \in [0,1], j = 1, \cdots n \right)$ and a pair of cases e_p and e_q, equation (1) defines a weighted distance measure $d_{pq}^{(w)}$ and equation (2) defines a similarity measure $SM_{pq}^{(w)}$.

$$d_{pq}^{(w)} = d^{(w)}(e_p, e_q) = \left(\sum_{j=1}^{n} w_j^2 (x_{pj} - x_{qj})^2 \right)^{1/2} = \left(\sum_{j=1}^{n} w_j^2 \chi_j^2 \right)^{1/2} \tag{1}$$

where $\chi_j^2 = (x_{pj} - x_{qj})^2$. When all the weights are equal to 1, the distance metric defined above degenerates to the Euclidean measure, denoted by $d_{pq}^{(1)}$, in short, denoted by d_{pq}.

$$SM_{pq}^{(w)} = \frac{1}{1 + \alpha \cdot d_{pq}^{(w)}} \tag{2}$$

where α is a positive parameter. When all the weights take value 1, the similarity measure is denoted by $SM_{pq}^{(1)}$.

A feature evaluation index E is defined as

$$E(w) = \frac{2 * [\sum\limits_{p} \sum\limits_{q(q < p)} \left(SM_{pq}^{(w)} (1 - SM_{pq}^{(1)}) + SM_{pq}^{(1)} (1 - SM_{pq}^{(w)}) \right)]}{N * (N - 1)} \tag{3}$$

where N is the number of cases in the case base.

To minimize equation (3), we use a gradient descent technique. The change in w_j (i.e. Δw_j) is computed as

$$\Delta w_j = -\eta \frac{\partial E}{\partial w_j}, \tag{4}$$

for $j = 1, \cdots, n$, where η is the learning rate.

The training algorithm is described as follows:

Step 1. Select the parameter α and the learning rate η.
Step 2. Initialize w_j with random values in [0, 1].

Step 3. Compute Δw_j for each j using equation (4).

Step 4. Update w_j with $w_j + \Delta w_j$ for each j.

Step 5. Repeat step 3 and step 4 until convergence, i.e., until the value of E becomes less than or equal to a given threshold or until the number of iterations exceeds a certain predefined number.

2.2 Phase Two - Partitioning the Case Library into Several Clusters

This section attempts to partition the case library into several clusters by using the weighted distance metric with the weights learned in section 2.1. Since the considered features are considered to be real-valued, many methods, such as K-Means clustering [15] and Kohonen's self-organizing network [16], can be used to partition the case library. However in this paper, in order to compare the fuzzy decision tree and fuzzy-rough approaches in mining adaptation rules, we take the similarity matrix clustering method in [1].

2.3 Phase Three - Mining Adaptation Rules by Fuzzy-Rough Approach

For each cluster $L = \{e_1, e_2, \cdots, e_m\}$, we denote its cases in the form of $e_i = (x_{i1}, x_{i2}, \cdots, x_{in}, c_i)$, where x_{ij} corresponds to the value of feature $F_j (1 \le j \le n)$ and c_i corresponds to the action $(i = 1, \cdots, m)$. Arbitrarily taking a case $e_k (1 \le k \le m)$ in the cluster L, a set of vectors, namely $\{f_i \mid f_i \in R^{n+1}, i = 1,2, \cdots, m\}$, can be computed in the following way:

$$f_i = e_i - e_k = (x_{i1} - x_{k1}, x_{i2} - x_{k2}, \cdots, x_{in} - x_{kn}, c_i - c_k) =$$
$$\{y_{i1}, y_{i2}, \cdots, y_{in}, u_i\}$$

We attempt to find several adaptation rules with respect to the case $e_k (1 \le k \le m)$ from the set of vectors $\{f_i \mid f_i \in R^{n+1}, i = 1,2, \cdots, m\}$ by fuzzy rules.

Consider a problem of learning from examples in which there are n+1 numerical attributes, $\{Attr^{(1)}, Attr^{(2)}, \cdots, Attr^{(n)}, Attr^{(n+1)}\}$ ($Attr^{(n+1)}$) is the classification attribute). Then $\{f_i \mid i = 1,2, \cdots, m\}$ can be regarded as m examples described by the n+1 attributes. We first fuzzify these n+1 numerical attributes into linguistic terms.

The number of linguistic terms for each attribute is assumed to be five (which can be enlarged or reduced if it is needed in a real problem). These five linguistic terms are Negative Big, Negative Small, Zero, Positive Small, and Positive Big, in short, NB,NS, ZE, PS and PB respectively. Their membership functions are supposed to have triangular form and are shown in Figure 1. For each attribute (the k-th attribute $Attr^{(k)}$, $1 \le k \le n+1$) with the attribute-values $Range\ (Attr^{(k)}) = \left\{ y_{1k}, y_{2k}, \cdots, y_{mk} \right\}$, the two parameters in Figure 1, a and b, are defined by

$$a = \sum_{y \in N} y \big/ Card(N) \quad \text{and} \quad b = \sum_{y \in P} y \big/ Card(P) \qquad (5)$$

in which $N = \left\{ y \mid y \in Rang\ (Attr^{(k)}), y < 0 \right\}$,

$P = Range\ (Attr^{(k)}) - N$ and Card(E) denotes the cardinality of a crisp set E.

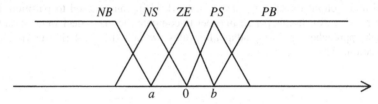

Fig. 1. Five membership functions

After the process of fuzzification, we transform the crisp cases in the case library to fuzzy cases successfully. Each fuzzy case is considered to be a fuzzy set defined on the non-fuzzy label space consisting of all values of attributes, where the non-fuzzy label space consists of the linguistic terms of each attribute. Consider each fuzzy case as an initial fuzzy rule. We then apply the rough set technique to these fuzzy rules and get a subset of those fuzzy rules, which covers all fuzzy cases, and the cardinality of the subset is approximately minimal. The fuzzy-rough algorithm is divided into three tasks to be fulfilled [1]: (1) in search of a minimal reduct for each initial fuzzy rule, (2) in search of a family of minimal reducts for the i th ($1 \le i \le M$, where M is the number of fuzzy cases)fuzzy case such that each reduct inside of this family covers the i th fuzzy case, and (3) in search of a subset of those fuzzy rules which covers all fuzzy cases and the cardinality of the subset is minimal.

We first introduce the definitions used in the fuzzy-rough approach.

In order to transfer the fuzzy data into fuzzy rules, firstly we introduce fuzzy knowledge base concept, Table 1 is said to be a fuzzy knowledge base, where there are n rows and m attributes. $Attr_j (j = 1,2,...,n)$. A_{ij} $(i = 1,2,...,n; j = 1,2,...,m)$ are all fuzzy sets defined on the same universe $U = \{1,2,...,n\}$, and it can be regarded as the value of the ith fuzzy case for the jth attribute. C_i is the classification result of the ith fuzzy example, the ith row is explained to be an initial fuzzy rule taking a form

$\bigcap_{p=1}^{m} A_{ip} \Rightarrow C_i$ with true degree α_i (see **Definition 1**) and inconsistent degree β_i (see **Definition 2**).

A fuzzy knowledge base can be generated by selecting the maximal membership of each attribute over its range of non-fuzzy label values from the fuzzy data.

Table 1. Fuzzy Knowledge Base

No.	Attr$_1$	Attr$_2$	...	Attr$_m$	Class	True Degree	Inconsistency
r_1	A_{11}	A_{12}	...	A_{1m}	C_1	α_1	β_1
r_2	A_{21}	A_{22}	...	A_{2m}	C_2	α_2	β_2
$\vdots$	$\vdots$	$\vdots$	$\vdots$	$\vdots$	$\vdots$	$\vdots$	$\vdots$
r_n	A_{n1}	A_{n2}	...	A_{nm}	C_n	α_n	β_n

From the ith initial fuzzy rule, many fuzzy rules can be generated such as $\bigcap_{l=1}^{k} A_{ij_l} \Rightarrow C_i$ with a true degree and an inconsistent degree, where $\{ j_1, j_2,..., j_k \} \subset \{1,2,...,m\}$. Let S=$\{ Attrj_1, Attrj_2,..., Attrj_k \}$ be a subset of condition attributes($k \le m$). We denote the fuzzy rule $\bigcap_{l=1}^{k} Attr_{ij_l} \Rightarrow C_i$ with a true degree α_i and an inconsistent degree β_i, in short, by $Attr\Big|_{S}^{i} \Rightarrow C_i [\alpha_i, \beta_i]$.

Definition 1. (Yuan and Shaw [17]) The true degree of fuzzy rule $A \Rightarrow B$ is defined to be $\alpha = \sum_{u \in U} \min(u_A(u), u_B(u)) / \sum_{u \in U} u_A(u)$, where A and B are two fuzzy sets defined on the same universe U.

Definition 2. (Wang and Hong [2]) The inconsistent degree of a given fuzzy rule is defined by $|E|$ where E=$\{ j \mid Attr\big|_{S}^{i} = Attr\big|_{S}^{j}, C_i \ne C_j \}$, $|E|$ denotes the number of elements of the set E.

Definition 3. (Wang and Hong [2]) For a given fuzzy rule $Attr\Big|_{S}^{i} \Rightarrow C_i [\alpha_i, \beta_i]$, an attribute $A (A \in S)$ is said to be dispensable in the fuzzy rule if $Attr\Big|_{S-\{A\}}^{i} \Rightarrow C_i$ has a true degree greater than or equal to σ (a given threshold) and an inconsistent degree less than or equal to β_i. Otherwise, attribute A is indispensable in the rule.

Definition 4. (Wang and Hong [2]) For a given fuzzy rule $Attr\Big|_{S}^{i} \Rightarrow C_i [\alpha_i, \beta_i]$, if all attributes in S are indispensable, this rule is called independent.

Definition 5. (Wang and Hong [2]) A subset of attributes $R(R \subset S)$ is called a reduct of the rule $Attr\Big|_S^i \Rightarrow C_i$ if $Attr\Big|_R^i \Rightarrow C_i$ is independent and has a true degree greater than or equal to σ (a given threshold) and an inconsistent degree less than or equal to β_i .The set of attributes, which are indispensable in the initial rule, $Attr\Big|_C^i \Rightarrow C_i$ is called the core of the initial fuzzy rule.

Definition 6. (Wang and Hong [2]) A reduct of an initial fuzzy rule $Attr\Big|_C^i \Rightarrow C_i$, R is said to be minimal, if S is not a reduct of the initial fuzzy rule for each set S with $S \subset R$ and $S \neq R$.

Definition 7. (Wang and Hong [2]) A fuzzy rule $Attr\Big|_S^i \Rightarrow C_i[\alpha_i, \beta_i]$ is said to cover a fuzzy example if the membership of attributes and the membership of classification for the example are all greater than or equal to η (a threshold).

The detailed algorithms of each task are described as follows:

Task 1 algorithm [2]: It can be divided into six steps:

Step1: for the i th initial fuzzy rule $(1 \leq i \leq m)$, the core K can be given by verifying whether an attribute is dispensable in the attribute set. K can be empty.

Set $\Gamma := 1$

Step 2: Take Γ attributes $Attr_1, Attr_2, ..., Attr_\Gamma$ from $C - K$

Step 3: Add $Attr_1, Attr_2, ..., Attr_\Gamma$ to K.

Step 4: compute the true degree and the inconsistent degree of the fuzzy rule $Attr\Big|_K^i \Rightarrow C_i$,

Step 5: if K is a reduct then exit successfully, else new Γ attributes $Attr_1, Attr_2, ..., Attr_\Gamma$ are taken from $C - K$, goto Step 3.

Step 6: if all combinations of elements of $C - K$ have been used and a reduct does not appear, $\Gamma := \Gamma + 1$, goto step 2.

Task 2 algorithm [2]: For each i $(1 \leq i \leq m)$, R_i, a subset of R= $\{r_1, r_2, ..., r_m\}$, where r_i is the minimal reduct of the i th initial rule, can be determined by checking whether the rule covers the example f_i:

$$R_i = \{r_j | r_j \in R, r_j \, covers \, f_i\}(i = 1, 2, ...m)$$

Task 3algorithm [2]:

Take $\Omega = \{R_1, R_2, ..., R_m\}$, R_i from the second task. The initial value of R^* is supposed to be an empty set. Repeat the following three steps:

Step1: for each $r \in R$, compute the number of times that r appears in the family Ω.

Step2: select r^*, such that the number times of r^* appears in the family Ω is maximum.

Step3: for i=1,2,...m, remove R_i from Ω if $r^* \in R_i$ and replace R^* with $\{r^*\} \cup R^*$ until Ω becomes empty.

R^* is then the fuzzy rule we need. For each case of a considered cluster, a set of adaptation rules is generated.

With respect to the generated adaptation rules, we need a reasoning mechanism to predict the amount of adjustment for the solution of non-representative cases. We propose our fuzzy reasoning mechanism as in [1].

As a result of this phase, for each case of a considered cluster, a set of adaptation rules (fuzzy production rules) is generated, and a reasoning mechanism for this set of fuzzy rules is given.

2.4 Selecting Representative Cases

This phase aims to select representative cases from each cluster according to the adaptation rules obtained in phase three. Our selection strategy uses the method in [1], which is based on a ε-coverage concept. Instead of the deletion, [1] proposes a selection strategy which makes use of Smyth's proposed concepts of coverage and reachability with some changes (called ε-coverage and ε-reachability respectively).

Let L be a cluster in which each case e is accompanied by a set of adaptation rules AR(e), ε be a small positive number, and $e_p = (x_{p1}, x_{p2}, \cdots, x_{pn}, v_p)$ and $e_q = (x_{q1}, x_{q2}, \cdots, x_{pn}, v_q)$ be two cases in the cluster L. According to the reasoning mechanism established in phase 3, an adjustment amount Δ of the solution for case e_q can be obtained by matching $(x_{q1} - x_{p1}, \cdots, x_{qn} - x_{pn})$ against $AR(e_p)$. If $v_q + \Delta \in (v_p - \varepsilon, v_p + \varepsilon)$, then e_p is said to ε-cover with e_q. The ε-coverage and ε-reachability of the case e_p are defined by

$$\text{Coverage}(e_p) = \{e \mid e \in L, e \text{ is } \varepsilon\text{-covered by } e_p\} \qquad (6)$$

and

$$\text{Reachability}(e_p) = \{e \mid e \in L, e \ \varepsilon\text{-covers with } e_p\} \text{ respectively} \qquad (7)$$

3 Experimental Analysis

This section presents the experimental analysis of our approach on a real-world problem, i.e. the rice taste (RT) problem. The RT data consist of five inputs and a single output whose values are associated with subjective evaluations of the flavor, appearance, taste, stickiness, toughness and overall evaluation of 105 different kinds of rice (Table 2 shows some typical records).

Table 2. Rice taste datat sizes of headings

Flavor	Appearance	Taste	Stickiness	Toughness	Overall Evaluation
0.699	1.543	1.76	1.944	-0.875	1.706
-0.593	-0.898	-0.883	-0.647	0.323	-1.235
0.158	0.163	0.03	0.359	-0.128	0.135

After applying the learning feature weights algorithm mentioned in section 2.1 to these cases, the feature weight results shown in Table 3 are obtained (learning iterations = 10000 cycles).

Table 3. Feature weights of the problem features

Flavor	Appearance	Taste	Stickiness	Toughness	Overall evaluation
0.02	0.03	0.54	0.03	0.04	2.68

Phase two is the same as the one in [1], readers can refer to that paper. As a result of this phase, the cases are partitioned into 14 classes. Some of these classes are shown in Table 4. We label classes with less than 10 records as Odd classes and the rest Not-odd classes. The learning of fuzzy adaptation rules is carried out on the Not-odd classes.

Table 4. Clusters of the rice case-base

Cluster no.	Number of cases	Odd or Not-Odd class
1	34	Not-Odd
2	30	Not-Odd
3	13	Not-Odd
4	7	Odd
5	5	Odd
6	1	Odd

For the first five problem features, i.e. Flavor, Appearance, Taste, Stickiness and Toughness (see Table 1), we fuzzify them into three linguistic variables: small, medium, big. For the solution feature, i.e. overall evaluation, we fuzzify it into five linguistic variables, i.e. Negative Big, Negative Small, Zero, Positive Small, Positive Big.

The general form of a fuzzy adaptation rule generated from the fuzzy decision tree is as follows:

IF the change of X1 is [Small I Medium I Big]
      [AND the change of X2 is [Small I Medium I Big]
        [AND the change of X3 is [Small I Medium I Big]]]
THEN the change of overall evaluation is [Negative Big I Negative Small I Zero I Positive Small I Positive Big].
Where X = {Flavor, Appearance, Taste, Stickiness, Toughness}.

For example, in cluster 3, which consists of 13 cases, one of the adaptation rules is:
      Rule: IF the change of Flavor is medium and the change of Appearance is medium, THEN the change of overall evaluation is Positive Small.

Table 5. Reachability and coverage of each case in cluster 3 of the rice case-base

Case number (x)	Number of cases which are covered by case(x)	The actual cases which are covered by case(x)	No. of adaptation rules
0	2	3,9	4
1	4	2,3,6,9	4
2	1	1	4
3	0		5
4	3	5,7,10	7
5	1	4	5
6	5	1,2,3,9,10	5
7	4	4,8,11,12	5
8	3	5,7,12	7
9	2	1,11	3
10	1	4	5
11	0		5
12	4	4,5,8,10	4

According to the case selecting strategy defined in section 2.4, we select cases {6,7,0,5,10} as the representative cases in this cluster 3 (see Table 5, the specific ε =0.05). As a result of this selection, a total of 24 fuzzy adaptation rules are also selected (i.e. each case has five adaptation rules on average).

Table 6. Selection of representative cases in all the Not-Odd clusters

Cluster No.	Number of cases	No. of representative cases	No. of deleted cases	The average relative error of the deleted cases
1	34	9	25	2.39%
2	30	7	23	7.76%
3	13	5	8	5.62%
	Total 77	Total 21	Total 56	Overall Average 5.14%

After applying the case selection strategy to each not-odd cluster, 56 cases are deleted (see Table 6), in other words, the number of cases in rice taste case base can be reduced by 53%.

Comparing with that of the fuzzy decision tree method [19], the result generated by fuzzy rough approach is quite positive. There are 56 cases are deleted by using fuzzy rough approach while only 39 cases are deleted by using fuzzy decision tree method. And the number of adaptation rules for each case generated by the fuzzy-rough method is much less than that of the fuzzy decision tree method (listed in the second column of Table 7).

In order to evaluate the overall problem solving ability, we apply those deleted cases as new coming cases to the smaller case base and its associated adaptation rules generated by our maintenance approach for solving, the results shows that fuzzy rough approach is also much better than fuzzy decision tree method. Table 8 demonstrates the comparison results of those two methods.

Table 7. Comparison the number of adaptation rules between the fuzzy decision tree and fuzzy-rough method

	Average Number of Adaptation Rules	Generate Decision Tree
Fuzzy Decision Tree	11.8	Yes
Fuzzy-Rough Method	8.7	No

Table 8. Average error after deletion

Cluster No	The average relative error of the deleted cases by the fuzzy-rough method	The average relative error of the deleted cases by the fuzzy decision tree method
1	2.39%	8.76%
2	7.76%	14.86%
3	5.62%	3.48%
Average error	5.41%	10.26%

So the overall selection result based on the adaptation rules generated by fuzzy-rough method is better than those based on the rules generated by the fuzzy decision tree. We can therefore say the overall performance of the fuzzy-rough approach is better than that of the fuzzy decision tree induction method.

4 Summary and Future Works

In this paper, we have developed a fuzzy-rough approach to maintaining case-based reasoning systems and compared the results with on that used fuzzy decision tree induction [1]. The main idea is to mine the adaptation knowledge by the fuzzy-rough approach, i.e., taking the fuzzy cases as fuzzy rules, then applying the rough set technique to those fuzzy rules, and generating a group of adaptation rules. A case selection strategy is then implemented based on these adaptation rules, and finally the original case library is replaced with a small case library plus adaptation knowledge. This adaptation knowledge plays the role of complementing the reduction of cases. The experimental analysis of our method showed promising results. Future work includes(1) a large scale testing of our methodology using different case-bases, (2) the refining of the fuzzy-rough algorithms,   (3) a comprehensive analysis of the complexity of the case base maintenance and reasoning algorithm in time and space, and (4) future comparison with other methods, such as fuzzy decision tree, C4.5, genetic algorithm and so on. We are also very interested in building a framework of the case base maintenance, including a reasoning scheme, retaining new cases, and on-line or periodic updating.

Acknowledgement. We would like to express our thanks to the three anonymous reviewers who have given us a lot of valuable comments on this work.
This project is supported by the Hong Kong Polytechnic University MPhil research studentship grant G-V957 and small research grant G-T144

References

[1] Shiu C.K. , Sun. C. H., Wang X.Z. and Yeung S., "Transferring Case Knowledge to Adaptation Knowledge: An Approach for Case Base Maintenance", *Computational Intelligence*, Volume 17, Number 2, 2001.

[2] Wang X.Z., Hong, J.R., "Learning optimization in simplifying fuzzy rules", *Fuzzy Sets and Systems* 106, 1999.

[3] Kitano, H. and Shimazu, H. "The experience sharing architecture: A case study in corporate-wide case-based software quality control", In *Case-Based Reasoning: Experiences, Lessons, and Future Directions*. Edited by Leake, D. Menlo Park, CA, AAAI Press, pp. 235-268, 1996.

[4] Cheetham, W. and Graf, J., "Case-based reasoning in color matching", In *Proceedings of the Second International Conference on Case-Based Reasoning*, ICCBR-97, pp. 1-12, 1997.

[5] Deangdej, J., Lukose, D., Tshui, E., Beinat, P. and Prophet, L., " Dynamically creating indices for two million cases: A real world problem", In *Proceedings of the 3rd European Workshop of Case-Based Reasoning*, EWCBR-96, pp. 105-119,1996.

[6] Leake, D.B. and Wilson, D.C. "Categorizing Case-Base Maintenance: Dimensions and Directions", *In Proceedings of the 4th European Workshop of Case-Based Reasoning*, EWCBR-98, pp. 196-207,1998.

[7] Smyth, B. and Keane, M.T., "Remembering to Forget: A Competence-Preserving Case Deletion Policy for Case-based Reasoning systems", In *Proceedings of the 14th International Joint Conference on Artificial Intelligence*, IJCAI-95, pp. 377-382, 1995.

[8] Smyth, B. and Mckenna, E. , "Modeling the Competence of Case-bases", In *Proceedings of the 4th European Workshop of Case-Based Reasoning*, EWCBR-98, pp. 23-25, 1998.

[9] Anand, S.S., Patterson, D., Hughes, J.G. and Bell D.A., "Discovering Case Knowledge using Data Mining", In *Proceedings of the 2nd Pacific Asia Conference on Knowledge Discovery and Data Mining* : Current Issues and New Applications, PAKDD-98, pp. 25-35, 1998.

[10] Richter, M. M. , "The Knowledge Contained in Similarity Measures", *Invited Talk at ICCBR-95*. http://wwwagr.informatil.uni-kl.de/~lsa/CBR/Richtericcbr95remarks.html.

[11] Richter, M. M. , "Chapter one: Introduction", In *Case-Based Reasoning Technology: From Foundations to Applications*. Edited by Lena, M., Bartsch-Sporl, B., Burkhard, H.D. and Wess, S., Springer-Verlag, Berlin, Germany, pp. 1-15, 1998.

[12] Zadeh L.A., "Fuzzy Sets", *Information and Control*, Vol.8, 1965.

[13] Drwal G., "Rough, and Fuzzy Rough Classification Methods Implemented in RClass System", ?,?.

[14] Pawlak Z., "Rough Set", *International Journal of Computer and Information Sciences*, 1982.

[15] Bezdek, J. C. , "Pattern recognition with fuzzy objective function algorithms," Plenum, NewYork, 1981

[16] Kohonen, T., "Self-Organization and Associate Memory", Springer, Berlin, 1988.

[17] Yuan. Y, Shaw M.J., "Induction of fuzzy decision trees", *Fuzzy Sets and Systems 69*, pp.125-139, 1995.

[18] Nozaki, K., Ishibuchi, H. and Tanaka, H, "A simple but powerful heuristic method for generating fuzzy rules from numerical data," in *Fuzzy Sets and Systems*, FSS 86, pp.251-270, 1997.

[19] Shiu C.K., Sun. C. H., Wang X.Z. and Yeung S., "Maintaining Case-Based Reasoning Systems Using Fuzzy Decision Trees", In *Proceedings of the 5rd European Workshop of Case-Based Reasoning*, EWCBR-00, pp285-296, 2000.

Learning and Applying Case-Based Adaptation Knowledge*

Susan Craw[1], Jacek Jarmulak[1], and Ray Rowe[2]

[1] School of Computer and Mathematical Sciences
The Robert Gordon University
Aberdeen AB25 1HG, Scotland, UK
s.craw@scms.rgu.ac.uk
http://www.scms.rgu.ac.uk
[2] AstraZeneca, Silk Road Business Park
Macclesfield, Cheshire, SK10 2NA, UK
http://www.astrazeneca.com

Abstract. Adaptation is an important step in CBR when applied to design tasks. However adaptation knowledge can be difficult to acquire directly from an expert. Nevertheless, CBR tools provide few facilities to assist with the acquisition of adaptation knowledge. This paper considers a special class of design task, where a component-based solution can be developed in stages, and suggests adaptation knowledge that is suited to CBR systems for component-based design. A case-based adaptation is proposed where the adaptation cases are generated from the original problem-solving case-base, and so knowledge acquisition is automated. Both numeric and nominal targets are adapted, although a different case-based adaptation is applied for each. The gains of adaptation are presented for a tablet formulation application, although the approach is suited for other formulation and configuration tasks that apply a component-based approach to design. The learned adaptation knowledge is understandable to the expert, with the effect that he can criticise the content and refine the knowledge if necessary. Results are promising but the case-based adaptation systems offer many opportunities for optimisation and further learning.

1 Introduction

Case-Based Reasoning (CBR) is a useful form of problem-solving because it can re-use previous problem-solving in new circumstances. Its approach is attractive because human problem-solving is often case-based and so the user can recognise the justification it uses to support its solutions. It is also popular because its major knowledge source is case-based data that may already have been collected, and so acquisition of this knowledge may be eased. However, some types of problem-solving demand significant knowledge engineering effort for the knowledge containers other than those directly associated with the case-base [5].

---

* This work is supported by EPSRC grant GR/L98015 awarded to Susan Craw.

D.W. Aha and I. Watson (Eds.): ICCBR 2001, LNAI 2080, pp. 131–145, 2001.

CBR design applications are particularly demanding. Specialised retrieval knowledge may be needed to identify relevant cases in the case-base. Furthermore, the open-ended nature of design tasks means that the case-base cannot contain representatives of all designs. Hence, adaptation is often necessary to apply a retrieved design in new circumstances. Knowledge to effect the required adaptation is essential in this case. Therefore, although the acquisition of case-knowledge for CBR systems may be more easily acquired than knowledge for other forms of knowledge-based system (e.g. rules), acquisition of similarity and adaptation knowledge may still be difficult and time-consuming.

This paper investigates the automated acquisition of adaptation knowledge, the second part of a larger project that looks broadly at automated knowledge engineering techniques for the whole CBR process. The motivation for the project is the realisation that despite the importance of retrieval and adaptation for many tasks, CBR tools provide few facilities to ease knowledge acquisition. Earlier work [8,3] acquired retrieval knowledge by learning relevant features for a CBR index and the relative importance of features for the similarity measure. We used a "knowledge light" approach [18] with the retrieval knowledge being learned from existing CBR knowledge – the case-base. Our approach to acquiring adaptation knowledge is similar, since we again learn adaptations that are applied to solve case-base problems from *other* cases already in the case-base.

Three forms of adaptation have been identified [14]. *Substitutional* adaptation alters the value of a component of the solution; e.g. increasing the price of a house because it has more rooms than an otherwise similar property. *Transformational* adaptation changes the structure of the solution; e.g. the repairs CHEF applies to failed recipes [6]. *Generative* adaptation repeats the reasoning that achieved the solution from the retrieved case with the appropriate steps for the new problem. These three adaptation methods are increasingly sophisticated, apply increasingly complex adaptation knowledge, and are required for increasingly demanding problem-solving. In this paper we look at automating the acquisition of knowledge for substitutional adaptation; more complex adaptations are likely to need significant expert intervention in knowledge acquisition.

An earlier paper [9] presented an overview of our general approach of extracting different types of adaptation knowledge from the existing case-base data. Here we concentrate on case-based adaptation where an adaptation CBR_A system is the adaptation phase of the standard CBR problem-solving cycle. We focus on the details of the content of our various CBR_A systems and highlight application issues surrounding the contribution of various sources of adaptation knowledge during the assembly of an adapation.

We illustrate our approach on our tablet formulation application [4], but it is more generally applicable to other component-based design tasks that use substitutional adaptation. Examples include other formulation problems (e.g. rubber formulation [2]) and customisation for component-based configuration tasks [16]. Tablet formulation is particularly challenging because the formulation task is demanding, the formulation for a tablet is not unique, and most importantly we have relatively small amounts of formulation data.

This paper starts with an overview of knowledge acquisition for adaptation in Section 2 and then Section 3 outlines the key features of component-based design as applied in formulation and configuration tasks. Section 4 describes how adaptation cases are built from the existing case-data. We compare the different approaches we use for adaptation of numeric and nominal targets in Sections 5 & 6. Our experimental results for tablet formulation and a simple house-pricing application appear in Sections 7 & 8.

2   Related Work on Adaptation Knowledge

Much of the research on knowledge acquisition and refinement for CBR systems is devoted to case-knowledge (e.g. [1,15]), and relatively little has appeared for retrieval or adaptation knowledge. This is perhaps explained by the dominance of classification in early CBR systems, and the more recent understanding of CBR for non-classification tasks [17] that highlights the importance of the retrieval and adaptation knowledge containers. Once retrieval and adaptation knowledge become essential, then tools to assist with acquisition are important.

Adaptation is often used to reflect the feature differences between the new problem and the retrieved cases. In this circumstance the adaptation knowledge must convert the problem differences into adaptations for the retrieved solutions. McSherry's CREST system [11] adapts the most closely matching case by applying the same correction as used between a pair of stored cases that have the same feature difference. Therefore the adaptation knowledge for CREST is whether the type of relationship between the feature and target values is linear, multiplicative, etc, and whether the relationship changes in different locations of the feature space. Currently this is selected for each application, although it could be learned from the case-base data.

Wilke et al. [18] learn adaptation knowledge from case-base data. In one application they optimise k for k-nearest neighbour weighted voting algorithms. Our CBR retrieval optimisation [8] also optimises k, as well as choosing feature weightings, although we regard it as learning retrieval knowledge. Wilke et al. further propose a generic "knowledge light" framework containing a pre-processor that assembles adaptation training data from the case-base data, and a learning algorithm that generates the knowledge for the adaptation container. This framework also covers the process used by Hanney & Keane [7] to induce adaptation rules from the feature and target differences between pairs of stored cases. In a similar way to CREST, Hanney & Keane's approach works well when there are only a few feature differences that must be reflected in the adaptation.

Leake et al.'s DIAL [10] also applies adaptation cases but these are acquired when effective adaptations are applied. Thus knowledge acquisition occurs as the standard CBR retain phase for the *adaptation* CBR system that they apply within the CBR problem-solving cycle. The adaptation cases are generated from manual adaptation, adaptation from a rule-based repair theory, or by retrieving (and adapting) previous adaptation cases.

Our approach fits Wilke et al.'s generic knowledge light framework because we assemble training data from the case-base data, use these to form cases for an adaptation CBR system CBR_A, and apply CBR_A and its adaptation case knowledge as a major part of the adaptation in the original CBR problem-solving.

3   Component-Based Design

Design problems can often be solved by decomposing the solution into several component parts and then finding compatible sub-solutions by solving each component. Although the full solution can be found in a single CBR problem-solving cycle, decomposition offers the possibility of solving the design sub-tasks individually and combining the sub-solutions. Multiple cases are used at different stages to solve the design sub-tasks and this can be advantageous with sparse case-bases, a common feature of design CBR systems. Instead of generating sub-solutions in parallel it is often advantageous to solve the sub-problems sequentially, when the sub-solution for earlier components can guide the problem-solving for later components.

This incremental approach is used by Déjà Vu [13] for software design, and EADOCS [12] for designing composite structures. In both, initial designs are refined using repeated retrievals with increasingly instantiated problems. Stahl & Bergmann [16] also view repeated retrieval as important for their customisation in PC configuration. Unlike the bottom-up retrievals in Déjà Vu and EADOCS, Stahl & Bergmann apply a recursive retrieval where the design is generated in a top-down manner.

Our tablet formulation domain [4] (and other formulation tasks like formulating rubber for Pirelli racing tyres [2]), fits into this component-based design and is suited to incremental retrieval. Creating a tablet for a new drug involves choosing additional inert excipients to mix with the drug so that the tablet can be manufactured in a robust form and contains the required dose of the drug. The additional tablet components that are needed are filler, binder, lubricant, disintegrant and surfactant that balance the physical properties of the drug and satisfy chemical stability constraints with the drug. The formulation identifies a suitable excipient for each of these components and the quantity of each that should be added. Formulation practice suggests that the design task can be decomposed into a sequence of subtasks from the most constrained filler component to the least constrained surfactant.

4   Learning Adaptation Knowledge from Case-Base Data

We apply a case-based adaptation system where the adaptation knowledge is the case-base of adaptation cases. In the following we adopt the convention that CBR_A is the adaptation system and CBR refers to the original case-based problem-solver for the task in hand; e.g. tablet formulation. Thus CBR retrieves cases from its case-base as normal to propose an initial solution. CBR_A then decides if any adaptation is required by retrieving and applying adaptation cases from the CBR_A case-base.

CBR_A's adaptation cases capture the circumstances under which adaptation is necessary and the adaptation that should be applied. Adaptation experience is not necessarily familiar to the domain expert, and equally, we do not want to run the CBR system repeatedly with the expert giving feedback on its faulty problem-solving. Instead, we exploit the knowledge already in the CBR cases to learn the case-based adaptation knowledge for CBR_A.

Figure 1 shows how adaptation knowledge is extracted from the CBR system. CBR's case-base CB is repeatedly partitioned into a small set of probe cases and a much larger set of cases that will be used as the case-base CB- in a less competent CBR system. Each probe retrieves k similar cases from CB-, and each retrieved case creates an adaptation case. CBR_A cases contain features of the probe and the retrieved problem to indicate the circumstances under which adaptation is required, together with the information about the retrieved and actual formulations – remember, this is known because the probe originated as a formulation in CB. Thus each case in CB is used to generate k CBR_A adaptation cases, but those that contain the same proposed solution for a probe are pruned to retain the CBR_A case from the most similar CB- case.

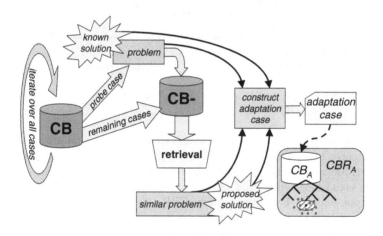

Fig. 1. Constructing adaptation cases for CBR_A

In our tablet formulation domain, it is common for tablets of several doses of the same drug to have formulations that are quite similar. Therefore, we use a leave-one-drug out partition where the different doses for one drug are used as probes for a CBR system containing the formulations for the other drugs. Similarly in experiments, whenever cases are partitioned, we always keep formulations for the same drug together; i.e. a leave-N-drug-out test, or n-fold cross-validation where different doses of the same drug appear in a *single* fold.

5   Adaptation for Numeric Targets

For numeric targets, CBR_A echoes the standard view of adaptation; it exploits the differences between the probe and retrieved cases to suggest a solution update. With numeric features and targets the concept of difference is clear and for nominal features we use the CBR feature similarity S to express the difference D as $1 - S$. Figure 2 illustrates the content of CBR_A cases for numerical targets. Each adaptation case contains the feature differences between the probe and the retrieved problem, and the difference between the proposed numerical value as retrieved from CB- and the probe's actual value. In addition, since the local shape of the solution space may change according to the location in the space, the adaptation case also contains the feature values of the probe and the proposed solution.

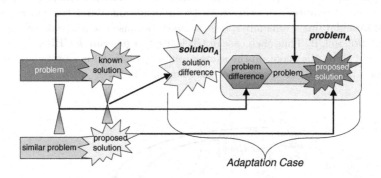

Fig. 2. Adaptation cases for numeric targets

In practice we have found that a single CBR_A system that tries to capture the differences in all feature values produces over-fitting; i.e. the adaptations do not generalise well to new problems. Instead, we create many CBR_A systems, each one containing adaptation cases that concentrate on the differences for a single input feature. From these many CBR_A systems, we select those whose decision tree indexes have a higher than average predictive accuracy.

Figure 3 illustrates how the selected CBR_A systems are used to suggest corrections to the initial solution proposed by the CBR problem-solver. A CBR_A probe for each CBR_A system is constructed from the CBR probe and the CBR retrieved case. The CBR_A probe has the same format as the CBR_A adaptation case in Figure 2, except that the solution difference is unfilled – it is the target.

Figure 4 indicates how these corrections are generated, and subsequently combined and applied to the initial CBR solution. The CBR system firstly retrieves k cases and creates the initial predicted value S for the numerical target using the average of the solutions S_i, weighted according to the degree of similarity match sim_i of the retrieved case. An adaptation correction δ_{ij} is proposed for each retrieved solution S_i by each feature-based CBR_A system CBR_{Af_j}. In

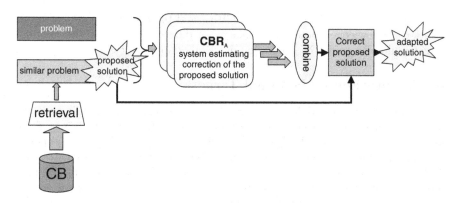

Fig. 3. Adaptation for numeric targets

addition to the correction δ_{ij}, CBR_{Af_j} also generates a confidence in its correction C_{ij} (described below). The adapted value S' is the average of the corrected values weighted according to the similarity of the CBR retrieved case S_i and the confidence in the correction C_{ij}:

$$S' = \frac{\Sigma_{ij} sim_i * C_{ij} * (S_i + \delta_{ij})}{\Sigma_{ij} sim_i * C_{ij}}$$

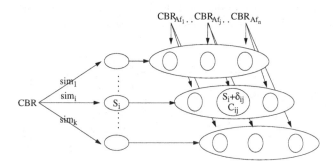

Fig. 4. Corrected values for numeric targets

C_{ij} indicates the confidence of the CBR_A for feature f_j in its predicted correction δ_{ij} for S_i. We feel that this should reflect both the average predictive accuracy of the CBR_A decision tree leaf node for δ_{ij} and the similarity of the CBR_A probe and the retrieved adaptation cases. Currently we use the product of the CBR_A accuracy and similarity, but more experimentation is needed to find better ways to combine these.

This adaptation approach could also be applied to nominal targets: the CBR_A adaptation cases would contain the corrected solution, and weighted voting would replace weighted average in CBR_A and the combination of corrected solutions. Knowledge about the similarity of different values for the nominal target could also guide the generation of useful adaptation cases.

6   Adaptation for Nominal Targets

We adopt a completely different approach to numerical adaptation in order to provide feedback on incorrect predictions. Repeated CBR retrievals suggest alternative solutions and the CBR_A system predicts the correctness of each proposed solution and the confidence in the predicted correctness. Figure 5 illustrates a CBR_A case which now captures features associated with the problem, the proposed solution, and the target feature is whether this solution is correct or not. An adaptation case also contains additional, features: *related* features can be evaluated once the proposed solution is known, and *estimated* features can be predicted from the problem features and the proposed solution. In filler prediction a related feature is the drug-filler-stability: once the excipient F is chosen as the filler, then the value of the problem feature that captures the stability of the drug with F can be copied to the drug-filler-stability feature. Estimated features are the tablet properties like tablet-strain-rate-sensitivity (tSRS) and tablet-yield-pressure (tYP) that can be estimated from the problem features of the drug and the properties of the proposed filler. These examples of related and estimated features are based on tablet formulation but their counterparts exist in formulation, configuration and design more generally. Related features are consequences of the design choices to date, where a feature of the design is filled by its value for the chosen design part. Estimated features are often constraints or metrics that indicate the suitability of the design choices to date.

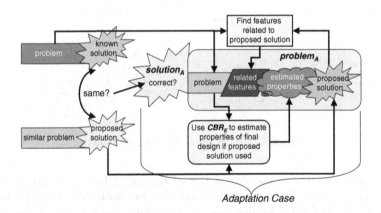

Fig. 5. Adaptation cases for nominal targets

As Figure 5 suggests, we use a case-based reasoning system (CBR_E) to predict values for estimated features. CBR_E cases contain the same features as the

CBR cases but the values for the CBR_E targets are added. Approaches other than CBR could be used to make predictions for the estimated values; e.g. rule-based systems, mathematical or logical formulae, etc.

CBR_A for nominal targets no longer predicts a correction but simply indicates whether the proposed solution is likely to be correct or not. Over-fitting with nominal CBR_A is reduced by limiting the features used in the CBR_A index to the related and estimated features and the proposed solution, and so for nominal targets we use a single CBR_A system. Figure 6 shows that adaptation is achieved by applying repeated CBR problem solving where, in each cycle, the cases containing previously proposed solutions are ignored during CBR retrieval. For each CBR solution proposed, the CBR_A system predicts its correctness and the confidence in its predicted correctness.

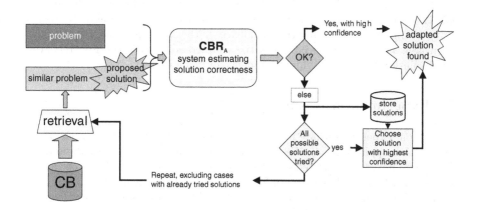

Fig. 6. Adaptation for nominal targets

Figure 7 indicates how the prediction from each repeated CBR retrieval is subjected to analysis by CBR_A, and how CBR_A's correctness predictions are used to choose the adapted solution from those nominated by repeated CBR retrievals. The CBR system in cycle j firstly retrieves k cases and creates the initial predicted value S_j for the nominal target as the weighted vote of the retrieved solutions σ_i, weighted according to the case similarity sim_i. A CBR_A probe is created for the initial solution S_j and CBR_A retrieves n adaptation cases each containing a (binary) correctness prediction C_{jk}. CBR_A returns a correctness prediction C_j for S_j: the weighted vote of the correctness predictions C_{jk} weighted according to the degree of CBR_A similarity match $Asim_{jk}$. The confidence ($Conf_j$) in the correctness prediction C_j again reflects the CBR_A similarity and leaf-node accuracy (A_{jk}) for the correctness predictions:

$$Conf_j = \frac{\Sigma_{k,C_{jk}=C_j} Asim_{jk} * A_{jk}}{\Sigma_k Asim_{jk} * A_{jk}}$$

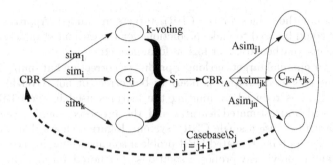

Fig. 7. Correctness of nominal targets

The adapted CBR solution is the retrieved CBR solution with the highest CBR_A confidence of being correct. The confidences $Conf_j$ are actually scaled using a ramp function so that the confidences in the correctness of CBR solutions from later cycles are reduced. Thus the adapted solution is the first retrieved CBR solution with a fairly high confidence of being correct.

7 Experimental Results

Most of our experiments have been acquiring adaptation knowledge for our tablet formulation application [4]. We have a complete dataset of 156 formulations for 39 drugs. The results reported below are from sets of cross-validation experiments where the CBR case-bases are built from leave-N-drug-out partitions and each N-drug fold is used as the source of test problems. Adaptation knowledge is acquired for each leave-N-drug-out CBR system by creating CBR_A adaptation cases from the formulations for the $39 - N$ drugs in the CBR case-base.

We employ an accuracy measure that counts as correct numerical predictions within 10% of the actual quantity and nominal predictions whose excipient similarity with the actual component is at least 90%. Our domain expert has provided excipient similarity scores based on excipient properties where 90% agreement is sufficient to indicate that the excipients are interchangeable, and excipients with similarity less than 50% are considered incompatible. He also maintains that a 10% quantity error is within manufacturing limits.

We apply sequential CBR problem-solving where the filler is chosen using only the drug and excipient features, the binder prediction is based also on the already chosen filler and its quantity, and so on, until the choice of surfactant has access to all the other components. The quantities are handled similarly with the excipient choice for each also being known. We omit results for lubricant prediction, and the amounts for disintegrant and surfactant where non-optimised retrieval already achieves 100% accuracy. We additionally show results for filler\$ where the filler is predicted last after the other four components and quantities.

Table 1 presents the gains in accuracy when case-based adaptation knowledge is learned from, and applied to, tablet formulation CBR systems without/with optimisation of the CBR retrieval. Particularly good gains were achieved for filler amount, although optimisation of the CBR retrieval was also effective (row 6). Smaller adaptation gains were made for disintegrant prediction, despite the accuracy before adaptation being already quite high (row 3). Adaptation even made a small gain for optimised CBR despite disintegrant prediction being already very close to 100% (col 3/4). Otherwise, whenever the accuracy of non-adapted solutions was already above 90% (rows 4,7,8), virtually no adaptation gains were made, although in each case optimisation of the retrieval (col 3) improved the accuracies over non-optimised retrieval (col 1). This perhaps indicates the flexibility to choose alternative excipients from those that have similar properties of differing importance, and the need to emphasise certain features when predicting quantities rather than feature differences.

Table 1. Gains from adaptation with tablet formulation CBR systems

	Non-Opt CBR	Adaptation Gain	Opt CBR	Adaptation Gain
Filler Prediction	69.0%	no gain	82.1%	no gain
Binder Prediction	26.6%	**4.7%**	*40.7%*	**0.6%**
Disintegrant Prediction	93.1%	**2.0%**	97.3%	**0.7%**
Surfactant Prediction	98.7%	no gain	100%	0.0%
Filler$ Prediction	64.6%	1.5%	–	–
Filler Amount	84.9%	**13.8%**	*100.0%*	0.0%
Binder Amount	94.2%	no gain	99.9%	0.0%
Lubricant Amount	90.4%	no gain	97.4%	no gain
Tablet-SRS	78.2%	no gain	76.2%	**1.6%**
Tablet-YP	81.2%	**1.9%**	*96.4%*	0.3%

The reasonable gain for binder prediction is still relatively modest given the very low accuracy of non-optimised binder prediction (row 2). Optimisation had a much bigger effect and was further improved by adaptation slightly, but is still below 50% (col 3/4). In [9] we compared case-based adaptation for nominal targets with another repeated CBR retrieval where the preference for a retrieved solution was profiled using probabilistic curves generated from the values of the related and estimated features in the CBR case-base. This preference profile approach worked well for binder giving 5% gains on both non-optimised and optimised retrieval.

The lack of improvement from adaptation for filler prediction is also disappointing (row 1); preference profiling also showed no gains. Since it is the first component to be predicted, we experimented with re-predicting the filler after the rest of the formulation (except filler quantity) is completed (row 5). Although adaptation now produces a small gain, the initial predictions are less accurate than from the normal problem-solving sequence for filler (row 1). However, a larger gain of 7.6% is achieved in *exact accuracy* for Filler$ (not shown) and so it is clear that some of the similar fillers proposed initially have been adapted to give exactly the right filler.

The final two rows show the gains from adaptation in CBR_E systems to predict the estimated tablet features tSRS and tYP. The effectiveness of these CBR_E systems is important as one step in the application of CBR_A adaptation to nominal targets. Optimisation had degraded the prediction of tSRS but adaptation has almost entirely retrieved this situation. A similar adaptation gain was achieved for non-optimised tYP estimation, and, although optimisation had given a major improvement, adaptation nevertheless gives a slight further gain.

8   Adaptation Knowledge

The adaptation knowledge we have acquired is represented in the adaptation cases and applied by the various CBR_A systems. We explored the adaptation knowledge we had acquired for filler prediction because the adaptations had resulted in no gain. Our expert has warned us that this is a relatively hard subtasks because the filler, being the majority tablet component, is most responsible for ensuring that the drug's physical properties are correctly balanced by the rest of the tablet.

The decision tree index for CBR_A highlights the features that are important for selecting relevant adaptation cases to predict the correctness of the selected filler. The expert approved many of the decisions in the tree; e.g. formulations with a low estimated tablet SRS are likely to contain the correct filler, with the threshold being dependent on the chosen filler because of its contribution to SRS. The faulty decision nodes were mainly caused by a lack of training data for adaptation. For one particular filler, choosing it was always predicted to be wrong, because the adaptation training did not contain a CBR system that correctly predicted this filler. Conversely, the choice of another filler was always predicted to be correct, again caused by limited training experiences. Another fault wrongly preferred a low drug-filler stability when a particular filler was chosen and the tablet SRS was too high; again this is caused by not having enough adaptation evidence with this filler choice.

It seems that the failure of good adaptation knowledge for filler prediction stems from the relatively small tablet formulation case-base which does not capture enough adaptation evidence for fillers to provide effective training. For binder the problem is further exacerbated by a relatively restricted set of binders, so that partitioning of the formulations can lead to biased case-bases without a particular binder. In both situations the scarcity of available formulations is blamed, although data for 39 drugs is deemed to be realistic by our expert.

We have also run some experiments with a simple house pricing CBR system. It contains 125 properties in central Aberdeen ranging in price from £17K to £195K extracted from the Aberdeen Solicitors' Property Centre website (www.aspc.co.uk), and each is represented by 14 features. This is a simpler problem with fewer features and so we do not face the same over-fitting problems caused by the lack of available data in tablet formulation. Non-optimised CBR retrieval achieved 61.9% accuracy and adaptation afforded a gain of 6.4%. The CBR_A index partitions the adaptation cases according to similar price changes. The features highlighted in the adaptation index were indicative of house price adjustments: differences in location or property type; having central heating or double glazing (this is Scotland!); having a garage, parking, or a garden; and the number of additional rooms of varying types.

In addition to the availability of training data, several other things affect the CBR_A systems that can be built. We are not convinced that we have made the correct choices in what features are represented in the various adaptation cases. For example, we were forced down to single feature CBR_A systems for numeric adaptation because of the over-fitting with our data. Also, we have not yet made any attempt to optimise the CBR_A systems and in this way learn which CBR_A features are important. In addition, there are parameter settings for the indexing and nearest neighbour algorithms in CBR_A. The experience we gained from optimising the tablet formulation CBR problem solvers does not help in this different, adaptation, domain. The initial experiments for case-based adaptation reported in [9] applied naive parameter settings and a simple combination of evidence. We are still at the stage of experimenting with different parameters and monitoring how the adaptations go wrong, and this is indicated by the improvements, but also some deteriorations, in the adaptation gains of Table 1. There are clearly many opportunities for learning, perhaps by comparing the adaptations from different CBR_A systems and applying consensual changes rather than combining all of their suggestions.

Further tailoring, specific to CBR_A systems, is desirable, including the way that confidence is calculated and applied. For numeric adaptation we select CBR_A systems with higher than average confidence and combine all their suggested changes according to confidence. Perhaps we should apply higher selectivity of CBR_A systems, or use all CBR_A systems but with more selectivity of the predicted changes. With nominal adaptation we have experimented with different ways to handle the confidence of correct predictions. On the one hand, we give all correct predictions the same positive score so that the first CBR solution predicted to be correct is used. Alternatively, we use the ramped confidences of correct predictions so that the prediction with the highest ramped confidence of being correct is applied. In both scenarios, if no CBR solution is predicted correct, then the CBR solution with the least ramped confidence score for being *incorrect* is used.

9   Conclusions

We have presented case-based adaptation for CBR systems. The main contribution of this work is that the adaptation knowledge can be acquired from the case-data already in the CBR system. We have developed case-based adaptation for both numeric and nominal components. Adaptation of numeric targets applies a standard case-based approach to propose corrections for the proposed solution. Several CBR_A systems can be created, each concentrating on corrections based around a particular set of features. Nominal adaptation adopts a different approach where the CBR_A system predicts the correctness of the proposed nominal solution. Repeated CBR retrievals are undertaken until a sufficient confidence in the prediction is achieved by CBR_A. In both numeric and nominal case-based adaptation, an important feature is the confidence of the CBR_A system in its correction or correctness prediction.

We have applied adaptation to both non-optimised and optimised CBR retrieval. Gains can be made in either situation, although gains on optimised retrieval are harder, since the problem-solving is already more accurate. It is interesting to compare the gains of adaptation and optimisation for non-optimised retrieval. The retrieval and adaptation knowledge containers complement each other; adaptation knowledge can partially replace retrieval knowledge, but adaptation knowledge also complements retrieval knowledge.

A decision tree index for the CBR_A case-base proved to be a useful way to present adaptation knowledge to the domain expert. He found its knowledge easy to understand and was able to provide useful criticisms. Automated acquisition of adaptation knowledge may be a useful way to start to develop adaptation knowledge that can be reviewed and improved by a human expert.

Our results for tablet formulation are promising – the accuracy of some formulation components are improved. However, our case-based adaptation, and its knowledge acquisition, is more generally applicable, in particular to design applications that have component based solutions. We are constantly facing the problem of over-fitting in our tablet formulation domain, not only in the case-based formulation task, but also in the adaptation of formulations. We always have many parameters that we are trying to learn but have access to only a small amount of training data. However this is an important part of our project since the lack of data is inherent in drug development.

CBR_A systems have many opportunities to exploit. The adaptation task is different from the problem-solving task and we are not convinced that we have the correct CBR_A parameterisation for this altered task. We have suggested several sources of adaptation, but we have not yet exploited the redundancy in these sources to achieve the improved learning that this multiplicity offers.

Acknowledgements. We acknowledge ISoft's software contribution to the project.

References

1. D. W. Aha and L. A. Breslow. Refining conversational case libraries. In D. B. Leake and E. Plaza, editors, *Proceedings of the 2nd International Conference on CBR*, LNAI 1226, Providence, RI, 1997. Springer.

2. S. Bandini and S. Manzoni. A support system based on CBR for the design of rubber compounds in motor racing. In E. Blanzieri and L. Portinale, editors, *Proceedings of the 5th European Workshop on Case-Based Reasoning (EWCBR 2k)*, LNAI 1898, pages 348–357, Trento, Italy, 2000. Springer.
3. S. Craw, J. Jarmulak, and R. Rowe. Maintaining retrieval knowledge in a case-based reasoning system. *Computational Intelligence*, 17(2):346–363, 2001.
4. S. Craw, N. Wiratunga, and R. Rowe. Case-based design for tablet formulation. In *Advances in Case-Based Reasoning, Proceedings of the 4th European Workshop on Case-Based Reasoning*, LNCS 1488, pages 358–369, Dublin, Eire, 1998. Springer.
5. P. Cunningham and A. Bonzano. Knowledge engineering issues in developing a case-based reasoning application. *Knowledge Based Systems*, 12:371–379, 1999.
6. K. J. Hammond. Explaining and repairing plans that fail. *AI*, 45(1–2):173–228, 1990.
7. K. Hanney and M. T. Keane. The adaptation knowledge bottleneck: How to ease it by learning from cases. In D. B. Leake and E. Plaza, editors, *Proceedings of the 2nd International Conference on CBR*, LNAI 1226, pages 359–370, Providence, RI, 1997. Springer.
8. J. Jarmulak, S. Craw, and R. Rowe. Genetic algorithms to optimise CBR retrieval. In *Proceedings of the 5th European Workshop on Case-Based Reasoning (EWCBR 2k)*, LNAI 1898, pages 136–147, Trento, Italy, 2000. Springer.
9. J. Jarmulak, S. Craw, and R. Rowe. Using case-base data to learn adaptation knowledge for design. In *Proceedings of the 17th International Joint Conference on Artificial Intelligence (IJCAI 01)*, Seattle, WA, 2001.
10. D. B. Leake, A. Kinley, and D. Wilson. Acquiring case adaptation knowledge: A hybrid approach. In *Proceedings of the Thirteenth National Conference on Artificial Intelligence*. AAAI Press, 1996.
11. D. McSherry. An adaptation heuristic for case-based estimation. In *Proceedings of the 4th European Workshop on Case-Based Reasoning (EWCBR 98)*, LNCS 1488, pages 184–195, Dublin, Eire, 1998. Springer.
12. B. D. Netten and R. A. Vingerhoeds. Incremental adaptation for conceptual design in EADOCS. In *ECAI Workshop on Adaptation in Case-Based Reasoning*, Budapest, Hungary, 1996.
13. B. Smyth and P. Cunningham. Déjà Vu: A hierarchical case-based reasoning system for software design. In B. Neumann, editor, *Proceedings of the ECAI92 Conference*, pages 587–589, Vienna, Austria, 1992. Wiley.
14. B. Smyth and P. Cunningham. Complexity of adaptation in real-world case-based reasoning systems. In *Proceedings of 6th Irish Conference on Artificial Intelligence & Cognitive Science*, Ireland, 1993.
15. B. Smyth and E. McKenna. Building compact competent case-bases. In K.-D. Althoff, R. Bergmann, and L. K. Branting, editors, *Proceedings of the 3rd International Conference on CBR*, LNAI 1650, pages 329–342. Springer, 1999.
16. A. Stahl and R. Bergmann. Applying recursive CBR to the customisation of structured products in an electronic shop. In E. Blanzieri and L. Portinale, editors, *Proceedings of the 5th European Workshop on Case-Based Reasoning (EWCBR 2k)*, LNAI 1898, pages 297–308, Trento, Italy, 2000. Springer.
17. D. Wettschereck and D. W. Aha, editors. *Proceedings of the ECML-97 Workshop on Case-Based Learning: Beyond Classification of Feature Vectors*, 1997.
18. W. Wilke, I. Vollrath, K.-D. Althoff, and R. Bergmann. A framework for learning adaptation knowledge based on knowledge light approaches. In *5th German Workshop on Case-Based Reasoning (GWCBR'97)*, 1997.

Case Representation Issues for Case-Based Reasoning from Ensemble Research

Pádraig Cunningham and Gabriele Zenobi

Department of Computer Science
Trinity College Dublin
Padraig.Cunningham@tcd.ie

Abstract. Ensembles of classifiers will produce lower errors than the member classifiers if there is diversity in the ensemble. One means of producing this diversity in nearest neighbour classifiers is to base the member classifiers on different feature subsets. In this paper we show four examples where this is the case. This has implications for the practice of feature subset selection (an important issue in CBR and data-mining) because it shows that, in some situations, there is no single *best* feature subset to represent a problem. We show that if diversity is emphasised in the development of the ensemble that the ensemble members appear to be local learners specializing in sub-domains of the problem space. The paper concludes with some proposals on how analysis of ensembles of local learners might provide insight on problem-space decomposition for hierarchical CBR.

1. Introduction

The idea of Case-Based Reasoning (CBR) has strong appeal because it is recognised that much of human expertise is experienced based and CBR is considered to capture this idea. Practitioners recognise that, while CBR does involve reuse of previous problem solving episodes in solving new problems, it is a limited imitation of the versatility of reuse that humans exhibit in problem solving. An important aspect of this shortcoming is the reliance of CBR on feature-vector representations of cases. This approach is firmly based in the symbolic AI paradigm (Newell & Simon, 1976) but it is recognised to have shortcomings. In 1997 an ECML workshop entitled "Case-Based Learning: Beyond Classification of Feature Vectors" (Wettschereck & Aha, 1997) was organised to advance the state of knowledge representation in CBR. However, it is fair to state that current CBR practice is still strongly dependent on cases represented as feature vectors.

In this paper we present an example of the shortcomings of a case representation based on a single feature-value vector. We present four examples of ensembles of k-Nearest Neighbour (k-NN) classifiers that outperform a single k-NN classifier based on the best single feature subset available. The ensemble incorporates several individual k-NN classifiers based on different feature subsets and *aggregates* their results. Based on our analysis of the ensembling process we will propose that its power derives from the aggregation of several *local* specialists.

While this illustrates the shortcomings of a solution based on a single global representation it is important to point out that approaches exist to address this within

D.W. Aha and I. Watson (Eds.): ICCBR 2001, LNAI 2080, pp. 146-157, 2001.

the CBR paradigm. The obvious solution is to have local weights that vary across the solution space and this approach has been explored in the lazy learning literature (Wettschereck, Aha, & Mohri, 1997; Bonzano, Cunningham & Smyth, 1997) The difficulty with this approach is the problem of determining appropriate feature weights. It is well known that learning feature weights from examples is subject to overfitting. Kohavi, Langley & Yun,(1997) show that binary weights (i.e. feature selection) are often better than more fine grained weights due to the potential for overfitting. This problem is greatly exacerbated in local weighting because of the significant increase in the number of weights to be learned.

Another approach to this global representation problem within the CBR paradigm would be a hierarchical CBR approach where the problem space is partitioned with different sub-case-bases covering the different partitions. In fact, research on hierarchical CBR has focused on *problem* decomposition rather than *problem-space* decomposition (Smyth & Cunningham, 1992; Smyth et al., 2000). This is perhaps because of the difficulty in determining appropriate decompositions of the problem space. In the conclusion to this paper we propose that hierarchical CBR and problem-space decomposition may be the means to bring the performance of CBR systems up to that of ensembles. We outline how the analysis of ensemble solutions can provide guidance on problem-space decomposition.

The ensemble technique described in this paper achieves this decomposition implicitly with different members of the ensemble acting as specialists in different parts of the domain. While this approach is still a lazy learning technique with processing deferred to run time, it lacks the interpretability of CBR because of the large number of cases retrieved in the solution process. There is not a small number of cases that can be used as a starting point for adaptation or in explaining the answer.

In this paper we describe the operation of ensembles of nearest neighbour classifiers based on different feature subsets and show how such ensembles can perform better than any single classifier. We discuss the ramifications of this for CBR research. In the next section we describe ensembles in general and introduce the idea of ensembles based on different feature subsets. In section 3 we show how ensembles based on different feature subsets can outperform a classifier based on a single feature subset. Then the ramifications of this for CBR are discussed in section 4.

2. Ensembles

The key idea in ensemble research is; if a classifier or predictor is unstable then an ensemble of such classifiers voting on the outcome will produce better results – better in terms of stability and accuracy. While the use of ensembles in Machine Learning (ML) research is fairly new, the idea that aggregating the opinions of a committee of experts will increase accuracy is not new. The Codorcet Jury Theorem states that:

If each voter has a probability p of being correct and the probability of a majority of voters being correct is M, then p > 0.5 implies M > p. In the limit, M approaches 1, for all p > 0.5, as the number of voters approaches infinity.

This theorem was proposed by the Marquis of Condorcet in 1784 (Condorcet, 1784) – a more accessible reference is (Nitzan & Paroush, 1985). We know now that M will be greater than p only if there is diversity in the pool of voters. And we know that the probability of the ensemble being correct will only increase as the ensemble grows if the diversity in the ensemble continues to grow as well. Typically the diversity of the ensemble will plateau as will the accuracy of the ensemble at some size between 10 and 50 members.

In ML research it is well known that ensembling will improve the performance of unstable learners. Unstable learners are learners where small changes in the training data can produce quite different models and thus different predictions. Thus, a ready source of diversity is to train models on different subsets of the training data. This approach has been applied with great success in eager learning systems such as Neural Networks (Hansen & Salamon, 1992) or Decision Trees (Breiman, 1996) This research shows that, for difficult classification and regression tasks, ensembling will improve the performance of unstable learning techniques such as Neural Networks and Decision Trees. Ensembling will also improve the accuracy of lazy learners such as k-Nearest Neighbour (k-NN) classifiers, however k-NNs are relatively stable in the face of changes in training data so other sources of diversity must be employed (Ho,1998a;1998b; Cunningham & Carney, 2000).

2.1. Ensembles and Lazy Learning

To an extent the strength of the ensemble idea is bad news for lazy learning research because, with the ensemble approach, several learners have to be consulted at run-time and lazy learners do all their work at run-time. With lazy learners there has been little or no offline processing of the training data to build a hypothesis or model – this work is deferred to run-time.

If the ensemble approach poses problems for lazy learning in general then it proposes fundamental problems for Case-Based Reasoning (CBR) in particular. The key idea in CBR is that a single case or a small number of cases are retrieved during problem solving and these cases are reused to produce a solution for the new problem. Thus, as a problem solving technique, CBR has the special advantage of interpretability. The motivation in ensemble research is quite different; instead of there being a single line of reasoning in the problem solving process there are several parallel lines of enquiry and the results of these parallel efforts are aggregated to form a single solution. Thus it is difficult to *explain* the output of an ensemble. For this reason it appears difficult to bring the advantages of the ensemble idea to CBR without losing the interpretability advantages of CBR.

A further threat to the CBR idea arises from ensembles where the diversity in the ensemble is achieved by having different problem representations in the ensemble components. Research shows that ensembles of classifiers based on different feature subsets can produce better performance than a single classifier with a fixed feature set. (Cunningham & Carney, 2000; van der Laar & Heskes, 2000; Ho,1998a;1998b; Guerra-Salcedo & Whitley,1999a; 1999b). The important point here is that this improved performance is not based on a single problem representation but on a variety of different representations. The ensemble might be considered to embody a distributed problem representation. Alternatively it might better be viewed as a committee of local problem solvers using a variety of local representations. This contrasts with the fixed representations that are common in case-based reasoning. In Richter's knowledge container terms (Richter, 1998), the vocabulary knowledge container is difficult to characterise in these ensembles based on different feature subsets.

2.2. The Importance of Diversity

Krogh & Vedelsby (1995) have shown that the reduction in error due to an ensemble is directly proportionate to the diversity or ambiguity in the predictions of the components of the ensemble as measured by variance. It is difficult to show such a direct relationship for classification tasks but it is clear that the *uplift* due to the ensemble depends on the diversity in the ensemble members. Cunningham and Carney (2000) propose that this diversity can be quantified using entropy.

Colloquially, we can say that; if the ensemble members are more likely on average to be right, and when they are wrong they are wrong at different points, then their decisions by majority voting are more likely to be right than that of individual members. But they must be more likely on average to be right and when they are wrong they must be wrong in different ways.

The example in Figure 1, if a little contrived, illustrates these principles in action. The test set is shown at the top of the figure and the five component classifiers have an average accuracy of 65% on this. The ensemble decision is by simple voting and the ensemble has an accuracy of 100% on the test data. If the four voting scenarios are examined it is clear that the tendency to be right coupled with the tendency to be wrong in different ways accounts for the improvement due to the ensemble.

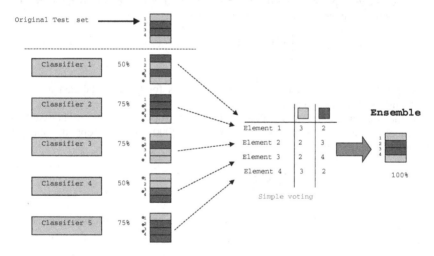

Fig. 1. An example showing how diversity in the ensemble leads to better classification.

Different Sources of Diversity

Several ways to differentiate members of an ensemble of classifiers have been proposed in the literature. The most common source of diversity is by training members on different subsets of the data. This can be done systematically of by bootstrapping (sampling with replacement) different training sets from the training data. However, since this will not produce diversity in a stable (low variance) predictor such as k-NN (Breiman, 1996) it is of no use here.

Another popular technique is to use different feature subsets in the different classifiers – this is the approach that we are concerned with here. Other approaches such as different output targets and different learning hypothesis have also been considered.

Different Measures of Diversity

There are a variety of ways to quantify ensemble diversity – usually associated with a particular error measure. In a regression problem (continuous output problem) it is normal to measure accuracy by the squared error so, as suggested by (Krogh & Vedelsby, 1995), a diversity measure can be variance, defined as:

$$a_i(x) = \left[V_i(x) - \overline{V}(x)\right]^2 \tag{1}$$

where a_i is the ambiguity of the ith classifier on example x, while V_i and $\overline{V}$ are, respectively the ith classifier and the ensemble predictions.

For a classification problem the most commonly used error measure is a simple 0/1 loss function, so a measure of ambiguity in this case is:

$$a_i(x) = \begin{cases} 0 \text{ if } classV_i(x) = class\overline{V}(x) \\ 1 \text{ otherwise.} \end{cases} \tag{2}$$

where this time the classifier and ensemble outputs for the case labeled as x are classes instead of real numbers.

Another measure, associated with a conditional-entropy error measure, is based on the concept of entropy (Cunningham & Carney, 2000). This entropy measure of diversity can be defined as:

$$\tilde{A} = \frac{1}{M} \sum_{x=1}^{M} \sum_{k=1}^{K} - P_k^x \log(P_k^x) \tag{3}$$

This quantifies the overall entropy of an ensemble on a test set of M cases where there are K possible classes and P_k^x is the proportion of predictions of class k for case x. While this is an useful measure of diversity it does not allow us to gauge the contribution of an *individual* to diversity so we will not use it here; instead we will use the 0/1 based approach as described in (2).

2.2. Ensembles of Different Feature Subsets

In this paper we focus on ensembles based on different feature subsets. The feature subset selection problem is very well studied in Machine Learning for a single classifier: it consists in finding the subset of features $F_s \subseteq F$ that maximizes performance. This is important when some of the features are irrelevant or redundant and consequently introduce some noise in the space of the instances. The main reasons why it's useful to perform feature subset selection are:

i)   to build better predictors: better quality classifiers can be built by removing irrelevant and redundant features. This is particularly important for lazy learning systems;

ii)   to achieve economy of representation and allow problems/phenomena to be represented as succinctly as possible;

iii)   for knowledge discovery: to discover what features are and are not influential in weak theory domains.

A few studies have been done on the use of feature selection to create an ensemble of classifiers; among them those ones made by Cherkauer (1995), Ho (1998a, 1998b), Guerra-Salcedo and Whitney (1999a, 1999b) Tumer and Ghosh (1996) and Cunningham and Carney (2000) give the most promising results. However, if the use of ensembles improves the performance from one side, from one another it reduces the other benefits of the feature selection strategy. It is quite intuitive that an ensemble of feature subsets affects the goal of economy of representation (ii) and also dramatically worsens the knowledge discovery (iii), mainly because we cannot say anymore that the outcome of a phenomenon depends on a particular subset of features.

Emphasizing Diversity

A very simple approach to selecting an ensemble of classifiers consists of two separate steps: first a group of independently "good" classifiers is selected, then they are aggregated to form an ensemble. Such an approach has the advantage of simplicity, both conceptually and computationally, but the main disadvantage is that the classifiers are selected for the results they obtain singly and not for their contribution in the context of the ensemble. Following the work of Krogh and Vedlsby (1995), which demonstrated the crucial role played by the disagreement (Ambiguity) in the final prediction of an ensemble, other less straightforward approaches have been proposed to build an ensemble of good classifiers that have a high degree of disagreement. Among them the most relevant results were obtained by Liu (1999), who introduced a negative correlation penalty term to train ensembles of neural networks, and that by Optiz and Shavlik (1996), who used the notion of ambiguity to find a diverse ensemble of neural networks using a genetic algorithm.

In this paper we provide some results for ensembles that are obtained with an algorithm based on a hill-climbing strategy that makes use of the concept of ambiguity (Zenobi & Cunningham, 2001). The results show that this technique outperforms the classic two-steps strategy for selecting ensembles via hill-climbing search. We give here only a brief description of it; a more detailed one can be found in the paper mentioned above.

In a classic hill climbing strategy that performs feature selection (Cunningham & Carney, 2000) a "good" classifier is selected by flipping each bit of the feature mask and accepting this flip if the classifier error decreases. (A feature subset is a mask on the full feature set.) This process is repeated until no further improvements are possible – i.e. a local minimum in the feature set space is reached. The error is measured using leave-one-out testing. To produce an ensemble this process is repeated for each classifier and at the end all the classifiers are aggregated to form the ensemble. This is the approach used to produce the results shown in Table 1.

The algorithm used to produce the results in Table 2 goes one step further; it considers instead every classifier in the context of the ensemble, and at each step accepts or rejects the flip depending on two parameters: the classifier error and the classifier ambiguity, using a variance measure as shown in equation (2). If the improvement of one of the two parameters leads to a "substantial" deterioration of the other, then the flip is rejected (see Figure 2). With "substantial" here we mean that a threshold is given for the highest acceptable deterioration. This technique allows us to avoid the selection of a set of good classifiers that make mistakes over the same subspace of the instances

```
    generate a random ensemble of feature subsets;

  do {
   for every classifier i in the ensemble {
        calculate initial error E_i and contribution to ambiguity A_i;
        for every bit j of the mask {
      flip j^{th} bit of i^{th} mask;
      calculate new E_i' and new A_i';
      if {   { [ E_i'< E_i] AND
         [    [( E_i'≤(1-Thresh ) × E_i ) AND (A_i'≥(1-Thresh) × A_i)] OR
              [( E_i' >(1-Thresh ) × E_i ) AND (A_i'≥ E_i'/E_i × A_i) ]      ] } OR
         { [A_i' >A_i] AND
         [    [( A_i'≥ (1+Thresh )× A_i ) AND (E_i'≤(1+Thresh )×E_i )] OR
              [( A_i' < (1+Thresh )× A_i) AND (E_i'≤A_i'/ A_i ×E_i ) ]      ] }      }
      E_i= E_i' ; A_i = A_i';  //flip accepted
      else flip back j^{th} bit of i^{th} mask; //flip rejected
        }
   }
  } while there are changes in the masks AND not  maximum number of iterations;

calculate final ensemble prediction;
```

Fig. 2. The algorithm for generating ensembles while emphasising diversity in ensemble members.

Here we are not particularly interested in the difference in accuracy resulting from these two techniques. What is of interest is that the focus on diversity in the second technique appears to produce local learners.

3. Evaluation

The objective of this evaluation is to show that ensembles of k-NN classifiers can outperform the best single k-NN classifier available. We also show that if the ensemble members are forced to be diverse then very good ensemble accuracy can be achieved with ensemble members that have poor overall accuracy. These diverse ensemble members also prove to have fewer features than ensemble members selected without consideration for diversity.

We start with two data-sets, an InVitro Fertilisation (IVF) data-set presented in (Cunningham & Carney, 2000) and the Hepatitis data from the UCI repository. The IVF data has 53 features and Hepatitis has 19 features so it is not practicable to search through the full space of feature subsets to find the best mask. In each case 100 good masks are found using hill-climbing search as described above; see also (Cunningham & Carney, 2000). Six ensembles of size 20 are produced using these masks and the error figures are shown in Table 1. This size of 20 was chosen because ensembles larger than this were found to produce little added benefit. The ensembles outperform the best masks found.

Table 1. An error comparison of ensembles of k-NN classifiers compared with best single k-NN classifiers found using hill-climbing search.

Dataset	Average Mask	Best Mask Found	Average Ensemble	Best Ensemble
IVF	41.1%	38.3%	35.7%	35.5%
Hepatitis	20.7%	17.4%	16.8%	15.5%

In the next evaluation two data-sets are chosen with few enough features to perform an exhaustive search of the space of feature masks. These are the Pima and Abalone data-sets from the UCI repository and each has 8 input features. The Abalone data is converted to a classification format by partitioning the outcome variable into two classes (age 7&8 → Class 1; age 11,12&13 → Class 2). In this case ensembles are produced using the algorithm presented in Figure 2 that emphasizes diversity. These ensembles are compared using 5-fold cross validation with the best masks that have been found by exhaustive search. Using a one tailed paired t-test the ensemble is better than the best mask with 80% confidence for the Pima data and 90% confidence for the Abalone. In the 5-fold cross validation the data is divided into 5 parts and the ensemble is tested on each part in turn having been trained on the other 4 parts. The scoring of the masks in determining the best mask is done in the same fashion.

Table 2. An error comparison of ensembles of k-NN classifiers compared with best single k-NN classifiers.

Dataset	All Features	Best Mask	Ensemble	Average Ens. Mask
Pima	23.9%	23.8%	22.5%	30.7%
Abalone	18.1%	16.5%	15.9%	22.5%

The final part of the evaluation compares these ensembles with ensembles built considering error only (see Table 3). The overall error figures are slightly better when diversity is considered – however that is not the important point. The increase in ambiguity (diversity) comes at the cost of significantly higher errors in the ensemble members. It seems to us that the only way to account for this small improvement in overall performance in the face of deterioration of the ensemble members is that the members are local specialists. This view is reinforced by the fact that the ensemble members produced using diversity have fewer features on average than the others (3.4 v's 4.6 for Pima and 3.7 v's 4.7 for Abalone). It seems reasonable that fewer features are required to discriminate in these local regions.

Table 3. A comparison of ensembles of k-NN classifiers trained using error and ambiguity and error only.

	Pima			Abalone		
	Average Error	Amb.	Ensemble Error	Average Error	Amb.	Ensemble Error
Error & Amb.	30.7%	21.5%	22.5%	22.5%	15.0%	15.9%
Error Only	26.9%	14.0%	23.9%	17.8%	5.6%	16.3%

3.1. Implications for CBR

From the results shown above we can make some observations. When we train an ensemble of classifiers we are able to obtain a better performance than any possible single classifier. This brings into question the practice of feature subset selection and illustrates some shortcomings of the feature vector representation of cases. Searching for *the* predictive feature subsets is questionable because a combination of feature subsets, maybe poorly predictive if taken singularly, can give a better prediction when aggregated in an ensemble. In other words, in a case-based reasoning system a single classifier (in this case, a single feature subset) might have an upper limit to its performance that can be raised by the use of an ensemble.

This result suggests the hypothesis that the search space is "adapted" by a single classifier (dropping some of the features) in order to fit better to its intrinsic metric (usually the Euclidean one). A single classifier uses a "global adaptation" of the space, while in the case of an ensemble we have a number of different "adaptations" that can be seen as making errors in different regions of the search space.

So in terms of the interpretability of the knowledge representation in the ensemble, at the extreme, there are two possibilities:
1. The ensemble embodies a distributed knowledge representation, similar to a neural network, and is not readily interpretable.
2. The ensemble is a set of local specialists and these specialists are locally interpretable.

Clearly, we are inclined to this second view. In our algorithm for generating diverse ensembles shown in Figure 2, by forcing the ensemble to be diverse the accuracy of the ensemble is increased but the average overall accuracy of the ensemble members is decreased. Coupled with this is the curious effect that the average number of features in the ensemble members is reduced compared to ensemble members that are optimized for accuracy only (see (Zenobi & Cunningham, 2001) for more details on this. We would suggest that this poor overall accuracy and small "specialized" feature set indicates that the ensemble members are local specialists.

This evaluation shows that an ensemble of lazy learners outperforms the best single lazy learner. The advantage of ensembling derives from aggregating diverse models. This advantage seems incompatible with CBR because if case-based learners are aggregated then the interpretability of CBR is lost.

In the future work section of this paper we propose a line of research whereby an ensemble of lazy learners would be used to discover a problem space decomposition that would allow for a hierarchical CBR solution that would have a performance comparable to that of the ensemble and better than a single CBR system.

4. Future Work and Conclusions

If, as suggested in section 4, the ensemble members are local specialists then the ensemble should be locally interpretable – the question is how to access this?

In this scenario local specialists are combining to ensure that elements in their locality are classified correctly. So one way to discover the problem decomposition implicit in the ensemble would be to cluster the data elements based on the classifiers that correctly classify them. For the problems presented in section 3 the classifiers that correctly classify the test data elements become *descriptors* of those data elements. Clustering the data according to these descriptors should produce clusters corresponding to the problem decomposition embodied in the ensemble.

These clusters should represent homogenous regions of the problem space where a single problem representation would work well. This suggests that a hierarchical CBR system that implements problem decomposition based on the problem decomposition implicit in the ensemble should perform better than a single CBR system operating over the whole problem domain.

4.1. Conclusion

In this paper we show how an ensemble of lazy learners based on different feature subset can perform better than a single lazy learner based on the best feature subset available. This brings into question the practice of searching for a single best feature subset, an issue that has received a lot of attention in CBR and in data-mining. This may indicate a fundamental shortcoming of symbolic representations or, more likely, it simply shows that a single representation across the whole problem space is not adequate

We show that if diversity is emphasized in the ensemble that the ensemble members act as local learners specializing in sub-regions of the problem space. We propose that an analysis of the performance of the ensemble may provide an insight into how the problem space should be partitioned to develop a hierarchical CBR system that implements problem space decomposition.

References

Aha, D.W. (1998) Feature weighting for lazy learning algorithms. In: H.Liu and H. Motoda (Eds.) *Feature Extraction, Construction and Selection: A Data Mining Perspective.* Norwell MA: Kluwer.

Bonzano, A., Cunningham, P., Smyth, B., (1997) Using introspective learning to improve retrieval in CBR: A case study in air traffic control *International Conference on Case-Based Reasoning,* Providence, Lecture Notes in Computer Science, SpringerVerlag, E. Plaza & D. Leake (eds), pp291-302.

Breiman, L., (1996) Bagging predictors. *Machine Learning,* 24:123-140.

Cherkauer, K.J. (1995) Stuffing Mind into Computer: Knowledge and Learning for Intelligent Systems. *Informatica* 19:4 (501-511) Nov. 1995

Condorcet, Marquis J. A. (1781) Sur les elections par scrutiny, *Histoire de l'Academie Royale des Sciences*, 31-34.

Cunningham, P., Carney, J., (2000) Diversity versus Quality in Classification Ensembles based on Feature Selection, *11th European Conference on Machine Learning (ECML 2000)*, Lecture Notes in Artificial Intelligence, R. López de Mántaras and E. Plaza, (eds) pp109-116, Springer Verlag.

Guerra-Salcedo, C., Whitley, D., (1999a). Genetic Approach for Feature Selection for Ensemble Creation. *in GECCO-99: Proceedings of the Genetic and Evolutionary Computation Conference*, Banzhaf, W., Daida, J., Eiben, A. E., Garzon, M. H., Honavar, V., Jakiela, M., & Smith, R. E. (eds.). Orlando, Florida USA, pp236-243, San Francisco, CA: Morgan Kaufmann.

Guerra-Salcedo, C., Whitley, D., (1999b). Feature Selection Mechanisms for Ensemble Creation: A Genetic Search Perspective, in *Data Mining with Evolutionary Algorithms: Research Directions. Papers from the AAAI Workshop*. Alex A. Freitas (Ed.) Technical Report WS-99-06. AAAI Press, 1999.

Hansen, L.K., Salamon, P., (1990) Neural Network Ensembles, *IEEE Pattern Analysis and Machine Intelligence*, 1990. **12**, 10, 993-1001.

Ho, T.K., (1998a) The Random Subspace Method for Constructing Decision Forests, *IEEE Transactions on Pattern Analysis and Machine Intelligence*, **20**, 8, 832-844.

Ho, T.K., (1998b) Nearest Neighbours in Random Subspaces, *Proc. Of 2nd International Workshop on Statistical Techniques in Pattern Recognition*, A. Amin, D. Dori, P. Puil, H. Freeman, (eds.) pp640-648, Springer Verlag LNCS 1451.

Kohavi, P. Langley, Y. Yun, (1997) The Utility of Feature Weighting in NearestNeighbor Algorithms, *European Conference on Machine Learning, ECML'97*, Prague, Czech Republic, 1997, poster.

Krogh, A., Vedelsby, J., (1995) Neural Network Ensembles, Cross Validation and Active Learning, in *Advances in Neural Information Processing Systems 7*, G. Tesauro, D. S. Touretsky, T. K. Leen, eds., pp231-238, MIT Press, Cambridge MA.

Liu Y., Yao X. (1999) Ensemble learning via negative correlation, *Neural Networks* 12, 1999.

Newell, A., & Simon, H.A., (1976) Computer Science as Empirical Enquiry: Symbols and Search. *Communications of ACM*, 19(3), 1976, pp.113-126.

Nitzan, S.I., Paroush, J., (1985) *Collective Decision Making*. Cambridge: Cambridge University Press.

Opitz D., Shavlik J., (1996) Generating Accurate and diverse members of a Neural Network Ensemble, *Advances in Neural Information Processing Systems*, pp. 535-543, Denver, CO. MIT Press. 1996.

Richter, M. M. (1998). Introduction (to Case-Based Reasoning). in *Case-based reasoning technology: from foundations to applications*, Lenz, M., Bartsch-Spörl, B., Burkhard, H.-D. & Wess, S. (eds.) (1998). Springer-Verlag, LNAI 1400, pp1-16.

Smyth B., Cunningham P., (1992) Déjà Vu: A Hierarchical Case-Based Reasoning System for Software Design, in Proceedings of *European Conference on Artificial Intelligence*, ed. Bernd Neumann, John Wiley, pp587-589, Vienna Austria, August 1992.

Smyth, B., Keane, M., & Cunningham, P., (2000) Hierarchical Case-Based Reasoning: Integrating Case-Based and Decompositional Problem-Solving Techniques for Plant-Control Software Design, *to appear in IEEE Transactions on Knowledge and Data Engineering*.

Tumer, K., and Ghosh, J., (1996) Error Correlation and Error Reduction in Ensemble Classifiers, *Connection Science, Special issue on combining artificial neural networks: ensemble approaches*, Vol. 8, No. 3 & 4, pp 385-404.

van de Laar, P., Heskes, T., (2000) Input selection based on an ensemble, *Neurocomputing*, 34:227-238.

Wettschereck, D., & Aha, D. W. (Eds.) (1997). ECML-97 MLNet Workshop Notes: *Case-Based Learning: Beyond Classification of Feature Vectors* (Technical Report AIC-97-005). Washington, DC: Naval Research Laboratory, Navy Center for Applied Research in Artificial Intelligence.

Wettschereck, D., Aha, D. W., & Mohri, T. (1997). A review and comparative evaluation of feature weighting methods for lazy learning algorithms. *Artificial Intelligence Review, 11*, 273-314.

Zenobi, G., & Cunningham, P., (2001) Using ambiguity in preparing ensembles of classifiers based on different feature subsets to minimize generalization error, *submitted to ECML 2001.*

A Declarative Similarity Framework for Knowledge Intensive CBR*

Belén Díaz-Agudo and Pedro A. González-Calero

Dep. Sistemas Informáticos y Programación
Universidad Complutense de Madrid
{belend,pedro}@sip.ucm.es

Abstract. This paper focuses on the design of knowledge intensive CBR systems and introduces a domain-independent architecture to help it. Our approach is based on acquiring the domain knowledge by reusing knowledge from a library of ontologies and integrating it with CBROnto, a task based ontology comprising common CBR terminology. In this paper we focus in retrieval and similarity assessment processes taking advantage of this domain knowledge. We describe our CBROnto based similarity representation framework and explain how it is used to represent similarity measures and retrieval processes.

1 Introduction

Any knowledge-based system achieves its reasoning power through the explicit representation and use of different kinds of knowledge about a certain domain. Although in a CBR system the main source of knowledge is the set of previous experiences, our approach to CBR is towards integrated applications that combine case specific knowledge with models of general domain knowledge, mainly about the domain terminology.

Our overall goal is the development of a CBR shell, which provides support to design knowledge intensive CBR applications. In knowledge rich CBR, the domain knowledge is used to reason and provide with more sophisticated CBR processes. The core of our architecture is CBROnto an ontology incorporating common CBR terminology. The CBROnto terminology helps defining generic and domain independent CBR processes that access the domain terminology by term classification through the CBROnto terms.

In this paper we are interested in the representation of semantic similarity measures where the domain knowledge influences similarity. After describing, in Section 2, CBROnto key ideas, Section 3 presents the proposed framework for similarity representation. Sections 4 through 7 describe similarity assessment and retrieval choices currently available within the framework, and, finally, Section 8 concludes and presents future work.

---

* Supported by the Spanish Committee of Science & Technology (CICYT TIC98-0733)

D.W. Aha and I. Watson (Eds.): ICCBR 2001, LNAI 2080, pp. 158–172, 2001.

2   CBROnto

Our approach to CBR is towards integrated applications that combine various knowledge types and reasoning methods. Besides the cases, we work with explicit models of general domain knowledge, mainly about the domain terminology. The major problem associated with this knowledge intensive CBR approach is the so called knowledge acquisition bottleneck.

We state that ontologies can be useful for designing knowledge intensive CBR applications because they allow the knowledge engineer to use knowledge already acquired, conceptualized and implemented in a formal language, reducing considerably the knowledge acquisition bottleneck. Moreover, the reuse of ontologies from a library also benefits from their reliability and consistency. Our approach proposes the use of an ontology library (Ontology Server) to build the domain model for knowledge rich CBR applications [5]. To take advantage of this domain knowledge, the CBR knowledge needed by the processes, or at least part of it, should be expressed in a similar way. We have developed an ontology for CBR (CBROnto) that provides the vocabulary for describing the elements involved in the CBR processes. CBROnto serves two purposes: the integration between the domain ontologies and the CBR process knowledge; and as a domain-independent framework to design CBR applications. CBROnto aims to unify case specific and general domain knowledge representational needs. The main reasoning mechanism underlying this unification process is classification as provided by Description Logics (DL).

Description Logics is considered one of the most important knowledge representation formalism unifying and giving a logical basis to the well known traditions of Frame-based systems, Semantic Networks and KL-ONE-like languages, Object-Oriented representations, Semantic data models, and Type systems. In DL, there are three types of formal objects: *concepts* and *relations*, descriptions with a potentially complex structure, formed by composing a limited set of description-forming operators; and *individuals*, simple formal constructs intended to directly represent objects in the domain of interest, which may be recognized as concept instances, and related to other individuals through relation instances. DL reasoning mechanisms are based on *subsumption*, to determine whether a description –concept or relation– is more general than another, and *instance recognition*, to determine the concepts that an individual satisfies and the relations that a tuple of individuals satisfies. Subsumption supports classification, i.e., the ability of automatically classifying a new description within a –semi– lattice of previously classified descriptions; and instance recognition supports completion, i.e., the ability of drawing logical consequences of assertions about individuals, based on those descriptions they are recognized as instances of. Contradiction detection, both for descriptions and assertions about individuals, completes the basic set of reasoning mechanisms provided by DL systems.

We use LOOM [7], a particular DL implementation, as the supporting system on top of which our shell is built. Within this architecture, different knowledge sources for a CBR application can be integrated:

- General knowledge about domain concepts and relationships, acquired by reusing ontologies.
- CBROnto provides a vocabulary for describing terms involved in the CBR problem-solving processes, and domain knowledge integration with CBROnto allows CBR processes having semantic CBR information about the domain terminology. CBR processes are domain-independent but they are guided by the domain terminology organized below (in the subsumption hierarchies) the CBROnto terms.
- Cases described using this domain knowledge and CBROnto terms as the case representation language.
- Knowledge extracted from the case base using inductive techniques as FCA.

With this representational schema CBROnto helps in structuring the domain knowledge within the cases. Nevertheless, we do not use the domain model as the case organization structure. By now, we use a simple case organization below the CBROnto CASE subconcepts (representing different case types in the case base). We are studying other case organization structures to improve the retrieval process [6] but they are out of the scope of this paper. In this paper we use the domain terminology to get semantic similarity measures where the domain knowledge influences similarity. We have defined a similarity framework to represent similarity measures for structured case representation where individuals are concept instances and concepts are organized in a hierarchy with inheritance. This approach requires similarity assessment processes that allow comparing two differently structured individuals and that take into account the influence of the domain term hierarchies over similarity [3,4].

3   Similarity Framework

What we propose is a way of representing the similarity choices for a CBR shell in a coherent framework that is used by the retrieval and similarity assessment processes. The framework allows representing and coexisting different case similarity measures in the same case base. Given two cases, our system provides with a general retrieval process that accesses the represented knowledge to get the type of retrieval and similarity measure to be used. The framework offers some initial options, although other similarity measures can be easily integrated into it. Four are the retrieval mechanisms our framework supports:

Relevance criteria. One straight possibility with our representational scheme is the use of the LOOM query language to enable the user to describe the current situation and interests.
Similarity terms. Another approach, when working with knowledge organized in hierarchies, is to explicitly compute and automatically classify a similarity concept, representing, in a declarative way, the similarity and differences between the cases.
Representational approach. This approach assigns similarity meaning to the path joining two individuals in the case organization structure and retrieval

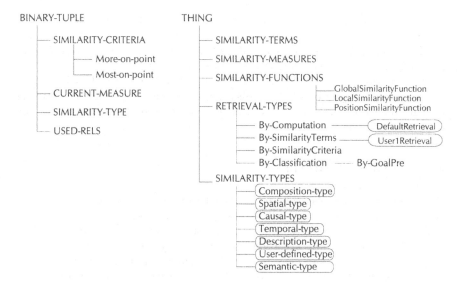

Fig. 1. CBROnto similarity terms.

is accomplished by traversing that structure starting from the position of the query.

Computational approach. The most straightforward CBR approach to retrieval is the one that computes all the similarity values during the retrieval process.

Figure 1 shows the CBROnto terms needed to represent the similarity knowledge. The RETRIEVAL-TYPES concept is used to classify other concepts representing each one of the retrieval types offered by our system: BY-SIMILARITYTERMS, BY-SIMILARITYCRITERIA, BY-CLASSIFICATION, and BY-COMPUTATION. In this figure THING is the top level concept, root of the concept hierarchy, while BINARY-TUPLE is the root of the relation hierarchy. These terms will be described in the following sections, although most of them are needed to represent numerical similarity measures for structured case representations –used mainly in the computational approach.

The type of retrieval is represented by an individual classified below one of the RETRIEVAL-TYPES subconcepts. The default retrieval type must be specified by the application designer and is represented by a distinguished instance named DEFAULTRETRIEVAL that is classified below the concept determining the default retrieval type. Besides –if the designer activates this option– each user could define the type of retrieval she wants to use by an instance name USER$_i$RETRIEVAL that is used as the retrieval type during this user session but it is destroyed when the user finishes the session. The first step the retrieval process performs is accessing the type of retrieval and depending on it the rest of the process is decided.

Besides the retrieval mechanism, CBROnto terms –mainly through its relation hierarchy– allow to define different similarity types depending on a semantic classification of the attributes –i.e., the relations–: the structural similarity will be computed based on the composition relations, the semantics similarity is due to all the concepts and relations describing the meaning of the case, the temporal similarity depends on the temporal relations, and so on.

Next sections describe the similarity assessment and retrieval choices to be offered to the designer of a CBR application using our shell. While prototyping a CBR application different choices can be incorporated and tested so that the more successful ones are chosen.

4   Relevance Criteria

Our representational schema based on the CBROnto terminology and the LOOM instance definition language, allows the use of the LOOM query language to enable the user to describe the current situation and interests. Relevance criteria are defined as the criteria according to which the system asserts that a case is relevant to a problem and more relevant than any other cases.

In [2] relevance criteria are expressed in first order logic using LOOM. That allows complex retrieval processes and an interactive use of the CBR system where the user makes a possibly complex description of the case/s she needs and can judge the quality of the retrieved cases and make changes to the query if needed. This approach to CBR relates also with [9] where the user defines both the query and the similarity criteria expressing what she means by similar. That allows the system to perform different goals for different users.

The user formulates a query using the LOOM query language. The LOOM interpreter receives the query and finds the individuals satisfying the given definition. If the user query is an interesting one, a new relevance criteria can be created by defining a relation whose :satisfies clause contains the interesting query. That way the query becomes a relevance criteria that can be used later by the same or other user.

So, relevance criteria are represented by using LOOM relations defined with a :satisfies clause, i.e., giving explicitly the properties satisfied by the relation tupla. Within this approach many relevance criteria can be pre-defined during the system design to facilitate the user query formulation process. Each user query can include –or not– previous relations representing relevance criteria.

For example, the *more-on-point* relation in Figure 2 defines a relevance criteria (predefined in the system) that could be included in a user query. It is adapted from [2], and represents which case in the base shares more properties with a given situation. The tupla $(c1, c2, problem)$ belongs to the *more-on-point* relation if the case $c1$ has more shared properties than the case $c2$ with the case *problem*. Based on the *more-on-point* criteria the criteria *most-on-point* is easily defined as a binary relation whose tuples $(c, problem)$ satisfy that c is the case with more shared properties with the *problem* case, i.e., there is no other case $c1$ with more shared properties with *problem* than c. The following query uses the *most-on-point* criteria to retrieve cases:

    (retrieve ?c (:and (Case ?c) (most-on-point ?c problem)))

```
(defrelation more-on-point
 :constraints (domains Case Case)
 :range Case
 :is (:satisfies (?c1 ?c2 ?cfs)
       (:and (Case ?c1)
             (Case ?c2)
             (Case ?cfs)
             (neq ?c1 ?cfs)
             (:for-all ?p (:implies (:and (Property ?p)
                                          (shared-Property ?c2 ?cfs ?p))
                             (applicable-Property ?c1 ?p)))
             (:for-some ?p (:and (Property ?p)
                           (shared-Property ?c1 ?cfs ?p)
                           (:not (applicable-Property ?c2 ?p)))))))
```

Case $?c1$ is more on point than case $?c2$ relative to situation $?cfs$ if: $?c1$ has all the properties that $?c2$ shares with $?cfs$; and shares at least one additional common property with $?cfs$.

```
(defrelation most-on-point
 :domain Case
 :range Case
 :is (:satisfies (?c  ?cfs)
       (:and (Case ?c)
             (Case ?cfs)
             (neq ?c ?cfs)
             (:for-all ?c1 (:implies
                             (:and (Case ?c1)
                                   (neq ?c1 ?cfs))
                             (:not (more-on-point ?c1 ?c ?cfs)))))))
```

Case $?c$ is the most on point case relative to situation $?cfs$ if: for any other case $?c1$ it is not more-on-point than $?c$.

Fig. 2. *more-on-point* and *most-on-point* relevance criteria [2].

In a CBR application, predefined similarity criteria are offered to facilitate the user query formulation process. Our shell proposes and facilitates the similarity criteria incorporation during a CBR application design. The designer can incorporate general similarity criteria proposed by our shell (as the *more-on-point* and *most-on-point*), or define domain specific criteria. CBROnto includes a primitive relation named SIMILARITY-CRITERIA so that the relation classification mechanism can access directly all the similarity criteria defined in the system.

We have incorporated also other more complex criteria where a case is relevant depending not only on the case itself, but on the relations with other cases. Complex conditions that involve any number of cases interrelated by multiple relationships can be expressed with this logical representation.

Our shell offers this approach for CBR applications to get complex retrieval processes comprising relations among cases and the retrieval of a set a cases related in a certain way, and not only the retrieval of isolated cases similar to a simple query. With this approach case retrieval does not compute a similarity value but is a process based on finding the cases satisfying a certain complex declarative relevance criteria that can be pre-defined or user defined.

5   Similarity Terms

There is another similarity and retrieval choice taking advantage of the LOOM reasoning mechanisms, and fitting our representational schema. It works in the line of [10,12] where a similarity term (concept) is explicitly computed to represent with the domain terms, in a declarative way, the similarity and differences between the cases.

With this approach, similarity is characterized by the most specific concept (called least common subsumer –LCS–, which can be obtained through disjunction in DL) which subsumes the two compared cases. Since the similarity is represented by using a concept it is automatically classified in the hierarchy using the subsumption relationship.

This way, retrieval is accomplished by comparing the query instance with every instance representing a case, and computing the corresponding similarity concept. CBROnto includes a concept SIMILARITY-TERMS such that all the similarity concepts are classified below it, i.e. it is the root of the similarity taxonomy for every retrieval process. In the taxonomy of similarities the most specific concepts correspond to the cases that are the most similar to the query case because they have more common properties with the query individual. The instances of the most specific similarity concepts will be retrieved.

One of the main advantage of this approach is that the similarity term can be used to justify the result and to explain, by means of the domain terminology, why the retrieved cases are similar in a declarative way. As its main drawback we cite the not satisfaction of a desirable property for DL representations, namely a static TBox (the set of concepts and relations). Since new concepts are defined in every retrieval process, the similarity taxonomy should be recomputed for each retrieval interaction.

6   Representational Approach

Another choice for a CBR application designer using our shell, is the use of a representational approach that assigns similarity meaning to the path joining two individuals in a case organization structure or in the domain terminology. (note we use rich domain taxonomies). With this approach A is more similar to B than C to B iff A is closer to B than C. By now, we only have applied this approach using the subsumption links in the domain taxonomies to define the distance between two individuals. The goodness of this kind of approach will strongly depend on the knowledge structure where the cases are located. We use

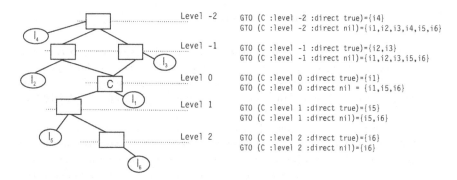

Fig. 3. The Generic Travel Operator (GTO).

certain operators to retrieve cases based on the distance along the subsumption links. We have defined a Generic Travel Operator (GTO) that retrieves instances in the knowledge base within different levels. It takes a concept C as the starting point and the level used to retrieve the instances. Negative level numbers means upwards paths in the hierarchy and positive numbers means downwards paths. The last argument is a Boolean value that is true if only direct instances should be retrieved. Figure 3 shows the use of GTO.

Similar retrieval operations, based on instance recognition and concept classification, have been proposed in the literature [8,12] that can be seen as a particularization of GTO.

Instance recognition. Retrieval is defined as a classification process where the queries are represented as DL instances. Given a query individual q, the retrieval process finds the most specific concepts q is an instance of $[C_1, \ldots, C_n]$, and returns their instances:

$\text{GTO}(C_1 : \text{level } 0) \cup \text{GTO}(C_2 : \text{level } 0) \cup \ldots \cup \text{GTO}(C_n : \text{level } 0)$

Instead of just retrieve cases classified below at least one of them, the conjunction concept can be computed to get instances belonging to all the concepts:

$\text{GTO}((\text{compute-conjunction-concept } C_1 \ldots C_n) : \text{level } 0)$

Concept classification. Queries are represented as DL concepts and the classification module puts the concept in its correct place at the hierarchy. Retrieval process returns the case instances that are recognized as the query concept instances:

$\text{GTO}(\text{query-concept} : \text{level } 0)$

Within the representation approach, retrieval is accomplished as a sequence of GTO invocations associated with a particular By-Classification instance. The elements of the given sequence will be applied and the retrieved instances returned.

7   Pure Computational Approach

Our similarity framework allows representing several alternatives to compute numerical similarity values for complex case representations in an homogeneous manner. This section describes the similarity assessment and retrieval as general processes that access the domain specific knowledge through the CBROnto terms.

The Nearest Neighbour (NN) algorithm searches through every case in memory, applies a similarity measure and returns the case or cases most similar to the query. The NN algorithm assumes cases described by characteristics and a similarity metric takes into account the common characteristics between the query and each one of the stored cases.

The classical scheme to define (global) similarity measures between two object- oriented represented cases o_1 and o_2, is recursive and bottom-up: take each simple common attribute and use a local similarity measure to determine the similarity between the two attribute fillers (values or slotless individuals). For each common relational attribute recursively use a global similarity measure to compare the two related sub-objects. The similarity values resulting from the local and global similarity measures applied to the common attributes are aggregated (e.g. by a weighted sum) to the similarity value of the objects being compared.

With this approach, only attributes and values contribute to the similarity but the result does not take into account the concepts the individuals belong to. Intuitively the class hierarchy contains similarity knowledge that should participate in the similarity assessment. Apart from the concrete values filling the common attributes, closer objects in the hierarchy should be more similar that further ones.

Taking this consideration into account there should be two components in the similarity result: one due to the closeness in the class hierarchy and other due to the attribute values. In [3] these two components are recognized as *intra-class* and *inter-class* similarity and both results are multiplied to get the final similarity result. The intra-class similarity combines the similarity among the fillers in the common attributes, that are determined by the most specific common class between the two objects. The inter-class similarity component is due to the objects position in the hierarchy and is independent of the attribute values[1]. The deeper in the hierarchy the most specific common class is, the more similar the objects are. That represents a qualitative measure, so to get a quantitative similarity result the nodes are annotated with a similarity value that is bigger with the hierarchy depth. Bergmann's approach allows comparing objects of different classes while considering the knowledge contained in the class hierarchy itself. The proposals of [10,12] also take into account the concept hierarchy to compute the similarity value but contrasting with Bergmann's approach they do not get a numerical similarity value but an structured object to explicitly represent it.

---

[1] Although the attribute fillers will affect the object position within the hierarchy.

```
(defconcept similarity-measures
  :is-primitive
    (:and (:the contents          similarity-functions)
          (:the structure         similarity-functions)
          (:the combination       similarity-functions)
          (:the similarity-type   similarity-types)      )
  :annotations
    ((documentation
      "the class of all the individuals representing
       a similarity measure to compare instances of a concept.")))

(defconcept similarity-functions
  :is-primitive
    (:and (:exactly 1 function-name)
          (:all parameters function-parameter))
  :annotations
    ((documentation
      "the class of all the individuals representing
       a similarity function to compute a similarity value.")))
```

Fig. 4. LOOM representation for similarity measures.

As we want the taxonomy to take part in the similarity assessment, in the line of Bergmann we consider the numerical similarity measures are represented by means of two components one due to the attribute values (sim-intra or *contents similarity*) and the other due to the individuals position in the hierarchy (sim-inter or *position similarity*). CBROnto includes a primitive concept SIMILARITY-MEASURES such that each particular similarity measure is represented as one of its instances. Although the particular similarity measures are used to compute a similarity value between two instances, they are linked to concepts. A similarity measure is annotated in a concept by using the CBROnto CURRENT-MEASURE relation. Annotations in LOOM imply that the relation will not be inherited by the concept instances, but it is a concept level relationship with a similarity measure individual, representing the way of computing the similarity between every two instances of the concept.

Figure 4 shows the LOOM definition for a similarity measure. A SIMILARITY-MEASURES instance includes knowledge about which function is being used for each similarity component (contents and position), which function is being used to combine both results, and also the type of similarity according to the contributing terms. Three CBROnto relations named CONTENTS, STRUCTURE and COMBINATION relate the similarity measure instance with instances representing the similarity functions. The CBROnto relation named SIMILARITY-TYPE relates the similarity measure instance with the instance representing the information about the type of contributing attributes. Next sections describe similarity functions, similarity types and how the pieces are put together.

7.1   Similarity Functions

CBROnto includes a primitive concept SIMILARITY-FUNCTIONS (cf. Figure 1, whose instances represent the similarity functions associated to the similarity measures. Similarity functions are classified as local, global and structural by the three SIMILARITY-FUNCTIONS subconcepts: LOCALSIMILARITYFUNCTION, GLOBALSIMILARITYFUNCTION and POSITIONSIMILARITYFUNCTION. Similarity function instances are described by the FUNCTION-NAME and the list of PARAMETERS apart from the individuals being compared that are implicit arguments.

Local functions are typically associated to "types", and used to compare the similarity between two values of that type. In our representational scheme with DL, local functions are associated to concepts whose instances are slotless. The general similarity assessment process retrieves the function name and the list of parameters (if any), and applies the function to the parameters and the two compared individuals.

The framework includes a number of standard similarity functions but it is a general framework in the sense of new functions can be included and associated to the domain concepts.

Global functions define the way of combining the result of the local similarity function application to the fillers of the common attributes between the compared individuals. They can be used to define both the contents or combination components of a certain similarity measure. The general process applies the function to the list of parameters (if any) and the list of similarity values to be combined.

Weight vectors can be used as parameters in the similarity function, i.e. they are fixed during the application design, either manually or extracted from the cases.

The position similarity functions are used to compute the similarity (sim-inter) between two individuals independently of their attribute values, but dependent on the position in the hierarchy of the most specific concepts containing both individuals. The general process applies the function to the parameters and the two compared individuals

The framework includes, for example, functions that compute the depth of the least common subsumer between the two individuals, or the number of common superconcepts between them, and more sophisticated computations based on the vector space model.

7.2   Similarity Types According to the Contributing Terms

We complete our similarity representation framework with mechanisms to express different similarity types depending on the contributing terms. Similarity types are represented by instances classified below the SIMILARITY-TYPES concept. Each SIMILARITY-TYPES instance has a link (through the USED-RELS relation) with the list of relations contributing this type of similarity. Moreover all the relation classified below any of them will contribute in the similarity assessment. The basic mechanism we are using here is the relation hierarchy and the knowledge integration between the CBROnto and domain terms. The SIMILARITY-TYPES instances shown in Figure 1 are some of the predefined types, but the system designer can include new types by selecting a different set of contributing terms. We introduce some examples of the predefined similarity types offered to the designer to be linked to the similarity-measure instances.

The structural similarity between two cases is computed taking into account only the composition relations (part-of, has-part) represented by the composition-type individual. The semantics similarity (SEMANTIC-TYPE instance) is due to all the concepts and relations describing the meaning of the case. The causal similarity (CAUSAL-TYPE instance) uses the causing relations (depends-on, cause, explains). The temporal similarity (TEMPORAL-TYPE instance) will use the temporal relations (during, before, after). The description similarity (DESCRIPTION-TYPE instance) will use the descriptive relations (any relation classified below DESCRIPTION-PROPERTY).

7.3   Retrieval

When the RETRIEVAL-TYPE instance is classified below the BY-COMPUTATION concept, first thing to do when computing the similarity between any two individuals i_1 and i_2 is to obtain the most specific concept C containing both i_1 and i_2, and access the similarity measure instance INS-SIM that is linked to C through the CURRENT-MEASURE relation. INST-SIM gives access to the content, position and combination similarity function names, and if needed also to their parameters, along with the similarity type available through the SIMILARITY-TYPE relation.

The similarity assessment process applies the combination function to the result of applying the content function to i_1 and i_2 and the result of applying the position function to i_1 and i_2. If i_1 and i_2 are slotless individuals the content function will be local and not recursive. If i_1 and i_2 are structured individuals the content function will be global and the similarity assessment process is recursively applied for the fillers of a certain list of slots that depends on the similarity type instance.

This general method of obtaining the similarity measure to compare two individuals i_1 and i_2 through the most specific concept C containing both poses two problems: numerical values and multiple inheritance.

Suppose, for example, the values 100,000 and 120,000 represent the price value for two CAR instances we are comparing. Although the domain taxonomy classifies the concept PRICE as a subconcept of NUMBER, the DL recognition module does not recognize them as PRICE instances but NUMBER instances (because there are not evidence the numbers are representing prices and not any other characteristic), so we do not have access to the similarity measure instance linked to the PRICE concept. The information about the number meaning is given by the slot they are filling, i.e., the SALE-PRICE relation and its range, the PRICE concept. That is why we use a complementary method to access the similarity

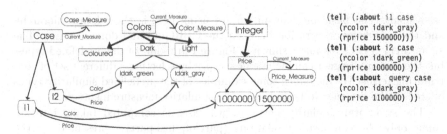

Fig. 5. A retrieval example.

measure instance using both the individuals we are comparing and the relation they are filling.

The second problem is due to the multiple inheritance that makes the concept most specific containing both individuals not unique so we could obtain different applicable similarity measure instances. That could be considered a design flaw, and we consider to let the user decide which measure instance should be used, or even to select the measure instance depending on the concrete query values.

7.4   A Retrieval Example

Suppose we have the two cases i_1 and i_2 represented in Figure 5, where the similarity measure instances CASE-MEASURE, COLOR-MEASURE and PRICE-MEASURE are the ones represented in Figure 6. The CASE-MEASURE individual represents the way of computing the similarity between i_1 and i_2.

The similarity assessment process applies the combination function (average) to the result of applying the content function (average) to i_1 and i_2 and the result of applying the position similarity function (estrul) to i_1 and i_2. Note that as i_1 and i_2 are structured objects the content function is global and the similarity assessment process is recursively applied for the fillers of the list of slots depending on the similarity type instance. For the example, the terms contributing similarity between cases are all the relations classified below DESCRIPTION-PROPERTY in the relation hierarchy, i.e., all the domain relations classified as descriptive during the knowledge integration phase. We consider price and color have been both classified as case descriptive relations.

The COLOR-MEASURE individual represents the way of computing the similarity between the COLOR concept instances, and the PRICE-MEASURE individual represents the way of computing the similarity between the PRICE concept instances. Note, that in both cases the content function is local and the similarity assessment process compute the similarity value finishing the recursion.

The similarity results for this simple example are:

(|I|query |I|I1 7/8) (|I|query |I|I2 41/48)

CASE-MEASURE is the similarity measure instance used to compare query with i_1 and i_2. COLOR-MEASURE is used to compare IDARK-GRAY and IDARK-GRAY and IDARK-GRAY and IDARK-GREEN, filling the color relation; and PRICE-

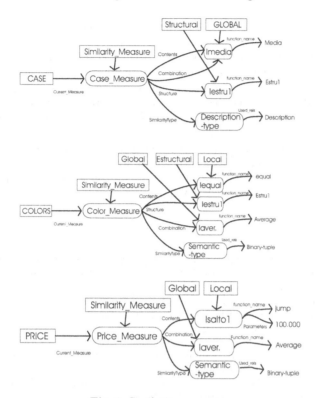

Fig. 6. Similarity measures.

MEASURE is used to compare 1,100,000 with 150,000, and 1,100,000 with 100,000 filling the price relation.

8   Conclusions

We use a knowledge rich CBR approach where the domain knowledge should undoubtedly influence the similarity metric of a case-based reasoning system [3,4]. In this paper we have described a framework to be used within knowledge intensive CBR systems, to represent semantic similarity measures where the domain knowledge influences similarity. We have described the CBROnto terminology related to the similarity representation and the use of this terminology to define different types of similarity and retrieval. A general similarity assessment process accesses the knowledge described with the similarity representation framework. Our domain independent similarity assessment process refers only to CBROnto terms but let the domain taxonomy to influence the similarity result.

Regarding related work, we should mention the one described in [1] where a frame-based knowledge representation system aimed at unifying case-specific and general domain knowledge within a single representation system is presented. The main differences with the work here presented are, first, the underlying technology for knowledge representation –frame-based vs. classification-based– and, second, our interest on integrating available ontologies.

Although none of the described approaches to retrieval and similarity assessment are new, we consider that two are the main contributions of the work here presented. First, we have shown how these heterogeneous approaches can be integrated into our knowledge intensive CBR framework. And, second this integration is accomplished in a declarative way, by means of CBROnto terminology, that facilitates experimentation and prototyping in the development of a CBR system. Our framework is easily extensible and allows representing other similarity measure choices. As a future work we are planning the incorporation of other similarity models as the one in [9], along with further experimentation and development within the CBROnto framework.

References

1. Aamodt, A., 1994. "A Knowledge Representation System for Integration of General Knowledge and Case-Specific Knowledge". In *Procs. Int. Conf. on Tools with Artificial Intelligence,* – (IEEE TAI'94).
2. Ashley, K.D., Aleven, V., 1993. "A logical representation for relevance criteria". In Wess, S., Althoff, K.D., Richter, M.M., (eds.), *Topics in Case-Based Reasoning* – (EWCBR'93), Springer-Verlag.
3. Bergmann, R., Stahl, S., 1998. "Similarity Measures for Object-Oriented Case Representations". In SmythB., Cunningham, P. (eds.), *Advances in Case-Based Reasoning* – (EWCBR'98), Springer-Verlag.
4. Cain, R., Pazzani, M., Silverstein, G. 1991. "Using domain knowledge to influence similarity judgments". In *Procs. EWCBR'91.*
5. Díaz-Agudo, B., González-Calero, P.A., 2000. "An Architecture for Knowledge Intensive CBR Systems". In *Advances in Case-Based Reasoning* – (EWCBR'00), Springer-Verlag.
6. Díaz-Agudo, B., González-Calero, P.A., 2000. "Formal Concept Analysis as a Support Technique for CBR". In *Procs. of the Twentieth SGES International Conference on Knowledge Based Systems and Applied Artificial Intelligence* – (ES'2000), Springer-Verlag.
7. Mac Gregor, R., Bates, R., 1987. "The Loom Knowledge Representation Language". *ISI Reprint Series, ISI/RS-87-188,* Univ. of Southern California.
8. Napoli, A., Lieber, J., Simon A., 1997. "A Classification-Based Approach to Case-Based Reasoning", In *Procs Int. Workshop on Description Logics* – (DL'97).
9. Osborne, H., Bridge, D.G., 1997. "Similarity metrics: a formal unification of Cardinal and not cardinal similarity measures", In Leake, D.B., Plaza, E., (eds.), *Case Based Reasoning Research & Development,* – (ICCBR'97), Springer-Verlag.
10. Plaza, E., 1995. "Cases as Terms: A feature term approach to the structured representation of cases". In Veloso, M., Aamodt, A., (eds.), *Case Based Reasoning Research and Development,* – (ICCBR'95), Springer-Verlag.
11. Porter, B.W., 1989. "Similarity Assessment: computation vs. representation". In *Procs. of DARPA CBR Workshop,* Morgan Kaufmann, 1989.
12. Salotti, S., Ventos, V., 1998. "Study and Formalization of a Case-Based Reasoning System using a Description Logic". In Smyth, B., Cunningham, P., (eds.), *Advances in Case-Based Reasoning* – (EWCBR'98), Springer-Verlag.

Classification Based Retrieval Using Formal Concept Analysis*

Belén Díaz-Agudo and Pedro A. González-Calero

Dep. Sistemas Informáticos y Programación
Universidad Complutense de Madrid, Spain
{belend, pedro}@sip.ucm.es

Abstract. This paper shows how the use of Formal Concept Analysis (FCA) can support CBR application designers, in the task of discovering knowledge embedded in a case base. FCA application provides an internal sight of the case base conceptual structure and allows finding regularity patterns among the cases. Moreover, it extracts dependence rules between the attributes describing the cases, that will be used to guide the query formulation process. In this paper we focus in classification based retrieval and the utility of Galois lattices as structures to classify and retrieve cases.

1 Introduction

Our approach to CBR is towards integrated applications that combine case specific knowledge with models of general domain knowledge, mainly about the domain terminology and we are developing a CBR shell, supporting the design process of knowledge intensive CBR applications [2]. In this paper, we use specific knowledge extracted from the concrete cases to complement general knowledge about the domain.

Structured domains are characterized by the fact that there is an intrinsic dependency between certain elements in the domain. Considering these dependencies leads to better performance of CBR systems and it is an important factor for determining the relevance of the cases stored in a case base [6]. We consider that a case library contains useful knowledge more than the individual specific pieces of problem solving experiences to be reused, and although dependency knowledge could be manually identified for a domain expert, we propose extracting them from the case base.

We use Formal Concept Analysis (FCA) as an inductive technique that elicits knowledge embedded in a concrete case library. Moreover the concept lattice resultant from FCA application, can be used as a case organization structure. In [3] we have seen how specific knowledge extracted from the concrete cases can be used to complement the general domain knowledge already acquired by other techniques of domain modelling. The dependency knowledge implicitly contained in the case base is captured during the FCA process in the form of dependency

---

* Supported by the Spanish Committee of Science & Technology (CICYT TIC98-0733)

D.W. Aha and I. Watson (Eds.): ICCBR 2001, LNAI 2080, pp. 173–188, 2001.
© Springer-Verlag Berlin Heidelberg 2001

rules among the attributes describing the cases, that will guide the CBR query formulation process.

Although our system provides with other retrieval processes that intensively use the general domain knowledge, in this paper we want to point up a kind of semantic retrieval in the context of case based planning systems, that takes advantage of the concept lattice resultant from FCA application.

Section 2 introduces our knowledge representation approach using description logics. Section 3 sketches the case organization we propose based on Formal Concept Analysis, and describes the basics of the technique. Section 4 describes classification based retrieval and the advantages of using classification based retrieval over the FCA lattices. Section 5 and 6 conclude and describe related and future work.

2 Knowledge Representation

Our approach to CBR is towards integrated applications that combine various knowledge types and reasoning methods. Besides the cases, we work with explicit models of general domain knowledge. We state that ontologies can be useful for designing knowledge intensive CBR applications because they allow the knowledge engineer to use knowledge already acquired, conceptualized and implemented in a formal language, reducing considerably the knowledge acquisition bottleneck. Besides, we have developed an ontology for CBR (CBROnto) that provides the vocabulary for describing the elements involved in the CBR processes. CBROnto serves two purposes: the integration between the domain ontologies and the CBR process knowledge; and as a domain-independent framework to design CBR applications. CBROnto aims to unify case specific and general domain knowledge representational needs [2].

Description Logic based languages (DLs) are commonly used to implement ontologies, and it is the technology we use in our model to formalize aspects of representation and reasoning. We use a DLs system, LOOM [8]. DLs capture the meaning of the data by concentrating on entities (grouped into classes or concepts) related by relationships. This intuition is shared by formalisms such as semantic data models, semantic networks or frame systems. More important than the DLs representational characteristics are its reasoning mechanisms. The most important characteristic is the checking of incoherencies and the organization of the concepts on a taxonomy that the system automatically builds from the concept definitions. This is possible because of the clear and precise semantic of concept definitions that avoid the user to put the concepts in the correct place of the hierarchy (as in frame systems, which provide inheritance but not classification).

DLs reasoning mechanisms and deductive inferences are based on *subsumption* and *instance recognition*. Subsumption determines if a term is or not more general than another, and instance recognition finds all the concepts that an individual satisfies. Furthermore, completion mechanisms perform logical consequences like inheritance, combination of restrictions, restriction propagation, contradiction detection, and incoherent term detection. In our approach, these mechanisms are used, in general, as the base for all the CBR processes.

Case Representation

Cases in the case base should be described somehow by mean of the domain vocabulary. The issue of case representation involves deciding the type and the structure of the domain knowledge within the cases. As our system is intended to be suitable for different types of CBR, our aim is to propose a framework to represent cases based on the terminology from CBROnto together with a reasoning system that works with such representations. Although CBROnto provides with a wide range of possibilities to represent cases, in this paper we consider cases described by the goals satisfied by the solution and the precondition properties needed to apply the case solution. This approach is related to case-based planning where given a set of goals, a planner finds an applicable plan in memory that makes the best goal match [5].

An Example

When using our architecture, the first step is the domain knowledge representation phase. As an example, we describe an abstract domain identifying basic goals, properties, actions and entities. We are supposing all goals and properties are primitive, and for each concrete case it is explicitly asserted (and not inferred) the corresponding goals and preconditions.

```
Domain primitive goals (CBROnto GOAL subconcepts): A, B, C, D, E
Domain properties (CBROnto PROPERTY subconcepts): X, Y, Z, T
```

In our example, $Case_i$ description is related with a precondition individual (Pre_i) representing the properties needed to apply $Case_i$ solution. Besides, $Case_i$ description is related with a goal individual ($Goal_i$) representing the set of goals satisfied after applying $Case_i$ solution to a situation that satisfies $Case_i$ precondition. Our example case base is made up of 6 simple test cases.

```
Case₁ description: (Pre₁) X,Y      (Goal₁) A,B,C
Case₂ description: (Pre₂) X,Y,Z    (Goal₂) A,C
Case₃ description: (Pre₃) Z         (Goal₃) A,B,D,E
Case₄ description: (Pre₄) Y,Z       (Goal₄) A,B
Case₅ description: (Pre₅) X,Y,Z,T  (Goal₅) D,E
Case₆ description: (Pre₆) Y,T       (Goal₆) A,C
```

Lets suppose the following query is posed to our system:

```
Query: query_descr X Y Z query_goals A B C
```

$Query_{descr}$ individual describes the current situation, i.e., the state of the world when the query occurs. With this description we can decide which are the applicable cases. In this example $Case_1$, $Case_2$, $Case_3$ and $Case_4$ solutions could be applied.

$Query_{goals}$ individual describes the goals that are wanted to be fulfilled. In this example $Case_1$ solution will be the only one leading to a situation where all the required goals are satisfied. So, $Case_1$ is the best case to be retrieved, because it is applicable and gets all the required goals.

Next section describes the FCA technique and applies it to this example. Section 4 shows the utility of the lattice structures obtained by FCA application, to organize the case base and guide an intelligent retrieval process that takes into account the semantic meaning of the case description composing parts.

3   Case Organization

With our approach many possibilities are suitable to organize the case base. The straight one is the use of the domain terminology as the case organization structure. However, although the domain knowledge acquired by reusing ontologies terms and integrating them with CBROnto, in a certain sense organizes the cases, it is not an optimized structure to effectively classify and retrieve cases (representational retrieval approach). Typically, it will be a good structure only when appropriate index concepts have been manually added by a domain expert. Approaches like [9,10] let the system designer explicitly define indexes as new concepts and organize the case base around them. However index concepts are difficult to acquire and force the designer to anticipate the queries that will be posed to the system. The domain knowledge base is useful to compute semantic numeric similarity measures (computational retrieval approach).

In this paper we propose an organization structure using an inductive technique over the case base, that is guided by the domain knowledge. FCA application to a case library provides with a conceptual hierarchy, because it extracts the formal concepts and the hierarchical relations among them, where related cases are clustered according to their shared properties. Concepts in the lattice represent maximal groupings of cases with shared properties, and for a given query, we can access all the cases that share properties with the query at the same time so that they are grouped under the same concept. The order between concepts allows structuring the library according to the attributes describing the cases. The lower in the graph, the more characteristics can be said about the cases; i.e. the more general concepts are higher up than the more specific ones.

3.1   Formal Concept Analysis

FCA is a mathematical approach to data analysis based on the lattice theory of Garret Birkhoff [1]. It provides a way to identify groupings of objects with shared properties. FCA is especially well suited when we have to deal with a collection of items described by properties. This is a clear characteristic of the case libraries where there are cases described by features. A *formal context* is defined as a triple $\langle G, M, I \rangle$ where there are two sets G (of objects) and M (of attributes), and a binary (incidence) relation $I \subseteq GxM$, expressing which attributes describe each object (or which objects are described using an attribute), i.e., $(g, m) \in I$ if the object g carries the attribute m, or m is a descriptor of the object g. With a general perspective, a concept represents a group of objects and is described by using *attributes* (its intent) and *objects* (its extent). The extent covers all objects belonging to the concept while the intent comprises all attributes (properties) shared by all those objects. With $A \subseteq G$ and $B \subseteq M$ the following operator (*prime*) is defined as:

$$A\prime = \{m \in M \mid (\forall g \in A)(g, m) \in I\}$$
$$B\prime = \{g \in G \mid (\forall m \in B)(g, m) \in I\}$$

A pair (A,B) where $A \subseteq G$ and $B \subseteq M$, is said to be a *formal concept* of the context $\langle G, M, I \rangle$ if $A' = B$ and $B' = A$. A and B are called the *extent* and the *intent* of the concept, respectively.

It can also be observed that, for a concept (A, B), $A'' = A$ and $B'' = B$, what means that all objects of the extent of a formal concept, have all the attributes of the intent of the concept, and that there is no other object in the set G having all the attributes of (the intent of) the concept.

The set of all the formal concepts of a context $\langle G, M, I \rangle$ is denoted by $\beta(G, M, I)$. The most important structure on $\beta(G, M, I)$ is given by the subconcept-superconcept order relation denoted by $\leq$ and defined as follows: $(A1, B1) \leq (A2, B2)$ if $A1 \subseteq A2$ (which is equivalent to $B2 \subseteq B1$ see [4]).

Basic Theorem for Concept Lattices [13]

Let $\langle G, M, I \rangle$ be a context. Then $\langle \beta(G, M, I), \leq \rangle$ is a complete lattice, called the concept lattice of the context $\langle G, M, I \rangle$, for which infimum and supremum can be described as follows:

$$Inf\beta(G, M, I) = \left[\bigwedge_\alpha (A_\alpha, B_\alpha) = \bigcap_\alpha A_\alpha, \left(\bigcup_\alpha B_\alpha \right)'' \right]$$

$$Sup\beta(G, M, I) = \left[\bigvee_\alpha (A_\alpha, B_\alpha) = \left(\bigcup_\alpha A_\alpha \right)'', \bigcap_\alpha B_\alpha \right]$$

Graphically, contexts are usually described by cross-tables while concept lattices are visualized by Hasse diagrams. The following sections illustrate how FCA is applied to our simple example, and how the dependency knowledge is extracted from the concept lattice interpretation.

3.2   FCA Application Example

We propose the application of FCA as an automatic technique to elicit the attribute co-appearance knowledge inside a case library. In this paper we apply FCA to compute two separated concept lattices that are appropriately travelled through the retrieval process. The *goal lattice* captures formal concepts representing the co-appearance of goals solved by the concrete cases. The *precondition lattice* captures the co-appearance of properties in the concrete case preconditions. We consider the primitive goals and properties, and the simple case base described in section 2. Goals and preconditions in the cases can be interpreted as formal contexts, and represented by using the incidence tables in Fig. 1.

Besides the cross table representation, there is a graphical representation of formal contexts using Hasse diagrams. Fig. 2 shows Hasse diagrams of the concept lattices associated to the contexts in Fig. 1. Each node in the diagram represents a formal concept of the context, and the ascending paths of line segments represent the subconcept-superconcept relation. Each lattice (Fig. 2) contains exactly the same information that the cross table (Fig. 1), so that the incidence relation I can always be reconstructed from the lattice.

In the Hasse Diagram, labels meaning attributes from the intent are marked by [ ] and labels meaning object from the extent are marked by {}. A lattice node is labelled with the attribute m∈M if it is the upper node having m in its

	X	Y	Z	T
Case1 (Pre1)	☑	☑		
Case2 (Pre2)	☑	☑	☑	
Case3 (Pre3)			☑	
Case4 (Pre4)		☑	☑	
Case5 (Pre5)	☑	☑	☑	☑
Case6 (Pre6)		☑		☑

	A	B	C	D	E
Case1 (Goal1)	☑	☑	☑		
Case2 (Goal2)	☑		☑		
Case3 (Goal3)	☑	☑		☑	☑
Case4 (Goal4)	☑	☑			
Case5 (Goal5)				☑	☑
Case6 (Goal6)	☑		☑		

Case Precondition Cross Table   Case Goals Cross Table

Fig. 1. Case base formal contexts

intent; and a lattice node is labelled with the object $g \in G$ if it is the lower node having g in its extent. Using this labelling, each label (attribute or object name) is used exactly once in the diagram. If a node C is labelled by the attribute $[m]$ and the object $\{g\}$ then all the concepts greater than C (above C in the graph) have the object g in their extents, and all the concepts smaller than C (below C in the graph) have the attribute m in their intents. In a Hasse diagram, the intent of a concept can be obtained as the union of the attributes in its label [ ] and attributes in the labels [ ] of the concepts above it in the lattice. Conversely, the extent of a concept, is obtained as the union of the objects in its label {} and attributes in the labels {} of the concepts below it in the lattice.

To reconstruct a row of the original incidence relations in Fig. 1, look for the unique concept C which label {} contains the object name heading the row and mark with a cross (in the row we are reconstructing) the column of each one of the attributes of the intent of C. For example, to reconstruct the cross table row of Case6 (Goals6), mark with a cross the columns corresponding to the intent of concept O3 in the goal lattice: [A, C]. Dually, to reconstruct a table column, look for the concept C which label [ ] contains the attribute name heading the column, and mark with a cross the row of each one of the objects of the extent of C. For example, to reconstruct the column named Y in the precondition cross table, mark the rows corresponding to the concept P2 extent: Case4(Pre4), Case1(Pre1), Case6(Pre6), Case2(Pre2), Case5(Pre5).

Besides the hierarchical conceptual clustering of the cases, the concept lattice provides with a set of implications between attributes: *dependence rules* [3]. A dependence rule between two attribute sets (written $M1 \rightarrow M2$, where $M1, M2 \subseteq M$) means that any object having all attributes in $M1$ has also all attributes in $M2$. We can read the dependence rules in the graph as follows:

- Each line between nodes labelled with attributes means a dependence rule between the attributes from the lower node to the upper one.
- When there are several attributes in the same label it means that there is a co-appearance of all these attributes for all the cases in the sample.

For example, the two attributes label in the goal lattice [D,E] means that in the case base all cases that fulfill goal D also fulfill goal E viceversa, i.e. goals D and E appear always together in the cases. It induces a bidirectional dependence

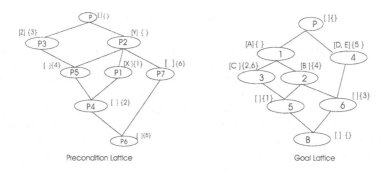

Fig. 2. Formal Concept Lattices

rule in the form D $\leftrightarrow$ E, that is separated in the two dependence rules $D \rightarrow E$ and $E \rightarrow D$. We can read the following set of dependence rules in Fig. 2:
Goal Dependence Rules: { D → E; E → D; B → A; C → A}
Precondition Dependence Rules: { X → Y; T → Y }

Dependence rules will help the query definition process and are naturally represented using DLs concept representation language. A rule associated to a concept means properties not between the definitional part of the concept (sufficient properties), but incidental (necessary) properties that do not correspond to the intrinsic concept meaning and do not participate in the classification or instance recognition mechanisms. We apply FCA as a complementary way of knowledge acquisition and although it is not general knowledge about the domain, but knowledge associated to this concrete case base, it suggests concepts and rules to be added to the general domain model.

4   Classification Based Retrieval

Classification based retrieval [9] is typically implemented as a three steps process: first, query is represented as a concept or an individual and is classified or recognized in its corresponding place in a certain hierarchy; second a number of individuals are retrieved and, third, one (or more) of them can be chosen by applying a selection function or by the user. There are two different methods to implement retrieval using the reasoning mechanisms available in DLs:

- Retrieval based on *concept classification*, where a concept description c_q is built using the restrictions specified in the query. This concept is then classified, and finally all its instances are retrieved.
- Retrieval based on *instance recognition*, where an individual is built and a number of assertions are made about it based on the query features. Instance recognition retrieves the most specific concepts of which this individual is an instance, and then all the instances of these concepts are retrieved.

There are two main differences between these two methods:

- The type of restrictions that can be included, since concept description language and assertion language are different. Concept description language is richer because restrictions about role type and cardinality can be included.
- Instance completion. There are a number of inferences that are only applied to individuals because DLs systems do not enrich concept descriptions with inferred constraints. On the other hand, when an individual is recognized as instance of a given concept, based on the sufficient conditions for belonging to that concept, then necessary conditions on the concept definition are automatically asserted on the individual.

So, both approaches have its pros and cons, namely expressiveness vs. completion. We have decided to implement retrieval as an instance recognition process mainly for one reason: instance completion accomplishes a kind of query completion where additional constraints can be automatically inferred from those explicitly asserted by the user. In this way, we have a straightforward method to let the domain knowledge and the cases themselves assist in the crucial process of query formulation, using the dependence rules extracted from FCA.

Classification based retrieval on the domain taxonomy considers retrieval as a classification process over a hierarchy of terms representing domain knowledge. In our framework, the domain knowledge base is acquired by reusing ontologies terms and integrating them with CBROnto. We have experienced that it is not an optimized structure to effectively retrieve similar cases based on classification: i.e classify a query individual and retrieve cases near it at this hierarchy. Results are better when goals and properties are organized in a hierarchy (constructed manually during domain modelling) that can be used to determine the relative utility of different cases with respect to a given set of goals or preconditions. That way, ad hoc hierarchies are built to do classification based retrieval on them. However, index concepts are difficult to acquire and force the designer to anticipate the queries that will be posed to the system.

Classification based retrieval on the formal concept lattices makes use of the case library to guide the search. Lattice properties justify how this approach always finds the *best* case according to the current situation and the required goals, without travelling through all cases, but taking advantage of the DLs classification mechanism to find the formal concepts clustering the cases.

As we have two lattice structures, we can consider how retrieval performs when we use only the query goal requirements over the goal lattice, only the precondition requirements over the precondition lattice, or combine the use of the two organization lattice structures. That offers the user the possibility of different kind of queries: providing a set of goals to retrieve cases that fulfill them, providing a description of the current situation to retrieve the applicable cases, giving both to retrieve applicable cases fulfilling the required goals.

Query Formulation Guided by Dependencies

As we have described, FCA applied on a case library allows capturing its specific dependencies, i.e. it detects regularities satisfied by all the cases in the library. We propose an interactive query definition process where the user is guided towards the definition of "good" queries for this case base. During the incremental query description process, the user provides with certain descriptors, either goals or properties, while the system proposes other properties by using the dependence rules captured during the FCA. It begins a conversation where the system asks the user using the knowledge extracted from the case library, so the cases themselves are guiding the query formulation process.

Generic Travel Operator (GTO). To formulate classification based retrieval, we have defined a generic operator based on DLs classification and instance recognition. The generic travel operator (GTO) takes a concept C and an integer number (level) and returns *direct* instances of concepts at distance *level* from C. *Direct* instances of a concept C_i are those individuals that belong to C_i, but not to any of its subconcepts. Negative levels mean travelling upwards in the concept hierarchy and positive levels mean travelling downwards. Using zero level, direct instances of C_i are retrieved. Function *depth* gives a concept depth in the lattice, where $depth(TOP) = 0$, and $depth(BOTTOM) =$ maximum lattice depth.

Classification Based Retrieval over the Goal Lattice

Retrieval by goals aims finding cases simultaneously fulfilling all the required goals and not superfluous (not required) goals. The process classifies $query_{goals}$ individual with regard to the goal lattice, obtaining a set of concepts recognizing $query_{goals}:\{O_1, .., O_n\}$. Next, *direct* instances of these concepts are retrieved. If there are not direct instances, approximate retrieval tries to retrieve, first, cases satisfying all the required goals although other (not required) goals are also fulfilled, and second, cases maximizing the number of required goals although some of them are not fulfilled. Lattice properties assure that the following process retrieves the best cases (regarding the goal criterion) in order:

- GoalStep1: retrieve cases satisfying the maximum number (possibly all) of query goals and no superfluous goals, if there are any. They are obtained getting the union of the *direct* instances of $\{O_1, .., O_n\}$: $\bigcup_{i=1}^{n} GTO(O_i, 0)$
- GoalStep2: retrieve cases satisfying the maximum number (all when possible) the query goals and some superfluous goals. We travel through O_i *subconcepts* level by level downwards, we get cases satisfying the required goals, ordered by minimizing the number of superfluous goals:
$\bigcup_{j=1}^{depth(Bottom)-depth(O_i)} \bigcup_{i=1}^{n} GTO(O_i, j)$
When using this kind of retrieval, results from each level are shown to the user incrementally and only go down to the next level, when none of the already retrieved cases is chosen.
- GoalStep3: retrieve cases fulfilling the maximum number of required goals (although not all). If we travel through O_i *superconcepts* level by level upwards, we obtain more general concepts to get cases ordered by minimizing the number of not satisfied goals:
$\bigcup_{j=-1}^{-depth(O_i)} \bigcup_{i=1}^{n} GTO(O_i, j)$

The three goal steps are done sequentially and, typically only if one step returns no cases or by user request, we try next step. Next examples illustrate the process. See also Fig. 2.

Example 1: User asserts $query_{goals}$: A, B and C
Classify $query_{goals}$: (get-types $query_{goals}$) = O5

- GoalStep 1: GTO(O5, 0) = (get-direct-instances O5)= $Goal_1$
  $Case_1$ is retrieved as the only case fulfilling *exactly* the query goals.

- GoalStep 2: depth(BOT)=4 ; depth(O5)=3;
  GTO(O5, 1) = (get-direct-instances BOT)= none
  There are not other cases fulfilling *all* the query goals.

- GoalStep 3: GTO(O5, -1) $\cup$ GTO(O5, -2) $\cup$ GTO(O5, -3)=
  (get-direct-instances O3) $\cup$ (get-direct-instances O2) $\cup$
  (get-direct-instances O1)$\cup$(get-direct-instances TOP)= $Goal_2$, $Goal_6$, $Goal_4$
  $Case_2$, $Case_6$, $Case_4$ satisfy *some* of the required goals A, B, C.

Besides the retrieval process based on classification over the goal lattice, next examples also illustrate the *query formulation process* as an incremental process, where the user provides with certain goals, while the system proposes others by using the dependence rules captured during the FCA.

Example 2: User asserts $query_{goals}$: B
Applicable dependence rules: B $\rightarrow$ A
Using the applicable dependence rules, the system suggests completing query goals with A. If the user rejects the suggestion, no search is needed because the lattice properties assure that there are no cases fulfilling B and not A. If the user accepts the suggestion, we get the new query $query_{goals}$: B, A, and retrieve similar cases by classification as follows:
Classify $query_{goals}$: (get-types $query_{goals}$) = O2

- GoalStep 1: GTO(O2, 0) = (get-direct-instances O2)= $Goal_4$
  $Case_4$ is retrieved as the only case fulfilling *exactly* the query goals.

- GoalStep 2: depth(BOT)=4 ; depth(O2)=2;
  GTO(O2, 1) $\cup$ GTO(O2, 2)= (get-direct-instances O5) $\cup$
  (get-direct-instances O6)$\cup$(get-direct-instances BOT)= $Goal_1$, $Goal_3$
  $Case_1$, $Case_3$ satisfy all the required goals (A and B), although they satisfy other not required goals, and could need adaptation.

- GoalStep 3: GTO(O2, -1) $\cup$ GTO(O2, -2) =
  (get-direct-instances O1) $\cup$ (get-direct-instances TOP)= none
  No other cases are retrieved.

Example 3: User asserts $query_{goals}$: B, C, D
Applicable dependence rules: D $\rightarrow$ E ; B $\rightarrow$ A ; C $\rightarrow$ A

The system notifies that goals E and A will be also fulfilled. If the user accepts the suggestion, we get the new query $query_{goals}$: A, B, C, D, E and retrieve similar cases by classification as follows:

Classify $query_{goals}$: (get-types $query_{goals}$) = BOT

- GoalStep 1: GTO(BOT, 0) = (get-direct-instances BOT)= none
  There are not cases fulfilling *exactly* the query goals.

- GoalStep 2: $\emptyset$. There are not cases satisfying *all* the required goals

- GoalStep 3: GTO(BOT,-1) $\cup$ GTO(BOT,-2) $\cup$ GTO(BOT,-3) $\cup$ GTO(BOT,-4)=
  $Goal_1$, $Goal_3$, $Goal_2$, $Goal_6$, $Goal_4$, $Goal_5$

$Case_1$, $Case_3$, $Case_2$, $Case_6$, $Case_4$, $Case_5$ are retrieved because they satisfy *some* of the required goals. Note they are ordered maximizing the number of shared goals, and we could stop after the first level obtaining cases $Case_1$ and $Case_3$.

Classification Based Retrieval over the Precondition Lattice

Retrieval by precondition aims finding applicable cases, i.e. cases whose precondition is fulfilled by the query situation. The process classifies the $query_{desc}$ individual with regard to the precondition lattice, obtaining a set of concepts recognizing $query_{desc}$:$\{P_1, .., P_n\}$. Next, *direct* instances of these concepts are retrieved. If there are not direct instances, approximate retrieval tries to retrieve, first, other applicable cases, and second, other not applicable cases maximizing the number of precondition properties fulfilled by the query situation.

Lattice properties assure that, the following process retrieves cases whose precondition is satisfied by the query described situation, and use the maximum number of properties. If there are not applicable cases, the process retrieves cases sharing the maximum number of properties with the query situation.

- PreStep 1: try to retrieve cases whose precondition includes all the query properties and no other property, if there are any. They are obtained getting the union of the *direct* instances of $\{P_1, .., P_n\}$: $\bigcup_{i=1}^{n} GTO(P_i, 0)$
- PreStep 2: retrieve other applicable cases, i.e whose precondition properties are a subset of the query properties, if there are any. If we travel through P_i *superconcepts* level by level upwards, we get cases ordered by maximizing the number of satisfied properties: $\bigcup_{j=-1}^{-depth(P_i)} \bigcup_{i=1}^{n} GTO(P_i, j)$
  Note this process is dual to the process performed in the goal lattice. In the precondition lattice we first go upwards to get cases with weaker (more general) preconditions that could be applicable to the query situation. In the goal lattice we first go downwards to get cases fulfilling more goals so that the query required goals could be achieved.
- PreStep 3: retrieve not applicable cases, i.e. cases whose precondition properties are not satisfied by the query situation. If we travel through P_i *subconcepts* level by level downwards, we get cases ordered by minimizing the number of not satisfied properties: $\bigcup_{j=1}^{depth(Bot)-depth(P_i)} \bigcup_{i=1}^{n} GTO(P_i, j)$

The three steps are done sequentially, and typically only if one step returns no cases, we try next step.

Example 4:
$query_{desc}$: X, Z i.e. current situation satisfies properties X, Y and Z.
Applicable rules: X → Y

The system asks if the query situation also satisfies the Y property. If the user refuses it, search is not needed because the lattice properties assure that there are no cases fulfilling X and not Y. If the user accepts the suggestion, we get the new query: $query_{desc}$: X, Y, Z and retrieve similar cases by classification as follows:

Classify $query_{desc}$: (get-types $query_{desc}$) = P4

- PreStep 1: GTO(P4, 0) = (get-direct-instances P4)= Pre_2
  $Case_2$ is retrieved as the best case, because its precondition exactly matches the query situation (X, Y and Z).

- PreStep 2: depth(P4)=3;
  GTO(P4, -1) ∪ GTO(P4, -2) ∪ GTO(P4, -3)= (get-direct-instances P5) ∪ (get-direct-instances P1)∪ (get-direct-instances P3) ∪ (get-direct-instances P2) ∪ (get-direct-instances TOP)= Pre_4, Pre_1, Pre_3
  $Case_4$, $Case_1$, $Case_3$, are retrieved as applicable cases. Their precondition set is contained in the set of query properties. Note they are ordered by maximizing the number of query properties used in the precondition.

- PreStep 3: depth(BOT)=4; depth(P4)=3;
  GTO(P4, 1) = (get-direct-instances P6) = Pre_5
  $Case_5$ is not applicable but shares properties with the query situation.

Note PreStep 3, retrieves cases not totally applicable, that surely will need later adaptation. Besides, following level by level the concept hierarchy, the retrieved cases are ordered by the number of properties shared with the query situation.

Classification Based Retrieval Based on the Pre and Goal Lattices
Depending on the query, retrieval by goal/precondition could be used independently or their results could be combined. When the query includes both, required goals and properties describing the current situation, best possible retrieval tries to find applicable cases satisfying all the required goals. Lattice properties assure that (if there are any) these cases are found retrieving *direct* instances for both, retrieval by precondition and by goal, and intersecting the results. If the intersection were empty, then the approximate retrieval process finds the best cases although they are not completely applicable or satisfying more or less of the required goals. We use two strategies:

- Strategy 1 considers that cases satisfying all the required goals, although they are not applicable, are better that applicable cases not fulfilling all the required goals. This strategy travels through the precondition lattice, searching first between the applicable cases (steps 1, 2) and second between not applicable cases (step 3).

for j=1 to 3
   for i=1 to 3
      retrievedCases=retrievedCases ∪ (PreStepi ∩ GoalStepj);

– Strategy 2 considers that applicable cases, although they do not fulfill all the required goals, are better that not applicable cases fulfilling all the required goals.

for i=1 to 3
   for j=1 to 3
      retrievedCases=retrievedCases ∪ (PreStepi ∩ GoalStepj);

Strategies define the order to travel completely through the lattices, however as soon as we get any case retrieved it is shown to user, who decides if the process should continue or not. Next examples illustrate the process.

Example 5:
$query_{desc}$: X, Y, Z
$query_{goals}$: A B C
Strategy 1:
PreStep1 ∩ GoalStep1 = $\{Case_2\} \cap \{Case_1\} = \oslash$
PreStep2 ∩ GoalStep1 = $\{Case_1, Case_4, Case_3\} \cap Case_1 = Case_1$
$Case_1$ is retrieved as the best case, it is *applicable* and fulfills *all* the required goals.
Strategy 2:
PreStep1 ∩ GoalStep1 = $\oslash$
PreStep1 ∩ GoalStep2 = $\oslash$
PreStep1 ∩ GoalStep2 = $Case_2$
$Case_2$ is retrieved as the best case, it exactly matches the query situation and fulfills *some* of the required goals.

Example 6: $query_{desc}$: T
Using the dependence rule (T → Y) is completed to: T, Y
$query_{goals}$: A, C
Both strategies retrieve $Case_6$ as the best case. It exactly matches the query.
PreStep1 ∩ GoalStep1 = $\{Case_6\} \cap \{Case_2, Case_6\} = Case_6$

We find the following advantages of this kind of *intelligent* retrieval based on goal and precondition fulfillment:

– It does not travel through every case in the case base.
– It makes use of the case library itself to guide the search.
– It is formally well-founded.
– The lattice properties will assure that the retrieved cases are those with the maximum number of common descriptors with the query.

Note that in the simple example we have used to illustrate our proposal in this paper, the goals and properties are organized in a flat structure under the CBROnto **GOAL** and **PROPERTY** concepts, but deep taxonomic structures could be used to organize and select goals and properties.

5   Related and Future Work

In the context of planning and design, retrieval means searching for adaptable cases [7,11], thus any retrieval process should measure the adaptation effort of the cases with respect to a query problem. Although we will study this topic further, we think that our retrieval approach minimizes the adaptation effort in the sense that maximizes the number of shared goals and retrieves applicable cases when possible.

Our approach is related to PRODIGY/ANALOGY [12] where the retrieval process finds cases satisfying all the goals of the new problem, and whose *footprints* matches the initial state of the new problem with a certain accuracy (footprint based similarity [12,6,7]). The footprint of a goal are the features in the initial state that contributed to achieve the goal, and the footprint of a set of goals is the union of the footprints for each individual goal in the set. The idea of footprint is related with our use of preconditions. In the first retrieval step, a case will be searched for that covers all the goals of the new problem. If that fails, PRODIGY/ANALOGY will try to find cases in two groups: cases that covers all the goals but one, and others covering the remain goal. If this does not work, then the decomposition process will continue. At last PRODIGY/ANALOGY will try to cover each goal independently from the others. Note that, our retrieval over the goal lattice, meets the same requirements using classification.

As the PRODIGY/ANALOGY matching process between sets of goals is quite expensive, in [6] an alternate architecture is proposed that explicitly considers structural dependencies between goals to get a better performance. CA-PLAN/CBC [6] considers domains where there are dependencies between goals that are included in the problem description, and that can be determined before the planning process begins. An example of dependencies is the order between steps for achieving a set of goals, that establishes a partial order between the goals. The order constraints for achieving the goals during the planning process is used during retrieval as an additional constraint that must be meet by cases in order to be retrieved.

Our approach also represents an alternate architecture, as formal concepts in the goal (and precondition) lattices facilitate the matching between sets of goals (and preconditions) using classification in an un-expensive way. Our dependencies are not explicitly provided as part of the query description (as in [6]) but extracted from the case base; besides in our approach, dependency knowledge refers to the co-appearance of goals and features in the cases of the particular case library and does not take into account the goal order. CAPLAN/CBC organization is not well suited for domains without structural dependencies between goals. Our approach using FCA is domain independent and flexible to be applied to any case base.

At present, our approach doesn't consider some goals or properties having more importance than others, and quantitatively maximizes the number of goals or properties satisfied, but not qualitatively maximizes the case utility. However, usually not all features have the same importance to a solution. Weighted foot-printed similarity metric [7] counts feature weights and recompute these weights according to the performance of cases during problem solving episodes. As future work we will consider to incorporate these ideas in our framework.

6   Conclusions

FCA has been successfully used in many data analysis applications but we don't know of any use in the CBR area. We use it as a complementary technique to enrich the domain taxonomy, providing an alternative organization of the case library that facilitates a direct and guided access to the cases. FCA application provides an internal sight of the case base conceptual structure and allows finding patterns and regularities among the cases. With our approach the knowledge structures are easy to acquire as we don't want to be forced to do a big domain knowledge engineering effort to define good indexes to retrieve cases using classification. We use the case base itself to extract patterns of goal and preconditions co-appearance patterns among the cases in the particular case base we are using. Actually, Formal Concepts behave as a kind of indexes for retrieval, but they are automatically extracted from the cases and are used to cluster cases.

DLs reasoning mechanisms are useful to automatically organize the concept lattice and to keep the cases automatically organized under them. Besides the instance recognition and classification mechanisms are used during retrieval.

We have defined a retrieval process based on classification over the goal and precondition lattices acquired applying FCA, that makes use of the case library itself to guide the search of good cases and is formally well-founded.

References

1. Birkhoff, G., 1973: Lattice Theory, third editon. American Math. Society Coll. Publ. 25, Providence, R.I.
2. Díaz-Agudo, B., González-Calero, P.A., 2000: "An Architecture for Knowledge Intensive CBR Systems". In *Advances in Case-Based Reasoning (EWCBR 2000)*, LNAI 1898, Springer.
3. Díaz-Agudo, B., González-Calero, P.A., 2000: "Formal Concept Analysis as a Support Technique for CBR". In *Procs. International Conference on Knowledge Based Systems and Applied Artificial Intelligence, ES2000*. Springer.
4. Ganter, B., & Wille, R., 1997. Formal Concept Analysis. Mathematical Foundations. ISBN 3-540-62771-5 Springer Verlag.
5. Hammond K.J., 1989: Case-Based Planning: Viewing Planning as a Memory Task. Academic Press.
6. Muñoz-Avila H., Hüllen J., 1995: "Retrieving Cases in Structured Domains by Using Goal Dependencies". in *CBR Research and development, (ICCBR'95)*, Springer.
7. Muñoz-Avila H., Hüllen J., 1995: "Feature Weighting by Explaining Case-based Planning Episodes". In *Advances in CBR (EWCBR'96)*, Springer-Verlag.
8. Mac Gregor R., & Bates R., 1987: "The Loom Knowledge Representation Language". ISI Reprint Series, ISI/RS-87-188, Univ. of Southern California.

9. Napoli A., Lieber J., & Courien R., 1996: "Classification-Based Problem Solving in CBR", in *Advances in CBR (EWCBR'96)*, Springer.
10. Salotti S. & Ventos V., 1998: "Study and Formalization of a CBR System using a Description logic", in *Advances in CBR (EWCBR'98)*, Springer-Verlag.
11. Smyth B. & Keane M., 1994:"Retrieving adaptable cases", in *Advances in CBR (EWCBR'93)*, Springer-Verlag.
12. Veloso M. "Planning and learning by analogical reasoning", LNAI 886 Springer.
13. Wille, R., 1982. "Restructuring Lattice Theory: an approach based on hierarchies of concepts". In Rival, I., (ed.), Ordered Sets.

Conversational Case-Based Planning for Agent Team Coordination

Joseph A. Giampapa and Katia Sycara

The Robotics Institute
Carnegie Mellon University
5000 Forbes Avenue
Pittsburgh, PA 15213–3890 (U.S.A.)
{garof, katia}+@cs.cmu.edu
http://www.cs.cmu.edu/~{garof, katia, softagents}

Abstract. This paper describes a prototype in which a conversational case-based reasoner, NaCoDAE, was agentified and inserted in the RETSINA multi-agent system. Its task was to determine agent roles within a heterogeneous society of agents, where the agents may use capability-based or team-oriented agent coordination strategies. There were three reasons for assigning this task to NaCoDAE: (1) to relieve the agents of the overhead of determining, for themselves, if they should be involved in the task, or not; (2) to convert seemingly unrelated data into contextually relevant knowledge — as a case-based reasoning system, NaCoDAE is particularly suited for applying apparently incoherent data to a wide variety of domain-specific situations; and (3) as a conversational CBR system, to both unobtrusively listen to human statements and to proactively dialogue with other agents in a more goal-directed approach to gathering relevant information. The cases maintained by NaCoDAE have *question* and *answer* components, which were originally intended to maintain the textual representations of questions and answers for humans. By associating agent capability descriptions and queries with the case questions, NaCoDAE also assumed the team role of a capability-based coordinator. By encoding fragments of HTN plan objectives in its case actions, we were able to convert NaCoDAE into a conversational case-based planner that served compositionally-generated HTN plan objectives, already populated with situation-relevant knowledge, for use by the RETSINA team-oriented agents.[1]

---

[1] The authors are grateful to the Naval Research Labs for providing the sources to NaCoDAE. Matthew W. Easterday made a significant contribution to this project by adapting NaCoDAE to operate in an agent context. Many thanks to Alex Rudnicky for allowing us to agentify Sphinx and for providing us with technical support. On a personal note, Joseph Giampapa would like to thank David Aha for his encouragement and helpful suggestions. This research was sponsored in part by the Office of Naval Research Grant N-00014-96-16-1-1222 and by DARPA Grant F-30602-98-2-0138.

D.W. Aha and I. Watson (Eds.): ICCBR 2001, LNAI 2080, pp. 189–203, 2001.
© Springer-Verlag Berlin Heidelberg 2001

1   Introduction

Complex tasks are often solved by teams because no one individual has the collective expertise, information, or resources required for effective performance. Team problem solving involves a multitude of activities such as gathering, interpreting and exchanging information, creating and identifying alternative courses of action, choosing among alternatives by becoming aware of differing and often conflicting preferences of action by team members, and ultimately implementing a choice, determining how incremental progress will be measured, and monitoring its evolution. There have been many attempts and views in the agent community as to how intelligent software agents should organize themselves into teams. The work of this paper was inspired by the *joint intentions* theory of Cohen and Levesque [5,14], the *shared plans* theory proposed by Barbara Grosz [12], and Milind Tambe's research based on the *TEAMCORE* [19,28] multi-agent software system.

In the joint intentions theory, a team is composed of agents that jointly commit to the achievement of a *joint persistent goal*, or JPG. Agents desiring to be part of a team must communicate their intention to each other that they intend to commit to that goal. A team is formed once every agent has committed to a goal and has received a communication that all the other agents have committed to it, as well. The team remains a team as long as: (a) no agent has a reason to believe that the goal is unachievable; (b) no agent decides, on its own, to de-commit from the team goal; (c) the goal is not yet achieved and all agents remain convinced that it is still achievable; and (d) no agent perceives that another agent has de-committed from the team goal. Team goals are formed by an individual agent nominating a task as a proposed team goal, and communicating that intention until consensus is formed that the nominee is worth pursuing as a team goal. The joint intentions theory is significant because it is a formal model of what motivates agent communications about teamwork. Further, it has enjoyed broad recognition within the agent community as making pertinent claims and observations about team-oriented behaviors. But the theory does not address: (1) the problems of how agents acquire a team goal; (2) how agents identify the roles that contribute to the fulfillment of a team goal, and identify those roles for themselves; (3) how agents relate the roles of their individual goals to the overall goal of the team; and (4) how the agents know when to break commitments to their individual goals while still maintaining the team goal.

The shared plan theory [12] emphasizes the need for a common high-level team model that allows agents to understand all requirements for plans that might achieve a team goal, even if the individuals may not know the specific details of the plans or how the requirements will be met. This allows team members to map their capabilities to a plan to achieve a team goal, assign roles to themselves, and measure their progress at achieving their overall team objective. Like joint intentions theory, shared plan theory is based on observations of human forms of teamwork.

TEAMCORE is an agent architecture that implements many of the basic principles of joint intention theory. TEAMCORE application scenarios are usually situated in the military and robotic soccer domains, where the team-oriented agents are homogeneous and their roles typically represent either authority relations, such as military rank, or high-level capability descriptions, such as *transport* or *escort* helicopters. But once individual TEAMCORE agents commit to being part of a team, they cannot dynamically add or subtract members to or from their team so as to adapt to a new situation, while executing their plan.

Within human-machine teams, intelligent software agents can play a variety of roles that help reduce some of the overhead of teamwork, as well as help solve team problems. By means of their autonomy, agents can: get information requested by a human; self-activate and present unsolicited important information to a human user; suggest solutions to a problem; actively monitor the environment and cache relevant information so as to provide quick updates to "situation knowledge" if required; and recombine, as needed, with other agents to adapt to the particular task requirements over time.

To coordinate agents into teams effectively in dynamic environments, our research thrust has been in line with the following principles: (1) we make open world assumptions about the nature of tasks and the strategies for solving them — a multi-agent solution to a problem will most likely involve agents of different architectures and abilities, available at different times; (2) we subscribe to the belief that there are meta rules that describe the nature of teamwork, that are independent of the specific task being performed [8,18,21], and that it is possible to reuse this knowledge in different application domains; and (3) that individual roles and objectives of agents within the team may need to change in order to maintain and achieve the full team goal.

In this paper we describe a prototype, implemented in our RETSINA[2] multi-agent infrastructure, in which agents interact with each other via capability-based [23] and team-oriented coordination. For the team-oriented agent coordination to be effective, we propose a model of teamwork based on the joint intentions theory for agent communications about their intended commitments, combined with the shared plans strategy of expressing descriptions of roles and context-specific requirements for those roles. We enhance this proposal by adding our own characterizations of role and subgoal relations in software agent teamwork, and show how the software agents can acquire this information from their operating environment during execution time. The acquisition and maintenance of the contextual information that determines the plan requirements is performed by NaCoDAE, a conversational case-based reasoner, which is used to compositionally generate Hierarchical Task Network [HTN] plan [9,16] objectives for the RETSINA team agents. We show that the unobtrusive and invisible use of NaCoDAE as the primary means by which human and agent information is gathered and merged can eliminate any information overload that might result from the conscious interactions of humans with their intelligent agents.

In the sections that follow, we present RETSINA, NaCoDAE, the interacting NaCoDAE and RETSINA prototype, and a command and control scenario that we used as a case study for NaCoDAE's effectiveness as an agentified conversational case-based planner. After a brief review of related work, we conclude with some ideas for future work in this area.

---

[2] **R**eusable **E**nvironment for **T**ask-**S**tructured **I**ntelligent **N**etwork **A**gents

2   The RETSINA Multi-agent System

The RETSINA multi-agent system (MAS) is a collection of heterogeneous software entities that collaborate with each other to either provide a result or service to other software entities or to an end user. As a society, RETSINA agents can be described in terms of the *RETSINA Functional Architecture* [27,24], illustrated by Figure 1, which categorizes agents as belonging to any of four agent types:

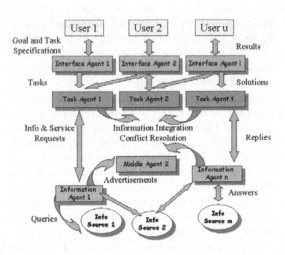

Fig. 1. The RETSINA Functional Architecture

Interface agents present agent results to the user, or solicit input from the user. In addition, they could learn from user actions [4]. Interface agents typically represent specific modes of input or output, such as a *VoiceRecognition* agent or a *SpeechGeneration* agent, or can be associated with different device types such as *PDA*, *Phone*, or *E-Mail* agents. Interface agent behaviors can also be associated with *task agents*.

Task agents encapsulate task-specific knowledge and use that knowledge as the criterion for requesting or performing services for other agents or humans. In this respect, they are the typical agent coordinators of a multi-agent system.

Middle agents [29,10] provide infrastructure for other agents. A typical instance of a middle agent is the *Matchmaker* [25,26], or *Yellow Pages* agent. Requesting agents submit a *capability* request to the Matchmaker, which will then locate the appropriate service-providing agents based upon their published *capability descriptions*, known as *advertisements*.

Information agents model the information world to the agent society, and can monitor any data- or event-producing source for user-supplied conditions. Information agents may be *single source* if they only model one information source, or may be *multi-source* if one information agent represents multiple information sources. Information agents can also update external data stores, such as databases, if appropriate.

By classifying agents functionally, we believe that it is possible to uniformly define agent behaviors [6] that are consistent with their functional description. For example, information agents implement four behaviors for interacting with the data sources that they model: *ask once, monitor actively, monitor passively,* and *update.* RETSINA agents typically use the capability-based coordination [23] technique to task each other, which means that one agent will dynamically discover and interact with other agents based on their capability descriptions. RETSINA agents also support other forms of coordination techniques, such as the team-oriented coordination that is described later in this paper.

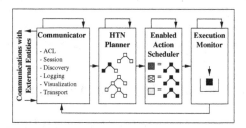

Fig. 2. Schematic diagram of the RETSINA Agent Architecture. The boxes represent concurrent threads and the arrows represent control and data flow. The "external entities" may be agent or non-agent software components.

The *RETSINA Individual Agent Architecture* [24,3,6] is illustrated by Figure 2. This agent architecture implements Hierarchical Task Network (HTN) Planning [9,16] in three parallel execution threads. A fourth thread, the *Communicator* [20], provides the means by which the agent communicates with the networked world. The Communicator provides a level of abstraction that insulates the planning component from issues of agent communication language (ACL), communication session management, the location of agent services via discovery, the logging and visualization of agent messages and state information, and the communication transport being used (e.g. infrared, telephone, base band, etc.). The *HTN Planner* thread receives HTN plan *objectives* from the Communicator, extracts the information and instructions contained therein, and attempts to apply the extracted data to all the plans in its plan library. Plan actions are partially *enabled* as the data is applied to them, and once all actions of a plan are completely enabled, they are scheduled by the *Scheduler*. The Scheduler maintains the enabled actions in a priority queue, and works with the *Execution Monitor*, which actually executes the enabled actions. The coordination among the three planning modules is done in such a way that high-priority actions can interrupt those being executed by the Execution Monitor, if those being executed are of a lower priority.

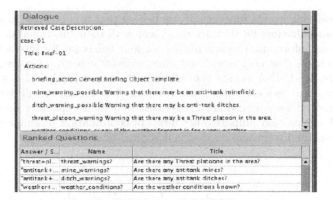

Fig. 3. Case and question areas of the NaCoDAE GUI

3 Navy Conversational Decision Aiding Environment

NaCoDAE [2] is a *conversational case-based reasoning* (CCBR) system that helps a user decide a course of action by engaging him in a dialogue in which he must describe the problem or situation. A conversational session begins with the user providing an initial partial description of the problem that he is trying to solve. NaCoDAE responds by providing a ranked *solution* display, which lists the solutions of stored cases whose problem descriptions best match the user's problem descriptions, and a ranked *question* display, which lists the unanswered questions in these cases. The user interacts with these displays, either refining their problem description by answering select questions, or by directly selecting a solution to apply. By presenting questions in a ranked list, NaCoDAE attempts to help guide the user to a rapid description of the problem by asking what it perceives to be the most relevant questions, given the information provided.

Figure 3 illustrates the way in which NaCoDAE presents its solutions to the user. It displays the case as a bundle of *actions* to take, a textual description of what the case means, a list of the questions, their responses, and the case that resulted from their selection. To make case authoring easier, NaCoDAE also contains a module named *CLiRe* [1][3], that refines case libraries so as to enforce specific case authoring guidelines. CLiRe uses a machine learning technique to refine case libraries.

There were three features of NaCoDAE that made it suitable for team co-ordination and interaction with RETSINA agents. First, NaCoDAE can work with partial descriptions of the problem and use them for initiating a dialogue. This could allow one to encode a general strategy of, "always knowing the strategy for how to get more information, if nothing else is known" — a technique inspired by one of Barbara Grosz's motivations for shared plans [12]. Second, NaCoDAE can continually revise its list of most likely candidate cases, as data is provided to the system by either an agent or the user. This feature lends itself

---

[3] Case Library Revisor

to a form of coherent, compositional and incremental construction of knowledge structures, such as HTN plan objectives and representations of situational or contextual knowledge. This knowledge can be accessed even if time and the lack of specific information do not allow for a description to be completely specified. Third, the cases can be modified to store any type of textual data, including agent capabilities and queries.

4   The RETSINA Model of Teamwork

Teamwork must be motivated by an overall description of a goal that merits solution by a team, and a description of a shared plan that can achieve the goal. As permitted by the shared plan theory, the plans can be fully or partially specified. A team-oriented individual must possess three types of knowledge: his capabilities, the team plan requirements, and social parameters for role assessment, such as knowledge of his authority to address team plan requirements, and knowledge of social structure, such as superior, peer, and subordinate relationships. To be able to act on that knowledge, a team-oriented individual should also know how to perform certain types of assessments, such as: how to match his individual capabilities to plan requirements; how to evaluate if his authority allows him to apply his capabilities to the plan requirements; how to assess the impact of his and his teammates' roles on achieving the overall team goal, so that he may offer more appropriate role proposals when situations change; how to monitor progress when executing a plan; and how to map social structure to plan requirements, such as knowing to report to an immediate superior or that only particular team members have the authority to assign certain tasks.

The acquisition of situation-specific knowledge serves to "update" an individual's beliefs about the three types of team knowledge, mentioned above. Individuals should attempt to become aware of as much situation-specific knowledge as is necessary, both in the stage of forming a team and committing to roles in the team plan, and while executing the team plan. Some situation-specific knowledge may fill gaps in the partial shared plan and transform it into a full shared plan. Other situation-specific knowledge may modify the individual's knowledge of his capability, social status, or of his authority. Still, another form of situation-specific knowledge is that which is communicated by teammates at consensually-determined *checkpoints* so as to indicate individual progress in relation to the overall team plan.

As requirements of the task change, subgoals are achieved, or as individuals change their capabilities, individuals must communicate these changes to the appropriate teammates. These communications have been found to be critical in human high performance teams [8,18,21]. If an individual discovers that he is no longer capable of performing a role, then he must communicate this knowledge to his teammates and superiors (if appropriate) and break with his subgoal commitment. Alternatively, the individual may opt to stay with the subgoal commitment if it does not impede progress to achieving the overall team goal and there is no reason or request to assume another role.

An individual determines candidate roles for himself by matching his individual capabilities to the requirements of the overall team goal within the constraints of his authority and other social parameters.[4] If there are no candidate roles, then the individual has the following options: (1) to attempt to further refine the requirements of the overall team plan; (2) to attempt to acquire those capabilities that match the plan requirements; (3) to attempt to acquire the authority for applying the capability to the plan requirements; and (4) if it is not possible to either specify the requirements, acquire the capability or the authority to generate a candidate role in the team plan, then the individual should not commit to the team plan. If the individual were successful at generating candidate roles, however, then the individual should select the candidate roles that he feels comfortable with committing to — by whatever evaluation metric at his disposition (e.g. most commitments, least commitments, those that are the best for a certain metric, etc.) — and communicate them to his teammates.

An individual with candidate roles must communicate them to the other team members as proposals for his role in the team plan. Similarly, the individual must receive the proposals for roles of the other team members, and evaluate if all plan requirements are covered by all the proposals that were generated or received by the individual. If all role proposals cover all plan requirements without conflicts, then the individual may commit to the team plan and to his roles. If there are no role proposal conflicts but not all plan requirements are met, then the individual must evaluate if the requirements must be met as a precondition to executing the plan. If they are, then the individual should reconsider if he has the capability for addressing the non-assigned plan requirement, since he might have withheld proposing the role for cost reasons. If he does have the capability, and the benefit of achieving the team goal outweighs the cost of committing to that role, then the individual should propose it. If he does not have a capability to respond to the requirement, then he must wait until all other teammates have attempted to bid on it. If the requirement is eventually covered, then the team can commit to the shared plan. If the requirement is not covered, then the team members cannot commit to the shared plan, but they may actively recruit new team members that could cover the requirement.

If there are any conflicts, then only those agents with conflicting role proposals must renegotiate their role proposals in a generate-and-repropose cycle. If the conflicting parties cannot resolve their differences, they should enlarge the circle of participants to include non-conflicting individuals, in the hope that new members of the conflict resolution group may have capabilities that can permit a reassigning of proposed roles so as to avoid the conflict. Once conflicts have been resolved by the conflicted individuals, the proposed roles must be recommunicated to all team members to form a shared mental model of the team plan, so that all members can commit to it.

---

[4] Since individuals may be committed to roles for the entire duration of the full team plan, or for less time, we often call roles, *subgoals*, as well, and use the two terms interchangeably.

5   The Interaction of NaCoDAE in RETSINA

We placed the agentified version of NaCoDAE, now a RETSINA task agent, in a group of other RETSINA agents that had to organize themselves so as to perform a mission in the *ModSAF* simulation environment [7][5]. There were other agents in that community, but the group that was relevant to the mission was composed of:

BriefingAgent a task agent that, together with NaCoDAE, maintains the domain-specific knowledge of the full and partial shared plans for the MissionAgents, and performs agent-to-agent conversations on behalf of NaCoDAE. It also assembles shared plans from the actions of NaCoDAE cases, and finds MissionAgents to execute these plans by querying the Matchmakers with the platoon capability descriptions as preferences.

DemoDisplay an interface agent that monitors the MessageLogger so as to provide visualization of agent-to-agent communications for humans monitoring the agent system.

Matchmakers there are two types of matchmakers, Gin [25] and LARKS [26], that are capable of different forms of semantic matching. A matchmaker is a middle agent that enables agents to find each other based on their capabilities.

MessageLogger an information agent to which agents send copies of the messages they send to other agents.

MineSweepingTeam a team of task agents that use their own team-oriented coordination strategies to clear a path through a minefield as quickly as possible. [22]

MissionAgents three team-oriented task agents that must plan their joint mission with each other. Each one monitors and commands a platoon on behalf of the human platoon commanders, in the ModSAF simulation environment.

ModSAF_Proxy a task agent that models ModSAF behaviors to the other RETSINA agents, and allows those agents to interact with the ModSAF environment.

MokSAF / PalmSAF three interface agents, installed on three different portable hardware platforms, such as pen tablets or PDAs, that present human users with shared plan proposals for team coordination. The proposals show the coordinated planned routes on a ModSAF map. They also solicit the commanders' approval or rejection of the proposed team plans. [17] PalmSAF is a version of MokSAF for the PalmPilot^{TM}.

NaCoDAE a task agent that, together with the BriefingAgent, maintains the knowledge that a superior commanding officer is likely to impart and require from the three platoon commanders. It merges information that is provided by both humans and agents to compositionally generate HTN plan objectives that the plan shared by the MissionAgents aims to fulfill.

NarratorAgent a special type of task agent that, given the number of SpeechAgents in audible range of each other, assigns them different voices, and paces the tasking of SpeechAgents so that their speech does not interfere with each other.

---

[5] ModSAF is an acronym for **Mod**ular **S**emi-**A**utomated **F**orces.

RoutePlanningAgents three task agents, one dedicated to each MissionAgent, that plots routes for the platoons given characteristics of the terrain, the vehicle composition of the platoon, and constraints imposed by the mission and human commanders, such as the need for some routes to be mutually reinforcing. [17]

SpeechAgents three speech generation interface agents that synthesize audible speech from text provided by subscriber agents.

VisualReconnaissance an information agent that scans the ModSAF map and notifies its subscribers of the location of a Threat Platoon when it finds one.

VoiceAgent a voice recognition interface agent that is based on the Sphinx [13] speech recognizer. The VoiceAgent provides a dictation service to any agent that subscribes to it. The service provides the subscriber with a textual representation of what it recognizes from the human user's speech.

WeatherAgents three information agents that permit requesting agents to learn about the current weather conditions from the web sites of: USA Today, CNN, and Intellicast.

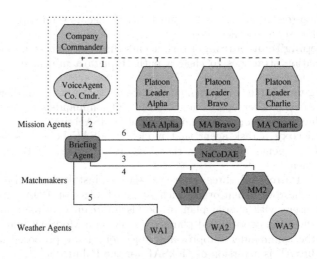

Fig. 4. Agent communications that involved the *BriefingAgent* and *NaCoDAE*

Figure 4 illustrates the types of agent communications that involve the BriefingAgent and NaCoDAE. The human figures of the scenario are represented by the irregular hexagonal shapes at the top of the diagram, and their communications by the dashed line, (1). As the Company Commander speaks, his speech is translated into text by his VoiceAgent. The BriefingAgent receives those textual translations, as represented by line (2), and attempts to match the text of the Commander's speech with the textual answers to questions that were posed by

NaCoDAE.[6] If there is a match, then the BriefingAgent will send that answer to NaCoDAE, as shown by (3). If NaCoDAE can use that answer to complete a case, then it will return a case to the BriefingAgent (3), otherwise return a regenerated ranked list of questions and their associated answers (3). If NaCo-DAE's questions contain agent queries, the BriefingAgent will directly query the provider agent if it is known (5), or first ask either or both of the Matchmakers for the identity of a provider agent (4), and then contact it (5). Upon request of the MissionAgents (6), or upon the completion of a case by NaCoDAE (3), the BriefingAgent will assemble a shared plan from the case actions and send it to the MissionAgents (6). During the execution of the scenario, the MissionAgents may also provide the BriefingAgent with updates to their capabilities (6), which the BriefingAgent can forward to NaCoDAE (3).

6 Description of the Scenario

In the scenario, our model of teamwork is implemented by the MissionAgents, knowledge of the shared plans is maintained by NaCoDAE and the BriefingAgent, and the shared plans are represented by *briefing_cases* that contain *briefing_actions* similar to the one in Figure 5. Information that should be part of the briefing is stored in the case-base: map data, additional resources allocated to the team such as mine sweepers and intelligence reports, warnings, information on the adversary, and reminders for the type of information to monitor during the execution of the plan. In the descriptions that follow, references to shared plan content that is represented in Figure 5 will appear in a different font.

```
BEGIN ACTION briefing_action                    TITLE "Briefing Object"
TEXT "(briefing_object :brief_type captains-orders
  :goal (goal :type (1 2 primary-goal)
  :1 (description :do move :what your-platoons :to horizontal_line_500)
  :2 (description :do force :what Threat_Platoon :to (behind :landmark
  :primary-goal both)              horizontal_line_500) :mode if-found)
  :map-checkpoints
  (map-checkpoints :type (Xcoords-Ohio Ycoords-Ohio width-Ohio
    Xcoords-Texas Ycoords-Texas width-Texas
    Xcoords-Utah Ycoords-Utah width-Utah
    checkpoint-1  [...]  checkpoint-11  map-reference)          [...]
  :plan-requirements (requirements :type (names ohio texas utah distribution)
    :names (ohio texas utah)              :ohio (maneuverability :rating 3-6)
    :texas (maneuverability :rating 6-8)      :utah (maneuverability :rating 3-6)
    :distribution (description :quantity 1 :assigned negotiate)        )
  :team-capability (team :type (capability-1 capability-2 capability-3)
    :capability-1 (description :maneuverability 5 :firepower 6 [...]      )
  :warning ()   )"
TOOLBOOK                                        END ACTION
```

Fig. 5. Part of the *Briefing Object*, encoded as a NaCoDAE case action

---

[6] The BriefingAgent uses a token subset matching algorithm to permit matches despite variations in word order and phrase length.

The scenario begins with a Company Commander briefing three human platoon leaders. As he speaks, the BriefingAgent eavesdrops on the Commander's discourse via the VoiceAgent. When he describes the composition of the platoons, the BriefingAgent matches that information to some of the anticipated answers to questions that NaCoDAE had ranked as highly likely, and passes that information to NaCoDAE, which then selects cases with descriptions of platoons having the same composition. NaCoDAE sends a revised ranked question list to the BriefingAgent: *Will the platoons have scouts? Is this a nighttime mission? What will the weather conditions be? Are there any known anti-tank mines?* etc. Since the question about the weather also contains a query for agents, the BriefingAgent queries the Matchmakers for WeatherAgents, finds some, and queries them for the weather conditions, while the Commander continues with his description of the mission. The WeatherAgents reply "rainy", and NaCoDAE immediately refines its list of solution cases to those which include the action representing the constraint, *plan platoon routes to avoid soft soil areas.*

At the conclusion of the Commander's briefing, the BriefingAgent finds the MissionAgents by querying the Matchmakers for agents with knowledge of team coordination for the command of platoons in ModSAF. Upon receipt of a list of four MissionAgents, the BriefingAgent selects three and then assigns one platoon to each of them. All three MissionAgents receive the same description of the task that requires teamwork in the form of an HTN plan objective, with the briefing_object as the data segment. The goals are: (a) to scout the terrain up to landmark `horizontal_line_500`; (b) to force `Threat_Platoon`, if encountered, behind the landmark; and (c) the team goals are conjunctive: `:primary-goal both`.

A team member's capabilities are those of the platoon that it represents. Since the platoon's composition is provided by the Company Commander, the team members initially learn of their capabilities via the briefing_object, for example, `:team-capability-1 (description :maneuverability 5 :firepower 6 ...)`. During the execution of the mission, if any component of a MissionAgent's platoon suffers damage, or needs to share resources, then the MissionAgent will perceive the change to its own capabilities and communicate that knowledge to the other team members, and to the supervising commanding officer via the BriefingAgent.

The plan requirements are represented in the briefing_object as the three corridors, `ohio texas utah`. There is also a `distribution` requirement that one platoon should patrol one corridor, but leaves it up to the MissionAgents to `negotiate` their assignment to a corridor. Each corridor has its own `maneuverability :rating` requirement, which the MissionAgents match to their own `maneuverability :rating` capabilities to generate candidate roles. The MissionAgents propose, two of them negotiate a conflict, they seek and receive approval from the human commanders, and commit to their plans and begin executing the mission.

In the course of the mission, one of the platoon's advance scouts discovers an anti-tank minefield in their path. The robotic mine sweeping team is already committed to one of the other platoons, so the MissionAgent for this platoon announces his desire for any unassigned mine sweeping groups, to the whole team, while it continues to execute its role in the team plan. Shortly afterwards, the lead tank of the platoon with the mine sweepers assigned to it falls into an anti-tank trap and breaks a track. Its MissionAgent notifies the BriefingAgent and the other MissionAgents about its change in capability, and that its new subgoal is to wait for an Armored Repair Vehicle. Remembering the new plan requirement of the first MissionAgent, the mine sweeping team asks both MissionAgents (current and requesting) and the BriefingAgent, if they can be assigned to the first platoon. Both of the MissionAgents, and the BriefingAgent agree to the request, and the mine sweepers change platoons and roles.

7   Related Work

We demonstrate a proof of concept conversational case-based planning system for the team coordination of independent, intelligent software agents. From a literature review, the *SiN* [15] algorithm, which integrates a generative planner, *SHOP*, with a conversational case retriever, *NaCoDAE/HTN*, appears to be very similar to the overall MAS configuration of NaCoDAE, the BriefingAgent, and the MissionAgents in the context of a multi-agent system application. SHOP provides generalized domain knowledge that can be applied to a variety of domain problems. NaCoDAE/HTN interacts with humans to gather information specific to the domain problems. The SiN algorithm manages the matching of NaCoDAE/HTN task decompositions to SHOP plans, and the alternation of control between the two systems. The reason for integrating the two planning systems is to significantly reduce the plan space of the NaCoDAE/HTN planner, if it were used in isolation, and to allow for more interactivity with humans, if SHOP were used in isolation. Future work could investigate if the RETSINA agent HTN plan space is comparable to the NaCoDAE/HTN plan space in isolation, or to the plan space of the total SiN system.

A novel aspect of our work was to use the conversational model of NaCoDAE as a way of merging the asynchronous human- and agent-provided information into cases. To our knowledge, this is the first instance of a conversational CBR system that conversed directly with software agents. New agent queries or interactions were triggered by the regeneration of NaCoDAE's ranked list of questions in response to new input, which in turn triggered more agent responses.

Although others have used speech recognition as front-ends to conversational CBR systems [11], we did not direct any of NaCoDAE's responses back to the human user, thus NaCoDAE did not dialogue directly with the human. Rather, so as to not cognitively overload the user and to be as unobtrusive as possible, the NaCoDAE GUI was not visible, and the CCBP system passively listened to the textual transcription of human statements, attempting to extract information from the human conversation by matching their statements with the answers associated to the ranked list of questions.

8   Conclusions

The work that we have presented in this paper is significant in four ways. First, we have introduced a technique by which information technologies can be elevated to a level of accessibility that is closer to humans. Namely, by deploying NaCoDAE as a passive listener to human conversations, and by agentifying it so that it can actively dialogue with intelligent software agents in order to fill the gaps of unspecified knowledge, we showed that we can avoid overloading the human with detailed questioning while still allowing him to specify relevant information. Second, we have demonstrated the flexibility of conversational case-based reasoning at combining knowledge from many sources in a dynamic and ever-changing situation into meaningful knowledge. We do this by mapping information from human and disparate agent sources into case actions, which can then be assembled into team plans and descriptions of the environment. Also, by performing this mapping asynchronously and incrementally, NaCoDAE has demonstrated that its conversational nature is well-suited for agent information gathering domains. Third, from the perspective of team-oriented agent research, we have provided principles for developing and supporting agent teams, and tested them by applying these principles to a scenario that involved software agent teams operating in a simulated environment. Through such tests, we contribute to the understanding of agent roles and human-agent interactions in teams composed of humans and intelligent software agents. Fourth, we have provided an innovative technique to the agent community that illustrates how to access multimodal information that includes structured data as well as speech, text, and agent responses.

References

1. D. W. Aha and L. A. Breslow. Refining conversational case libraries. In *Proceedings of the Second International Conference on Case-Based Reasoning*, 1997.
2. D. W. Aha, L. A. Breslow, and T. Maney. Supporting conversational case-based reasoning in an integrated reasoning framework. *Case-Based Reasoning Integrations: Papers from the 1998 Workshop*, 1998.
3. D. Brugali and K. Sycara. Agent technology: A new frontier for the development of application frameworks? In *Object-Oriented Application Frameworks*. Wiley, 1998.
4. L. Chen and K. Sycara. Webmate: A personal agent for browsing and searching. In *Agents 1998*, May 1998.
5. P. R. Cohen and H. J. Levesque. Teamwork. *Noûs*, 25(4):487–512, 1991.
6. K. Decker, A. Pannu, K. Sycara, and M. Williamson. Designing behaviors for information agents. In *Agents 1997*, February 1997.
7. Defense Modeling, Simulation, and Tactical Technology Information Analysis Center. *ModSAF Kit C*, ModSAF 5.0 edition. http://www.modsaf.org.
8. D. J. Dwyer, J. E. Fowlkes, R. L. Oser, E. Salas, and N. E. Lane. *Team Performance Assessment and Measurement: Theory, Methods and Applications*. Erlbaum, 1997.
9. K. Erol, J. Hendler, and D. S. Nau. HTN planning: Complexity and expressivity. In *Proceedings of AAAI-94*, 1994.
10. J. A. Giampapa, M. Paolucci, and K. Sycara. Agent interoperation across multagent system boundaries. In *Agents 2000*, June 2000.
11. M. Göker and C. Thompson. Personalized conversational case-based recommendation. In *EWCBR 2000*, September 2000.
12. B. Grosz and S. Kraus. Collaborative plans for complex group action. *Artificial Intelligence*, 86(2):269–357, 1996.

13. K.-F. Lee, H.-W. Hon, and R. Reddy. An overview of the Sphinx recognition system. In *IEEE ASSP-38*, volume 1, pages 35–45, January 1990.

14. H. J. Levesque, P. R. Cohen, and J. H. T. Nunes. On acting together. Technical Note 485, AI Center, SRI International, May 1990.

15. H. Muñoz-Avila, D. W. Aha, L. A. Breslow, D. Nau, and R. Weber. Integrating conversational case retrieval with generative planning. In *Proceedings of the Fifth European Workshop on Case-Based Reasoning*.

16. M. Paolucci, O. Shehory, and K. Sycara. Interleaving planning and execution in a multiagent team planning environment. Technical Report CMU-RI-TR-00-01.

17. T. Payne, K. Sycara, M. Lewis, T. L. Lenox, and S. K. Hahn. Varying the user interaction within multi-agent systems. In *Agents 2000*, June 2000.

18. C. Prince, D. P. Baker, L. Shrestha, and E. Salas. Situation awareness in team performance. *Human Factors*, 37:123–136, 1995.

19. D. V. Pynadath, M. Tambe, N. Chauvat, and L. Cavedon. Toward team-oriented programming. In *Intelligent Agents VI: ATAL, N.R.*, pages 233–247, 1999.

20. O. Shehory and K. Sycara. The RETSINA communicator. In *Agents 2000*.

21. R. J. Stout and E. Salas. The role of planning in coordination team decision making: Implications for training. In *Human Factor and Ergonomics Society* 37th *Annual Meeting*, pages 1238–1242, 1993.

22. G. Sukthankar. Team-aware multirobot strategy for cooperative path clearing. In *AAAI-2000*, July 2000.

23. K. Sycara. Multiagent systems. *AI Magazine*, 19(2):79–92, Summer 1998.

24. K. Sycara, K. Decker, A. Pannu, M. Williamson, and D. Zeng. Distributed intelligent agents. *IEEE Expert*, 11(6):36–45, 1996.

25. K. Sycara, K. Decker, and M. Williamson. Middle-agents for the internet. In *IJCAI-97*, 23–29 August 1997.

26. K. Sycara, M. Klusch, S. Widoff, and J. Lu. Dynamic service matchmaking among agents in open information environments. *Journal ACM SIGMOD Record, A. Ouksel, A. Sheth (Eds.)*, 28(1):47–53, March 1999.

27. K. Sycara and D. Zeng. Coordination of multiple intelligent software agents. *IJI-CIS*, 5(2 and 3):181–211, 1996.

28. M. Tambe, D. V. Pynadath, N. Chauvat, A. Das, and G. A. Kaminka. Adaptive agent architectures for heterogeneous team members. In *ICMAS-2000*, pages 301–308, 10–12 July 2000.

29. H.-C. Wong and K. Sycara. A taxonomy of middle-agents for the internet. In *ICMAS 2000*, pages 465–466, 10–12 July 2000.

A Hybrid Approach for the Management of FAQ Documents in Latin Languages

Christiane Gresse von Wangenheim[1], Andre Bortolon[2], and Aldo von Wangenheim[2]

[1]Universidade do Vale do Itajaí, Computer Science
São José, Brazil
gresse@sj.univali.br

[2]Federal University of Santa Catarina - Production Engineering/Computer Science
Florianópolis, Brazil
bortolon@eps.ufsc.br, awangenh@inf.ufsc.br

Abstract. Essential for the success of FAQ systems is their ability to systematically manage knowledge, including the intelligent retrieval of useful FAQ documents and the continuous evolution of the knowledge base. Based on our experience, we propose a hybrid approach for the management of FAQ documents on programming languages written in Portuguese, Spanish or other latin languages. Our approach integrates various types of knowledge and provides intelligent mechanisms for knowledge access as well as the continuous evolution and improvement of the FAQ system throughout its life cycle. The principal strength of this approach lies in the integration of Case-Based Reasoning and Information Retrieval techniques, customized to the specific requirements and characteristics of FAQ document management. Our work is currently being implemented and evaluated in the context of an international research project.

Keywords. Text Retrieval, Case-based Reasoning, Natural Language Processing, Knowledge Management

1 Introduction

In order to efficiently implement high-quality software systems, programmers require up-to-date, detailed and broad knowledge with respect to programming language(s). However, since the software domain is characterized by rapid technological advances and frequent changes, it is a challenge to support the learning of new programming languages. In this context, tacit knowledge describing concrete experiences obtained by individuals, through the observation of attempts and mistakes for example, has been shown to be an important knowledge source that contributes to an effective learning process. A possible form of representing and communicating this type of knowledge are lists of *Frequently Asked Questions* (FAQ), which state a question and its answer provided by a specialist. These lists explicitly capture know-how and solution strategies to support finding adequate solutions for given problems. Thus, they make know-how available on commonly asked questions, which otherwise would be asked again and again to an expert.

In this context, we developed a software system for the management of FAQ documents related to programming languages. To this end, the system has to store FAQ

D.W. Aha and I. Watson (Eds.): ICCBR 2001, LNAI 2080, pp. 204–218, 2001.

documents in a structured form, retrieve relevant documents for given questions and support the continuous evolution of the knowledge base. Regarding the specific application domain, the system must be able to handle experiential knowledge in form of FAQ documents, extract information from textual documents and map it into a structured representation of cases and similarity-based mechanisms in order to allow the retrieval of documents with similar but not necessarily identical questions [5]. Furthermore, the system has to be able to deal with queries and documents in natural language. This requires mechanisms for spelling correction, normalization of verbs, nouns and adjectives as well as the automatic extraction of relevant terms. Although in our test application the principal language used is Brazilian Portuguese, our approach has been developed to fit a whole set of modern latin languages. In addition, the system has to be able to handle queries which may be mixed with English jargon of the specific application domain (e.g., "O que é class?"[1]). If the system is unable to provide a satisfactory answer based on the existing knowledge base, support has to be provided for the manual answer process via an expert. In order to enable the continuous evolution of the knowledge base, the acquisition and integration of new FAQ documents must be supported. This requires mechanisms for the semi-automatic indexation of new FAQ documents as well as the continuous enhancement and update of general domain knowledge.

Today, many FAQ repositories exist, mainly in newsgroups or in text form as part of a technical manual. However, most FAQ repositories do not provide efficient access to the knowledge contained in the documents. In general, there are two basic methods for accessing this knowledge: visualization and search. Visualization methods offer an organized collection of information that can be explored by the user, such as in newsgroups. The problem is that it can be quite time-consuming to find an answer to a specific question. On the other hand, search methods provide a mechanism that allows users to explicitly express requirements and obtain the best results found in the FAQ repository. Traditionally, Information Retrieval (IR) techniques or key-word searches are used, e.g., by Internet search engines. However, this method often either overwhelms the user by the amount of information retrieved or by not returning any useful information. Another problem is the inadequate indexing of vocabulary, which results from the diversity of expertise and backgrounds of the system users. Recently, various systems have been developed which address the problem of handling textual documents by means of knowledge-based techniques, in particular Case-Based Reasoning (CBR) [2]. The principal advantages of CBR in this context are the similarity based retrieval of cases and the incremental evolution of the knowledge base. Specific textual CBR techniques have been developed in order to handle textual cases (e.g., [3, 4, 9, 13]). They facilitate the integration of any type of general domain knowledge and, thus, allow content-oriented document search strategies which perform much better than traditional IR approaches. However, the existing approaches focus on the handling of documents in English. Today, in this specific application domain, there does not yet exist a general approach for dealing with queries and documents in latin languages, which are morphologically much more complex than the English language.

1.in English: What is a class?

Another aspect generally not supported, is the continuous evolution of the FAQ repository. Exceptions include, for example, [1,12], which supports organizational memory by routing a question for which the system cannot find an answer to a human expert. However, the acquisition and integration of the new cases and the appropriate update of the general domain knowledge have to be intertwined in order to comprehensively support the evolution of the knowledge base.

In this paper, we present a hybrid approach that is able to deal with these problems. It integrates techniques from Case-Based Reasoning and Information Retrieval adapted to the specific application domain.

2   Requirements for Intelligent Text Retrieval in Portuguese and Other Modern Latin Languages

Besides a few isolated efforts aimed at specific languages, much work in the field of content-oriented document search strategies has been done in English. Very little systematic work has been performed that is oriented toward the development of general strategies capable of handling a whole family of languages. Strategies developed for the English Language cannot be generalized, nor can other for modern anglo-saxon languages based upon analytical grammars, such as Dutch. This is because most modern indo-european languages have morphological and syntactic rules that are much more complex than those of English, even though these languages are similar in the general structure. For example, they contain variations in verb form spectrums or gender/number dependent morphologic modifications of nouns and adjectives. To develop a FAQ retrieval system that goes beyond simple keyword search, those morphological and syntactic rules have to be taken at least partly into consideration.

However, there exists a set of modern indo-european languages of the family of Latin Languages that share syntactic and morphological rules and are candidates for an integrated approach: Portuguese, Spanish[1], Italian, Galician, Catalonian and Reto-Roman. These languages have sufficiently similar syntactic structures that allow the translation from one into another by substituting the words and applying the appropriate morphological rules. These languages have the following principal characteristics in common [8,14,16]:

1. Syntactic structures are based upon true analytical grammars and do not possess any kind of surface cases[2], not even degenerated genitive or possessive. All semantic relations between noun phrases (NP) are defined by the preposition at the beginning of the NP. The rules governing the generation of phrase structures are also very formal and shared[3] between these languages.

2. The verbal spectrum of the Latin Language is maintained, with all different verbal modi such as the subjunctive mode and the gerundium mode still in everyday usage. Most verbal modi have a full set of simple verb tenses, which, in the indica-

---

1. Following the international tendency, we call here the Castilian Spanish Language, *Castellano*, simply as "Spanish", in contrast to Galician Spanish and Catalonian Spanish.
2. For a detailed discussion on surface cases versus deep cases and Linguistic Universals see [10].
3. See [6] for a discussion on syntax rules of natural languages.

tive mode can be 6 different simple tenses (1 present, 3 past and 2 future). Since there are 3 different regular conjugations depending on the infinitive form of the verb and each of the 6 simple tenses conjugates each of the 6 persons differently, there are 108 different morphological rules only for the regular verbs of the indicative mode. The other modi similar but simpler.

3. Adjectives and articles undergo fully morphological modification in gender and number by the noun or nouns they refer to. Here the terminal symbols are different among languages, but the morphological rules are the same. E.g., in Portuguese the suffix rule for regular adjectives is "o" if the noun referenced is masculine singular, "os" if masculine plural, "a" if feminine and "as" if feminine plural; in Italian the respective terminal symbols are "o", "i", "a" and "e", but the rule is the same. Nouns that can change gender obey a similar rule: e.g., the word "cat" has 4 different forms (in Spanish: *gato, gata, gatos, gatas*).

4. Double negation[1] is not used.

These grammar rule characteristics are, obviously an enormous advantage in natural language processing of these languages, since the detailed verbal structures and the morphological interdependencies convey much semantic information that gives context sensitivity to the parsing of phrases and makes discourse analysis easier. However, in order to build a FAQ system, we need something between a simple keyword search and a full discourse analysis. The appropriate approach should be able to capture the semantics of key expressions in the question text, and therefore must also be able to deal with the full morphological variety of these languages, but does not need to perform a full semantic mapping of the NPs of the query.

The approach we have developed has focused on the Portuguese Language as a testbed, but can be applied to any other of the latin languages cited above.

Regarding our application on the management of FAQ documents on programming languages, we can further state the following specific characteristics and requirements regarding the analysis of the queries and FAQ documents:

- useful answers depend on the type of question, e.g., the question *"O que é o controller?"*(What is a controller?) asks for a different type of answer than the question *"Como implementar um controller?"* (How to implement a controller?).

- English jargon is intermixed with the Portuguese question. These are principally names of standard classes or methods (e.g., *"OrderedCollection"* or *"addAll"*) or technical standard terms related to object-oriented programming, such as *"object"*. The English terms, in general, are not derived or inflected in the queries. However, a specific characteristic of class or method names is that the individual words may be concatenated into one term. Thus, a frequent spelling error is the separation of those terms by inserting blanks between the individual words (e.g., *"Ordered Collection"*).

- frequently observed types of spelling errors in the Portuguese terms of queries are:
  - missing character (e.g., *"eviar"* instead of *"enviar"*)
  - extra characters (e.g., *"eenviar"* instead of *"enviar"*)
  - erroneous character (e.g., *"enfiar"* instead of *"enviar"*)
  - pair of transposed characters (e.g., *"envira"* instead of *"enviar"*)
  - missing accents (e.g., *"colecao"* instead of *"coleção"*)

1.Like in the French Language: "ne ... pas".

- normalization regarding the inflection of Portuguese nouns, verbs and adjectives is required, in order to identify morphological variants. For example, if plural forms of nouns are not normalized, it may be impossible to find a related case with the respective noun in singular form, or vice versa. According to Brazilian Gramatical Nomenclature [8] the normal form is defined as follows:
  - nouns: singular,   masculine   form   (i.e.,   regular   plural   generation: *"objetos"*⇨*"objeto"* and irregular plural generation: *"imagens"*⇨*"imagem"*)
  - verbs: infinitive form (i.e., regular forms: *"evita"*⇨*"evitar"*, *"evitando*⇨*"evitar"* and irregular forms: *"posso"*⇨*"poder"*, *"feito"*⇨*"fazer"*)
  - adjectives: singular, masculine form (i.e., *"profundas"*⇨*"profundo"*)

Normalization is facilitated in our specific application, as queries are always written in present tense and verbs only occur in 1. person singular, 3. person singular or 1. person plural. Prefixes are important for the semantic meaning of the question and therefore may not be separated from the word root (e.g. *"desabilitar"* (*disable*) and *"habilitar"* (*enable*)).

These requirements show that sophisticated support is required for analyzing the natural language queries in order to allow intelligent retrieval and to support the continuous integration of new documents.

3   A Hybrid Approach: The FAQ@System

The objective of the FAQ@System is to provide a tool that, for a given query formulated in Portuguese, finds related FAQ documents stored in a case base in order to help professionals to solve problems and questions arising during the programming of a software system.

As input to the system, the user formulates a programming language question in Portuguese. Relevant terms are extracted automatically from the given query (including the correction of orthographic errors and normalization of verbs, nouns and adjectives). Based on the terms extracted from the given query, the case base of FAQ documents is queried. Relevant documents are identified based on a set of indexes referencing the content of the FAQ document. By matching the cases with the query using similarity measures, a partial order is induced among the cases of the base. Upon a first try, the most similar case is suggested to the user. If this case does not satisfactory answer the stated question, the user can request and explore the next ten most similar cases. If the system fails to provide a sufficiently similar case or all cases retrieved do not satisfactory answer the question, the user can request the support of an expert. The user's question is then stored in the knowledge base (marked as still unresponded). An expert is informed via e-mail about the open question and asked to provide an answer. Once the answer is available, it is forwarded to the user and in combination with the query captured as a new case into the knowledge base. The new case is automatically indexed and mapped into its structured representation. The results of the indexing process are revised by a domain expert, and if necessary, enhanced, for example, by modifying indexes or adding new terms to the general domain knowledge.

The principal aspects of our approach, including knowledge representation, natural language text analysis and extraction, similarity based retrieval and continuous evolution are described in the following sections.

3.1   Knowledge Representation

The information and knowledge in the FAQ documents is represented in the form of cases. In order to represent the FAQ documents in an accessible way, the textual description is mapped into a structured representation, which consists of the question text, the answer text, a set of indexes and a question type (see Figure 1).

Case 007	
Question	Como ordenar uma coleção?
Answer	Enviando a mensagem sort para esta coleção
Indexes	ordenar, coleção
Type	modo (tipo 3)

Fig. 1. Example of case representation

The indexes indicate the terms of the question text which are relevant for the retrieval of useful cases in the specific application domain, enabling efficient access to the documents. The classification of the cases per type of question generates the need for different types of answers. Here, the following categories of questions have been identified [5]:

- Definition: questions beginning with "*O que*", e.g., "*O que é uma coleção?*" (What is a collection?).
- Nature or quantity: questions beginning with "*Qual*", e.g., "*Quais tipos de mensagens existem?*" (Which message types exist?)
- Modal: questions beginning with "*Como*", e.g., "*Como executar um programa?*" (How to execute a program?)
- Utility: questions beginning with "*Para que*", e.g., "*Para que serve o método hash?*" (What purpose does the hash method serve?)
- Example: questions beginning with "*Exemplifique*", e.g., "*Exemplifique a utilização de uma janela.*" (Give an example for the usage of a window)
- Others: questions beginning with any other term, e.g., "*Classes são objetos?*" (Classes are objects?)

Besides the knowledge represented in cases, general domain knowledge is represented in order to provide support for automatic text extraction, spelling correction and similarity-based retrieval. This includes:

Domain specific vocabulary, which defines indicative expressions for a predictive indexation by restricting normative key-terms that represent terms and common terminology with respect to the specific application domain (e.g., "*classe*", "*executar*", "*rápido*"). The domain specific vocabulary is used in order to automatically extract relevant terms from the query and FAQ documents. Two types of domain specific vocabularies have been separated, one on class names (e.g., "*collection*") and one on commonly used method names (e.g., "*initialize*") with respect to the specific programming language.

Domain specific English-Portuguese dictionary, which contains terms in English used as technical jargon in the specific application domain. In order to enable the automatic translation of these terms into Portuguese, the dictionary represents the English terms and their Portuguese translation (e.g., *"class"* ⇨ *"classe"*).

Domain specific thesaurus, which represents relations between domain specific terms, such as hierarchical relations (e.g., *"OrderedCollection"*⇨*"Collection"*), associative relations (e.g., *"objeto"*⇨*"classe"*) and abbreviations (e.g., *"mvc"* ⇨{*"modelo"*, *"visão"*, *"controlador"*}). The thesaurus enables the consideration of local similarities at index level.

The domain specific vocabularies, dictionary and thesaurus include only terms which are related to the specific application domain.

Normalization rules, which are used for removing or modifying suffixes (e.g., *"...ns"* ⇨*"...m"*, as in *"imagens"*⇨*"imagem"*), changes of genus (e.g., *"...oa"*⇨*"...ão"*, as in *"leoa"*⇨*"leão"*) and conjugation of irregular verbs (e.g., *"faço"* ⇨*"fazer"*) in order to identify morphological variants.

General Portuguese vocabulary, which represents a general vocabulary of the Portuguese Language including more than 20.000 terms based on [11]. The vocabulary is used in the spelling correction and normalization process.

Stop list, which includes about 200 words, such as *"aqui"*, *"acima"*, *"para"*[1], which are very common in the language and, thus, having a low descriptive potential. The stop list is used in the evolution of the domain specific vocabularies in order to exclude domain irrelevant terms.

3.2   Natural Language Text Analysis and Extraction

The query is described by the user by formulating a question in natural language, e.g., *"Como posso ordenar uma Ordered Collection"* (How can I order an Ordered Collection?). The query is automatically analyzed and mapped to an internal representation. The objective of this step is to extract all relevant terms from the question as indexes and to classify the type of question. This includes the following steps:

Tokenization. The tokenization aims at splitting the text into strings of characters delimited by blanks (e.g., {*"como"*, *"posso"*, *"ordenar"*, *"uma"*, *"Ordered"*, *"Collection"*}).

Classification of question type. The classification is done based on the interrogative pronoun or the adverb used at the beginning of the question. For example, a question starting with *"Como"* is classified as a modal question, asking for the explanation on how to do something.

Extraction of English domain-specific terms. The automatic extraction of English domain-specific terms is enabled through the usage of the domain specific vocabularies on class and method names and the domain specific English-Portuguese dictionary (see Section 3.1). Regarding the specific characteristics of the application domain, the extraction is done by iteratively concatenating subsequent terms (e.g., *"Ordered"* and *"Collection"* to *"OrderedCollection"*) and verifying the resulting terms against the domain vocabularies or the dictionary.

1.in English: here, above, to

Spelling correction. The spelling correction is based on comparing terms with the general portuguese vocabulary. Any near miss with at least 60% similarity is used to substitute the original term in the query. This optimistic strategy has been chosen in order to prevent the omission of any correct term. For example, if the character "*n*" is missing in "*enviar*", another potential candidate could also be the word "*evitar*", with the same degree of similarity to the wrong spelled word "*eviar*".

Normalization. This step aims at the normalization of terms in documents and queries so that morphological variants between the query and a case will match. Through the normalization process each word is converted into its normal form (e.g., "*posso*"⇨"*poder*"). This is accomplished by an iterative process based on a rule-based reduction of words and a verification of the newly created term in accordance to general Portuguese vocabulary. The defined rules (see Section 3.1) basically undo the spelling rules for adding affixes, covering the generation of plurals and other inflections such as verb endings. Exceptions of the rule, e.g., irregular verbs, are listed explicitly.

Extraction of relevant portuguese terms. The extraction of Portuguese terms is done by comparing each corrected and normalized word of the query against the domain specific vocabulary.

Query	
Question text	Como posso ordenar uma Ordered Collection?
Indexes	{poder, ordenar, OrderedCollection}
Type	modo (tipo 3)

Fig. 2. Example of analysis result

For example, the internal representation of the query "*Como posso ordenar uma Ordered Collection?*" as result of the analysis is illustrated in Figure 2.

3.3   Similarity-Based Retrieval

With respect to the indexes and the question type of the query, for all cases in the base a similarity value is computed. This is done by partially matching the indexes and question type using similarity measures on different levels.

Global similarity. The global similarity of a case c_k of the case base with respect to the given query q is calculated by:

$$sim(q, c_k) = \frac{\left(\sum_{(i = 1)}^{n} simLoc(q_i, c_k) \right) + simType(q, c_k)}{n + 1}$$

where $simLoc(q_i, c_k)$ is the local similarity, $simType(q, c_k)$ is the similarity of the question type and n the total number of indexes of the query q. Any case with a similarity above a threshold is considered as a potential answer candidate for the query.

Local similarity. The determination of the similarity between the query and a case is further enhanced through the integration of the domain-specific thesaurus. This allows the consideration of similar, but not necessarily equal index values. The local similarity $simLoc(q_i, c_k)$ of the ith index q_i of the query q and the case c_k is determined by the maximum local similarity value $simLoc_j(q_i, c_{kj})$ of the index q_i with all indexes c_{kj} of the case c_k:

$$simLoc(q_i, c_{kj}) = \max \; simLoc_j(q_i, c_{kj}) \qquad 0 \le j \le m$$

where m is the total number of indexes of the case c_k.

$simLoc_j(q_i, c_{kj})$ is calculated by comparing the index q_i to the jth index of the case c_k, considering also the set s_i of similar terms to the index q_i based on the domain-specific thesaurus:

$$simLoc_j(q_i, c_{kj}) = \begin{cases} 1.0 & \text{if } (\exists (x \in c_{kj})): x = q_i \\ 0.9 & \text{if } ((((\neg\exists(x \in c_{kj}))): x = q_i) \wedge ((\exists(y \in s_i)): y = q_i)) \\ 0 & \text{if } ((((\neg\exists(x \in c_{kj}))): x = q_i) \wedge ((\neg\exists(y \in s_i)): y = q_i)) \end{cases}$$

Type similarity. The similarity of the question types $simType(q, c_k)$ is determined by comparing the question type $type_q$ of the query q and $type_{ck}$ of a case c_k of the case base in accordance to the question types defined in Section 3.1.

$$simType(q, c_k) = \begin{cases} 1.0 & \text{if } type_q = type_{c_k} \\ 0 & \text{if } type_q \ne type_{c_k} \end{cases}$$

Untying similarity. Using the global similarity measure described above, a partial order is induced among the cases of the case base. However, using this global similarity measure, various cases can have the same maximum similarity to the given query. For example, given the following situation as illustrated in Figure 3, the global similarity of case1 and case2 is 95%, as they both have the index "controlador" (the Portuguese translation of "controller") and are of the same question type as the query.

	Query	Case 1	Case 2
Question	O que é controller?	O que é um controlador?	O que é um controlador de janela?
Answer		Controlador é um ...	Controlador de janela é um ...
Indexes	{controller}	{controlador}	{controlador, janela}
Type	1	1	1

Fig. 3. Example for untying similarity

However, as the primary goal of the FAQ system is to retrieve one unique answer, the untying similarity measure is used in order to refine the similarity calculation if upon using the global similarity measure more than one case has the maximum similarity value. For example, case1 which is more similar to the stated query should be retrieved as an answer to the query. The selection of such a case is done by a different type of normalization. The resulting $simUntying(q, c_k)$ does not only include the total number of indexes of the query but considers also the total number of indexes of the case:

$$simUntying(q, c_k) = \frac{\left(\sum_{(i=1)}^{n} simLoc(q_i, c_k) \right) + simType(q, c_k)}{\frac{n+m}{2} + 1}$$

where n is the total number of indexes of query q and m the total number of indexes of case c_k.

Continuing with the example above, using the untying similarity measure, case1 is considered as more similar to the query (simUntying(query,case1)=0,95) than case2 with simUntying(query,case2)=0,76. The untying measure is only used when more than one case has the same maximum global similarity. Otherwise, for example, the substitution of the global similarity measure, would significantly reduce recall.

3.4   Continuous Evolution of the FAQ@System

In order to continuously improve the FAQ@System and to update the knowledge base, new cases have to be acquired and integrated in the case base. Furthermore, the similarity measure and the general domain knowledge have to be improved and adapted based on feedback from its application in practice.

3.4.1 Acquisition of Cases

Each time a query is manually answered by an expert, a new case is acquired, enabling the continuous evolution and actualization of the case base. The new case is based on the question stated by the user and the answer given by the expert. In order to facilitate the integration of the new case into the existing case base, the indexing process is done by automatically extracting relevant terms based on the existing general domain knowledge, using techniques as described in Section 3.2. The created case is then revised by the domain expert, who can add, change or delete assigned indexes based on the question text of the case. If new terms which are not yet included in the general domain knowledge become relevant for the description of a case, the domain specific vocabularies, dictionary and thesaurus have to be updated accordingly, as described in the following sections.

3.4.2 Evolution of the Domain Vocabulary

In order to adapt to changes in the application environment, domain specific vocabularies have to be updated each time new domain relevant terms become available. In order to keep the required manual effort for the identification of new relevant terms as low as possible, new acquired cases are pre-processed in order to point out potential candidate terms. The objective of this pre-processing is to identify candidate terms in a document by determining their descriptive power in the case base. Among the many probabilistic techniques that have been developed, those which typically incorporate term frequency and inverse document frequency [15] have been found to be simple and yet very useful [7]. The basic rationales underlying these two measures are that terms which appear more frequently in a document should be assigned higher weights (term frequency) and terms which appear in fewer documents in the whole case base (the more specific terms) should have higher weights (inverse document frequency).

These weights are determined for each term in the question text of the new case which is not yet indexed by the following procedure: Using a stop list (see Section 3.1) any non-semantic bearing terms are filtered. The remaining terms are ranked by using the inverse document frequency, where the weight of the term k in document i is represented by:

$$weight_{ik} = tf_{ik} \cdot (\log_2 n - \log_2 df_k + 1)$$

where tf_{ik} is the frequency of term k in document i, df_k the number of documents in which term k occurs and n the total number of cases in the case base. This weight induces a partial order among the terms of the question text, guiding the manual investigation by the domain expert, who finally decides if a term should be added to the domain-specific vocabularies or dictionary.

3.4.3 Evolution of Domain Specific Thesaurus

Each time a new term is added to the domain specific vocabularies, it may also be necessary to update the domain specific thesaurus if the new term is related to any already existing term. However, the major impediment to the usage of thesauri has been the cost of their manual creation and evolution. Therefore, pre-processing is performed in order to point out potentially related terms. Virtually all techniques for automatic thesaurus generation are based on the statistical co-occurrence of word types in text [15], where similarity coefficients are obtained between pairs of distinct terms based on coincidences in term assignments to the documents of the collection.

Thus, each time a new term k is included into the domain specific vocabulary, a term co-occurrence analysis is performed. Therefore, the documents of the case base are represented by a matrix such as shown in Table 1 based on the vector space model:

Table 1. Term assignment matrix

	T_1	T_2	...	T_k	...	T_m
D_1	tf_{11}	tf_{12}	...	tf_{1k}	...	tf_{1m}
...	...	...	...	...	...	...
D_n	tf_{n1}	tf_{n2}	...	tf_{nk}	...	tf_{nm}

where the rows of the matrix represent the individual document vectors and the columns identify the term assignments to the cases. Then, the similarity between the new term k and any other term l can be measured based on the respective pairs of columns of the matrix. A similarity measure may be defined as [15]:

$$sim(TERM_k, TERM_l) = \frac{\sum_{i=1}^{n} tf_{ik} \cdot tf_{il}}{\sum_{i=1}^{n} tf_{ik}^2 + \sum_{i=1}^{n} tf_{il}^2 - \sum_{i=1}^{n} tf_{ik} \cdot tf_{il}}$$

given term vectors in the form of $TERM_k = (tf_{1k}, ...,)$ where tf_{ik} indicates the frequency of $TERM_k$ in case i and assuming n cases in the base. As a result a $term_k$-term association vector T_k is computed expressing the similarity of term k with every term l of the domain specific vocabulary through $sim(TERM_k, TERM_l)$.

All relations with a similarity measure above a threshold are considered as potential candidates and are ordered by their similarity value. This is revised by the expert, who, if appropriate, adds new associations to the domain specific thesaurus.

3.4.4 Continuous Improvement through Feedback

Due to the fact that the FAQ document content area and relevant terms may change over time, the domain knowledge and similarity measure for retrieval requires continuous tailoring during the whole life cycle of a FAQ system. This tailoring is performed by careful analysis of system performance and possible changes in application context. To support this maintenance, protocols documenting user´s (re-) actions (e.g., the percentage of acceptance of the first answer provided) and feedback (e.g., on the general experienced usefulness) can be used by the knowledge engineer. Based upon the analysis of occurring problems the system is adapted accordingly, for example, by increasing the global similarity threshold or revising the domain specific vocabulary.

4 Implementation

Based on the approach presented in this paper, a prototypical implementation has been developed for the management of FAQ documents on the programming language Smalltalk [5]. The system allows the retrieval of FAQ documents via queries stated in natural language, supports the manual response of questions and provides facilities for enhancing the stored domain knowledge.

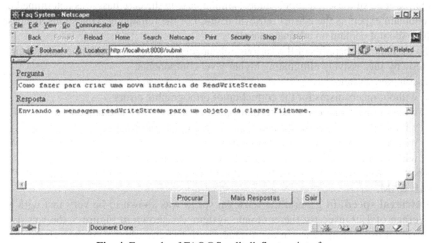

Fig. 4. Example of FAQ@Smalltalk System interface

The tool is basically a client-server architecture consisting of three logical layers: presentation, application, and data storage. All knowledge, including the FAQ document cases, as well as domain knowledge (e.g., vocabularies) is stored in a file system. The initial case base contains 200 FAQ documents. The domain-specific vocabulary includes 647 terms related to the programming language Smalltalk, 2.612

class names and 100 method names with respect to a standard Smalltalk image. The domain-specific English-Portuguese dictionary includes 51 terms; the thesaurus 510 terms, initially defined through the analysis of the application domain. The application layer provides support tools for the retrieval of FAQ documents, the manual answer process (by automatically contacting experts and users via e-mail), the acquisition of new cases as well as the enhancement of the domain knowledge. The system is accessed through web browsers and e-mail systems via Internet.

The tool is platform independent, developed in Smalltalk using VisualWorks 5i.2.

5 Evaluation

We evaluated our approach based on the FAQ@Smalltalk System by adapting the evaluation techniques of CBR and IR systems [13]. Regarding the specific focus of FAQ systems to return one unique answer to the query instead of various potential candidates [4], the following criteria have been evaluated:

- Retrieval speed: the time required for performing the retrieval.
- Recall: the percent of questions for which the system returns a correct answer, if one exists (considering only the first answer provided).

The common IR metric precision is not evaluated, as the primary objective of the FAQ system is to return one unique answer and, therefore, there is presumed to be only a single correct answer to every query, rendering precision undefined.

The evaluation was conducted with 40 test questions (including orthographic errors, etc.). For 35 of these questions, a most similar case in the case base was determined by a domain expert as the correct retrieval result. For the remaining 5 questions, the case base did not contain an adequate answer.

To evaluate the benefits of the various enhancements made, we performed an ablation study by successively eliminating higher level components:

1. complete system
2. without mechanisms for the correction of orthographic errors
3. without mechanisms for the normalization of nouns, verbs and adjectives
4. without mechanisms for the automatic extraction of information
5. without consideration of local similarity
6. without consideration of global similarity (perfect matching only)

The tests were run using a case base with 200 cases on a Pentium III 800 Mhz with 128 MB RAM.

Retrieval speed. In general the retrieval speed was shown to be very fast with an average of 129 msec for the complete system. As shown in Figure 5, the speed of retrieval did not increase in accordance with the complexity of the system. For example, we observed a reduction of retrieval time when including information extraction mechanisms. This can be explained by the fact that during tests 4,5, and 6 more indexes had to be processed (e.g., including irrelevant terms such as articles, pronouns etc.) than during tests 1,2, and 3. As a result, the integration of the information extraction mechanisms reduced significantly the retrieval time, resulting in almost the same retrieval time as of a system based on a perfect matching. It also has been shown that depending on the respective need for spelling correction and normalization, the retrieval speed of the complete system can vary significantly from average.

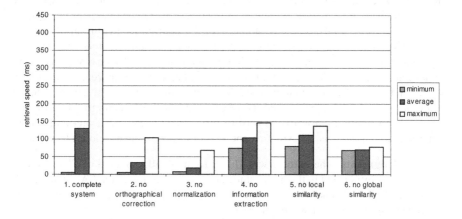

Fig. 5. Retrieval speed

Recall. The obtained recall of the approach was high with about 83% of the queries correctly responded by the complete system. 50% of the questions not correctly responded were not covered by the case base. This means that the system returned an answer in a situation where it should not have returned any.

Comparing the different components of the system, the largest increase of recall was obtained through the integration of the local similarity measure and the domain specific thesaurus (see Figure 6). Regarding the other components (tests 1,2,3,4) a continuous recall increase of about 10% as observed from each new component added.

Our evaluation shows that better results in retrieval speed and recall can be obtained through the integration of various techniques than by techniques used individually.

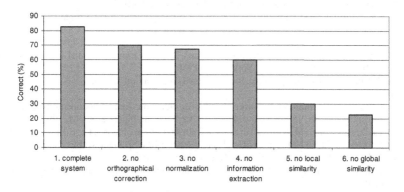

Fig. 6. Recall

6 Conclusion

In this paper we describe a hybrid approach for the management of FAQ documents in Portuguese by integrating techniques from Case-Based Reasoning and Information Retrieval. In comparison to other existing approaches, this work contributes especially to the automatic information extraction of queries or FAQ documents in Portuguese language and the semi-automatic support for the continuous evolution of domain knowledge. The techniques developed do not only offer an effective and efficient approach for the retrieval of documents in Portuguese, but can also be easily adapted to other Latin languages. The prototypical implementation of this approach is currently being undertaken by the Cyclops research group at the Federal University of Santa Catarina. Based on feedback from its usage in practice, we intend to direct further research on the extension of the tool to other FAQ areas (e.g., medical image interpretation) as well as the evolution and generalization of the developed techniques.

Acknowledgments. The authors would like to thank all members of The Cyclops Project who participated in the initial study and the application of the FAQ@Smalltalk System as well as the anonymous reviewers for their helpful comments and Leslie Paas for reviewing the final version of the paper.

References

[1] M. S. Ackerman. Augmenting the Organizational Memory: A Field Study of Answer Garden. Proc. of the ACM Conference on Computer Supported Cooperative Work,1994.

[2] A. Aamodt, E. Plaza. Case-Based Reasoning: Foundational Issues, Methodological Variations, and System Approaches. AI Communications, 17(1), 1994.

[3] K. Ashley. Progress in Text-Based Case-Based Reasoning. International Conference on Case-Based Reasoning, Germany, 1999.

[4] R. Burke, K. Hammond, V. Kulyukin, S. Lytinen, N. Tomuro, S. Schoenberg.. Question Answering from Frequently Asked Question Files. AI Magazine, 18(2), 1997.

[5] A. Bortolon. Desenvolvimento e Implementação de uma Abordagem Hibrida para a Gerência de Documentos FAQ em Portugues. Master Thesis, Production Engineering, Federal University of Santa Catarina, 2001.

[6] N. Chomsky. Aspects of the Theory of Syntax. MIT Press, Cambridge, USA, 1965.

[7] H. Chen, K. J. Lynch, K. Basu, T. Ng. Generating, Integrating, and Activating Thesauri for Concept-based Document Retrieval. IEEE Expert, 8(2), April 1993.

[8] L. F. L. Cintra. Nova Gramatica do Portugues Contemporaneo, Nova Fronteira,1979.

[9] J. J. Daniels, E. L. Rissland. What You Saw Is What You Want: Using Cases to Seed Information. Proc. of the Int. Conference on Case-Based Reasoning, Rhode Island,1997.

[10] J. Fillmore. The Case for Case. In Bach, E. Harms, R.T. (eds.), Universals in Linguistic Theory, Holt, Rinehart & Winston, New York, USA, 1968.

[11] G. H. Kuenning,R.U. Karpischek. International Ispell Version 3.1.20. (ftp://ftp.cs.ucla.edu)

[12] V. Kulyukin, K. Hammond, R. Burke, Answering Questions for an Organization Online. Proceedings of the 15th National Conference on Artificial Intelligence, AAAI, 1998.

[13] M. Lenz, A. Hübner, M. Kunze. Textual CBR. In M. Lenz et al (eds.), Case-Based Reasoning Technology. Lecture Notes in Artificial Intelligence 1400. Springer Verlag, 1998.

[14] E. A. Llorach. Gramática Estructural, Editorial Gredos,1991.

[15] G. Salton, M. J. McGill. Introduction to Modern Information Retrieval. New York: McGraw Hill, 1983.

[16] Nicola Zingarelli. Vocabulario Della Ligua Italian. French & European Publication,1994.

Taxonomic Conversational Case-Based Reasoning

Kalyan Moy Gupta[1,2]

[1]ITT Industries, AES Division, Alexandria, VA 22303
[2]Navy Center for Applied Research in Artificial Intelligence,
Naval Research Laboratory, Washington, DC 20375
gupta@aic.nrl.navy.mil

Abstract. Conversational Case-Based Reasoning (CCBR) systems engage a user in a series of questions and answers to retrieve cases that solve his/her current problem. Help-desk and interactive troubleshooting systems are among the most popular implementations of the CCBR methodology. As in traditional CBR systems, features in a CCBR system can be expressed at varying levels of abstraction. In this paper, we identify the sources of abstraction and argue that they are uncontrollable in applications typically targeted by CCBR systems. We contend that ignoring abstraction in CCBR can cause representational inconsistencies, adversely affect retrieval and conversation performance, and lead to case indexing and maintenance problems. We propose an integrated methodology called *Taxonomic CCBR* that uses feature taxonomies for handling abstraction to correct these problems. We describe the benefits and limitations of our approach and examine issues for future research.

1 Introduction

Case-Based Reasoning (CBR) systems support problem-solving by recalling and applying those experiences or cases that are similar to the problem at hand (Kolodner, 1993). A wide range of applications has been developed using CBR methodology. By far, the most frequently developed real-world applications of CBR include help-desk, interactive troubleshooting, and equipment maintenance systems. These systems engage a user in a series of questions and answers to retrieve cases that solve his/her problem. They have been referred to in the literature as *Conversational CBR* (CCBR) systems (Aha *et al.*, 2001).

A pervasive issue in CCBR case bases, and case bases in general, is that the case contents and their features may be expressed at different levels of abstraction (Baudin & Waterman, 1998; Kolodner, 1993; Shimazu, 1998). For example, a feature in a printer troubleshooting application could be expressed generally as "My printer is showing an error message" or more specifically as "My printer is showing a paper out error." Ignoring abstraction can create unique problems for end users, case base developers, and the CCBR system.

In this paper, we note that the existing CCBR approaches only partially address abstraction. We propose that CCBR systems should be designed with an integrated approach for supporting abstraction. The remainder of the paper is organized as follows. In Section 2, we identify the problems that result when abstraction is ignored in CCBR. In Section 3, we develop an integrated methodology called *Taxonomic*

D.W. Aha and I. Watson (Eds.): ICCBR 2001, LNAI 2080, pp. 219–233, 2001.

CCBR to overcome these problems. Section 4 summarizes the benefits and limitations of our approach. Section 5 presents related work on CCBR systems. Section 6 concludes the paper.

2 Abstraction in CCBR Systems

Features of a CCBR system may be expressed at different levels of abstraction. For example, a problem in the domain where weather is a factor in decision-making (e.g., a Noncombatant Evacuation Operation Planning (DoD, 1997)) may record weather conditions at the following levels of abstraction:

    (1.) The weather was bad

        (1.1) The weather was stormy

            (1.1.1) The wind speed was very high

                (1.1.1.1) The wind speed was over 90 mi./hr.

Abstraction affects interactive decision support systems in two ways: (1) The communication between a human user and the system becomes problematic (Furnas *et al.*, 1987), and (2) the design, development, and maintenance of systems for optimal performance becomes a problem (Pedrycz & Vukovich, 2000). CBR systems are prone to the same problems.

In general, CBR systems have dealt with abstraction in a limited way (Kolodner, 1993; See for example Alterman (1986)). For traditional CBR systems that are highly structured and do not engage in a conversation, the communication between human user and the system is usually not a problem. In these systems, the approach has been to design abstraction into them. For example, Bergmann and Wilke (1996) and Branting and Aha (1995) have used cases and features at   predefined levels of abstraction to reduce the representational complexity and to improve the retrieval efficiency of case bases. Likewise, Drastal and Czako (1989) compute an abstract representational feature space for inductive learning to improve the learning and classification accuracy of their system. These systems are restricted to well-defined application domains such as hierarchical planning and do not require conversation. The assumption that system developers can define feature spaces at suitable levels of abstraction for optimal system performance is unrealistic for a highly dynamic CCBR application. In CCBR, not only can case features occur at multiple levels of abstraction, but neither the feature set nor their levels of abstraction can be determined with certainty in advance and over the life-cycle of the case base. The problem is that the domain is often both ill structured and dynamic (i.e., features and cases continue to be added over the life cycle of the case base). In addition, end users have different backgrounds and degrees of expertise than case authors. In the following subsections, we examine the sources of abstraction and the ways in which it affects CCBR systems.

2.1   Sources of Abstraction

We identify the following sources of abstraction:

1. *Variations in the level of domain expertise between users and developers*: The level of domain expertise is the dominant factor in a user's ability to describe and formulate problems (i.e., specify features and their values). Experts can be very

precise, complete, or very abstract in their description, whereas non-experts' description are usually imprecise, incomplete, or ambiguous (Arocha & Patel, 1995). Consequently, there can be significant differences in the levels of abstraction between users and developers.

2. *Variations in information availability and the cost of its acquisition*: Lack of information or the expense of acquiring it at the desired level of abstraction (i.e., detail) can limit a user's ability to provide it. For example, in the description of a weather condition described above, the wind speed information may not be available or it may be too expensive to acquire because it may require a setup of measuring instruments. This is particularly true of customer support and troubleshooting applications where information may be unavailable or may only become available in the future. Variations in information availability and the cost of acquisition affect the level of abstraction.

3. *Variations in decision-making needs*: The most appropriate level of abstraction depends on user's decision-making and problem solving needs (Rosch, 1978). Often the information is available at a higher level of precision (i.e., lower level of abstraction), however, information at a lower level of precision (i.e., higher level of abstraction) may be sufficient. Variations and differences in decision-making needs affect the appropriate level of abstraction.

These sources are to a large extent uncontrollable and CCBR systems must be capable of tolerating their effects. Ignoring them can result in problems discussed in the following section.

2.2   Problems Due to Ignoring Abstraction

Abstraction has not been addressed adequately in CCBR systems. However, the issue of vocabulary differences between end users and case authors has been recognized (Shimazu, 1999). Such differences adversely impact the user system communication and limit the effective use of a CCBR system. Still, the connection between abstraction as a source of vocabulary differences and its adverse impact on CCBR performance has not been established. In a CCBR system, abstract features are frequently used to classify a problem into a case (Trott & Leng, 1997). However, a common over simplification is mixing the abstract features with the more specific case features into a single level (e.g., a list of question answer pairs, (Aha *et al.*, 1998)). This leads to the following problems:

1. *Unwanted correlation among features*: Placing abstract and specific features in the same level introduces significant unwanted correlation among them. This can be problematic for nearest-neighbor matching functions that assume independent uncorrelated features. Often, artful weighting of questions is required to address such feature correlation (Trott & Leng, 1997).

2. *Limited ability to assess similarity*: Ignoring abstract relations between features is in effect ignoring their similarity. In systems that ignore abstraction, two cases describing the same problem using different features related by abstraction cannot be assessed as similar. This leads to redundancy and inconsistency among cases (Everett & Bobrow, 2000; Racine &Yang, 2001).

3. *Redundant questions are generated during conversation*: Depending on the user's approach to problem description, redundant and irrelevant questions are presented by the conversation algorithm. Often, this is a result of ignoring the abstract relations between questions. Background knowledge in the form of rules and models can be used to answer other questions and overcome the problem (Aha *et al.*, 1998). Question selection algorithms using frequency or information theoretic measures are likely to be misled by abstraction (e.g., Aha et al., 1998, Yang & Wu, 2001), as are those that use probabilistic or belief net strategies (e.g., Montazemi & Gupta, 1996; McSherry, 2001).

4. *Loss of decisional information due to feature generalization*: When a single level of feature abstraction is encoded, often abstract features are retained over specific features to improve the applicability of a case to new problems. This can be problematic because discarding specific features during indexing can cause loss of vital information needed for discriminating cases (Kolodner, 1993).

5. *Difficulty of assigning indices*: Not unlike authors of scientific publications who assign keywords to their paper, case authors face a difficult problem of indexing, without the benefit of a predefined question list. A case author often tends to index a case using multiple features that express the same semantic feature at different levels of abstraction. This is done to improve the recall and to manage conversation (Trott & Leng, 1997).

6. *Inconsistencies develop in case representation when new features are added:* Introducing new generalized features without the ability to accommodate abstraction relationships among them can yield situations where related cases are expressed and represented with a combination of features that are conflicting or at inconsistent levels of abstraction.

In the following section, we propose an integrated methodology to handle abstraction in CCBR systems. To this end, we recognize abstract relations between features and explicitly structure them into taxonomies. We exploit these taxonomies to develop a new case representation scheme. We call a CCBR system that incorporates this methodology as a *Taxonomic CCBR* system.

3   Proposed Taxonomic CCBR System

3.1   Case Representation with Feature Taxonomies

CCBR tools that support problem solving typically use a case representation structure that includes a problem description and a solution. The problem is described by a set of question-answer (i.e., feature and a value) pair, which is the basis of case retrieval (Aha *et al.* 1998; Gupta, 1998).   For example, a printer troubleshooting CCBR application may have the following question answer pair: "Do you have a print quality problem?=*Yes.*"

We assume that the Taxonomic CCBR includes the following:
1. A *set of questions* Q that are used for indexing cases. The ith member of Q is denoted by q_i $(0 < i \leq n$, where n = number of questions in the case base) and has

a set of answers $\boldsymbol{a}_i$ applicable to it. The jth member of $\boldsymbol{a}_i$ is denoted by $a_{i,j}$ $(0 < j \leq m_i,$ where m_i = number of possible answers for q_i). We denote a specific question answer pair $(q_i, a_{i,j})$ by $qa_{i,j}$. We denote the set of all possible question answer pairs by $\boldsymbol{QA}$. For example, in a printer troubleshooting CCBR application, a question in the set $\boldsymbol{Q}$ regarding the nature of print quality problems could be "What does the print quality look like?" with "*Black Streaks*", "*Faded*", and "*No Problem*" as potential answers. For simplicity, we consider only binary and nominal valued questions. Our experience shows that, in CCBR applications, a disproportionately large number of questions are binary and nominal valued (Gupta, 1998).

2. *Feature Taxonomies*: We define a feature taxonomy $\boldsymbol{T}$ to be an acyclic directed graph comprising nodes t_j $(0 < j \leq l,$ where l = number of nodes in the taxonomy). A node t_j in a taxonomy includes a question-answer pair drawn from the set $\boldsymbol{QA}$. It is related to a set of parent nodes π_j. The relationships between node t_j and its parents are either of type *is-a-type-of* or *is-a-part-of*. If the set π_j is empty t_j is the *root node* of the taxonomy. The node t_j is also related to a set of child nodes denoted by χ_j. If the set χ_i is empty, t_j is *a leaf node* in $\boldsymbol{T}$. The relationships between nodes are transitive. If a node t_i is a ancestor of t_j we denote this relationship by $t_i = \pi(t_j)$. Also, an ancestor node is said to *subsume* all its descendent nodes. Figure 1 shows a subset of the taxonomy from a CCBR application for printer troubleshooting.   In this figure, the node t_2 representing question-answer pair "Print quality problem?=*Yes*" has one parent node t_1 and two child nodes t_5 and t_6.

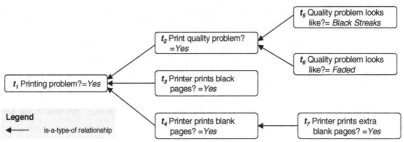

Fig. 1. Subset of a feature taxonomy from a printer troubleshooting application

A Taxonomic CCBR includes a set of taxonomies each representing a family of question-answer pairs interrelated by abstract relations.

3. *A set of cases* $\boldsymbol{C}$: We define a case C_k $(0 < k \leq r,$ where r = number of cases in the case base) to include the following:
   a. *Problem State*: This is a set of question-answer pairs $\boldsymbol{P}_k$. The members of $\boldsymbol{P}_k$ are drawn from the set of question-answer pairs $\boldsymbol{QA}$ in the case base and are denoted by $p_{k,i}$ $(0 < i \leq r_k,$ where r_k = number of question answer pairs in $\boldsymbol{P}_k$). We apply the following representational rules to the question-answer pairs in $p_{k,i}$:
      i. **Only one question-answer pair from a taxonomy can be included in a case**: No two question-answer pairs in a case refer to the same question and no two pairs are related by an abstract relation. This representational rule eliminates redundant indexing and correlation among features in a

case. For example, referring to the Figure 1, a case cannot simultaneously include question answer pairs t_2 and t_6, but may include either t_2 or t_6.

ii. **The most specific available and applicable question-answer pair is used to represent the case**: This representational rule is based on the assumption that specific question-answer pairs are more likely to include the necessary information required to discriminate cases. For example, referring to Figure 1, if t_6 applies to the case and is known at the time of indexing the case, t_6 should be included in it.

b. *Solution*: We denote a solution in case C_k by S_k. The solution includes a sequence of actions that corrects the problem described by the problem state.

Table 1 compares the Taxonomic CCBR case representation with a current approach (e.g., Aha *et al.*, 1998). Taxonomic CCBR eliminates redundant indexing and reduces the number of features used for representing the case. Further, the textual problem description in cases is eliminated by our search technique presented in Section 3.2.

Table 1. Comparison of the Taxonomic CCBR case representation with a typical CCBR case representation for a printer troubleshooting application

Case Representation	Example Text	Taxonomic CCBR	CCBR
Case Title	Ink cartridge is damaged causing black streaks.	Included	Included
Text Description	Vertical black streaks or smears appear on successive pages	*Excluded*	Included
qa pairs	Do you have a print quality problem? = *Yes*	*Excluded*	Included
	What does the print quality look like? = *Black streaks*	Included	Included
	Does cleaning the printer with cleaning paper remove problem? = *No*	Included	Included
Solution	Check toner cartridge and replace if it is low in toner or damaged. For toner level, check the indicator on the left side of the cartridge.	Included	Included

For simplicity, we ignore feature weighting that is typically included in CCBR systems.

3.2   Taxonomic CCBR Processes

A problem solving session with a CCBR system proceeds as follows (Aha *et al.*, 1998; Gupta, 1999) (See Figure 2). The user *describes* a problem with a short textual description. Next, the system *retrieves* cases by *search*ing, *match*ing, and *rank*ing (Gupta & Montazemi, 1997). The user and the system engage in a *conversation* where the system selects, rank orders, and presents questions to the user and the user refines his/her problem description by selecting and answering questions from those presented by the system. The conversation and retrieval iterate until the user finds a case that solves his/her problem or determines that no existing case solves his/her problem. Depending on the situation the user may select a case and apply its solution or trigger new case acquisition.

Consider a user query description Q. It includes the following:

1. *Textual problem description (QT)*: Search for potentially relevant cases is initiated by the textual problem description.

2. *Problem description represented by a set of question answer pairs QP*. The members of *QP* are drawn from the set of question answer pairs *QA* in the case base and are denoted by qp_i ($0 < i \leq w_k$, where w_k = number of question answer pairs in *QP*).

Using this notation, we present our methodologies for case retrieval, conversation, and acquisition.

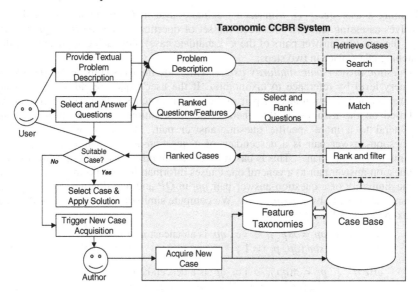

Fig. 2. User interactions with a Taxonomic CCBR system

Case Retrieval. Case retrieval includes searching, matching, ranking and selection steps.

Step I-Search

Search for potentially relevant cases is initiated by *QT*. The search includes the following steps:

1. *Question-answer pair identification*: The system matches the textual problem description *QT* with question answer pairs in *QA* to identify the question answer pair that is most similar to the users textual description. One of the many available string and text matching algorithms can be used for this purpose (e.g., using n-grams). We denote this initially identified question-answer pair as qp_1. This step is only performed once in a problem solving session and it eliminates the need for a text problem description in a case.

2. *Search scope expansion by taxonomy traversal*: For each member qp_i in *QP* traverse its corresponding taxonomy T_i to identify all its descendants. This step expands the search scope.

3. *Candidate cases selection*: For all the descendant nodes identify their associated cases. An inverted index could be used for this purpose or the cases can be indexed directly on the taxonomies. We denote the candidate set of cases for a query Q by C_Q.

Step II-Match

Matching a user query Q with each candidate case in C_Q establishes its rank. It involves assessing similarity between the set of question-answer pairs in QP and P_k (i.e., the question-answer pairs of the kth candidate case). For each candidate case, the matching takes place in two steps:

1. *Question answer pair similarity assessment*: This involves considering the user's query level by reference to taxonomies. If the user's question-answer pair is an ancestor of a question-answer pair in the case, it matches with a score of 1. This is based on the assumption that there is no information loss when moving from general to a more specific question-answer pair. However, when the user's question-answer pair is a descendant of a question-answer pair in the case, the similarity is less than 1. This is based on the assumption that moving from specific question-answer pair to a general one causes information loss. Formally, we denote the similarity of a question-answer pair qp_i in QP and question-answer pair p_{kj} in candidate case C_k by $sim_k(qp_i, p_{kj})$. We compute similarity between two nodes in a taxonomy as follows:

if $qp_i = \pi(p_{kj})$,   i.e., qp_i is an ancestor of p_{kj}
$$sim_k(qp_i, p_{kj}) = 1 ; \tag{1}$$

else if $p_{kj} = \pi(qp_i)$,   i.e., qp_i is a descendant of p_{kj}
$$sim_k(qp_i, p_{kj}) = (n+1-m)/(n+1+m); \tag{2}$$

where, n = the number of links between qp_i and the root of the taxonomy
m = is the number of links between p_{kj} and qp_i.
Otherwise $sim_k(qp_i, p_{kj}) = 0;$ $\tag{3}$

Note that the similarity metric is asymmetric because of its reference to the user's query level. Furthermore, the metric in equation 2 considers the depth and the density of the taxonomy to establish a notion of semantic distance by including a normalizing factor in the denominator. For the same m, the similarity of nodes at deeper levels of the taxonomy is higher. Table 2 shows an example similarity computation by referring to the taxonomy shown in Figure 1.

Table 2. Example of question-answer pair similarity assessment

(qp_i, p_{kj})	Applicable Condition	sim_k
t_2, t_6	qp_i is an ancestor of p_{kj}	1.0
t_6, t_2	qp_i is a descendant of p_{kj}, $n=2$, $m=1$	0.5
t_6, t_1	qp_i is a descendant of p_{kj}, $n=2$, $m=2$	0.2
t_4, t_6	Otherwise	0.0

2. *Aggregate similarity score assessment using a similarity metric*: We compute the overall similarity of a user query QP with a case problem description P_k denoted by $Sim_k(QP, P_k)$ by adapting the Rogers and Tanimoto (1960) similarity coefficient to include graded similarity as follows:

$$Sim_k(QP, P_k) = \frac{\sum_{i \in QP, j \in P_k} sim_k(qp_i, p_{k,j})}{T} \qquad (3)$$

Where T is the number of taxonomies common to the question-answer pairs of QP and P_k.

Step III-Rank and Select

A set of retrieved cases C_R that is a subset of candidate cases C_Q is presented to the user ranked in descending order by the similarity score.

Conversation. Conversation involves presenting the user with a rank ordered set of questions derived from C_R. We denote such a set presented in response to user query description Q by Q^Q. We select and rank order the members of Q^Q in the following steps:

1. *Taxonomy selection*: By reference to C_R, select the applicable taxonomies based on their question-answer pairs.
2. *Question scoring and selection:* To select an ordered list of questions, by reference to applicable taxonomies selected in step 1, we first score each question-answer pair in the taxonomies and then score the corresponding questions as follows:
   a. Question-answer pair and taxonomy scoring: The score at a node t_i in a taxonomy T is denoted by $s(t_i)$. It is the sum of scores of all its child nodes and the aggregate similarity scores of those retrieved cases that are indexed by it. We perform a backward pass on the taxonomy to compute all its node scores. Consider the example shown in Figure 3. It shows an extension of the printing problem taxonomy with example case similarities and node scores. We assume that the user's problem description contains a question-answer pair t_1 based on which the cases 1,2,3,7, and 11 were retrieved with scores as shown. For example, we compute the $s(t_4)$ as follows:
   $$(s(t_4) = 0.6) = (Sim_{11} = 0.2) + (s(t_7) = 0.4)$$
   We denote the score of the root node as the taxonomy score $s(T)$. In the example, $s(T) = 2.0$.
   b. Question selection and scoring: If the user problem description already contains a question-answer pair from the taxonomy, then we select its children. By reference to Figure 3 in our previous example, given that the user had selected t_1, we select nodes t_2, t_3, and t_4 for presenting questions. If the user problem description does not contain any question-answer pair from the taxonomy, then we select the most specific node that subsumes the set of retrieved cases C_R. Consider the following example scenario by reference to the taxonomy shown in Figure 3. We assume that C_R consists of only case 1 ($Sim_1 = 0.5$) and case 2 ($Sim_2 = 0.5$). We also assume that the cases 3,7, and 11 are not retrieved because their scores were below the specified threshold (e.g., ≤ 0). In this scenario, the most specific node subsuming C_R is t_2 with a score $s(t_2) = 0.9$.

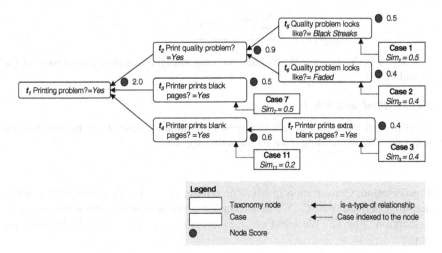

Fig. 3. An example of question-answer pair scoring using the backward pass algorithm.

3. *Question ranking:* The score of a question q_i, denoted by $s(q_i)$ is a tuple '< >' with two values: taxonomy score $s(T)$, and sum of its corresponding question-answer pair scores. For example, the score for the question "print quality problem" is $s(q) = <2.0, 0.9>$. The members of Q^Q are sorted in descending order on their taxonomy score followed by the question-answer score.

During a problem solving session, if the user selects more than one question-answer pair from the same taxonomy, the most specific question-answer pair is retained in *QP*. For the example taxonomy shown in Figure 1, if the user selects t_1 (Printing Problem?=*Yes*) and t_2 (Print Quality Problem=*Yes*), t_2 is retained and t_1 is discarded. This rule is the same as the one that applies to the case representation to enforce representational consistency.

We illustrate the advantages of the question selection and ranking technique by the following two examples. We assume that users interact with a Taxonomic CCBR system to troubleshoot printers, parts of which have been presented earlier.

Example 1, Abstract problem description: Consider a scenario where the user starts with a textual problem description *QT* such as "I am having printing problems." The CCBR application determines using search step 1 that the corresponding question-answer pair is "Printing Problem?=*Yes*." Based on this question-answer pair, the search expands the query to include all its descendents using the taxonomy presented in Figure 3 and retrieves cases 1,2,3,7, and 11. Let us assume that the overall similarity scores were the same as presented earlier. The user is presented with the following questions in order (for simplicity, we exclude other questions that might be derived from the candidate cases):

> Do you have a print quality problem?
> Is the printer printing blank pages?
> Is the printer printing black pages?

We assume that the user answers the question "Print quality problem?" with a *Yes*. Consequently, the question answer pair "Print quality problem?=*Yes*" is used to replace the earlier general question "Printing problem?=*Yes*." The traversal on taxonomy from node t_2 (i.e., search step 2) implies that only cases 1 and 2 are retrieved with scores 0.5 and 0.4. In this iteration, only the nodes t_1, t_2, t_5, and t_6 have scores greater than 0. The nodes that are subordinate to t_2 are t_5 and t_6. Therefore, the question presented is "What does the quality problem look like?" This example illustrates how the conversation guides a user in refining his/her problem description when the query is expressed at an abstract level.

Example 2, Specific problem description: Consider a scenario where the user starts with a textual problem description QT such as "I have black streaks on my printout." Taxonomic CCBR application determines using search step 1 that the corresponding question-answer pair is "Printing quality problem?=*Black Streaks*." Since this question-answer pair does not have any descendents, the search only retrieves case 1 and there is no further conversation.

Comparing examples 1 and 2, we note that the retrieval and conversation appropriately respond to the abstraction level of user's problem description. On the one hand, when a user expresses his/her query at an abstract level, s/he is guided in progressively refining his/her query. On the other hand, when the user expresses a query at a concrete or specific level s/he is spared irrelevant general questions and presented with a set of cases with high precision.

Case Acquisition. During a problem solving session, if no suitable cases are presented to the user, s/he can trigger new case acquisition. Typically, in such a scenario, the unsolved problem session comprising the user's problem description is complemented with a solution by a case author. The case author then adds the new case to the case base by following these steps:

1. Add new questions to the case base. Depending on the availability of information in a new case, the case author has the flexibility to retain and create new question-answer pairs at appropriate levels of abstraction. Our proposed methodology does not force an author to generalize or specialize a new question to one that already exists as would happen in CCBR system where abstraction is ignored.
2. Add the corresponding question-answer pairs to existing taxonomies or create new taxonomies.
3. Index the new case with appropriate question-answer pairs.

4 Advantages of Taxonomic CCBR

The following are the benefits of Taxonomic CCBR:
1. *Consistent and efficient representation*: Taxonomic CCBR methodology ensures representational *consistency* in user queries and stored cases. That is, a case or query cannot be indexed by more than one question-answer pair that belong to the same taxonomy. It also makes the case representation *efficient* since it is indexed by *fewer* and only the most specific question-answer pairs available at the time of indexing. There is no need for redundant indexing with a combination of general

and specific features because the taxonomic search appropriately expands the search scope.

2. *Accurate and responsive retrieval:* Representational consistency eliminates any unwanted correlation among features that could result from inherent abstract relationships between question-answer pairs. This simplifies and improves matching. The retrieval is responsive to the abstraction level in the user's query since it appropriately expands or contracts search scope using taxonomic traversal.

3. *Responsive conversation with reduced information load*: The conversation is responsive to the level of abstraction in a user's query. Furthermore, the information load during the conversation is reduced since only the questions from the most appropriate level of abstraction are selected.

4. *Simplified and flexible case maintenance*: Since the representational consistency can be enforced by feature taxonomies, error prone and redundant indexing of cases is eliminated. Case maintenance is simplified as new features are introduced because only the taxonomies need to be maintained. In addition, the taxonomic CCBR methodology affords *indexing flexibility* by allowing case authors to create new question-answer pairs at appropriate levels of abstraction thereby preserving information at the level of abstraction at which it was originally expressed.

These benefits, however, come at an expense (See Table 3). First, the computational complexity is increased by taxonomic traversal during retrieval and conversation. A worst-case scenario analysis shows that this increase is linear with the maximum number of nodes in any taxonomy (i.e., m). However, the gains in representational efficiency ($\hat{q} \leq q$) can partially offset this increase. Second, the space requirement in Taxonomic CCBR increases linearly with the number of question-answer pairs in the case base $O(Q.A)$. Third, additional knowledge engineering is needed to develop and maintain feature taxonomies, which is not discussed here.

Table 3. Computation and Space Complexity Comparison

Complexity	CCBR	Taxonomic CCBR
Computation	$O(Cq^2)$	$O(C\hat{q}^2 m)$
Space	$O(CQ + QA)$ Cases + Question answers	$= O(CQ + QA)$ Cases + Taxonomies
C= number of cases in the case base Q= total number of questions in the case base A= Maximum number of possible answers per question q = Maximum number of questions per case in regular CCBR $\hat{q}$ = Maximum number of questions per case in Taxonomic CCBR ($\hat{q} \leq q$) m = Maximum number of nodes in a taxonomy		

Nonetheless, we conjecture that our claimed benefits are likely to outweigh the above expenses. As presented in Section 6, we intend to empirically investigate this conjecture in our future research. We plan to compare the existing CCBR performance with Taxonomic CCBR in terms of representational efficiency, retrieval accuracy, conversational efficiency, and development and maintenance effort (e.g., taxonomies).

5 Related Work

The commercial success of CCBR applications has been particularly noteworthy in troubleshooting and help-desk tasks. However, the performance of these systems can be significantly affected by the extent of their scope, complexity, and application domain dynamics. This issue presents opportunities for formalizing and improving CCBR. For example, Montazemi and Gupta (1996) presented a diagnostic CBR application for troubleshooting AC motors called TRAAC. TRAAC used an adaptive agent to converse with a troubleshooter. The conversation was generated using a belief net to assist the troubleshooter in the identification of potential hypotheses and tests. The user selections were used to retrieve appropriate cases. While this approach was effective, it required the development and the maintenance of belief nets. Furthermore, they did not recognize the abstract relations among features (e.g., "Motor vibration" and "Drive-end motor vibration"). This research recognizes such abstract relations and exploits it for retrieval and conversation. However, we do not consider causal and evidential relationship among features that might be pertinent to troubleshooting applications.

Aha *et al.* (1998) addressed the problem of redundant questions in conversation by means of their CCBR tool NaCoDAE. They examined rule-based and model-based approaches to automatically answer questions. Their approach led to more efficient conversation and retrieval. In their example application to printer troubleshooting, they include abstraction as *instance-of* and *implies* relations. However, unlike the Taxonomic CCBR, their approach was not explicitly motivated by abstraction. Aha *et al.* (2001) present problems of representational redundancies arising from case design guidelines that promote the use of general and specific features to index cases. They correct these inconsistencies in part by automatically revising case libraries. In contrast, we exploit the abstract relations in the feature taxonomies to create a robust representation framework that eliminates representational inconsistencies and simplifies similarity assessment. Instead of automatically answering questions we exploit the taxonomy to tailor the conversation and retrieval to the level of abstraction in the user's problem description.

McSherry (2001) addressed user interface issues in CCBR application for sequential diagnosis. His research focused on determining an optimal conversation strategy based on an attribute's ability to confirm or disconfirm candidate hypotheses. Our research differs from his in terms of assumptions we make about the domain. We assume heterogeneous case structures where abstraction is an issue combined with the domain dynamics as opposed to homogeneous case structures at a single-level of abstraction. Consequently, our research focuses on feature taxonomies to support the differences in conceptual level of end users. It conducts conversation and retrieval that is responsive to these differences.

Carrick *et al.* (1999) addressed the problem of trivial or repeated questions that CCBR systems prompts a user. They reduce the number of questions asked of the user by accessing other information sources that can be used to answer them. Their question generation strategy considers information quality together with the cost of acquiring information from additional sources to conduct the conversation. Their notion of information quality is very similar to our question-answer score. However, they did not consider feature abstraction in their system nor do they address the representational problems that arise from it.

6 Conclusion

In this paper, we established that sources of variation and differences in levels of abstraction are, in large part, uncontrollable in application domains typically targeted by CCBR systems such as help-desk and troubleshooting. Because CCBR systems are mixed-initiative systems their performance can be adversely affected when abstraction among features is ignored. We argued that ignoring abstraction could cause representational inconsistencies, redundant conversations, poor case retrieval performance, and numerous indexing and case maintenance problems.

We presented an integrated methodology called Taxonomic CCBR that explicitly represents abstract relations in taxonomies. We showed that the methodology eliminates representational inconsistencies, generates non-redundant conversation that adapts to the abstraction level of a user's problem description, and dramatically simplifies case indexing and case base maintenance. In our future work, we plan to empirically assess the benefits and limitations of Taxonomic CCBR. We recognize that the success of Taxonomic CCBR could be limited by the availability of tools and methodologies for acquisition and maintenance of taxonomies. We will investigate these methodologies in future research.

While we contend that the Taxonomic CCBR methodologies can improve the performance of existing CCBR systems, there can be other kinds of relationships among features that could be pertinent to CCBR systems and were not included in our methodology. For example, troubleshooting and diagnostic domains can include causal and evidential relations among features (e.g., Montazemi & Gupta (1995); McSherry, 2001). We intend to explore this issue further in our research.

Finally, we believe that this research is relevant to textual CBR systems that retrieve short text documents (Ashley & Lenz, 1998). In such systems, document cases do not undergo extensive knowledge engineering and abstraction is a common problem. A problem resulting from abstraction is that of case redundancy and inconsistency (Everett & Bobrow, 2000; Racine &Yang, 2001). In our future work, we will examine the applications of this research to textual CBR.

Acknowledgements. This research was funded by the Design For Safety Program of the NASA Ames Research Center, Naval Research Laboratory, and the Office of Naval Research. Thanks to David Aha, Karl Branting, David McSherry, Len Breslow, and the three anonymous reviewers for their helpful comments on an earlier version of this paper.

References

Aha, D.W., Breslow, L.A., & Munoz-Avila, H., (2001), Conversational Case-Based Reasoning, *Applied Intelligence*, 14(1), pp. 9-31.

Aha, D.W., Maney, T., & Breslow, L.A., (1998), Supporting Dialogue Inferencing in Conversational Case-Based Reasoning, *Advances in Case-Based Reasoning* (B. Smyth and P. Cunningham (Eds.)), 4th European Workshop EWCBR-98, Dublin, Ireland, pp. 262-273.

Alterman, R., Griffin, D., (1994), Remembering Episodes of Question Answering, *Proceedings of the Second European Workshop on Case-Based Reasoning*, EWCBR-94, M. Keane, J.P. Haton, M. Manago (Eds.), pp. 235-242.

Arocha, J.F. & Patel, V.L., (1995), Diagnostic Reasoning by Novices: Accounting For Evidence, *Journal of Learning Sciences*, 4(4), pp. 355-384.

Ashley, K.D., & Lenz, M. (Eds.), (1998), Textual Case-Based Reasoning, Papers from the AAAI-98 Workshop, AAAI Tech. Rep. WS-98-12, *AAAI Press*, Melno Park, CA.

Baudin, C., & Waterman, S., (1998), From Text to Cases: Machine Aided Text Categorization for Capturing Business Reengineering Cases, *Proceedings of the AAAI Workshop on Textual Case-Based Reasoning, Technical Report WS-98-12*, pp. 51-57.

Bergmann, R., & Wilke, W., (1996), On the Role of Abstraction in Case-Based Reasoning, (I. Smith and B. Faltings (Eds.)), Advances in Case-Based Reasoning, *EWCBR-96*, pp. 28-43.

Branting, K.L., & Aha, D.W., (1995), Stratified Case-Based Reasoning: Reusing Hierarchical Problem Solving Episodes, *IJCAI* 1995, Vol. 1, pp. 384-390.

Carrick, C., Yang, Q., Abi-Zeid, I., & Lamontagne, L., (1999), Activating CBR systems through autonomous information gathering. *Proceedings of the Third International Conference on Case-Based Reasoning*, Munich, Germany: Springer, pp. 74-86.

DoD (1997). *Joint tactics, techniques and procedures for noncombatant evacuation operations* (Joint Report 3-07.51). Washington, DC: Department of Defense, Joint Chiefs of Staff.

Drastal, G., & Czako, G., (1989), Induction in an abstraction space: A Form of Constructive Induction," *Proceedings of the Eleventh International Joint Conference on AI*, Vol.1, pp. 708 –712.

Everett, J.O., Bobrow, D.G., (2000), Resolving Redundancy: A Recurring Problem in a Lessons Learned System, *Intelligent Lessons Learned Systems: Papers from the AAAI Workshop (Technical Report AIC-00-005)*, Washington DC: Naval Research Laboratory, Navy Center for Applied Research in Artificial Intelligence, pp. 12-16.

Furnas, G.W., Landauer, T.K., Gomez, L.M., & Dumais, S.T., (1987), The Vocabulary Problem in Human-System Communication, *The Communications of the ACM*, 30(10), pp. 964-971.

Gupta, K.M., & Montazemi, A.R., (1997), Empirical Evaluation of Retrieval in Case-Based Reasoning Systems using Modified Cosine Matching Function, *IEEE Transactions on Systems, Man, and Cybernetics*, 27(5), pp. 601-612.

Gupta, K.M., (1998), Knowledge-Based System For Troubleshooting Complex Equipment, *International Journal of Information and Computing Science*, 1(1), pp. 29-41.

Kolodner, J.L., (1993), Case-Based Reasoning, *Morgan Kaufman*, San Mateo, CA.

McSherry, D., (2001), Interactive Case-Based Reasoning in Sequential Diagnosis, *Applied Intelligence*, 14(1), pp. 65-76.

Montazemi A.R., & Gupta K.M., (1996), An Adaptive Agent for Case Description in Diagnostic CBR Systems, *Computers in Industry*, 29(3), pp. 209-224.

Pedrycz, W., & Vukovich, G., (2000), Granular Worlds: Representation and Communication Problems, *International Journal of Intelligent Systems*, 15(11), pp. 1015-1026,

Racine, C., and Yang. Q., (2001), Redundancy and Inconsistency Detection in Large and Semi-Structured Case Bases, *IEEE Transactions on Knowledge and Data Engineering*, To appear.

Rogers, D.J., & Tanimoto, T.T., (1960), A Computer Program for Classifying Plants, *Science*, Vol. 1332, pp.1115-1118

Rosch, E., (1978), Principals of Categorization, in Cognition and Categorization, E. Rosch and B. Llyod, (Eds.) *Lawrence Earlbaum Associates Publishers*, Hillsdale, New Jersey, NJ, pp. 28-48.

Shimazu, H., (1999), Translation of Tacit Knowledge into Explicit knowledge: Analyses of Recorded Conversations between Customers and Human Agents, *Exploring Synergies of Knowledge Management and Case-Based Reasoning*, Papers from the AAAI Workshop, TR WS-99-10, pp. 81-85.

Trott, J.R., Leng, B., (1997), An Engineering Approach for Troubleshooting Case Bases, *Case-Based Reasoning Research and Development*, (Eds.) D.B. Leake and E. Plaza, ICCBR-97, pp.178-189.

Yang, Q., & Wu, J., (2001), Enhancing the Effectiveness of Interactive Case-Based Reasoning with Clustering and Decision Forests, *Applied Intelligence*, 14(1), pp. 49-64.

A Case-Based Reasoning View of Automated Collaborative Filtering

Conor Hayes[1], Pádraig Cunningham[1], and Barry Smyth[2]

[1]Trinity College Dublin
Conor.Hayes@tcd.ie
Padraig.Cunningham@tcd.ie

[2]University College Dublin
Barry.Smyth@ucd.ie

Abstract. From some perspectives Automated Collaborative Filtering (ACF) appears quite similar to Case-Based Reasoning (CBR). It works on data organised around users and assets that might be considered case descriptions. In addition, in some versions of ACF, much of the induction is deferred to run time – in the *lazy* learning spirit of CBR. On the other hand, because of its lack of semantic descriptions it seems to be the antithesis of case-based reasoning – a learning approach *based* on case representations. This paper analyses the characteristics shared by ACF and CBR, it highlights the differences between the two approaches and attempts to answer the question "When is it useful or valid to consider ACF as CBR?". We argue that a CBR perspective on ACF can only be useful if it offers insights into the ACF process and supports a transfer of techniques. In conclusion we present a case retrieval net model of ACF and show how it allows for enhancements to the basic ACF idea.

1. Introduction

In recent years there has been some discussion on whether Automated Collaborative Filtering (ACF) should be considered a form of Case-Based Reasoning (CBR). It appears that many see CBR-like characteristics in ACF. For instance, entities (users and assets) can be considered to be cases. In addition, some of the reasoning is often deferred to run-time in the lazy manner of CBR. In contrast, others view ACF as a very different approach to CBR, considering ACF to be 'representationless' in contrast to the semantic descriptions in a case representation (Smyth & Cotter, 1999) (Balbanović & Shoham, 1997).

In this paper, we present brief descriptions of case-based reasoning, content-based recommendation and automated collaborative filtering. Then the shared characteristics and differences between ACF and CBR are considered with a view to answering the question "When is it useful or valid to consider ACF as CBR?"

The conclusion of the paper is that this CBR perspective on ACF is useful and this is illustrated in section 5 where we illustrate how ACF may be implemented using a case retrieval net.

D.W. Aha and I. Watson (Eds.): ICCBR 2001, LNAI 2080, pp. 234-248, 2001.

2. Characteristics of CBR

CBR is a problem solving technique that reuses previous problem solving episodes in solving new problems. Previous problem solving episodes are stored as cases in a case-base and typically each case has a case specification part and a solution part. In a diagnosis domain for instance, the specification might describe fault symptoms and fault context and the solution describes the cause of the fault. CBR can also be used in situations where this problem-solving vocabulary is not appropriate. More generally, it can be viewed as a means of determining outcomes associated with situation descriptions. With CBR, instead of attempting to model the causal interactions that link outputs to inputs the idea is to retrieve and adapt cases when solving new problems. This is described in Figure 1 where SP is a specification of a problem that needs to be solved, SL is a solution to that problem and FP is some hypothetical First Principles reasoning that would infer the appropriate solution for the problem description SP. The idea in CBR is to avoid having to model this First Principles reasoning by instead retrieving a case with a similar description SP'and adapting the solution to that case (SL') to fit the problem in hand. The implication is that this retrieval and adaptation process is simpler to implement than the First Principles reasoning.

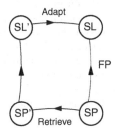

Fig. 1. The case based reasoning process; SP is a specification of a target problem and SL is a solution to that problem, SP' and SL' form a case that is retrieved to solve for this new problem (Cunningham, Finn & Slattery, 1994).

In this view, the special thing about CBR is its ability to avoid the knowledge engineering problem of modeling FP. Instead the problem solving knowledge is stored in the cases.

2.1 CBR as Lazy Learning

In the context of ACF, the other important characteristic of case-based reasoning is that it is a lazy learning technique. This means that induction is delayed to run-time, a factor that can have some important benefits. For instance, in dynamic environments where data is changing continuously, alternative eager approaches have the disadvantage that models (e.g. d-trees or neural nets) can quickly go out of date. Whereas, with the lazy approach of CBR, the induction at run-time reflects the latest data available. Also the lazy approach of CBR has the advantage that it can model local phenomena well compared to eager techniques that tend to focus on more global models. It will be clear in section 3 that these two advantages of CBR are shared by ACF.

2.2 CBR as Case Completion

The key idea in CBR is that similar problems have similar solutions. This has led to a tendency to view cases as being composed of two parts – a problem specification part and a distinct solution part. This representation is usually adequate for problem scenarios where the problem part is fully specified for a target case and the goal is to retrieve cases with similar problem specifications and use or adapt their solutions for the target problem. This model suggests that the problem specifications are available all at once and that there is no dependency on the order in which problem features are used.

In dialog based CBR there is recognition that a complete problem specification may not be available, and that the order in which the descriptors make themselves available may be important. An example of dialog – based CBR would be the CBR-NET system (Doyle & Cunningham, 2000) where the online user is posed a series of discriminating questions based on the information tendered to date. The system's goal is classification – to recommend a laptop based on the constraints incrementally tendered by the user. In the Nodal system, electronic fault diagnosis is performed by having the tester incrementally perform and submit diagnostic tests. (Cunningham, Smyth & Bonzano, 1998) In both cases the system suggests the next test to perform by carrying out an information theoretic analysis on the subset of cases remaining after submission of the previous test result.

This type of dialogue based CBR is not very different from the conventional model described above. Cases still have distinct specification and solution parts, the difference is that the specification part is filled out during the problem solving process.

Dialog Driven CBR

However, for certain types of dialog driven CBR the eliciting of a series of problem features is not only a pre-requisite but is in fact the goal or solution. In these domains the CBR system is a tool to aid problem-solving processes where the objective is to find the next step in a process considering the steps taken to date. An initial case would represent a task or process where very little information is available initially. The CBR system must suggest the steps whereby the task may be completed and the target case filled out.

Burkhard has defined CBR case completion as an elaboration of the target task by collecting case relevant information (Burkhard, 1998). This definition highlights the interactive nature of the case completion process and the requirement for incremental feedback from the real world. The feedback in this scenario is of course an extended example of the *revise* phase of the typical CBR cycle (Aamodt & Plaza, 1994). In case completion the CBR cycle is traversed several times, each period having a *retrieve, reuse* and *revise* phase until the target case is complete. The retain phase will not be engaged (if at all) until case completion is achieved.

An interesting specialization on case completion is that of *information completion* where the information to complete the case is gathered only from cases in the case base (Lenz et al., 1998) (Waszkiewicz et al., 1999). In both examples the target case represents an instance in time of a process and the goal is to find cases that suggest possible completion scenarios. Whereas in dialog based CBR the user provides the information to complete the cases, in this case completion process the information to complete the cases is inferred from the case-base.

It should be obvious that the typical case representation of problem part and solution part is inappropriate for cases where case completion is the goal. If the objective is to find the next step in a problem solving process with consideration of the steps taken to date it does not make sense to have a specified solution part. There will be no case solution that is distinct from the case specification.

Case Completion Process

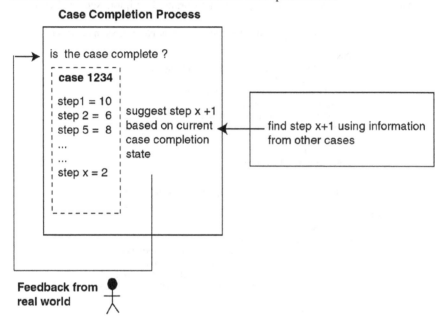

Fig. 2. A general view of the case completion process.

For case completion scenarios Burkhard and Lenz suggest that case representation should not be confined by the standard specification-solution structure. They propose a case as a *view* upon the raw data. They define the term an *Information Entity* as the basic unit of information in a case. A case is composed of a number of information entities, one of which may be designated as a solution. This representation caters for cases where information is missing, and where case completion is the goal.

2.3 Content-Based Recommendation

In the next section ACF, a *representation-less* recommendation process, is introduced; before that, we will describe a CBR-like content-based recommendation system that we can use for comparison purposes.

Table 1 shows a case-like description of a film (movie) and Table 2 shows the corresponding description of a user of the recommendation system. In this scenario recommendation is based on how well a film matches a user's profile. In producing recommendations for a user, the matching score for each film in turn would be determined and the highest scoring films not already viewed would be recommended. As will be clear in the next section, this process has advantages over ACF in working well for assets of minority interest or for new assets and users. However, the major drawback is the problem of coming up with appropriate descriptors such as Genre.

Table 1. A case-like description of a film for content based recommendation

4W&1F	
Title:	Four Weddings and a Funeral
Year:	1994
Genre:	Comedy, Romance
Director:	Mike Newell?
Starring:	Hugh Grant, Andie MacDowell
Runtime:	116
Country:	UK
Language:	English
Certification:	USA:R (UK:15)

Table 2. A case-like description of a user's interests

JB-7	
Name:	Joe Bloggs
Preferred Era:	1988 →
Genre:	Thriller, Comedy, War, Romance
Director:	S. Spielburg, F. F. Coppola.
Actors:	Sharon Stone, Sylvester Stallone, Julia Roberts, Keanu Reeves, Liam Neeson, Andie MacDowell
Runtime:	< 150
Country:	UK, US
Language:	English
Certification:	Any

3. Automated Collaborative Filtering

The basic idea of ACF can be shown using Figure 3. In this figure three users have all shown an interest in assets A, B & C (for instance they have all rented videos A B C). This high level of overlap indicates that these users have similar tastes. Further it seems a safe bet to recommend assets D and E to User 1 because they are 'endorsed' by Users 2 and 3 that have similar interests to User 1.

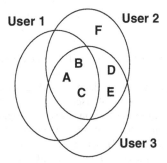

Fig. 3. A Venn diagram showing interests of three users in assets ABCDEF

One of the great strengths of ACF is that, if enough data is available, good quality recommendations can be produced without needing representations of the assets being recommended. The amount of data required depends to some extent on type of data available. In this context, there are two distinct approaches to the ACF idea that are termed *invasive* and *non-invasive*. With the invasive approach the user is explicitly asked to rate assets. This is the approach adopted by PTV (ptv.ucd.ie) for instance and clearly the data contains more information (see Table 3). Non-invasive data contains less information and can be noisy in the sense that customers may not like some of the items they have used. This can be seen in Table 4, which is a non-invasive version of Table 3. The information that User 2 dislikes asset D is lost in the non-invasive approach. Because of this data noise and loss of information more data is needed to produce good recommendations with the non-invasive approach.

Table 3. Data for use in ACF where users have explicitly rated assets.

	A	B	C	D	E	F	G
User 1	0.6	0.6	0.8			0.8	0.5
User 2		0.8	0.8	0.3	0.7		
User 3	0.6	0.6	0.3	0.5		0.7	0.5
User 4					0.7	0.8	0.7
User 5	0.6	0.6	0.8			0.7	
User 6		0.8	0.8	0.7	0.7		
User 7	0.7	0.5			0.7		
User 8					0.7	0.7	0.8

Table 4. ACF data from Table2 where users have not explicitly rated assets.

	A	B	C	D	E	F	G
User 1	1	1	1			1	1
User 2		1	1	1	1		
User 3	1	1	1	1		1	1
User 4					1	1	1
User 5	1	1	1			1	
User 6		1	1	1	1		
User 7	1	1			1		
User 8					1	1	1

Whether the data available is binary (non-invasive scenario) or contains an explicit rating, the basic structure of the recommendation process will have two distinct phases:
1. First the neighbourhood of users that will produce the recommendations must be determined.
2. Then recommendations must be produced based on the behaviour of these users.

Determining the neighbourhood of users requires a similarity metric and some examples are presented in the next section. This management of neighbourhoods can be done *eagerly* in an offline clustering process. Or it can be done *semi-eagerly* as in GroupLens (Konstan et al., 1997) where a correlations data-base of pair-wise similarities is maintained and used to identify neighbours and build recommendations at run-time. This correlation data-base is updated every 24 hours. In the next subsection we will show the detail of the operation of a lazy ACF system.

3.1 ACF – The Lazy Model

(Shardanand & Maes, 1995) evaluate a selection of similarity metrics that may be used for identifying neighbours in ACF. A simple similarity metric could be based on least-squares:

$$\sigma_{UJ} = 1 - \frac{1}{|InCommon|} \sum_{f \in InCommon} (U_f - J_f)^2 \tag{1}$$

where U_f and J_f represents user U's and user J's rating for asset f. This could be the basis for clustering users in an eager version of ACF or it could be used at run-time to identify neighbours within a threshold. These neighbours can then be used to produce ratings for a series of assets. The expected value of U's rating for asset x is:

$$U_x = \overline{U} + \frac{\sum_{J \in Raters\ of\ x} (J_x - \overline{J}) \sigma_{UJ}}{\sum_{J \in Raters\ of\ x} |\sigma_{UJ}|} \tag{2}$$

where the *Raters of x* are neighbours that have rated asset x, an asset that would be new to U. In this process an expected value for U's rating is aggregated from his neighbours. In the aggregation their ratings are normalized using their average rating, $\overline{J}$ and weighted using their similarity to U, σ_{UJ} (Billsus & Pazzani, 1998).

For binary data, the similarity of two users could be measured as:

$$\sigma_{UJ} = \frac{|InCommon(U, J)|}{|U| + |J|} \tag{3}$$

and the rating for an asset could be based on its frequency among neighbours identified with this metric. Clearly binary data is less rich and more data will be needed to produce good recommendations (compare Table 3 & Table 4).

ACF: Criticisms and Simple Extensions

"Amazon.com, the poster child of personalisation, will start recommending needlepoint books to you as soon as you order that ideal gift for your great aunt."

(www.shorewalker.com)

In fact Amazon.com does not make this mistake because the extreme representation-less view of ACF is unlikely to be pursued in practice. This mistake can be avoided by annotating assets with simple category descriptors in order to allow recommendations to be made in context. Such as simple extension will prevent knitting pattern recommendations *leaking* into a core interest in computing books for instance. This would also address the *latency* problem in ACF whereby new assets cannot be recommended until they have been rated by a number of users.

So the extreme representation-less version of ACF as described above is too restrictive. The addition of basic semantic tags adds considerable value and moves representation of assets and users (customers) more towards CBR-like cases.

ACF & CBR

So a continuum exists with extreme representation-less ACF at one end and CBR at the other. ACF can move toward CBR by attaching semantic descriptors to assets. Also, some *k*-Nearest Neighbour implementations will determine similarity with no reference to the semantics of the case features in a manner that is in the same spirit as the ACF similarity described above.

So the representation issue is not such a defining difference between ACF and CBR. The difference in representation is only one of degree. Each ACF user profile represents a history of that user's consumption along with either explicit or implicit ratings. Each ACF profile is a record of the users consumption of items to date, the goal being to recommend the next step the user should take in his/her listening or reading behaviour. This temporal perspective on ACF has been neglected to date. As such we suggest that ACF should be viewed as an attempt to model usage patterns where the goal is to suggest the next step in an ongoing process of use.

With these ideas in mind we have come to view ACF as analogous to a dialog driven CBR process. In the next sections we will present our ideas on how closely ACF parallels CBR, and describe our current work on developing a CBR based memory model for ACF. We will describe the benefits of such a system.

4. ACF as Dialog Driven CBR

ACF is a successful methodology for managing the long-term resource requirements of the online user. The user's interaction with an ACF based recommender system is usually of a sustained nature and may last from a few minutes to a few years in the case of a successful retail portal like Amazon.com. A target profile is much like a case – it is composed of a number of feature value pairs, where each feature refers to the item consumed and the rating assigned by the user. An ACF case is an incomplete one – it is essentially one row in the user–item matrix and will usually be quite sparsely populated. The key idea in viewing ACF as CBR is to recognize that the goal in ACF is case completion – an incremental elaboration of the user profile based on feedback given by the user. The system uses the information it has to hand to retrieve similar user profiles and extract completion information for the case profile which is then offered to the user. Negative user feedback may move the user toward a different set of neighbour profiles which are then used to make the next set of recommendations.

So in ACF we have an iterative recommendation process whereby the items recommended for inclusion in the user profile are determined by the feedback to date. The parallel with incremental case completion is obvious. Whilst incremental case completion might generally have a stopping point, in ACF the recommendation cycle is traversed indefinitely, each period having a *retrieve* (similar profiles), *reuse* and *revise* phase. Of course we work with the assumption that there are so many items that the user could not possibly review each, hence the recommendation cycle is repeated continuously.

The *adaptation* phase in the ACF system is the actual process of information completion, of choosing those components of neighbour profiles that are suitable for recommendation to the target user. As described in section 3.1 ACF uses weighted majority voting or the weighted aggregation of the scores of nearest neighbours to produce the recommended components for the target user profile. This may easily be compared to simple CBR adaptation techniques such as producing a solution by weighted majority voting of the k-nearest neighbours.

5. Using Case Retrieval Nets for ACF

In the previous section we examined how the typical ACF approach is similar to a lazy case completion process. Since the ACF process involves an extended dialog with many users the amount of information in the system will increase very quickly. Hence, it is appropriate to examine whether we should use our data to build eager structures that may work in conjunction with the lazy ACF process. In this section we introduce our design of an ACF memory model based on Case Retrieval Nets (CRNs). We will firstly describe basic case retrieval nets, then our implementation of them in an ACF context and finally we will describe why CRNs are an appropriate memory structure for extending ACF systems.

5.1 Case Retrieval Nets

Our initial investigation of CRNs was motivated by their use in domains where missing case information is typical and where the 'problem–solution' case representation is inappropriate. Indeed Lenz suggests that CRNs are designed specifically for information completion processes (Lenz et al., 1998). Secondly, new cases and case features can be added without having to rebuild the memory structure which is necessary for ACF where the user 'case base' and the case profiles themselves are growing. Firstly, we give a brief summary of CRNs. The reader is referred to Lenz (Lenz, 1999) for a formal definition of the CRN model.

A CRN is a memory model that builds a net instead of a tree from the case base. It uses organizational features derived from associative memory structures (Shank, 1982) and a spreading activation process similar to that used in connectionist models. In contrast to the latter, however, all the nodes and arcs in the net should have precise meaning.

The components of a basic case retrieval net are as follows:

Information Entities nodes: CRNs have a node for each Information Entity (IE) observed in the domain (see fig. 4). Information Entities are any basic knowledge item such as a particular attribute-value pair. Cases will typically be made up of a number of IEs. In order to facilitate the spreading activation process IE nodes are connected by *similarity arcs.*

Case nodes: each case in the case base has a case node which is reachable from its constituent IE nodes via *relevance arcs.*

By varying the arc weights we can express differing degrees of similarity and relevance between nodes. Case retrieval using a CRN has three stages:

1. *Initial Activation:* this involves activating the IEs in the query. Given the query, the initial activation is determined for all IE nodes.
2. *Similarity Propagation:* the second step involves incrementally propagating the activation through the net of IEs. The amount of activation depends on arc weights.
3. *Relevance Propagation:* the final step entails collecting the achieved activation in the associated case nodes. This is done using the relevance arcs which connects each case node to its constituent IE nodes.

The result of the retrieval process is a set of cases ranked in order of decreasing activation.

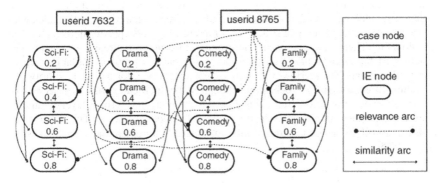

Fig. 4. A portion of a case retrieval net showing two case nodes and a selection of IE nodes. This illustrates the type of CBR data collected during the ptv project (Smyth & Cotter, 1999).

5.2 ACF and CRNs

If we view ACF profiles as incomplete cases as described in section 4 it is clear how we may implement a CRN based ACF system in which the Information Entities nodes represent item-value pairs and the case nodes represent the user profile identifiers. Figure 5 illustrates a simple example using a portion of a user profile in the *smart radio* domain (Hayes & Cunningham, 2000). What makes the spreading activation a little more complicated in ACF is that whereas in the CBR model similarity arcs tend to extend between IE nodes in which the feature descriptor part is the same, there is no reason why this should be the case in the ACF model. A similarity arc may extend between two different item types such as items 1959 and 1968 in figure 5.

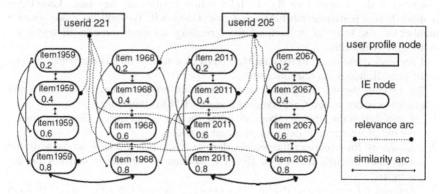

Fig. 5. ACF implemented as a CRN

However, figures 4 and 5 also illustrate the weakness of the basic CRN model we have outlined, namely the requirement for explicit similarity arcs between IE nodes. Where the number of nodes is large it may be infeasible to define similarity arcs in such a way. One way to address this is to replace direct connections to IE nodes with connections to a set of more abstract nodes representing concepts or micro-features in the domain. There may be some descriptive information already on hand. For instance, in the *smart radio* data there are some basic attributes available such as *artist, album* and *genre*. However, most genre category information is simply not discriminating enough (i.e. rock, pop), though some such categories such as *folk* or *electronic* may be a little better. This *free* information may form a layer of micro-feature nodes below the IE layer, linking several IE nodes in one go. This schema has a direct corollary in Lenz's description of micro-features in the Cabatta system (Lenz, 1999).

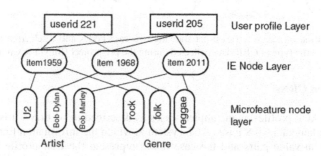

Fig. 6. Example of micro-features describing relationships between different IE nodes

5.3 Embedding Discovered Knowledge in CRNs

The standard ACF system learns in a very simple way – it collects use-data and lazily produces new recommendations. Since the relationship is an extended one, a smarter system would seek to learn the patterns informing a user's resource requirements at any time and to determine the relationships between assets that are not *apriori* given.
As we suggested at the top of this section it is possible to find rules and relationships between information entities in an ACF system using knowledge discovery techniques. The relatively *expensive* information found using these techniques may be incrementally added to the CRN memory structure without having to rebuild it.

We can do this using an extension to the basic case retrieval net model called *conceptual case retrieval nets* (Lenz, 1999). The key idea is to introduce additional nodes into the net which do not represent actual attribute-value pairs, but more abstract domain knowledge. These concept nodes allow us to link several IE nodes as shown in fig 8. During the retrieval process the initially activated nodes pass activation according to their *similarity functions* as usual, but also pass activation to connected concepts nodes, which in turn distribute activation to connected IE nodes. As such we begin to address the problem in CRNs of defining similarity relations between each pair of IE nodes. By reducing the explicit number of similarity relations between IE nodes we reduce maintenance and computational expense.

Some domain knowledge may in certain circumstances be freely available as mentioned in the previous section, but more generally it will require expert analysis of the domain to find deeper structures. However, it may be infeasible to have an expert keep track of the shifting concepts informing a particular domain. Where we have a lot of use-data it makes sense to employ well established knowledge discovery techniques to mine the concepts.

Fig. 7 presents three simple examples of concepts mined from *smart radio* data. These examples which relate artists in the data set were produced using Cobweb, Fisher's incremental concept formation algorithm (Fisher, 1987).

C410 ['Martyn, John', 'Orton, Beth', 'Guthrie, Arlo ']
C438 ['The Beatles', 'Raitt, Bonnie', 'Fitzgerald, Ella', 'Simone, Nina', 'Lennox, Annie', 'Amos, Tori']
C1066 ['Hill, Lauryn', 'Scott-Heron, Gil', 'Van Morrison', 'Getz-Gilberto', 'Evans, Bill']

Fig. 7. An example of some basic artist concepts found using Fisher's Cobweb algorithm on smart radio data.

A second source of information which can be used in the CRN model are *association rules*. Typically used in market basket analysis, the key idea is to find interesting relationships between different items in a given data set. By mining association rules we can build similarity arcs between associated IE nodes, thus boosting the activation of connected cases. This activation would not have spread to these cases without the use of discovered association rules.
In the *smart radio* domain (Hayes & Cunningham 2000), for instance, users build music playlists and are in turn recommended other people's playlists. Running the

Apriori algorithm on these lists allows us to find association rules between tracks and between artists (Agrawal et al. 1996).

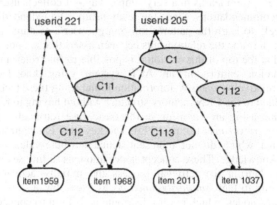

Fig. 8. Embedding concepts in an ACF CRN. The figure illustrates a hierarchal concept structure such as produced by a concept formation algorithm like Cobweb.

5.4 Benefits for ACF

A case retrieval net memory model caters to the unbounded nature of the ACF process. Initially, we can make recommendations using a sparse memory structure similar to that shown in figure 5. As the amount of information in the system grows we can incrementally derive rules and concepts which we can add to the case retrieval net as shown in figure 8. This eagerly derived information is used to augment the essentially lazy ACF recommendation process, particularly in areas where it is a weak such as the latency period mentioned in section 3. This sort of additional information is not fixed but shifting and would need to be run periodically to keep up with the level of activity in the community. Secondly, we surmise that this additional information will allow us to reduce the number of user profiles in the case retrieval net. Choosing which profiles are members would involve developing a theory of ACF *coverage*. In the concluding section we address some of the issues involved.

Finally, Lenz et al. propose that the CRN caters for a bottom up search which is appropriate in a situation where information is missing. Apart from the difficulties encountered with missing information with an inductively derived model, they argue that cognitive science would tend to support a memory model that is *reconstructive* rather than purely search oriented: i.e. humans tend to start with a sparse representation and gather more information until a clearer picture is built. (Lenz et al., 1998) These ideas can be found in memory models proposed for early CBR (Schank, 1982) (Kolodner, 1993). Whereas ACF has often been regarded as being on the periphery of AI, using a CRN approach pushes it much closer to the center.

6. Conclusions and Further Work

We have put forward the idea that ACF is very similar to dialog–driven CBR. Both approaches are involved in the process of case completion. We have then sought to unify both approaches by suggesting Case Retrieval Nets as a suitable memory structure for ACF. Since ACF involves an extended dialog with the user, CRNs offer the advantage of allowing us to incrementally add eagerly learned rules and content.

However, the amount of raw data generally required by ACF may complicate matters. The general claim for a reduction in knowledge engineering in CBR assumes that the case instances are readily available. A CBR system may require careful authoring of its cases which can require a substantial amount of 'expensive' knowledge (Aha, 2001, Aha 1997). If we are to consider ACF in CBR terms, we must examine whether we can author or 'prune' user profiles, and whether it is possible to apply techniques of problem space coverage to remove 'redundant' profiles.

Case base maintenance is an important issue in CBR both for reasons of efficient retrieval and to ensure the problem space is sufficiently covered. A key research issue is whether we can choose component user profiles of the CRN using case coverage criteria (Smyth & McKenna 1998). Thus, though all case profiles are kept in a case-base, the subset that best *covers* the user space *and* the asset space would be used in the Case Retrieval Net. We would need also to take into account a measure of which profiles consistently produce good recommendations. The idea of coverage in ACF is complicated by the fact that user profiles themselves are growing. We are left with the option to leave the 'raw data' of the profile alone and lazily make recommendations, or to seek to reduce this data into cases profiles. This would necessitate reducing the ACF profile by summarising some of the data, by finding key items that will differentiate one user group from another. Current coverage models assume a single-shot CBR system. A case either covers a problem or it does not. There is no partial coverage. Now in many CBR scenarios we have multiple-cases retrieved to solve a problem much as we do in ACF. A CBR coverage model that takes into account partial coverage situations would of course fit the ACF model very well.

References

Aamodt, A. and Plaza, E., (1994). Case Based Reasoning: foundational issues, methodological variations, and system approaches. AI Communications, 7(1):39-59

Agrawal, R., Manilla, H., Srikant, R., Toivonen, H., Verkamo, A.I. (1996) Fast discovery of association rules in Advances in Knowledge Discovery and Data mining, pp. 307-328, eds. Fayyad, U.M., Piateskty-Shapiro, G, Smyth, P., Uthurusamy, R. AAAI/MIT Press 1996.

Aha, D. W. (1997). A proposal for refining case libraries. In R. Bergmann & W.Wilke
(Eds.) Proceedings of the Fifth German Workshop on CBR (TR LSA-97-01E).

Aha, D., (1998) Reasoning and Learning: The Lazy-Eager Dimension, Invited Keynote Talk at EWCBR 1998, http://www.aic.nrl.navy.mil/~aha/

Aha, D., (2001). Conversational Case based Reasoning in Applied Intelligence (14:1), special issue on "Interactive CBR", Kluwer.

Arcos, J.L., R. Lopez de Mantaras; (1997); Perspectives: A declarative bias mechanism for case retrieval. In proceedings of ICCBR 1997, LNAI 1266. Springer-Verlag, pp. 279-290.

Balbanovi, M., Shoham, Y., (1997) Fab: Content-Based Collaborative Recommendation, Communications of the ACM, Vol. 40, No. 3, pp66-72.

Billsus, D., & Pazzani, M.J., (1998) Learning Collaborative Information Filters, in Proceedings of AAAI Workshop on Recommender Systems. AAAI Press, 24-28.

Burke, R., (2000) A Case-Based Approach to Collaborative Filtering, In: Proceedings of the EWCBR 2000, LNAI 1898, p. 370 - 379, Springer-Verlag, Berlin, 2000.

Burkhard, H-D., (1998) Extending Some concepts of CBR – Foundations of Case Retrieval Nets, in Case Based Reasoning Technology from foundations to applications, eds Lenz, M., Bartsch-Spörl B., Burkhard, H-D., Wess, S. , LNAI 1400, pp17 –50, Springer-Verlag.

Cunningham, P., (1998) CBR: Strengths and Weaknesses, in Proceedings of 11th International Conference on Industrial and Engineering Applications of Artificial Intelligence and Expert Systems, eds A. P. del Pobil, J. Mira & M. Ali, LNAI 1416, Vol. 2, pp517-523, Springer.

Cunningham P., Bonzano, A., (1999) Knowledge Engineering Issues in Developing a Case-Based Reasoning Application, Knowledge Based Systems Vol. 12, pp372-379.

Cunningham P., Finn D., Slattery S., (1994) Knowledge Engineering Requirements in Derivational Analogy in Topics in Case-Based Reasoning, LNAI, S. Wess, K-D Althoff, M. M. Richter eds., pp234-245, Springer Verlag.

Cunningham, P., Smyth, B., Bonzano, A., (1998) An incremental retrieval mechanism for case-based electronic fault diagnosis, Knowledge-Based Systems (11)3-4, pp. 239-248

Doyle, M., Cunningham, P., A Dynamic Approach to Reducing Dialog in On-Line Decision Guides, Proceedings of EWCBR 2000, LNAI 1898, E.Blanzieri, L. Portinale (eds.), pp49-60, Springer Verlag.

Fisher, D. H. (1987). Knowledge acquisition via incremental conceptual clustering. Machine Learning, 2, 139-172.

Hayes, C., Cunningham, P., (2000) Smart Radio - Building community based music radio, in Applications and Innovations in Intelligent Systems VIII, eds., Macintosh, A., Moulton, M., Coenen, F. , BCS Conference Series, Springer-Verlag.

Kolodner , J.L., (1993) Case Based Reasoning. Morgan Kaufmann, San Mateo.

Konstan, J.A., Miller, B.N., Maltz, M., Herlocker, J.L., Gordon, L.R., & Riedl, J., GroupLens: Applying collaborative filtering to Usenet News, CACM, Vol. 40, No. 3, pp77-87.

Lenz, M., Auriol E., Manago M., (1998) Diagnosis and Decision Support, in Case Based Reasoning Technology from foundations to applications, eds Lenz, M., Bartsch-Spörl B., Burkhard, H-D., Wess, S. , LNAI 1400, pp17 –50, Springer-Verlag.

Lenz, M., (1999) Case Retrieval Nets as a model for building flexible information systems. PhD dissertation, Humboldt University, Berlin. Faculty of Mathematics and Natural Sciences.

Richter, M. M. (1998). Introduction (to Case-Based Reasoning). in Case-based reasoning technology: from foundations to applications, Lenz, M., Bartsch-Spörl, B., Burkhard, H.-D. & Wess, S. (eds.) (1998). Springer-Verlag, LNAI 1400, pp1-16.

Schank, R.C., (1982) Dynamic Memory: A Theory of Learning in Computers and People. Cambridge University Press, New York.

Shardanand, U., and Mayes, P., (1995) Social Information Filtering: Algorithms for Automating 'Word of Mouth', in Proceedings of CHI95, 210-217.

Smyth, B. & McKenna E., (1998) Modeling the competence of case-bases. In Advances in Case-Based Reasoning: Proceedings of EWCBR 1998, LNAI 1488, pp196-207. eds.: Barry Smyth and Pádraig Cunningham. Springer-Verlag, Berlin, Germany, September 1998

Smyth, B. & Cotter, P., (1999) Surfing the Digital Wave: Generating Personalised TV Listings using Collaborative, Case-Based Recommendation, in Proceedings of ICCBR 1999, LNAI 1650, eds K-D. Althoff, R. Bergmann, L. K. Branting, , V pp561-571, Springer Verlag.

Waszkiewicz, P., Cunningham, P., Byrne, C., (1999) Case-based User Profiling in a Personal Travel Assistant, User Modeling: Proceedings of the 7th International Conference, UM99, Judy Kay, (ed).pp. 323-325, Springer-Wien-New York.

A Case-Based Approach to Tailoring Software Processes

Scott Henninger and Kurt Baumgarten

Department of Computer Science & Engineering
University of Nebraska-Lincoln
Lincoln, NE 68588-0115
scotth@cse.unl.edu

Abstract. Software development is a knowledge-intensive activity involving the integration of diverse knowledge sources that undergo constant change. The volatility of knowledge in software development demands approaches that retrieve episodic knowledge and support the continuous knowledge acquisition process. To address these issues, case-based technology is used in combination with an organizational learning process to create an approach that turns Standard Development Methodologies (SDM) into living documents that capture project experiences and emerging requirements as they are encountered in an organization. A rule-based system is used to tailor the SDM to meet the characteristics of individual projects and provide relevant development knowledge throughout the development lifecycle.

1 Case-Based Software Development Knowledge

Software process and process modeling has become a hot topic the software engineering community [2, 3, 13, 20, 21, 23]. The software development process in this view is treated as a set of high-level activities for planning software development activities, such as creating a requirements document, holding code an document reviews, and creating test plans, to name just a few. In many ways, these efforts represent critical knowledge about how large-scale software projects should be conducted. But this knowledge is often idealized and abstracted away from the realities of everyday work practices. In addition, the field has done little to resolve issues of how the knowledge embedded in software processes can be turned into a repository of proven practices that can be brought to bear on software development efforts. Further research is needed into the development of tools and techniques that capture specific guidelines, examples, deviations and other information that can become an integral and valuable tool for software developers.

The fact that knowledge in software development settings is both dynamic and situation-specific indicates that a case-based approach may be fruitful. The case-based decision support technique, which views cases as problem-specific solutions that can be retrieved to help augment human memory [14, 15, 22], is particularly appropriate in this setting, where no formalized or algorithmic solutions are available, or expected to appear any time soon.

D.W. Aha and I. Watson (Eds.): ICCBR 2001, LNAI 2080, pp. 249-262, 2001.
© Springer-Verlag Berlin Heidelberg 2001

In what follows, a set of case-based knowledge management tools for software development are presented. The traditional case-based reasoning paradigm needed to be augmented to meet our needs in a couple of ways. First, in a dynamic knowledge domain it is necessary to continuously update the repository. While it has been acknowledged that collecting cases is an incremental process [15], few methods are available to support this process [5]. Mechanisms and tools are needed to easily create new cases and organize them by resources and development projects. Second, a means of disseminating the software development process standard is needed. The activities in the process play the role of organizing principles. Individual projects create an instance of the process, creating the cases that contain project-specific information. In other words, general principles are captured in the activities defined in an organization's Standard Development Methodology (SDM) and cases capture situation-specific knowledge of actual practice. This helps turn SDMs into a resource, something that truly supports the development process as it is actually practiced, while adding necessary degrees of formal procedures to ensure high-quality products.

2 Capturing and Disseminating Best Practices in an Organizational Setting

Our early work in this area started with the design of a case-based repository for capturing software development knowledge [9]. An exploratory prototype, named BORE (Building an Organizational Repository of Experiences), was built to capture project experiences and search the repository for relevant cases [11]. The general idea has been to use case-based structures as an organizational memory [1], a way to capture the collective knowledge of the organization.

Early BORE prototypes were evaluated in two separate contexts. In the first, a pilot project in the IT department of a large transportation corporation evaluated BORE by documenting some cases and providing comments of how BORE can be improved to better meet their specific needs. The second evaluation context was a Software Engineering course consisting of seniors and graduate students. Students in this class developed small to medium scale software systems for clients external to the university system. Project assignments for requirements, design, implementation, and formal testing all required the use of BORE. The scope of the projects were rather small, with less than a semester to develop the software and 4-6 people on the project. Nonetheless, the six projects generated over 150 cases.

In both instances we were disappointed in the detail and amount of information provided by BORE users. Cases were not described adequately, solutions were often left blank, and cases seldom contained adequate information for subsequent users to re-use the knowledge. There was clearly a need to encourage users to provide higher quality information. It could be argued that better results would have been achieved in more structured settings where more emphasis was given on project documentation. While this argument has merit, our observations also indicate that any activity deemed as ancillary to the immediate goal of producing a working software product is often given short shrift. Because BORE was not intimately tied to these goals, people regarded using the system as supplemental documentation and not part of the critical path.

Through our studies, it became clear that if the potential benefits of an organizational learning approach [5, 6, 10, 26] were to be realized, people needed guidelines on the level and quality of information they needed to capture through support tools, such as BORE. Use of an organizational learning system needs to be *formalized* in the sense that its use is mandated in a documented process to ensure that proper information is collected. In addition, this requirement must be carefully balanced with adding documentation tasks to already burdened development staffs. Instead of treating the repository as a supplemental obligation with little to no immediate benefit, mechanisms are needed to turn the repository into the central planning and documentation repository for a project. This would both avoid duplication of effort and provide one place for projects to coordinate and document their work.

We began to conceptualize our solution in terms of a dynamic technology for Standard Development Methodology (SDM) documents that serve as a focal point for an organizational learning process. While software process modeling techniques, such as software process programming [2, 4, 19], have received a great deal of attention in the research community, most software development organizations still practice the use of Software Development Methodology (SDM) documents. These are usually found in a monolithic manual, although hypertext and Web-based versions are becoming popular. This research focuses on turning current SDMs into a *living document* designed to evolve and improve through use, drawing on the collective knowledge of the organization.

2.1 Towards a Defined, Extensible, SDM

Most traditional SDMs created by software organizations eventually fall into disuse for two reasons: 1) To accommodate diverse needs, the SDM is stated at a very high level and lacks the detail that can truly guide a project. Stating the need for "detailed design" is insufficient. There also needs to be specific guidelines, examples, and detailed procedures that help people create the design. I.e., to be successful, the SDM must provide valuable resources for development efforts. 2) The SDM quickly falls behind the rapid pace of technology and business needs. Even if SDM curators are appointed, it is difficult for a few people to keep pace with changes in large development organizations.

To reduce these problems, our process begins with a defined on-line SDM describing a standard work breakdown structure for the software development organization. Multiple paths through the SDM are designed to accommodate the different kinds of projects typically encountered in the organization [19]. Fig. 1 shows a diagram of the overall process of using and evolving the SDM. In this figure, the SDM (shown in the box marked "Process Schema" in the BORE repository) has three different paths. More complex structures are possible, and it is not expected that everyone should understand the SDM in its entirety. Instead, a decision support system is used to reduce the complexity by eliciting project characteristics, such as end-user, data and security requirements, whether an iterative or waterfall methodology should be used, etc.

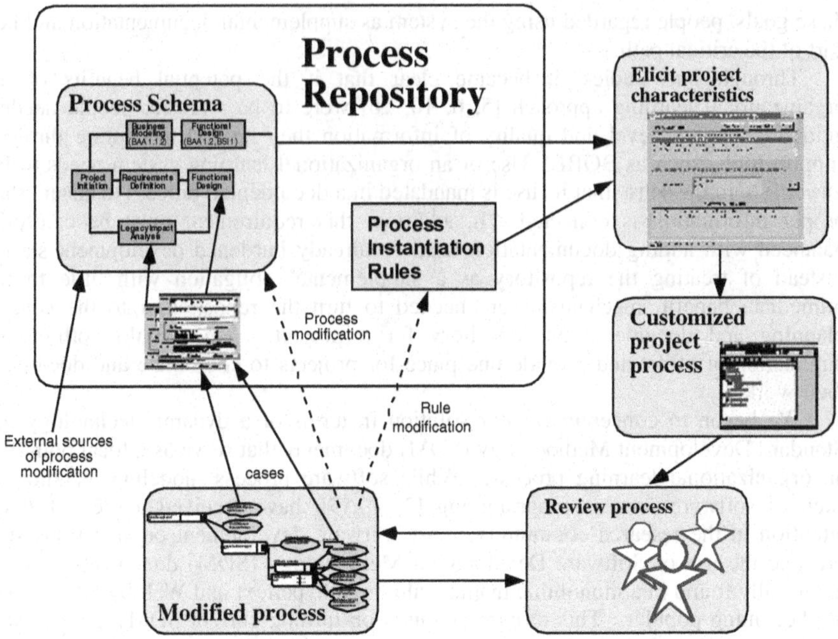

Fig. 1. Using and Evolving a case-based repository.

During various points in the software development effort, the decision support system steps project personnel through questions designed to elicit project characteristics. These characteristics are matched against requirements in the SDM to propose a customized process for the project. Developers can then modify this process to meet the project's needs. The end result is subjected to an approval review in which the answers provided to the decision support system and any modifications made to the resulting process are carefully examined. The outcome of the review can be one of three actions: 1) the project is required to re-visit some of the questions posed by the decision support system and potentially choose different options, 2) modifications are rejected and/or new modifications are proposed, or 3) the process is approved.

Upon approval of the process, a BORE project is created and the repository is changed in two ways. First, new cases are created for each project activity that is copied from defined SDM activities. Using case-based terminology, the defined SDM activity is the general principle, and each project creates a case to describe problem-specific issues and solutions. Second, exceptions to the SDM may involve adding new activities to the project's process. These are seen as "opportunities for learning" and can be added to the SDM. New rules are then created to identify the circumstances under which a given activity is applicable. In this way, new projects with similar needs can learn from the efforts of previous projects.

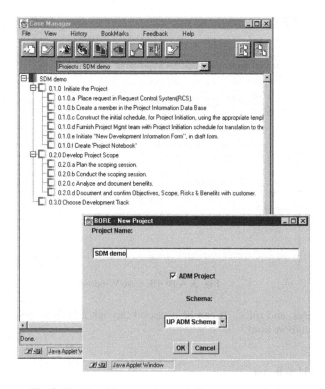

Fig. 2. The Case Manager view and Creating a new Project.

Process rigor is retained in this technique by forcing projects to base their activities on previous work, yet the process is able to support changing development needs by allowing deviations to provide feedback on the utility of specific process activities. Over time, the SDM will evolve to meet the needs of issues that recur in the organization [8], position the organization to take advantage of previous experiences and improve. Process complexity is managed through the decision support system, which prunes the SDM to only those activities the project needs to address.

3 Tools for Supporting SDM Tailoring and Modification

The process outlined in the previous section is designed to turn an organization's SDM into a living document that captures situation-specific knowledge and evolves and improves with use. The following sections use a BORE prototype to demonstrate how this is accomplished. There are two major components of this process: 1) The standard SDM is *tailored* to specific project requirements, and 2) if necessary, the SDM is *modified* to meet the emerging needs of development projects. The BORE prototype is a Web-enabled application that uses a database back-end to store

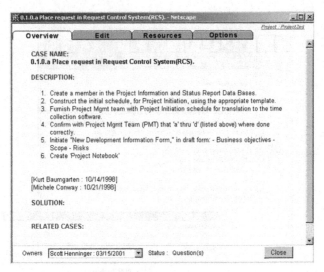

Fig. 3. A BORE Case Window.

activities, cases, and rules. It can be accessed through a Web browser at http://cse-ferg40.unl.edu/bore.html.[1]

3.1 The SDM Schema

One of the primary interfaces of the BORE prototype is the Case Manager, shown in **Fig. 2**. This interface displays a hierarchical work arrangement of cases that define the activities in a project's development process. For example, in **Fig. 2**, A project named "SDM demo" has been chosen from the list of resources in the drop-down menu that displays "Projects:". A set of cases are displayed in a hierarchical work breakdown that represent a set of activities in a software development project. Each of these activities are cases that contain project-specific information as shown in Fig. 3, which was obtained by double-clicking on the case named "0.1.0.a Place a Request in Request Control System (RCS)."

This is the case-based organizational memory paradigm of BORE [9]. Each case represents project-specific information that is used to help coordinate and disseminate project experiences. The significant difference is the addition of project "schemas" that create the tailoring and modification process shown in Fig. 1. The SDM "schema" is a set of cases and relationships between cases that define the software development process for all projects in the SDM schema, ranging from throwaway prototypes to in-house applications to shrink-wrap or custom-built software systems. Projects choose an appropriate subset of the schema cases to define its development process. We have chosen to call it a "schema" in the sense of data model schema,

---

[1] The system functions best when used by Netscape Communicator 4.x or later versions, or Internet Explorer 5.x or later versions. Java and Javascript must be turned on. Guest users may log in as 'guest' or request an account.

0.3.0 - Select Development Strategy

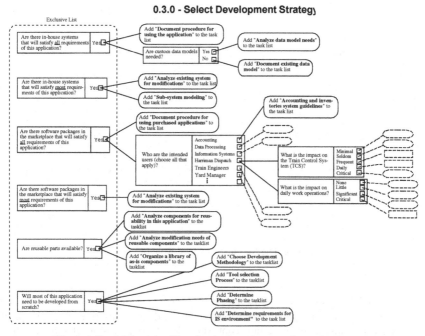

Fig. 4. A Partial Decision Tree for the Development Strategies Process.

where the SDM schema is the logical data model that is instantiated by the physical model and data contained in the database.

To tailor the SDM schema to create project cases requires a process by which developers and managers decide which processes are necessary and/or relevant for the requirements of the given project. While there are many valid approaches to this decision process, we have been experimenting with a semi-formal approach that utilizes decision trees such as the one shown in Fig. 4 that shows a partial decision tree for choosing a development strategy. These decision trees can be used at an arbitrary level of project detail, from high-level development processes such as whether business modeling or requirements definition is needed to specific corporate standards, such as which login screen should be used.

When creating a new project, the window in the lower right of **Fig. 2** is used to choose the schema from which the project's cases will be derived. In our example, the three major tasks of **Fig. 2** (see the cases numbered 0.1.0, 0.2.0, etc.) are assigned to the project in a partial development process that details project initiation steps. These cases can serve as a checklist of project tasks that document progress and coordinate efforts. BORE supports a color coding of the glyph to the left of the case name in the Case Manager to provide a visual means of identifying the status of cases -- whether the case is open, actively being worked on, resolved, and etc. The purpose of the case is to document how a given task was addressed by the project. The Overview, Resources, Attachments, and Related Cases tabs are used to document project-specific issues that arise when addressing the task (Fig. 3).

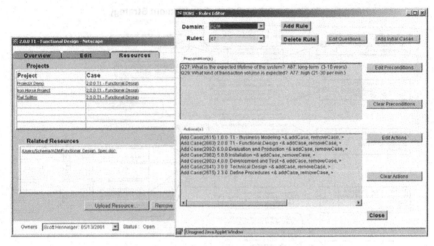

Fig. 5. The Resources tab and Rule Editor.

This is the essence of a case-based approach -- general principles (the SDM schema) are used as a guide for decision makers, and cases describe situation-specific problems that may arise in certain contexts [14]. In our version of this case-based paradigm, the SDM schema defines the canonical development process under a wide range of situations encountered in the organization. Cases describe some of the problems or necessary steps that must be taken to ensure that the process is properly followed. For example, a process step may dictate that the corporate standard login screen is used for an application. A project trying to follow this step may find that using the password database required a couple of work-arounds to fit their specific architecture. The project's case would reflect these problems and document how the problems were solved in the "Solution" field of BORE cases.

3.2 The Rule-Based System

In BORE, the process of tailoring the SDM schema to the specific characteristics of a project involves answering questions from a rule-based system. As opposed to traditional case-based systems, which retrieve cases from a repository, BORE uses rules to assign cases to projects. The rules define "applicability conditions" for the SDM activities, which become project-specific cases when assigned to a project. For example, a rule can be created stating that a project must perform a "Functional Design" activity when the "expected lifetime of the system" is "long term" and the "transaction volume" is "high". This describes part of the rule shown in Rule Editor window to the right in Fig. 5.

Each rule has a set of preconditions consisting of one or more question/answer pairs. When all preconditions evaluate to true, the rule "fires," causing a set of actions to be executed. Actions in BORE can take one of three forms: 1) A question can be removed from the question stack (displayed in the Option window of a case),

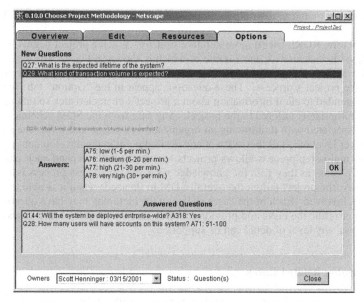

Fig. 6. Options Tab for Tailoring the SDM to Individual Projects.

2) a question can be added to the question stack, and 3) cases can be added to a project's activities. When adding cases, the hierarchical ordering of activities is preserved when copied to the project. Rule actions can be extended by adding Java methods to perform the actions and undo them. Backtracking of fired rules is supported, allowing questions to be re-answered or un-answered.

The production system provides the flexibility to implement complex decision trees. While AND relationships are inherent in the precondition/action structure of the rules, OR relationships are easily represented by having two rules with different preconditions and the same action. Combinations can be created by mixing these strategies as needed. This flexibility comes at the price of complexity, though, and future efforts will look at improving interfaces and checks on the system to ensure the integrity of the rule base. To facilitate rules permanence (see next section), questions and answers are represented in a SQL compatible database back-end.

3.3 Iterative Disclosure of Detail

One approach to capturing project requirements with the questions and answers would be to require a long question-answer session at the beginning of a project that would construct a plan from beginning to end. We found this kind of approach to be unappealing for a number of reasons. First, we want BORE to support a number of different levels of decision making, from choosing whether the project is enterprise-wide or local to what kind of database should be used all the way to choosing reusable code, such as back-up and recovery schemes and other coding standards. Secondly, if a system spans these levels of support, and indeed it must to be called an organizational memory, it would be impossible to anticipate the answers to all quests up-front.

Therefore, BORE uses a more iterative strategy. When a project begins, an initial set of cases is instantiated, an example of which is shown in **Fig. 2**. The cases copied from the SDM schema can contain questions that are used to further refine and expand the project's process. These questions appear in the "Option" tab (see Fig. 6) and are intended to elicit information about a project's characteristics so that the SDM can be appropriately tailored to the project. Any case from the SDM schema can have options associated with it, allowing an organization to define and refine their process to whatever level of detail they wish at any desired point in the development process.

This multi-step process allows projects to incrementally expand each part of the project's process as they gain the knowledge necessary to address process issues [19]. In this way, the project tailors the overall SDM to its needs when it is able to address the issues involved. Each of the cases shown in the hierarchy may have questions that will further refine the tasks and provide resources for the project. Since cases control this process, any level of detail can be supported.

3.4 Accessing Related Cases

Cases that are created from the SDM schema are automatically cross-referenced to each other. The Resources tab is shown in the left window of Fig. 5. The "Projects" frame show a list of all cases that were created from the SDM schema activity named "2.0.0 – T1 Functional Design". Clicking on the case name, which is the same in all projects because it was created from the SDM schema activity, opens the case for that specific project. Clicking on the project name will display the project cases in the Case Manager. The "Related Resources" frame displays documents that are associated with the case. In this instance, the Functional Design SDM activity has a functional design specification associated with it. Whenever a case is instantiated from this activity, a link to the template is copied into the case. Users can now download the document (via HTTP), edit it, and upload the edited version. . These resources can provide valuable information for subsequent development efforts, automatically indexed by the SDM activity, thus providing an opportunity to disseminate best practices. Project personnel assigned a given process element can easily check the repository to see cases documenting how other projects accomplished the process goals and potentially reuse their solutions [12, 24].

3.5 Modifying the SDM

As shown in Fig. 1, the SDM is refined in two ways. First, a new case is instantiated for each process element assigned to the project. As described in the previous section, this case will document how the project met the requirements of the given process activity. The second modification the activities and rules that define the SDM. Modifying the SDM involves creating new decision points and process elements in the SDM and integrating new questions and answers to existing questions into BORE. Rules are edited through an interface (Fig. 5) that displays preconditions and actions for a given rule. Tasks are added to the SDM Schema through the Case

Manager, which supports a view for editing the SDM schema in the same way that BORE cases can be edited.

Modifying the SDM consists of either or both adding tasks to the SDM and editing the rules for adding tasks to a project. For example, suppose a project is amongst the first to create Java applets, and designs a method to use JDBC to access Oracle tables. To do this means deviating from the SDM because certain issues of creating a Web-based database server haven't been addressed before in this organization. The project goes through the review process, is approved, and engages in mandated documentation to pave a path for projects with similar characteristics. The project creates a number of tasks and subtasks that must now be added to the SDM. A process expert is assigned to add these tasks and insert new questions into the repository that ensures that future Web-based project can take advantage of, and improve on, the procedures created by this ground breaking project.

There are some authorization considerations associated with changing the schema and rules. Whereas editing cases can and should be the responsibility of individual projects, editing the SDM involves some policy decisions on whether individual projects should be allowed to make changes or whether some curator or administrative body controls the SDM. Note that in Fig. 1 changes are made to the SDM repository only after undergoing a review process. Following this kind of process will ensure that decisions are appropriate for future development efforts. There is also the issue of creating rules so they are not inconsistent, contradictory, or incomplete. Personnel with expertise in rule-based systems are needed to create and test new rules before they are placed in the repository.

4 Open Issues and Future Directions

The general goal of this approach is to try to split the gap between overly-restrictive procedures and not following a defined process. Currently, the industry standard is to define a SDM and then ignore it in its entirety or follow it enough to justify it to certification authorities. We wish to turn SDMs into something that truly supports the development process as it is actually practiced, while adding necessary degrees of formal procedures to ensure high-quality products. This involves not only defining a process, but also using feedback from projects using the SDM to refine and improve its procedures.

More research is needed to investigate case-based approaches to software processes, and project planning in general. One area of research that has received little attention in the software engineering community is using planning approaches to the software development process. Applying AI planners, particularly case-based planning [7, 18] has the potential for significant impact in the software engineering field. Hierarchical planners seem particularly suited to the problem of creating development plans, as hierarchical task breakdowns are often used. We are particularly interested in approaches that combine rule-based systems with CBR [7, 16] and use conversational dialogues to retrieve cases [17]. BORE uses both a conversational CBR dialogue and a rule-based system for case retrieval, and seems poised to further investigate how case-based planners can be applied to the problem. An interesting complication to case-based planning is the mixture of hard and soft matching criteria in the software development domain. Some rules may retrieve activities that are required by the standard ("if system integration is needed then an integration test plan must be created"), while others may be optional or marked as possible solutions (for ex. an activity to create a user logon screen could lead to many possible solutions that could potentially be applied).

5 Conclusions

Centering the information around a single repository through an ongoing process of capturing project experiences [1] can prevent the duplication of efforts, avoid repeating common mistakes, and help streamline the development process. Case-based architectures can further improve such repositories by helping people find situation specific solutions to problems. A defined development process is used to structure cases into a work breakdown hierarchy defined in a standard development methodology (SDM). Each project creates their own instance of the SDM, tailors it through rules that match project characteristics to SDM activities, and creates a project-specific case for each SDM activity assigned to the project. The cases are then used to describe project-specific solutions to the defined activity.

Just as important as the definition of the SDM and cases are procedures to keep the process current in the face of changing development needs, methods, techniques, and changing technologies. This mandates a strong tie between technology and process in which using the technology must become part of routine work activities.

To accomplish these goals, we have coupled process and technology to turn SDM documents into dynamic "living" resources that can be extended and improved as new project needs and application requirements emerge. As the repository accumulates through principled evolution of the SDM, the accumulated cases improve the repository to handle a wider range of circumstances [14], while evolving toward answers to problems that fit the organization's technical and business context. Similar projects have shown that design repositories will be used by development personnel, provided it contains relevant, useful and up-to-date information [25]. We are currently working with some software development organizations to use and further evaluate this approach.

Acknowledgments. I gratefully acknowledge the efforts a number of graduate students that have helped develop GUIDE and BORE, including Kurt Baumgarten, Kyle Haynes, Charrise Lu, and Roger Van Andel. This research has been funded by the National Science Foundation (CCR-9502461, CCR-9988540, and ITR/SEL-0085788), and Union Pacific Railroad.

References

1. K. Althoff, A. Birk, S. Hartkopf, and W. Müller, "Managing Software Engineering Experience for Comprehehensive Reuse," *Proc. 11th International Conference on Software Engineering and Knowledge Engineering*, Kaiserslautern, Germany, pp. 10-19, 1999.

2. V. Ambriola, R. Conradi, and A. Fuggetta, "Assessing Process-Centered Software Engineering Environments," *ACM Transactions of Software Engineering and Methodology*, vol. 6, pp. 283-328, 1997.
3. G. Cugola, "Tolerating Deviations in Process Support Systems via Flexible Enactment of Process Models," *IEEE Transactions on Software Engineering*, vol. 24, pp. 982-1000, 1998.
4. B. Curtis, M. I. Kellner, and J. Over, "Process Modeling," *Communications of the ACM*, vol. 35, pp. 75-90, 1992.
5. B. Decker, K.-D. Althoff, M. Nick, and T. C., "Integrating Business Process and Lessons Learned with an Experience Factory," *1st German Conference on Professional Knowledge Management*, 1998.
6. E. Ellmer, "Organizational Learning in Software Engineering: An Approach and Experimental Results," *Proc. International Symposium on Applied Corporate Computing*, Monterrey, Mexico, 1996.
7. A. Golding and P. S. Rosenbloom, "Improving Rule-Based Systems Through Case-Based Reasoning," *Proc. 9th National Conference on Artificial Intelligence*, Anaheim, CA, pp. 22-27, 1991.
8. S. Henninger, "Accelerating the Successful Reuse of Problem Solving Knowledge Through the Domain Lifecycle," *Fourth International Conference on Software Reuse*, Orlando, FL, pp. 124-133, 1996.
9. S. Henninger, "Case-Based Knowledge Management Tools for Software Development," *Journal of Automated Software Engineering*, vol. 4, pp. 319-340, 1997.
10. S. Henninger, "Supporting Software Development with Organizational Memory Tools," *International Journal of Applied Software Technology*, vol. 2, pp. 61-84, 1996.
11. S. Henninger, K. Lappala, and A. Raghavendran, "An Organizational Learning Approach to Domain Analysis," *17th International Conference on Software Engineering*, Seattle, WA, pp. 95-104, 1995.
12. P. Katalagarios and Y. Vassiliou, "On the Reuse of Sotware: a Case-Based Approach Employing a Repository," *Automated Software Engineering*, vol. 2, pp. 55-86, 1995.
13. R. Kehoe and A. Jarvis, ISO 9000-3 : A Tool for Software Product and Process Improvement. New York: Springer, 1996.
14. J. L. Kolodner, *Case-Based Reasoning*: Morgan-Kaufman, San Mateo, CA, 1993.
15. J. L. Kolodner, "Improving Human Decision Making through Case-Based Decision Aiding," *AI Magazine*, vol. 12, pp. 52-68, 1991.
16. S. W. Mitchell, "A Hybrid Architecture for Real-Time Mixed Initiative Planning and Control," *Proc. 9th Conference on Innovative Applications of AI*, Providence, RI, pp. 1032-1037, 1997.
17. H. Muñoz-Avila, D. W. Aha, L. A. Breslow, D. S. Nau, and R. Weber, "Integrating Conversational Case Retrieval with Generative Planning," *Proc. 5th European Workshop on Case Based Reasoning*, Trento, Italy, pp. 322-334, 2000.
18. D. Nau, Y. Cao, A. Lotem, and H. Muñoz-Avila, "SHOP: Simple Hierarchical Ordered Planner," *Proc. 16th International Conference on Case-Based Reasoning*, Stockholm, pp. 968-973, 1999.
19. L. Osterweil, "Software Processes are Software Too," *Ninth International Conference on Software Engineering*, Monterey, CA, pp. 2-13, 1987.
20. L. Osterweil, "Software Processes are Software Too, Revisited," *Proc. Nineteenth International Conference on Software Engineering*, Boston, MA, pp. 540-548, 1997.
21. M. C. Paulk, B. Curtis, M. Chrissis, and C. V. Weber, "Capability Maturity Model, Version 1.1," *IEEE Software*, vol. 10, pp. 18-27, 1993.
22. M. Pearce, A. K. Goel, J. L. Kolodner, C. Zimring, L. Sentosa, and R. Billington, "Case-Based Design Support: A Case Study in Architectural Design," *IEEE Expert*, vol. 7, pp. 14-20, 1992.

23. B. Ramesh and V. Dahr, "Representing and Maintaining Process Knowledge for Large-Scale Systems Development," *IEEE Expert*, vol. 9, pp. 54-59, 1994.
24. C. Tautz and K.-D. Althoff, "Using Case-Based Reasoning for Reusing Software Knowledge," *Proc. 2nd International Conference on Case-Based Reasoning (ICCBR'97)*, pp. 156-165, 1997.
25. L. G. Terveen, P. G. Selfridge, and M. D. Long, "Living Design Memory' - Framework, Implementation, Lessons Learned," *Human-Computer Interaction*, vol. 10, pp. 1-37, 1995.
26. J. V. Vandeville, "Organizational Learning Through the Collection of "Lessons Learned"," *Informing Science*, vol. 3, pp. 127-133, 2000.

The Conflict Graph for Maintaining Case–Based Reasoning Systems

Ioannis Iglezakis

DaimlerChrysler AG, Research & Technology, FT3/AD,
P.O. Box 2360, 89013 Ulm, Germany
ioannis.iglezakis@daimlerchrysler.com

Abstract. The maintenance of case–based reasoning systems is remarkably important for the continuous working ability of case–based reasoning applications. To ensure the utility of these applications case properties like correctness, consistency, incoherence, minimality, and uniqueness are applied to measure the quality of the underlying case base. Based on the case properties, the conflict graph presents a novel visualization of conflicts between cases and provides a technique on how to eliminate these conflicts and therefore maintain the quality of a case base. An evaluation on ten real world case bases shows the applicability of the introduced technique.

1 Introduction

During the last years, the research in the realm of case–based reasoning (CBR) systems in general and maintaining of case–based reasoning systems in particular has become a main topic for many researchers. In the field of maintaining case–based reasoning systems various measures like coverage and reachability [14,17] and thereby case competence [15] are modeling the competence of a case base. The use of case properties which show the relations within cases and between cases [11] is an other way to measure the quality of a case base. Compared to the standard case–based reasoning cycle [1], the case properties are embedded in an extended case–based reasoning cycle [12] with the two additional steps: *review* and *restore*. The review step detects conflicts within and between cases with the help of the case properties. These conflicts are then monitored and the decision is made when to maintain and therefore trigger the restore step. The restore step suggests the necessary changes for the contents of the case base to reestablish the quality.

This paper focuses on the monitor task of the review step and how it can be used to restore the quality of the case base. It introduces a new visualization for the conflicts between cases — the conflict graph — and shows how this conflict graph can be used to find a subset of cases which must be changed in order to restore the quality of a case base. Therefore the needed case properties are revisited in section 2. The concept of a conflict graph is defined in section 3, followed by results of an evaluation in section 4. Section 5 discusses the related work. Finally, section 6 concludes the paper with a summary and issues of further work.

D.W. Aha and I. Watson (Eds.): ICCBR 2001, LNAI 2080, pp. 263–275, 2001.
© Springer-Verlag Berlin Heidelberg 2001

2 The Case Properties Revisited

As explained above, the review step in the extended case–based reasoning cycle has among other things like monitoring the quality of the case base the duty of measuring the case base through case properties. These measures are disjunct and used for quality indication within cases or between cases. The formal definition of the case properties which are used here can be found in [11]. In this section only an informal description of the case properties *correctness, consistency, uniqueness, minimality,* and *incoherence* is given to motivate them for further use in the next sections.

2.1 Correctness

There are two kinds of case properties: *isolated* and *comparative*. Correctness is the only isolated property, because the correctness of a case can be recognized without considering any other case. A case is believed to be correct if and only if the problem description of the case corresponds to the given solution. This implies that the solution solves the problem that is described by the problem description. Note that for the following descriptions of case properties and experiment the correctness of the cases is assumed.

2.2 Consistency

The first of the comparative case properties is consistency. A given case is called consistent if and only if there is no other case whose problem description is a subset or the same of the given case's problem description and their solutions are different. Hence, consistency covers situations where the subset relation between problem description with different solutions reports that there possibly is an absence of some attributes or values to make the two cases distinctive.

Table 1 illustrates a counter–example from the help–desk domain when two cases are not consistent. This example shows two cases with the same operating system, the

Table 1. Example for (in-) consistency

Operating System	Printer	Printing	Paper	Ink	Solution
WinNT	HP840c	No	Yes	Yes	*Update Driver*
WinNT	HP840c	No	—	—	*Second Level*

same printer and no printing. In addition, the first case has more information about the paper and ink situation than the second. Note that the value "—" for the paper and ink attribute in the second case means the these values are unknown. Thus, with regard to the above description the second case is not consistent, because the problem description of the second case is a real subset of the first case and the solutions are different.

In general, consistency contains the occurrence of alternatives. It is assumed that for each capable problem description there exists a "best" solution. As a matter of course, the case base should only consist of cases that have "best" solutions. Thus, no alternative solutions are allowed neither as an alternative in the same case nor as a further case with the same or a more general problem description and a different solution.

Note that it is possible for some domains to have equivalent solutions for the same or more general problem description. The travel domain is a good example for this kind of domain and it is up to the case base administrator to decide whether these alternatives are admitted or not.

2.3   Uniqueness

Another comparative case property is uniqueness. A given case is called unique if and only if the problem description and corresponding solution of each other case in the case base is different. A counter–example from the help–desk domain is displayed in table 2. It describes the fact when the given case property uniqueness is violated.

Table 2. Example for (not) unique

Operating System	Printer	Printing	Paper	Ink	Solution
WinNT	HP840c	No	Yes	Yes	Update Driver
WinNT	HP840c	No	Yes	Yes	Update Driver

For both cases in this example, the problem descriptions and solutions are exactly the same. With the above description of uniqueness follows that both cases are evidently not unique.

2.4   Minimality

The third comparative case property is minimality which means the opposite of subsumption. A given case is called minimal if and only if there is no other case for which the problem description is a real subset of the given case and the solutions are identical. This concept is clarified by the counter–example in table 3 which contains an example when two cases are not minimal.

In this table both cases are identical besides the value for the operating system. The first case contains a value for the operating system while the second case does not. This disobeys the definition of minimality because the problem description of the second case is a real subset of the first case's problem description and the solution for both cases are equal.

Table 3. Example for (not) minimal

Operating System	Printer	Printing	Paper	Ink	Solution
WinNT	HP840c	No	Yes	Yes	Update Driver
—	HP840c	No	Yes	Yes	Update Driver

2.5 Incoherence

Finally, the last comparative case property is incoherence. A given case is incoherent if and only if each other case with the same solution as the given case has the same problem description with the exception of a specific (small) number (Δ) of attributes whose values are different. To illustrate this case property in table 4 once more a counter–example is used.

Table 4. Example for (not) incoherent (for $\Delta = 1$)

Operating System	Printer	Printing	Paper	Ink	Solution
WinNT	HP840c	No	Yes	Yes	Update Driver
Win95	HP840c	No	Yes	Yes	Update Driver

Both cases in table 4 have the same solution and differ only in the value for the operating system and in contrast to the minimality example in both cases these values exist. With the assumption that $\Delta = 1$ and the above description it follows that these two cases have a conflict with the definition of incoherent and are therefore not incoherent.

This section gave an informal description of the case properties in combination with examples from the help–desk domain. With these descriptions it is possible to build case base properties in which the case properties are assigned to a whole case base. For example, if each case in a case base is minimal, then the entire case base is by definition also minimal. To receive a better granularity of assessment, the case properties can be measured in degrees within the case base. The measurement for each case property is computed by counting the number of cases which fulfill this property divided by the total number of cases in the case base. This mapping of sets to numbers offers a more sophisticated way to measure the quality of the case base. Finally, quality measures are defined as a function over the degrees of case properties. For example, a weighted sum could respresent one usable function. More information on the subject of quality measures for case base maintenance can be found in [11]. In the following section, the notion of the conflict graph is introduced. This notion can help to visualize the conflicts between cases and decide which cases should be changed in order to restore the quality of a case base.

3   The Conflict Graph

After measuring the quality of the case base with the help of the case properties, the next step is to monitor these results. This section will introduce a novel method to display conflicts between cases which are indicated by case properties and how this representation can be used in order to maintain a case base.

When applying the described case properties from the previous section to the case base it is usually that not all properties are satisfied and thus the degree of case properties is below 100%. This means that for some cases a case property is not fulfilled. The purpose of the *single conflict indicators* in definition 1 is to test two cases for a particular case property and to indicate a possible conflict.

Definition 1 (Single Conflict Indicator). *Assume a case base C with two cases $c_i, c_j \in C$ and $i \neq j$.*

(i) $cInd_1 : C \times C \mapsto \{\neg\, consistent, \emptyset\}$,

$$cInd_1(c_i, c_j) := \begin{cases} \neg\, consistent, & if\ c_i\ is\ not\ consistent\ with\ c_j \\ \emptyset\ else \end{cases}$$

(ii) $cInd_2 : C \times C \mapsto \{\neg\, incoherent, \emptyset\}$,

$$cInd_2(c_i, c_j) := \begin{cases} \neg\, incoherent, & if\ c_i\ is\ not\ incoherent\ with\ c_j \\ \emptyset\ else \end{cases}$$

(iii) $cInd_3 : C \times C \mapsto \{\neg\, minimal, \emptyset\}$,

$$cInd_3(c_i, c_j) := \begin{cases} \neg\, minimal, & if\ c_i\ is\ not\ minimal\ with\ c_j \\ \emptyset\ else \end{cases}$$

(iv) $cInd_4 : C \times C \mapsto \{\neg\, unique, \emptyset\}$,

$$cInd_4(c_i, c_j) := \begin{cases} \neg\, unique, & if\ c_i\ is\ not\ unique\ with\ c_j \\ \emptyset\ else \end{cases}$$

To explain the above as well as the following definitions an exemplary case base is designed. Table 5 shows this case base with seven cases. Each case c_i contains the solution s_i and the problem description p_i which encloses the attribute–value pairs v_{ij}.

Table 5. Example case base with seven cases

c_i	p_i			s_i
c_1	v_{11}			s_1
c_2	v_{12}	v_{22}		s_1
c_3	v_{11}	v_{22}		s_1
c_4	v_{12}	v_{22}	v_{33}	s_2
c_5	v_{11}	v_{23}	v_{35}	s_1
c_6	v_{11}	v_{23}	v_{34}	s_1
c_7	v_{11}			s_1

Example 1 (Single Conflict Indicator). Assume the cases c_1 and c_6 from the case base given in table 5 and the single conflict indicators $cInd_1$ and $cInd_3$. The results are: $cInd_1(c_1, c_6) = \emptyset$ and $cInd_3(c_1, c_6) = \neg \, minimal$.

After defining the single conflict indicators the next step is to define the *conflict indicator set* which is then used to build the *conflict indicator*.

Definition 2 (Conflict Indicator Set). *Assume the indices of all single conflict indicators $I = \{1, \ldots, n\}$, where n is the maximum number of single conflict indicators, and $I^{\subseteq}$ the set of all subsets of I. The conflict indicator set M is defined as $M \in I^{\subseteq}$ with $M \neq \emptyset$ and $m_l \in M$ where l denotes the l-th element of M.*

The purpose of the conflict indicator set is to choose which single conflict indicators are used to configure a conflict indicator. Note that for the single conflict indicators given in definition 1 the maximum number n of single conflict indicators is $n = 4$ which limits the possible number of different conflict indicator sets to $2^n - 1 = 15$.

Definition 3 (Conflict Indicator). *Assume a case base C with two cases $c_i, c_j \in C$ and $i \neq j$, and M is a conflict indicator set.*

$$cInd : I^{\subseteq} \times C \times C \mapsto \{\neg \, consistent, \neg \, incoherent, \neg \, minimal, \neg \, unique, \emptyset\},$$
$$cInd(M, c_i, c_j) := \bigcup_{l=1}^{|M|} cInd_{m_l}(c_i, c_j)$$

Note that for the given single conflict indicators $cInd_k$ in definition 1 the value of $|cInd(M, c_i, c_j)|$ is 0 or 1 for all conflict indicator sets M and pairs of cases c_i, c_j.

The conflict indicator is a composition of the single conflict indicators. The conflict indicator set M determines the configuration of which single conflict indicators are used. The results are the kind of conflicts between two cases or the empty set if all case properties are satisfied. Example 2 illustrates this behavior.

Example 2 (Conflict Indicator). Assume the cases c_1 and c_6 from the case base given in table 5 and the conflict indicator set $M = \{1, 2\}$ and $M' = \{3, 4\}$. Then results are $cInd(M, c_1, c_6) = \emptyset$, and $cInd(M', c_1, c_6) = \neg \, minimal$.

The *conflict graph* creates a graphical representation of conflicts between two cases within a case base which are indicated through the conflict indicator. This means that the conflict graph contains all the cases which have conflicts detected by the case properties and connects these cases with a labeled edge. The label depends on the kind of property violation. Definition 4 formalizes this in a more detailed form.

Definition 4 (Conflict Graph). *Assume a case base $C = \{c_1, \ldots, c_i\}$, a conflict indicator set M, a set of nodes $N \in C^{\subseteq}$ where $C^{\subseteq}$ is the set of all subsets of C, and a set of edges $E \subseteq N \times N$ with $e_{jk} \in E$ and e_{jk} defines an edge from node of case c_j to node of case c_k with label $cInd(M, c_j, c_k)$ if and only if $cInd(M, c_j, c_k) \neq \emptyset$. The conflict graph $G = (N, E, M)$ is a directed Graph with labeled edges and $\forall c_j \in N, \exists c_k \in N : cInd(M, c_j, c_k) \neq \emptyset$ and $\forall c_j \in C \setminus N, \forall c_k \in C : cInd(M, c_j, c_k) = \emptyset$.*

Note that for some case bases it is possible to have more than one conflict graph which are not connected. For example, if a case base has four cases $\{c_1, \ldots, c_4\}$ and c_1 has only an inconsistency conflict with case c_2, case c_3 has only a minimality conflict with case c_4 and no other conflicts are detected, then the result would be two conflict graphs with the cases c_1 and c_2 in the one and the cases c_3 and c_4 in the other graph.

Figure 1 shows the conflict graph for the example case base given in table 5. The graph displays thirteen conflicts within the case base. One consistency conflict (c_2, c_4), four incoherence conflicts $(c_2, c_3), (c_3, c_2), (c_5, c_6), (c_6, c_5)$, six minimality conflicts $(c_1, c_3), (c_1, c_5), (c_1, c_6), (c_7, c_3), (c_7, c_5), (c_7, c_6)$, and two uniqueness conflicts which are (c_1, c_7) and (c_7, c_1). Note that with the increasing number of cases the conflict graph

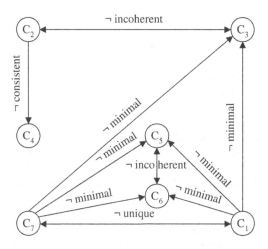

Fig. 1. The conflict graph for table 5

can confuse a human observer like the case base administrator. However it is possible to cluster groups of conflict cases and present these groups first with the ability to navigate into these groups.

The advantage of the conflict graph in comparison to other representations like adjacent lists is the ability to display the cases which do not satisfy the defined case properties in a compact manner. Thus, the case base administrator can decide which cases have to be modified to restore the quality of the case base. However this decision is very complex because the goal is to modify at least as possible cases dependable on the arising costs. The following definitions do support the case base administrator within this task by identifying the cases which should be modified. Hence, the following definitions can help to automate the parts of the restore step within the extended case base reasoning cycle.

Definition 5 (Independent Graph). *A Graph $G = (N, E, M)$ with conflict indicator set M is independent if and only if there is no pair of nodes $n_i, n_j \in N$ for which G defines an Edge $e_{ij} \in E$.*

Graph $G = (N, E, M)$ is independent :$\iff E = \emptyset$

An *independent graph* is the result after the decision is made which cases have to be modified. It is a graph in which the nodes have no edges and therefore no conflicts which each other. For example, if the cases $\{c_1, c_3, c_4, c_5, c_6\}$ are removed from the conflict graph in figure 1 then the resulting graph would be independent. However it is not appropriate to remove too many cases because of the unnecessary loss of knowledge and the costs which appear with each modification of the case base. Note that instead of removing a case other modify operators are possible. For simplicity, in this paper only the remove operator is considered. A list of more sophisticated modify operators can be found in [12].

Definition 6 (Optimal Subset). *Assume the conflict graph $G = (N, E, M)$, the set $N^\subseteq$ of all subsets of N, the conflict indicator set M, the cost function cost : $N^\subseteq \mapsto [0; 1]$, $N' \in N^\subseteq$, and the graph $G' = (N', E', M)$ is independent.*

N' is the optimal subset within $N^\subseteq$:$\iff \nexists N'' \in N^\subseteq : cost(N') > cost(N'')$ and the graph $G'' = (N'', E'', M)$ is independent.

Definition 6 states that the optimal subset of a conflict graph creates an independent graph and is mainly dependable of a cost function. The cost function is an arbitrary function which describes the optimization goal. Example 3 introduces a cost function for which the search for an optimal subset becomes equivalent to the search for a maximum independent set.

Example 3 (Maximum Independent Set). Assume a conflict graph $G = (N, E, M)$, a node subset $N' \in N^\subseteq$, and a cost function $cost : N^\subseteq \mapsto [0; 1], cost(N') := |N'|/|N|$. Then the search for an optimal subset is equivalent to the search for a maximum independent set. For the conflict graph in figure 1 the maximum independent set is (c_3, c_4, c_5), or (c_3, c_4, c_6). Note that the search for a maximum independent set is $\mathcal{NP} - complete$ [13].

The case base administrator can control the search for an optimal subset on three different ways. If there exists more than one solution for the optimal subset like in example 3 then the first way is to decide which of the possible solution is adequate for the actual situation. The second way is to mark the cases which should be put in the optimal subset. This can totally change the behavior of the algorithm which searches for the optimal subset. For example, if case c_1 is marked for the conflict graph in figure 1, then the optimal subset with the same cost function as in example 3 is (c_1, c_2) or (c_1, c_4) and hence different from the optimal subset without any interaction. Finally, the third way is to mark the cases which should not be included in the optimal subset. Again, this would change the manner of how to search for the optimal subset. For example, if case c_5 is marked for the conflict graph in figure 1, then the optimal subset with cost function like in example 3 is (c_3, c_4, c_5).

4 Evaluation

The last section introduced the conflict graph and how it can be used to indicate a subset of cases which should be changed to restore the quality of the case base. This section will present an evaluation of these conflict graph related techniques for the maintenance of case–based reasoning systems.

4.1 Experimental Procedure

To perform the experiments, the data set of cases is divided into a training set and a test set. The training set becomes the case base and is then used for the case–based reasoning algorithm. Then each case from the test set is tested against the case base within a case–based reasoning algorithm. This implements the benchmark for the other experiments and a certain accuracy and case base size is acquired. To achieve the remaining experiments the training case base is optimized. Thus, the conflict indicator is configured with the following conflict indicator sets $\{\{1\}, \{2\}, \{3\}, \{4\}, \{1, 2, 3, 4\}\}$. This means that each single case property was applied on its own as a conflict indicator and then all properties together. For the optimization the same cost function is chosen as in example 3: $cost : N^{\subseteq} \mapsto [0; 1], cost(N') := |N'|/|N|$ where N denotes the Nodes in the conflict graph and $N' \in N^{\subseteq}$. This means that the search for the optimal subset is $\mathcal{NP} - complete$. Algorithm 1 is a heuristics to calculate a not necessarily optimal solution of the optimal subset for a given graph. The algorithm returns a nodes–collection which is then viewed as the optimal subset and the graph which can build from the nodes–collection is guaranteed to be independent.

Algorithm 1 (Heuristic to calculate the optimal subset for a given graph).
nodes–collection := nodes of graph
while *(nodes–collection does not build an independent graph)*
  n := node with the maximum number of incoming and outgoing edges
  remove node n from nodes–collection
end while
return *nodes–collection*

Furthermore, the optimization's modify operator is remove and the optimization is done automatically without human interaction. After optimizing the case base the test cases are applied to the case base, a level of accuracy is reached, and the case base size is registered.

4.2 Experimental Results

The aim of the predefined benchmarks and experiments is to show that the representation of the conflict graph and the following search for the optimal subset is applicable for maintaining case–based reasoning systems.

To accomplish this, data of the UCI Machine Learning Repository [6] is taken. Namely, the following case bases are used: *Annealing* (797 cases), *Audiology* (200 cases), *Australian* (690 cases), *Credit Screening* (690 cases), *Housing* (506 cases), *Letter Recognition* (16000 cases), *Pima* (768 cases), *Soybean* (307 cases), *Voting Records* (435 cases), and *Zoo* (101 cases). To achieve the results that are presented below, a five–fold cross validation with a basic optimistic nearest neighbor algorithm is used. If numerical attributes did occur they have been pre–processed by a standard equal–width discretization.

Table 6. Results

case base	benchmark size acc.	consistency size acc.	incoherence size acc.	minimality size acc.	uniqueness size acc.	all properties size acc.
Annealing	637.6 0.97	622.8 0.97	416.0 0.97	532.6 0.97	574.8 0.97	335.6 0.97
Audiology	160.0 0.70	160.0 0.70	144.2 0.70	156.0 0.70	145.2 0.69	128.6 0.70
Australian	552.0 0.81	550.6 0.81	509.4 0.80	552.0 0.81	548.6 0.81	506.0 0.80
Credit S.	552.0 0.80	550.6 0.80	508.8 0.79	551.4 0.80	549.0 0.79	505.6 0.78
Housing	404.8 0.31	404.2 0.31	391.2 0.30	404.8 0.31	401.4 0.30	387.2 0.30
Letter R.	16000.0 0.88	16000.0 0.88	14787.8 0.88	16000.0 0.88	15081.4 0.88	14044.6 0.88
Pima	614.4 0.65	614.4 0.65	575.6 0.65	614.4 0.65	612.0 0.65	573.0 0.65
Soybean	245.6 0.92	244.8 0.92	217.0 0.92	245.0 0.92	243.2 0.92	213.2 0.92
Voting R.	348.0 0.93	344.4 0.92	257.6 0.93	271.6 0.93	280.6 0.93	191.8 0.93
Zoo	80.8 0.95	80.8 0.95	53.8 0.95	80.8 0.95	50.4 0.95	33.4 0.95

Table 6 shows that optimization through the case properties keeps the case base consistent, incoherent, minimal, and unique and reduces the case base size while preserving the prediction accuracy.

For the single case properties as conflict indicators, the case base size is reduced up to 34.8% from the original case base for incoherence in the annealing case base and the reduction for all properties as conflict indicator is up to 58.7% while the prediction accuracy remains the same as in the benchmark. The combination of all case properties gives each time a better case reduction result than the single case properties. The results vary from 0.5% between incoherence and all properties in the pima case base and 33.7% between uniqueness and all properties in the zoo case base.

In addition, the letter recognition case base with 16000 cases shows that the described technique is applicable for large case bases, too.

Furthermore, in comparison with the results in [8] which uses a different kind of optimization the results for the prediction accuracy were better and thus more robust against the used case base domain. Moreover, this evaluation used combinations of the case properties while the earlier did not. Another advantage of the optimization used in this evaluation is that it is possible to have an interaction with the case base administrator.

This shows that with the help of the conflict graph and the search of an optimal subset within this graph it is possible to maintain a case base reasoning system. Furthermore with the interactive help of a case base administrator the results should improve.

5   Related Work

The formal definitions of the case properties used for the conflict graph can be found in Reinartz et al. [11]. Several additional measures like case base properties, degrees of case properties, and quality measures are defined there, too. Evaluations showing that case properties are valueable for maintaining case–based reasoning systems have been done by Iglezakis et al. [7,8]. The extension of the standard case–based reasoning cycle and the definitions of the modify operators were first proposed by Reinartz et al. [12].

The use of graphs to maintain conversational case libraries (CCL) has been presented by Aha [3] and Aha and Breslow [4,5]. The CCL is applied to a transformation process which produces hierarchies. Then the hierarchies are pruned with the help of some design guidelines provided by case–based reasoning vendors. The resulting hierarchies are transformed back into cases of the CCL.

Over the years there where different kinds of measures for the maintenance of case–based reasoning systems published. Racine and Yang [9,10] proposed the measures for inconsistency and redundancy for the maintenance of large and unstructured case bases. Furthermore, with the access and use of background knowledge it is possible to differentiate between intra–case and inter–case measures. Smyth and Keane [14] described two different measures — coverage and reachability. The coverage of a case is the set of all problems in the problem area which can be solved by this case through adaptation. The reachability of a case is the set of all cases which are used to solve this case through adaptation. These two measures lead to different strategies how to preserve the competence of the used case base, namely case deletion by Smyth and Keane, and case addition introduced by Zhu and Yang [17]. In addition, Smyth and McKenna [15] presented the measures for case density and group density for modeling competent case–based reasoning systems which are case addition strategies, too. More strategies on how to decide which cases should be stored are proposed by the DROP1–DROP5 and DEL Algorithms by Wilson and Martinez [16], and Aha's CBL1–CBL4 algorithms [2].

6   Conclusions

With the help of case properties it is possible to create consistent, incoherent, minimal, and unique case bases. These properties have been shown to be valuable in the field of maintaining case–based reasoning systems. The application of these properties is the first step in a framework for maintaining case–based reasoning systems, to monitor the properties and then if necessary to restore the quality of the case base are the next steps.

This paper introduced a novel method to visualize conflicts between cases which are detected by the case properties and how to use this presentation to maintain a case base. This is accomplished by formal definitions of the conflict graph and the optimal subset. The subsequent evaluations showed that the proposed concepts and methods are useful for maintaining case–based reasoning systems, by reducing the size of the evaluated case bases and preserve the prediction accuracy while satisfy the case properties.

Further tasks appear on both sides of the review–restore chain of the extended case–based reasoning cycle. At the beginning of the chain, the case properties can be extended by the use of the similarity measures. This would allow the application of the case properties more flexibility in use. On the other side of the chain the use of other modify operators than remove (cf. Reinartz et al.[12]) provides a strong technique for not only reducing the case base size but also for changing the cases which have conflicts and therefore increasing the quality of the case base. This would yield to an approach which does improve the cases rather than remove them.

Acknowledgments. The author is grateful to Thomas Reinartz (DaimlerChrysler, Research & Technology, FT3/AD) and Thomas Roth–Berghofer (tec:inno — empolis knowledge management GmbH) for the fruitful discussions and continual support.

References

1. Agnar Aamodt and Enric Plaza. Case–based reasoning: Foundational issues, methodological variations, and system approaches. *AI Communications*, 7(1):39–59, 1994.
2. David W. Aha. Case–based learning algorithms. In *Proceedings of the DARPA Case–Based Reasoning Workshop*, pages 147–158. Morgan Kaufmann, 1991.
3. David W. Aha. A proposal for refining case libraries. In *Proceedings of the 5th German Workshop on Case–Based Reasoning (GWCBR)*, 1997.
4. David W. Aha and Leonard A. Breslow. Learning to refine case libraries: Initial results. Technical Report AIC–97–003, Navy Center for Applied Research in AI, 1997.
5. David W. Aha and Leonard A. Breslow. Refining conversational case libraries. In *Proceedings of the Second International Conference on Case–Based Reasoning*, pages 267–278, 1997.
6. Catherine L. Blake and Christopher J. Merz. UCI repository of machine learning databases, 1998.
7. Ioannis Iglezakis and Christina E. Anderson. Towards the use of case properties for maintaining case based reasoning systems. In *Proceedings of the Pacific Knowledge Acquisition Workshop (PKAW)*, pages 135–146, 2000.
8. Ioannis Iglezakis, Thomas Roth–Berghofer, and Christina E. Anderson. The application of case properties in maintaining case–based reasoning systems. In *Professionelles Wissensmanagement: Erfahrungen und Visionen (includes the Proceedings of the 9th German Workshop on Case–Based Reasoning (GWCBR))*, pages 209–219. Shaker Verlag, 2001.
9. Kirsti Racine and Qiang Yang. On the consistency management of large case bases: the case for validation. In *Proceedings of the AAAI–96 Workshop on Knowledge Base Validation, American Association for Artificial Intelligence (AAAI)*, pages 84–90, 1996.
10. Kirsti Racine and Qiang Yang. Maintaining unstructured case bases. In *Proceedings of the 2nd International Conference on Case–Based Reasoning (ICCBR)*, pages 553–564. Springer–Verlag, 1997.
11. Thomas Reinartz, Ioannis Iglezakis, and Thomas Roth–Berghofer. On quality measures for case base maintenance. In *Proceedings of the 5th European Workshop on Case–Based Reasoning*, pages 247–259. Springer–Verlag, 2000.
12. Thomas Reinartz, Ioannis Iglezakis, and Thomas Roth–Berghofer. Review and restore for case–base maintenance. *Computational Intelligence: special issue on maintaining CBR systems*, 17(2):214–234, 2001.
13. Steven S. Skiena. *The Algorithm Design Manual*. Springer–Verlag, 1998.
14. Barry Smyth and Mark T. Keane. Remembering to forget: A competence–preserving deletion policy for case–based reasoning systems. In *Proceedings of the 14th International Joint Conference on Artificial Intelligence*, pages 377–382, 1995.

15. Barry Smyth and Elizabeth McKenna. A portrait of case competence: Modelling the competence of case–based reasoning systems. In *Proceedings of the 4th European Workshop on Case–Based Reasoning.*, pages 208–220. Springer–Verlag, 1998.
16. D. Randall Wilson and Tony R. Martinez. Reduction techniques for exemplar-based learning algorithms. *Machine Learning*, 38(3):257–286, 2000.
17. Jun Zhu and Qiang Yang. Remembering to add: Competence–preserving case addition policies for case base maintenance. In *Proceedings of the International Joint Conference in Artificial Intelligence (IJCAI)*, pages 234–239, 1999.

Issues on the Effective Use of CBR Technology for Software Project Prediction

Gada Kadoda[1], Michelle Cartwright, and Martin Shepperd

Empirical Software Engineering Research Group
School of Design, Engineering and Computing
Bournemouth University
Talbot Campus
Poole, BH12 5BB, UK
{gkadoda, mcartwri, mshepper}@bournemouth.ac.uk

Abstract. This paper explores some of the practical issues associated with the use of case-based reasoning (CBR) or estimation by analogy for software project effort prediction. Different research teams have reported varying experiences with this technology. We take the view that the problems hindering the effective use of CBR technology are twofold. First, the underlying characteristics of the datasets play a major role in determining *which* prediction technique is likely to be most effective. Second, when CBR is that technique, we find that configuring a CBR system can also have a significant impact upon predictive capabilities. In this paper we examine the performance of CBR when applied to various datasets using stepwise regression (SWR) as a benchmark. We also explore the impact of the choice of number of analogies and the size of the training dataset when making predictions.

This paper is submitted as a research paper.

1 Background

The software development community acknowledges that timely, accurate estimates of development effort are important to the success of major software projects. Estimates are used when tendering bids, for evaluating risk, resource scheduling and progress monitoring. Inaccurate estimates have implications for all these activities, and so, ultimately, the success or failure of a project. Many projects fail or run over budget. Although investigations of such failed projects reveal a number of issues, including problems with requirements and faulty software, difficulties associated with poor effort estimation, such as unrealistic budgets and timescales will almost invariably be found to have contributed to the problem.

Over the years a variety of techniques have been proposed to help solve the problem of making accurate, yet early, software project predictions. Many of these techniques involve the use of historical data in order to develop prediction systems. An example is statistical regression. Other approaches involve the use of general

---

[1] Corresponding Author

D.W. Aha and I. Watson (Eds.): ICCBR 2001, LNAI 2080, pp. 276-290, 2001.

models or prediction systems that are parameterised to account for differences between project environments. Examples include COCOMO [1], and proprietary methods such as SLIM [2]. Often the disadvantage with such approaches is the need for quantifiable inputs that are not available at the early stages of a project, such as the bidding stage, yet the accuracy of an estimate has implications for the rest of the project.

There are a number of aspects of the software project effort prediction problem that make it quite challenging. First, software development organisations typically have little systematic data on past projects so this leads to very small training sets or case bases. Indeed it is not unusual to have as few as 20 cases. Second, the data is frequently complex with many features, both continuous and categorical, and exhibiting strong tendencies for multi-collinearity but nevertheless with many underlying dimensions. Third, the relationships between the predicted features – typically effort and duration – and the independent features are not well understood. Fourth, the data is often subject to considerable measurement error. For example, even defining what constitutes project effort in a large organisation is a non-trivial problem. Moreover, there are often reasons such as politics why the resultant data may only bear an approximate resemblance to reality. Finally, there are significant problems of heterogeneity both within datasets and certainly between different measurement environments. For this reason it has seldom been efficacious to merge training sets.

Unfortunately, as a result of the above problems, no prediction technique has proved consistently accurate, even when we relax the accuracy criterion to merely require that a technique generates *useful* predictions. Worse still some techniques have proved consistently unsuccessful. For this reason there has been growing interest in recent years in exploring a variety of machine learning (ML) techniques either as a complement, or an alternative, to existing techniques. Examples the use of artificial neural nets [2], rule induction [3] and case based reasoning or analogy [4]. Although, on occasions researchers report impressive results, what is often less visible is the amount of hidden effort to configure a ML system. Typically there is a large search space – since many decisions must be made – and little theory to guide the would-be predictor. Consequently, searching for an effective prediction system frequently degenerates into an exercise of trial and error.

The Empirical Software Engineering Research Group at Bournemouth have been involved in the development of case based reasoning (CBR) techniques and tools to build software effort prediction systems for more than five years. Over this period we have had some success in producing more accurate results than traditional regression based techniques [5, 4, 7]. Subsequently, other research groups have reported more mixed experiences. We believe that the reasons why this may be so are twofold. First, effectiveness of any prediction technique depends upon characteristics of the dataset. For example, regression will do well if the majority of datapoints lie upon, or are close to, some hyperplane. Conversely, CBR may well be favoured when discontinuities exist in any underlying relationship between effort and other independent variables. Second, there are a variety of decisions that must be made when utilising CBR techniques. Such decisions include feature subset selection, the number of analogies to utilise and choice of adaptation strategy. This paper is intended to provide some experimental data to assist with the more effective use of

CBR techniques for building prediction systems in the problem domain of software project effort, although it is hoped that some of the issues will be pertinent to a wider class of prediction problem. It also considers some of the issues involved in making comparisons between competing prediction systems.

The remainder of the paper is structured as follows. The next section (2) describes CBR in more detail and discusses the various experiences of different research teams. In section 3 we outline our experimental method and provide some background on the datasets. Section 4 analyses the impact of the underlying dataset model on the accuracy of predictions. In section 5, we consider the impact of the size of the training set on accuracy. Finally, we test whether the same results are obtained if different training sets (sampled from the same dataset) are used. Section 6 considers the impact of both the choice of the number of analogies and the underlying model on CBR performance.

2 Related Work

The use of analogies as a possible technique for software project effort prediction was first suggested by Bohem [1] almost 20 years ago and restated by Cowderoy and Jenkins [8] a few years later. However, no formal mechanisms for selecting analogies were proposed. It was Vicinanza et al. [9, 10, 11] who suggested that developments from the machine learning community in the form of CBR might be usefully adapted to help make better software project predictions. Case-based reasoning is one of the most recent approaches to problem solving and learning by combining information retrieval and decision support. A more comprehensive study of CBR technology can be found in Aamodt and Plaza [12]. Reports on activities involving CBR technology have shown that its use has grown and broadened considerably over the last few years. For example, CBR technology was used in the SaxEx system which generates expressive musical performances [13], CADET is a case-based design tool that aids conceptual design of electromechanical devices [14], and ProtoISIS is reported to have been successfully applied to the selection of diagnostic imaging procedures and could potentially be helpful in clinical decision support [15]. In software engineering, CBR technology implementations vary in their use of quantitative and/or qualitative data. ANGEL [7], for instance, can use either continuous or categorical features. On the other hand, CBR-PEB implementing concepts of the Experience Factory Model mostly looks at quantitative data by considering experiences gained when building CBR applications and tools [16, 17].

The approach of Vicinanza et al. [11] is to use domain specific similarity measures coupled with rule based adaptation. They found their technique outperforms COCOMO and FPs for Kemerer's [18] dataset of project effort augmented with an additional 7 cases. One disadvantage of this approach is that it is very specific to the particular dataset, since the rules and similarity measures are defined in terms of features available. It is unclear how this approach could be easily generalised. Bisio and Malabocchia [19] report accuracy levels in the region of MMRE^2 = 40 to 50%, for CBR again using the COCOMO dataset, however, the system was only able to make predictions for 46 out 63 projects. Some recent work by Delany and Cunningham [26] presents an example of case features available early in the lifecycle and criticises reliance on size-based measures such as LOC and Function Points as drivers for effort estimation. Instead they propose that available features be used to derive a measure of productivity.

Our approach contrasts with that of Vicinanza *et al.* in that we were seeking to develop a more general means of building prediction systems. Our belief is that collecting historical data is sufficiently challenging as it stands without the additional requirement of having predetermined feature sets. We prefer to allow estimators the freedom to utilise those features that they believe best characterise their projects and are most appropriate to their environments. Typically this might include features that describe the task such as the number of individual requirements, application domain or interfaces, features that describe the process such as development method, and features that describe the technology such as target processor and programming language(s). Note, however, no particular features are prescribed. Consequently, we use Euclidean distance in p-dimensional feature space as a means of measuring similarity between cases. Categorical features are treated as either identical or completely dissimilar. We adopt a simple analogy adaptation strategy of the mean of the k nearest neighbours, where k is an integer such that $0 < k \le n$ and n is the total number of cases in the case base. When $k=1$ then the technique is a simple nearest neighbour method. As k tends towards n so the prediction approach tends towards merely using the sample mean. The choice of k is determined by the estimator.

Our analogy based approach to project estimation is implemented in a software tool known as ANGEL. Using ANGEL we were able to compare the levels of accuracy we obtained with stepwise regression (SWR). We found that for all nine (independent) datasets we studied, ANGEL generated better results than SWR with the exception of one dataset where results were equally good (see Shepperd and Schofield [4]). Subsequently other research groups endeavoured to replicate these findings, with more mixed results. Niessink and van Vliet [20] reported that CBR out performed SWR, and Finnie *et al.* [10] found that CBR outperformed regression analysis. By contrast, Briand *et al.* [22] and Stensrud and Myrtveit [23] reported that regression based analysis generated more accurate models than CBR. Why should this be the case? As we have already stated there is likely to be a strong interaction between the accuracy of a given prediction system and underlying characteristics of the dataset it is applied to. Briand *et al.* report very high adjusted R-squared values for their regression based prediction system. The obvious conclusion is that majority of datapoints fall close to a hyperplane. Such circumstances will favour regression since it will sensibly interpolate and extrapolate. Conversely, an analogy based approach tends to explore what *existing* datapoint, or clump of datapoints, is most similar to the target case. In this paper, we look into 8 different models simulated into large datasets.

---

^{2} MMRE or mean magnitude of relative error is due to Conte *et al.* [5] and is the mean absolute percentage error.

The review of these results indicates CBR is a more complex technology involving more design decisions than might initially be supposed. In this paper we consider the impact of: distribution of the dataset; type of the underlying model for the dependent variable on the accuracy of predictions (CBR compared with SWR); size of the training set on accuracy of predictions; and choice of the number of analogies.

With reference to the number of analogies, ANGEL allows the estimator to choose the number of analogies. In our published results we used between one and three analogies. Briand *et al.* use a single analogy. Which is "best"? How can we know? This area has not been systematically explored, in particular given the interaction that one might expect between k and n.

To summarise this section and reiterate the issues discussed in this paper, we note that different research groups have had varying experiences using CBR to predict software project effort. We posit that there are two, probably complementary, explanations. The first is that underlying dataset characteristics will be influential in favouring or inhibiting different techniques for building prediction systems. CBR is no exception. We have already undertaken research into this topic [25]. The second explanation is that design decisions when building a CBR prediction system are also influential upon the results.

3 Method

Our analysis is partly based on a public domain dataset collected by a Canadian software company. However, the greater part was based on project effort data created by means of simulation. This meant we had control over the underlying model and a possibility to generate large validation datasets. To test the hypothesis that dataset characteristics play an important role in choosing the most suitable prediction system, we use stepwise regression (SWR) as a benchmark. We chose SWR since it is widely regarded as a strong prediction technique for software project effort [26], and also to allow us to make comparisons with previous work. The following sub-sections outline the main features of the datasets used and how the analysis of the results was performed.

3.1 Simulated Data

The aim of this investigation is to explore which dataset properties favour the case-based reasoning prediction technique. To be able to identify what are the typical characteristics that may be found in a software project dataset, we studied a number of publicly available datasets. This will guide the choice of what characteristics to use for simulating representative datasets and inform our investigation of the relationship between dataset characteristics and prediction system performance. Our conclusion from this informal survey is that the use of categorical features is rare, and second, every dataset in the table exhibits both outliers and multicollinearity.

The use of simulated rather than real datasets is motivated by a number of factors. First, using simulated datasets allows us to control the combinations of the characteristics we wish to examine. Second, it is difficult to determine how much of the various characteristics that are of interest to us naturally occurring datasets possess. For instance, it is quite difficult to distinguish between some, e.g. heteroscedasticity and outliers - more so with smaller datasets. Third, assessing prediction systems on small datasets is difficult since we do not know what the "true" model is. Lastly, the small number of cases in these datasets prevent the possibility of large validation sets even when applying techniques such as jack knife or bootstrap [27], without running the risk of very unreliable results. We discuss below the number of characteristics — typical of software datasets — that we used to artificially generate the datasets. Building the datasets was done blind, so that the researcher building the prediction systems was unaware of the built in characteristics of the dataset or of the underlying model.

Training set size
We used two 2 different sizes of training set (n) small with $n = 20$ and large with $n = 100$. We sampled 2 training sets for each size to establish the reliability of results obtained. Having a large training set was also useful especially in datasets where outliers were introduced.

Features in training set (p)
The number of features in the training set was kept at a low value of 4 variables although we shall consider increasing that number in future work.

Distribution of independent variables
• *normal*: value were generated by randomly sampling from a normal distribution with mean set at 500 and the standard deviation at 25% of the mean, i.e.125. In the case of negative values, they are reset to 1.
• *outliers*: we applied an increasing scaling function to the values that fall above the mean of a normal distribution to positively skew the distribution. The Skewness coefficient (which measures the degree of asymmetry of the distribution) was tested and found to exceed 5.0 for all variables.
• *collinearity*: this is achieved by randomly generating functions using a simple grammar to build a relationship between the variables. In this case, three of the independent variables were functionally related to the fourth variable with a minimum correlation of r = 0.7. However, it appears that it would have been more effective had we used an external variable in place of X_1.
• *outliers plus collinearity*: both procedures described above were applied.

Dependent variable models - "true model"
We built two types of models into each dataset, namely a continuous (Y1) and discontinuous (Y2) model. The grammar used was sufficient to generate models of arbitrary length, use arbitrary subsets of the available independent variables $X_1 \ldots X_n$ and arbitrary operators available from a spreadsheet package. The only restriction imposed was that the models generated comprise a continuous and a discontinuous model. We also associated error terms with the independent variables that were generated in the form of: $Y_x = f(X_1, \ldots, X_n)$, where $X'_1 = X_1 + \varepsilon_1, \ldots, X'_n + \varepsilon_n$. These were generated from a normal distribution with a mean of zero and $\sigma = 10\%$ of the standard deviation of the sample of X_i. In retrospect, we feel we should have

considered a different distribution such as Gamma since there is considerable evidence that errors tend to have a positive skew since many features cannot have a negative value.

Validation set

We generated a large validation set of 1000 cases that are used to test the accuracy of the prediction system but, of course, not used to generate it. This was particularly important for later on in the analysis as it allowed us to test for significance at $\alpha=0.01$. There are a number of factors that will be considered for future work, such as, introducing more feature types and investigate more types of distribution of values. However, we consider the listed characteristics to be sufficient to test our ideas considering the large amount of time simulation work requires.

Assessment of prediction systems accuracy

The estimator was supplied with four unlabelled datasets, each with different properties, e.g. normal, with outliers, etc. ANGEL and SPSS were used to generate prediction systems for the two dependent variables Y1 and Y2. The results were then validated them on the validation set of 1000 cases for that particular dataset.

First, we used the MMRE value that is generally easier to interpret, particularly across different datasets. However, this disadvantages SWR since ANGEL optimises on MMRE [28] whilst SWR minimises the sum of squares of the residuals. Therefore, we used the absolute residuals accuracy measure, which that is less vulnerable to bias.

We tested the normality of the absolute residuals using the Kolmogorov-Smirnov test for non-Normality and found that they were heavily skewed which meant using non-parametric tests. In our analysis, we used the Kruskal-Wallis test for comparing the variance, and to compare the differences in location between two populations, we used the Wilcoxon Signed Rank test when the data was naturally paired and the Mann-Whitney U test otherwise.

3.2 Real Data

The first data set has been collected from a Canadian software house [29]. We chose this dataset since it is publicly available, it is reasonably large by software engineering standards (81 cases, of which 77 are complete) and combines both continuous and categorical features (8 continuous or discrete and 1 categorical). These factors were important since we required some flexibility for our experimentation into the interaction between different CBR strategies and the dataset characteristics. The only pre-processing was to discard the incomplete cases.

Table 1. A case example in the Desharnais dataset

Project Name	Actual Effort	Exp Equip	Exp ProjMan	Transactions	Raw FPs	Adj. Factor	Adj. FPs	Dev. Env.	Year Fin.	Entities
1	5152	1	4	253	30	34	30	1	85	52

Table 2. Summary Statistics for the Dependent Variable (Effort)

	Mean	Median	Min	Max	Skewne
Desharnai	4833.91	3542	546	23940	1.998

Table 2 indicates that Desharnais is positively skewed and is rather heterogeneous with an almost 20-fold variation in the dependent variable (effort). In order to generate predictions we adopted a jack-knifing procedure for each dataset as a means of avoiding very small validation sets. Consequently for each dataset there are n predictions each based upon the remaining n-1 cases. For each prediction there is a corresponding residual, or error, i.e. the difference between actual and predicted.

Table 3. Desharnais MMRE values using CBR and SWR [28]

Data Set	MMRE – using CBR	MMRE – using SWR
Desharnais	37%	66%

Table 3 indicates that CBR (or nearest neighbour) was more accurate than SWR. However, Schofield [28] found that using three analogies to be the most accurate for this dataset. Although, only the MMRE accuracy indicator was used in this table, our preference is for mean absolute residual since it is a symmetric[3] measure, however, it is dataset dependent so it is essential to provide the more conventional MMRE indicator to allow some comparability with other results. The mean absolute residual is provided in the following section to compare results of CBR and SWR using simulated datasets. We would warn the reader though, that the two indicators can potentially provide contradictory results. In such circumstances we consider the mean absolute residual to be a better guide. A more detailed discussion of merits and demerits of different prediction accuracy indicators can be found [30].

4 Dataset Characteristics and Accuracy

We now consider the results from our simulation study. Table 4 provides MMRE percentage accuracy figures for all types of datasets using CBR. Each cell contains two values representing results from two different training sets sampled from the dataset. The shaded cells contain the corresponding MMRE values obtained when SWR was applied. Note also, the asterisks indicate where terms were forced into the prediction system procedure, since the procedure rejected all features. We do not provide accuracy figures in such circumstances.

The results in table 4 compare the prediction system in two distinct ways. First, based on dataset characteristics, it can be observed that CBR yielded more accurate predictions in terms of the MMRE indicator with messier data. Second, based on the built-in "true model", the severe deterioration between Y1 and Y2 is very evident and in many cases much larger than that between CBR and SWR or other dataset characteristics. This would mean that when dealing with very heterogeneous data, it would be more effective to partition the data into smaller more homogeneous datasets.

We pointed out earlier that in some cases SWR was only able to generate predictions when entry of terms into the regression equation was forced. In contrast, CBR will always try to generate a prediction whatever the circumstances. However,

---

[3] By symmetric we mean an accuracy indicator that doesn't penalise under and over estimates differently.

we have reported elsewhere that SWR is just as vulnerable when we tested different prediction systems over random data [25]. However, using SWR as a benchmark is still useful as it is widely regarded as a top prediction technique [26] Moreover, it will enable us to compare the results obtained to some of - our or other researchers - previous work.

Table 4. Analysis of accuracy (MMRE) for continuous and discontinuous models

Dataset	Continuous model Y1				Discontinuous model Y1			
Training sets	**small**		**large**		**small**		**large**	
Prediction system	CBR	SWR	CBR	SWR	CBR	SWR	CBR	SWR
Normal	20.03	9.90	17.90	9.77	640.74	711.05	212.03	447.37
	22.14	10.32	17.80	9.31	198.01	484.59	157.43	404.95
Normal + outliers	205.04	36.57	37.62	51.33	572.68	295.67	245.99	296.17
	57.64	63.95	34.39	40.19	206.13	313.54	166.38	258.12
Normal + multicollinearity	26.03	11.11	24.65	17.87	960.78	645.29	180.29	437.33
	34.07	20.65	21.33	12.04	770.92	1087.4	147.14	427.40
Normal + outliers + multicollinearity	26.14	285.7	13.71	172.14	361.49	*	417.84	498.66
	22.50	140.5	14.55	148.22	405.00	*	277.13	248.30

So do the characteristics of the dataset matter? Using the Kruskal-Wallis test on absolute residuals suggests that there is a significant interaction between dataset characteristic and technique ($\alpha=0.01$). The test also suggested that differences between prediction systems for a *given* dataset were also significant.

5 Multiple Training Sets, Size, and Accuracy

The two questions addressed here are (i) do larger training sets improve prediction accuracy (ii) are the same results replicable when using more than one training set sampled from the dataset? To answer the first part, we compared the absolute residuals of predictions made using the small (20 cases) with the large (100 cases) training set. We tested for differences using the Wilcoxon Signed Rank test once again setting the confidence limit at $\alpha=0.01$. Table 5 shows where a larger training set size *significantly* improved predictions using absolute residuals as the accuracy indicator.

Table 5. Multiple training sets sample and size – impact on accuracy

Dataset	Size				Multiple Training Sets							
	CBR		SWR		CBR				SWR			
					Small		Large		Small		Large	
	Y1	Y2	Y1	Y2	Y1	Y2	Y1	Y2	Y1	Y2	Y1	Y2
Normal	Y	Y		Y	Y	Y		Y	Y	Y		
Normal + outliers	Y	Y		Y	Y	Y			Y	Y		
Normal + multicollinearity	Y	Y			Y	Y	Y		Y	Y	Y	
Normal + outliers + multico	Y	Y	Y	Y	Y				Y	Y		Y

In general, we found having a larger training set always had a positive effect on the accuracy of predictions. Furthermore, it can be observed that this gain is clearer for

CBR. SWR regression seems to benefit when the data is messy (Normal + outliers + multicollinearity) but could easily identify a useful hyperplane in small training sets when the data is well behaved. The second part of the table considers the question of whether the same results could be replicated if a different training set was sampled from the overall dataset. In other words how reliable are the results? Typically, the overall dataset is partitioned into a training set and validation set often using a two thirds: one third split. This is done randomly. The question is, supposing the training set comprised different cases would we still obtain the same results. We try to answer this question by performing each prediction twice using different training sets sampled from the same underlying dataset. We then compare the resulting pairs of predictions using a Wilcoxon Signed Rank test. It can be seen that in many cases there were significant differences. The indication that sampling several training sets may give different results implies is a key issue when considering the robustness of a prediction system. We therefore believe that it is very important to repeat any evaluation of prediction techniques several times using different validation sets, especially when comparing different prediction systems since it indicates robustness.

6 Number of Analogies Selection and Accuracy

In this section we organise the results by data source and then by the following two questions: does the choice of the number of analogies (k) make any practical difference? And if so, how can we a priori determine a value for k?

6.1 Analysis Using Real Data Desharnais Dataset

(a) Does the choice of (k) make any significant difference?

We answer this question by performing a Kruskal-Wallis test[4] on the absolute residuals of all the predictions arising from $k=1$ to 5 (and also predicting using the sample mean so as to establish CBR adds some value). We find that there is slight evidence that accuracy improves using more analogies, but we are unable to show statistical significance ($p = 0.439$).

(b) How can we a priori determine a value for k?

This part of our investigation is concerned with the relationship between the number of analogies (k) and the size of the dataset (n). We consider two approaches to determining k. First, it can be set to some constant value. We explore values in the range 1-5. Second, it can be determined dynamically as the number of cases that fall within distance d, of the target case. This has the effect that sometimes no prediction is possible since no analogies fall within the specified distance especially when dealing with very small case bases.

---

[4] This is a non-parametric version of ANOVA and is necessitated by the fact that we use absolute residuals.

Table 6. Accuracy by Number of Analogies for Desharnais

Accuracy Indicator	k=1	k=2	k=3	k=4	k=5	Sample Mean
MMRE %	60.9	55.3	52.5	47.6	49.3	119.3
Mean abs. res.	2598	2417	2192	1979	1989	3008

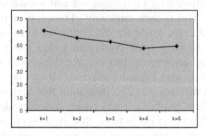

Fig. 1. Lineplot of k vs MMRE

Figure 1 summarises Table 6 in a graphical form. We note there is some tendency in for accuracy to improve between $k=1$ and $k=4$ and thereafter to flatten out. Our analysis of the differences in accuracy is rather subjective. The question remains as to the significance of any of these differences. As we indicated in the previous section we turn to the residuals to answer this question. For the purposes of this analysis we do not care about the direction of an error – an overestimate is deemed to be equivalent to an underestimate – consequently we use absolute residuals. The next step is to assess whether any of the differences in accuracy shown by Table 6 and Figure 1 are significant. Using the Wilcoxon Signed Rank test we find even with the worst predictor (using $k=1$) that we still have a median error that is significantly lower than using the sample mean approach (p=0.0126). With a dataset of this size we are at last able to show some differences between the prediction systems. We can also establish the following order of preference $k=4$, $5 < k=3 < k=1$, $k=2$ where $x<y$ denotes x has a smaller mean absolute residual value than y. It would seem that a larger number of analogies tends to be more effective for prediction purposes.

6.2 Analysis Using Simulated Data Sets

We now turn to our simulated data sets to explore what impact some of the underlying characteristics of the data set have upon the relationship between k and accuracy. We chose two of the simulated datasets (i) *normal* (small) and (ii) *normal* with *outliers* and *multicollinearity* (small). We felt that these were sufficient to test our ideas given the labour-intensive simulation work requires – especially when considering the size of the simulated datasets.

(a) Does the choice of the number of analogies k *make any practical difference?*

As per the Desharnais data set we answered this question by performing a Kruskal-Wallis test on the absolute residuals of all the predictions by data set and model. We found that in all cases, other than for the continuous model of the (Normal + outliers + multicollinearity) dataset, it does make a significant difference as to what value is selected for k. This means trying to better understand how to determine k a priori is an important research question. We are uncertain why this was an exception although the explanation may lie in the complex nature of the dataset and the relatively small size of the training set.

(b) How can we a priori *determine a value for* k*?*

Having determined that the value of k is important we now examine how two factors influence this relationship, namely (i) the type of distribution of the data set and (ii) the type of underlying model for the dependent variable.

Comparing Figures 2 and 3 (below) we see that, unsurprisingly, the predictions are substantially poorer when the underlying model is discontinuous in nature. For the continuous model we also see better predictions where the data is normally distributed. This again is unsurprising. Less expectedly we see the reverse for the discontinuous model. Probably the only conclusion we can easily draw is that both the model and the *messy* dataset have complex properties that interact in ways that are not always intuitive. This reinforces the need for further systematic exploration of this type of prediction since unfortunately it better represents the real world than the continuous model and normally distributed data.

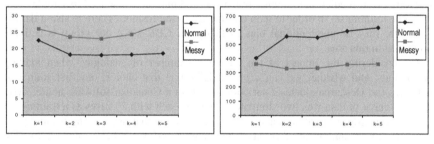

Fig. 2. & Fig. 3. Lineplots of k vs MMRE for the Continuous & Discontinuous Models respectively

In Figure 2 (with the continuous model) we see some evidence for $k=2$ being preferable to other values of k. The p values are: 0.000, 0.044, 0.043, 0.000 when compared with 1, 3, 4 and 5 analogies respectively. Also in Figure 4 (the discontinuous model), $k=1$ is preferable, although only significant when compared with values for 4 and 5 analogies with p values of 0.006 and 0.000 respectively. It is interesting to see that k is lower for the simulation studies than for Desharnais, almost certainly because the training set is much smaller. A more detailed investigation [31] found support for such a relationship between k and n, the number of cases in the training set.

Unfortunately there are few other clear patterns. We believe this because we are studying complex phenomena and considerable further work is required to explore all the different interactions between predictive performance, how to configure the CBR system and underlying characteristics of the data set.

288   G. Kadoda, M. Cartwright, and M. Shepperd

7 Conclusions

In this paper we have discussed some of our experiences in investigating the problems that either other research groups or we ourselves see as hindering the effective use of CBR technology for software project effort prediction. In particular, we examine the performance of CBR when applied to differently distributed datasets using stepwise regressing as a benchmark. We also explore the impact of the choice of number of analogies and the size of the training dataset when making predictions. Our analysis is partly based on a public domain dataset collected by a Canadian software company. However, the greater part was based on project effort data created by means of simulation. Use of simulated data for evaluating software models was first proposed by Pickard *et al.* [6]. We believe this to be essential if we are to systematically explore the impact of different dataset characteristics upon predictions.

We found that there is a strong relationship between the characteristics of the prediction problem such as training set size, nature of the "cost" function and general characteristics of the dataset and the success of a particular technique. Although, this might have been a predictable result, it provides a strong argument against the idea of seeking the "best" prediction technique. It also helps explain why different research groups have had different degrees of success in using CBR as a means of developing software effort prediction systems. We also found that there is a need to sample more than one training set in order to gain confidence in the results. There is also a danger that there may be unintentional bias in favour of CBR since our group is actively interested in this area.

In considering the impact of the choice of number of analogies when making predictions, and whether we can *a priori* determine that choice, our first source of data was the Desharnais dataset set collected from a Canadian software house. The second source of data was two simulated datasets, each with 20 cases as a training set and a 1000 cases as a validation set. The results show that using a larger number of analogies for a training set of 76 cases generated significantly better predictions. On the other hand, the nearest neighbour is observed to be the better predictor for a training set of 20 cases. We also found that the underlying distribution of the dataset does have a significant impact on the choice of the number of analogies. Moreover, predictions are substantially poorer when the underlying model is discontinuous in nature. It was difficult to identify patterns for datasets with complex distribution properties so we anticipate that a considerable amount of further work will be required to understand the relationship between the properties of the dataset and configuring a CBR system.

Acknowledgements. The authors are grateful to Jean-Marc Desharnais for making his dataset available.

References

[1]   Boehm, B.W., Software Engineering Economics. Prentice-Hall: Englewood Cliffs, N.J., (1981)

[2]   Putnam, L. H., 'A General Empirical Solution to the Macro Sizing and Estimating Problem.' IEEE Transactions on Software Engineering, 4(4), (1978) 345-36

[3]   Mair, C., et al., 'An investigation of machine learning based prediction systems', J. of Syst. Softw, 53, , (2000), 23-29

[4]   Shepperd, M.J. and C. Schofield, 'Estimating software project effort using analogies', IEEE Trans. on Softw. Eng. , 23(11), (1997), 736-743

[5]   Atkinson, K. and M.J. Shepperd. 'The use of function points to find cost analogies', in Proc. European Software Cost Modelling Meeting. Ivrea - Italy, (1994)

[6]   Pickard, L., et al. 'An investigation of analysis techniques for software datasets', in Proc. 6th IEEE Intl. Software Metrics Symposium. Boca Raton, FL: IEEE Computer Society, 1999.

[7]   Shepperd, M.J., et al. 'Effort estimation using analogy', in Proc. 18th Intl. Conf. on Softw. Eng. Berlin: IEEE Computer Press, (1996)

[8]   Cowderoy, A.J.C. and J.O. Jenkins. 'Cost estimation by analogy as a good management practice', in Proc. Software Engineering 88 . Liverpool: IEE/BCS, (1988)

[9]   Mukhopadhyay, T., et al., 'Examining the feasibility of a case-based reasoning model for software effort estimation', MIS Quarterly, 16(June), , (1992),155-71

[10] Prietula, M.J., et al., 'Software Effort Estimation With a Case-Based Reasoner', J. Experimental & Theoretical Artificial Intelligence, 8, (1996), 341 - 363

[11] Vicinanza, S., et al.. 'Case-based reasoning in effort estimation', in Proc. 11th Intl. Conf. on Info. Syst. (1990)

[12] Aamodt, A., Plaza, E. 'Case-Based Reasoning: Foundational Issues, Methodological Variations, and System Approaches', AI Communications, 7(1), (1994), 39-59

[13] Arcos, J., et al. ' SaxEx: a case-based reasoning system for generating expressive musical performances, Proceedings of the Int. Computer Music Conference, (1997)

[14] Sycara, K. et al., 'CADET: a case-based Synthesis Tool for Engineering Design', Int. Journal of Expert Systems, 4(2), (1992)

[15] Kahn, C.E., Anderson G.M. 'Case-based reasoning and imaging procedure selection', Investigative Radiology, 29, (1994), 643-647

[16] Althoff, K. et al., 'CBR-FEB: A Tool for Implementing Reuse Concepts of the Experience Factory for CBR-System Development', Proc. of the 7th German Conference on Knowledge-Based Systems, available online atwww.iese.fhg.de/home/althoff/ documents/, (1999)

[17] Carsten, T. et al., 'A Case-Based Reasoning Approach for Managing Qualitative Experience', 17th National Conference on AI (AAAI-00) Workshop on Intelligent Lessons Learnt Systems, available online at: www.iese.fhg.de /home/ althoff/ documents/, (2000)

[18] Kemerer, C.F., 'An empirical validation of software cost estimation models', CACM, 30 (5), (1987), 416-429

[19] Bisio, R. and F. Malabocchia. 'Cost estimation of software projects through case base reasoning', in Proc. 1st Intl. Conf. on Case-Based Reasoning Research & Development . Springer-Verlag, (1995)

[20] Niessink, F. and H. van Vliet. 'Predicting maintenance effort with function points', in Proc. Intl. Conf. on Softw. Maint. Bari, Italy: IEEE Computer Society, (1997)

[21] Finnie, G.R., et al., 'A comparison of software effort estimation techniques using function points with neural networks, case based reasoning and regression models', J. of Syst. Softw., 39, (1997), 281-289

[22] Briand, L., T. et al.. 'Using the European Space Agency data set: a replicated assessment and comparison of common software cost modeling techniques', in Proc. 22nd IEEE Intl. Conf. on Softw. Eng. Limerick, Ireland: Computer Society Press, (2000)

[23] Myrtveit, I. and E. Stensrud, 'A controlled experiment to assess the benefits of estimating with analogy and regression models', IEEE Trans. on Softw. Eng., 25(4), (1999), 510-525

[24] Delany, S. J., Cunningham, P. 'The Application of Case-Based Reasoning to Early Software Project Cost Estimate and Risk Assessment', Technical Report no. TCD-CS-2000-10, available online at www.cs.tcd.ie/research_groups/aig/, (2000)

[25] Shepperd, M. Kadoda, G., "Using Simulation to Evaluate Prediction Techniques", 7th IEEE Intl. Metrics Symp., London, UK, April 4-6, (2001)

[26] Kok, P., , et al. (1990). The MERMAID approach to software cost estimation. Esprit Technical Week.

[27] Efron, B. and G. Gong, 'A leisurely look at the bootstrap, the jackknife and cross-validation', Amer. Stat., 37(1), (1983), 36-48

[28] Scholfield, C., An Empirical Investigation into software Effort Estimation by Analogy, PhD Thesis, Bournemouth University, UK, (1998)

[29] Desharnais, J.M., Analyse statistique de la productivitie des projets informatique a partie de la technique des point des fonction . 1989, University of Montreal:

[30] Kitchenham, B.A., et al., 'Assessing Prediction Systems', IEEE Transactions on Software Engineering (submitted), 1999.

[31] Kadoda, G., Cartwright, M. H., Chen, L. and Shepperd, M. J., 'Experiences Using Case-Based Reasoning to Predict Software Project Effort, ESERG Technical Report No. 00-09, Bournemouth University, (2000) - also published in the Proceedings of EASE 2000

Incremental Case-Based Plan Recognition Using State Indices

Boris Kerkez and Michael T. Cox

Department of Computer Science and Engineering
College of Engineering & CS
Wright State University
Dayton, OH 45435-0001

{bkerkez;mcox}@cs.wright.edu

Abstract. We describe a case-based approach to the keyhole plan-recognition task where the observed agent is a state-space planner whose world states can be monitored. Case-based approach provides means for automatically constructing the plan library from observations, minimizing the number of extraneous plans in the library. We show that the knowledge about the states of the observed agent's world can be effectively used to recognize agent's plans and goals, given no direct knowledge about the planner's internal decision cycle. Cases (plans) containing state knowledge enable the recognizer to cope with novel situations for which no plans exist in the plan library, and to further assist in effective discrimination among competing plan hypothesis.

1. Introduction

In plan recognition systems, the main performance task is recognition of an observed agent's plans and goals, based on agent's planning behavior. Recognition can be *intended*, as in natural language dialogue [1, 6], where the observed agent is aware of the recognizer, and tries to assist (cooperative) or obstruct (adversarial) the plan recognition task. During *keyhole* plan recognition the observed agent does not participate in the recognition process; the recognizer determines the goals of the planner based solely on available observations of planner's behavior. In order to infer the plans and goals of the observed agent, the recognizer typically compares the observations of planner's behavior with possible plans contained in its *plan library*, and tries to find the plan(s) from the library that would account for observed behavior.

In a large number of plan recognition systems [4, 11], the plan library is specified for the recognizer *a priori*, by some external agent who is often the system designer. This limits the plan recognition process in that only the plans known in advance can be recognized, and novel plans will not be accounted for. Furthermore, it is often required that the plan library be complete [4, 17], i.e., the plan library contains all of the possible plans an observed agent may pursue. This approach is suitable in situations where possible plans can be enumerated in advance. However, enumerating

D.W. Aha and I. Watson (Eds.): ICCBR 2001, LNAI 2080, pp. 291-305, 2001.

all of the plans in large domains can be a difficult knowledge acquisition task, as the number of possible plans may be very large. Furthermore, this enumeration may include those plans that the planner never uses. [12] shows how the presence of extraneous plans in the plan library can impact the efficiency of the recognizer. They also introduce techniques to automate the process of constructing the plan library by synthesizing possible actor's plans and goals through plan and goal biases. The automatic plan library construction methods suffer from the same problem as the hand-coded plan libraries, since the plans that are automatically generated may be extraneous (even though the biases will minimize their occurrence).

We present a case-based approach to keyhole plan recognition applicable to state-space planners where world states of the planner can be monitored and where states are represented using the first-order predicate calculus. We focus not only on the knowledge about the actions the planner performs, but also on the states of the world the planner finds itself in during the planning. We show that the knowledge about the world states increases the efficiency of the recognizer in planning domains with wealth of the state information. Cases rich in state knowledge enable more informed predictions for recognition systems in which the planner's internal decision cycle (i.e. reasons for taking actions) is not exposed. We propose a scheme intrinsic in the case-based approach, in which a plan recognition system is able to learn about novel plans and incorporate them in its plan library for future use, thus incrementally improving its recognition process. By employing a case-based approach to plan recognition along with the knowledge about planner's world states, our system may be able to predict the agent's behavior even when the actions and states observed are not consistent with any plans in the plan library. This is because our system is able to partially match past cases, which guide the recognition process when exact matches are not available. This approach greatly improves the robustness and flexibility of a plan recognition system.

The next section describes the motivation behind our work. Section 3 deals with the benefits of retaining state knowledge, which is used in section 4 where concepts of indexing and case similarity are explored. Section 5 presents implementation and recognition examples. Finally, we conclude with the summary of presented topics in section 6.

2. Motivation and Related Work

In our opinion, the case-based approach comes as a natural reasoning paradigm for the plan recognition task. The plan library contains instances of plans an observed agent may pursue. Planning episodes in the plan library can be viewed as cases, and the recognition process can utilize these past plans (cases) to generate predictions. The main focus in the context of plan recognition is on retrieval of cases that account for the observed behavior, and not on the adaptation of the retrieved cases to solve planning problems. While most traditional plan recognition systems [11] are able to recognize only those plans whose steps are exact matches to the plans in the plan library, a pure case-based approach to plan recognition allows the recognizer to partially match cases (plans) from the library with its observations. A case-based recognizer can therefore recognize plans that are not exact matches to the plans from the library, but instead are similar to the description of a current situation, based on the observed planning steps.

In our system, cases (plans) contain not only knowledge about actions, but also the knowledge about the states of the world seen during the planning. Such state knowledge can be of great utility for case-based plan recognition, because, cases retrieved on a basis of matched planning actions can further be narrowed down by their applicability, given the current state of the world. Bares and his colleagues [5] explore the concept of case-based plan recognition, but, their cases do not represent explored world states like our system does.

A case-based plan recognizer can efficiently overcome difficulties of requiring a complete plan library specified for the recognizer *a priori*. The recognizer can start the recognition process with an incomplete (or empty) plan library and accumulate the plans from observations of the planner's behavior. The observed plans themselves constitute contextualized pieces of knowledge useful for future predictions from observations. The main disadvantage of this approach is that some of the plans observed for the first time may not be recognized by the system initially, because relevant plans may be absent from the plan library. However, the observed plans are then learned and used by the recognizer in subsequent plan observations. The ability to incorporate novel plans into a plan library makes a case-based recognizer applicable to a wide variety of different applications, especially to those where all of the plans may not be known in advance and therefore cannot be enumerated (e.g. recognizing military maneuvers of enemy ground troops).

The ability of a plan recognition system to deal with an incomplete plan library is important, because, constructing a complete plan library can be a difficult knowledge acquisition task. Enumeration of all of the plans in the library can impact the efficiency of the recognizer, because, such an enumeration may include extraneous plans, which the planner will never execute and the recognizer will need not to predict. The methods for automatic plan library construction may suffer from the same problem. Our incremental construction of the plan library ensures that only the plans that were actually observed during the planning process are used in the recognition process, and therefore minimizes the number of extraneous plans in the library. If we assume that the planner is a goal-oriented expert (all performed planning steps are necessary to reach the goal), we are guaranteed that the plan library will contain no extraneous plans.

3. State Knowledge

The focus of our research is to incorporate the knowledge about the states of the world in which the planner finds itself during the planning and the plan recognition processes. Traditionally a plan is simply a sequence of actions that transform the initial state into the goal state. However our system represents a case (i.e., a plan) as a sequence of action-state pairs. Such pairs encode both the action and the new state that results from an action. Note that using this representation, the initial pair in a plan is always the *null* action that "results" in the initial state, and, the final pair is the action that results in the goal state.

The knowledge about the world states allows for more informed recognition of a planner's goals than if the system relied on past actions alone. Competing hypothesis about possible pursued plans and goals based on past actions can further be discriminated on the basis of the current state of the world, as some consistent plans may not be applicable in the current world state. As an example, consider the logistics planning domain, where packages are supposed to be transported to their destinations, which can be either a post office or an airport on an island. Airplanes fly between islands (e.g., from an airport on one island to another), and, trucks transport packages within islands (e.g., between an airport and a post office). In this domain, for example, plans anticipating packages to be loaded into an airplane as the next step may be eliminated from the set of possible hypothesis, given a world state in which no packages are present on an island at which the airplane is. Other researchers have explored the role of the state knowledge to a limited degree. Albrecht and his colleagues show different Bayesian net recognition models, one of which recognizes plans based on the state knowledge. They postulate that such a model would be applicable in domains with limited number of actions [2][1]. Their work is different from ours in that the states they encounter are simplified[2] and the number of different states is relatively small (about 4000).

In order to be able to observe the state of the world during the planning, we focus on state-space planners in which actions change the state of the world [8]. States are represented as sets of instantiated first-order logical predicates (or *ground literals*). For example in the blocksworld domain, {(clear B), (on B A), (on A C), (on-table C), (arm-empty)} represents the state depicted in figure 1.

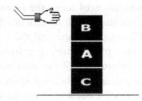

Fig. 1. Example of a blocksworld state {(clear B), (on B A), (on A C), (on-table C), (arm-empty)}.

The most common notion of a plan is an ordered sequence of actions that transforms an initial state of the world to some distinguished goal state. Each action is represented by an operator that has preconditions and effects. Preconditions establish applicability criteria, and, effects change the state of the world. Furthermore, each action starts in a certain state of the world and results in a change from the current state to another one We extend the notion of a plan to a sequence of state changes, where the state changes are caused by the actions the planner performs. Although

---

[1] We are referring to *locationModel*.

[2] States in their research are locations of a player in the context of online dungeon game. These states lack the detail of information provided by combinations of literals corresponding to sensory information.

world state changes in the real-world systems can be caused by exogenous events and external agents [e.g., 3, 16], we do not deal with this issue here.

Many planning systems (case-based or otherwise) [10, 13, 14, 15] also keep track of the world states; however, they commonly focus on a limited set of only two states explored by the planner. That is, planners concentrate on the initial state of the world and a specification of the goal state. Case-based planners are usually given a *partial* representation of the goal state in which the truth values of only some of all of the possible instantiated state predicates (literals) are specified. For example, a goal from the blocksworld domain {(on blockB blockA)} lacks specifications for other state literals, such as positions of other blocks in the problem in hand. Such a *full* specification of a goal state allows for versatility and goal-directed planning, and permits more than one world state to achieve a goal (figure 2).

In our research, we assume that the plan recognition system is given no initial knowledge about partial goals of the planner. Because we focus on keyhole plan recognition, we are limited by available observations of the planner's activity during problem solving. Since state-space planners search the state-space during problem solving, we modified the PRODIGY planning cycle [7] to monitor the world states after the planner performs an action[3] to perform keyhole-like observation of the planner's behavior. Our cases contain all of the world states visited during the planning, along with all of the actions performed by the planner. The goal states in our system are described fully. Therefore, a keyhole-like observation of a goal state treats the goal as just another observed state.

Fig. 2. Both pictures depicted represent a state of the blocksworld domain in which the partial goal *{(on B A)}* is satisfied. The complete state specification for the state on the left is {(on B A), (on D C), (clear B), (clear D), (on-table A), (on-table C), (arm-empty)}, while the state on the right is uniquely determined by {(on B A), (clear B), (clear C), (clear D), (on-table A), (on-table C), (on-table D), (arm-empty)} combination of literals. Eleven other world states, not depicted here, also satisfy goal *{(on B A)}*.

In the next section, we describe a scheme that is able to transform the observed states into their abstracted representation, retaining the knowledge about the structure of a type-generalized world state. The abstracted representation of world states allows us to focus the plan recognition process on the relevant features of the states, within much smaller abstract state-space.

A full representation of a goal state that accounts for state predicates other than ones explicitly given as traditional (partial) planning goals has another advantage

---

[3] We keep track of PRODIGY's *applied operators* during problem solving episodes; we focus only on those applied operators along the solution path. The monitoring is not implemented as those monitors described in [16].

in both case-based planning and plan recognition. A case-based planner may not be able to successfully retrieve a solution to the current problem when only partial goal state predicates are specified. For example, if we assume that the planner encounters a goal specification {(NOT (clear blockA))} for the first time, matching this goal state with states depicted in figure 2 would fail, even if problems in figure 2 were already solved. However, both states in figure 2 implicitly contain state predicates, which define a goal state for the newly seen problem; storing all of the state predicates for goal states would yield successful matches.

Although knowledge about the world states is beneficial for the plan recognition process in state-space planners, the number of possible states in the complete state-space may be quite large. The exact number depends on the domain theory as well as on the instances of objects a particular problem definition may entail. To gain understanding of how large the state-space may be, let us introduce

$$P^i = \{ p \mid p \in D \wedge p \text{ is a predicate} \wedge \mid \arg s(p) \mid = i \}$$

a set of all predicates from the domain theory D that have arity i. Each predicate p has arguments of certain types from the type hierarchy of the domain theory, and, predicates instantiate into ground literals of appropriate types at planning time. For a given problem, let n be the number of different instances, and to account for the worst-case scenario, assume that all n instances are of the same type. We operate under a closed-world assumption, where if a predicate is not known to be *true*, than it is explicitly assumed that the truth-value of a predicate is *false*.

The representation of state-space that accounts for the complete states may be expensive. Given

$$P^0, P^1, ..., P^q, \text{ where } q = \max \mid \arg s(p_i) \mid, \forall p_i \in D$$

the size of a feature bit vector representing a state without any loss of state information in the state-space is

$$\mid \vec{F} \mid = P^0 + nP^1 + n^2 P^2 + ... + n^q P^q = \sum_{i=1}^{q} n^i P^i$$

and the size of the state-space

$$\mid SS \mid = 2^{\mid \vec{F} \mid}.$$

In the blocksworld domain, given only 10 different blocks to work with, the feature vector size is 19, and the state-space size is 524,288. Therefore the approaches based on pruning a fully constructed state-space [e.g. 9] are computationally extremely expensive, because the state-space size prohibits efficient pruning. Such approaches are promising only if they are able to prune large regions of the state-space at one time.

However, except for the simplest domains with small number of possible states, planners tend not to explore all of the state-space during the planning. In fact, the number of states a planner encounters is domain dependent and often constitutes only a fraction of the number of all possible states it may explore, as our experimental results show. Moreover, some of the states in the state-space are simply impossible to achieve. For example, having two blocks stacked on top of each other prohibits both of them from being *clear*. Likewise, a block cannot be on top of itself. Such anomalous states can never be reached. Finally, some of the states may not be useful to the planner, although they may be possible to achieve. If several solutions to some task exist (one of which is the best) then the planner may always opt to prefer the best solution and ignore the traversal of the state-space along sub-optimal paths, thus never encountering any of the states traversed along the sub-optimal solution paths.

Our approach implements incremental construction of the state-space, rather than the pruning of the complete state-space. To ensure that only the states that are useful for the planner are present, we start with empty state-space, monitor the states in which the planner finds itself, and incrementally expand our state-space to include nodes representing only the observed states. The space savings in our approach are significant, because the recognizer ignores the states that are not useful to the planner.

4. Indexing and Similarity

Two of the most important components of any case-based system are its indexing and retrieval mechanisms. The importance is amplified in the context of the plan recognition task, where a case-based recognizer typically does not try to adapt the cases for problem solving, but rather tries to recognize plans that are consistent with observed planning behavior. As described in Section 3, plans are equivalent to cases in our system. Each case describes the temporal ordering of actions in the plan, as well as the world states before and after each action is performed, which represents all of the information we are able to observe during the keyhole state-space planning. Although it would be very interesting to incorporate knowledge about the planning failures, our initial work focuses on the situation where observed plans achieve their goals, and, the recognizer deals only with the actions and world states along the solution path ignoring the rest of the planner's unsuccessful search. Such an approach mimics the behavior of an expert planning agent. It also enables the system to minimize the number of world states of which it needs to keep track, although knowledge of situations in which planning failures occurred would be useful in recognizing such subsequent failures (e.g. Hammond's failure anticipation). Our future research efforts will explore this aspect of failure-driven learning.

The indexing mechanism in our system is based on matching the current state of the world with the world states observed previously during planning. One can think of the world states (and actions taken) as the recognizer's sensory inputs, which describe a specific situation in which the planner finds itself. When the planner encounters a similar situation in the future, the recognizer can draw predictions given the knowledge about planner's behavior in known similar situations. As the number of states explored by the planner can be quite large, the naïve indexing-scheme in which a state is compared with every other state, can prove to be very inefficient. Our indexing scheme employs a simple abstraction, at level of which states can be more efficiently compared and retrieved.

The plan recognition algorithm observes the planner's current state of the world as well as the current action that produced the world state. Based on these observations and a partial plan observed so far, the recognizer retrieves the plans (cases) that account for the observations, and predicts possible goals and plans that the planner may be pursuing. The retrieved cases are ranked by their relevance. Once the goal state is reached, we collect information about system's predictions and evaluate its usefulness.

The case base consists of a few hash tables for indexing purposes and a graph-based representation of the abstracted state-space that is constructed from the observations of planner's search. To increase indexing efficiency, we employ a simple abstraction scheme in which states of the world are abstracted to their type-generalized state predicates [14][4]. The abstract state representation is a non-negative integer vector in which each dimension represents a number of instances of a single type-generalized state predicate. For instance, the dimensions of abstract state feature vectors in the blocksworld planning domain are depicted in fig. 3. Abstract states constitute vertices of the abstracted state-space graph, in which an edge from one abstract state to another indicates the observation of an action that changed the former world state into the latter one. Each case can be abstracted to represent a path in the abstracted state-space graph.

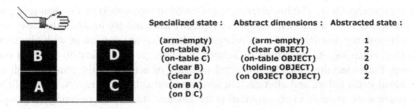

Specialized state :	Abstract dimensions :	Abstracted state :
(arm-empty)	(arm-empty)	1
(on-table A)	(clear OBJECT)	2
(on-table C)	(on-table OBJECT)	2
(clear B)	(holding OBJECT)	0
(clear D)	(on OBJECT OBJECT)	2
(on B A)		
(on D C)		

Fig. 3. An example of a blocksworld planning domain state of the world and its representations. State predicates, whose truth values are false, are not shown in the *specialized state*.

A case is indexed by its abstracted state representation. Each abstract state points to a set of specialized world states (i.e., ground literals) indexed by it. These in turn point to the cases that contain them. Because we utilize hash tables for indexing cases and world states by abstract state representations, this scheme allows us to retrieve the initial set of matching cases very efficiently. When the recognizer tries to retrieve cases that match with observed plan steps, it first uses the abstract representation of the current state of the world to retrieve those cases that contain the current abstract state. If the current abstract state has never been observed before, the recognizer tries to find *similar* abstract states and returns the cases containing these states. If the recognizer cannot retrieve any such cases (i.e. no situations similar to the current one were observed in the past), it is unable to make predictions at this time and opts to wait for observations of subsequent planning steps. The use of abstract world

---

[4] State literal from the logistics planning domain, such as (at-obj A-300.1 JFK_NY.1) would be type-generalized to (at-obj AIRPLANE AIRPORT), because the type of instances A-300.1 and JFK_NY.1 are AIRPLANE and AIRPORT respectively.

states is an efficient indexing scheme at the top level, as the number of abstract states is much smaller than the number of specialized world states, and the distribution of specialized states into bins indexed by their abstracted representation provides means to eliminate a large number of possible hypothesis and focus the recognition process on the relevant cases.

More specifically, if no exact matches are found for the current abstract state, the recognizer attempts to find nodes in the state-space graph that are similar to the current abstract state as follows. Since abstract states are represented as feature vectors of positive integers, our system uses a modified nearest neighbor similarity metric, where the neighbor states considered are those which differ from the current abstract state by some distance in each dimension[5]. Similar abstract states are then ranked by their distance, and the abstract state at the shortest distance is used for retrieval.

After cases that matched at the abstract level are retrieved, the abstract states from the retrieved cases that matched with the current abstracted world state are compared at the specialized level (i.e. at the *ground literal* level). The similarity metric we currently use to match states is the same metric used in [14][6]. Note that the indexing scheme at the level of abstracted world states ensures that all of the cases potentially similar at the specialized level will be considered. We are currently investigating the matching of cases at the specialized level by using a graph representation, where the specialized world states are encoded as directed graphs, and case matching is equivalent to the graph-isomorphism problem. This will increase the efficiency of the recognizer, because the complexity of the current approach is $O(n!)$. In contrast, there exist polynomial-time algorithms for graph-isomorphism for certain classes of graphs. Furthermore, since graph-isomorphism is an equivalence relation, the specialized world states corresponding to a single abstracted world state can further be indexed by their equivalence classes, thus reducing the amount of search during the retrieval.

If the set of possible plan hypothesis consists of a single case at this point, the case is used to guide the recognition process and form predictions. If more than one case is still a match, the recognizer uses the knowledge about the actions and past states in the matched cases to prefer the cases whose actions and states are more consistent with the plan observed so far. At present time, the matching scheme employs a graph matching algorithm, where cases can be abstracted into their abstract paths and matched among themselves.

The abstraction scheme provides a means of rapid access to the specialized world states indexed by their abstract representation. It is a one-to-many relation, because an abstract state may index several specialized states. The result is a smaller set of first level indexes, which ensures similarity at the level of specialized states. The exact space savings of such an abstraction scheme depend on the domain theory. In general, the number of possible abstract states for a given domain theory is

$$\prod_{i=1}^{d} m_i$$

---

[5] To increase matching efficiency, only the states that were actually observed within a ball with given radius are considered.

[6] The threshold we used in our similarity matching scheme was 2.

where d is the number of abstract dimensions, and m_i is the maximum possible value in abstract dimension i. Given n object instances, abstract dimensions corresponding to i-ary predicates may possibly have values from 0 to n^i. For example, in the case of the blocksworld domain, the abstracted state feature vector size is five (i.e., the number of abstract dimensions), and number of possible abstract states for ten object instances is 48,884. This represents a considerable savings when compared to the number of all possible specialized states (see section 3). As stated before, not all of these states are possible; in the blocksworld domain, there cannot be more than n-1 instances of the *on* state predicate, because no more than n-1 blocks can be stacked directly on top of other blocks. Also, the only possible values for the abstracted *holding* state predicate are zero and one, since the domain theory restricts resources to only one robot arm with which the blocks can be picked up. Effectively, this reduces the possible abstract state-space to 4,840 possible states. Some of the remaining abstract states are still not possible. For example, abstract state that has a nine as a value of *on* state predicate dimension, cannot have more than a value of one in either *clear* or *ontable* dimensions (assuming ten object instances). The incremental construction of the case library assures that the number of both abstract and specialized states actually stored is minimal.

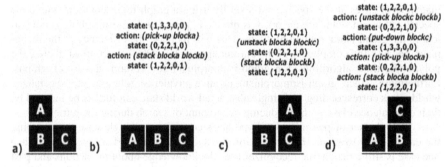

Fig. 4. a) The goal state reached by all of the problems. b-d) The initial states and abstracted plans, for problems *p1* (b), *p2* (c), and *p3* (d).

5. Implementation

To illustrate the approach discussed above, we will discuss two examples of the plan recognition task, implemented in the blocksworld planning domain. The observed planning agent is the PRODIGY nonlinear state-space planner whose execution cycle was slightly modified in order to observe the world states traversed along the solution path. Plans for problems successfully solved by the planner are then augmented to contain the state information and are passed to the recognizer for observation of simulated plan execution.

We first show how the knowledge about the world states can enable the recognizer to cope with situations in which a completely new action is encountered. Consider the problems in figure 4 where the planner's partial goal is to have blockA on top of blockB. We start with an empty plan library, observe the very first plan (*p1*), and store this plan in the case library. The contents of the library after the first plan is observed are depicted in figure 5. During observations of the second plan (*p2*), the first action performed by the planner is *unstack*, which has not been seen before. However, the world state reached after *unstack* action was already explored in the past (the second state in plan *p1*). The recognizer makes predictions based on the planner's decisions in the matched situation, and is able to correctly predict the next world state and planner's goal as depicted in figure 6a. The same scenario happens when the recognizer observes plan *p3*, because action *put-down* is seen for the first time. Again, the recognizer forms correct predictions based on the decisions made in a similar situation (the first world state in plan *p1*) as depicted in figure 6b.

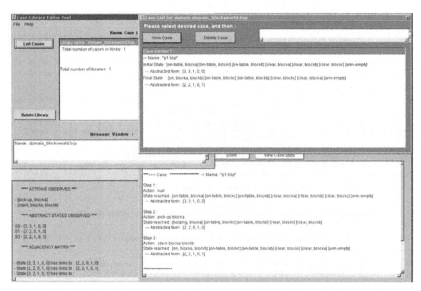

Fig. 5. The contents of the plan library after a single plan *p1* is observed.

The case-based nature of the plan recognition system enables it to form predictions even in completely new situations, because the situations from past plans (cases) can facilitate partial matches of those cases with the current situation. To illustrate this point, assume that the only plans observed by the recognizer are the plans described in the previous example and the initial world state of a new plan (*p4* of figure 1), having all three blocks stacked in a tower) has just been observed. The recognizer first abstracts the observed world state into its abstract state vector representation of (1,1,1,0,2), and attempts to find cases indexed by this abstract state in its library. As this abstract state is a completely new one, this first retrieval phase finds no matches to the current abstracted situation. The recognizer next searches its state-space graph for neighbor states, and successfully finds the abstract state (1,2,2,0,1) at the shortest distance from the current abstract state. Three states are indexed by the matched abstract state, and one of these states is the goal state. The matched goal state is eliminated, because the planner made no subsequent decisions after this state was observed. At this point, the recognizer is able to use two specialized states to

```
...
                    Observing the next plan step...
          - Action observed : [unstack, blocka, blockc]
                       - Current state  :
[[holding, blocka], [on-table, blockc], [on-table, blockb], [clear, blockc], [clear, blockb]]
          ********** Abstracted state : [2, 2, 0, 1, 0]

          Retrieve_Matches : EXACT MATCHES AT ABSTRACT STATE LEVEL !!!!
For state [2, 2, 1, 0, 1] following cases were found : [PlanRecogni-tion.Case@1ba640]
                    ...
                    Observing the next plan step...
          - Action observed :  [stack, blocka, blockb]
                       - Current state  :
[[on, blocka, blockb], [on-table, blockc], [on-table, blockb], [clear, blockc], [clear, blocka], [arm-empty]]
          ********** Abstracted state : [2, 2, 1, 0, 1]

          Verifying the predictions made at the previous planning step :

          Predicted next state correctly : true, predicted state was :
[on, blocka, blockb] [on-table, blockc] [on-table, blockb] [clear, blockc] [clear, blocka] [arm-empty]
--- Abstracted form : [2, 2, 1, 0, 1], Predicted abstract state was [2, 2, 1, 0, 1]

          Predicted next action correctly : true, predicted action was "stack blocka blockb"


                           6a)


                    ...
                    Observing the next plan step...
          - Action observed :  [put-down, blockc]
                       - Current state  :
[[on-table, blockc], [on-table, blocka], [on-table, blockb], [clear, blockb], [clear, blocka], [clear, blockc], [arm-empty]]
          ********** Abstracted state : [3, 3, 1, 0, 0]

          Retrieve_Matches : EXACT MATCHES AT ABSTRACT STATE LEVEL !!!!
For state [3, 3, 1, 0, 0] following cases were found : [PlanRecogni-tion.Case@1ba640]
          Adding an edge into state-space graph...
                    ...
                    Observing the next plan step...
          - Action observed :  [pick-up, blocka]
                       - Current state  :
[[holding, blocka], [on-table, blockc], [on-table, blockb], [clear, blockb], [clear, blockc]]
          ********** Abstracted state : [2, 2, 0, 1, 0]

          Verifying the predictions made at the previous planning step :

          Predicted next state correctly : true, predicted state was :
[holding, blocka] [on-table, blockc] [on-table, blockb] [clear, blockb] [clear, blockc]
--- Abstracted form : [2, 2, 0, 1, 0], Predicted abstract state was [2, 2, 0, 1, 0]

          Predicted next action correctly : true, predicted action was "pick-up blocka"


                           6b)
```

Fig. 6. The predictions made by the recognizer in light of unknown actions. a) Predictions after action *unstack* in plan p2 is observed for the first time; b) Predictions after a new action *put-down* in plan p3 is observed.

form predictions. As both matched states were followed by an *unstack* action, the recognizer successfully predicts planner's next action of unstacking blockC off of the block it is on. The goal prediction in this particular case is trivial, given a match and only one goal state observed. The recognizer then observes the next plan step consisting of an *unstack* action and abstract state (0,1,1,1,1), also seen for the first time. Nevertheless, predictions can be formed again, in the same fashion as done before.

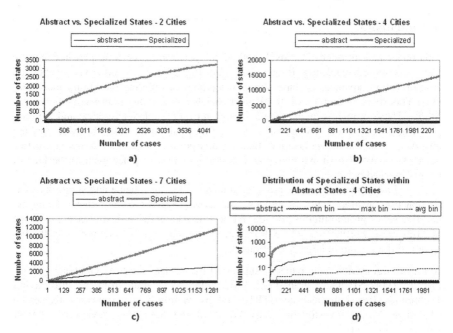

Fig. 7. a) – c) represent the number of abstract versus specialized world states in the logistics planning domain for 2, 4, and 7 cities respectively. d) is a logarithmic plot of the distribution of specialized world states indexed by their abstract state "bins".

In order to experimentally determine the number of possible abstract world states for a given domain, we randomly generated problem sets in the logistics planning domain. Each problems set contained 3000 problems and a fixed number of cities. The number of cities ranged from 2 to 9, for a total of 8 problem sets. We executed the problems using PRODIGY, with a time-bound of 16 seconds. The planner successfully generated solutions (plans) to about 80% of the problems (some did not finish in the time allowed). We then considered the generated plans as inputs to the plan recognition system in order to determine the ratio of abstract states versus the specialized states, as well as the distribution of specialized states into "bins" indexed by abstract states. As we can see from figure 7[7], the number of abstract states observed is much smaller than the number of specialized states, and the rate at which new abstract states are recognized is also considerably smaller than the recognition rate of abstract world states. Figure 7(d) shows a logarithmic plot of the number of abstract states (first-level indexes) and the statistics for the specialized states which they index. The minimum (1) and the maximum (201) bin sizes represent extremes, while the average bin size reaches 16 specialized states for the plans collected. These results are very encouraging. Our future research efforts will experimentally determine the asymptotic abstract state-space behavior for other planning domains.

---

[7] Due to a lack of space, not all of the results are depicted in figure 7.

6. Conclusion

This paper has introduced a novel method for performing keyhole plan recognition using case-based reasoning. Rather than requiring a hand- (or otherwise) generated case library in advance, we have shown a method for building the library incrementally. This solves a number of problems associated with many plan recognition algorithms. These problems include the assumption of a complete case-base and the danger of irrelevant cases. By incrementally adding plans to the case library as they are observed, we avoid the inclusion of theoretically possible cases that do not in practice occur. We have also shown how plan recognition can take place even in the face of novel observed behavior.

Furthermore, we have provided a novel indexing scheme and similarity metric that uses abstract states as indices. The use of abstract states rather than an exhaustive set of ground literals provides a tractable means for retrieval when a large set of cases exist. Further research will produce empirical results to demonstrate the behavior of the system in large case libraries.

Acknowledgements. This paper is supported by the Dayton Area Graduate Studies Institute (DAGSI) under grant #HE-WSU-99-09, by a grant from the Information Technology Research Institute (ITRI), and by Wright State University (Research Challenge: Young Investigator grant). We thank the anonymous reviewers for their valuable comments.

References

1. Allen, J. F., and Perrault, C. R.: Analyzing intention in dialogues. *Artificial Intelligence* 15(3) (1980) 143-- 178.
2. Albrecht, D. W., Zukerman, I, and Nicholson, A. E.: Bayesian models for keyhole plan recognition in an adventure game. *User Modeling and User-Adapted Interaction*, 8 (1998) 5--47.
3. Blythe, J.: Planning under uncertainty. *Doctoral thesis. Technical Report, CMU-CS-98-147*. Computer Science Dept., Carnegie Mellon University (1998).
4. Bauer, M.: Machine learning for user modeling and plan recognition. In V. Moustakis J. Herrmann, editor, *Proc. ICML'96 Workshop "Machine Learning meets Human Computer Interaction"* (1996) 5--16.
5. Bares, M., Canamero, D., Delannoy, J.-F., and Kodratoff, Y.: *XPlans: Case-Based Reasoning for Plan Recognition*. Applied Artificial Intelligence 8 (1994) 617—643.
6. Carberry, S.: *Plan Recognition in Natural Language Dialogue*. MIT Press (1990).
7. Carbonell, J. G., Blythe, J., Etzioni, O., Gil, Y., Joseph, J., Kahn, D., Knoblock, C., Minton, S., Perez, A., Reilly, S., Veloso, M., and Wang, X.: Prodigy4.0: The Manual and Tutorial. *Technical Report, CMU-CS-92-150*. Computer Science Dept., Carnegie Mellon University (1992).
8. Fikes, R. and Nilsson, N.: STRIPS: A new approach to the application of theorem prov*ing to problem solving*. In James Allen, James Hendler, and Austin Tate, editors, Readings in Planning. Morgan Kaufmann (1990).
9. Fish, D.: A Dynamic Memory Organization for Case-Based Reasoning Supporting Case Similarity Determination and Learning Via Local Clustering. *Masters Thesis*. Computer Science Dept., University of Connecticut (1995).

10. Hammond, C.: *Case-Based Planning: Viewing Planning as a Memory Task.* Academic Press, San Diego (1989).
11. Kautz, H.: A formal theory of plan recognition and its implementation. In J. Allen, H. Kautz, R. Pelavin and J. Tenenberg, *Reasoning about plans*, Morgan Kaufmann (1991).
12. Lesh, N., and Etzioni, E.: Scaling up goal recognition. In *Proceedings of the 5th International Conference on Principles of knowledge Representation and Reasoning* (1996) 178--189.
13. Penberthy, J. S., and Weld, D. S.: *UCPOP: A sound, complete, partial order planner for ADL.* In Proceedings of KR-92 (1992) 103--114.
14. Veloso, M.: Planning and learning by analogical reasoning. Springer-Verlag (1994).
15. Veloso, M., Carbonell, J., Perez, A., Borrajo, D., Fink, E. and Blythe, J.: Integrating planning and learning: The PRODIGY architecture. *Journal of Theoretical and Experimental Artificial Intelligence.* 7(1) (1995) 81--120.
16. Veloso, M. M., Pollack, M. E., and Cox, M. T.: Rationale-based monitoring for continuous planning in dynamic environments. In R. Simmons, M. Veloso, & S. Smith (Eds.), *Proceedings of the Fourth International Conference on Artificial Intelligence Planning Systems.* Menlo Park, AAAI Press (1998) 171--177.
17. Weida, R. and Litman, D.: *Terminological plan reasoning and recognition.* In Proceedings of the Third International Workshop on User Modeling (1992) 177--191.

A Similarity-Based Approach to Attribute Selection in User-Adaptive Sales Dialogs

Andreas Kohlmaier, Sascha Schmitt, and Ralph Bergmann

Artificial Intelligence – Knowledge-Based Systems Group
Department of Computer Science, University of Kaiserslautern
67653 Kaiserslautern, Germany
{kohlma|sschmitt|bergmann}@informatik.uni-kl.de

Abstract. For dynamic sales dialogs in electronic commerce scenarios, approaches based on an information gain measure used for attribute selection have been suggested. These measures consider the distribution of attribute values in the case base and are focused on the reduction of dialog length. The implicit knowledge contained in the similarity measures is neglected. Another important aspect that has not been investigated either is the quality of the produced dialogs, i.e. if the retrieval result is appropriate to the customer's demands. Our approach takes the more direct way to the target products by asking the attributes that induce the maximum change of similarity distribution amongst the candidate cases, thereby faster discriminating the case base in similar and dissimilar cases. Evaluations show that this approach produces dialogs that reach the expected retrieval result with fewer questions. In real world scenarios, it is possible that the customer cannot answer a question. To nevertheless reach satisfactory results, one has to balance between a high information gain and the probability that the question will not be answered. We use a Bayesian Network to estimate these probabilities.

1. Introduction

Online customers need information adequate to their demands instead of pure data. They want personalized advice and product offerings instead of simple possibilities for product search [15]. Gaining sufficient information from the customer but also providing her/him with information at the right place is the key. Resulting from this fact, an automated communication process is needed that simulates the sales dialog between customers and sales persons.

Especially in electronic commerce (EC) scenarios, it is very important to ask as few questions as possible adapted to the customers' knowledge about the product space. It has to be taken into account that online customers are very quickly annoyed and/or bored and the next e-shop is only one mouse click away.

Recently, a couple of CBR approaches to automated sales dialogs have been suggested [5,14]. The ideas that can be found have in common that their aim is the reduction of the number of questions (dialog length) a customer is asked by the sales system. Most of the approaches are based on an information gain measure that is used to select the next attribute to ask which is maximally discriminating the product

D.W. Aha and I. Watson (Eds.): ICCBR 2001, LNAI 2080, pp. 306-320, 2001.

database, i.e. limits the number of product cases. Unfortunately, a couple of problems can be found in those approaches:

- The system-inherent similarity information is neglected and stays unused in this context. Attributes with a statistically high information gain might not contribute to a similar solution (product). A straightforward counterexample is the unique product ID, which certainly discriminates the case base perfectly. If a customer knew the ID of the desired product it would be found with a single question.
- Online sales have to deal with different kinds of customers with different knowledge about the products. An unanswered question or one that is not understood by the customer is of no practical use in the electronic sales process.
- It has not been considered that each question entails certain costs with the effect that the customer can terminate the sales dialog without buying as soon as a certain satisfaction level is undergone.
- The assessment of these approaches is only concentrated on dialog length. It is not considered how well does the retrieval result fit (quality of the dialog) with respect to the information gained by the dialog.

In this paper, a new attribute selection strategy especially tailored to EC scenarios is presented, which replaces the proposed information gain measures by a similarity influence measure. Furthermore, the attribute selection also depends on a probability estimation of the customers' ability to answer this question. A Bayesian Network is used that also adapts to the current customer's behavior to manage these probabilities. To finally select an attribute, utility values are derived from combination of the probabilities and the similarity variance, *simVar*. To emphasize the advantages gained by our approach, we made a detailed evaluation considering various influence factors of a dynamically interpreted dialog strategy focussing on the quality in terms of correctness with respect to a reference retrieval and the length of the produced dialogs. We compared the results to an entropy information gain measure. The case base used for our tests contained personal computer systems.

Section 2 describes the principle of a dynamically interpreted dialog strategy and presents several influencing factors of the produced dialog. An attribute selection strategy based on similarity influence that overcomes the problem of unlabelled data and utilizes the knowledge contained in similarity measures is presented in section 3. Section 4 deals with the necessity to dynamically adapt to the customer during the dialog as not all questions have the same answering cost for everyone. Section 5 presents a comprehensive evaluation of the different influence factors focusing on the quality of the produced dialogs. We end with related work and conclusions as well as an outlook on future work.

2. Dynamically Interpreted Dialog Strategies

In our sense, a dynamically interpreted dialog strategy [12] does not process a previously generated decision tree but also decides which attribute to ask next during the dialog [1,2]. This has the dual benefit of being more flexible to adapt to the current customer and to avoid the construction of an exhaustive decision tree, which can be problematic for unlabelled data and continuous value ranges [9,14].

Input: CaseBase
Output: Set of Retrieved Cases

Procedure Dialog (CaseBase)
Candidate_Cases := CaseBase;
Query := Empty_Query;
While not **Terminate** do {
                Attribute := **Select_Attribute** (Candidate_Cases, Query);
                Value := Ask_Question (Attribute);
                Query := Assign_Value (Query, Attribute, Value);
                Candidate_Cases := **Partition** (Candidate_Cases, Query); }
end;

Fig. 1. Algorithm for a dynamically interpreted dialog strategy. (In a meta-language notation.)

Figure 1 presents the principle algorithm for a dialog strategy to be computed at runtime. The strategy starts with an empty problem description (Query) and chooses a first question (Attribute) according to the attribute selection strategy. Depending on the answer to the proposed question, the set of candidate cases is reduced and the process is iterated until a termination criterion is fulfilled. Three different aspects can be identified that influence the dialog strategy:

1.   The **attribute selection strategy** determines which attribute to ask next and influences the *dialog length*. A good questioning strategy leads to minimal dialogs with optimal results. Section 3 explains in more detail how to determine an optimal result.

2.   The **termination criterion** determines when enough information has been gathered. It therefore influences the *quality of the result* and the dialog length. A perfect termination criterion should continue asking questions until the optimal result is reached. Since it is not known in advance what the optimal solution is, several possible termination criteria can be examined. E.g., Doyle & Cunningham [5] suggest continuing asking questions until a manageable set of n cases remains (e.g., $n = 20$) or all attributes are asked. A more suitable way for EC is to check if the expected information gain for all remaining attributes falls below a given threshold. Section 5 investigates in detail the influence of the termination criterion on the quality of the dialog.

3.   The **partitioning strategy** is used to reduce the search space to the best matching candidate cases. A partitioning strategy traditionally used in the construction of decision tress is to exclude all cases that do not exactly match the given attribute. This approach can be broadened to exclude all cases that do not reach a certain threshold of similarity. It has to be investigated how the partitioning strategy affects the recall of the dialog, i.e. how many possible solutions are erratically excluded from the search space. However, in this paper, the influence of partitioning will not be further investigated. We chose a sufficiently high threshold and in tests with our criterion for correctness of dialogs (cf. Section 5) it turned out that we do not lose any solutions. (We used this same partitioning strategy for all tests.)

Section 5 gives experimental data that measures the influences of the described factors on the length and quality of the produced dialogs.

3.   A Similarity Influence Measure for Attribute Selection

Attributes asked to the customer should be selected on the basis of how much information they contribute to select possible cases from the case base. Most attribute selection strategies evaluate the information gain for a given attribute on the basis of the distribution of attribute values to distinct classes. The most commonly known strategy is the measure of expected information gain introduced by Quinlan [9] in the ID3 algorithm for the construction of decision trees.

To apply the measure of expected information gain on unclassified cases which occur in an online product guide, it is either necessary to pre-cluster the case base to generate an artificial classification or to directly use the case identifier as the class label [5].

A different approach that is better tailored to deal with unlabelled cases is to select attributes not on the basis of their information gain but on the basis of the influence of a known value on the similarity of a given set of cases. In an online shop, it is desirable to present the customer a selection of products most similar to her/his query. It is therefore a reasonable strategy to first ask the attributes that have the highest influence on the similarity of the cases (products) stored in the case base.

3.1   The Variance of Similarities

A way to measure the influence on similarities is to calculate the variance Var of similarities a query q induces on the set of candidate cases C:

$$Var(q,C) = \frac{1}{|C|} \cdot \sum_{c \in C} (sim(q,c) - \mu)^2 \qquad \text{(Variance of Similarities for a Query)}$$

Here, $sim(q,c)$ denotes the similarity of the query q and the case c, μ denotes the average value of all similarities.

When asking a question the assigned value is not known in advance. It is therefore necessary to select the attribute only on the expected similarity influence $simVar$, which depends on the probability p_v that the value v is chosen for the attribute A:

$$simVar(q,A,C) = \sum_v p_v \cdot Var(q_{A \leftarrow v}, C) \qquad \text{(Expected Similarity Influence of an Attribute)}$$

$Var(q_{A \leftarrow v}, C)$ defines the similarity influence of assigning a value v to an attribute A of the query q. To simplify the computation of $simVar(q,A,C)$ it is possible to consider only the attribute values v that occur in the case set C. Then, the probability p_v for the value v can be calculated from the sample of cases in C, i.e. $p_v = |C^v| / |C|$. (Here, it has to be remarked that at present the calculation of p_v only follows a heuristic. The distribution of values in the case base is certainly not the same like for the real customer buying behavior of products. However, without loss of generality this function can easily be exchanged.)

In a dialog situation, the attribute with the highest expected similarity influence on the set of candidate cases is selected. This strategy leads to the highest increase of knowledge about similarity thereby faster discriminating the case base in similar and dissimilar cases.

3.2 Why Variance of Similarities as a Heuristic?

Bergmann et al. [3] examined the (classical) role of similarity in CBR and suggested to ask about the intuitive meaning of a similarity measure. In contrast to, e.g., equality, similarity is not an elementary concept with a well-defined semantics and it would be appreciated if it could be reduced to such a concept. In [3], it was pointed out that similarity measures always try to approximate some form of utility. Referring to that, the *simVar* measure interprets similarity as an estimation of the probability that the customer is contented with the retrieved products, under the conditions of the information given by the dialog performed so far. This information significantly influences the procedure to select the next attribute to ask for. *simVar* tries to optimize the degree of customer satisfaction. It should be clear that the aim of optimization is not to find the absolute best products but to find one which satisfies the customer's wishes in a sufficient way.

The aim of a good selection strategy should be to select an attribute to be set in the query by which the similarity for product candidates is increased in the average. This aim is reached when *simVar* is maximal on the current set on candidate cases. With this method, in addition candidates with an already high similarity are preferred. It should be noted that *simVar* only calculates the *a priori* (expected) variance. Depending on the customer's answer to the question, the *a posteriori* variance may decrease.

An aspect that is not considered by other proposed approaches for attribute selection strategies is that the amount of information provided by customers also depends on their background knowledge of the product domain. The ensuing section deals with this issue.

4.   Answering Cost Estimation

In diagnostic domains it is common practice to consider the cost of every examination. Current approaches for EC implicitly assume that every question has the same cost. This assumption is fairly accurate as long as every customer can and is willing to answer every posed question. But in a real world EC scenario, it is quite possible that a customer does not answer a question, either because s/he does not care about the proposed attribute or s/he does not understand the meaning of the attribute. Traditional attribute selection strategies can be misleading in this situation because they do not take into account that asking a question may not result in the assignment of a value to an attribute. It is therefore necessary to model in more detail the possible outcomes of asking a question and to define a *utility* for the different outcomes. During the dialog situation, the question with the highest expected utility will be asked. An additionally very important factor is the customers' degree of satisfaction during the dialog. According to Raskutti & Zuckerman's nuisance factor [10], we introduced a satisfaction level to mirror this aspect. This level is decreased dependent on the questions posed and the customers' action respectively. This level is decreased dependent on the questions posed and the customers' action respectively. Usually, a customer will not answer any desired number of questions, especially if the questions are not understood or s/he does not care about the attribute asked.

4.1   Integrating Question Answering Costs

The *expected utility EU* of an action A^1 with the possible results *Result(A)* is defined by the probability $p(a|E)$ that a is the outcome of A based on the current knowledge E of the world and the utility of the outcome a, as suggested by Russell & Norvig [11]. Utilities model a preference relation between the different outcomes of A. An outcome a with a higher utility is preferred to an outcome with lower utility. The expected utility of an action A can be defined as:

$$EU(A \mid E) := \sum_{a \in Result(A)} U(a_A) \cdot p(a_A \mid E) \qquad \textbf{(Expected Utility of an Action)}$$

We will now discuss in detail the possible outcomes of the proposal of a question and their utility with respect to constructing a dialog that leads to customers' buying decision.

The most preferred outcome of a posed question is that the user answers the question, i.e. a value is assigned to the respective attribute. The utility of this outcome depends on the average discrimination power of the attribute.

It is also possible that the customer does not want to assign a value to this attribute, because it is of no importance to her/him. Although the discrimination power of this attribute can be very high, there is no actual gain in knowledge[2] for this outcome, because no value can be assigned to the attribute. Such an outcome should be avoided, because it unnecessarily increases the dialog length.

Another possible outcome is that the customer cannot assign a value to the attribute because s/he does not understand the question. This situation is astonishingly common, as most decision guides ask very technical questions that cannot be answered by a novice user. This outcome has the lowest possible utility as it does not only result in an information gain of zero but also in frustration of the user, that could lead to unsuccessful cancellation of the dialog.

It is possible to model the intermediate outcome that the customer was only able to answer the question with significant difficulties. A possible indicator for this can be that the customer has consulted some sort of help pages provided by the system. The utility of this outcome also depends on the discrimination power of the attribute but is

---

[1] In our case, there is only one action A for an Attribute A, namely asking the attribute's value. E.g., Shimazu [13] suggests navigation by proposing as further action.

[2] It can however be possible to conclude the importance of other attributes from this outcome, so that there is some gain in knowledge.

lower than a direct answer of the question, as it may lead to customers' frustration, too. Table 1 summarizes the possible outcomes of questions and their utility.

To assign exact numerical values to the utility of each outcome depending on the expected information gain (*info*) of the attribute, the following function $U: Result(A) \rightarrow [-1,1]$ is used:

$$
U(a_A) := \begin{cases}
info(A) & \text{if } a_A = \text{"answered without help"} \\
info(A) - d & \text{if } a_A = \text{"answered with help"} \\
0 & \text{if } a_A = \text{"don't care"} \\
0 - 2d & \text{if } a_A = \text{"don't understand"}
\end{cases}
$$

Here d denotes the penalty for lost information because a question cannot be asked because of the decrease in user satisfaction. To assign a value to d, it is necessary to assess the *a priori* information gain of the chance to ask a question. Since the information gain of future questions is not known in advance, a plausible estimation is to give d half the information gain of the current question. Of course, it is conceivable to choose d differently, e.g., dependent on each one of the customer classes. More utility functions have to be investigated in the future.

To compute the overall utility of a question, the probabilities $p(a|E)$ are needed. These probabilities differ for every customer and strongly depend on her/his background knowledge of the given domain. We use a Bayesian Network to assess the customers' background knowledge.

Table 1. Possible outcomes of posing a question and their expected utility.

Event	Description	Effect	Utility
answered without problems	the question was answered without aid of the help function	the attribute is assigned a value, information is gained	high, depending on the gained information
answered with help	the question was confusing, but the customer managed to answer the question after studying the built-in help system	the attribute is assigned a value, information is gained, the customer is bothered	medium, depending on the gained information
don't care	the customer understands the meaning of the question, but its result is of no importance to her/him	no value is assigned, inform. on the importance of attributes is gained	none
don't understand	the customer could not answer the question	no information gain, the customer is frustrated	negative, because of information loss

4.2   Calculation of Outcome Probabilities Using a Bayesian Network

A Bayesian Network is a representation of causal relationships (links) between random variables (nodes), which allows inference on the variables. Associated with each node is a distribution of values for the random variable. Associated with each link is a conditional probability table, describing the probability distribution of the random variable dependent on the probability distribution of the parent node. Using the information contained in these tables, it is possible to propagate probability distributions over the network. If the probability distribution of one random variable is known, the distribution of the linked random variables can be calculated (cf. [8,7]).

In the EC scenario, there is a random variable that represents the customers' background knowledge of the domain and a variable for each possible question. The question variables are directly dependent on the customers' knowledge.

The shop owner has to supply the *a priori* distribution of customers according to their knowledge of the domain, and the conditional probability tables describing the probability of each question outcome depending on the background knowledge of the user. Table 2 gives an example of a conditional probability table for the attributes CPU Speed and CPU Front Side Bus in the domain of a personal computer (PC) e-shop.

Table 2. Example for a conditional probability tables for CPU Speed and CPU Front Side Bus.

CPU Speed	without help	with help	don´t care	don´t understand
Professional	0.90	0.05	0.05	0.0
Intermediate	0.70	0.10	0.15	0.05
Beginner	0.50	0.20	0.20	0.10

CPU FSB	without help	with help	don´t care	don´t understand
Professional	0.50	0.30	0.10	0.10
Intermediate	0.30	0.40	0.20	0.10
Beginner	0.05	0.10	0.20	0.65

At the beginning of a dialog, only the *a priori* distribution of users in classes according to their background knowledge as assessed by the shop owner is known. This gives the unconditional probability that a customer has a certain degree of knowledge about the domain, if nothing else is known about the customer. With this information and the conditional probability tables associated with each link, the probabilities of every outcome of each question can be inferred. And, with this information the question that has the highest expected utility can be selected according to what is currently known about the customer. Then, during the execution of the dialog this question is posed, and the result is given as evidence to the Bayesian Network. This evidence is used to better assess the customers' domain knowledge by inferring the new distribution of the domain knowledge variable. This new information is then propagated through the network to every question node, so that the probability distributions of each question are modified to include the newly acquired information about the customer. So, as more and more information about the customer is acquired the utilities for each question change and therefore the attribute selection strategy is adapted to the customer.

At the end of each dialog, all the accumulated evidence can be used to train the behavior of the Bayesian Network. There exist a variety of learning algorithms for Bayesian Networks that learn the conditional probability tables and unconditional probability distributions. Such algorithms can be found in, e.g., [8,7].

5. Evaluation of Dynamic Dialog Strategies

To test the different aspects of our approach for a dynamic dialog system, we used a domain of 217 cases describing PC systems. Each case consisted of 28 attributes ranging from more generally known attributes to highly technical ones. The cases were generated by a PC configuration system [14].

5.1   Test Environment

We employed the *leave one out* strategy for each test 200 times. A single case was removed from the case base and used as the reference query, describing the completely known customer's demands. This reference query was used for retrieval on the case base and returned the ideal result, i.e. the best possible result when all information is available. The result consists of an ordered list of the 10 cases with highest similarity to the reference query. We used a *customer agent* to simulate the behavior of a real customer. The customer agent was repetitiously asked questions by the system and supplied one by one the attribute values of the reference query. We implemented two different kinds of agents, an ideal customer agent that can answer every question and a real life customer agent that can only answer questions with a certain probability. After each question, a retrieval with the partially filled query was performed and this result was compared to the ideal retrieval result of the reference query. The result of the retrieval was considered successful if the three best cases of the current retrieval result could be found amongst the five best cases of the ideal retrieval result (reference retrieval). In our experiments, we measured how many dialogs out of the total number of 200 were successful for a given dialog length. This result is a good measure for the quality of the dialog strategy as it measures how quality of the result increases with the length of the dialog.

For retrieval, we used the commercial CBR system *orenge* from tec:inno[3]. To compare our approach to the entropy selection strategy, we adapted the built-in *orenge*:dialog component. We connected the orenge system via an API to *Netica* from Norsys[4], a commercial product for defining and processing Bayesian Networks.

5.2   Evaluation of the Attribute Selection Strategy

The most significant influence on the quality of the dialog lies in the attribute selection strategy. In the first test, we compared the *similarity variance measure* simVar to an *entropy-based* one as a traditional representative of an information gain measure. We used an ideal customer agent that can answer every question. The second test shows how these strategies behave in a real world environment using the real world customer agent and shows the benefit of considering question-answering costs in real world situations.

---

[3] http://www.tecinno.com/
[4] http://www.norsys.com/

To avoid the influence of the termination criterion, we let the questioning continue until all questions had been asked. It was recorded how many out of the total of 200 performed dialogs were successful at a given dialog length.

Attribute Selection Strategy

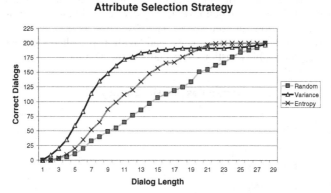

Fig. 2. Comparison of *random*, *simVar*, and *entropy* attribute selection strategies.

5.2.1   Test 1: Ideal User Agent

The chart in Fig. 2 depicts the result for an ideal user agent acting in a sales dialog environment for *random*, *similarity variance (simVar)*, and *entropy* attribute selection strategies.

It can be seen that our *simVar* strategy rises steeper and faster than the other two. This stems from the fact that *simVar* poses the most relevant questions right at the beginning phase of the dialog.

Maximizing the variance is generally a good strategy to separate the best cases, however, it is sometimes necessary to tolerate decrease in variance when most cases have already been excluded from the candidate set. While a strategy like ours that strictly maximizes the variance avoids such questions and leads to a leveling of the curve, such a heuristic is nevertheless justified by the maximum likelihood principle.

Compared to the random method which shows only a linear progression and the steeply rising entropy method, *simVar* is the best strategy.

5.2.2   Test 2: Real World Agent

The second series of tests simulated a real world scenario of an e-shop. Therefore, it was executed with customer agents that could not answer all questions. Each agent simulated a customer with certain knowledge of the problem domain. That means an agent either had expert, intermediate, or little (beginner) knowledge of PCs. When an agent was asked a question it could answer the question with a certain probability depending on its knowledge level. This probability was looked up in the conditional probability tables stored with each question. This implicitly assumes that the Bayesian Network was optimally trained as the simulated customer behaved exactly as modeled in the network. So, the results represent an upper bound of what can possibly be gained considering question answering costs.

Two test series were carried out for each customer class separately. Series No. 1 (see Fig. 3) tested the pure entropy strategy against pure attribute selection based on the probabilities to answer a question and the utility combination, which considered answering costs in the entropy strategy. Series No. 2 (see Fig. 4) followed the same proceeding but with the difference that the entropy strategy was exchanged with the *simVar* strategy. The satisfaction level introduced in section 4 was set up for a dialog abort after 12 questions in both series. Thereby, answers of "don't understand" had more damaging effect than "don't care" and "with help". This was important for not asking incomprehensible questions, especially to the beginners.

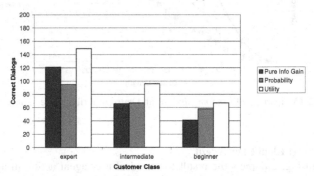

Fig. 3. Series No.1: Entropy strategy tested with a real world agent for each customer class.

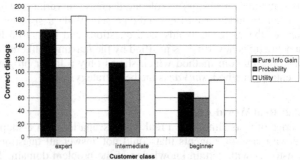

Fig. 4. Series No. 2. *SimVar* strategy tested with a real world agent for each customer class.

Fig 3 shows that the entropy strategy can be drastically improved by considering utility. This is the case, because questions preferred by the entropy strategy are those with the greatest distribution of values, which can be difficult to answer. This is also reflected by the fact that the probability approach produces better results than the pure entropy one for beginner customers.

The increase for the variance strategy, as depicted in Fig. 4, is not so high. This can be explained by the fact that the variance strategy already prefers questions that are easy to answer. The questions chosen by *simVar* have the highest weight in the similarity calculation. These are most likely the key features of the product (such as price or processor speed), which can easily be understood by most customers. This also justifies the poor performance of the pure probability strategy.

Analyzing Figures 4 and 5, it can be seen that all *simVar* strategy methods clearly reach better results in terms of correct dialogs than their entropy competitors.

5.3   Evaluation of the Termination Criteria

To measure the quality of a termination criteria for a given attribute selection strategy, every dialog is executed until it is ended by the termination criteria. The retrieved cases are then compared with the ideal result obtained within the reference retrieval. Again, we compared the entropy and *simVar* strategies. For the entropy approach, the dialog ended when a manageable set of 20 cases remained (cf. [5]). For the *simVar* attribute selection strategy, the termination criterion considered the utility, namely termination was reached if no more information could be gained, i.e. no question had positive utility. An important difference of the termination tests compared to the other tests is the fact that the customers' satisfaction level was not considered, i.e. the customer could not abort the dialog. This was done because the possibility of aborting could have falsified the results for the termination criterion only.

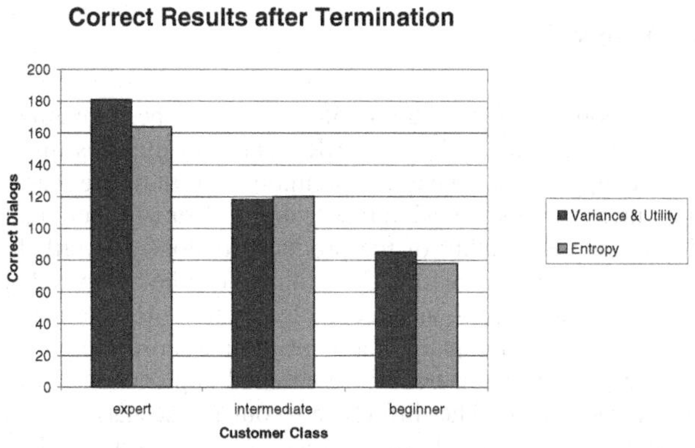

Fig. 5. Comparison of termination criterion for *simVar* and entropy.

Figure 5 shows the results of the examination of correctness. It can be seen that both strategies perform equally in terms of correct dialogs. However, Fig. 6 brings to light that *simVar* reduces the average dialog length for all customer classes, while maintaining constant quality. This is most noticeable considering the results for beginners. The entropy-based strategy continues asking questions which cannot be answered by the customer, leading to very long dialogs with relatively few answered questions. The utility-based approach recognizes the fact that the customer will most likely not be able to answer difficult questions and therefore terminates the dialog when all easy questions have been answered. This leads to the best possible results for beginners, requiring only half the number of questions.

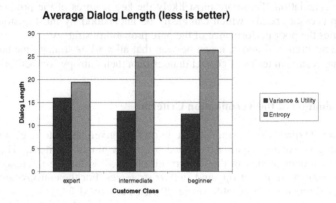

Fig. 6. Comparison of average dialog length for *simVar* and entropy.

Summarizing, we can state that our approach produces significantly shorter dialogs by keeping a high quality of the retrieval results. This final test used the strategy for attribute selection that joined the *simVar* measure and the idea of considering a utility.

6. Related Work

From the scientific point of view, many publications have been dealing with the topic of attribute selection in the field of CBR. Their origin lies in diagnosis and classification. The approaches have in common that they are based on entropy information gain measures and decision tree learning. None of them neither considers the described costs nor the quality of the produced dialogs. Nevertheless, dialogs in diagnostic situations and dialogs with EC customers can be compared. The answer to each query is a step to advance to an acceptable solution [4]. The general strategy in classification is to select such a query that approves the most likely hypothesis. Here, further developments of decision trees or combined approaches can be found (e.g., TDIDT, INRECA trees [1,2]). The difference to our EC scenario is that our ultimate goal is not to find a correct (or almost correct) classification but the most suitable product. Furthermore, an annoyed customer may interrupt the dialog. This situation does not occur as frequently in diagnostic processes.

Concentrating on EC, currently most relevant to our approach is the work of Doyle & Cunningham [5], but their approach bases on a classification of the cases. Shimazu [13] proposes navigation methods in combination with an attribute selection strategy. Göker & Thompson [6] follow an unconventional way with a rule-based approach with dialog operators.

A couple of commercial systems providing dialog functionality for EC systems are on the market but to our best knowledge none of them follows an approach like ours. Examples for such systems are *orenge* and its former version *CBR-Works* from tec:inno, both with an entropy-based approach. Furthermore, there is the *Pathways* system from IMS MAXIMS[5] that only allows defining static decision trees. The often cited PersonaLogic[6] system asks a large number of questions, not adapting to the customer at all. However, the search process is integrated in the dialog filtering the current candidate cases.

7. Conclusions and Future Work

We developed a new approach for attribute selection especially tailored to EC scenarios and compared it to the traditional entropy-based proceeding. It turned out that sensible dialogs are generated by always selecting the combination of the most important and easiest to answer question. Of course, *simVar* as a heuristic is only a first step. We will further investigate in other possibilities.

As we have mentioned, there are many parallels between diagnosis and EC. E.g., it is sufficient to find an adequate product and not the best one. A diagnostic process also has to be advanced as long it has an influence on the therapy. However, one of the main differences between diagnosis and EC scenarios lies in the fact that information from the customer in EC scenarios represents needs or wishes, which can be discussed in principle. Observations in a diagnostic process cannot be changed because they represent a true fact. The answers given by a customer depend on her/his product knowledge. Therefore, the computation of the information gain does not have to look for an optimal answer but has to take into account the answer given by the customer. It may be necessary to first give some information to the customer before posing the question, which can be an advantage compared to diagnosis, too. Thereby, the information gain can be increased before asking a question. In the diagnostic process, it can happen that certain questions cannot be answered. Then, this will not be due to the lack of knowledge but due to the fact that certain tests and objective observations cannot be made (e.g., because they refer to some event in the past).

A couple of open questions have already been raised in this paper. They are currently under investigation. Here, we only want to hint on a few more aspects. Our approach does not guarantee an optimal or logical ordering of questions from a customer's point of view. This issue could be addressed by another influence factor for our utility calculation, which we get, e.g., out of an extension of our Bayesian Network. An important next step will be the training of the Bayesian Network with real user data from an e-shop. Therefore, we have to optimize the processing of *simVar* to deploy it in live scenarios. A more technical aspect of *simVar* lies in the threshold mentioned in Section 3.2. It will be examined in the near future in how far dynamic adaptation could be useful.

---

[5] http://www.cykopaths.com/

[6] http://www.personalogic.com/

References

[1]   E. Auriol, M. Manago, K.-D. Althoff, S. Wess, S. Dittrich. (1994). Integrating Induction and Case-Based Reasoning: Methodological Approach and First Evaluations. In J.-P. Haton, M. Keane, M. Manago (Eds.): *Advances in Case-Based Reasoning. Proc. of the 2ⁿᵈ European Workshop on Case-Based Reasoning, EWCBR'94*, Chantilly, France. LNAI 984, Springer.

[2]   E. Auriol, S. Wess, M. Manago, K.-D. Althoff, R. Traphöner. (1995). INRECA. A Seamlessly Integrated System Based on Inductive Inference and Case-Based Reasoning. In: M. Veloso, A. Aamodt (Eds.): Case-Based Reasoning Research and Development. *Proc. of the 1ˢᵗ Internat. Conf. on Case-Based Reasoning, ICCBR'95*, Sesimbra, Portugal. LNAI 1010, Springer.

[3]   R. Bergmann, M. M. Richter, S. Schmitt, A. Stahl, I. Vollrath. (2001). Utility-Oriented Matching: A New Research Direction for Case-Based Reasoning. *Proc. of the 9ᵗʰ German Workshop on Case-Based Reasoning, GWCBR'01*, Baden-Baden, Germany. In: H.-P. Schnurr et al. (Eds.): Professionelles Wissensmanagement. Shaker Verlag.

[4]   P. Cunningham, B. Smyth. (1994). A Comparison of model-based and incremental case-based approaches to electronic fault diagnosis. In: *Proc. of the Case-Based Reasoning Workshop, AAAI-1994*.

[5]   M. Doyle, P. Cunningham. (2000). A Dynamic Approach to Reducing Dialog in On-Line Decision Guides. In: E. Blanzieri, L. Protinale (Eds.): *Advances in Case-Based Reasoning. Proc. of the 5ᵗʰ European Workshop on Case-Based Reasoning, EWCBR 2000*, Trento, Italy. LNAI 1898, Springer.

[6]   M. H. Göker, C. A. Thompson. (2000). Personalized Conversational Case-Based Recommendation. In: E. Blanzieri, L. Protinale (Eds.): *Advances in Case-Based Reasoning. Proc. of the 5ᵗʰ European Workshop on Case-Based Reasoning, EWCBR 2000*, Trento, Italy. LNAI 1898, Springer.

[7]   T. M. Mitchell. (1997). Machine Learning. McGraw-Hill.

[8]   J. Pearl. (1988). Probabilistic Reasoning in Intelligent Systems. Morgan Kaufmann Publishers.

[9]   J. R. Quinlan. (1993). C4.5 Programs for Machine Learning. Morgan Kaufmann Publishers.

[10] B. Raskutti, I. Zuckerman. (1997). Generating Queries and Replies during Information seeking Interactions. In: *Internat. Journal of Human Computer Studies*, 47(6).

[11] S. Russell, P. Norvig. (1995). Artificial Intelligence: A Modern Approach. Prentice Hall International Editions.

[12] S. Schmitt, R. Bergmann. (2001). A Formal Approach to Dialogs with Online Customers. To appear in: *Proc. of the 14ᵗʰ Bled Electronic Commerce Conference*, Bled, Slovenia.

[13] H. Shimazu. (2001). ExpertClerk: Navigating Shoppers' Buying Process with the Combination of Asking and Proposing. To appear in: *Proc. of the 17ᵗʰ Internat. Joint Conference on Artificial Intelligence, IJCAI-01*, Seattle, Washington, USA.

[14] A. Stahl, R. Bergmann. (2000). Applying Recursive CBR for the Customization of Structured Products in an Electronic Shop. In: E. Blanzieri, L. Protinale (Eds.): *Advances in Case-Based Reasoning. Proc. of the 5ᵗʰ European Workshop on Case-Based Reasoning, EWCBR 2000*, Trento, Italy. LNAI 1898, Springer.

[15] M. Stolpmann, S. Wess. (1999). Optimierung der Kundenbeziehung mit CBR-Systemen. Addison-Wesley.

When Two Case Bases Are Better than One: Exploiting Multiple Case Bases

David B. Leake[1] and Raja Sooriamurthi[2]

[1] Computer Science Department, Indiana University, Lindley Hall 215
150 S. Woodlawn Avenue, Bloomington, IN 47405, U.S.A.
leake@cs.indiana.edu
[2] Department of Computer Science, University of West Florida
11000 University Parkway, Pensacola, FL 32514, U.S.A
sraja@cs.uwf.edu

Abstract. Much current CBR research focuses on how to compact, re-fine, and augment the contents of individual case bases, in order to distill needed information into a single concise and authoritative source. However, as deployed case-based reasoning systems become increasingly prevalent, opportunities will arise for supplementing local case bases on demand, by drawing on the case bases of other CBR systems addressing related tasks. Taking full advantage of these case bases will require *multi-case-base* reasoning: Reasoning not only about how to apply cases, but also about when and how to draw on particular case bases. This paper begins by considering tradeoffs of attempting to merge individual case bases into a single source, versus retaining them individually, and argues that retaining multiple case bases can benefit both performance and maintenance. However, achieving the benefits requires methods for *case dispatching*—deciding when to retrieve from external case bases, and which case bases to select—and for *cross-case-base adaptation* to revise suggested solutions from one context to apply in another. The paper presents initial experiments illustrating how these procedures may affect the benefits of using multiple case bases, and closes by delineating key research issues for multi-case-base reasoning.

1 Introduction

One of the early inspirations for case-based reasoning research was the desire to model how experiences affect individual human reasoning: how individual memories are organized, retrieved, and re-applied [Schank, 1982]. Likewise, most CBR systems in research and applications capture knowledge as independent, individual systems, and studies of how to improve systems' access to good cases focus on single, unified case bases. For example, all the papers in the forthcoming *Computational Intelligence* special issue *Maintaining Case-Based Reasoning Systems* [Leake *et al.*, 2001] address issues in maintaining independent systems that each access a single case base. Drawing on a single well-maintained case base can significantly facilitate knowledge access. However, when numerous independent systems collect individual case bases, merging them into a single case

D.W. Aha and I. Watson (Eds.): ICCBR 2001, LNAI 2080, pp. 321–335, 2001.
© Springer-Verlag Berlin Heidelberg 2001

source may not be practical, and case base sharing raises its own issues: Case bases may reflect differences in their tasks, task environments, and even case representations, complicating the knowledge sharing process. This paper argues for the importance of developing methods to exploit the information available in multiple case libraries that may have been collected under differing circumstances. It surveys the issues and opportunities involved, and demonstrates that under some circumstances, two case bases can be better than one: Retaining multiple case bases can improve performance and provide useful information to aid case base maintenance.

Case-based reasoning is a natural method to support knowledge capture and reuse. Riesbeck (1996), for example, argues for the promise of CBR for intelligent components, integrated in other systems, and numerous stand-alone CBR applications exist for tasks such as diagnosis and help-desk support (e.g., [Auriol et al., 2000]). The accumulation of individual case bases in these systems provides an opportunity for future CBR systems to draw not only on their own stored cases, but also on external case bases for related tasks. Just as thousands of topic-specific information sources are now available on the Web, multiple case bases may eventually provide a large-scale distributed, sharable information resource.

Previous research (e.g., [Hayes et al., 1998; Martin et al., 1999]) has addressed fundamental issues for distributed case bases, when those case bases are standardized. *Multi-case-base reasoning* strategically accesses and applies case bases that may have been accumulated in other contexts, for somewhat different tasks, but that still can be useful to augment the CBR system's own competence. Multi-case-base reasoning requires supplementing the "eager" case base generation and refinement methods from case base maintenance research with a "lazy" approach to case base building: augmenting the local case base as needed by retrieving new cases from other case bases, and adjusting their solutions in light of overall differences between case bases.

Making effective use of cases from multiple idiosyncratic case bases depends on reasoning not only about the cases, but also about case properties that can be inferred from knowledge of their sources. It depends on developing methods for *case dispatching*—deciding when to retrieve from external case bases, and which case bases to select. It also depends on developing methods to address a new type of adaptation problem, *cross-case-base adaptation*, to adapt suggested solutions from one case base to apply to the needs of another. This paper examines the issues, opportunities, and tradeoffs of drawing on multiple case bases developed under differing circumstances. It first describes the motivations for this approach and the possible benefits of augmenting the information provided by individual cases with contextual information about the case bases from which they were drawn. It next presents experimental results demonstrating that when a local case base is sufficiently sparse, accessing a more competent external case base can improve performance, even if that case base reflects a different task and only simple cross-case-base adaptation is available. It closes with a proposal for key areas for future research in managing multiple case bases.

2   Problems for Case Base Combination

Most case-based reasoning systems are envisioned as reasoning based on a single case base; the goal of case-base maintenance is to assure the competence (e.g., [Smyth and McKenna, 1999a; Zhu and Yang, 1999]) and performance (e.g., [Leake and Wilson, 2000; Portinale *et al.*, 1999]) of this case base. This suggests that the natural approach to multiple case bases is to merge them into a single authoritative resource. Unfortunately, however, when multiple agents generate case bases, the practicality and benefits of merging may be decreased by problems of availability, efficiency, standardization, and maintenance.

Availability problems may arise if case bases are proprietary, requiring permission to access an entire case base to combine it. For example, in e-commerce, suppliers such as Amazon.com are willing to provide individual cases, such as records of books, to users, but not their entire case base.

Efficiency problems may arise if storing all cases locally results in the swamping utility problem for case retrieval, or if excessive case size causes space efficiency problems. If individual systems keep their own local case bases, tailored to their frequent needs, and access other case sources for individual supplementary cases as needed, these problems are avoided.

Standardization problems may arise if case features that are unspecified in the individual case bases become crucial when cases are shared. Even for closely related tasks, similar cases in different case bases may have different relevance to particular problems, because each one may implicitly reflect its different task circumstances. The AI-CBR travel case base, one of the standard benchmarks used by the CBR community, provides an example. That case base contains records of travel packages, with the information needed to match customer preferences (means of travel, destination, purpose, hotel, price of the package, etc.). It is possible to imagine world-wide travel agencies collecting sets of these types of cases individually, and combining them into a single centralized case base of recommendations. However, the cases omit a key contextual feature, without which the cases in the combined case base would be useless: the origin of the trip. Thus a client asking for the price of a trip to Paris would receive the same estimate, regardless of whether flying to Paris from London, or from Japan.

Even if two travel agencies are located within a single town, so that their locations may be similar enough not to affect the applicability of their cases, implicit aspects of their case collection process may be important to the appropriateness of their solutions. For example, if one agency has a wealthy clientele, its travel cases may tend to suggest luxurious options, so that combining its case base with the cases from an economy agency could increase the chance of a mis-match between client needs and retrieved cases. Such differences in task environments arise in many domains. For example, the advice provided by a system to diagnose engine problems and guide repairs must depend not only on the problem, but on factors such as the availability of tools, resources, and expertise to conduct the repairs. If case bases are combined, useful retrievals will depend on representing these factors, but it may be difficult to identify all the factors relevant to case applicability in order to add explicit annotations to the case base.

Maintenance problems may also arise from combining and standardizing individual case bases. First, the combined case base may lose access to updates of the case bases from which it is drawn. In e-commerce, for example, if a collection of product case bases from different suppliers is combined into a standardized, centralized case base, it may rapidly become obsolete as the combined case base misses subsequent additions and revisions (e.g., price changes). Second, even if the original case bases remain static, a standardized version of the combined case base may become obsolete as the relationships between individual case bases change. In international e-commerce, one case base might quote prices in euros, and another in dollars. If these are combined into a case base with standardized prices in a single currency, cases become more comprehensible to the public for which they were standardized, but currency fluctuations would introduce errors after the fact.

All of the previous problems suggest difficulties that may be avoided by retaining multiple distinct case bases. In the following section, we consider the benefits that multiple case bases can provide beyond their cases alone.

3   Benefits of Multiple Idiosyncratic Case Bases

In case-based problem-solvers, the case base provides one type of information: its cases. The most basic way to exploit additional case bases is to retrieve and apply their cases, supplementing the competence of the local case base and providing a source of cases to be stored locally. If all case bases were developed in a standardized form, for standardized problems, this would be their only benefit. However, when different case bases reflect systematic differences, such as different tasks, domains, problem environments, case collection and validation procedures, or maintenance procedures, knowledge of a case's sources can enable a reasoner to make useful additional inferences that cannot be generated from the case in isolation. Because of the potential value of these inferences, the value of access to multiple idiosyncratic case bases may exceed the value of the union of the cases that they contain.

The knowledge that may be available from an external case base falls into three general categories. The first is simply *individual cases,* which supplement local competence and may be added to the local case base. The second is case base *descriptions and histories*, which provide information on the generation, previous use, and maintenance of the case base: how cases were collected, the types of problems and environment they were collected for, performance statistics, and how the case base was maintained. The third is *data for comparative analysis*, providing a source for identifying systematic differences in the contents of local and external case bases. The following sections discuss in more detail how each of these may be used.

3.1   Individual Cases

The most obvious potential benefit of accessing external case bases is to provide additional cases to augment those of the local case base, to solve problems outside its competence and possibly store those cases for future use. Another potential advantage, however, is to bring to bear additional cases even when solutions can be generated locally, in order to improve performance. In the machine learning community, research on ensemble learning has shown that combining ensembles of classifiers by weighted votes can often result in substantially better performance than the individual classifiers [Dietterich, 2000]. The ramifications of ensemble methods for CBR are comparatively unexplored, but are potentially promising (for example, see [Cunningham and Zenobi, 2001] for a recent study of insights that they may provide for case representation). A necessary condition for the success of ensemble methods is that the individual classifiers be diverse, making their errors on different examples. Here not only the access to external cases, but also their diversity arising from case base differences, may be advantageous.

3.2   Case Base Descriptions and Histories

Pre-compiled descriptive information about a case base can provide a valuable guide to when its cases may apply. For example, knowledge about the source of a case base (e.g., the organization that generated it) can be used to assess its trustworthiness. If more detailed information is available, such as detailed task descriptions or information about how cases are collected, that information can also be used to determine the likely applicability of cases. Likewise, information on maintenance policies and the maintenance schedule can help in assessing the timeliness of the case base and can provide additional information about its likely reliability. All this information provides value to a system developer or maintainer beyond the value of the cases out of context. Ideally, this information could be made available to an automated case base selection process, to support large-scale case base sharing. To do so, however, will require methods for standardized branding and descriptions of case base contents and characteristics.

3.3   Data for Comparative Analysis

When two distinct case bases are available, analysis of their differences can provide additional useful information for guiding case base maintenance and standardization. When the two case bases are each internally consistent, and each is reasonably homogeneous (e.g., reflecting, the solution preferences of a single user), their systematic differences may reflect important general case base characteristics. Multiple case bases may have three main types of differences:

1. Differences in their indices and case representations (here we focus on differing domain content, rather than differing forms).

2. Differences in their competence or problem distributions.
3. Differences in the solutions they suggest for problems in the intersection of their coverage, given consistent indexing schemes and fixed adaptation knowledge.

Detecting these types of differences can provide important information during the maintenance process. Although the differences are not guaranteed to be significant, they are a useful focusing device for determining whether case base maintenance is needed and how it should be applied, as well as for guiding cross-case-base knowledge application. For example, case base comparison may be useful for:

1. **Assessing case base reliability:** When a new case base overlaps with one whose trustworthiness is already known, comparison of the solutions for the overlapping cases can provide a reliability estimate for the new case base, which can then be extrapolated to non-overlapping case regions.
2. **Guiding standardization:** When two case bases use different representations and feature sets, but produce similar solutions, differences in their representations may reflect alternative representations of equivalent features. This suggests the potential for re-representation in standard form, or for the development of translation criteria for rerepresenting cases for transfer from one case base to another.
3. **Suggesting case base applicability conditions:** Differences in competence or problem distributions can provide information about the types of problems that tend to occur in different task environments, in turn suggesting problem distributions for which a particular case base is likely to be a useful resource. For example, if a particular travel agent has an extensive case base applicable to one region, that information may be useful for characterizing the case base, in order to facilitate its selection for problems relevant to that area.
4. **Guiding feature discovery:** When two case bases are both believed reliable, but provide divergent solutions on similar problems, their divergence suggests a possible gap in case representation: that relevant features of the task or environment in which the case bases were applied were left unstated. When both case bases use different feature sets, those differences provide a first suggestion of additional features to examine. For example, if two case bases have differing problem representations, and one case base provides greater accuracy, a useful heuristic is to consider whether the problem descriptions used in that case base are more appropriate.
5. **Guiding case discovery:** The existence of problems in one case base but not in another provides information about real problems that are not covered, suggesting possible competence gaps to fill.
6. **Guiding cross-case-base adaptation:** Once systematic differences have been identified between case bases, they may enable automatic conversion of cases from one case base to apply in another context. For example, if one product case base states prices in euros, and another in dollars, comparing

average prices (or prices for similar items) may provide an approximate euro-dollar conversion factor, enabling the system to use cases from one case base to predict the prices for missing items in the other. We demonstrate a simple application of this type of derived adaptation knowledge in the next section.

Fully exploiting solution relationships requires explaining whether observed patterns are actually significant—whether they can be explained in terms of the task or environment. In general, this may be difficult. For example, some case-based travel planners might accept plans with little margin for error if they conserve resources (e.g., accept travel plans with tight connections); others might favor more forgiving routings. When differences arise and cannot be explained internally, case pairs reflecting differences can be presented to a user or maintainer to explain (cf. [Shimazu and Takashima, 1996], which applies a similar approach to identify problems within a single case base).

However, it may sometimes be possible to reason from correlations, even without explanations. In the following experiments, we show how a simple calculation of the difference in ranges of numerical predictions can be used to improve performance by cross-case-base adaptation in the travel domain.

4   Experiments

To illustrate the issues involved in reasoning from multiple case bases, we performed initial experiments on the benefits of drawing on related but distinct case bases. Our goal was to explore how CBR system performance is affected by the interaction of (1) the competence of the local case base, (2) the case dispatching criteria used, (3) the availability of cross-case-base adaptation, and (4) the use of solution combination to exploit the availability of diverse case sources.

The system's reasoning task was predicting the prices of travel packages. The data used were drawn from the AI-CBR travel case base at www.ai-cbr.org, which contains 1470 instances. Because the indicated prices vary widely for similar trips, after defining feature weightings for distance-weighted k-NN retrieval we selected a 681-case subset with reasonable problem-solution regularity. We defined a very simple case adaptation function: The prices of prior packages were adjusted proportionate to differences in their duration and number of travelers. More refined feature weights and adaptation criteria would have improved predictions, but because our goal was comparative, to study relative effects of drawing on an external case base, we did not tune the basic system.

To generate two case bases for related but distinct task contexts, we divided the travel cases according to hotel star ratings, simulating the division in travel packages that might arise for cases collected by two travel agencies, one catering to luxury and the other to economy travelers. The luxury (3–5 stars) case base, CB_1, contained 352 cases. The economy (1–2 stars) case base, CB_2, contained 329 cases. In the following runs the star weighting was suppressed by giving that feature a zero weighting.

4.1 Performance of Individual and Combined Case Bases

We first compared the predictive accuracy of CB_1, CB_2, and $CB_1 \cup CB_2$, each tested on itself by leave-one-out cross validation for distance-weighted 3-NN retrieval. This compares the performance of processing cases in the most appropriate individual case base, versus in a combined version. Performance was measured in two ways, (1) the prediction accuracy—defined as the percent of problems whose prices were predicted within 20% of the correct price—and (2) the average percent error of predicted prices. We expected that performance for each individual case base would be superior to the performance of $CB_1 \cup CB_2$, but that differences would be comparatively small, due to the availability of other features in the case representation (e.g., the hotel name) that should correlate with the luxury of the trip. In fact, the result was more marked than expected. When all cases were processed by $CB_1 \cup CB_2$, 61% of the cases were predicted with accuracy within 20% of the correct values, and the average percent error for predictions was 28%. When problems were dispatched to their corresponding case base, accuracy was 83% with an average percent error of 13% for the luxury case base, and 72% with 17% percent error for the economy case base. This illustrates how case base combination may impair performance by blurring distinctions in the task environment (for this example, the types of trips considered). Its main interest, however, is as a backdrop for the next experiment. That experiment will show that despite this performance drop from combining CB_1 and CB_2, strategically drawing on CB_2 to augment the knowledge in CB_1 can actually *improve* performance compared to using CB_1 alone.

4.2 Augmenting a Local Case Base with External Retrievals

When multiple idiosyncratic case bases are available, a central question is whether those case bases can be used effectively. Because drawing on external case bases may be especially important when the local case base has limited competence (e.g., in the early phases of a CBR system or when case storage space is limited), we explored the effects of case dispatching starting from a set of local case bases of different sizes. Starting from CB_1, we generated a series of case bases $CB_1^\star$, of varying sizes, each consisting of a randomly-selected subset of CB_1. $CB_1^\star$ simulates an incomplete "local" case base of a growing system.

In our tests, CB_2 (the economy travel case base) functions as an external case base that can be drawn on as a supplement to $CB_1^\star$ (a sparse version of the luxury travel case base). Problems from CB_1 (the full luxury travel case base) are used to test the predictive accuracy of $CB_1^\star$ by leave-one-out cross validation. Test problems from CB_1 are first directed to $CB_1^\star$, which can either handle the query locally or dispatch it to CB_2. The decision whether to dispatch a problem to CB_2 is made by calculating its average distance from the k closest cases in $CB_1^\star$. If this distance exceeds a fixed threshold, the problem is dispatched to CB_2. If CB_2 contains a closer case, the case from CB_2 is used, possibly with cross-case-base adaptation; otherwise, the system reverts to the solution from $CB_1^\star$. Our tests used a very simple cross-case-base adaptation method: The range of prices from CB_2 was linearly interpolated to map to the range of prices in CB_1, and predictions from CB_2 were adjusted for case base differences by multiplying them by the corresponding scale factor.

We expected that results would be superior when most problems were solved directly by $CB_1^\star$, because both $CB_1^\star$ and the input test cases from CB_1 involve luxury travel. However, when luxury travel problems are solved using the economy case base, it may be possible to compensate somewhat by performing cross-case-base adaptation on estimates from CB_2, to correct for the generally lower prices of the economy travel.

Our tests compared the predictive accuracy of:

1. **$CB_1^\star$**: Predicting using only $CB_1^\star$.
2. **$CB_1^\star$ + CB_2**: Predicting using $CB_1^\star$ if the input problem is within a fixed distance threshold of a case in $CB_1^\star$; else dispatching the problem to be solved by CB_2 if CB_2 contains a case closer to the current problem.
3. **$CB_1^\star$ + CB_2 + cross-CB adaptation**: Predicting as in (2), except that cross-case-base adaptation is applied to the solutions from CB_2.
4. **Combined solution**: Predicting by averaging the prediction from method (2) with the prediction from method (3).

Because the results of methods 3–4 depend on the dispatching threshold, we tested 11 different distance thresholds defined so that the dispatch rates ranged from 100% (i.e., all cases sent to CB_2) to 0% (i.e., all problems solved locally by $CB_1^\star$), in decrements of 10%. Testing was done with random $CB_1^\star$s of sizes 60%, 20%, 5%, 2%, and 0.5% the size of CB_1. The full experimental setup consisted of 30 random $CB_1^\star$s (in 3 groups of 10 each) for each of the 5 case sizes and 11 distance thresholds, for a total of 1650 runs. The results across each group of 10 case bases were averaged.

As mentioned in Section 3.1, a potential advantage of access to multiple case bases is providing a diverse set of predictions that may be suitable for ensemble methods. Method (4) above, the combined method, tests a very simple form of combining results from two case bases with divergent characteristics.

Figures 1 and 2 illustrate the averaged results of 10 runs for different sparsity levels for random $CB_1^\star$. When CB_1 (the luxury case base) is tested on its own problems by leave-one-out cross validation, its prediction accuracy is 75%. In the left-hand graph of Figure 1, $CB_1^\star$ has 60% the size of CB_1 and on average can correctly solve 73% of the cases in CB_1—Drops in average accuracy levels as case bases become smaller reflect the expected decrease in competence when fewer cases are available. For this case base size, none of the methods match the performance of $CB_1^\star$ at any dispatching rate. However, even the simple cross-case adaptation strategy improves average performance compared to simply drawing on the supplementary case base. Despite the simplicity of the cross-case-base adaptation method used, its benefit compared to dispatching alone was highly consistent across all trials. The right-hand graph shows the average performance for $CB_1^\star$ with 20% of the cases, for which CB_1 alone achieves 64% predictive accuracy. Here the proportionate benefit of cross-case-base adaptation is greater. Also, the combined method slightly outperforms $CB_1^\star$.

The left-hand side of Figure 2 shows average performance for a set of 10 $CB_1^{\star}$s selected to contain 2% of the cases in CB_1. Though the average accuracy of $CB_1^{\star}$ drops to 47%, due to the sparser case base, cross-case-base adaptation has a more pronounced effect, sometimes resulting in performance slightly superior to $CB_1^{\star}$, and the combined prediction method markedly outperforms $CB_1^{\star}$. In the right-hand side, for an even sparser case base that solves an average of 32% of the test problems, all alternative methods surpass the original case base for some dispatching rates, and both dispatching with cross-case-base adaptation and the combined method do consistently better than $CB_1^{\star}$ for high dispatching rates. The small peak at 70% of cases dispatched may illustrate the balance between problem similarity and cross-case-base differences. When larger percentages are dispatched, cases in $CB_1^{\star}$ that would give better predictions than cross-case-base adaptation are being bypassed; when smaller percentages are dispatched, the error in predicting from distant cases in $CB_1^{\star}$ is greater than the error introduced by case base differences. We have observed similar but more marked peaks for $CB_1^{\star}+CB_2+$cross-CB adaptation in individual runs.

Figure 3 illustrates two specific examples for the 5% $CB_1^{\star}$, which is able to solve 53% of the problems. In the left-hand graph, the combined prediction method is again best, followed by $CB_1^{\star}+CB_2+$cross-CB-adaptation, both of which noticeably outperform $CB_1^{\star}$ and $CB_1^{\star}+CB_2$. In the right-hand graph, both dispatching with cross-case-base adaptation and the combined method outperform $CB_1^{\star}$ alone, with slightly superior performance from $CB_1^{\star}+CB_2+$cross-CB-adaptation.

We believe that the variation in results of individual runs is accounted for by our very simple linear cross-case-base adaptation function. When the range of values in $CB_1^{\star}$ corresponds naturally to the range in CB_2, performance is maximized. When it does not, performance suffers. We expect that case dispatching would be more helpful for denser case bases if this function were refined. We are also investigating methods for assessing the quality of cross-case-base adaptation during processing, to predict when (and whether) dispatching will be useful, in order to adjust dispatching criteria.

Even with the present cross-case-base adaptation function, the results suggest that in the early phases of a CBR system, when its case base is sparse, dispatching selected cases to a denser external case base can improve performance, even if the external case base is suboptimal for the task. Because the combined method consistently outperformed $CB_1^{\star}$, they also suggest the potential value of using multiple case bases with cross-case-base adaptation to provide diverse data sources for ensemble predictions.

5   Towards "Case Boutiques:" A Research Agenda

The previous discussion argues that comparing multiple case bases can provide valuable information for case base maintenance, and the experiments show that drawing on even a sub-optimal external case base can help supplement a system's own case base. Exploiting multiple case bases, however, depends first on their

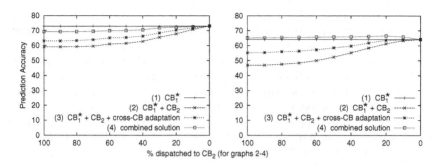

Fig. 1. Predictive accuracy for $CB_1^\star$ containing 60% (left) and 20% (right) of the cases in CB_1, averaged over 10 runs.

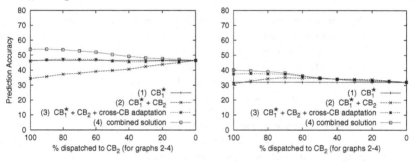

Fig. 2. Predictive accuracy for $CB_1^\star$ containing 2% (left) and .5% (right) of the cases in CB_1, averaged over 10 runs.

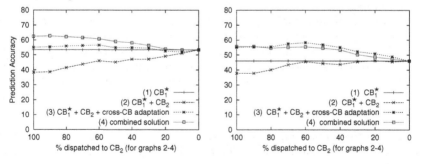

Fig. 3. Sample individual results for $CB_1^\star$ containing 5% of the cases in CB_1.

availability. Thus a central research issue is how to build up sharable task-based case libraries and to describe their contents in a way that will permit the right case bases to be identified efficiently. Data warehousing research and applications suggest a useful parallel. With terabyte storage now available, storage of available data is not a major issue, but effective access is. This has led to the development of "data boutiques" that provide specialized applications for particular tasks. Analogously, "case boutiques" can be developed to provide similar access.

The idea of case base sharing is not new; as early as 1995, Inference Corporation formed a knowledge publishing division to sell case bases for particular tasks. However, this approach was viewed as a means for a one-time "jump start" to building an individual case base, rather than part of a supplemental resource to augment a local case base on demand. Exploiting multiple case bases on demand requires addressing new multi-case-base issues for steps that parallel the basic steps of CBR, but that apply to case bases as a whole, rather than to individual cases:

- **Situation assessment:** Determining the general task context in which a particular problem is being solved, to express it in a vocabulary compatible with the case base description vocabulary.
- **Case base indexing:** Characterizing the types of task contexts and problems for which a particular case base may be useful. This requires a vocabulary to describe overall task types and solution characteristics, competence characteristics (e.g., areas of high density), representations used, etc.
- **Multi-source retrieval:** Determining when to dispatch cases to external case bases, which sources are most appropriate, and how to convert indices to apply to the external case base's own retrieval mechanisms.
- **Cross-case-base adaptation:** Revising retrieved cases' representations and contents based on general characteristics of the cases in the external case base.
- **Multi-case-base maintenance:** Determining how to distribute cases—when to split, merge, or standardize collections of cases. Case deletion in standard case base maintenance research may be replaceable by export of cases to new case bases; and case discovery by importation of new cases from other case bases. Multi-case-base maintenance issues also include determining how to apply comparative information to focus the maintenance process for individual cases.

We believe that addressing these issues, thus developing a foundation for "case boutiques," is a promising way to leverage the independent knowledge of individual CBR systems.

6   Related Work

6.1   Hierarchical Retrieval and Web Source Selection

The idea of dispatching cases to particular case bases is related to research on hierarchical retrieval [Watson and Perera, 1997] and footprint similarity

[Smyth and McKenna, 1999b]. Both of these methods can be seen as determining a region to which to dispatch an input case, within a single case base. Likewise, the potential growth of sharable independent case bases has parallels to the increasing availability of specialized information sources on the web, and the issues involved in developing methods to determine which web sources to access for a particular query (e.g., [Leake and Scherle, 2001; Sugiura and Etzioni, 2000]). Just as Apple's Sherlock XML-style plug-ins encode wrapper information about search engines, analogous methods could be used to facilitate access to external case bases.

Some existing web data, such as FAQ files, already provide a resource that has been used for on-demand exploitation by textual CBR techniques [Burke *et al.*, 1997]. Issues in how to convert between different representations for information are being addressed in work on ontologies on the *wrapper generation problem* (e.g., [Ashish and Knoblock, 1997]).

6.2   Relationship to Multi-agent and Distributed CBR

[Prasad *et al.*, 1996] describe an approach in which multiple agents each cooperatively access their individual case bases to contribute subparts of a solution. [Martin *et al.*, 1999] describes an approach to knowledge reuse in which peer agents each maintain independent cases and share them as needed. Both these situations differ from the current task in assuming that all cases have a consistent representation and consistent solutions, removing the need for cross-case-base adaptation and the need for comparative inferences. [Hayes *et al.*, 1998] present methods for efficient distributed CBR when using a single standardized case format, and propose a potential method to facilitate case communication: CBML, an XML application to serve as a standard for large-scale case distribution. Of work on distributed CBR, the most closely related is [McGinty and Smyth, 2001], in which retrievals from multiple case bases are used to compensate for experience gaps when recommending travel routes reflecting individual preferences.

6.3   Relationship to Case Base Maintenance

Current case base maintenance research focuses on the issues of generating high-quality individual case bases, with the aim of producing a unified, consistent body of cases for a given problem class. These methods provide a valuable means to improve the quality of the case bases to be exploited by multiple-case-base methods. However, they are based on the fundamental assumption that all cases are available for combination, that all are collected for a single task and environment, and that the goal is to eagerly process cases. Multi-case-base reasoning must instead address the issues of facilitating lazy case access on demand. Thus it is crucially concerned not only with assuring the quality of cases, but also the quality of information about case bases as a whole. As described in section 3.3, however, case base comparison may prove a valuable tool for focusing maintenance of individual case bases.

7 Conclusion

The increasing use of CBR systems and web-based communication provides an opportunity to improve the performance of case-based reasoners by developing methods for strategically combining their local case information with cases drawn from external sources containing similar cases, even if those case bases may be designed for different task environments. This paper has considered the benefits and difficulties of using multiple case bases that may reflect different tasks and environments. It has illustrated that the ability to dispatch cases to an alternative case base—even when that case base reflects systematic task differences—can help improve system performance, provided that solution transfer is supported by cross-case-base adaptation.

Making effective use of external case bases requires developing methods for *case dispatching*—deciding when a problem should be handled by retrieval from an external case base, and which external case base to select—and for performing *cross-case-base adaptation* to transform solutions to fit new contexts. By combining these operations with the standard case-based reasoning process, a CBR system may supplement its competence through just-in-time knowledge access from external knowledge sources.

Acknowledgments. David Leake's research is supported in part by NASA under awards NCC 2-1035 and NCC 2-1216. Raja Sooriamurthi's research is supported in part by a professional development leave from the University of West Florida. The authors would like to thank the anonymous reviewers for their helpful comments.

References

[Ashish and Knoblock, 1997] N. Ashish and C. Knoblock. Wrapper generation for semi-structured internet sources. In *SIGMOD Record*, volume 26, pages 8–15, 1997.

[Auriol et al., 2000] E. Auriol, P. Avesani, B. Bartsch-Spoerl, M. Goeker, M. Manago, K. Pulaski, and W. Wilke, editors. *Workshop Notes, Workshop on Innovative Customer Centered Applications (ICCA)*, Trento, Italy, 2000. EWCBR-2K.

[Burke et al., 1997] R. Burke, K. Hammond, V. Kulyukin, S. Lytinen, N. Tomuro, and S. Schoenberg. Question answering from frequently asked question files: Experiences with the FAQFinder system. *AI Magazine*, 18(2):57–66, Summer 1997.

[Cunningham and Zenobi, 2001] P. Cunningham and G. Zenobi. Case representation issues for case-based reasoning from ensemble research. In *Case-Based Reasoning Research and Development: Proceedings of the Fourth International Conference on Case-Based Reasoning*, Berlin, 2001. Springer Verlag. In press.

[Dietterich, 2000] T. Dietterich. Ensemble methods in machine learning. In *Proceedings of the First International Workshop on Multiple Classifier Systems*, pages 1–15, Berlin, 2000. Springer Verlag.

[Hayes et al., 1998] Conor Hayes, Pádraig Cunningham, and Michelle Doyle. Distributed CBR using XML. In *Proceedings of the KI-98 Workshop on Intelligent Systems and Electronic Commerce*, 1998.

[Leake and Scherle, 2001] D. Leake and R. Scherle. Towards context-based search engine selection. In *Proceedings of the 2001 International Conference on Intelligent User Interfaces*, pages 109–112, 2001.

[Leake and Wilson, 2000] D. Leake and D. Wilson. Remembering why to remember: Performance-guided case-base maintenance. In E. Blanzieri and L. Portinale, editors, *Proceedings of the Fifth European Workshop on Case-Based Reasoning*, pages 161–172, Berlin, 2000. Springer Verlag.

[Leake et al., 2001] D. Leake, B. Smyth, Q. Yang, and D. Wilson, editors. *Maintaining Case-Based Reasoning Systems*. Blackwell, 2001. Special issue of *Computational Intelligence*. In press.

[Martin et al., 1999] F. Martin, E. Plaza, and J.-L. Arcos. Knowledge and experience reuse through communications among competent (peer) agents. *International Journal of Software Engineering and Knowledge Engineering*, 9(3):319–341, 1999.

[McGinty and Smyth, 2001] L. McGinty and B. Smyth. Collaborative case-based reasoning: Applications in personalised route planning. In *Case-Based Reasoning Research and Development: Proceedings of the Fourth International Conference on Case-Based Reasoning*, Berlin, 2001. Springer Verlag. In press.

[Portinale et al., 1999] L. Portinale, P. Torasso, and P. Tavano. Speed-up, quality, and competence in multi-modal reasoning. In *Proceedings of the Third International Conference on Case-Based Reasoning*, pages 303–317, Berlin, 1999. Springer Verlag.

[Prasad et al., 1996] M. V. Nagendra Prasad, V. Lesser, and S. Lander. Reasoning and retrieval in distributed case bases. *Journal of Visual Communication and Image Representation*, 7(1):74–87, 1996.

[Riesbeck, 1996] C. Riesbeck. What next? The future of CBR in postmodern AI. In D. Leake, editor, *Case-Based Reasoning: Experiences, Lessons, and Future Directions*, pages 371–388. AAAI Press, Menlo Park, CA, 1996.

[Schank, 1982] R.C. Schank. *Dynamic Memory: A Theory of Learning in Computers and People*. Cambridge University Press, Cambridge, England, 1982.

[Shimazu and Takashima, 1996] H. Shimazu and Y. Takashima. Detecting discontinuities in case-bases. In *Proceedings of the Thirteenth National Conference on Artifical Intelligence*, volume 1, pages 690–695, Menlo Park, CA, 1996. AAAI Press.

[Smyth and McKenna, 1999a] B. Smyth and E. McKenna. Building compact competent case-bases. In *Proceedings of the Third International Conference on Case-Based Reasoning*, pages 329–342, Berlin, 1999. Springer Verlag.

[Smyth and McKenna, 1999b] B. Smyth and E. McKenna. Footprint-based retrieval. In *Proceedings of the Third International Conference on Case-Based Reasoning*, pages 343–357, Berlin, 1999. Springer Verlag.

[Sugiura and Etzioni, 2000] A. Sugiura and O. Etzioni. Query routing for web search engines: Architechture and experiments. In *Proceedings of Proceedings of the Ninth World Wide Web Conference (WWW9)*, pages 417–429, 2000.

[Watson and Perera, 1997] I. Watson and R. Perera. The evaluation of a hierarchical case representation using context guided retrieval. In *Proceedings of the Second International Conference on Case-Based Reasoning*, pages 255–266, Berlin, 1997. Springer Verlag.

[Zhu and Yang, 1999] Jun Zhu and Qiang Yang. Remembering to add: Competence-preserving case-addition policies for case base maintenance. In *Proceedings of the Fifteenth International Joint Conference on Artificial Intelligence*, pages 234–241. Morgan Kaufmann, 1999.

COBRA: A CBR-Based Approach for Predicting Users Actions in a Web Site

Maria Malek[1] and Rushed Kanawati[2]

[1]LAPI-EISTI, Av. du Parc, F-95011 Cergy
maria.malek@eisti.fr
[2]LIPN-CNRS UMR Q 7030, Av. J. B. Clément, F-93430 Villetaneuse
rushed.kanawati@lipn.univ-paris13.fr

Abstract. In this paper we describe an original case-based reasoning (CBR) approach, called Cobra, that aims at predicting users requests in a web site. The basic idea underlying the Cobra approach is to model users navigational behavior in a web site by a set of *cases*. Typically, in a CBR system a case is composed of at least two parts: the situation or the problem part and the solution one. In the Cobra approach the situation part of a case captures a navigation experience within a user navigation session. The solution part is composed of a set of *actions* that *may* explain the transition (i.e. the move from one page to another) which follows the navigation experience described in the case situation part. The proposed case structure and the reuse phase enable to predict the access to pages that have never been visited before by any user. This is a very useful feature that matches prediction requirements in *real* web sites where the structure and the content change frequently over time.

1. Introduction

Designing a hypermedia (i.e. a web site) that can readily yields its information for its users is now known to be a complex and a tricky task. Different visitors of a web site may have distinct goals and different backgrounds. Knowledge about both site content and organization may differ from one visitor to another. In addition the same visitor may seek different goals at different visits to the same site. Web site designers can not imagine a priori how the site will *be used* by he different visitors. This design problem has give birth to a new trend in the area of hypermedia and web site development: adaptive hypermedia systems (AHS) development. Works reported in [2, 6, 8, 12] present the general problem of AHS system design. In this paper we address the specific problem of how to automatically learn from users access patterns to a web site in order to personalize the structure of this web site. A first step towards personalizing the structure of a web site consists on predicting user actions in the site [8, 10, 13]. Prediction results can be used to recommend links (or pages) to the site visitor. Different techniques have been proposed in the literature to coop with this problem (see section 2.2). In this paper we propose a new approach, called the COBRA approach (for CBR-based Collaborative Browsing Advisor), that is based on using the case-based reasoning problem solving methodology. In our approach, a case refers to an experience of navigation in the site. Past navigations are used to extract

D.W. Aha and I. Watson (Eds.): ICCBR 2001, LNAI 2080, pp. 336–346, 2001.

basic navigation behaviors in the studied site. Given an on-going navigation session, the system extracts from the navigation base, behaviors that are similar to the current observed one. Actions taken in past similar behaviors are evaluated in the context of the current navigation. Pages resulting from the evaluation process form, after a filtering process, the set of predicted pages to be visited next in the current navigation.

The reminder of this paper is organized as follows. In section 2 we introduce some notations that help to describe the general problem of predicting users actions in a web site by learning from past user access patterns. Existing works are described in section 2.2. The Cobra approach is described in section 3. An informal presentation of the approach is first made in section 3.1. Basic concepts and definitions are given in section 3.2. The CBR cycle implemented by the Cobra approach is detailed in section 3.3. A conclusion is given in section 4.

2. Predicting Actions by Learning from User Access Patterns

In this section, we define the problem of predicting users actions in a web site by learning from user access patterns. A brief review of works that have addressed the above-cited problem is also presented.

2.1 Problem Definition

For sake of clarity, we start by introducing some notations that are used later in this paper.

Web page (P). A web page P is defined as a triple $P = <U, L, I>$. Where U is the page address (i.e. the page URL), L is the list of links contained in the page P, and I is some information record about the page (i.e. the record I may contain a description of the page content, the page author, etc). We denote by $L(P)$ (respectively $U(P)$ and $I(P)$) the U (respectively L and I) component of the page P.

Web site (S). A web site, denoted S, is a set of n web pages. We write $S = \{P_i, 0<i<= n\}$.

Navigation (N). A user navigation session in a site S denoted N, is a *sequence* of steps s_i. We write $N = [s_i]_{i=0..m}$ where m is the navigation length.

Step (s). A step s is defined as a couple $s = <P_i \in S, SI>$ where P_i is a web page, and SI is some information structure about the step. The SI structure can contain entries about request result (i.e. successful access, page not found, etc), page visualization time, user satisfaction from the page, etc. The ith step in a navigation N_j is designated by $N_j[i] = s_i^j$. We use the notation $P(s_i^j)$ (respectively $I(s_i^j)$) to designate the page (respectively information) component of a step.

Transition (T). We call a *transition* T^j_i a sequence of two pages visited sequentially in navigation N_j at steps i and $i+1$. Formally, we write $T^j_i = [P(s^j_i), P(s^j_{i+1})]$.

Navigation Base (NB). We define a navigation base *NB* as a set of past navigation sessions that have occurred in the site *S*.

Using the above-defined notations, the problem of predicting users actions in a web site can be expressed as follows: How to construct a function F that: given the site description *(S)*, the set of past navigations that have occurred in the site *(NB)*, and a current navigation session N_c, the function F returns pages in S that to be visited next (with some probability)? Formally we define the function F as follows:

$$F: (BS, S, N_c, P_l) \rightarrow \{P_j, j<m\} \subset S$$ where P_l is the last page visited in N_c, $\{P_j\}$ is the set of pages from the site S that the user is *likely* to visit in the next step.

2.2 Existing Systems

Recently, different approaches have been proposed in the literature dealing with the problem of predicting user actions in a web site based on mining web server log files. The different systems have different final goals and use different techniques. Clustering techniques are used in [4, 10, 13, 17]. Markovian prediction techniques are experimented in [18] for predicting future user's requests, which can be used for network and proxy caching. Data mining techniques (mining paths, association rules, etc.) are used in [11, 14]; for the purpose of deriving marketing intelligence. Simple statistical approach is applied in [16] in order to trace a usage map of navigations in a given site. Case-based reasoning methodology is used in [7, 15] for recommending links in a web site basing on user behavior similarity. All these approaches share the same drawback of being unable to predict pages that have never been visited before. Hence, if new pages are added to a web site, these pages can not be considered by the previous systems. Our approach is conceived to coop with this problem (see next section).

Other related works are navigation browsing assistants such as *Letizia* [9] and the *PageGather* algorithm proposed in [12]. The first systems tries to build a dynamic user profile by analyzing pages visited by the user. Other pages in the site are evaluated in function of the learned user profile. Links are added to pages that match the most this profile. The second system aims to automatically constructing index pages for web sites by learning from user access patterns.

3. The COBRA Approach

3.1 Overview

The basic idea underlying the *Cobra* approach is to model users navigational behavior in a web site by a set of *cases*. Typically, in a case-based reasoning system [1] a case is composed of at least two parts: the situation or the problem part and the solution one. In Cobra, the situation part of a case captures a navigation experience within a user navigation session. The solution part is composed of a set of *actions* that *may* explain the transition (i.e. the move from one page to another) which follows the navigation experience described in the case situation part. In order to predict pages that will be visited in an on-going navigation the following steps are made:

1. First, a target case is elaborated from the on-going navigation. The target case situation part is composed of a set of indices that model the *history* of the navigation session. The solution part is the empty set.

2. We search the set of cases that have the most similar history as the target case. Each case proposes a set of actions as a solution.

3. Actions that are proposed by cases retained from the previous step are *evaluated* in the context of the on-going navigation. An action evaluation results in indicating a set of web pages. A ranking algorithm is applied to sort pages resulting from the evaluation process. The top ranked pages are taken to be the predicted pages.

4. The user behavior is observed in order to revise the proposed solutions. Cases that have proposed actions that result in a *good* prediction (i.e. prediction confirmed by the user) will have their confidence increased. Others will witness some diminution in their confidence.

3.2 Definitions and Notations

In this section we introduce new concepts and definitions that will be later used in sections 3.3 while exposing the design concepts of the Cobra approach.

Navigation action template & navigation actions. We define a navigation action template, denoted NAT_k, as a generator of *hypothesis* that can explain a transition T_i^j occurring in navigation N_j. The set of all used templates is denoted by NAT. The composition of the NAT set is *site-dependent*. Next, we give some examples of different templates based only on the definition of a hypermedia navigation process. The given list is far from being exhaustive and it should be taken just as a simple example of hypothesis we can generate to explain transitions in a navigation. The four examples are the following:

1. NAT_1 : *Follow a link.* If page P_i contains a hypertext link that points to P_{i+1}, then one plausible hypothesis that can explain the transition from P_i to P_{i+1} is that the user has clicked that link. Two sub-types can be derived from NAT_1 type:

    • NAT_{11}: *Follow a link with anchor A.* One possible explanation of the choice of a link by a user is that the link's anchor is relevant to the user information need.

    • NAT_{12}: *Follow a link with rank X.* Another possible explanation for choosing a link is the rank of that link in the page P_i. For example, if page P_i presents search results returned by a web-searching engine, then a link rank can be a plausible explanation for choosing that link.

Other types can be derived from the NAT_1 type such following a link whose context is C, or following a recommended link R, etc.

2. *NAT$_2$. Move backward.* If page P_{i+1} has already been visited in the same navigation then a plausible transition explanation would be that the user has made a backward move. Once again, we can derive several sub-types of that action type such as moving backward n steps, moving up to the start, etc.
3. *NAT$_3$. Page Reload.* If page P_{i+1} is the same as P_i then one plausible explanation is that the user has reloaded the same page.
4. *NAT$_4$. Follow an URL.* A simple transition explanation is that the user has simply typed the address (i.e. the URL) of the page P_{i+1} after visiting page P_i.

The application of a template, NAT_i, on navigation N_j allows to generate for each transition T_i^j a set of *hypothetical* actions, defined by the template NAT_i that may explain the transition. Let A_i be the set of concrete actions from type NAT_i that can explain the transition T_i^j, we write: $A_i = Apply(N_j, NAT_i, T_i^j)$

The generated navigation action set can be the empty set. For example consider the web site illustrated on figure 1. Consider a navigation N_j in that site. N_j is composed of the following steps:

$$N_j = [<P1, SI1>, <P3, SI2>, <P4, SI3>, <P4, SI5>]$$

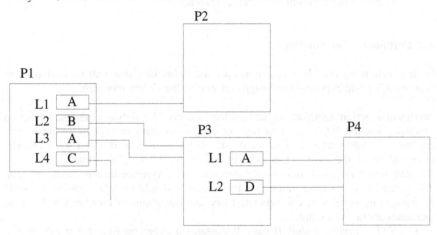

Fig. 1. Example of a simple Web site

The following table illustrates the result of applying the different templates defined above on each simple transition in the navigation N_j.

Table 1. Example of generated actions by applying navigation action templates

Transition	NAT$_{11}$	NAT1$_2$	NAT$_3$	NAT$_4$
Nj[1,2]	follow link with anchor B	follow link 2	-	follow URL: P3
	follow link with anchor A	follow link 3		
Nj[2,3]	follow link with anchor A	follow link 1	-	follow URL P4
	follow link wit anchor D	follow link 2		
Nj[3,4]	-	-	Reload	follow URL P4

Action evaluation function (Eval). We define the function of action evaluation as follows:

$$\texttt{eval : A x NB x S} \rightarrow \wp\texttt{(S)}$$

Where A is the set of all actions, NB is the navigation base and S is the web site. The evaluation of an action $a \in A$ is made in the context of a given navigation $N_i \in NB$ and on a given page $P_i \in S$. The result of the evaluation is either a set web page $\{P_k\} \subseteq S$ or the null (ϕ) value. For example consider the action A_x: *follow link with anchor equal to "A"* to be evaluated for each page in the navigation example given above (figure 1). Evaluation results are given in the following table.

Table 2. Evaluation of action : follow link with anchor A in the context of the example illustrated on figure 1.

Page	Evaluation result
P_1	$\{P_2, P_3\}$
P_2	ϕ
P_3	$\{P_4\}$
P_4	ϕ

Elementary behavior (EB). Given a navigation N_j. With each step $s^j_i \in N_j$ we can associate an elementary behavior EB^j_i, defined as follows: $EB^j_i = <s^j_i, LA_i, CF_i>$ where:

- LA_i is the set of all actions from all types that verify the following condition: $\forall a_j \in LA_i : eval\ (a_j, N_j, P(s^j_i)) = P(s^j_{i+1})$.
- CF_i is a vector that represents the system confidence in each action listed in LA_i.

Using the concept of elementary behavior we can now represent a navigation session N_j as a sequence of elementary behaviors $N_j = [EB_i]_{i=0..N}$ where each EB_i represents the elementary behavior associated to the step s^j_i in N_j.

Similarity functions. A page similarity function SIM_p, is defined as follows:

$$\texttt{SIMp : (S x S)} \rightarrow \texttt{[0,1]}$$

Different page similarity functions are proposed in the literature. Examples are similarity based on URLs similarity [7] or page content similarity [8].

Another required similarity function is $SIMs$ that measures the similarity between two steps. Again the result is obtained in the interval [0,1]

3.3 Cobra-Enabled Web Site Architecture

Figure 2 illustrates the architecture of a Cobra-enabled Web site.

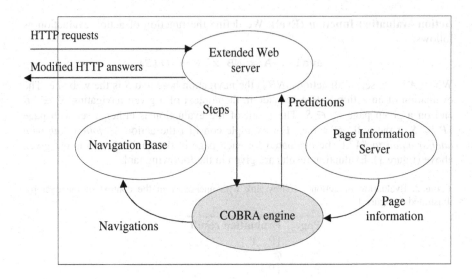

Fig. 2. Cobra-enabled Web site architecture.

The system is composed of four modules:

1. **A web server.** This is an extended web server program. In addition to the classical functions of a web server (i.e. execution of the http protocol), this web server performs the following tasks:
   - *Identification of user navigation sessions.* In the current developed prototype this function is ensured by using a Java *servlet* and link-rewriting technology. Each new step in each on-going navigation is sent to the Cobra server. The Web server has the charge to detect navigation termination.
   - *Web page reformatting.* For each page requested by a client the server applies the following modifications:
     a) Firstly, as proposed in [13] the server inserts an invisible Java applet that send events to the server when the page is displayed by a client, even if the page is loaded from the client cache memory. This simple technique allows tracing users navigations in the site despite of the use of cache memory. In addition it allows to compute the page visualization time without taking into consideration the file transfer time over the network.
     b) Secondly, the server integrates the page prediction results provided by the Cobra server in the web page returned to the client. In the current prototype, each web page is formed of two frames: the first contains the initial page while the second displays links to pages the system has predicted. This decomposition allows delivering basic required information as soon as possible without adding time penalties due to the prediction computation time.

2. **Navigation-base**. This module saves the set of terminated navigations in the site. The decision whether to save a navigation or not is taken by the Cobra engine.

3. **Page information base**. For each page $P_i \in S$, this module provides the following information: the information record $I(P_i)$ *and the list of links* $L(P_i)$ contained in the page. The later list is required in order to compute the different action that may explain transitions (see here after).

4. **The Cobra engine**. This module implements the Cobra user's action prediction approach. It executes the following tasks: First, the Cobra engine codes on-going navigation as a sequence of elementary behaviors (see section 3.2). Given an ongoing navigation N_o which is composed of m steps $N_o = [s_1, ..., s_m]$, when the Cobra engine receives the description of a new step in navigation N_o; (i.e. the step s_{m+1}) it starts by completing the computation elementary behavior EBm. The following algorithm is executed:

`LA ←Φ;`	// LA the list of actions
`For each NAT_i ∈ NAT do:`	// Computing all action of all types that
`    A = Apply(NAT_i,N_o,T_o^m)`	// can explain the transition T_o^m
`    LA ← LA ∪ A`	
`N = |LA|`	// N is the number of found actions
`For i=0 to N do:`	// Computing the default confidence in
`    CF[i]=1/N`	// each action
`EB = <S_m, LA,CF>`	// Setting the elementary behavior of rank
`N_o[m] = EB`	// m in navigation No.

After computing the elementary behavior EB^o_m, the Cobra engine executes the reasoning steps described hereafter in order to predict next pages to be visited in the navigation N_o.

3.4 Reasoning Cycle

Given an on-going navigation $Nc=[EB_1, EB_2, ..., EB'_m]$ in the site S, the goal of the reasoning process is predict the page taht will be visited is step s_{m+1}. Recall that on requesting the page P_m the system will be able to compute the actual value of EB_{m-1}. The reasoning cycle applied by the Cobra approach is composed of the following phases: a) *Target case elaboration.* b) The *retrieval phase.* c) The reuse phase. d) The learning phase. We discuss next the each of these phases.

Target case elaboration. The goal of this phase is to build a case that models the actual user behavior in the navigation N_c. In the Cobra approach, a case references a precise navigation experience within a navigation session. As usual a case in a CBR system is composed a problem part that defines situations where the case is usable and a solution part that gives the solution proposed by the case. When elaborating a target case, only the problem part is defined. The solution part is the result of the reasoning cycle. Given an on-going navigation $N_c=[EB_1^c, ..., EB_m^c]$, we model the user behavior by the sequence of the last observed elementary behaviors: $[EB_{m-l+1}, EB_{m-l+2}, ..., EB'_m]$. l is a system parameter. In the current prototype l is fixed to 3. The searched solution is the set PP = {P$_i$ i<k} of the K predicted pages to be visited next in the navigation N$_c$. Once the target case is constructed the Cobra engine executes the next phase.

The retrieval phase. The goal of this phase is to retrieve from the navigation base, NB, situations that are similar to the behavior modeled in the problem part of the target case. Unlike most existing CBR systems, No concrete case base is used in the Cobra approach. Source cases are extracted from the set of raw data, here the navigation base, upon their similarity with the target case. Given that *l=3*, and given the sequence: *[EB$_{m-2}$, EB$_{m-1}$, EB'$_m$]*, representing the problem part of the target case, the retrieval phase consists on extracting from *NB* sequences of the form *[EB$_i$*,EB$_j$*,EB$_k$]* such that:

- All three elementary behaviors are extracted from the same navigation N$_x$, and that i<j<k. * is a wildcard indicating that any length of elementary behavior sequences can separate behaviors *i* and *j* as well as *j* and *k*.
- The sequence *[EB$_i$*,EB$_j$*,EB$_k$]* is *similar* to the sequence *[EB$_{m-2}$, EB$_{m-1}$,EB'$_m$]*. Two sequences are similar if the step associated to EB$_k$ (respectively EB$_j$ and EB$_i$) is similar, using the step similarity function *SIMs*, to the step associated to EB'$_m$ (respectively EB$_{m-1}$ and EB$_{m-2}$) and k-j ≈ 1, k-i ≈2 and j-i ≈1.

Extracted sequences which similarity with the target case is above a given threshold τ are retained. The solution part proposed by an extracted case (i.e. sequence *[EB$_i$*,EB$_j$*,EB$_k$]*) is the couple <LA$_k$, CF$_k$> of actions and system confidence in actions associated to the elementary behavior EB$_k$.

The reuse phase. Given the set of couples *SOL=<LA$_k$, CF$_k$>* of solutions proposed by the cases retained in the retrieval phase the reuse phase applies the following algorithm:

```
PP ←Φ                            // PP is the list of predicted pages.
PF={}                            // PF is a dictionary that counts the
                                 // number of prediction of a page p.
For each LAk∈ SOL do :           // We evaluate each action proposed by
    For each a ∈ LAk do:         // the extracted case in the context
        P= eval(a,Nc,P(sm^c))    // of the on-going navigation.
        if P ≠φ:                 // For each predicted page we count the
            PP = PP ∪ P          number of times it is predicted
            for each p in P:
                if !exist PF(p):
                    PF{p}=1
                else:
                    PF{p} = PF{p}+1
Return the k top ranked pages    // Pages are ranked according to their
in PF.                           // frequency of prediction
```

The reuse algorithm consists on evaluating each action proposed by cases returned by the retrieval phase in the context of the on-going navigation session N$_c$. As described in section 3.2, the action evaluation function returns either a set of pages or null. Different actions extracted from the same or from different past navigations can return the same page after evaluation. We need to use a ranking method that allows estimating the system confidence in the predicted page. In the current prototype, we use a simple ranking method that ranks pages according to their frequency of being predicted. However, we believe that other factors should be considered when ranking predicted pages such the system confidence in the evaluated action, the similarity between the extracted case and the target case, etc.

The learning phase. This phase has two goals: to define a strategy for feeding the systems experience base and to modify the system knowledge in order to enhance the prediction quality. Traditionally, in a CBR system, one first learning task consists on deciding whether to memorize the solved target case or not [1]. In our approach, where no concrete case base is used, the question becomes whether to add an on-going navigation to the case base or not. Another important question is the following: How to modify the system confidence in actions explaining transitions in saved navigations?

Currently we use a simple heuristic that consists on adding all navigations whose lengths exceed l elementary behaviors, where l is the sequence length that form the problem part of a target case (see section: target section elaboration). The second problem stills an open one. Some heuristics have been defined in order to change the system confidence in an action a depending whether the user has followed a predicted page resulting form action a evaluation. However, we believe that this question defines an interesting research axe that needs further investigations.

4. Conclusion

In this paper, we have presented Cobra, an approach for predicting user actions in a web site based on reusing past navigations occurred in the same site. The prediction method is used in order to adapt dynamically the structure of a web site by adding dynamic links to predicted pages. Unlike most existing user action prediction, our approach presents the originality of being able to predict pages that have never been visited before by any user. This is achieved by modeling user navigation behaviors as a sequence of elementary behavior actions. Actions can be evaluated in the context of a new navigation in order to predict the next pages to be visited. This feature is a capital advantage of our approach since web sites configuration change from day to day. A prediction system should be able to cope with this dynamic aspect.

The proposed approach presents new ideas for developing CBR systems such as integrating the source case extraction from raw data in the reasoning cycle. The case base is a virtual base. Source cases are extracted in function of their similarity with the target case. Two important issues need to be studied further in order to increase the efficiency of the proposed approach:
1. How to accelerate the retrieval phase?
2. And how to cope efficiently with the huge amount of data composed of the log file of web server?

Another important issue is the learning phase that needs to be enhanced. We are working now on the above-mentioned issues. Solution elements are already developed using novel CBR-maintenance strategy that will be described in a coming publication.

References

1. A. Aamodt, E. Plaza. Case-Based Reasoning: Foundational Issues, Methodological Variations and Systems; AI Communications, Vol. 7:1, pp. 36-59, 1994.
2. R. Barrett, P. Maglo and D.C. Kellem. How to Personalise the Web. Proceedings of the International Joint Conference of Artificial Intelligence (IJCAI'97), Morgan Kaufmanns, pp. 770-775, 1997
3. J. Borges and M. Levene. Mining navigation patterns with hypertext probabilistic grammars. Research Note RN/99/08, Department of Computer Science, University College London, Gower Street, London, UK, February 1999.
4. E. Danna and A. Laroche. Auditing Web sites Using Their Access Patterns. In proceedings of the 9th International World Wide Web conference, Amsterdam, May 15 - 19, 2000
5. P. De Bra, Design Issues in Adaptive Web-Site Development, Proceedings of the Second Workshop on Adaptive Systems and User Modelling on the World Wide Web, pp. 29-39, Toronto and Banff, Canada, 1999. (Editors P. Brusilovsky and P. De Bra, available as CSN 99/07, TUE, or at http://wwwis.win.tue.nl/asum99/) 1999.
6. P. Bursilovsky, Methods and Techniques of Adaptive Hypermedia. In User Modelling and User-Adapted Interaction 6: 87-129, Kluwer academic publishers, 1996.
7. M. Jaczynski and B. Trousse. WWW Assisted Browsing by Reusing Past Navigations of a Group of Users. In proceedings of EWCBR'98. 1998.
8. R. Kanawati, M. Malek, COBRA : Une approche d'adaptation structurelle de sites Web fondée sur une technique d'apprentissage à partir des traces d'accès utilisateurs et utilisant la méthodologie de raisonnement à partir de cas, NTIC'2000 (In french)
9. H. Liberman, Letizia: An Agent that Assists Web Browsing, In Proceedings of the 4th International Joint Conference on Artificial Intelligence (IJCAI'95), Morgan Kaufmann Publishers pp. 924-929, 1995
10. A. Mobasher, R. Cooley and J. Srivastava. Creating Adaptive Web sites Through Usage-Based Clustering of URLs. In IEEE Knowledge and Data Engineering Workshop (KDEX'99), 1999.
11. J. Pei, J. Han, B. Mortazavi and H. Zhu. Mining Access Patterns Eficiently from Web Logs. In proceedings of Pacific-Asia Conference on knowledge Discovery and Data Mining, pp. 396-407, 2000 (available on citeseer.nj.nec.com/article/pei00mining.html)
12. M. Perkowitz and O. Etzioni, Towards Adaptive Web Sites: Conceptual Framework and Case Study, In proceedings of 8th International Conference on the World Wide Web (WWW'8), Toronto. 1999
13. Shahabi, A. M. Zarkesh, J. Adibi and V. Shah. Knowledge Discovery from Users Web-Page Navigation, IEEE RIDE, 1997
14. M. Spiliopoulou, C. Pohle and L. C. Faulstich. Improving the Effectiveness of a Web Site with Web Usage Mining. In proceedings of KDD workshop WebKDD'99, San Diego, August 1999.
15. B. Trousse, M. Jaczynski, and R. Kanawati. Using User Behaviour Similarity for Recommendation Computation: The Broadway Approach. In H-J Bullinger and J. Ziegler, editors, proceedings of the HCI International (HCI'99), Munich. pp 85-89. Lawrence Erlbaum Associates, august 1999
16. Wexelblat and P. Maes, P. Footprints: History-rich Web Browsing. In Proceedings of International Conference on Computer-Assisted Information Retrieval (RIAO'97), Montréal, pp. 75-84, 1997.
17. T. W. Yan, M. Jacobsen, H. Gracia-Molina and U. Dayal. From User Access Patterns to Dynamic Hypertext Linking. In proceedings of the 5th International World Wide Web Conference. Paris May 6-10, 1999, Computer Network and ISDN systems 28:1007-1014. 1999.
18. I. Zukerman, David W. Albrecht, Ann E. Nicholson, Predicting users' requests on the WWW, Proceedings of the Seventh International Conference on User Modelling, 1999.

Similarity vs. Diversity

Barry Smyth[1,2] and Paul McClave[1]

[1] Smart Media Institute, University College Dublin,
Dublin, Ireland
[2] ChangingWorlds, University College Dublin
Dublin, Ireland
Barry.Smyth@ChangingWorlds.com

Abstract. Case-based reasoning systems usually accept the conventional similarity assumption during retrieval, preferring to retrieve a set of cases that are maximally similar to the target problem. While we accept that this works well in many domains, we suggest that in others it is misplaced. In particular, we argue that often diversity can be as important as similarity. This is especially true in case-based recommender systems. In this paper we propose and evaluate strategies for improving retrieval diversity in CBR systems without compromising similarity or efficiency.

1 Introduction

Case-based reasoning (CBR) systems solve new problems by reusing the solutions to problems that have been previously solved and stored as cases in a case-base. The success of any CBR system depends on its ability to select the right case for the right target problem [1,8,13]. The conventional wisdom is that the right case is among those that are the most similar to the target problem, and thus considerable research effort has been invested into techniques and strategies for evaluating case similarity (eg. [5,8,10,14]).

Recently it has become clear that traditional notions of similarity are not always ideal, inspiring many researchers to look for alternative ways to judge the *utility* of a case in a given problem solving context (eg. [2,3,7,6,11,13]). For example, researchers have looked at the importance of adaptability alongside similarity, arguing that while a case may appear to be similar to a target problem, this does not mean it can be successfully adapted for this target (see [11,13]).

In this paper we question the similarity assumption for a new reason. We suggest that in many application scenarios, where multiple cases are retrieved for a given target situation, the *diversity* of these cases (relative to each other), as well as their similarity (relative to the target), must be explicitly considered. We argue that this diversity is particularly important in so-called *recommender systems* [4,9,12] (Section 2). In Section 3, we propose a number of different retrieval strategies that are designed to improve diversity while maintaining similarity. Moreover these strategies can be implemented without any additional knowledge-engineering effort - all that is required is access to the existing similarity metric. In Section 4 we evaluate the effectiveness of these different approaches.

D.W. Aha and I. Watson (Eds.): ICCBR 2001, LNAI 2080, pp. 347–361, 2001.
© Springer-Verlag Berlin Heidelberg 2001

We demonstrate that it is possible to improve retrieval diversity substantially compared to standard similarity-based retrieval methods. Moreover, we focus on the usual trade-off that exists between similarity and diversity and explore the relative merits of the different retrieval strategies in optimising this trade-off.

2 Background

The Internet is now almost synonymous with the so-called *information overload* problem as users find it more and more difficult to locate the right information at the right time. Recently a new type of information system called the *recommender system* has been developed to better serve the information needs of individual users. Recommender systems combine techniques from information retrieval, artificial intelligence, and user profiling to proactively predict the needs of individual users and provide more personalised information services.

Many recommender systems, such as Entrée [4], employ a CBR strategy, selecting the most similar cases for a given query. Entrée operates in the restaurant domain and allows users to query the restaurant case-base using features such as *cuisine type*, *price* etc. By design, Entrée returns a single best case but allows the user to *tweak* this result, if they are unhappy with the case, to produce a refined query for a new search.

Very often a recommender system will be designed to return a number of similar cases in order to provide the user with a choice of recommendations. For example, popular applications such as travel or property recommenders typically return the k best cases (holiday packages or apartment listings) for a user query. The objective is to satisfy user needs with a single search, hence the retrieval of multiple cases, and to maximise the likelihood of relevant cases appearing high up in the result list, hence the priority given to similarity.

We believe that this standard *pure* similarity-based retrieval strategy is flawed in some application domains. Consider a travel recommender: a user submits a query for a 2-week vacation for two in the sun, costing less than $750, within 3 hours flying time of Ireland, and with good night-life and recreation facilities on-site. The top recommendation returned is for an apartment in the Hercules complex in the Costa Del Sol, Spain, for the first two weeks in July. A good recommendation by all accounts, but what if the second, third, and fourth recommendations are from the same apartment block, albeit perhaps for different two-week periods during the summer? While the k best recommendations are all very similar to the target query, they are also very similar to each other. The user will not have received a useful set of alternatives if the first recommendation is unsuitable. For instance, in this example, if the user decides to avoid the Costa Del Sol, then none of the alternative recommendations will suffice and she will have to initiate a new search.

By prioritising similarity during retrieval a standard case-based approach will implicitly ignore the importance of retrieval diversity, and this may reduce the quality of the retrieval results. Often, it is not good enough for a recommender to return only the most similar cases. It should also return a diverse set of cases in order to provide the user with optimal coverage of the information space in the vicinity of their query. This diversity problem is a recognised shortcoming of case-based or content-based recommendation techniques [12]. Indeed one common solution is to consider alternative recommendation techniques, such as automated collaborative filtering, that are less susceptible to the diversity problem. For example, PTV operates in the TV listings domain, recommending TV programmes to users based on their learned viewing preferences [12]. PTV combines case-based recommendation with collaborative filtering in order to help guarantee that each user is delivered a diverse set of recommendations, rather than swamping sci-fi buffs with the likes of Star Trek and the X-Files, for example.

In this paper we are interested in ways of solving this diversity problem while remaining within the CBR paradigm. But before moving on it is worthwhile briefly mentioning how new developments in the area of mobile information access further highlight the need for recommender systems that attempt to optimise both similarity and diversity. Current mobile computing devices such as PDAs and WAP-enabled mobile phones have a screen size that is a fraction of that found on a typical PC; a mobile phone screen can be 200 times smaller than a PC screen. This reduces the number of recommendations that can be returned in a single search, and since users dislike scrolling the goal has to be to return a result list that will fit on a single screen page. On a WAP-device this means a list of only 3 or 4 cases. If all of these cases are essentially the same (such as vacations in the same apartment block) then the chances of satisfying the user in a single search are greatly reduced. However, if the recommendations are relevant (similar to the target query) *and* diverse then there is a much greater chance of success.

3   Combining Similarity and Diversity

In case-based recommenders, the normal approach to measuring the similarity between a case c and target query t, is to use a weighted-sum metric (Equation 1). Selecting the k most similar cases usually results in a characteristic similarity profile where average similarity of the result set reduces gradually for increasing values of k (see Section 4.1).

$$Similarity(t, c) = \frac{\sum_{i=1..n} w_i * sim(t_i, c_i)}{\sum_{i=1..n} w_i} \qquad (1)$$

We define the diversity of a set of cases, $c_1, ...c_n$, to be the average *dissimilarity* between all pairs of cases in the case-set (Equation 2). Standard case-based recommenders also display a characteristic diversity profile with diversity increasing for larger result sets (see Section 4.1). Thus the trade-off between similarity and diversity is simple: for low values of k, while similarity tends to be high, diversity tends to be very low, highlighting the fundamental problem that exists with case-based recommenders.

$$Diversity(c_1, ...c_n) = \frac{\sum_{i=1..n} \sum_{j=i..n}(1 - Similarity(c_i, c_j))}{\frac{n}{2} * (n - 1)} \qquad (2)$$

In practice, improving the diversity characteristics of a fixed-size recommendation list means sacrificing similarity. Our goal is to develop a strategy that optimises this similarity-diversity trade-off, delivering recommendation sets that are diverse without compromising their similarity to the target query. We will describe three different strategies for retrieving k cases from a case-base C, given a target query t, each focusing on a different way of increasing the diversity of the recommendation set.

```
t: target query, C: case-base, k: # results, b: bound

1.    define BoundedRandomSelection (t, C, k, b)
2.    begin
3.        C' := bk cases in C that are most similar to t
3.        R := k random cases from C'
4.        return R
5.    end

1.    define GreedySelection (t, C, k)
2.    begin
3.        R := {}
4.        For i := 1 to k
5.            Sort C by Quality(t,c,R) for each c in C
6.            R := R + First(C)
7.            C := C - First(C)
8.        EndFor
9.    return R
10.   end

1.    define BoundedGreedySelection (t, C, k, b)
2.    begin
3.        C' := bk cases in C that are most similar to t
4.        R := {}
5.        For i := 1 to k
6.            Sort C' by Quality(t,c,R) for each c in C'
7.            R  := R + First(C')
8.            C' := C' - First(C')
9.        EndFor
10.   return R
11.   end
```

Fig. 1. Diversity preserving algorithms: Bounded Random Selection; Greedy Selection; Bounded Greedy Selection.

3.1   Diversity 1 - Bounded Random Selection

The simplest strategy for increasing the diversity of a set of k cases is the bounded random selection method (Random): select the k cases at random from a larger set of the bk most similar cases to the target, with $b > 1$ (see Figure 1).

Of course as $bk \to n$, Random becomes ineffective as a retrieval method since similarity is essentially ignored. While the retrieved cases may be diverse they are unlikely to be similar to the target. Nevertheless this algorithm does serve as a benchmark against which to evaluate more principled strategies, and for lower values of b it will at least limit the similarity sacrifices albeit perhaps with only modest diversity improvements.

3.2   Diversity 2 - Greedy Selection

A more principled approach to improving diversity, while at the same time maintaining similarity, is to explicitly consider both diversity and similarity during retrieval. The greedy selection algorithm (Greedy) in Figure 1 achieves this by incrementally building a retrieval set, R. During each step the remaining cases are ordered according to their *quality* with the highest quality case added to R.

The key to this algorithm is a quality metric that combines diversity and similarity (Equation 3). The quality of a case c is proportional to the similarity between c and the current target t, and to the diversity of c *relative* to those cases so far selected, $R = \{r_1, ..., r_m\}$; see Section 5.3 for alternative quality metrics. The *relative diversity* metric shown in Equation 4 is a variation of the diversity metric from Equation 2.

$$Quality(t, c, R) = Similarity(t, c) * RelDiversity(c, R) \qquad (3)$$

$$RelDiversity(c, R) = 0 \ if \ R = \{\};$$
$$= \frac{\sum_{i=1..m}(1 - Similarity(c, r_i))}{m}, otherwise \qquad (4)$$

The first case to be selected is always the one with the highest similarity to the target. During each subsequent iteration, the case selected is the one with the highest combination of similarity to the target and diversity with respect to the set of cases selected during the previous iteration.

As it stands this algorithm is expensive. For a case-base of n cases, during each of the k iterations we must calculate the diversity of each remaining case relative to those so far selected. This means an average of $\frac{n-k}{2}$ relative diversity calculations, each one consisting of an average of $\frac{k}{2}$ similarity calculations. This gives an average total cost of $k * \frac{n-k}{2} * \frac{k}{2}$ similarity computations per retrieval. For example, for a case-base of 1000 cases, retrieving the top 3 cases can mean approximately 2250 similarity computations.

3.3   Diversity 3 - Bounded Greedy Selection

To reduce the complexity of the greedy selection algorithm we can implement a bounded version in the same spirit as the bounded random selection algorithm. The bounded greedy selection algorithm (Bounded Greedy)(see Figure 1) first selects the best bk cases according to their similarity to the target query (line 3) and then applies the greedy selection method to these (lines 4 - 11).

This new algorithm has a greatly reduced retrieval cost since k cases are selected from bk cases instead of from n cases and $bk \ll n$ for typical low values of b and k. This means a total of $k * \frac{k(b-1)}{2} * \frac{k}{2}$ extra similarity computations on top of the normal retrieval cost. For example, for a 1000 case case-base, retrieving the 3 best cases with $b = 2$ will now require about 7 extra similarity computations on top of the standard similarity-based retrieval cost.

Of course this improved efficiency comes at a cost: because we are no longer examining all of the remaining cases we may miss a case with a marginally lower similarity value than the best bk cases but with a significantly better diversity value. Even if such a case has a higher overall quality value it will not be added to the retrieved set because it is not one of the best bk cases. However, the likelihood of this happening decreases with case similarity so that for suitable values of b it becomes unlikely.

4   Experimental Analysis

Our position is this: in many application scenarios, especially recommender systems, similarity and diversity *both* have roles to play in retrieval. However, trade-offs do exist. Increasing retrieval diversity means decreasing the similarity of the retrieved cases to the target query. Our objective has been to develop an efficient retrieval strategy that is capable of maximally improving diversity while minimally compromising similarity.

We use a standard benchmark case-base for our evaluation, the Travel case-base (www.ai-cbr.org). This case-base contains cases from the travel domain - each describing an vacation in terms of features such as *location, duration*, etc. Four recommender systems are implemented, each designed to return the k best travel cases for a given query according to one of the following retrieval methods:

- **Similarity**: standard similarity-based retrieval;
- **Random**: retrieval using the bounded random selection algorithm ($b = 2$);
- **Greedy**: retrieval using the greedy selection algorithm;
- **Bounded Greedy**: retrieval using the bounded greedy selection algorithm ($b = 2$).

4.1   Similarity vs. Diversity

The most important issue is the trade-off between similarity and diversity in the various retrieval algorithms - is there an increase in retrieval diversity, and if so what is the associated similarity cost?

To investigate this we run a series of retrievals using each recommender system for various values of k. 400 cases are chosen at random from the Travel case-base as queries, with the remaining cases serving as the case-base. For each retrieval we measure the average similarity and overall diversity of the k results. This is repeated 100 times for different sets of 400 queries and from the resulting similarity and diversity measurements we compute an overall average similarity and diversity value for each value of k.

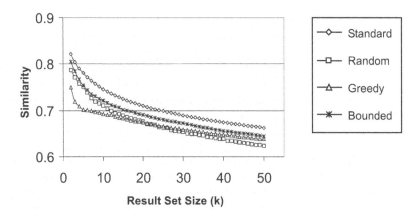

Fig. 2. The similarity characteristics of the retrieval algorithms relative to the retrieval set size (k).

The results are shown in Figures 2 and 3 as graphs of average similarity and diversity against k, respectively. The characteristic similarity and diversity profiles predicted in Section 3 are clearly seen for each retrieval strategy: in Figure 2 average similarity drops off with k; and in Figure 3 average diversity increases with k.

As expected, from a similarity viewpoint, the Standard strategy works best across all values of k. For example, for $k = 5$ the average similarity for the Standard strategy is 0.78, compared to 0.753, 0.748, 0.7 for the Bounded Greedy, Random, and Greedy techniques, respectively. The Greedy technique fairs worst for values of $k < 20$, after which the Random approach begins to suffer the most (although Random does achieve good similarity for low values of k). Overall the Bounded Greedy technique performs well from a similarity standpoint, achieving over 97% of the optimal (Standard) similarity level on average across all values of k - in comparison, on average the Greedy and Random techniques achieve only 94.5% and 94.7% of the optimal similarity level.

From a diversity point of view, the Greedy strategy delivers the best diversity characteristics across all values of k. For example, for $k = 5$ the average diversity for the Greedy strategy is 0.458, compared to 0.375, 0.326, 0.289 for the Bounded Greedy, Random, and Standard techniques respectively. If we consider

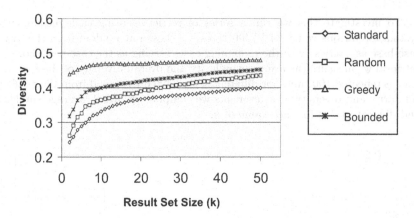

Fig. 3. The diversity characteristics of the retrieval algorithms relative to the retrieval set size (k).

the Greedy algorithm to deliver *optimal* diversity then the Bounded Greedy technique performs very well, achieving 90% of optimal diversity on average across all values of k - by comparison, the Standard and Random techniques achieve, on average, only 76% and 83% of the Greedy diversity values. Even for low values of k, such as $k = 5$, Bounded Greedy achieves over 80% of the Greedy diversity, compared to 74% and 69% for the Random and Standard methods, respectively.

Another way to look at these results is to consider the number of cases that need to be retrieved in order to achieve a certain level of diversity. The Bounded Greedy algorithm achieves a mean diversity of 0.4 for $k = 10$, with a corresponding mean similarity of 0.72. The Random method only achieves this diversity at $k = 23$, and the Standard method only achieves it at $k = 46$, with similarities that have fallen to 0.66 and 0.67, respectively. This ability of the Bounded Greedy method to achieve high diversity and similarity with small retrieval sets is an important advantage in recommender systems.

Overall it seems clear that the Bounded Greedy algorithm offers the best performance, with near optimal similarity and diversity characteristics across all values of k. In contrast, the Greedy and Random strategies suffer from more significant similarity compromises, while the Standard and Random techniques suffer from significant diversity compromises.

4.2 Relative Benefits

The precise trade-offs between similarity and diversity are not yet clear. For example, at the $k = 5$ level the Bounded Greedy algorithm generates retrieval sets with an average similarity of 0.753 and an average diversity of 0.375. The similarity is lower than the Standard similarity value at this level (0.78), but the diversity is higher than the Standard diversity (0.289).

In general how does the increase in diversity relate to the loss in similarity? In this experiment we attempt to answer this question by measuring increases in diversity relative to decreases in similarity for the three diversity preserving algorithms (Random, Greedy, and Bounded Greedy). For each of the three algorithms, and each value of k, we measure the *relative benefit* of the algorithm in question by dividing the difference in diversity (compared to Standard), by the difference in similarity (compared to Standard). For example, a relative benefit of 1 means that every unit increase in diversity is accompanied by a corresponding unit drop in similarity - the similarity and diversity trade-off is perfectly balanced. For an algorithm to perform well it should offer relative benefit values greater than one; that is, decreases in similarity should be compensated for by greater increases in diversity.

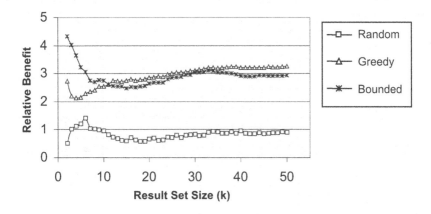

Fig. 4. The relative benefits of the diversity preserving algorithms.

The results are shown in Figure 4 as a graph of relative benefit against k. The Random strategy performs poorly with a relative benefit less than one for most values of k, and an average relative benefit of 0.83. In contrast, the Greedy and Bounded Greedy algorithms perform very well with relative benefits greater than one across all values of k, and average relative benefits of 2.9. In other words, on average, a unit drop in similarity can be traded for almost 3 units of diversity using the Greedy and Bounded Greedy algorithms.

Importantly, the Greedy and Bounded Greedy algorithms both perform very well for low values of k. For example, the Bounded Greedy method has a relative benefit of 3.6 for $k = 3$. This is important since many recommenders are designed to return small result lists (typically $k < 10$) and so it is useful that these algorithms deliver maximal relative benefits when k is small. In general, the Bounded Greedy algorithm has higher relative benefits than the Greedy algorithm for $k < 11$.

4.3 Efficiency

Of course in any real-time CBR system, the efficiency of the retrieval algorithm is just as important as the quality of the retrieved cases. So far we have seen that the Greedy and Bounded Greedy algorithms benefit from improved diversity characteristics, but these benefits are only useful if they can be achieved without significant additional retrieval cost.

In CBR the typical nearest-neighbour approach to retrieval compares the target to every case in the case-base - this is the retrieval method used in our Standard strategy. In this experiment we evaluate the efficiency of the Random, Greedy, and Bounded Greedy methods in the light of this benchmark efficiency. We set $k = 6$ and measure retrieval cost as the number of similarity computations required for the four retrieval techniques. For each set of 400 target queries we compute and average the retrieval times over different case-base sizes from 100 cases to 1000 cases.

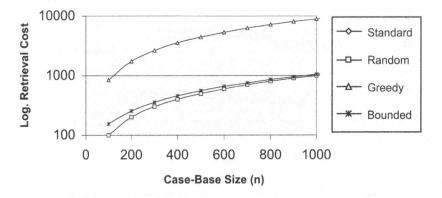

Fig. 5. The retrieval costs versus case-base size (n) for the test algorithms. Note that the Standard curve is overwritten exactly by Random.

The results are graphed in Figure 5 as the logarithm of retrieval cost against case-base size, and in Figure 6 as the relative retrieval cost increase of each algorithm compared to Standard, against case-base size. Clearly, the Greedy algorithm performs poorly, with high retrieval costs across all case-base sizes, backing up our complexity analysis from Section 3. For example, for a case-base of 1000 cases, the Greedy algorithm requires an average of nearly 9000 similarity computations for each retrieval at $k = 6$ (a relative cost increase of 9). The other algorithms perform a lot better. The Standard and Random methods have the same benchmark efficiency characteristics, and the Bounded Greedy algorithm suffers from only a minor reduction in efficiency compared to Standard, again supporting the complexity analysis in Section 3. For example, for a 1000 case case-base, the Bounded Greedy algorithm (with $k = 6$ & $b = 2$) requires only 1054 similarity computations, representing a 5% increase in relative retrieval

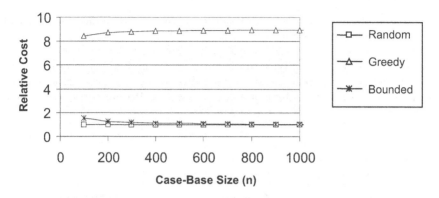

Fig. 6. The relative cost of the diversity preserving algorithms compared to the Standard algorithm.

cost over the Standard method (an extra 54 similarity computations). Moreover this increase is independent of case-base size, since it depends on k & b only.

4.4 Evaluation Summary

These experiments demonstrate that, in our test domain at least, the Greedy and Bounded Greedy algorithms allow retrieval diversity to be improved without sacrificing retrieval similarity; we have carried out similar experiments in the movie domain with similar results. However, the positive performance of the Greedy algorithm is offset by its very high retrieval costs, but the Bounded Greedy algorithm provides a more cost effective solution, with only a minor decrease in efficiency compared to standard retrieval. In fact, Bounded Greedy out-performs Greedy, not only in efficiency, but also in the way that it trades-off similarity for diversity for reasonable values of k.

5   Discussion

We have argued for the importance of diversity as a retrieval constraint in many CBR scenarios. We are not advocating an across the board change in the way that we approach case retrieval. Sometimes diversity is important and sometimes it is not. If it is important then we now offer a way to factor diversity in to existing retrieval strategies without the need for additional knowledge.

5.1   Prototype Application

Our original motivation for this work was application-driven: to develop a movie recommendation system designed for use on WAP-enabled mobile phones. Because of the limited capabilities of these devices, such as reduced screen sizes and restricted input options, it became clear that a standard, similarity-driven

case-based recommender would not succeed because of the limited diversity of
the recommendation results. For instance, a typical interaction might see a user
with an interest in sci-fi and drama, and a preference for Stephen Spielberg
films, being recommended Back to the Future 1, 2, and 3 as the top suggestions
- a limited choice indeed. Clearly a more diverse set of recommendations (such
as Back to the Future 1, Jurassic Park, and Saving Private Ryan) might be a
better bet.

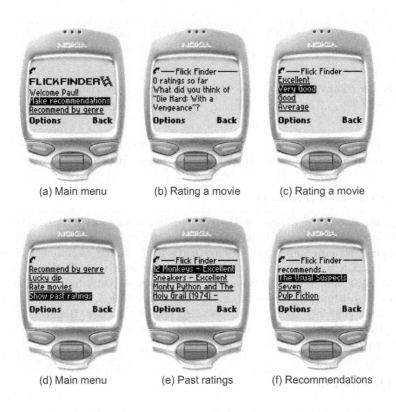

(a) Main menu   (b) Rating a movie   (c) Rating a movie

(d) Main menu   (e) Past ratings   (f) Recommendations

Fig. 7. The FlickFinder WAP-based movie recommender benefits from the diversity-
preserving characteristics of the bounded greedy selection technique.

By using our bounded greedy diversity technique it has been possible to
develop a WAP-based movie recommender that is capable of delivering more
diverse and more appropriate recommendations. Unfortunately due to space
restrictions we cannot describe the resulting FlickFinder application here but
screenshots are shown in Figure 7 for reference.

5.2 Diversity Beyond Case-Based Reasoning

CBR is just one of a number of similarity-based reasoning paradigms. In recommender systems, for example, automated collaborative filtering (ACF) is a related strategy [9,12] based on the retrieval and reuse of user profiles rather than solution cases. User profiles are composed of previous content item ratings, and the ratings contained within the profiles of the selected similar users are used as a source of ranked recommendations for the target user.

Very often ACF techniques are also guilty of blindly following the similarity assumption. A retrieved set of similar user profiles may all be very similar to each other. Thus, they may contain ratings for the same narrow set of content items thereby limiting the possible recommendations. The bounded greedy algorithm can be used in any similarity-based reasoning system, including ACF systems. Instead of retrieving a set of k profiles that are maximally similar to the target user, select profiles that are similar to the target while at the same time different from each other. Once again all that is required is the existing profile similarity metric. The resulting profiles will tend to cover a larger space of rated content items and so offer a more diverse recommendation source.

5.3 Alternative Quality Metrics

In this paper we have proposed one quality metric (Equation 3) to drive our diversity preserving algorithms. Our current work focuses on other metrics such as, for example, Equations 5 and 6. Equation 5 allows for the relative importance of similarity and diversity to be controlled by modifying α, which may be useful at the application level. Equation 6 defines quality as the harmonic mean of the similarity and relative diversity values. A weighted harmonic mean is also possible to provide for a way of balancing the relative importance of similarity and diversity as in Equation 5; this is related to the F-measure in information retrieval research.

$$Quality(t, c, R) = \alpha * Similarity(t, c) + (1 - \alpha) * RelDiversity(c, R) \quad (5)$$

$$Quality(t, c, R) = 2/(\frac{1}{Similarity(t, c)} + \frac{1}{RelDiversity(c, R)}) \quad (6)$$

One common question is: why use a separate quality metric at all? This question is motivated by the hypothesis that poor retrieval diversity is really the result of a poor similarity metric, and that by developing a better similarity metric it will be possible to improve similarity and diversity. This is simply not true. Similarity and diversity are orthogonal measures. Similarity is a local function of two cases, the target and a candidate, and the similarity of a case with respect to a target does not depend on the similarity of any other case. In contrast, the relative diversity of a case depends on previous similarity computations (and case selections). For this reason it is not possible to fold diversity in to a single similarity computation.

5.4   General Applicability

When is diversity important and what is needed for our proposed technique to work? We have already suggested that diversity is important in recommender systems. More generally we argue that diversity is important in CBR applications where vague target queries are the norm, and thus where the retrieval results must provide broad query coverage. This is especially true in many interactive CBR settings where an end-user is provided with a set of candidate cases and is expected to chose from this set in order to solve the target problem. Recommender systems are good examples of this as are help-desk systems and many conversational case-based reasoning systems.

The bounded greedy technique is generally applicable, and only requires access to the existing similarity metric. Of course our ability to maximise diversity does depend on certain characteristics of the case-base in question, such as the distribution of its cases. For example, diversity can be improved significantly with minimal similarity sacrifices in highly clustered case-bases where ordinarily the risk of retrieving cases with poor diversity characteristics greatly increases.

6   Conclusions

We have argued that blindly following the similarity assumption in case-based reasoning can have an adverse effect on the diversity of the retrieved cases. This can be particularly important in case-based recommender systems where broad or incomplete target queries often demand the retrieval of a diverse set of similar cases in order to provide users with good coverage of the information space in the vicinity of their query. Case-based recommenders are often faulted for the limited diversity of their recommendations.

In this paper we have described a number of techniques for improving the diversity of case-based recommenders. Increasing the diversity of recommendations generally means reducing their similarity to the target query. The key is to understand this trade-off and to develop a technique that allows the right balance to be achieved. We have demonstrated empirically that this is possible. The bounded greedy algorithm improves diversity without significantly compromising similarity, and it does so without adversely affecting retrieval time. Moreover, this technique is generally applicable across all case retrieval systems - all that is required is a standard similarity metric. Indeed, we have argued that it can even be used to good effect in other similarity-based reasoning frameworks, such as collaborative filtering.

Of course it is true that, in many CBR applications, diversity is not be an important consideration. Sometimes similarity is king. However, very often diversity is important, and in the past, in these situations it has been necessary to consider alternatives to case-base reasoning. Our point is that it is now possible to improve the diversity characteristics of CBR without resorting to other recommendation techniques, thereby broadening the scope and general applicability of the case-based reasoning method.

References

1. Aamodt, A. and Plaza, E.: Case-Based Reasoning: Foundational Issues, Methodological Variations, and System Approaches. *AI Communications*, 7(1):39–52, 1994.
2. Bergmann, R., Richter, M., Schmitt, S., Stahl, A. and Vollrath, I.: Utility-Oriented Matching: A New Research Direction for Case-Based Reasoning. In: *Proceedings of the German Workshop on Case-Based Reasoning*, 2001.
3. Burke, R.: Conceptual Indexing and Active Retrieval of Video for Interactive Learning Environments. *Knowledge-Based Systems*, 9(8):491–499, 1996.
4. Burke, R.: A case-based approach to collaborative filtering. In: *Proceedings of the 5th European Workshop on Case-Based Reasoning*. Springer-Verlag, 2000.
5. Faltings, B.: Probabilistic Indexing for Case-Based Prediction. In: *Proceedings of the 2nd International Conference on Case-Based Reasoning*, pages 611–622. Springer-Verlag, 1997.
6. S. Fox, S. and Leake, D.B.: Using Introspective Reasoning to Refine Indexing. In: *Proceedings of the 14th International Joint Conference on Artificial Intelligence*, pages 391 – 397. Morgan Kaufmann, 1995.
7. Kolodner, J.: Judging which is the "best" case for a case-based reasoner. In: *Proceedings of the Second Workshop on Case-Based Reasoning*, pages 77–81. Morgan Kaufmann, 1989.
8. Kolodner, J.: *Case-Based Reasoning*. Morgan Kaufmann, 1993.
9. Konstan, J.A., Miller, B.N., Maltz, D., Herlocker, J.L., Gorgan, L.R., and J. Riedl.: GroupLens: Applying collaborative filtering to Usenet news. *Communications of the ACM*, 40(3):77–87, 1997.
10. Leake, D. B.: *Case-Based Reasoning: Experiences,Lessons and Future Directions*. AAAI/MIT Press, 1996.
11. Leake, D. B.: Constructive Similarity Assessment: Using Stored Cases to Define New Situations. In: *Proceedings of the 14th Annual Conference of the Cognitive Science Society*, pages 313–318. Lawrence Earlbaum Associates, 1992.
12. Smyth, B. and Cotter, P.: A Personalized TV Listings Service for the Digital TV Age. *Journal of Knowledge-Based Systems*, 13(2-3):53–59, 2000.
13. Smyth, B.: and Keane, M.: Adaptation-Guided Retrieval: Questioning the Similarity Assumption in Reasoning. *Artificial Intelligence*, 102:249–293, 1998.
14. Smyth, B.: and McKenna, E.: Incremental Footprint-Based Retrieval. In: *Proceedings of the 21st SGES International Conference on Knowledge Based Systems and Applied Artificial Intelligence* , pages 89–101. Springer Verlag, 2000.

Collaborative Case-Based Reasoning: Applications in Personalised Route Planning[*]

Lorraine Mc Ginty[1] and Barry Smyth[1,2]

[1] Smart Media Institute, University College Dublin, Dublin 4, Ireland.
{Lorraine.McGinty@ucd.ie}
[2] ChangingWorlds Ltd., South County Business Park, Dublin 18, Ireland.
{Barry.Smyth@ChangingWorlds.com}

Abstract. Distributed case-based reasoning architectures have the potential to improve the overall performance of case-based reasoning systems. In this paper we describe a collaborative case-based reasoning architecture, which allows problem solving experiences to be shared among multiple agents. We demonstrate how this technique can be used successfully to solve an important challenge in the area of personalised route planning; the problem of how to generate route plans that conform to a user's implicit travel preferences in an unfamiliar map territory.

1 Introduction

Distributed case-based reasoning strategies, where problems are solved by the combined effort of multiple, independent CBR agents, have the potential to improve the performance and maintainability of real-world case-based systems [10, 11,12]. For example, efficiency can be improved by distributing problem solving effort across multiple independent agents operating in parallel. Also, any single CBR system or agent will have limited coverage characteristics, but by combining multiple agents, with independent or overlapping coverage contributions, overall system coverage can be improved. Similarly, solution quality can be enhanced by pooling the solutions offered by each CBR agent. And finally, since each individual agent can be treated as an independent problem solving entity, overall system maintenance is made easier - agents may be locally adapted independently of the other agents.

In this paper we propose a distributed case-based reasoning framework called collaborative case-based reasoning (CCBR) where problem solving experience and responsibility is distributed among multiple CBR agents. Individual agents are capable of directly solving problems that fall within their area of expertise, but draw on the experience of other agents for problems that do not.

The CCBR framework is motivated by realistic challenges faced in the area of personalised route planning; that is, the problem of how to generate routes that not only satisfy a specific travel goal, but that also respect the implicit

---

[*] This research was funded in part by grant N00014-00-1-0021 from the US Office of Naval Research.

D.W. Aha and I. Watson (Eds.): ICCBR 2001, LNAI 2080, pp. 362–376, 2001.
© Springer-Verlag Berlin Heidelberg 2001

route planning preferences of an individual user. Researchers have shown that during route planning different users can be influenced by very different preference models, and in fact that individual users may not even be aware of their own planning preferences [14,16]. Hence, unlike related work [6,9,14], in our research we have developed a case-based approach that operates without explicitly modeling these preferences according to some fixed preference model [7,8].

One of the shortcomings of our previous work is that it is limited to generating personalised route plans in regions of a map where the target user has some prior planning experience. As such, it is not possible to personalise routes from an unfamiliar territory. CCBR provides a solution to this problem. Each user's route planning needs are addressed by a single CBR agent with a case-base of preferred route plans for that user. In the situation, where a given user needs to plan a route in an unfamiliar territory, the user's agent will seek to locate and reuse the case-base of another agent with experience in the target territory *and* with similar preferences.

In the remainder of this paper, after outlining related work in the area of distributed CBR (Section 2), we will focus our attention on collaborative CBR. Section 3 details the CCBR framework and in Sections 4 and 5 we describe and evaluate how CCBR can be used in the domain of personalised route planning.

2   Background

The term *distributed case-based reasoning* can be used in two different contexts. First, it can be used to refer to *single-agent* case-based reasoning systems where case experience is distributed across multiple case-bases, but where there is a single problem solving agent with access to these case-bases. For example the work of Aha & Branting [2] and Smyth & Cunningham [18] focuses on CBR systems with access to multiple, hierarchical case-bases that contain problem cases at different levels of abstraction. New problems are solved in a top-down fashion by selecting and combining multiple cases to solve the sub-parts of the target problem; similar approaches are described by [1,13].

Alternatively, *multi-agent* distributed case-based reasoning systems distribute case knowledge and problem solving effort across multiple CBR agents. For example, Nagendra Prasad et al. [11] describe the CBR-TEAM system that uses a set of heterogeneous cooperative agents in a parametric design task (steam-condenser component design). Each agent is responsible for a particular component design task and the agents cooperate to resolve design conflicts as each new design is constructed from the contribution of the individual agents.

Nagendra Prasad & Plaza [12] introduce the *Federated Peer Learning* (FPL) framework, which aims to study different models of cooperation within multi-agent distributed CBR frameworks, and in particular looks at the situation where an individual agent can leverage the learning capabilities or past experience of other agents. Unlike the work described above, the agents in the FPL framework are usually capable of solving the overall target problem, rather than specialising in solving individual sub-problems. The authors introduce two different modes of cooperation within the FPL framework: (1) an agent A_i transmits the target problem to another agent A_j and transfers problem solving authority to this other agent; (2) an agent A_i transmits the target problem and a method for solving it, to another agent A_j, and thus A_i benefits from A_j's accumulated experience but maintains control of how the target problem should be solved.

Collaborative Case-Based Reasoning can be viewed as a form of Federated Peer Learning. It describes a multi-agent CBR system in which individual agents can leverage the problem solving experience of others. However, CCBR differs from other FPL cooperation models in the sense that each agent retains problem solving authority by solving each target problem locally. When a given agent, A_i, does not have the experience to solve the target problem, A_i cooperates with other agents by *borrowing* their problem solving experience.

3   The Collaborative Case-Based Reasoning Architecture

The CCBR architecture, shown in Figure 1, consists of a collection of homogeneous CBR agents, $A_1, ..., A_n$. The agents have the same CBR capabilities, but differ in their problem solving experiences. An agent case-base, CB_i, may focus on specific regions of the target problem space, and thus each agent may differ in their problem solving coverage, thereby allowing different agents to solve different problem types. Alternatively, the agent case-bases may cover similar problem solving regions but differ in their solution biases, thus allowing different agents to solve the same problems in different ways.

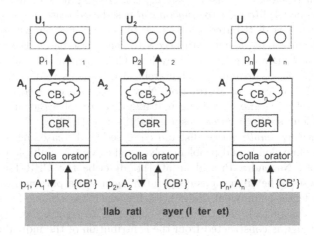

Fig. 1. The Collaborative Case-Based Reasoning Architecture

For our personalised route planning requirement each agent corresponds to an individual user and the CBR component consists of a personalised case-based route planner with a case-base of their preferred route planning experiences. The current architecture functions on the basic assumption that this set of positive routing plans exists and is not concerned with its origins. One possibility is that the case-base holds routes frequently followed by a user. These routes could be collected by manual user-specification or non-intrusively through an in-car GPS navigation system. Each agent will cover a particular route planning territory according to a specific user preference model, and thus different agents will solve the same problems in different ways according to their user's preferences. Of course, in general each CCBR agent may be associated with a set of users rather than a single user, depending on the application setting. For example, in a call-centre or help-desk scenario [4] a given CCBR agent may cover a particular set of product types and service the requests of many users that have purchased the corresponding products.

Very briefly, new target problems, p_i, are presented to the appropriate agents, A_i. Each agent is assumed to be equipped with a capability model which allows it to determine the coverage capabilities of its own local case-base. If A_i can solve p_i the solution plan s_i is generated locally and returned to the originating user. Otherwise, A_i broadcasts the current problem to the other agents, along with a representation of any local problem solving constraints A_i'. Each remote agent is responsible for evaluating whether p falls within its capability given the constraints. When a suitable agent, A_j, exists, its relevant cases, CB_j', are returned to A_i where they are used to solve the target. It may be that more than one suitable collaborating agent is found for A_i in which case more than one set of cases, $\{CB_i'\}$, can be returned to A_i. In the next section we will take a closer look at the CCBR concept with a particular focus on the personalised route planning application.

4   CCBR for Personalised Route Planning

Our research is motivated by the need for better route planning systems. These systems should efficiently generate route plans to solve a target problem while respecting the implicit travel preferences of a target user. There are two interesting types of route-planning scenarios: *Type 1*, solving an unfamiliar problem in a familiar territory; or *Type 2*, solving an unfamiliar problem in an unfamiliar territory. As mentioned earlier we have previously demonstrated the benefits of a case-based approach to deal with Type 1 problems [7,8], but this approach fails to adequately handle Type 2 problems, since by definition the user will not have access to relevant cases from the unfamiliar territory. By implementing a collaborative case-based reasoning system, where each user is associated with an individual route-planning agent, we can leverage the experience of other agents with the relevant planning expertise, in order to deal with Type 2 challenges. This notion of sharing the experience of similar users has been widely practised with tremendous success by collaborative filtering systems [3,5,17], but has largely been ignored in the pure CBR context.

The top-level CCBR agent algorithm is illustrated in Figure 2. Upon receiving a target route planning problem, p (consisting of a start and goal location), the target agent A_i first determines if p falls within its area of expertise. In the

context of route planning this capability check determines whether any of the
junctions that make up the routes in the target agent's case-base are near to the
start and goal locations of p. If this is the case then the target user agent has
planning experience in the problem territory and their own case-base is used to
generate a routing solution to the target problem. In short, where p is covered
by A_i, planning proceeds using the agent's local CBR Planner (see Figure 3).

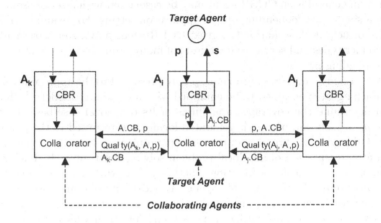

Fig. 2. The top-level CCBR agent algorithm.

If p is not covered by A_i then the collaborative component seeks to locate
cases from a set of similar users that do have the required planning experience
with A_i, and solves p using these *borrowed* cases. Specifically, A_i broadcasts p
to each remote agent (A_j and A_k in Figure 2) and selects that agent with the
highest quality score (see Section 4.2). In Figure 2 the agent A_j is selected as
the *best quality agent* for A_i.

4.1   The Case-Based Component

The core case-based route planning algorithm is shown in Figure 3. This technique has been described and analysed in detail in earlier work [7,8], but we
outline it here for completeness and because it serves as the core problem solving capability of each collaborative case-based reasoning agent. Very briefly, each
new route is generated recursively by retrieving and adapting multiple cases to
fit the current problem. Each recursive call attempts to solve a particular part
of the overall target problem by reusing a case section such that the remaining
uncovered distance is maximally reduced. If at any stage a suitable case cannot
be found, or if the distance between the current start and goal locations is below
a set threshold, the standard distance-based A* planning algorithm is used to
complete the route.

In addition, a geometric case indexing scheme is employed in which a route
case, C is abstracted as a straight line segment, C', connecting the case's start

```
RoutePlan(start, end, CB, threshold)
1    If Dist(start,end) < threshold then
2        route ← A*(start,end)
3    Else if
4        case    ← RetrieveCase(start, end, CB)
5        If case then
6            section ← AdaptCase(start, end, case)
7            route ← RoutePlan(start, Start(section),CB,threshold)
                    + section + RoutePlan(End(section),end,CB,threshold)
8        Else route ← A*(start,end)
9    End if
10   Return(route)

RetrieveCase(start, end, CB)
10 For each case C∈CB
11     C.X'← junction in C with min Dist(start,X')
12     C.Y'← junction in C with min Dist(Y',end)
13 End For
14 C ← case with min Dist(start,C.X')+Dist(C.Y',end)
15 Return(C)

AdaptCase(start, end, C)
16 C.X'← junction in C with min Dist(start,X')
17 C.Y'← junction in C with min Dist(Y',end)
18 section ← road segments in C from C.X' to C.Y'
19 Return(section)
```

Fig. 3. The CBR route planning algorithm.

and goal locations (see Figure 4). This so-called *fast-indexing* strategy facilitates a very efficient retrieval mechanism whereby problem-case similarity is estimated to be the sum of the perpendicular distances from the start (s) and goal (g) locations to the case line segment. This is illustrated in Figure 4, where the problem-case similarity is computed as $|s, x| + |g, y|$. This *fast-indexing* scheme is preferred to the *standard* approach in which a case is indexed according to its individual junctions, with problem-case similarity computed as the sum of the distances between the start and goal and their nearest case junctions. Clearly this standard approach is far more computationally expensive at retrieval time since each case junction must be examined in turn. A more detailed account of these indexing stategies can be found in a previous paper [7].

It is important to understand that, unlike many traditional approaches to personalised route-planning, this case-based approach makes no strong assumptions regarding the structure of user preference models. In fact we assume that such knowledge is not available. We argue that routes that have been liked by a user have been preferred because they conform to that user's preference model, whatever it might be. We have previously shown that this case-based approach

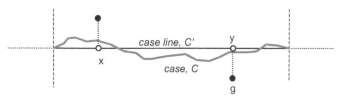

Fig. 4. The fast-indexing technique treats individual routes as simple line segments to facilitate an efficient indexing and retrieval scheme.

allows us to reuse and re-combine these preferred routes to generate new routes that also respect the users planning preferences, and in a fraction of the time taken by traditional approaches [7,8].

4.2   The Collaborator Component

As we have already mentioned, while the pure CBR approach to route planning works well, it is limited to Type 1 route-planning problems (problems from familiar territories). To deal with Type 2 problems (problems from unfamiliar territories) a target user agent A_i must be provided with access to relevant cases from another user, who does have the necessary experience. The key to success then, is the identification of agents that not only have experience in the target problem territory, but that also have similar route-planning preferences to the target user. As mentioned previously, in Section 3, each agent, A_j, is equipped with a *collaborator component*, whose job it is to assess whether it is capable of solving the current target problem, p, and whether its preference model is similar to some A_i.

The overall quality of an agent A_j with respect to a particular target route-planning problem p for a target agent A_i depends on the coverage that A_j provides of p and the similarity of A_i to A_j. The quality metric used is shown in Equation 1, which allows the relative weight of user similarity and problem coverage to be adjusted; in our experiments we have found $w = 0.75$ to deliver the best results.

$$Quality(A_j, A_i, p) =$$
$$(1 - w) * ProblemCoverage(A_j, p) + w * AgentSimilarity(A_j, A_i) \quad (1)$$

After the target agent A_i has broadcast the target problem p and its case-base to the other collaborative agents, it receives a set of quality scores from each of these. A_i then selects the best agent and merges their case-base with its own local case-base in order to solve the target problem. Alternative selection strategies may be used, such as the selection of the top k agents for example.

Problem Coverage: The problem coverage metric is designed to evaluate the likelihood that a user agent A_j will adequately cover the target problem p; that is, the likelihood that A_j's case-base will contain cases that are useful in constructing a route that satisfies p. We compare the junctions in A_j's case-base to the set of junctions, $Region(p)$, in the region of p, and compute the overlap according to Equation 2. We calculate $Region(p)$ according to Equation 3, which computes all junctions that fall between the start and goal locations of p.

$$ProblemCoverage(A_j, p) = \frac{Junctions(A_j) \cap Region(p)}{|Region(p)|} \quad (2)$$

$$Region(p) = \{j : Distance(start(p), j) < Distance(start(p), goal(p))$$
$$\wedge\, Distance(j, goal(p)) < Distance(start(p), goal(p))\} \quad (3)$$

Agent Similarity - Shared Problems: To determine whether the preference models of the two agents are similar the collaborator compares its local case-base to the case-base of the target agent. The agent similarity metric is designed to evaluate the similarity between the preference models that underpin the route-planning experience of two users. Of course we do not have direct access to these models, but we do have access to the route plans that they helped to build. Thus, we can estimate the similarity between the target and a local agent by comparing their case-bases in two steps: step 1 identifies route-planning problems that the agents have in common, their *shared problems*; and step 2 evaluates the similarity of their solutions to these shared problems. Two cases c_i and c_j have a shared problem, $p = (s, g)$, if both cases contain a maximal continuous sequence of junctions that start at s and end at g - see Equation 4. For example, Figure 5 shows an example with two cases, c_i from agent A_i and c_j from agent A_j. These agents share a common problem $p = (J - 46, J - 200)$.

$$SharedProblem(A_i, A_j, s, g) \leftrightarrow$$
$$\exists c_i \in A_i : \{s, x_1...x_n, g\} \subseteq c_i \ \wedge$$
$$\exists c_j \in A_j : \{s, y_1...y_m, g\} \subseteq c_j \ \wedge$$
$$\neg \exists s', g' \in \{x_1...x_n\} : SharedProblem(A_i, A_j, s', g') \quad (4)$$

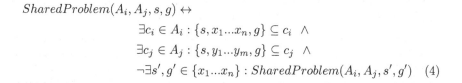

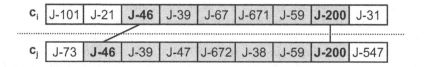

Fig. 5. Cases c_i and c_j share a route-planning problem from J-46 to J-200.

Agent Similarity - Solution Overlap: Two users are similar if they solve their shared problems in a similar way, that is, if the same route segments are chosen for their solutions to the same problems. If two users share many problems, and consistently agree in the way that they solve these problems, then these users must have very similar underlying preference models. Thus, to measure the similarity between two user agents, A_i and A_j, we compute the average solution overlap between their shared problems. That is, if $SP(A_i, A_j) = \{p_1, ...p_n\}$ is the set of problems shared between A_i and A_j, and if $SS_{ij}(k)$ is A_i's solution to the kth shared problem between A_i and A_j, then the similarity between these agents is given by Equation 5. For instance, taking our earlier example (see Figure 5, the solution overlap between c_i and c_j is $\frac{4}{9}$.

$$Similarity(A_i, A_j) = \frac{\sum_{k=1...n} \frac{SS_{ij}(k) \cap SS_{ji}(k)}{SS_{ij}(k) \cup SS_{ji}(k)}}{n} \quad (5)$$

5   Experimental Evaluation

So far we have argued that collaborative case-based reasoning allows us to solve a significant shortcoming of our previous work in personalised route planning, namely, how to generate personalised route plans for a given user in unfamiliar territory. Collaborative CBR achieves this by facilitating the sharing of agent experience, and in the context of route planning this means that it is possible for an agent to solve a target problem from an unfamiliar territory by borrowing cases from a similar agent. The key questions now relate to solution quality and problem solving efficiency and in this section we examine these issues in detail.

5.1   Set-Up

We compare the performance of three route planning algorithms:

Distance-Based A*: standard A* planner with a distance based cost function;
CCBR-STD: a collaborative, case-based planner with standard case indexing;
CCBR-FI: a collaborative, case-based planner with fast-indexing;

Some may argue that a purely distance-based cost heuristic for A* (our benchmark for comparison) is less appropriate than one based on a measure of traffic flow or scenic value. This may well be true, but unfortunately many digital maps lack this sort of information. Thus, the distance-based A* method has been largely adopted by a majority of the existing route planning technologies.

As mentioned earlier, we have previously developed a pure CBR route planning approach that generates routing plans for a user based on their past routing patterns [7,8]. In this work we investigated the two methods of case-indexing; the standard indexing approach (CBR-STD) and the fast-indexing approach (CCBR-FI), as outlined in Section 4.1. Our evaluations confirmed that our CBR-STD approach made significant efficiency sacrifices in order to produce high quality routing solutions but the CBR-FI approach was capable of generating high quality routing plans in a fraction of the time taken by the traditional A* approach. Testing the previous CBR-STD technique with our new collaborative planner (CCBR-STD) serves as a benchmark, to ensure that the solution quality difference between the CBR-STD and CBR-FI techniques is acceptable.

Ideally we would like to evaluate our techniques using real users with real case-bases generated over time. Unfortunately, real users are hard to come by and were not available for the study at hand. Instead we chose to simulate users by defining artificial cost functions and generate case-bases that conform to these functions; this is similar to the *dummy profile* strategy described in [15]. We define a user cost function by assigning random weights to the road segments of our digital map, and the cost of an individual road segment is computed according to the cost function shown in Equation 6.

$$Cost(segment) = length(segment) * weight(segment) \qquad (6)$$

One can view these weights as being inversely proportional to the *desirability* of the road segment for a given user, where desirability is based on some complex and hidden user preference model. Road segments with a high weighting have a low desirability and present with a higher cost than similar length road segments with a low weight (high desirability). Now we can generate arbitrarily large user case-bases for given user by using their specific cost function in association with an A* planner to solve a set of selected route planning problems. This will guarantee to generate a case-base of routes that minimize the user's cost function. These are the ideal routes for the user, the routes that the user would prefer in a real-life route-planning scenario. We also localise each case-base to a specific map territory by selecting the route problems from this territory acording to a specific probability function.

5.2 Method

A set of 260 test users is generated, each with a different preference model (cost function). In general, these preference models are generated such that they display varying degrees of similarity. The similarity values exhibited between pairs of users ranges from 0 to 1, with an average of 0.81 and a standard deviation of 0.13. For each user we generate a case-base of 200 cases in a target territory and 60 test problems outside of this territory. The levels of coverage overlap between user case-bases ranges from 0 to 0.77, with a mean pairwise coverage overlap of 0.3 and a standard deviation of 0.155. It is important to note here that user profiles are constructed such that the users personal cost function is not correlated with the distance-based A* cost function. In this way, we are assuming a minimal relationship between the A* distance-based cost heuritic and the users preference model. The optimal route for each target problem and user is calculated such that the cost function for that user is minimised. These optimal routes are the routes that would be ideally chosen by the user and serve as a benchmark against which to evaluate the routes produced by our planner, which of course do not have access to the actual cost functions.

Each target problem is solved by the three test algorithms, using different sized profile case-bases for each user, ranging from 50 to 200 cases. The mean problem solving efficiency and solution quality is measured for the resulting target solutions. The above is repeated across all 260 users and the efficiency and quality results are averaged for each of the case-base sizes tested.

5.3 Planning Efficiency

The efficiency of each of the three planning algorithms is measured in terms of the mean total problem solving time for the target problems. Note that the total problem solving time of an agent for a given target problem includes the execution time for the collaborator component plus the execution time for the target agent's case-based planner. The execution time for the collaborator component is essentially the average time it takes a remote agent to evaluate its similarity to the target agent and identify those cases needed by the target problem.

The overall efficiency results are shown in figure 6 as a plot of mean problem solving time time versus case-base size. The results are positive showing that

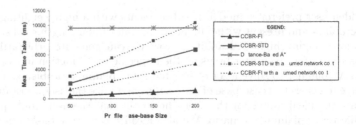

Fig. 6. Mean problem solving time versus case-base size.

the efficiency of both versions of the CCBR planner (CCBR-STD and CCBR-FI) enjoy superior problem solving efficiency than the standard A* planner. The CCBR-STD does not perform as well as CCBR-FI, due to its expensive indexing and retrieval methods. Indeed, the CCBR-FI technique solves target problems between 9 and 23 times faster than the A* method, and between 5 and 7 times faster than CCBR-STD. As expected, we find that the efficiency of both case-base methods is linearly related to case-base size, although the CCBR-FI method is far less susceptible to increasing case-bases, and its mean problem solving time is unlikely to overtake A* for reasonable profile case-base sizes. In contrast, after the 300 case mark the CCBR-STD method is set to experience problem solving times that are greater than those needed by A*. A fundamental issue in distributed computation is the tradeoff between processor and network load. In figure 6 the dashed lines indicate the efficiency cost experienced by the compared planners assuming a low network bandwidth of 56 kilobits per second. We accounted for the trade-off by calculating the average size of a case-base over 56K and adjusting the efficiency times accordingly. Of course in reality we would expect the bandwidth to be much higher.

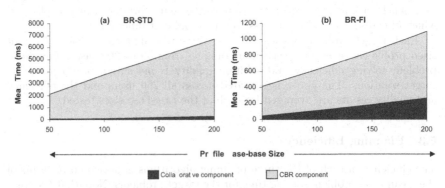

Fig. 7. Computational efficiency comparison showing the mean breakdown in execution times for the collaborative, case-based route planning algorithms.

Figure 7 shows the computational breakdown for the CCBR-STD and CCBR-FI methods. Clearly the majority of the problem solving time is associated with the CBR component, since the task of ranking potential collaborators is distributed across multiple agents. For both algorithms the collaborator component represents an average of 250 msecs of the total problem solving time at the 200 case level, with the CBR component taking approximately 6400 msecs on average for CCBR-STD versus only 820 msecs for CCBR-FI.

In summary our collaborative case-based reasoning method has the potential to offer an efficient case-based planning framework. Overall the CCBR-FI method is capable of delivering personalised route plans in a fraction of the time taken by a standard first-principles approach such as A*.

5.4   Solution Quality

Our main reason for developing the CCBR concept is as a way of extending the coverage of a case-base route planner. Planning efficiency is just part of the evaluation equation. Ultimately, the collaborative case-based reasoning approach can only viewed as being successful if high quality routes are generated. Therefore, the important question is: do the CCBR planners generate routes that respect the planning preferences of the target users, even though the routes are created from the route planning experience of other similar users? Furthermore, we are concerned with the level of variance exhibited between routes generated by the distance-based A* method and those generated by our collaborative approach.

In our earlier work we demonstrated that a single-agent case-based planner is capable of generating high quality routes when its case-base provides adequate coverage of the target territory. But of course it is by no means a given that this will hold true if routes are generated from the case-bases of other users, even if these other users appear to be similar to the target user. For a start, our user similarity metric is unlikely to be perfect, and hence reliability in identifying similar users is far from simple. And there are no guarantees that relevant, similar users will always be available for a given target agent and problem.

After solving each of the 60 target problems for the 260 target users we measure the quality of the resulting solutions by comparison to the optimal solution, which is already known. Two quality metrics are used. First, we compute the segment overlap between each target solution and the optimal solution. An overlap value of 70% means that the target solution correctly incorporates 70% of the actual road segments present in the optimal solution. Second, we compute the true cost of the target solutions with reference to the target user's underlying cost model and compare this to the true cost of the optimal solutions.

The results are shown in Figure 8(a&b) where we plot overlap against casebase size for each of the test planning algorithms. The results are extremely positive. They show that both CCBR methods are capable of generating route plans that share more road segments with their corresponding optimal route than the routes generated by A*. For example, these results indicate that, on average, A* produces target routes that share approximately 38% of their road segments with the corresponding optimal route. In contrast, the CCBR-STD and CCBR-FI methods exhibit overlap values of between 50% and 66% depending on casebase size. As expected, the CCBR-STD methods performs better than CCBR-FI, since CCBR-FI's fast-indexing strategy results in minor quality sacrifices compared to the more expensive standard indexing method.

We also find that the overlap tends to increase slowly with the case-base size. This is to be expected because the case-base size refers to the average case-base size of all of the agents in the CCBR system, and the availability of larger case-bases improves the likelihood that a collaborating agent will exist with the right cases to solve the current target problem. But also, the larger case-bases will lead to more reliable agent similarity estimates.

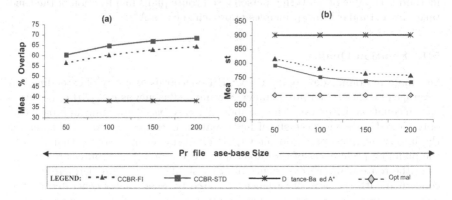

Fig. 8. Quality comparison showing the mean overlap values (a) and mean route costs (b) for each of the comparative route planning algorithms with the optimal route.

Similar characteristics are observed for our second route quality measure, mean route cost, as shown in Figure 8(b). Both CCBR methods are seen to approach the mean cost of the optimal routes. For example, at the 200 case level the mean optimal route cost is approximately 690 units while the CCBR-FI and CCBR-STD methods generates routes with mean costs of approximately 740 and 760 units respectively. This is compared to 902 units for the routes produced by the standard A* approach. In other words, the CCBR methods generate routes that are only 7% - 15% more costly than the optimal route, compared to a relative cost increase of 30% for the A* methods. In general then, these cost results indicate that while the CCBR methods are generating routes with 55% - 70% segment overlap with the optimal routes, the missing segments are being replaced by other high quality road segments. Once again, the CCBR-STD method consistently produces routes that are closer to optimal than the CCBR-FI technique, although the difference is minor (approximately 4%).

5.5   Summary Analysis

Our central hypothesis has been that it is possible to generate route plans that reflect the implicit preferences of individual users in unfamiliar map territories, by borrowing and reusing the cases of relevant similar users. Our results confirm this hypothesis. We have shown that on average the quality of the route plans generated by the CCBR methods is a significant improvement over the quality of the routes produced by the standard non-personalised A* method. In other words route planning experience can be sucessfully transferred between similar users. Moreover we have demonstrated that these results can be achieved in an efficient manner. In fact, the CCBR-FI is capable of delivering high-quality routes in a fraction of the time that it takes A* or even CCBR-STD methods.

6 Conclusions

Distributed case-based reasoning systems have the potential to benefit from improved performance characteristics compared to single-agent, centralised systems, both in terms of problem solving efficiency, problem coverage, and solution quality. In this paper we have described a particular type of distributed case-based reasoning strategy called collaborative case-based reasoning (CCBR), in which individual problem solving agents can collaborate and share their problem solving experiences by trading cases.

Our research has been motivated by the need to solve an important challenge in personalised route planning, namely how to generate route plans from an unfamiliar map territory that are personalised for an individual user. The collaborative case-based reasoning strategy promises a solution by allowing a given user agent to *borrow* cases from similar agents that are familiar with the target territory. We have described how similar agents can be located by comparing agent case-bases and demonstrated empirically that by transferring relevant cases to the target agent high-quality, personalised routes can be generated.

There is a tradeoff between agent similarity and their case-base coverage. That is, a remote agent is useful to a target agent if it has a different coverage, but to be considered similar they must share a set of common problems. In the future, we intend to investigate and propose measures to manage this tradeoff.

In summary then there are two main contributions in this paper. First and foremost, we have now developed a case-based route planning technique that is capable of generating highly personalised routes in familiar and unfamiliar map territories that reflect the implicit preference models of individual users. Secondly, the collaborative case-based reasoning framework that has made this possible is domain and task independent and, we believe, holds promise in a wide variety of application scenarios.

References

1. R. Barletta and W. Mark. Breaking cases into pieces. In *Proceedings of the AAAI Case-Based Reasoning Workshop*, pages 12–17. St. Paul,MN, 1988.
2. L. Branting and D. Aha. Stratified Case-Based Reasoning: Reusing hierarchical problem solving episodes. In *Proceedings of the Fourteenth International Joint Conference on Artificial Intelligence*, pages 384–390. Morgan Kaufmann, 1995.
3. R. Burke. Integrating Knowledge-based and Collaborative-filtering Recommender Systems. In *Proceedings of the Workshop on Artificial Intelligence and Electronic Commerce (AAAI99)*. AAAI Press/MIT Press, 1999.

4. Mehmet Goker. The Development of HOMER: A Case-Based CAD/CAM Help-Desk Support Tool. In B. Smyth and P. Cunningham, editors, *Proceedings of the Fourth European Workshop on Case-Based Reasoning: Advances in Case-Based Reasoning*, pages 346–357. Springer, 1998.

5. J.A. Konstan, B.N Miller, D. Maltz, J.L. Herlocker, L.R. Gorgan, and J. Riedl. GroupLens: Applying collaborative filtering to Usenet news. *Communications of the ACM*, 40(3):77–87, 1997.

6. B. Liu. Intelligent Route Finding: Combining Knowledge, Cases and An Efficient Search Algorithm. In *Proceedings of the 12th European Conference on Artificial Intelligence*, pages 380–384, 1996.

7. L. McGinty and B. Smyth. Personalised Route Planning: A Case-Based Approach. In E. Blanzieri and L. Portinale, editors, *Advances in Case-Based Reasoning: Proceedings of the Fifth European Workshop of Case-Based Reasoning*, pages 431–442. Springer-Verlag, 2000.

8. L. McGinty and B. Smyth. Turas: A Personalised Route Planning System. In *Proceedings of the Sixth Pacific Rim International Conference on AI*, 2000.

9. T. Payne, T. L. Lenox, S.K. Hahn, M. Lewis, and K. Sycara. Agents-Based Team Aiding in a Time Critical Task. In *Proceedings of the Thirty-Third Annual Hawaii International Conference on System Sciences*. IEEE Computer Society, 2000.

10. M.V. Nagendra Prasad, V. Lesser, and S. Lander. On retrieval and reasoning in distributed case bases. In *1995 IEEE International Conference on Systems Man and Cybernetics*, 1995.

11. M.V. Nagendra Prasad, V. Lesser, and S. Lander. Retrieval and reasoning in distributed case bases. *Journal of Visual Communication and Image Representation, Special Issue on Digital Libraries*, 7(1):74–87, 1996.

12. M.V. Nagendra Prasad and E. Plaza. Corporate Memories as Distributed Case Libraries. In *Proceedings of the Corporate Memory and Enterprise Modeling Track in the Tenth Knowledge Acquisition Workshop*. Banff, Canada, 1996.

13. M. Redmond. Distributed cases for case-based reasoning: Facilitating use of multiple cases. In *Proceedings of AAAI*, pages 304–309. AAAI Press/MIT Press, 1990.

14. S. Rogers, C. Fiechter, and P. Langley. An Adaptive Interactive Agent for Route Advice. In *Proceedings of the Third International Conference on Autonomous Agents*, pages 198–205. Seattle, W.A, 1999.

15. S. Rogers and P. Langley. Personalized Driving Route Recommendations. In *Proceedings of the American Association of Artificial Intelligence Workshop on Recommender Systems*, pages 96–100. Madison,WI, 1998.

16. J. Rottengatter. Road User Attitudes and Behaviour. In G.B. Grayson, editor, *Behavioural Research in Road Safety*. Transport Research Laboratory, UK, 1993.

17. B. Smyth and P. Cotter. Surfing the Digital Wave: Generating Personalized Television Guides Using Collaborative, Case-based Recommendation. In *Proceedings of the Third International Conference on Case-based Reasoning*, 1999.

18. B. Smyth and P. Cunningham. The Utility Problem Analysed: A Case-Based Reasoning Perspective. In I. Smith and B. Faltings, editors, *Proceedings o f the American Association of Artificial Intelligence Spring Symposium on Agents with Adjustable Autonomy*, pages 392–399. Springer-Verlag, 1996.

Helping a CBR Program Know What It Knows

Bruce M. McLaren[1] and Kevin D. Ashley[2]

[1] OpenWebs Corporation
2403 Sidney Street
Pittsburgh, Pennsylvania 15203-2116
bmclaren@openwebs.com

[2] University of Pittsburgh
Intelligent Systems Program
3939 O'Hara Street
Pittsburgh, PA 15260
ashley+@pitt.edu

Abstract. Case-based reasoning systems need to know the limitations of their expertise. Having found the known source cases most relevant to a target problem, they must assess whether those cases are similar enough to the problem to warrant venturing advice. In experimenting with SIROCCO, a two-stage case-based retrieval program that uses structural mapping to analyze and provide advice on engineering ethics cases, we concluded that it would sometimes be better for the program to admit that it lacks the knowledge to suggest relevant codes and past source cases. We identified and encoded three strategic metarules to help it decide. The metarules leverage incrementally deeper knowledge about SIROCCO's matching algorithm to help the program "know what it knows." Experiments demonstrate that the metarules can improve the program's overall advice-giving performance.

Introduction

Humans typically know the limits of their own expertise. They can recognize when they have seen problems before and whether the solutions to the past problems are likely to lead to a solution in a new situation. Self-knowledge of the limitations of ones expertise is a hallmark of intelligence and a characteristic that would greatly benefit expert systems, especially case-based ones.

Earlier work in AI addressed the issue of an expert system's knowing the limits of its expertise using *meta-knowledge* [Lenat *et al.*, 1983, chapter 7; Davis and Buchanan, 1985]. In that work, one could "draw upon a very useful body of knowledge: [a] model of what it is you do and do not know, what tasks you can and cannot tackle, and how long it would take you to solve some problem." [Lenat *et al.*, 1983, p. 234] A program so equipped could respond to some situations by simply admitting its ignorance instead of venturing risky advice. This line of research led to the development of systems such as TEIRESIAS [Davis, 1982].

D.W. Aha and I. Watson (Eds.): ICCBR 2001, LNAI 2080, pp. 377-391, 2001.

While the problem of imbuing a program with strategic knowledge of its own limitations is still important, it has been largely ignored in recent years. In particular, the case-based reasoning community has focused little attention on the issue. This may be due, in part, to the goal of many CBR systems to provide "quick-and-dirty" solutions: such an objective does not appear to comport well with the overhead of employing deeper strategic knowledge. It may also be a result of the emphasis by most CBR programs on finding the most relevant past case or cases, given a current case base. A past case may be the most similar of *known* cases, but it still may not be similar enough at a deeper level to warrant its use as the basis of a solution. Providing criteria for making that decision, however, may require representing more knowledge than is customary in most CBR approaches.

In applying CBR techniques in sensitive or dangerous domains, such as medicine or air traffic control, knowing what one knows is a particularly important characteristic. It is one thing to take a "best guess" at a real estate assessment, quite another to suggest a dangerous medical procedure on the basis of a weakly supported diagnosis. A CBR program operating in the latter domain would be well advised to admit to its uncertainty in such situations.

One could use techniques to construct and maintain "competent" case bases, which cover a range of cases that might be presented to a system [Smyth and Keane, 1995; Smyth and McKenna, 1999]. The case base essentially becomes a sample distribution of possible target problems. This approach relies on techniques for deleting from and editing a case base so that the case base itself defines what the program "knows." Competent case bases appear to be useful in domains in which the retrieval technique is well understood (e.g., nearest neighbor) and in which a single "best case" is retrieved, but they may have less import in domains in which retrieval is performed at both a surface and structural level and in which multiple cases support a result. In such situations, computing competence may be a prohibitively difficult task.

We have been working with a problem domain, engineering ethics, in which incorrect suggestions could be considered sensitive and damaging. Engineering ethics deals with ethical dilemmas and problems that occur in professional engineering, and these problems typically involve delicate issues such as public safety, confidentiality between an engineer and a client, and duty to an employer [Harris *et al.*, 1999]. We have developed a CBR program, SIROCCO, which provides advice for engineering ethics problems by applying a two-stage retrieval algorithm [McLaren, 1999; McLaren and Ashley, 2000]. Because of its sensitive nature, our chosen domain could clearly benefit from a program that knows its limitations. At the same time our two-stage retrieval algorithm, which involves both surface and structural mapping, requires an approach other than competent case bases.

After analyzing and experimenting with SIROCCO's retrieval algorithm and representation, we have devised certain metarules to assess whether a given retrieval has been successful. Given the most relevant known cases, the metarules assess whether the program has previously encountered cases enough like the problem to warrant giving advice. The metarules leverage strategic knowledge about the operation of the retrieval algorithm and about what successful retrievals look like.

As noted, SIROCCO's two-stage algorithm matches at two levels: a surface level and a deeper structural level. In addition, the algorithm depends on collecting a *set* of reasonably matched cases rather than a single best match. This led to defining three metarules. Given a target case and a set of retrieved source cases, each rule provides evidence that the program cannot suggest advice for the target case:

- **Metarule 1**: If the best superficial match between the target and source cases is a weak surface-level match of critical and questioned facts, then SIROCCO may be inadequate for the task.

- **Metarule 2**: If the top N superficially-matched source cases do not share enough citations to the same underlying ethical principles (i.e., codes), then SIROCCO may be inadequate for the task.

- **Metarule 3**: If the best deep match between the target and source cases is a weak structural match, then SIROCCO may be inadequate for the task.

The rules are listed in order of increasing sensitivity to depth of analysis. The first assesses the surface-level match with respect to certain important facts. The second accounts for how well the source cases overlap conceptually with respect to underlying ethical principles. The third assesses the quality of the structural mapping to source cases. While we believed that the third rule provides SIROCCO with the strongest evidence of the limitations of its knowledge, we also believed that the first two rules could provide useful evidence.

We constructed specific implementations for each metarule and performed a series of experiments to better understand their potential benefits, alone and in various combinations. In the remainder of this paper, we describe our program, provide examples of the usefulness of the metarules in deciding when to provide advice, and report the results of our experiments.

Overview of SIROCCO

SIROCCO, an interpretive CBR program, extends techniques that have been applied to the legal domain [Ashley, 1990; Branting, 1991, Rissland *et al.*, 1996] to the domain of engineering ethics. SIROCCO contributes a detailed, narrative case representation, including temporal relations between facts, and an extensional model of general principles and cited cases. It can retrieve cases over a wider range of factual scenarios than the AI & Law programs, but unlike those programs it does not make arguments for or against a conclusion. Rather, it provides suggestions that can help a human construct a reasoned argument.

The program accepts a target case expressed in the Ethics Transcription Language (ETL) and produces suggestions about relevant code provisions and past cases. A sample target case is shown in Figure 1; it deals with an engineer who has discovered structural defects in an apartment building but has been told he must keep that information confidential. SIROCCO's output for the case is shown in Figure 2, at the top of which is a textual description of the case facts. SIROCCO's output is essentially a series of "possibly relevant" codes and past cases that the engineer should consider in analyzing the target case.

1. Apartment Building **<may be hazardous to safety>**.	Pre-existing fact
2. Apartment Building Owner **<owns>** Apartment Building.	Occurs during 1
3. Residents of Apartment Building **<reside in>** Apartment Building.	Occurs during 1, 2
4. Residents of Apartment Building **<file a lawsuit or arbitration action against>** Apartment Building Owner **<because>** (Apartment Building **<may be hazardous to safety>**).	Occurs during 3
5. Apartment Building Owner **<is legally represented by>** Owner's Attorney.	Occurs during 4
6. Owner's Attorney **<hires the services of>** Engineer A **<for>** (Engineer A **<inspects>** Apartment Building).	Occurs during 4, 5
7. Engineer A **<inspects>** Apartment Building.	Occurs during 6
8. Engineer A **<discovers that>** (Apartment Building **<fails standards and may be hazardous to safety>**).	Occurs during 7
9. Engineer A **<knows>** (Government Authority **<should be informed about the hazard or potential hazard>**).	Occurs during 8
10. Engineer A **<informs>** Owner's Attorney **<that>** (Apartment Building **<fails standards and may be hazardous to safety>**).	Immediately after the conclusion of 8
11. Owner's Attorney **<instructs>** Engineer A **<to>** (Engineer A **<withholds information from>** Anyone Else **<regarding>** Apartment Building).	After the conclusion of 10
12. Engineer A **<does not inform>** Anyone Else **<that>** (Apartment Building **<fails standards and may be hazardous to safety>**). *[Questioned fact]*	After the conclusion of 11

Fig. 1. The Fact Chronology of Case 90-5-1

***   SIROCCO is analyzing Case 90-5-1

Facts: Tenants of an apartment building sue the owner to force him to repair many defects in the building that affect the quality of use. The owner's attorney hires Engineer A to inspect the building and give expert testimony in support of the owner. Engineer A discovers serious structural defects in the building, which he believes constitute an immediate threat to the safety of the tenants. The tenants' suit has not mentioned these safety-related defects. Upon reporting the findings to the attorney, Engineer A is told he must maintain this information as confidential as it is part of a lawsuit. Engineer A complies with the request of the attorney.

Question: Was it ethical for Engineer A to conceal his knowledge of the safety-related defects in view of the fact that it was an attorney who told him he was legally bound to maintain confidentiality?

***   SIROCCO's suggestions for evaluating Case 90-5-1:

*** *Possibly Relevant Codes:*
> I-4: Act as a Faithful Agent or Trustee
> III-4: Do not Disclose Confidential Info. Without Consent
> I-1: Safety, Health, and Welfare of Public is Paramount
> II-1-A: Primary Obligation is to Protect Public (Notify Authority if Judgment is Overruled). ...
> II-1-C: Do not Reveal Confidential Info. Without Consent
> III-2-B: Do not Complete or Sign Documents that are not Safe for Public ...

*** *Possibly Relevant Cases:*
> 76-4-1: Public Welfare - Knowledge of Information Damaging to Client's Interest
> 89-7-1: Duty To Report Safety Violations
> 84-5-1: Engineer's Recommendation For Full-Time, On-Site Project Representative

Fig. 2. SIROCCO's Output for Case 90-5-1 (excerpts)

SIROCCO represents ethics cases as narratives, expressed in a limited language. As shown in Figure 1, ETL represents the actions and events of a scenario as an ordered list (i.e., a *Fact Chronology*) of individual sentences (i.e., *Facts*), each consisting of:

1. *Actors and Objects*, instances of general actors and objects which appear in the scenario (e.g., "Owner's Attorney," "Engineer A," "Apartment Building"),
2. a *Fact Primitive*, the action/event in which the actors/objects participated (e.g., "owns," "inspects," "discovers that"), and
3. a *Time Qualifier*, a temporal relation between the Fact and other Facts (e.g., "Occurs during," "After the conclusion of").

At least one Fact in the Fact Chronology is designated as a Questioned Fact; this is an action or event corresponding to an ethical question raised in the scenario. ETL conforms to the well-formed grammar defined in [McLaren and Ashley, 1999].

The *Time Qualifiers* are disjunctive compositions of Allen's temporal constraints [1983], and SIROCCO uses a time propagation system, TIMELOGIC [Koomen 1989], to compute time relations not explicitly provided.

SIROCCO's source cases (i.e., the cases in its case base) are represented as Fact Chronologies together with templates that represent the case analysis. Each analysis comes from the text of a large corpus of cases published by the National Society of Professional Engineers Board of Ethical Review (NSPE BER). Each template contains attributes for the conclusion (i.e., ethical, unethical, or undecided), the protagonist whose action is questioned, the general argument structure, and information about each code or past case cited in the analysis of the case. Figure 3 shows part of the template filled in for Code II.1.a.[1], cited in Case 90-5-1.

Code	II.1.a
Code Status	Violated
...	**...**
Why relevant	Engineer's judgment is overruled in a particular professional circumstance. [11]
	Overruling the Engineer's judgment may lead to the endangerment of the safety, health, property or welfare of the public [8, 9]
Why violated, not violated,...	In the given situation, Engineer does not hold paramount the safety, health, property, and welfare of the public. [12]

Fig. 3. Extracts from the template for Code II.1.a in Case 90-5-1

A key aspect of SIROCCO is its use of operationalization techniques. Case analyses provide extensional definitions of ethical principles and case citations, and SIROCCO operationalizes those definitions to help it focus on the most important facts of cases. *Code* and *case instantiations*, the two most important of the nine techniques used by SIROCCO, relate a questioned fact, critical facts, and the temporal sequence of those facts in the citing case to the cited code or case. For instance, in Figure 3, Code II.1.a. is operationalized. The numbers in brackets in the last two rows refer to the facts of Case 90-5-1 (Figure 1) that are critical to the code's application

---

[1] Code II.1.a. states: "Engineers shall hold paramount the safety, health, and welfare of the public. If engineers' judgment is overruled ... they shall notify their employer or client and such authority as may be appropriate."

and explain why it was violated (or not). Code II.1.a. is thus connected extensionally to a real case's relevant facts and chronology in a way that SIROCCO can reuse.

The program uses two abstraction hierarchies to determine similarities between Facts and Codes. The *Action/Event Hierarchy* clusters and generalizes similar Fact Primitives. The *Code Hierarchy* clusters codes dealing with similar issues.

SIROCCO's case base consists of 242 cases. 184 of the cases are referred to as the *foundational cases*. These were used to design, implement, and refine the program. The other 58 are *trial cases*. These were represented by independent case enterers and were used to run earlier experiments, reported in [McLaren, 1999; McLaren and Ashley, 2000], in which we compared SIROCCO's capabilities to a full-text retrieval program and an ablated version of the program. (SIROCCO performed significantly better than both the full-text retrieval system and the ablated version of the program in those experiments.) The cases deal with a variety of issues including public safety, confidential information, duty to employer, credit for engineering work, proprietary interests, and honesty in reports and public statements.

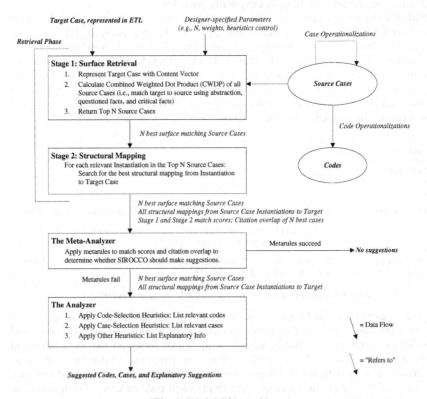

Fig. 4. SIROCCO's Architecture

SIROCCO's Two-Stage Retrieval Process

As indicated in Figure 4, once SIROCCO receives a target case represented in ETL, it engages in a two-stage process to retrieve relevant code provisions and source cases from its database. Stage 1 rapidly matches the Fact Primitives of the target case to those of all possible source cases. Stage 2, employs A* search in a more-refined structural mapping.

In both stages, the code and case instantiations help SIROCCO focus attention on the most critical facts. Stage 1's accuracy improves by giving more weight to the instantiations' Fact Primitives. Focusing on only a subset of a source case's Facts, those critical Facts cited in an instantiation, makes Stage 2's structural mapping routine more efficient and accurate.

For Stage 1, the target case and all of the source cases are represented as content vectors [Forbus *et al.*, 1994]. Each vector summarizes the Fact Chronology of a single case. It specifies the Fact Primitives, and their abstractions, and a count of how many times each one appears. Figure 5 shows two content vectors for Case 90-5-1. The content vector on the left represents the lowest level of abstraction; the vector on the right is one level higher in the Action/Event Hierarchy. There are a total of four predefined levels in the hierarchy. The facts with three asterisks ("***") correspond to the questioned fact(s) of the case.

Fact-Primitive-CV:	Fact-Group-CV:
(May -be-Hazardous-to-Safety 1)	(Deal-with-Potential-Dangers-or-Hazards 1)
(Owns 1)	(Own-Something 1)
(Resides-in 1)	(Specify-Location-of-Residence 1)
(Files-a-Lawsuit-or-Arbitration-Action-Against 1)	(Initiate-Legal-or-Arbitration-Proceedings 1)
(Is-Legally-Represented-by 1)	(Has-Legal-Representation 1)
(Hires-the-Services-of 1)	(Work-as-an-Employed-or-Contract-Professional-Engineer 1)
(Inspects 1)	(Perform-Engineering-Analysis-Review-or-Testing-Work 1)
(Discovers-That 1) (Knows 1)	(Know-or-Believe-Something 2)
(Informs-That 2) ***	(Disclose-Information 2) ***
(Instructs-to 1)	(Order-Subordinate-to-Perform-Task 1)

Fig. 5. Two of the Content Vectors for Case 90-5-1

Stage 1 computes a *combined weighted dot product* (CWDP) for every source case and outputs a list of the top N source cases (experimentation reported in [McLaren, 1999] determined N = 6 to be optimal) ranked by descending CWDP scores. Predefined weights are assigned as parameters to matches at the four abstraction levels and to matches of a source case's critical and questioned facts.

Since, as described in the next section, our implementation of metarule #1 deals with CWDPs, it is worth explaining them in some detail. Given a target case (T) and a source case (S_n), the CWDP for S_n is:

$$CWDP = WDP + (QFW_x * MWDP) + (CFW_y * MWDP) \qquad (1)$$

$$WDP = (W_1 * DP_1 / MDP_1) + (W_2 * DP_2 / MDP_2) + (W_3 * DP_3 / MDP_3) + (W_4 \qquad (2)$$
$$* DP_4 / MDP_4)$$

Where:
- WDP is the weighted dot product; $0 <= WDP <= 1.0$
- QFW_x is the pre-defined questioned fact weight at the most specific match level; $QFW_x <= 1.0$
- CFW_y is the pre-defined critical fact weight at the most specific match level; $CFW_y <= 1.0$
- MWDP is the maximum weighted dot product (WDP) over all source cases.
- $W_1 + W_2 + W_3 + W_4 = 1.0$ (Pre-defined weights corresponding to each abstraction level).
- $DP_1 \ldots DP_4$ are the normalized dot products of T and S_n at each abstraction level.
- $MDP_1 \ldots MDP_4$ are the maximum dot products at each abstraction level over all source cases.

The dot products (i.e., DP_1 to DP_4) are calculated as in standard vector arithmetic, by summing the product of matching vector elements. Since the calculation tends to favor long fact chronologies, the dot products are normalized by dividing by the sum of the content vector elements, which is roughly the length of a fact chronology. Each dot product is also normalized by dividing it by the maximum dot product (MDP_1 to MDP_4) over all source cases at that abstraction level.

Here is the intuition behind the CWDP. The weighted dot product (WDP) captures how well facts of two cases match both exactly and at more abstract fact levels. The contribution of an exact match is more than that of an abstract match (the standard weights applied by SIROCCO are $W_1 = 0.53$, $W_2 = 0.27$, $W_3 = 0.14$, and $W_4 = 0.06$, each level twice the weight of the previous level, considering rounding). The combined weighted dot product (CWDP) accounts for matching of questioned and critical facts between the target and source case. For both questioned and critical facts an extra element is added to the WDP that is equivalent to the best WDP over all source cases, times a weight that corresponds to the abstraction level of the match. Questioned facts are considered more important than critical facts since they are the focus of the ethical analysis of a case. This difference in relative importance is reflected in the standard abstraction-level weights: 1.0, 0.5, 0.25, and 0.125 for questioned facts, 0.333, 0.111, 0.036, and 0.012 for critical facts. Matching a questioned fact can have a dramatic effect; the weighting factor is applied to the *highest* WDP over *all* source cases.

Given SIROCCO's standard weights, the maximum possible CWDP is 2.333: 1.0 for the WDP, 1.0 for the questioned fact addend ($QFW_x * MWDP$), and 0.333 for the critical fact addend ($CFW_y * MWDP$). The CWDP only occasionally exceeds 2.0. For the example case (Figure 1), one on which SIROCCO performs well, the top 6 CWDP scores ranged from 1.97 to 2.27. A more typical range is 1.2 to 1.9.

Stage 2 employs a heuristic A* search for each target case / candidate source case instantiation pair to attempt a structural mapping between the two. Unlike the use of A* search in GREBE [Branting 1991], SIROCCO takes temporal relations into account and supports abstract matches. The goal is to map each of the Facts of the source instantiation to a corresponding Fact in the target case while maintaining a one-to-one and consistent mapping between Actors and Objects across the cases.

Since, as described below, our implementation of metarule #3 tests values of the cost function, $f(n)$, of the A* search, we describe in some detail how it is calculated. The initial node of the search space maps the source's questioned Actor to the target's. Each subsequent node corresponds to a new mapping of a Fact in the source instantiation to a Fact in the target. The solution depth is equal to the number of Facts in the source instantiation. Expanding a new node requires four conditions to be met: (1) a match of a pair of Facts at the same level of abstraction, one from the source instantiation and one from the target, (2) preservation of a one-to-one Fact mapping between the source and target (i.e., no Fact can be mapped more than once), (3) preservation of a one-to-one, consistent set of Actor and Object mappings entailed by the Fact mappings, and (4) consistent temporal relations between mapped Facts of the source and target. Temporal relations are consistent if the Allen relations of every pair of mapped source Facts intersect with the Allen relations of the corresponding pair of target Facts.

As new nodes are expanded a *mismatch score* is calculated for each. The score is based on the abstraction level at which the target and source Facts match: 0.0 is assigned for an exact match, 0.4 for a match at the first abstraction level, 0.6 for the second level, 0.9 for the third level, and 1.0 for a complete mismatch. The mismatch score at a node is cumulative; it sums all of the mismatched values between target and source Facts along the current search path. The mismatch score is used by the A* cost function, $f(n) = g(n) + h'(n)$, to calculate the "goodness" of a node. The $g(n)$ function is the mismatch score divided by the current search depth. The $h'(n)$ function provides the most optimistic possible completion of the mapping from node n to the goal node; it is the mismatch score divided by the solution depth.

The goal node is reached when the current depth equals the solution depth and either the current node has the lowest $f(n)$ score of all open nodes or the nodes list is empty.

Mapping Level	Facts of Source Case Inst. III.4. (Case 76-4-1)	Mapped Target Facts (Case 90-5-1)
1ˢᵗ abstraction level	2. Engineer Doe **<reviews and analyzes>** Discharge	7. Engineer A **<inspects>** Apartment Building
Exact Match	3. Engineer Doe **<discovers that>** (Discharge **<fails standards and may be hazardous to safety>**).	8. Engineer A **<discovers that>** (Apartment Building **<fails standards and may be hazardous to safety>**).
Exact Match	11. Engineer Doe **<does not inform>** Control Authority **<that>** (Discharge **<fails standards and may be hazardous to safety>**).	12. Engineer A **<does not inform>** Anyone Else **<that>** (Apartment Building **<fails standards and may be hazardous to safety>**).

Fig. 6. Mapping of Code Instantiation III.4. of Case 76-4-1 to Case 90-5-1

Consider the search node in Figure 6, showing a mapping of a source instantiation, Code III.4, to the example target case in Figure 1. SIROCCO has succeeded in mapping all three Facts of the instantiation. In fact, the node in this figure represents the goal node that was reached in this search. Only one of the three Facts was not matched exactly, the 1ˢᵗ abstraction level match of the first Fact, and, since this is a goal node, the current depth and solution depth are both equal to 3. Thus, the cost function for this node is $(0.4 / 3) + (0.4 / 3) = 0.27$. It is usually more convenient to think of f(n) as a *match percentage*. Because 0.27 measures mismatch and the maximum possible mismatch is 2.0, the match percentage of an instantiation is $(2.0 - f(n)) / 2.0$. Thus, the match percentage of the node in Figure 6 is $1.73 / 2.0 = 86.7\%$.

The Meta-analyzer and Analyzer

SIROCCO's decision to provide advice based on how well the target matches the source cases is made in the Meta-Analysis step of the SIROCCO architecture depicted in Figure 4. As described in the next section, this step applies the metarules.

Assuming that SIROCCO decides to provide suggestions, i.e., the metarules fail, its final stage (the Analyzer shown in Figure 4) uses other knowledge to decide which codes to suggest to the user. For instance, the Code-Selection Heuristic "Good Match to Questioned Facts of Code Instantiation" is satisfied if the f(n) is sufficiently low (<= 1.0) and a Questioned Fact in the source and/or target is matched. Because the example mapping of Figure 6 meets this criterion (step 11 of Case 76-4-1 and step 12 of Case 90-5-1 are Questioned Facts of their respective cases), SIROCCO suggests Code III.4 as relevant (see Figure 2).

SIROCCO blends the results of multiple source cases into its output, rather than relying on a single best match. It attempts to find a structural mapping to the instantiations of *all* the top N superficially matched source cases, and can provide suggestions based on all of them. Another of SIROCCO's Code-Selection Heuristics, "Frequent Occurrences in the Top Cases," is based on this feature. If a code is cited by 33% of the top N cases, evidence accumulates for the selection of this code in SIROCCO's suggestions. As described below, the implementation of metarule #2 also employs common code citations as evidence of whether the program has found good source cases for a target.

Helping SIROCCO Know What It Knows

To imbue SIROCCO with the knowledge of its limitations we carefully considered its architecture, experimented with the foundational cases, and added a new step, the Meta-Analyzer, to the program (Figure 4). Our goal was to determine which results from the retrieval phase provide the best indicators of when the program should or should not provide advice for a case.

Our hunch was that SIROCCO's deepest knowledge, i.e., the results it generates in the second stage, would be the most useful. However, it is clear that even the program's first stage contains some deeper knowledge, since the dot product algorithm accounts for abstract matches and matches to critical and questioned facts. Moreover, we wanted to test whether the program could make use of critical information across the top cases it retrieves, such as shared code and case citations.

To explore these issues we identified 30 foundational cases that SIROCCO processed correctly (i.e., cases for which the program made accurate code and case suggestions, according to the experiment described in [McLaren and Ashley, 2000]) and 28 foundational cases that SIROCCO processed incorrectly. We collected data about SIROCCO's processing of each of these target cases, including the stage 1 scores of the top 6 matching source cases, the amount of code and case citation overlap between the top 6 stage 1 source cases, and the top stage 2 scores. By analyzing and experimenting with a number of variants, we came up with the following three metarules, which are implementations of the general metarules discussed previously. These are the rules applied in the Meta-Analysis step depicted in Figure 4.

- **Metarule 1**: If the best Stage 1 CWDP <= 1.2, then SIROCCO may not have good enough source cases for this target case.
- **Metarule 2**: If at least 3 of the top 6 Stage 1 cases do not share a code citation, then SIROCCO may not have good enough source cases for this target case.
- **Metarule 3**: If the best match percentage of a source instantiation < 80%, then SIROCCO may not have good enough source cases for this target case.

These rules screened out a reasonably high percentage of the target cases for which there were no sufficiently good source cases, while at the same time not eliminating many of the targets for which there were good source cases. While comparing internally-computed values against thresholds is a simple way of applying and testing meta-knowledge, the important contribution of the above rules is the identification of the important aspects of the problem solver to be monitored and tested.

As an illustration of how the metarules can help, consider the effect of some variations of the example case in Figure 1. SIROCCO handles Case 90-5-1 well, and thus one would expect that none of the metarules would block the program from providing suggestions. In fact, none of the three metarules fires for the original version of Case 90-5-1.

Suppose, however, that we scramble Case 90-5-1 such that all of the same Facts are used but their time ordering is reversed. For instance, Fact 12 becomes a Pre-existing fact, Fact 11 occurs "After the conclusion of 12," Fact 10 occurs "After the conclusion of 11," and so on. This obviously produces a nonsensical, but superficially similar, version of the original case. Because of the identical Facts in the two cases, SIROCCO's Stage 1 process retrieves the same set of source cases and assigns the same CWDP scores for the scrambled case as for the original case. Thus, metarules 1 and 2 do not fire. However, because the temporal sequence has been altered in the new case, SIROCCO is not able to find a strong structural mapping to any source case instantiation. As a result, metarule 3 fires, correctly suggesting that SIROCCO should not attempt to make suggestions for this case.

Now consider a plausible variation of Case 90-5-1 in which the time sequence of the Facts is not perturbed, but new Facts are added and the Questioned Fact is changed. Engineer B is a fellow employee of Engineer A at Company X. Instead of the owner's attorney hiring Engineer A directly, the attorney hires Company X. As in the original scenario, Engineer A discovers problems with the apartment building but does not inform anyone, including his colleague Engineer B. Since Engineer B does not know about the defects, he obviously does not inform anyone of them either. However, Engineer B's action of "not informing" is questioned in the new version of the case. In this variation, the scenario is clearly plausible, but the ethical question raised (i.e., whether an engineer who doesn't know something should report what he doesn't know) is probably not what one would expect to see in the case base. Again, metarules 1 and 2 do not fire, because of the substantial amount of superficial Fact overlap between the original and variant case. However, changing the Questioned

Fact from Engineer A's action to Engineer B's action substantially alters SIROCCO's search process, and no source case instantiation provides a good match to the variant target case. Again, the deepest metarule, rule 3, correctly fires, providing evidence that SIROCCO should not suggest codes and source case citations for this target case.

These examples focus on metarule 3 and, in fact, this rule appears to have the greatest utility. However, the intuitions underlying metarules 1 and 2 are fairly clear. Metarule 1 can eliminate target cases that lack abstract, questioned fact, or critical fact matches that may still have enough structural match to qualify under metarule 3. In practice (and in the experiments reported below), however, we found this metarule makes a fairly small contribution. Metarule 2 takes into account two key aspects of SIROCCO's approach: using multiple cases in a solution and using common citations to underlying code provisions as evidence that the source cases deal with a relevant issue. The experiments showed that this rule has more utility than metarule 1.

Evaluation of SIROCCO's Ability to Know What It Knows

Two series of experiments were performed to test the capabilities of the metarules: one series that tested them against the foundational cases and the other tested them against the trial cases. Each series compared the results of tests of six combinations of the metarules with the experimental results reported in [McLaren and Ashley, 2000], and with a test in which SIROCCO rejected target cases at random. In each of the six metarule tests, a different combination of metarules was used to screen out targets for which there were no good source cases. For the foundational tests, each of the 184 cases was run as a target case with the remaining cases as source cases. For the trial tests, each of the 58 cases was run as a target against 241 source cases, the remaining 57 trial cases plus the 184 foundational cases. The six metarule tests were: three tests in which each of the rules was applied by itself (eliminating the target case if satisfied), a test in which rules 2 and 3 were applied (eliminating the target case if either rule was satisfied), a test in which all three rules were applied (eliminating the target case if any rule was satisfied), and a test in which all three rules were applied, but at least 2 of the 3 rules would have to be satisfied to eliminate the target case. The random test consisted of running all target cases through SIROCCO 10 times, with 1 of every 3 cases randomly eliminated during each of the 10 runs. The random result was calculated as an average of the 10 runs.

SIROCCO's performance for each target case was quantified by calculating overlap of the program's suggested codes and cases with the NSPE BER's code and case citations for the same case. We used the *F-measure*, an information retrieval metric that combines precision P and recall R: $F = (\beta^2 + 1)PR / (\beta^2 P + R)$ with $\beta = 1.0$ [Lewis et al., 1996]. Two F-Measure values were computed for each target case, one representing exact matches of codes and source cases between SIROCCO's solution and the Board's and one representing inexact matches. Inexact matches of codes were determined using the Code Hierarchy. Inexact matches of source cases were determined using a citation overlap metric, inversely related to the shortest citation path between two cases.

The results are shown in Figures 7 and 8. The tables show the mean exact and inexact F-Measure for each test, the number of target cases that remained after applying the metarules, the number of target cases that were eliminated by the metarules, and the mean exact and inexact F-Measures for the eliminated cases. (For experimental purposes, SIROCCO always provided suggestions – and we calculated F-Measures – even for the "eliminated" cases.) In Figure 7 note that there are only 179 foundational cases (target cases remaining plus cases eliminated); five cases were dropped from the original 184 because the board cited either no code or obsolete codes.

Metarules Applied	Mean Exact F-Measure (Remaining)	Mean Inexact F-Measure (Remaining)	Target Cases Remaining	Target Cases Eliminated	Mean Exact F-Meas. (Eliminated)	Mean Inexact F-Measure (Eliminated)
MR 2 & 3	0.368	0.552	67	112	0.246	0.426
MR 1, 2, & 3	0.368	0.552	67	112	0.246	0.426
MR 3	0.331	0.538	95	84	0.247	0.4
2 of 3 MR	0.316	0.501	149	30	0.168	0.336
MR 2	0.324	0.49	128	51	0.211	0.43
MR 1	0.304	0.491	167	12	0.125	0.226
Random	0.292	0.473	118.2	60.7	0.287	0.469
No metarules	0.292	0.473	179	0	NA	NA

Fig. 7. Results of Applying Metarules to the Foundational Cases

Metarules Applied	Mean Exact F-Measure (Remaining)	Mean Inexact F-Measure (Remaining)	Target Cases Remaining	Target Cases Eliminated	Mean Exact F-Measure (Eliminated)	Mean Inexact F-Measure (Eliminated)
MR 2 & 3	0.238	0.541	30	28	0.184	0.378
MR 1, 2, & 3	0.217	0.539	27	31	0.208	0.396
MR 3	0.233	0.501	36	22	0.178	0.4
2 of 3 MR	0.227	0.476	52	6	0.078	0.342
MR 2	0.221	0.496	50	8	0.155	0.255
MR 1	0.215	0.471	49	9	0.194	0.415
Random	0.218	0.466	36.9	21.1	0.200	0.451
No metarules	0.212	0.462	58	0	NA	NA

Fig. 8. Results of Applying Metarules to the Trial Cases

Discussion

It is clear from the tables in Figures 7 and 8 that the metarules had a positive effect. Every metarule test improved SIROCCO's F-Measures as compared to SIROCCO running without metarules and SIROCCO running with random elimination of cases.

The results also indicate that the combination of metarules 2 and 3 yield the best results. For the foundational cases, MR 2 & 3 led to approximately a 26% improvement in exact matching and a 16% improvement in inexact matching over SIROCCO running with no metarules. For the trial cases, the improvement was 12%

and 17%. Since the test of the trial cases had a bigger case base, one would expect the coverage to be greater and thus the elimination of fewer target cases. In fact, notice that while MR 2 & 3 eliminated approximately 2/3 of the foundational cases, only 1/2 of the targets were eliminated in the trial cases version of this test.

Perhaps not surprisingly, adding metarule 1 to metarules 2 and 3 produces little effect (see the first two rows of the tables in both Figures 7 and 8). The latter two rules take into account a deeper level of knowledge, so adding rule 1 to the mix does not help SIROCCO better identify cases it cannot properly handle. Metarule 1 used alone, however, does lead to a small improvement over the use of no metarules.

The contrasting F-Measure results between the remaining and eliminated cases for every test indicate that SIROCCO is making more good choices than bad in deciding whether to eliminate cases. In particular, for every test the mean F-Measures of remaining cases are higher than the corresponding F-Measures of the eliminated cases. On the other hand, the numbers indicate a trade-off. Since the F-Measures of the remaining cases are not dramatically higher than the corresponding F-Measures of the eliminated cases, it is clear that SIROCCO sometimes makes the mistake of eliminating a target case for which it could have provided good suggestions.

Another trade-off is apparent. The versions of SIROCCO that achieve higher F-Measures (e.g., MR 2 & 3, MR 1, 2, & 3, MR in both tables) eliminate the most cases. Arguably, this is a deleterious side effect. If the program can provide suggestions for only 47% of the problems it is provided, as is the case with MR 1, 2, & 3 in the trial test, users may be disinclined to use the program. At this time, however, we do not know that this figure is unreasonable given our case base, whose coverage may well be less than we imagined. Since SIROCCO's Mean F-Measures on the eliminated cases for this test are not dramatically below the remaining cases, it appears that SIROCCO could have correctly processed at least some of the eliminated targets. Thus, in some instances, metarule 3 by itself or the "2 of 3" metarules approach might be preferred, since both eliminate far fewer cases yet still achieve better scores than SIROCCO without metarules. Yet these approaches also appear to eliminate some good targets.

Conclusion

This work addresses the question of how a CBR system can know the limitations of its expertise. Having found the known source cases most relevant to a target problem, how can a system assess whether those cases are similar enough to the target to warrant venturing advice? We have devised, implemented and evaluated three metarules to help the SIROCCO program make this assessment. The metarules leverage strategic knowledge of how the retrieval algorithm operates and of what successful retrievals look like. Our evaluation confirms that the rules make a positive contribution to SIROCCO's retrieval ability, subject to some tradeoffs.

Our approach addresses some of the same concerns as the use of competent case bases [Smyth and Keane, 1995; Smyth and McKenna, 1999] but is more appropriate for less well-structured domains like ethics, which require the kind of case representation and retrieval mechanisms in SIROCCO. The retrieval algorithm is multi-staged and based on mapping complex data structures, rather than nearest neighbor matching and attribute-value pairs. The cases provide explanations that cite other cases and general rules. Also, SIROCCO doesn't rely on a single best match. Instead, it uses a set of similar cases to help it produce a solution. It benefits from having redundant (i.e., similar) cases in its case base in a domain in which it is not easy to define what a "correct" solution is.

References

[Allen 1983] James F. Allen. Maintaining Knowledge about Temporal Intervals. In the *Communications of the ACM* 26(11), 832-843.

[Ashley 1990] K. D. Ashley. *Modeling Legal Argument: Reasoning with Cases and Hypotheticals*. Cambridge: MIT Press.

[Branting 1991] L. K. Branting. Building Explanations from Rules and Structured Cases. *Int'l Journal of Man-Machine Studies*, 34 (6): 797-837.

[Davis 1982] R. Davis. Expert Systems: Where Are We? And Where Do We Go From Here? *AI Magazine* 3, no. 2:3-22.

[Davis and Buchanan 1985] R. Davis and B. Buchanan. "Meta-Level Knowledge," chapter 28 in B. Buchanan and E. Shortliffe (ed.)*Rule-Based Expert Systems*, pp. 507-530. Addison-Wesley: Reading, MA.

[Forbus *et al.* 1994] K. D. Forbus, D. Gentner, and K. Law. MAC/FAC: A Model of Similarity-based Retrieval. *Cognitive Science* 19, 141-205, Norwood, NJ: Ablex Publ.

[Harris *et al.* 1999] C. E. Harris, M. S. Pritchard, and M. J. Rabins. *Engineering Ethics: Concepts and Cases*. Belmont, CA: Wadsworth, 2nd edition.

[Koomen 1989] J. A. G. M. Koomen. *The TIMELOGIC Temporal Reasoning System*. Tech. Report 231, Computer Science Dept., University of Rochester, NY.

[Lenat *et al.* 1983] D. Lenat, R. Davis, J. Doyle, M. Genesereth, I. Goldstein, and H. Schrobe. "Reasoning about Reasoning," chapter 7 in F. Hayes-Roth, *et al.* ed. *Building Expert Systems*, pp. 219-239. Addison-Wesley: Reading, MA.

[Lewis *et al.* 1996] D. D. Lewis, R. E. Schapire, J. P. Callan, and R. Papka. Training Algorithms for Linear Text Classifiers. In: *Proceedings of the 19th International ACM-SIGIR Conf. on Res. and Dev. in Information Retrieval*. Zurich.

[McLaren 1999] B. M. McLaren. *Assessing the Relevance of Cases and Principles Using Operationalization Techniques*. Ph.D. Dissertation, University of Pittsburgh, PA.

[McLaren and Ashley 1999] B. M. McLaren and K. D. Ashley. Case Representation, Acquisition, and Retrieval in SIROCCO. In: *Proc. of the 3rd International Conference on Case-Based Reasoning*, 248-262.

[McLaren and Ashley 2000] B. M. McLaren and K. D. Ashley. Assessing Relevance With Extensionally Defined Principles and Cases. In: *Proc. of the 17th National Conference on Artificial Intelligence*, 316-322.

[Rissland *et al.* 1996] E. L. Rissland, D. B. Skalak, and M. T. Friedman. BankXX: Supporting Legal Arguments through Heuristic Retrieval. *AI and Law* Volume 4. Kluwer.

[Smyth and Keane 1995] B. Smyth and M. T. Keane. Remembering to Forget: A Competence Preserving Deletion Policy for Case-Based Reasoning Systems. In: *Proc. of the 14th International Conference on Artificial Intelligence*, 377-382.

[Smyth and McKenna 1999] B. Smyth and E. McKenna. Building Compact Competent Case-Bases. In: *Proc. of the 3rd International Conference on Case-Based Reasoning*, 329-342.

Precision and Recall in Interactive Case-Based Reasoning

David McSherry

School of Information and Software Engineering, University
of Ulster, Coleraine BT52 1SA, Northern Ireland
dmg.mcsherry@ulst.ac.uk

Abstract. Often in interactive case-based reasoning (CBR), the case library is *irreducible* in the sense that the deletion of a single case means that a unique product or fault is no longer represented in the case library. We present empirical measures of precision and recall for irreducible case libraries, identify sources of imperfect precision and recall, and establish an upper bound for the level of precision that can be achieved with any retrieval strategy. Finally, we present a retrieval strategy for irreducible case libraries that gives better precision and recall than inductive retrieval or nearest-neighbour retrieval based on the number of matching features in a target case.

1 Introduction

While many CBR systems are appropriately evaluated in terms of classification accuracy, efficiency and precision of retrieval are often more relevant in *interactive* CBR applications such as fault diagnosis, help-desk support, and on-line decision guides [1,3,5,8]. Typically in these applications, each of the faults to be identified, or products to be selected, is represented by a single case in the case library. Such case libraries are *irreducible* in the sense that the deletion of a single case means that a unique product or fault is no longer represented in the case library. Our previous work focused on efficiency of retrieval in irreducible case libraries [5]. We showed that information gain [7] is often more effective than other splitting criteria in reducing the *average path length* of the decision tree, or equivalently the average number of questions required to identify a fault, or product that meets the requirements of the user.

In this paper, we focus on precision and *recall* in interactive case-based reasoning. While precision has received more attention as a measure of retrieval performance in CBR research, we argue that recall is also an important measure and should not be neglected. In Section 2, we define empirical measures of precision and recall for irreducible case libraries. In Section 3, we identify common sources of imperfect precision and recall, and establish an upper bound for the level of precision that can be achieved with any retrieval strategy. In Section 4, we present a retrieval strategy for irreducible case libraries that gives better precision and recall than inductive retrieval or nearest-neighbour (NN) retrieval based on the number of matching features in a target case.

D.W. Aha and I. Watson (Eds.): ICCBR 2001, LNAI 2080, pp. 392-406, 2001.

In Section 5, we examine the effects of missing values on retrieval performance in irreducible case libraries. Our conclusions are presented in Section 6.

2 Measures of Precision and Recall

When a target case (or problem) is presented to a CBR system for solution, the cases retrieved depend on the attribute values in the target case, the available cases, and the retrieval strategy used by the system. Common retrieval strategies include inductive retrieval and NN retrieval, either of which can be applied to irreducible case libraries as we show in Section 3. However, as each case in an irreducible case library has a unique solution, the k-NN technique [6] of selecting a majority class from the k most similar cases is inapplicable in an irreducible case library. On the other hand, two or more library cases may be maximally similar to a target case, and therefore equally eligible for retrieval. We assume that when NN is applied to an irreducible case library, the retrieved cases are those that are maximally similar to the target case according to the chosen similarity measure. In inductive retrieval, a decision tree induced from stored cases is used to guide the retrieval process [10]. The cases retrieved for a given target case are those at the leaf node of the decision tree, if any, reached by following the path determined by the attribute values in the target case. As in NN retrieval, more than one case may be retrieved.

Definition 1. *Given a case library L, target case C_t, and retrieval strategy S, we denote by rCases(C_t, S, L) the set of cases that are retrieved when S is applied to L with C_t as the target case.*

In the context of information retrieval, precision is defined as the percentage of retrieved documents that are relevant, while recall is the percentage of relevant documents that are retrieved [9]. While precision and recall are also useful measures of retrieval performance in CBR, an important difference is that the aim in CBR is usually to retrieve a single case that solves a target problem rather than a set of relevant documents as in information retrieval. Moreover, it is often true that at most one case in an irreducible case library can provide the correct solution for a target case. An example of this is a case library for fault diagnosis in which every case has a unique solution. Similarly in an identification task, an object is either correctly identified or it is not.

Our approach to the evaluation of retrieval performance in irreducible case libraries is based on the assumption that the case library contains a single case that meets the requirements of the user, or explains the reported symptoms in fault diagnosis, better than any other case. We also assume that if more than one case is retrieved, then one of the retrieved cases is selected at random and its solution is applied to the target problem. Similar assumptions are implicit in Aha et al.'s [1] *leave-one-in* approach to the evaluation of retrieval performance in conversational case libraries. In their approach, each available case is used as a test case but without removing it from the case library during testing. Precision is measured in terms of the number of times the solution for the most similar case matches the solution for the test case.

Our empirical measures of precision and recall are based on a modified version of leave-one-in in which any missing values in a test case are "filled in" before the case is presented to the CBR system as a target case. Of course, this is possible only if the values that were missing are known to the investigator. This is ensured by the experimental techniques we describe in Section 5. Given a test case C, we denote by C^* the intact version of C that is presented as a target case to the CBR system. Below we define the individual contributions of a single test case to precision and recall.

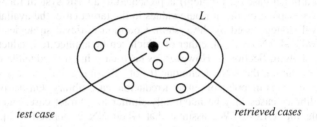

Fig. 1. Retrieval of a test case from an irreducible case library

Definition 2. *Given a test case $C \in L$ and retrieval strategy S, we define $r(C, S, L) = 1$ if $C \in rCases(C^*, S, L)$; otherwise we define $r(C, S, L) = 0$.*

Definition 3. *Given a test case $C \in L$ and retrieval strategy S, we define $p(C, S, L)$*

$$= \frac{1}{\left| rCases(C^*, S, L) \right|} \quad \text{if } C \in rCases(C^*, S, L); \text{ otherwise, we define } p(C, S, L) = 0.$$

An example of the retrieval of a test case C from an irreducible case library L is illustrated in Fig. 1. As C has been retrieved, $r(C, S, L) = 1$, where S is the (unspecified) retrieval strategy. As two "unwanted" cases have also been retrieved, $p(C, S, L) = \frac{1}{3}$. If the retrieved cases did not include C, then both $r(C, S, L)$ and $p(C, S, L)$ would be 0. We now define overall measures of precision and recall for a given retrieval strategy when applied to an irreducible case library.

Definition 4. *For any irreducible case library L and retrieval strategy S, we define*

$$recall(S, L) = \frac{\sum_{C \in L} r(C, S, L)}{|L|} \times 100$$

$$precision(S, L) = \frac{\sum_{C \in L} p(C, S, L)}{|L|} \times 100$$

It is worth noting that our measure of recall is equivalent to the percentage of queries in which the test case is among the retrieved cases. Our measure of precision is the probability that a target case is correctly solved in leave-one-in if, as we assume, one of the retrieved cases is selected at random and its solution is applied to the target case. As the following theorem shows, precision can never exceed recall in an irreducible case library, and so perfect precision implies perfect recall.

Theorem 1. *For any irreducible case library L and retrieval strategy S, precision(S, L) ≤ recall(S, L).*

Proof. It can be seen that $p(C, S, L) \leq r(C, S, L)$ for any test case $C \in L$ such that $C \in rCases(C^*, S, L)$. On the other hand, if $C \notin rCases(C^*, S, L)$ then $p(C, S, L) = r(C, S, L) = 0$. It follows that $precision(S, L) \leq recall(S, L)$ as required.

While precision may be the more important of the two measures, retrieval performance cannot be assessed adequately in terms of precision alone. For example, 50% precision can be achieved by retrieving only the test case in one half of all queries and failing to retrieve the test case in the other half. The same level of precision can be achieved by retrieving two cases that include the test case in every query. In the first of these scenarios, recall is only 50%. In the second, it is 100%. It is also worth noting that perfect recall can always be achieved, at the expense of minimal precision, by retrieving all cases in the case library. Both measures must therefore be considered in the assessment of retrieval performance.

3 Sources of Imperfect Precision and Recall

When applied to an irreducible case library, a retrieval strategy gives perfect precision and recall if the test case is always retrieved and no unwanted case is ever retrieved. However, perfect precision and recall are unlikely to be possible in other than ideal conditions. In this section we examine common sources of imperfect precision and recall in interactive CBR.

3.1 Inseparability

A common cause of imperfect precision is that the case attributes may not be adequate to distinguish a test case from other cases. This problem, which we refer to as *inseparability*, is common in recommender systems [3,5]. A similar problem that arises in decision-tree learning is the inadequacy of attributes to distinguish between examples in a given data set [7]. We say that two cases are *inseparable* if they have the same known value, or both have missing values, for every case attribute. A point we would like to emphasize is that irreducibility does not imply the absence of inseparability. For example, it is not unusual in product recommendation for two distinct products to have the same values for all attributes including price range.

Definition 5. *Given an irreducible case library L, we define* $iCases(C, L) = \{C^o \in L : C$ *and* C^o *are inseparable*\}.

A property shared by all the retrieval strategies examined in this paper is that if one of two inseparable cases is retrieved, then the other is also retrieved. We will say that a retrieval strategy is *consistent* if it has this property. It can be seen that $iCases(C, L) \subseteq rCases(C^*, S, L)$ for any irreducible case library L, consistent retrieval strategy S, and test case $C \in L$ such that $C \in rCases(C^*, S, L)$. Below we describe an approach to quantifying the effects of inseparability on precision. First we introduce the complementary notion of *separability*.

Definition 6. *Given an irreducible case library L, we define*

$$separability \ (L) = \frac{\displaystyle\sum_{C \in L} \frac{1}{|iCases(C, L)|}}{|L|} \times 100$$

Separability is a measurable characteristic of a case library that is independent of the retrieval strategy used by the CBR system. In Section 2, we showed that precision can never exceed recall in an irreducible case library. As the following theorem shows, the separability of an irreducible case library also provides an upper bound for the level of precision that can be achieved with any consistent retrieval strategy.

Theorem 2. *For any irreducible case library L and consistent retrieval strategy S, precision(S, L) ≤ separability(L).*

Proof. It can be seen that $p(C, S, L) \le \dfrac{1}{|iCases(C, L)|}$ for any test case $C \in L$ such that $C \in rCases(C^*, S, L)$. The same is clearly true for any test case that is not retrieved by S, and so $precision(S, L) \le separability(L)$ as required.

3.2 Missing Values

Missing values in library cases are common in interactive CBR and can adversely affect both precision and recall. In product recommendation, the descriptions of available products are often incomplete [3]. In fault diagnosis, it is seldom necessary for all possible tests to be performed. Even if the result of an omitted test can be inferred from other available data, it is unlikely to be recorded in the case description. For example, if the problem reported to a help-desk operator is that there are strange characters on a computer screen, the operator has no need to ask if the power light is on and is unlikely to record this detail in the case description.

Precision and recall may also be affected by *incomplete data* in the target problem. However, the causes of incomplete data and missing values are often different. In fault diagnosis, there are often questions that the user cannot answer, for example because the answer requires an expensive test that the user is reluctant to perform [4]. In product recommendation, the user may be indifferent to the values of certain attributes.

In our view, missing values in library cases and incomplete data are different problems and require different solutions. One solution to the problem of incomplete data in lazy approaches to inductive retrieval [3, 4] is to select the next most useful attribute when the user is unable (or declines) to answer the question considered most useful by the system. However, the effects of incomplete data on retrieval performance is an important issue to be addressed by further research. In this paper, we assume that there are no missing values in the target case.

Table 1. Example case library with 25% missing values

	mpg	cyl	disp	hp	wt	acc	yr	or
toyota carina	20-24	4	< 100	50-99	2000-2499	15-19	73	3
audi 100ls	20-24	4	100-149	50-99	2500-2999	15-19	75	2
amc concord dl 6	20-24	6	200-249	50-99	?	15-19	?	?
oldsmobile omega	?	8	350-399	150-199	3500-3599	10-14	73	1
amc matador	15-19	?	250-299	100-149	?	15-19	75	?
datsun 710	?	?	100-149	50-99	2500-2999	15-19	75	3
ford mustang gl	25-29	4	?	50-99	?	?	?	?
pontiac j2000 se hatchback	30-34	4	100-149	50-99	2500-2999	15-19	?	?
buick century luxus (sw)	10-14	?	350-399	150-199	4500-4999	15-19	?	1
mazda rx2 coupe	15-19	3	?	50-99	2000-2499	10-14	?	3

Table 2. Example target case

datsun 710*	20-24	4	100-149	50-99	2500-2999	15-19	75	3

An irreducible case library containing 10 cases from the AutoMPG data set [2] is shown in Table 1. Many of the attributes in the data set resemble those that one might expect to see in a CBR system for recommending previously-owned automobiles. Three of the attributes in the data set (*cylinders, year* and *origin*) have discrete values. Continuous attributes in the data set (*mpg, displacement, horsepower, weight* and *acceleration*) were discretized by dividing their ranges into intervals that seemed most natural for the expression of user preferences. Twenty attribute values in the example case library are missing. The missing values were introduced by randomly selecting 25% of the 80 attribute values in the ten cases, none of which has missing values in the original data set. The example target case shown in Table 2 is the intact case corresponding to the test case *datsun 710*.

Unlike the data set from which it originates, the example case library is perfectly separable; that is, no two cases have the same values for all attributes. As we shall see in Section 4, however, different retrieval strategies produce quite different results when applied to the example case library.

3.3 Heterogeneity

A problem related to missing values is *heterogeneity* in the case library arising from the use of different features to describe cases [1,8,10]. In fault diagnosis, for example, certain test results may not be relevant for every case. Heterogeneity can sometimes be eliminated by extending the case representation to include all attributes for every case, and inserting missing values for those attributes in a case that were not recorded in the original case library [11]. The result is a homogeneous case structure albeit with a high frequency of missing values in the case library. However, a problem that remains to be addressed is that certain attributes may not be *meaningful* for every case. A possible solution that we propose to investigate in future research involves a case representation that distinguishes between attributes whose values are missing and those that are *inapplicable* for a given case. In this paper, we assume a homogeneous case structure.

3.4 Noise

Retrieval performance in interactive CBR is likely to be adversely affected if *noise* is present in the case library. In large-scale applications, it can be very difficult to ensure the absence of errors in library cases. Retrieval failure may also be caused by errors in the problem data provided by the user. In its present form, however, the leave-one-in technique on which our approach to the evaluation of retrieval performance is based implicitly assumes the absence of noise. The use of library cases as test cases not only eliminates the potential for user error but also ensures that any errors that may be present in library cases cannot affect the apparent retrieval performance. The effects of noise on retrieval performance is therefore an important issue to be addressed by further research [1].

4 Retrieval Strategies for Irreducible Case Libraries

In this section, we examine possible retrieval strategies for irreducible case libraries including inductive retrieval and NN retrieval based on three similarity measures. We show that NN retrieval based on one of these measures is equivalent to inductive retrieval in some aspects of its retrieval behaviour. Finally, we present a retrieval strategy for irreducible case libraries that gives better precision and recall than inductive retrieval or NN retrieval based on the number of matching features in a target case. The similarity measures on which we focus do not rely on semantic assessments of similarity or importance weights. One reason for this is to place NN retrieval on an equal footing with inductive retrieval, in which a minimum of domain knowledge is required. Exclusion of more sophisticated similarity measures from the analysis also has the advantage of ensuring that our theoretical results are domain independent.

4.1 NN Retrieval

In NN retrieval, we assume that the retrieved cases are those that are maximally similar to the target case according to a given similarity measure. That is, for any case library L, similarity measure Sim, and target case L

$$rCases(C_t, NN, L) = \{C \in L : \text{for all } C^o \in L - \{C\}, Sim(C_t, C) \geq Sim(C_t, C^o)\}$$

Three similarity measures are defined below for any cases C_1 and C_2.

$Sim_1(C_1, C_2) = K^+$, where K^+ is the number of attributes for which C_1 and C_2 have the same known value

$Sim_2(C_1, C_2) = K^+ - K^-$ where K^- is the number of attributes for which C_1 and C_2 have different known values

$$Sim_3(C_1, C_2) = \frac{K^+ - K^-}{K^+ + K^-}$$

Where necessary to clarify which cases are being compared, we will write $K^+(C_1, C_2)$ and $K^-(C_1, C_2)$ rather than simply K^+ and K^-.

Sim_1 is perhaps the simplest possible measure of similarity between two cases. Sim_3 is the similarity measure used by Aha et al. [1] to evaluate retrieval performance in conversational case libraries. In this measure, a point is awarded for each attribute for which C_1 and C_2 have the same known (i.e. not missing) value and a point is deducted for each attribute for which C_1 and C_2 have different known values. The resulting score is normalized by the number of attributes that have known values in both cases. Sim_2 is a modified version of Sim_3 in which the normalization step is omitted.

Table 3. Similarity of library cases to the target case *datsun 710**

	K^+	K^-	Sim_1	Sim_2	Sim_3
toyota carina	5	3	5	2	0.25
audi 100ls	7	1	7	6	0.75
amc concord dl 6	3	2	3	1	0.2
oldsmobile omega	0	7	0	-7	-1
amc matador	2	3	2	-1	-0.2
datsun 710	6	0	6	6	1
ford mustang gl	2	1	2	1	0.33
pontiac j2000 se hatchback	5	1	5	4	0.67
buick century luxus (sw)	1	5	1	-4	-0.67
mazda rx2 coupe	2	4	2	-2	-0.33

We will refer to NN retrieval with Sim_1, Sim_2 and Sim_3 as the similarity measure as NN_1, NN_2 and NN_3 respectively. These retrieval strategies, which we evaluate more rigorously in Section 5, give different results when applied to the example case library in Table 1. For example, Table 3 shows the similarity scores of the library cases with *datsun 710** (the intact version of the test case *datsun 710*) as the target case. According to Sim_1, *audi 100ls* is more similar to the target case than *datsun 710*, so NN_1 fails to retrieve the test case. According to Sim_2, *audi 100ls* and *datsun 710* are equally (and maximally) similar to the target case, so NN_2 retrieves the test case and one unwanted case. According to Sim_3, however, the test case is more similar to the target case than any other case; so only the test case is retrieved by NN_3.

4.2 Inductive Retrieval

We refer to a decision tree used to guide retrieval in an irreducible case library as an *identification* tree [5]. In product recommendation, for example, identification trees are often used to identify a product that meets the requirements of the user by asking as few questions as possible [3,5]. Our algorithm for building identification trees from irreducible case libraries, called *Identify*, works in a similar way to algorithms for top-down induction of decision trees and can be used with any splitting criterion. It recursively partitions the case library until a subset is reached that contains only a single case, or none of the remaining attributes can distinguish between the cases surviving in the current subset.

Identify differs from most decision-tree algorithms in the way it handles missing values in library cases. To illustrate the approach, let X be the current subset of the case library, and let A be the attribute selected to partition X. If no case in X has a missing value for A, then a subset is created for each value of A that occurs in X and the assignment of cases to these subsets proceeds in the usual way. On the other hand, if any case $C \in X$ has a missing value for A, then a subset of X is created for *every* value of A and C is assigned to all these subsets along with any other cases that have missing values for A. Cases that have known values for A are assigned to the subsets of X corresponding to their known values in the usual way.

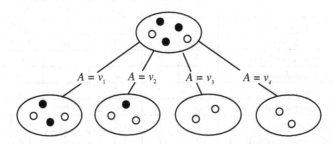

Fig. 2. Partitioning a subset of an irreducible data set

In the example shown in Fig. 2, an attribute A with four possible values is used to partition the current subset X of an irreducible case library. Two of the 5 cases in X, shown as unfilled circles, have missing values for A. As this example illustrates, an overhead associated with missing values is that the tree tends to grow very rapidly in *breadth* as the data set is partitioned. In the absence of missing values, the number of *represented* values of an attribute tends to reduce as a case library is partitioned [5], a phenomenon that helps to contain the otherwise exponential rate of increase in breadth of the tree. Although only two values of A are represented in X, the presence of two cases (in fact one would be enough) with missing values for A means that a subset must be constructed for every value of A.

However, a partial solution to this problem follows from the fact that our tree-building procedure results in the creation of a *duplicate* sub-tree for each value, if more than one, of the selected attribute that is represented only by a missing value in the current subset. We can avoid this duplication by grouping the affected values together as a single relabelled value. In Fig. 2, for example, the two branches labelled $A = v_3$ and $A = v_4$ can be replaced by a single branch labelled $A = other$. This is the strategy used in Identify.

We will refer to the strategy of inductive retrieval based on an identification tree constructed by Identify as IR.

Theorem 3. *For any irreducible case library L and test case $C \in L$, rCases(C^*, IR, L) = \{$C^\circ \in L : K(C^*, C^\circ) = 0$\}.*

Proof If $C^\circ \in L$ and $K(C^*, C^\circ) = 0$, then C° must be one of the cases stored at the leaf node of the identification tree reached by following the path determined by the attribute values in C^*; that is, $C^\circ \in rCases(C^*, IR, L)$. On the other hand, if $K(C^*, C^\circ) \neq 0$, then the existence of an attribute for which C^* and C° have different known values ensures that C° cannot be one of the cases stored at the leaf node; that is $C^\circ \notin rCases(C^*, IR, L)$.

Since $K(C^*, C) = 0$ for any test case $C \in L$, it follows from the above theorem that IR always gives perfect recall as measured by the leave-one-in technique. Another important corollary of the theorem is that precision and recall in IR are independent of the splitting criterion used to construct the identification tree. On the other hand, the efficiency of retrieval very much depends on the splitting criterion, and the effects of missing values on the performance of splitting criteria for irreducible data sets is an important issue to be addressed by further research [5]. Though we are mainly concerned here with precision and recall, we briefly mention a splitting criterion that is often very effective in reducing the average path length of identification trees for irreducible case libraries in which missing values are numerous. Used by Aha et al. [1] to build decision trees from conversational case libraries, it gives priority to the attribute that has fewest missing values. For the example case library in Table 1, the most useful attribute is *horsepower*, as it has no missing values. Fig. 3 shows the identification tree constructed by Identify from the example case library in Table 1 with fewest missing values as the splitting criterion.

The numbers at the leaf nodes may be ignored for the purposes of the present discussion. One point to note is that although there are more leaf nodes than there are cases in the case library, not all are reachable with library cases as test cases. For example, *datsun 710* appears at seven leaf nodes, two of which it shares with other cases. However, when *datsun 710** (the intact version of *datsun 710* shown in Table 2) is presented as a target case, the path determined by its attribute values leads to the

horsepower = 100 to 149 : *amc matador* (1)
horsepower = 150 to 199
  weight = 3500 to 3999 : *oldsmobile omega* (2)
  weight = 4500 to 4999 : *buick century luxus (sw)* (2)
horsepower = 50 to 99
  mpg = 15 to 19
    weight = 2000 to 2499 : *mazda rx2 coupe* (3)
    weight = 2500 to 2999 : *datsun 710* (2)
  mpg = 20 to 24
    displacement = 100 to 149
      origin = 2 : *audi 100ls* (4)
      origin = 3 : *datsun 710* (3)
    displacement = 200 to 249 : *amc concord dl 6* (3)
    displacement = less than 100 : *toyota carina* (3)
  mpg = 25 to 29
    cylinders = 4
      displacement = 100 to 149
        weight = 2500 to 2999
          acceleration = 15 to 19
            year = 75
              origin = 3 : *ford mustang gl* (3) *datsun 710* (6)
              origin = other : *ford mustang gl* (3)
            year = other : *ford mustang gl* (3)
          acceleration = other : *ford mustang gl* (3)
        weight = other : *ford mustang gl* (3)
      displacement = other : *ford mustang gl* (3)
    cylinders = other : *datsun 710* (1)
  mpg = 30 to 34
    cylinders = 4
      year = 75
        origin = 3 : *datsun 710* (3) *pontiac j2000 se hatchback* (3)
        origin = other : *pontiac j2000 se hatchback* (3)
      year = other : *pontiac j2000 se hatchback* (3)
    cylinders = other : *datsun 710* (1)
  mpg = other : *datsun 710* (1)

Fig. 3. Identification tree for the example case library

leaf node shown in bold, at which the test case *datsun 710* is the only case. In fact, the same is true for all test cases in the leave-one-in technique, so IR gives perfect precision for the example case library. Thus perfect precision may be possible in IR even when missing values are present in considerable numbers.

4.3 Retrieval Characteristics of NN$_3$

As the following theorem shows, NN$_3$ is equivalent to IR in terms of precision and recall when applied to an irreducible case library.

Theorem 4. *For any irreducible case library L and test case C $\in$ L, rCases(C*, NN$_3$, L) = rCases(C*, IR, L).*

Proof. It suffices by Theorem 3 to show that for any test case $C \in L$, $rCases(C^*,$ NN$_3$, $L) = \{C^\circ \in L : K(C^*, C^\circ) = 0\}$. If $C^\circ \in L$ and $K(C^*, C^\circ) = 0$, then $Sim_3(C^*, C^\circ) = \dfrac{K^+ - K^-}{K^+ + K^-} = 1$. As this is the maximum possible value of Sim_3, it follows that $C^\circ \in rCases(C^*, NN_3, L)$. On the other hand, if $K(C^*, C^\circ) \neq 0$, then $Sim_3(C^*, C^\circ) < 1$. As $Sim_3(C^*, C) = 1$, it follows that $C^\circ \notin rCases(C^*, NN_3, L)$.

Of course, we do not suggest that NN$_3$ and IR are equivalent. NN$_3$ assigns a similarity score to every library case, whereas no similarity scores are assigned in IR. In conversational CBR, the similarity scores produced by NN$_3$ are used to rank cases in order of non-increasing similarity to the target case [1]. However, if all cases except those that are maximally similar to the target case are discarded, as we assume in this paper, then NN$_3$ is equivalent to IR in its retrieval behaviour.

4.4 Inductive Retrieval with Ranking

We now present a retrieval strategy for irreducible case libraries called *inductive retrieval with ranking* (IRR). In this strategy, the cases retrieved for a given target case are those cases retrieved by IR that are maximally similar to the target case according to Sim_1. That is, for any case library L and target case C_t

$rCases(C_t, IRR, L) = \{C \in L : K(C_t, C) = 0$ and for all $C^\circ \in L - \{C\}$, $Sim_1(C_t, C) \geq Sim_1(C_t, C^\circ)\}$

As in IR, retrieval is guided in IRR by an identification tree. The retrieved cases in IRR are *selected* from the cases at the leaf node, if any, reached by following the path determined by the attribute values in the target case. In practice, only the attributes on the path to the leaf node need contribute to the ranking of cases retrieved by IR in order of non-increasing similarity to the target case. For any other attributes, the cases at the leaf node must all have the same values. Another point to note is that the similarity scores can be computed at the time when the identification tree is constructed. For any case at a leaf node reached by a path determined by the attribute values in a given target case, the required Sim_1 score is simply the number of attributes on the path for which the leaf-node case has a known value. The Sim_1 scores that determine which cases, if any, are retrieved for a given target case are shown at the leaf nodes of the example identification tree in Fig. 3. For example, if the path determined by the attribute values in a given target case leads to the leaf node at which *ford mustang gl* (3) and *datsun 710* (6) are stored, then the only case retrieved by IRR would be *datsun 710*.

In the following theorems we show that when they differ in retrieval performance, IRR gives better precision and recall than NN_2, and NN_2 gives better precision and recall than NN_1.

Theorem 5. *For any irreducible case library L, recall(NN_1, L) $\leq$ recall(NN_2, L) $\leq$ recall(IRR, L).*

Proof. If $C \in L$ is a test case such that $C \notin rCases(C^*, IRR, L)$, there must be another case $C^\circ \in L$ such that $K^-(C^*, C^\circ) = 0$ and $Sim_1(C^*, C^\circ) > Sim_1(C^*, C)$. That is, $K^+(C^*, C^\circ) > K^+(C^*, C)$. Thus $Sim_2(C^*, C^\circ) = K^+(C^*, C^\circ) - K^-(C^*, C^\circ) = K^+(C^*, C^\circ) > K^+(C^*, C) = K^+(C^*, C) - K^-(C^*, C) = Sim_2(C^*, C)$. So $C \notin rCases(C^*, NN_2, L)$. Thus any test case that is retrieved by NN_2 must also be retrieved by IRR and so $recall(NN_2, L) \leq recall(IRR, L)$ as required. The proof that $recall(NN_1, L) \leq recall(NN_2, L)$ follows similar lines.

Theorem 6. *For any irreducible case library L, precision(NN_1, L) $\leq$ precision(NN_2, L) $\leq$ precision(IRR, L).*

Proof. To show that $precision(NN_2, L) \leq precision(IRR, L)$ it suffices to show that $p(C, NN_2, L) \leq p(C, IRR, L)$ for any test case $C \in L$. If a test case C is not retrieved by IRR then it is not retrieved by NN_2, and so $p(C, NN_2, L) = p(C, IRR, L) = 0$. On the other hand, if C is retrieved by IRR but not by NN_2, then $p(C, NN_2, L) < p(C, IRR, L)$. Now let $C \in L$ be a test case that is retrieved by both IRR and NN_2, and let $C^\circ \in L$ be such that $C^\circ \notin rCases(C^*, NN_2, L)$. As C is retrieved by NN_2 and C° is not, $K^+(C^*, C^\circ) - K^-(C^*, C^\circ) < K^+(C^*, C) - K^-(C^*, C)$. If $K^-(C^*, C^\circ) \neq 0$ then $C^\circ \notin rCases(C^*, IRR, L)$. On the other hand, if $K^-(C^*, C^\circ) = 0$, then $Sim_1(C^*, C^\circ) = K^+(C^*, C^\circ) < K^+(C^*, C) - K^-(C^*, C) = K^+(C^*, C) = Sim_1(C^*, C)$. Again it follows that $C^\circ \notin rCases(C^*, IRR, L)$. So $p(C, NN_2, L) \leq p(C, IRR, L)$ as required. The proof that $precision(NN_1, L) \leq precision(NN_2, L)$ follows similar lines.

5 Comparison of Retrieval Strategies

We now present the results of experiments in which we examine the effects of missing values on precision and recall in four retrieval strategies for irreducible case libraries. The retrieval strategies to be evaluated are NN_1, NN_2, IR and IRR. As NN_3 is equivalent to IR in terms of precision and recall by Theorem 4, it need not be included in the evaluation. The irreducible case libraries used in our experiments were generated from the AutoMPG data set [2]. First we removed the 6 examples in the data set that already have missing values to provide a case library containing 392 cases with no missing values. Separability of this case library is 84%. As shown in Section 3, this means that the precision achieved with any consistent retrieval strategy cannot exceed 84%.

We then constructed eight case libraries with frequencies of missing values ranging from 10 to 80 per cent. Each case library was independently constructed by adding missing values at random to the first case library subject to the constraint that at least one value remained intact in each case.

5.1 How Do Missing Values Affect Recall?

By Theorem 3, IR always gives perfect recall regardless of missing values. Fig. 4 compares the performance of NN_1, NN_2, and IRR in terms of recall on case libraries with frequencies of missing values ranging from 0 to 80 per cent. The results shown for the case libraries with missing values are averages over 10 repeated trials. As predicted by our theoretical results, recall is always lower in NN_2 than in IRR (when not the same) and higher than in NN_1 (when not the same). IRR shows slightly greater tolerance to missing values than NN_2, particularly in the missing value range from 20% to 60%. Both strategies give considerably better recall than NN_1, in which recall has fallen to about 50% when the frequency of missing values reaches 30%.

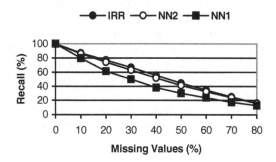

Fig. 4. Comparison of three retrieval strategies in terms of recall on irreducible case libraries with increasing frequencies of missing values

5.2 How Do Missing Values Affect Precision?

Fig. 5 compares the performance of IR, NN_1, NN_2, and IRR in terms of precision on case libraries with frequencies of missing values ranging from 0 to 80 per cent. As before, the results shown are averages over 10 repeated trials. Again as predicted by our theoretical results, precision is always lower in NN_2 than in IRR (if not the same)

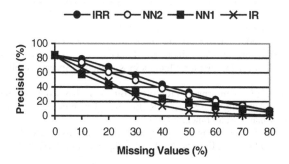

Fig. 5. Comparison of four retrieval strategies in terms of precision on irreducible case libraries with increasing frequencies of missing values

and higher than in NN₁ (if not the same). What is most striking, though, is the poor performance of IR in terms of precision for frequencies of missing values of 20% and higher. When the frequency of missing values reaches 20%, precision in IR has fallen below 50%. This equates to the retrieval of one unwanted case, on average, with every test case. Beyond this point, IR is consistently outperformed by the other retrieval strategies.

6 Conclusions

We have presented empirical measures of precision and recall for the irreducible case libraries that are typical in interactive CBR. Evaluation of retrieval performance is based on the leave-one-in technique [1]. We have examined sources of imperfect precision and recall and the effects of missing values on precision and recall. Our results suggest that while IR always gives perfect recall, its performance in terms of precision may not be acceptable for irreducible case libraries in which missing values are numerous. We have presented a retrieval strategy for irreducible case libraries that gives better precision and recall than inductive retrieval or NN retrieval based on the number of matching features in a target case. Issues to be addressed by further research include the effects of incomplete data and noise on retrieval performance in general, and the effects of missing values on retrieval efficiency.

References

1. Aha, D.W., Breslow, L.A., Muñoz-Avila, H.: Conversational Case-Based Reasoning. Applied Intelligence **14** (2001) 9-32
2. Blake, C., Merz, C.: UCI Repository of Machine Learning Databases. Department of Information and Computer Science, University of California, Irvine, California (1998)
3. Doyle, M., Cunningham, P.: A Dynamic Approach to Reducing Dialog in On-Line Decision Guides. In: Blanzieri, E., Portinale, L. (eds): Advances in Case-Based Reasoning. LNAI, Vol. 1898. Springer-Verlag, Berlin Heidelberg (2000) 49-60
4. McSherry, D.: Interactive Case-Based Reasoning in Sequential Diagnosis. Applied Intelligence **14** (2001) 65-76
5. McSherry, D.: Minimizing Dialog Length in Interactive Case-Based Reasoning. Proceedings of the Seventeenth International Joint Conference on Artificial Intelligence. International Joint Conferences on Artificial Intelligence (2001)
6. Mitchell, T.: Machine Learning. McGraw-Hill (1997)
7. Quinlan, J.R.: Induction of Decision Trees. Machine Learning **1** (1986) 81-106
8. Shimazu, H., Shibata, A., Nihei, K.: ExpertGuide: A Conversational Case-Based Reasoning Tool for Developing Mentors in Knowledge Spaces. Applied Intelligence **14** (2001) 33-48
9. van Rijsbergen, C.J.: Information Retreival. Butterworth & Co, London (1979)
10. Watson, I.: Applying Case-Based Reasoning: Techniques for Enterprise Systems. Morgan Kaufmann, San Francisco (1997)
11. Yang, Q., Wu, J.: Enhancing the Effectiveness of Interactive Case-Based Reasoning with Clustering and Decision Forests. Applied Intelligence **14** (2001) 49-64

Meta-case-Based Reasoning: Using Functional Models to Adapt Case-Based Agents

J. William Murdock and Ashok K. Goel

College of Computing
Georgia Institute of Technology
Atlanta, GA 30332-0280
{murdock,goel}@cc.gatech.edu

Abstract. It is useful for an intelligent software agent to be able to adapt to new demands from an environment. Such adaptation can be viewed as a redesign problem; an agent has some original functionality but the environment demands an agent with a slightly different functionality, so the agent redesigns itself. It is possible to take a case-based approach to this redesign task. Furthermore, one class of agents which can be amenable to redesign of this sort is case-based reasoners. These facts suggest the notion of "meta-case-based reasoning," i.e., the application of case-based redesign techniques to the problem of adapting a case-based reasoning process. Of course, meta-case-based reasoning is a very broad topic. In this paper we focus on a more specific issue within meta-case-based reasoning: balancing the use of relatively efficient but knowledge intensive symbolic techniques with relatively flexible but computationally costly numerical techniques. In particular, we propose a mechanism whereby qualitative functional models are used to efficiently propose a set of design alternatives to specific elements within a meta-case and then reinforcement learning is used to select among these alternatives. We describe an experiment in which this mechanism is applied to a case-based disassembly agent. The results of this experiment show that the combination of model-based adaptation and reinforcement learning can address meta-case-based reasoning problems which are not effectively addressed by either approach in isolation.

1 Issues

Case-based reasoning systems are inherently flexible. As long as a new problem sufficiently resembles an old problem, the case-based reasoner can address that problem. Furthermore, case-based reasoners tend to become increasingly flexible over time. As they develop experience, they build an increasingly large case library and thus may have an increasingly broad range of similar problems that they are able to address. However, some kinds of environments demand an additional kind of flexibility: the ability to reason not only about the cases but also about the case-based reasoning processes themselves.

Consider an intelligent agent which disassembles physical devices using case-based reasoning to adapt disassembly plans. When it is asked to disassemble a

D.W. Aha and I. Watson (Eds.): ICCBR 2001, LNAI 2080, pp. 407–421, 2001.

new device, it simply retrieves an existing plan to disassemble a similar device, adapts that plan, and then executes it. However, if such an agent is given a new sort of request, it is likely to be completely unsuccessful at satisfying that request. For example, if the disassembly system is asked to assemble a device instead of disassembling it, that system is unlikely to be able to address the problem at all; some or all of its processes for plan retrieval, adaptation, execution, etc. are likely to be specifically constructed for disassembly and thus should be unsuited to the task of assembly. However, the necessary processes for assembly may be similar to those which are used for disassembly. Thus it may be possible to adapt the disassembly processes so that they can be used for assembly.

There is some work which has shown that adaptation of reasoning can be facilitated by a functional model that specifies how the elements of an agent's design combine to achieve its functions [4,13,14]. Furthermore, models of this sort have been shown to be useful for encoding "meta-cases" [8], i.e., cases of case-based reasoning. Unfortunately, existing mechanisms for adaptation using functional models are effective for only a limited range of problems [12]. In particular, this approach can address those problems for which there is an existing strategy that solves a similar problem and the functional differences in the problems are particularly simple. If the functional differences are complex, then the information in the model may not be sufficient to completely determine all of the characteristics of the final solution. There are less knowledge intensive reasoning techniques which can be employed to address issues which model-based adaptation leaves unresolved. Of course, less knowledge intensive techniques tend to be more computationally costly, particularly for large problems. However, if the knowledge in the models is thorough enough to provide large pieces of the solution and to identify which elements of the solution still need to be resolved, then the portion of the problem left for a less knowledge intensive technique may be much smaller. Completing the solution can thus provide relatively small challenges to sub-symbolic reasoning techniques such as reinforcement learning and thus may be tractably completed by these techniques even when the complete problems themselves cannot be.

2   Functional Models as Meta-cases

A *model* is an explicit representation of a phenomenon which supports inferences about both static and dynamic properties of that phenomenon. A *functional model* is a model in which function, i.e., the intended effect of a system, plays a central role. For example, functional models of physical devices are useful for representing and organizing design cases and supporting case retrieval and adaptation [5,7]. The use of functional models as meta-cases requires models that encode abstract, computational devices, i.e., reasoning processes. These models of reasoning processes can serve an analogous role in meta-case-based reasoning to the role that is served by models of physical devices in design reasoning.

One approach to functional modeling of reasoning processes is TMK (Task Method Knowledge). TMK models provide information about the function of agents and their elements (i.e., the tasks that they address) and the behavior of those agents and elements (i.e., the methods that they use) using explicit representations of the information that these elements process (i.e., the knowledge that they apply). TMK has been used to model many types of reasoning processes, including not only case-based reasoning [8], but also scheduling using search [12], scientific discovery using analogy [9], and many others. In this paper we concentrate on the use of TMK in the context of case-based reasoning.

We have built a reasoning shell, called REM (Reflective Evolutionary Mind), which provides capabilities for executing and adapting agents represented by TMK models. The specific implementation of the TMK modeling approach encoded in REM is called TMKL. Like all variations of TMK, TMKL breaks down into three major portions: tasks, methods, and knowledge. TMKL instantiates these three portions in the following ways:

Tasks: Tasks are functional elements: a description of a task encodes what that piece of computation is intended to do. A task in TMKL is described by the kinds of knowledge used as inputs and outputs as well as logical assertions which are required to hold before and after the task executes. The assertions involve concepts and relations, which are defined in the knowledge portion of the TMKL model. In addition, some tasks contain information about how they are implemented. TMKL allows three types of tasks, categorized by the information that they contain about implementation:

- **Non-primitive tasks** have a slot which contains a list of methods which can accomplish that task.
- **Primitive tasks** have some direct representation of the effects of the task. TMKL allows several different ways to specify primitive tasks including links to LISP procedures which accomplish the effect and logical assertions which the execution of the task forces to be true.
- **Unimplemented tasks** have no information about how they are to be accomplished, either in the form of methods or in the form of primitive information such as logical assertions. Such tasks cannot be immediately executed; they must, instead, be adapted into either non-primitive tasks or primitive tasks.

Methods: Methods are behavioral elements: a description of a method encodes how that piece of computation works. A method description contains a state-transition machine which describes the operation of the method. The machine contains links to lower level tasks which are required to create the overall effect of the method. Thus tasks and methods are arranged in a hierarchy: tasks refer to methods which accomplish them and methods refer to tasks which are a part of them, all the way down to primitive tasks which have a direct specification of their effects.

Knowledge: Knowledge is the foundation on which tasks and methods are built. A description of a task or a method is inherently interconnected with the description of the knowledge that it manipulates. REM uses Loom [3,11] as its underlying mechanism for knowledge representation. Loom provides many of the basic capabilities which are common to many knowledge representation formalisms, e.g., concepts, instances, relations, etc. The knowledge portion of TMKL begins with the basic Loom syntax and ontology and adds additional forms and terms for integrating this knowledge with information about the tasks and methods of an agent. Of particular value to REM is Loom's ability to represent knowledge about knowledge such as relations which describe properties of other relations. The adaptation of tasks and methods in REM is facilitated by abstract knowledge about the kinds of knowledge that these tasks and methods manipulate; the relation mapping algorithm in Section 4 provides an example of this sort of reasoning.

3   Illustrative Example

We have conducted experiments using REM on a variety of agents. A key element of these experiments involves the comparison of the combined effects of generative planning, reinforcement learning, and model-based reasoning with the effects of the separate approaches in isolation. One particularly noteworthy set of experiments involves the use of REM on ADDAM [6], a case-based agent which plans and executes (in simulation) the disassembly of physical devices. In this section we describe ADDAM and REM's use of it. The first subsection describes ADDAM itself, using REM's model of ADDAM. The second subsection then explains how REM uses this model to adapt ADDAM to assemble (rather than disassemble) devices. Finally, the last subsection describes the results of an experiment with REM and ADDAM involving the assembly problem.

3.1   The ADDAM Case-Based Disassembly Agent

Figure 1 shows some of the tasks and methods of ADDAM. Note that the TMKL model of ADDAM encoded in REM contains about twice as many tasks and methods as are shown here. In the interests of succinctness, we are only presenting the pieces of ADDAM which are directly relevant to this paper. The omitted elements occur in between and around the ones presented; they are largely focussed on supporting ADDAM's complex hierarchical structures for plans and devices.

The top level task of ADDAM is Disassemble. This task is implemented by ADDAM's process of planning and then executing disassembly. Planning in ADDAM involves taking an existing plan for disassembling a similar device and adapting it into a plan for the new device. ADDAM's planning is divided into two major portions: Make Plan Hierarchy and Map Dependencies. Make Plan Hierarchy involves constructing plan steps, e.g., screw Screw-2-1 into Board-2-1 and Board-2-2. The heart of this process is the creation of a node for the hierarchical plan structure and the addition of that node into that structure. Map Dependencies involves imposing ordering dependencies on steps in the plan, e.g., the two boards must be put into position before they can be screwed together. The heart of this process is the selection a potential ordering dependency and the assertion of that dependency for that plan. Dependencies are much simpler than plan nodes; a dependency is just a binary relation over two nodes while a node involves an action type, some objects, and information about is position in the hierarchy. The relative simplicity of dependencies is reflected in the implementation of the primitive task which asserts them; this task is implemented by a simple logical assertion which says that the given dependency holds. In contrast, the tasks which make a plan node and add it to a plan are implemented by procedures.

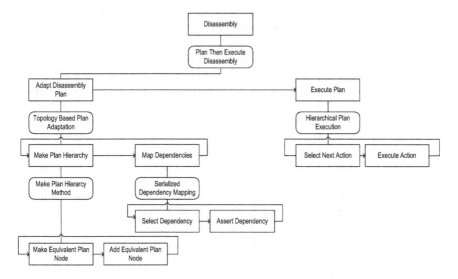

Fig. 1. A diagram of some of the tasks and methods of ADDAM. Rectangular boxes represent tasks, and rounded boxes represent methods.

Given the collection of plan steps and ordering dependencies which the AD-DAM planning process produces, the ADDAM execution process is able to perform these actions in a simulated physical environment. Execution involves repeatedly selecting an action from the plan (obeying the ordering dependencies) and then executing that action. If the plan is correct, the ultimate result of the execution process is the complete disassembly of the simulated physical object.

3.2   Meta-case-Based Assembly with ADDAM in REM

ADDAM is able to perform disassembly on its own without any use of meta-cases. However, if ADDAM alone were given an assembly problem, it would be completely helpless. In contrast, when ADDAM is explicitly modeled within the REM reasoning shell, REM treats its model of ADDAM as a meta-case. When REM receives a request for assembly, it searches its meta-case memory for an implemented task which is similar to assembly. Because disassembly and assembly are similar, REM retrieves ADDAM's disassembly task. At that point, REM can attempt to adapt that disassembly task to satisfy the new requirement: assembly.

REM is able to perform this adaptation using a combination of both model-based and non-symbolic techniques. In particular, REM applies model-based adaptation to ADDAM to provide an incomplete (underconstrained) assembly agent and then runs that agent repeatedly using reinforcement learning to produce a final, fully operational version of the assembly system. We have contrasted this approach with two other ways of addressing the same assembly problems; both of these alternative approaches are also performed by REM. The first alternative involves planning assembly through pure generative planning. This alternative is implemented by exporting the relevant facts and operations to Graphplan [2], a popular generative planning system. The second alternative involves performing assembly through pure reinforcement learning, i.e., beginning by simply attempting random actions on random objects and eventually learning which sorts of actions lead to successful assembly. This approach is implemented using the well-known Q-learning[1] algorithm [17].

When REM operating on ADDAM is asked to solve the assembly task, it is not given an implementation for that task. However, it is given the other portions of the TMKL model for a task: the inputs and outputs and the assertions which hold before and after the task executes. This information can be used to retrieve a similar task. In particular, the background knowledge in REM's model of ADDAM provides a relation, inverse-of, and an assertion that this relation holds between the states referred to in the output conditions of assembly and disassembly. This allows REM's meta-case retrieval mechanism to find the disassembly task.

REM has multiple strategies for adapting meta-cases. The one which is relevant to the assembly example is called relation mapping; it involves propagating a relation which holds between the desired task and the retrieved task through the implementation of the later to produce an implementation of the former. REM's relation mapping mechanism is a complex adaptation strategy involving changes to several different tasks within the overall structure of ADDAM. Furthermore, the process is not an entirely complete or reliable one; it involves suggesting a variety of modifications but some of these changes are only tentative and may conflict with each other. These incomplete modifications are resolved later in the reasoning process.

---

[1] Although Q-learning is a powerful and easy to use technique for decision making, it does have extensive competition, and there is undoubtedly some benefit to other decision making approaches. For example, TD(λ) [15] is a reinforcement technique which is particularly well-suited to situations in which rewards are often delayed, which is typically the case in running a TMK model (since the reward comes at the end, when it is possible to observe whether the desired result of the specified task has been accomplished). Alternatively, one could envision abandoning reinforcement learning altogether and simply using a search process to make decisions. The benefits and drawbacks of using different techniques is an important area for future research.

Figure 2 presents the effects of relation mapping over ADDAM in the assembly example, again focusing on those elements which are relevant to this discussion. After the disassembly process is copied, there are three major changes made to the copied version of the model:

1. The **Make Plan Hierarchy** process is modified to adjust the type of actions produced. Because the primitive tasks which manipulate plan nodes are implemented by procedures, REM is not able to directly modify their implementation. Instead, it inserts a new mapping task in between the primitive tasks. The mapping task alters an action after it is created but before it is included in the plan. This newly constructed task asserts that the action type of the new node is the one mapped by the **inverse-of** relation to the old action type; for example, an **unscrew** action in an old disassembly plan would be mapped to a **screw** action in a new assembly plan.

2. The portion of the **Map Dependencies** process which asserts a dependency is modified. Because the primitive task for asserting dependencies is implemented as a simple logical assertion, it is possible to impose the **inverse-of** relation on top of that assertion. If one action was to occur before another action in the old disassembly plan then the related action in the new assembly occurs after the other related action (because **inverse-of** holds between the relations indicating before and after). For example, if an old disassembly plan requires that boards be unscrewed before they can be removed, the new assembly plan will require that they be placed before they can be screwed together.

3. The execution process is modified to adjust the type of actions executed. This adjustment is done by an inserted task which maps an action type to its inverse. For example, if a **screw** action is selected, an **unscrew** action is performed.

Obviously the first and third modifications conflict with each other; if the system inverts the actions when they are produced *and* when they are used, then the result will involve executing the original actions. In principle, if the TMKL model of ADDAM were precise and detailed enough, it might be possible for REM to deduce from the model that it was inverting the same actions twice. However, the model does not contain the level of detail required to deduce that the actions being produced in the early portion of the process are the same ones being executed in the later portion. Even if the information were there, it would be in the form of logical expressions about the requirements and results of all of the intervening tasks (which are moderately numerous, since these inversions take place in greatly separated portions of the system); reasoning about whether a particular knowledge item were being inverted twice for this problem would be a form of theorem proving over a large number of complex expressions, which can frequently be intractable.

Fortunately, it is not necessary for REM's model-based adaptation technique to deductively prove that any particular combination of suggestions is consistent. Instead, REM can simply execute the adapted system with the particular decisions about which modifications to use left unspecified. In the example, REM

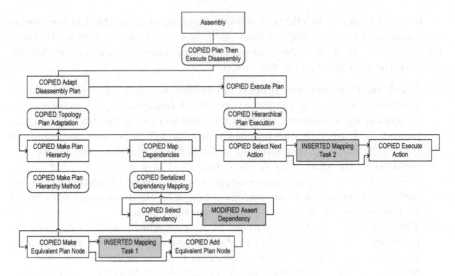

Fig. 2. Tasks and methods produced for the assembly process by adapting ADDAM. Tasks which were added or modified are highlighted in grey.

makes the two inserted mapping tasks optional, i.e., the state-transition machine for the modified methods has one transition which goes into the inserted task and one which goes around it. During execution, a decision making process selects among these two transitions; this decision making process uses Q-learning to resolve ambiguities in the model such as the optional mapping tasks. For the assembly problem, this decision making process develops a policy of including either of the inserted mapping tasks but not both.

Note that REM is using exactly the same decision making component here that it uses to perform this task by pure Q-learning; however, here this component is being used *only* to decide among the options which model-based adaptation left unspecified. In contrast, the pure Q-learning approach uses the decision maker to select from *all* possible actions at *every* step in the process. The Q-learning that needs to be done to complete the model-based adaptation process occurs over a much smaller state-space than the Q-learning for the original problem (particularly if the original problem is, itself, complex); this fact is strongly reflected in the results.

3.3   Results

We have used REM on ADDAM for disassembly and assembly of a variety of devices such as cameras, computers, and furniture. One particularly interesting design which REM on ADDAM has been applied to is a nested roof design in which the placement of the upper level boards blocks access to the connections among the lower level boards. This design can be extended by adding more and more boards, thereby nesting the roof arbitrarily deep. This characteristic is useful from an experimental perspective because it allows us to track the behavior of different approaches to assembly as the number of components increases.

Figure 3 shows the performance of REM on the roof assembly problem. Two of the lines indicate the performance of REM without access to ADDAM and the model thereof; one of these attempts uses Graphplan and the other uses Q-learning alone. The remaining line shows the performance of REM when it does use ADDAM, using the model to invert the system and then using reinforcement learning to fully specify the details of the inversion. The key observation about these results is that both Graphplan and Q-learning undergo an enormous explosion in the cost of execution (several orders of magnitude) with respect to the number of boards; in contrast, REM's model-based adaptation (with assistance from Q-learning) shows relatively steady performance. The reason for the steady performance is that much of the work done with this approach involves adapting the agent itself. The cost of the model adaptation process is completely unaffected by the complexity of the particular object (in this case, the roof) being assembled because it does not access that information in any way; i.e., it inverts the existing specialized disassembly agent to be a specialized assembly agent. The next part of the process *uses* that specialized assembly agent to perform the assembly of the given roof design; the cost of this part of the process is affected by the complexity of the roof design, but to a much smaller extent than generative planning or reinforcement learning techniques are.

4   Algorithms

The previous section contains a detailed example of the execution of REM for a specific problem. This section provides a more abstract view of the processes that are involved in that example. Table 1 shows a high-level overview of the main algorithm for REM. Note that this algorithm is essentially a case-based one: when there is a request for a task for which no method is available, a similar task is retrieved, the method for that task is adapted, the new method is stored for later reuse, and the new method is also verified through execution (and further adapted if needed).

REM has two inputs: main-task and initial-condition. In the earlier example, the main-task is assembly and the initial-condition describes the design of the device to be assembled (in this case, a roof) and the initial state of the world (that nothing is connected to anything else). If the task is unimplemented then a new method needs to be developed for it. In this situation, if there is some existing task which has a known implementation and is similar to the main task then we can try to adapt the implementation of the known task to address the new task (this process is described in more detail below). If no such existing task is available, then a method can be built from scratch, either by using a generative planner or by deferring the decisions about action selection until execution, thus reasoning purely by reinforcement learning. These three alternatives (adapting a method, building a method from scratch using generative planning,

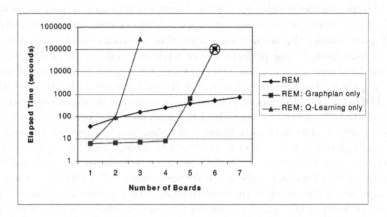

Fig. 3. Logarithmic scale graph of the relative performances of different techniques within REM on the roof assembly example for a varying number of boards. The Graphplan and Q-learning lines show the performance of these techniques used in isolation without any model information (the "X" through the last point on the Graphplan line indicates that the program, using Graphplan, ran up to that point and then terminated unsuccessfully, apparently due to memory management problems either with Graphplan or with REM's use of it). The other line shows the combined effect of REM's redesign of the model of ADDAM (which uses both model-based adaptation and Q-learning). Of particular note is the relatively steady performance of model-based adaptation, compared to the explosions in execution time from the other approaches.

Table 1. Main algorithm for REM

Algorithm do-task(main-task, initial-condition)	
Inputs:	main-task: A task to be executed
	initial-condition: The input knowledge for the main-task
Effects:	The task has been executed.

```
IF [main-task does not have a known implementation] THEN
    IF [there is a known-task which is similar to main-task] THEN
        [adapt the methods of that known-task to perform main-task]
    ELSE
        [build a method for main-task from scratch]

REPEAT
    [execute main-task under initial-condition]
    IF [execution has failed] THEN
        [modify the implementation of main-task]
UNTIL [execution has succeeded]
```

building a method from scratch using reinforcement learning) are contrasted in the experimental results presented in the previous section.

Once the main-task has an implementation, it can be executed in the context of the initial-condition. Decisions (such as method selection) which are left unresolved by the model are addressed through reinforcement learning during this execution process. When executing a method developed for pure reinforcement learning, all possible actions on all possible objects are available as separate methods for each step of the process; consequently, the decision making process is responsible for all of the control in this situation. In contrast, when REM's generative planning module (using Graphplan) has been used to build the method, a complete, ordered specification of exactly which actions to perform is available so that *no* decision making is needed during execution. Executing a method which was developed by model-based adaptation lies between the two extremes; many control decisions are specified by the adapted model, but a few are left open and must be resolved by the reinforcement learning process.

If execution is unsuccessful, REM can try to modify the implementation of the task and try again. If the task involves decisions which are being made through reinforcement learning, this modification can simply involve providing negative reinforcement to the last action taken by the agent (since it directly lead to failure). In other circumstances, REM is able to use model-based techniques to further adapt the implementation using the results of the execution and even user feedback (when available). No post-execution model-based adaptation is done in the ADDAM roof example, but we have conducted other experiments which do use these mechanisms. If additional modification is done, the REM process then starts over at the beginning, this time with an implemented task (so it can immediately start executing).

Recall that one of the steps described in the main algorithm of REM involves adapting the methods of a known task to perform main-task. This step is a complicated part of the process and there are many strategies which can be used for this step. Table 2 presents the algorithm for the particular adaptation strategy which is used in the ADDAM inversion example: relation mapping.

The relation mapping algorithm takes as input main-task and an existing known-task for which at least one method is already available (i.e., a task which the existing agent already knows how to perform). The algorithm begins by copying the methods (including the methods' subtasks and those subtasks' methods) for known-task and asserts that these copied methods are new methods for main-task; the remaining steps of the algorithm then modify these copied methods so that they are suited to main-task.

In the next step in the adaptation process, the system finds a relation which provides a mapping between the effects of main-task and the effects of known-task. In the experiment described in this paper, the relation which is used is inverse-of. This relation is selected by REM because (i) the task of disassembly has the intended effect that the object is disassembled, (ii) the task of assembly has the intended effect that the object is assembled, and (iii) the relation inverse-of holds between the assembled and disassembled world states. These three facts

Table 2. Algorithm for relation mapping, the adaptation strategy used in the assembly example.

Algorithm **relation - mapping** (main-task, known-task)	
Inputs:	main-task: An unimplemented task
	known-task: An existing implemented task which is similar to main-task
Effects:	There is an implementation for main-task.

[copy methods for known-task to main-task]
map-relation = [relation which connects results of known-task to results of main-task]
mappable-relations = [all relations for which map-relation holds with some relation]
mappable-concepts = [all concepts for which map-relation holds with some concept]
relevant-relations = mappable-relations + [all relations over mappable-concepts]
relevant-manipulable-relations = [relevant-relations which are internal state relations]
candidate-tasks = [all tasks which affect relevant-manipulable-relations]
FOR candidate-task IN candidate-tasks DO
    IF [candidate-task directly asserts a relevant-manipulable-relations] THEN
        [invert the assertion for that candidate task]
    ELSE IF [candidate-task has mappable output] THEN
        [insert an optional inversion task after candidate-task]

are explicitly encoded in the TMK model of ADDAM. Note that there are other relationships besides inversion which could potentially be used by this algorithm or one similar to it. Some examples include specialization, generalization, composition, similarity, etc.; additional research is needed to fully explore the space of relations which can be used here and how those relations interact with the steps of this algorithm.

Once the mapping relation has been found, the next steps involve identifying aspects of the agent's knowledge which are relevant to modifying the agent with respect to that relation. The system constructs lists of relations and concepts for which the mapping relation holds. For example, ADDAM, being a hierarchical planner, has relations node-precedes and node-follows which indicate ordering relations among nodes in a hierarchical plan; these relations are the inverse of each other so both are considered mappable relations. A list of relevant relations is computed which contains not only the mappable relations but also the relations over mappable concepts. For example, the assembled and disassembled world states are inverse of each other (making that concept a mappable concept) and thus some relations for the world state concept are also included as relevant relations. The list of relevant relations is then filtered to include only those which can be *directly* modified by the agent, i.e., those which involve the internal state of the agent. For example, node-precedes and node-follows involve connections between plan nodes which are knowledge items internal to the system. In contrast, the assembled and disassembled states are external. The system cannot make a device assembled simply by asserting that it is; it needs to perform actions which

cause this change to take place, i.e., inverting the process of creating a **disassembled** state needs to be done implicitly by inverting internal information which
leads to this state (such as plan node ordering information). Thus **node-precedes**
and **node-follows** are included in the list of relevant manipulable relations while
relations over world states are not.

Given this list of relevant manipulable relations, it is possible to determine
the tasks which involve these relations and to modify these tasks accordingly.
For example, the **Assert Dependency** task in the ADDAM disassembly planning
process directly asserts that a plan node precedes another plan node; this task
is inverted in the assembly planning process to directly assert that the node
follows the other node instead. Another example in ADDAM is the portions of
the system which involve the types of actions in the plan (e.g., screwing is the
inverse of unscrewing); in these situations, new tasks need to be inserted in the
model to invert the output of those steps which produce this information. As
noted in the previous section, these inserted tasks can conflict with each other
so they need to be made optional; when the **main-task** is later executed, the
inclusion or exclusion of these optional tasks is resolved through trial and error
(via Q-learning).

5 Discussion

One obvious alternative to using REM in combination with a specialized task-
specific case-based planner such as ADDAM is to simply use a general-purpose
case-based planner. However, note that the assembly plans produced by REM
and ADDAM bear virtually no superficial resemblance to the original disassembly plans upon which they were based: there is typically no overlap at all in the
operators used (since all of the operators are inverted) and while the objects
of those operators are similar, they are manipulated in the reverse order. Case-
based reasoning is generally suited to the types of problems for which similar
requirements lead to similar results; clearly the adaptation of disassembly plans
into assembly plans does not meet that criterion. However, the processes by
which the disassembly plans and assembly plans are produced are very similar
(as evidenced by the relatively small differences between the models illustrated
in Figures 1 and 2). Consequently, while this problem is ill-suited to traditional
case-based reasoning, it is well-suited to meta-case-based reasoning. We claim
that meta-case-based reasoning is also appropriate for many other problems for
which similar requirements lead to radically different solutions but do so through
relatively similar processes.

There are other case-based reasoning approaches which explicitly reason
about process. For example, case-based adaptation [10] considers the reuse of
adaptation processes within case-based reasoning. Case-based adaptation does
not use complex models of reasoning, because it restricts its reasoning about
processes to a single portion of case-based reasoning (adaptation) and assumes a
single strategy (rule-based search). This limits the applicability of the approach
to the (admittedly quite large) set of problems for which adaptation by rule-

based search can be effectively reused. It does provide an advantage over our approach in that it does not require a functional model and does not require any representation of the other portions of the case-based reasoning process. However, given that that case-based reasoning systems are designed and built by humans in the first place, information about the function and composition of these systems should be available to their builders (or a separate analyst who has access to documentation describing the architecture of the system) [1]. Thus while our approach does impose a significant extra knowledge requirement, that requirement is evidently often attainable, at least for well-organized and well-understood agents.

Another approach to using knowledge of process within case-based reasoning is derivational analogy [16]. Derivational analogy focuses not on abstract models of how reasoning can occur but rather on concrete traces of specific instances of reasoning. This can be an advantage in that these traces can be automatically generated and thus do not necessarily require any prior knowledge engineering. However, to the extent that the traces are automatically generated, derivational analogy is limited to kinds of problems which are already adequately solved by other approaches (typically generative planning). This can be effective if the agent first encounters relatively small examples which can be solved relatively efficiently using generative planning and then only encounters larger problems after it has built up some experience. However, if the environment provides a relatively complex example immediately, then derivational analogy is essentially helpless. In contrast, our meta-case-based reasoning approach is able to immediately address complex problems by leveraging the relative efficiency of some specialized case-based technique even on a distinct (but similar) task from the one for which that technique was designed.

Experiments with REM, such as the one presented in Section 3, show that meta-case-based reasoning using the combination of model-based adaptation and reinforcement learning is often computationally much less costly than reinforcement learning alone (and also less costly than generative planning). Note that reasoning about models does involve some processing overhead, and for very simple problems this overhead can exceed the benefits provided by model-based adaptation. However, if an agent is being built for a complex environment, its designer can expect that it will face complex problems, at least some of the time, and the enormous benefits provided by model-based adaptation for those problems should outweigh the additional costs for very simple problems. We, therefore, conclude that meta-case-based reasoning via a combination of model-based adaptation and reinforcement learning represents a reasonable and useful compromise among flexibility, knowledge requirements and computational cost.

References

1. Gregory Abowd, Ashok K. Goel, Dean F. Jerding, Michael McCracken, Melody Moore, J. William Murdock, Colin Potts, Spencer Rugaber, and Linda Wills. MORALE – Mission oriented architectural legacy evolution. In *Proceedings International Conference on Software Maintenance 97*, Bari, Italy, 1997.

2. Avrim Blum and Merrick L. Furst. Fast planning through planning graph analysis. *Aritificial Intelligence*, 90:281–300, 1997.
3. David Brill. Loom reference manual. *http://www.isi.edu/isd/LOOM/ documentation/manual/ quickguide.html*, December 1993. Accessed August 1999.
4. Michael Freed, Bruce Krulwich, Lawrence Birnbaum, and Gregg Collins. Reasoning about performance intentions. In *Proceedings of the Fourteenth Annual Conference of the Cognitive Science Society*, pages 7–12, 1992.
5. Ashok K. Goel. A model-based approach to case adaptation. pages 143–148, August 1991.
6. Ashok K. Goel, Ethan Beisher, and David Rosen. Adaptive process planning. Poster Session of the 10th International Symposium on Methodologies for Intelligent Systems, 1997.
7. Ashok K. Goel, Sambasiva R. Bhatta, and Eleni Stroulia. Kritik: An early case-based design system. In M. L. Maher and P. Pu, editors, *Issues and Applications of Case-Based Reasoning to Design*. Lawrence Erlbaum Associates, 1997.
8. Ashok K. Goel and J. William Murdock. Meta-cases: Explaining case-based reasoning. In I. Smith and B. Faltings, editors, *Proceedings of the Third European Workshop on Case-Based Reasoning - EWCBR-96*, Lausanne, Switzerland, November 1996. Springer.
9. Todd Griffith and J. William Murdock. The role of reflection in scientific exploration. In *Proceedings of the Twentieth Annual Conference of the Cognitive Science Society*, 1998.
10. David B. Leake, Andrew Kinley, and David Wilson. Learning to improve case adaptation by intropsective reasoning and cbr. In *Proceedings of the First International Conference on Case-Based Reasoning - ICCBR-95*, Sesimbra, Portugal, 1995.
11. Robert MacGregor. Retrospective on Loom. *http://www.isi.edu/ isd/ LOOM/ papers/ macgregor/ Loom_Retrospective.html*, 1999. Accessed August 1999.
12. J. William Murdock and Ashok K. Goel. An adaptive meeting scheduling agent. In *Proceedings of the First Asia-Pacific Conference on Intelligent Agent Technology - IAT-99*, Hong Kong, 1999.
13. Eleni Stroulia and Ashok K. Goel. A model-based approach to blame assignment: Revising the reasoning steps of problem solvers. In *Proceedings of the National Conference on Artificial Intelligence - AAAI-96*, Portland, Oregon, August 1996.
14. Eleni Stroulia and Ashok K. Goel. Redesigning a problem-solver's operators to improve solution quality. In *Proceedings of the 15th International Joint Conference on Artificial Intelligence - IJCAI-97*, pages 562–567, San Francisco, August 23–29 1997. Morgan Kaufmann Publishers.
15. Richard Sutton. Learning to predict by the methods of temporal differences. *Machine Learning*, 3:9–44, 1988.
16. Manuela Veloso. PRODIGY / ANALOGY: Analogical reasoning in general problem solving. In *Topics in Case-Based Reasoning*, pages 33–50. Springer Verlag, 1994.
17. Christopher Watkins. *Learning from delayed rewards.* Ph.D. thesis, Cambridge University, Psychology Dept., Cambridge, UK, 1989.

Exploiting Interchangeabilities for Case Adaptation

Nicoleta Neagu and Boi Faltings

Artificial Intelligence Laboratory (LIA),
Computer Science Department, Swiss Federal Institute of Technology (EPFL)
CH-1015 Ecublens, Switzerland
{neagu, faltings}@lia.di.epfl.ch http://liawww.epfl.ch/

Abstract. While there are many general methods for case retrieval, case adaptation usually requires problem-specific knowledge and it is still an open problem. In this paper we propose a general method for solving case adaptation problems for the large class of problems which can be formulated as *Constraint Satisfaction Problems*. This method is based on the concept of *interchangeability* between values in problem solutions. The method is able to determine how change propagates in a solution set and generate a minimal set of choices which need to be changed to *adapt* an existing solution to a new problem.

The paper presents the proposed method, algorithms and test results for a resource allocation domain.

Keywords: case-based reasoning, case adaptation, constraint satisfaction problems, interchangeability.

1 Introduction

Case-based reasoning (CBR) for solving problems can be broken down into two important steps: case *retrieval* and case *adaptation* [1]. While there are many general methods for case retrieval, solutions to case adaptation remain highly domain specific, requiring detailed problem-specific knowledge.

Although it may be unrealistic to hope for generic methods to solve all adaptation problems, one class of problems which may be addressed is problems which can be formulated as *Constraint Satisfaction Problems* (CSPs) [2]. CSPs consist of a number of choices that need to be made (variables), each of which has an associated number of options (the variable domain) and a set of relationships between choices (constraints). A valid solution to a CSP is an assignment of a value to each variable from its domain with the total set of assignments respecting all the problem constraints. The CSP model can therefore be applied to a very wide range of problems [3], well known examples are: diagnosis [4], planning [5], scheduling [6], robot control [7] and configuration [8].

This flexibility makes CSP problems a valuable class of problems for CBR adaptation methods. Solutions which can be shown to apply to CSP type problems can be applied to a wide range of problems.

This paper presents a method based on the concepts of interchangeability [9] and neighbourhood partial interchangeability (NPI) [10]. These methods can be used to

D.W. Aha and I. Watson (Eds.): ICCBR 2001, LNAI 2080, pp. 422–436, 2001.
© Springer-Verlag Berlin Heidelberg 2001

capture equivalence among values of a variable in a discrete CSP (original interchangeability) and localise the effect of modifications to some variables and determine relations between close solutions.

These techniques are applied and extended to case adaptation to enable a CBR system to determine a minimal change in the solution of the retrieved case. The main contributions of this paper are:

- A model for the application of Interchangeability techniques to a large class of CBR adaptation problems (Section 3).
- An algorithm for computing minimal neighbourhood partial interchangeability; it determines how change propagates in a solution set and generates a minimal set of choices which need to be changed in order to *adapt* an existing solution to a new problem. (Section 3.4).
- Test results and initial analysis of the effectiveness of the adaptation technique (Section 4).

Additionally, in Section 2 we recall the main definitions of interchangeability that are of interest to us while conclusions and further work can be found in Section 6.

2 Definitions

Definition 1 (CSP). *A CSP is defined by $P = (V, D, C)$, where $V = \{ V_1, V_2, ..., V_n \}$ is the set of variables, $D = \{ D_{V1}, D_{V2}, ..., D_{Vn} \}$ the set of domains (i.e., sets of values) associated with the variables, and C is the set of constraints that apply to the variables.*

In other words, Constraint Satisfaction Problems (CSPs) involve finding values for variables subject to constraints on which combination of values are permitted. The work presented here is currently restricted to problems which can be modelled as discrete binary CSPs. These are problems where each domain contains a finite set of discrete values and constraints are never between more than two variables. Although this is a restriction, this is the most common class of CSPs and covers a large range of problems. In these work it was considered that the constraints are *hard*, where for specific values assigned to the variables involved in the constraint, the constraint can be satisfied or not. In further work, we intend to investigate how our algorithms for detecting minimal changes apply CSP with fuzzy constraints [11], where different tuples satisfy the given constraint to a different degree.

The concept of Interchangeability formalises equivalence relations among objects, respectively the values of the variables in a CSP. The concept of interchangeability was first introduced by Freuder in [9]. Among others, Freuder defines the following three kinds of interchangeability:

Definition 2 (Full Interchangeability - FI). *Values $V_i = a$ and $V_i = b$ are fully interchangeable if for any solution where $V_i = a$, there is an otherwise identical solution where $V_i = b$, and vice versa.*

This means that by exchanging values a and b for variable V_i in a given solution, the solution will remain a valid solution of the CSP (without requiring changes to the other variable assignments). There is no efficient general algorithm for computing FI values in a CSP; this might require computing all solutions [9].

Definition 3 (Neighbourhood Interchangeability - NI). *Values $V_i = a$ and $V_i = b$ are neighbourhood interchangeable if for every constraint involving V_i, for every tuple that admits $V_i = a$ there is otherwise an identical tuple that admits $V_i = b$, and vice-versa.*

Neighbourhood Interchangeability considers only local interactions and thus can be efficiently computed. Freuder proposes a polynomial-time algorithm for computing NI values [9].

Definition 4 (Partial Interchangeability - PI). *Values $V_i = a$ and $V_i = b$ are partially interchangeable with respect to a set of variables S if for any solution where $V_i = a$, there is another solution where $V_i = b$ which otherwise differs only in values assigned to variables in S, and vice versa.*

Partial Interchangeability exploits the idea that values for a subset of variables from the CSP may differ among themselves, but stay fully interchangeable with the rest of the CSP. We can therefore identify groups of partial solutions. Equivalent solutions can be generated by modifying the values of the indicated variables only.

Again, there is no efficient algorithm for computing PI set. A localised algorithm has however been proposed for computing Neighbourhood Partial Interchangeability (NPI) sets of variables with the corresponding NPI values [10].

Definition 5 (Neighbourhood Partial Interchangeability - NPI). *Values $V_i = a$ and $V_i = b$ are neighbourhood partial interchangeable (NPI) with respect to a set of variables S if for every constraint between V_i and the neighbourhood of set S, for every tuple that admits $V_i = a$ there is otherwise an identical tuple that admits $V_i = b$, and vice-versa, (where this change can affect the variables from set S), while the same condition applies also for all the other variables from S.*

NPI is a localised form of PI where the propagation of the change is computed by looking 'through' the neighbourhood of the set S.

NPI interchangeability classes are computed by the use of the **Joint Discrimination Tree (JDT)** algorithm, as described in [10], where the annotations of the JDT of a set S = $\{V_1, V_2, ..., V_k\}$ contains NPI values as follows:

$$\text{NPI(S)} = \{\ \{\ (V_1, d_{m1}), (V_2, d_{m2}), ..., (V_k, d_{mk})\}$$
$$\text{such that } (\forall\ 1 \leq i \leq k, d_{mi} \neq \Phi\ ) \bigwedge (\exists\ 1 \leq i \leq k, |\ d_{mi}\ | > 1)\ \}$$

Definition 6 (Minimal Neighbourhood Partial Interchangeability Set - MNPIS). *For $\forall\ V_i$ belonging to a NPI set S, $\forall\ v_{ijk}, v_{ijl} \in d_{ij}$ in a NPI set exchanging v_{ijk} with v_{ijl} implies $\exists\ V_n \in S$ which has to change its value (only in the domain d_{nj} of the interchangeability class of the current NPI set) such that the constraint in the set S are satisfied and the solution maintained.*

In other words, exchanging the value of one variable V_i contained in a NPI set S, has to affect at least one of the other variables of the set S.

Definition 7 (Minimum Neighbourhood Partial Interchangeability Set - mNPIS). *A minimum NPI set for a variable V_i is the minimal NPI set which contains the minimum number of variables, including the starting variable V_i. (take here into consideration that the sets are constructed starting from a variable and enlarging its environment by following its constraints and including the neighbors in the constructed set)*

3   Adaptation Model Based on Interchangeability

In previous work [12], the authors applied a restricted interchangeability framework to case adaptation problems in car configuration. This previous approach was able to identify NI values for CSP values and therefore determine individal choices in a solution which could be adapted. The work here extends this idea to include adaptation over complete NPI sets to find minimal sets of variables which might be changed to generate adapted solutions. The framework is illustrated through an example application to a generic resource allocation problem.

The resource allocation problem used is defined as a CSP in the following way:

- tasks $(T_1, T_2, ..., T_n)$ are considered as the variables of the CSP where their values are resources.
- domains of variables are sets of resouces by which the tasks can be executed.
- constraints among variables denote mutual exclusion with respect to the values. That means that two tasks overlapping in time cannot be carried out by the same resource.

Since the main contribution of this work relates to the adaptation step of the CBR process, retrieval is done use a simple metric which picks out the closest previous case.

3.1   CBR Model

The framework presented in the figure 1 solves new resource allocation problems by retrieving and adapting previous solutions. The problem solving process proceeds as follows:

1. A new problem (defined in terms of tasks and resources to allocate as above) arrives in the system.
2. The problem is matched to a single previous case.
3. The adaptation phase of the process therefore receives the following inputs:
   - The solution of the retrieved case.
   - The corresponding CSP retrieved from the CSP base according to the tasks contained in the new problem.
   - The differences between the problem at hand and the one expressed in the indexing parameters of the retrieved case[1] (see Figure 1).
4. The adaptation module applies the minimal NPI algorithm (Section 3.4) to this input to generate the closest solution to the new problem.

The adaptation phase of the process therefore has an extra form of information available to it which is the CSP model corresponding to the new problem. The domain knowledge is represented as a CSP problem. It is this that allows us to apply the interchangeability algorithms. The most common algorithm for performing systematic search in a CSP is backtracking but in large CSPs it might be expensive. Thus, inffering a new solution from an already known one by studying local changes based on interchangeability, have a linear cost and can be used as a reliable adaptation method.

---

[1] The requirements can also be imposed by the user.

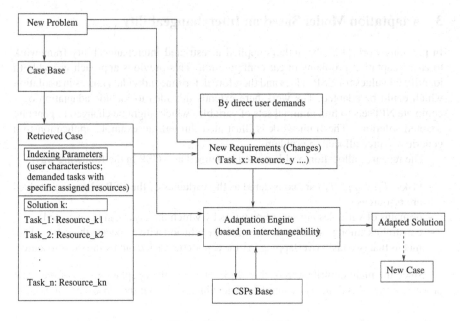

Fig. 1. Adaptation Model

For the tasks with their corresponding exchanging values, provided by the new requirements module, the adaptation engine applies the minimal NPI algorithm (Section 3.4) in order to find the NI or NPI values for adapting solutions. For an input as single task, it might find that the values proposed to be exchanged are NI, and thus the new solution keeps all the same values for all the other tasks and exchanges only the NI values of the task asked to be changed. In other cases the algorithm might find an NPI set of variables which have to be changed in order to get a solution for the new requirements. Thus the constraints between the variables of the NPI set have to be solved, while all the others variables of the solution stay unchanged. We notice that the computational effort is here restricted to the NPI set and one does not have to solve the whole problem from scratch. If the minimal NPI set finding algorithm does not find any NPI set, it means that there are no solutions for the new requirements in the limited threshold of number of variables which might be changed imposed in the minimal NPI algorithm. In this situation, it might be necessary to solve the problem from scratch.

In the CSP base we store the knowledge about the domain in the form of CSPs. In our previous work, the car configuration system [12] there we had only one CSP which modeled all possible configurations. For increasing the generality, we propose now to represent the knowledge by several CSP, which modell different resource allocation problems.

3.2   Example of Applying Neighborhood Interchangeability (NI) to Case Adaptation

As presented in previous work, the simplest way to apply interchangability to case adaption is to find NI sets of values for a variables of the CSP. Figure 2 shows an example of this for a resource allocation problem. The resource allocation problem is modelled as a discrete CSP in which the constraints are binary and denotes mutual exclusion with respect to the values. The nodes of the CSP represents the tasks to be executed, and their values are sets of resources by which these tasks can be executed. Arcs links tasks that overlap in time and have at least one resource in common.

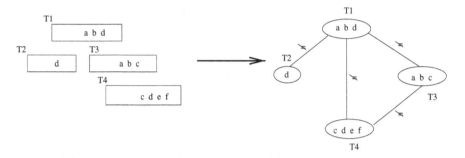

Fig. 2. Simple example of how resource allocation is modelled as CSP

Following the sequence described in the previous section a new problem might match a solution such as:

Sol1 = { T1 = a, T2 = d, T3 = b, T4 = e}

but impose the new requirements to allocate resource f to task T4. Normally this requirement could have a knock on effect on all or many other choices but in this case the values e and f of variable T4 are NI. Thus the exchange does not affect the other variables and it stays a solution of the CSP (and hence a valid solution to the whole problem). Formulation of the problem as a CSP and applying the algorithm for detecting NI allows us to detect and prove this (which may be non-trivial in other representations).

3.3   Example of Applying Neighborhood Partial Interchangeability (NPI) to Case Adaptation

Applying NI is useful but only allows single values to be exchanged in a solution. This makes a very strong requirement that zero other choices are impacted by changing an assignment. NPI is a weaker form of NI and thus more frequent in any given solution since several interdependent choices can be varied together while leaving the rest of the problem unchanged. The consequence is to isolate the effect of modification to a subproblem of the CSP. It identifies qualitatively equivalent solutions which can be generated by modifying the values of the indicated variables only.

Since NPI is more frequent in a solution, it increases the flexibility and utility of the adaptation module. The example given in Figure 2 illustrates how the adaptation module works when using NPI interchangeability.

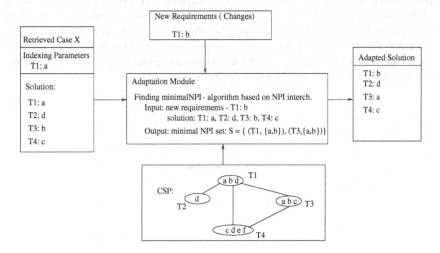

Fig. 3. Example of how the adaptation module use the NPI intercahgeability for case adaptation

The Adaptation module receives as input the solution of the retrieved case, the CSP corresponding to the current solution and of course the requirements which it has to adapt according to the requirements from the user or not matching with the indexing parameters. Indexing parametes contain previous user requirements (tasks with the corresponding resources). Similarity measure used in computing the closest case is only on simple matching between the new requirements and the previous requirements which are now the indexing parametes of the case. The differences between requirements (T1=a have to become T1=b) gives the input for the minimal NPI algorithm Section 3.4.

As we can see in figure 3, by 'adapting' the task T1 from resource a to resource b we have to change also the task T3 from resource b to resource a to stay a solution, while all the other tasks remain the same. Change across two variable is therefore detected as leaving the rest of the solution valid. Although this is a simple example, the NPI algorithm can be used to detect invariance over subproblems of size N. The system also works when several changes are required at once.

Once the NPI sets have been identified the adaptation module can check to see if it can find a valid solution, which respects the changes imposed by the new problem w.r.t. the retrieved case.

The key to being able to apply NPI set information is the algorithm for detecting these sets in the solution case to be adapted - this algorithm is presented in the next section.

3.4   Algorithm for Finding Minimal NPI Sets

The method applied for detecting NPI sets uses an algorithm which was adapted from the Joint Discrimination Tree (JDT) for computing the NPI values proposed by Choueiry and Noubir in [10]. As it is an important base to our algorithm we recall the JDT algorithm below. The complexity of this algorithm is $O(s(n\text{-}s)d^2)$, where n is the size of CSP, s is the size of set S for which we compute the JDT and d the size of the largest domain.

Algorithm 1: JDT for S= $\{V_1, V_2, ..., V_k\}$ (D_{Vi} , Neigh(S)):
Create root of the Joint Discrimination tree
Repeat for each variable $V_i \in$ S
   Repeat for each value $v_{il} \in D_{Vi}$
     Repeat for each variable $V_j \in$ Neigh(S)
       Repeat for each value $v_{jk} \in D_{Vj}$
         If there is a child node coresponding to '$V_j = v_{jk}$'
         Then move to it,
         Otherwise, construct such a node and move to it.
   Add 'V_i, v_{il}' to annotation of the node (or root)
   Go back to the root of the discrimination tree.

The JDT algorithm is applied to a set S of variables in order to identify how these variables (when considered together and regardless of the constraints that apply among them) interact through the neighborhood with the rest of the CSP.

In the adaptation process our main interest is in seeing how much change propagates through the CSP when values are substituted for a variable. The objective is therefore to identify how many variables must change for a solution to remain valid after adaptation. The basic method is as follows:

– Start by constructing the Discrimination Tree (DT), which is the JDT applied to a set which contains a single variable, for the given values which we have to exchange.
– If the values are not in the annotation of the same branch, we reconstruct the JDT of a set formed by the starting variable and the variables found to make the difference in the branches for the considered values.
– Check if the actual JDT contains NPI values: if there exist annotations of the branches which contain at least one value for each variable from the input set and if there exists at least one variable which has at least two values (see Definition 5)
– If this is not the case, we try further to reconstruct the JDT for a new set S which includes the former S and the variables which make difference between the branches and separate some variables from the considered set to arrive with values in the annotation of the branch which contains the values of starting variable.

For the moment we have as a heuristic for choosing between branches: the algorithm selects the branch with the smallest differences to the refering branch and contains the starting variable with its set of pair values. So the basic principle is: whenever two values are not NPI values, we see where the branches in the tree differ. Those are variables one need to include in the set S (and thus take out of the tree) in order to create the NPI.

The algorithm was further extended so it could be applied to a set of starting variables with their corresponding pair of values in order to identify minimal NPI set.[2] In the following algorithm, the idea stays the same: we try to bring in the annotation of the same branch all the variables from the input with the corresponding values-pairs by including in the set the variables which make the difference between the branches.

Algorithm for Searching Minimal NPI Set(Inputset=$\{(V_1, d_k \in D_1), ..., (V_l, d_l \in D_l)\}$):
S = Inputset
repeat
   Construct JDT(S)
   Construct set DIFF = S \ A (set of variables from S which are not in the annotation of the branch B)
   Consider a variable $V_k \in$ DIFF
   Take from JDT(S) the branch which contains in the annotation V_k and has minimal difference relatively to B
   Add to set S the variables which makes the differences between these branches.
until DIFF!=0
Procedure Test Minimality (JDT(S), Inputset) return minimal NPI set
return minimal NPI set for values v_{i0} and v_{i1} of variable V_i.

The procedure *Test Minimality* checks if the NPI set found is minimal and if not returns the minimal one. It is implemented as follows: once we have created the NPI we look for a minimal set by successively adding to the tree variables taken out from the set S. When nothing can be added to the tree without destroying the NPI, we have a minimal NPI set.

For a given input set there might exist more then one minimal NPI set. This algorithm is complete in the sense that if there exists minimal NPI set for a given input set, it will find at least one of them.[3] Given a set S of size s, the time complexity of the algorithm is $O(n\,s\,(n\text{-}s)\,d^2)$, where n is the size of the CSP, and d is the size of the largest domain.

By applying the algorithm on the simple example from Figure 2 we obtain the following results:

From V_1 found: NPI: $V_1 = \{a, b\}$ $V_3 = \{a, b\}$	From V_2 found: –
From V_3 found: NPI: $V_1 = \{a, b\}$ $V_3 = \{a, b\}$ NPI: $V_3 = \{c\}$ $V_4 = \{c, e, f\}$ NPI: $V_3 = \{a, c\}$ $V_1 = \{a, b\}$ $V_4 = \{c, d, e, f\}$	From V_4 found: NI: $V_4 = \{e, f\}$ NPI: $V_3 = \{c\}$ $V_4 = \{c, e, f\}$ NPI: $V_4 = \{c, d, e, f\}$ $V_1 = \{a, b\}$ $V_3 = \{a, b, c\}$

---

[2] The generalization to a set of variables as a starting point is straightforward and obtained by replacing the input with the set of variables and their corresponding values pair and followed by constructing the JDT for this input set.
[3] All can be found by eliminating sets as they are found.

Minimal NPI set characteristics:

- In a CSP there are more minimal NPI sets for two given v_{i1} and v_{i2} values of a given variable V_i.
- To have a minimal NPI set by building the JDT for a given set of variables S we have to reach with all the variables in an annotation of the tree (end of one branch) such that all contain at least one value and at least one variable has more than one value (see Definition 5).
- The branch contains all the neighbor variables with at least one value; otherwise this NPI set does not interest as it means that there is no solution for the CSP.
- The set of the NPI variables has to be connected.
  Proof:
  Suppose we have a minimal NPI set S = { V_i, V_j, V_k } with NPI values NPI(S) = { $(V_i, \{ v_{i1}, v_{i2} \})$, $(V_j, \{ v_{j1}, v_{j2} ...\})$, $(V_k, \{ v_{k1}, v_{k2} ...\})$)} and variable V_k has no constraints with any of the other two variables. As there are no constraints that means that all the values of V_i and V_j are compatible with all the values of V_k. That means that there exists NPI values for the set S'={V_i, V_j } $\in$ S. That proves that S is not a minimal NPI set for the values v_{i1}, v_{i2} of the variable V_i.

4 Evaluation of NPI Sets

The performance of the algorithm for finding a minimal NPI set depends very much on the structure of the CSP problem. The following results are from tests analysing the number and *coverage* (size) of NPI sets detected w.r.t. varying CSP *configuration* (structure) by:

1. size of the problem: the number of variables.
2. the domains sizes of the variables.
3. the *density* of the problem: the ratio of the number of constraints relatively to the minimum and maximum number of constraints allowed in the given CSP, measured on a scale of 0.0 - 1.0.

As the current application is over mutual exclusion CSPs, the tightness of the constraints, the fraction of the combinatorially possible pairs that are allowed by the constraint between two variables, is not taken into consideration. It will be an interesting issue in further work for more general CSPs.

The number and coverage of NPI sets found for solutions is a critical measure of the potential performance of the adaptation engine since it indicates the degree of freedom the engine will have in adapting a particular solution. It therefore gives a general indication of the general difficulty of the case adaptation problem for certain problem characteristics.

An accurate study of evaluation of NI sets has been done by Choueiry, Faltings and Weigel in [13]. This study measured the occurrence of NI sets depending on the configuration of the CSP and found that:

- Only problems with low density allow NI values; the number of NI values become near to 0 for a density higher then 0.4 (this also corresponds to Benson and Freuder's results in [14]).
- For problems with low density the number of NI values increases with the number of resources.
- In general, the number of NI values decreases with the size of the problem.

These results indicate that NI interchangability is quite restricted in its domain of applicability and is one of the major reasons for attempting solutions based upon NPI sets (which are more likely to occur).

Performance is evaluated on randomly generated problems. Many CSP researchers use random instances to evaluate their constraint satisfaction algorithms.

Following the model of measuring the NI set as [13], we report the results only for problem sizes n = 10 and n = 20, while varying the density (dens-csp) in $\{0.1, 0.2, ..., 1\}$ of the CSP and the maximum domain size dom-size = $\{\frac{n}{10}, \frac{2n}{10}, ..., \frac{9n}{10}, n\}$. For each case, ten random problems were generated and then graphically represented by considering the measures described below.

Lets consider the CSP problem G = (V, E) as a constraint graph where V represents the vertices (variables) and E edges (constraints), and

- The density of the problem is: dens-csp = $\frac{e - e\_min}{e\_max - e\_min}$, where e represents the number of edges in the current CSP, e_min = $n - 1$ and e_max = $\frac{n(n-1)}{2}$, where n is the size of the problem CSP.
- nNPI(V_i) is the number of minimal NPI sets for variable V_i where we computed a minimal NPI set for each pair of values from the domain of V_i.
- avNPI(V_i) = $\frac{\sum_{k=1}^{nNPI} size(k)}{nNPI}$ is the average size of an minimal NPI set for variable V_i, where size(k) representes the number of variables in the current NPI set.
- $\|V\|$ is the number of variables which has minimal NPI sets over their entire domain (all possible pair values).

In the following we introduce the three criteria we used to measure the existence and maximality of NPI sets in the CSP.

Coverage: maximality of the NPI sets. m1 measures the "maximality" of the neighbourhood partial interchangeability (NPI sets) in the sense that we computed the average size of the minimal NPI set in a given CSP:

$$m1 = \frac{\sum_{k=1}^{\|V\|} avNPI(Vk)}{\|V\|}$$

We have the graphical representation in the figure 4 for problems of size 10 and in the figure 5 for problem of size 20. We can see that for problems with low density the coverage tends to 0. This means as expected that in low density problems exchanging the values of one variable do not propagate too much in the CSP (corresponds to NI, interestingly the threshold corresponds to the results cited above). This indicates that NI adaptation could be successfully applied here. Coverage increases with the number of resources.

The two metrics applied to measuring the number of NPI occurrences were as follows:

Occurrence 1: existence of the NPI sets. m2 measures the "occurrence" of NPI sets in a given CSP in the sense that it computes how many variables have minimal NPI set in rapport to the size of the problem.

$$m2 = \frac{\|V\|}{n}$$

Looking at the figures 6 and 7 we have the proof that NPI occurs often in any CSP configuration and increases with the density of the CSP as well as with the number of resources.

Occurrence 2: existence of the NPI sets. m3 measures the "occurrence" of NPI sets in the sense that it computes the average number of NPI sets per variable.

$$m3 = \frac{\sum_{k=1}^{\|V\|} nNPI(Vk)}{n}$$

The average number of NPI sets per variable depends in the same way as Occurrence1 on the configuration of the CSP, but is a better indicator w.r.t the density of the problem and highly dependent on the number of resources, see 8 and 9.

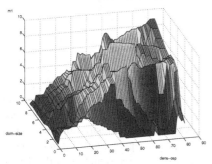

Fig. 4. Coverage of NPI sets for random generated CSPs with size 10.

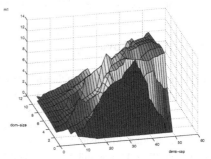

Fig. 5. Coverage of NPI sets for random generated CSP with size 20.

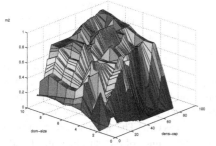

Fig. 6. Occurrence of NPI sets per variable in random CSPs with size 10.

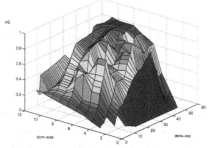

Fig. 7. Occurrence of NPI sets per variable in random CSPs with size 20.

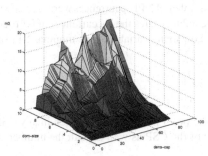   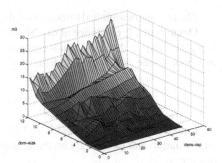

Fig. 8. Average number of NPI sets per variable in random CSPs with size 10.   **Fig. 9.** Average number of NPI sets per variable in random CSPs with size 20.

From the results we can conclude that on higher density problems the occurrence of NPI increases and thus the range of the adaptation increases as well with it, but in the same time the coverage is enlarged over the variables of the CSP. When the coverage enlarges, the effect of a change propagates further. Thus at a certain point, searching the NPI sets should be stopped. When the NPI set becomes too large, it might not bring any profit anymore as it would be equivalent to or even more costly than solving the problem from scratch. In a further work we will study how much a change should maximally propagate in a CSP to keep NPI profitable.

5   Related Work

There are some other approaches to seeing the adaptation problem as a constraint satisfaction problem. The solution of a new problem is built by satisfying the new constraints and by transforming a memorised solution. Hua, Faltings and Smith [15] proposed a case-based reasoner for architectural design where constraints restrict numerical relationships among dimensions. CADRE introduced the concept of *dimensional reduction*: before attempting to adapt a case, it constructs an explicit representation of the degrees of freedom available for adaptation. However, CADRE defined this approach only for numeric constraints. The adaptation method based on *dimensional reduction* has been tested successfully in the IDIOM project [16].

In the domain of discrete variables, the adaptation space is less obvious. We proposed here a method based on interchangeability which localise changes in discrete spaces and thus offers a reliable method for determining the closest solution.

Another approach for adaptation based on constraints over discrete domains was done by Purvis and Pu [17] in a case-based design problem solving domain. Their methodology formalises the case adaptation process in the sense of combining multiple cases in order to achieve the solution of the new problem, by applying repair-based CSP algorithm [18]. Our method do not rely only on the knowledge accumulated in the case base but also on the domain knowledge formulated as CSP. The approaches are different as by their method the constraints between specific values of the variables are stored in the case and we consider in the case only the solution of the new problem, while the constraints between variables are hold in an external module which contains the domain knowledge. We believe that our approach gives more flexibility to adaptation module but we will study in the future how to combine the two methods for improving the adaptation process.

6   Conclusions

Up until now, interchangeability has mostly been applied as a technique for enhancing search and backtracking, see [19] and [20]. It had not been effectively exploited as a technique for updating solutions. In this work we have studied how interchangeability can be applied for updating solutions with the goal of using it further in case adaptation. The work makes the following main contributions:

- A complete algorithm for detecting NPI sets which can be used to provide more flexible adaptation than NI based approach would.
- An evaluation of how far changes propagate in solutions to be adapted according to problem structure (investigating impact of density and size of the problem.) indicating:
  - Strong dependency on the density parameter of the CSP where NPI are more frequent in CSPs with high density.
  - Weak dependency on the domain sizes where NPI increases with the number of resources.
- Presentation of NPI based adaptation as a good candidate for general case adaptation strategies on a large class of problems

On the basis of this work we believe that Neighbourhood Partial Interchangeability has strong potential as an important strategy for identifying classes of equivalent solution as a basis for adaptation.

7   Further Work

Interesting future directions include:

- Detecting minimum set of changes in a given solution (the smallest from all the possible minimal NPIs).
- It is claimed that random problems are not very relevant in proving the results; so we consider as a step forward testing these algorithms and strategies on real-world problems.
- Improving the optimisation strategies for the finding minimal NPI set algorithm.
- Developing new algorithms for finding NPI values by decomposing the problem into different subproblems.
- Investigating the distribution of NPI sets in a solution by size of coverage (small coverage sets are useful to minimise overhead in adaptation).
- Classifying case bases of solutions by how re-usable ("adaptable") their solutions are according to density and other CSP configuration measures.

Acknowledgements. The authors are indebted to Steve Willmott and Djamila Sam-Haraud for valuable discussions and comments.

References

1. D. Leake. Case-Based Reasoning: Experiences, Lessons and Future Directions. In *AAAI Press*, 1996.
2. E. Freuder. *Constraint-based Reasoning*. MIT Press, 1994.
3. Van Hentenryck. Generality versus Specificity: An Experience with AI and OR Techniques. *In AAAI-88: Proceedings National Conference on Artificial Intelligence*, pages 660–664, 1988.
4. R. Dechter Y. El Fattah. Diagnosing tree-decomposable circuits. *In Proc. of the 14 th IJCAI, pg. 1742-1748*, 1995.
5. H. Krautz and B. Selman. Planning as Satisfiability. *In Proc. of the 10 th Ecai, pages 359-363*, Vienna, Austria, 1992.
6. M. Wallace. Applying constraints for scheduling. *In Constraint Programming, volume 131 of NATO ASI Series Advanced Science Institute Series. Springer Verlag*, 1994.
7. A. Mackworth. Constraint-based Design of Embeded Intelligent Systems. *In Constraints 2(1), pages 83-86, Vienna, Austria*, 1992.
8. R. Weigel and B. Faltings. Interchangeability for Case Adaptation in Configuration Problems. *In Proceedings of the AAAI98 Spring Symposium on Multimodal Reasoning, Stanford, CA, TR SS-98-04.*, 1998.
9. E. C. Freuder. Eliminating Interchangeable Values in Constraint Satisfaction Problems. In *In Proc. of AAAI-91*, pages 227–233, Anaheim, CA, 1991.
10. B. Y. Choueiry and G. Noubir. On the Computation of Local Interchangeability in Discrete Constraint Satisfaction Problems. In *Proc. of AAAI-98*, pages 326–333, Madison, Wiscowsin, 1998.
11. Z. Ruttkay. Fuzzy Constraint Satisfaction. *In 3rd IEEE Int. Conf. on Fuzzy Systems*, pages 1263–1268, 1994.
12. N. Neagu and B. Faltings. Constraint Satisfaction for Case Adaptation. *Proceedings of the Workshops at ICCBR'99*, pages III–35–III–41, 1999.
13. B. Choueiry B. Faltings, R. Weigel. Abstraction by Interchangeability in Resource Allocation. In *Proc. of the 14 th IJCAI-95*, pages 1694–1701, Montreal, Canada, 1995.
14. B.W. Benson and E. Freuder. Interchangeability Preprocessing can Improve Forward Checking Search. *In Proc. of the 10 th Ecai, pages 28-30, Vienna, Austria*, 1992.
15. B. Faltings K. Hua and I. Smith. CADRE: case-based geometric design. *In Artificial Intelligence in Engineering 10, pages 171-183*, 1996.
16. C. Lottaz I. Smith and B.Faltings. Spatial composition using cases: IDIOM. *In Proc. of the 1st International Conference in CBR, pages 88-97*, 1995.
17. L. Purvis and P. Pu. Adaptation using Constraint Satisfaction Techniques. *In Proc. of the 1st International Conference in CBR, pages 88-97*, 1995.
18. A. Philips S. Minton, M. Johnson and P. Laird. Minimizing Conflicts: A Heuristic Repair Method for Constraint Satisfaction and Scheduling Problems. *In Artificial Intelligence 58, pages 88-97*, 1995.
19. E. C. Freuder and D. Sabin. Interchangeability Supports Abstraction and Reformulation for Multi-Dimensional Constraint Satisfaction. In *In Proc. of AAAI-96*, pages 191–196, Portland, 1991.
20. A. Haselbock. Exploiting Interchangeabilities in Constraint Satisfaction Problems. *In Proc. of the 13 th IJCAI*, pages 282–287, 1993.

Ensemble Case-Based Reasoning: Collaboration Policies for Multiagent Cooperative CBR

Enric Plaza and Santiago Ontañón

IIIA, Artificial Intelligence Research Institute
CSIC, Spanish Council for Scientific Research
Campus UAB, 08193 Bellaterra, Catalonia (Spain).
{enric,santi}@iiia.csic.es, http://www.iiia.csic.es

Abstract. Multiagent systems offer a new paradigm to organize AI applications. Our goal is to develop techniques to integrate CBR into applications that are developed as multiagent systems. CBR offers the multiagent systems paradigm the capability of autonomously learning from experience. In this paper we present a framework for collaboration among agents that use CBR and some experiments illustrating the framework. We focus on three collaboration policies for CBR agents: Peer Counsel, Bounded Counsel and Committee policies. The experiments show that the CBR agents improve their individual performance collaborating with other agents without compromising the privacy of their own cases. We analyze the three policies concerning accuracy, cost, and robustness with respect to number of agents and case base size.

1 Introduction

Multiagent systems offer a new paradigm to organize AI applications. Our goal is to develop techniques to integrate CBR into applications that are developed as multiagent systems. Learning is a capability that together with autonomy is always defined as a feature needed for full-fledged agents. CBR offers the multiagent systems paradigm the capability of autonomously learning from experience. In this paper we present a framework for collaboration among agents that use CBR and some experiments illustrating the framework.

A distributed approach for CBR makes sense in different scenarios. Our purpose in this paper is to present a multiagent system approach for distributed case bases that can support these different scenarios. A first scenario is one where cases themselves are owned by different partners or organizations. This organizations can consider their cases as assets and they may not be willing to give them to a centralized "case repository" where CBR can be used. In our approach each organization keeps their private cases while providing a CBR agent that works with them. Moreover, the agents can collaborate with other agents if they keep the case privacy intact an they can improve their performance by cooperating. Another scenario involves scalability: it might be impractical to have a centralized case base when the data is too big.

D.W. Aha and I. Watson (Eds.): ICCBR 2001, LNAI 2080, pp. 437–451, 2001.
© Springer-Verlag Berlin Heidelberg 2001

Our research focuses on the scenario of separate case bases that we want to use in a decentralized fashion by means of a multiagent system, that is to say a collection of CBR agents that manage individual case bases and can communicate (and collaborate) with other CBR agents. In this paper we focus on three collaboration policies that improve the individual performance of CBR agents without compromising the agent's autonomy and the privacy of the case bases. These collaboration policies are a refinement of the general multiagent scenario of *Cooperative CBR* proposed in [9]. Particularly, CoopCBR established two cooperation modes, namely DistCBR and ColCBR[1]. The collaboration policies presented here are strategies that CBR agents can follow to improve their individual performance in the framework of the DistCBR cooperation mode.

The structure of the paper is as follows. Section 2 presents three policies the CBR agents can follow to improve their performance cooperating with other agents in a multiagent system. Then, section 3 presents the CBR method that the agents use in our current experiments. The experiments themselves are explained in section 4. The paper closes with related work and conclusion sections.

2 Policies for Cooperative CBR

A multiagent CBR ($\mathcal{MAC}$) system $\mathcal{M} = \{(A_i, C_i)\}_{i=1...n}$ is composed of n agents, where each agent A_i has a case base C_i. In the experiments reported here we assume the case bases are disjunct ($\forall A_i, A_j \in \mathcal{MAC} : C_i \cap C_j = \emptyset$), i.e. there is no case shared by two agent's case bases. This is just an experimental option and not a restriction on our model. In this framework we restrict ourselves to analytical tasks, i.e. tasks (like classification) where the solution is achieved by selecting from an enumerated set of solutions $K = \{S_1 ... S_K\}$. A case base $C_i = \{(P_j, S_k)\}_{j=1...N}$ is a collection of pairs problem/solution.

When an agent A_i asks another agent A_j help to solve a problem the interaction protocol is as follows. First, A_i sends a problem description P to A_j. Second, after A_j has tried to solve P using its case base C_j, it sends back a message that is either :sorry (if it cannot solve P) or a solution endorsement record (SER). A SER has the form $\langle \{(S_k, E_k^j)\}, P, A_j \rangle$, where the collection of *endorsing pairs* (S_k, E_k^j) mean that the agent A_j has found E_k^j cases in case base C_j endorsing solution S_k—i.e. there are a number E_k^j of cases that are relevant (similar) for endorsing S_k as a solution for P. Each agent A_j is free to send one or more endorsing pairs in a SER.

Before presenting the three policies for cooperative CBR, *Committee*, *Peer Counsel* and *Bounded Counsel* policies, we will introduce the voting mechanism.

---

[1] Summarily, in the DistCBR mode each CBR agent uses its own similarity assessment to retrieve cases while in the ColCBR cooperation mode an agent sends to other agents the *method* to assess the similarity in the process of case retrieval.

2.1 Voting Scheme

The voting scheme defines the mechanism by which an agent reaches an aggregate solution from a collection of SERs coming from other agents. The principle behind the voting scheme is that the agents vote for solution classes depending on the number of cases they found endorsing those classes. However, we do not want that agents having more number of endorsing cases may have an unbounded number of votes regardless of the votes of the other agents. Thus, we will define a normalization function so that each agent has one vote that can be for a unique solution class or fractionally assigned to a number of classes depending on the number of endorsing cases.

Formally, let $\mathcal{A}^t$ the set of agents that have submitted their SERs to agent A_i for problem P. We will consider that $A_i \in \mathcal{A}^t$ and the result of A_i trying to solve P is also reified as a SER. The vote of an agent $A_j \in \mathcal{A}^t$ for class S_k is

$$Vote(S_k, A_j) = \frac{E_k^j}{c + \sum_{r=1...K} E_r^j}$$

where c is a constant that on our experiments is set to 1. It is easy to see that an agent can cast a fractional vote that is always less or equal than 1. Aggregating the votes from different agents for a class S_k we have ballot

$$Ballot^t(S_k, \mathcal{A}^t) = \sum_{A_j \in \mathcal{A}^t} Vote(S_k, A_j)$$

and therefore the winning solution class is

$$Sol^t(P, \mathcal{A}^t) = arg \max_{k=1...K} Ballot(S_k, \mathcal{A}^t)$$

i.e., the class with more votes in total. We will show now three collaboration policies that use this voting scheme.

2.2 Committee Policy

In this policy the agents member of a $\mathcal{M}$AC system $\mathcal{M}$ are viewed as a committee. A CBR agent A_i that has to solve a problem P broadcast P to the other CBR agents in $\mathcal{M}$. Each CBR agent A_j sends a solution endorsement record $\langle\{(S_k, E_k^j)\}, P, A_j\rangle$ to A_i. The initiating agent uses the voting scheme above upon all SERs, i.e. its own SER and the SERs of all agents in the multiagent system. The final solution is the class with maximum number of votes.

The next two policies, *Peer Counsel* and *Bounded Counsel*, are based on the notion that an agent A_i tries to solve a problem P by himself and if A_i "fails" to find a "good" solution then A_i asks counsel to other agents in the $\mathcal{M}$AC system $\mathcal{M}$. Let $E_P^i = \{(S_k, E_k^i)\}$ the endorsement pairs the agent A_i computes to solve problem P. For an agent A_i to decide when it "fails" we require that each agent in $\mathcal{M}$ has a predicate *Self-competent*(P, E_P^i). This predicate determines whether or not the solutions endorsed in E_P^i allow the agent to conclude that there is a good enough solution for P.

2.3   Peer Counsel Policy

In this policy the agents member of a $\mathcal{MAC}$ system $\mathcal{M}$ try first to solve the problems they receive by themselves. Thus, if agent A_i receives a problem P and finds a solution that is satisfactory according to its own *Self-competent* predicate, the solution found is the final solution. However, if an agent A_i assesses that it is not capable of finding a reliable solution, then it asks the other agents in $\mathcal{M}$ to also solve the problem P.

The agents in $\mathcal{M}$ return to A_i their solution(s) inside their solution endorsement records and (as done in the committee policy) the final solution is the class with maximum number of votes.

2.4   Bounded Counsel Policy

In this policy the agents member of a $\mathcal{MAC}$ system $\mathcal{M}$ try first to solve the problems they receive by themselves, as in the previous *Peer Counsel* policy. However, when an agent A_i assesses that its own solution is not reliable, the *Bounded Counsel* Policy tries to minimize the number of questions asked to other agents in $\mathcal{M}$. Specifically, agent A_i asks counsel only to one agent, say agent A_j. When the answer of A_j arrives the agent A_i implements a termination check. If the termination check is true the result of the voting scheme is the global result, otherwise A_i asks counsel to another agent—if there is one left to ask, if not the process terminates and the voting scheme determines the global solution.

The termination check works, at any point in time t of the *Bounded Counsel* Policy process, upon the collection of solution endorsement records (SER) received by the initiating agent A_i at time t. Using the same voting scheme as before, Agent A_i has at any point in time t a plausible solution given by the winner class of the votes cast so far. Let V_{max}^t be the votes cast for the current plausible solution, $V_{max}^t = Ballot^t(Sol^t(P, \mathcal{A}^t), \mathcal{A}^t)$, the termination check $TC(V_{max}^t, \mathcal{A}^t)$ is a boolean function that determines whether there is enough difference between the majority votes and the rest to stop and obtain a final solution. In the experiments reported here the termination check function (applied when there are votes for more than one solution class) is the following

$$TC(V_{max}^t, \mathcal{A}^t) = \frac{V_{max}^t}{\left(\sum_{S_k \in K} Ballot(S_k, \mathcal{A}^t)\right) - V_{max}^t} \geq \eta$$

i.e. it checks whether the majority vote V_{max}^t is η times bigger than the rest of the ballots. After termination the global solution is the class with maximum number of votes at that time.

Policy Varieties. There may be small variations on this policies that follow the same overall schema. For instance, we are assuming that the global solution implies selecting a single alternative $S_k \in K$. However, depending on the task at hand, a ranked list of possible solutions might be a better option. We can easily adapt the present policies for tasks with ranked solutions: the final step in voting that takes the solution with maximum number of votes can be substituted by yielding k highest solutions ranked by their respective number of votes. Nevertheless, for the experiments reported later, it is more convenient for comparisons purposes to work with the hypothesis that a single solution is required.

We call this framework *Ensemble CBR* since a meaning of *ensemble* (Oxford Dictionary) is this: *"(Math) a group of systems with the same constitution but possibly with different states"*. From the point of view of the $\mathcal{MAC}$ framework, a system $\mathcal{M} = \{(A_i, C_i)\}_{i=1...n}$ performs Ensemble CBR when the CBR agents $A_1 \ldots A_n$ work with the CBR method but they have different experience (different case bases $C_1 \ldots C_n$).

The collaboration policies described here have been implemented on the **Noos** Agent Platform [8]. NAP consists of **Noos**, a representation language with support for case management and retrieval [1], and FIPA-compliant utilities for agent interaction. A multiagent system in NAP consists of the individual agents capabilities (like CBR) plus a specification of the agent roles and interaction protocols in the framework of agent-mediated institutions [8]. Cases are represented as feature terms in **Noos** and the next section introduces the CBR method used in our CBR agents.

3   Case-Based Reasoning Agents

In the following section we will introduce the concepts needed to explain LID [2], the CBR method used by the agents. First we will introduce feature terms, the representation used for cases; then we will explain the heuristic measure used by LID, and finally the LID algorithm will be described.

3.1   Representation of the Cases

LID handles cases represented as feature terms. *Feature Terms* (also called feature structures or ψ-terms) are a generalization of first order terms. The difference between feature terms and first order terms is the following: a first order term, e.g. $f(x, y, g(x, y))$ can be formally described as a tree and a fixed tree-traversal order. In other words, parameters are identified by position. The intuition behind a feature term is that it can be described as a labelled graph i.e. parameters are identified by name. A formal definition of feature terms is the following:

Given a signature $\Sigma = \langle S, \mathcal{F}, \leq \rangle$ (where S is a set of sort symbols that includes $\perp$; $\mathcal{F}$ is a set of feature symbols; and $\leq$ is a decidable partial order on S such that $\perp$ is the least element) and a set ϑ of variables, we define *feature terms* as an expression of the form:

$$\psi ::= X : s[f_1 \doteq \Psi_1 \ldots f_n \doteq \Psi_n] \tag{1}$$

where X is a variable in ϑ called the *root* of the feature term, s is a sort in S, the function *root(ψ)* returns the sort of the root, $f_1 \ldots f_n$ are features in $\mathcal{F}$,

$n \geq 0$, and each Ψ_i is a set of feature terms and variables. When $n = 0$ we are defining a variable without features. The set of variables occurring in ψ is noted as ϑ_ψ.

Sorts have an informational order relation ($\leq$) among them, where $\psi \leq \psi'$ means that ψ has less information than ψ' Nor equivalently that ψ is more general than ψ'. The minimal element ($\bot$) is called *any* and it represents the minimum information. When a feature has an unknown value it is represented as having the value *any*. All other sorts are more specific that *any*.

A *path* $\rho(X, f_i)$ is defined as a sequence of features going from the variable X to the feature f_i.

There is a *path equality* when two paths point to the same value. Path equality is equivalent to variable equality in first order terms.

The *depth* of a feature f in a feature term ψ with root X is the number of features that compose the path from the root X to f, including f, with no repeated nodes.

Given a particular maximum feature depth k, a *leaf feature* of a feature term is a feature f_i such that either 1) the depth of f_i is k or 2) the value of f_i is a term without features.

3.2   Heuristic Assessment of Feature Relevance

The heuristic used in LID is the minimization of the RLM distance [5]. The RLM distance assesses how similar are two partitions over a set of cases (in the sense that the lesser the distance the more similar they are). On the one hand, we have the correct partition given by the classified cases in the case base $C_i = \{(P_j, S_k)\}_{j=1...N_i}$ of agent A_i. Formally, the *correct partition* is the collection of sets $\Pi_C(C_i) = \{\pi_{S_k}\}_{k=1...K}$ where $\pi_{S_k} = \{P_z | (P_z, S_k) \in C_i\}$. On the other hand, each feature f that has legal values $v_1 ... v_{n^f}$ induces also a partition over the case base, namely a partition whose sets are formed by those cases that have the same value for feature f. Formally, the induced partition is the collection of sets $\Pi_f(C_i) = \{\pi_{v_j}^f\}_{j=1...n^f}$ where a set is $\pi_{v_j}^f = \{P_w | \exists S_k : (P_w, S_k) \in C_i \wedge P_w.f = v_j\}$.

In the following, we will use RLM distance over a variable case base B and not over the whole case base C_i. For a partition $\Pi_f(B)$ induced by a feature f, LID computes the RLM distance to the correct partition $\Pi_c(B)$. Given two partitions Π_f and Π_c of the case base B, the RLM distance between them is computed as follows:

$$RLM(\Pi_f, \Pi_c) = 2 - \frac{I(\Pi_f) + I(\Pi_c)}{I(\Pi_f \cap \Pi_c)}$$

where $I(\Pi_f)$ and $I(\Pi_c)$ measure the information contained in the partition Π_f and Π_c respectively and $I(\Pi_f \cap \Pi_c)$ is the mutual information of the two partitions.

Let Π_c be the correct partition and Π_f and $\Pi_{f'}$ the partitions induced by features f and f' respectively. We say that the feature f is *more discriminatory*

Function LID $(\mathcal{S}_\mathcal{D}, P, \mathcal{D}, K)$
   if stopping-condition$(\mathcal{S}_\mathcal{D})$
      then return $SER(\mathcal{S}_\mathcal{D}, P)$
      else $f_d :=$ Select-leaf $(p, \mathcal{S}_\mathcal{D}, K$)
            $\mathcal{D}' :=$ Add-path$(\rho(root(P), f_d), \mathcal{D})$
            $\mathcal{S}_{\mathcal{D}'} :=$ Discriminatory-set $(\mathcal{D}, \mathcal{S}_\mathcal{D})$
            LID $(\mathcal{S}_{\mathcal{D}'}, P, \mathcal{D}', C)$
   end-if
end-function

Fig. 1. The LID algorithm. $\mathcal{D}$ is the similitude term, $\mathcal{S}_\mathcal{D}$ is the discriminatory set of $\mathcal{D}$, K is the set of solution classes, $SER(\mathcal{S}_\mathcal{D}, P)$ constructs the Solution Endorsement Record of problem P.

than the feature f' if $RLM(\Pi_f, \Pi_c) < RLM(\Pi_{f'}, \Pi_c)$. In other words, when a feature f is more discriminatory than another feature f' the partition that f induces in B is closer to the correct partition Π_c than the partition induced by f'. Intuitively, the most discriminatory feature classifies the cases in B in a more similar way to the correct classification of cases.

3.3   The LID Method

The main steps of the LID algorithm are shown in Figure 1. Initially, LID of agent A_i receives as parameter $\mathcal{S}_\mathcal{D}$ the whole case base C_i and parameter $\mathcal{D}$ is empty.

The top down process of LID specializes the similitude term $\mathcal{D}$ by adding features to it. In principle, any of the features used to describe the cases could be a good candidate. Nevertheless, LID uses two biases to obtain the set F_l of features candidate to specialize the current similitude term $\mathcal{D}$. First, of all possible features in the domain $\mathcal{F}$, LID will consider only those features present in the problem P to be classified. As a consequence, any feature that is not present in P will not be considered as candidate to specialize $\mathcal{D}$. The second bias is to consider as candidates for specializing $\mathcal{D}$ only those features that are leaf features of P—i.e. a feature f_i such that either 1) the depth of f_i is equal to a depth threshold k or 2) the value of f_i is a term without features.

The next step of LID is the selection of a leaf feature $f_d \in F_l$ to specialize the similitude term $\mathcal{D}$. Let F_l be the set of leaf features candidates to specialize $\mathcal{D}$. Selecting the most discriminatory leaf feature in the set F_l is heuristically done using the RLM distance which is explained in section 3.2. Let us call the most discriminatory feature f_d.

The feature f_d is the leaf feature of path $\rho(root(P), f_d)$ in problem P. The specialization step of LID defines a new similitude term $\mathcal{D}'$ by adding to the current similitude term $\mathcal{D}$ the sequence of features specified by $\rho(root(P), f_d)$. After this addition $\mathcal{D}'$ has a new path $\rho(root(\mathcal{D}'), f_d)$ with all the features in the path taking the same value that they take in P. After adding the path ρ to $\mathcal{D}$, the new similitude term $\mathcal{D}' = \mathcal{D} + \rho$ subsumes a subset of cases in $\mathcal{S}_\mathcal{D}$, namely the discriminatory set $\mathcal{S}_{\mathcal{D}'}$ (the subset of cases subsumed by $\mathcal{D}'$).

Next, LID is recursively called with the discriminatory set $\mathcal{S}_{\mathcal{D}'}$ and the similitude term $\mathcal{D}'$. The recursive call of LID has $\mathcal{S}_{\mathcal{D}'}$ as first parameter (instead of $\mathcal{S}_\mathcal{D}$) because the cases that are not subsumed by $\mathcal{D}'$ will not be subsumed by further specialization. The process of specialization reduces the discriminatory set $\mathcal{S}_\mathcal{D}^n \subseteq \mathcal{S}_\mathcal{D}^{n-1} \subseteq \ldots \subseteq \mathcal{S}_\mathcal{D}^0$ at each step.

The result of LID solving a problem P is a Solution Endorsement Record $\langle \{(S_k, E_k^j)\}, P, A_j \rangle$. When the termination condition is that all cases in the discriminatory set $\mathcal{S}_\mathcal{D}$ belong to only one solution S_k, the SER is simply $\langle (S_k, M_k), P, A_j \rangle$, where $M_k = |\mathcal{S}_\mathcal{D}|$. Otherwise, the SER is built in a similar way for each solution class in $\mathcal{S}_\mathcal{D}$ computing the number of cases endorsing each class $M_k = |\{(P_i, S_k) \in \mathcal{S}_\mathcal{D}\}|$

4   Experiments

We use the marine sponge identification (classification) problem as our testbed. Sponge classification is interesting because the difficulties arise from the morphological plasticity of the species, and from the incomplete knowledge of many of their biological and cytological features. Moreover, benthological specialists are distributed around the world and they have experienced different benthos that spawn species with different characteristics due to the local habitat conditions. Therefore the task of marine sponge identification is inherently distributed among agents that have a non-complete experience of their domain of expertise. We have chosen to follow this scenario in our experiments. specifically we use a sample of marine sponges that will be distributed among a number of agents' cases bases in such a way that they are disjoint (no specimen is in more than one case base).

This scenario is quite different from other multimodel classification approaches where different (classifier) agents have access to all the examples and propose candidate classifications that later are aggregated into a global solution (see §5).

In order to compare the performance of the three policies, we have designed an experimental suite with a case base of 280 marine sponges pertaining to three different orders of the *Demospongiae* class (*Astrophorida, Hadromerida* and *Axinellida*). The goal of the agents is to identify the correct biological order given the description of a new sponge.

We have experimented with 3, 4, 5, 6 and 7 agents using LID as its CBR method. The results presented here are the result of the average of 5 10-fold cross validation runs. Therefore, as we have 280 sponges in our case base, in each run 252 sponges will form the training set and 28 will form the test set.

In an experimental run, training cases are randomly distributed to the agents (without repetitions, i.e. each case will belong to only one agent case base). Thus, if we have n agents and m examples in the training set, each agent should have about m/n exampes in its case base. Therefore increasing the number of agents

Table 1. Average precision and standard deviation for a case base of 280 sponges pertaining to three classes. All the results are obtained using a 10-fold cross validation.

Policy	3 Agents		4 Agents		5 Agents		6 Agents		7 Agents	
	μ	σ	μ	σ	μ	σ	μ	σ	μ	σ
Isolated Agents	83.21	6.71	82.50	6.44	79.43	8.44	77.93	7.55	75.78	6.82
Bounded Counsel	87.29	6.1	86.71	6.47	85.07	6.29	85.00	7.25	84.14	7.04
Peer Counsel	87.28	5.72	86.79	6.67	85.85	6.68	85.50	5.86	84.71	6.75
Committee	88.36	5.98	88.29	5.72	88.36	5.41	88.14	6.04	87.93	5.86

in our experiments their case-base size decreases. When all the examples in the training set have been distributed, the test phase starts.

In the test phase, for each problem P in the test set, we randomly choose an agent A_i and send P to A_i. Thus, every agent will only solve a subset of the whole test set. If testing the isolated agents scenario, A_i will solve the problem by itself without help of the other agents. And if testing any of the collaboraton policies, A_i will send P to some other agents.

4.1 Experimental Results

We can see (Table 1) that in all the cases we obtain some gain in accuracy compared to the isolated agents scenario. The Committee policy is always better than the others; however this precision has a higher cost since a problem is always solved by every agent. We evaluate costs later in this section. If we look at the cheaper policies *Bounded Counsel* and *Peer Counsel*, we can see that their accuracy are very similar. They both are much better than the isolated agents, and slightly worse than the Committee policy.

A small detriment of the system's performance is observable when we increase the number of agents. This is due to the fact that the agents have a more reduced number of training cases in their case bases. A smaller case base has the effect of obtaining less reliable individual solutions. However, the global effect of reducing accuracy appears on *Bounded Counsel* and *Peer Counsel* policies but not on the Committee policy. Thus, the Committee policy is quite robust to the effect of diminishing reliability individual solutions due to smaller case bases. This result is reasonable since the Committee policy always uses the information available from all agents.

In order to assess that *Committee*, *Peer Counsel* and *Bounded Counsel* policies obtain better accuracies that the isolated agents scenario, we have tested the statistical significance of the gains achieved by the collaboration policies. We have used the *signed rank* test with a confidence of 99% — meaning that we can be sure of the results with a confidence of the 99%. This test tells us when a method obtains numeric accuracies higher than another, and thus we can use it to compare the accuracies obtained by our collaboration policies. The results obtained are that all the collaboration policies are always significantly better than the isolated agents. *Committee* policy is always significantly better than

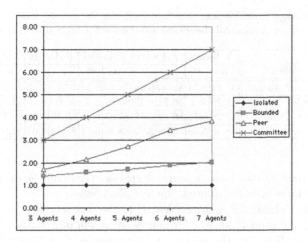

Fig. 2. Average cost (in euros) of solving a problem depending on the policy and number of agents.

Peer Counsel and *Bounded Counsel*. And the diferences between *Peer Counsel* and *Bounded Counsel* are not statistically significant.

A more realistic scenario in multiagent systems is to take into account the cost of cooperation among agents. Assuming that solving a problem has a cost, we have made some experiments where the nominal price for an agent solving a problem is 1 euro. Thus, an agent solving a problem by itself will have a cost of 1 euro—but if it asks two other agents to help the cost will be 3 euro. Having a cost on questions allows us to see how the different policies minimize the global cost and its tradeoff with accuracy. Figure 2 shows the average cost per problem in different policies and with a $\mathcal{MAC}$ composed of 3 to 7 agents. The cost is calculated over the same 5 10-fold cross validation runs. In the isolated agents scenario the cost for solving a problem is always 1 euro because only one agent is involved per problem. On the other side we have the Committee policy, where all the agents are asked to solve each problem; in this policy the cost increases linearly with the number of agents, i.e.: if we have 5 agents the cost is 5 euros. With the *Peer Counsel* policy the cost per problem is lower and increases much more slowly than in the Committee policy— with only a small detriment of the accuracy. Finally, the cost of *Bounded Counsel* policy is lower than the *Peer Counsel* policy —and also increases much slowly. This outcome is as expected since Bounded Counsel tries to minimize questions asked to other agents. Moreover, since the accuracy of *Peer Counsel* is not statistically different than *Bounded Counsel*, we should prefer *Bounded Counsel* for having a lower cost.

Related to the cost in euros we have the computational cost of solving a problem. Figure 3 shows the cost in computation time, specifically it shows the average time spent to solve a problem when all the agents are running in the same machine. We can see that there is a direct relation between the computational cost (time) and the cost in euros. As before the cheapest policy is *Bounded Counsel* (except for the isolated agents scenario) and the most expensive is the Committee policy. Now, observing Figure 3 it is apparent that having more agents reduces the time needed to compute a solution. This occurs in all policies except for the Committee policy where it's constant. The computation time has two components: the average retrieval time (in an agent) and the number of retrieval processes performed to solve a problem (the number of agents involved in solving a problem). The general trend in the reduction of computational time is due to the first component: the bigger the number of agents, the smaller the number of cases in a case base and, thus, the faster the retrieval process implemented by LID. On the other side, the number of retrieval processes involved can vary with the policy and the number of agents involved.

For instance, if we look with some detail the Figure 3 we may notice that *Peer Counsel* first starts decreasing and in the 6 and 7 agents columns it slightly increases again. If we look at the policy with detail, we can see that it's not so surprising. The fact is that when an agent has very few cases in the case base then more often its self-competence assessment indicates that the individual results are not reliable enough and has to ask counsel to the other peer agents. This effect is particularly noticeable in the *Peer Counsel* policy since it implies the agent will ask all the other agents. However, the *Bounded Counsel* is more robust; even though an agent with less cases tends to ask more often counsel we see in Figure 3 that the computation time is decreasing. The fact is that the first component (retrieval time) keeps decreasing with smaller case bases and the increasing number of counsels that are required are sufficiently restricted by the *Bounded Counsel* policy to prevent a worsening of the cost in computation time.

We have also tested the system with a subset of the whole case base consisting in 120 sponges pertaining to the same three biological orders. Given the reduced number of cases, in these experiments we have only considered a 3 agents system. As we can see in table 2 the results are similar to those obtained using 280 cases, including the cost reduction of the *Bounded Counsel* and *Peer Counsel* compared to Committee. The gain in efficiency is also observable in this case, and we can compare the time spent per problem using the Committee policy (1.88 sec) with the lower one needed by the *Bounded Counsel* policy (0.93 sec), that is very close to the time need in the isolated agents scenario.

Finally, as an extreme scenario of agents with very few cases we tested the Committee policy (being the most robust) with 16 agents. In this scenario, with 280 sponges using 10-fold cross-validation, an agent's case base has only about 17 sponges—i.e. about 5.6 examples that randomly belong to 3 solution classes. In this scenario the Committee policy still has an accuracy of about 83% while the isolated agents are only capable of about 64% accuracy. If we move towards a scenario of 25 agents (with about 11 cases per case base) the Committee policy still has an accuracy of about 82% while the isolated agents are only capable of about 60% accuracy. Clearly, in these extreme scenarios the other policies

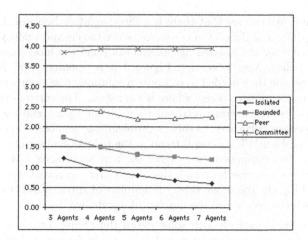

Fig. 3. Average time needed (in seconds) to solve a problem in the reported experiments.

(*Bounded Counsel* and *Peer Counsel*) are not appropriate. In fact, they can only make sense if the agents always assess their lack of self-competence and ask the other agents (that also will have very low self-competence assessments)—i.e. if both policies tend to work as the Committee policy asking counsel for every case to every agent.

5   Related Work

A general result on multiple model learning [4] demonstrated that if uncorrelated classifiers with error rate lower than 0.5 are combined then the resulting error rate must be lower than the one made by the individual classifiers. The BEM (*Basic Ensemble Method*) is presented in [7] as a basic way to combine continuous estimators, and since then many other methods have been proposed: *Stacking generalization, Cascade generalization, Bagging* or *Boosting* are some examples. However, all these methods do not deal with the issue of "partitioned examples" among different classifiers as we do—they rely on aggregating results

Table 2. Average precision and standard deviation for 3 agents and a case base of 120 sponges pertaining to three classes. All the results are obtained using a 10-fold cross validation.

Policy	μ	σ	Time	Cost
Isolated Agents	82.00	12.84	0.64 sec	1.00
Bounded Counsel	87.99	10.29	0.93 sec	1.48
Peer Counsel	88.83	9.40	1.08 sec	1.71
Committee	88.99	8.40	1.88 sec	3.00

from multiple classifiers that have access to *all* data. Their goal is to use multiplicity of classifiers to increase accuracy of existing classification methods. Our goal is to combine the decisions of autonomous classifiers (each one corresponding to one agent), and to see how can they cooperate to achieve a better behavior than when they work alone.

Usually, lazy learners (e.g. Nearest Neighbour) don't get benefited by any of the combination methods like *Bagging* or *Boosting*. Ricci and Aha propose in [10] a method to combine the decision of lazy learners. They create various NN classifiers, each one considering a different subset of features and then combine their results using ECOCs(Error-Correcting Output Codes). However, the case-base is not partitioned and each classifier works with all instances in the case-base.

When trying to combine decision through a voting scheme, the simplest way is a non-weighted voting combination, where all the agents have the same strength in the decision. The Naive Bayesian Classifiers (NBC) committees [12] proposal trains various NBC with the same training set but using different subsets of attributes, and then combine their predictions using some strategy (majority, etc). Again this approach does not deal with "partitioned examples". Moreover, usually the agent members of a committee can only cast a vote for one of the solution classes. The *Committee* CBR Policy is innovative in that the agents following it assign a fractional vote to each solution class in function of the number of relevant precedent cases found endorsing them.

The meta-learning approach in [3] is applied to partitioned data. They experiment with a collection of classifiers which have only a subset of the whole case base and they learn new meta-classifiers whose training data are based on predictions of the collection of (base) classifiers. They compare their meta-learning approach results with weighted voting techniques. The final result is an *arbitrator tree*, a centralized and complex method whose goal is to improve classification accuracy. We also work on "partitioned examples" but we assume no central method that aggregates results; moreover we assume a multiagent approach where communication and cooperation may have a cost that has to be taken into account.

Smyth and McKenna [11] propose a method to assess the competence of a case-base based on case coverage, case-base size and distribution of the cases. They measure the competence by finding *Competence Groups* (clusters of related cases) and measuring how each *Competence Group* is covered in the case-base. In our experiments, each agent compute its *self-competence* as a function of the number of cases endorsing the possible solution classes returned. That is because agents only need to assess the confidence degree of the answer to a specific problem. In [6] we propose an inductive technique that allows each agent to learn autonomously an individual *self-conpetence* function.

6   Conclusions and Future Work

We have presented a framework for cooperative CBR in multiagent systems. The framework is cooperative in that the CBR agents help each other to improve their individual performance. Since the agents improve with respect to their performance as isolated individual, cooperating is also in their individual interest—specially since the framework allows them to keep confidential their own cases. A major theme in multiagent systems is the *autonomy* of the agents. In our framework the agent autonomy is mainly ensured by two facts: i) the capability of each agent to determine whether or not itself is competent to solve a problem, and ii) the capability of each agent to integrate into a global solution for a problem the counsels given by other agents. In the experiments we have presented all agents used the same methods to implement these two capabilities. However, this option is just an experiment design decision, and a particular application that requires different biases by different agents is compatible with our framework.

Another issue is the generality of the cooperation policies and their dependence upon the CBR agents using LID. The cooperation policies depend only on the CBR agents being able to provide SERs (Solution Endorsement Records), so any CBR method that can provide that is compatible. For instance, CBR agent using k-nearest neighbour as a retrieval method could provide a SER for the k closest cases.

A natural evolution of this experimental setting is moving towards case-bases with higher volume in which learning *competence models* [9] of the involved agents is necessary. In higher volume case-bases the need for a distributed multiagent approach seems more practical than a completely centralized schema. A major difference from our current experimental setting is that the hypothesis that all agents have an unbiased sample of the data no longer holds. That is to say, with higher volume case-bases a CBR agent may be biased towards solving accurately a subset of all possible problems. For instance, a particular agent may solve often sponge identification problems *inside* the order of Astroforida—and very seldom problems inside the order of Axinellida. In this setting future work will investigate how CBR agents can learn *competence models* of other agents—e.g. which agent is competent in identifying a sponge inside the order of Astroforida. Competence models can guide an agent into asking counsel only (or mainly) to competent agents and to have this information into account when integrating solutions proposed by several agents. A relevant question here is whether it is possible to adapt the method in [11] to obtain the competence models of the other agents keeping the autonomy and the privacy of the individual case-bases.

Finally, we plan to lift the restriction of the case bases of the agents in a $\mathcal{MAC}$ system being disjunct. Basically, our idea is that agents could incorporate in their case bases some cases originally owned by other agents. The interesting question here is this: what strategy of case sharing can improve the overall $\mathcal{MAC}$ system performance —without every agent having in their case base every case known to the $\mathcal{MAC}$ system.

Acknowledgements. The authors thank Josep-Lluís Arcos and Eva Armengol of the IIIA-CSIC for their support and for the development of the Noos agent platform and the LID CBR method respectively. Support for this work came from CIRIT FI/FAP 2001 grant and projects TIC2000-1414 "eInstitutor" and IST-1999-19005 "IBROW".

References

[1] Josep Lluís Arcos and Ramon López de Mántaras. Perspectives: a declarative bias mechanism for case retrieval. In David Leake and Enric Plaza, editors, *Case-Based Reasoning. Research and Development*, number 1266 in Lecture Notes in Artificial Intelligence, pages 279–290. Springer-Verlag, 1997.

[2] E. Armengol and E. Plaza. Lazy induction of descriptions for relational case-based learning. In *Submitted*, 2001.

[3] Philip K. Chan and Salvatore J. Stolfo. A comparative evaluation of voting and meta-learning on partitioned data. In *Proc. 12th International Conference on Machine Learning*, pages 90–98. Morgan Kaufmann, 1995.

[4] L. K. Hansen and P. Salamon. Neural networks ensembles. *IEEE Transactions on Pattern Analysis and Machine Intelligence*, (12):993–1001, 1990.

[5] Ramon López de Mántaras. A distance-based attribute selection measure for decision tree induction. *Machine Learning*, 6:81–92, 1991.

[6] S. Ontañón and E. Plaza. Learning when to collaborate among learning agents. In *Submitted*, 2001.

[7] M. P. Perrone and L. N. Cooper. When networks disagree: Ensemble methods for hydrid neural networks. In *Artificial Neural Networks for Speech and Vision*. Chapman-Hall, 1993.

[8] E. Plaza, J. L. Arcos, P. Noriega, and C. Sierra. Competing agents in agent-mediated institutions. *Journal of Personal Technologies*, 2:212–220, 1998.

[9] Enric Plaza, Josep Lluís Arcos, and Francisco Martín. Cooperative case-based reasoning. In Gerhard Weiss, editor, *Distributed Artificial Intelligence Meets Machine Learning. Learning in Multi-Agent Environments*, number 1221 in Lecture Notes in Artificial Intelligence, pages 180–201. Springer-Verlag, 1997.

[10] Francesco Ricci and David W. Aha. Error-correcting output codes for local learners. In *European Conference on Machine Learning*, pages 280–291, 1998.

[11] Barry Smyth and Elizabeth McKenna. Modelling the competence of case-bases. In *EWCBR*, pages 208–220, 1998.

[12] Z. Zheng. Naive bayesian classifier committees. In *Proceedings of the 10th European Conference on Machine Learning, ECML'98*, volume 1398 of *LNAI*, pages 196–207. Springer Verlag, 1998.

MaMa: A Maintenance Manual for Case–Based Reasoning Systems

Thomas Roth–Berghofer[1] and Thomas Reinartz[2]

[1] tec:inno — empolis knowledge management GmbH,
Sauerwiesen 2, 67661 Kaiserslautern, Germany
thomas.roth-berghofer@empolis.com
[2] DaimlerChrysler AG, Research & Technology, FT3/AD,
P.O. Box 2360, 89013 Ulm, Germany
thomas.reinartz@daimlerchrysler.com

Abstract. In this paper, we consider Case–Based Reasoning (CBR) as a complex process. In order to perform such a complex process in a specific project, we argue that an appropriate process model helps to accomplish the process in a well–structured manner. We briefly review some existing process models to define the necessary concepts to specify a process model for CBR. Thereby, we identify several levels of abstraction for process definitions, and explain the role of concrete manuals at one of these levels. For one particular phase of the CBR process, namely the maintenance phase, we outline a maintenance manual and characterize some of its components. Initial experiences with the maintenance manual called MaMa illustrate the purpose of such a manual and indicate the usefulness of its application in specific projects.

Keywords: Case–Based Reasoning, CBR process, process model, maintenance, maintenance manual, methodology

1 Introduction

When Aamodt and Plaza defined the four–step cycle of Case–Based Reasoning (CBR) back in 1994 [1], CBR was still more a young art than a well–established engineering discipline. The four steps in their cycle, i.e., retrieve, reuse, revise, and retain, were sufficiently able to cover issues arising in early CBR applications, and already indicated directions for future research by that time. Since then, CBR has evolved from this state of a young art to a well–established engineering discipline which became available and applicable across many applications. Several tools for deployment of CBR solutions into practice exist, and many efforts have elaborated the different aspects of CBR including the discussion of broader perspectives on CBR in an engineering sense.

As CBR is now an engineering discipline, it is also reasonable to compare CBR to other engineering disciplines, and to make use of experiences in such related fields. One of the most intuitive analogies to other engineering disciplines is the relation of CBR to software engineering. The crucial point in this analogy — from our point of view — is the idea of a (software development) *process*. A well–structured process with clear descriptions of tasks and deliverables as well as the control flow between them enables practitioners to deploy solutions from engineering disciplines into their application.

D.W. Aha and I. Watson (Eds.): ICCBR 2001, LNAI 2080, pp. 452–466, 2001.
© Springer-Verlag Berlin Heidelberg 2001

Hence, we argue that it is necessary to define a well–structured CBR process in order to enable appropriate deployment of CBR solutions into practice.

In the light of this argumentation, we view Aamodt and Plaza's paper on the four–step CBR cycle as one of the early initiatives to define such a process for CBR (of course, there were earlier process descriptions, like a CBR flowchart by Riesbeck and Bain reprinted in [17]). By now, other research contributed to definitions of the CBR process, too. The possibly most important contribution to these efforts are the results of the two European projects INRECA I and II [3]. In the data mining community, we have seen a very similar history ending up in the CRoss–Industry Standard Process model for Data Mining (CRISP–DM) [4]. Both efforts share their attempt to transform these disciplines from art to well–structured engineering processes.

In this paper, we start to follow up this tradition of transition from less structured research ideas to well–established and well–specified techniques that are applicable in practice. Thereby, we focus on one particular aspect of CBR which is currently one of the most important research issues in CBR: maintenance.[1] The particular reason why we emphasize the maintenance aspect of CBR is that we feel that there is not yet a well–structured process description for CBR maintenance. However, as previous experience shows, we have to define such a process which clearly describes "what to do" and "how to do it" in maintenance of CBR systems if we expect practitioners to be able to deploy techniques in this area of CBR research.

We start the rest of the paper by a brief summary of concepts in two previous attempts to define process models, namely INRECA and CRISP–DM. We consolidate these concepts and adopt their characterization for our own purposes. Thereafter, we introduce a short broader perspective on CBR to show how maintenance in CBR fits into the overall CBR process. Then, we outline a process model for maintenance in CBR and exemplify its detailed description for a specific step in the maintenance phase. The fourth section is devoted to the maintenance manual for one particular class of CBR projects and initial experiences with this manual in a concrete project. Finally, we conclude the paper with a summary of this work and an outlook of issues for future work.

2   General Concepts for the Definition of Process Models

In this section, we briefly review the concepts of two different process models for two different disciplines. The INRECA methodology provides general process descriptions and example processes for CBR, whereas the CRISP–DM process model contains advice for performing data mining projects. Although the two processes specify the foundations for different disciplines, it is interesting to recognize the amount of overlapping ideas and the number of similar concepts. We consolidate the concepts of both approaches by re–using the best aspects of both INRECA and CRISP–DM for our own purpose of defining a maintenance manual for CBR.

2.1   INRECA and CRISP–DM

The INRECA methodology provides a data analysis framework for developing CBR solutions for successful applications in real–world industrial contexts [3]. It mainly con-

---

[1] Several workshops were dedicated totally or in part to this topic (e.g., [16], [20], or [9]). It is also an issue in software engineering, especially in the field of experience bases [10].

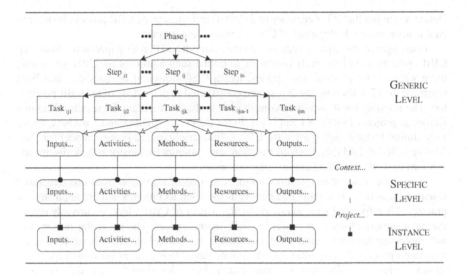

Fig. 1. Different Components of Process Definitions

sists of a collection of CBR development experiences, represented as software process models [19] and stored in an experience base of an experience factory [2].

In a similar vein, the CRISP–DM process model is a step–by–step guide to data mining. It mainly describes the life cycle of data mining projects at different levels of granularity. Thereby, CRISP–DM focuses more on the general applicable description of the entire process but does not provide specific application examples. In this way, CRISP–DM presents a more complete picture of data mining than INRECA does for CBR, but INRECA provides more details as it outlines several projects that were realized using the INRECA methodology.

Both approaches, INRECA and CRISP–DM, rely on descriptions at different levels of abstraction or generality, and both approaches divide the various stages of the CBR and data mining process, respectively, into smaller units which in turn are characterized by different components. We consolidate these two common aspects of both efforts in the following two subsections, and thereby introduce the concepts for the definition of the maintenance phase in CBR.

2.2   Different Levels of Abstraction — Hierarchical Breakdown

Both initiatives, INRECA and CRISP–DM, describe processes at different levels of abstraction; figure 1 presents the hierarchical breakdown into three different levels: *generic*, *specific*, and *instance*.

The top level of a process model is the *generic* level. We call the top level generic, because it is intended to be general enough to cover all possible project situations. The descriptions at the generic level are as complete and stable as possible. Complete means covering both the whole process and all possible applications. Stable means that the process model should be valid for yet unseen developments like new techniques. Note that in this section we are reporting on general concepts for process descriptions independent of the considered discipline. For INRECA, this discipline is CBR, whereas for CRISP–DM this discipline is data mining. For the purpose of this paper, this discipline is maintenance in CBR. However, examples in this section are all in the context of CBR.

The second level of a process model is the *specific* level. This level is the place to describe how actions of the generic level are carried out in certain specific situations. For example, if there exists a generic task called "add case" at the top level, the specific level describes different ways of executing this task in different situations. Hence, the specific level already makes specific assumptions about the class of projects and distinguishes different descriptions for different assumptions. We call a set of such assumptions *context* (see below).

Finally, the bottom level of the hierarchical breakdown is the *instance* level. It describes how tasks are (or were) performed and which results they produce (or produced) in a particular engagement. Following the example of "add case" above, the instance level contains the concrete description of how this task is (or was) performed in a specific project, i.e., how the case is (or was) actually added in this project. The instance level serves two different roles. First, it is the instance level where concrete project documentation takes place. And second, if new projects look for specific experiences for re–use, they search for descriptions at the instance level.

2.3 Mapping between Different Levels of Abstraction

The relation between the three different levels of abstraction is characterized by the *context* between generic and specific level and by a concrete *project* between specific and instance level.

The *context* consists of instantiations of one or more of the following dimensions: *type of CBR*, *type of CBR application*, *CBR tool*, and *affected knowledge containers*.

The *type of CBR* describes if we use a structural, textual, or conversational CBR approach (for an overview of this distinction, see [3]). The second dimension specifies the *type of CBR application*, e.g., diagnosis, help–desk, product search, etc. The *CBR tool* dimension states which CBR system is used, e.g., orenge, CBR–Works[2], eGain Knowledge[3], or Kaidara Commerce.[4] Finally, the fourth dimension informs which of the four *affected knowledge containers* of a CBR system, i.e., vocabulary, similarity measures, adaptation knowledge, or case base is involved [13].

Any instantiation of any of these dimensions builds a concrete context. For example, if you are an employee of a company which only uses CBR systems from tec:inno, your context is either using the CBR tool orenge or CBR–Works. This restriction makes some choices or alternatives at the generic level impossible. For instance, if a generic task "choose appropriate CBR tool" asks the project for a decision for a specific product

---

[2] orenge and CBR–Works are CBR shells from tec:inno — empolis knowledge management GmbH; see http://www.tecinno.com.

[3] eGain Knowledge (formerly k–Commerce Support Enterprise) is a product of eGain (formerly Inference); see http://www.egain.com.

[4] Kaidara Commerce (formerly part of the KATE suite) is one of the CBR systems sold by Kaidara; see http://www.kaidara.com.

to apply, then given the context above, this task is "choose between orenge and CBR–Works" at the specific level. The more information about the context becomes available, the more specific is the advice of a process model at the specific level.

The concrete facts within a project give even more insight and allow an even more specific re–use of experience. For example, if we are in the same context of the example above but we know that our project budget for the CBR tool of choice is fixed, this possibly leads to a choice of a CBR tool based on its price. So, if we randomly (!) assume orenge is twice as expensive as CBR–Works and our budget is able to cover the costs for CBR–Works but not for orenge, we automatically get to an instance level, where the specialized task "choose between orenge and CBR–Works" is obsolete. Consequently, the mapping from the specific to the instance level is driven by certain *project* constraints.

2.4   Components of Process Descriptions — Phases, Steps, and Tasks

INRECA as well as CRISP–DM use different components to build entities of a process model, and both approaches describe some entities at varying levels of granularity. For this paper, we make use of the following concepts.

At the top level, a process model is organized into a number of phases (see figure 1). Each *phase* covers a set of related steps. And each *step* again consists of several tasks. A *task* is the atomic unit of the description of a process model. Tasks appear at all levels of abstraction, whereas phases and steps (and their names) are only generic terms to group related issues at the next lower level of granularity.

Besides its name and its overall goal description, each task at each level of abstraction has several components: *inputs, activities, methods, resources,* and *outputs*. The *inputs* component describes whatever is necessary before a project can start with the respective task. Inputs cover "physical" objects such as data, documents, or available resources, as well as "logical" circumstances such as approved budget, successful review, or project out of its time plan. Similarly, the *outputs* of a task contain whatever a task produces or whatever the result of a task is. As for inputs, outputs are "physical" or "logical" outcomes.

Between inputs and outputs, a task comprises a series of *activities* that explain how to perform this task, i.e., how to get from the inputs component to the desired outputs component. Activities are basically more detailed actions that describe the contents of a task more precisely and that elaborate on the goal description of a task.

The *methods* component specifies concrete mechanisms that help to perform a single activity or a set of activities. For example, the Euclidian distance as a means of dissimilarity is a typical method. Of course, such methods are not necessarily technical methods but also management or organizational techniques. For example, a task possibly suggests utilizing specific project management control mechanisms to ensure the overall project success.

Finally, each task has a component for *resources*. Resources are required to perform a task. We distinguish between two types of resources. A resource is either a human resource (called *agent* in the INRECA methodology) which actively carries out activities within a task and which is responsible for producing the outputs, or alternatively a resource is a (software) *tool* which helps a human resource and which implements specific methods. For example, if we have a method Euclidian distance, we possibly also have a specific tool which supports an implementation of the Euclidian distance

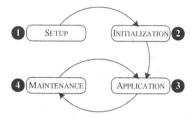

Fig. 2. A Global View on Case-Based Reasoning

to realize a similarity measure based on the Euclidian distance. Note that we do not replicate information on methods and resources as part of the inputs component although the availability of appropriate methods and sufficient resources to perform a task is also an important prerequisite before the project is able to start to work on a task.

We consider these five task components as the core elements of task descriptions. For each of these components, there exist various aspects that additionally play an important role when performing a task in the context of a concrete project. For example, for many methods and their implementations it is important to take into account the costs of computation. In some situations, limited resources, for instance, possibly make the application of some methods impossible since the respective implementations are too computationally expensive.

3 The Maintenance Process Model

In this section, we describe the maintenance phase of the CBR process model in terms of the concepts introduced in the previous section. In order to get an idea how the maintenance phase fits into the overall CBR process, we start this description by a short outline of a broader perspective on the entire CBR process which will better support the application of software engineering techniques.

3.1 A Broader Perspective on Case–Based Reasoning

The four–step CBR cycle presented by Aamodt and Plaza [1] describes deployed CBR systems. It does not include any phases or steps that explain how to build a success-ful CBR application or how to implement an appropriate CBR system. These aspects are partly covered in the INRECA methodology. For example, chapter four of the IN-RECA book describes nine specific guidelines for developing CBR applications ([3], p. 65ff). Thereby, the guidelines focus on management issues rather than organizational or technical challenges. From our point of view, these guidelines are an example for task descriptions of phases within the CBR process that appear before the deployment of a CBR system, and hence that come before the four steps of the CBR cycle by Aamodt and Plaza.

Figure 2 outlines a broader perspective on the CBR process that covers two specific phases to deal with all issues that come before the deployment of a CBR system. All in all, we identify four different phases at the top level of this more global CBR process model: *Setup, Initialization, Application,* and *Maintenance*. We call this process model the *SIAM* methodology for CBR.[5]

The *setup* phase in CBR contains all issues which a CBR project has to deal with in its early stages. For example, the INRECA methodology names specific tasks such as "define clear objectives", "aim at the customer", "make a purposive system design", "take maintenance seriously" etc. In CRISP–DM, the corresponding phase is business understanding and contains tasks such as "determine business objectives", "assess situation", "determine data mining goals", and "produce project plan". Other possible tasks within the setup phase include activities such as "build project team", "identify an internal sponsor", "select an appropriate CBR tool", "identify internal processes that affect the CBR project" etc. Basically, the setup phase incorporates all activities that are necessary to work on before the implementation of the CBR system starts.

The *initialization* phase then intends to implement the CBR system and to initially fill all the knowledge containers appropriately. Here, we can think of tasks such as "adapt user interface to customer's needs", "build an initial domain model", "acquire knowledge to create cases", "build an initial case base" and so on. At the end of this initialization phase, the CBR system is ready for real usage in the application domain.

At this stage of a CBR project, the two main and regularly iterating phases of the CBR process begin: application and maintenance. The *application* phase consists of the steps retrieve, reuse, and revise, whereas the *maintenance* phase comprises the steps retain, review and restore [15].

At this point, it is important to mention two essential points:

- For the first three phases of the CBR process, we also see the need for defining a complete process model using the concepts introduced above. However, we strongly believe that there exists enough material related to the concrete specification of these three phases — including the INRECA and CRISP–DM efforts among others — and that it is consequently more interesting to reason about the fourth phase which is not yet clearly defined at all.
- It is neither the purpose of this paper to define the three phases setup, initialization, and application in detail, nor do we claim that this distinction of these four phases is the final and best choice for separating issues occurring in a CBR project. The short description of the broader perspective above only emphasizes that there is a CBR process before and after the traditional four steps retrieve, reuse, revise, and retain.

Subsequently, we concentrate on the maintenance phase and outline the CBR process model for this phase in more detail. Particularly, we specify the review step and two of its tasks as part of the maintenance phase in order to exemplify how the concepts are used to define each step within the maintenance phase precisely.

3.2   The Maintenance Phase in Case–Based Reasoning — An Overview

One of the main motivations to deal with the maintenance phase in CBR in more detail and to define a more elaborated process for this phase of the CBR process, is the insight

---

[5] The metaphorical meaning of SIAM emphasizes that the two phases application and maintenance within CBR live together in a CBR project as Siamese twins.

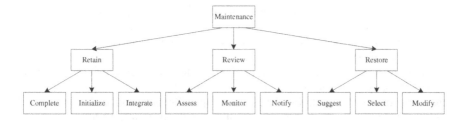

Fig. 3. Steps and Tasks at the Generic Level of the Maintenance Phase

that the INRECA methodology explicitly emphasizes the importance of maintenance but does neither provide specific task descriptions for maintenance nor does it contain any suggestions for methods how to perform these tasks.

In terms of the concepts introduced above, each step of the maintenance phase consists of three tasks. In order to perform a step, we have to accomplish all tasks of the given step. Figure 3 shows all steps and tasks of the maintenance phase at the generic level in their intended order of execution from left to right. This intended order of execution defines an idealized sequence which we recommend for applications. However, in specific contexts other orders or iterations between several tasks are possible as well. At this level of description (and throughout the rest of this paper), we do not further discuss the control flow between several different tasks.

Subsequently, we instead focus on a brief introduction of each task. Thereafter, we present more detailed task descriptions for the review step at both the generic and the specific level as an example of complete task specifications.

The Retain Step. Within the retain step, new knowledge enters the CBR system, and we have to incorporate this new knowledge into the appropriate knowledge containers. The new knowledge is either a result of the revise step or it is the outcome of any other part of the process that leads to new knowledge. The retain step comprises the tasks *complete*, *initialize*, and *integrate*.

The *complete* task ensures that the new knowledge is as complete as possible. For example, in a help–desk application, the complete task makes sure that a new help–desk case contains all necessary attachments. The complete task also covers the activities of extract as defined in [1]. The goal of these extract activities is to learn from the revise step. For example, you learn to remember why a proposed solution failed to solve the given problem.

After completion of the new knowledge item, its quality information is set up properly. This is the main goal of the *initialize* task.

Finally, the *integrate* task within the retain step of maintenance takes care of the correct index of the new knowledge item according to the knowledge structure of the CBR system [1]. Integrate also covers activities to actually store the new knowledge item in the respective knowledge container of the CBR system.

The Review Step. The overall purpose of the review step is to consider the current state of the CBR system, to assess its quality, and to invoke the next step within the maintenance phase if necessary. Therefore, the review step contains three different tasks: *assess*, *monitor*, and *notify*.

The *assess* task evaluates the quality of one of the knowledge containers of a CBR system. Usually, this evaluation requires computing values for some quality measures that are normally chosen during the phases setup and initialization earlier in the CBR process. Note that for the computation of such quality measures, we have to consider their execution costs.

One of the primary purposes of the *monitor* task is to display or visualize the results of the assess task. The monitor task occurs at regular intervals, ad hoc (e.g., if the user decides to accomplish this task right now), or according to pre-defined conditions [7]. Another important issue within the monitor task is to compare the assessment outcome with thresholds set up during the initialization phase, or to detect some trends using data mining technologies. Any statistical methods are possible candidates for methods to perform activities within this task.

At the end of the review step, it is the goal of the *notify* task to act on the results of the monitor task. One of the activities of the notify task is to decide whom to inform about necessary maintenance operations. For example, there are possibly defects of the CBR system that maintenance methods repair automatically, and there are possibly other issues that require a human to react on. Another activity of the notify task is to decide if there needs to be a repair operation immediately or if there is still time to wait for the next routine inspection.

The Restore Step. The restore step of the maintenance phase actually changes the contents of the CBR system to get back to a desired level of quality. If there is no need to go to the restore step since the quality values are still in good shape, we simply return to the next iteration of application and maintenance within the entire CBR process. The restore step also consists of three tasks: *suggest*, *select*, and *modify*.

The *suggest* task as the first task of the restore step computes potential restore operations that are able to modify the affected knowledge container in order to get back to the desired level of quality. Thereby, the result of the suggest task omits to propose operations that either do not solve the quality problem at hand or that are not possible within the given situation.

The first activity of the *select* task is to rank the suggested restore operations. One possible criterion for such a ranking are computational costs or the total number of operations that are necessary to return to a usable system state. Possibly, there are operations which the specific process is able to perform closely together to reduce maintenance costs. For example, if you have two cases, one is more general than the other, it does not make sense to generalize the more specific one such that the two cases become identical since then the restore operation introduces a new potential quality problem of two redundant cases.

Finally, the goal of the *modify* task as the last task within the maintenance phase of CBR is the execution of the selected restore operations using the suggested methods. As part of this modification, one particular activity of the modify task updates and adapts the quality information of the respective knowledge item or items. Thereafter, it is advisable

Table 1. The Assess Task at the Generic Level

Phase Maintenance	Step Review	Task Assess	Level Generic
Assess new knowledge items and the knowledge containers with quality measures.			

Inputs	– Knowledge item(s) related to the knowledge containers – Knowledge container(s)	Outputs	– Quality assessment of the knowledge containers
Activities	– Assess quality of the new knowledge item(s) – Assess quality of the new knowledge item(s) in relation to knowledge container(s) – Assess knowledge container(s)		
Methods	– Quality measures	Resources	– Maintenance engineer – Software tools which implement the methods

to return to the review step in order to check if the system is now in the desired state, or if there is still a need for repair operations.

3.3 Review as a Maintenance Step — Generic Task Descriptions

In order to exemplify concrete task descriptions and how we propose to structure their descriptions, we present two example tasks of the review step within the maintenance phase of CBR, namely, assess and monitor. For each of the remaining seven tasks in maintenance, we created task descriptions in a similar way. However, their contents are beyond the scope of this paper.

Table 1 and 2 show the task descriptions of assess and monitor at the generic level. Task descriptions share the same structure, and we recommend using a tabular presentation for the sake of an easy and quick access to the relevant information. Besides the task name, the top row classifies each task according to the corresponding phase, step, and level. The second row contains a short description of the task which states the overall purpose of the task. The third row provides the inputs and outputs of the task. In the fourth row, the project staff finds the activities which they have to accomplish in order to produce the outputs given the inputs. Finally, the bottom row indicates which methods and resources the project needs to perform the activities.

Note that we currently do not distinguish between different roles like the roles of the CBR administrator and the case author in the INRECA methodology. For a discussion of those roles during the development of a CBR application, we refer to [3] or [5]. For the moment, we only mention the role of a maintenance engineer as a resource who is responsible for setting up a maintenance plan and who executes this plan accordingly. In our view, a maintenance engineer is a skilled user but not necessarily an expert.

Table 2. The Monitor Task at the Generic Level

PHASE Maintenance	STEP Review	TASK Monitor	LEVEL Generic
Analyze quality assessment results.			
INPUTS: – Quality assessment results – Thresholds		OUTPUTS: – Analysis of quality assessment results	
ACTIVITIES: – Display quality assessment results – Visualize quality assessment results – Compare quality assessment results with thresholds – Analyze trends			
METHODS: – Monitor operators – Visualization techniques		RESOURCES: – Maintenance engineer – Software tools which implement the methods	

4   MAMA: A Maintenance Manual for CBR

In this section, we present the same two tasks, assess and monitor, of the review step in maintenance as examples of specific task descriptions that build the basic units to set up a concrete maintenance manual. [6]

4.1   On the Role of a Manual

In general, a manual (or handbook) provides concise information about a certain subject. A maintenance manual provides guidance in setting up maintenance, in our case, guidance for the maintenance of CBR systems. Such a manual must supply a step–by–step guide on how and when to perform tasks in order to get the CBR system back to a desired level of quality. Step–by–step means that it must help its user from setting up maintenance and initializing all necessary parameters up to performing the appropriate activities in certain situations. The designated user of the maintenance manual is the maintenance engineer mentioned above.

In contrast to the generic descriptions at the generic level, a manual appears at the specific level, and hence a manual is related to a specific context. This context is necessary since otherwise a manual is not able to provide concrete guidelines how to perform tasks of a process.

The SIAM methodology covers generic descriptions across all levels of abstraction. It defines the skeleton for the CBR process, for different manuals according to different contexts, as well as for instantiated project documentations. MAMA is one specific example of a manual for a concrete context.

---

[6] We keep the examples short due to the limited space in this paper. The complete task descriptions contain more details and elaborated textual characterizations of each item within a task.

Table 3. The Assess Task at the Specific Level

PHASE Maintenance	STEP Review	TASK Assess	LEVEL Specific
Assess new cases and the case base with quality measures.			
INPUTS	– New case(s) – Case base	OUTPUTS	– Quality assessment of the case base
ACTIVITIES	– Assess quality of the new case(s) – Assess quality of the new case(s) in relation to the case base – Assess the case base		
METHODS	– domain–dependent (e.g., competence, case base density, case base distribution [18]) and domain–independent (e.g., redundancy, consistency, minimality, and incoherence [11]) quality measures	RESOURCES	– Maintenance engineer – Dr. orenge [8]

4.2   MaMa for Orenge in Help–Desk Applications — Specific Task Descriptions

For the two task description examples of MaMa, we emphasize the following aspects of the respective context: type of CBR is textual CBR, type of CBR application is help–desk support, CBR tool is orenge, and the case base is the affected knowledge container.

Table 3 presents a possible specific description of the assess task with example methods for the measurement of the case and case base quality within the given context. We separate the example quality measurement methods into domain–dependent and domain–independent quality measures. Domain–dependent means that these quality measures use domain knowledge of the measured system for the computation of the quality values (e.g., similarity measures and adaptation knowledge), whereas domain–independent quality measures do not use any domain knowledge for the computation. Obviously, using domain knowledge for the computation of the quality of the assessed system bears some risks.

Table 4 provides a specific description of the monitor task with sample monitor operators taken from [12].

The two examples of specific task descriptions of MaMa use the same tabular templates as the generic ones. We are aware that the specific descriptions of assess and monitor are not necessarily complete in the sense that there exist other approaches to support the activities within these tasks. We imagine a toolbox for all tasks occurring during the maintenance phase of CBR that incorporates more methods. Note also that for each task at the generic level there exist many specializations at the specific level for varying contexts as well as many instantiations at the instance level for specific CBR projects.

Table 4. The Monitor Task at the Specific Level

PHASE Maintenance	STEP Review	TASK Monitor	LEVEL Specific
Analyze quality assessment results.			
INPUTS – Quality assessment results – Threshold τ		**OUTPUTS** – Analysis of quality assessment results	
ACTIVITIES – Display quality assessment results – Visualize quality assessment results – Compare quality assessment results with thresholds – Analyze trends			
METHODS – Monitor operators M_1, M_2, and M_3 [12]		**RESOURCES** – Maintenance engineer – Dr. orenge [8]	

4.3 Initial Experiences with MAMA

We developed the maintenance manual called MAMA presented in this paper within the context of a DaimlerChrysler research project [14]. In this project, the overall goal was to build an integrated multi–level help–desk support system that offers the benefits of structural and textual CBR as well as text mining technologies in combination. As the CBR tool of choice, we utilized two different systems, namely eGain's eGain Knowledge and tec:inno's orenge.

Another important aim of this project was the development of processes and methods to support the maintenance phase of CBR. Thereby, we focused our attention on the case base [6]. Consequently, the overall context within this project consists of the following instantiations of the context dimensions: structural and textual CBR, help–desk support, eGain Knowledge and orenge, and the case base. The outlined examples of MAMA in the previous section further emphasized aspects of textual CBR and the CBR tool orenge.

For the first phases of the SIAM methodology — setup, initialization, and application — we refer to Göker's contribution to the INRECA book (see [3], chapter 7, especially section 7.4, p. 123ff). This contribution exactly describes the tasks of the first three phases within this project at the specific level. Hence, we consider this chapter of the INRECA book as sort of an example of a manual for setup, initialization, and application, although this manual uses different concepts and formats to describe the contents of each task and the context is more general since it only focuses on CBR application type help–desk support.

For the maintenance phase, we developed and used the manual outlined in this paper. The specified tasks helped to organize the maintenance phase in a well–structured way, and with the help of the manual it was possible to optimize the case base of the integrated multi–level help–desk support system in cooperation with the CBR team at the application partner, debis SH PCM Computer AG. We presented specific maintenance methods and maintenance results in [12].

In summary, the maintenance manual called MaMa proved its purpose as a strong and helpful support to efficiently and effectively perform the maintenance phase of the CBR process.

5 Conclusions

In this paper, we presented an outline of MaMa, a maintenance manual for CBR in help–desk applications using the orenge CBR system. A manual is a specialization of a process model which describes different phases as well as their steps and tasks at a more abstract level that is applicable across all different contexts in CBR. Initial experiences with MaMa showed that such manuals are helpful to conduct concrete CBR projects, especially, to perform the not yet well–structured maintenance phase in CBR.

All concepts that were used to specify the manual were based on existing efforts to define process models. In particular, we reviewed the INRECA methodology for CBR and the CRISP–DM standard for data mining. We strongly believe that the presented view on CBR is an important contribution to make CBR an engineering discipline that is suitable for real–world applications and projects.

Future work includes efforts to continue the complete definition of different maintenance manuals for distinct contexts. Another crucial line of research is a closer link between the defined tasks and activities to available techniques. In this area, the manual possibly helps to detect where novel techniques are necessary since no method is yet accessible to work on some tasks. All in all, we encourage the CBR community to further discuss the CBR process, the broader perspective on CBR in general, and the maintenance phase in particular.

Acknowledgments. We thank the anonymous reviewers for their insights and helpful comments. We tried to incorporate their feedback in preparing this version of the paper. We consider their more fundamental remarks as valuable hints for future directions of this research.

References

1. Agnar Aamodt and Enric Plaza. Case–based reasoning: Foundational issues, methodological variations, and system approaches. *AI Communications*, 7(1):39–59, 1994.
2. V. R. Basili, G. Caldiera, and H. D. Rombach. The experience factory. In J. Marciniak, editor, *Encyclopedia of Software Engineering*, pages 469–476. Wiley, New York, 1994.
3. R. Bergmann, S. Breen, M. Göker, M. Manago, and S. Wess. *Developing Industrial Case–Based Resoning Applications: The INRECA Methodology*. Lecture Notes in Artificial Intelligence, LNAI 1612. Springer–Verlag, Berlin, 1999.
4. P. Chapman, J. Clinton, R. Kerber, Th. Khabaza, Th. Reinartz, C. Shearer, and R. Wirth. *CRISP–DM 1.0: Step–by–Step Data Mining Guide*. CRISP-DM consortium: NCR Systems Engineering Copenhagen (USA and Denmark) DaimlerChrysler AG (Germany), SPSS Inc. (USA) and OHRA Verzekeringen en Bank Groep B.V (The Netherlands), 2000.

5. Mehmet H. Göker and Thomas Roth-Berghofer. The development and utilization of the case–based help–desk support system HOMER. *Engineering Applications of Artificial Intelligence*, 12(6):665–680, December 1999.

6. Ioannis Iglezakis and Thomas Roth-Berghofer. A survey regarding the central role of the case base for maintenance in case–based reasoning. In Mirjam Minor, editor, *ECAI Workshop Notes*, pages 22–28, Berlin, 2000. Humboldt–University.

7. David B. Leake and David C. Wilson. Categorizing Case–Base Maintenance: Dimensions and Directions. In B. Smyth and P. Cunningham, editors, *Advances in Case–Based Reasoning, Proceedings of the 4th European Workshop on Case–Based Reasoning EWCBR 98*, pages 196–207. Springer–Verlag, 1998.

8. Rainer Maximini. Basesystem for maintenance of a case–based reasoning system. Diploma thesis, University of Kaiserslautern, 2001.

9. Mirjam Minor, editor. *Flexible Strategies for Maintaining Knowledge Containers, ECAI 2000 Workshop Notes*, Berlin, 2000. Humboldt University.

10. Markus Nick and Klaus-Dieter Althoff. Systematic evaluation and maintenance of experience bases. In Mirjam Minor, editor, *ECAI Workshop Notes – Flexible Strategies for Maintaining Knowledge Containers*, pages 14–21, Berlin, 2000. Humboldt University.

11. Thomas Reinartz, Ioannis Iglezakis, and Thomas Roth-Berghofer. On quality measures in case base maintenance. In Enrico Blanzieri and Luigi Portinale, editors, *Advances in Case–Based Reasoning, Proceedings of the 5th European Workshop on Case–Based Reasoning EWCBR 2000*, pages 247–259. Springer–Verlag, 2000.

12. Thomas Reinartz, Ioannis Iglezakis, and Thomas Roth-Berghofer. Review and restore for case base maintenance. *Computational Intelligence: Special issue on maintaining case–based reasoning systems*, 17(2):214–234, 2001.

13. Michael M. Richter. The knowledge contained in similarity measures. Invited Talk at the IC-CBR'95, 1995. http://wwwagr.informatik.uni-kl.de/~lsa/CBR/Richtericcbr95remarks.html.

14. Thomas Roth-Berghofer and Ioannis Iglezakis. Developing an integrated multilevel help–desk support system. In Mehmet H. Göker, editor, *Proceedings of the 8th German Workshop on Case–Based Reasoning*, pages 145–155, DaimlerChrysler, FT3/KL, 2000.

15. Thomas Roth-Berghofer and Ioannis Iglezakis. Six steps in case–based reasoning: Towards a maintenance methodology for case–based reasoning systems. In Hans-Peter Schnurr, Steffen Staab, Rudi Studer, Gerd Stumme, and York Sure, editors, *Professionelles Wissensmanagement — Erfahrungen und Visionen*, pages 198–208, Aachen, 2001. Shaker–Verlag.

16. Sascha Schmitt and Ivo Vollrath, editors. *Challenges for Case–Based Reasoning — Proceedings of the ICCBR'99 Workshops*. Centre for Learning Systems and Applications, University of Kaiserslautern, 1999.

17. Stephen Slade. CBR: A research paradigm. *AI Magazine*, 12(1):42–55, 1991.

18. Barry Smyth and Elizabeth McKenna. Modelling the competence of case–bases. In B. Smyth and P. Cunningham, editors, *Advances in Case–Based Reasoning, Proceedings of the 4th European Workshop on Case-Based Reasoning EWCBR 98*, pages 208–220. Springer-Verlag, 1998.

19. M. Verlage and H. D. Rombach. Directions in software process research. *Advances in Computers*, 41:1–61, 1995.

20. Ian Watson. Workshop on automating the construction of case–based reasoners at IJCAI'99, 1999. http://www.ai--cbr.org/ijcai99/workshop.html.

Rough Sets Reduction Techniques for Case-Based Reasoning

Maria Salamó and Elisabet Golobardes

Enginyeria i Arquitectura La Salle, Universitat Ramon Llull,
Psg. Bonanova 8, 08022 Barcelona, Spain
{mariasal,elisabet}@salleurl.edu

Abstract. Case Based Reasoning systems are often faced with the problem of deciding which instances should be stored in the case base. An accurate selection of the best cases could avoid the system being sensitive to noise, having a large memory storage requirements and, having a slow execution speed. This paper proposes two reduction techniques based on Rough Sets theory: Accuracy Rough Sets Case Memory (AccurCM) and Class Rough Sets Case Memory (ClassCM). Both techniques reduce the case base by analysing the representativity of each case of the initial case base and applying a different policy to select the best set of cases. The first one extracts the degree of completeness of our knowledge. The second one obtains the quality of approximation of each case. Experiments using different domains, most of them from the UCI repository, show that the reduction techniques maintain accuracy obtained when not using them. The results obtained are compared with those obtained using well-known reduction techniques.

1 Introduction and Motivation

Case-Based Reasoning (CBR) systems solve problems by reusing the solutions to similar problems stored as cases in a case memory [19] (also known as case-base). However, these systems are sensitive to the cases present in the case memory and often its good accuracy rate depends on the significant cases stored. Therefore, in CBR systems it is important to reduce the case memory in order to remove noisy cases. This reduction allows us to achieve a good generalisation accuracy.

In this paper we present an initial approach to two different reduction techniques based on Rough Sets theory. Both reduction techniques was introduced into our Case-Based Classifier System called BASTIAN. Case-Based Reasoning and Rough Sets theory have usually been used separately in the literature.

The first one, Case-Based Reasoning [19,10], is used in a wide variety of fields and applications (e.g. diagnosis, planning, language understanding). We use Case-Based Reasoning as an automatic classification system.

On the other hand, Rough Sets theory [16] is a Data Mining technique. The main research trends in Rough Sets theory -which tries to extend the capabilities of reasoning systems- are: (1) the treatment of incomplete knowledge; (2) the management of inconsistent pieces of information; and (3) the manipulation of

D.W. Aha and I. Watson (Eds.): ICCBR 2001, LNAI 2080, pp. 467–482, 2001.

various levels of representation, moving from refined universes of discourse to coarser ones and conversely.

The reduction techniques proposed are: Accuracy Rough Sets Case Memory (AccurCM) and Class Rough Sets Case Memory (ClassCM). Both Rough Sets reduction techniques use the reduction of various levels of information. From those levels of information we extract relevant cases. The first technique, AccurCM, extracts an accuracy measure to capture the degree of completeness of our knowledge. The second one, ClassCM, obtains the quality of approximation of each case. It expresses the percentage of possible correct decisions when the case classifies new cases.

The paper is structured as follows: section 2 introduces related work; next, section 3 explains the Rough Sets theory; section 4 details the proposed Rough Sets reduction techniques; section 5 describes the Case-Based Classifier System used in this study; section 6 exposes the testbed of the experiments and the results obtained; and finally, section 7 presents the conclusions and further work.

2   Related Work

Case-Based Reasoning systems solve problems by reusing a corpus of previous solving experience stored (set of training instances or cases T) as a case memory of solved cases t. Reduction techniques are applied in Case-Based Reasoning systems for two main reasons: (1) to reduce storage requirements by increasing execution speed, and (2) to avoid sensitivity to noise. Thus, a performance goal for any CBR system is the maintenance of a case memory T maximizing coverage and minimizing case memory storage requirements. Reduction techniques remove instances of T obtaining a new training set S, $S \subseteq T$, that aims to maintain the generalization performance as well as reduce the storage requirements.

Many researchers have addressed the problem of case memory reduction [26]. Related work on pruning a set of cases comes from the pattern recognition and machine learning community, most of them through studies of *nearest neighbour algorithm* (NNA), and *Instance-Based Learning* (IBL) methods.

The first kind of approaches to the reduction of the case memory are commonly known as *nearest neighbours editing* rules. Most algorithms look for a subset of cases S of the original case memory T. The first approach was *Condensed Nearest Neighbour* (CNN) [9], which ensures that all cases in T are classified correctly, though it does not guarantee a minimal set and it is sensitive to noise. *Selective Nearest Neighbour* (SNN) [20] extends CNN such that every member of T must be closer to a member of S of the same class than to any member of T (instead of S) of a different class. SNN is more complex than other reduction techniques and its learning time is significantly greater; it is also sensitive to noise. *Reduced Nearest Neighbour* (RENN) [6] removes an instance from S if any other instance in T is misclassified by the instances remaining in S. RENN is computationally more expensive than CNN, but it is able to remove noisy instances while retaining border cases (i.e. cases that are placed at the boundaries of two classes). *Edited Nearest Neighbour* rule (ENN)[26], removes noisy instances, and maintains internal cases and close border ones. *Variable Similarity Metric* (VSM)[13], removes instances depending on a confidence level and all the K nearest neighbours. VSM is able to remove noisy instances and internal instances and retains border ones.

The second kind of approaches are related to Instance Based Learning Algorithms (IBL) [1]. IB1 is a simple implementation of NNA. IB2 is an incremental algorithm that does not necessarily classify all the instances correctly because it is sensitive to noise. IB2 is similar to CNN; it retains border points while it eliminates cases that are surrounded by members of the same class. IB3 improves IB2 retaining only those cases that have *acceptable* bounds. IB3 produces higher reduction than IB2 and higher accuracy. It also reduces sensitivity to noise. IB4 extends IB3, by building a set of attribute weights for each class.

There is another way to approach this problem. There are systems that modify the instances themselves, instead of simply deciding which ones to keep. RISE [3] treats each instance as a rule that can be generalised. EACH [23] introduced the *Nested Generalized Exemplars* (NGE) theory, in which hyperrectangles are used to replace one or more instances, thus reducing the original training set.

Another approach to instance pruning systems are those that take into account the order in which instances are removed [26]. DROP1 is similar to RNN and RISE, with some differences. DROP1 removes an instance from S (where $S = T$ originally) if at least as many of its associates in S would be classified correctly without it. This heuristic has some problems with noisy instances, which DROP2 tries to solve by removing an instance from S if at least as many of its associates in T would be classified correctly without it. DROP3 is designed to filter noise before sorting the instances. DROP4 is a more careful noise filter. Finally, DROP5 modifies DROP2 trying to smooth the decision boundary.

Finally, researchers have also focused on increasing the overall competence, *the range of target problems that can be successfully solved*, of the case memory through case deletion [24]. Strategies have been developed for controlling case memory growth through methods such as competence-preserving deletion [24] and failure-driven deletion [18], as well as for generating compact case memories through competence-based case addition [25,28]. Leake and Wilson [11] examine the benefits of using fine-grained performance metrics to directly guide case addition or deletion. This method is specially important for task domains with non-uniform problem distributions. Finally, a case-base maintenance method that avoids building sophisticated structures around a case-base or complex operations is presented by Yang and Wu [27]. Their method partitions cases into clusters where the cases in the same cluster are more similar than cases in other clusters. Clusters can be converted to new smaller case-bases.

3   Rough Sets Theory

Zdzislaw Pawlak introduced Rough Sets theory in 1982 [16,17]. The idea of Rough Sets consists of the approximation of a set by a pair of sets, called the lower and the upper approximation of this set. In fact, these approximations are inner and closure operations in a certain topology. These approximations are generated by the available data about the elements of the set. The nature of Rough Sets theory makes them useful for reducing knowledge, extracting dependencies in knowledge, reasoning about knowledge, pattern recognition, etc.

We use Rough Sets theory for reducing and extracting the dependencies in knowledge. This reduction of knowledge is the basis for computing the relevance of instances into the Case-Based Classifier System. We use that relevance in two different ways. The first one is **Accuracy Rough Sets Case Memory** and the second one is **Class Rough Sets Case Memory**.

First of all, we incorporate some concepts and definitions. Then, we explain how to obtain the dependencies, in order to select the set of instances.

Basic Concepts and Definitions

We have a **Universe** (U) (finite not null set of objects that describes our problem, i.e. the case memory). We compute from our universe the **concepts** (objects or cases) that form partitions. The union of all the *concepts* make the entire Universe. Using *all the concepts* we can describe all the **equivalence relations** (R) over the universe U. Let an equivalence relation be a *set of features* that describe a specific concept. U/R is the family of all **equivalence classes** of R.

The universe and the relations form the **knowledge base** (K), defined as $K = < U, \hat{R} >$. Where $\hat{R}$ is the family of equivalence relations over U. Every relation over the universe is an elementary concept in the knowledge base. All the concepts are formed by a set of equivalence relations that describe them. Thus, we search for the minimal set of equivalence relations that defines the same concept as the initial set.

DEFINITION 1 (INDISCERNIBILITY RELATIONS)
$IND(\hat{P}) = \bigcap \hat{R}$ where $\hat{P} \subseteq \hat{R}$. The indiscernibility relation is an equivalence relation over U. Hence, it partitions the concepts (cases) into equivalence classes. These sets of classes are sets of instances indiscernible with respect to the features in P. Such a partition is denoted as $U/IND(P)$. In supervised machine learning, the sets of cases indiscernible with respect to the class attribute contain the cases of each class.

4   Rough Sets as Reduction Techniques

In this section we explain how to reduce the case memory using the Rough Sets theory. We obtain a minimal case memory unifying two concepts: (1) approximation sets of knowledge and (2) reduction of search space. These two concepts are the basis for the AccurCM and ClassCM reduction techniques.

Both reduction techniques deal with cases containing continuous, nominal and missing features. Rough Sets reduction techniques perform search approximating sets by other sets and both proposals are global. Global means that we select the representative knowledge without taking into account which class the cases classify. AccurCM computes an accuracy measure. ClassCM computes the classification accuracy measure of each case in the representative knowledge. We want to remark that AccurCM and ClassCM can be used in multiclass tasks.

First of all, this section explains how to approximate and reduce knowledge. Next, it describes the unification of both concepts to extract the reduced set of cases using two policies: (1) Accuracy Rough Sets Case Memory (AccurCM), and Class Rough Sets Case Memory (ClassCM).

4.1   Approximating and Reducing the Knowledge

Approximations of Set. This is the main idea of Rough Sets, to approximate a set by other sets. The condition set contains all cases present in the case memory. The decision set presents all the classes that the condition set has to classify. We are searching for a subset of the condition set able to classify the same as the initial set, so it approximates the same decision set. The following definitions explain this idea.

Let $K =< U, \hat{R} >$ be a knowledge base. For any subset of cases $X \subseteq U$ and an equivalence relation $R \subseteq IND(K)$ we associate two subsets called: Lower $\underline{R}X$; and Upper $\overline{R}X$ approximations. If $\underline{R}X=\overline{R}X$ then X is an *exact set* (definable using subset R), otherwise X is a **rough set** with respect to R.

DEFINITION 2 (LOWER APPROXIMATION)
The lower approximation, defined as: $\underline{R}X = \bigcup\{Y \in U/R : Y \subseteq X\}$ is the set of all elements of U which can certainly be classified as elements of X in knowledge R.

DEFINITION 3 (UPPER APPROXIMATION)
The upper approximation, $\overline{R}X = \bigcup\{Y \in U/R : X \bigcap Y \neq \emptyset\}$ is the set of elements of U which can possibly be classified as elements of X, employing knowledge R.

EXAMPLE 1
If we consider a set of 8 objects in our Universe, $U = \{x_1, x_2, x_3, x_4, x_5, x_6, x_7, x_8\}$, using $\hat{R} = (A, B, C, D)$ as a family of equivalence relations over U. Where $A = \{x_1, x_4, x_8\}$, $B = \{x_2, x_5, x_7\}$, $C = \{x_3\}$ and $D = \{x_6\}$. And we also consider 3 subsets of knowledge X_1, X_2, X_3. Where $X_1 = \{x_1, x_4, x_5\}$, $X_2 = \{x_3, x_5\}$, $X_3 = \{x_3, x_6, x_8\}$.

The lower and upper approximations are:
$\underline{R}X_1 = \emptyset$ and $\overline{R}X_1 = A \bigcup B = \{x_1, x_2, x_4, x_5, x_7, x_8\}$
$\underline{R}X_2 = C = \{x_3\}$ and $\overline{R}X_2 = B \bigcup C = \{x_2, x_3, x_5, x_7\}$
$\underline{R}X_3 = C \bigcup D = \{x_3, x_6\}$ and $\overline{R}X_3 = A \bigcup C \bigcup D = \{x_1, x_3, x_4, x_6, x_8\}$

Reduct and Core of knowledge. This part is related to the concept of reduction of the search space. We are looking for a reduction in the feature search space that defines the initial knowledge base. Next, reduction techniques apply this new space to extract the set of cases that represents the new case memory.

Intuitively, a **reduct** of knowledge is its essential part, which suffices to define all concepts occurring in the considered knowledge, whereas the **core** is the most important part of the knowledge.

Let $\hat{R}$ be a family of equivalence relations and $R \in \hat{R}$. We will say that:

- R is *indispensable* if $IND(\hat{R}) \neq IND(\hat{R} - \{R\})$; otherwise it is *dispensable*. $IND(\hat{R} - \{R\})$ is the family of equivalence $\hat{R}$ extracting R.
- The family $\hat{R}$ is *independent* if each $R \in \hat{R}$ is *indispensable* in R; otherwise it is *dependent*.

DEFINITION 4 (REDUCT)
$\hat{Q} \in \hat{R}$ is a reduct of $\hat{R}$ if : $\hat{Q}$ is *independent* and $IND(\hat{Q}) = IND(\hat{R})$. Obviously, $\hat{R}$ may have many reducts. Using $\hat{Q}$ it is possible to approximate the same as using $\hat{R}$. Each reduct has the property that a feature can not be removed from it without changing the indiscernibility relation.

DEFINITION 5 (CORE)
The set of all indispensable relations in $\hat{R}$ will be called the *core* of $\hat{R}$, and will be denoted as: $CORE(\hat{R}) = \bigcap RED(\hat{R})$. Where $RED(\hat{R})$ is the family of all reducts of $\hat{R}$. The core can be interpreted as the set of the most characteristic part of knowledge, which can not be eliminated when reducing the knowledge.

EXAMPLE 2
If we consider a set of 8 objects in our Universe, $U = \{x_1, x_2, x_3, x_4, x_5, x_6, x_7, x_8\}$, using $\hat{R} = \{P, Q, S\}$ as a family of equivalence relations over U. Where P can be colours (green, blue, red, yellow); Q can be sizes (small, large, medium); and S can be shapes (square, round, triangular, rectangular). For example, we can suppose that the equivalence classes are:
$U/P = \{ (x_1, x_4, x_5), (x_2, x_8), (x_3), (x_6, x_7) \}$
$U/Q = \{ (x_1, x_3, x_5), (x_6), (x_2, x_4, x_7, x_8) \}$
$U/S = \{ (x_1, x_5), (x_6), (x_2, x_7, x_8), (x_3, x_4) \}$
As can be seen, every equivalence class divides the Universe in a different way. Thus the relation $IND(R)$ has the following equivalence classes:
$U/IND(\hat{R}) = \{(x_1, x_5), (x_2, x_8), (x_3), (x_4), (x_6), (x_7)\}$
The relation P is indispensable in $\hat{R}$, since:
$U/IND(\hat{R} - \{P\}) = \{ (x_1, x_5), (x_2, x_7, x_8), (x_3), (x_4), (x_6) \} \neq U/IND(\hat{R})$.
The information obtained removing relation Q is equal, so it is dispensable in $\hat{R}$.
$U/IND(\hat{R} - \{Q\}) = \{ (x_1, x_5), (x_2, x_8), (x_3), (x_4), (x_6), (x_7) \} = U/IND(\hat{R})$.
Hence the relation S is also dispensable in R.
$U/IND(\hat{R} - \{S\}) = \{ (x_1, x_5), (x_2, x_8), (x_3), (x_4), (x_6), (x_7) \} = U/IND(\hat{R})$.
That means that the classification defined by the set of three equivalence relations P, Q and S is the same as the classification defined by relation P and Q or P and S. Thus, the reducts and the core are: $RED(\hat{R}) = \{(P, Q), (P, S)\}$ and $CORE(\hat{R}) = \{P\}$.

4.2   Reducing the Set of Cases

Accuracy Rough Sets Case Memory and Class Rough Sets Case Memory, the methods which we propose, use the information of reducts and core to select the cases that are maintained in the case memory.

Accuracy Rough Sets Case Memory. This reduction technique computes the *Accuracy reducts* coefficient (AccurCM) of each case in the knowledge base (case memory). The coefficient $\mu(t)$ is computed as:

$$For\ each\ instance\ t\ \in\ T\ it\ computes:$$

$$\mu(t) = \frac{card\ (\ \underline{P}(t))}{card\ (\ \overline{P}\ (t))} \tag{1}$$

Where $\mu(t)$ is the relevance of the instance t; P is the set that contains the reducts and core obtained from the original data; T is the condition set; *card* is the cardinality of one set; and finally $\underline{P}$ and $\overline{P}$ are the lower and upper approximations, respectively.

For each case we apply the following algorithm, where the confidenceLevel is the $\mu(t)$ value computed:

1. *Algorithm SelectCases*
2.   *confidenceLevel = 0.0*
3.   *for each case*
4.   *select the case if it accomplishes this confidenceLevel*
5.   *end for*
6. *end Algorithm*

In this algorithm the *confidenceLevel* is set at to zero, in order to only select the set of cases that accomplishes this space region. Inexactness of a set of cases is due to the existence of a borderline region. The greater a borderline region of a set, the lower the accuracy of the set. The accuracy measure expresses the degree of completeness of our knowledge about the set P. This reduction technique obtains the minimal set of instances present in the original case memory. The accuracy coefficient explains if an instance is needed or not, so $\mu(t)$ is a binary value. When the value $\mu(t)= 0$ it means an internal case, and a $\mu(t) =1$ means a borderline case. This technique does not guarantee that all classes will be present in the set of instances selected. However, it guarantees that all the internal points that represent a class will be included. The accuracy expresses the percentage of possible correct decisions when classifying cases employing knowledge P. This measure approximates the *coverage* of each case.

Class Rough Sets Case Memory. In this reduction technique we use the *quality of classification* coefficient (ClassCM), computed using the core and reducts of information. The classification accuracy coefficient $\mu(t)$ is computed as:

$$For\ each\ instance\ t\ \in\ T\ it\ computes:$$

$$\mu(t) = \frac{card\ (\ \underline{P}(t))}{card\ (\ all\ instances)} \tag{2}$$

Where $\mu(t)$ is the relevance of the instance t; P is the set that contains the reducts and core obtained from the original data; T is the condition set; *card* is the cardinality of one set; and finally $\underline{P}$ is the lower approximation.

The ClassCM coefficient expresses the percentage of cases which can be correctly classified employing the knowledge t. This coefficient ($\mu(t)$) has a range of values between 0 to 1, where 0 means that the instance classifies incorrectly the range of cases that belong to its class and a value of 1 means an instance that classifies correctly the range of cases that belong to its class. In this reduction technique the cases that obtain a higher value of $\mu(t)$ represent cases that classify correctly the cases, but these cases are to be found on the search space boundaries.

This reduction technique guarantees a minimal set of instances of each class also applying the following algorithm, where the *confidenceLevel* is the $\mu(t)$ computed previously:

1. *Algorithm SelectCases*
2.   *confidenceLevel = 1.0 and freeLevel = ConstantTuned (set at 0.01)*
3.   *select all possible cases that accomplish this confidenceLevel*
4.   *while all classes are not selected*
5.   *confidenceLevel = confidenceLevel - freeLevel*
6.   *select all possible cases that accomplish this confidenceLevel*
7.   *end while*
8. *end Algorithm*

Due to the range of values, it is possible to select not only the best set of instances as ClassCM computes. We select a set of instances depending on the confidence level of $\mu(t)$ that we compute. The confidence level is reduced until all the classes have a minimum of one instance present in the new case memory.

The introduction of these techniques into a CBR system is explained in section 5.1.

5   Description of the BASTIAN System

The study described in this paper was carried out in the context of BASTIAN, a *case-BAsed SysTem In clAssificatioN* [22,21]. This section details two points: (1) the main capabilities of the BASTIAN platform used in the study carried out in this paper, in order to understand what kind of CBR cycle has been applied in the experimental analysis; (2) how to introduce the Rough Sets reduction techniques into a Case-Based Reasoning System.

The BASTIAN system is an extension of CaB-CS (**C**ase-**B**ased **C**lassifier **S**ystem) system [5]. The BASTIAN system allows the user to test several variants of CBR (e.g. different retrieval or retain phases, different similarity functions and weighting methods). For details related to the BASTIAN platform see [22]. BASTIAN has been developed in JAVA language and the system is being improved with new capabilities.

BASTIAN Platform Capabilities

The system capabilities are developed to work separately and independently in co-operation with the rest. Each capability described in the general structure has a description of the general behaviour that it has to achieve. The main goal is to obtain a general structure that could change dynamically depending on the type of Case-Based Reasoner we want to develop. The main capabilities are:

- The *CaseMemory* defines the behaviour for different case memory organizations. In this study, we use a list of cases. Our main goal in this paper is to reduce the case memory; for this reason, we have not focus on the representation used by the system.
- The *SimilarityFunctionInterface* concentrates on all the characteristics related to similarity functions. It allows us to change the similarity function dynamically within the system. In this paper, we use the *K*-Nearest Neighbour similarity function.
- The *WeightingInterface* contains the main abilities to compute the feature relevance in a Case-Based Classifier System [22]. It is related to the *RetrievalInterface* and the *SimilarityFunctionInterface*. This paper does not use them in order to test the reliability of our new reduction techniques. Further work will consist of testing the union of both proposals.
- The {*Retrieval, Reuse, Revise, Retain*}*Interface* are the four phases of the CBR cycle. These interfaces describe the behaviour of each phase.
  - *Retrieval interface* is applied using *K=1* and *K=3* values in the *K*-NN policy.
  - {*Reuse, Revise, Retain*} *interface* are applied choosing a standard configuration for the system, in order to analyse only the reduction techniques.

Our aim, is to improve the generalisation accuracy of our system by reducing the case memory in order to remove the noisy instances and maintain border points [26].

5.1   Rough Sets Inside the BASTIAN Platform

Figure 1 shows the meta-level process when incorporating the Rough Sets into the CBR system. The Rough Sets process is divided into three steps:

The first one discretises the instances, it is necessary to find the most relevant information using the Rough Sets theory. In that case, we discretise continuous features using [4] algorithm. The second step searches for the reducts and the core of knowledge using the Rough Sets theory, as was described in section 4. Finally, the third step uses the core and the reducts of knowledge to decide which cases are maintained in the case memory using AccurCM and ClassCM techniques, as explained in 4.2.

Rough Sets theory has been introduced as reduction techniques in two phases of the CBR cycle. The first phase is the *start-up* phase and the second one is the *retain* phase. The system adds a previous phase *Startup*, which is not in the Case-Based Reasoning cycle.

This initial phase prepares the initial start-up of the system. It computes the new initial case memory from the training case memory; this new case memory is used by the retrieval phase later. The retain phase computes a new case memory from the case memory if a new case is stored. In this paper, we focus our reduction techniques on the retrieval phase. The code of Rough Sets theory in the Case-Based Reasoning has been implemented using a public Rough Sets Library [7].

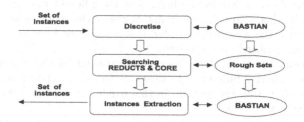

Fig. 1. High level process of *Rough Sets*.

6   Empirical Study

This section is structured as follows: first, we describe the testbed used in the empirical study; then we discuss the results obtained from the reduction techniques based on Rough Sets. We compare the results compared to CBR system working with the original case memory. And finally, we also compare the results with some related learning systems.

6.1   Testbed

In order to evaluate the performance rate, we use twelve datasets. Datasets can be grouped in two ways: *public* and *private*. The datasets and their characteristics are listed in table 1.

Public datasets are obtained from the UCI repository [15]. They are: *breast cancer Wisconsin (breast-w), glass, ionosphere, iris, sonar and vehicle.* **Private datasets** comes from our own repository. They deal with *diagnosis* of breast cancer and *synthetic* datasets. Datasets related to diagnosis are *biopsy* and *mammogram. Biopsy* [5] is the result of digitally processed biopsy images, whereas *mammogram* consists of detecting breast cancer using the microcalcifications present in a mammogram [14,8]. In *mammogram* each example contains the description of several μCa present in the image; in other words, the input information used is a set of real valued matrices. On the other hand, we use two *synthetic* datasets to tune up the learning algorithms, because we knew their solutions in advance. *MX11* is the eleven input multiplexer. TAO-*grid* is a dataset obtained from sampling the TAO figure using a grid [12].

These datasets were chosen in order to provide a wide variety of application areas, sizes, combinations of feature types, and difficulty as measured by the accuracy achieved on them by current algorithms. The choice was also made with the goal of having enough data points to extract conclusions.

All systems were run using the same parameters for all datasets. The percentage of correct classifications has been averaged over stratified ten-fold cross-validation runs, with their corresponding standard deviations. To study the performance we use paired t-test on these runs.

Table 1. Datasets and their characteristics used in the empirical study.

	Dataset	Reference	Samples	Numeric feats.	Simbolic feats.	Classes	Inconsistent
1	*Biopsy*	BI	1027	24	-	2	Yes
2	*Breast-w*	BC	699	9	-	2	Yes
3	*Glass*	GL	214	9	-	6	No
4	*Ionosphere*	IO	351	34	-	2	No
5	*Iris*	IR	150	4	-	3	No
6	*Mammogram*	MA	216	23	-	2	Yes
7	*MX11*	MX	2048	-	11	2	No
8	*Sonar*	SO	208	60	-	2	No
9	*TAO-Grid*	TG	1888	2	-	2	No
10	*Vehicle*	VE	846	18	-	4	No

6.2 Experimental Analysis of Reduction Techniques

Table 2 shows the experimental results for each dataset using CBR system Rough Sets reduction techniques: AccurCM and ClassCM, IB2, IB3 and IB4 [1]. This table contains the mean percentage of correct classifications (%PA)(*competence of the system*) and the mean storage size (%MC). We want to compare the results obtained using the proposed ClassCM reduction technique with those obtained by these classifier systems. Time performance is beyond the scope of this paper.

Both Rough Sets reduction techniques have the same initial concept: to use the reduction of knowledge to measure the accuracy (AccurCM) or the quality of classification (ClassCM).

Although reduction is important, we decided to use these two different policies in order to maintain or even improve, if possible, prediction accuracy when classifying a new case. That fact is detected in the results. For example, the *vehicle* dataset obtains good accuracy as well as reduces the case memory, in both techniques. However, the case memory reduction is not large.

There are some datasets that obtain a higher reduction of the case memory but decrease the prediction accuracy, although this reduction in not significant.

Table 2. Mean percentage of correct classifications and mean storage size. Two-sided paired t-test (p = 0.1) is performed, where a • and ○ stand for a significant improvement or degradation of our ClassCM approach related to the system compared. Bold font indicates the best prediction accuracy.

Ref.	CBR		AccurCM		ClassCM		IB2		IB3		IB4	
	%PA	%CM	%PA	%CM	%PA	%CM	%PA	%CM	%PA	%CM	%PA	%CM
BI	83.15	100.0	75.15•	2.75	**84.41**	1.73	75.77○	26.65	78.51•	13.62	76.46•	12.82
BC	96.28	100.0	94.56	58.76	**96.42**	43.95	91.86•	8.18	94.98	2.86	94.86	2.65
GL	**72.42**	100.0	58.60•	23.88	71.12	76.11	62.53•	42.99	65.56•	44.34	66.40•	39.40
IO	90.59	100.0	88.60•	38.98	**92.59**	61.00	86.61•	15.82	90.62	13.89	90.35	15.44
IR	96.0	100.0	94.00○	96.50	87.40	8.85	93.98○	9.85	91.33	11.26	**96.66**	12.00
MA	64.81	100.0	**66.34•**	81.56	59.34	37.50	66.19	42.28	60.16	14.30	60.03	21.55
MX	78.61	100.0	68.00•	0.54	78.74	99.90	**87.07○**	18.99	81.59	15.76	81.34	15.84
SO	84.61	100.0	75.48•	33.01	**86.05**	67.05	80.72	27.30	62.11•	22.70	63.06•	22.92
TG	95.76	100.0	**96.34○**	95.39	86.97	13.14	94.87○	7.38	95.04○	5.63	93.96○	5.79
VE	67.37	100.0	64.18•	34.75	**68.42**	65.23	65.46•	40.01	63.21•	33.36	63.68•	31.66

Comparing AccurCM and ClassCM, the most regular behaviour is achieved using ClassCM. This behaviour is due to its own nature, because it introduces all the border cases classifying the class correctly into the reduced case memory, as well as the internal cases needed to complete all classes. AccurCM calculates the border points of the case memory. AccurCM calculates the degree of completeness of our knowledge, which can be seen as the *coverage* [25]. AccurCM points out the relevance of classification of each case.

ClassMC reduction technique obtains on average a higher generalisation accuracy than IBL, as can be seen in table 2. There are some datasets where ClassCM shows a significant increase in the prediction accuracy. The performance of IBL algorithms declines when case memory is reduced. CBR obtains on average higher prediction accuracy than IB2, IB3 and IB4.

On the other hand, the mean storage size obtained for ClassCM is higher than that obtained when using IBL schemes (see table 2). IBL algorithms obtain a higher reduction of the case memory. However, IBL performance declines, in almost all datasets (e.g. *Breast-w*, *Biopsy*). This degradation is significant in some datasets, as happens with the *sonar* dataset. Our initial purpose for the reduction techniques was to reduce the case memory as much as possible, maintaining the generalisation accuracy. We should continue working to obtain a higher reduction on the case memory.

To finish the empirical study, we also run additional well-known reduction schemes on the previous data sets. The reduction algorithms are: CNN, SNN, DEL, ENN, RENN, DROP1, DROP2, DROP3, DROP4 and DROP5 (a complete explanation of them can be found in [26]). We use the same data sets described above but with different ten-fold cross validation sets. We want to compare the results obtained using the proposed ClassCM reduction technique with those obtained by these reduction techniques. Tables 3 and 4 show the mean prediction accuracy and the mean storage size for all systems in all datasets, respectively.

Table 3 shows the behaviour of our ClassCM reduction technique in comparison with CNN, SNN, DEL, ENN and RENN techniques. The results are on average better than those obtained by the reduction techniques studied. RENN

Table 3. Mean percentage of correct classifications and mean storage size. Two-sided paired t-test (p = 0.1) is performed, where a • and ○ stand for a significant improvement or degradation of our ClassCM approach related to the system compared. Bold font indicates the best prediction accuracy.

Ref.	ClassCM		CNN		SNN		DEL		ENN		RENN	
	%PA	%CM	%PA	%CM	%PA	%CM	%PA	%CM	%PA	%CM	%PA	%CM
BI	**84.41**	1.73	79.57•	17.82	78.41•	14.51	82.79•	0.35	77.82•	16.52	81.03•	84.51
BC	96.42	43.95	95.57	5.87	95.42	3.72	**96.57○**	0.32	95.28	3.61	**97.00○**	96.34
GL	**71.12**	76.11	67.64	24.97	67.73	20.51	64.87•	4.47	68.23	19.32	68.66	72.90
IO	**92.59**	61.00	88.89•	9.94	85.75•	7.00	80.34•	1.01	88.31•	7.79	85.18•	86.39
IR	87.40	8.85	**96.00○**	14.00	94.00○	9.93	**96.00○**	2.52	91.33	8.59	**96.00○**	94.44
MA	59.34	37.50	61.04	25.06	63.42○	18.05	62.53○	1.03	63.85○	21.66	**65.32○**	66.92
MX	78.74	99.90	89.01○	37.17	89.01○	37.15	68.99•	0.55	85.05○	32.54	**99.80○**	99.89
SO	**86.05**	67.05	83.26	23.45	80.38	20.52	77.45•	1.12	85.62	19.34	82.74	86.49
TG	86.97	13.14	94.39○	7.15	94.76○	6.38	87.66	0.26	**96.77○**	3.75	95.18○	96.51
VE	68.42	65.23	**69.74**	23.30	69.27	19.90	62.29•	2.55	66.91	20.70	68.67	74.56

improves the results of ClassCM in some data sets (e.g. *Breast-w*) but its reduction on the case memory is lower than ClassCM.

Table 4. Mean percentage of correct classifications and mean storage size. Two-sided paired t-test (p = 0.1) is performed, where a • and ○ stand for a significant improvement or degradation of our ClassCM approach related to the system compared. Bold font indicates best prediction accuracy.

Ref.	ClassCM		DROP1		DROP2		DROP3		DROP4		DROP5	
	%PA	%CM	%PA	%CM	%PA	%CM	%PA	%CM	%PA	%CM	%PA	%CM
BI	**84.41**	1.73	76.36•	26.84	76.95•	29.38	77.34•	15.16	76.16•	28.11	76.17•	27.03
BC	**96.42**	43.95	93.28	8.79	92.56	8.35	96.28	2.70	95.00	4.37	93.28	8.79
GL	**71.12**	76.11	66.39	40.86	69.57	42.94	67.27	33.28	69.18	43.30	65.02•	40.65
IO	**92.59**	61.00	81.20•	23.04	87.73•	19.21	88.89	14.24	88.02•	15.83	81.20•	23.04
IR	87.40	8.85	91.33	12.44	90.00	14.07	**92.66**	12.07	88.67	7.93	91.33	12.44
MA	59.34	37.50	**61.60**	42.69	58.33	51.34	58.51	12.60	58.29	50.77	**61.60**	42.64
MX	78.74	99.90	87.94○	19.02	**100.00○**	98.37	82.37	17.10	86.52	25.47	86.52	18.89
SO	86.05	67.05	84.64	25.05	**87.07**	28.26	76.57•	16.93	84.64	26.82	84.64	25.11
TG	86.97	13.14	94.76○	8.03	**95.23○**	8.95	94.49•	6.76	89.41•	2.18	94.76○	8.03
VE	**68.42**	65.23	64.66•	38.69	67.16	43.21	66.21	29.42	68.21	43.85	64.66•	38.69

In table 4 the results obtained using ClassCM and DROP algorithms are compared. ClassCM shows better competence for some data sets (e.g. *biopsy, breast-w, glass*), although its results are also worse in others (e.g. *multiplexer*). The behaviour of these reduction techniques are similar to the previously studied. ClassCM obtains a balance behaviour between competence and size. There are some reduction techniques that obtain best competence for some data sets reducing less the case memory size.

All the experiments (tables 2, 3 and 4) point to some interesting observations. First, it is worth noting that the individual AccurCM and ClassCM works well in all data sets, obtaining better results on ClassCM because the reduction is smaller. Second, the mean storage obtained using AccurCM and ClassCM suggest complementary behaviour. This effect can be seen on the *tao-grid* data

M. Salamó and E. Golobardes

set, where AccurCM obtains a 95.39% mean storage and ClassCM 13.14%. We want to remember that ClassCM complete the case memory in order to obtain at least one case of each class. This complementary behaviour suggests that they can be used together in order to improve the competence and maximise the reduction of the case memory. Finally, the results on all tables suggest that all the reduction techniques work well in some, but not all, domains. This has been termed the *selective superiority problem* [2]. Consequently, future work consists of combining both approaches in order to exploit the strength of each one.

7 Conclusions and Further Work

This paper introduces two new reduction techniques based on the Rough Sets theory. Both reduction techniques have a different nature: AccurCM reduces the case memory maintaining the internal cases; and ClassCM obtains a reduced set of border cases, increasing that set of cases with the most relevant classifier cases. Empirical studies show that these reduction techniques produce a higher or equal generalisation accuracy on classification tasks. We conclude that Rough Sets reduction techniques should be improved in some ways. That fact focus our further work. First, the algorithm *selectCases* should be changed in order to select a most reduced set of cases. In this way, we want to modifiy the algorithm selecting only the most representative K-nearest neighbour cases that accomplishing the *confidenceLevel*. Second, we should search for new discretisation methods in order to improve the pre-processing of the data. Finally, we want to analyse the influence of the weighting methods in these reduction techniques.

Acknowledgements. This work is supported by the *Ministerio de Sanidad y Consumo, Instituto de Salud Carlos III, Fondo de Investigación Sanitaria* of Spain, Grant No. 00/0033-02. The results of this study have been obtained using the equipment co-funded by the *Direcció de Recerca de la Generalitat de Catalunya* (D.O.G.C 30/12/1997). We wish to thank *Enginyeria i Arquitectura La Salle* (Ramon Llull University) for their support of our Research Group in Intelligent Systems. We also wish to thank: D. Aha for providing the IBL code and D. Randall Wilson and Tony R. Martinez who provided the code of the other reduction techniques. Finally, we wish to thank the anonymous reviewers for their useful comments during the preparation of this paper.

References

1. D. Aha and D. Kibler. Instance-based learning algorithms. *Machine Learning*, *Vol. 6*, pages 37–66, 1991.
2. C.E. Brodley. Addressing the selective superiority problem: Automatic algorithm/model class selection. In *Proceedings of the 10th International Conference on Machine Learning*, pages 17–24, 1993.
3. P. Domingos. Context-sensitive feature selection for lazy learners. In *AI Review*, volume 11, pages 227–253, 1997.

4. U.M. Fayyad and K.B. Irani. Multi-interval discretization of continuous-valued attributes for classification learning. In *19th International Joint Conference on Artificial Intelligence*, pages 1022–1027, 1993.

5. J.M. Garrell, E. Golobardes, E. Bernadó, and X. Llorà. Automatic diagnosis with Genetic Algorithms and Case-Based Reasoning. *Elsevier Science Ltd. ISSN 0954-1810*, 13:367–362, 1999.

6. G.W. Gates. The reduced nearest neighbor rule. In *IEEE Transactions on Information Theory*, volume 18(3), pages 431–433, 1972.

7. M. Gawry's and J. Sienkiewicz. Rough Set Library user's Manual. Technical Report 00-665, Computer Science Institute, Warsaw University of Technology, 1993.

8. E. Golobardes, X. Llorà, M. Salamó, and J. Martí. Computer Aided Diagnosis with Case-Based Reasoning and Genetic Algorithms. *Knowledge Based Systems (In Press)*, 2001.

9. P.E. Hart. The condensed nearest neighbour rule. *IEEE Transactions on Information Theory*, 14:515–516, 1968.

10. J. Kolodner. *Case-Based Reasoning*. Morgan Kaufmann Publishers, Inc., 1993.

11. D. Leake and D. Wilson. Remembering Why to Remember:Performance-Guided Case-Base Maintenance. In *Proceedings of the Fifth European Workshop on Case-Based Reasoning*, 2000.

12. X. Llorà and J.M. Garrell. Inducing partially-defined instances with Evolutionary Algorithms. In *Proceedings of the 18th International Conference on Machine Learning (*To Appear*)*, 2001.

13. D.G. Lowe. Similarity Metric Learning for a Variable-Kernel Classifier. In *Neural Computation*, volume 7(1), pages 72–85, 1995.

14. J. Martí, J. Español, E. Golobardes, J. Freixenet, R. García, and M. Salamó. Classification of microcalcifications in digital mammograms using case-based reasonig. In *International Workshop on digital Mammography*, 2000.

15. C. J. Merz and P. M. Murphy. UCI Repository for Machine Learning Data-Bases [http://www.ics.uci.edu/~mlearn/MLRepository.html]. *Irvine, CA: University of California, Department of Information and Computer Science*, 1998.

16. Z. Pawlak. Rough Sets. In *International Journal of Information and Computer Science*, volume 11, 1982.

17. Z. Pawlak. *Rough Sets: Theoretical Aspects of Reasoning about Data*. Kluwer Academic Publishers, 1991.

18. L. Portinale, P. Torasso, and P. Tavano. Speed-up, quality and competence in multi-modal reasoning. In *Proceedings of the Third International Conference on Case-Based Reasoning*, pages 303–317, 1999.

19. C.K. Riesbeck and R.C. Schank. *Inside Case-Based Reasoning*. Lawrence Erlbaum Associates, Hillsdale, NJ, US, 1989.

20. G.L. Ritter, H.B. Woodruff, S.R. Lowry, and T.L. Isenhour. An algorithm for a selective nearest neighbor decision rule. In *IEEE Transactions on Information Theory*, volume 21(6), pages 665–669, 1975.

21. M. Salamó and E. Golobardes. BASTIAN: Incorporating the Rough Sets theory into a Case-Based Classifier System. In *III Congrés Català d'Intel·ligència Artificial*, pages 284–293, October 2000.

22. M. Salamó, E. Golobardes, D. Vernet, and M. Nieto. Weighting methods for a Case-Based Classifier System. In *LEARNING'00*, Madrid, Spain, 2000. IEEE.

23. S. Salzberg. A nearest hyperrectangle learning method. *Machine Learning*, 6:277–309, 1991.

482   M. Salamó and E. Golobardes

24. B. Smyth and M. Keane. Remembering to forget: A competence-preserving case deletion policy for case-based reasoning systems. In *Proceedings of the Thirteen International Joint Conference on Artificial Intelligence*, pages 377–382, 1995.
25. B. Smyth and E. McKenna. Building compact competent case-bases. In *Proceedings of the Third International Conference on Case-Based Reasoning*, 1999.
26. D.R. Wilson and T.R. Martinez. Reduction techniques for Instance-Based Learning Algorithms. *Machine Learning, 38*, pages 257–286, 2000.
27. Q. Yang and J. Wu. Keep it Simple: A Case-Base Maintenance Policy Based on Clustering and Information Theory. In *Proc. of the Canadian AI Conference*, 2000.
28. J. Zhu and Q. Yang. Remembering to add: Competence-preserving case-addition policies for case base maintenance. In *Proceedings of the Fifteenth International Joint Conference on Artificial Intelligence*, 1999.

Sequential Instance-Based Learning for Planning in the Context of an Imperfect Information Game

Jenngang Shih

Department of Computer Science
The Graduate School of The City University of New York
365 Fifth Avenue, New York, NY 10016
jshih@gc.cuny.edu[*]

Abstract. Finding sequential concepts, as in planning, is a complex task because of the exponential size of the search space. Empirical learning can be an effective way to find sequential concepts from observations. Sequential Instance-Based Learning (SIBL), which is presented here, is an empirical learning paradigm, modeled after Instance-Based Learning (IBL) that learns sequential concepts, ordered sequences of state-action pairs to perform a synthesis task. SIBL is highly effective and learns expert-level knowledge. SIBL demonstrates the feasibility of using an empirical learning approach to discover sequential concepts. In addition, this approach suggests a general framework that systematically extends empirical learning to learning sequential concepts. SIBL is tested on the domain of bridge.

Introduction

This paper describes an approach to apply empirical learning to synthesis problems. Empirical learning is most often used to address a classification problem [Quinlan 1986; Breiman et al. 1984], whereas a synthesis problem requires the construction of sequences of actions to achieve a goal [Clancey 1985]. A classification problem addressed by an empirical learning paradigm usually does not involve a state change from one problem to the next. On the other hand, a synthesis problem typically involves a state change from one action to the next. The approach described in this paper takes advantage of the empirical learning paradigm to address the problem of constructing sequences of actions.

To bridge the gap between empirical learning and constructive problem solving, the method proposed here views a synthesis problem as a sequence of sequentially related classification problems, such that a classification yields an action selection in a sequence of problems. Therefore, given a set of examples each represents a problem solving sequence, the proposed method is to construct a model by discovering sequential concepts from the input examples. The hypothesis is that sequential problem solving experience may be represented in an example suitable for empirical learning, and that a weak-theory approach may be used to support sequential concept discovery.

---

[*] The author's new postal and email addresses are: 4476 Hock Maple Ct. Concord, CA 94521, USA. jenngang@ix.netcom.com

D.W. Aha and I. Watson (Eds.): ICCBR 2001, LNAI 2080, pp. 483–501, 2001.
© Springer-Verlag Berlin Heidelberg 2001

484   J. Shih

In particular, the thrust of this paper has the following two perspectives. First, the idea of sequential dependency (SD), which views a sequence of events as sequentially dependent, may be used to clarify superficially similar yet intrinsically different events. Second, empirical learning (e.g., IBL [Aha 1992; Salzberg 1991]) may be extended to handle input examples from which sequential concepts may be discovered.

The remainder of this paper justifies the application of SD for a synthesis problem, rationalizes SIBL as an approach to learning synthesis tasks, presents the result of SIBL with a set of experiments on the bridge domain, surveys related work, and concludes with the strengths and weak-nesses of SIBL.

Sequential Dependency

In [Epstein and Shih, 1998], we first described SD as a means to disambiguate the identity of a state in a sequence of states by using a multi-state context. For a synthesis task, where actions are selected in a sequence of states, a multi-state context will reduce the ambiguity introduced when a state is derived from two different paths. Particularly, SD views a sequence of state-action pairs as sequentially dependent. These state-action pairs may be found in a *transition sequence* – contiguous sequence of state-action pairs that achieve a goal. SD identifies within the transition sequence a sub-string of consecutive states called *sequential concept* – contiguous subsequence of state-action pairs that establishes a subgoal. Viewing a synthesis task in terms of SD enables a problem solver to find the correct action more often by distinguishing between two otherwise identical states derived from two different sequential concepts.

As shown in Fig. 1, without additional information, one may not be able to recognize the identity of the *Current* state to correctly derive the *Next* state. The multi-state context of sequential concepts is often useful here.

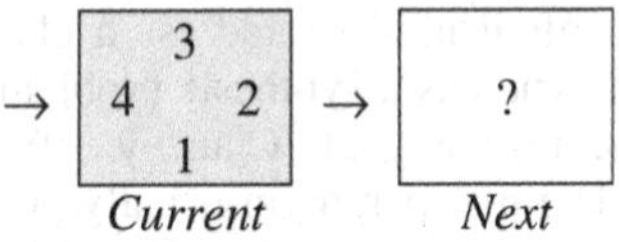

Fig. 1. Figuring out the next state from the current state.

Consider the transition sequence *TS* in Fig. 2, which consists of four known states, s_1 ... s_4, where state s_4 is the current state. Embedded in *TS* is a sequential concept, *sc*, states s_2 ... s_4. Since *sc* embodies the concept that the numbers rotate *clockwise* from one state to the next, it becomes straightforward to figure out what the next state might be.

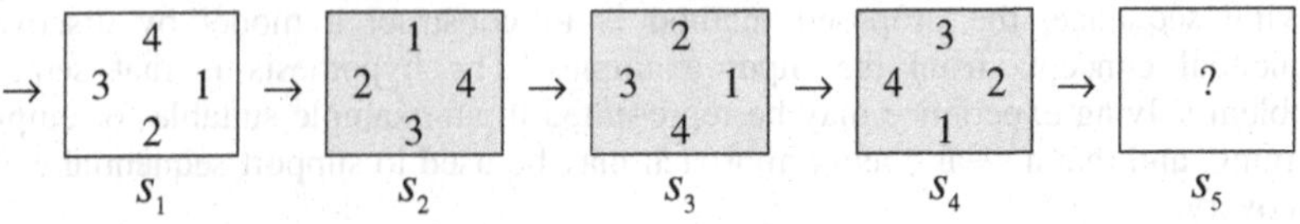

Fig. 2. Transition sequence *TS* contains a sequential concept *sc*, (s_2, s_3, s_4), where the numbers rotate clockwise from on state to the next.

Similarly, the transition sequence TS' in Fig. 3 includes a sequential concept sc', states $s'_2 \ldots s'_4$. Here the numbers rotate *counter clockwise* from one state to the next. Again, given the nature of the sequential concept sc', it is straightforward to predict what state s'_5 would be.

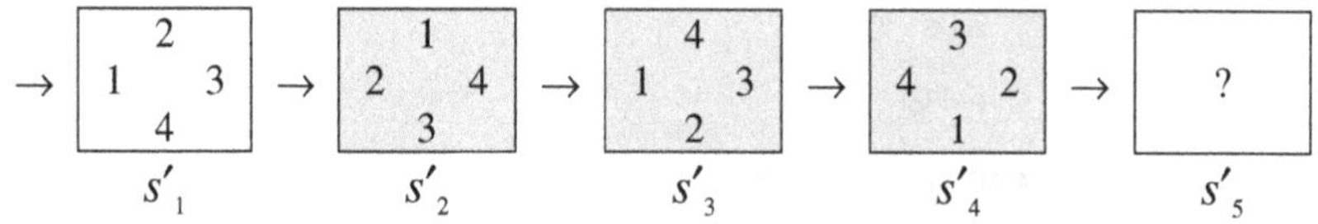

Fig. 3. Transition sequence TS' contains a sequential concept sc', (s'_2, s'_3, s'_4), where the numbers rotate counter clockwise from one state to the next.

Although the current states, s_4 and s'_4, in TS and TS' are identical, their contexts as the third state in the sequential concepts, sc and sc', predict different next states. In other words, a multi-state context in terms of sequential concepts may be used to disambiguate a current state by the additional information provided by a sequential concept. This is because in a synthesis domain, adjacent states are often sequentially related and searching for a correct action is more effective with associated sequential concepts.

Sequential Instance-Based Learning

Sequential Instance-Based Learning (SIBL), an extension to Instance-Based Learning (IBL) paradigm, incorporates sequential dependency to learn sequential concepts for synthesis domains. In particular, the IB4 algorithm [Aha 1992] is employed here to demonstrate an adaptation of empirical learning approach to learning sequential concepts. As shown in Table 1, the adapted algorithm, called SIB4, has a similar high-level algorithm, except that sequential examples, which contain contextual information beyond the current state in a transition sequence, are used.

More specifically, the input to SIB4 is a set T of sequential instances (s-instances) $\langle x^w, a \rangle$ of w states as the independent variables, in which a relevant action a is the dependent variable, and w is a predefined *window* for a transition sequence. The output is a set of sequential concept descriptions CD in terms of prototypical s-instances used for the selection of an action given an unseen s-instance. Each s-instance x^w in T consists of a set of partial s-instances x^i, each of which contains a context of i states, $1 \leq i \leq w$. In other words, x^i is a subsequence of x^w with length i. For each subsequence x^i of x^w, the most similar s-instance y^i_{max} of length i is calculated using the *similarity* function on the two same-length partial s-instances, x^i and y^i in CD. Every y^i_{max} is added to a candidate set C for sequential similarity calculations. The action of the most sequentially similar candidate a_{max} is calculated by the *findSequentialSimilarity* function. This is facilitated by using a set of sequential similarity metrics described in Table 2. Finally, if the action a associated with the input x^w is not the same as a_{max}, then x^w is stored in CD as a new prototypical instance.

Table 1. Top-level SIB4 algorithm.

```
 1. SIB4(T, CD)

 2.      CD ← Ø

 3.      for <x", a>∈ T

 4.           C ← Ø

 5.           for 1 ≤ i ≤ w

 6.                for y^i ∈ CD

 7.                     y^i_max ← similarity(x^i, y^i)

 8.                     C ← C ∪ y^i_max

 9.                a_max ← findSequentialSimilarity(x", C)

10.           if a ≠ a_max then

11.                CD ← CD ∪ {x"}
```

As in IB4, the *similarity* function on line 7 in Table 1 calculates the similarity between two instances with respect to their attributes, in this case, the same-length *s*-instances. First, the difference of each attribute k (f_k) within a state is calculated with $diff_k$ shown in (1). The function $diff_k$ uses Euclidean distance for numeric features and Hamming distance for symbolic features.

$$diff_k(x^i,c^i) = \begin{cases} \left| f_k(x^i) - f_k(c^i) \right|, \text{if } f_k \text{ is numeric.} \\ 1, \text{if } f_k \text{ is discrete and } f_k(x^i) \neq f_k(c^i). \\ 0, \text{otherwise.} \end{cases} \quad (1)$$

Second, the state difference at state j is calculated with the function $sdiff_j$ shown in [2]. Let each state be represented by a set of m features. Given the attribute differences calculated by $diff_k$, $1 \leq k \leq m$, the state difference between two sub-sequences x_j^i and c_j^i at state j is defined as

$$sdiff_j(x^i,c^i) = \sum_{k=1}^{m} diff_k(x_j^i,c_j^i)^2 \quad (2)$$

Finally, the distance between two partial *s*-instances is calculated with $dist_i$ shown in (3). Let each partial *s*-instance contain i states. Given the state differences calculated by $sdiff_j$, $1 \leq j \leq i$, the function $dist_i$ that computes the distance between x^i and c^i up to i states is defined as

$$dist_i(x^i, c^i) = \sqrt{\sum_{j=1}^{i} sdiff_j(x^i, c^i)} \qquad (3)$$

The distance metric just described is the basis for sequential similarity metrics (SSM) used in the *findSequentialSimilarity* function on line 10 in Table 1, for calculating the similarity between two   *s*-instances. *Procedurally*, rather than computing similarity with all states involved in one shot, SSM starts with the similarity calculation with only the current state, and progressively includes prior states. As a result, the current state is included in every similarity calculation. *Declaratively*, SSM consists of a set of sequential similarity metrics that calculates the similarity between two partial *s*-instances with increasing details, namely, their *distance, convergence, consistency,* and *recency*.

As shown in Table 2, the *findSequentialSimilarity* function iteratively compares two partial *s*-instances with increasing number of states *i* (context) until a metric can distinguish among the set of candidates. Let B and B' be partial *s*-instances whose differences for metric m from a partial *s*-instance A is represented as $m(A, B)$ and $m(A, B')$. A metric m is said to *distinguish* between B and B' with respect to A if and only if $m(A, B) \neq m(A, B')$ to some precision, say, the nearest tenth. As an example, if $m(A, B) = .04$, and $m(A, B') = .10$, then m distinguishes between B and B' to the nearest tenth. If, on the other hand, $m(A, B) = .06$, but $m(A, B') = .10$, then m does not distinguish between B and B' with respect to A to the nearest tenth. When the candidates are not distinguishable for given metric, additional state (context) is added in the next iteration. If the number of states has been exhausted, a more elaborate metric will be used.

Table 2. The function that finds majority for set of sequential instances.

```
1.   findSequentialSimilarity(xʷ, C) returns aₘₐₓ

2.   while 1 ≤ i ≤ w

3.        X ← X ∪ xⁱ

4.        for all <cⁱ, a> ∈ C

5.             for m ∈ SSM

6.                  if m(X, cⁱ) is distinguishable then aₘₐₓ ← a; return

7.                  Otherwise, i ← i +1; continue
```

The richness in the representation makes similarity comparisons for sequential instances possible. These metrics range from a simple distance measure to increasingly more elaborate ones. They exploit sequential characteristics of a transition sequence, so that each metric examines one aspect of such a transition sequence. The intuition here is that the more sequential characteristics two transition sequences share, the more the two transition sequences are alike. In additional to the *distance* metric described above, the *convergence* metric measures reduction of sequential distance, the distance from one end of a sequence of states to another; the *consistency* metric counts the number of consecutive reductions in convergences; and the *recency* metric records the most recent reduction of sequential distance.

The *convergence* metric quantifies the change in the state difference between partial *s*-instances, measured from their least recent states to their current states. In particular, the convergence for x^i and c^i from the least recent state s_i to the currents state s_1 is shown in (4),

$$convergence(x^i, c^i) = dist_i^i(x^i, c^i) - dist_c^i(x^i, c^i) \qquad (4)$$

where $dist_i^i(x^i, c^i)$ is the distance between x^i and c^i for up to i states and $dist_c^i(x^i, c^i)$ is the distance between x^i and c^i at the current state s_c.

For each input partial *s*-instance and the candidate retrieved for it, the *consistency* metric tallies the number of consecutive positive reduction in convergence for all adjacent states for two partial *s*-instances x^i and c^i. Reduction in convergence $\Delta_{j, j+1}$ between state j and state $j + 1$ may be calculated in terms of convergence, that is, $\Delta_{j, j+1} = conv(x_{j+1}^i, c_{j+1}^i) - conv(x_j^i, c_j^i)$. Therefore, consistency between x^i and c^i may be measured by (5):

$consistency(x^i, c^i)$ = the largest t in $[1, n\text{-}1]$ such that

$$ \qquad (5)$$

$$conv(x_{j+1}^i, c_{j+1}^i) > conv(x_j^i, c_j^i) \text{ for } j = 1 \text{ to } t \text{ where } 1 \leq j < n$$

where *conv* (x_{j+1}^i, c_{j+1}^i) is strictly larger than *conv* (x_j^i, c_j^i), t counts the number of consecutive reductions in convergence (positive convergence) between two adjacent states, t is the largest such number in the range from 1 to n-1, and n is the total number of states.

The *recency* metric identifies the most recent point in the sequence where a reduction in convergence has occurred between two partial *s*-instances x^i and c^i as defined in (6).

$recency(x^i, c^i)$ = the greatest j in $[1, n - 1]$ such that

$$ \qquad (6)$$

$$conv(x_j^i, c_j^i) > conv(x_{j+1}^i, c_{j+1}^i)$$

Reduction in convergence at state j occurs when $\Delta_{j\text{-}1, j}$ the reduction in convergence from state $j - 1$ to j is greater than $\Delta_{j, j+1}$ the reduction in convergence from state j to $j + 1$.

As the states are being included incrementally in the SSM calculation, the decision boundary is being adjusted as a result. This is similar to the way the decision boundary is being adjusted by modifying the attribute weights. During sequential similarity calculation, the attribute weight is modified by favoring the attribute that represents the most recent state over the attribute that represents the least recent state. In other words, on average, the attributes representing the states closer to the current state have more weight than those representing previous states. As a result, the decision boundary will change as well. As shown in   Fig. 4(a), when the attribute weight associated with the y-axis is decreased, the new decision boundary rotates counter clockwise with a steeper slope (dashed-line). Also, as the SSM are being selected successively to measure the similarity between two *s*-instances, the decision boundaries are also being refined as a result. This happens when a new metric is being incorporated in SSM calculation. As shown in Fig. 4(b), when only one attribute is used alone the *x*-axis, the decision boundary is a vertical line dividing the instance space into two partitions. When adding an SSM to the similarity calculation, the instance space increases its dimension by one, and the new decision boundary is now formed by two lines and divides the instance space up to four partitions.

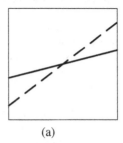 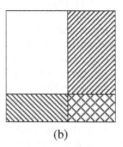

(a)   (b)

Fig. 4. (a) A change in a decision boundary due to a change in attribute weights. As the attribute weight associated with the y-axis decreases, the decision boundary rotates counter clockwise; (b) decision boundary is refined with an additional feature.

Experimental Design and Results

This section describes the research domain, representation of examples, knowledge discovery steps, and the experimental results in a series of experiments performed on SIB4. The game of bridge is the target domain because it is sequential in nature and challenging. It involves synthesizing a sequence of actions to achieve the goal of winning a contest. Although I chose the game of bridge as the target domain, other domains that involve sequence synthesis (e.g., the game of hearts) may also be used. In terms of knowledge representation, the syntactic aspect is typically dictated by the chosen learning paradigm. Since IBL is chosen here, the representation is based on attribute value pairs, a common representation. The semantic aspect of knowledge representation is influenced by the amount of domain knowledge used. The more the domain knowledge, the less flexible it is for transferring the method to a new domain. This research minimizes the use of domain-specific knowledge to keep the proposed learning method flexible. Instead, a multi-state context is added in an input example to enable sequential concept disambiguation.

Bridge

The game of bridge was chosen as the research domain because it is a sufficiently complex game, and because the result of a bridge problem solver can be evaluated by standard criteria. In short, bridge is a four-player game that consists of bidding followed by play. During bidding, a specific number of tricks for winning (the *contract*) are determined. During play, the players try to make or break the contract by playing the cards in a specific order. To begin, a deck of 52 cards is distributed evenly to four players; each holds 13 cards called a *hand*. In each round, each player plays a card. Together, the four cards played during each round are called a *trick*. All players must play a card of the suit led, unless they have no card in that suit (*void*). In that case, the player may play a card in another suit (*drop*) or play a trump card, a card in the trump suit, which is determined during the bidding phase. The bidding determines the player who plays the first card, and play proceeds clockwise. In each trick, the player who plays the highest rank of the suit wins the trick and leads a card to begin the next trick.

This work concentrates only on the playing phase. The problem of bridge play is to design a sequence of actions (card plays) that guides a bridge player to reach a specific goal (e.g., make or break a contract). Also, the focus here will be to guide a particular player, the *declarer*, who first named the contract suit during bidding. The declarer also decides which card to play for its partner (the *dummy*), whose cards are exposed on the table for all to see after the first lead (first card play) by the opponent. Since 13 cards are dealt to each player, the declarer makes 26 card plays in a deal. In other words, each deal provides 26 examples of declarer play. Given a set of such examples, the learning algorithm is expected to identify bridge playing sequences for the side of the declarer and dummy.

Like many other large sequential domains, bridge's search space is intractable. The search space consists of two factors: static descriptions and dynamic plays. For static descriptions, with a 52-card deck, there are

$$S = \binom{52}{13} * \binom{39}{13} * \binom{26}{13} * \binom{13}{13} = 5.36E + 28 \qquad (7)$$

possible deals (descriptions). For dynamic plays, the branching factor is $n*(n/4)^3$ for each trick, where n is the number of cards currently remaining in each hand (i.e., the number of choices the lead player of a trick has to play a card), and $n/4$ is the average number of choices the other three players have to play a card among the four possible suits. For a complete deal, the number of possible plays will be

$$D = \prod_{n=1}^{13} n*(n/4)^3 = 1.27E + 18 \qquad (8)$$

Taking both static descriptions and dynamic plays into consideration, there are

$$S * D = 6.83E + 46 \qquad (9)$$

possible states in bridge. With such an enormous search space, the game of bridge has become an active research domain in recent years.

Finally, the game of bridge is a domain with many sub-problems. A particular contract, say three no trump, is viewed as a unique problem because it dictates the strategies and tactics to be used. In this example, the number "three" determines the number of tricks needed to win a contest. Since the base number for trick counting is six, "three" means winning nine tricks (6 + 3) out of a total of thirteen tricks. The term "no trump" (NT) means that no suit has any privilege over the other suits, and only the ranks of the suit led are used to decide win or lose. The number of tricks needed to win and the rules governs the natures of suits and ranks determine different strategies. In the following experiments, I concentrated on one of the most popular contracts – 3 No Trump (3NT).

Representation

The representation consists of mainly the card distributions among the players. As depicted in Fig. 5, each of the four players has a total of thirteen cards in four different suits. At any given time, a player is either leading a suit at the beginning of a trick, or following a suit led in the middle of a trick. As a convention, the declarer is at South (S) and the dummy is at North (N). This leaves West (W) and East (E) as the opponents. For example, if West leads the 9 of spades (♠), this will focus a bridge state on the spade suit, since bridge requires that one follows suit, and a no trump contract removes the threat of being trumped. Therefore, only the cards in the spade suit are represented in a state; the cards in the other suits may be ignored.

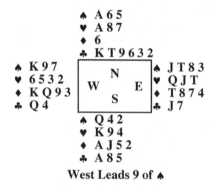

West Leads 9 of ♠

Fig. 5. A bridge example with a complete suit description.

Such a suit-oriented representation effectively reduces the search space. For example, in a hand-oriented representation, all 52 cards are needed to represent a bridge state. Since each may be held by one of four players, the size of the instance space is 5.36E+28 as discussed earlier. With a suit-oriented representation, there are only 13 cards to represent among the four players. For example, the hand most evenly distributed among suits is 4-3-3-3. The number of possible deals for this distribution is only 1.67E+10, which is calculated as

$$\binom{13}{4}\binom{13}{3}\binom{13}{3}\binom{13}{3}*4 \tag{10}$$

Thus, domain knowledge effectively streamlines the representation and limits the search.

More specifically, each example is represented as a state-action pair $<s, a>$. The state consists of *independent* attributes that represent the context in which the player (declarer or dummy) is to play a card, and the action is the *dependent* attribute that represents the play executed in this context. Fig. 6 shows an example of the context in which North is to play a card. The actual card played (one of A 6 5) by North is the *action*.

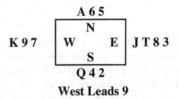

West Leads 9

Fig. 6. A bridge example with a single suit description.

The attributes for a state s include bookkeeping information and card distribution information. As summarized in Table 3, the *bookkeeping information* keeps track of the contest in progress, with information such as the trick number and play number in a contest, the leading player of the trick, the current player, and the card(s) played thus far in a trick. More specifically, the bookkeeping information includes:

Table 3. Attributes for representing bridge states. The bookkeeping and distribution information describes the context in which a player is to play a card. The action attribute represents such card played.

	Name	Description	Type	Domain
Bookkeeping Information	Trick number	i^{th} trick in a contest	Integer	[1, 13]
	Play number	j^{th} play in a contest	Integer	[1, 26]
	Leader	The leader of a trick	Discrete	$\Omega = \{$West, North, East, South$\}$
	Current player	The current player	Discrete	$\Omega = \{$West, North, East, South$\}$
	Current trick	Cards played in a trick	String	$\{w \in \Sigma^4$, where $\Sigma = [A, K, Q, J, T, 9, x, -]\}$
Distribution Information	West hand	Cards played by West	String	$\{w \in \Sigma^{13}$, where $\Sigma = [A, K, Q, J, T, 9, x, -]\}$
	North hand	Cards held by North	String	$\{w \in \Sigma^{13}$, where $\Sigma = [A, K, Q, J, T, 9, x, -]\}$
	East hand	Cards played by East	String	$\{w \in \Sigma^{13}$, where $\Sigma = [A, K, Q, J, T, 9, x, -]\}$
	South hand	Cards held by South	String	$\{w \in \Sigma^{13}$, where $\Sigma = [A, K, Q, J, T, 9, x, -]\}$
Action	Card played	Target attribute	Discrete	$\{A, K, Q, J, T, 9, x\}$

- *trick number* indicates the ith trick in a contest. It is an integer value i in [1, 13].
- *play number* indicates the jth play in a contest. It an integer value j in [1, 26]. Note that this is the decision number by the declarer, and is less than the number of total cards played in the hand.
- *leader of a trick* identifies the player who plays the first card on a trick. It is a discrete value in $\Omega = \{$West, North, East, South$\}$.
- *current player* is a discrete value in Ω that corresponds to the player who is to play the next card
- *current trick* is a string of four elements, one for each player. The entries in this string represent the card played by West, North, East, and South, respectively, always in that order. Each element is from the set $\Sigma = \{A, K, Q, J, T, 9, x, -\}$, where "x" represents any card that is smaller than a 9 because smaller cards are indistinguishable with respect to the result. A card played from a different suit, because that player had no card in the suit led, is also represented as an "x." The symbol "-" means that the player has not yet played in this trick. As an example,

the string "A-xx" means that West played an ace, North has not yet played, and East and South played low cards (x's).

The *distribution information* consists of the cards *held* by the declarer and the dummy, and those *played* (exposed) by the two opponents (West and East). A *hand* includes a single *suit*, which is represented as a string of up to 7 possible ranks from the set Σ, and '-' means an empty hand. As an example, Fig. 6 shows that North holds A 6 5 and South holds Q 4 2. If the representation included K 9 7 for West and J T 8 3 for East, however, that would mean that they had already played those cards before the current trick. That is, the representation would record '-' for both East and West before any card in the suit is played. Finally, action *a* is the dependent attribute, whose value serves as the teacher during training and as the critic during testing. The action is a discrete value from the set $\Sigma - \{-\}$, that is, every element in Σ except '-'.

Although the difference function for the integer and the discrete attributes, shown in (1), is well defined, the difference for a string attribute, such as a player's hand, is not. A simple string difference may be defined by treating the entire string as a discrete symbol, and performing an exact match, like that for a discrete attribute. This approach, however, imposes an overly strict constraint. A more relaxed approach employed here, which adopts the *n*-gram approach to measure the string difference. In this approach, only a sub-string of *n* symbols in two strings are compared at a time, and the result of the comparison is used to compute the difference. For example, to find the difference between the string *x* = "bank" and the string *y* = "bunk" with *n* = 3, first, each string generates a set of *n*-grams, sub-strings of length *n* = 3 with one non-overlapping symbol in the adjacent *n*-grams as shown in Table 4. Both strings generate six *n*-grams. To calculate the difference between *x* and *y*, first, the cardinality of the intersection of the *n*-grams between *x* and *y* is counted. In this case, the cardinality is three because there are three exact matches (- - b, n k -, k - -). Then, the count is scaled between 0 and 1 based on the number of *n*-grams for the longer of the two strings as follows:

$$difference\ (x, y) = 1 - \frac{\#\ of\ identical\ n\text{-}grams\ between\ x\ and\ y}{\#\ of\ total\ n\text{-}grams\ of\ the\ longer\ of\ the\ two\ strings} \tag{11}$$

If no identical *n*-grams exist, the difference will be 1; if all *n*-grams are identical, the difference will be 0. Also, the larger the number of identical *n*-grams between *x* and *y*, the smaller the difference. In this example, the difference value is 1 − (3/6), or 0.5. The *n*-gram approach accounts for more details in comparing two strings, and has a smoother difference computation.

Table 4. Two strings, "bank" and "bunk", with their corresponding n-grams, sub-strings of length n, for n = 3.

String	*n*-grams
bank	- - b, - b a, b a n, a n k, n k -, k - -
bunk	- - b, - b u, b u n, u n k, n k -, k - -

With this representation, Table 5 shows a sequence of five instances representing the bridge sequence in Fig. 7. In the first instance, the trick number is 2 (column 1) and the play number is 5 (column 2). The leader of the trick is North (column 3) and the current player is South (column 4). In this trick, three low cards have already been played (column 5). On tricks prior to this one, West played a low card (column 6), North now holds the ace and T (column 7), East has already played the king and a low card (column 8), and South holds the queen and three low cards (column 9). Finally, play x (column 10) is the dependent attribute that represents the action taken. Since there are 13 tricks in a contest and two instances, one for North and one for South, are recorded for each trick, there are 26 instances in a contest.

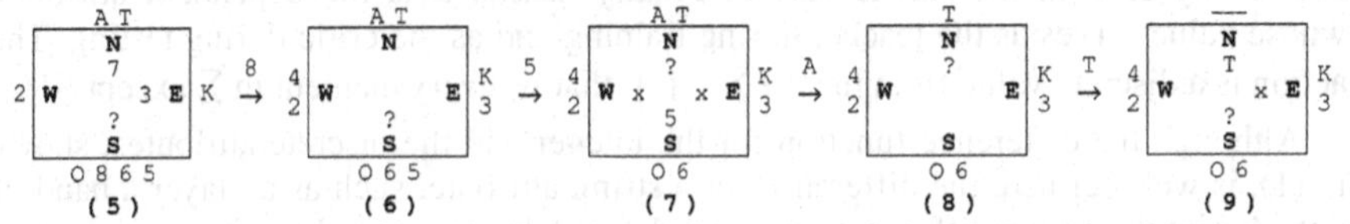

Fig. 7. An example of a bridge sequence from state (5) to the current state (9). In state (5), North led the 7, East played 3, and South is to play next (?). South played 8 followed by West's 4. In state (6), South is to lead (?) and played the 5. In state (7), West is void in the suit and played a card (x) from a different suit, and North is to play next (?). North played the A followed by East's card from a different suit (x). In state (8), North is to lead and played the T. In state (9), East played a card from a different suit (x), and South is to play next (?).

Table 5. A representation of the bridge sequence in Fig. 7.

State									Action
Trick number	**Play number**	**Lead player**	**Current Player**	**Trick**	**West**	**North**	**East**	**South**	**Play**
2	5	N	S	xxx-	x	AT	Kx	Qxxx	x
3	6	S	S	----	xx	AT	Kx	Qxx	x
3	7	S	N	x--x	xx	AT	Kx	Qx	A
4	8	N	N	----	xx	T	Kx	Qx	T
4	9	N	S	-Tx-	xx	---	Kx	Qx	?

Knowledge Discovery

The experiment follows a typical knowledge discovery process that collects relevant data, preprocess the data to suit the learning algorithm, iterates the search through the concept space defined by the attributes of the data, and post-process the search results into a meaningful form [Fayyad et al. 1996].

In bridge, a useful data source is the bridge hands that appear in daily newspaper bridge columns. Almost all daily newspapers in the United States carry a bridge column. The deals in these bridge columns are typically instructive and challenging. Therefore, they are suitable for knowledge discovery. Using a newspaper bridge column as the main source of my data collection, I collected 200 3NT deals from the San Francisco Chronicle for the experiment.

The next task was to transform them into computer readable form. There are a number of computer programs available on the World Wide Web to facilitate automatic data generation. The one written by Matt Ginsberg at Oregon University, called GIB [Ginsberg 1999], is used here because the source code available. This permitted me to build an interactive training and testing program by integrating GIB with the learning algorithm. Each hand produces a series of 13 tricks out of which 26 plays (examples) are generated for two players – 13 for the declarer and 13 for the dummy. The 200 collected 3NT deals produced 5,200 examples.

As shown in Table 6, 5,200 examples were randomly divided into a training set with 90% and a test set with 10% of the total examples in each experiment. To measure the performance accurately, a 10-fold cross validation was performed to produce an averaged performance [Kibler and Langley 1988]. On a *run*, one subset was selected for testing with all the others used for training. Ten runs, each with a different test set, constitute a *sub-experiment*. In addition, the examples were partitioned so that all examples from the same deal fell in the same subset. This prevented training and testing with examples from the same deal. A known caveat for an incremental learning method, such as IBL, is that the experimental results may depend on the order of the examples in the training set. For this reason, each cross validation sub-experiment was replicated ten times, randomizing the order of the examples. This produced ten variations on each cross validation sub-experiment, training 10 times on differently ordered but otherwise equivalent sets of examples.

Table 6. Total number of training and test examples and their uses with a 10-fold cross validation, each with 10 runs.

	#Examples per set	#Sub-experiments	#Total examples	#Variations	#Total references
Total	5,200	10	52,000		520,000
Train	4,680		46,800	10	468,000
Test	520		5,200		52,000

Table 7 describes the experiments performed. IB4-*n* represents a series of experiments that use a fixed context of various sizes. These experiments demonstrate the benefit of using context in an example for a sequential domain, while exposes the weaknesses of using a fixed-context. Unlike IB4-*n*, SIB4 uses a variable context in sequential similarity calculation. As will be shown later, it demonstrates that the context of a relevant candidate for an input example does not have to be fixed at a certain number of states.

Table 7. A list of experiments based on instance-based learning approach.

IB4-*n*	Fixed size multi-state context, $n = 1, 2, 3, 4, 5$
SIB4	Quality approach to context selection

Experimental Results

Fig. 8(a) shows the results of the IB4-*n* algorithms in term of their ratio of correct action selection, measured on a scale from 0 to 1 along the y-axis. For example, IB4-1 selected on average 64 out of 100 times correctly, while IB4-5 averaged at 79. Overall, a gain of 23% is achieved from using one state as the context in an example (IB4-1) to five states as the context in an example (IB4-5).

The performance advantage of IB4-5 over IB4-1 is attributed to the phenomenon of class noise reduction. When two examples are similar but are associated with different actions, a context with only the current state may not be sufficient to determine the relevance among a set of candidate examples. In particular, each training example used by IB4-1 is a snapshot of a single state in a sequence. As discussed earlier, such an example does not have sufficient context to disambiguate itself from similar examples because the same example derived from different contexts may require a different action.

Furthermore, IB4-n also suffers from context noise, where a fixed-size context mandates that each state should be affected by exactly the same context. IB4-n uses examples that always have the same number of states and attributes. When the number of relevant states differs from one situation to another, context noise occurs. In a sequential domain like the game of bridge, the execution of similar tactics may depend on different context sizes (different number of historical states). The execution of finesse, for example, may rely on a varying number of historical states given different situations (e.g., simple finesse[1] verses double finesse[2]). This underscores the need to use variable context sizes in examples to represent different situations.

The performance of SIBL4 is compared with those of the IB4-n algorithms and SIBL-Vote in Fig. 8(b). The correct action ratio of .83 is respectably better than those of IB4-n.

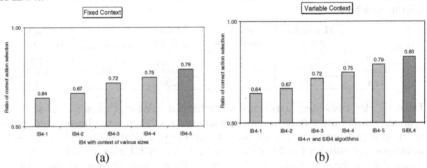

(a)   (b)

Fig. 8. A performance comparison of IB4-n that is based on the ratio of correct action selection. A gain of 23% is achieved from using one state in the context of an example (IB4-1) to five states in the context of an example (IB4-5); (b) A performance comparison of SIBL4 IB4-n in terms of correct action selection. With SIBL-SSM, a gain of 5% is achieved over IB4-n by using a set of sequential similarity metrics.

A breakdown of the ways decisions were made and their correct action selection ratio is shown in Fig. 9. In a total of 520 test instances, the candidates of various context sizes agree 40% of the time (unanimous) with a correct action selection ratio of .89. The distance metric makes 46% of the decisions with a correct ratio of .78. The convergence metric makes of 11% of the decisions with a correct ratio of .83. The consistency and recency metrics make 1% of the decisions each, with correct ratios of .86 and .67, respectively. The remaining 1% of action selections is done randomly with a correct ratio of .67.

---

[1] A simple finesse is one against only one missing card.
[2] A double finesse is one against two missing cards.

From Fig. 9, it may seem that the recency metric is useless because it has the same correct ratio as random selection. Also, the order in which the sequential similarity metrics are applied is based on the rationale that simpler metric is used first. A lesion study can be used to provide empirical explanation for the two observations. A *lesion study* is one where components of an algorithm are individually disabled to determine their contribution to the full algorithm's performance. [Kibler and Langley 1988]. Here, two sets of experiment are performed on SSM. The first set tests combined performance within the SSM, and the second set tests the individual components (metrics) of SSM.

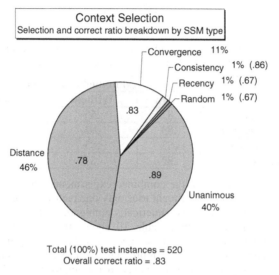

Context Selection
Selection and correct ratio breakdown by SSM type

Convergence   11%
Consistency   1% (.86)
Recency   1% (.67)
Random   1% (.67)

.83

Distance
46%   .78

.89

Unanimous
40%

Total (100%) test instances = 520
Overall correct ratio = .83

Fig. 9. SIBL-SSM action selection breakdown by SSM type. In a total of 520 test instances, 46% selects by distance, 40% are unanimous, 11% select by convergence, and selections by consistency, recency and random selection are each 1%. The correct selection ratios are .78, .89, .83, .86, .67 and .67, respectively.

In the *combined* experiments, all four metrics are applied in a sequence from the most simple (distance) to the most elaborate one (recency) in an effort to mitigate ambiguity discussed earlier. In the subsequent experiments, the most elaborate metric is removed to examine the contribution of that metric. Table 8 shows the five experiments in the combined experiments.

Table 9 shows the combined experiments' performance results both with or without a particular metric. The change in percent represents the contribution of a given metric. For example, when the distance metric is included, it contributed a performance improvement of 26.15% from .65 to .82, or (.82 − .65) / .65. As shown in the following table, except for the distance metric, the contributions are unimpressive. In fact, there is no improvement from consistency or recency. This is due to the small (1%) population of input examples used for the two metrics. As a result, the combined experiment does not show the full impact of each metric.

Table 8. Five experiments performed in the lesion study. A metric is examined by excluding the metric from the experiment.

	Metrics included	Metric examined
1	Distance, Convergence, Consistency, Recency, Random	N/A
2	Distance, Convergence, Consistency, Random	Recency
3	Distance, Convergence, Random	Consistency
4	Distance, Random	Convergence
5	Random	Distance

Table 9. Performance results both with and without a particular metric. The change is the improvement in terms of correct action selection ratio.

	Combined experiment		
	With	Without	Change
Distance	.82	.65	+26.15%
Convergence	.83	.82	+1.22%
Consistency	.83	.83	0.00%
Recency	.83	.83	0.00%

To mitigate the limitations of the combined experiments, individual experiments are performed. An *individual* experiment uses only one metric for the entire data set, with random selection if the metric is numerically ambiguous. The purpose here is to show the full impact of each metric. Table 10 shows the performance results of the individual experiments. As in the combined experiments, the correct action selection ratio of the distance metric at .82 represents a 26.15% improvement over random selection at .65. Similarly, the convergence metric improved 24.62%, the consistency and recency metric both improved 23.08%.

Table 10. Performance results both with and without a particular metric in an individual experiment where only one sequential similarity metric is used. The change is the improvement in terms of correct action selection ratio.

	Individual experiment		
	With	Random	Change
Distance	.82		26.15%
Convergence	.81	.65	24.62%
Consistency	.80		23.08%
Recency	.80		23.08%

Related Work

Sequence categorization (*SC*) assigns a category to a finite sequence, a string of elements of a fixed length. The function for category assignment is defined in a model that maps a sequence to a category from a finite set of categories. DNA secondary structure prediction is an example of SC. It predicts the category of the secondary structure of a DNA chain. A DNA chain is a sequence of amino acids, each of which is one of the 20 types of amino acids, represented by a set of 20 alphabetic letters [Qian and Sejnowski, 1988]. The model maps a DNA chain to one of three secondary structure categories, alpha helix (α), beta sheet (β), or coil (χ). An example of a DNA chain is (KQPEEPWFα), where α is the category of the secondary structure at the last amino acid F. Because the elements involved are singleton objects rather than more states, the search space for a synthesis problem is several orders of magnitude larger than that for a SC problem. A sequence of n elements, each from a set of m symbols, for example, has a search space of n^m. In DNA sequence prediction, for example, a sequence of $n = 7$ symbols, each may be one of $m = 20$ symbols, has a search space of 7^{20}. With a sequence of complex elements, the search space is much larger. In the game of bridge, for example, a play sequence of $n' = 7$ states, each from one of $m' = 446$ state descriptions, the search space is $7^{446} \gg 7^{20}$. The disparity in search space underscores the difference between SC and SIBL.

Sequence prediction (*SP*) predicts the most likely element that is preceded by a sequence of elements. Typically, SP relies on well-defined probability distribution for elements and state transitions in a time series. Given a finite number of elements and a state transition model, the probability distribution for the elements at each state, and the state transition probabilities can be calculated. The most likely next element in the sequence is the one with the highest probability and the most likely next state has the highest transition probability [Rabiner 1989]. SP using HMM requires a good estimation of the probability distributions to work well. It is usually applied to sequential problems with a finite set of states. When the number of states increases, it is less likely to have complete probability distributions because of insufficient samples. In a planning problem such as the game of bridge, the number of states could reach 10^{28} because there are 5.36E+28 possible deals as discussed above. In such a large state space, it is not feasible to estimate the probability distributions. For this reason, HMM and similar approaches is not feasible for sequential concept discovery. SD, the alternative investigated here, does not use a finite state transition model. Rather, it uses a multi-state context to provide context-related information to limit the search for a sequence.

Reinforcement Learning (RL) learns a mapping from states to actions with trial-and-error [Kaelbling et al. 1996]. RL consists of an environment of states, a reinforcement function, and a value function. A *reinforcement function* defines the reinforcement (reward/penalty) for a state transition, and maps state/action pairs to reinforcements. A *value function* defines state values (utilities) in terms of reinforcements with respect to terminal (goal) states. Most RL algorithms are used in a knowledge-poor context. Many RL algorithms have been applied to solve the robot perception problem. For example, *Utile Suffix Memory* (USM) is an RL algorithm that uses short-term memory to overcome *perceptual aliasing*: the mapping between states of the world and sensory inputs is not one-to-one in robot's perception [McCallum 1995]. In addition, USM uses memory-based (instance-based) techniques to uncover hidden states. Although the USM algorithm can reduce the number of training steps with minimal memory usage, the basic mechanism for an RL algorithm is the action-percept-reward cycle, where a reward can be explicitly expressed. Such a step-by-step reward may not be clear in incomplete information domains, such as bridge, where rewards for actions (card plays) typically come only at the end of a contest rather than at each step. In such a domain, credit (or penalty) assignments are often domain-specific rather than domain-independent.

More recently, an active research topic in knowledge discovery in databases and data mining (*KDD*) is sequential pattern mining (*SPM*) [Agrawal and Srikant, 1995]. The input is a *data sequence*, which is a list of elements, called an itemset. An itemset is a compound object, which contains one or more events. A *sequential pattern* is a subsequence of the data sequence such that the percentage of data sequences that contain the sequential pattern, called *support*, is greater than a predefined threshold. Detection of a sequential pattern establishes a link among the itemsets in the sequential pattern within a data sequence. A sequence in SPM is an ordered, but not necessarily contiguous, list of elements, or itemsets. In addition, an element in an SPM sequential pattern is marked by the time of occurrence, so that the time interval between the occurrences of two elements may be used for inference. The search space for SPM sequential patterns, however, is relatively small compared to that for problems like planning. This is because, like SC, an element in a SPM sequence is a single object that maps to a relatively small set of items. Furthermore, SPM assumes that the context in which a sequential pattern occurs has no bearing on the presence of the sequential pattern. In other words, the elements in an SPM sequence are static rather than dynamic, and it does not transition from one state to the next, which is an important characteristic for a synthesis problem.

Conclusion

The primary contribution of this work is the adoption of sequential dependency to learning and reasoning with sequential information. In terms of reasoning, sequential dependency uses a multi-state context to disambiguate a given state in a transition sequence. In terms of learning, sequential dependency provides the basis for creating a model for synthesis problem solving. The experimental results show that the learned model can effectively solve a synthesis task.

SIBL's strengths stem from the use of sequential dependency as a way to disambiguate two states with different derivations, and its systematic extension to an empirical learning approach to learn a synthesis task. The ability to distinguish between two otherwise ambiguous states improves the quality of action selection. In an application to the bridge domain, with only the knowledge for representing an example, action selection accuracy exceeds 80%. The weakness of SIBL is partly due to a duplication of state information within the attributes of an *s*-instance, i.e., the frame problem [McCarthy and Hayes, 1969]. The existence of such an attribute inevitably perturbs the difference calculation between two examples. Although a complete state specification is useful for analyzing the state differences between two examples, avoiding duplicated difference calculations for unchanged states increases the potential to improve the overall performance.

References

Agrawal, R., Srikant, R. (1995). "Mining Sequential Patterns." In *Proceedings of the Eleventh International Conference on Data Engineering (ICDE'95)*, Taipei, Taiwan, 3-14.

Aha, D. W. (1992). "Tolerating noisy, irrelevant and novel attributes in instance-based learning algorithm." *International Journal of Man-Machine Studies*, 36, 267-287.

Breiman, L., Friedman, J., Olshen, R., Stone, C. (1984). *Classification and Regression Trees*, Wadsworth International Group.

Clancey, W. J. (1985). "Heuristic Classification." *Artificial Intelligence*, 27, 289-350.

Epstein, S. L. and Shih, J. (1998). "." In *Proceedings 12th Biennial Conference of the Canadian Society for Computational Studies of intelligence (AI'98)*, Vancouver, BC, Canada, 442-454.

Fayyad, U. M., Piatetsky-Shapiro, G., Smyth, P., and Uthurusamy, R., eds. (1996). *Advances in Knowledge Discovery and Data Mining*: AAAI Press.

Ginsberg, M. (1999). "GIB: Steps towards an expert-level bridge-playing program." In *Proceedings of the Sixteenth International Joint Conference on Artificial Intelligence (IJCAI-99)*, Stockholm, Sweden, 584-590.

Kaelbling, L. P., Littman, M. L., and Moore, A. W. (1996). "Reinforcement Learning: A Survey." *Journal of Artificial Intelligence Research*, 4, 237-285.

Kibler, D., and Langley, P. (1988). "Machine Learning as an Experimental Science." *Machine Learning*, 3(1), 5-8.

McCallum, R. A. (1995). "Instance-Based Utile Distinctions for Reinforcement Learning with Hidden State." In *Proceedings of the Twelfth International Conference on Machine Learning*, Tahoe City, CA.

McCarthy, J. and Patrick J. Hayes, 1969. Some philosophical problems from the standpoint of artificial intelligence. In *Machine Intelligence 4*, ed. B.Meltzer and D. Michie. Edinburgh: Edinburgh University Press.

Qian, N., Sejnowski, T.J. (1988). "Predicting the secondary structure of globular proteins using neural network models." *Journal of Molecular Biology*, 202, 865-884.

Quinlan, J. R. (1986). "Induction of Decision Trees." *Machine Learning*, 1, 81-106.

Rabiner, L. R. (1989). "A tutorial on Hidden Markov Models and selected applications in speech recognition." *Proceedings of the IEEE*, 77(2), 257-285.

Salzberg, S. L. (1991). "A nearest hyperrectangle learning method." *Machine Learning*, 6, 251-276.

Winston, P. H. (1975). "Learning structural descriptions from examples." *The Psychology of Computer Vision*, P. H. Winston, ed., McGraw-Hill, New York.

Learning Feature Weights from Case Order Feedback

Armin Stahl

University of Kaiserslautern, Computer Science Department
Artificial Intelligence - Knowledge-Based Systems Group
67653 Kaiserslautern, Germany
stahl@informatik.uni-kl.de

Abstract. Defining adequate similarity measures is one of the most difficult tasks when developing CBR applications. Unfortunately, only a limited number of techniques for supporting this task by using machine learning techniques have been developed up to now. In this paper, a new framework for learning similarity measures is presented. The main advantage of this approach is its generality, because its application is not restricted to classification tasks in contrast to other already known algorithms. A first refinement of the introduced framework for learning feature weights is described and finally some preliminary experimental results are presented.

1 Introduction

Anyone who has implemented a case-based application knows that the definition of an adequate similarity measure is one of the most important tasks, but unfortunately, one of the most difficult tasks, too. Although similarity measures are often defined on a syntactical level only, the experience has shown that these similarity measures do not usually provide the best results. This means, one has to encode particular domain knowledge into the similarity measure to guarantee a suitable case retrieval. However, the definition of such semantic-oriented similarity measures is much more difficult than defining pure syntactical measures. One difficulty is the fact that the necessary domain knowledge is usually only available in form of a human domain expert. Nevertheless, such a domain expert has often problems to describe his knowledge in an explicit way as required for the definition of a similarity measure. One way to overcome this problem is a close collaboration of the domain expert with a CBR expert with the necessary experience to elicit the required knowledge form the domain expert. However, such close collaboration is time consuming work and leads to high development costs for the CBR application.

An additional problem arises if the intended CBR application is required to perform case adaptation. Then it is not enough to concentrate on the semantic similarity between the query and the case. As described in [9], one has to consider the adaptation procedure during the definition of the similarity measure

D.W. Aha and I. Watson (Eds.): ICCBR 2001, LNAI 2080, pp. 502–516, 2001.
© Springer-Verlag Berlin Heidelberg 2001

to guarantee the retrieval of 'adaptable' cases. However, the particular adaptation method to be used does usually not reflect the domain experts way of thinking. In this case, the domain expert can probably not give useful advise how to modify the semantic similarity measure regarding the adaptation procedure. Nevertheless, he should be able to evaluate the result of the adaptation procedure and to give useful feedback about the quality of the final solution.

In principle, such feedback can be used to simplify the acquisition of the similarity measure for a retrieval only system, too. Here, the domain expert can give some feedback on the quality of the retrieval result determined by an initial similarity measure. In this paper, we develop a new framework how to use such a kind of feedback to learn similarity measures more or less automatically.

In the next section we will present the basic framework for learning similarity measures by introducing an abstract concept, called 'similarity teacher'. We will discuss possible ways in which the role of the teacher might be filled. In the remainder of the paper we will apply this framework on learning feature weights which are one important part of almost every similarity measure. Therefore, we describe a new feature weight learning algorithm whose application is not limited to classification tasks as similar algorithms developed in the past. Due to the fact that many actual CBR applications go beyond simple classification systems, this is a crucial advantage of our learning framework. To demonstrate the basic capability of our approach, we present the results of a first basic evaluation. Finally, we will close with a short discussion of related work and further research objectives respecting the learning of similarity measures.

2   A Framework for Learning Similarity Measures

Several approaches for applying machine learning techniques in Case-Based Reasoning have been investigated in the past. Nevertheless, the primary focus was on the retain phase of the CBR cycle, i.e., the learning of new cases [1]. However, according to [8], the case base is not the only important *knowledge container* for a CBR system. Another very important knowledge carrier is the similarity measure, of course. Unfortunately, most approaches to learning the content of this knowledge container suffer from limited applicability because they strictly assume a CBR system used for classification [12,1,13,6,5,4]. Basically, the functionality of these learning algorithms requires a set of pre-classified cases. Due to this fact they are unable to handle cases with a non-classification solution part. Nevertheless, many currently successful commercial CBR systems do not perform pure classification, for example, the recommendation systems applied in e-Commerce [11].

In the following we will introduce a new framework for learning similarity measures, avoiding the requirement of the availability of pre-classified cases. The need for such a more general framework was already discussed in [2].

2.1   Similarity versus Utility

As discussed in [3], one can notice a difference in the semantics of the two concepts *similarity* and *utility* of cases. Basically, the similarity is only defined between the problem parts of two cases. In contrast, the utility is defined between a problem (usually called query) and the (known) solution part of a case, i.e., the utility is a measure for the usefulness of a solution for solving a given problem. Because the utility function is an a-posteriori criterion and often only partially known, in CBR the similarity function is used to approximate the utility function a-priori. However, a pure syntactical similarity considering only the problem part of a case is often not sufficient to obtain optimal retrieval results. This leads to the need of utility-oriented similarity measures that take the solution part of the case into account, too.

2.2   The Similarity Teacher

Consider the typical situation when using a CBR system as illustrated in Fig. 1. Given is a *query* representing a new problem of the application environment to be solved. Then, the retrieval function retrieves a set of cases from the *case base* by using the defined *similarity measure*. The *retrieval result*, i.e., a set of cases ordered by their similarity to the query, is finally presented to the user.

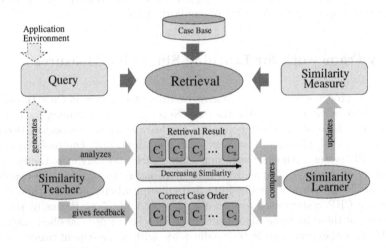

Fig. 1. A Framework for Learning Similarity Measures

The central element of our framework for learning similarity measures is a concept that we call *similarity teacher*. The job of this teacher is the evaluation of the determined retrieval result. Therefore, we assume that he possesses some implicit knowledge about the utility function described in Section 2.1. Due to this knowledge he can determine a kind of correct retrieval result, given through the *correct case order*. This means, we do not assume that he is able to correct the 'wrong' similarity values calculated by the similarity measure directly. Nevertheless, he should be able to order the retrieved cases correctly with respect to their utility for the query. This feedback information is then used by the *similarity learner* to update the previously used similarity measure. Therefore, the similarity learner has to compare the wrong retrieval result with the correct case order given by the teacher. During a similarity training phase, one can consider that the teacher generates special queries in order to obtain an optimal learning result. Depending on the concrete application scenario the similarity teacher can be realized differently. In the following we describe three typical examples.

Human domain expert. An obvious way to realize the similarity teacher is a human domain expert. As already mentioned before, a crucial problem during the development of a CBR system is the acquisition of the knowledge to be encoded in the similarity measure. The reason is the inability of many domain experts to formulate their knowledge in a formal way. However, they are usually able to give examples and to compare them. Therefore, we can assume that they can give the required feedback on the retrieval result, represented by the correct case order.

Customer in e-Commerce. Another situation occurs in many case-based e-Commerce applications. Here, it is often impossible to define an optimal similarity measure during the development of the application. The reason is that 'the optimal' similarity measure is usually determined by the preferences of the customers that are not known in advance by the developers of the e-Commerce system. This means that the system has to learn these preferences online to improve a pre-defined initial similarity measure. Of course, it is not very realistic to expect a customer to give explicit feedback about the complete retrieval result. However, due to his buying patterns he gives the system feedback in an implicit way. For example, if he finally buys a product with a lower similarity score than other recommended products, he partially defines the correct case order.

Adaptation procedure. The similarity teachers described in the two previous sections are both represented by human beings. However, the role of the similarity teacher can also be taken by an arbitrary adaptation procedure. As already mentioned in the introduction, the application of adaptation in CBR requires a special similarity measure because the utility of cases also depends on the adaptation method used. Thus utility can also be characterized as 'adaptability' [9]. Unfortunately, this complicates the definition of 'good' similarity measures enormously. However, the presented framework can help to overcome this problem. Therefore, we have to apply the given adaptation procedure on a set of retrieved cases. After that, the results of these adaptation attempts have to be evaluated, i.e., they have to be ordered respecting their utility for solving the problem specified by the query. The resulting case list can then again be interpreted as the correct case order on the originally retrieved cases. If we assume two different similarity measures, one for the basic case retrieval and one for the evaluation of the adaptation results, it is even possible to learn the first similarity measure in an automated way. In this way, the adaptation procedure coupled with the *evaluation similarity measure* that has not to consider the adaptability of cases, can be regarded as the similarity teacher. Here, the basic idea is the assumption that it is easier to define the evaluation measure than the adaptation-dependent retrieval measure. Of course, our approach can be applied without such an evaluation measure if the correct case order is determined by a human domain expert again. Nevertheless, one can imagine within our framework an approach in which the evaluation measure is first learned from a domain expert.

2.3 The Similarity Learner

Concerning the similarity learner, we suppose an arbitrary learning algorithm that is able to perform the kind of supervised learning described before. Depending on the structure of the similarity measures to be used, this algorithm may apply different machine learning techniques. In the following we assume attribute-value based case representations and a similarity measure consisting of three major parts:

1. a number of *local similarity measures* used to compare the values of single attributes
2. a number of *feature weights* representing the relative importance of each attribute
3. a *global similarity measure* responsible for the computation of a final similarity value base on the local similarities and feature weights

In the next section we will describe a first refinement of our similarity learning framework. Due to the fact that the learning of feature weights is an established area in machine learning, we will focus on this part of the similarity measure in the remainder of this paper. Therefore, we show how to implement an algorithm using the conjugate gradient method respecting the introduced learning framework.

3   Learning Feature Weights

3.1   Basics

To apply our feature weight learning approach we assume a flat attribute-value based case representation, i.e., a case $c = (v_1^c, \ldots, v_n^c)$ can be described as a vector with n values where v_i^c is the value of feature f_i. With respect to the similarity computation between a query and a case we introduce the following definition:

Definition 1 (Similarity). *Given a query* $q = (v_1^q, \ldots, v_n^q)$ *and a case* $c = (v_1^c, \ldots, v_n^c)$, *the similarity between* q *and* c *is defined as follows:*

$$Sim(q,c) = \sum_{i=1}^{n} w_i \cdot sim_i(v_i^q, v_i^c) = \sum_{i=1}^{n} w_i \cdot sim_i(q,c)$$

where $w_i \in [0,1]$ *is the weight, and* sim_i *is the local similarity measure of feature* f_i. *It holds* $\sum_{i=1}^{n} w_i = 1$ *and* $sim_i(v_i^q, v_i^c) \in [0,1]$, *and therefore, it holds* $Sim(q,c) \in [0,1]$, *too. To simplify the notation we write* $sim_i(q,c)$ *instead of* $sim_i(v_i^q, v_i^c)$ *in the following.*

Because we are mainly interested in the result of a retrieval, i.e., the similarity computation between a query and a set of cases, we now give a definition for the *retrieval result*.

Definition 2 (Retrieval Result). *Given a case base* $CB = \{c_1, \ldots, c_m\}$, *a query* q *and a similarity function* Sim, *we define the corresponding retrieval result as*

$$C_r^{Sim}(q, CB) = (c_1, \ldots, c_r)$$

where $c_i \in CB$ *and* $Sim(q, c_i) \geq Sim(q, c_j) \; \forall i,j$ *with* $1 \leq i < j \leq r$.

This means, the retrieval result $C_r^{Sim}(q, CB)$ consists of a subset of r cases out of the case base CB (partially) ordered by their similarity to the given query q. We do not explicitly define which cases have to appear in the retrieval result, i.e., the retrieval result can contain an arbitrary case selection out of the case base. A possible selection may consist of the r most similar cases with $r \leq m$.

The case order in the retrieval result is determined by the similarity measure Sim representing an approximation of the utility function (see Section 2.1). Because the core of our interest is the difference between these two functions, we now introduce the concept of the *feedback function*:

Definition 3 (Feedback Function). *Let* Q *be the set of all queries. The function* $fb : Q \times (CB \times CB) \rightarrow \{0,1\}$ *defined as*

$$fb(q, (c_1, c_2)) := \begin{cases} 1 & if \quad U(q, c_2) > U(q, c_1) \\ 0 & otherwise \end{cases}$$

is called the feedback function. $U(q, c_i)$ *is supposed to be a (possibly informal) measure of the utility of a case* c_i *with respect to a query* q.

The feedback function fb evaluates the utility of two cases given by the tuple (c_1, c_2) with respect to a query q. If c_2 has a higher utility than c_1 it returns a 1, otherwise it returns a 0. Because the utility function U is possibly an informal measure we do not necessarily suppose that $U(q, c_i)$ is computable. However, we assume the existence of a 'teacher' who is able to compare two cases (c_1, c_2) with respect to their utility for a given query q. This means, the teacher can give feedback regarding which of the two cases has the higher utility for q.

By using the feedback function fb we are now able to give a definition for the *correct case order*:

Definition 4 (Correct Case Order). *Let $CB = \{c_1, \ldots, c_m\}$ be a case base and q be a query. The correct case order is defined as*

$$C^U(q, CB) = (c_1, \ldots, c_m)$$

where $c_i \in CB$ and $fb(q, (c_i, c_j)) = 0\ \forall i, j$ with $1 \le i < j \le m$.

Because in the following we suppose a constant case base CB, we simply write $C_r^{Sim}(q)$ instead of $C_r^{Sim}(q, CB)$ and $C^U(q)$ instead of $C^U(q, CB)$.

After the introduction of these basic definitions, we will now discuss the core aspect of our weight learning approach, namely the error function used by the conjugate gradient learning algorithm to be described in Section 3.3.

3.2   Definition of the Error Function

As already described in Section 2, the goal of our similarity learner is to optimize the similarity measure in such a way that the case order in the retrieval result is equal to the correct case order given by the teacher. To be able to measure the difference between the correct case order C^U and the retrieval result C_r^{Sim} determined by the similarity measure Sim, we can define a special error function. A first attempt for the definition of such an error function is the *index error*:

Definition 5 (Index Error). *Consider a query q, a similarity function Sim and the corresponding retrieval result $C_r^{Sim}(q)$. We define the index error as*

$$E_I(q, C_r^{Sim}(q)) = \sum_{k=1}^{r-1} \sum_{l=k+1}^{r} fb(q, (c_k, c_l))$$

The index error can be interpreted as a measure for the 'disorder' in the retrieval result C_r^{Sim} in comparison to the correct case order C^U. If the two partial orders $C_r^{Sim}(q)$ and $C^U(q)$ are equal, it can be seen that $E_I = 0$. The maximum possible index error is obtained if $C_r^{Sim}(q)$ is the reverse order of $C^U(q)$.

However, if we want to apply a conjugate gradient algorithm for learning feature weights, the previously introduced error function is not usable. The reason for this is that the index error E_I is not partially derivable w.r.t. a weight w_i. In the following we define an alternative error function in order to overcome this problem. First, we give a definition for the *similarity error for a case pair*:

Definition 6 (Similarity Error for a Case Pair). *Let q be a query, Sim be a similarity measure, and (c_1, c_2) be a case pair with $Sim(q, c_1) \ge Sim(q, c_2)$. We define the similarity error for the case pair as*

$$E_{Sim}(q, (c_1, c_2)) = (Sim(q, c_1) - Sim(q, c_2)) \cdot fb(q, (c_1, c_2))$$

$$= (\sum_{i=1}^{n} w_i \cdot (sim_i(q, c_1) - sim_i(q, c_2))) \cdot fb(q, (c_1, c_2))$$

In the next step we extend this definition to a *similarity error for a retrieval result*:

Definition 7 (Similarity Error for a Retrieval Result). *Let q be a query and $C_r^{Sim}(q)$ be the corresponding retrieval result. The similarity error of the retrieval result is defined as*

$$E_{Sim}^{\alpha}(q, C_r^{Sim}(q)) = \sum_{k=1}^{r-1} \sum_{l=k+1}^{r} E_{Sim}(q, (c_k, c_l)) \cdot (l - k)^{\alpha}$$

where $(l - k)^{\alpha}$ is called the index-distance weight which can be influenced by the parameter $\alpha \geq 0$.

The index-distance weight influenced by the parameter α can be used to manipulate the similarity error depending on the degree of 'disorder' in the retrieval result compared with the correct case order. Generally, a greater α leads to an increased impact of the disorder on the similarity error.

If we are able to change the similarity measure Sim in such a way that the similarity error $E_{Sim}^{\alpha}(q, C_r^{Sim}(q))$ for a query q becomes 0, then we have reached our goal - but only for this particular query q. However, we want to optimize the similarity measure Sim in a more global manner, i.e., we are searching for a similarity measure Sim leading to a similarity error $E_{Sim}^{\alpha}(q_i, C_r^{Sim}(q_i)) = 0$ for any arbitrary query q_i. This leads us to the following definitions:

Definition 8 (Retrieval Collection). *Let $Q_s = \{q_1, \ldots, q_s\}$ be a set of queries. The set*

$$\hat{C}^{Sim}(Q_s) = \{(q_1, C_{r_1}^{Sim}(q_1)), \ldots, (q_s, C_{r_s}^{Sim}(q_s))\}$$

is called the retrieval collection for Q_s where $C_{r_j}^{Sim}(q_j) = \{c_{1_j}, \ldots, c_{r_j}\}$ is the corresponding retrieval result for query q_j.

Definition 9 (Average Similarity Error). *The average similarity error for a retrieval collection $\hat{C}^{Sim}(Q_s)$ is defined as*

$$\hat{E}_{Sim}^{\alpha}(\hat{C}^{Sim}(Q_s)) = \frac{1}{s} \cdot \sum_{j=1}^{s} E_{Sim}^{\alpha}(q_j, C_{r_j}^{Sim}(q_j))$$

$$= \frac{1}{s} \cdot \sum_{j=1}^{s} \sum_{k=1}^{r_j - 1} \sum_{l=k+1}^{r_j} E_{Sim}(q_j, (c_{k_j}, c_{l_j})) \cdot (l - k)^{\alpha} \qquad (1)$$

Now we are able to describe our learning goal by using the average similarity error $\hat{E}_{Sim}^{\alpha}$. Suppose that we have a set of queries $Q_s = \{q_1, \ldots, q_s\}$. To get an adequate similarity measure Sim with respect to the utility function given by the teacher, we have to minimize the average similarity error $\hat{E}_{Sim}^{\alpha}(\hat{C}^{Sim}(Q_s))$. If we are able to construct a Sim leading to an average similarity error of $\hat{E}_{Sim}^{\alpha} = 0$, we can call Sim an *optimal similarity measure* respecting Q_s.

From the machine learning point of view we can characterize the set of queries Q_s together with the corresponding correct case orders $C^U(q_i)$ given by the teacher as the *training data* for our learning algorithm.

3.3   The Learning Algorithm

After the introduction of the average similarity error $\hat{E}^{\alpha}_{Sim}$ we will now describe an algorithm that tries to minimize this error function by adjusting the feature weights w_i as part of the similarity measure Sim. Therefore, we use a conjugate gradient algorithm performing an iterative search for a local minimum of our error function $\hat{E}^{\alpha}_{Sim}$. To apply this algorithm we assume a starting situation given by:

- initial similarity measure Sim with feature weight-vector $w = (w_1, \ldots, w_n)$
- query set Q_s
- case base CB
- a 'similarity teacher' (see Section 2.2)
- a fixed value $\alpha \geq 0$

We assume that the similarity teacher is able to give the algorithm his knowledge about the utility function U by realizing the feedback function fb introduced in definition 3. Assuming this starting situation we can describe the basic learning algorithm as follows:

1. Initialize weight-vector w
2. Start retrieval procedure for Q_s to determine $\hat{C}^{Sim}(Q_s)$
3. Compute average similarity error $\hat{E}^{\alpha}_{Sim}(\hat{C}^{Sim}(Q_s))$
4. Initialize learning rate λ
5. **While** stop-predicate = false **do**
   a) Generate new Sim': $\forall i \; w'_i := w_i - \frac{\partial \hat{E}^{\alpha}_{Sim}(\hat{C}^{Sim}(Q_s))}{\partial w_i} \cdot \lambda$
   b) Normalize $w'_i := \frac{w_i}{\sum_{j=1}^{n} w_j}$
   c) Start retrieval procedure for Q_s to determine $\hat{C}^{Sim'}(Q_s)$
   d) Compute average similarity error $\hat{E}^{\alpha}_{Sim'}(\hat{C}^{Sim'}(Q_s))$
   e) **If** $\hat{E}^{\alpha}_{Sim'}(\hat{C}^{Sim'}(Q_s)) < \hat{E}^{\alpha}_{Sim}(\hat{C}^{Sim}(Q_s))$
      then $Sim := Sim'$
      else $\lambda := \frac{\lambda}{2}$
6. Output: New similarity measure Sim

Basically, the algorithm can be separated into two phases which are iteratively repeated until the stop-predicate becomes true. In the first phase the algorithm performs the retrievals for the given query set Q_s by using the actual similarity measure Sim including the actual weight-vector w. In the second phase the algorithm uses the feedback of the teacher to calculate the error function $\hat{E}^{\alpha}_{Sim}$. Depending on the result of this error function a new similarity measure Sim' with a new weight-vector w' is computed. If the next iteration shows an improvement in the error function, Sim' is accepted, i.e., $Sim := Sim'$. Else the learning rate is decreased by $\lambda := \frac{\lambda}{2}$.

As typical for a conjugate gradient algorithm, it uses the derivation of the error function to update the feature weights. According to equation 1, the partial derivation of the average similarity error $\hat{E}^{\alpha}_{Sim}$ w.r.t. the weight w_i is as follows:

$$\frac{\partial \hat{E}^\alpha_{Sim}(\hat{C}^{Sim}(Q_s))}{\partial w_i} = \frac{1}{s} \cdot \sum_{j=1}^{s} \sum_{k=1}^{r_j-1} \sum_{l=k+1}^{r_j} (sim_i(q_j, c_{k_j}) - sim_i(q_j, c_{l_j})) \cdot$$
$$\cdot fb(q, (c_{k_j}, c_{l_j})) \cdot (l-k)^\alpha$$

Initialization of feature weights. As in other algorithms that apply a conjugate gradient method, the initialization of the start point, here given by the initial weights, is important for the success of the approach. In general, it cannot be guaranteed that the algorithm is able to find the global minimum of the error function. However, a 'good' initialization of w can enable the algorithm to find the global minimum or at least a relatively low local minimum. Basically, one can distinguish between three possible approaches to initialize w:

1. use an uniform weight-vector, i.e., $\forall i \ w_i = \frac{1}{n}$
2. initialize the weights randomly
3. a domain expert defines the initial weights

Of course, the third approach is usually the best choice because a domain expert should be able to initialize the weights in a more 'intelligent' way by using his domain knowledge.

The role of the learning rate. Similar to other machine learning approaches, the choice of the learning rate λ is crucial for the outcome of the algorithm. Generally, we can notice a tradeoff between a very small and a too large λ. A quite small λ leads to a poor convergence speed, however, the advantage of a small λ is a higher probability of finding the next local minimum with respect to w. This is important if the weights were initialized by a domain expert because this local minimum should normally correspond to a very accurate weight-vector. On the other hand, if λ is too large, the algorithm will 'jump over' this nearby minimum. This leads to the risk that the algorithm will 'get caught' in another local minimum corresponding to a much higher error value.

To simplify the selection of an appropriate initial learning rate, we have introduced a normalization with respect to the resulting change of the weights in the first learning step. We allow the user of the learning algorithm to determine a maximal change in one of the weights w_i represented by $\Delta_{max}w$. The corresponding initial learning rate λ is then computed as follows:

$$\lambda = \frac{\Delta_{max}w}{max\{\Delta w_i\}} \quad \text{where} \quad \Delta w_i = \frac{\partial \hat{E}^\alpha_{Sim}}{\partial w_i}$$

Consider the example of a domain with four features and an initial weight-vector $w = (0.25, 0.25, 0.25, 0.25)$. If the user determines $\Delta_{max}w = 0.05$, the new weight-vector computed in the first learning step will at least contain one weight w_i with $w_i = 0.2$ or $w_i = 0.3$. For all other weights w_j holds $w_j \in [0.2, 0.3]$.

A further improvement with respect to the determination of an appropriate learning rate is the introduction of a *dynamic learning rate* adapted for every single learning step. Up to now, we have assumed that the initial learning rate is only changed if a learning step increases the value of the error function, i.e., $\hat{E}^\alpha_{Sim'} > \hat{E}^\alpha_{Sim}$. Then the learning rate is halved to guarantee the convergence of the learning algorithm. During the experiments we have made the observation that we can improve the learning efficiency by using a dynamic learning rate that depends on the actual value of $\hat{E}^\alpha_{Sim}$. The basic idea of this approach is the following heuristic: the larger the error $\hat{E}^\alpha_{Sim}$, the more the weights have to be changed. This heuristic can be realized by replacing λ by $\lambda \cdot \hat{E}^\alpha_{Sim}$ in step 5.a of the algorithm. Of course, then we have also to update the normalization of the initial learning rate with respect to the additional factor $\hat{E}^\alpha_{Sim}$.

The stop-predicate. To guarantee the termination of the algorithm we have to introduce a stop-predicate. Generally, various possibilities to realize this stop-predicate exist [13]. For our experiments we have selected a minimal change of the error function.

4 Experiments

The primary motivation for the development of the introduced approach for learning similarity measures was the perception that any sophisticated adaptation approach requires a special similarity measure to retrieve the best adaptable cases. In [10] for example, we have presented a compositional adaptation method used to perform case-based configuration of personal computers. However, for a first evaluation of our learning algorithm we have decided to use a very simple artificial test domain, due to the huge complexity of the PC-domain. Nevertheless, we think that the results obtained from this test domain are sufficient to demonstrate the basic capability of our approach.

4.1 An Artificial Test Domain

The used case structure consists of 5 attributes, each of which has a value range of [0,100]. The local similarity measure for each attribute is a quite simple distance-based function:

$$sim_i(q, c) = sim_i(v_i^q, v_i^c) := 1 - \frac{|v_i^q - v_i^c|}{100}$$

The global similarity measure is a weighted sum as defined in Definition 1 with the particular weight-vector $w = (w_1, w_2, w_3, w_4, w_5)$. For the initial weights we have chosen a uniform w^I, i.e., $\forall i \ w_i^I = 0.2$. To get the necessary case base CB we have generated 100 cases randomly. All cases are completely filled, i.e., every attribute has been assigned a random value between 0 and 100.

4.2   The Test Scenario

For our experiments we have realized the similarity teacher in the form of a pre-defined *target weight-vector* w^T. This means, the assumed similarity measure with this special weight-vector determines the correct case order for a given query. Of course, this situation will not appear in real world application scenarios due to the not explicitly known learning target. However, it enabled us to perform the experiments automatically and without using a complex adaptation procedure. Another advantage of this approach is the possibility to compare the learned weight-vectors with the correct target weights.

To get an impression of the amount of training data needed to obtain satisfactory learning results, we have performed a large number of learning cycles with a varying size s of the query sets Q_s. Further, we have varied the size r of the retrieval results $C_r^{Sim}(q, CB)$ used by the learning algorithm. Therefore, we have selected some cases out of the retrieval result (complete CB) returned by CBR-Works, the CBR tool used in our experiments. To simulate a realistic application scenario, we have restricted the retrieval result to between 5 and 25 cases. This corresponds to the necessary procedure if one wants to apply our learning approach in a real world application. On the one hand, a domain expert could not be expected to determine the correct case order for all cases in a large case base. On the other hand, the application of a sophisticated adaptation procedure on all cases would perhaps be limited by computational complexity. The concrete selection of the cases to be used in our experiments was again realized randomly with the restriction that the most and the least similar cases are always selected.

For the different combinations of s and r we recorded the finally learned weight-vectors w^L, i.e., the weight-vectors calculated so far when the stop-predicate became true. To evaluate the quality of these weight-vectors, we used two measures:

1. the *average index error* $\hat{E}_I(Q_{1000}^T) = \frac{1}{1000} \sum_{j=1}^{1000} E_I(q_j, C_m^{Sim}(q_j))$ (see definition 5) for a fixed test query set Q_{1000}^T consisting of 1000 randomly generated queries and $m = |CB|$. To get meaningful evaluation results, the test query set is different from the training query sets used during the learning phase.
2. an additional *weight error* $E_W(w^L, w^T) = \sum_{i=1}^{n} |w_i^T - w_i^L|$

Because the quality of the results varies for different query sets (especially for small s) we have repeated our experiments several times with different randomly generated Q_s. Finally, we determined the *best*, the *average* and the *worst learning result* for each combination of s and r. Due to the lower variance for large s, we decreased the number of iterations while increasing s. Concerning the different learning parameters introduced in section 3.3, we selected the following values: $\Delta_{max}w = 0.1$ and $\alpha = 1$.

4.3   Results

Fig. 2 shows the resulting average index error $\hat{E}_I(Q_{1000}^T)$ for three different values of r and four different values of s. A legend like '100x10' states that the results were obtained by repeating the learning procedure for 100 different query sets Q_s with $s = 10$, i.e., the first number represents the number of experiments while the second number represents the size of the query set used. Additionally, we have shown the value of $\hat{E}_I(Q_{1000}^T)$ for the initial weights w^I.

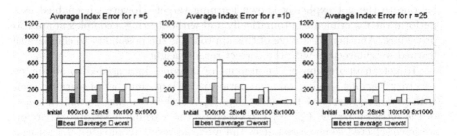

Fig. 2. Evaluation Results

One expected result is the fact that larger query sets and larger retrieval results lead to much better learning results because then the algorithm gets more information to find a globally valid weight-vector.

Another very important observation is the wide variation in the results of different identical experiments especially for small s. For example, the best index error for the '100x10/r=5' experiment is 144 while the worst index error is 1041. This suggests that the efficiency of the learning algorithm could significantly be improved by using 'good' Q_s instead of randomly generated ones.

The results for the three different values for r show that smaller retrieval results require a significant larger number of queries to obtain comparable results as with large retrieval results. In principle, a domain expert has to perform the same number of case-pair comparisons for the '$s=10/r=10$' and the '$s=45/r=5$' experiment. And in fact, the observed learning results are very similar. Therefore, dependent on the particular application, it is possible to obtain the necessary training data either by a large number of queries or by a large number of analyzed cases, i.e., by the determination of the correct case order for many cases.

Finally, in Table 1 we have summarized some of the learned weight-vectors in comparison to the target weights w^T and the initial weights w^I. The last two rows of the table contain the weight errors E_W for the particular learned weights or the average weight error $\emptyset E_W$ for all weight-vectors of one experiment respectively. Here, we can notice similar results as in the diagrams discussed before. Again, the size and the quality of the query set Q_s and the value of r are the major criteria for obtaining weight-vectors that are close to the target weights. Another observation is the lower precision in the learning results for the relative small weights. This can be explained with their minor impact on the error function.

Table 1. Comparison of Learned Weight-Vectors

			Learned Weight-Vectors									
			r=5				r=10				r=25	
			100×10		25×45		100×10		25×45		5×1000	
w_i	w^T	w^I	best	worst	best	worst	best	worst	best	worst	best	worst
w_1	**0.033**	0.2	0.046	0.2	0.045	0.124	0.046	0.082	0.028	0.07	0.03	0.032
w_2	**0.33**	0.2	0.36	0.2	0.299	0.258	0.316	0.325	0.327	0.296	0.334	0.334
w_3	**0.033**	0.2	0.05	0.2	0.056	0.087	0.04	0.073	0.047	0.107	0.04	0.046
w_4	**0.2**	0.2	0.169	0.2	0.208	0.241	0.204	0.175	0.197	0.19	0.199	0.189
w_5	**0.4**	0.2	0.375	0.2	0.388	0.291	0.393	0.345	0.4	0.336	0.396	0.399
E_W	0.0	0.667	0.11	0.667	0.092	0.369	0.087	0.45	0.029	0.221	0.015	0.027
$\emptyset E_W$	-	-	0.345		0.193		0.206		0.076		0.02	

5 Related Work and Outlook

Some basic considerations concerning the learning of similarity measures can be found in [7]. Particularly, the learning of feature weights is a classic topic in the area of machine learning. A very good overview of different approaches used in CBR is given in [12]. Another very interesting approach that learns asymmetric similarity measures by adjusting two different weight-vectors (one for every 'side' of each local measure) is described in [6]. An algorithm that considers the costs of the decisions made with the learned weights is proposed in [13]. An approach that uses only 'boolean' feedback, i.e. the information whether the solution of a retrieved case is the same as the target solution or not, is described in [4]. However, all these approaches are restricted to classification tasks.

A more general approach is presented in [14]. Here, the teacher is able to give the system feedback about the desired score of a case. Nevertheless, the use of a special two-layer network architecture to model a case-base leads to some limitations. For example, only discrete feature value ranges can be represented and no local similarity measures to compare feature values are supported.

In this paper we have presented a framework for learning similarity measures independent of the application task. Further, we have described a first application of our framework for learning feature weights. Due to the evaluation results, we have seen that 'good' query sets are one crucial factor affecting the quality of the obtained learning results. Therefore, we are planning to investigate how to determine such 'good' queries. Additionally, it will be helpful to apply our algorithm to real-world problems and to perform more sophisticated evaluation experiments. Further, it is our goal to apply the framework to learning local similarity measures instead of learning feature weights only.

In our view, the ability to learn similarity measures more or less automatically will be a significant advance in the application of Case-Based Reasoning in real world applications. However, due to the lack of generally applicable approaches, we see an urgent need for further research in this area.

Acknowledgements. The author would like to thank Ralph Bergmann for the helpful discussions during the development of the presented approach. This work was funded by the European Commission (GROWTH programme, contract number GRD1-1999-10385, the FIORES-II project: Character Preservation and Modelling in Aesthetic and Engineering Design).

References

1. D. Aha. Case-based learning algorithms. In *Proceedings of the DARPA Case-Based Reasoning Workshop*, pages 147–158. Morgan Kaufmann, 1991.
2. D. W. Aha and D Wettschereck. Case-based learning: Beyond classification of feature vectors. In *Proceedings of the 9th European Conference on Machine Learning (ECML'97)*. Springer, 1997.
3. R. Bergmann, M. Michael Richter, S. Schmitt, A. Stahl, and I. Vollrath. Utility-oriented matching: A new research direction for Case-Based Reasoning. In *Professionelles Wissensmanagement: Erfahrungen und Visionen. Proceedings of the 1st Conference on Professional Knowledge Management*. Shaker, 2001.
4. A. Bonzano, P. Cunningham, and B. Smyth. Using introspective learning to improve retrieval in CBR: A case study in air traffic control. In *Proceedings of the 2nd International Conference on Case-Based Reasoning (ICCBR-97)*. Springer, 1997.
5. Igor Kononenko. Estimating attributes: Analysis and extensions of RELIEF. In *Proceedings of the European Conference on Machine Learning*, pages 171–182, 1994.
6. F. Ricci and P. Avesani. Learning a local similarity metric for case-based reasoning. In *Proceeding of the 1st International Conference on Case-Based Reasoning (ICCBR'95)*, pages 301–312. Springer, 1995.
7. Michael M. Richter. Classification and learning of similarity measures. Technical Report SR-92-18, 1992.
8. Michael M. Richter. The knowledge contained in similarity measures. Invited Talk at ICCBR-95, 1995.
9. B. Smyth and M. T. Keane. Retrieving adaptable cases: The role of adaptation knowledge in case retrieval. In *Proceedings of the 1st European Workshop on Case-Based Reasoning*. Springer, 1993.
10. A. Stahl and R. Bergmann. Applying recursive CBR for the customization of structured products in an electronic shop. In *Proceedings of the 5th European Workshop on Case-Based Reasoning*. Springer, 2000.
11. M. Stolpmann and S. Wess. *Optimierung der Kundenbeziehung mit CBR-Systemen*. Business and Computing. Addison-Wesley, 1999.
12. Dietrich Wettschereck and David W. Aha. Weighting features. In *Proceeding of the 1st International Conference on Case-Based Reasoning (ICCBR'95)*, pages 347–358. Springer Verlag, 1995.
13. W. Wilke and R. Bergmann. Considering decision cost during learning of feature weights. In *Proceedings of the 3rd European Workshop on Case-Based Reasoning*. Springer, 1996.
14. Z. Zhang and Q. Yang. Dynamic refiniement of feature weights using quantitative introspective learning. In *Proceedings of the 16th International Joint Conference on Artificial Intelligence (IJCAI 99)*, 1999.

Adaptation by Applying Behavior Routines and Motion Strategies in Autonomous Navigation

Haris Supic[1] and Slobodan Ribaric[2]

[1] Faculty of Electrical Engineering, University of Sarajevo,
Skenderija 70, 71000 Sarajevo, Bosnia and Herzegovina
hsupic@utic.net.ba
[2] Faculty of Electrical Engineering and Computing, University of Zagreb,
Unska 3, 10 000 Zagreb, Croatia
slobodan.ribaric@fer.hr

Abstract. This paper presents our current efforts toward development of high-level behavior routines and motion strategies for the stepwise case-based reasoning (SCBR) approach. The SCBR approach provides an appropriate architectural framework for autonomous navigation system in which *situation cases* are used to support the situation module, and *route cases* are used to support the high-level route planning module. In the SCBR approach, adaptation knowledge comes in the form of high-level behavior routines and motion strategies. The SCBR system determines next action based on an analysis of the generated view in terms of positions of relevant objects. Thus, higher-level case-based symbolic reasoning intervenes at the action selection points to determine which action vector is appropriate to control the SCBR system. In order to qualitatively evaluate the SCBR approach, we have developed a simulation environment. This simulation environment allows us to visually evaluate the progress of an SCBR system while it runs through a predefined virtual world.

1 Introduction

Case-based reasoning systems have traditionally been used to perform high-level reasoning in problem domains that can be adequately described using discrete, symbolic representations. Many real-world problem domains, such as autonomous robotic navigation, require continuous performance, such as online sensorimotor interaction with the environment, and continuous adaptation and learning during the performance task. Continuous problem domains require different representations and place additional constraints on the problem solving process [1]. An example of system that uses case-based methods in continuous environment is the ACBARR system [2]. The ACBARR system uses a case-based method for on-line selection of robotic control behaviors, and on-line adaptation of selected behaviors to the immediate demands of the environment, within a reactive approach to autonomous robotic control. Context-mediated behavior (CMB) is mechanism for ensuring that an agent behaves appropriately for its context [3]. There have been several efforts to apply case-based reasoning to route-planning problems. Haigh and Veloso have described

D.W. Aha and I. Watson (Eds.): ICCBR 2001, LNAI 2080, pp. 517–530, 2001.

an approach to applying case-based reasoning methods to route planning [4]. Smyth and Cunningham have investigated the utility problem in CBR using a case-based route planner [5]. Stratified case-based reasoning is an approach in which abstract solutions produced during hierarchical problem solving are used to assist case-based retrieval, matching, and adaptation [6]. A route-finding task is used to demonstrate the utility of this approach.

There is a considerable amount of work addressing issues related to autonomous robot system architectures. A categorization, which seems to be accepted by the research community, divides system architectures into the following groups: planning (deliberative), reactive and hybrid. The architecture of a system built using the planning approach consists of the following functional blocks: sensing, building a model of the state of the world, planning and actuator control modules. In reactive systems, intelligent behavior is achived through using a set of behaviors. Each behavior connects perception to action. Example of such system is Brooks' subsumption architecture [7]. Hybrid architectures integrate the planning and the reactive approaches. They combine the high-level planning activities of the planning approach with the activities of the low-level reactive approach.

The ability to learn is often achieved by using reinforcement learning, neural network or genetic algorithms and is mostly implemented in a local environment. The work on the SCBR approach is primarily motivated by the desire to develop intelligent system that integrate local observations and global environment structures. Case-based reasoning in such problem domains requires significant enhancements to the basic case-based reasoning methods used in traditional case-based reasoning systems.

2   An Overview of the SCBR Approach

Case-based reasoning is a paradigm based on remembering previous experience (cases) [8, 9]. The stepwise case-based reasoning (SCBR) approach provides an appropriate architectural framework for autonomous navigation system in which *situation cases* are used to support the situation module, and *route cases* are used to support the high-level route planning module (see figure 1).

Position and orientation of system is described by state vector S_{ij}:

$$S_{ij} = [x_{ij}, y_{ij}, \theta_{ij}]^T .$$

This indicates the system is at position (x_{ij}, y_{ij}) and orientation θ_{ij} with respect to a Cartesian frame of reference. Index i corresponds to situation i and index j corresponds to step j for the current situation.

System actions are applicable commands of the system's effectors. An SCBR system is commanded with a desired translational speed, v_{ij}, and a desired turning rate, ω_{ij}:

$$a_{ij} = [v_{ij}, \omega_{ij}]^T .$$

The route planning module generates high-level sketchy plans, based on route cases. The route case retrieved from casebase is used as a resource to guide the sequencing of the route. This module cannot construct a detailed plan. Actions in the route plan will have to be left unspecified until the situation in which they are required arises and relevant details of the local environment can be determined by direct observation. The route planning module is accessible via a user interface allowing a human operator to monitor the navigation process or make their own suggestions, thus forcing the system to follow some particular route.

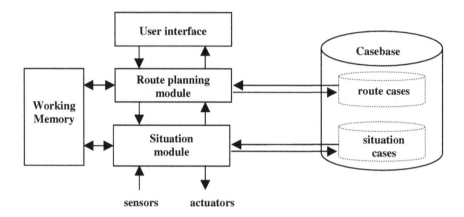

Fig. 1. An SCBR system architecture. Situation cases are used to support the situation module, and route cases are used to support the high-level route planning module

The route planning module poses tasks to a situation module as a sequence of subgoals. The situation module is then responsible for reaching the subgoal location while avoiding obstacles. If the situation module fails to reach the subgoal location, the route has to be replanned by the route planning module. The situation module interacts with sensors, the actuators, the casebase and the working memory in a bidirectional way. This module is responsible for situation assessment, behavior selection and behavior execution. The situation module controls the sequence of the actions based on actual situation case.

Route cases. A route case is a description of the route, holding the source and destination of the route. Let R denote the set of all possible routes in the environment. A route R $(P_s, P_d) \in$ R from the source place P_s to the destination place P_d is specified as an ordered set of concrete situation cases P_i:

$$R (P_s, P_d) = \{P_s, \ldots, P_i, \ldots, P_d\} .$$

Situation cases. Each situation case represents a particular context, that is, a particular class of problem situations. The term situation refers to any identifiable structure (configuration) of the local environment. Situation cases include not only a description of the current situation, but also information about how to behave in it. A situation case is defined by situation properties some of which are represented on the level of concrete situation cases, others, those that are shared by several concrete situation cases, are reflected by abstract situation cases. Examples of concrete situation cases are illustrated in figure 7.

3 The SCBR's Execution Cycles

The execution of an SCBR autonomous navigation task proceeds through a number of cycles.

Table 1. An overall simplified algorithm depicting SCBR's execution cycles

```
/*Input: Start sit. case (SC) and start state vector*/
/*Output: Goal sit. case (GC) and goal state vector*/

Main_SCBR_Cycle {
current_route_case=Select_Route_Case (SC, GC);
FOR i =1 to N DO
  current_situation_case=current_route_case[i];
  use_situation_case(current_situation_case);
}
/*use_situation_case procedure*/

use_situation_case(current_situation_case)
{
next_subgoal=current_route_case[i+1];
ms = motion_strategy for next_subgoal;
N  = number of sit. cases in current_route_case;
FOR  j =1 to N  step 2 DO
{
    current_behavior=ms[j];current_landmark=ms[j+1];
    DO
    current_view = Observe at the current state;
    Compute clutter scale parameter (s_c);
    Compute open space scale parameter (s_os);
    If (danger of collision = TRUE) {
      Vf=[f1,..fn]=Focus_View(current_view);
      a_ij=Obstacle_Avoidance(Vf);
    else
      Vf=[f1,…, fn]=Focus_View(current_view);
      a_ij=current_behavior(Vf);}
    Compute ΔTa;
    Output action a_ij during ΔTa; Generate new state;
    Add new state (S_ij)and a_ij to the working memory;
      UNTIL (current_landmark reached or max_steps reached)
}
return  to Main_SCBR_Cycle;
}
```

Autonomous navigation task is defined as the task of finding a path along which a system can move safely from a source point to a destination point. A source point and a destination point are specified directly by the user. A destination point determines a location in the environment, that the SCBR system is commanded to navigate towards. An overall simplified algorithm depicting SCBR's execution cycles is presented in table 1.

The route case *current_route_case* retrieved from casebase is used as a resource to guide the sequencing of the route. This case is not a detailed plan. Actions have to be left unspecified until the situation in which they are required arises and selected features of the local environment can be observed by direct perception. The *current_route_case* can be viewed as a set of subgoals to be achieved. Each subgoal represents a concrete situation case. The SCBR execution cycle poses tasks to the *use_situation_case* procedure as a sequence of subgoals (see table 1). As *use_situation_case* procedure runs, it is trying to apply appropriate motion strategy, until the subgoal has been achieved. During a particular segment of selected behavior, the system moves through the environment by setting its action vector in response to focused view inputs according to the selected behavior routine.

4   Adaptation by Applying Behaviors and Motion Strategies

In the SCBR approach, adaptation knowledge comes in the form of behavior routines and motion strategies.

4.1   Behavior Routines

Behavior routines are elements of the adaptation knowledge that enable a system to construct actions. Each behavior connects perception to action. Based on carefully selected sensory information, each behavior produces actions to control the system:

$$a_{ij} = [v_x, v_y, \omega] = B_i (f_1, .. f_n) .$$

where:

v_x, v_y, ω components of action vector a $_{ij}$,

$f_1, ... f_n$ selected features from actual view.

In our present system the following set of behavior routines is used:

- *Door_localize (DL)*. This behavior initiates process that searches for a doorway (to be used for movement into another room).
- *Open_space_localize (OSL)*. This behavior initiates actions that search for an open space. It is used to find the orientation directly facing an open space.
- *Door_traversal (DT)*. This behavior routine traverses a door way.
- *Left_wall_following (LWF)*. This behavior makes the system move at a constant distance from a left wall.
- *Right_wall_following (RWF)*. This behavior makes the system move at a constant distance from a right wall.

- *Middle_line_following (MLF)*. This behavior is for motion at an equal distance from left and right walls.
- *Safe_advance (SA)*. This behavior is designed to move the system forward at maximum speed V_{max}.
- *Left_parabolic_turn (LPT)*. This behavior serves to trace a left directed parabolic trajectory.
- *Right_parabolic_turn (RPT)*. This behavior serves to trace a right directed parabolic trajectory.
- *Move_to_object (MTO)*. This behavior is used to approach an object in the current view.
- *Obstacle_avoidance (OA)*. The objective of this behavior is to move the system at a safe distance from obstacles.

All of these behaviors assume specific perceivable objects in the local environment. An attention during the behavior execution is focused to objects relevant for the current situation. These objects provide suggestions of how behavioral parameters should be set. The selected behavior routine uses the focused perceptual data to compute next actions.

4.2 Motion Strategies

Within the SCBR approach, an SCBR system motion results from the execution of motion strategies. A motion strategy represents an alternating sequence of behaviors and landmarks:

$$ms = [B_1, L_1, B_2, L_2 \ldots B_n, L_n]$$

where:

$B_1..B_n$ Behavior routines,

$L_1..L_n$ Landmarks.

Landmarks are distinctive features of the environment, which help the system to apply motion strategies. In the SCBR approach, a landmark can also be a condition that indicates successful termination of a behavior application. The SCBR system uses a sequence of landmarks. This sequence is retrieved from a concrete situation case. To navigate using landmarks, all the system has to do is to constantly approach the next landmark in the sequence retrieved from a concrete situation case. An example of a motion strategy is the sequence:

<B_1 = Door_localize, L_1 = door, B_2 = Move to_object, L_2=door is reached , B_3 = Door_traversal, L_3 = H_1 is reached>

to arrive at situation case H_1 (hallway) from situation case R_1 (room) (see figure 7).

In an SCBR system, intelligent motion is achieved through coordination of a set of purposive *behaviors*. The sequence typically begins with an identification of relevant objects. Once the motion strategy is retrieved, the SCBR system makes use of it in step-by-step movement from one concrete situation case to another.

4.3 Calculating the Actions

An action vector computation can be generalized as:

1. Select behavior specific features from current view,
2. Compute desired θ_d based on selected features,
3. Compute action vector components as follows:

$$v_x = s_v \cdot v_i \cdot \sin \theta_d$$

$$v_y = s_v \cdot v_i \cdot \cos \theta_d$$

$$\omega = \begin{cases} 0 & \text{if} \quad B_i \quad \text{is} \quad DT \text{ or } LWF \text{ or } RWF \text{ or } MLF \text{ or } SA \text{ or } MTO \\ \omega_i & \text{if} \quad B_i \quad \text{is} \quad LPT \text{ or } RPT \text{ or } DL \text{ or } OSL \text{ or } OA \ . \end{cases}$$

where:

v_i translational speed property from situation case,

ω_i turning rate property from situation case,

s_v scale parameter specified by situation case.

Figure 2 illustrate use of relevant objects, selected behavior specific features and computation of desired direction (θ_d).

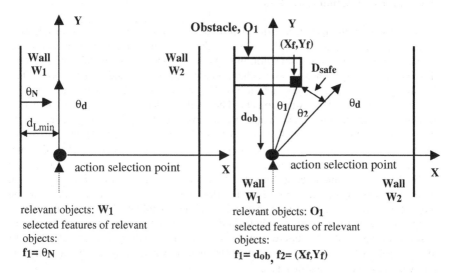

relevant objects: W_1
selected features of relevant objects:
$f_1 = \theta_N$

relevant objects: O_1
selected features of relevant objects:
$f_1 = d_{ob}, f_2 = (X_f, Y_f)$

Fig. 2. The left part of the figure outlines computation of a desired direction when left wall following behavior is selected from motion strategy. The right part of the figure shows computation of a desired direction when obstacle avoidance behavior is selected

The left part of the figure 2 outlines computation of a desired direction when *left wall following* behavior is selected from motion strategy. The desired direction is computed as follows:

$$\theta_d = \theta_N + \frac{\pi}{2}.$$

where:

θ_N normal vector to an observed wall plane.

The right part of the figure 2 shows computation of a desired direction when *obstacle avoidance* behavior is selected. In this situation case, the desired direction is computed as follows:

$$\theta_d = \theta_1 + \theta_2 = \arccos\frac{d_{ob}}{\sqrt{x_f^2 + y_f^2}} + \arcsin\frac{D_{safe}}{\sqrt{x_f^2 + y_f^2}}.$$

where:

d_{ob} observed distance from the obstacle,

x_f, y_f observed coordinates of the selected feature,

D_{safe} situation case property that indicates safe distance from an obstacle.

4.4 Control of Action Execution

A critical step in our approach is the identification of a discrete set of action selection points within a continuous environments. A discrete action selection point is a place in the environment where a selection must be made among actions. Whenever a new discrete action selection point is reached, a new view is generated for the point. The SCBR system determines next action based on an analysis of the generated view in terms of positions of relevant objects. The analysis determines whether there is a frontal obstacle straight ahead. Thus, higher-level symbolic reasoning intervenes at the action selection points to determine which action vector is appropriate to control the SCBR system. Next action selection point is determined based on selected action vector and computed parameter called *action time interval* (ΔTi). This parameter is used to determine time interval for safe execution of selected action. For example, in a situation case with very few obstacles (free space), the system should focus on moving towards the goal rather than worry about avoiding obstacles. This would allow the system to proceed directly towards the goal without any delay. However, in a situation case with a cluttered space, the system should pay more attention to avoiding obstacles and slow down its movement towards the goal. An action time interval (ΔT) can be generalized as:

$$\Delta T = \max\left(\Delta T_{min}, \Delta T_{max} \cdot s_c \cdot s_{os}\right).$$

where:

$\Delta T_{min}, \Delta T_{max}$ situation case properties,

s_c clutter scale parameter,

s_{os} open space scale parameter.

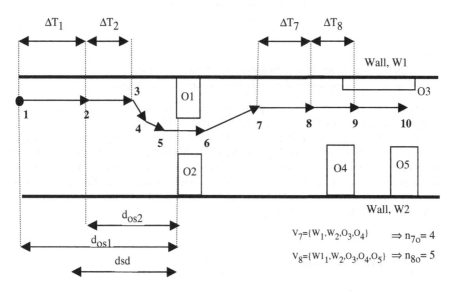

d_{sd} sit. case property; V_7, V_8 are view descriptions; d_{os1}, d_{os2} are observed open spaces

Fig. 3. Next action selection point is determined based on selected action and computed parameter called action time interval (ΔT_i). This parameter is used to determine time interval for safe execution of selected action

In our present system a clutter scale parameter s_c is computed as:

$$s_c = \begin{cases} 1 & \text{for} \quad n_o < n_{sc} \\ \dfrac{n_{sc}}{n_o} & \text{for} \quad n_o \geq n_{sc} . \end{cases}$$

where:

n_{sc} threshold value defined as situation case property,

n_o represents the number of objects in current view.

Figure 3 shows nine action time intervals and ten action selection points. For example, let $n_{sc}=4$ then scale parameter $s_c=1$ at selection point labeled as 7 (because $n_o=4$), and $s_c=0.8$ at action selection point labeled as 8 (because $n_o=5$).

An open space scale parameter is computed as:

$$
s_{os} = \begin{cases} 1 & for \quad d_{osi} > d_{sd} \\ \dfrac{d_{osi}}{d_{sd}} & for \quad d_{osi} \leq d_{sd} . \end{cases}
$$

where:

d_{osi} observed distance from an obstacle at step i,

d_{sd} threshold value defined as situation case property.

For example, at action selection point labeled as 1, $s_{os}=1$ (because $d_{os1}>d_{sd}$). At action selection point labeled as 2, $s_{os}<1$ (because $d_{os2} < d_{sd}$).

As outlined in the algorithm in table 1, the SCBR system first checks the actual view (*current_view*) to see if there is any immediate danger of collision. If there is then the system selects *avoid_obstacle* behavior to avoid collision. If there is no immediate danger of collision, the system selects actual behavior from motion strategy. Thus, *avoid_obstacle* behavior is guaranteed to take precedence over behaviors from motion strategies.

5 Simulation Results

5.1 Simulation Environment

In order to qualitatively evaluate the SCBR approach, we have developed a simulation environment. Physically-based simulation software is commonly used for developing and evaluating low-level system control algorithms. In order to facilitate the development and evaluation of higher-level system behaviors, we have developed simulation environment that provides us to test the SCBR algorithms. This simulation environment allows us to visually evaluate the progress of an SCBR system while it runs through a predefined virtual world. The first step to validating algorithms is observing them in action. Hence, the goals of the simulation environment are:

- Visualize the system movement in a simulated 3D virtual world,
- Provide a tool for the development and evaluation of system algorithms.

Relationships among real world, virtual world and an SCBR system are shown in figure 4.

The simulation environment separates high-level reasoning and low-level control, and provides a model of interaction between the system and the environment. The SCBR system acquires image data from a scene, and the scene is graphically rendered from the system's point of view (see figures 5 and 6). The key idea is to somehow realistically model the flow of image sequences from the environment to the SCBR system. In our simulation environment, we have developed an approximate model for synthetic vision that is suitable for simulation purposes. Once the action vector and action time interval have been computed, the state vector is integrated forward discretely by the time step Δt. Thus, while the technology used in real robots will improve in the future, the high-level software support to control them can potentially be developed at the present time.

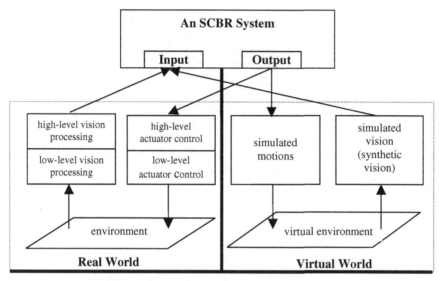

Fig. 4. Relationships among a real world, a virtual world and an SCBR system. The simulation environment separates high-level reasoning and low-level control

Objects are the building blocks of the virtual world. Examples of objects include walls, doors, floors, tables, chairs etc. The surface is assumed to be flat in the implementation described here (see figure 5).

5.2 Approximate Synthetic Vision

Simulated visual perception, also known as synthetic vision, can provide an appropriate means for an SCBR system to reason based on what it perceives. Simulated visual perception generally involves determining which object surfaces in the environment are currently visible to an SCBR system. This problem can be viewed as calculating all visible surfaces from a particular viewpoint given a collection of objects in 3D. The SCBR system has a limited perceptual range. Thus, computing the view object from a system's current location involves intersecting all environment geometry with the system's cone of vision and performing removal of hidden surfaces to determine which objects are visible. There have been several proposals for simulated visual perception [10,11,12]. Tu and Terzopoulos implemented a model of synthetic vision for their artificial fishes based on ray casting. We adopt an approach to synthetic vision similar to the one described by Tu and Terzopoulos.

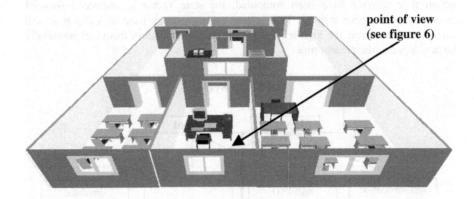

point of view
(see figure 6)

Fig. 5. The virtual environment. Objects are the building blocks of the virtual environment. Examples of objects include walls, doors, floors, tables, chairs etc. The surface is assumed to be flat in the implementation described here

Fig. 6. A simulated vision from system's point of view (see figure 5)

It is also important to model the basic limitations of system's perception capabilities. The perceptual range is limited to a spherical angle extending to an effective radius R_V [10]. The spherical angle and the effective radius R_V define a view volume within which objects can be seen. The radius of the view volume R_V should be influenced by the size of the object. An object in the distance d_1 may be too far to be seen, but this may not be the case if a much larger object is placed at the same distance. We associate size parameter S_i with each object O_i in the virtual environment. The parameter $S_i=1$ represents the standard size, while $S_i >1$ represents larger sizes. When R_V is used for determining whether object O_i is visible, R_V is scaled by the size parameter S_i. When a system observes the environment, simulated vision returns the set of objects that are currently visible.

5.3 An Example of Navigation Task Execution

Figure 7 illustrate an example of a navigation task execution. The SCBR system is here commanded to go from the room R_1 to the room R_2. The SCBR system applies route case R={R_1, H_1, LJ_1, H_2, LJ_2, H_3, R_2}. As the system navigates this virtual world, a line is drawn indicating the system's progress from start location to goal location. The resulting sequence of rooms, hallways and junctions specifies thus an overall plan for carrying out navigation task, while motion strategies associated with each situation case specify the behaviors to be invoked to reach subgoal location. From the example it is obvious that the system is successful in carrying out the navigational task.

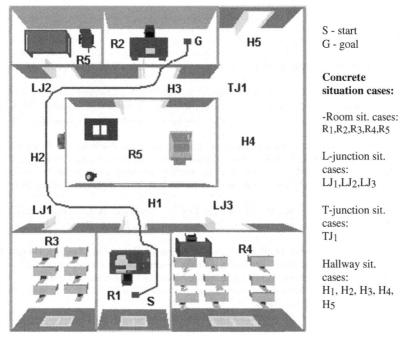

S - start
G - goal

Concrete situation cases:

-Room sit. cases:
R_1,R_2,R_3,R_4,R_5

L-junction sit. cases:
LJ_1,LJ_2,LJ_3

T-junction sit. cases:
TJ_1

Hallway sit. cases:
H_1, H_2, H_3, H_4, H_5

Fig. 7. The simulated SCBR system applies route case and situation cases (top view). As the system navigates this virtual world, a line is drawn indicating the system's progress from start location to goal location

6 Conclusion and Future Work

In this paper, we have presented application of the behavior routines and motion strategies as adaptation knowledge for the SCBR approach. A critical step in our approach is the identification of a discrete set of action selection points within a continuous environments. An SCBR system's navigation task is a decision-making procedure. The SCBR system determines next action based on an analysis of the generated view in terms of positions of relevant objects and selected features. Higher-level reasoning intervenes at the action selection points to determine which action vector is appropriate to control the SCBR system. We have also developed a simulation environment for qualitatively evaluating high-level control algorithms. Visualization tool allow us to qualitatively evaluate progress of an SCBR system. This paper presents some preliminary results using a prototype simulation environment. For future work our goal is to incrementally build the more complete simulation environment that will allow us more capabilities to evaluate the stepwise case-based reasoning approach. As our work progresses, we will carry out a proper experimental analysis and evaluate the SCBR approach.

References

1. G.F. DeJong, Learning to Plan in Continous Domains, Artificial Intelligence 65 (1), 71-141, 1994.
2. Ram, A., Arkin, R.C.: Case-based reactive navigation: A case-based method for on-line selection and adaptation of reactive control parameters in autonomous systems. Tech. Rep. GIT-CC-92/57,College of Computing, Georgia Institute of Technology, Atlanta, USA,1992.
3. Turner, R., Context-mediated behavior, Lecture Notes in Artificial Intelligence 1415, Methodology and Tools in Knowledge-Based Systems, Springer Verlag, New York, 1998.
4. Haigh, K., Veloso, M.: Route Planning by Analogy. Learning Systems. In Proceedings of the 1st International Conference on Case-Based Reasoning, Springer Verlag. Sesimbra, Portugal, 1995.
5. Smyth, B., Cunningham, P.: The Utility Problem Analyzed: A Case-Based Reasoning Perspective. Third European Workshop on Case-Based Reasoning. Lausanne, Switzerland, 1996.
6. Branting, L. K., Aha, D. W.: Stratified Case-Based Reasoning: Reusing Hierarchical Problem Solving Episodes Proceedings of the Fourteenth International Joint Conference on Artificial Intelligence, Morgan Kaufmann, Montreal, Canada, pp. 384-390, 1995.
7. Brooks, R. A.: A Robust Layered Control System for a Mobile Robot. Autonomous Mobile Robots, 152-161, 1990.
8. Kolodner, J.L.: *Case–Based Reasoning*. Morgan K. Publishers, Inc., San Mateo, CA, 1993
9. Aamodt, A., Plaza, E.: Case-Based Reasoning: Foundational Issues, Methodological Variations and System Approaches, in *AICOM* , vol 7(1), 39-59, 1994.
10. Tu X. and Terzopouls D. Artificial fishes: Physics, locomotion, perception, behavior. In A. Glassner, editor, Proc. SIGGRAPH 1994, Computer Graphics Proceedings, Annual Conferences Series, pages 43-50., 1994.
11. Terzopoulos D and Rabie T. Animat vision: Active vision in artificial animals. In Proc. Fifth Int. Conf. on Computer Vision , 1995, pages 801-808, Cambridge, MA, 1995.
12. Renault O., Thalmann N.M., and Thalmann D. A vision-based approach to behavioral animation. Visualization and Computer Animation, 1:18-21, 1990.

An Accurate Adaptation-Guided Similarity Metric for Case-Based Planning[*]

Flavio Tonidandel [1] and Márcio Rillo [1,2]

[1] Universidade de São Paulo - Escola Politécnica
Av. Luciano Gualberto 158, trav3
05508-900 - São Paulo - SP - Brazil
[2] Faculdade de Engenharia Industrial
Av. Humberto de A. Castelo Branco, 3972
09850-901 - São Bernardo do Campo - SP - Brazil
flavio@lac.usp.br ; rillo@lsi.usp.br
phone: +55 11 3818 5530

Abstract. In this paper, we present an adaptation-guided similarity metric based on the estimate of the number of actions between states, called ADG (*Action Distance-Guided*). It is determined by using a heuristic calculation extracted from the heuristic search planning, called FF, which was the fastest planner in the AIPS'2000 competition. This heuristic provides an accurate estimate of the distance between states that is appropriated for similarity measures. Consequently, the ADG becomes a new approach, suitable for domain independent case-based planning systems that perform state-space search.

1 Introduction

The purpose of Case-based Reasoning (CBR) systems is to improve efficiency by using stored cases to solve problems. However, there are many efficiency *bottlenecks* in CBR systems. Two of them, which are concerned with the retrieval phase, are: the space of cases where the search engine is performed, and the similarity metric that is responsible for determining how much similar the cases are to a new problem. The researches in former topic are concerned with locating the best case in a reduced space of search [13,15]. In the latter, the researches are concerned with how to design a suitable similarity metric that provides an accurate measure. Better approaches for this topic have been the measurement of the similarity of cases based on adaptation effort [8,11,16]. The less effort, the better is the case to be retrieved.

This paper focuses on developing a similarity metric that may predict the adaptation effort of a case by the estimate of the distance between states in case-based planning (CBP) systems. We mean by CBP a general problem solver where plans are a sequence of actions. It is different from route planning [14] and episode-based planning [8], which are particular samples of CBP systems, and consequently, they have specific features that can be explored in order to improve the system efficiency.

---

[*] This work is supported by FAPESP under contract no. 98/15835-9.

D.W. Aha and I. Watson (Eds.): ICCBR 2001, LNAI 2080, pp. 531-545, 2001.
© Springer-Verlag Berlin Heidelberg 2001

As the plans are a sequence of actions, a suitable similarity can be found through the distance given by the possible number of actions between states. However, the similarity metrics, until now, would find a similarity by the number of differences between states [7,19].

The ADG (*Action Distance Guided*) similarity here proposed is a new similarity metric based on the estimate of the number of actions. It is extracted from the heuristic used by the FF planning system [4,6] to estimate the number of actions between the current state and the final state. The FF was the fastest planner in the AIPS'2000 competition [1] by using this heuristic method to guide the search engine at each step.

The proposed similarity metric is suitable to be applied in conjunction with any method that reduces the search space of cases, as [15], or with in any method of case-base maintenance based on the adaptation effort. For example, the ADG similarity can be used in RP-CNN [9], which is a measure based on the adaptation costs. It needs a suitable similarity metric to edit case-bases and to preserve the efficiency of the system. The RP-CNN assumes "*that the similarity metric will accurately select the most adaptable case for any problem*" ([9] p. 166), and the ADG can be this similarity metric.

This paper is organized as follow. Section 2 presents some related works. Section 3 presents the Transaction Logic that is used to formalize actions, plans and cases. Section 4 presents the relaxed fixpoint extracted from [4] and defines the ADG similarity. Section 5 presents some experiments. Finally, some discussions are presented in section 6 and conclusions in section 7.

2 Related Works

Although the case-base competence is important, the efficiency is really the main factor that affects the performance in environments where case-based systems have intensive domain knowledge, which can provide a solution *from scratch*.

The retrieval phase critically affects the systems performance. It must search in a space of cases in order to choose a proper one that will allow the system to solve a new problem easily. In order to improve efficiency in the retrieval phase, it is necessary either to reduce the search space or to design an accurate similarity metric. Reducing the search space will let available only a suitable subset of cases for the search process and an accurate similarity metric will choose the most similar case to decrease the adaptation phase effort. Some works present interesting approaches that reduce the search space of cases (e.g [13,15]).

In this paper, we are concerned with similarity metric. Much attention has been given to researches that design suitable similarity metrics. They focus on choosing the most adaptable case as the most similar one, such as DIAL [8], DéjàVu [16] and ADAPtER [11] systems. DIAL system is a case-based planner that works in disaster domains where cases are schema-based episodes. It uses a similarity assessment approach, called RCR, which considers an adaptability estimate to choose cases in the retrieval phase. Similarly, Déjà Vu system operates in design domains and uses an adaptation-guided retrieval (AGR) to choose cases that are easier to be adapted. ADAPtER is a diagnostic system that calculates an estimate of adaptability of a solution to supply a pivoting-based retrieval with the capacity to choose a group of relevant cases between an upper and a lower bound.

The adaptation-based metric presented by this paper, called ADG (*Action Distance-Guide*), differs from those presented in ADAPtER and DéjàVu systems. It is designed to be applied in case-based planning systems that operate with actions. The action-based planning is a general problem solver that finds a sequence of actions to transform the initial state into a desirable final state [4,6,7,12,17,18,19]. This approach is slightly different from route planning [14] and episode-based planning [8], which are specific planners and have specific features that can be used to improve the efficiency of the system.

The ADG similarity differs from the AGR approach because it does not use any domain knowledge besides those obtained from actions and states, which are the minimal knowledge that is required to define a domain for planning systems. The AGR approach in DéjàVu system uses additional domain knowledge, called *capability knowledge*, which is similar to what *critics* used to determine and solve conflicts in partial-order planning systems. This additional knowledge allows identifying the type and the functionality of a set of transformations, which are performed by actions, through a collection of *agents* called *specialists* and *strategies*. It must be well specified in order to maximize the AGR performance.

The ADG similarity differs from RCR method, used by DIAL system. It is based on domain knowledge that is available in action definitions, while the RCR method uses the experience learned from the adaptation of previous utilization of cases. They also differ in their applicability because the RCR method considers cases as episodes in disaster domains; the ADG approach considers it as a sequence of actions, suitable for domain independent planning systems.

There are many domain independent case-based planning systems (e.g. [2,7,10,19]). A great number of them use a search engine based on a space of states [7,19]. Most of the state-space planning systems use a similarity rule that only confronts *(I)* - the initial state and *(G)*- the final state of a stored case with *(I')* – current state and *(G')* - goal state of the new problem. If I subsumes I' and G subsumes G' under some limits, the case is appropriate to be retrieved. All retrieved cases are then ordered following this subsumption. However, this approach is not a suitable measure to improve the adaptation phase efficiency because it is not a good measure of the real similarity.

An alternative approach to planning with states is the plan-space planning systems [2,10]. They search in a space of plans and they have no goals, but only tasks to be achieved. Since tasks are semantically different from goals, the similarity metric designed for plan-space based CBP systems is also different from the similarity rules designed for state-space based CBP systems.

An interesting similarity rule in plan-space approach is presented in the CAPLAN/CBC system [10]. It extends the similarity rule introduced by the PRODIGY/ANALOGY system [19] by using feature weights in order to reduce the errors in the retrieval phase. These feature weights are learned and recomputed according to the performance of the previous retrieved cases. This approach is similar to RCR method used by DIAL system in disaster domains.

There are two important differences between ADG and CAPLAN/CBC's similarity rule. One difference is that the former is designed for state-space planning and the latter for plan-space planning. Another difference is that the ADG similarity does not need to learn any knowledge to present an accurate estimate. As highlighted before, the ADG similarity only needs the knowledge that can be extracted from actions.

The purpose of this paper is, therefore, to develop an adaptation-based similarity rule that estimates the adaptation effort of each case for general and domain independent case-based planning systems with state-space search.

3 The Transaction Logic in Planning

The Transaction Logic (TR) [3], in its serial-Horn version, is an extension of the first-order logic, by the introduction of the serial conjunction operator ($\otimes$), e.g., $\alpha \otimes \beta$, which means "first execute α, and then execute β".

It uses the following notation to describe a transaction: $P, D_0,...,D_n \models \phi$, where ϕ is a transaction formula and P is a set of TR formulas called transaction base. Each D_i is a database state that is a set of first-order formulas. Intuitively, P is a set of transaction definitions, ϕ is an invocation of some of these transactions; $D_0,...,D_n$ is a sequence of databases that represents an updating made by ϕ. On the other hand, a situation of a query is not given by a sequence of databases, but by just one state. For example, $P,D_k \models qry(c)$, where c is true in D_k.

To perform an updating, TR works with a transition oracle (O^t) that is a mapping between two states and a set of atomic formulas. For our purposes, it is only necessary to define two formulas: $ins(\_)$ and $del(\_)$ in the transition oracle framework. To formally execute both formulas, for example $ins(c)$ and $del(d)$, a possible satisfaction can be: $P,D,D_1,D_2 \models ins(c) \otimes del(d)$. It happens if and only if $ins(c) \in O^t(D,D+\{c\})$; $del(d) \in O^t(D,D-\{d\})$; $D_1 = D+\{c\}$ and $D_2 = D+\{c\}-\{d\}$.

With all these formal features, TR is a suitable logic to describe actions and plans for planning systems, as can be seen with some uses of TR in planning formalization [12,17,18]. As TR is suitable for planning, it is suitable for CBP system components as well, because the case memory is a collection of plans.

In order to define the planning components in a TR framework, we will follow in accordance with Santos and Rillo's work [12]. Considering L a language defined in serial-Horn version of TR, the components of a planning system can be defined as:

Definition 1 (State): *The state D is a finite set of first-logic predicates and it is represented in TR as a database state. Each $d \in D$ is called literal.*

Two examples of state definition are given in Figure 1. States can be modified by actions, which are defined as:

Definition 2 (Strips-like Actions): *Considering $A \subseteq L$ as a set of action definitions, each α, $\alpha \in A$, has the following structure:*

$$\alpha \leftarrow pre(\alpha) \otimes delete(\alpha) \otimes add(\alpha)$$

where
- *$pre(\alpha)$ is a TR formula that is composed by $qry(\_)$ predicates that represents the preconditions of the action α.*

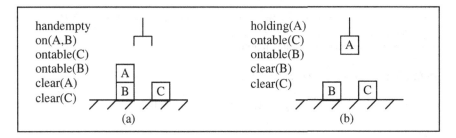

Fig. 1. Two examples of state definition in block-world domain.

- *delete(α) is the delete list of the action α. It is a TR formula in accordance with transition oracle and it represents all predicates that will not be true after the action execution.*
- *add(α) is the add list of the action α. It is a TR formula in accordance with transition oracle and it represents all predicates that will be true after the action execution.*

The result of an action execution is an updated state D' from D after the deletion and the inserting of the delete and add lists respectively. Any action α just can be executed from a state D if pre(α) $\subseteq D$. For example, consider the following action in the well-known blocks-world domain:

unstack (x,y) $\Leftarrow$ *qry(handempty(x))* $\otimes$ *qry(clear(x))* $\otimes$ *qry(on(x,y))* $\otimes$ *del(clear(x))* $\otimes$ *del(handempty)* $\otimes$ *del(on(x,y))* $\otimes$ *ins(holding(x))* $\otimes$ *ins(clear(y))*.

which means to get the block *x* from the top of block *y*. We can observe that:

pre(unstack(x,y)) = qry(handempty(x)) $\otimes$ *qry(clear(x))* $\otimes$ *qry(on(x,y))*.
delete(unstack(x,y)) = del(clear(x)) $\otimes$ *del(handempty)* $\otimes$ *del(on(x,y))*.
add(unstack(x,y)) = ins(holding(x)) $\otimes$ *ins(clear(y))*.

Consider now a state D_0 as the state described in Figure 1a and the state *Df* as the state described in Figure 1b. Thus, *unstack(A,B)* can be satisfied in TR as:

$$P, D_0..Df \models unstack(A,B)$$

Where *P* is the set of actions *A* and $<D_0..Df>$ is the state path from D_0 to *Df* by the application of *del* and *ins* predicates contained in formula *unstack(A,B)*. Therefore, TR permits to perform formally an action in planning.

With the definitions of actions and state, it is possible, following [17], to define plans, goals, and cases with the use of the TR:

Definition 3: (Plan) *A plan* $\delta = \alpha_1 \otimes ... \otimes \alpha_n$ *is a TR formula, where* $\alpha_i \in A$; $1 \leq i \leq n$.

Definition 4: (Goal) *A goal Df is a TR formula and it is a set of queries that represents the desirable final state.*

When the planner finds a desirable sequence of actions in order to reach Df, the plan can become a case to be stored for future uses. A case is a modified plan by the insertion of initial and final states features:

Definition 5: *(Case) A case η is a TR rule:*

$$\eta \leftarrow Wi \otimes \alpha_1 \otimes ... \otimes \alpha_n \otimes Wf,$$

where:

- η *is a TR rule that represents a stored case.*
- $\alpha_i \in A$; $1 \leq i \leq n$, *a plan defined by the planner that satisfies a proposed goal.*
- *Wi is a set of queries in TR that represents the precondition of the case.*
- *Wf is a set of queries in TR that represents the pos-condition of the case.*

Intuitively, *Wi* is a set of those literals that are deleted by the plan. It is equal to the result of the foot-printing method used by PRODIGY/ANALOGY system [19] and it represents the pre-condition of the plan. The process of foot-printing the initial state is described in [19].

With respect to *Wf*, it is a set of those literals that are inserted by the plan and will be presented in the final state after the plan execution. There is no correspondence to other cases features in any case-based planning system.

4 The Similarity Rule

Once we have *Wi* and *Wf*, we will be able to define values of similarity between a new problem, described by a goal formula (def. 4), and a case. It can be made through two comparisons. One is with the current initial state, denoted by D_0, and with the initial state features from the case, denoted by *Wi*. This comparison is called *initial similarity value* (δ_I). Another comparison is between the desirable final state (Df) from the goal and the final state features (Wf) from the case. This comparison is called *goal similarity value* (δ_G). Both similarity values are obtained after the determination of a state-fixpoint from a relaxed planning problem.

4.1 The State-Fixpoint

The process of estimating the distance between two states is the main part of a heuristic-search planning systems, as FF [4,6]. In fact, we use the same heuristic, which is used by FF planner to guide the search, to estimate the similarity between the current situation and stored cases.

The first step of heuristic determination is to create a graph for a relaxed planning problem. Hoffmann and Nebel [6] explain that this relaxing is obtained by ignoring the delete list of actions. It allows the graph to find a relaxed fixpoint that is composed by all predicates that are reached from the initial state.

As defined by Hoffmann [4], the graph is constituted by layers that comprise alternative facts and actions. The first fact layer is the initial state (D_0). The first action layer contains all actions whose preconditions are satisfied in D_0. Then, the add lists of these actions are inserted in the next fact layer together with all predicates from the previous fact layer, which leads to the next action layer, and so on. The process keeps going on until it finds a relaxed fixpoint, i.e., when there are no more fact layers that are different from previous fact layers.

These layers show in how many steps, at least, a predicate can be reached, or an action can be applied, from D_0. The algorithm in Figure 2 shows this process, and it can be performed as an off-line process or as a startup process of the retrieval phase. It can be off-line because it uses only information from the initial state (D_0) and the actions that are available before the retriever starts. In addition, it is performed only once, so it can be performed as a startup process of the retrieval phase.

Some useful information can be determined from the relaxed fixpoint process. Following [4,6], they are:

Definition 6: *levelpred(d) := min {i | d ∈ F_i, where F_i is the ith layer of facts }*

Definition 7: *levelpred(α) := min {i | α ∈ O_i, where O_i is the ith layer of actions }*

Definition 8: *difficulty (α) := $\sum_{d \in pre(\alpha)}$ levelpred(d)*

The definitions 6 and 7 provide the order number of the layer where each literal or action appears first. It means that each literal, or action, is a membership of its first appearance in the fact layer or in the action layer respectively.

The definition 8 presents a heuristic that calculates the difficulty of an action in respect of its first preconditions appearance. As highlighted in Hoffmann and Nebel's work, *"this heuristic works good in situations where there are several ways to achieve one fact, but some ways need less effort than others."* [6].

With the graph generated, it is possible to find a relaxed solution for any state that can be reached from D_0. This relaxed solution, improved by the difficulty measure, provides an estimate for the optimal length of the not-relaxed solution [6]. This relaxed solution will give us the *initial similarity value (δ_I)* and the *goal similarity value (δ_G)*.

4.2 The Initial Similarity Value

For a stored case, one important measure that must be estimated is the distance between the initial state (D_0) and the features of the case initial state (Wi). This distance estimation can be obtained by the second step of the FF's estimate heuristic: the relaxed solution [6].

The process of obtaining the relaxed solution for a target-state (Wi) from initial state (D_0), as described in [6] uses the generated graph. First, each predicate in the target-state is initialized as a goal in its correspondent layer, determined by *levelpred(_)* value. The process is then performed from the last layer to the first layer, finding and selecting actions in layer *i-1* which their add-list contains one or more of goals initialized in layer *i*. Then, the preconditions of the selected actions are initialized as new goals in their correspondent layer.

```
F₀ := D₀;
k:=0;
fixpoint:=False;
while   fixpoint=False do
    Oₖ := {α ∈ A | pre(α) ⊆ Fₖ}
    Fₖ₊₁ := ∪α ∈ ok add(α)
    if Fₖ₊₁ = Fₖ then fixpoint:=True;
    k:=k+1;
endwhile
max:=k;
```

Fig. 2. The algorithm that computes the relaxed fixpoint from the initial state. It is extracted from [4].

The process stops when all unsatisfied goals are in the first layer, which is exactly the initial state. The estimate number of action between initial state and the target-state is the number of action selected to satisfy the goals in each layer.

The algorithm to compute the relaxed solution is shown in Figure 3. The variable h is used to count the number of selected actions. The initialization of each goal is made by an array and each predicate has a mark that can be true or false.

With the algorithm in Figure 3, it is possible to find the *Initial Similarity Value*, that is the result h from the function **relaxed_initial_length (Wi)** after *setting all marks of all predicates as false*:

$$\delta_I = h$$

The value of δ_I is the estimate of the distance between D_0 and Wi, and configures the first part of our similarity metric. The second part is obtained by the estimate of the distance between Wf and Df, which is presented below.

4.3 The Goal Similarity Value

So far, the similarity measure only used the FF´s estimate heuristic without any changes in its original concept. In fact, we had needed only to calculate the distance from D_0, and the direct application of the FF´s heuristic is enough. Now, we have to introduce some modifications in the FF´s heuristic concept in order to calculate the distance from Wf to Df using the generated graph.

The generated graph is suitable to estimate the distance from D_0. In this case, the distance between Wf and Df cannot be estimated by simply calculating the distance of Df from D_0 and then diminishing the number of actions in the case and the δ_I value. This is because the solution trace from D_0 is different from the other solution traces that consider the actions in the case. It leads us to force the solution trace from D_0 to use the sequence of actions in the case.

```
relaxed_initial_length(G)

clear all Gi
for i:= 1 ... max do
  Gi := {g ∈ G |levelpred(g) = i};
endfor
h:=0;
for i:= max ... 1 do
  for all g ∈ Gi, g not marked TRUE at time i do
    select α_levelpred=i-1; minimal difficulty; g ∈ add(α);
    h:=h+1;
    for all d_levelpred ≠ 0 ∈ pre(α), not marked True at i-1 do
        G_levelpred(d) := G_levelpred(d) ∪ {d};
    endfor
    for all d ∈ add(α) do
        mark d as True at time i-1 and i;
    endfor
  endfor
endfor
return h;
```

Fig. 3. The algorithm that computes the relaxed solution from a relaxed fixpoint, where G is the target-state. It is extracted from [6].

To force the estimate of the distance of *Df* from D_0 considering the case actions, it is necessary to maintain the values of each mark of each predicate, after the performing of the *Initial Similarity Value* calculation. It means that we will call the function *relaxed_final_length(Wi,Wf,Df)* (Figure 4) using the marks changed by the *relaxed_initial_length(Wi)*.

However, keeping the marks unchanged is not enough. It is also necessary to change some truth predicate values of *Wi* and *Wf*. First, we must set all marks of all predicates in *Wi* as false. Then, we have to mark as true each predicate in *Wf* in their correspondent layer. All these changes are necessary because *Wi* indicates the predicates that the case will delete, and the *Wf* indicates the predicates that will be true after the case execution.

In addition, it is also necessary to initialize *Wi* as a goal, because the trace must be calculated through the actions of the case.

The reason to keep unchanged all marks from δ_I calculation is to avoid that the calculation of the *Goal Similarity Value* incorporates redundant values like the number of actions between D_0 and *Wi*.

With the result *h'* from the function *relaxed_final_length(Df)* of the algorithm presented in Figure 4, we can define the *Goal Similarity Value*, that is the second part of our similarity metric:

$$\delta_F = h'$$

With all parts defined, it is possible to determine the similarity value of a case.

```
relaxed_final_length(Wi,Wf,Df)

G:=Df;
for each d ∈ Wi do
    mark d as False at all levels;
    G:=G+{d};
endfor
for each d ∈ Wf do
     mark True at levelpred(d) and levelpred(d)-1
endfor
h':=relaxed_initial_length(G);
return h';
```

Fig. 4. The algorithm that extracts the distance between *Wf* and *Df* by considering the marks from relaxed_initial_length(*Wi*).

4.4 The Action Distance-Guided Similarity

Finally, the similarity metric can be defined joining the two values: δ_I and δ_F. This similarity metric, that we call *Action Distance-Guided* (ADG), is a measure of the adaptation effort for constructing a plan from D_0 to *Wi* and from *Wf* to *Df*. It is the sum of both values:

$$ADG = \delta_I + \delta_F$$

It is important to note that ADG is a domain independent approach and it is also designed to be used in any retrieval phase of a state-space CBP system with action-based cases, i.e., where cases and plans are sequence of actions.

A case is useful when the ADG value is less than the direct distance between D_0 and *Df*, that can be calculated with the FF's heuristic. If this distance is less than the ADG value of any stored case, a generative planner, as FF [4,6], can be performed without the use of any retrieved case.

Otherwise, if the ADG value is less than the direct distance between D_0 and *Df*, it is preferable to use a retrieved case than plan *from scratch*. It means that, for example, the ADG value of a case with 10 actions is 7 and the distance between D_0 and *Df* directly is 15. It is preferable to avoid any kind of modification in the case structure and to plan a sequence of 7 actions, and finding a solution with 17 actions, than plan *from scratch* and have to find a sequence of 15 actions. This preference is based on the generative planner effort, which is less if it is requested to find a sequence of 7 actions than a sequence of 15 actions.

Some CBP systems incorporate a modification phase that can change the actions in the case in order to find a solution near to optimal. However, this process is more time expensive than the approach that does not perform any modification in the case structure. Therefore, the generative planning is used to *complete* the retrieved case by finding a sequence of actions that links D_0 to the case and another sequence that links the case to *Df*. It is considered in the experiments below.

5 Experiments

Some empirical tests are necessary in order to analyze the performance and results that the ADG similarity can produce. The experiments are performed with two case-bases with 100 cases each, in two different domains: Block-world and Logistic domains. The former is a well know domain in the planning area, and the latter is a simplified version of UCPOP domain. Both were used in AIPS'2000 competition [1].

In order to compare the results from ADG, we will consider the similarity rules used by some case-based planning systems, such as MRL's subsuming similarity [7] and Prodigy's footprint similarity [19]. We will also consider the standard normalized Nearest Neighborhood (NN) rule as a generic similarity rule.

However, the NN rule and MRL's subsuming similarity used in the tests are improved by Wi and Wf information from the stored cases. It means that the accuracy improvement obtained by Prodigy's footprint similarity over the standard Nearest Neighborhood does not exist anymore. It happens because the improvement was mainly based on the consideration of information about initial and goal states of the cases, and this information is already described in Wi and Wf. On the other hand, the time used by Prodigy's similarity to compute the footprint initial states, which takes $O(n^2)$ for a case with n actions [19], is not necessary because Wi is already computed in all stored cases. Consequently, Prodigy's similarity takes the same processing time as MRL's subsuming and standard Nearest Neighborhood.

Considering the fact that Prodigy's similarity rule does not calculate normalized values of similarities, and that MRL's subsuming does not consider the case initial state features to rank similar cases, it is expected that the normalized standard NN performs better than both in the experiments, but worse than AGR.

The experiments are performed in a *Pentium*® III computer with 450 MHz and 128 Mbytes of memory, in *Microsoft*® *Windows* environment.

5.1 Experiment 1 – The Accuracy of Each Similarity Rule

In the first experiment (Figure 5a), each test considers a couple of cases. We performed 600 tests with couple of different cases in different initial and final states. Initial states, final states and cases are chosen randomly for each case base in blocks and logistic domains.

At each test, the time used by a generative planning to *complete* the cases is annotated. The case that requested less effort to find a solution is considered the most similar one. The cases are considered equally similar if the difference time between both is less than 0.3 seconds. Then, each similarity rule is applied. The results of each method are confronted with the correct answer. The percentage of correct results from each similarity rule is presented in Figure 5a.

The results show that the ADG is better than the common similarity rules used by some CBP systems. It leads us to conclude that ADG is suitable for any adaptation-guided similarity rule applied in CBP systems with state-space search.

However, this accuracy is obtained to the detriment of processing time, as we can see in the processing time experiment.

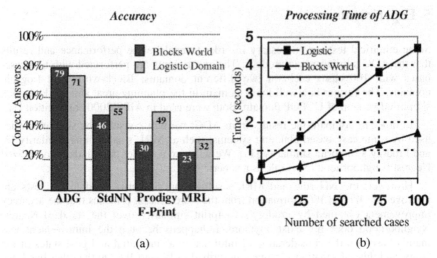

Fig. 5. The performance of the ADG compared with other methods by accuracy (a) and its processing time (b).

5.2 Experiment 2 – Processing Time

This experiment shows the processing time behavior of ADG similarity in different domains. As the ADG is a process that calculates a relaxed solution, it is more time expensive than the other methods, which take a processing time less than 0.3 second for a case-base with 100 cases.

The purpose of this experiment is to verify if the time curve from ADG similarity calculation presents any exponential average time behavior that can invalidate the benefit obtained by the similarity accuracy. The curve is plotted in Figure 5b.

The test is performed by determining the processing time to calculate the ADG value for different quantities of cases in each domain. The result is an average time value.

The result of the tests lead us to conclude that the ADG similarity calculation presents a linear behavior in the average, even though it varies from domain to domain.

The difference in processing times occurs because domains have different complexities. Any generic system presents different processing times for different complexities, because it does not have any specific domain features or any particular heuristic methods that can improve the system efficiency in such domains.

For being a generic similarity rule, ADG presents the same different processing times for different domains like any domain independent generative planner. Therefore, we claim that the time expended to find a similar case in the case-base is proportional to that presented by a generic generative planner as a result from planning from scratch. The accuracy of the ADG can provide efficiency to the system by the fact that the time wasted in the retrieval phase can be compensated in the adaptation phase.

The efficiency of the system can be improved by a combination of an accurate similarity rule, such as ADG, and a method that reduces the space of cases in the retrieval searching process [15].

6 Discussion & Future Works

The actions defined in section 3 are STRIPS-like. However, as the FF's heuristic can also be calculated from actions in ADL-style [6], our similarity metric can be applied to ADL-style as well.

The meaningful improvement introduced by the ADG similarity metric is the use of FF's heuristic that calculates a solution length, not necessarily optimal, for the relaxed problem. It provides an informative estimate of the difficulty for planning. This heuristic is well used by FF planning to escape from local minima and plateaus in a local search engine combined with a breadth first search [4,5,6]. The use of this heuristic permits that the FF works well in most of planning domains, as shown by the results in AIPS'2000 competition [1]. An excellent and deep analysis of the reasons that lead the FF to work well in planning domains is presented in [5].

As ADG is an estimate of the difficulty in planning to complete the retrieved case in order to solve a problem, it is suitable for systems that have the purpose to use the case without any or with less modification. The idea is to retrieve a case that can decrease the number of actions that the system has to find and arrange to solve the problem.

For a little group of cases, it is possible to investigate the intermediary states of each case, and decide if any modification, like adding, deleting or replacing actions, can be performed. The ADG similarity can be used to estimate the distance between the current initial state and these intermediary states, and consequently, it can discover if there are superfluous actions and states in a case composition. If they exist, they can be eliminated.

However, only ADG similarity is not sufficient to perform a modification phase, because this phase can become a time expensive process, and in most situations, some of heuristic-search planning systems, such as FF planner, could be faster than it. Therefore, other heuristic methods should be researched in order to perform the modification phase efficiently.

The ADG similarity is suitable to be used in CBP systems with state-space search, and it cannot be applied in plan-space approaches as it is presented in this paper. However, with some modifications, the ADG similarity could operate with tasks instead of states and be appropriate to be used in domain independent case-based planning with plan-space search. In addition, it can be mixed with techniques of learning and feature weights, as CAPLAN/CBC's similarity rule. All these advances will be left for future works.

7 Conclusions

This paper presents a similarity metric for case-based planning systems based on the number of actions necessary to transform one state into another state. We called this similarity rule ADG (*Action Distance-Guided*).

The ADG similarity estimates the distance among the stored case and the initial and final states. Consequently, the ADG similarity presented a better accuracy than the usual similarity rules applied in generic case-based planning.

Although the processing time is higher than in other methods, the retrieved case is much more accurate, and consequently, it will require less effort from the adaptation phase.

As far as the processing time is concerned, many methods can reduce the space search of cases in the case-base, reducing the processing time [15]. As mentioned before, this paper is concerned with the accuracy of the similarity rule, which, if applied with any reducing space search method, can provide a CBP system with a fast and accurate retrieval phase.

References

1.   Bacchus, F. AIPS-2000 Planning Competition Results. Available in: http://www.cs.toronto.edu/aips2000/.
2.   Bergmann, R., Wilke, W. Building and Refining Abstract Planning Cases by Change of Representation Language. Journal of Artificial Intelligence Research, 3. (1995). 53-118.
3.   Bonner, A.J., Kifer, M.: Transaction logic programming. Technical Report, CSRI-323, Department of Computer Science, University of Toronto (1995).
4.   Hoffman, J. A Heuristic for Domain Independent Planning and its Use in an Enforced Hill-climbing Algorithm. In: Proceedings of 12th International Symposia on Methodologies for Intelligent Systems. North Carolina, USA. (2000).
5.   Hoffman, J. Local Search Topology in Planning Benchmarks: An Empirical Analysis. In: Proceedings of the 17th International Joint Conference on Artificial Intelligence IJCAI'01. Morgan Kaufmann Publishers (2001).
6.   Hoffman, J., Nebel, B. The FF Planning System: Fast Plan Generation Through Heuristic Search. In: Journal or Artificial Intelligence Research. To appear.
7.   Koehler, J. Planning from Second Principles. Artificial Intelligence, 87. Elsevier Science. (1996).148-187.
8.   Leake, D., Kinley, A., Wilson, D. Case-Based Similarity Assessment: Estimating Adaptability from Experience. In: Proceedings of 14th National Conference on Artificial Intelligence – AAAI'97. AAAI Press. (1997).
9.   Leake, D., Wilson, D. Remembering Why to Remember: Performance-Guided Case-Base Maintenance. In: Blanzieri,E., Portinale, L. (Eds.) Proceedings of the 5th European Workshop on Case-Based Reasoning (EWCBR2K). Lecture Notes in Artificial Intelligence, Vol 1898. Springer-Verlag. (2000) 161-172.
10.   Muñoz-Avila, H.,Hüllen, J. Feature Weighting by Explaining Case-Based Planning Episodes. In: Smith, I., Faltings, B. (Eds) Proceedings of 3rd European Workshop on Case-Based Reasoning (EWCBR'96). Lecture Notes in Artificial Intelligence, Vol 1168. Springer-Verlag. (1996) 280-294.
11.   Portinali, L., Torasso, P., Magro, D. Selecting Most Adaptable Diagnostic Solutions through Pivoting-Based Retrieval. In: Leake,D.,Plaza,E. (Eds) Proceedings of the 2nd International Conference on Case-Based Reasoning – ICCBR'97. Lecture Notes in Artificial Intelligence, Vol 1266. Springer-Verlag. (1997). 393-402.
12.   Santos, M., Rillo, M. Approaching the *Plans are Programs* Paradigm using Transaction Logic. In: Steel, S., Alami,R (Eds) Proceedings of 4th European Conference on Planning – ECP'97. Lecture Notes in Artificial Intelligence, vol. 1348. Springer-Verlag. (1997) 377-389.

13. Schaaf, J. Fish and Shrink: A Next Step Towards Efficient Case Retrieval in Large-Scale Case-Bases. In: Smith, I., Faltings, B. (eds): Advances in case-Based Reasoning. Lecture Notes in Artificial Intelligence, Vol 1168. Springer-Verlag, (1996) 362-376.
14. Smyth, B. , McGinty, L. Personalised Route Planning: A Case-Based Approach. In: Blanzieri,E., Portinale, L. (Eds.) Proceedings of the 5th European Workshop on Case-Based Reasoning (EWCBR2K). Lecture Notes in Artificial Intelligence, Vol 1898. Springer-Verlag. (2000).431-442.
15. Smyth, B.,   McKenna, E. Footprint-Based Retrieval. In: Althouff, K., Bergmann, R., Branting, K. (Eds.) Proceedings of the 3rd International Conference in Case-Based Reasoning. ICCBR'99. Lecture Notes in Artificial Intelligence, Vol 1650. Springer-Verlag. (1999).343-357.
16. Smyth, B., Keane, M. Adaptation-Guided Retrieval: Questioning the Similarity Assumption in Reasoning. In: Journal of Artificial Intelligence, 102(2). (1998). 249-293.
17. Tonidandel, F, Rillo, M. Case-Based Planning in Transaction Logic Framework. In: Proceedings of Workshop on Intelligent Manufacturing Systems (IMS'98). Elsevier Science. (1998). 281-286.
18. Tonidandel, F., Rillo, M. Handling Cases and the Coverage in a Limited Quantity of Memory for Case-Based Planning Systems. In: Sichman, J., Monard, C. (Eds). Proceedings of IBERAMIA/SBIA 2000. Lecture Notes in Artificial Intelligence, Vol 1952. Springer-Verlag. (2000) 23-32.
19. Veloso, M. Planning and Learning by Analogical Reasoning. Lecture Notes in Artificial Intelligence, Vol 886. Springer-Verlag. (1994).

Releasing Memory Space through a Case-Deletion Policy with a Lower Bound for Residual Competence*

Flavio Tonidandel [1] and Márcio Rillo [1,2]

[1] Universidade de São Paulo - Escola Politécnica
Av. Luciano Gualberto 158, trav3
05508-900 - São Paulo - SP - Brazil
[2] Faculdade de Engenharia Industrial
Av. Humberto de A. Castelo Branco, 3972
09850-901 - São Bernardo do Campo - SP - Brazil
flavio@lac.usp.br ; rillo@lsi.usp.br - phone: +55 11 3818 5530

Abstract. The number of techniques that focuses on how to create compact case-base in case-base maintenance has been increasing over the last few years. However, while those techniques are concerned with choosing suitable cases to improve the system performance, they do not deal with the problem of a limited memory space, which may affect the performance as well. Even when a CBR system admits only a limited number of stored cases in memory, there will still exist the *storage-space problem* if it has cases that vary in size, as in most of case-based planning domains. This paper focuses on case-deletion policy to release space in the case memory, which can guarantee the competence-preserving property and establish a theoretical lower bound for residual competence.

1 Introduction

The importance of case-base maintenance has been increasing in the CBR community since it is essential to improve the performance of a system that gets information from a case-base. Recent works have shown that the system performance is affected by the competence - "*the range of target problems that can be successfully solved*" [7] - and the efficiency - "*the computational costs of solving a set of target problems*" [7] - of a case-base.

The main factor that affects the competence and the efficiency, and consequently the performance, of a CBR system is the size of the case memory. Much significant researches are concerned with reducing the size of the case-base. Some of them focus on developing methods that limit the number of cases and concerns about competence-preserving [12,7] or efficiency-preserving [2].

The competence and the efficiency can be extremely affected if the memory is full. In fact, how is it possible to improve the competence when there is no space left for a new case with high competence? And how is it possible to improve the efficiency when the memory is full and a new case, if it could be inserted, would solve many target problems of other cases? The *storage-space problem*, as we call the problem

---

* This work is supported by FAPESP under contract no. 98/15835-9.

D.W. Aha and I. Watson (Eds.): ICCBR 2001, LNAI 2080, pp. 546-560, 2001.

that arises when the memory becomes full, may affect drastically the improvement of the system performance.

This paper is a detailed extension of [10]. It differs from previous approaches since it considers the possibility of cases varying in size and deals with the *storage-space problem* by releasing enough space for a useful new case. A case becomes useful when it improves the competence or even the efficiency of the system. To release space, a case-deletion policy is designed to choose cases to delete in order to ensure a lower bound for residual competence, similar to that one presented in [12].

This paper is organized as follow. Section 2 presents an overview of the case-base maintenance area and related works. Section 3 proposes a case-deletion policy and a lower bound for residual competence. Section 4 presents some experiments and finally section 5 concludes this paper.

2 Related Works in Case-Base Maintenance

In recent years, a great amount of interest has been paid to Case-Base maintenance (CBM), a CBR research branch.. The reason of that rises from the desire to improve the performance of CBR systems. Recent work highlighted the importance of the maintenance in a CBR process proposing a new CBR cycle that includes some maintenance steps - Review and Restore [6]. An excellent definition of CBM can be found in [3]:

> *A case-base maintenance implements policies for revising the organization or contents of the case-base in order to facilitate future reasoning for a particular set of performance objectives.*

This definition shows that case-base maintenance is concerned with performance improvement, and two factors affect it significantly: the competence of the case-base and the efficiency. This is because none of CBR system can improve the performance if the case-base cannot solve efficiently a great number of problems.

However, increasing the competence does not mean increase the number of cases, otherwise the system efficiency can be degraded rather than improved. Therefore, strategies that are concerned with reducing the case-base size have been the focus of the case-base maintenance research.

Different strategies have been developed. One of these is the *selective deletion*. It deletes cases according to a case-deletion policy. It can be made with techniques involving the utility of each case [4,5] or involving the overall competence of a case-base [9]. Smyth and Keane's work [9] introduces a competence-preserving approach that guides their case-deletion policy through a classification of types of cases.

Another strategy is the *selective utilization*. It tries to improve the efficiency by making available just a subset of the case-base to the retrieval process [7,11,12].

The methods employed in each strategy are also different. They can consider the competence of each case [7,12], or the adaptation effort that each case can request [2].

Instead of guiding the development of other *selective deletion* techniques, the competence-preserving approach has been used to guide some *selective utilization* policies [7,12] that choose cases with more competence from the case-base and make them available for the search engine. An interesting approach is RC-CNN [7], which is a *selective utilization* policy that constructs compact case-bases with high competence. It is based on the *CNN (Condensed Nearest Neighbor)* method with a suitable measurement called *Relative Coverage*.

Another *selective utilization* approach is the case-addition policy proposed by Zhu and Yang [12]. They achieved a lower bound that is around 63% of the relation between the optimal choices of cases and the choices made by their algorithm.

Similar to competence-preserving approach, efficiency-preserving techniques can also improve the performance of a CBR system, but they are concerned with the adaptation costs. Leake and Wilson [2] recently addressed an efficiency-preserving algorithm called RP-CNN. The approach is similar to RC-CNN, but it focuses on preserving the efficiency of the original case-base through a measurement called *Relative Performance*. It takes into account the relative adaptation costs of each case.

However, none of these strategies addresses the problem that may arise when limited space is available for storing cases. This limitation can also create a barrier for a case-based system and its performance, and we call it *storage-space problem*. Even when a limited number of stored cases are defined, the problem can still appear. This is because there are many domains where cases vary in size and therefore use different amounts of memory. One example of these domains is a case-based planning systems domain, where cases are a sequence of actions, and they can have different numbers of actions in their composition [10,11].

One could argue that there is no problem because the quantity of memory can be augmented. However, the quantity of memory will always be limited to the store case capacity. Additionally, depending on the complexity of the domain and how many problems the domain has, the *storage-space problem* persists.

In fact, memory space limitation requires that some cases should be deleted. The previous deletion-based approaches do not present good results when applied to solve the *storage-space problem*. In addition, although the *selective utilization* approaches [7,12] present good results and a lower bound for residual competence [12], they are not efficient for releasing space in memory, because in almost all situations the number of cases to be deleted is smaller than the number of cases to be retained.

Therefore, one way is to use a *selective deletion*. However, the Smyth and Keane's deletion-based policy [9], as shown in [12], cannot guarantee a lower bound for residual competence and does not perform as well as *selective utilization* approaches, as shown empirically in some experiments in section 4.

This paper does differ from previous approach in considering the possibility of cases having varied sizes. In addition, it proposes a competence-preserving case-deletion policy that can be applied to release space in order to permit the storage of new cases. As shown in section 4, in some circumstances, this case-deletion policy can preserve the competence as high as the *selective utilization* approaches can do but ten times faster.

3   A Case-Deletion Policy

After the adaptation phase succeeds, a CBR system can find a solution to a target problem. This solution might be a new case and, consequently, will have the possibility of being stored in the memory for future use. A new case will be stored if it is useful, i.e., if it increases the total competence of the case-base. However, when the memory is full, a new case is stored in the memory only if the lost competence imposed by the deletion of some cases is less than the competence increasing resulted by the storage of a new case.

Therefore, it is necessary to design a case-deletion policy which releases enough space only if a new case can increase the competence of the case-base.

3.1 Case Competence

The competence, or coverage, is the set of problems that a case, or case-base, can solve [7,9]. The same notion is given in [12], that also highlights the importance of determining the competence through adaptation costs and a similarity metric.

For competence definition, we will use the definition $CoverageSet(c \in C) = \{t \in T: Solves(c,t)\}$, from [7], with the definition of neighborhood function $N(x)$, from [12]. In this paper, we consider the $N(x)$ formula equal to the set $CoverageSet(c \in C)$, where x and c are the same case in the set of cases C for the same target problem t in the space of problem T. Considering a set $M \subseteq C$ of cases in the case-base, we can establish the following definition for competence of a group of cases $X \subseteq M$:

$$Competence(X) = |N(X)| \tag{1}$$

where:

$$N(X) = \bigcup_{x \in X} N(x)$$

With the above definition, we can define the shared competence among cases in the case-base:

$$Shared(X,Y) = \{t \in N(X) : N(X) \cap N(Y)\} \tag{2}$$

The shared competence is the set of target problems that a group of cases X and a group of cases Y can solve together. Conversely, it is possible to define, as in [7], a set of cases that can be used to solve a specific target problem:

$$ReachabilitySet\ (t \in T) = \{c \in C \mid t \in N(c)\} \tag{3}$$

These definitions are used to redefine the **benefit** formula proposed in [12]. It calculates the number of target problems that only the case x can solve with respect to a set W of chosen cases. Assuming the frequency function $P(x)$ equal to 1, the **benefit** becomes:

$$Bft(x) = |N(x) - Shared(x,W)| \tag{4}$$

Following the same idea of benefit formula, the **injury** of a set of cases X is defined:

$$Injury(X \in M) = |N(X) - Shared(X,M-X)| \tag{5}$$

The **injury** is calculated by the analysis of the damage that can be caused in the total competence if X is removed from the case-base. It is the competence of X minus the competence of X that is reached by other cases in $M-X$. This **injury** formula calculates the competence that the case decreases from the case-base when deleted.

```
func Recalc(c)

for each t ∈ N(c) do
    Determine ReachabilitySet(t)
    if |ReachabilitySet(t)|=1 then
          Injury(c'∈ ReachabilitySet(t))= Injury(c') + 1
    endif
endfor
```

Fig. 1. The **Recalc(_)** algorithm, where c is a deleted case

However, formula 5 is not useful to be computationally implemented, because it will takes many cases in the shared set to calculate the *injury* of a single case. Another feasible way to determine the *injury* is calculating the variation of the *injury* of a case c' caused by a deletion of a case c. It is made by the **Recalc (c)** algorithm presented in figure 1. It recalculates the *injury* of cases after the deletion of a case c.

The complexity when recalculating the *injury* through **Recalc(_)** algorithm and the *benefit* in Zhu and Yang's case-addition algorithm, are similar. The difference between both is that the *injury* is recalculated with respect to the retained cases in the memory, and the *benefit* is recalculated with respect to the chosen cases.

Until now, we have been concerned with the competence and *injury* of cases; from this point we will be concerned with the total competence of a case-base as well. However, the determination of the total competence is not a trivial process because any case can share competence with a great number of other cases in the case-base. Therefore, the following simple Lemma can be stated for the total competence, *TC* (*M*) for a case-base *M*:

Lemma: $TC(M) \leq \sum_{x \in M} Competence(x)$

The Lemma above states that the total competence, *TC*, is at most, the summation of the competence of each case in the case-base. The proof can be obtained directly from formula 1 and the union of cases. This Lemma will be useful in Theorems ahead.

3.2 The Case-Deletion Algorithm

There are different types of cases. Smyth and Keane [9] classify four types of cases: (1) pivotal cases are the ones which cannot be solved by other cases; (2) spanning cases are the ones that share the competence independently covered by other cases; (3) auxiliary cases are the ones whose competence is subsumed by other cases competence; and (4) support cases are redundant cases that solve the same problems and, consequently, have the same competence.

According to formula 5, auxiliary cases, support cases and some spanning cases can result in *Injury*(*x*) = 0. Thus, it is necessary to identify which cases with same *injury* should be deleted. As highlighted in [9], some spanning cases can turn to pivotal cases if some auxiliary cases are deleted; so deleting a spanning case in this circumstance is not a good choice.

```
func minimal-injury (c´, M): set_cases

1. set Mb = available(memory);
2. While size(c´) > Mb  and  M has auxiliary cases
   2.1. Select an auxiliary case y with larger size;
   2.2. Recalc (y).
   2.3. M = M - y;
   2.4 Mb = available(memory)
3. While size(c´) > Mb
   3.1. Select a case c with the minimal injury.
   3.2. Recalc (c).
   3.3. M = M - c;
   3.4. Mb = available (memory)
4. return (M);
```

Fig. 2. The case-deletion algorithm, where c' is a new case and M is a set of stored cases.

To avoid wrong choices, a heuristic method is used to delete auxiliary cases first. This is because by their definition, they do not cause any competence decreasing when removed.

The auxiliary cases can be labeled together with the determination of the competence of each case. There is no need to do the process of labeling and determining the competence each time the deletion algorithm is performed. When a case c is deleted, it is just necessary to recalculate the competence and the shared groups with respect to this case c. Therefore, the process to determine auxiliary cases, shared groups and competence for each case are done just one time and off-line.

The case-deletion algorithm is presented in Figure 2. It incorporates a heuristic method that considers the deletion of auxiliary cases first. Consequently, the first choices of the case-deletion algorithm, called *minimal-injury*, are identical to the first choices of the Smyth and Keane's algorithm [9]. However, instead of using all types of cases, the proposed case-deletion algorithm uses only the auxiliary type. It avoids the re-labeling of cases as Smyth and Keane's approach, because the deletion of an auxiliary case does not change the type of any other auxiliary case in the case-base.

Some other heuristic methods are also performed by *minimal-injury* algorithm. One of them chooses the case with larger size among auxiliary cases and cases with the same *injury*. It also considers support cases as a special case of a pivotal case with some auxiliary cases inside.

The case-deletion algorithm presented in Figure 2 is a greedy algorithm that, at each step, chooses a case with minimal *injury* to be deleted. The algorithm will mark cases to be deleted until it releases enough space. However, if the lost competence is bigger than the benefit of a new case, the algorithm will stop the process and will not delete the marked cases. If at that point enough space is already released, the marked cases will be deleted in order to allow the system inserting the new case.

The implementation of the case-deletion algorithm has its complexity imposed on by the recalculation of the *injury,* similar to the recalculation of the *benefit* in Zhu and Yang´s algorithm [12]. If we do not assume the *representativeness assumption* [7], the performance of both algorithms becomes dependent of the case-base concentration, as we see in the empirical results in section 4.

The *minimal-injury* algorithm performs the best choice at each step because it is a greedy algorithm, although it does not guarantee the resulting set of selected cases to be optimal. However, it is possible to define, similar to Zhu and Yang's work [12], a lower bound for the residual competence.

3.3 Establishing a Lower Bound

Let $\Im$ be the set of cases that remain following the deletion of a set $\overline{\Im}$ of cases from the case-base M. In this notation, $B \cup \overline{B} = A \cup \overline{A} = M$, where $\overline{B}$ is the optimal set of cases for deletion and $\overline{A}$ is the set of cases selected for deletion by the algorithm. Any X and $\overline{X}$ are always disjoint sets. Thus, the notation for competence is:

Definition 1: $X^C = Competence(X) = |N(X)|$

The set $N(X)$ allows the calculation of the competence of cases group X. Similarly, we can define the calculation of the lost competence from the disjoint set of $N(X)$:

Definition 2: $\overline{X}^{LC} = LostCompetence(\overline{X},M) = |N(M) - N(X)|$

The lost competence is the total competence M minus the competence remaining after the deletion of cases in the set $\overline{X}$. These definitions allow that the total competence may be the sum of the competence X^C and the lost competence $\overline{X}^{LC}$.

However, although the definition of **injury** is different of **Lost Competence** definition, we can prove that the calculation of the **injury** is correct with respect to definition 2 directly by some sets operations, i.e., considering that $\overline{X}$ is a set of deleted cases from M, **Injury**$(\overline{X}) = Lost\ Competence(\overline{X},M)$.

It shows that the calculation of the **injury** is accurate and that it really represents the competence that is lost after the deletion of cases.

The **injury** formula is used by the case-deletion algorithm presented in Figure 2. As emphasized before, this algorithm is a greedy algorithm and does not perform the optimal choice at each step. However, it is possible to find a lower bound for the optimal choices for deletion and the choices performed by the algorithm.

In order to define a lower bound for residual competence, denoted by A^c, we must proof some theorems and derive algebraically a formula for A^C/M^C.

Focusing on lost competence, the following Theorem shows the relation between the r choices of the deletion algorithm and the optimal deletion of r cases.

Theorem 1: *The optimal lost competence for r cases is at least 58% of the lost competence resulting from the case-deletion algorithm after the deletion of r cases.*

According to the Theorem above, we have $\overline{B}^{LC}/\overline{A}^{LC} \geq 0.58$. In fact, the competence of the case-base decreases from M^C to A^C after the deletion of cases chosen by the algorithm (see Figure 3). Thus, the most important is to establish a lower bound for the relation between A^C and M^C. If we now let $G = \overline{B}^{LC}/\overline{A}^{LC}$, we will obtain the following formula.

$$G = \frac{M^c - B^c}{M^c - A^c}$$

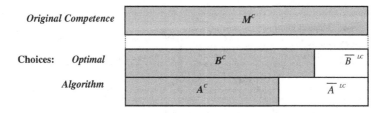

Fig. 3. The meaning of all competences involved in this paper.

Developing the equation and dividing both sides by M^c, and considering that B^c is a percentage of M^c, i.e., $B^c = z.M^c$, the formula becomes:

$$\frac{A^c}{M^c} = \frac{(G-1+z)}{G} \qquad (6)$$

The formula above expresses the value obtained by the relation between M^c and A^c, with respect to G, that represents the relation between $\overline{B}^{LC}$ and $\overline{A}^{LC}$, and the percentage $z = B^c/M^c$.

However, the percentage z must have a lower bound with respect to the percentage of cases that will be deleted in order to achieve a lower bound for A^c/M^c.

In some case-based systems, as in case-based planning, cases have different sizes and occupy different quantities of memory in their storage. However, in most domains, it is possible to calculate the maximal number of cases that will be deleted in order to release space in memory. The worst case is when a case with the maximal size is required to be stored and we must delete cases with minimal size. So, the maximal number of cases to be deleted is:

$$r = \left\lceil \frac{C_{max}}{C_{min}} \right\rceil \qquad (7)$$

Where C_{max} is the maximal size that a case can have in a certain domain, and C_{min} is the minimal size. With the formula 7, we can define, in the worst-case scenario, the percentage of deleted cases from a case-base with m cases:

$$D = \frac{r}{m} \qquad (8)$$

This percentage of deleted cases permits the determination of a lower bound for the optimal residual competence B^c when it is necessary to delete the maximal number of cases, r, from the case-base. First, we must prove the following Theorem:

Theorem 2 : *A competence KC for optimal k choices from m cases with competence MC, with k<m, is KC $\geq$ k/m MC.*

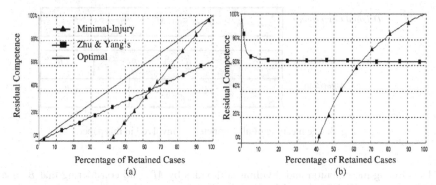

Fig. 4. Plotting of *Minimal-Injury* and Zhu & Yang's lower bounds with respect to total competence (a) and optimal lower bound (b).

The following Corollary provides a lower bound for z in terms of D:

Corollary: *If BC = z.MC, and D=r/m, then z>=1-D.*

This Corollary defines a lower bound for z relating to D. Now we have a lower bound for the optimal residual competence in the worst-case scenario, when r cases with minimal size must be deleted in order to release space for a case with maximal size. With this lower bound for z, and the results from Theorem 1, it is possible to find a generic lower bound for the residual competence from the algorithm, A^c, and the total competence M^c, for the worst-case scenario. It is obtained substituting the result of Corollary in (6):

$$\frac{A^c}{M^c} \geq \frac{(G-D)}{G} \qquad (9)$$

$$\text{where} \qquad G \geq \frac{1}{\left(\dfrac{r+1}{r}\right)^r - 1} \quad \text{and} \quad D = \frac{r}{m}.$$

This lower bound is similar to that one established by Zhu and Yang [12], however, it is dependent on D (percentage of deleted cases*)*, and can achieve, for some values of D, better results than Zhu and Yang's lower bound. Figure 4 shows Zhu and Yang's and *Minimal-Injury* lower bounds for each percentage of retained cases (1-D).

By formula 9, the lower bound depends only on r and m. The r is constant in a specific domain, and m depends on the quantity of memory, where the worst-case scenario is m cases with C_{max}. Thus, for a certain domain, it is possible to define the quantity of memory that is necessary to achieve a specific lower bound, or the inverse, determine the lower bound for a specific quantity of memory.

It is important to note that the heuristic of choosing first the auxiliary cases for deletion does not alter the lower bound achieved above. This heuristic just improves the results of the algorithm.

4 Empirical Results

To validate our case-deletion policy, some empirical tests need to be performed. These tests were not performed in a specific domain framework, but use a case-base that is composed of by hypothetical cases that are randomly created by a case-base seeding system. Instead of considering the *representativeness assumption*, the competence is calculated by taking into consideration some hypothetical target problems that are distributed randomly by the seeding system.

With this generic framework, it is possible to create different case-bases with different concentrations. Concentration is calculated by the relation between the total competence and the sum of the competence of each case. It means that a high concentrated case-base has more target problems that can be solved by a great number of cases. Consequently, it also has more spanning and auxiliary cases compared to a low concentration case-base that has a great number of pivotal cases.

The tests were performed in opposite situations. We generated 10 different low concentration case-bases with 250 cases, and 10 high concentration case-bases with 250 cases. The presented results are the best representation of the average result for each concentration. These tests exploit the case-addition policy from [12], the compact competence case-base from [7] and the case-deletion from [9]. They are referred to as Max-Benef, RC-CNN and Type-based respectively. We named our approach in the experiments as Min-Injury. Although RC-CNN is an editing algorithm that preserves the competence of a case-base, we use it as an addition-based algorithm that chooses cases until a determined number of cases or amount of space is achieved.

It is important to note that each method has some incorporated heuristic in order to maximize their results. For example, Max-Benef chooses the case that occupies less space among cases with the same benefit measure. RC-CNN and Type-based have similar heuristic.

4.1 Experiment 1

The first experiment takes into account case-bases with low concentration. It is concerned with the competence decreasing observation when it performs the deletion of determined number of cases and releases a specific quantity of memory space. The processing time of each method in this experiment takes less than 0.05 seconds.

The results show that the Min-Injury, Max-Benef and RC-CNN have similar performance when concentration is low, either deleting a determined number of cases (Figure 5a) or releasing space in memory (Figure 5b).

In our experiments, the Type-based had the best performance when the space to be released is bigger than 75% of the total memory. In other conditions, it proved to be the worst. Two reasons explain the performance of the Type-based approach. One is the heuristic that chooses the case with larger size among cases with the same type, and another is the low concentration of the case-base, which has a great number of pivotal cases. When 75% of memory space is released by the Type-based approach, almost all cases in a low concentration case-base are pivotal cases. In this circumstance, the Type-based approach performs choices that are near to optimal.

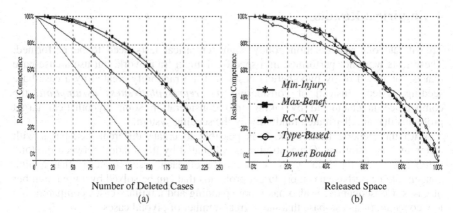

Number of Deleted Cases
(a)

Released Space
(b)

Fig. 5. Competence results after deleting a specific number of cases (a) and after releasing a percentage of memory space (b) in a case-base with low concentration.

The positive results obtained by Min-Injury lead us to conclude that it is a valid method to decrease the number of cases and to release space in memory, although it has a similar performance to other case-addition approaches.

4.2 Experiment 2

The second experiment is similar to the first experiment, but it focuses on high concentration case-bases. In high concentrations, the time of each method is different (Figure 6). The time is normalized according to the higher processing time presented in the test.

The results show that Min-Injury and Max-Benefit perform better than RC-CNN and Type-Based approach, either deleting a determined number of cases (Figure 6a) or releasing space in memory (Figure 6b). However, Min-Injury and Type-Based methods - case-deletion approaches - are more efficient in processing time than case-addition approaches when the purpose is to decrease the number of cases or to release less than 70% of the total space.

Each method has its own processing time *bottleneck*. For Min-Injury, it is the recalculation of the *injury*. For Max-Benefit, it is the recalculation of the benefit. For RC-CNN, it is the determination of the resulted case-base that solves cases in the training set, and for Type-based approach, it is the necessity to re-label the types of cases. The curves plotted in figure 6 are influenced by these *bottlenecks*.

This leads us to conclude that in spite of presenting the same results as Max-Benefit for residual competence, the Min-injury is faster when the purpose is to delete cases or release less than 70% of the space.

It certifies that Min-Injury is a useful approach, not only for releasing space to store a new case, but also for decreasing the number of cases in a case-base or even for advanced editing techniques.

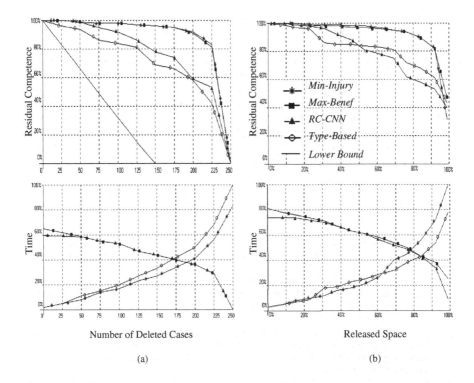

Fig. 6. Competence and Time results after (a) deleting a determined number of cases; and (b) releasing a percentage of memory space. Both are performed in a case-base with high concentration

5 Conclusion

A competence-preserving deletion based algorithm is proposed to release space in case memory. It allows the user to define a lower bound for residual competence for each domain based on the available space to store cases. It is useful for the systems that have cases varying in size as case-based planning systems. It might also be applied in systems and as a policy that is concerned with reducing the size of case-base. The achieved results show that the *minimal-injury* policy can perform as well as *selective utilization* methods, but when the number of retained cases is more than half of total cases - mainly if it is more than 30% - the *minimal-injury* can be faster.

The *minimal-injury* approach maximizes its results by a heuristic method based on auxiliary cases that can be labeled off-line. A definition of such heuristic method in addition-based policy is heavily dependent on case-base features, and thus, it is difficult to be generally designed.

This paper concludes that case-deletion approach can be useful, and sometimes more efficient, than any *selective utilization* approach, to preserve the competence in some specific circumstances such as releasing memory space.

As our point of view, case-addition approaches and deletion-based algorithms are not concurrent, but complementary, and a suitable mix of both methods would probably improve the results.

The competence was chosen to be the main factor of our policy instead of adaptation costs in an efficient-preserving method, as [2], due to the fact that the dichotomy between competence and efficiency is not yet defined or proved to exist. We believe that if the competence measure were designed to take into consideration the adaptation costs, as in [12], the competence-preserving approach would approximate the efficiency-preserving property. However, it is not well known beyond some empirical tests, and probably many researches will arise in order to combine competence and efficient in one single approach.

References

1. Harinarayan, V., Rajaraman, A., Ullman J.D. Implementing Data Cubes Efficiently. In: Proceedings of ACM-SIGMOD. Computing Machinery, Montreal, Canada. (1996) 311-320.
2. Leake, D., Wilson, D. Remembering Why to Remember: Performance-Guided Case-Base Maintenance. In: Blanzieri,E., Portinale, L. (Eds.) Proceedings of the 5th European Workshop on Case-Based Reasoning (EWCBR2K). Lecture Notes in Artificial Intelligence, Vol 1898. Springer-Verlag (2000). 161-172.
3. Leake, D.B., Wilson, D.C. Categorizing Case-Base Maintenance: Dimensions and Directions. In: Smyth, B., Cunningham, P. (Eds.): 4th European Workshop on Case-Based Reasoning EWCBR-98. Lecture Notes in Artificial Intelligence, Vol 1488. Springer-Verlag (1998) 196-207.
4. Markovich, S., Scott, P. The Role of Forgetting in Learning. In: Proceedings of the Fifth International Conference on Machine Learning. Morgan Kaufmann Publishers. (1988) 459-465.
5. Minton, S. Qualitative Results Concerning the Utility of Explanation-based Learning. Artificial Intelligence, 42. AAAI Press. (1990) 363-391.
6. Reinartz, T., Iglezakis, I., Roth-Berghofer, T. On Quality Measures for Case-Base Maintenance. In: Blanzieri,E., Portinale, L (Eds.) Proceedings of the 5th European Workshop on Case-Based Reasoning (EWCBR2K). Lecture Notes in Artificial Intelligence, Vol 1898. Springer-Verlag (2000) 247-259.
7. Smyth, B., McKenna, E. Building Compact Competent Case-Bases. In: Althouff, K., Bergmann, R., Branting, K. (Eds.) Proceedings of the 3rd International Conference in Case-Based Reasoning. ICCBR'99. Lecture Notes in Artificial Intelligence, Vol 1650. Springer-Verlag (1999) 329-342.
8. Smyth, B., McKenna, E. Competence-Guided Case-Base Editing Techniques. In: Blanzieri,E., Portinale, L (Eds.) Proceedings of the 5th European Workshop on Case-Based Reasoning (EWCBR2K). Lecture Notes in Artificial Intelligence, Vol 1898. Springer-Verlag (2000) 186-197.
9. Smyth, B., Keane, M. Remembering to Forget: A Competence-preserving Case-deletion Policy for Case-based Reasoning Systems. In: Proceedings of the 14th International Joint Conference on Artificial Intelligence IJCAI'95. Morgan Kaufmann Publishers (1995) 377-382.
10. Tonidandel, F., Rillo, M. Handling Cases and the Coverage in a Limited Quantity of Memory for Case-Based Planning Systems. In: Sichman, J., Monard, C. (Eds). Proceedings of IBERAMIA/SBIA 2000. Lecture Notes in Artificial Intelligence, Vol 1952. Springer-Verlag (2000) 23-32.

11. Veloso, M. Planning and Learning by Analogical Reasoning. Lecture Notes in Artificial Intelligence, Vol 886. Springer-Verlag (1994).
12. Zhu J., Yang Q. Remembering to Add: Competence-preserving Case-Addition Policies for Case-Base Maintenance. In: Proceedings of the 16th International Joint Conference on Artificial Intelligence IJCAI'99. Morgan Kaufmann Publishers (1999).

Appendix: Proofs

Theorem 1: The optimal lost competence for r cases is at least 58% of the lost competence resulting from the case-deletion algorithm after the deletion of r cases.

Proof: Following the algorithm described in Figure 2, we have:
1. *According to the definition of auxiliary cases, the deletion of an auxiliary case at step 2 does not affect the competence of the case-base.*
2. *According to step 3 of the algorithm, the proof is similar to that one for datacubes [1] and similar to that one for case-addition algorithm [12]. Due to space limitations, the proof is summarized and details can be obtained in [1]. Let m be the total number of cases, suppose that r cases are deleted and that $a_1 \leq a_2 \leq ... \leq a_r$ are the injury of each case numbered in order of selection. Suppose that $b_1 \leq b_2 \leq ... \leq b_r$ are the injury of each optimal case for deletion. Consider $x_{ij} = |N(y_i) \cap N(x_j)|$, i.e., the number of problems solved by the optimal case y_i and by the case x_j chosen by the algorithm. Thus, the following formulas can be written:*

$$\overline{A}^{LC} \geq \sum_{i=1}^{r} a_i; \quad \overline{B}^{LC} \geq \sum_{i=1}^{r} b_i \quad and \quad \sum_{i=1}^{r} x_{ij} \leq a_j.$$

Thus, for each choice:
(1). For all i at the first choice: $b_i \geq a_1$
(2). For all i at the second choice: $b_i + x_{i1} \geq a_2$
...
(n). For all i at the nth choice: $b_i + x_{i1} + x_{i2} + ... + x_{i(n-1)} \geq a_n$

if we sum each above equations, the following inequalities are obtained:

(1). $b_i \geq a_1$ ➔ $\sum_{i=1}^{r} b_i \geq \sum_{i=1}^{r} a_1$ ➔ $\overline{B}^{LC} \geq r.a_1$

(2). $b_i + x_{i1} \geq a2$ ➔ $\sum_{i=1}^{r} b_i + \sum_{i=1}^{r} x_{i1} \geq \sum_{i=1}^{r} a_2$ ➔ $\overline{B}^{LC} \geq r.a_2 - a_1$

...

(r). $\overline{B}^{LC} \geq r.a_r - a_1 - a_2 - ... - a_{r-1}$

Observe that the step $i^{th} = r.a_i - a_1 - a_2 - ... - a_{i-1}$ and $(i+1)^{th} = r.a_{i+1} - a_1 - a_2 - ... - a_i$. Thus, the difference between i^{th} and $(i+1)^{th}$ is: $r.a_{i+1} - (r+1)a_i$. Since this difference must be 0, the equality becomes: $a_i = \dfrac{r}{r+1} a_{i+1}$. Thus, $\overline{A}^{LC} = \sum_{i=0}^{r-1} \left(\dfrac{r}{r+1}\right)^i .a_r$ and

$$\overline{B}^{LC} \geq r. \left(\frac{r}{r+1}\right)^{r-1}.a, \text{The relation becomes: } \frac{\overline{B}^{LC}}{\overline{A}^{LC}} \geq \frac{1}{\left(\frac{r+1}{r}\right)^r - 1}.$$

With $r \to \infty$, the relation becomes: $\quad \dfrac{\overline{B}^{LC}}{\overline{A}^{LC}} \geq \dfrac{1}{e-1} = 0.58.$ ∎

Theorem 2 : A competence KC for optimal k choices from m cases with competence MC, with k<m, is KC ≥ k/m MC.

Proof: *By Lemma, the total competence is less or equal to the summation of individual case competence. The maximal competence is obtained when the cases are disjointed. Thus, the proof is an induction in k. Due to space, it is summarized as follow:*

- *K=0, KC=0; It results in KC ≥ k/m MC;*
- *K=1, if each case does not share any competence with another case and has a competence KC < 1/m MC, the summation of each case competence does not result in total competence MC. Therefore, one case, at least, must have KC ≥ 1/m MC, that would be the optimal choice for k=1. It results in KC ≥ k/m MC;*
- *K=2, considering that the cases are disjointed, any group of 2 cases will have KC < 2/m MC with at least 1 case y with KC ≥ 1/m MC; otherwise it would be the step K=1. The case y would have YC = 1/m MC + ε and any other case would have the competence less than 1/m MC - ε. The summation of the competence would be 1/mMC + ε + (m-1).(1/mMC - ε), that is equal to MC + 2ε - m.ε. The initial condition says that k<m, thus, m>2 and the summation does not result in MC. Therefore, one group of 2 cases, at least, must have KC ≥ 2/m MC, that would be the optimal choice for k=2. It results in KC ≥ k/m MC;*
- *K=n, considering that the cases are disjointed, any group of n cases will have KC < n/m MC with at least a group y of n-1 cases with KC ≥ (n-1)/m MC; otherwise it would be the step K=n-1. The group y would have YC = (n-1)/m MC + ε and any other case would have the competence less than (n-1)/m MC - ε. The summation of the competence would be (n-1)/mMC + ε + (m-n).((n-1)/mMC - ε), that is equal to MC + nε - m.ε. As m>n, the summation does not result in MC. Therefore, one group of n cases, at least, must have KC ≥ n/m MC, that would be the optimal choice for k=n. It results in KC ≥ k/m MC.*

Thus, for k from 0 to n<m the competence is KC ≥ k/m MC. ∎

Corollary: If BC = z.MC, and D=r/m, then z>=1-D.

Proof: *If r cases are deleted, then k cases will be left in the case-base, where k=(1-D)m. By Theorem 2, the optimal choices of k cases have the competence of KC ≥ k/m MC. As KC = BC by definition, we can conclude that z ≥ k/m = 1-D.* ∎

Using Description Logics for Designing the Case Base in a Hybrid Approach for Diagnosis Integrating Model and Case-Based Reasoning

Yacine Zeghib, François De Beuvron, and Martina Kullmann

LIIA, ENSAIS, 24, bld de la Victoire,
67084 Strasbourg, France
zeghib@liia.u-strasbg.fr

Abstract. In this paper we propose an approach of how to use description logics for modeling the case base for case-based reasoning. We illustrate our approach by applying it to hybrid diagnosis. Integrating model-based and case-based reasoning for diagnostic problem solving we contribute to the domain of real time diagnosis. We describe the architecture of this approach, and present some preliminary experimental results. The case-based reasoning component of the hybrid diagnosis system is enabled to exploit description logic inferences for classifying and querying the case base. As description logic interpreter we use the system CICLOP, whereas the diagnosis system is implemented in G2. The description logic system runs as a server application and can thus be queried by the diagnosis system.

1 Introduction

The complexity of industrial plants requires the development of performed and practical diagnosis systems. The tasks of diagnosis consist in the detection and localization of the system's failures, which can be divided into three categories: components failure, controllers failure, and sensors failure. Several diagnosis systems have been developed based on heuristic knowledge (Shallow Knowledge). These approaches have some disadvantages like incompleteness and none-transportability [1]. In order to eliminate these inconveniences a new approach based on the correct behavior of the system has been developed [1]. The main idea is to compare the observed behavior of the system and the predicted one. If they differ then the diagnostic problem is to determine, which system elements being components, sensor and controllers failed. The main difficulty of these approaches is to obtain a complete and correct model of the system. To solve this problem, several methods were proposed such as qualitative physics [2], Fuzzy Logic [3], hierarchical models [4], etc. Recent research uses both analytical and heuristic knowledge ([5], [6]). In this paper a DL-based approach is proposed. In Sect. 2 we present the architecture of the hybrid diagnosis system [7]. We use a case-based reasoning system that interacts with the main diagnosis module in order to execute the diagnosis task. An overview of the model and the diagnostic modules is given. Section 3 is devoted to the development of the case-based reasoning module: First we give an overview of description logics. Then we present the case base model and it's description logic implementation. For the implementation of the

D.W. Aha and I. Watson (Eds.): ICCBR 2001, LNAI 2080, pp. 561–575, 2001.

CBR system we use the description logic system CICLOP (Customizable Inference and Concept Language for Object Processing) [8]. Besides, the main tasks and the general behavior of the CBR system are developed. In Sect. 4 an example to illustrate our method is given. Finally, we draw some conclusions and discuss the remaining problems on which we will work in the future

2 The Hybrid Diagnosis System

The hybrid diagnosis system (HDS) incorporates the flexibility and the power of model-based reasoning, as well as the rapidity of case-based reasoning.
The main motivations for the development of an HDS can be summarized as follows:
- Taking the advantages from both of the approaches
- Combining complementary approaches, namely analytical and heuristic methods
- Possibly increasing the performance of the diagnosis system by using all the available knowledge from both of the sources.

In this paper, we suppose that all the failures are visible, i.e. we do not consider the hidden failures.

2.1 Outline of the System Architecture

The general architecture of the hybrid diagnosis system is presented in Fig. 1. The general approach can be described as follows: The analytical knowledge and the heuristic knowledge are first used off-line for building the model of the system and the case base, respectively. The diagnostic module uses the observed variables of the system in order to perform the following tasks: supervision, simulation, and diagnosis. During the diagnosis session, the diagnosis module uses simultaneously the model of the device and the case base to generate the hypotheses of the diagnosis and the breakdown actions. The different modules, given in Fig. 1, are briefly described in the following sections.

2.2 Modeling

Based on the literature, we distinguish eight types of models [9]: structural, behavioral, functional, topological, causal, temporal, hierarchical, and taxonomical ones. In our approach we take into account the first three types mentioned above which are briefly described below. We make the assumption that the system can be hierarchically decomposed.
- Structural model: A structural model describes the physical structure of a device, i.e. it's physical components and connections between the components.
- Behavioral model: A behavioral model describes the components behavior, i.e. the physical relation between the component's variables.
- Hierarchical model: A hierarchical model is meant to capture the different levels of aggregation that are distinguished in the real world, i.e. describes how constituents are composed of sub-constituents.

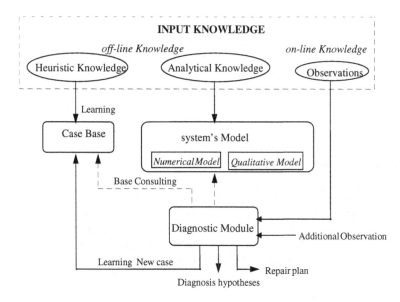

Fig. 1. System architecture

Fig. 2 shows the hierarchical representation of the system, which represents the hierarchical aspects of the system.

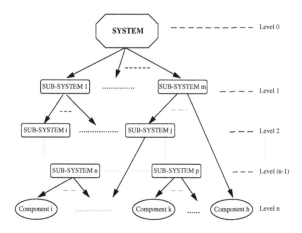

Fig. 2. The hierarchical representation of the system

We define the different parts of the model that show the structural and behavioral aspects of the system [10]:

- Component definition:

```
(COMPONENT <component-class-name>
    (INPUT-VARIABLE <variable-name>
                    <variable-description>)
    (OUTPUT-VARIABLE <variable-name>
                     <variable-description>)
    (PARAMETER <parameter-name> <parameter-description>)
    (BEHAVIORAL-MODE <mode-name> (<numerical-behavior>)
                     (<qualitative-behavior>)))
```

- System definition:

```
(SYSTEM <system-name>
    (SUB-SYSTEMS <sub-systems-names>)
    (INPUT-VARIABLE <subsystem-name-variable-id>)
    (OUTPUT-VARIABLE <subsystem-name-variable-id>)
    (CONNECTIONS <subsystem-name-variable-id
         subsystem-name-variable-id name-variable-id>)
    (ABNORMAL-MODES <mode-name> <mode-description>))
```

- Subsystem definition:

```
(SUB-SYSTEM_level(i) <sub-system-name>
    (SUPER-SUB-SYSTEM_level(i-1)
            <sub-system_level(i-1)-name>)
    (SUB-SYSTEMS_level(i+1)
            <sub-systems_level(i+1)-names>)
    (COMPONENTS <components-names>)
    (INPUT-VARIABLE <subsystem-name-variable-id>|
                    <component-name-variable-id>)
    (OUTPUT-VARIABLE <subsystem-name-variable-id>|
                     <component-name-variable-id>)
    (CONNECTIONS <sub-system-name-variable-id
                  sub-system-name-variable-id>|
                 <sub-system-name-variable-id
                  component-name-variable-id>|
                 <component-name-variable-id
                  sub-system-name-variable-id>)
    (ABNORMAL-MODES <mode-name> <mode-description>))
```

For more detail about the corresponding implementation of this model see [7].

2.3   Diagnostic Module

The reasoning algorithm of the diagnostic module is as follows. At every simulation step and after acquiring the value of the input variables a supervision procedure is done. The aim of this procedure is to detect any anomaly in the system's input variables like an aberrant value, or abnormal behavioral mode, etc. When the input variables are validated, a simulation session of the normal behavior of the system takes place. If the diagnostic module detects a failure, it tries to assume for the system at least a deteriorated behavioral mode and at the same time it starts the failure's research processes. The case base component of the hybrid diagnosis system is developed in the following section.

3 The Case Base

Case-based reasoning is a problem solving paradigm, in which a new problem is solved by exploiting similar previous cases [3]. The four processes of the CBR-Cycle, which are illustrated in Fig. 3, are briefly described in the following (see also [4], [5]):

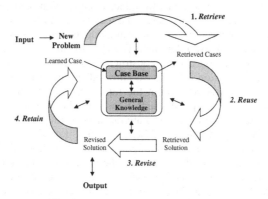

Fig. 3. The case-based reasoning cycle

- Retrieve: The retrieve task starts with a (partial) problem description, and ends when a best matching previous case has been found.
- Reuse: The reuse of the retrieved case solution in the context of the new case focuses on two aspects: (a) the differences among the past and the current case and (b) which part of a retrieved case can be mapped to the new case.
- Revise: Case revision consists of two tasks: (a) evaluate the case solution generated by reuse. If successful, learning from the success (case retainment), (b) otherwise, repair the case solution using domain-specific knowledge.
- Retain: This is the process of incorporating into the existing knowledge what is useful to retain from the new problem-solving episode.

The heuristic knowledge about the behavior of the system is implemented as a case base with a description logic (DL) representation. The use of DLs has the following advantages:
- The abstraction process is clearly defined.
- The cases are represented in a language with a clear semantics.
- The indexing process is done automatically by the CBR system. More precisely, DLs allow for an automatic classification of concepts, i.e. for the calculation of a specialization hierarchy.

- The automatic classification of concepts facilitates incrementally changing the concept hierarchy.

In the following paragraph we introduce the description logic formalism.

3.1 Description Logics

Description logics (DLs) are a class of knowledge representation formalisms (see [12] for more details). They can be used to construct a knowledge base, containing knowledge about a specific application. In this paper we propose a DL model for the case base. The DL formalism consists of two parts. The terminological formalism enables defining the abstract conceptual frame through which the real world is to be seen. Using this formalism concepts can be introduced and relations can be defined. By the assertional formalism concrete facts about the real world can be described, i.e. knowledge about particular objects, the so-called individuals. Individuals are defined to be instances of concepts, and also relations between individuals can be introduced. So, a world description (or ABox) can be constructed based on a given terminology (or TBox). Besides, a description logic-based knowledge representation supports several inference methods for reasoning about the represented knowledge. They automatically can make knowledge explicit which is only implicitly represented in a knowledge base. The basic reasoning facilities are the satisfiability and the consistency test. They allow for checking, whether a description logic knowledge base is contradiction-free. The subsumption inference computes the subsumption relation between two concepts, and can thus be used to organize the concepts of the knowledge base in taxonomical order, i.e. to classify the concepts. A concept C subsumes a concept D if C is more general than or equal to D, i.e. the set of individuals denoted by D, is included in or equal to the set of individuals denoted by C. Besides, the realization inference calculates the set of most specific concepts in the TBox for a given individual.

3.2 Organization and Implementation of the Case Base Model

The hybrid diagnosis system proposed in [7], uses a CBR system containing a set of cases, i.e. failure examples, which represent the state of the system when the failure occurs. A case is described by the quadruple <PROB, CTX, CONS, SOL>, where:

- PROB = {*(Variable, qualitative-value, tendency)*}, the set of abnormal variables (variables with abnormal values) which characterize the considered case.

- CTX = {*(Constituant, mode); (Variable, qualitative-value, tendency)*}; the state of the system when the problem occurs.

- CONS = {*(Variable, qualitative-value, tendency)*}, the set of variables that are observed to be affected by the abnormal variables.

- SOL = {*Diagnostic* <*(Constituant, failure-mode), (breakdown-actions)*>}, the corresponding diagnosis and breakdown actions of the case.

The stored real world cases are represented as individuals in the ABox and their conceptual counterpart cases as concepts in the TBox. The taxonomy of cases is automatically computed using the corresponding DL inference. Individual cases are automatically matched to their corresponding concept cases using the realization inference [13]. As mentioned above, we use the DL system CICLOP [8] for the implementation of the CBR system. In our model we use the DL expressiveness ALCF (Attributive Language with Complements and Features) with strings which comprises the language constructors AND, OR, SOME, ALL, NOT and string concept descriptions. For more details see [8] and [16].

We define the following terminology. Variables are defined to take the qualitative values big, medium, or small. The tendency of the variables can be decreasing, increasing, or stable. For the definition of the variables, we use the two attributes has-Qualitative-Value and has-Tendency. The problem is characterized by a set of abnormal variables. Its consequences are defined using the role has-variable. After that, we define the context using the has-component-state role. The definition of the solution consists of the diagnosis part, which is composed by the set of the failed components and the actions of the breakdown service. Finally, we give the complete definition of the case. A graphical interpretation of the described terminology is given in Fig. 4.

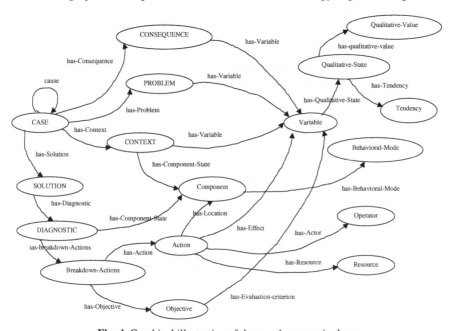

Fig. 4. Graphical illustration of the case base terminology

```
(define-concept Qualitative-Value
    (aset big medium small))

(define-concept Tendency
    (aset increasing stable decreasing))
(define-concept Qualitative-State (AND
    (SOME has-Qualitative-Value Qualitative-Value)
    (ALL  has-Qualitative-Value Qualitative-Value)
```

```
            (SOME has-Tendency Tendency)
            (ALL  has-Tendency Tendency)))

    (define-concept Variable (AND
        (SOME has-Qualitative-State Qualitative-State)
        (ALL has-Qualitative-State Qualitative-State )))

    (define-concept PROBLEM (AND
        (SOME has-Variable Variable)
        (ALL has-Variable Variable)))

    (define-primitive-concept Component (AND
        (SOME has-Behavioral-Mode Behavioral-Mode)
        (ALL has-Behavioral-Mode Behavioral-Mode)))

    (define-concept CONTEXT (AND
        (ALL has-Variable Variable)
        (SOME has-Component-State Component)
        (ALL has-Component-State Component)))

    (define-concept CONSEQUENCE (AND
        (SOME has-Variable Variable)
        (ALL has-Variable Variable)))

    (define-concept SOLUTION (AND
        (SOME has-Diagnostic DIAGNOSTIC)
        (ALL has-Diagnostic DIAGNOSTIC)))

    (define-concept DIAGNOSTIC (AND
        (SOME has-Component-State Component)
        (ALL has-Component-State Component)
        (SOME has-breakdown-Actions breakdown-Actions)
        (ALL has-breakdown-Actions breakdown-Actions)))

    (define-concept Breakdown-Actions (AND
        (SOME has-Objective Objective)
        (ALL has-Objective Objective)
        (SOME has-Action Action)(ALL has-Action Action)))

    (define-concept Objective (AND
        (ALL has-Objective Objective)
        (SOME has-Evaluation-criterion Variable)
        (ALL has-Evaluation-criterion Variable)))

    (define-concept Action (AND
        (SOME has-Begin-Time real)(ALL has-Begin-Time real)
        (SOME has-End-Time (>=(path has-Begin-Time)))
        (SOME has-Duration
```

```
          (=(-(path has-Begin-Time)(path has-End-Time))))
     (SOME has-Location Component)
     (ALL has-Location Component)
     (ALL has-Effect Variable)
     (SOME has-Actor Operator)(ALL has-Actor Operator)
     (SOME has-Resource Resource)
     (ALL has-Resource Resource)))

(define-concept CASE (AND
     (SOME has-Problem PROBLEM)(ALL has-Problem PROBLEM)
     (SOME has-Context CONTEXT)(ALL has-Context CONTEXT)
     (ALL has-Consequence CONSEQUENCE)
     (ALL has-Solution SOLUTION)
     (ALL cause CASE)))
```

3.3 Case-Based Reasoning Tasks

The CBR tasks presented in Sect 3.1 are developed in the following:

Retrieve

The role of the retrieve task is first, to determine the concepts parents of the current concept case C_c. This is done based on the concept taxonomy. Second, it computes among its individuals cases the most similar to the current individual case one by using the case-based learning (CBL) algorithm CBL1 [14], which defines the similarity of the cases C_1 and C_2 as:

$$Similarity(C_1, C_2, p) = \frac{1}{\sqrt{\sum_{i \in P} Feature\_dissimilarity(C_{1i}, C_{2i})}}, \qquad (1)$$

$$0 < Similarity \leq 1,$$

where P is the set of predictor features which are the abnormal variables and their values in our case. The feature dissimilarity is calculated as follows:

$$Feature\_dissimilarity(C_{1i}, C_{2i}) \begin{cases} 0, \text{ if } C_{1i} = C_{2i}, \\ 1, \text{ otherwise.} \end{cases} \qquad (2)$$

If there are more cases with the same similarity, we use the coverage criteria (see [15])

$$Coverage \; AC_i = \frac{Number\_of\_individuals\_of\_AC_i}{Total\_number\_of\_individuals\_in\_the\_case\_base}, \qquad (3)$$

$$0 < Coverage \leq 1.$$

This value compares the amount of individual cases of a certain case with the total number of cases in the case base. It therefore reflects the importance of a given case.

Reuse
- If an identical concept case is found the solution of its most similar individual case is directly applied to the current case.
- If no identical concept case is found, the CBR system uses the procedure described in Fig. 5 to propose a solution.

```
                        /* start from the set selected cases */
BEGIN
1. select the solution (DIAG1)of the case with the highest similarity values;
2. create case: non-resolved-part;
3. if non-resolved-part exists then
      begin
      for c = each case do compute similarity(c, non-resolved-part);
      select the solution (DIAG2) of the
      most similar case;
      DIAGcurrent-case = DIAG1 U DIAG2
      end;
4. if non-resolved-part does not exist then
      begin
            compute the set of the children of non-resolved-part;
            select the children which that their ABN is a subset of the ABN of
            the abstract-current-case;
            if exists then
               begin
                  for c = each case do
                  compute similarity(c, non-resolved-part);
                  end;
                  select the solution (DIAG2) of the most similar case;
                  DIAGcurrent-case = DIAG1 U DIAG2;
               end;
            else
            DIAGcurrent-case = DIAG1;
      end;
END
```

Fig. 5. The reuse procedure

Revise
The revise task consists of validating the proposed solution by simulation using the model of the system. This task is realized by the hybrid diagnosis system, and its description is out of the purpose of this paper.

Retain
The new learned conceptual case is automatically introduced into the case base by classification, if it does not exist already. Furthermore, the corresponding individual case is defined to instantiate its concept case.

3.4   General Algorithm

When the HDS detects a fault it creates a current case and its abstract case. Then it starts the CBR process by sending the corresponding commands to the system CIC-LOP. For this task CICLOP is run as a server and communicates with its client via a simple, text file-based protocol. In our application the client is the hybrid diagnosis system implemented with G2 [17]. The general procedure of the behavior of the CBR system is described in Fig. 6. The interaction between the HDS and the CICLOP server is realized as described in Fig. 7.

```
                    /* start from the given current*/
BEGIN
1. if the current case is a failed case then go to END
2. if the current-case exists then
   begin
       select its individual cases;
           for c = each individual case do
               compute similarity (c, current-case);
           end;
       select the most similar case mc;
       copy the solution of mc to the current-case;
       go to END;
   end;
3. if the current -case does note exist then
   begin
       Compute the set of the parents of the current case;
       Reuse the solution of the retrieved cases to the current-case;
       Revise the proposed solution by simulation;
   if success then
       retain the new case;
       go to END
   end;
END
```

Fig. 6. The general procedure

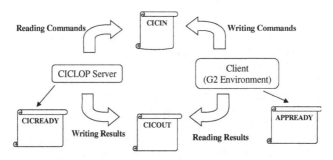

Fig. 7. The CICLOP server protocol

4 An Application Example

An example of an application is described in Fig. 8.

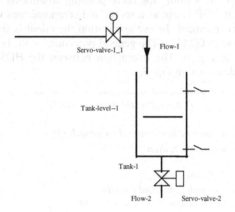

Fig. 8. The thank example

Suppose we have the two following cases in the case base:
Case-1:
    PROB = {(flow-1, medium, decreasing)}
    CTX = {(servo-valve-1, Open), (Tank-1, Normal-Tank), (servo-valve-2, Open)}
    CONS = {(tank-level-1, medium, decreasing)}
    SOL = { <(servo-valve-1, blocked)>, <(close-servo-valve-2>)}
Case-2:
    PROB = {(tank-level-1, decreasing)}
    CTX = {(servo-valve-1, Open), (servo-valve-2, Open)}
    SOL = { <(tank-1, tank-leakage)>, <(close-servo-valve-2>)}

and the new current case:
Current-case:
    PROB = {(tank-level-1, big, decreasing)}
    CTX = {(servo-valve-1, Open), (servo-valve-2, Open),(flow-1, medium,stable)}

The DL representation of these cases is illustrated in the following. The concepts
flow-1, flow-2, and tank-level-1 denote variables and. The concepts servo-valve-1,
servo-valve-2, and Tank-1 denote components.

```
(define-concept Case-1
 (AND CASE
  (SOME has-Problem(AND PROBLEM(SOME has-Variable
   (AND flow-1(SOME has-Qualitative-State
    (AND Qualitative-State
     (SOME has-Qualitative-Value (aset medium))
     (SOME has-Tendency (aset decreasing))))))))
  (SOME has-Context(AND CONTEXT
   (SOME has-Component-State (AND servo-valve-1
```

```
      (SOME has-Behavioral-Mode Open)))
      (SOME has-Component-State (AND Tank-1
      (SOME has-Behavioral-Mode Normal-Tank)))
      (SOME has-Component-State (AND servo-valve-2
      (SOME has-Behavioral-Mode Open)))))
    (SOME has-Consequence (AND CONSEQUENCE
      (SOME has-Variable (AND tank-level-1
      (SOME has-Qualitative-State (AND Qualitative-State
      (SOME has-Qualitative-Value (aset medium))
      (SOME has-Tendency (aset decreasing))))))))
    (SOME has-Solution (AND SOLUTION (SOME has-Diagnostic
      (AND Diagnostic
      (SOME has-Component-State(AND servo-valve-1
      (SOME has-Behavioral-Mode blocked)))
      (SOME has-breakdown-Actions
                          close-servo-valve-2)))))))

(define-concept Case-2
 (AND CASE
  (SOME has-Problem(AND PROBLEM(SOME has-Variable
   (AND tank-level-1 (SOME has-Qualitative-State
   (AND Qualitative-State
   (SOME has-Tendency (aset decreasing)))))))))
  (SOME has-Context(AND CONTEXT
   (SOME has-Component-State (AND servo-valve-1
   (SOME has-Behavioral-Mode Open)))
   (SOME has-Component-State (AND servo-valve-2
   (SOME has-Behavioral-Mode Open)))
  (SOME has-Solution (AND SOLUTION (SOME has-Diagnostic
   (AND Diagnostic
   (SOME has-Component-State(AND Tank-1
   (SOME has-Behavioral-Mode tank-leakage)))
   (SOME has-breakdown-Actions
                       close-servo-valve-2)))))))

(define-concept Current-case
 (AND CASE
  (SOME has-Problem(AND PROBLEM(SOME has-Variable
   (AND tank-level-1 (SOME has-Qualitative-State
   (AND Qualitative-State
    (SOME has-Qualitative-Value (aset big))
    (SOME has-Tendency (aset decreasing)))))))))
  (SOME has-Context(AND CONTEXT
   (SOME has-Component-State (AND servo-valve-1
   (SOME has-Behavioral-Mode Open)))
   (SOME has-Component-State (AND servo-valve-2
   (SOME has-Behavioral-Mode Open)))
  (SOME has-Variable (AND flow-1
```

```
(SOME has-Qualitative-State (AND Qualitative-State
(SOME has-Qualitative-Value (aset medium))
(SOME has-Tendency (aset stable)))))))))))
```
The classification of the four cases is given in Fig. 9.

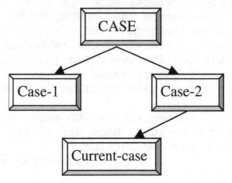

Fig. 9. The graphical representation of the case base

5   Conclusion and Future Work

In this paper we propose how to design a case-based reasoning system using description logics. The formal DL representation enables the use of corresponding inference methods, and thus provides efficient means for classifying and querying the case base. We have described the main processes of the CBR cycle and how they have been realized in our approach. The work which remains to be done is first, to improve the retrieve task, by using the set of the normal variables which influence the value of the abnormal ones. In fact, we want use more efficient similarity measures to better being able to distinguish between the cases. Second, it remains to improve the reuse task, by using more efficient techniques like taking into account the knowledge about the diagnosis of the case or/and, the failure mode of the components, for instance.

References

1.   Reiter, R.: A theory of Diagnosis from First Principles. Elsevier Science Publishers (1987)
2.   Winston, H. A., Clark, R. T., Buchina, G.: AGETS MBR: An application of Model-Based Reasoning to Gas Turbine Diagnostics. American Association for Artificial Intelligence, Winter (1995)
3.   Frank, P.: Fuzzy Supervision - Application of Fuzzy Logic to Process Supervision and Fault Diagnosis. International Workshop on Fuzzy Technologies in Automation and Intelligent Systems, Duisbourg (1994)
4.   El Ayeb, B.: Towards systematic construction of diagnostic systems for large industrial plants: Methods, Language, and Tools. IEEE, Vol. 6 N° 5, October (1994)

5. Portinale, P., Torasso, P., Ortalda, C., Giardino, A.:.Using Case-Based Reasoning to focus Model-Based Diagnostic problem solving. Lecture Notes in Artificial Intelligence 837, PP 325-337, (1994)
6. Stamos, T., Feyock, S.: An Integration of Case-Based and Model-Based Reasoning and its Application to Physical System Faults. Lecture Notes in Artificial Intelligence 604, F. Belli and F. J. Radermacher (Eds), Springer-Verlag, (1994)
7. Zeghib, Y., Rousselot, F., Keith, B.: Building a Diagnostic System for Large Industrial Plants: Using Symbolic and Numerical Knowledge. IAR 98, MULHOUSE (1998) 46-52
8. De Bertrand de Beuvron, F., Rousselot, F., Grathwohl, M., Rudloff, D., Schlick, M.: CIC-LOP. System Comparison of the International Workshop on Description Logics '99, Linköping, Sweden (1999)
9. Benjamins, R., Heijst, G. V.: Modeling Multiple Models". SWI , University of Amsterdam
10. Schen, Q, Leitch R. R, and Steele A. D. A Generic Harness for the Systematic Generation of Multiple Models. Heriot-Watt University, Department of Computing and Electrical Engineering (1994)
11. Lenz, M., Bartsch-Spörl,.B., Burkhard, H.-D., Wess, S.: Case-Based Reasoning Technology: From Foundations to Applications. Springer-Verlag, Berlin Heidelberg (1998)
12. F. Baader. Logic-Based Knowledge Representation. In M.J. Wooldridge and M. Veloso, editors, Artificial Intelligence Today, Recent Trends and Developments, number 1600 in Lecture Notes in Computer Science, pages 13-41. Springer Verlag, (1999)
13. Salotti, S., Ventos, V.: Study and Formalization of a Case-Based Reasoning System with a Description logic. LIPN-CNRS URA 1507, Université Paris-Nord France (1997)
14. Aha, W. D.: Case-Based Learning Algorithms. Case-Based Reasoning Workshop. Morgan Kaufmann (1991)
15. Maria, M. :Etudes des aspects liés au contenu et à l'organisation de la memoire dans le RàPs. Ecole de Mines, Paris (1998) (In French)
16. Schlick, M. : CICLOP: Description Logics for configuration. Phd Thesis, LIIA, ENSAIS, Strasbourg, France, (1999)
17. Gensym Intelligent Real-Time Systems : G2 Reference Manual, Version 4.0, (1995)

T-Air: A Case-Based Reasoning System for Designing Chemical Absorption Plants

Josep Lluís Arcos

IIIA, Artificial Intelligence Research Institute
CSIC, Spanish Council for Scientific Research
Campus UAB, 08193 Bellaterra, Catalonia, Spain.
arcos@iiia.csic.es, http://www.iiia.csic.es

Abstract. In this paper we describe a case-based reasoning application developed for aiding engineers in the design of chemical absorption plants. Based on the notion of flow sheet, the paper describes how the application uses a highly structured representation of cases and similarity criteria based on chemical knowledge for designing solutions following an interactive case-based reasoning approach.

1 Introduction

TECNIUM is an engineering company that designs and sells installations and equipments for gas treatment around the world. The gas treatment is required in many and diverse industrial processes such as:

- *Control of the atmospheric pollution* due to corrosive residual gases which contain vapours, mists, and dusts of industrial origin;
- *Industrial gas purification*, as a stage of a production process;
- *Recovery* of product manufacture, starting from gaseous sources;
- *Degassing* of liquids which contain vapours or gases in solution;
- *Dust removal* of particles mixed in a gas.

Examples of gas treatments are the absorption of gases and vapours such as SO_2, CLH, or CL_2; the absorption of NO_x with recovering of HNO_3; the absorption of drops and fogs such as PO_4H_3 or $ClNH_4$; dust removal in metalic oxides; and elimination of odours from organic origin.

The main problem in designing gas treatment plants is that the diversity of possible problems is as high as the diversity of industrial processes while the experimental models about them is small. The knowledge acquired by engineers with their practical experience is the main tool used for solving new problems. In TECNIUM, the most important presentation card is its more than thirty five years of experience.

An additional issue with gas treatment is that there are many customers sending consultations for analyzing their specific problem but not many of them finally make an order. This issue forces TECNIUM to spend many efforts in designing proposals without profit. Moreover, the proposals have to be analyzed in

D.W. Aha and I. Watson (Eds.): ICCBR 2001, LNAI 2080, pp. 576–588, 2001.
© Springer-Verlag Berlin Heidelberg 2001

detail because the economical assesments of the offer are binding. For instance, during the last year the amount of offers exceeded thirty millions of euros while the order ratio was around the twenty per cent. This issue motivated the first contacts for providing computer tools for helping in the design of gas treatment plants.

Because the experience accumulated along the years is the main knowledge used in the design of gas treatment plants, the chances for using a case-based reasoning approach were very high. Moreover, the different existing case-based reasoning commercial applications have demonstrated the viability of the CBR approach [9] for solving complex problems and, specifically, for design support [6,7].

Given these initial hypotheses and our previous expertise in developing case-based reasoning systems [2,4] with the use of knowledge intensive methods for modeling similarities in complex structured cases, we decided to start a project of six month duration for developing and testing a CBR application.

For focusing the problem only the chemical absorption (most than 80 %) was covered by the *T-Air* application and we excluded other currently used technologies such as oxi-redox reactions or biofilters. Moreover, the plastic material used for constructing the equipments—they are using more than eight different plastic combinations as well as some metal materials—is determined by the expert except in some predefined problems.

For the design of gas treatment plants about forty different types of main equipments have been covered. We also started with a database of a thousand of solved problems involving, each of them, from two to twenty different equipments.

The organization of this paper is as follows. In Section 2 we briefly present the working principles of chemical gas treatment for illustrating the design process and the design decisions where the use of case-based reasoning techniques can help to the experts. Section 3 describes the *T-Air* application and the case-based reasoning techniques used. Finally, in Section 4 we present the conclusions and future directions of the work.

2   Working Principles of Chemical Gas Treatment

The chemical gas treatment is based on applying to a gas current (the contaminant) another liquid current (the solvent) in a parallel or opposite direction for obtaining a resulting clear gas plus a residual liquid and/or dust useful for another industrial process—or, at least, a liquid that can be eliminated more easily. There are different equipments for achieving this goal each of them based in a different principle such as the mass transfer, the venturi effect, or cyclones. Any chemical absorption plant is designed by determining a *flow sheet* (see Figure 1) composed of a collection of washing elements, tanks for storing the solvents, fans for aspirating the polluted gas, and pumps for circulating the washing liquids. Moreover, for each equipment a specific model and the values of its working pa-

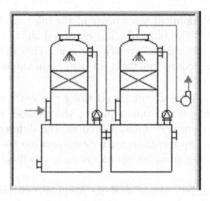

Fig. 1. An example of a simple flow sheet generated by *T-Air* with two scrubbers, each of them on top of a tank with a pump that sucks the washing liquid from the tank to the scrubber, and one fan at the end of the process.

rameters have to be determined. Below we briefly summarize the two main used principles.

Removal of gaseous pollutants by counter-current *Flow Packed Scrubbers* is based on the principle of mass transfer. This is defined as the transfer, in mass, of gaseous polluting molecules from the air stream into the scrubbing liquid. Transfer is achieved by a combination of diffusion, physical absorption, and/or chemical reaction. Highly soluble gases are transferred from an air stream into water by diffusion and physical absorption. Medium or low solubility gases are often scrubbed by absorption, followed by chemical reaction with the treated scrubbing liquid.

The selection of the required equipment and dimensions is determined by two parameters: the number of mass transfer units N_{OG} and the height of transfer unit H_{OG}. The number of mass transfer units is determined given the concentration of the incoming polluted gas and the desired pollution concentration of the outcome gas. The height of transfer unit H_{OG} is determined experimentally depending on factors such as the solubility, concentration, and temperature of the polluting gas. There are only reported H_{OG} values for some prototypical gas-liquid configurations—such as $NH_3 - air - H_2O$, or $Cl_2 - air - NaOH$. For the other cases the value of H_{OG} is determined using the chemical similarity among gases and the experience of previously built installations.

In washers using the *Ventury* effect, the absorption of gas and the collected of particles or vesicles is performed in a gas-liquid parallel current with high energy and turbulence. In the zone of the ventury throat, the liquid is injected in the form of fine droplets which presents a large surface to moisten and facilitates the diffusion of the liquid into the gas. At the same time, an agglomeration and increasing of the mass of the solid particles is produced, being afterwards separated in a cyclonic separator or in a liquid-gas impingement separator, both

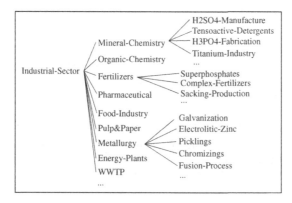

Fig. 2. A portion of the hierarchy for Industrial Sectors.

provided with a high efficiency mist-eliminators of low pressure drop, so avoiding an eventual droplets emission to the atmosphere.

The selection of the adequate configuration of basic equipments for each problem is made bearing chiefly in mind the following data:

- The industrial sector of the customer (see Figure 2).
- Provenance of gas (the industrial process that originates the gas);
- Composition of gas;
- Gas flow to be treated (a range from 100 to 100.000 m^3/h. can be washed with an efficiency of 99 %);
- Temperature (from -10 to 1.000 $°C$);
- Concentration and solubility of the polluting gas;
- Solids and/or vesicles contents;
- Granulometry;
- Pressure drop to be admitted;
- Efficiency or maximum emission desired.

As a summary of this brief description of the working principles of chemical gas treating, we want to emphasize that there are many experimental parameters involved. These parameters are mainly determined from the past experience using the knowledge about the common issues present in different industrial processes and the similarity among the chemical properties of different gases. This was the original working hypothesis for developing an application based on case-based reasoning techniques.

3   System Description

T-Air is implemented in *Noos* [2,5], an object-centered representation language designed to support knowledge modeling of problem solving and learning. *Noos* was developed using the notion of *episodic memory* and provides a collection

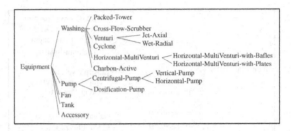

Fig. 3. A portion of the hierarchy for equipments used in Absorption systems. There are four main equipments: gas-washing units, pumps, fans, and tanks. Examples of accessories are spray-nozzles, valves, or demisters.

of components for case-based reasoning such as retrieval perspectives [3] and adaptors [8]. *T-Air* is currently running in Windows computers in the TECNIUM intranet.

In the development of the system two engineers from TECNIUM were involved as domain experts and main users of the system, an additional engineer was consulted for technical issues, and a AI-CBR researcher was the project manager and programmer. The development has taken six months and the utility of the system has exceeded the initial expectatives of TECNIUM. An extension covering the aspects excluded in this initial phase is planed to start in the next months.

We have covered forty different types of equipments organized in five categories: gas-washing units, pumps, fans, tanks, and accessories (see Figure 3). Each equipment has in turn around twenty different models.

3.1 Modeling Chemical Knowledge

In *T-Air*, we have modeled the chemical knowledge that is the basis for determining the similarity between a gas composition in a new problem and those treated previously and stored in the case base. Moreover, since we are mixing a polluted gas with a washing liquid, we also have modeled the properties of the washing liquids, the compatibility among gases and liquids, and some chemical reactions involved.

First of all, the basic substances contained in the periodical table were codified with their main properties such as molar mass, critical temperature, and critical pressure, the groups they belong (metals, non-metals, halogens, ...) and the main properties of these groups.

The second component modeled was gas compounds with their properties such as critical temperatures and pressures or solubilities. The gas compounds are organized in a hierarchy of compounds grouped by chemical notions such as organic compounds, inorganic-compounds, acids, oxides, alcohols, etc. Because the number of possible gas compounds is extremately high, only those present in the case base have been modeled initially. The design decision was that the knowledge about new gas compounds will be acquired when a new problem requires it. The approach we have adopted is close to work of capturing expert design knowledge through "concept mapping" [7]. As we will describe later, when the engineer is analyzing a problem involving a gas not previously covered, the engineer uses the navigation interactive capabilities of *T-Air* for determining the possible characteristics of the gas and improves the chemical knowledge of the system by means of completing the information.

The third component modeled was liquid compounds (solvents). We have followed the same approach taken for gas compounds: only those present in the case base have been modeled. As in gases the navigation capabilities of *T-Air* are used for capturing new knowledge during the analysis of new problems.

The last component modeled was the chemical reactions such as oxidation or reduction. An example of property modeled is the exothermic or endothermic process associated to a reaction.

3.2 Case Representation

Solved problems are represented as structured cases embodying four different kinds of knowledge;

- The *Input Knowledge* embodies data about the customer such as the industrial sector it belongs or the industrial process that originates the polluting gas; data about the working conditions of the installation such as temperature or gas flow; data about the composition and concentration of input polluted gas; and data about the desired concentration in the output emission. Additionally, the customer may constrain the solution desired—for instance proposing a washing liquid that results from another process of the customer.
- The *Chemical Case-Model* embodies a graph structure, generated by *T-Air* using the chemical knowledge, modeling the main characteristics of the input gas. The chemical case-model extends the input knowledge and fixes the thresholds for the working conditions, the main issues to be analyzed, and the kind of gas treatment required. The typology of gas treatment covered by *T-Air* is absorption, dust removal, elimination of fogs and mists, degassing, and elimination of odours. The solution for a specific problem can involve several of them.
- The *Flow Sheet* describes the solution designed for cleaning a polluted gas. As shown in Figure 1, the flow sheet specifies a collection of required equipment (mainly scrubbers, pumps, tanks, and fans), the design and working parameters for each equipment, and the topology of the installation (the gas circuit and the liquid circuits). The flow sheet is also represented as a graph structure.
- *Annotations* are meta-information that describes the reasons for a given decision. Examples of annotations are the design decisions forced by the user requirements (such as the washing liquid), over-dimensionated parameters either because security or unknown input data, different laws in different countries, or spatial requirements. The use of these annotations is important for discriminating different solutions given the similar input information, or for focusing an initial flow sheet when there is unknown data.

An important remark about the cases is the different level of detailed information given in the input knowledge and in the chemical model. This fact is motivated because the different nature of gases. For instance, in gases with highly known solubility with water the exact concentration is not essential for determining a solution. In the opposite side, gases with low solubility or risking parameters (such as originators of exothermic reactions) have to be analyzed in more detail before taking decisions about the flow sheet.

3.3   The Case Base

The Case-Base is composed of three different kinds of cases: performed installations, proposed installations, and pilot experiments.

Performed installations are the collection of designed and constructed installations developed by TECNIUM during the last ten years. The information was obtained from an existing database used by TECNIUM for reporting performed installations. The information contained in the database was incomplete and a the generation of cases involved the participation of the engineers. After, this process, the database was not longer used and *T-Air* is now used for storing all the information about performed installations. Because we are storing all the constructed installations developed during the last ten years, there are cases—such as those involving the use of biological solutions—out of the scope of the current system. Nevertheless, this cases have an special annotation and are used just for presenting the solutions to the engineer and the engineer has to decide all the parameters (only price lists have been included in *T-Air*).

Proposed installations are customer consultations that have been analyzed for offering a solution where there is no customer order for effectively construct them—either because the customer is studying the proposal or because is not interested in making an order. All the proposed installations are stored in the system but only those considered as relevant are used in case retrieval (see subsections 3.6 and 3.7). When a customer decides to order a previously proposed installation, the engineer can retrieve the proposed solution and complete it using the *T-Air* in the same way.

Pilot Experiments are tests performed either by TECNIUM or by universities with some prototypical gas-liquid configurations. The goal of these experiments is twofold: i) collect experimental information by means of systematically studying different range of gas features (pressure, flow, and concentration) in different gas-liquid configurations, and ii) optimize the design parameters of equipments for minimizing dimensions and costs of equipments. This optimization knowledge is mainly used by *T-Air* in the adaptation phase (see subsection 3.5).

Cases are stored in an external database and accessed by SQL queries. The application started with a thousand of performed installations, zero proposed installations, and 200 initial pilot experiments. TECNIUM expects to incorporate five hundred proposed installations in a year where at least one hundred will become performed installations.

3.4   Case Retrieval

T-Air fulfills two different tasks: the analysis of customer consultations and the detailed design of an installation. In the first task the main goal is to determine the cost of a proposal minimizing the risk with the unknown information. When we have to effectively construct an installation, all the parameters in the flow sheet have to be determined even though some of them do not have cost implications.

Because sometimes there is unknown information or some data is only required in some problems, we decide to follow the interactive case-based reasoning approach [1,4]. First of all, an initial form is presented to the engineer and he decides the information initially provided. Given that information the *T-Air* proposes a first solution or presents the alternatives supported by the different retrieved cases and the chemical case-model. Then, the user can introduce more data either by directly filling them or navigating through of the cases or the chemical case-model. At this second stage, the system is working in the background monitoring the decisions of the user and preventing possible issues—like conflicting parameters, risk working conditions of equipments, or uncovered problems—by means of warning messages. An important goal in this stage is to monitor the decisions of the user for acquiring meta-information in the form of annotations.

Like in [10], case retrieval is a two stage process. First, the input data is relaxed to ensure that a minimum number of relevant cases are retrieved from the database. In a second stage, additional similarity criteria are used for ranking the precedents. The process of relaxing the input data uses the hierarchy of industrial sectors or chemical concept hierarchies. For the numerical features we also use the notion of range [10]. Examples of numerical features are the temperature and the gas flow.

The second stage is a process where an initial flow sheet is incrementally refined by using domain criteria, the retrieved cases, and the interaction with the user. This stage is based on the use of *perspectives* [3]—a powerful mechanism for describing declarative biases for case retrieval in structured representations of cases—and on the notion of support sets. Excluding the trivial problem where the user is just designing a new problem that has been previously solved by the system, the usual circumstance is that a new problem is solved by using parts of solutions coming from different cases. In this context the procedure of *T-Air* is to present a flow sheet with different cases supporting different design parameters. For instance, the presence of dust supports the decision of including a ventury in the installation, the kind of industry can support the use of different washing liquids, and the amount of gas flow can support the use of different fan models. After achieving an initial flow sheet with their support sets, the adaptation phase starts.

Let us present a simplified trace of the retrieval phase: the engineer enters a new problem into the system by defining a gas compound generated in a "Fine Chemistry" industrial process with the presence of fogs and a high concentration of sulfates. The first retrieval step, is the identification of the important features of the new problem and the construction of the initial *chemical case-model*. Given the chemical case-model and the input knowledge, *T-Air* performs three initial

SQL queries: i) a first query for retrieving cases about similar industrial sectors using the hierarchy of industrial sectors for generalizing "Fine Chemistry" and ranking the obtained cases using this hierarchy; ii) a second query regarding cases involving sulfates using the hierarchy of gas compounds in a similar way; and iii) a third query is performed using the chemical case-model about the washing processes involved. The final step of the retrieval phase is to build an initial flow sheet with their support sets (the cases supporting design decisions and their similarity with the current problem). It is important to notice that we are performing different SQL queries because there are features of the problems that influence different parts of the design. The goal of the adaptation phase is to check for possible incompatibilities or for overestimated parameters due to the presence of equipments that can help each other.

3.5 Case Adaptation

The goal of the case adaptation is to determine precise models and parameter values for all the equipments involved in the flow sheet. Parameters only known by experience are determined using a collection of domain adaptors developed with the experts that specified when criteria such as mean, maximum or minimum can be used for adapting the values from cases. Moreover we have an equational model for each equipment that allows to determine non-experimental values using the values from cases. Finally, the adaptation knowledge is also charged of determining possible conflicts between different support sets.

The construction of a new solution for a given problem by combining parts of the solutions of different cases is performed in the following way: First of all we have to determine the parts of the solution in each case relevant for our problem. For instance, if one of the tasks in a given problem is the problem of dust removal, using the chemical knowledge and the models about the equipments, we can determine the equipments relevant for this task. Then, given the collection of partial solutions to our problem, and our adaptation knowledge about the general principles of design of absorption plants, we connect all the partial solutions with a high support set, each of them solving a part of the problem, and link each of them to the possible alternatives (those partial solutions with a low support set). After that, the process of refinement of the solution starts by determining possible conflicts between different support sets or the presence of equipments that can help each other. For instance, increasing the dimensions of a given scrubber we can eliminate another one.

An important remark about partial solutions is that T-Air presents only one flow sheet with bullets pointing to the engineer the places where there are alternatives and the engineer can inspect and select some of them. The final decision is performed by the engineer and the goal of the adaptation phase in T-Air is to present a flow sheet and the possible alternatives and provide an easy mechanism for allowing the final design decisions.

Cases retrieved from pilot experiments are mainly used in the adaptation phase. Pilot experiments allow to optimize the values of equipment parameters—especially in experimental parameters—for minimizing dimensions and costs. For instance, when there is a five years old case supporting a value of 0.6 for H_{OG}

for the same gas in the problem, and a two years old case pilot experiment supporting a value of 0.4 for H_{OG} with a similar gas, taking into account the degree of similarity, we can decrease the final value to 0.5.

3.6 Case Storage

All the installations designed by the system have to be stored because *T-Air* is also the repository of designs proposed/performed by the company. Moreover, when a customer makes a consultation not covered by the system, the engineers want to explore the existing case base in an exhaustive way using a collection of criteria such as navigating through the chemical hierarchy an inspecting to the solutions designed in the cases.

The current storage policies in *T-Air* are very simple: i) preliminary consultations are not used in retrieval until the experts marks them as fully analyzed; and ii) when there are several equal cases solved with an equivalent design, only the latest is indexed for retrieval with an additional annotation that marks the number of equal cases. The experience with the use of the system also confirms our initial hypothesis that cases representing proposed installations with many unknown values are rarely retrieved.

The case storage is an open issue in *T-Air* that requires further analysis. Nevertheless, the main issue now is not an efficiency problem. Discussing with the experts, the main problem is how to minimize the amount of information that the engineer has to manage for identifying the important issues in each problem.

3.7 User Interface

T-Air has been developed in *Noos* for Windows computers running in an Intranet. An important issue with the graphical interface was to find the most appropriate way of displaying the design parameters because of the high amount of data and taking into account that the expert was interested in modifying any of them.

Another important issue was to provide useful navigation tools for inspecting the chemical knowledge and the case base. This requirement is crucial when the expert is trying to design the solution for a problem that is not covered with the current knowledge of the system. In those cases, during the testing phase we had to tune some interactive mechanisms of acquiring new chemical information.

An example of the procedure followed by the expert with a not covered problem is the following: the expert starts navigating through the hierarchy of industrial sectors, then follows the hierarchy of industrial processes involved and then, the kind of gases previously treated. Suppose that in our hypothetical problem we have acids from organic origin, the important properties of these gases are listed and the expert consults to his bibliography about our specific problem. This information is introduced in the system and the retrieval starts. After the

---

[1] The system interface has been developed in Catalan but for helping to the comprehensibility of the system the labels have been translated to English.

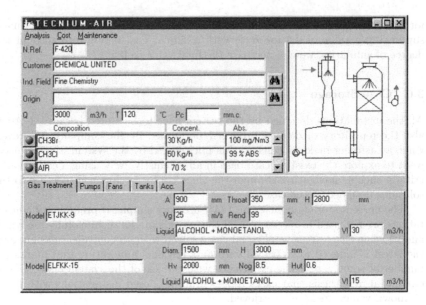

Fig. 4. A snapshot of the T-Air system[1].

retrieval, either there is an initial proposal or the expert has to determine an initial flow sheet. At this point the interaction between *T-Air* and the expert is the same as in covered problems. A sample screen of the *T-Air* application is shown in Figure 4.

4   Conclusions

The utility of the *T-Air* system has exceeded the initial expectatives of TEC-NIUM. The first indicator of success was that we advanced the delivery of a first prototype of the system because just with some preliminary similarity criteria and the possibility of manipulating the design parameters the experts were able to decrease the time for analyzing customer consultations. A second measure of success is the request of connecting the information provided by *T-Air* with other existing applications used for construct the installations. For instance, since the engineers have determined the elements and many dimensional features of an installation, this information can be used by analysts that elaborate the detailed list of required materials and can be also used by the draftsman responsible of the technical drawing. The last successful criterion is that we are planning an extension of the application for covering the aspects not addressed in this initial initial phase.

A side effect of the use of *T-Air* is that now all the proposed installations are stored in the TECNIUM server and not only the information about performed installations as before. This is important for the performance of *T-Air* but is also very important for the company.

Another important aspect discovered during the field testing phase is the facility that the system provides to the engineer of changing any design parameter. Moreover, this changing facility has increased the reliance on the use of system and has demonstrated that for many problems the expert is not really changing them. Moreover this feature allows engineers to test more than one design alternative for a given problem, capability that was impractical without the use of the system because of the high amount of information and calculus required for designing each plant.

Related with the use of meta-information as annotations, the initial approach was to ask an explanation to the engineer when some decisions monitored by *T-Air* were not supported by the current knowledge. Nevertheless, this was demostrated a wrong strategy because we are trying to minimize the design time and the engineer is usually busy in many issues at the same time. The current approach we are exploring is how to periodically analyze the knowledge of the system for detecting these unsupported decisions and develop a specific tool for this purpose.

Acknowledgements. The research reported in this paper was supported by the *T-Air* project financed by the TECNIUMcompany. Any possible mistake or error in the description of the working principles of chemical gas treatment is the sole responsability of the author.

References

1. David W. Aha, Leonard A. Breslow, and Héctor Mu noz Avila. Conversational case-based reasoning. *Applied Intelligence*, 14(1):9–32, 2001.
2. Josep Lluís Arcos. *The Noos representation language*. PhD thesis, Universitat Politècnica de Catalunya, 1997. online at www.iiia.csic.es/~arcos/Phd.html.
3. Josep Lluís Arcos and Ramon López de Mántaras. Perspectives: a declarative bias mechanism for case retrieval. In David Leake and Enric Plaza, editors, *Case-Based Reasoning. Research and Development*, number 1266 in Lecture Notes in Artificial Intelligence, pages 279–290. Springer-Verlag, 1997.
4. Josep Lluís Arcos and Ramon López de Mántaras. An interactive case-based reasoning approach for generating expressive music. *Applied Intelligence*, 14(1):115–129, 2001.
5. Josep Lluís Arcos and Enric Plaza. Inference and reflection in the object-centered representation language Noos. *Journal of Future Generation Computer Systems*, 12:173–188, 1996.
6. D. Hinkle and C. Toomey. Applying case-based reasoning to manufacturing. *AI Magazine*, 16(1):65–73, 1995.
7. David B. Leake and David C. Wilson. Combining cbr with interactive knowledge acquisition, manipulation and reuse. In *Proceedings of the Third International Conference on Case-Based Reasoning (ICCBR-99)*, pages "218–232", Berlin, 1999. Springer-Verlag.
8. Enric Plaza and Josep Lluís Arcos. Towards a software architecture for case-based reasoning systems. In Z. Ras and S. Ohsuga, editors, *Foundations of Intelligent Systems, 12th International Symposium, ISMIS 2000*, number 1932 in Lecture Notes in Artificial Intelligence, pages 601–609. Springer-Verlag, 2000.

9. Ian Watson. *Applying Case-Based Reasoning: Techniques for enterprise systems.* Morgan Kaufmann Publishers Inc. San Francisco, CA, 1997.
10. Ian Watson and Dan Gardingen. A distributed case-based reasoning application for engineering sales support. In *Proc. 16th Int. Joint Conf. on Artificial Intelligence (IJCAI-99)*, pages 600–605, 1999.

Benefits of Case-Based Reasoning in Color Matching

William Cheetham

General Electric Company, 1 Research Circle, Niskayuna, NY, 12309, USA
(cheetham@crd.ge.com)

Abstract. GE Plastics has a case-based reasoning tool that determines color formulas which match requested colors that has been in use since 1995. This tool, called FormTool, has saved GE millions of dollars in productivity and colorant costs. The technology developed in FormTool has been used to create an on-line color selection tool for our customers called, ColorXpress Select. A customer innovation center has been developed around the FormTool software.

1 Introduction

General Electric (GE) is one of the world's largest producers of plastics. The plastic GE creates can be made any color that is requested by a customer. Plastic is colored by adding pigments while the plastic is manufactured [2]. In order to determine the correct formulas for our customers, three different approaches have been created. They are an internal productivity tool for custom color matches called FormTool, a web based e-commerce tool for the customer called ColorXpress Select, and a customer collaboration center called ColorXpress. The approaches are based on the case-based reasoning (CBR) methodology [6]. This paper will describe these approaches.

2 Custom Color Matches

The first approach is to have the customer submit a sample of the color and a GE employee select the correct pigments to create a formula for that color. This section will describe the non-automated custom color match approach, show how that approach was automated, and then list the benefits of the automation.

2.1 Non-automated Approach

Before 1995, the selection of pigments was primarily a manual process. A GE employee, called a color matcher, used the following process to perform a color match.

1. Look at color standard submitted by customer.
2. Go to filing cabinet filled with previously created colored plastic chips and their formulas. Select the chips for any similar colors that have already been created.

D.W. Aha and I. Watson (Eds.): ICCBR 2001, LNAI 2080, pp. 589-596, 2001.

3. Determine if one of these previous chips matches the customer color standard. If yes, the color match is done, else continue.
4. Adapt the amount of one or more pigments in the formula.
5. Make a small batch of the plastic and mold it into a chip. [This takes about 3 hours]
6. Determine if the new chip matches the customer color standard. If not, go to step 4.
7. Save the chip in the filing cabinet. The color match is done.

This process follows the CBR Methodology [1,7]. The case-base is a filing cabinet. The Retrieval phase is opening a drawer and pulling out a chip. The Reuse phase is experience or a commercially available software tool adapting the loading of the pigments. The Revise phase is determining if the newly created chip matches the customers' standard. The Retain phase is putting any new chips into the appropriate drawer in the filing cabinet.

CBR is a good methodology for this application because it is difficult to predict the color produced by a given set of pigments, but it is easier to predict what effect a slight change in a pigment will have. This means that adapting previous solutions can produce a formula more quickly than creating one from scratch.

2.2 Automated Approach - FormTool

In 1994 a tool to automate the above formula creation process was started. This formula creation tool is called FormTool. The case-base for FormTool consisted of a problem/solution pair for each chip in the filing cabinet. The problem is a numerical representation of the color. The solution is the formula that was used for the chip. The color of a chip can be read numerically by a machine called a spectrophotometer. The case-base was stored in a Microsoft Access® database. The FormTool application was written using the Microsoft VisualBasic® programming language. FormTool used the following process to perform a color match.

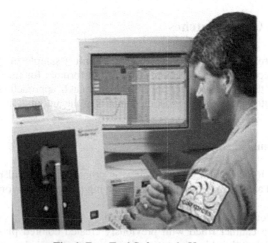

Fig. 1. FormTool Software in Use

1. Use the spectrophotometer to read the color standard submitted by customer
2. Select the cases for any similar colors that have already been created from the case-base.
3. Determine if one of these previous cases matches the customer color standard. If yes, the color match is done. Else continue.
4. Use adaptation algorithm to change the amount of one or more pigments.
5. Make a small batch of the plastic and mold it into a chip. [This takes about 3 hours]
6. Determine if the new chip matches the customer color standard. If not, go to step 4.
7. Save the chip in the case-base. The color match is done.

The details of case selection and adaptation are given in [4]. Figure 1 shows a color matcher using FormTool. The machine on the left is a spectrophotometer.

2.3 FormTool Benefits

FormTool has been in constant use since its introduction in 1995. During 2000 it was used for an average of 120 custom color matches per week. The following benefits have resulted from using FormTool.

2.3.1 Color Matcher Productivity
The average number of test chips that are created (step 5 above) per color match has decreased from 4.2 to 2.7.   This is an average reduction of 4.5 hours per color match. Since over 5000 color matches are performed per year, this saves 22,500 hours of work per year. The custom color match is a free service for our customers, so the cost of these 22,500 hours would directly reduce our earnings. A reasonable estimate of the burdened cost of a color matcher is $100 per hour, so the time savings resulted in a dollar savings of $2.25 million per year.

2.3.2 Pigment Cost Reduction
Pigments are the most expensive component in plastic. If the amount of pigment that is needed can be reduced then the difference in the cost of the pigment and the cost of the plastic would be saved. This could be a few cents per pound. FormTool's adaptation algorithms were designed to determine the minimum pigment loading that would allow for correct manufacturing of the color desired.

Another way to reduce pigment cost is to use cheaper pigments. Different pigments have different properties and different costs. For example, some red pigments are twice as expensive as other red pigments. The most expensive pigments are usually the easiest to use in a color match. FormTool's case selection algorithms select the best previous match based on cost, and other factors, in addition to the color of the case.

Part of the testing for FormTool that was conducted in 1994 was re-matching 100 colors that had already been matched but still were being manufactured. FormTool found lower cost matches for 64 of the 100 colors. The new formulas were substituted for the old, more costly, formulas. For each of these colors we tracked the number of pounds that were manufactured with the new formula. The cost savings can be calculated by multiplying the difference in cost by the volume for each color then taking the sum for all 64 colors. This was done near the end of 1994. The cost savings were $200,000 in 1994, $1.2 million in 1995, and $1.5 million in 1996. FormTool was used for new matches from 1995 onward. The colorant cost savings for years after 1996 are conservatively estimated at an average of $2.4 million per year.

2.3.3 Global Color Consistency
GE has plastics manufacturing sites throughout the world. The consistency of the colors we produce across the world is important to our customers. FormTool has been used to share color formulas. Also, if some pigments are not available in one location, FormTool's case selection can automatically substitute the unavailable pigments with the closest available pigments. This has helped provide globally consistent colors.

A separate tool was created to allow the color matchers to manage the case-base and list of available colors. The manager tool allows the following functionality.
- Import a case base from another location
- Numerically determine the visual properties of a pigment for use in adaptation
- Specify which pigments are available for use
- Specify the price of each pigment

2.3.4 Other Tool Development
The case adaptation algorithms were used to create a tool for controlling the color produced by a manufacturing line, called LineTool. When colors are manufactured they do not always come out as planned because of many factors. LineTool can determine how to adjust a color that is not exactly on target. It produces a list of pigments that should be added to bring the manufacturing line back on target.

2.3.5 Speed of Color Match
The speed of the color match was very important to many of our customers. For example, if a cell phone maker needed to add a month of time to their development cycle in order to get the various pieces of plastic in the casing to match they might miss their target date for product release. FormTool reduced the time needed for a color match. This allowed the color matchers to eliminate the backlog of color matches. Since less experience was needed to perform a color match, resources could easily be added when a spike in demand was received and shifted to other work when there was low demand. Because of the benefits mentioned, the average time from receiving a color match request to creating the formula was reduced by two thirds.

3 ColorXpress Select

Having a tool that creates lower cost color matches faster is good, but it is better to completely eliminate the need for a color match. Since we had already created the case-base and selection algorithms so that they were easy to use, why not allow our customers to select their own colors from our case-base? This has been done by transforming FormTool into a web-based e-commerce tool [3,5]. This section will describe the web-based version of FormTool, called ColorXpress Select, which was designed to be used by GE's customers.

ColorXpress Select, www.gecolorxpress.com, is a web site that offers customers an opportunity to both color match and order standards on-line. In the past, our customers used a variety of ways to select the color for their products then sent us a sample of the color in order that we could perform a custom color match. Now, ColorXpress Select can be used to select their colors. Any item selected has already been matched in a previous color request and a sample can be mailed to the customer in less than 48 hours. This both increase the speed of the match and eliminates the need for many custom matches. Since computer monitors do not always reproduce a reliable representation of a color we need to mail out a sample for the final approval. Third party software is suggested for calibrating a users monitor before ColorXpress Select is used.

The case-base from FormTool is used as the set of colors that can be selected and the case selection algorithm is used to find the colors that can satisfy the customers needs. The web page for selecting a formula is shown in Figure 2.

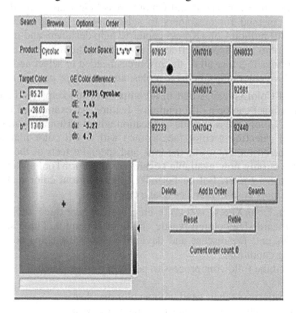

Fig. 2. ColorXpress Select Web Page

In order to select a formula a customer would first select the resin type of plastic required from the "Product" pull-down list in the top left of the screen. Different resins have different colors that have been created. Next, either a numeric value of the color desired can be entered below the "Product" pull-down list, or a point in the rainbow display at the bottom left can be selected. For those of you who do not have a color version of this paper, the large square in the bottom left displays every possible color to a given resolution. If a numeric color value is entered, the corresponding point in the rainbow display is selected. If a point in the rainbow display is selected, the values of that point are placed in the numeric color value boxes. Next, when the search button is clicked the case selection algorithm will be executed and the chip display in the top right will show the nine closest matches to the desired color. Finally, to view the color difference between the desired color and a specific chip, a user should click on one of the nine closest matches. The difference will be displayed in the "GE Color Difference" area. If a satisfactory match can not be found then a custom match request can be submitted. The formula created for the custom match will eventually be available on ColorXpress Select.

ColorXpress Select has been in use since 1999. It is one of the first customer service tools that GE Plastics has made available over the web. Tools like this have simplified the process for customers to submit orders over the web. GE now leads the plastic industry in on-line sales.

4 ColorXpress

The cost savings from FormTool and ColorXpress Select allowed GE Plastics to invest in another method for customers to select colors. In early 2000 GE Plastics opened a new $10 million ColorXpress center to help designers and marketers quickly create custom colors and special effects for plastics. The 4000 square foot center in Selkirk, N.Y. brings together all of the resources needed to select and develop custom colors and produce color chips, pellet samples, and prototype parts in a single day.

The idea behind ColorXpress is that in a competitive marketplace the color, texture, and style of a product can be a differentiating feature. An example of this is the Apple iMac computer. ColorXpress provides a location where customers can go through the CBR process of selecting a color face-to-face with a GE color matcher. The color matcher helps the customers refine the look and special effects of their products. This one-day service is only now available because of the FormTool system, which is the key tool used in the center. Before FormTool most custom color matches took over two days. Now, most custom matches take a day or less.

The case-base in ColorXpress is a color-chip room where three walls are filled with 20,000 baseball-card size colored plastic chips, see Figure 3. Three sets of overhead lights - incandescent, fluorescent and daylight – show the chips color varies under different lighting conditions.

ColorXpress used the following process to perform a color match.

1. The customer discusses their need with a color matcher
2. The customer selects a few samples from the chip room
3. The customer determines if one of these previous chips meets their needs. If yes, the color match is done. Else continue.
4. Use FormTool to adapt the amount of one or more pigments in the formula.
5. Make a small batch of the plastic and mold it into a chip. [This takes about 3 hours]
6. The customer determines if the new chip meets their needs. If not and there is enough time before the customers visit is over, go to 4.
Save the chip in the case-base and chip room. If the color is not done, submit a custom color match request

Fig. 3. ColorXpress Chip Room

There has been a constant flow of customers through the ColorXpress. The customer feedback from the face-to-face CBR has been very useful. GE researchers are trying to develop new effects such as speckles and marbling to meet new customer requests. The new product ideas that have been developed by the customers during these sessions have been very creative. One recent customer developed removable cell phone faceplates that match women's fingernail polish colors.

5 Summary and Future Work

We have found that in customer service organizations, like color services, it is useful to have internal productivity tools (FormTool), on-line services available to the customer (ColorXpress Select), and customer collaboration centers (ColorXpress). The CBR Methodology can be the basis for all three of these customer service opportunities.

We are currently working on two new CBR tools. The first system allows customers to select the appropriate type of plastic that meets all engineering requirements for a need. The second system will help GE researchers develop new plastics by providing a common repository for sharing experiments and designing new experiments.

References

1. Aamodt, A., Case-Based Reasoning: Foundational Issues, Methodological Variations, and System Approaches, AICOM, Vol. 7, No. 1, (March 1994)
2. Billmeyer, F., Principles of Color Technology: Second Edition, John Wiley & Sons, New York (1981)
3. Burke, R., The Wasabi Personal Shopper: A Case-Based Recommender System, In Proceedings of the 11th National Conference on Innovative Applications of Artificial Intelligence, pages 844-849, AAAI, 1999
4. Cheetham, W., Graf, J., Case-Based Reasoning in Color Matching, Lecture Notes in Computer Science, Vol. 1266. Springer-Verlag, Berlin Heidelberg New York (1997) 1–12
5. Cunningham, P., Intelligent Support for E-Commerce, Invited Talk, International Conference on Case-Based Reasoning, Monastery Seeon, Bavaria Germany, 1999
6. Watson, I., Applying Case-Based Reasoning: Techniques for Enterprise Systems, San Francisco, Cal.: Morgan Kaufmann Publishers (1997)
7. Watson, I., CBR is a methodology not a technology. In, Research & Development in Expert Systems XV. Miles, R., Moulton, M., & Bramer, M. (Eds.), Springer, London (1998) 213-223

CBR for Dimensional Management in a Manufacturing Plant

Alexander P. Morgan, John A. Cafeo, Diane I. Gibbons, Ronald M. Lesperance,
Gülcin H. Sengir, and Andrea M. Simon

General Motors R&D and Planning Center
Mail Code 480-106-359
Warren, MI 48090-9055
810-986-2157, 810-986-0574 fax
alexander.p.morgan@gm.com

Abstract. Dimensional management is a form of quality assurance for the manufacture of mechanical structures, such as vehicle bodies. Establishing and maintaining dimensional control is a process of adjusting complex machinery for environmental and material changes to manufacture product to specifications within very small tolerances. It involves constant monitoring of the process as well as responding to crises. A good deal of undocumented "folk wisdom" is built up by the dimensional management teams on how to diagnosis and cure problems, but this knowledge tends to be lost over time (people can't remember, people move on) and is rarely shared from shop to shop. Our project involves establishing a case-based diagnostic system for dimensional-management problems, which can also serve as a system for systematically documenting solved dimensional-control problems. It is intended that this documentation should be meaningful over time and be shareable between plants. The project includes defining a workable case structure and matching ontology, especially to establish the context and generic language to accomplish this. A prototype system has been launched in a vehicle assembly plant.

1 Introduction

A basic vehicle body (the frame or "body-in-white") is measured in meters but must meet its nominal tolerances to within a few millimeters (ideally, to a fraction of a millimeter). Otherwise, difficult-to-diagnose-and-cure problems arise in the final build, such as wind noise, water leaks, and a host of "fit and finish" issues. Typically, stamped sheet metal is welded together into the basic frame in the part of the plant known as "the body shop." Parts and paint are then added to this basic frame to create the finished vehicle. The basic frame, however, is the critical part of the build for dimensional integrity. Minute deviations in the tooling which holds the metal for welding, or in the thickness of the metal, or in the wear on the weld-gun tips, or in many other process elements, can significantly affect dimensional-control. When a problem is detected "downstream" in the process, it can be very challenging to discover quickly the source of the problem and find a cure. Working with

D.W. Aha and I. Watson (Eds.): ICCBR 2001, LNAI 2080, pp. 597-610, 2001.

measurements at various stages of the process, as well as other information about the build, a dimensional management (DM) team hypothesizes cause from effect to create a short list of most likely problems, makes visual inspections to refine the list, and makes process adjustments to solve the problem. Sometimes the problem is directly observed and fixed, sometimes a "cause" is inferred from a "fix" suggested by the list, and sometimes problems are not solved.

The members of the DM Team generally know the process very well. This knowledge tends to be very specific, is sometimes documented in process documents but often is not, and involves a great deal of three-dimensional intuitive reasoning, as well as experience with the basic materials and machines that make up the process. Because the DM team members can consider questions such as "If the tooling in a particular station is defective in a particular way, what particular problems will this cause later in the process?" one might be lead to consider a rule-based approach to capturing this knowledge. However, there are several key aspects that suggest "cases" rather than "rules." The most important is coverage; that is, it is difficult to imagine a complete set of rules for such a high-dimensional problem space. A related issue is capturing the three-dimensional and the pictorial nature of the knowledge; that is, part of the reason the problem space is so high-dimensional is that the knowledge and reasoning process are expressed in terms of (pictures of) three-dimensional structures. In a case-based system, we can evoke the powerful ability of expert humans to interpret and use such knowledge. The reasoning doesn't have to be "automated." In their own problem-solving process, the DM team members work from previous experiences in a way that strongly suggests a case-based approach. Only the most trivial problems are solved via pure "if-then" reasoning.

The goals of our project were to develop a prototype system that could provide a problem-solving memory for generating reports and diagnosing new problems. A case-based approach seemed best to fit the application area and our goals. The system has a good deal in common with lessons-learned systems [1], as well as CBR diagnostic systems, such as GE's ICARUS for locomotive diagnosis [2]. This latter reference also includes a nice summary of other CBR diagnostic systems. See [3, 4] for more general descriptions of CBR systems. Since we also introduced a "daily log" as an adjunct to the case-based system, to provide for peer-to-peer sharing, our system has elements of standard knowledge management, too [5]. Plant management has begun to take an interest in creating reference books of potential problems and solutions for specific assembly lines. These books consist of brief text descriptions with many digital pictures of details of process elements to illustrate potential issues. We have considered integrating this material also into our system, based somewhat on the way The Stamping Design Adviser described in [6] integrates other knowledge sources. Our first approach is via the "analytical cases" noted at the end of Section 3.

Aspects of this work include developing an ontology for dimensional management in automotive assembly plants, designing a case structure for archival lessons that would satisfy reporting needs and at the same time facilitate a case-based retrieval mechanism, and designing a user interface that would be acceptable to the process engineers and technicians. Our project is in its early stages, but preliminary reactions from plant personnel are positive. An earlier report on this project was given in [7].

We considered using several widely distributed CBR tools for our prototype development. We decided not to use any of them for the following reasons. Our core need has been to facilitate rapid and effective case authoring, with a focus on ontology and the associated user-interface issues. Our cases are naturally complex.

They include chains of symptoms (including the results of tests) in no fixed order and of no fixed length, with much of the essential information in the form of pictures. Our cases will be read by persons and used for training and management review, as well as for diagnosis. The CBR software we considered did not seem to offer much help with our core need. In fact, this software seemed most natural for "feature vector" cases [8] but not complex-structure cases. In [9] complex cases are mapped to indices, so that the indices are feature-vector cases. We may adopt a similar idea in the future. However, indexing and retrieval have been secondary to our core need and may never be much of an issue in this application.

We are aware of some of the current efforts in developing ontologies for manufacturing (such as NIST's PSL project [10]), but we did not attempt to exploit them. Our main ontological focus so far has been on supporting the user interface and clarifying person-to-person communication. In fact, since our approach to case generation has been "fill-in-the-blank sentences with pull-down menus," we have been committed to generating a person-to-person ontology as a core deliverable. The resulting body of material might be viewed as background material from which a formal ontology could be constructed. However, whether we take that step or not, constructing our current ontology was a critical and necessary part of our project for which a formal ontology would not have substituted.

2   Dimensional Control and Variation Reduction

In a body shop, a collection of stamped metal parts is converted into a basic vehicle frame, which we will refer to as the BIW (body-in-white). The parts are joined in clusters into subassemblies, the subassemblies are themselves joined into larger subassemblies, and so on, until the process ends with the BIW. Parts to be joined at every stage in this process are held in place by *tooling* (clamps, pins, blocks) and, for efficiency, the parts and subassemblies are moved from one configuration of tooling to another in the process. If the tooling and joining equipment in every station is perfectly in tune, if the parts and subassemblies are moved from station to station flawlessly, if the measuring lasers and check-fixtures are freshly calibrated, then the process works as intended and the BIW is built to specifications. Current best practices allow very little deviation from the ideal. Many important customer-satisfaction issues, such as wind noise, water leaks, door-closing effort, and "fit and finish," can be related to the dimensional integrity of the BIW.

2.1 Variation

It may seem counterintuitive that the main focus of dimensional management is on reducing variation. The logic is that, if each BIW is the same (zero variation), then it is easy to tune the various process elements to correct any deviation from *nominal* (that is, the ideal). On the other hand, if the BIW's vary a great deal in their measurements ("the process has high variation"), then it is impossible to know how to tune the process. Essentially, *variation reduction* must be accomplished first. In practice, almost all the time spent by the DM team solving problems is devoted to variation reduction. The acceptable variation is currently a "95% six-sigma" of 2mm. This criterion is developed as follows: for each measurement location on the BIW, compute 6 times the standard deviation (six-sigma) of the measurements; order the six-sigma values from smallest to largest; and verify that 95% of the six-sigma values are less than the 2mm cutoff. While the ideal situation is to have each of the six-sigma values less than 2mm, the 95% six-sigma criterion is used in practice. For comparison, a US dime is 2mm thick.

Since it can be confusing, let us say a bit more about this six-sigma measurement goal. The BIW is measured at a number of points, selected because they are judged to be key to the dimensional integrity of the vehicle. At each of these points, the deviation from nominal for each assembly is measured, and over some fixed time period (like a shift or a week), the standard deviation of these measurements is computed. The set of these standard deviations is expected to meet the six-sigma criterion. When it does not, then the DM team will want to find out why. Generally, the measurements at the high variation points will be examined through statistical analysis to begin a search for patterns that will lead to the process fault.

2.2 DM Problems and Solutions

There are various ways to test the dimensional integrity of the build at various stages in the manufacturing plant. There are laser measurement stations in which all assemblies are measured (100% sample). There are portable measuring machines, which can be set up where needed, and there are especially accurate measuring instruments to which a small sample of assemblies might be taken. There are check fixtures, which are mechanical devices for testing dimensional integrity. If any of the measurements from these devices has a higher than desired variation or deviation from nominal, then this may trigger a problem-solving process by the DM team.

There is another way that the DM team may be triggered into action; there can be a "call from downstream." At later stages in the build process, problems with assembly may be attributed to the early stage of assembly; *i.e.*, the body shop. This can sometimes take the character of a crisis: the doors are not hanging properly, the trim doesn't look right. The problem needs to be fixed immediately.

The DM problem-solving process follows a general sequential pattern but not a fixed format. If the triggering event involves the analysis of measurement data, then the first step is generally to do further data analyses. Sometimes, more data is collected, sometimes with alternative measurement devices. If the triggering event is not a data event, then relevant data might be collected and analyzed. The next step is to make a list of possible causes. Each item on this list will include, at least implicitly, what to look for in the field to confirm the hypothesis. Sometimes, there is no non-intrusive test or inspection; the item is investigated by adjusting the process to see if the triggering problem goes away. The problem-solving process ends with a confirming data test that shows the high variation or deviation from nominal has gone away, or the triggering problem itself has gone away. There is no prescription of what data analyses must be done or in what order or what inspections or tunings follow from specific triggers. The team values and uses its own judgment in such matters.

3   Case Structure and Ontology

It is important to note that context and purpose determine our approach to case structure and ontology. The body shop of a vehicle manufacturing plant is an environment of large machines, in which the DM team members must guide the process to stay within minute tolerances. The daily problem list is full of routine, but important, tasks, which must be addressed immediately. There are other issues whose solution leads to the "continuous improvement" which is the constant long-term goal of dimensional management. Our purpose is to address this second set of more subtle problems, for which there never seems to be enough time.

In most of the plants we are studying, there are no records or logs which are sufficient to use as a core of already available cases. Usually, progress reports are given to management weekly, but these briefings are not archived for general use. Following general principles of knowledge management, we decided there were several needs to be addressed:

- Peer-to-peer sharing needed to be enhanced with a simple log, to improve local sharing and provide the DM team with a "short-term memory."

- A mechanism for identifying significant problems, facilitating their solution, and archiving the problem-solution-outcome information needed to be developed. Further, this needed to be in the workflow of the team, and the resulting archive needed to be meaningful when shared over time and with other plants.   It would have a dual use: problem solving and report generation.

The DM team already uses a statistical computer package to analyze measurement data. We could create some sense of "in the workflow" by linking the daily log to this package, then linking the archival system to that.

The decision to capture knowledge via cases involved the following considerations:

1. Providing a meaningful utility via report generation.
2. Filling in the gap created by the lack of an existing process for archiving and sharing lessons learned.
3. Reducing the knowledge-acquisition time frame, especially to get started.
4. Dealing with the high-dimensional problem space, especially the "picture knowledge" and sensitivity of solution details to problem details.

Items 1 and 2 are important because they serve a need in the plant which is immediately recognized and useful.   The templates and ontology we devised (described below) allow for reasonably quick report generation as well as a reasonably uniform report format. No free-text need be generated, although text annotations are allowed. Relevant pictures of subassemblies can be quickly selected from a picture library, annotated as needed, and attached to the report. Statistical summaries of the common analyses of measurement data, and the related charts and graphs, can be also attached easily. The reports generated from cases can be used for management briefings and other such purposes, which helps motivate case authoring. The other use of the cases, providing the core of a case-based diagnostic system, need not motivate the initial case collection. This is helpful, since the benefits of the diagnostic system are difficult to demonstrate until a set of cases with sufficient coverage of the problem space has been collected.

Item 3 was critical to our need to convince the DM team that this would be a meaningful effort. The "customer" did not ask us to construct a system; rather, we wanted to demonstrate what such a system might do. A reasonably rapid return on time invested was important. It is difficult to quantify item 4, but it is an important element of this environment. We brought together three experts in the DM area at our pilot plant to consider some hypothetical problems. It was sometimes difficult to get consensus on solution approaches. One reason is that our problem descriptions often did not contain the kind of physical details that trigger the solution process for them. Further, their thought processes are not "generic" but rather specific: not just which type of machine, but literally which machine, could make a difference in their analyses. Thus, a case can be constructed from a problem-solving episode, but there is a strong sense of "incomplete hypotheses" to these cases. They are more like stories, which require interpretation to apply again, than they are like rules. Put another way, the knowledge of "which machine the story is about" and "which machine a new problem might involve" evokes a judgment of the strength of the matching, when these experts are reviewing the situation, which is difficult to imagine reducing to rules. However, we are open to discovering and exploiting patterns, if our case base ultimately reveals them.

In the light of these (and other) considerations, we have developed the following case structure. A case consists of an arbitrary number of "observations." There are 26 types of observations. Each type has a fixed structure, essentially a fixed set of attributes, although we allow lists of values for some attributes. Thus, two observations of the same type from two different cases may be compared with each other in a one-to-one manner, as long as some way of comparing lists of values for the same attribute is available. Only a few types of attributes are important for similarity. However, all are significant for case capture and reporting.

The observation templates are organized around "menu selection" rather than "authoring." The ontology consists of a rather complete set of plant-floor object names with verbs and verb phrases which express process elements, faults with process elements, tests, results of tests, and other such objects. These are partially organized taxonomically, somewhat like the hierarchical domain model for the diagnostic support application described in [11, chapter 9]. There is also a library of pictures showing, in particular, the relevant parts, components, sub-assemblies, and assemblies. These pictures are mostly design diagrams generated in the course of planning the build, but made active for point-and-click selection of specific parts and assemblies. They have a natural taxonomic classification derived from the parts breakdown of the build. A small number of the pictures describe the body-shop layout. Their taxonomy follows the factory-floor organization by zones, stations, and machines. All of these pictures can be used to annotate observations. Observations can be annotated by text as well as pictures, but text annotations are optional. Some multimedia objects would also be relevant for diagnosis and might be attached to observations in the future; for example, principal-component analysis animations [12], virtual reality presentations showing how the assemblies should fit into the tooling and interact with the machines, the sound of specific machine faults, etc. Finally, the DM team has a digital camera, and pictures are taken "in the moment" to illustrate problems and solutions. These pictures are also used to annotate case observations.

Note that various aspects of this environment lead us not to expect to identify a fixed set of attributes whose values define a definite problem and unique solution. The diagnostic process can involve many data tests and physical tests, and the technicians want the freedom to decide which tests to run and the order in which they are done. (This point was made in [9], where a case structure with some elements in common with ours is described.) Further, a good deal of the "knowledge content" of the case history is in the chain of causation and the chain of discovery. Representing every possible fault in a fixed set of attributes or organizing diagnosis around a small number of questions linked to attribute values (as described in [3, Chapter 7]) is not reasonable here. In particular, each case may have a different number of relevant attributes, and the approach to comparing cases for similarity must take this into account. The "information completion" framework described in [13] in a context of "case retrieval nets" does provide a formal structure which we might use, but the practical issues of dealing with "mismatching cases" and developing a workable similarity function remain. We should also note that similarity is not our only concern. The lessons-learned case structure must be capable of generating reports which express the problem and solution in terms that are meaningful to the DM team members. Thus, some items of data which might be discarded to generate a case index must be preserved in the cases themselves.

One interesting element of manufacturing applications is the product-process duality of expression which is commonly used. In other words, process problems and their corresponding effects on the product are often referred to interchangeably and with a certain ambiguity. For example, the following sentences are (hypothetically) all saying essentially the same thing:

- "The Station A build is off in the down direction."
- "The pins in Station A are low."
- "The left front fender needs to be moved up 1mm."
- "The pins in station A need to be moved up 1mm."

We see that an additional element of ambiguity can be added by referencing a process fault and an action to correct the fault interchangeably. We can imagine cases with these kinds of variations of expression which we would want to match during similarity search. Part of the motivation for using observation templates and a limited ontology is to control the number of ways of saying the same thing. We have not tried to eliminate the product-process duality of language, however, as this is too much a part of standard assembly-plant usage. Rather, we have tagged dual expressions to be similar.

Here are a few additional notes on ontology:

- Our ontology provides, in essence, a "local domain model," where what is missing is as significant as what is included. For example, the sentences "Weld sequence is faulty" and "Measurement system is faulty" are included, but "Tooling is faulty" is not. Given that "Tooling is broken," "Tooling is missing," "Tooling is worn," "Tooling is missing," and others are included, we wondered why "Tooling is faulty" shouldn't be. The domain experts explain that they always know more than "Tooling is faulty." It is not a description they would use.

- Much of the information content of cases in this domain are pictures and charts. Excluding graphic information from our ontology is a shortcoming of our approach, where all indexing is though the templated text. Put another way, the human experts could make do with the pictures without the text to understand the problem and the solution of the case, given that the full graphic library of parts and process are available, free use of a digital camera is allowed for identifying process problems, and the results of data tests are almost always displayed as charts. The experts would prefer "having only pictures" to "having only words," but the "computer part" of our system would have no way of dealing with purely graphical cases. Further, it appears that any techniques currently available to "automatically" extract features from pictures to index cases would require a massive (textual!) ontology to provide enough context to give such an approach a chance to work. The only practical approach to indexing and classification is to have the expert humans add text to the pictures, mostly for the convenience of non-expert humans and the computer system itself.

Analytical cases were created to seed the case base, in an exercise with the DM team in which we visited each station, talked about what could go wrong with process elements in that station and what effects on the build each fault might cause and where these faults would most likely be detected. This information was synthesized into a set of about 50 analytical cases, which serve as an independent resource (*e.g.*, they can be browsed) as well as being seed cases for the CBR system.

4   User Interface

The observations are essentially fill-in-the-blank sentences, which can be completed using pull-down menus that select objects from the ontology. Choices are limited to what makes sense for the particular slot being filled in. Additional information is often included with the observation's basic sentence, such as descriptions of relevant data filters and vehicle model numbers. The 26 types of observation are organized under 8 tabs:

- *data test*, meaning the results of simple statistical tests,
- *data analysis*, the results of more complex statistical tests,
- *correlation*, the results of various correlation tests,
- *fit problems with final assembly*, an indication of problems "downstream,"
- *possible problem location*, a problem hypothesis focusing on a process location,
- *problem found/action taken*, *e.g.*, bent pin replaced,
- *comparison*, *e.g.*, of data tests before & after corrective action taken,
- *root cause*, an identification of a "problem found" to be the root cause.

Figure 1 shows the "Observation Maker" screen after a tab has been chosen. It includes several graphic attachments to the observation being constructed.

The DM team is fairly picky about language and generally dislikes generic nouns and verbs. This was noted at the end of the previous section. Here are a few more examples: "possible problem location" is preferred over "root cause hypothesis" and "fit problems with final assembly" is preferred over "product problems." Behind the scenes, however, generic information (*e.g.*, the inner leaves of ontology taxonomies) are used in the way the pull-down choices are organized, for similarity computations, and for generating summary statistics over all cases. The pictures are organized for selection using the taxonomies noted above.

The DM team uses a specialized in-house statistical package to analyze the data from the vision stations. This data analysis generates statistical information including graphs and charts, which can be cut and pasted into observations as annotations. In the spirit of fast prototyping and easy integration, we used Microsoft Access and Visual Basic to build our system. The similarity function is written in C^{++}.

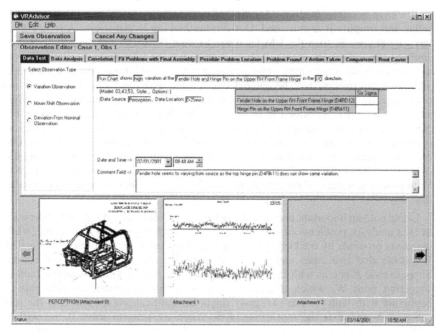

Fig. 1. "Observation Maker" screen, showing the basic sentence for a data test, additional information on the vehicle model and the data filter, a comment ("text attachment"), and several graphic attachments.

5 Similarity and Case-Based Retrieval

Similarity is developed by considering case relevance from the point of view of the specific DM team problem-solving process. In other words, when the team is considering a new case, what sorts of reference cases would it want to be reminded of? There are several natural focal points:

- Similarity of location, in terms of the geography of the plant; *e.g.*, cases may involve the same zone, the same station, or contiguous zones or stations.

- Similarity of location, in terms of the geography of the body; *e.g.*, involve the roof line, involve the left front part of the body.

- Similarity of structure, in terms of the vehicle body; *e.g.*, the roofline and the door ring are both boundary regions whose dimensional control is critical.

- Similarity of process, *e.g.*, two welding processes or (more generally) two joining processes.

- Similarity of tools, *e.g.*, pins and clamps, or robots, or glue guns.

We have not done much field testing of our similarity function, and we expect to refine and simplify it as it is used. Our current thinking is that if case A *is similar in any way* to case B, then the DM team would want the cases and the nature of their similarity brought to its attention. Our system is not for a "naïve user." Rather it is to aid the diagnostic reasoning of human experts. As a new case is "being completed," additional information will be entered but "... the additional information may not come directly from the most similar cases, [but rather these similar cases] might suggest tests to be performed in order to obtain [the] new information." [13, p. 65] Note, too, that this is an application which will always have only a "few" cases, as opposed, say, to certain web-based or e-business applications. Significant DM problems occur at the rate of about one a week in a body shop. Even multiplying this over 20 assembly plants and 10 years, the number of cases is on the order of 10,000. With proper case-base management, the number should remain considerably smaller than this.

Let us note an important point for the definition of similarity. As is well understood in fault analysis, problems cascade "downstream" until a symptom is observed, while diagnosis proceeds by tracking symptoms "upstream" until the root cause is revealed. It follows that two cases can be similar, but have entirely different root causes. Suppose case A begins with fault X, which then causes fault Y, itself causing fault Z, triggering fault W, which directly creates the initial symptom. Imagine case B beginning with fault Y. The two cases might be identical, except that X is the root cause of A and Y is the root cause of B. When we want to solve B, we will be particularly interested in seeing A. This means that our similarity function will need to consider sub-case similarity in a way that strongly favors sub-case matching, while not penalizing the parts that don't match. This is not a typical "similarity function," as described for example in [3].

6   Factory Experiences

In the "shift log" free-text comments can be made, organized by date, shift, and factory zone. These notes are read by one shift to see what the last few shifts have been working on. They include direct messages from one shift to the next. Thus, they perform the function of a simple bulletin board for the team. Shift log entries can be used to identify problems that will become cases, but many of them do not.

It is interesting to examine the use of the shift log. Within one month, this simple tool became a part of both shifts' routines. Each engineer on both shifts uses this bulletin board to communicate important information across shifts. This is analogous to what occurs in a typical hospital when the nursing staff changes shifts. Each nurse does a brief oral report to a counterpart, but most of the important information is passed along in the patients' charts. This allows an orderly and efficient shift change to occur. The same thing occurs in the assembly plant.

At the beginning of each shift, the engineers print out the shift log entries for the previous four shifts or so. They then refer to this list when issues come up, to see if they are new or ongoing. Figure 2 illustrates the type of messages in the shift log. It is a set of actual consecutive entries spanning about 1.5 shifts. It has been lightly edited; in particular, the names of DM team members have been changed.

Let us consider some general observations on Figure 2. Entries 6 and 8 are a question and an answer between shifts. Entries 3 and 7 represent the skeleton of complete cases. They need only some supporting details. Entries 4 and 12 are about updating the manufacturing process with some new tools.

Although the case-based system and the shift log are distinct, there are some linkages that are natural and that we are exploring. First, while creating a case in the midst of a problem-solving process, it is natural to imagine the analyst wanting to check a process element to test a hypothesis. Perhaps it isn't quite clear what the problem is yet, but comparison with similar cases suggests, say, a particular process location to check. We have provided the function to link this "hypothesis" observation into the shift log, with a request that someone check (and fix, if feasible) the process. The reply in the shift log is then linked back into the observation as a text annotation, and the case can be continued with this additional information.

Another type of case-log linkage that we are considering is the ability to attach a thread of related shift entries to observations of a case. This is merely a particular kind of text annotation, but, given the richness of the daily log, it makes sense to facilitate including this material as desired.

Further analysis and some imagination leads us to consider the possibility of text mining the daily log to automatically generate templated observations for cases and to discover unexpected patterns. This is not a part of our current project. Even a glance at Figure 2 shows that the text is rather incomplete and "dirty." The best bet here might be to organize the mining via domain-specific concepts developed from our ontology. In fact, when we consider Figure 2, we see clearly why we want to archive cases with a carefully focused ontology in the first place. Note the use of "local" language and lack of contextual explanations in the text. Of course, the log performs its primary function of "peer-to-peer sharing" very well. It isn't clear that this material would be very meaningful in another plant, or five years from now in any plant.

The case-based ("archival") portion of the system is slowly gaining favor at the assembly plant. We are spending significant time in the plant entering cases with the DM team, both as training and to provide us with feedback. We have struggled through the initial phases of re-structuring the ontology to more closely match the way that the DM team works.

1	Horatio - Moved the left and right doors forward .5mm. Gaps door to B pillar tight on final and the M1 deck.
2	Horatio - Rhett and Miles the electrician modified the robot program for the left front door in station 210 today for the window opening. We were getting alarms for being too narrow. Also I had Leto put the alarm back to its original limit.
3	Had problems with right side inner to outer load in T zone. When we loaded the inner to the outer we were scraping the adhesive off onto the inner skin leaving a mess on the door. WE reprogramed 30 R2 load on the right side door load and it is fine
4	Tried the new battery guns for the striker tonight on final line. The left fitter likes the big 90 degree gun and the right fitter likes the small pistol grip. I locked the guns in the gf cabinet where we store the lap tops. the chargers and extra batteries.
5	Pulled a BIW for metrology tonite
6	When do you think we will have our new report format for dvc jobs completed?
7	Had problems with the shot pin sticking in T zone right hemmer found that it had a lot of fine weld dust on it . We cleaned it and flushed it out with break free and it is working fine now. Rhett is going to clean all the shot pins on both hemmers tonite.
8	Horatio - Samson has the new cmm Report for the full BIWs done. I will leave one for you in your mail box. Samson is now working on a system so that the new report will automatically come out after the cmm check is completed.
9	Worked in left P-zone today on fender variation at hood hinge hole. I/O variation has been high on this hole only on the left fenders. I slowed the pierce units down. I also found that the pierce was jerking the hood attachment
10	Worked in main line today. Station 25 the head board on the left side was not held tight in the tooling. See shim log for details.
11	Horatio - Samson used the vvm in x-zone today as you requested. He will leave you a message about the results when he gets the data analyzed.
12	Horatio - Tried the power tools on final and both fitters liked the small pistol grip. I ran into some problems with GA tooling and higher ups. They wanted us to verify with the click wrench, every job done by the gun. We weren't doing that.
13	Got the striker tools hung up in trim today. Operators are happy with them and they seem to be working well.

Fig. 2. Consecutive entries in the shift log over one and a half shifts.

There have been some interesting discoveries here. In our initial contacts, the DM team members wanted our system to be formally linked to some other databases and tools that they use. This sounded reasonable to us but outside the scope of our prototype project. Now, we are finding that the "cut-and-paste" functionality, which we do provide, may actually be preferable. In more detail: recall that a case is made up of a sequence of observations. Each observation has a set of fill-in-the-blank attributes, but we also provide the ability to capture any number of pictures and attach them to an observation. This is effected merely by copying screen shots from any other tool into the computer clipboard, which can then be pasted into the observation. The DM team seems to like this, because it can use familiar tools and because it can capture and store electronically the large amount data and process pictures that they use as a matter of course. These screen shots provide for the team a summary of a vast amount of information. It has, in the past, been cumbersome for the team to save all these screen shots for reuse. This minor function, essentially an electronic file cabinet, is received as a huge benefit by the team. Note that our structured ontology and similarity function facilitate this by providing a basis for indexing.

7 Current Status

Most of our time last year has been spent in learning how to approach the ontological engineering and in building a good working relationship with the plant. We have entered a fairly complete starter set of analytical cases, and we are getting a good deal of feedback from the DM team. The comments are positive, but the number of modifications requested is large. This is as expected in prototype development. The number of cases captured so far makes premature any assessment of our approach to similarity. One issue of current interest is how to manage the linkage between the daily log and the case base. There has been some discussion of "automatically" generating cases from log entries.

8 Summary and Conclusions

We have launched a case-based system for diagnosing and solving dimensional management problems in vehicle assembly plants. This includes
- a "daily log" to facilitate peer-to-peer sharing (short-term memory) and
- a case-based lessons-learned system (long term memory).
- This latter is intended to be useful over time and from plant to plant.

When the number of cases grows to a large enough number, we will test our similarity strategy. We expect to modify and simplify, but we do not anticipate this to be a roadblock to completion of the project.

The long term intent is to link all assembly plants to the same case base, so that lessons learned in plant A can benefit plant B. There are (essentially) no ontological issues for several plants building the same product. For different products, the ontological issues have to do with "lifting" the specific language favored by the DM teams to generic language which could suggest solutions across different types of vehicles. This is our eventual goal.

References

1. Weber, R., Aha, D., Munoz-Avila, H., and Breslow, L.: Active Delivery for Lessons-Learned Systems. In: Blanzieri, E. and Portinale, L. (eds.): Advances in Case-Based Reasoning: 5th European Workshop, EWCBR 2000, Trento, Italy, September 2000, Proceedings, Lecture Notes in Artificial Intelligence 1898, Springer-Verlag, Berlin (2000) 322-334
2. Varma, A.: ICARUS: Design and Deployment of a Case-Based Reasoning System for Locomotive Diagnostics. In: Althoff, K-D., Bergmann, R., and Branting L. (eds.): Case-Based Reasoning Research and Development: Third International Conference on Case-Based Reasoning, ICCBR-99, Seeon Monastery, Germany, July 1999, Proceedings, Lecture Notes in Artificial Intelligence 1650, Springer-Verlag, Berlin (1999) 581-595
3. Watson, I.: Applying Case-Based Reasoning: Techniques for Enterprise Systems. Morgan Kaufmann, San Francisco (1997)
4. Leake, D. (ed.): Case-Based Reasoning: Experiences, Lessons, & Future Directions. AAAI Press, Menlo Park, California and The MIT Press, Cambridge, Massachusetts (1996)
5. Smith, R. G., and Farquhar, A.: The Road Ahead for Knowledge Management: An AI Perspective. AI Magazine vol. 21, No. 4 (Winter 2000), 17-40.
6. Leake, D., Birnbaum, L., Hammond, K., Marlow, C., Yang, H.: Integrating Information Resources: A Case Study of Engineering Design Support. In: Althoff, K-D., Bergmann, R., and Branting L. (eds.) Case-Based Reasoning Research and Development: Third International Conference on Case-Based Reasoning, ICCBR-99, Seeon Monastery, Germany, July 1999, Proceedings, Lecture Notes in Artificial Intelligence 1650, Springer-Verlag, Berlin (1999) 482-496
7. Cafeo, J., Gibbons, D., Lesperance, R., Morgan, A., Sengir, G., and Simon, A.: Capturing Lessons Learned for Variation Reduction in an Automotive Assembly Plant, Proceedings of FLAIRS (Florida Artificial Intelligence Research Society) 2001, to appear (2001)
8. Wettschereck, D., and Aha, D. W.: Case-Based Learning: Beyond Classification of Feature Vectors, An ECML-97 MLNet Workshop (26 April 1997, Prague). Proceedings available at www.aic.nrl.navy.mil/~aha/ecml97-wkshp/ (1997)
9. Hamilton, A., and Gomes, B.: Failure Analysis of Semi-conductor Products. Presented at Innovative Customer Centered Applications, Trento, Italy (2000) oral only
10. Schlenoff, C., Ivester, R., and Knutilla, A.: A Robust Process Ontology for Manufacturing Systems Integration, National Institute of Standards and Technology, Gaithersburg, MD 20899. Available at www.ontology.org/main/papers/psl.html (1998)
11. Bergmann, R., Breen, S., Göker, M., Manago, M., and Wess, S. (eds.): Developing Industrial Case-Based Reasoning Applications: The INRECA Methodology, Lecture Notes in Artificial Intelligence 1612, Springer-Verlag, Berlin (1999)
12. Hu, S. J., and Wu, S. M.: Identifying Root Causes of Variation in Automobile Body Assembly Using Principal Component Analysis, Transactions of North American Manufacturing Research Institution, Vol. XX (1992), 311-316
13. Lenz, M., Bartsch-Spörl, B., Burkhard, H.-D., Wess, S. (eds.): Case-based Reasoning Technology. Lecture Notes in Artificial Intelligence 1400, Springer-Verlag, Berlin (1998)

Real-Time Creation of Frequently Asked Questions

Hideo Shimazu and Dai Kusui

NEC Laboratories, NEC Corporation,
8916-47, Takayama, Ikoma, Nara 630-0101, Japan,
(shimazu@ccm.cl.nec.co.jp, kusui@ccm.cl.nec.co.jp)

Abstract. This paper analyzes the case duration of product defects in high-tech product customer support. User inquiries about new defects often increase very rapidly within a few weeks. They continue to increase until corresponding solutions are provided or new versions appear. Typical user inquiries are added into FAQ (frequently-asked questions) case bases using conventional case-based reasoning (CBR) tools by expert engineers later on. However, some additions take too much time. Such knowledge may really be necessary within a few weeks after a problem first appears. This paper describes SignFinder, which analyzes textual user inquiries stored in a database of a call tracking system and extracts remarkably increasing cases between two user-specified time periods. If SignFinder is given a problem description, it displays a list of recently increasing keywords in the cases that include the problem description. These keywords can signal new defects. An empirical experiment shows that such increasing keywords can become salient features for retrieving signs of new defects not yet recognized by expert engineers. SignFinder is not a general-purpose case retriever. It only retrieves frequency-increasing similar-looking cases to a user's problem description. SignFinder fills in the time gap between the first appearing time of a new defect and the time when the defect and its solution are added into a FAQ case base using a conventional CBR system.

1 Introduction

This paper describes the interactive case retrieval tool SignFinder. The tool analyzes chronological changes in a case base and extracts remarkably increasing cases during given time periods. Such cases sometimes include important signs of possible defects not yet recognized by expert engineers.

The motivation behind this research was two-fold. First, the authors recognized that the instant creation of FAQ case bases is important. In conventional CBR systems, it is hard for busy agents in high-tech product customer support to keep their case bases always fresh. FAQ case bases are typically revised every month. However, inquiries about high-tech product defects often appear and increase very rapidly within a few weeks. Obviously, revising case bases monthly in such cases is too late. It is hard for agents to share knowledge only by face-to-face communications. If an organization is large, this problem becomes more

D.W. Aha and I. Watson (Eds.): ICCBR 2001, LNAI 2080, pp. 611–621, 2001.
© Springer-Verlag Berlin Heidelberg 2001

serious. Actually, the authors have been working with a large-scale customer support organization and observed the difficulty of gathering all of the agents and providing them with new knowledge. Our solution is to create a pseudo FAQ case base in real time so that agents can immediately share all new knowledge.

Second, the authors understood that it is very important to detect signs of a serious product defect at a very early stage of its appearance. Empirical analysis has taught us that signs of a defect appear before the problem is reported in a newspaper. Such signs are often regarded as exceptional cases caused by user misuse or because of a specific poor-quality product module. Such assertions are right in most cases, but serious defects should not be overlooked. Product-recall-level defects can cause serious damage to vendors and brand names. The discovery of such defects by customer support can minimize the damage.

The authors have developed SignFinder. SignFinder receives a problem description and two specific time periods from a user, and retrieves a list of increasing keywords in the cases that include the problem description between the two time periods. Some of the keywords possibly indicate signs of new defects. SignFinder users can continue to narrow down the keyword list by selecting one of the increasing keywords and find frequency-increasing similar-looking cases to the problem description. An experiment has shown that such keywords can sometimes become salient features for retrieving signs of new defects not yet recognized by expert engineers.

2   Lifetime of a Defect Case

This section introduces an example of the lifetime of a reported defect.

Example: OLEDLG.dll Case

A user ran a software virus checking software called VirusScan. The application detected a virus and advised the user to delete contaminated files. The user followed the advice. After deleting the files, however, the user was unable to run another program (not all programs). The reason was because VirusScan regarded OLEDLG.DLL to be contaminated and advised the user to delete it. But the DLL file was not contaminated. Because of this, the application program using OLEDLG.DLL could no longer run. The defect was solved when the vendor released a new version.

This case had two difficulties in analyzing the cause. First, many of the users who called did not remember the names of the deleted files. Second, not all application programs were unable to run after the virus checking process. Before this defect case was reported by an expert engineer and added into a FAQ case base, some agents already knew the cause and effect because they solved this problem by themselves. Other agents did not know about the cause and effect and therefore had difficulty trying to answer the inquiry. Furthermore, many of the agents did not know that the number of defects was increasing remarkably.

Fig. 1 shows a typical example of the lifetime of a defect case. The number of defect inquiries rapidly increased from the third week of the first month to the second week of the second month. New FAQ records were added into the FAQ case base several times two months after the first appearance of the problem. The number of inquiries suddenly decreased at the third week of the third month. This was because a free patch program was offered for download from the vendor's Web page and a new software version appeared which fixed the problem. After the fourth week of the fourth month, the lifetime of this defect could be described as almost dead because no one asked about this problem any more. Between the third week of the first month and the third week of the second month, there was no FAQ case related to this defect. Agents had to solve this defect without corresponding FAQ case bases.

The authors understood the need for a novel case retrieval tool to help agents solve a problem at an early stage of its appearance. SignFinder was the result. This tool, however, is not a general-purpose case retriever but only retrieves frequency-increasing similar-looking cases to a user's problem description. It works like a *stand-in* by filling in the time gap of a defect between the first appearing time of a new defect and the time when the defect and its solution are added into a FAQ case base using a conventional CBR system.

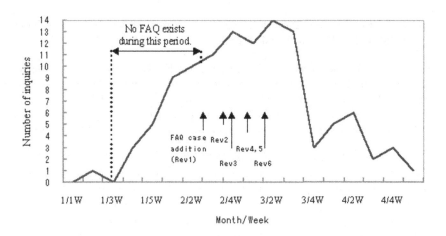

Fig. 1. The lifetime of a specific defect

3   SignFinder Design Decision

This section describes the design decision of SignFinder.

Direct use of inquiry databases of call tracking systems: User inquiries are stored in a call tracking system database. Because signs of a new defect only

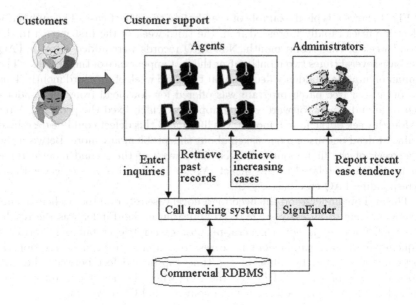

Fig. 2. SignFinder and a call tracking system

appear in users' textual inquiries, SignFinder directly refers to the database of a call tracking system as shown in Fig. 2.

Complement of conventional CBR tools: SignFinder is not a general-purpose case retriever. It only retrieves frequency-increasing similar-looking cases to a user's problem description to extract signs of future-reported defect cases as their predictors. Because such signs have been ignored as case indices by conventional CBR tools, SignFinder works complementary with conventional CBR tools.

Comparison of the frequency of keywords between two time periods: A user specifies two separate time periods besides a problem description. Among the cases generated during the two time periods, SignFinder retrieves only those that match the problem description and counts the frequency of keywords in the cases. SignFinder then compares the frequency differences of each keyword between the two time periods. A keyword is judged as an *increasing keyword* if the following condition is satisfied,

$$(N_2/C_2)/P_2 - (N_1/C_1)/P_1 \geq N_{threshold} \tag{1}$$

where N_1 is the number of appearances of a keyword K, C_1 is the number of created cases during the time period P_1, N_2 is the number of appearances of a keyword K, C_2 is the number of created cases during the time period P_2, and $N_{threshold}$ is the predefined threshold value to judge if the difference is remarkable.

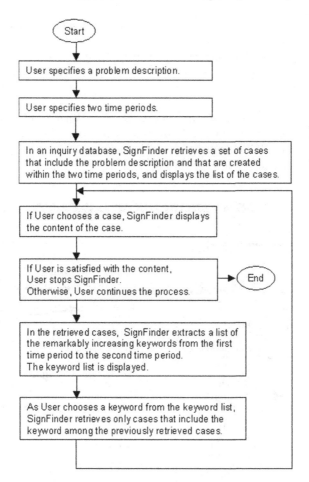

Fig. 3. A conversation between a user and SignFinder

Interactive case narrowing down: The user interface of SignFinder was designed to narrow down cases interactively. Fig. 3 shows the conversation flow between a user and SignFinder. The user activates SignFinder when he/she wants to know if there are signs of a newly appearing defect not yet reported in a FAQ case base but related to a problem he/she is facing. First, the user inputs a problem description and two separate time periods. SignFinder analyzes textual inquiries stored in a database of a call tracking system, retrieves a set of cases that include the problem description and that are created during the two time periods, and displays a list of the cases. If the user chooses a case from the list, SignFinder displays the content of the case. If the user is satisfied with the content, he/she stops SignFinder. Otherwise, the user continues the retrieval process. In the retrieved cases, SignFinder extracts a list of keywords remarkably increasing from the first time period to the second time period. The keyword list is displayed. As the user chooses a keyword from the keyword list, SignFinder retrieves only cases that include the keyword among the previously retrieved cases. The retrieval process is repeated until cases or keywords are sufficiently narrowed down.

Automatic sign detection and warning generation: When SignFinder is running in the background, it automatically slides the time window and analyzes the call tracking database. If it detects keywords that are notably increasing in frequency, it reports them to an expert for review.

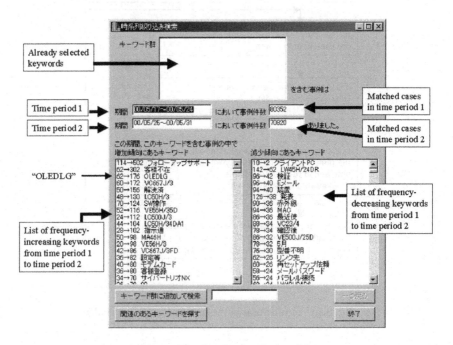

Fig. 4. The SignFinder Screen (1)

4   SignFinder User Interface

Fig. 4, 5, and 6 show screen shots of SignFinder when an agent is using it while talking with a user. Fig. 4 shows the initial screen just after the agent inputs two time periods; the first period is between 2000/05/17 and 2000/05/24 and the second period is between 2000/05/25 and 2000/05/31. 80352 cases exist within the first period and 70820 cases exist within the second period. The top text box displays the user's problem descriptions. It is empty because the agent has

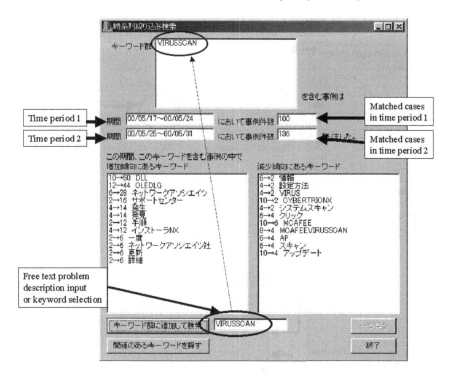

Fig. 5. The SignFinder Screen (2)

not yet specified anything. The bottom left text box shows the list of increasing keywords. Each row displays the number difference from the first period to the second period and an increasing keyword. "OLEDLG" can be seen in the third row. It appeared 62 times within the first period and 176 times within the second period. "VirusScan" had not yet appeared high on the keyword list. During this time, neither the user nor the agent recognized that "OLEDLG" played an important role among corresponding inquiries. This is because the user told the agent that a trouble occurred after running the VirusScan program, and the agent responded by inputting "VirusScan".

In Fig. 5, the top text box displays VirusScan. The agent can see the list of increasing keywords. The first one is "DLL", the second is "OLEDLG", and the third is "Network Associates". Now, the agent can recognize that a possible sign of the cause is OLEDLG. The agent then inputs "OLEDLG". The screen changes to Fig. 6. The number of cases including VirusScan and OLEDLG increases from 8 to 36. The agent reads the contents of these cases, and understands that the user's inquiry is the same as these previous cases.

The bottom right text box in each window displays a list of decreasing keywords. The authors have not yet found cases of decreasing keywords becoming salient indices for retrieving sign cases. However, because each case has its life-

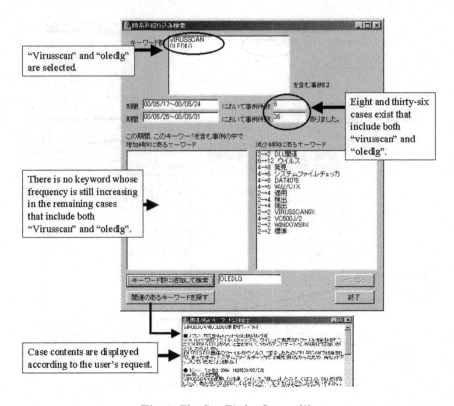

Fig. 6. The SignFinder Screen (3)

time as shown in Fig. 1, the authors believe that old cases should be removed from a case base when their lifetimes expire. In order to recognize the lifetime of a case, analyzing decreasing keywords may be useful. This is one of the future research issues of SignFinder.

5   Evaluation

Readers may be skeptical about whether recently increasing keywords extracted by SignFinder can be useful keywords to detect signs of future defects. Fig. 7 shows the types of increasing keywords extracted by SignFinder between 2000/05/17 and 2000/05/31. Product names appear most frequently. These product names are quite diversified. The quoted words are specific single keywords. These quoted words are useful indices for narrowing down similar cases. A top 10 keyword analysis of different time periods should generate similar results. The authors believe that SignFinder sufficiently retrieves signs from important keywords.

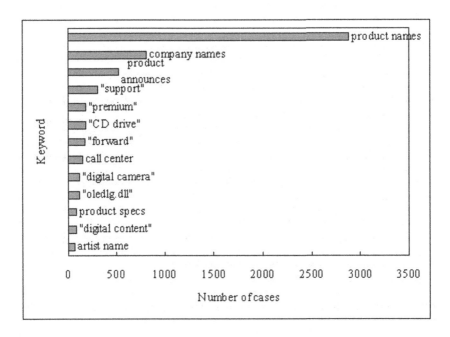

Fig. 7. Top 10 keywords and topics of a specific time period

Fig. 8 shows an example of how a sign about a serious defect appears before and after a related article is described in a newspaper. The X-axis of Fig. 8 shows the relative date of the newspaper appearance. The "0" date is the date when the article appears in the newspaper. The Y-axis shows the number of cases that include a specific text expression. Before the article appears, the product name appears frequently because it is a popular product. Even though the number of appearances of "smoking" is small, inquiries related to "smoking" exist; they appear several days before the article. If SignFinder can find such a sign of a serious defect at an early stage, a serious situation can be avoided.

6   Related Research

Textual CBR is a research direction that addresses the issue of textual document retrieval and reuse from a CBR perspective. FALLQ [Lenz et al. 1998] uses FAQ documents to help customer support agents solve problems. FAQFinder [Burke et al.1997] also retrieves FAQ documents. In fact, there are many other approaches that deal with the retrieval of FAQ documents that have already been created by someone else. On the other hand, SignFinder does not require the pre-existence of a FAQ database. Instead, it creates a pseudo FAQ case base from raw documents in real time according to the user preferences of time periods and viewpoints.

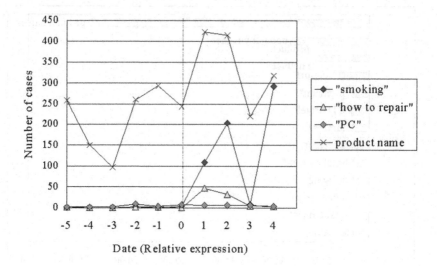

Fig. 8. Changes in inquiry numbers before and after newspaper articles about defects

Situation assessment [Kolodner 1993] is one of the important aspects of CBR. The situation assessment of SignFinder is unique because it deals with *situations at being prevalent* by analyzing the high frequency, increasing frequency, and decreasing frequency of texts in cases at given time periods.

Conversational CBR [Aha & Breslow 1997] research projects have focused on user-interface issues. FindMe [Hammond et al.1996] and Wasabi [Burke 1999] combine instance-based browsing and tweaking by difference. These systems show the user an example of retrieved results. By critiquing the example, the user then indicates his/her preferences and controls the system's retrieval strategies. NaCoDAE [Aha et al 1998] has a dialogue-inference mechanism to improve the conversational efficiency. It infers the details of a user's problem from his/her incomplete text description by using model-based reasoning. SignFinder is a kind of conversational CBR, but it is unique because it repeatedly narrows down cases by using the keyword frequency changes in the cases as indices.

7   Conclusion

In this paper, the authors introduced a concept about the case lifetime of product defects in high-tech product customer support. The authors observed that chronological keyword frequency changes in cases can be important indices in case retrieval, and designed SignFinder based on this assumption. SignFinder analyzes textual user inquiries stored in a database of a call tracking system, and extracts remarkably increasing cases during the given time periods. If SignFinder is given a problem description, it displays a list of recently increasing keywords in the cases that include the problem description. These keywords can signal new defects. An empirical experiment shows that increasing keywords can become salient features for retrieving signs of new defects not yet recognized. SignFinder is not a general-purpose case retriever. It only retrieves frequency-increasing similar-looking cases to a user's problem description. SignFinder fills in the time gap between the first appearing time of a new defect and the time when the defect and its solution are defined in a FAQ case base using a conventional CBR system.

References

[Aha & Breslow 1997] Aha, D.W., and Breslow, L.A.: 1997, Refining conversational case libraries, Proceedings of the Second International Conference on Case-Based Reasoning, pp. 267 – 278.

[Aha et al 1998] Aha, D.W., Maney, T., and Breslow, L.A.: 1998, Supporting dialogue inferencing in conversational case-based reasoning, Proceedings of the Fourth European Workshop on Case-Based Reasoning, pp. 267 – 278. Berlin: Springer.

[Burke et al.1997] Burke, R.D., Hammond, K., Kulyukin, V., Lytinen, S, Tomuro, S., and Schoenberg, S., : 1997, Question Answering from Frequently Asked Question Files. AI Magazine, 18(2): 57-66.

[Burke 1999] Burke, R.D.: 1999, The Wasabi Personal Shopper: A Case-Based Recommender System, Proceedings of the 11th National Conference on Innovative Applications of Artificial Intelligence, pp. 844 – 849, Menlo Park, CA: AAAI Press.

[Hammond et al.1996] Hammond, K.J., Burke, R., and Schumitt, K.: 1996, A case-based approach to knowledge navigation, in: Leake, D.B. (Eds.): *Case-Based Reasoning Experiences, Lessons, & Future Directions*, pp. 125 – 136. Menlo Park, CA: AAAI Press.

[Kolodner 1993] Kolodner, J.: 1993. Case-Based Reasoning. San Francisco, CA: Morgan Kaufmann.

[Lenz et al. 1998] Lenz, M., Hübner, A., and Kunze, M.: 1998. Textual CBR in: Lenz, M., Bartsch-Spörl, B., Burkhard, H-D., and Wess, S. (Eds.): *Case-Based Reasoning Technology, From Foundations to Applications*, pp. 115 – 138. Menlo Park, CA: AAAI Press.

Managing Diagnostic Knowledge in Text Cases

Anil Varma

Information & Decision Technology Laboratory
One Research Circle, Niskayuna, NY 12309. USA.
varma@crd.ge.com

Abstract. A valuable source of field diagnostic information for equipment service resides in the text notes generated during service calls. Intelligent knowledge extraction from such textual information is a challenging task. The notes are characterized by misspelled words, incomplete information, cryptic technical terms, and non-standard abbreviations. In addition, very few of the total number of notes generated may be diagnostically useful. We present an approach for identifying diagnostically relevant notes from the many raw field service notes and information is presented in this paper. N-gram matching and supervised learning techniques are used to generate recommendations for the diagnostic significance of incoming service notes. These techniques have potential applications in generating relevant indices for textual CBR.

1 Introduction

Case Based Reasoning relies on the fact that experiential knowledge (memory of past experiences - or cases) is an important component of human problem solving. Presenting information as cases can provide deeper context and guidance than rules and guidelines. This is especially true in diagnostic tasks associated with servicing consumer and professional equipment. Tools that embody domain knowledge and deploy it to offer expert level assistance to field engineers performing diagnostic tasks can significantly enhance the effectiveness of a service oriented organization.

Equipment troubleshooting and service is a prime application area for case-based reasoning technologies since what constitutes a case is usually a well-defined and repetitive event. A typical diagnostics case is a distinct troubleshooting incident composed of symptoms, troubleshooting steps and a solution. The application addressed in this paper is in the domain of servicing medical imaging machines. GE Medical Systems employs a team of field engineers to service and support a large installed base of several thousand GE and non-GE imaging equipment. Each visit results in a text description of the symptom and the solution being recorded.

Such cases composed of short technical descriptions are extremely valuable sources of corporate knowledge. The text descriptions can provide an informed field engineer with immediate relevant technical information that he/she can interpret and apply. In

D.W. Aha and I. Watson (Eds.): ICCBR 2001, LNAI 2080, pp. 622-633, 2001.

this regard, a well-chosen text case describing a previous troubleshooting experience is extremely valuable in a new diagnostic situation. The challenge of extracting diagnostic case information from free text typically occurs in any distributed repair and service oriented operation where the service personnel enter a repair summary as free text. From an overall organizational viewpoint, corporate retention and utilization of such information is also valuable since it represents mature, field validated knowledge about the failure modes of the equipment under consideration that goes beyond troubleshooting manuals and can provide valuable inputs into the design and prioritization of future enhancements and upgrades.

However, the knowledge embedded within such text cases is not easy to analyze, extract or compare. The text notes are characterized by misspelled words, incomplete information, cryptic technical terms, and non-standard abbreviations. In addition, only a small fraction of notes generated contain non-trivial and non-routine information of value. This paper describes a project whose objective was to create a textual case-based tool by mining the several hundred megabytes of archived text notes. The tool would be deployed on a laptop for field engineers to use on troubleshooting calls. The experience of the project provided valuable insights and research directions into some of the challenges of dealing with text cases.

The approach underlying this project was generic in nature and applicable across diverse businesses - especially in the service field.

2 Related Work

There are several perspectives from which such a project can be viewed. We shall focus on text-based diagnostics or self-help systems, and then on related work in text based CBR. We shall not attempt to cover the wider area of information retrieval.

A variety of hybrid approaches have been used in the process of dealing with case based diagnostic system development. Uthurusamy et al. (1993) focus on improving the retrievability of free text service notes from General Motor's Technical Assistance Database. These researchers focus on natural-language processing techniques to correct, standardize and grammatically and semantically improve the source text. They then utilize a natural language parser to construct constraint rules from the input text. This approach is focused on supporting centralized technical assistance centers that respond to service calls. Creecy et al. (1992), present the PACE system, which classifies free-text responses to US Census Bureau forms into hundreds of pre-determined categories and uses a knowledge base of over 100000 manually, classified returns as the reasoning base. It uses the nearest neighbor technique with feature weighing. Liu et al. (1995) apply case-based diagnostics using fuzzy neural networks (FNN) to the task to recalling help-desk call logs. To allow for the FNN to work, the call logs need to be mapped from an unstructured to a structured format with defined attributes and fuzzy if-then rules using linguistic properties are associated with each attribute. This approach uses pre-processing of incoming data to produce a well-defined case structure. Varma et al. (1996) post-process responses to a user query to a structured case base to create flexible meta-information that allows the user to refine the case attribute definition. Both the approaches provide some flexibility in interacting with the data but only by mapping the data to distinct attributes in either a pre or post processing stage.

Textual CBR has been a growing and active research area in recent years. Lenz (1998) makes the point that CBR's basis of using 'experiences' leads it naturally to text documents where many such experiences have been traditionally stored. In comparison to general information retrieval, CBR may be a more promising approach for domain specific applications. Wilson and Bradshaw (1999) present an overview of textual CBR and examine how textual features can be used for case similarity. Brüninghaus and Ashley (1998) discuss the issue of evaluating the performance of text-based CBR systems, with context from the measures used in traditional information retrieval.

Brüninghaus and Ashley (1997) also present work towards indexing full-text legal opinions by the relevant factors by considering the task as a classification problem using a learning approach. Nigam et al. (1998) present a probabilistic framework for classifying text from labeled and unlabeled documents. They use labeled data to train the classifier (based on naïve Bayes). Their domain of application is the World Wide Web and they make the assumption that the number of labeled examples required to train the classifier adequately can be prohibitively large. Our experience is that this may not be the case in narrowly defined, domain specific applications.

Finally, in a paper entitled 'How machine learning can be useful for textual case-based reasoning', Brüninghaus and Ashley (1998) explicitly address the relationship between machine learning and textual case-based reasoning. They recognize the valuable role machine learning techniques can play in 'bootstrapping' a text-based CBR system.

3 Problem Description

Each visit by a field engineer in response to a customer call results in a problem-solution note being generated. Several hundred thousand such notes are generated each year. These are archived in a database. The input software restricts the length of each note. There was general agreement among the experts at GE Medical Systems that some of the best diagnostic knowledge in that business was buried in these notes. The objective of this project was to try to create a limited number of useful 'cases' that could form the core of knowledge-based tool.

A sample problem-solution pair is shown in Figure 1. The language is concise and technical. Spelling errors are very frequent, as is the use of technical and general abbreviations. The example shown would be considered a 'good' case since is relatively descriptive and has useful content in both the symptom and solution text.

Symptom Text: KEYBOARD IS NOT WORKING/TIME OUT MEASUREMENT ERROR QUE OVERRUN ERROR
Solution Text: SYSTEM HAD COMMUNICATION INTERFERENCE LIKE BEFORE BETWEEN FUNCTION KEYS AND HOST COMPUTER SWAPPED FIBER OPTIC COMM LINES BETWEEN KEYBOARD AND FUNCTION KEYS. PROBLEM FIXED.

Fig. 1. Sample symptom-solution text note

The content in the notes varied widely. A majority of notes were unsuitable for being reused as solutions because they were either incomplete, near impossible to interpret or the text in the solution box did not really address the symptom. An example of useful solutions is given in Figure 2. 'xxxxx', where present, represents masked proprietary information.

● PROBLEM FOUND TO BE WITH "xxxxx" CONNECTOR FROM POWER SUPPLY CONNECTOR CHANGED BY xxxxxx ON xxxxx, PROBLEM CORRECTED.

● PERFORMED EXTENSIVE TESTING TO PROVE THAT CUT-OFF IS CAUSEDBY MIS-ALIGNMENT OF FILMSCREENS INSIDE xxxxxx CASSETTES NOT AN OBSTRUCTION IN THE X-RAY FIELD.

● FILM APPEARS TO BE HANGING ON THE NIP ROLLER AS IT ENTERS THE RECEIVER MAGAZINE ORDERED NIP ROLLER AND DRIVE BELTS. INSTALLED NIP ROLLER AND DRIVE BELTS. OK FOR NOW BUT BELIEVE SPRING STEEL TENSIONER IS WEAK AND NEEDS REPLACEMENT.

Fig. 2. Useful Solutions

In contrast, a randomly picked sample of notes that needed to be eliminated from the knowledge base is given below. Only the solution text is shown in figure 3.

● DID NOT FIND ANY PROBLEMS

● TESTED XXXX BUT COULD NOT FIND ANY PROBLEMS RETURNED TO SERVICE.

● CHECKED SYSTEM OPERATION AND DID NOT FIND ANY PROBLEM

● CHECKED IMAGE DID NOT FIND ANY   PROBLEMS.

● THIS IS A BOGUS DISPATCH

● COULD NOT REPRODUCE PROBLEM ADJUSTED TABLE BUCKY CONTACTS.

● COULD NOT REPRODUCE PROBLEM TURNED PROBLEM OVER TO TABLE LOCKS WERE WORKING AND COULD NOT REPRODUCE PROBLEM

● PERFORMED PMBILL NATIONAL MD FOR 6 5 HRS LABOR & 1 HR TRAVEL TOTAL CHARGE

Fig. 3. Non-Useful Solutions

The approach presented in this paper was developed to accommodate a business situation where the volume of service notes generated was extremely high with not all service dispatches necessarily containing diagnostic information. The diagnostic tool containing service notes was required to be deployed on field service engineers laptops with limited memory and processor speed. Thus there was a need to weed through the central database of service notes and select only a small percentage. Due to the large volume of new notes generated daily, the process for picking 'good' solutions had to be entirely automated! An additional task was to clean the quality of the text and provide a pick list of keywords that would provide starting points for accessing relevant service notes. This information was then to be incorporated into an Microsoft Access based tool that was released to the field service engineers with periodic updates provided as new information was analyzed.

4 Understanding the Utility of a Text Note

Due to the volume of text notes generated each year, it was absolutely necessary to come up with an automated way of deciding which note contained potentially useful information. The desired process is shown in Fig 4. A preliminary analysis of the text in the notes showed that spelling errors, abbreviations and domain specific terms made it very hard to 'understand' the content of the notes based on natural language techniques.

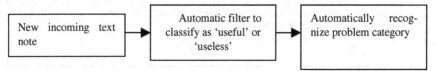

Fig. 4. Desired automated process for classifying new text notes

A significant decision was taken to try to use plain pattern matching to achieve the filtering. The text in the note was viewed as a pattern of alphabets and we tried to learn if significant patterns could be extracted which would help indicate a note's utility. A long-term continuing goal is to be able to automatically assign a note to the appropriate failure mode of the machine.

A supervised learning approach was taken to train the system to try to predict whether a service note is diagnostically significant. This process is shown in Figure 5. A user is required to accept or reject a few service notes as being diagnostically relevant. Once a training set of accepted and rejected service notes is created, it is used to score new incoming service notes automatically as diagnostically relevant or irrelevant. The scoring is carried out on fixed length text fragments called N-grams, which are explained in more detail in the next section. Suffice it to say that the score indicates what word fragments, occur to a greater extent in one class of notes (useful vs. useless) than another. There are two advantages to learning this. First, this can be used to identify the 'key' word fragments that are meaningful in a text case. As a heuristic, these can be used as case features in preference to other text fragments that do not seem directly relevant to the text note's meaning. For example, as shown in figure 5, the word 'void' strongly indicates that a note is not useful. The fragment 'the' predictably is assigned a low significance since it occurs evenly in the two classes of notes.

Now it one were to try to calculate a 'closeness' index between two cases, it would be reasonable to use strongly meaningful fragments like 'voi' and 'fix' as indices to compare on, independent of their sign, in preference to a fragment like 'the'.

Secondly, these significances, used with their sign could independently be used to classify a new note. Broadly, if a majority of word fragments in a new note have a negative significance, it may be concluded that the note may be rejected. These are the ideas between the 'case based' and the 'summing' approaches described later in the paper.

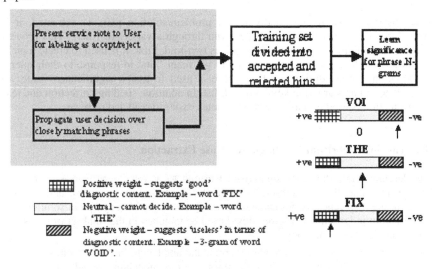

Fig. 5. Process for supervised learning of N-gram significances

A basic technique used in this paper is N-Gram matching. An N-gram refers to a fragment of N consecutive letters of a text phrase. For a given text phrase of length L, there are (L-N +1) N-grams, the first having as its first letter the first letter of the phrase, the second the second letter and so on. For example, the 3-grams (or trigrams) for the word diagnose would be {dia, iag,agn,gno,nos,ose}.

For each phrase that is labeled by the user in the training mode, all distinct N-grams are generated. A master list of distinct N-grams encountered so far is maintained along with two counts associated with each N-gram. The first count indicates how often this N-gram occurred in a phrase that was labeled as accept by the user and the second count indicated the number of times a phrase containing this N-gram was rejected.

N-grams are utilized to generate a similarity score between two text phrases. We refer to a parent phrase as one that has been assigned a label by the user and a candidate phrase is one that whose degree of similarity needs to be assessed with respect to the parent phrase. In its simplest version, this looks like

Simple n-gram similarity index $= \dfrac{[\,\#\,P_i \cap \#\,C_i\,]^2}{\#\,P_i \times \#\,C_i}$

where

$\#P_i$ = Number of unique n-grams in Parent text note
$\#C_i$ = Number unique n-grams in Candidate text note

Fig. 6. Simple N-gram similarity

Once the subset of diagnostically useful problem/solution pairs is extracted, it is parsed into individual keywords that are run through a variety of filters. This process is shown in Figure 2. The purpose of this is two-fold. First, it is used to create a pick-list of keywords that users are assured will get them 'hits' in response to their query. Information learned during the first phase is used to assign significance values to terms that will appear in the keyword pick list. In addition, spelling correction and text reformulation is used to make the service notes easier to read and retrieve.

4.1 Learning Algorithm for Diagnostic Case Extraction

The learning algorithm uses supervised learning to assign "significance factors" to phrase fragments that are subsets of the text constituting the symptom and solution fields in the dispatches. A domain expert was presented with a symptom/solution pair and asked to judge simply whether this should be included in the final set of cases that constitute the data in the tool.

The system operates in a dual mode - incremental and batch. In the batch mode, every time a user labels a phrase, It uses simple n-gram matching to pull up symptom phrases that are extremely similar and assign to them, the same decision given to the parent phrase. This serves to present the minimum number of phrases for judgment to the user by ensuring that they are sufficiently distinct from phrases he/she has already encountered. To enforce this, the level of similarity needed for this to happen is assigned a relatively high value. This constitutes the batch mode of operation for the learning cycle.

Simultaneously, at every decision point, all the phrases that have had a decision associated with them are polled. They are split into all distinct n-grams and a count is maintained for each as to provide a relative frequency of occurrence in acceptable and rejected symptom/solution texts. By default, at the beginning of the process, all n-grams are assigned a weight of 1. A user-defined threshold determines how many occurrences of a particular N-gram in a phrase should be seen before its weights are sought to be adapted.

It is desirable that if N-grams are to be used to assess similarity between phrases, only those that provide distinguishing information regarding an 'accept' or 'reject' decision be utilized. For example, the word "the" is seldom indicative of whether the service note is useful whereas the word 'void' in the data set strongly indicates that the service note should be rejected. For this purpose, a "significance" was calculated for each N-gram. This was obtained by examining if the occurrence of a N-gram in a phrase is strongly skewed towards either of a "accept" or "reject" diagnosis. Specifically, the significance weight was calculated as

$$\frac{\text{\#Accepted - \#Rejected}}{\text{\#Total}}$$

\# Accepted = Number of accepted Service notes in which N-gram occurs
\#Rejected = Number of Service notes in which N-gram occurs
\#Total = Total number of distinct service notes in which N-gram occurs
Phrases that do not provide evidence of a significant (user controllable) skew are thresholded out to a weight of zero. The weights of the remaining n-grams are updated to the actual weight. Once all the training phrases have been presented to the user, the system is ready for automatically assigning an accept/reject recommendation to new service notes.

4.2 Selecting Relevant Notes

Once a sufficient number of service notes have been presented to the user (typically 5-10%), the learned weights for the N-grams are used for determining incoming service note relevance. We discuss two approaches for doing this.

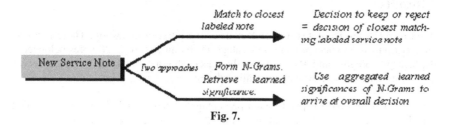

Fig. 7.

4.3 Case Based Approach

If a service note is considered a text based diagnostic case, then the traditional practice would be to compare the incoming service note with all available labeled service notes and calculate the degree of match with each. The decision associated with the closest matching labeled service note would be assigned to the incoming note. The match index using learned N-gram weights is calculated as:

Weighed n-gram match index $=$
$$\frac{[\Sigma W_{Ni}]^2, \ Ni \in (\ Pi \cap Ci)}{\Sigma W_{Pi} \times \Sigma W_{Ci}}$$

where
P_i = unique n-grams in Parent phrase
C_i = unique n-grams in Candidate phrase
W_{Pi} = Learned weight of $P_i \in (0,1)$
W_{Ci} = Learned weight of $C_i \in (0,1)$

The drawback with this approach is that each incoming service note needs to be compared to the entire archive of labeled service notes. As the volume of incoming notes as well as the archive is quite large, this quickly becomes very time consuming and inefficient.

4.4 Direct Summing Approach

An alternate approach was devised to overcome the problem with the case based approach. The basis for the direct summing approach is that the weight associated with each N-gram is a signed number between 0 and 1. The sign of the number indicates whether the N-gram indicates an accept (+ve) or reject (-ve) decision and the magnitude indicates relative strength of that recommendation. A first cut approach involved summing up the N-gram weights for the new service note. If the sum was above a certain limit, an automatic assignment of 'accept' was given. Similarly, if it was below a certain limit, an automatic assignment of 'reject' was given. The intermediate band between the definitely accept and definitely reject limit was used as an indicator that the system was inconclusive in its recommendation and human intervention was required. Since only learned N-gram weights corresponding to the new service note were required to be retrieved, this process was much faster.

5 Results

A set of 6975 service notes was collected for the purpose of testing. These had been already divided into accept and reject categories by an expert. 2428 notes belonged to the 'accept' category and 4547 notes to the reject category. Fig 4 shows typical service note comments considered diagnostically relevant.

The user was allowed to specify what percentage of these would be used for training. The default value was 70% for training and 30% for testing. The results were averaged over ten cross-validation runs. Training consisted of learning weights for N-grams culled from the service notes in the training set based upon the pre-assigned labels. A partial table of results is given below for reference. In general, the system was able to correctly sort between 80% and 90% of the service notes which was considered acceptable for the business application.

Table 1. Service note classification performance

Trial	Size of N-gram	Overall accuracy %	% of accepted notes correctly classified	% of rejected notes correctly classified	% training set
1	3	84	90	80	70
2	4	87	94	83	70
3	5	81	88	77	70
4	4	88	95	84	80

The above numbers are computed only from the service notes on which the system actually gave a decision and not those that were referred for human judgment.

The 3-grams were 'reconstituted' into words by summing the significances of a word's 3-grams. This resulted in a weight allocation as shown in figure 8. As previously mentioned, this highlights that the learning procedure has been able to weigh the 'features' i.e. text fragments in a manner approximately related to their diagnostic significance.

```
CONNECTOR      2.6264
GREASE         0.4797
BEAR           0.0000
ALLOW          0.0000
COST           0.0000
TRANSMISSION   2.2856
DETECTOR       2.3476
BILLING       -3.4435
VOID          -1.7765
```

Fig. 8. Sample significances learned for words

When the words are further reconstituted into the whole text of a diagnostic case, we see different parts of the text highlighting different decisions. The words in **bold** represent fragments that suggest that the text is diagnostically useful while the words in *italics* suggests the opposite, with the underlined text being judgment neutral. There are many obvious criteria one may use for arriving at an overall decision. These can be selected based on experimental validation based on the nature of data.

OPTICAL DISK IS **MECHANICALLY JAMMED**
WILL NOT ACCEPT **DISK.REPLACE** WITH *PART FROM INVENTORY*
HP UNIT. TEST PASSED.

Fig. 9. Different fragments of text note suggest different decisions

6 Conclusions and Future Work

Textual information is often the preferred format in which diagnostic information is captured due to its simplicity. This paper has presented a simple approach towards being able to 'mine' large amounts of text service information to extract small percentage of service notes with the most valuable diagnostic information. This reduced subset may now be forwarded for further cleaning and processing. An advantage of this approach is that minimal user interaction of a yes/no nature is all that is required by a person that is not necessarily require a domain expert. As time goes by, the database of labeled phrases is continually enhanced and the quality of automated decisions progressively improves. Variable thresholds can be set to control the quality of information as well as the user interaction required. A high threshold for the diagnostic score generated by the system for new phrases will result in good quality information at the risk of excluding some valuable information, and vice versa. If the user does not wish to spend a large amount of time providing judgements, he/she may engage the automated decision process earlier and its performance will be correspondingly somewhat decreased in quality since the system has had less information to learn over. Since this approach is not domain specific, it can be quickly applied to service notes from any business to improve the quality of text-based diagnostic information available. A tool based upon this approach has been deployed within GE Medical Systems service business for the past two years.

The research that is presented in the paper was carried out with a specific practical purpose – to distinguish good text notes from bad – in a diagnostic sense, and to do so in an automated way. We believe that its relevance in the context of CBR is not so much in what was completed, but in the potential of what could be done further. The freedom of not having to worry about the natural language aspects of text data opens up new possibilities for experimentation with text and CBR. Here are some thoughts from our perspective. As industry researchers, being able to tabulate the most frequently occurring failure modes from field text data would be a great advantage. This suggests extending this from a 2-class classification to an N-class situation. Secondly, we have worked with text fragments of a fixed size – 3 and 4 in our case. Using genetic algorithms to evolve significant text phrases of variable size is another extension we would like to pursue in the future.

References

Uthurusamy, R., Means, L.G., Godden, K.S. and Lytinen, S.L., "Extracting Knowledge from Diagnostic Databases" ,1993, IEEE Expert pp.27-37.
Creecy, R.H., Masand B.M., Smith S.J., Waltz D.L., "Tradimg MIPS and Memory for Knowledge Engineering: Automatic classification of Census Returns on a Massively Parallel Supercomputer", Communications of the ACM, 1992, pp 48-64, V. 35 (8).
Varma, Anil, Wood,W.H. and Agogino, Alice M., " A Machine Learning Approach to Automated Design Classification, Association and Retrieval", Published in the Proceedings of the Fourth International Conference on Artificial Intelligence in Design, June 24-27, 1996, Stanford,CA
Liu, ZQ and Yan, F, "Case-based diagnostic systems using fuzzy neural network" , in IEEE International Conference on Neural Networks. 1995, IEEE: Perth, WA, Australia. pp. 3107-3112.
Mario Lenz, `Textual CBR and Information Retrieval -- A Comparison', in Proc. 6th German Workshop on CBR, 1998.
Wilson, D., and Bradshaw, S. (1999). CBR Textuality. In Proceedings of the Fourth UK Case-Based Reasoning Workshop
Brüninghaus, S., and Ashley, K. 1998. Developing Mapping and Evaluation Techniques for Textual Case-Based Reasoning. In Workshop Notes of the AAAI-98 Workshop on Textual CBR.

Stefanie Brüninghaus and Kevin D. Ashley (1998) Evaluation of Textual CBR Approaches. In: *Proceedings of the AAAI-98 Workshop on Textual Case-Based Reasoning (AAAI Technical Report WS-98-12)*. Pages 30-34. Madison, WI. Copyright 1998 by AAAI.

Kamal Nigam, Andrew McCallum, Sebastian Thrun, and Tom Mitchell. *Learning to Classify Text from Labeled and Unlabled Documents*. AAAI-98, 1998.

Stefanie Brüninghaus and Kevin D. Ashley (1997) Finding Factors: Learning to Classify Case Opinions Under Abstract Fact Categories. In: L. Karl Branting (editor). *Proceedings of the 6th International Conference on Artificial Intelligence and Law (ICAIL-97)*. Pages 123-131. Melbourne, Australia. Copyright 1997 by ACM, Inc.

Stefanie Brüninghaus and Kevin D. Ashley (1998) How Machine Learning Can be Beneficial for Textual Case-Based Reasoning. In: *Proceedings of the AAAI-98/ICML-98 Workshop on Learning for Text Categorization (AAAI Technical Report WS-98-05)*. Pages 71-74. Madison, WI. Copyright 1998 by AAAI.

CBR Adaptation for Chemical Formulation

Stefania Bandini and Sara Manzoni

Department of Computer Science, Systems, and Communication
University of Milan - Bicocca
via Bicocca degli Arcimboldi, 8 - 20126 - Milan (Italy)
tel +39 02 64487835 - fax +39 02 64487839
bandini,manzoni@disco.unimib.it

Abstract. Solution adaptation of previously solved cases to fit new situations is one of the basic tasks of the Case-Based Reasoning (CBR) approach for problem solving. The central issue of the paper is to present a formal computational model for the chemical formulation as innovative adaptation of previously developed products for new scenario and/or constraints in product design process. This general model (called Abstract Compound Machine - ACM) allows knowledge about chemical formulation to be explicitly represented, computed, integrated and performed in a CBR architecture. The specific domain that is presented as an example for the implementation of the ACM model regards the creation of rubber compounds. Its generality allows it to be adopted in cases of chemical formulation where basic ingredients are expressed in discrete quantities.

1 Introduction

Solution adaptation of previously solved cases to fit new situations is one of the basic tasks of the Case–Based Reasoning (CBR) approach for problem solving. The problem of defining adaptation rules is crucial in the development of the complete cycle of CBR [1], but the definition of specific rules is not a simple task. One of the most evident reasons of this difficulty lies in the very nature of the problem–solving approach addressed by CBR. Episodic and experiential knowledge is the key issue of CBR, and it largely fits domains where models cannot be formalized or created at all. Paradoxically, the development of adaptation mechanisms for CBR requires a change of perspective about the involved knowledge: from fragmentary to well formalized knowledge, in order to reproduce, in some sense, the very core ability of human problem–solvers, that is adapting previously adopted solutions to new situations. From a human viewpoint, the development of adaptation abilities is dynamical in its nature and requires many experiences to be accumulated from the solution of many problems. It is the very art of combining experiential knowledge and formal rules/models. The development of CBR systems without any form of adaptation has been successful, because the representation and retrieve process of episodic knowledge allowes the creation of several innovative methods and techniques dealing with complex knowledge domains (reasoning by analogy, similarity measurement, incremental learning, and

D.W. Aha and I. Watson (Eds.): ICCBR 2001, LNAI 2080, pp. 634–647, 2001.

so on). Adaptation is the challenge both in the development of complete performing CBR cycle and in the study of cognitive models to be computationally supported in order to handle with complex problems.

The design of products that in some step of their production process requires *chemical formulation* is a very complex problem, involving different competencies, experience (positive and negative) accumulated in the time, and a constant perspective in innovation and knowledge creation. The CBR approach in this area is very promising and a certain number of formal and application proposals have been developed [2,3,4,5,6]. This approach fits very well to the traditional tasks to be executed by all the competencies involved, and the adaptation of previously adopted solutions to new situation is the routine in their practical performance. Moreover, the storage of all the episodes representing solved cases (both negative and positive) allows the problem of *failure removal* to be tackled, and previously adopted negative solution to be retrieved, reprocessed, and adapted to new cases.

The central issue of this paper is the study of chemical formulation as innovative adaptation of previously developed products for new scenario and/or constraints in product design process. A general model for chemical formulation has been developed by the creation of the representation formalism called Abstract Compound Machine (ACM). It allows knowledge about the chemical formulation to be explicitly represented, computed, integrated, and performed in a CBR architecture. ACM is inspired by the CHAM (CHemical Abstract Machine) formalism [7]. The specific domain that will be presented as an example for the implementation of the ACM model regards the creation of rubber compounds. Its generality allows it to be adopted also in other cases of chemical formulations where basic ingredients are expressed in discrete quantities.

The general architecture of the developed CBR–based system will be outlined in the next section. In particular Subsection 2.1 presents the ACM Adapter component, supporting the adaptation step of the entire CBR cycle and performing the chemical formulation mechanism. A sample application of the approach to the problem of the chemical formulation in the design of rubber compounds for tires will be presented in Section 3.

2   General Architecture

In Figure 1 is outlined a high level representation of the CBR–based approach applied to the design of products requiring chemical formulation as adaptation of previously developed products. It can be divided into three main conceptual parts (drawn by dotted lines in the figure). Part A contains the main components devoted to the collection and the representation of cases: a dedicated user interface designed in order to access various domain knowledge containers (e.g. enterprise databases), an Indexing component which composes data and structures them into cases.

Part B is the CBR core; its main component is the Retrieval module, which computes similarity between the current problem description and all cases con-

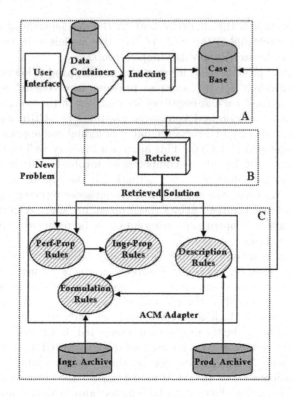

Fig. 1. The role of the ACM Adapter in the CBR–based approach

tained in the Case Base. The Retrieved Solution and the new problem description
are used in the Adaptation process (part C in Figure 1) to identify what should
be modified and what should be maintained in order to fit the old solution to
the current situation. Available ingredients descriptions and already developed
products (reported in Figure 1 as *Ingr. Archive* and *Prod. Archive*) are the main
data used during this step. The Retrieved Solution is represented through a set
of attributes, which identify and to characterize it. For instance, a subset of the
attributes describes the outcome deriving from the application of the solution to
the past problem. In the following subsection the ACM component for chemical
formulation will be illustrated.

2.1   The ACM–Based Adaptation

The main part of the ACM–based Adaptation module is dedicated to the design
of a chemical compound, that is, the generation of the chemical formulation of
a specific "recipe".

The Abstract Compound Machine (ACM) is a model created for the representation and computation of the knowledge involved in the chemical formulation of a compound. In this model, a *recipe* of n ingredients is a finite non ordered set $\{Q_1, ..., Q_n\}$, where each Q_i represents the quantity of the i-th ingredient. A given ingredient belongs to one or more families of ingredients. Each family F_k is described by a set $\{A_1^k, ..., A_m^k\}$ of attributes representing properties. Therefore, each element i of a family F_k (an ingredient) is described by a value V_{ij}^k for each of its own attributes A_j^k. If an ingredient i does not belong to the family F_k, the corresponding values V_{ij}^k are undefined. Starting from a recipe R, a *modified recipe R'* is a recipe where some quantities have been changed. A set of tolerance constants T_j^k has been introduced for the comparison of attribute values. The necessity of these constants is due to the empiric nature of attribute values and to take care of errors introduced by empirical measurement processes (e.g. lab tests measurements). Modifications follow the application of four sets of rules, where rules take the form of productions:

1. *Description Rules*, describing a product already developed whose specification is contained in some archive as a recipe according to the ACM model, that is as a vector of quantities of ingredients.
2. *Performance–Properties Rules*, defining which changes are needed in the properties of the recipe, in order to obtain a change in performance.
3. *Ingredients–Properties Rules*, defining which attributes of the ingredients of a recipe are involved in the modification of the properties of the product.
4. *Formulation Rules*, generating a modified recipe R' starting from R. Three types of formulation rules have been defined:

   – *Substitution*, replacing the quantity of an ingredient i with an equal quantity of another ingredient l of the same family F_k (chosen by the Ingredients–Properties Rules), in order to change the value of one or more attributes (V_{ij}^k):

   $$if \ (Q_i \neq 0); \ (i \in F_k); \ (l \in F_k); (|V_{ij}^k - V_{lj}^k| > T_j^k)$$

   $$then$$

   $$\{Q_1, Q_2, \ldots, Q_{i-1}, Q_i, Q_{i+1}, \ldots, Q_l, \ldots, Q_n\} \rightarrow$$

   $$\{Q_1, Q_2, \ldots, Q_{i-1}, 0, Q_{i+1}, \ldots, Q_i + Q_l, \ldots, Q_n\}$$

   – *Increase in quantity*, adding to the quantity of an ingredient a given constant U_k, defined according to the family F_k of the ingredient:

   $$if \ (i \in F_k) \ then$$

   $$\{Q_1, Q_2, \ldots, Q_{i-1}, Q_i, Q_{i+1}, \ldots, Q_n\} \rightarrow$$

   $$\{Q_1, Q_2, \ldots, Q_{i-1}, Q_i + U_k, Q_{i+1}, \ldots, Q_n\}$$

- *Reduction in quantity*, decreasing the quantity of an ingredient by a constant U_k, defined as in the previous point:

$$if\ (i \in F_k);\ (Q_i > U_k)\ then$$

$$\{Q_1, Q_2, \ldots, Q_{i-1}, Q_i, Q_{i+1}, \ldots, Q_n\} \rightarrow$$

$$\{Q_1, Q_2, \ldots, Q_{i-1}, Q_i - U_k, Q_{i+1}, \ldots, Q_n\}$$

$$if\ (i \in F_k);\ (Q_i < U_k)\ then$$

$$\{Q_1, Q_2, \ldots, Q_{i-1}, Q_i, Q_{i+1}, \ldots, Q_n\} \rightarrow$$

$$\{Q_1, Q_2, \ldots, Q_{i-1}, 0, Q_{i+1}, \ldots, Q_n\}$$

For chemical formulation the rules activation order is domain dependent and determines how the recipe is adapted to the current case. The application of this CBR–based approach to the design of tread batches for motorsports races will be described in the next section. In particular subsection 3.3 describes the ACM–based component dedicated to adaptation of rubber compounds formulation.

3   The Design of Rubber Compounds

A rubber compound (in jargon *batch*) is made by a *recipe*, a chemical formulation that determines its major properties. Each batch comprises a set of ingredients (in the case of rubber compounds for tires: artificial or natural elastomers, active fillers, accelerants, oils, and others), all of which are essential for the acquisition of the desired chemical–physical properties determining the needed performance. The evaluation of the performances of a rubber compound is not absolute, but depends on several factors. In the case of tires dedicated to car racing, for example, the most important, *characterizing each single race*, concern car set–up, road ground, geometrical profile and severity of the tracks, weather conditions, and racing team. Quite obviously, the skills of the people involved in designing motor racing tires (race engineers, tire designers and rubber compound designers) consist of their experience in the field and their knowledge about a very complex decision making problem. Since their choice has to be made for each single race (where a specific product has been designed and developed ad hoc), it is usually strongly related to performances (grip, warm–up, thermal and mechanical stability, resistance to wear) and results obtained in previous races on 'similar' tracks (usually in previous seasons of the championship, such as Sports Racing World Cup (SRWC), American Le Mans Series (ALMS), or others). Moreover, the evaluation of unsuccessful adoptions of some rubber compound (e.g., lost race) can be useful for both the creation of new future products and its adaptation in 'similar' situations, without losing information. The general problem solving mechanism used by race engineers and compound designers is strongly based on reasoning about past cases in order to solve a new case. Also, the use of *episodic knowledge* is one of the main characteristics determining the choice of the rubber compound. The modalities that allow obtaining solutions from the reasoning about past cases in this specific case are:

- *reuse* of a solution previously adopted, e.g., the same tread batch used in some previous race of a championship;
- *adaptation* of a solution previously adopted, i.e. the design of a new compound, where some elements in the recipe of the batch are modified, in order to improve its expected performances.

It is possible to roughly split into two main roles all the knowledge involved in this problem–solving process. The first concerns to capture the similarity between cases (past and current), while the second regards the adaptation of a retrieved solution to the new case (i.e., the chemical formulation of the rubber compound). We are in presence of two very different competencies in their nature. For the first one, no model can be created (if we follow the example of car racing, it is impossible to create a formal model representing the knowledge of a race engineer: a classical CBR approach is the best one for capturing the episodic knowledge characterizing this problem). For the second one, the creation of a formal model based on the chemical formulation knowledge owned by professional chemical competence is possible. On the contrary, a pure CBR approach (where each recipe is a case) does not allow capturing the core abstract and formal knowledge of the expert. Moreover, following the rubber compound example, the chemical formulation knowledge in tire production does not change if the required product design is for car racing or for large scale production (namely, cars, trucks or motorbikes).

3.1   The CBR Approach Applied to Rubber Compounds Design (P-Race System)

The general CBR architecture presented in Section 2 has been exploited in the implementation of P-Race system. It produces chemical formulation of rubber compounds supporting race engineers and compound designers in the main steps of their decisional activity concerning the adoption of rubber compounds for car racing tires (slick). Schematically, they can be divided into: analysis of past experiences on racing or testing tracks; adoption or modification of previously used rubber compounds; identification of needed properties in order to be competitive; choice of right interventions on the ingredients of rubber compounds in order to adapt the resulting recipe to the needed properties; actions towards the production process; storing all the information about races or track test to be used in the future. The P-Race system assists in a very "natural" way the knowledge process involved in this decisional cycle in a general CBR approach. Its main components are listed below (it is quite intuitive to map these components on the general architecture sketched in Figure 1).

Applying the CBR approach described in Section 2 to the problem of rubber compounds design for car racing tires we have obtained:

- a *Case Base*, where each case represents a set of domain data: for instance chronometrical measurements concerning races and trials (meaningful events) are considered in the construction of a case. As in any CBR system, the three major parts of a case are problem/situation description, solution, and outcome [8]. The outline of the problem contains descriptive information (date, time and location of an event) and a set of parameters used by the system to retrieve from the Case Base the most similar cases (the description of this set of parameters could be both quantitative and qualitative, that is, expressed by fuzzy representation). The solution for a case describes the coded recipe of the rubber compound for that case, while the outcome represents the resulting state in terms of performances obtained when the solution was applied.
- the *Case Memory Manager* able to retrieve solutions from the Case Base and to evaluate the similarity between the current case and the stored ones (see section 3.2 for more details about the similarity function). Both the solution and the outcome of a retrieved case must be controlled by the compound designer, who activates the Adaptation module.
- the *ACM Adapter*, that adapts retrieved solutions to the current problem. It activates the integration interface with the recipes archive in order to provide to the ACM component the decoded recipe expressed in terms of quantity of ingredients (*Description Rules*). That is, it modifies the recipe of the proposed rubber compound in order to improve the performance observed in the outcomes of the past case, or to obtain new performances in relation with the description of the new case (see section 3.3).

The reasoning process starts with the representation of the current problem as a case to be solved. Starting from the new description, the system examines the Case Base containing past cases already solved, and proposes a list of solutions (the most similar cases). The main task of the retrieval algorithm is to apply a function giving a measurement of similarity between cases. The list of solutions proposed by the system could, at this point, include a feasible solution for the problem at hand that could be directly applied. Otherwise, an adaptation process has to modify one of the proposed solutions. Adaptation could be necessary when the proposed solution contains ingredients no longer available for the tire production or when the past use of the solution had shown undesired outcomes.

The list of proposed solutions could, at this point, include feasible solution for the problem at hand that could be directly applied. The system supports users in feasibility evaluation, reporting in a structured way the outcomes of proposed cases. They comprise all documents associated to the case (comments filled by race engineers and drivers after race or test on track; quality-values vectors stating results in terms of performances obtained applying the solution; and so on), namely, the view of all the current conditions the user needs to make his decision on which performance must be reached. Within this framework, if some modification to the basic recipe is needed, in order to improve or obtain some desired performance, adaptation process is invoked.

3.2   The Case Memory Manager

A fuzzy approach has been integrated in the Case Memory Manager in order to index data acquired from the user in form of cases. Fuzzy rules have also an important role in the evaluation of the similarity between the current case and the stored ones. We have chosen this kind of description because the knowledge representation task of real problems needs to consider flexibility aspects. In these situations the problem description may comprise preferences of the expert between characteristics, and it may also regards incomplete, imprecise and uncertain data [9] due to nature of the problem. More details about the role of the fuzzy approach used for the development of the Case Memory Manager will be outlined in next two subsections.

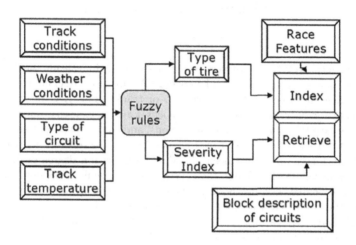

Fig. 2. The Case Memory Manager

Fuzzy Indexing of the Case Base. In Figure 2 is shown the role of the set of fuzzy rules in the flexible interpretation process of the inputs given by the race engineer. As previously mentioned, the information the race engineer considers in order to decide the tire tread to be adopted in a race mainly regards morphological features of tracks, characteristics of the track surface, thermal variation from a straight stretch to a bend (and vice versa), weather and track conditions, and temperature of the track surface.

The involved knowledge is formalized through formal models not always explicit. Moreover, conventional models are often described by using natural language, that codes experience and knowledge of all the Motorsports Department team. For instance, the formal (geometrical) description of a track is not always useful,

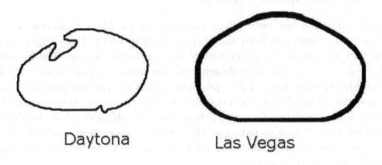

Daytona   Las Vegas

Fig. 3. Daytona and Las Vegas Circuits

while the interpretation of drivers comments several times leads the decisions to be made. It has been developed a Knowledge Acquisition (KA) module dedicated to the race engineer for the description of tracks. The KA module allows a representation of tracks decomposed in *blocks*. Each block is characterized mainly by a type (stretch, bend, chicane, and so on), and by the level of stress tires have to withstand (determined also by the road ground), expressed with numerical quantities. Fuzzy rules have been introduced to derive a degree of membership to classes of values that define the severity of the circuit. This first set of rules defines the degree to which a circuit belongs to the fuzzy set of severe circuits. Race engineers would describe morphological severe circuits as characterized by a lot of sharp curves and with a frequent changes in speed. Fuzzy sets have been constructed across these concepts. The result is a representation of the tracks that captures the experience and the knowledge of the race engineer in terms of crucial information about the track. This representation allows the user to compare tracks according to their morphological profiles. For instance the circuits of Daytona and Las Vegas (shown in figure 3) are considered by experts belonging to the same concept frame ("medium severity"). This opinion is related to the similarity of road grounds (both "quite smooth") and of the morphological profile of the track (both synthetically described as "oval circuit with a fast chicane"). So, in the selection of the proper tire for a race which took place in these locations, race engineers would consider this information and could choice a batch even if its resistance to wear is low.

A second set of fuzzy rules has been integrated in order to handle uncertainty involved in the description of the target problem. In particular, during the description of the target problem the race engineer has to give a prediction about weather and road conditions for the day of the race. These predictions influence the decision, for instance, about the type of tires (slick, rain or intermediate) to propose to racing teams. For instance, suppose a situation where, weather forecasts say that the day of the race will be moderately rainy but the race engineer predicts to have dry road ground. The race engineer indicates as "moderately rainy" a day in which the degree of sun irradiation is comprised between 15 $Watt/m^2$ and 44 $Watt/m^2$. Moreover "dry" for the road ground means that less than 16 for the percentage of humidity. Under this conditions the race engineer would decide to use slick tires. The P–Race system through fuzzy membership function for temperature, weather and track conditions can have a correct description of the target problem and propose a correct solution to the race engineer. An example of the representation with fuzzy rules for the description of the target problem features is outlined in Figure 4. For instance in the figure is shown the way in which the system interprets track conditions through the percentage of humidity of the soil, that is:

if $\%humidity \leq 16 \rightarrow$ track(dry) = 1 and track(damp) = track(wet) = 0
if $\%humidity \geq 45 \rightarrow$ track(wet) = 1 and track(damp) = track(dry) = 0
if $16 < \%humidity < 45 \rightarrow$ degree of membership for track conditions to 'dry', 'damp' and 'wet' sets are all greater than zero.

Fuzzy Retrieval of Similar Cases. Usually, a Case–Based Reasoner must find a set of cases similar to the target problem. Indeed most CBR systems are based on similarity relations between the target and the cases. These relations are vague by nature. In the CBR cycle, during the analysis of the similarity among cases (Initially Match Process during the Retrieve Step [8]), crisp classification methods can not always be used in order to improve the performance and the efficiency of the CBR system. The retrieval of previously solved problems similar to the current one is a two–step process. The Initially Matching process can be described as a function with a domain represented by the Case Base and the target problem specification, and a co–domain represented by the collection of cases with severity index belonging to the same set of values as the target problem (three–valued severity range has been defined for this purpose: low, medium and high severity). The task of this function is to filter the Case Base and to isolate interesting cases. During this step it is performed a reduction of the set of cases to be compared to the current case in the second step of the similarity computation (*Similarity Function*). In order to compute this function, Similarity Metrics have been developed. A fuzzy approach is introduced also in this step of the CBR cycle, in order to perform a method for the measurement of similarity among cases. The main concern in the approach to the design of the similarity algorithm regards the implementation of the membership function. It has as inputs two cases (the target problem and another case). It computes the Similarity Degree between the two cases as a value between 0 and 1. More in detail, the Similarity Function between the case $c = (f_1^c, f_2^c, \ldots, f_n^c)$ and the target problem $t = (f_1^t, f_2^t, \ldots, f_n^t)$ is given by the weighted sum

$$\sum_{i=1}^{n} \frac{w_i \cdot SIM(f_i^t, f_i^c)}{\sum_{i=1}^{n} w_i} \tag{1}$$

where w_i is the weight for the i-th feature. It can assume two values:

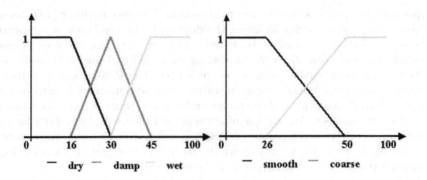

Fig. 4. Membership functions for track conditions and road ground

MatchWeight, if $SIM(f_i^t, f_i^c)$ is greater than a *Similarity Threshold* and *NoMatchWeight* otherwise. A *NoValueWeight* has also been introduced for features with value not specified by the user. *MatchWeight*, *NoMatchWeight*, *NoValueWeight* and *Similarity Threshold* are constants. $SIM(f_i^t, f_i^c)$ is the measurement of the difference between the i-th feature of the target problem and the i-th feature of the compared case. To compute this value, the system builds a gaussian curve with mean value f_i^t and fixed standard deviation σ:

$$SIM(f_i^t, x) = e^{-\frac{(x-f_i^t)^2}{\sigma^2}} \qquad (2)$$

$SIM(f_i^t, f_i^c)$ is the value of the gaussian curve for f_i^c.

3.3 ACM Adapter

As previously mentioned, suggested solutions often require adaptation in order to be used for a new situation. Materials evolution, minor but not trivial differences in the current situation or unsatisfying results (e.g. bad race times due to not perfect tire) are the main motivations of this requirement. The adaptation step of the CBR cycle is represented by the invocation of the ACM Adapter component (Figure 1). It receives as input the recipe/solution of the retrieved case and the performance that the race engineer would like to improve. The core task of this component is to provide the new chemical formulation applying ACM-like rules and producing the entire new recipe.

Chemical formulation of rubber compounds can be represented according to the ACM model as a recipe. Each element of the ACM representation identifies the quantity of a compound ingredient. All the rules, the consequent actions and the execution procedure of rules have been designed and implemented after knowledge acquisition interviews involving Pirelli Tires experts. The general structure of knowledge representation following the ACM model is sketched below.

- A code of a *recipe* represents a rubber compound (e.g. HSRXX);
- A not ordered set of quantity of ingredients represents the recipe associated to each code (e.g. {100, 20, 1.2, ..., 5});
- Each element of the set represents quantity value of an ingredient belonging to the recipe and refers to standard measurements;
- Ingredients are classified into families (polymer, resin, oil, filler, and so on);
- A specific set of attributes characterizes each family (in the case of the 'oil' family some attributes are Viscosity, Transition Glass and Hysteresis Level), and for each attribute related values are assigned. As a consequence, each ingredient belonging to a family is represented in term of attribute/value pairs.

Compounds adaptation follows the application of ACM rules. Rules implementation has been developed in a Java production rules environment. The knowledge base has been partitioned into *knowledge sources* corresponding to ACM rules (marked by ovals in Figure 1). As shown in Figure 5, knowledge sources activation starts from the application of Description Rules, that split the coded batch representing the solution for the retrieved case into the quantities of its ingredients. This step invokes the integration interface to Pirelli Tires Archive. Then, the Performance–Properties Rules knowledge source is activated, in order to determine the needed properties of the product starting from the required performance. From the global properties of the product, the Ingredients–Properties Rules knowledge source finds out which ingredients are involved in order to obtain a variation of the properties satisfying the required performance. Then the Formulation Rules knowledge source formulates the modified recipe applying Substitution, Increase in quantity or Decrease in quantity Rules.

To conclude, some sample rules developed for the chemical formulation of rubber compounds for car racing are listed below in natural language:

- *Description Rules*:
  ```
  if compound(HSRXX)
  then recipe(get recipe(HSRXX))
  ```
  ('it retrieves from the enterprise product archive the chemical formulation for compound HSRXX and produces the representation that will be used by the others sets of rules').
- *Performance–Properties Rules*:
  ```
  if desired_performance(increase_thermal_stability)
  then desired_property(high_increase_hysteresis)
  ```
  ('in order to increase thermal stability, hysteresis must be decreased').
- *Ingredients–Properties Rules*:
  ```
  if desired_property(high_increase_hysteresis)
  then interested_ingredient(polymer)
  and interested_property(transition_glass)
  ```
  ('in order to increase hysteresis, transition glass of polymer is involved').
- *Substitution Rules*, one of the types of *Formulation Rules*:
  ```
  if higher(transition_glass, new_polymer, old_polymer)
  ```

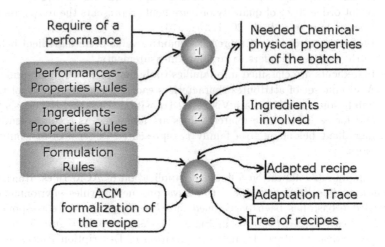

Fig. 5. Rules activation order

then insert(new_polymer) and delete(old_polymer)
('if it is available a polymer which could increase hysteresis more than the
one now present, apply substitution').
- *Increase in quantity*, another type of *Formulation Rules*:
if quantity(ingredient, q) and increase(hysteresis,
ingredient)
then increase_quantity(ingredient, q)
('if the recipe contains an ingredient which could increase hysteresis,
increase its quantity').

4   Concluding Remarks

The chemical formulation model proposed here as adapter of a CBR system has
been applied in the development of a real industrial application: the *P–Race system*, a Case–Based Reasoning system developed for the Motorsports Department
of Pirelli Tires where it is currently in use (for more details about application
benefits of P–Race see [6]). Nowadays, P–Race supports the decision making
process for the main championships where Pirelli Tires takes part. The chemical
formulation component has been adopted after an experimental campaign carried out in order to test the quality of system responses based on past solutions.
The campaign was structured into two stages. In the first one, the chemical formulations (recipes) suggested by the system have been tested on a set of 250
cases. Cases have been selected from two entire championships (about 30 races

from American Le Mans Series, Ferrari Challange and Sports Racing World Championship), focusing on some of the most competitive teams (Ferrari 333 SP, Riley & Scott, Porsche GT3R, Lola). The recipes adopted by the Motorsport Dept. in these real cases have been compared with those proposed by the system. The suggestions about the adoption of some ingredients of the recipes satisfied experts and no macroscopic mistakes have been detected. This first stage also allowed the tuning of adaptation rules to be completed.

The second stage of the campaign has been used in order to evaluate the system support to race engineers and compound designers in their decision making processes about tires selection and chemical formulation. The second stage was carried out during the same championships and the results have been judged very good.

The future development of the system will include the integration of P–Race with software systems devoted to the acquisition and the description of track data with telemetric devices in order to support rallies. The general ACM model will be used for the design of rubber compounds in large–scale production of tires dedicated to trucks.

References

1. D. B. Leake, *Combining Rules and Cases to Learn Case Adaptation*, Proc. of the Seventeenth Annual Conference of the Cognitive Science Society, 1995.
2. M.L. Maher, M. Balachandran, D.M. Zhang, *Case–Based Reasoning in Design*, Laurence Erlbaum Ass. Pu., Hove, UK, 1985
3. K. Börner, *CBR for Design*, in M. Lenz, B. Bartsch-Spörl, H. Burkhard, S. Wess (Eds.), Case–Based Reasoning Technology, Lecture Notes in Artificial Intelligence 1400, Springer, pp 201-233, 1998.
4. W. Cheetham, J. Graf, *Case–Based Reasoning in Color Matching*, in D.B. Leake, E. Plaza (Eds.), Case–Based Reasoning Research and Development, Proceedings of the 2nd International Conference on Case–Based Reasoning, Springer-Verlag, Berlin, 1997.
5. S. Craw, N. Wiratunga, R. Rowe, *Case–Based Design for Tablet Formulation*, Proceedings of the 4th European Workshop on Case–Based Reasoning, Springer-Verlag, Berlin, pp 358-369, 1998.
6. S. Bandini, S. Manzoni, *A Support System Based on CBR for the Design of Rubber Compounds in Motor Racing*, 5th European Workshop on Case–Based Reasoning, Trento 2000, LNCS/LNAI 1898, Springer Verlag, Berlin, 2000.
7. G.Berry, G.Boudol, *The Chemical Abstract Machine*,TCS 96, Elsevier, 1992, 217-248
8. J. Kolodner, *Case–Based Reasoning*, Morgan Kaufmann Pu., San Mateo (CA), 1993.
9. M. Jaczynski and B. Trousse. Fuzzy logic for the retrieval step of a case–based reasoner. *Proceedings Second European Conference on Case–Based Reasoning*, pages 313–322, 1994.

A Case-Based Reasoning Approach for Due-Date Assignment in a Wafer Fabrication Factory

Pei-Chann Chang[1], Jih-Chang Hsieh[1], and T. Warren Liao[2]

[1] Industrial Engineering and Management Department
Yuan Ze University, Nei-Li, Taoyuan, Taiwan
iepchang@saturn.yzu.edu.tw
[2] Industrial and Manufacturing System Engineering Department
Louisiana State University
Baton Rouge, Louisiana, USA
ieliao@unix1.sncc.lsu.edu

Abstract. This study explores a new application of Case-Based Reasoning (CBR) in the due-date assignment problem of the wafer fabrication factory. Owing to the complexity of the wafer fabrication, the manufacturing processes of the wafer are very complicated and time-consuming. Thus, the due-date assignment of each order presents a challenging problem to the production planning and scheduling people. Since the product of each order is closely related to the products manufactured before, the CBR approach provides a good tool for us to apply it to the due-date assignment problem. The CBR system could potentially replace the human decision in the estimation of the due-date. Therefore, a CBR system is developed in this study using the similarity coefficient of each order with previous orders. The experimental results show that the proposed approach is very effective and comparable with a neural network approach.

1. Introduction

The manufacturing processes of the wafer are very complicated and time-consuming. The processing steps of each wafer depend on the layout of workstations, production capacity of the shop floor, types of orders. We assume that the readers are somewhat familiar with the production steps of wafer manufacturing and the details are omitted. Basically, the wafer manufacturing processes can be divided into two sections, i.e., the front-end and the back-end processes. In the front-end, bare wafers are processed and packaged. A flowchart of the basic front-end processes is described in Figure 1.

Fig. 1. Basic Front-End Processes

In the front-end processes, they include (1) photolithography, (2) thermal processes, (3) implantation, (4) chemical vapor deposition, (5) etching, (6) physical vapor deposition, (7) chemical mechanical polishing, (8) process diagnostics and control (metrology), and (9) cleaning. The production steps introduced above are just

D.W. Aha and I. Watson (Eds.): ICCBR 2001, LNAI 2080, pp. 648-659, 2001.

a step-by-step process. Real floor shop manufacturing processes are more complicated with many detailed processing procedures.

After the front-end processes, wafers are fed into the back-end processes. A simple flowchart of the back-end processes is also shown in Figure 2.

Fig. 2. Basic Back-End Processes

The main production steps in the back-end include (1) test, (2) wafer dicing, (3) die attach, (4) wire bonding, and (5) encapsulation.

The production characteristics of wafer factories are different from the traditional job shops in the following characteristics: (1) reentry, (2) rework, (3) lot sizing, (4) common machines, (5) work-in-process (WIP) control, (6) random yield, (7) multi-function machines, and (8) diversities of machine types. Owing to the complicated production steps and attributes, due-date assignment becomes a great challenge to the production planning and scheduling department.

From the above description, we know that the due-date of each product in the wafer fabrication factory is greatly affected by the following factors: (1) routing of the product, (2) order quantities, (3) current shop loading, (4) jobs in the queue of the bottleneck machine, and so on. Traditionally, the due-date of each order is assigned by the production planning and control people based on their knowledge of the manufacturing processes. However, they may not be able to take all these factors into consideration. Therefore, the CBR approach provides a very encouraging motivation for the due-date assignment problem in the wafer fabrication factory. Moreover, as we know, backpropagation neural network (BPN) is also very prevailing in forecasting. Finally, experimental results obtained from CBR approach and BPN will be compared and concluded.

2. Literature Review

Recently, case-based-reasoning (CBR) has become very popular for a variety of application areas. Successful applications as reported by Watson and Marir [10] include areas such as academic demonstrators; knowledge acquisition; legal reasoning; expansion of anomalies; diagnosis; arbitration; design; planning; repair and adaptation; and tutoring.

In due-date assignment, production planning and scheduling people usually estimates the flowtime of each order by the product they produced before. If the specification of the product is exactly the same, then a flowtime can be derived and the due-date of the product is assigned. However, the status of the shop floor such as jobs in system, shop loading and jobs in the bottleneck machine,…, etc., may not be all the same. As a result, the estimation of the due-date could not be accurate and subject to errors.

In this study, we will adopt the case-based reasoning approach to solve the problem that originally is provided by human experts in experience-intensive application domains. Two innovative CBR researches and applications developed, namely INRECA in Auriol, et al. [1] and Bisio and Malabocchia [2], are the major driving forces to enable us to perform this new application.

In the early periods, different rules as listed in Cheng and Gupta [3] have been proposed for due-date assignment, i.e., TWK (total processing time), NOP (number of operations), CON (constant allowance), and RDM (random allowance) rules. As soon as the processing times are estimated by these rules, the due-date is equal to the order release time plus the estimated processing time, i.e.,

$$d_i = r_i + p_i \qquad (1)$$

where d_i is the due-date of the ith order, r_i and p_i are the release time and processing time of order i respectively.

Many other discussions are concentrated on the relationships between the shop status information and due-dates. Several significant effective factors, for example, jobs-in-queue (JIQ), jobs-in-system (JIS), delay-in-queue (DIQ), and processing plus waiting times (PPW) were explored. Conway, *et al.* [4] revealed that due-date rules incorporating job characteristics performed better than that which ignored job characteristics.

Recent successful applications of the CBR system in bankruptcy prediction by Jo *et al.* [6], document retrieval system by Watson and Watson [11], identifying failure mechanisms by Liao, et al. [7], and engineering sales support by Watson and Gardingen [9] also inspire this research. Finnie and Witting [5] applied the case-based reasoning technique to the software estimation which performs somewhat superior to the regression models based on the same data.

A CBR system is proposed to estimate the due-date of a new order by retrieving the features influential to flowtime from the previous order according to the global similarity coefficient in measuring the closeness between these two orders. Therefore, a similar case of the order to be processed can be retrieved and a new due-date of the order can be assigned.

3. Overview of the Simulated Wafer Fabrication Factory

Owing to the complexity of the production process, the history data of each order is only partially available in the factory. Information for the previous orders such as the JIQ, JIS, and waiting time, is not that easy to be collected on the shop floor. Therefore, a simulation model is built to simulate the manufacturing process of a real wafer fabrication factory. Then, the case base can be derived from the shop floor status collected from the simulation model.

The basic configuration of the simulated wafer factory is the same as a real-world wafer fabrication factory which is located in the Science Park of Hsin-Chu, Taiwan, R.O.C.. There are 66 single-server or multiple-server workstations in the factory. The program of the simulated wafer fabrication model is coded using the Microsoft Visual FoxPro 6.0. The summarized data about the workstations are given in Table 1, and the basic information of each workstation include: (1) workstation number, (2) mean processing time (hour), (3) number of lots per batch, and (4) number of machines in each workstation. The routing of a sample product is shown in Table 2. The gray-shaded cells (i.e., MT39) represent the workstation of furnace. As we can observe from the routing, the sample product passes through the furnace 9 times. The singular production characteristic "reentry" of the semiconductor industry is clearly reflected in the example. It also shows the difficulty for the production planning and scheduling people to provide an accurate due-date for the product with such a complicated routing.

Table 1. Parameter Values of the Simulated Wafer Fabrication Factory

Workstation No.	MPT (Hour)	Lots per Batch	# of Machines	Workstation No.	MPT (Hour)	Lots per Batch	# of Machines
MT01	0.31	1	2	MT34	0.22	1	1
MT02	0.28	1	4	MT35	5.52	6	1
MT03	0.28	1	9	MT36	1.4	1	4
MT04	1.65	6	4	MT37	1.77	1	2
MT05	0.36	1	6	MT38	1.16	1	6
MT06	1.7	6	3	MT39	1.15	1	5
MT07	3.3	6	2	MT40	0.23	6	2
MT08	0.31	1	3	MT41	0.26	1	2
MT09	1.1	1	4	MT42	1.68	1	6
MT10	0.77	1	6	MT43	0.63	1	2
MT11	1.65	1	2	MT44	0.23	1	3
MT12	0.26	1	3	MT45	4.88	6	3
MT13	0.23	6	3	MT46	1.35	1	1
MT14	2.4	1	2	MT47	1.32	1	6
MT15	0.45	1	3	MT48	13.3	6	3
MT16	4.37	6	1	MT49	4.01	1	2
MT17	0.27	1	2	MT50	0.29	1	8
MT18	1.3	1	1	MT51	3.15	6	2
MT19	0.29	1	2	MT52	0.25	1	1
MT20	5.17	6	1	MT53	0.32	1	8
MT21	5.88	6	5	MT54	0.38	1	2
MT22	0.31	1	6	MT55	1.49	1	6
MT23	0.29	1	10	MT56	0.77	1	1
MT24	5.31	6	1	MT57	0.33	1	2
MT25	0.81	1	3	MT58	1.29	1	1
MT26	1.22	6	1	MT59	0.56	1	1
MT27	0.25	1	6	MT60	0.93	1	2
MT28	0.9	1	3	MT61	0.28	6	3
MT29	0.55	1	2	MT62	0.3	1	2
MT30	0.63	1	2	MT63	7.87	6	4
MT31	1.15	1	8	MT64	4.23	6	1
MT32	1.18	1	1	MT65	1.58	1	1
MT33	6.6	6	1	MT66	0.35	1	2

Besides the parameter values and routing of products, there are some basic assumptions about this model, which include:
(1) The machines within a workstation are all identical.
(2) The average production capacity is 20000 pieces of wafers per month.
(3) The mean time between order's arrival follows exponential distribution with parameter λ equals to 144 hours.
(4) All orders are processed and distributed to available machines according to production steps and no preemption is allowed.

Table 2. Routing of a Sample Product

Steps	WS No.	Steps	WS No.	Steps	WS No.	Steps	WS No.	Steps	WS No.
1	MT01	41	MT05	81	MT03	121	MT57	161	MT06
2	MT07	42	MT66	82	MT27	122	MT13	162	MT59
3	MT63	43	MT03	83	MT53	123	MT23	163	MT39
4	MT12	44	MT08	84	MT61	124	MT52	164	MT02
5	MT62	45	MT07	85	MT09	125	MT23	165	MT27
6	MT17	46	MT24	86	MT21	126	MT08	166	MT36
7	MT02	47	MT16	87	MT66	127	MT66	167	MT03
8	MT02	48	MT07	88	MT58	128	MT03	168	MT44
9	MT15	49	MT16	89	MT66	129	MT39	169	MT05
10	MT08	50	MT39	90	MT61	130	MT02	170	MT03
11	MT27	51	MT02	91	MT33	131	MT53	171	MT04
12	MT54	52	MT53	92	MT61	132	MT34	172	MT41
13	MT05	53	MT34	93	MT64	133	MT27	173	MT62
14	MT66	54	MT27	94	MT16	134	MT31	174	MT41
15	MT03	55	MT43	95	MT61	135	MT44	175	MT02
16	MT29	56	MT03	96	MT64	136	MT44	176	MT40
17	MT50	57	MT05	97	MT39	137	MT03	177	MT05
18	MT39	58	MT08	98	MT02	138	MT27	178	MT39
19	MT02	59	MT66	99	MT53	139	MT53	179	MT02
20	MT30	60	MT03	100	MT34	140	MT28	180	MT30
21	MT05	61	MT27	101	MT27	141	MT49	181	MT05
22	MT66	62	MT53	102	MT46	142	MT28	182	MT08
23	MT03	63	MT30	103	MT03	143	MT57	183	MT66
24	MT07	64	MT61	104	MT05	144	MT13	184	MT14
25	MT48	65	MT64	105	MT66	145	MT50	185	MT21
26	MT08	66	MT58	106	MT03	146	MT23	186	MT66
27	MT23	67	MT61	107	MT25	147	MT52	187	MT05
28	MT07	68	MT51	108	MT61	148	MT23	188	MT08
29	MT35	69	MT39	109	MT16	149	MT28	189	MT03
30	MT27	70	MT02	110	MT39	150	MT39		
31	MT53	71	MT55	111	MT02	151	MT02		
32	MT07	72	MT05	112	MT53	152	MT53		
33	MT20	73	MT66	113	MT27	153	MT34		
34	MT18	74	MT03	114	MT43	154	MT27		
35	MT08	75	MT39	115	MT03	155	MT15		
36	MT07	76	MT02	116	MT05	156	MT08		
37	MT35	77	MT53	117	MT66	157	MT27		
38	MT08	78	MT27	118	MT03	158	MT65		
39	MT07	79	MT43	119	MT61	159	MT03		
40	MT35	80	MT03	120	MT38	160	MT44		

(5) The dispatching rule is first in first out (FIFO).

(6) The basic processing unit is "lot" and each lot contains 25 pieces of wafers. Each workstation may process the multiples of lot at a time.

(7) Pull production system is assumed.

(8) The system will not stop until all the orders are processed.

(9) The system output includes information such as order no, order type, order production quantity, arrival time, maximum queuing length, average queuing length, maximum waiting time, average waiting time, makespan, flowtime, work-in-process, bottleneck utilization, total works, number of operations, jobs-in-queue, jobs-in-system. These output information is collected for the purpose of flowtime forecasting.

The time series plot of 100 simulated flowtime data is shown in Figure 3. As we can observe here, the pattern of the flowtime is not stable and very non-stationary. The traditional approach by human decision is very inaccurate and very prone to failure when the shop status is totally different even for the same product.

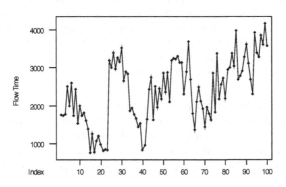

Fig. 3. Time Series Plot of Flow Time

4. Case-Based Reasoning Due-Date Assignment Model

A CBR based due-date assignment model is developed and compared with a back-propagation neural network in this study. These comparisons will be shown in Sec 5.1.

4.1 CBR Model

CBR is one of the rising approaches for designing expert systems. There are many advantages of CBR approach, the most important feature of which is that it resembles the way people solve problems in the real world. Typically, there are five steps in CBR:

1. presentation of a new case
2. retrieval of the most similar cases from the case base

3. adaptation of the selected cases
4. validation of the current solution given by CBR
5. updating of the system by adding the verified solution to the case base

The above-mentioned steps constitute the CBR cycle.

In this study, CBR is used to forecast the flowtime of each order. Therefore, historical analogous cases are often used to forecast the flowtime of new cases. As discussed earlier in section 2, there are many factors (i.e. order's attributes) may affect the flow time of each order. Some are influential to the flow time but some are not. Key factors affected the flow time significantly must be first identified with respect to the viewpoint of effectiveness. Backward elimination of regression analysis is a well-known tool to identify the influential factors. Once the influential factors are identified, the CBR due-date assignment procedure is implemented as follows.

4.1.1 Case Representation

The case of each order is represented by its influential attributes. For example, an order with average queuing length 1.043, processing time 331.07, jobs-in-system 58, job-in-queue 7, the shop loading 80% and flowtime 1729.38 can be represented using the row vector [1.043, 331.07, 58, 7, 80%, 1729.38]. Therefore, the case base will be a list of such vectors including all the orders received earlier with their product type and shop status information stored in the database.

4.1.2 Case Retrieval by Similarity Measurement

Analogous cases are retrieved to forecast order's flowtime on the basis of similarity. Hence, the similarity measurement should be defined first. To measure the similarity of the new order with the previous orders, a distance-based approach is applied. The measurement calculates the Euclidian distance between case $a = (a_1, a_2, \cdots\cdots, a_n)$ and case $b = (b_1, b_2, \cdots\cdots, b_n)$ as follows:

$$\overline{ab} = \sqrt{\sum_{i=1}^{n}(a_i - b_i)^2} \tag{2}$$

That is, the inter-case distances are measured using this formula. As we can observe that the small distances lead to the large similarities. There exists an inverse proportion relationship between the distances and similarities. But we hope the similarities can be reflected in the weights of combining influential attributes to forecast the flowtime. Thus, a simple inverse transformation should be taken to the distances. The exponential decay function is used to transform the distance into similarity. The representation of the exponential decay function is shown as (3)

$$S_{ab} = e^{-\overline{ab}}, \text{ for all } \overline{ab} \tag{3}$$

4.1.3   Generating a Forecast of the Flowtime

Jo et al. [5] derived the model from the context model of classification proposed by Medin and Schaffer [8]. In the model, the expected target value (TV_t) of the target case is obtained as follows:

$$E(TV_t | \{S_{tb}\}_{t=1,n}) = \sum_{b=1}^{n} P(TV_k = TV_b | \{S_{tb}\}_{t=1,n}) \; TV_b$$

$$= \sum_{b=1}^{n} \left(\frac{S_{tb}}{\sum_{i=1}^{n} S_{ti}} \right) TV_b \qquad (4)$$

Note that n is the number of cases selected to generate the forecasts; S_{tb} is the similarity between the new target t and the base case b; and TV_b is the flowtime of base b. The similarity ratio (i.e. similarity of each base case with the new target case over the sum of the similarities of all the cases) is used as the case's weight in the model. Thus, the forecast on the target value of the new case (TV_t) is represented as a linear combination of the target values of base cases, weighted in proportion to their relative similarities to the new case. The overall flow of the CBR due-date assignment model is depicted in Figure 4.

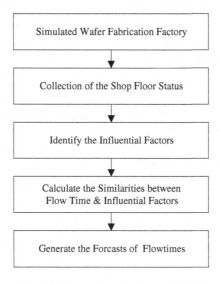

Fig. 4. CBR Due-Date Assignment Model

4.2 Backpropagation Neural Network

BPN is the most commonly used technique to apply neural network to the forecasting problem. The BPN is actually a gradient steepest descent method to minimize the total square error of the output computed by the net. The training of BPN includes three stages: (1) the feedforward of the input training pattern, (2) the calculation of the associated error, and (3) the adjustment of the weights. System parameters in the three-layer BPN should be set in the initial step and these values are listed in the following table.

Table 3. Architecture and Parameters of the BPN

Number of input nodes	According to experimental settings
Number of hidden layers	One
Number of nodes in hidden layer	The number of input nodes
Number of output nodes	One
Learning rule	Delta rule
Activation function	Sigmoid function

5. Experimental Results

The simulated wafer fabrication factory was executed and 900 data sets were collected from a steady-state simulated factory. Each datum provides information about order's attributes include number, type, production quantity, arrival time, maximum queuing length, average queuing length, maximum waiting time, average waiting time, makespan, flowtime, processing time, TWK, NOP, JIQ, JIS...etc.

The backward elimination of regression analysis is a common used tool to identify influential factors. Input the attribute "flowtime" as the response variable and the remaining attributes are taken as the explanatory variables. The backward elimination will take the least influential variable out and repeat the elimination steps till all the variables are influential to the response variable. After the iterative steps implemented with the aid of the statistical software "Minitab", eight variables are identified as the influential ones. They are order quantity, maximum queuing length, average queuing length, total queuing length, average shop workload when the order arrived, WIP, processing time, and JIQ.

Since the influential factors are identified, the cases can be represented by these influential variables and the flowtime. Take the first output record as an example, i.e., [7, 12, 1.043, 194, 10.606, 17812, 331.07, 1828.82, 1729.38]. To reduce the variation caused by the unit of measurement, data are pre-processed by normalization. Among the 900 data sets, 600 sets are randomly selected as the training data and the remaining ones are used as the test data to check the generalization capability in the BPN algorithm. The CBR approach uses the same 600 data sets of the training data as the base cases and the 300 test data sets are regarded as the new cases to be forecasted. Finally, the root mean square error (RMSE) is performed to measure the performances of the CBR and BPN approaches.

5.1 Numerical Comparisons of BPN and CBR

Three rules, TWK, NOP, and JIQ are used to evaluate the performances of CBR and BPN. In the TWK rule, cases are consisted of the factors "total work" and "flowtime". In the NOP rule, cases are consisted of the factors " number of operation" and "flowtime". And in the JIQ rule cases are consisted of the factors 'job-in-queue" and "flowtime". For the CBR approach, randomly selected 600 data sets are taken as the base case and top 20 similar cases are retrieved for case adaptation to forecast the flowtime of the remaining 300 data sets. The estimation errors depend on the sample size used for prediction (i.e., the number of retrieved cases). To study the performance of BPN based on the equal sample size, 20 data sets are randomly selected as the training data for BPN. With the aid of the software NeuralWork Professional II, the BPN algorithm is employed to forecast the flowtime. The forecasting accuracy and results are shown in Table 4. The differences (Diff (%)) of RMSE between BPN and CBR were calculated. As we can see in Table 4, the CBR is more accuracy than the BPN. The results also reflect that the CBR method is more efficient than BPN. This is an encouraging outcome to the CBR due-date assignment approach. Small prediction error (RMSE) is usually required in the forecasting problem. Consequently, CBR seems more powerful in forecasting the flowtime than the BPN does.

Table 4. Comparison II of BPN and CBR

RMSE	BPN	CBR	Diff (%)
TWK	611.74	590.49	3.60%
NOP	782.23	617.58	26.66%
JIQ	543.01	466.00	16.53%

5.2 Optimal Design of CBR Model

The implementation of CBR model follows the steps that are introduced from subsection 4.1.1 to 4.1.3. The evaluation in last section demostrates the effectiveness of CBR. However, the idea coming from the moving average mothod indicates that the number of retrieved cases will affect the smoothness of the forecasts. Usually, large number of retrieved cases leads to smooth forecasting behavior and small number of retrieved comes out the sharply varied forecasts. Therefore, another topic to be addressed is " how many cases should be retrieved? ". The experiment is designed as using k similar cases to forecast the flowtimes of new cases. The top k similar cases of the base case consisted of eight identified influential variables and the flowtime. The values of k are 1, 2, 3, 4, 5, 6, 7, 8, 9, 10, 20, 30, 40, and 50. The value of k is selected with the smallest RMSE. The exhaustive enumeration is used to examine fourteen specified numbers of retrieved cases and the results are plotted in Figure 5. And the numerical results are shown in Table 5. The best performance is 231.00 with retrieving seven cases to forecast the flowtime.

Since the optimal number of retrieved cases is determined, we turn back to the comparisons of BPN and CBR in Subsec. 5.1. BPN algorithm will randomly select 7 data sets for training the network to minimize the total squared error of the output. As soon as the network is well-trained, the test data will be recalled to monitor the training process to reach maximum generalization capability. The RMSE of test data is recorded in Table 6. Top 7 similar cases will be retrieved in the base case to forecast the flowtime of new cases in the CBR due-date approach. For comparison with the BPN algorithm, the RMSE is also recorded in Table 6. It has clearly shown in Table 6 that when the k (number of retrieved cases) is varied, the performance of CBR seems more stable than BPN. On average, the Diff(%) of using different k causes great fluctuation in forecasting by BPN. Therefore, it reveals that CBR is a robust tool in this study.

Table 5. The Corresponding RMSE of # of Retrieved Cases

No.	# of retrieved cases	RMSE
1	1	304.28
2	2	267.66
3	3	255.97
4	4	242.08
5	5	236.90
6	6	231.90
7	7	231.00
8	8	235.14
9	9	234.01
10	10	235.69
11	20	253.47
12	30	266.02
13	40	276.45
14	50	291.33

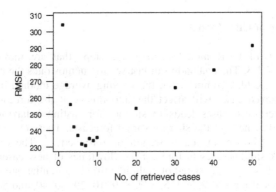

Fig. 5. The Relationship of # of retrieved cases and RMSE

Table 6. Comparison III of CBR and BPN

RMSE	BPN			CBR		
k	7	20	Diff(%)	7	20	Diff(%)
TWK	634.47	611.74	3.72%	629.58	590.49	6.62%
NOP	837.31	782.23	7.04%	641.64	617.58	3.90%
JIQ	678.77	543.01	25.00%	485.53	466.00	4.19%

6. Conclusions and Future Directions

This implementation has shown how a due-date assignment CBR system can be created using similarity measurement and case adaptive method. And the optimal number of cases to be retrieved in this study is determined. Traditionally, the due-date is assigned by the production planning and scheduling people. The department only takes the product specification into consideration to assign the due-date by adding the estimated flowtime with the release date. However, the flowtime is very much dependent on the current shop status such as the TWK, NOP, JIQ, and shop loading. That is the reason why most of the due-date assigned cannot be met by production department. Using the CBR approach as proposed in this study, the performance is comparable to that of the BPN algorithm. This is a very encouraging start for this study and we suggest that the flowtime adaptive method can be further improved by a better design of the CBR model or the fuzzy adaptive network. Since the shop loading can be expressed by using light, middle or heavy, and the similarity of the product can be discriminated by the number of critical resources passed instead of the total number of processing steps. In addition, more sophisticated learning algorithm can be applied in the reuse process. Also, we would like to explore more applications of CBR system in different manufacturing areas.

References

[1]   Auriol, E., Wess, S., Manago, M., Althoff, D-D., and Traphoner, R. Integrating Induction and Case-Based Reasoning: Methodological Approach and First Evaluations, Proc. 1st International Conference on Case-based Reasoning, Springer Verlag Berlin. 1995.

[2]   Bisio, R. and Malabocchia, F. Cost Estimation of Software Projects Through Case-Based Reasoning, Proc. 1st International Conference on Case-based Reasoning, Springer Verlag Berlin. (1995).

[3]   Cheng, T. C., and Gupta, E. Survey of Scheduling Research Involving Due-Date Determination Decisions. European Journal of Operational Research, 36(11):1017-1026, 1985..

[4]   Conway, R.W., Maxwell, W. L., and Miller, L. W. Theory of Scheduling. Massachusetts: Addison-Wesley 1967.

[5]   Finnie, G. R. and Witting, G. E. Estimating Software Development Effort with Case-Based Reasoning. Proc. 2st International Conference on Case-based Reasoning, Springer Verlag. (1995).

[6]   Jo, H., Han, I., and Lee, H. Bankruptcy Prediction Using Case-Based Reasoning, Neural Networks and Discriminant Analysis. Expert Systems and Applications, 13: 97-108, 1997.

[7]   Liao, T. W., Zhang, Z. M., and Mount, C.R. A Case-Based Reasoning System for Identifying Failure Mechanisms, Engineering Applications of Artificial Intelligence 13:199-213, 2000.

[8]   Medin, D. L. and Schaffer, M. M. Context Theory of Classification Learning. Psychological Review, 85:207-238, 1978.

[9]   Watson, I. and Gardingen, D., A Distributed Cased-Based Reasoning Application for Engineering Sales Support, In, Proc. 16th Int. Joint Conf. on Artificial Intelligence (IJCAI-99), Vol. 1:600-605, 1999.

[10] Watson, and Marir. Case-based reasoning: A Review. Knowledge Engineering Review. 9(4): 327-354, 1994.

[11] Watson, I. and Watson, H. CAIRN: A Case-Based Document Retrieval System, In, Proc. of the 3rd United Kingdom Case-Based Reasoning Wrokshop. University of Manchester, Filer, N & Watson, I (Eds) 1997.

DubLet: An Online CBR System for Rental Property Recommendation

Gareth Hurley and David C. Wilson

Smart Media Institute, Department of Computer Science
University College Dublin, Belfield, Dublin 4, Ireland
hurleyg@netsoc.ucd.ie,david.wilson@ucd.ie

Abstract. Searching for accommodation in Dublin's fast-moving rental market can be a difficult and frustrating process. Ideally, the accommodation seeker would have access to a support system that could consolidate available rental information, recommend suitable properties, and always be at hand with the most current information. This paper describes the fully implemented DubLet system to provide just such support. DubLet is an application that employs core CBR methods to recommend rental properties drawn from a number of online sources using Information Extraction techniques. User interaction is provided both via web-browser and via WAP mobile phone. The paper gives an overview of the DubLet system implementation, presents an evaluation of the extraction and recommendation methods, and describes future system directions.

1 Introduction

Searching for rental accommodation can be a difficult and frustrating process. In Dublin's fast-moving rental market, properties are often let within a matter of hours, and it is crucial for the accommodation-seeker to have the most complete and current market information possible. Typically, however, many hours or days must be spent searching through numerous disparate sources of property advertisements in order to locate suitable candidates. Moreover, the constraints and uncertainty in scheduling property viewings can result in missed opportunities (when viewings clash) and wasted time (when a property has already been let). Ideally, the accommodation-seeker would have access to a support system that could consolidate available rental information, recommend suitable properties, and always be at hand with the most current information.

We aim to provide just such support with DubLet, an applied case-based reasoning system for rental property recommendation, currently focused on properties in Dublin, Ireland. DubLet uses CBR as its core recommendation methodology in order to deliver personalised property listings both via a standard web-browser interface and via a WAP mobile phone interface. DubLet draws its property information from a number of online sources, allowing for one-stop property viewing. The web interface provides maximum usability, while the WAP interface enables maximum flexibility on the go. If a user has just arrived at a property

D.W. Aha and I. Watson (Eds.): ICCBR 2001, LNAI 2080, pp. 660–674, 2001.

to find it has already been let, they have the opportunity to dial up and find a better flat around the corner that may have just been listed.

In order to build its case library, DubLet makes use of Information Extraction (IE) techniques to obtain case data from a number of online sources. The source-specific extraction modules feed into a common XML case representation that facilitates end-to-end communication between system components and provides a high degree of flexibility in result presentation. Rental properties are represented by a set of features such as cost and location, and recommendations are made using a nearest-neighbour type similarity measure with a flexible feature-weighting scheme. While properties themselves are not amenable to adaptation, DubLet allows adaptation of user queries—in effect, navigation through the information space—via a set of conceptual buttons for adjustments such as cheaper, nicer, and closer to city centre.

This paper gives an overview of the fully implemented DubLet application and presents an evaluation of the extraction and recommendation components. Section 2 describes the system architecture. Section 3 presents the case representation, and section 4 describes the similarity and adaptation mechanisms involved in recommendation. An evaluation of DubLet is presented in section 5, and related work is discussed in section 6. The paper concludes with a discussion of future system directions.

2   DubLet System Architecture

DubLet is designed to be a fully online system, and it follows the *three-tier* model commonly used in building web applications [11]:

- The *Graphical User Interface* that runs on the user's computer, WAP Phone, PDA, etc. for interaction and presentation (Tier 1).
- The *Business Logic* or application program that runs on the web server and deals with the actual data processing (Tier 2).
- The *Backend Storage System* that stores the data used by the business logic, typically a database management system (Tier 3).

This breakdown also corresponds to the "Model View Controller" design described in [5].

DubLet is comprised of four primary modules that implement case-base construction, property recommendation, and result presentation:

1. Data Gatherer(s)—parallel set of source-specific modules that extract rental property information from online sources of rental property ads (typically HTML). Each source added to the system has a corresponding data gatherer.
2. Case-Base Builder—converts data extracted by the Data-Gatherer(s) into a set of uniformly represented rental property cases, thus integrating consistent data (represented in XML) from idiosyncratic original data sources.
3. Recommender—performs case-retrieval based on user queries and returns a ranked set of similarity scores and recommended properties.

4. User Interface(s)—parallel set of client-specific modules that tailor user interaction with the recommender to individual client platforms (e.g., HTML for web-browsers and WML for WAP mobile phones).

The User Interface module provides a link between client user interfaces and the rest of the system (Tier 1, presentation layer). The Data Gatherer and Case-Builder modules provide the case-library, stored in XML format (Tier 3, persistent data storage layer), while the Recommender module provides the intelligent core of the system (Tier 2, business logic).

3 Building the Case Base

There were two primary concerns in building the DubLet case-base: case-structure and case-data. In this section we first describe how cases are structured, both at the implementation level (XML) and at the representation level (features such as monthly rent). Second, we discuss how cases themselves (the knowledge level) are acquired from various online data sources (IE techniques).

3.1 Case Implementation

It was essential that the fundamental case implementation format facilitate communication between system modules, as well as promote system flexibility and extensibility. In particular, it was important to meet those goals in the context of a web-based application [15]. Thus, from the outset, XML (eXtensible Markup Language) was chosen as the medium for case implementation. XML provides a widely-supported standard for defining customised and extensible data markup (meta-data) that divides data into logical and semantically meaningful components in hierarchy. XML tag sets are specified using a Document Type Definition (DTD), so that different system components and applications have a common reference for "understanding" the markup. HTML is one of the most commonly used markup languages today (for presentation of web information), and HTML is only one example of a tag set that can be fully specified using XML.

XML has a number of advantages. As a text-based representation format, XML markup can pass through network firewalls using the *http* protocol and can be easily delivered over standard web channels using existing network transport protocols. XML provides a simple but powerful storage of tree-structured data, and it facilitates application-independent exchange of data, given the representation DTD. One of the significant benefits of XML in DubLet is the ease of transforming result data into various presentation formats (currently HTML and WML) using standard XML Stylesheet Language Transformation (XSLT) tools.

The markup used in DubLet, RPLML (Rental Property Listing Markup Language), draws both on current industry standards and application needs for its DTD. RELML (Real Estate Listing Markup Language) has been developed as an industry standard format for storing the Real Estate data of North American estate agents. RELML, however, does not address completely the specific requirements of DubLet (e.g., in supporting Irish currency). As a result, RPLML is derived from but is no longer fully compatible with RPLML. They maintain significant overlap, however, to facilitate future knowledge exchange via straightforward transformation from one DTD to the other [2]. The entire case-base itself is stored as an XML document, with each individual RPLML case added as an element of the case-base document.

3.2   Case Representation

In order to determine appropriate features for case representation, we carried out a domain analysis, examining typical features used in describing rental properties from the available sources in the Dublin area, both on- and off-line, as well as the feature set present in RELML. We identified index features that are useful for characterising or indexing properties (e.g., monthly rent), as well as features that provide important supplementary information (e.g., contact email address).

Predictably, almost all rental property ads were found to contain basic information on location, price, and number of bedrooms. Our aim, however, was to capture a richer set of features to enable more detailed user queries and refinements. Table 1 shows a representative subset of the property features used in DubLet, noting whether individual features are used as indices in the system. The features are listed in decreasing weight ranking, as employed by the recommender module discussed in section 4. In contrast, most of the current online rental property search facilities surveyed only allow location, price, and number of bedrooms. In order to provide maximum flexibility in the range of queries that can be specified via the user-interface, the overall property ad descriptions are used to match "keywords" entered by the user in a general keyword input field as part of a query.

3.3   Acquiring Case Knowledge

The online sources of rental property information currently used in DubLet make ads available as HTML documents. While the following discussion thus focuses on acquiring case knowledge from HTML sources, it should be noted that the architecture is designed to allow other source types (e.g., user entry or database/XML feeds) to be plugged-in using analogous modules within a common interface.

In order to build the case-base, the data-gatherer modules must fetch, parse, and extract data from the raw source HTML. To this end, the data-gatherer modules are composed of three main sub-components, each of which deals with a specific part of the information extraction task:

- The *Spider* traverses through a property site from the home-page, and returns the URLs of web-pages holding rental property ads.
- The *AdExtractor* receives a URL of a web-page featuring rental property ads, strips away the page header and footer, and extracts individual ads by matching structural patterns in the HTML source.

Table 1. Feature Subset of a DubLet Rental Property Case

Feature	Index?	Expected Value Type
Location	Yes	Text
Description	Yes	Text (Keywords)
Monthly Rent	Yes	Integer, Decimal
Number of Bedrooms	Yes	Integer
Type	Yes	Apartment, House, Studio, Shared
Number of Bathrooms	Yes	Integer
Garden, Balcony, etc.	Yes	Boolean
Fully Furnished	Yes	Boolean
Private Laundry	Yes	Boolean
Off-street parking	Yes	Boolean
Central Heating	Yes	Boolean
Cable TV	Yes	Boolean
Dishwasher	Yes	Boolean
Viewing Times	No	Text
Original URL of Ad	No	URL
Contact Number	No	Integer String
Contact E-mail	No	String (e-mail address)

- The *DataExtractor* takes HTML ad data and extracts individual feature values from the ads, returning a set of feature-value pairs for each ad.

This type of breakdown is fairly natural and has been employed in information extraction intensive systems, such as TheatreLoc [1].

The primary component of any Information Extraction module is a set of extraction patterns or rules to identify and extract relevant information from a document [14], and regular expression types of rules have often been employed for extraction from online sources [12,19,9,10]. In DubLet, the different characteristics of a given web source are identified by manually inspecting the site structure and HTML page layout(s). Extraction rules are hand-coded as regular expressions for each different source. Machine learning techniques for generating rules were investigated (e.g., [19,10,13]), but were not implemented due to concerns about granularity and accuracy of generated rules (given the variability among sources used). It should also be noted that the number of online sources of rental ads for Dublin is relatively small and many of the extraction rules were found to be reusable, so hand-coding extraction rules within this domain was considered a feasible approach.

The resulting regular expressions are similar in format to those used by the WHISK system [19]. Figure 1 shows a sample rule to extract an expiry date (e.g., of the form '22/8/2000') from a LetbyNet ad.

The main formats of textual information (with HTML sources) are structured text and unstructured free-text. In order to determine whether our extraction mechanism would be sufficient to cater for these contrasting text-formats, two very different sources were selected from which to extract data.

$$> Expir.*? < .*?([0-9] + /[0-9] + /[0-9]+) <$$

Fig. 1. Sample Regular Expression to Extract LetbyNet Ad Expiry Date

LetbyNet: Structured Source. Letbynet was chosen as a source, because its rental ads were laid out in a predictable and highly-structured HTML format, which clearly separated most individual textual feature values. For each (structured) data field within a Letbynet ad, a regular expression was constructed that identified the field based on predictable HTML delimiter patterns.

A serious problem encountered with this approach was the number of different variations possible for certain data fields. For example the following values were all used to represent monthly rent values: "1000pounds"; "1,000"; "1000"; "IR£1000"; "1000per month"; "one thousand pounds." Post-processing on the extracted data was required to allow for the normalisation of values. Currently all but the final variation ("one thousand pounds") are correctly interpreted by the data extractor.

Similarly, postal codes were often omitted in the original ads, so the codes had to be determined from placenames in the property address (e.g., Donnybrook → Dublin 4). These codes are the primary indicators of location, which, as described in section 5.2, are of great importance for the recommender.

DAFT: Free-Text Source. Adding "DAFT" as a data source considerably expanded the number of rental property ads stored by DubLet. The task of extracting information from DAFT ads, however, had to be approached in a very different manner to that of LetbyNet. While some structured fields are present in DAFT ads (e.g., rent and telephone number), most information is contained in a free-text property description. A *term-based* approach was used that involved compiling sets of terms commonly occurring in rental property ads, where each set corresponded to a particular feature value. This approach is similar to the semantic classes used in WHISK [19]. If any one of the terms in these sets of keywords was found in an ad, the canonical keyword value associated with that set was used. While this approach is not as sophisticated as the expectation-based parser used in the RentMe system [4], efforts were made to distinguish between phrases such as "furnished" and "unfurnished" by taking limited contextual information into account. Compilation of such keyword sets involves considerable domain analysis, but these mappings can be reused by other free text rental property sources.

4 Recommending Properties

The case-based recommender module in DubLet uses similarity metrics that are tailored to the rental property domain, with a flexible weighting scheme. DubLet also allows the user to navigate the information space via query adaptation. The

$$\{house, hse\} \rightarrow house$$
$$\{apt, apartment, aprtmnt\} \rightarrow apartment$$
$$\{3, three\} \rightarrow 3$$
$$\{bed, bd, bdrm\} \rightarrow bedroom$$

Fig. 2. Simplified Keyword Sets and Associated Canonical Keyword

interaction for initial query specification in the WAP mobile phone interface is shown in figure 3.

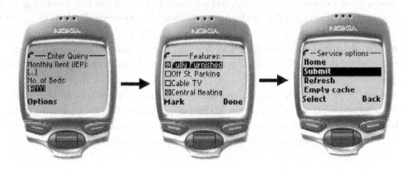

Fig. 3. Query Entry in WAP Interface

4.1 Similarity Measures

DubLet employs a weighted nearest-neighbour matching algorithm to determine similarity between cases, effectively a weighted-mean-sum of individual feature similarity scores. The overall similarity measure between case and query is always a value between 0 and 1. This is a common feature of many similarity metrics and allows easy conversion to a similarity percentage that can be presented to the user. Missing values in the query result in that feature being excluded from the similarity valuation, while missing values in a case are treated as the strongest possible mismatch. Table 2 gives a representative sample of the feature similarity measures currently employed.

An initial set of weightings is given to each indexing feature. In order to promote flexibility, a set of methods have been implemented to allow dynamic change of the weighting values. The weights may be updated over the course of a user's interaction with the system (as described in section 4.2) to reflect preferences from feedback on particular properties. In large part, the dynamic feature weighting scheme enables the query adaptation mechanism. The initial relative weightings of representative features are given in Table 1 (decreasing order).

Table 2. Representative Local Similarity Metrics

Feature	Local Similarity Metric
(Geographical) Area	If locality values are identical, 1.0. If the areas border one another, 0.5. Otherwise, 0.0.
Monthly Rent	A set of 'intervals' are created around the query price (e.g., within x%). Similarity is based on which interval a case rent value (if any) falls into. The function is deliberately biased so that cheaper case rent values typically get a higher similarity score than more expensive ones.
Bedrooms/Bathrooms	Measured as a function of the difference between the number of bedrooms/bathrooms.
Type (House etc.)	Maximum similarity (1.0) if the same, 0.0 otherwise.
Boolean (e.g Garden?)	Maximum similarity (1.0) only if the feature is present in the case AND user query.
Keywords	Function of number of query keywords matched in the stored case in relation to the total number of keywords supplied.

Once similarity scores have been computed, a ranked list of case results are passed to the User Interface module(s) for presentation to the user. Results are presented in blocks of 10 (entries for the web interface, WML cards for the WAP interface). Figure 4 shows the initial results listing for the web interface, as well as an individual result listing.

Fig. 4. Query Results and Ad Result Summary in Web Interface

4.2   Adaptation Metrics

DubLet currently offers a compromise between a pure query-based approach and an assisted-browsing approach. A set of "tweaking" buttons are provided to navigate the search space based on the results of the initial user query. Figure 4 shows the tweaking buttons for a sample result. On pressing one of the tweak buttons, a new user query is sent to the Recommender, resulting in an altered set of results. Four conceptual tweaks are currently implemented in DubLet:

Find Similar Properties. This tweak is intended as a means of providing positive feedback on a particular property. The features of the currently selected property are used to form the basis of a new query. If a feature had the same value in the current result and in the initial query, its weighting is increased to reflect its potentially greater relevance to the user. In general, a feature's weighting is increased if a certain value is consistently present in the currently selected ad, and gradually decreased otherwise. This tweak also has other effects, for example, any additional keywords found in the selected ad summary may be added to the list of user keywords.

Cheaper. This tweak operates in a very straightforward way. A new rent value is added to the user query that is a certain percentage (currently 15%) lower than that for the currently viewed ad summary. In addition, to reflect the user emphasis on price, the weighting of the Monthly Rent feature is increased.

Nicer. This tweak uses a range of heuristics to locate "nicer" properties. Niceness is clearly a highly subjective quality. However, a number of heuristics are employed to try and capture this elusive concept. The weightings of amenity features such as the presence of garden, parking, and cable TV are increased, while a further set of keywords such as "spacious," "pristine," and "all mod cons" are added to the search. The weighting on rent is also gradually decreased to reflect the potential tradeoff between niceness and price.

Closer to City Centre. This tweak also employs a straightforward heuristic. The area value of the currently displayed ad is noted, and an area immediately bordering the current area but closer to the city centre is added to the user search criteria. If the current ad does not contain a recognised area, then the user query area is set to "Dublin 2" (south city centre).

5   DubLet Evaluation

We performed three separate evaluations of DubLet. The first tested the effectiveness of the case-base building process. The second tested the system results using simulated user queries. The third collected user evaluations of DubLet's overall effectiveness and usability.

5.1   Data Gatherer

In order to evaluate the information extraction capabilities of the Data-Gatherer module(s), we evaluated precision, recall, and accuracy, after [19]. A random subset of the case-base was selected for examination. For each selected case, the stored values were compared by inspection with the actual values in the original ad.

For each case and original ad pair, the number of features falling into the following categories was first counted:

- True Positives (TP): Values in the case that exactly corresponded to those in the original ad.
- True Negatives (TN): Features for which no value was found both in the case and the original ad.
- False Positives (FP): Values in the case that differed from those in the original ad.
- False Negatives (FN): Values that were missing from the case but found in the original ad.

The following measures were then calculated based on the results obtained:

- Precision: TP / (TP + FP)
- Recall: TP / (TP + FN)
- Accuracy: (TP + TN) / (TP + TN + FP + FN)

From a case-base of 890 ads in total—801 from DAFT, 89 from LetbyNet—28 cases were randomly chosen in order to test the accuracy of the overall information extraction system. Additionally, in order to specifically test the extraction procedures for the two different sources, two restricted tests were carried out—the first with 20 random DAFT cases and the second with 10 LetbyNet cases. Table 3 shows the results of these tests.

Table 3. Information Extraction Results for a Sample of the Cases

	Sample Size	Precision	Recall	Accuracy
Full Case-Base	28	94%	96%	92%
DAFT Ads Only	20	94%	95%	92%
LetbyNet Ads Only	10	96%	99%	96%

The extraction rules for LetbyNet (structured) were more accurate overall than those for DAFT (structured/free-text), although by a small margin. Overall, the extraction module can be seen to perform extremely well. This success can be attributed in part to the generally predictable set of keywords for given features found in the ads, as well as to the careful crafting of the extraction knowledge.

5.2   Recommender Evaluation

The recommender was tested with simulated user queries, based on existing cases in the library. A target case was randomly selected from the case-base and converted into a set of potential queries that would target the original selected case. This set represented differing user query approaches to the same property goal. The four highest-weighted features by default (rent, number of bedrooms, type, and area) were taken to be the typical main features of user interest. Five "vague" queries were constructed by first removing all specified feature values except the main four. Then one of the 4 main features was set to "ANY." Seven "specific" queries (with all the main features present) were generated by selecting two additional non-main features at random. The values of these two features were then altered (e.g., boolean true switched to false, or number of bathrooms).

We tested 3360 query variations generated from 280 target cases. For both vague and specific queries, we calculated: (1) the average rank of the target in the list of properties returned; (2) the percentage of times the target fell within the top 10, 20, 30, and 40 returned cases; (3) the average difference in similarity score between the top score and the 10th, 20th, 30th, and 40th cases returned; and (4) the average similarity score returned for the target case. These values indicate how successful the system is in finding the target case and also give an idea as to how fine-grained the matching is. It was found that the average rank for the specific query was 3.8, while the average rank for the vague query was 9.1. The average similarity scores for the vague and specific queries were 99.9% and 95.5% respectively.

When there is a 'tie' (i.e. k results are returned with the same score) then the k results are arbitrarily ordered by the ranking function (based on the number of the case). Therefore it should be noted that a case returned with a similarity of 100% does not necessarily appear in the top 10. If the user query is detailed enough (and particularly if the criteria specified are atypical for the domain) the 'spread' of results returned should be significantly greater than if a very vague query is given.

As illustrated in figure 5, the recommender performed well in locating the target as a likely match, being in the top 10 results over 86% of the time, even for vague queries. As expected with the richer feature sets provided, more specific queries resulted in significantly higher target ranks and similarity score variation. Note, however, that tweaking could be used to refine an initially vague query, though the effectiveness of the tweaks remains to be tested in future experiments.

In addition, we calculated the average target rank for each of the five vague query types. These indicate the importance of the 4 main features in influencing the target case rank. Figure 6 illustrates how the omission of the main features can significantly affect the baseline target rank (no main features removed). In particular, omission of the location or monthly rent features results in a marked drop in target rank. As one might expect, these features are influential predictors of rank in the rental property domain.

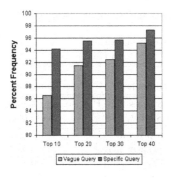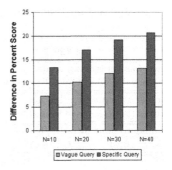

Fig. 5. Frequency that Target Case Falls Within Top n results, and Difference in Similarity Scores Between Top Match and nth Match

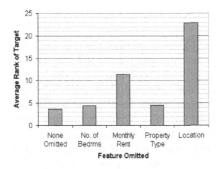

Fig. 6. Effect of Varying Omitted Features on Vague Queries

5.3 User Evaluation

User trials were carried out in order to obtain direct feedback on the effectiveness and usability of DubLet. A set of questionnaire forms was distributed to 1st, 3rd and 4th year undergraduate Science students with varying levels of computer literacy. Results are based on the 17 questionnaire forms returned. The tests were carried out with a total case-base size of approximately 900 over the course of a single day.

After briefly familiarising themselves with DubLet, the subjects, all of whom were resident in the Greater Dublin area, were instructed to use the system to find the property most similar to their own home/university residence. This was done in two ways that basically corresponded to the types of queries in section 5.2. First, the subjects were instructed to give as specific a query as they possibly could that reflected features of their own house or flat. Second, the subjects were instructed to enter only "vague" criteria (any three of no. of bedrooms, monthly rent, type and location) as an initial query and to use the tweaking buttons to further narrow down the search. In both cases the users were asked to evaluate the results obtained in terms of similarity to their own places of residence. The five questions and summary responses are shown in Table 4.

Table 4. User Evaluation Questions and Summary Responses

Have you ever used an online rental property site before?
Yes (29%)   No (71%)
How easy was the system to use?
Very Easy (76%)   Quite Easy (24%)   Difficult (0%)   Very Difficult (0%)
How similar to your own flat/house was the top result? (Precise, no tweaking)
Very (25%)   Quite (56%)   Slightly (19%)   Not (0%)
How similar to your own flat/house was the top result? (Vague, tweaking)
Very (6%)   Quite (57%)   Slightly (31%)   Not (6%)
Would you use this site in the future and/or recommend it to a friend?
Definitely (59%)   Probably(41%)   Probably Not(0%)   Definitely Not (0%)

There was a general consensus that the site was easy to use (even for first-time users). The quality of results returned was quite reasonable: 25% found a very similar property, while 56% found a quite similar property. This result reflects both case-base coverage and the quality of recommendations made. As regards the vaguer second query it is perhaps unsurprising that less similar results were generally obtained. In particular more extensive use of the tweaking buttons may be necessary to narrow down the vague search results sufficiently to get very similar properties, but this mechanism is not currently as powerful as the basic query system. Finally all respondents claimed that they would (or probably would) use the site again, and/or recommend it to a friend.

6   Related Work

A number of systems have addressed the rental property domain. The RentMe system recommends properties in the Chicago area [4]. RentMe uses an expectation based parser to extract property information from free-text classified ads. A standard database query provides a starting point for the user, followed by a dynamic constraint-based "assisted browsing phase" of navigation through that information space. As with other FindMe systems, RentMe emphasizes strong information browsing support from a more general starting point, which can require substantial domain knowledge to build the tweak set. DubLet places emphasis on a more strongly specified initial user query, and provides more knowledge-poor tweaks (inspired by RentMe) for refinement.

Hooke and MacDonald employ a case-based recommendation system called "Let on the Net[1]." This system has a more limited scope, since it is designed for a single agency.

The 'Apt Decision' agent [16] aids users in finding apartments in the Boston area. Apt Decision is more focused on profile building than DubLet, as it seeks

---

[1] http://www.hookemacdonald.com/letonthenet/index.htm

to iteratively learn a user's preferences on the basis of longer-term explicit feedback about the importance of individual features. This form of feedback, while detailed, is fairly complex and would be difficult to deploy using a WAP interface.

The Real Estate Visualizer (ReV) uses 'grammar induction' to convert a page of online rental-property ads into a set of grammar rules describing the page layout [8]. The rules capture common patterns in the (HTML) text, and rules covering specific patterns (e.g., whole ads, rent values) can be identified. ReV, however, is targeted at visualizing a whole space of properties at once, rather than recommending individual ones.

DubLet's XML representation follows other CBR/XML work (e.g., [6,7,17]), though its flexible architecture for data sources and presentation is perhaps closer to work on Information Management Assistants [3].

The WAP interface to DubLet is relatively novel, certainly among the property systems we have seen. PTV [18], a recommender system for television programmes, employs case-based reasoning for content-based recommendations (in addition to collaborative filtering) that are also delivered both via a web interface and a WAP phone interface. A longer term user-interaction would be expected with PTV than with DubLet, which has implications for the nature and quality of user profiles that could be gathered for DubLet.

The DubLet application has been designed very much in the spirit of CBR e-commerce systems, such as WEBSELL [20].

7 Conclusion and Future Work

We have described the DubLet system, a case-based recommender application for rental property in the Dublin area. DubLet provides reasonably good recommendations, even with limited domain knowledge and straightforward heuristics, and it provides these recommendations with ease-of-use and portability. Moreover, the end-to-end XML architecture provides significant flexibility and extensibility.

There is significant room for enhancing DubLet's recommendation capabilities. The acquisition of user profiles would allow for more on-point recommendations over longer periods of time, and would allow for auto-notification of suitable new property listings (e.g., via email or SMS message to the user). DubLet could clearly benefit from more sophisticated domain knowledge, such as knowledge of neighborhood qualities and transport links. Use of collaborative filtering techniques in a hybrid system, as in PTV, would enable recommendations based on other user experiences.

Finally, the rental property domain provides a rich target for a number of interesting research issues in CBR, such as textual CBR, case authoring and acquisition, case-adaptation techniques, and case-base maintenance within a rapidly changing environment.

References

1. G. Barish, Y. Chen, C.A. Knoblock, S. Minton, and C. Shahabi. The theaterloc virtual application. In *Proceedings of the Twelfth Annual Conference on Innovative Applications of Artificial Intelligence, IAAI-2000*, 2000.

2. N. Bradley. *The XML Companion.* Addison-Wesley, 2000.
3. J. Budzik, K. Hammond, and L. Birnbaum. Information access in context. *Knowledge Based Systems*, 14(1-2):37–53, 2001.
4. R. Burke, K. Hammond, and B. Young. Knowledge-based navigation of complex information spaces. In *Proceedings of the Thirteenth National Conference on Artifical Intelligence*, volume 1, pages 462–468, Menlo Park, CA, 1996. AAAI Press.
5. Michelle Doyle, Maria Angela Ferrario, Conor Hayes, Pádraig Cunningham, and Barry Smyth. CBR Net:- smart technology over a network. Technical Report TCD-CS-1998-07, Trinity College Dublin, 1998.
6. Dan Gardingen and Ian Watson. A web based case-based reasoning system for HVAC sales support. In *Applications & Innovations in Expert Systems VI.* Springer, 1998.
7. Conor Hayes, Pádraig Cunningham, and Michelle Doyle. Distributed CBR using XML. In *Proceedings of the KI-98 Workshop on Intelligent Systems and Electronic Commerce*, number LSA-98-03E. University of Kaiserslauten Computer Science Department, 1998.
8. T. Hong. Visualizing real estate property information on the web. In *Proceedings of the 1999 International Conference on Information Visualization*, 1999.
9. C. Hsu and M. Dung. Generating finite-state transducers for semi-structured data extraction from the web. *Journal of Information Systems*, 23(8):521–538, 1998.
10. N. Kushmerick, D. Weld, and B. Doorenbos. Wrapper induction for information extraction. In *Proceedings of IJCAI-97*, pages 729–735, 1997.
11. H. Maruyama, K. Tamura, and N. Uramato. *XML and Java—Developing Web Applications.* Addison Wesley, 1999.
12. I. Muslea, S. Minton, and C. Knoblock. A hierarchial approach to wrapper induction. In *Proceedings of the Third International Conference on Autonomous Agents*, 1999.
13. Ion Muslea. Extraction patterns: From information extraction to wrapper generation. Technical report, ISI-USC, 1998.
14. Ion Muslea. Extraction patterns for information extraction tasks: A survey. In *Proceedings of the AAAI-99 Workshop on Machine Learning for Information Extraction*, 1999.
15. Arijit Sengupta, David C. Wilson, and David B. Leake. On constructing the right sort of CBR implementation. In *Proceedings of the IJCAI-99 Workshop on Automating the Construction of Case Based Reasoners*, pages 68–72, 1999.
16. S. Shearin and H. Lieberman. Intelligent profiling by example. In *Proceedings of IUI-2001*, 2001.
17. Hideo Shimazu. A textual case-based reasoning system using XML on the worldwide web. In *Proceedings of the Fourth European Workshop on Case-Based Reasoning.* Springer, 1998.
18. Barry Smyth and Paul Cotter. PTV: intelligent personalised TV guides. In *Proceedings of IAAI-2000.* AAAI Press, 2000.
19. S. Soderland. Learning information extraction rules for semi-structured and free text. *Machine Learning*, 34(1):233–272, 1999.
20. I. Vollrath, W. Wilke, and R. Bergmann. Case-based reasoning support for online catalog sales. *IEEE Internet Computing*, 2(4):47–54, July-August 1998.

Improved Performance Support through an Integrated Task-Based Video Case Library

Christopher L. Johnson[1*], Larry Birnbaum[1], Ray Bareiss[2], and Tom Hinrichs[3]

[1]Northwestern University, Department of Computer Science
1890 Maple Avenue, Evanston, IL 60201
cj@mitre.org, birnbaum@ils.nwu.edu

[2]Cognitive Arts Corporation
115 E. 57th Street, 10th Floor, New York, NY 10022
bareiss@cognitivearts.com

[3]Cognitive Arts Corporation
1840 Oak Avenue, Evanston, IL 60201
thinrichs@cognitivearts.com

Abstract. Case-based retrieval and other decision support systems typically exist separately from the tools and tasks they support. Users are required to initiate searches and identify target case features manually, and as a result the systems are not used to their full extent. We describe an approach to integrating an ASK system—a type of video case library—with a performance support tool. This approach uses model-based task tracking to retrieve cases relevant to how a user is performing a task, not just to the artifacts that are created during the process.

1 Introduction

A common scenario for using case-based help retrieval begins with a person describing the particulars of a problem to a retrieval system, often by filling out a form or answering a series of questions. However, there are circumstances where this scenario is less than ideal. Requiring users to build a target case description in order to access help requires added effort which they may not be willing or able to give.

For instance, the hardest problem for large organizations implementing knowledge management initiatives is frequently cultural, not technical (e.g., [1]). Convincing members to add "extra" tools and processes to their already busy work schedule is one of the difficulties. As another example, users may be performing a time-critical task and unable to devote extra time to searching for help. Or the complexity of a task may require a relatively unreasonable amount of time to identify all relevant case features. At other times users don't even realize that they need help, much less that cases are available which apply to their current situation.

---

* Christopher Johnson currently works for The MITRE Corporation, Cognitive Science & Artificial Intelligence, 1820 Dolly Madison Blvd., McLean, VA, 22102.

D.W. Aha and I. Watson (Eds.): ICCBR 2001, LNAI 2080, pp. 675-689, 2001.

This paper describes a system we built to address this problem in the use of an ASK system, a type of video-based organizational memory. The Air Campaign Planning Advisor (ACPA) uses model-based task tracking to integrate an ASK system with a plan construction tool used by air campaign planners.

2 Issues with Non-integrated ASK Systems

Over the past several years, the Institute for the Learning Sciences at Northwestern University and the Cognitive Arts Corporation have developed an effective approach to creating organizational memories called ASK Systems [2]. This family of hypermedia systems aims at providing conversational access to large case libraries for training and performance support. Each ASK system contains a large number of 30-second to 2-minute video clips in which experts recount "war stories" of their actual experiences in these domains. These systems represent our attempts to develop organizational memories that capture the less tangible elements of human expertise.

One of the largest ASK systems we have built, Trans-ASK, contains 21 hours of video detailing the experiences of United States Transportation Command (USTRANSCOM) personnel in planning for Operations Desert Shield and Desert Storm, as well as the Somalia and Hurricane Andrew relief operations [3]. Shortly after Trans-ASK was completed, we tested it with novice transportation planners from USTRANSCOM for utility and usability. The test consisted of several exercises. Novices were given the same kinds of scenarios, constraints, information, and instructions that they would receive in real operations and were then asked to develop an acceptable transportation plan.

The test was a success: Trans-ASK did indeed provide natural and easy access to potentially useful information. Novices found it quite easy to navigate through the system to retrieve relevant answers to their questions. (Expert planners observing the test assessed the relevance of the information they retrieved.) However, during the assessment a few problems emerged which seemed to limit the potential utility of Trans-ASK. First, even though novice planners were able to find good answers to their questions, they weren't necessarily able to apply those answers to produce better transportation plans. Second, during focus group discussions following the exercises, participants agreed nearly unanimously that they would probably *not* use such a system in day-to-day operations—not because it wasn't valuable, but because it wasn't integrated with their normal work environment. To use Trans-ASK, planners would need to stop whatever they were doing, open a new application, and traverse a hierarchical menu system, specifying their current role, task, and problem to find a starting point in the case base—a time-consuming and distracting chore for someone in the midst of resolving a problem.

Finally, Trans-ASK presented one additional problem. Many of the experiences related in ASK systems deal with problems involved in performing a task. The best time for users to hear these experiences is when they are experiencing the same type of problem. But with a stand-alone ASK system, users first have to realize that they are having a problem before they can get help for that problem. Unfortunately, the nature of problems is that they are often not noticed until after the fact.

After observing these problems with Trans-ASK, we realized that, ultimately, organizational memory systems will be truly useful only if they are integrated with the tools that directly support users' tasks, i.e., performance support systems. Additional studies support this need. For instance, an extensive survey of *lessons learned systems* found that most systems were implemented with stand-alone retrieval tools, no deployed systems used active or proactive lesson dissemination, and systems generally failed to promote knowledge reuse and sharing [4].

3 Air Campaign Planning Advisor

ACPA is composed of a Web-based ASK system linked to a performance support tool through a model-based task tracking system. The ASK system itself contains approximately 1,000 video clips—about 20 hours—in which 12 expert air campaign planners relate their experiences in the Gulf War, Bosnia, Somalia, and Haiti, as well as several training exercises. The JFACC Planning Tool (JPT), to which the ASK system is linked, supports the authoring of hierarchical air campaign plans. (JPT, which was built by ISX Corporation, has been adopted by the US Air Force.) Finally, the task tracker that links them, which we call Argus, enables the entire system to provide contextual help and advice relevant to the current state of planners' planning process as they use JPT. The system is also capable of providing proactive critiques of the planning process as well as of the current plan itself. Figure 1 illustrates the basic architecture of ACPA.

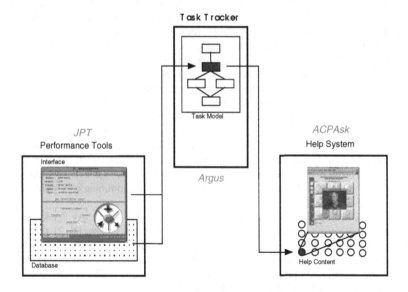

Fig. 1. An architecture for integrated performance support

The ACPA system embodies our vision of an intrinsic and integrated organizational memory. Our vision entails using performance support tools as a framework that helps ground the advice contained in the organizational memory. At the same time, by tracking users' progress through the task, such an integrated system could provide instantaneous access to relevant cases, thus relieving users of the burden of leaving the current task context to search for help. Again, our goal is to minimize the user's effort in obtaining guidance: any time spent away from the task in navigating, searching, or answering questions to identify appropriate case features for retrieval is too disruptive.

4 ACPA in Detail

The air campaign planning (ACP) task, greatly simplified, is the process of finding answers to three questions: What enemy targets need to be addressed? When do these targets need to be addressed? What resources should be used to address these targets? While answering these questions, planners should be guided by the dominant goals of the campaign. In other words, what would be the result of a successful military operation against an opponent? Each target should then directly support these goals. This is the task that ACPA was built to support.

4.1 Components of ACPA

The performance support tool in ACPA is the *JFACC Planning Tool* (JPT). JPT is an authoring tool for air campaign plans that also provides easy access to information and other tools required during the authoring process. The tool allows planners to create better air campaign plans more quickly and fosters greater collaboration and plan reuse. JPT is one of the actual tools that planners use to create air campaign plans today; it was developed to address planning problems encountered in the Gulf War and has been in active use since the first Bosnia operations.

The central activity of a planner using JPT is creating a six-level hierarchy of objectives and targets, ranging from national security objectives down to individual targets. This hierarchy of objectives is intended to both structure and archive the strategy behind a given list of targets, which allows others to better understand, critique, and modify the plan. As planners create objectives and targets, they often need to perform research or use additional software tools. To accommodate these needs, JPT also provides aids such as online access to commander's guidance and intelligence documents.

In ACPA, the Air Campaign Planning ASK system (for clarity, ACPAsk) plays the part of the organizational memory. We defer to previous papers [3, 2] for detailed discussions of the ASK concept. Specifically, ACPAsk is a Web-based ASK system that currently contains approximately 1,000 video clips—13.5 gigabytes worth—about air campaign planning, related by 12 experts. The clips are richly interconnected by approximately 28,500 links.

The two main activities involved in using an ASK system are *zooming* and *browsing*. When zooming, ACPAsk allows planners to navigate down through a graphical representation of our air campaign planning task model (Figure 2). When planners select a task in the model, ACPAsk either displays a more detailed model of the subtasks that form that task or, if the task has no subtasks, displays a set of questions related to the task. These questions are divided into three categories:

questions related to the *process* of performing the task, questions related to *concepts* associated with the task, and questions related to *problems* involved in performing the task.

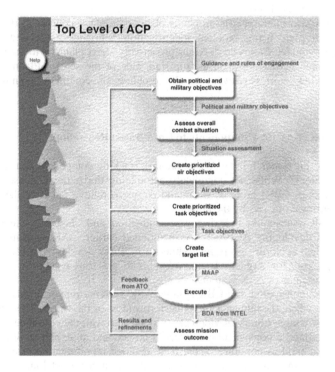

Fig. 2. Top level of the air campaign planning task model

Each question leads to a story page that allows planners to watch a video of an expert air campaign planner telling a story that addresses their question.

After listening to the story, planners can browse through related stories in ACPAsk by selecting one of eight relational links surrounding the story. In this manner, planners can choose to view other stories addressing follow-up questions they may have about *examples*, *alternatives*, *opportunities*, *warnings*, *causes*, *results*, *background information*, or *details* relative to the issues discussed in the story.

Each of these relational links leads to another set of questions, each question leads to another story, and each story has the same relational links that can lead to eight more sets of questions.

The final component of ACPA—the adhesive that binds planners' performance in JPT and the expertise in ACPAsk—is *Argus*. The purpose of Argus is to monitor planners as they create an air campaign plan using JPT and then to provide the most appropriate ACPAsk stories to them at the most appropriate times. To achieve this, Argus tracks planners' progress through the explicit model of air campaign planning as they work with JPT. By monitoring the actions that planners take, such as opening editors, selecting options from menus, or adding air objectives to their plan, Argus works to infer planners' current goals in the task model. Because stories in ACPAsk are also indexed by the task model, when planners ask for help, Argus can simply look at the task the planners are currently performing and give them the stories stored under that task in ACPAsk.

Argus can also infer specific problems planners might encounter as they build an air campaign plan, using problem identification heuristics associated with each subtask in the model. In this case, Argus proactively alerts planners to the problem by placing a small alert window on the top right side of the screen. Planners can then choose to view stories relevant to the problem or continue planning without interruption.

4.2 Relation of ACPA Components to Case-Based Reasoning

The focus of this research is on Argus, the task tracking component that links JPT to the ASK system. While not completely automating the retrieval phase of a case-based reasoning (CBR) process, we intend Argus to relieve much of the burden of initiating retrieval of cases by the human.

Other CBR issues—like indexing, case acquisition, and adaptation—tend to fall in the scope of developing ACPAsk. As mentioned earlier, ASK systems have been well established at Northwestern for awhile, so ACPAsk development played more of a supporting role for Argus. Again, we refer to previous papers [2, 3] for more detailed discussions of ASK systems.

But briefly, considered as a CBR system, ASK systems support a mixed-initiative CBR process where the human actually performs most of the work. The ASK system provides a browsable library of video cases to aid retrieval; the case index it provides is modeled around a conversation between a novice and an expert in order to make browsing as natural as possible. There is no detailed representation of an individual case, other than the way in which cases are linked to a task model and to each other (e.g., this case is related to task x and is an alternative to case y). Standard practice at Northwestern has been for groups of content specialists to index the ASK videos in this manner; there are tools that have been developed to assist them.

4.3 Sample Interaction with ACPA

Consider a novice air campaign planner using JPT to construct a plan. JPT itself looks and behaves no differently than it did without ACPA added. As mentioned earlier, the central activity supported by JPT is the creation of a six-level hierarchy of objectives and targets. Imagine that the planner has reached this point, and is in the middle of editing an air objective (we'll pretend that Major Jill Planner plays the part of our novice planner). Specifically, she has opened the Objectives Viewer by clicking on the *Objectives* button in the main control panel and chosen to create an air objective named *Destroy Libyan Computerized Networks for Information Transmittal*.

However, in the midst of creating this objective, the planner experiences a twinge of irritation. Why must she go through the trouble of filling out this complex hierarchy? She already has an idea of what the targets should be. What's the point?

She clicks the *Help* button. Because the objectives editor is open and is showing an air objective (one of five types of objectives in the hierarchy), ACPA has already inferred that the planner is currently involved in the task of *Creating Air Objectives.* ACPAsk opens and automatically loads a set of questions about creating air objectives. ACPAsk initially displays a set of questions on the process of creating air objectives (Figure 3), and Jill sees the question *Why must tasks be derived from an objective hierarchy?* This seems relevant, so she selects it.

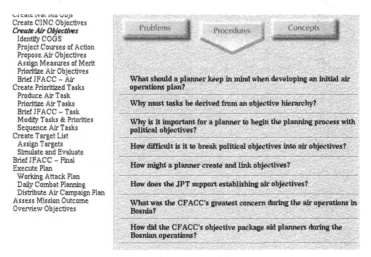

Fig. 3. A set of questions about procedures performing the task of creating air objectives

ACPAsk then opens the appropriate story page (Figure 4), and Jill can view an expert video, in which Lieutenant Colonel Joe Roberts talks about the importance of an objective hierarchy as a supporting rationale for the plan, thus avoiding wasted resources and possible failure of the entire campaign.

Jill still isn't satisfied. She would like to obtain more background on the nature of this "decomposition" process. She clicks the Background button, and ACPAsk displays a set of background questions. The question *How does a strategy to task review help a planner to identify targets?* looks interesting, so she selects it[1]. The appropriate story page opens and the planner watches a video of Col. Robert Plebanek discussing how this method allows planners to more quickly create plans with better emphasis on the important high level effects of an air campaign (e.g., leadership, communication), and because the supporting rationale is included, the plan can also be altered more quickly.

At this point, Jill decides that the time has come to return to JPT, so she minimizes ACPAsk and she's back at the objective editor. In fact, she also closes the objective editor in preparation for creating another objective. This creates a problem with her campaign plan. There are at least four components that every objective in an air campaign plan is supposed to have: a title, a center of gravity, a measure of merit, and

---

[1] The *strategy to task* approach advocates that each target should explicitly service at least one high-level goal [5]. JPT supports this approach by requiring targets to be directly linked to the highest level national security objective via a hierarchy of intermediate objectives.

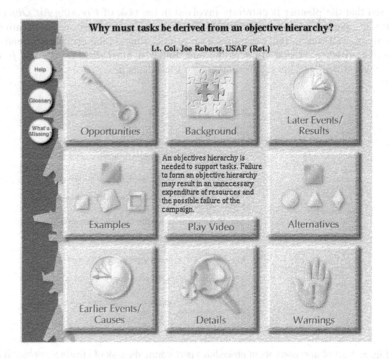

Fig. 4. A story page in ACPA. The user can either watch a video of the expert telling the story or click on one of the eight buttons surrounding the summary to see related questions and stories

links to parent objectives. When the planner closed the objective editor, she had yet to identify a center of gravity [6] for this objective.

In our scenario so far, we have seen one mode of support: the *reactive* help that ACPA provides when the planner explicitly requests it. However, ACPA provides another mode of help support as well: *proactive* help that ACPA presents automatically when it notices a problem with the planner's task. Here is just such a case.

When the planner closed the objective editor, ACPA assumed that she had finished with the Create Air Objectives task, but recognized that the objective she had been working on was missing a component. ACPA considers this to be a problem, and thus alerts the planner by displaying a small alert window. If the planner wishes not to be disturbed, she may ignore the alert window and it will quietly disappear in a minute. However, Jill is curious about what advice ACPA has to offer and clicks on the *Help* button located in the alert window.

ACPA appears and displays both the task problem that it thinks the planner is having and a set of questions related to that problem. In this case, the problem is *No Center of Gravity Identification* and only one question inhabits the set: *Should you ever skip analysis and COG identification because of time constraints?* Jill selects the question, which leads to a video in which Lt. Col. Roberts suggests that taking the time to perform situation analysis and center of gravity identification actually saves time in the long run.

This scenario, although clearly compressed and simplified, illustrates the type of interaction that linking an ASK system to a performance support tool like JPT, via a task-tracking mechanism, can provide.

5 Benefits of Task Tracking

In many instances, case features can be retrieved directly from the product—a design, a plan, etc.—that a user naturally generates as a result of performing a task. For example, textual case-based reasoning techniques attempt to derive features from the documents people produce [7]. INSPECT [8], another system that supports the task of air campaign planning, retrieves advice based on an analysis of the air campaign plan itself. These methods certainly represent good opportunities for integrating case libraries and other kinds of aids into performance support systems.

However, in other instances crucial case features reside in the user's task process. The stories told by the expert planners in ACPA are as much concerned with how planners go about generating a plan as they are concerned with the final air campaign plan itself. What are users doing right now? What have they done previously? What methods are being used? Are planners developing targets without first developing a strategy? Have they fully assessed the current situation? Did they really think about that information they just entered, or did they simply toss in a value?

Of course, an analysis of the task product can provide clues to the state of the task process; ACPA makes use of these clues to the extent that the air campaign plan generated by JPT contains explicit correlations to the planner's tasks. However, ACPA can also examine interface activity and the task model itself when these correlations don't exist or ambiguity does. We discuss some examples of task and problem tracking techniques in the last section.

Essentially, task tracking offers an opportunity for more precise, just-in-time advice, resulting in tighter integration with performance support tools. Instead of receiving a broad collection of advice about an entire design or plan, users can get help on precisely the tasks and problems they're currently thinking about.

6 General Architecture for Integrated Performance Support

Our approach to providing integrated performance support like that of ACPA is based on the use of an explicit task model to organize and guide task tracking, to represent the current state of the task, and to drive the initial access into the ASK system. Designing systems around task models is a central technique in cognitive engineering approaches (e.g., [9]). However, with our approach we want to further the notion by incorporating the task model as an actual, computer-manipulable part of the final system. Essentially, we are putting the main index of the ACPAsk case library to work as an interface between all components of the system. Rather than embedding and scattering task knowledge throughout the system, in a wizard here and an agent there, we wanted the task model to be the central component of the entire system.

Figure 1 illustrates not just the architecture of ACPA, but a general architecture for similar integrated performance support systems.

The first step in designing such a performance support system, then, is to define a task model that identifies steps in the process and associated information flows. Given this task model, the following items should then be defined for each subtask:

- A software "tool" that supports the information processing involved in performing the subtask. (*performance tools*).
- Recognition conditions that indicate when a user is taking part in the subtask. (*task tracker*).
- Recognition conditions that indicate when a user has made an error or encountered a problem while performing a subtask. These conditions could include not completing the subtask, attempting to perform the subtask prematurely, or performing the subtask inadequately (*task tracker*).
- Help and advice relevant to the subtask. This could include a broad range of aid such as background knowledge, step-by-step instructions, extended case studies, sample work products, common problems and solutions, and alternatives. The system could provide this information in various ways, such as entering an ASK system or invoking an intelligent information agent (*information sources*).

We believe that the use of explicit task models and task tracking to link organizational memory and performance support shows promise as a general performance support architecture. Potential advantages include the following.

- *Improved Task Monitoring.* Because the task model is explicit and centralized, task tracking agents can access knowledge that allows them to make better inferences about task state and provide more specific help to users.
- *Improved Organizational Memory Access.* The relatively natural access to information that ASK systems already provide can be improved further by using task models to track tasks and link ASK systems to a performance environment, which removes the burden of searching from the users.
- *Improved Human-Computer Communication.* By using explicit task models to create a shared context, a performance support system can support better communication and negotiation between computers and users. Because an explicit task model can be "understood" by both the systems and its users, the users can more easily see what the system is doing, and why, when it suggests advice or warns about a problem. Likewise, when the system makes a mistaken inference, users can more easily tell the system what they think the correct inference should have been.
- *Improved System Integration.* Explicit task models can act as an interface between components of a performance support system, resulting in better system integration. Instead of hard-coding particular stories, methods, or data objects to particular windows, interface actions, or tools, tasks can coordinate the interaction between these items. In turn, the performance support system becomes more flexible and adaptable.

7 Task Model Representation

Figure 2 illustrates the top level of our current air campaign planning task model. Many of the subtasks it contains are themselves complex tasks and are in turn broken down and modeled at a comparable level of detail. Task representations and their use have been extensively studied within the human factors and systems analysis communities, among others. Why did we choose to represent this particular content in this particular fashion? The simple answer is that we went with what worked for us— we based our model on empirical utility. Because our approach to organizational memory and performance support is grounded in case-based reasoning theory, with ASK systems playing a crucial role, our decisions were driven by how well the task model served as an indexing framework for the stories, information, advice, and tracking rules we had gathered and developed.

The result of this style of task modeling is a task model that seems relatively simple and intuitive. Several years ago, our research group pursued a more elaborate approach to the explicit modeling of planning tasks that resulted in an aggregation of complex predicate calculus clauses [10]. For this project, though, such complex and highly formal task representations appeared unnecessary for several reasons. First, such a model seemed likely to prove cumbersome when used to drive an application as dynamic as task tracking in a task as complex as air campaign planning.

Second, and more important, complex formal representations are difficult for typical users and designers to understand. And our project was not just about getting a computer to understand what users are doing, but about being able to communicate this understanding to users as well. In order to successfully collaborate with users, a performance support system must be *comprehensible* and *advisable*. Studies into interfaces and decision support for operators of complex, real-time, high-risk systems such as nuclear power plants have found similar needs [11]. Users must be able to trust and understand what the system is doing and why, and the system must be able to accept advice about what it did in a form that is natural to users. In other words, a user and a computer need to collaborate within a shared context. However, complex predicate calculus, or in fact any overly complex form of model, is not a natural basis for this shared context; rather than trust and understanding, it's more likely to foster confusion and frustration in the typical user.

The upshot is that our model of the air campaign planning task is represented in the form of a finite-state machine. There also are several levels representing the top level task and associated sub-tasks. Each level is composed of objects representing individual tasks (we used a simple frame system for our implementation) linked by sequencing information. Each task object is linked relevant cases and problem objects, which are also linked to relevant cases. Although we fully expect that it will ultimately be necessary to extend this approach, we believe that it provides an extremely useful start toward addressing the problems mentioned earlier. First, the simplicity of our approach translates well into simple graphical representations of tasks, which are easily understood by users and designers. Second, it encourages a comparably simple approach to task tracking, where tasks, problems, and transitions within the model are signaled by specific interface and database events. Third, it simplifies modification and extensions to the task model. Finally, the simplicity of the task model is naturally compatible with the mechanisms underlying many user interface management systems.

The most critical point, though, is this: it is the *content* of the task model, not its form, that drives the application. The model's power comes from the kinds of task and problem objects included, and how well they organize cases around a person's current context and thinking.

8 Techniques for Task Tracking

In ACPA, we were specifically interested in tracking two aspects of a task: the progress of users through the task, that is, what subtask a user is currently performing, and the problems encountered by users as they perform the task. These two categories also correspond to the two help modes of Argus: the reactive mode, in which a user explicitly asks for help and Argus responds, and the proactive mode, in which Argus notices a potential problem and notifies the user automatically.

8.1 Tracking Task Flow

While tracking task flow, we can analyze four kinds of information. First, we can look at *windows* (or agents, since windows are often simply manifestations of a specific tool), considering which are open, which are closed, which have "focus," which are visible, even which portions of a specific window are visible. Second, we can analyze *interface activity*—which buttons users click, which fields they type in, which text boxes they scroll, etc. Third, we can analyze *data activity* generated in the performance support tool's database by the users as they work. Fourth, we can analyze the *task history*, recording in the task model what users have achieved so far, and then using the task model itself as a source of information to guide inferences about their current location in the task.

These are the basics. There are also several other interesting task flow issues dealing with user perspective, task context, false starts, and so on, but in the remainder of this paper, we'd like to concentrate on tracking task problems.

8.2 Tracking Task Problems

Most of the especially interesting stories in ACPA—or any ASK system actually—concern problems. Failures are inherently interesting, and according to case-based reasoning theory, a crucial component of learning [12]. People are often most open to new knowledge and forming new cases when their expectations about the world around them fail. Consequently, explicit task problem representation and tracking compose a major part of our integrated performance support methodology.

When we began to investigate what problem recognition techniques might be, we knew that some problems would be easy to recognize, because the *syntax* inherent in the process of using JPT, or in the plan generated by JPT, directly reflected the *semantics* of the air campaign planning task. For instance, tracking whether or not a planner has skipped the *identify measure of merit task* could be cued by the absence of a value in the measure of merit space of the generated plan.

However, we also knew that there would also be a group of problems that didn't fit this pattern, and as a result, would be extremely difficult to track. For example, Table 1 lists the set of these problems types we found in ACPAsk related to developing strategy.

Table 1. A summary of air campaign planning problems that are difficult to track

Developing Strategy	
Not thinking strategically	Not addressing appropriate top priority
Objectives driven by measurables	Developing weak measurables
Objective too broad	Immediate creation of targets
Not thinking creatively	No viable solution
Failing to maintain perspective	Conflicting plan choices
Creating a serial rather than parallel plan	Failing to allow for uncertainty
Misinterpretation of standard domain concepts	

For us, then, the most interesting question became, Can we go beyond tracking the easy problems and help the planners with the difficult ones? In other words, how can we get these interesting, useful experiences stored in the organizational memory to planners when they really need them?

The answer we came up with is an idea we call *discount diagnosis*. Accepting the fact that we may not be able to identify a given problem with certainty, could we still look for simple clues that would indicate the possible presence of the problem, at least in some cases?

Not Thinking Strategically. For instance, consider the first problem listed in Table 1. One story in the air campaign planning ASK system talks about how, at a certain training exercise, a group of planners failed to develop a strategy—they "just started doing stuff." How can we detect this problem? The planners are using the planning tools, but how can we tell whether they are thinking strategically as they do so?

Several trackable features may indicate that this problem exists. For instance, we can look at the planner's task process, or how the planner performs the task. Perhaps a planner jumps directly from consulting the commander's guidance to creating targets. If the planner skips intermediate strategy-building tools, he may not be thinking strategically. Skipping tasks that support the development of strategy but are not used for directly recording strategy, such as situation assessment, may also indicate non-strategic thinking.

We can also look at the task product, or the items that are generated by the task process. For instance, in JPT, the air campaign plan's strategy is represented by a six-level hierarchy of objectives that connect top-level national security objectives and individual targets. If one of these objectives in the hierarchy is connected to too many parents or too many children, that objective may be "too broad," which in turn may mean that the planner is not thinking the situation through. Target ratios may also be an indication that the planner is not thinking strategically. For example, if a plan contains a large number of "low-impact" targets (e.g., anti-aircraft, ground forces) that have little impact on the plan's primary objectives, compared with "high-impact" targets (e.g., communications facilities, power plants), then the plan may not possess much of a strategy.

Patterns of Evidence. We have found the patterns of evidence listed in Table 2 useful for tracking these types of problems.

Table 2. Patterns of evidence for tracking task problems

Task order: Are there abnormal patterns that appear in the order of the subtasks? For instance, a user who jumps around in the task may be confused; a strategic planner who jumps immediately to creating target lists may not be thinking strategically.	*Quantities*: Is the user creating too much or too little of a particular type of component? Is the user performing too much or too little of a particular type of action?
Intervals: Has the user failed to do something after a certain interval of time?	*Key events*: Has the user done something or failed to do something after a certain event?
Ratios: Is there an imbalance in the quantity of one type of component in the work product compared to another type of component? Is there an imbalance in the number of times a user performs one type of action compared to another type of action?	*Modifications*: Has the user changed or failed to change something after a certain interval of time? Has the user selected a component from an archive of previous components and changed or failed to change it?
Searching: Does the user appear to be searching for long periods of time?	*Phrasing*: Is the user invoking words or phrases that indicate problematic or vague concepts?
Thrashing: Does the user appear to be moving quickly back and forth between a certain group of tools?	

9   Conclusions and Tools for the Future

Limited space prevents us from presenting a detailed comparison between ACPA and related work. However, ACPA is particularly distinguished by the fact that it retrieves cases based on features of a person's entire task process, not just features of a task product (e.g., a design, a plan, or a text). Furthermore, ACPA does this through integration with a performance tool and the use of task tracking to infer task features, without requiring the person to manually specify features to a stand-alone tool. Also, task tracking and case retrieval are supported by an explicit task model that is an internalized component of the final system.

As for future work, we believe that there exists a set of abstract, standardized, reusable task models, general enough to cover a wide variety of domains, and yet containing enough specific content to direct the construction of useful interfaces, performance support, and so forth. For example, the task of air campaign planning can be seen as a specific case of the more abstract task of strategic planning, which itself is the root of similar tasks in other domains. These tasks, such as strategic business planning, share common processes, common tools, and common problems.

We eventually hope to create a library of such task models, as well as development tools that are driven by them. We believe the result will be easy-to-use, easy-to-build, easy-to-modify, highly intelligent performance support and training systems.

Acknowledgements. We thank everyone at the United States Air Force, the ISX Corporation, and Northwestern University who helped in the development of ACPA. This work was supported in part by the Defense Advanced Research Projects Agency and Rome Laboratory under contract F30602-95-1-0019. Chris Johnson was supported in part by a graduate fellowship from the National Science Foundation.

References

1. Davenport, T.H., Prusak, L.: Working Knowledge: How Organizations Manage What They Know. Harvard Business School Press, Boston (1998)
2. Ferguson, W., Bareiss, R., Birnbaum, L., Osgood, R.: ASK Systems: An Approach to the Realization of Story-Based Teachers. The Journal of the Learning Sciences 1,2 (1992) 95-134
3. Bareiss, R., Osgood, R.: Applying AI Models to the Design of Exploratory Hypermedia Systems. Hypertext'93 (Seattle 1993). ACM Press 94-105
4. Weber, R., Aha, D.W., Becerra-Fernandez, I.: Intelligent Lessons Learned Systems. Expert Systems with Applications 20 (2001) 17-34
5. Thaler, D.E.: Strategies to Tasks: A Framework for Linking Means to Ends. RAND, Santa Monica, CA (1993)
6. Warden, Colonel J.F. III: 1989. The Air Campaign: Planning for Combat. Pergamon Press, Washington, DC (1989)
7. Lenz, M., Ashley, D.: Textual Case-Based Reasoning: Papers from the 1998 AAAI Workshop. AAAI Press, Menlo Park, CA (1998)
8. Valente, A., Blythe, J., Gil, Y., Swartout, W.: On the Role of Humans in Enterprise Control Systems: the Experience of INSPECT. DARPA-JFACC Symposium on Advances in Enterprise Control (San Diego 1999)
9. Rasmussen, J.R.: Information Processing and Human-Machine Interaction: An Approach to Cognitive Engineering. North-Holland, New York (1986)
10. Collins, G., Birnbaum, L., Krulwich, B., Freed, M.: The Role of Self-Models in Learning to Plan. In: Meyrowitz, A.L., Chipman, S. (eds.): Foundations of Knowledge Acquisition: Machine Learning. Kluwer, Boston (1993) 117-143
11. Mitchell, C.M.: Models for the Design of Human Interaction with Complex Dynamic Systems. Cognitive Engineering Systems in Process Control (Kyoto, Japan 1996)
12. Schank, R.: Dynamic Memory: A Theory of Reminding and Learning in Computers and People. Cambridge University Press, New York (1982)

Transforming Electronic Mail Folders into Case Bases

Dai Kusui and Hideo Shimazu

NEC Laboratories, NEC Corporation,
8916-47, Takayama-Cho, Ikoma, Nara 630-0101, Japan
(kusui@ccm.cl.nec.co.jp, shimazu@ccm.cl.nec.co.jp)

Abstract. This paper analyzes instant knowledge sharing among customer support agents. Customer support agents effectively exchange useful information through electronic mail and electronic bulletin board services. Empirical analyses have taught us that the direct use of electronic mail is the key towards instant knowledge sharing in busy organizations like high-tech product customer support organizations. The authors have developed "Interaction Viewer", an instant CBR tool that runs with commercial electronic mail management systems such as Microsoft Outlook Express. The tool analyzes the relations among electronic mail messages by tracing the body texts and extracting quotation descriptions inserted in the bodies. A pair of a question mail message and its answer mail message is integrated into a case. Because all mail messages are automatically modified into cases and mail folders are transformed into a case base, instant knowledge sharing is easily achieved. Although the case retrieval performance is not as good as more integrated CBR systems, the easy-to-adopt feature of the approach should be welcome by busy organizations. It should also be welcome by marketing divisions to analyze various customers opinions.

1 Introduction

This paper describes "Interaction viewer", a case-based retrieval system that directly uses electronic mail folders or electronic bulletin boards as its case storage.

The motivation behind this research was two-fold. First, conventional case-based reasoning (CBR) systems make it hard for busy agents in customer support organizations for high-tech products to maintain the case-bases everyday.

The authors have been working with internal customer support organizations and developing case-based retrieval systems for customer support using conversational case-based reasoning techniques [Aha & Breslow 1997]. "ExpertGuide" [Shimazu et al 2001] is the most recent commercial product of the authors. The system provides various indexing features that allow users to retrieve useful cases. It includes 1) Multi link retrieval, 2) Question selection by entropy, and 3) Indexing with scripts. Multi link retrieval provides a method for searching within a case library from several viewpoints. Question selection by entropy

D.W. Aha and I. Watson (Eds.): ICCBR 2001, LNAI 2080, pp. 690–701, 2001.
© Springer-Verlag Berlin Heidelberg 2001

finds the most effective questions by discriminating cases with information gain values of candidate questions. Indexing with scripts is a case-indexing method using scripts; it was proposed by Schank. Although ExpertGuide provides a case-authoring tool capable of being used by ordinary customer support agents, it is still hard for the agents to create new cases in their daily work routines. Extra skills and effort are required for the authoring of cases.

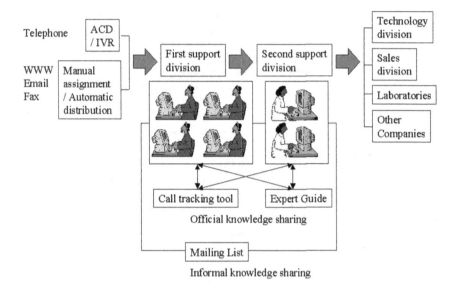

Fig. 1. Workflow in call centers

Second, the authors found that customer support agents often exchange information using electronic mail (email) and electronic bulletin board (BBS) services inside customer support organizations. The information includes bug fix news and frequently asked questions about new products. The information is not officially announced information from development divisions.

The agents often search through past email messages using the search functions provided by conventional mail systems such as Microsoft Outlook Express. The authors recognized that it is necessary to design an instant case-based retrieval system running on conventional mail systems. Unfortunately, there seems to be no CBR system that directly uses commercial email systems as its case storage.

This paper describes the design policy of Interaction Viewer and its basic functions. Interaction Viewer has been used as a customer opinion analysis tool in marketing divisions as well as a case-based retrieval tool in customer support organizations.

2   Email Conversations between Agents

This section analyzes aspects of email conversations between agents as shown in Figure 2. These conversations have the following characteristics:

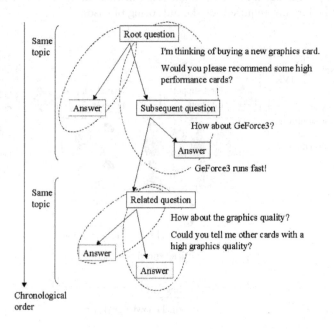

Fig. 2. Typical sequence in an email list

Email messages are grouped inside the same subjects. A first agent generates a new email message with a new subject in the mail header. The email message includes an initial question. Then, another agent replies to the message with a direct answer to the initial question. If the answer satisfies the initial question, the pair of a question message and its answer message constructs a case. If the second agent later asks a confirmation question like "did the PC recognize the CDROM at the device manager panel when you encountered the problem?", the first agent answers the confirmation question. Sometimes, a third person may ask a different question to clarify the point of the question. Such questions automatically construct a discrimination tree.

Quotations inside email messages construct relations among the messages. Basic relations among email messages can be traced by analyzing their header information such as the Subject, Message-Id, In-Reply-To, and References. Agents frequently include parts of another agent's message descriptions in quotation form. Such references express real relations between a referred message and a referring message. It is necessary to trace all of the texts in all of the email bodies to extract all quotations properly.

Email attributes include valuable information. An email header includes a sender name, receiver name, subject, and issued date and time. An email body often includes a sender signature. These attributes are used as the ingredients when building a human relationship database or who-knows-what directories.

Different topics may be included in email messages with the same subject. When many agents exchange email messages with the same subject, the discussion sometimes changes from the root question to a different question.

3 Design Decisions

The authors designed an instant CBR tool called "Interaction Viewer". This section describes the design decisions involving Interaction Viewer.

3.1 Defining the Model of an Email

An email message consists of a header section and a body section as shown in Figure 3. The header section has several attributes including a subject, sender, receiver, date and time, and so on. Each attribute is an index of the email. The body section consists of several pairs of a quotation part and a sentence part, and a signature part at the end.

There are two types of references. One is inserted in the header section. The subject often includes "Re:". This indicates that the message is a reply to a specific previous email. The in-reply-to attribute and reference attribute indicate the previous email message's message-id. The other type of reference includes quotation parts included in the email body. These quotation parts are copied from the previous email message. It is also an important index of the email. The keywords included in the quotation parts also become indices of the email.

3.2 Analyzing the Sequence of Email Messages

A first agent generates a new email message including an initial question with a new subject in the mail header. The initial question is called the *root question.* The replies of subsequent email messages are called *answers.* If an answer satisfies the root question, the pair of the question email and the answer email constructs a *case.* An answer email may at times include not only a partial answer but also a related question, like "what was the status of the device manager when you encountered the problem?" Such a question is asked to clarify the root question and called *subsequent question.* The sequence of subsequent questions automatically constructs a discrimination tree. Figure 2 shows relations among emails. A subsequent email sometimes includes a description that raises a new question related to the root question. Subsequent email messages might quote

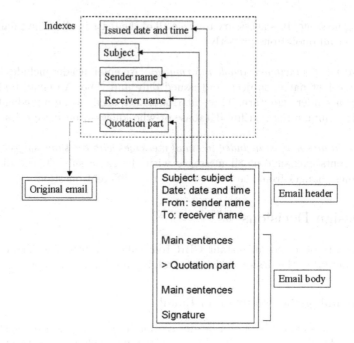

Fig. 3. An email structure

the new question instead of replying to the root question. This means that the main topic has been changed from the root question to the new question. The email starting the new question can be regarded as a new root question although the SUBJECT attribute includes the same description as the old root question email. It is difficult for a computer to find such a topic change in an email list automatically. A system has to be made to comprehend meanings to handle such a topic change.

3.3   Generating Multiple Viewpoints for an Email Sequence

Email messages can be sorted and grouped by different viewpoints. An original email sequence is placed in chronological order of the arriving time. The messages construct to a tree of referential relations. They are grouped by their contents described in the subject sections. For example, some of the messages including the keyword "USB" in the subject sections are grouped in the same category, and other email messages whose subject sections include the keyword "LAN" are grouped in another category. These categories are created based on the frequency of keyword appearances in the subject sections. Email messages are also grouped by sender name or issued date and time. Figure 4 shows how chronological ordered emails are sorted and grouped differently by subject and issued date and time.

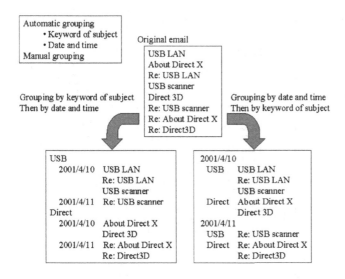

Fig. 4. Clustering email messages

4   Interaction Viewer

4.1   Outline of Interaction Viewer

Based on the results examined in section 3, we designed an instant CBR tool called "Interaction Viewer" as follows.

Interaction Viewer has two modes, i.e., *email list analysis mode* and *case view mode*. The email list analysis mode loads a list of email messages. Interaction Viewer analyzes the relationships among the email messages and displays a tree structure.

The typical use of Interaction Viewer is as follows. An agent uses the many messages it receives as a case base to answer a question-type message.

Figure 5 shows the initial screen of Interaction Viewer. The left-hand pane of the window is a list of original email folders. The middle-center pane of the window shows an arranged email-tree of referential relationships. An Interaction Viewer user can change the view of the tree structure to chronological order or can cluster email messages by subject, sender name, or issued date and time. If the user selects an email message in the pane, the contents of the email are shown in the bottom pane of the window. The top-right pane of the window shows a summary of the selected email message sequence.

The referential relationships among email messages can be displayed in another window like Figure 6. The figure shows messages with the email addresses of the senders using indentation.

The agent retrieves messages and understands their contexts through the referential relationships like Figure 6. If the agent finds a topic change from a root question to a new question within the referential relationships, the agent

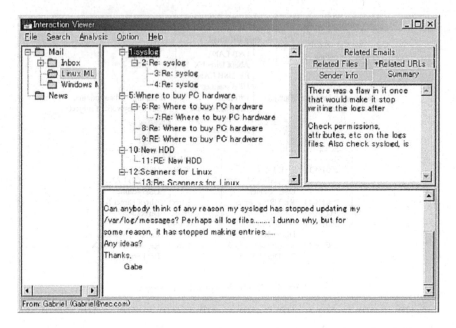

Fig. 5. The IV initial screen

Q & A tree expressing reference relationships among email messages

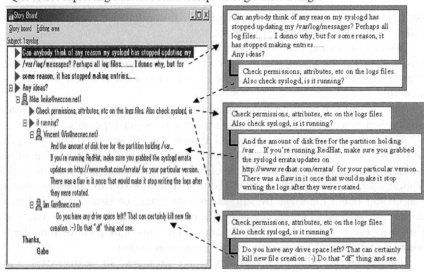

Fig. 6. Visualizing email flows

can cut the corresponding branch of the email tree list, connect it to the tree root, and store the new tree structure in the database. In this way, the case base is gradually regulated.

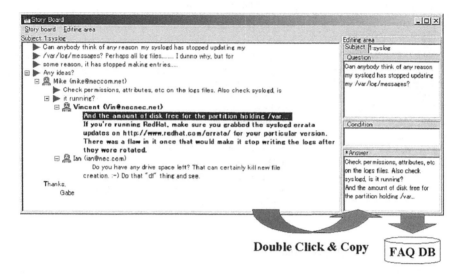

Fig. 7. Generating a new FAQ

If cases similar to a received question are abundant in the case base or if the question is judged to be a useful case, the agent generates a FAQ (Frequently Asked Question). A FAQ generation support tool is built into Interaction Viewer. When the agent accesses his/her email messages, if he/she finds a useful pair of a question and an answer, the agent can copy-and-paste the pair to generate a FAQ database like Figure 7.

All generated FAQs may be disclosed through the WWW. If end users can refer to the database of these FAQs through the WWW, they may be able to solve their problems themselves, and the agent can answer other questions.

The case base is also useful for analyzing various customer opinions in marketing divisions, product development divisions, and so on. An Interaction Viewer user can analyze the number of email topics, the number of email messages sent by a sender, and the message tendency of a sender (asks a lot, answers a lot, etc.). Interaction Viewer can generate a table of email topics and senders. This table includes the total email count of each topic (question and answer sequence) and sender, the number of a user's question-type email messages and the number of his/her answer-type email messages, a user's percentage of quotation parts in email bodies, and so on, like Figure 8. The FAQ database and the table of email topics and senders generated by Interaction Viewer are effective for this purpose.

In the case view mode, a user chooses a viewpoint before searching through topics. The viewpoints that the user can choose from are a chronological email

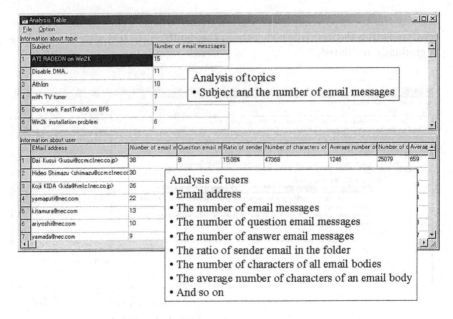

Fig. 8. Analyzing users in email communities

list, email tree of referential relationships, or categorized email group. The user can also set the search conditions such as the keyword combination, from-date time, to-date time, subject, sender, and receiver. The user can retry a search by changing the current viewpoint and search conditions until he/she reaches a satisfactory answer.

4.2   Evaluation

We carried out an experiment using 296 email messages. These messages were separated into 105 threads. A conventional mail reader using only email header information generated 82 threads. It had 23 isolation-failures and two connection-failures. The term isolation-failure means that a thread becomes connected to another thread although it should be isolated. The term connection-failure means that a thread becomes isolated although it should be connected to another thread. Interaction Viewer generated 105 threads. It had no isolation-failures and two connection-failures.

Interaction Viewer decreases the error rate in thread generation. The quality of the case base improves by decrease in the error rate. Interaction Viewer has already been adopted as a tool for analyzing various customer opinions in one marketing division. It is also under trial in five other divisions. Interaction Viewer has been highly evaluated by users because of its ability to save much time and labor.

5   Related Works

Nonaka assumes the existence of tacit knowledge and articulated knowledge in his theory of organizational knowledge creation [Nonaka 1991]. He explains that organizational knowledge spreads through the process of (1) socialization, (2) externalization, (3) combination, and (4) internalization. In the socialization process, unskilled members work with senior members to acquire skills on the job. Next, in the articulation process, the group documents these skills, so that some tacit knowledge is articulated. With a set of documents, new knowledge can be created by combining them and can spread beyond the group. In the fourth process, the knowledge acts on the basis of a new knowledge creation cycle.

The development of a conventional CBR system is defined as the process from externalization to combination. Before the externalization, the system designer designs the formalization of cases. Then, he/she assigns various indices to the cases. This is the combination process.

On the other hand, the development of an instant CBR system is defined as a process from socialization to externalization as shown in Figure 9. Mailing lists are just the place for such socialization. The instant CBR system directly modifies the socialization place into an externalization place.

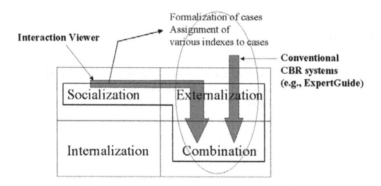

Fig. 9. The translation of tacit knowledge into explicit knowledge

This is a new and unique feature of instant CBR systems used with commercial email systems. The instant CBR system can save time and labor. Accordingly, it can be advantageous in busy organizations like high-tech product customer support organizations. For example, [Göker & Roth-Berghofer 1999] and [Thomas et al 1997] state the importance of CBR technology in customer support and help desk services.

Unlike conventional mail/news readers, Interaction Viewer provides a threaded list of messages based on their contents to make the reference more accurate. Conventional threaded mail/news readers, such as trn on Unix, generally make message threads using only message header information such as the message-id, in-reply-to, and reference attributes. However, these mail/news readers fail to make message threads if there are messages sent by several mail/news readers that do not add this header information. A user who has several mail addresses occasionally forwards received messages to other addresses. In such cases, the in-reply-to and reference attributes of answer-type messages for the forwarded messages differ from the original message's header information. As a result, message threads are not created. Interaction Viewer uses quotation parts included in the message bodies as well as header information to make message threads, so Interaction Viewer can successfully identify referential relationships even in such cases.

There are several software products that can handle email messages for their reuse in the customer support domain. Kana Response [Kana 2001] analyzes email messages and classifies them based on their urgency and priority levels. Kana Notify receives a user's query by an email message and automatically generates a reply email message using its template database. Solution Builder [Primus 2001] is a help desk support tool with which human agents describe customer inquiries with predefined tags and retrieve past inquiries using the tags. These tags are used to express important terms such as product names. A user can describe a query using tags like "retrieve an inquiry that includes X as the product name and Y as the symptom".

6   Conclusion

In this paper, we described how to achieve an instant knowledge sharing system. Empirical analysis has taught us that the direct use of email messages is the key towards instant knowledge sharing. The instant knowledge sharing system is useful in busy organizations like high-tech product customer support organizations because it saves time and labor. The authors analyzed aspects of email conversations among customer support agents, and investigated the characteristics involved.

We developed "Interaction Viewer", an instant CBR tool. Interaction Viewer directly uses email folders or electronic bulletin boards as its case storage, and provides reorganized viewpoints of cases. A user can retry a search by changing the viewpoint and search conditions. Interaction Viewer can show the referential relationships among email messages with a sender's email address. It also supports FAQ generation with the referential relationships. The user can analyze the number of email topics, the number of email messages sent by a sender, and the message tendency of a sender.

The analysis accuracy of Interaction Viewer makes it practically useful as a support tool for customer support divisions. The usefulness of Interaction Viewer in a customer support environment is explained in this paper. Interaction Viewer is also useful for analyzing various customer opinions in the marketing divisions of companies.

References

[Aha & Breslow 1997] Aha, D.W., and Breslow, L.A.: 1997, Refining conversational case libraries, *Proceedings of the Second International Conference on Case-Based Reasoning*, pp. 267 – 278.

[Aha et al 1998] Aha, D.W., Maney, T., and Breslow, L.A.: 1998, Supporting dialogue inferencing in conversational case-based reasoning, *Proceedings of the Fourth European Workshop on Case-Based Reasoning*, pp. 262 – 273, LNAI 1488, Springer Verlag, Berlin.

[Göker & Roth-Berghofer 1999] Göker, M. and Roth-Berghofer, T.: 1999, Development and Utilization of a Case-Based Help-Desk Support System in a Corporate Environment, *Case-Based Reasoning Research and Development, Proceedings of the ICCBR99*, pp. 132 – 146, LNAI 1650, Springer Verlag, Berlin.

[Kana 2001] Kana communications home page, (http://www.kana.com).

[Nonaka 1991] Nonaka, I.: 1991. *The Knowledge-Creating Company*. Cambridge, MA: Harvard Business Review.

[Primus 2001] PRIMUS home page, (http://www.primus.com).

[Shimazu et al 2001] Shimazu, H. and Shibata, A., and Nihei, K. : 2001. ExpertGuide: A Conversational Case-based Reasoning Tool for Developing Mentors in Knowledge Spaces *The International Journal of Artificial Intelligence, Neural Networks, and Complex Problem-Solving Technologies*, Vol. 14, Issue 1, January 2001. Kluwer Academic Publishers.

[Thomas et al 1997] Thomas, H., Foil, R., and Dacus, J.: 1997, New Technology Bliss and Pain in a Large Customer Service Center, *Case-Based Reasoning Research and Development, Proceedings of the ICCBR97* , pp. 166 – 177, LNAI 1266, Springer Verlag, Berlin.

Case-Based Reasoning in the Care of Alzheimer's Disease Patients

Cindy Marling[1] and Peter Whitehouse[2]

[1] School of Electrical Engineering and Computer Science
Ohio University, Athens, Ohio 45701, USA
marling@ohio.edu
[2] University Alzheimer Center and School of Medicine
Case Western Reserve University, Cleveland, Ohio 44106, USA
pjw3@po.cwru.edu

Abstract. Planning the ongoing care of Alzheimer's Disease (AD) patients is a complex task, marked by cases that change over time, multiple perspectives, and ethical issues. Geriatric interdisciplinary teams of physicians, nurses and social workers currently plan this care without computer assistance. Although AD is incurable, interventions are planned to improve the quality of life for patients and their families. Much of the reasoning involved is case-based, as clinicians look to case histories to learn which interventions are effective, to document clinical findings, and to train future health care professionals.

There is great variability among AD patients, and within the same patient over time. AD is not yet well enough understood for universally effective treatments to be available. The case-based reasoning (CBR) research paradigm complements the medical research approach of finding treatments effective for all patients by matching patients to treatments that were effective for similar patients in the past.

The Auguste Project is an effort to provide decision support for planning the ongoing care of AD patients, using CBR and other thought processes natural to members of geriatric interdisciplinary teams. System prototypes are used to explore the reasoning processes involved and to provide the forerunners of practical clinical tools. The first system prototype has just been completed. This prototype supports the decision to prescribe neuroleptic drugs to AD patients with behavioral problems. It uses CBR to determine if a neuroleptic drug should be prescribed and rule-based reasoning to select one of five approved neuroleptic drugs for a patient. The first system prototype serves as proof of concept that CBR is useful for planning ongoing care for AD patients. Additional prototypes are planned to explore the research issues raised.

1 Introduction

One hundred years ago, a fifty-one-year-old woman called Auguste D. was admitted to a clinic in Frankfurt, Germany. She had been suddenly beset by cognitive and personality changes, which were progressing insidiously. She was now jealous

D.W. Aha and I. Watson (Eds.): ICCBR 2001, LNAI 2080, pp. 702–715, 2001.
© Springer-Verlag Berlin Heidelberg 2001

of her husband, to whom she had been happily married for nearly thirty years. She had become careless with her household money, would make mistakes in preparing meals, and would put things away and forget where they were. Auguste D. spent the last four and a half years of her life at the clinic, where her condition steadily deteriorated. She became disoriented as to time and place, anxious, agitated, and uncooperative. At the end, she was wholly unresponsive and bedridden [18].

The psychiatrist who cared for her, unfamiliar with this disease process, carefully documented her progress. When she died, he autopsied her brain, discovering neuritic plaques and neurofibrillary tangles. He lectured and wrote, sharing his findings with the leading psychiatrists of his day. He concluded one paper,

> On the whole, it is evident that we are dealing with a peculiar, little-known disease process... We must not be satisfied to force it into the existing group of well-known disease patterns. It is clear that there exist many more mental diseases than our textbooks indicate. In many such cases, a further histological examination must be effected to determine the characteristics of each single case. [2][1]

Thus, Dr. Alois Alzheimer not only pioneered the investigation of the disease that bears his name, but also championed the use of case-based reasoning (CBR) in weak-theory domains.

Today, it is estimated that over twelve million people are afflicted with Alzheimer's Disease (AD) [11]. Case histories are still widely used to train health care professionals and to share clinical findings [17]. There is still no cure, but interventions are planned to improve the quality of life for patients and their family members. Due to the wide variability among patients, and within the same patient over time, these interventions must be painstakingly tailored to each patient. No computer-based assistance is available for this time-consuming task.

The Auguste Project was begun to investigate how case-based and multi-modal reasoning might model how health care professionals plan ongoing care for AD patients. Long-range goals are to:

1. gain a better understanding of the reasoning processes employed by health care professionals
2. learn what extensions are needed to CBR for a domain that includes:
   a) multiple, sometimes conflicting, perspectives of professionals from different disciplines
   b) cases that change over time
   c) ethical considerations and viewpoints
3. provide practical decision support tools for this difficult task

This paper describes the Auguste Project and its progress to date.

---

[1] This translation from the original was excerpted from [18].

2   The Auguste Project

The Auguste Project is a collaboration among case-based reasoning researchers and clinicians at the University Alzheimer Center, a U.S. Alzheimer's Disease Research Center (ADRC). The Center is one of twenty-six ADRCs sponsored by the National Institute of Aging (NIA), one of the National Institutes of Health (NIH). Clinicians at the Center work in geriatric interdisciplinary teams, including physicians, nurses and social workers, to collaboratively plan health care interventions for patients. The geriatric interdisciplinary team approach was instituted to improve the quality and cost-effectiveness of traditional patient care [13]. As the population ages and health care costs soar, it is important to find ways to minimize the time spent with each patient, while still providing high quality care. Teamwork has helped, by pooling the talents of different professionals. The focus of the Auguste Project is to further improve quality and efficiency, through case-based decision support tools. The ultimate goal is to build a virtual member of a geriatric interdisciplinary team. Such a system could not only support existing teams, but might also transfer the experience base of these geriatric specialists to the general practitioners who initially treat the majority of AD patients.

Many research issues must be investigated and resolved before the virtual team member can be built. Because of the great variability among patients, and within the same patient over time, standard medical quality assurance techniques, like critical care paths, do not readily apply. Current artificial intelligence (AI) technology is not yet ripe for this problem domain, because it is still unknown how to best represent and reason about: distributed, possibly conflicting, viewpoints; conditions that change over time, despite or because of planned interventions; and problems with solutions that depend on ethical perspective. However, geriatric interdisciplinary team members function effectively despite these difficulties, and their reasoning strategies may be modeled to shed light on these issues.

These issues are being explored in the Auguste Project by building and evaluating prototypical systems to support the various decisions that must be made for each AD patient. Many medical, social and nursing interventions are available, each of which may or may not benefit a particular patient at a given time. Although more issues have been raised than resolved to date, initial results are encouraging. The first system prototype has just been completed. This prototype supports the decision to prescribe neuroleptic drugs to control the behavioral problems that may beset AD patients.

3   The First System Prototype

Auguste D. once had to be isolated from the other patients at her clinic, because she was hitting them [18]. About half of all AD patients develop behavioral problems at some point during their disease, such as aggressiveness, disinhibition, or wandering away from home. These symptoms can be extremely stressful for family caregivers, as well as uncomfortable or unsafe for the patient. Some patients respond well to behavior management techniques. Other patients may respond to one of five different neuroleptic drugs approved by the U.S. Food and Drug Administration (FDA) [20,22,26]. Legally, the decision to prescribe a neuroleptic drug is the responsibility of the physician. The physician makes this decision with input from the nurse, social worker and family caregivers. The first system prototype helps the physician decide whether or not a patient would benefit from a neuroleptic drug, and if so, which one.

3.1   Case Representation

The first task in building the prototype was to represent a case. It was decided to make the case extensible, but to initially focus on just those features pertaining to the decision to prescribe a neuroleptic. The second author identified the factors considered by a physician in making this decision. Approximately 100 features were required to represent the problem description and solution for a case. The problem description depicts the patient in terms of medical history plus current physical, emotional, behavioral and cognitive status. It depicts the patient's environment in terms of caregivers, caregiver stress, available support services, safety concerns, and financial limitations. The solution tells whether or not a patient was prescribed a neuroleptic and, if so, which one. It also contains any other medication changes and behavioral interventions.

At the Center, information about patients is recorded on paper and maintained in patient charts. Hundreds of data points are recorded for each patient, in charts that contain from 25 to 50 pages apiece. Some of the data is semi-structured, in that it is handwritten on standard intake forms or transcribed from dictations following a standard format. Other information may vary in kind and in format, from chart to chart. The identified features were manually extracted from charts and organized hierarchically into cases. The top level organization of a case is shown in Figure 1. Twenty-eight cases were built and stored in the case base. The size of the case base was limited by the time required to extract the needed information from charts.

3.2   System Architecture

The architecture of the first system prototype is shown in Figure 2. This is a *master-slave* architecture, in the parlance of [1], in that an essentially CBR system has been enhanced by another reasoning modality. Here, CBR is used to decide whether or not a patient would benefit from a neuroleptic drug, and rule-based reasoning (RBR) is used to select one of the five available neuroleptic drugs for a patient.

The first step, upon receiving input for a new patient, is to see if the patient can quickly be screened out as a candidate for neuroleptic drugs. Patients without behavioral problems and patients already taking neuroleptics need not be considered further. One advantage of this initial screening is that it improves problem solving efficiency. It will also help to prevent brittleness as support for

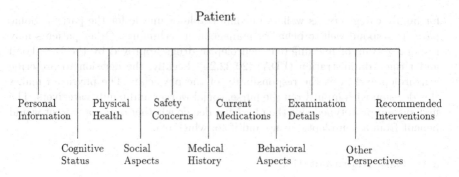

Fig. 1. Top Level View of a Case

more interventions is added to the system and each patient is considered for the most appropriate interventions.

The next step is to identify potentially similar cases within the case base. An initial discrimination is made based on Mini Mental Status Examination (MMSE) scores. The MMSE is a test of cognitive status. Patients with similar MMSE scores may be at similar stages of the disease, and thus may be treated similarly. This was the feature that most stood out as having discriminating power during tests of average disorder. Its usefulness was empirically validated by matching and ranking patients with and without initial discrimination on this feature.

Next, nearest neighbor matching is used to find the most similar case from among those initially identified. The biggest challenge in building the retrieval metric was determining which factors were most influential in defining patient similarity. A quick check of the number of features two patients share in common, not surprisingly, was worthless. A combination of physician input, average disorder analysis, and trial and error eventually led to the identification of nine salient features to include in the metric. These are: agitation; anxiety; hallucinations; paranoia; wandering; caregiver stress; external support services; concurrent Parkinson's disease or Parkinsonism; and problems with dressing, bathing, or transfer. These nine features are weighted equally in nearest neighbor matching.

As is standard practice in nearest neighbor matching, a domain dependent similarity function was developed for each feature. For binary valued features, such as whether or not a patient wanders, cases can only match or not match. For features with a range of values, like the number of external support services used, the degree of similarity between cases is computed. If data is missing for a feature, then cases are considered as not matching on that feature. A simple numeric cutoff is used to ensure that the system does not make an uninformed recommendation when no case in the case base is sufficiently similar to the new patient. The case with the highest match score above that cutoff is identified as the nearest neighbor.

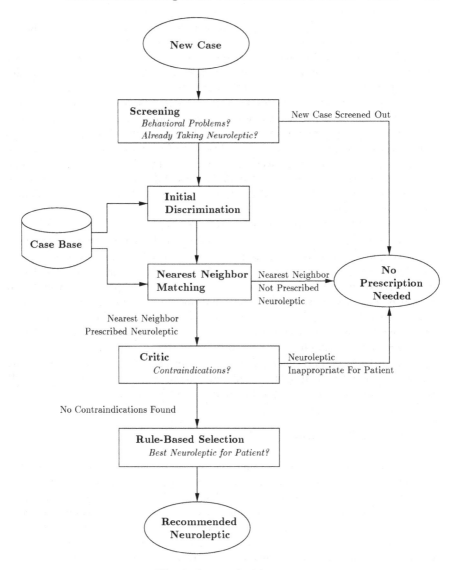

Fig. 2. System Architecture

If the new case's nearest neighbor has not been prescribed a neuroleptic, then no neuroleptic is recommended for the new patient. Otherwise, a critic is consulted, to make sure there are no contraindications to the new patient's taking a neuroleptic. For example, it is unsafe to prescribe a neuroleptic to a patient unless a caregiver is available to supervise handling of the medication. Allergies are also checked, although they occur infrequently for this type of drug.

Once the system determines that a neuroleptic is appropriate for the patient, an RBR module determines which of the five drugs would be best. RBR was initially selected for this part of the task because: the physician naturally described the prescription process in terms of rules; it was hoped that the rules could be easily modified as new neuroleptic drugs became available; and only a few good cases were available, as most AD patients do not take neuroleptic drugs. During knowledge acquisition for rule development, the physician at one point began using model-based reasoning, describing the effects of the various drugs on the cholinergic system of the brain. Unfortunately, this model did not extend to cover all relevant aspects of the decision. The disease process is not well enough understood to develop a complete physiological model. RBR proved to be a workable, pragmatic modality, although less than ideal, as will be explained in the next sections.

The primary system output is a recommendation for a specific neuroleptic for a patient. Additional recommendations may be displayed, when appropriate. For example, if a patient has trouble sleeping, the recommendation is made to administer the neuroleptic in the evening, to take advantage of its sedating effects. Recommendations are delivered via a password protected Web-based interface. The user may click on additional options for supporting information. If the user asks to see the basis of the patient comparison, the similarities and differences between the most similar past case and the current case are displayed. The user may request a full textual report on the most similar past case, in order to make further comparisons manually. The user may also ask for the reasoning behind the choice of neuroleptic. Explanations are not "rule chains" in the RBR sense, but informative messages prepared to explain the effects of the drugs.

3.3   System Evaluation

In addition to the continuous evaluation and refinement that characterizes the prototyping environment, the first system prototype was subjected to two types of evaluation as it neared completion. The first form of evaluation was a system test, in which test cases were input to see if the system's recommendations matched the recommendations actually made for the patient by health care professionals at the Center. The second form of evaluation was a system demonstration for clinicians at the Center, followed by an open feedback session and completion of structured feedback questionnaires.

For the system test, eight new cases were provided by the Center staff. Due to the difficulty of acquiring new cases, the test cases contained only the data needed to formulate a recommendation for the patient. There were approximately thirty data points needed by the reasoning modules. A Web-based interface was developed to facilitate entry of these data points. Had full cases been available, it would have been possible to generate textual reports for the new patients and to add the new cases to the case base to improve system coverage after the tests. The test cases were used only to compare system outputs to recommendations actually made for patients.

The test was conducted in two stages, to test the CBR and RBR modules as well as the final system output. All eight test cases were correctly classified by the CBR module as potentially needing or not needing a neuroleptic. However, one of the match scores was below the cutoff established to ensure a sufficient degree of match between cases. Neuroleptic drugs were recommended for three of the eight test cases. The neuroleptic recommended by the system matched that prescribed by the second author for only one of the three cases, despite the fact that he provided the rules for the system. In preliminary tests, in which cases were removed from the case base one at a time to serve as test cases, better agreement had been obtained. An analysis of the problem revealed two possible explanations: (a) errors or omissions in the charts may have caused important factors to be overlooked; (b) drugs may be favored when the latest evidence points to their effectiveness and then be less favored if results are disappointing or if new evidence suggests better alternatives.

After the system test, a demonstration and feedback session was held for clinicians at the Center. Clinicians were asked to anonymously complete structured feedback questionnaires, indicating their level of agreement with each of eleven statements. Eight of the twelve clinicians who attended the demo completed the questionnaire. Most people agreed that:

- The system seemed easy to use
- The system's suggestions were easy to understand
- The system's suggestions were comparable to those a knowledgeable clinician would make
- The comparison of two patients helped them understand why a neuroleptic was or was not prescribed
- The tool would be useful for training future health care professionals
- The tool would be useful to general practitioners
- The tool would be useful to geriatric interdisciplinary teams

Half of the respondents agreed, while half had mixed feelings, that:

- The report for a similar past patient helped them decide how to treat the current patient
- The explanation of the reasoning behind the choice of neuroleptic helped them evaluate if the suggested drug is right for the patient

Most respondents had mixed feelings about statements that:

- The system collects the right information needed to make informed decisions
- They would feel comfortable using the system's recommendations for their patients

Clinicians were also asked to note any other decisions they make for AD patients that could be facilitated by this type of system. Responses were:

- selecting drugs to treat agitation
- selecting anti-depressant drugs

- addressing competence/capacity issues, such as determining that a patient should no longer drive, manage their own finances, or manage their own health care
- detecting safety risks
- suggesting appropriate day care options
- providing caregiver support information

3.4 Discussion

The RBR module was the least successful part of the system prototype. As previously noted, system outputs did not always match physician recommendations. This was also the least popular part of the system in open discussion with Center clinicians. All physicians present at the demo were experts affiliated with a premier ADRC. These physicians do not all operate according to the same set of rules. The opinion was expressed, but not universally shared, that the CBR module seemed more evidence-based, and therefore more trustworthy, than the RBR module. The possibility of using a second CBR module to replace the RBR module will be explored.

Note that empirical evidence on which to base universally agreed upon rules is not readily available in this domain. In a recent study comparing four treatments for agitation, which often co-occurs with behavior problems, no significant differences were found among patients treated with a neuroleptic, an anti-depressant, behavior management techniques or a placebo [24]. Patients were randomly assigned to receive one of the four treatments, so that any differences noted could be ascribed solely to the effects of the treatments. This type of randomized, placebo-controlled clinical trial is a standard research paradigm in medical domains, where treatments are sought that can be universally applied. The CBR research paradigm complements this approach in the absence of universally applicable treatments. In [24], 34% of patients showed improvement after treatment. Each treatment helped some, but not most, patients. In CBR, patients can be matched to treatments that have helped other similar individuals. The hope is that this may lead to higher overall treatment success rates.

4   Future Work

The first system prototype serves as proof of concept that CBR can help provide decision support for planning the ongoing care of AD patients. Much work remains ahead before the virtual geriatric interdisciplinary team member becomes a reality. The hardest issues to resolve will be those of: integrating the multiple perspectives of team members from different disciplines; comparing cases that change over time; and incorporating ethical perspectives.

In the first system prototype, the physician had the primary responsibility for decision making. Input from the nurse, social worker and family caregiver were considered, but the multiple perspectives were complementary, or additive. For example, one factor considered in prescribing a neuroleptic is whether or not a patient is depressed. The patient may say he or she feels depressed, the family caregiver may report having observed signs of depression in the patient at home, and the nurse or social worker may sense and/or elicit confirmation of feelings of depression during a clinic visit. If depression is noted by anyone, then it is taken into account in deciding how to treat the patient. The larger problem is resolving issues where professionals disagree or recommendations conflict, as each focuses on different aspects of the problem or sees the same problem in a different way.

The initial discrimination on MMSE score during retrieval was a way of comparing patients at roughly the same point in the disease process. The longer range goal is for cases to extend over time, so that every case includes a picture of the same patient at different stages. Then, a current patient's state could be matched to the state of any patient in the case base when that patient was at the same stage of the disease. While AD patients do not all progress at the same rate, or even in the same ways, greater predictiveness might be achieved by extrapolating from the progression of similar patients over time.

Ethical perspectives did not play a role in the decision making process for prescribing neuroleptics. However, many important decisions in this domain do depend on ethical perspectives. These include: whether or not a patient's family members should undergo genetic testing for AD [21]; how a patient should be informed that he or she has AD; when an AD patient should be institutionalized; and when, if ever, life saving measures should be stopped for severely demented patients with life-threatening conditions. Research in a non-medical domain suggests that CBR can highlight points and counterpoints that enable individuals to make decisions based on their own ethical beliefs [19]. Integrating clinical evidence with ethical considerations in a CBR system is an important challenge to be addressed by further research.

Future plans are to build more prototypes to explore these issues and to transition laboratory prototypes into tools for practical use. The next focal points are: assisting family members in choosing whether or not to undergo genetic testing for AD; and supporting the decision to prescribe cognitive enhancement drugs. Additional prototypes may then be built to support the decisions suggested by clinicians, which were presented in Section 3.3.

5 Related Research

CBR has been used by researchers in medical domains ever since CASEY [14], which diagnosed heart failures, MEDIC [25], which diagnosed pulmonary disease, and PROTOS [3], which diagnosed audiological disorders. Diagnosis is not the only medical task that has been supported by CBR. CBR systems have been built to: educate users about sickle cell disease [4]; support the design of radiation therapy plans [6]; support the selection of diagnostic imaging procedures [12]; assist in the interpretation of radiological images [15]; support nursing diagnosis, prognosis and prescription [9]; and plan daily menus to meet special nutrition requirements [16].

The Auguste Project shares most in common with CBR and multimodal reasoning projects that support the ongoing therapy of long-term medical conditions. One such project is CARE-PARTNER [8]. CARE-PARTNER supports the long-term follow-up care of cancer patients who have had bone-marrow transplants. In this project, CBR was combined with RBR and information retrieval (IR) techniques to support evidence-based medical practice. In CARE-PARTNER, CBR reuses solutions to problems that were experienced by past patients. RBR incorporates standard practice guidelines and special care pathways developed by experts. IR provides integrated access to the relevant medical literature. As relatively few bone-marrow transplants have been performed to date, this system captures early experience that will help define standards for quality of care in the future.

Another system was recently fielded to support insulin dependent diabetes mellitis patient management [5]. Like AD, diabetes mellitis is an incurable disease, which must be managed on an ongoing basis. As in the Auguste Project, both CBR and RBR are applied to the task. A difference is that this system must handle less variability among patients. Every patient considered has problems related to blood sugar and uses insulin to control these problems. In contrast, only about half of AD patients ever exhibit behavior problems, and several different drugs and behavioral methods may be used to control them. Blood sugar is inherently more measurable than behavior, making it unnecessary to consider different perspectives on the problem.

ICONS uses CBR to advise physicians of suitable antibiotics to prescribe to intensive care patients with bacterial infections [10,23]. This work is highly germane in that CBR is used to recommend the best medications for patients. ICONS integrates CBR with other techniques, incorporating laboratory analyses of pathogens and statistical analyses of the effectiveness of therapies against pathogens. Some differences between ICONS and the Auguste Project are: ICONS uses patient prototypes as well as specific cases; and ICONS is able to adapt past patient prescriptions, instead of using RBR to choose appropriate drugs. The projects differ significantly in the time frames of the problem domains. ICONS must quickly provide a recommendation for a patient with an acute condition. The right therapy can quickly resolve the condition, once and for all. Efficiency is of the essence, but following the patient over a long period of time is unnecessary.

MNAOMIA operates in the domain of psychiatric eating disorders [7]. It assists clinicians with the cognitive tasks of diagnosis, treatment planning, patient follow-up and clinical research. It reasons from both actual and prototypical patient cases. It follows patients over time, using time points and intervals to detect patient trends, such as weight loss. MNAOMIA incorporates "points of view." However, in MNAOMIA, a viewpoint is not a different perspective on the same problem, as in this work, but a model of a single cognitive task, such as diagnosis.

6   Summary and Conclusion

The Auguste Project is an effort to provide decision support for planning the ongoing care of AD patients by modeling the thought processes of geriatric interdisciplinary teams. CBR is an apt paradigm for this research, because clinicians have focused on cases ever since Dr. Alois Alzheimer encountered the patient Auguste D. one hundred years ago. Computer-based tools to assist with the care planning task have not been available to clinicians. The task is complex because it involves the multiple perspectives of professionals from different health care disciplines, cases that change over time, and ethical points of view.

The first system prototype has just been completed. This prototype supports the decision to prescribe neuroleptic drugs to patients with behavioral problems. It uses a CBR module to determine whether or not a neuroleptic should be prescribed and an RBR module to choose among five available neuroleptic drugs. While there is still room to improve its performance, clinicians surveyed at an Alzheimer's Disease Research Center agreed that the system's suggestions were comparable to those a knowledgeable clinician would make. They also agreed that the tool would be useful to geriatric interdisciplinary teams and general practitioners, as well as for training future health care professionals. The prototype serves as proof of concept that CBR can help provide support for planning the ongoing care of AD patients. Much work remains ahead before the ultimate goal of creating a virtual member of a geriatric interdisciplinary team can be realized.

Acknowledgments. The authors gratefully acknowledge the contributions of the staff of the University Alzheimer Center, including Pat Brown, Pam Fioritto, Anna Gaydos, Dr. Marian Patterson, Julia Rajcan, Lauren Somple and Beth Wachter. Special thanks go to research assistants Amit Jain and Susie Sami. Their collaboration and assistance have made this work possible.

References

1. D. Aha and J. J. Daniels, editors. *Case-Based Reasoning Integrations: Papers from the 1998 Workshop*, Menlo Park, CA, 1998. AAAI Press.
2. A. Alzheimer. Über eine eigenartige erkrankung der hirnrinde. In E. Schultze and G. Suell, editors, *Allgemeine Zeitschrift für Psychiatrie und Psychisch-Gerichtliche Medizin*, volume 64, pages 146–148, Berlin, Germany, 1907. Georg Reimer.
3. R. Bareiss. *Exemplar-Based Knowledge Acquisition: A Unified Approach to Concept Representation, Classification, and Learning*. Academic Press, San Diego, CA, 1989.
4. B. Bell, R. Bareiss, and R. Beckwith. Sickle cell counselor: A prototype goal-based scenario for instruction in a museum environment. Technical Report 56, The Institute for the Learning Sciences, Evanston, IL, 1994.
5. R. Bellazi, S. Montani, L. Portinale, and A. Riva. Integrating rule-based and case-based decision making in diabetic patient management. In Althoff K. D., R. Bergmann, and L. K. Branting, editors, *Case-Based Reasoning Research and Development: Third International Conference on Case-Based Reasoning, ICCBR-99*, pages 386–400, Berlin, 1999. Springer.

6. J. Berger. Roentgen: Radiation therapy and case-based reasoning. In *Proceedings of the Tenth Conference on Artificial Intelligence for Applications*, Los Alamitos, CA, 1994. IEEE Computer Society Press.

7. I. Bichindaritz. MNAOMIA: Improving case-based reasoning for an application in psychiatry. In *Artificial Intelligence in Medicine: Applications of Current Technologies*, Stanford, CA, 1996. Working Notes of the AAAI-96 Spring Symposium.

8. I. Bichindaritz, E. Kansu, and K. M. Sullivan. Integrating case-based reasoning, rule-based reasoning and intelligent information retrieval for medical problemsolving. In D. Aha and J. J. Daniels, editors, *Case-Based Reasoning Integrations: Papers from the 1998 Workshop*, pages 22–27, Madison, WI, 1998.

9. C. Bradburn and J. Zeleznikow. The application of case-based reasoning to the tasks of health care planning. In S. Wess, K. D. Althoff, and M. M. Richter, editors, *Topics in Case-Based Reasoning: First European Workshop, EWCBR-93*, pages 365–378, Berlin, 1994. Springer-Verlag.

10. B. Heindl, R. Schmidt, G. Schmidt, M. Haller, P. Pfaller, L. Gierl, and B. Pollwein. A case-based consilarius for therapy recommendation (ICONS): Computer-based advice for calculated antibiotic therapy in intensive care medicine. *Computer Methods and Programs in Biomedicine*, 52:117–127, 1997.

11. Alzheimer's Disease International. World prevalence. London, UK, 2000. http://www.alz.co.uk/alz.

12. C. E. Kahn and G. M. Anderson. Case-based reasoning and imaging procedure selection. *Investigative Radiology*, 29:643–647, 1994.

13. S. Klein, editor. *A National Agenda for Geriatric Education: White Papers*. US Department of Health and Human Services, Health Resources and Services Administration, Bureau of Health Professions, Rockville, MD, 1995.

14. P. Koton. Reasoning about evidence in causal explanations. In *Proceedings AAAI-88*, pages 256–261, San Mateo, CA, 1988. Morgan Kaufmann.

15. R. T. Macura and K. J Macura. McRad: Radiology image resource with a casebased retrieval system. In M. Veloso and A. Aamodt, editors, *Case-Based Reasoning Research and Development: First International Conference, Proceedings ICCBR-95*, pages 43–54, Berlin, 1995. Springer-Verlag.

16. C. R. Marling, G. J. Petot, and L. S. Sterling. Integrating case-based and rulebased reasoning to meet multiple design constraints. *Computational Intelligence*, 15(3):308–332, 1999.

17. C. R. Marling, P. J. Whitehouse, P. A. Fioritto, and J. E. Bendis. Knowledge sharing and case-based reasoning in geriatric care. In *Exploring Synergies of Knowledge Management and Case-Based Reasoning: Papers from the AAAI 1999 Workshop*, Menlo Park, CA, 1999. AAAI Press.

18. K. Maurer, S. Volk, and H. Gerbaldo. Chapter 1: Auguste D. The history of Alois Alzheimer's first case. In P. J. Whitehouse, K. Maurer, and J. F. Ballenger, editors, *Concepts of Alzheimer Disease: Biological, Clinical and Cultural Perspectives*, Baltimore, MD, 2000. Johns Hopkins University Press.

19. B. McLaren and K.D. Ashley. Context sensitive case comparisons in practical ethics: Reasoning about reasons. In *Proceedings of the Fifth International Conference on Artificial Intelligence and Law*, pages 316–325, New York, NY, 1995. ACM Press.

20. M. R. Mendez, R. J. Martin, K. A. Smyth, and P. J. Whitehouse. Psychiatric symptoms associated with Alzheimer's disease. *Journal of Neuropsychiatry and Clinical Neurosciences*, 2:28–33, 1990.

21. S. Post and P. J. Whitehouse, editors. *Genetic Testing for Alzheimer Disease: Ethical and Clinical Issues*. Johns Hopkins University Press, Baltimore, MD, 1998.

22. M. A. Raskind. Psychopharmacology of noncognitive abnormal behaviors in Alzheimer's disease. *Journal of Clinical Psychiatry*, 59(9):28–32, 1998.
23. R. Schmidt, B. Pollwein, and L. Gierl. Case-based reasoning for antibiotics therapy advice. In Althoff K. D., R. Bergmann, and L. K. Branting, editors, *Case-Based Reasoning Research and Development: Third International Conference on Case-Based Reasoning, ICCBR-99*, pages 550–559, Berlin, 1999. Springer.
24. L. Teri, R. G. Logsdon, E. Peskind, M. Raskind, M. F. Weiner, R. E. Tractenberg, N. L. Foster, L. S. Schneider, M. Sano, P. Whitehouse, P. Tariot, A. M. Mellow, A. P. Auchus, M. Grundman, R. G. Thomas, K. Schafer, and L. J. Thal. Treatment of agitation in AD: A randomized, placebo-controlled clinical trial. *Neurology*, 55:1271–1278, 2000.
25. R. M. Turner. Using schemas for diagnosis. *Computer Methods and Programs in Biomedicine*, 30:199–208, 1989.
26. P. J. Whitehouse and D. S. Geldmacher. Pharmacotherapy for Alzheimer's disease. *Clinics in Geriatric Medicine*, 10(2):339–350, 1994.

Prototype of an Intelligent Failure Analysis System

Claude Mount[1] and T. Warren Liao[2]

[1]Claude Ray Mount, Inc., Jackson, LA 70748
CRM@CRMount.com
[2]Louisiana State University, Baton Rouge, LA 70803
ieliao@unix1.sncc.lsu.edu

Abstract. The investigation of commercial/industrial failures is a vital, but complex task. This paper presents an Intelligent Failure Analysis System (aIFAS). It is a system designed by a failure analyst with the goal of making failure investigation easier. The knowledge base for aIFAS comes from commercial laboratory reports. The methodologies employed represent the experience gained from over six years of development. One goal of aIFAS is to provide a case-based expert system tool to help find answers. Functionality ranges from matching a new case against stored example cases to extracting relational data from the aIFAS knowledge base.

1   Introduction

We are each one of us, from time to time, faced with the need to determine why something is not doing what it should. This might range from troubleshooting an air conditioner that quit cooling to dealing with a bed of wilting zinnias. In every sense, each such activity is a failure analysis. Magnify the scale of those problems to a size that can cost hundreds of thousands of dollars a day and you have an industrial/commercial failure analysis. That class of failure is the one considered by this work. Such failures demand thorough investigations that yield quality answers. In many instances, lives literally depend on the accuracy of the failure analysis process.

The practice of conducting failure analyses is not new. What is new is the notion of automating the process in an innovative fashion that capitalizes on the synergism of human-machine interaction. The description, prototype structure, and performance results for a knowledge system, dubbed as an Intelligent Failure Analysis System (aIFAS), are presented in this work.

1.1   Objectives

From a technical perspective, failure can be defined as the cessation of function or usefulness [48]. It follows that failure analysis is the process of investigating such a failure. This terse definition might sound overly broad in scope. It, however, quite accurately illustrates the character of the sort of failure analyses addressed by this work. Failure analysis, in its full and complete sense, is a wide-ranging knowledge

D.W. Aha and I. Watson (Eds.): ICCBR 2001, LNAI 2080, pp. 716-730, 2001.
© Springer-Verlag Berlin Heidelberg 2001

domain that encompasses many technical disciplines and a variety of fields of scientific or technical study.

A frequently used example for describing failure analysis is the familiar and generally well understood practice of medical diagnosis. The two methodologies closely parallel one another [1] in their cycle of operation, information requirements, and level of expertise for successful performance. The goal of either type of investigation is to apply knowledge of cause-and-effect relationships that will correctly link symptoms with their cause [8] for subsequent remediation.

Who can benefit from failure analysis? To a very large extent, the development of material science and engineering has resulted because of serious failures [12] (and their subsequent investigation). In the processing industries, plant operators depend on failure analysis results to efficiently and effectively control their systems [8]. In addition, many students in engineering courses would not be exposed to knowledge of how real-world systems work without the results of exemplar failure analyses.

Diagnostic tools very likely represent the largest area of application [38] for artificial intelligence systems. The sheer number of implementations serves to indicate their scientific and commercial importance. Those systems, however, are extremely focused in their application. Except for the work proximate to this project, no fully implemented system has been discovered that addresses the full breadth of failure analysis. That is, a system that can support a failure investigation and subsequent analysis to determine the primary cause of a failure in an unbounded operating environment.

1.2 Chronology

In the latter part of 1994, a project was begun to archive eighteen years of industrial failure analysis records. The initial intent was to simply catalog the modes of failure and group them by broad industrial classes. For example, how many fatigue-cracking failures occurred in rotating equipment that was operating within the power generation industry?

The sheer volume of available information pointed the investigation in another direction. The richness and variety of data would readily support the development of an expert system. A precursor system concept called an Intelligent Knowledge Engine (IKE) was presented at the Artificial Neural Networks in Engineering Conference (ANNIE '97) [40].

The current state of the project is more focused. A best-of-breed approach is being used to glean insights from earlier efforts. The goal is to produce an information resource tool for an individual; in particular, an independent consultant in the business of conducting failure analyses or when offering expert legal testimony [39].

2 Knowledge Acquisition

Knowledge acquisition can be interpreted as the transfer and transformation of problem-solving expertise from some knowledge sources to a computer program [32]. Gaining ownership of the knowledge is a major problem in building any knowledge-based system. acquisition is described in the literature as: the most difficult process [51]; one of the greatest difficulties [47]; the biggest bottleneck [43]; or, the most time-consuming task [32]. The magnitude of the issue is perhaps best expressed by the statement that few systems have progressed beyond the research or prototype phase mainly because of this inherent problem [29].

There are at least three reasons that explain the difficulties in knowledge acquisition. First is a lack of preparation. The knowledge domain may not have been researched in sufficient depth to support meaningful acquisition [9]. Second is a lack of effort. There seems to be a natural tendency to underestimate the difficulty [45] with attendant low levels of success because little effort is expended. Third is a lack of communication. Evidence suggests that experts organize concepts differently than those not familiar with the knowledge domain [43]. Simply put, if the expert and the knowledge engineer cannot effectively communicate, no knowledge is acquired.

In spite of the hindrances, knowledge acquisition remains a crucial element. The overall performance of a system literally depends upon the completeness of its knowledge base [33]. While the quality, or correctness, of the acquired knowledge determines the ultimate success of the system [45]

2.1   Methodology

There is no all-encompassing, unified theory of how to acquire knowledge, and probably never will be [59]. Devising a successful methodology is a complex problem. Consider the comment that "experts know what they know and what they do not know and can identity solution methods which will work or not work" [29]. Imagine facing the task of contriving a scheme to cope with that degree of variability in what information might be forthcoming.

Some general methods provide a basis for developing an approach tailored to meet the peculiarities of a chosen domain. Those methods can be grouped into five areas: direct (interviews); observational (shadowing); indirect (relational diagrams); machine learning (neural nets); and, document processing (data mining) [33]. Of the five, the direct and indirect methods have proven to be best suited to failure analysis.

Interviews. The direct approach of interviewing is good for obtaining a sense of the knowledge domain [29]. The interview process must be well directed to overcome a tendency by experts to describe interesting, complicated, or recent cases and omit the mundane and straightforward ones [25]. Other obstacles to be overcome during interviews are inarticulate experts, forgotten facts, omission of information presumed to be common knowledge, and the ambiguities of technical language [33]. In spite of the adversities, interviewing reveals the detailed structure of concepts better than other methods [10], yielding both general and specific information [25].

Cause-and-Effect Charts. A very fruitful technique is the production of cause-and-effect charts. This indirect method can be formalized into creating a two-dimensional matrix array of causal relationships [54]. This sort of information display is particularly good for forcing consideration of combinations that would not otherwise have come to mind, and identifying attributes that would never co-occur or have no relationship. A bonus comes from the insight into the nature of the domain provided by requesting explanations for non-occurrences of certain combinations.

2.2   Essential Elements

No one scheme of knowledge acquisition can sensibly be expected to suit all the circumstances arising in the failure analysis domain. It is equally important to remember that the process of knowledge acquisition cannot be rushed [49]. There are often demands for protracted interaction between domain experts and a knowledge engineer. Complex systems can take hundreds of person-days, or even years to finish the knowledge acquisition portion of their development [29]. However, a few elements are common to successful systems.

Standardized Terminology. Failure analysis is fraught with idiosyncratic terms related to particular industries. Some words can have three or four different alternative terms to describe the same thing [23]. Experts themselves are inconsistent. Two experts might use different terms to describe the same attribute or the same term for different attributes [33]. Each of these acquisition obstacles is related to the lack of standardized terminology.

Understandably, failure analysis is not the only knowledge domain that is affected. This comprehension/communication roadblock is as pervasive as it is owing to the nature of how knowledge is structured. An understanding of domain terminology is crucial to an optimal application of the domain knowledge [3]. The most direct approach to standardize terminology starts with the creation of a terminology glossary [3]; a data dictionary [25], a concept database [60], or whatever name one might coin in reference to a lexicon of the knowledge domain vernacular.

Attribute Set. As the information is collected, it must be indexed in such a way that it can be reused easily. An indexing scheme must satisfy two criteria: be general enough to apply to a large number of cases and specific enough to discriminate cases [4]. The indices that accomplish that important task of case classification will be referred to as attributes. Experts differentiate their selections in problem-solving situations with these measures. The characteristics of those attributes can be quite varied.

Attributes can convey predictive or descriptive information [61]. The data values for attributes can be continuous, discrete, nominal, or Boolean [15]. The very same case attribute in different analyses, or different stages of the same analysis, might have different relevance [36]. It is also a good prospect that even a carefully selected set of attributes will contain irrelevant or redundant members [15]. All these factors emphasize that the process of selecting appropriate attributes is a complex matter.

The attribute set must be sufficient in content to allow discrimination of subtly different cases, but compact enough to support efficient performance. What to pick as attributes and how to select attributes are not the only issues. Another, and much more elusive question, is the matter of deciding how many attributes is enough. Some resolution to the predicament comes by considering Pareto's Rule.

The 80-20 Pareto's Rule suggests that a small group of all possible attributes can describe most of the cases encountered. Combine that with a hierarchical system of attributes that can be easily augmented. The situation is now distilled to one of selecting a starting subset of all attributes that does not decrease accuracy and retains class distinctions for the complete domain.

Hierarchical Data. A system using a hierarchical representation of its information is reasonable and resource efficient [17]. Practically speaking, this organization of the knowledge base makes for answers that are more reliable. For example, if a lifting hook breaks, failure due to internal overpressurization is absurd [22]. No such combination would even be available for consideration with hierarchical data.

Functionally a hierarchical data structure for a knowledge base has merit, it also offers other advantages. A system design that organizes knowledge increases speed [46]. Furthermore, as the knowledge base grows and matures, multistage retrieval is an efficient means of dealing with large numbers of example cases [52].

Build Incrementally. Implementing a knowledge-based system is a difficult process, requiring special skills and often taking many person-years of effort [58]. The resulting mass of information can be overwhelming. Earlier efforts suffered from that sort of an information glut. The development process became bogged down. Worse yet, the data was sometimes imperfect, since experts do not always provide the knowledge needed in complete and consistent chunks [47].

Another approach for getting data to support system development came from a consideration of human learning. Knowledge acquisition (learning) is typically an iterative process [37]. It would seem reasonable, therefore, to have a system with an inherent incremental learning capability that would serve to expand its knowledge base and improve overall performance [33].

2.3   Sources

A common mistake that adversely affects the system performance is to collect knowledge from the first available or most convenient source. In most problem domains, relevant information is scattered through multiple sources that may require aggressive search efforts for their discovery. Knowledge in many domains is available only to experts and may never have been written down in structured form [45].

Being hard to find is one issue; data quality is another. Inconsistent or incomplete data can lead to difficulties in system development and performance [11]. Any data that is elicited must be reliable and valid – reliable in the sense that a similar acquisition would yield similar results; and valid in that the data obtained are accurate [54]. Creativity and experience are necessary for finding knowledge sources.

Historical files are a prime source of information for developing a failure analysis system [53]. This instance of aIFAS was developed by accessing report files from a commercial laboratory spanning 1989 to 1999, representing the work product of six failure analysts. Some twelve hundred reports are stored in electronic form; many with digitized graphics.

3   Implementation

Implementing an expert system to perform failure analysis is not a simple task. The system, however it is ultimately configured, must be able to provide expert problem-solving performance by exploiting a knowledge base and reasoning mechanism specific to the chosen domain [24]. That system's purpose is to meld the qualitative and non-quantifiable aspects of the problem-solving process with the fundamental or theoretical basis of the underlying knowledge domain [60].

3.1   Case-Based Reasoning

Case-based reasoning systems offer an intuitive attraction to users. People solve many problems by recalling their experiences. Only a novice would attempt to solve problems by applying rules or knowledge that has only recently been acquired. Since case-based reasoning systems rarely operate without human intervention, and actually encourage collaboration in the decision process, they are more readily welcomed by users as a problem-solving tool [58].

By using the knowledge embodied in past cases, the knowledge-acquisition bottleneck common to expert systems is at least widened [52]. Furthermore, proven systems already exist that can efficiently manage the large volumes of historical cases that may accumulate in the knowledge base [36]. To be considered successful, an expert system must be capable of generating adequate explanations. In case-based systems, the very information necessary to explain responses and justify answers is contained within the system [7].

A serendipitous realization is that as a case-based reasoning system acquires information it begins to reflect the personality of its user [58]. Case-based reasoning systems also offer a built in degree of flexibility. A considerable amount of modification can be accomplished by altering the indexing scheme for case selection without the necessity of completely rebuilding the system [7]. Finally, case-based reasoning systems can be developed much quicker, as much as four to eight times faster than other expert system implementation approaches [58].

Pragmatically, case-based systems are also strong contenders for representation of failure analysis domain knowledge. Work in that area showed 100% accuracy could be achieved for standard cases and as high as 71% accuracy for exceptional cases [35]. This level of performance comes with a price. Case-based systems usually consist of a large number of attributes to characterize an expansive case library. (Currently aIFAS has a library of 600 cases described by 144 attributes that can identify 95 failure modes.)

3.2   Knowledge Base Structure

A list containing 95 of the most-likely failure modes was constructed. Matrices showing cause-and-effect relationships were formed from that basis. One matrix used 144 independent, binary attributes to characterize the failure modes. A second matrix used the same attributes, but arranged them in 32 groups of multi-valued attributes.

In the resulting hierarchical structure, each of the original independent attributes was assigned a subjective interval value within one of the 32 groups. Only one sub-attribute within a group can be selected at a time. The group-attribute assumes the value of the sub-attribute that is selected, otherwise the group-attribute has a zero value. The sub-attribute values and groupings were based upon a ranking of the attributes by a failure analyst.

3.3   Metrics for Case Comparison

The size of the knowledge base for aIFAS has the potential of growing quite massive. As the system matures, there will be an ever-increasing set of failure modes with their particular attributes and simply more example cases. The algorithm chosen to retrieve cases that yield good solutions must be able to cope with those conditions. There is an imperative that the method not only discriminates well in the choices it makes, but is also computationally efficient. This is emphasized by an instance in which the computation of weightings for a genetic algorithm approach required 10 hours of computing time [61].

At present aIFAS can use any one of five different metrics for case selection. These represent more common approaches used for similarity measurement. The group includes the City Block (Manhattan) distance, Cosine Correlation similarity, Euclidean distance, and Hamming distance. A statistically based Knowledge Graph similarity measure [50] is also available.

4   System Framework

The goal of this reasoning system is not to replace the human, rather to provide a tool that allows the user to consistently obtain better results [6]. To date, there is no other computer-aided failure analysis systems that offers the features available with aIFAS.

Most systems are developed as design tools. Other such systems usually focus on a particular failure mechanism. For the most part, these systems tend to concentrate on predicting rather than analyzing failures. One such system is MIC.AB that finds examples of microbiologically influenced corrosion [22].

The Failure Analysis Diagnostic Expert System (FADES) was developed at Southampton University with a hybrid approach for developing solutions to problems. A limitation of FADES is the fact it can only resolve problems with eleven of the more common failure modes [23]. No subsequent reports on recent advances with that system have been found in the literature.

The aIFAS package makes available appropriate, adequate, and reliable support beyond what is obtainable elsewhere. The eventual coverage of aIFAS will include both common and unusual failures in industrial, commercial, or residential settings. The aIFAS program has the facility to offer multiple levels of detail to maintain adequate data granularity for rendering meaningful responses with the necessary particulars. An intuitive user interface is an integral element of aIFAS. To accommodate changing requirements, aIFAS is easily extensible. Above all, aIFAS is an effective research and learning tool.

4.1   Basic Structure

Real-world systems should strive for simplistic design [28]. Besides adhering to Ockham's Razor that the simplest answer is usually the best answer, reasoning systems need to exhibit acceptable performance levels. While meeting those criteria, the systems should also be usable and efficient [41]. In short, there are many factors to deal with while creating a viable reasoning system.

No system, however, will be accepted if it fails to yield understandable results [1]. Ultimately, users do not care whether a system uses sophisticated techniques or random guesses to generate results. What they care about most is ease-of-use and if the system provides them tangible benefits [26].

User Interface. In many cases, the disappointing history that reasoning systems have had can be traced to a lack of respect for the user [4]. The successful systems strive to use operational techniques and decision processes with which users are comfortable. Otherwise, frustrated users will shun the system and quickly return to their old way of doing thing [30].

What qualities, then, should the user interface have? The user interface must be at least able to display and update system messages or problem results comprehensibly [44]. A user interface that is so complex that deciphering it slows the problem-solution process is unusable [42]. Put more succinctly, good user interfaces for programs are invisible [14].

The aIFAS user is provided an informative interface that keeps them aware of system activity. Figure 1 is a typical view seen by a user. From this control panel, the various activities of aIFAS are managed.

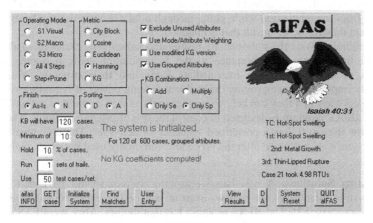

Fig. 1. The aIFAS User Interface.

Modular Architecture. While designing an expert system it must be kept in mind that even the highly efficient implementation of an invalid system is useless [41]. The aIFAS program construct is based upon architecture of specialized modules. That modular structure for aIFAS scales the task of implementation into several manageable parts [38].

There are secondary benefits to building a system from small pieces. Modular systems afford an advantage when maintenance is needed [56]; the logic of a small component is less convoluted than for a monolithic system. A modular system is also easier to reconfigure [20], only the affected part needs to be changed or replaced.

4.2   Individual Functions

Foremost, aIFAS is a human-support-oriented system. Its operation keeps well in mind the need (and value) of user interaction in the problem solving process [57]. This implementation of aIFAS marks a transition from a machine-centered to a user-centered computing, it attempts to not make undue assumptions about what users are going to request of it [4]. What aIFAS does instead, is provide basic support resources for directing a failure investigation or retrieving/displaying information.

Directing a Failure Analysis. The notion that human expertise can be divided into small chunks called rules, or instructions, suggests that a directed problem-solving methodology has advantages [56]. Furthermore, by compelling the examination and testing process to track a logical path, the number of time-consuming and costly tests necessary to provide an accurate solution can be greatly reduced.

Working through a problem in an orderly manner has other advantages. It is easier to recognize when the boundaries of the system knowledge are reached and thereby avoid making faulty decisions [18]. In addition, in the event a solution cannot be reached, why an unresolved case response occurs can be better understood [58].

Directing the course of an investigation can also have educational value. Not everyone interested in a failure has the same level or kind of training [19]. The insight gained from the interaction while going through a failure analysis may be even more important than the actual result that is obtained.

In failure analysis the intermediate results and subsequent decisions made during an investigation are of importance to the final solution. Few reasoning systems attempt to incorporate those intermediate steps into their structure. Yet, a task crucially important for improving the problem solving power of reasoning systems is to develop ways that they can behave smarter in the course of their operation [2].

The aIFAS program is designed to control the use of program features. The system forces the user to follow a prescribed sequence of activities. The individual steps of that sequence are patterned after the procedure commonly used in failure analyses.

Suggesting Solutions. A case-based reasoning system should be able to present listings of similar cases for review, even at any of the intermediate stages of the solution process [52]. The aIFAS program has that facility. Also, the aIFAS program, like other systems, intentionally does not choose a final answer. Instead, possibilities are offered, leaving the ultimate decision to the user [10]. What is presented is a list of most closely matching cases ordered by their degree of similarity [30].

The user interface, to be effective, should include numerical and verbal information about the cases that are being considered. The user can then elect to accept the results presented, reject the results and start over; or continue on to the next step of the investigation [27]. Figure 2 shows one of the two different results displays offered the user by aIFAS.

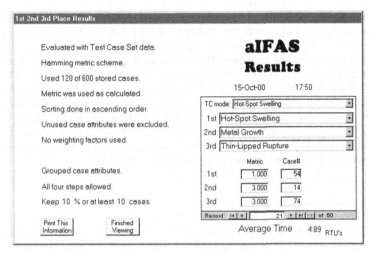

Fig. 2. Best Three Matches Results Display for aIFAS

Accessing Information. The minimum information to be stored by a system consists of the attributes needed to identify and describe the example case [52]. More flexibility is afforded if associated report documents and data spreadsheets can be included [13]. A special benefit comes with the inclusion of graphical objects in such form as diagrams, charts, photographs, or drawings [46].

Besides the obvious necessary data, all these types of supporting information are stored by the aIFAS program. They are accessible to the user via an assortment of pre-programmed queries. This is an ability of intangible value. Humans often depend on such prompts to initiate information retrieval; that is, solve problems.

5   Testing aIFAS

When considering how to test aIFAS, it was discovered that there is no generally accepted criterion for evaluating reasoning systems [55]. Further, of the various methods proposed for testing such programs, many are incomplete, poorly systematic, or not easily applied. Some thinking regarding system testing ran the risk of fashioning a measuring tool more complex than the system being evaluated [24]. The paradox in applying reasoning systems is that we want them to do perfectly things that are not really understood. They are expected to provide sound advice where errors may lead to damage of facilities and equipment, great economic loss, or even the loss of human life [31].

The testing plan finally decided upon for aIFAS does three things. First, it verifies that the system can do what it is supposed to do. Second, it measures the accuracy and performance. Third, it evaluates the ability of aIFAS to learn and grow.

5.1 The aIFAS Knowledge Base

A group of 1184 reports was ordered by date and report number. A set of 50 test cases was extracted from that list by choosing successive reports at a twenty-count interval. The reasoning behind that selection method was to produce a real world set of cases, similar to what might actually be encountered by aIFAS.

A set of 600 example cases for aIFAS was taken from the remaining reports. The knowledge base available for testing represented roughly five years of failure analyses as performed in a commercial laboratory. Those stored cases provide a representative mixture of failure modes that could be expected in a real world application of aIFAS.

In the main case library, all but 12 of the initial failure modes entered into the system had at least one representative. Some of those example cases could be uniquely identified with only one attribute. The maximum number of attributes used was eight and the average number of attributes used was four.

5.2 Verification

Verification is proof that the system does the job right [5]. For the most part, verification investigates aspects not open to subjective appraisal, so objectivity is generally not an issue [42]. Either a system does what is supposed to or it does not.

Verification testing of aIFAS considers two functions. First, does the system appropriately direct a failure investigation? Second, can the user explore the system information and auxiliary material stored in the system knowledge base?

Previous discussion addressed the issue of directing a failure investigation. That functionality is "hardwired" into the program and cannot be defeated by the user. The ability to explore the aIFAS knowledge base is more involved. There are some fifteen pre-programmed queries to display stored data; as well as, the ability to display results as they are produced during a case comparison search. Figure 3 shows information available about a case attribute.

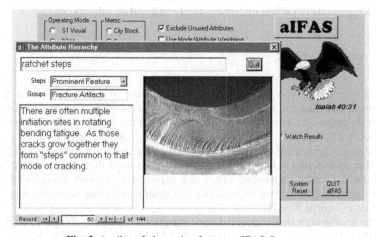

Fig. 3. Attribute Information from an aIFAS Query

5.3   Validation

Most definitions of reasoning systems mention their ability to perform close to human expert levels. Yet the testing to validate that performance is mostly ad hoc and of dubious value [43]. That is in contrast with the supposition that validation is the process of assuring a system is producing the desired result as sanctioned through systematic testing [5].

Obviously, reasoning systems cannot be expected to perform better than the human experts they mimic do, but no one places much value on the answers from a sometimes-correct failure analyst. The most reasonable approach is to define the level of expertise at which it should perform [42]. For aIFAS, literature and reason suggest that 90% accuracy, would be a reasonable lower bound for acceptable performance.

Testing is done two ways. All 50 of the test cases are considered only one time, assuming that subsequent testing would not yield different results. Conversely, 6 trials using sets of 15 test cases randomly chosen from the pool of 50 test cases are used to explore knowledge base diversity.

Three quantities are used to measure performance. The first is called the Correctness Ratio (CR), [21]. The CR is defined as a percentage ratio between the number of successful solutions and the number of attempts made trying to produce a solution. The second is called a Relative Time Unit (RTU). The RTU is defined as the ratio of measured time for an evaluation divided by the time to perform a standard looping operation. It creates a dimensionless quantity to remove execution time bias when running aIFAS on different platforms. The third is called the Performance Score (PS). The PS is defined as the CR value divided by the RTU value. It is proposed to combine the factors of accuracy and computational time.

With as few as 120 example cases in the knowledge base, aIFAS was able to achieve the desired 90% accuracy for the Correctness Ratio value. Increasing the number of example cases showed marginal improvement in accuracy, but a marked decrease in the Performance Score. (A parametric study of CR versus PS might be a means to determine an optimum number of example cases.)

5.4   Incremental Learning

As the case library expands and if the system is working as expected, its accuracy should improve. The aIFAS program was tested for that effect with ever increasing numbers of example cases. An initial group of 30 example cases produced a typical success rate of 66%. There was a roughly exponential improvement to 100% success with a group of 300 example cases. The improved performance was at the expense of rapidly increasing computational times.

6   Conclusions

The portion of the prototype that provides user information regarding the database and guided a failure investigation characterizes the goal of the project. The experienced user has access to knowledge base statistics to recall past work, or can enter attributes of a new case as they become available to aid in an investigation. The novice user can learn about failure modes and attributes, can read actual reports dealing with those issues, and can test hypothetical cases interactively.

Only a portion of the aIFAS prototype is discussed in this paper. The system supports not just the application-oriented functionality presented here, but is a viable tool for the investigation of case-based knowledge systems. Features not detailed include: easy exchange of the case library to explore a different knowledge domain; rapidly modify the model for case data representation; choose from a wide range of similarity measure algorithms, control the size of the example case library being exercised; modify the test case set used for assessments; perform single-shot or multiple-instance evaluations; store test conditions and results; and, perform automated parametric studies over combinations of features.

The aIFAS prototype as described does not represent a complete work, rather a lifework in progress. This paper, however, should offer sufficient information to indicate the possibilities of the concept.

References

1. Adlassnig, K., Fuzzy Set Theory in Medical Diagnosis, *IEEE Transactions on Systems, Man and Cybernetics*, Vol. SMC-16, 1986.
2. Agre, G., KBS Maintenance as Learning Two-Tiered Domain Representation, *Proceedings of the International Conference on Case-Based Reasoning Research and Development*, October 1995.
3. Ahmad, K., Fulford, H., Griffin, S., and Holmes-Higgin, P., Text-Based Knowledge Acquisition – A Language for Special Purposes Perspective, Research and Development in Expert Systems VIII, Cambridge University Press, 1991.
4. Allemang, D., Combining Case-Based Reasoning and Task-Specific Architectures, *IEEE Expert*, October 1994.
5. Andert, E.P., Integrated Knowledge-Based System Design and Validation for Solving Problems in Uncertain Environments, *International Journal of Man – Machine Studies*, 36, 1992.
6. Backer, E., Gerbrands, J.J., Reiber, J.H.C., Reijs, A.E.M., Krijgsman, H.J., and Van Den Herik, H.J., Modeling Uncertainty in ESATS by Classification Inference, *Pattern Recognition Letters*, #8, Elsevier Science Publishers, 1988.
7. Barletta, R., An Introduction to Case-Based Reasoning, *AI Expert*, August 1991.
8. Becraft, W.R., and Lee, P.L., An Integrated Neural Network/Expert System Approach for Fault Diagnosis, *Computers in Chemical Engineering*, Volume 17, 1993.
9. Bench-Capon, T., Coenen, F., Nwana, H., Paton, R., and Shave, M., Two Aspects of the Validation and Verification of Knowledge-Based Systems, *IEEE Expert*, June 1993.
10. Binaghi, E., A Fuzzy Logic Inference Model for a Rule-Based System in Medical Diagnosis, *Expert Systems*, Volume 7, 1990.
11. Bort, J., Data Mining's Midas Touch, *InfoWorld*, April 1996.
12. Brostow, W. and Corneliussen, R.D., Failure of Plastics, Hanser Publishers, 1986.
13. Churbuck, D.C., Learning by Example, *Forbes Magazine*, June 8, 1992.
14. Cooper, A., About Face: The Essentials of User Interface Design, IDG Books, 1995.
15. Dash, M., and Liu, H., Feature Selection For Classification, Intelligent Data Analysis, Elsevier Science, 1997.
16. Doherty, N.F., Kochhar, A.K., and Main, R., Knowledge-Based Approaches to Fault Diagnosis: A Practical Evaluation of the Relative Merits of Deep and Shallow Knowledge, *Proceedings of the Institution of Mechanical Engineers*, Volume 208, 1994.

17. Fink, P.K., Lusth, J.C. and Duran, J.W., A General Expert System Design for Diagnostic Problem Solving, *IEEE Transactions on Pattern Analysis and Machine Intelligence*, September 1985.
18. Fourali, C., Fuzzy Logic and the Quality of Assessment of Portfolios, *Fuzzy Sets and Systems 68*, Elsevier, 1994.
19. French, D.N., <u>Metallurgical Failures in Fossil Fired Boilers</u>, John Wiley & Sons, 1983.
20. Golding, A.R., and Rosenbloom, P.S., Improving Accuracy By Combining Rule-Based and Case-Based Reasoning, *Artificial Intelligence 87*, Elsevier, 1996.
21. Gonzalez, A.J., Xu, L., and Gupta, U.M., Validation Techniques for Case-Based Reasoning Systems, *IEEE Transactions on Systems, Man, and Cybernetics – Part A: Systems and Humans*, Volume 28, No. 4, July, 1998.
22. Graham-Jones, J., and Mellor, B.G., Expert and Knowledge-Based Systems in Failure Analysis, *Engineering Failure Analysis*, Volume 2, Elsevier, 1995.
23. Graham-Jones, J., and Mellor, B.G., The Development of a Generic Failure Analysis Expert System Based on Case-Based Reasoning, *Proceedings of Corrosion 96 Symposium*, Denver, CO, 1996.
24. Guida, G., and Mauri, G., Evaluating Performance and Quality of Knowledge Based Systems: Foundation and Methodology, *IEEE Transactions on Knowledge and Data Engineering*, April 1993.
25. Hart, A.E., The Role of Induction in Knowledge Elicitation, *Expert Systems*, January 1985.
26. Hinkle, D., and Toomey, C., Applying Case-Based Reasoning to Manufacturing, *AI Magazine*, Spring 1995.
27. Isaacson, D.R., Davis, T.J., and Robinson, J.E. III, Knowledge-Based Runway Assignment for Arrival Aircraft in the Terminal Area, *AIAA Guidance, Navigation, and Control Conference*, August 1997.
28. Jackson, A.H., Machine Learning, *Expert Systems*, Volume 5, 1988.
29. Johannsen, G. and Alty, J.L., Knowledge Engineering for Industrial Expert Systems, *Automatica*, Volume 27, 1991.
30. Klinger, D.W., A Decision Centered Design Approach to Case-Based Reasoning: Helping Engineers Prepare Bids and Solve Problems, <u>Advances in Agile Manufacturing</u>, IOS Press, 1994.
31. Lee, S., and O'Keefe, R.M., Developing a Strategy for Expert System Verification and Validation, *IEEE Transactions on Systems, Man, and Cybernetics*, April 1994.
32. Lee-Post, A., Knowledge Acquisition Automation: Research Issues and Directions, *Journal of Computer Information Systems*, Fall 1994.
33. Liao, T.W., Zhan, Z.H., Mount, C.R., An Integrated Database and Expert System for Failure Mechanism Identification: Part I – Automated Knowledge Acquisition, *Engineering Failure Analysis*, vol. 6, no. 6, 1999, 387-406.
34. Liao, T.W., Zhan, Z.H., Mount, C.R., An Integrated Database and Expert System for Failure Mechanism Identification: Part II – The System and Performance Testing, *Engineering Failure Analysis*, vol. 6, no. 6, 1999, 407-421.
35. Liao, T.W., Zhang, Z.M., and Mount, C.R., A Case-Based Reasoning Approach to Identifying Failure Mechanisms, *Engineering Applications of Artificial Intelligence*, vol. 13, no. 2, 2000, 199-213.
36. Liao, T.W., Zhang, Z.M., and Mount, C.R., Similarity Measures for Retrieval in Case-Based Reasoning Systems, *Applied Artificial Intelligence*, vol. 24, no. 4, 1998, 267-288.
37. Low, B.T., Lui, H.C., Tan, A.H., and Teh, H.H., Connectionist Expert System with Adaptive Learning Capability, *IEEE Transactions on Knowledge and Data Engineering*, June 1991.
38. Morales, E. and Garcia, H., A Modular Approach to Multiple Faults Diagnosis, <u>Artificial Intelligence in Process Engineering</u>, Academic Press, 1990.
39. Mount, C.R., An Intelligent Failure Analysis System, Ph.D. Dissertation, Louisiana State University, Baton Rouge, LA, 2000

40. Mount, C.R., Liao, T.W., and Chen, Y.S., Integrated Knowledge Engine for Failure Analysis, Smart Engineering Systems: Neural Networks, Fuzzy Logic, Data Mining, and Evolutionary Programming, ASME Press, 1997.
41. O'Keefe, R.M., Balci, O., and Smith, E.P., Validating Expert System Performance, *IEEE Expert*, Winter 1987.
42. O'Keefe, R.M., and O'Leary, D.E., Expert System Verification and Validation: A Survey and Tutorial, *Artificial Intelligence Review*, 7, 1993.
43. Olson, J.R., and Rueter, H.H., Extracting Expertise from Experts: Methods for Knowledge Acquisition, *Expert Systems*, August 1987.
44. Padalkar, S., Karsai, G., Biegl, C., Sztipanovits, J., Okuda, K., and Miyasaka, N., Real-Time Fault Diagnostics, *IEEE Expert*, June 1991.
45. Parsaye, K., and M. Chignell, Knowledge Acquisition and Validation, Expert Systems for Experts, John Wiley & Sons, 1988.
46. Perez, R.A., and Koh, S.W., Integrating Expert Systems with a Relational Database in Semiconductor Manufacturing, *IEEE Transactions on Semiconductor Manufacturing*, August 1993.
47. Polat, F., and Guvenir, H.A., UVT: A Unification-Based Tool for Knowledge Base Verification, *IEEE Expert*, June 1993.
48. Powell, G.W. and Mahmoud, S.E., Metals Handbook: Failure Analysis and Prevention, 9th Edition, V11, American Society for Metals, 1986.
49. Quinlan, J.R., Induction of Decision Trees, Machine Learning, Kluwer Academic Publishers, 1986.
50. Reategui, E.B., Campbell, J.A., and Leao, B.F., A Case-Based Model that Integrates Specific and General Knowledge in Reasoning, *Applied Intelligence*, July 1997.
51. Scott, R., Artificial Intelligence: Its Use in Medical Diagnosis, *Journal of Nuclear Medicine*, March 1993.
52. Stottler, R.H., CBR for Cost and Sales Prediction, *AI Expert*, August 1994.
53. Tan, A.H., Pan, Q., and Lui, H.C., The, H.H., Connectionist Expert System in Fault Diagnosis of Avionics Line Replaceable Units, *New Challenges in Aircraft Maintenance Conference*, Singapore, February 1990.
54. Tansley, D.S.W., and Hayball, C.C., Knowledge-Based Systems: Analysis and Design, Prentice-Hall, 1993.
55. Tzafestas, S., Palios, L. and Cholin, F., Diagnostic Expert System Inference Engine Based On the Certainty Factors Model, *Knowledge-Based Systems*, Volume 7, 1994.
56. Vargas, J.E., and Raj, S., Developing Maintainable Expert Systems Using Case-Base Reasoning, *Expert Systems*, November 1993.
57. Walton, H.W., Failure Diagnostics – Application of Expert Systems, *Conference Proceedings of the International Conference and Exhibits on Failure Analysis*, July 1991.
58. Watson, I., and Marir, F., Case-Based Reasoning: A Review, *The Knowledge Engineering Review*, Volume 9:4, 1994.
59. Witten, I.H., and MacDonald, B.A., Using Concept Learning for Knowledge Acquisition, *International Journal of Man-Machine Studies*, Volume 29, 1988.
60. Zahedi, F., Intelligent Systems for Business, Wadsworth, 1993.
61. Zhang, Z., Applying Case-Based Reasoning and Genetic Algorithms to Failure Analysis, A Thesis Submitted to the Louisiana State University Department of Industrial and Manufacturing Systems Engineering, Baton Rouge, LA, 1998.

Applying CBR and Object Database Techniques in Chemical Process Design

Timo Seuranen[1], Elina Pajula[2], and Markku Hurme[1]

[1] Helsinki University of Technology, Laboratory of Chemical Engineering and
Plant Design, P.O. Box 6100, FIN-02015 HUT, Finland
`timo.seuranen@hut.fi`
[2] Oy Keskuslaboratorio – Centrallaboratorium Ab, P.O. Box 70,
FIN-02151 ESPOO, Finland

Abstract. The aim of this paper is to introduce a new method for finding and
reusing process equipment design and inherently safer process configurations by
case-based reasoning (CBR) and object database techniques. CBR is based on
finding most alike existing solutions and applying the knowledge of their properties for solving new problems in the early phases of design. This supports design engineer's knowledge by allowing a systematic reuse of existing experience
in order to improve the quality and safety of new designs. The possibilities of
CBR and object database techniques in chemical process engineering field have
been illustrated by two prototype applications.

1. Introduction

Case-based reasoning (CBR) is a widely used problem solving technique, which has
been successfully applied to a large range of different tasks [1]. CBR is based on the
reuse of proven solutions when solving new problems. The current problem is defined
as a query by giving the essential parameters e.g. reactor type and relief system. Based
on these, the similarity is calculated and a user-defined number of the most similar
cases are retrieved. The user can select a case and launch adaptation routines, e.g.
scale-up calculations or adapt the case using other simulators. The more similar cases
can be found the fewer accurate simulations are needed because a large part of the
design can utilize data already available in the existing cases.

Process design applications like process synthesis are very complex problems and
currently available commercial CBR tools don't support all the properties needed. For
instance, the database engine of the tools is based on relational database technique,
which limits representing complex problems. An object-oriented database approach
would allow more flexible application developing [2].

CBR and object database prototype applications in this paper are developed with
C++ programming language and an object database programming language. The first
prototype application was developed to aid heat exchange equipment design. The

D.W. Aha and I. Watson (Eds.): ICCBR 2001, LNAI 2080, pp. 731-743, 2001.

program generates necessary input data including mechanical configuration for heat exchanger design simulators. The second prototype application was developed for conceptual process design, especially to find out if known inherently safer solutions to the current process design problem exist. The found safer alternatives can then be used as an evolutionary manner to substitute less safe process features in different levels of detail.

1.1 Case-Based Reasoning

The method presented is based on case-based reasoning (CBR) and an object database approach. The database contains collection design cases collected from open literature and existing process designs.

To find the nearest existing design a set of parameter values, e.g. reactor type, of all cases in the case base are compared to the input data given by the user. The retrieval phase uses several distance functions [1]. The idea is to define a distance between case values and input values. In case of numerical data types, distance can be determined following way [3]. If the input value is smaller than the minimum or greater than the maximum of the case values $C_{ij}(X_i < min\ C_{ij}\ or\ X_i > max\ C_{ij})$:

$$D_{i,j} = \left(\frac{C_{i,j} - X_i}{C_{i,j}}\right)^2 \tag{1}$$

where D_{ij} is distance between the case value and the input value, C_{ij} is value of parameter i of case j, and X_i is the input value of parameter i. If the input value is smaller than the minimum or greater than the maximum of the case values $C_{ij}(min\ C_{ij} \leq X_i \leq max\ C_{ij})$:

$$D_{i,j} = \left(\frac{C_{i,j} - X_i}{max\ C_{i,j} - min\ C_{i,j}}\right)^2 \tag{2}$$

Similarity between different cases can be presented with a normalized distance:

$$Y_{i,j} = 1 - \frac{D_{i,j}}{max\ D_{i,j}} \tag{3}$$

where Y_{ij} is similarity of the parameter i for the case j. In case of string data types similarity is simply:

$$X_{i,j} = C_{i,j} \Rightarrow Y_{i,j} = 1$$
$$X_{i,j} \neq C_{i,j} \Rightarrow Y_{i,j} = 0 \tag{4}$$

In case of linguistic type data types fuzzy set operations can be used for the determination of a similarity. Linguistic values can be transformed into membership functions, and the similarity can be expressed as an intersection of fuzzy sets: [3]

$$Y_{i,j} = \min\{\mu_x(z), \mu_c(z)\} \tag{5}$$

where μ_c is value of the linguistic parameter i for the case j.

The quality of reasoning increases if importance of selection parameters can be altered. In case of inherent safety in exothermic reactor design, reaction enthalpy and available heat transfer area may be more important selection parameters than type of impeller used. Weighted similarity can be expressed: [3]

$$R_{i,j} = W_i Y_{i,j} \tag{6}$$

where W_i is the weight factor of the selection parameter i evaluated by the user. Overall similarity can be calculated for a case j based on the number of parameters and based on parametric similarities:

$$S_j = \frac{\sum_{i=1}^{N} R_{i,j}}{N} \tag{7}$$

where N is number of parameters. Including an estimation of design quality for the case retrieval can also increase the quality of reasoning. Eq. (7) can be substituted with:

$$S_j = DQ_j \frac{\sum_{i=1}^{N} R_{i,j}}{N} \tag{8}$$

where DQ_j is design quality factor for case j.

1.2 Object Database

Chemical processes have very complex structure. The major problem in modeling such systems is the management of relationships between e.g. processes, equipment, components, and materials. Objects are well suited to the natural modeling of relationships. The semantic relationships among objects can be used to design programs that are modular, contain well-defined interfaces, and are structured along the lines of the problem to be solved. Using the object-oriented programming model intelligent way results in programs that are well structured and easier to understand [4].

An object database supports the object-oriented model. Like an object-oriented programming language, it is designed to express the relationships among data. Like a conventional database, it is designed to manage large amounts of data and perform fast value-based queries. In object database programming the system developer is not forced to use any pre-described data storing formalism. Domain specific, complex data can be declared as data types of their own [2]. This is benefit especially in conceptual process design since the process structure is complicated and a flexible data structure is needed to represent the information. In this presentation the data types are object classes identified as entities in the knowledge related to real world processes and process design. An object database is a collection of user defined object classes, e.g. reactor, heat exchanger, that are declared persistent.

A part of the basic structure of the persistent class diagram of the safety case-base (second application) is represented with UML-object modeling language (fig. 1).

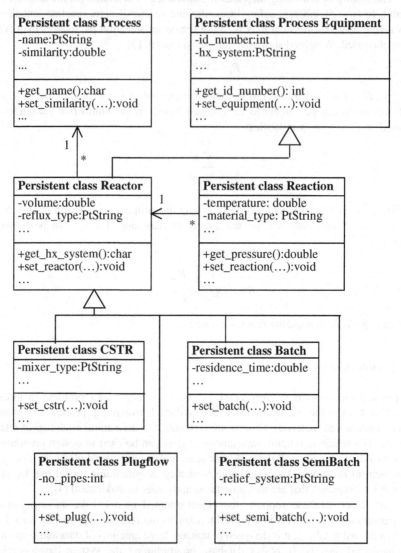

Fig. 1. A part of the persistent class diagram of the safety case-base.

2. Existing Process Design Approaches

The existing chemical process design approaches can be divided to:
1. Heuristic and engineering experience based methods which use often an hierarchical approach [5]
2. Optimization approaches using either mixed integer nonlinear programming (MINLP) [6] or genetic algorithms (GA) [7].
3. CBR methods where existing design cases are reused and adapted to solve new design problems. This approach has been used to some extent to equipment design in chemical engineering [8,9,10] but very little to process design.

The problem in heuristic approaches is that no computer-based support systems are usually available to support in heuristic conceptual methods. Therefore the approach relies totally on the designer.

The optimization-based methods require that an explicit objective function have to be defined for the method. However many design criteria such as safety or operability are difficult or impossible to quantify explicitly. The optimization approaches are not very interactive; the optimization cannot be interfered or guided easily by the user. For these reasons the optimization methods often lead to impractical or even impossible solutions. The use of optimization requires that the optimization alternatives and area has to limited by the user. This task called 'generation of superstructure' has to be done by the user and can be a tedious procedure, which if done improperly has a detrimental effect on the result.

Therefore the main differences of the approaches are related to the interaction with the user, requirement of superstructure and the possibility of combinatorial explosion. In MINLP and GA a superstructure is required for the optimization algorithm. To our experience the differences of methods can be summarized as follows:

	MINLP	GA	CBR
superstructure required	yes	yes	no
combinatorial explosion	yes	some	no
noninteractive method	yes	yes	no

3. The Prototype Application Programs

The prototype application programs have been built using MS Visual C++ 6.0 programming language. The object databases have been built by POET (Persistent Objects and Extended database Technology) an object database programming language and fully integrated with C++-language.

3.1 Shell-and-Tube Heat Exchanger Selection Application

The basic idea of the heat exchanger selection application is to use existing designs of heat exchangers for creating input parameters for heat exchanger design or dynamic process simulation programs. The most similar existing case is retrieved from the case-base. Results from retrieval are necessary input data to for example dynamic process simulators, which require information on the type and mechanical dimensions of the heat exchangers. Also a rigorous exchanger design, which is normally done by simulation programs such as HTRI or HTFS, can benefit from CBR by the reuse of design and operation information on the existing heat exchangers. Many aspects such as fouling and the feasible exchanger types are experience-based information. The detailed adaptation can be done using a heat exchanger simulator. Such simulator consists of necessary thermal design calculations for detailed heat exchanger design. The major benefit of CBR when applied in the equipment design is that it offers the experience of earlier designs needed in many engineering design tasks.

The heat exchanger model in the case-base is very detailed. Input parameters are in this case: fluid types, mass flows, operating pressures, possible phase changes, temperature differences between inflow and outflow and fluid temperatures of inflows etc. Output parameters define detailed fluid data, heat exchanger operating data, and heat exchanger mechanical design data including design quality. Retrieval calculations are constructed as described in section 1.1.

Results from retrieval are the TEMA type for heat exchangers, position (vertical/horizontal), shells per unit, number of units, and number of passes. The TEMA type defines front-end head types, rear end head types, and shell types of shell-and-tube heat exchangers.

The demonstration of the heat exchanger program is shown in Figs. 2, 3 and 4. The selected input parameters with weight factors are shown in Fig. 2. The results from the retrieval with input values are presented in Fig. 3. Heat exchanger configuration of the most similar case with a user given input data is used for heat exchanger simulator calculations, Fig. 4. The heat exchanger selection is done, when results from the simulation are satisfactory. The heat exchangers in the case-base can also be studied by built-in queries.

3.2 Emulsion Polymerization Process

Process design by case-based reasoning methods is a very new approach even it has an obviously potential. CBR would combine the traditional engineering experience-based methods with computer based design support systems, which enable the systematic reuse of exiting design information and hereby can form an institutional memory of a company. The systematic use of existing information and the feed back of the successful existing designs is a method of continuous improvement of engineering work in a company.

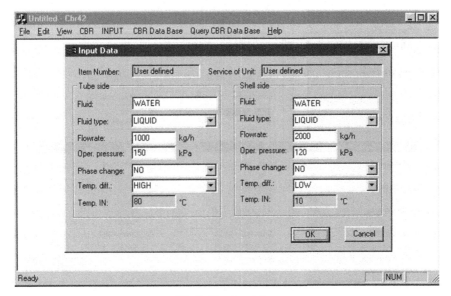

Fig. 2. User input data

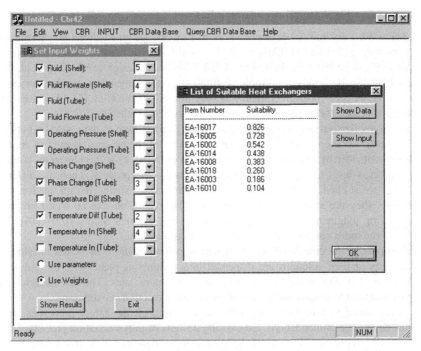

Fig. 3. Input parameters and weight factors for the query, and query result window.

738   T. Seuranen, E. Pajula, and M. Hurme

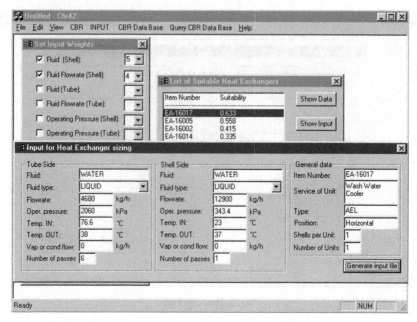

Fig. 4. Input data for dynamic heat exchanger design simulators.

There are very few CBR applications in process design in literature. Surma and Braunschweig [11] and Heikkilä et al. [12] used CBR for finding similar process designs in database but they did not use CBR for process design itself. King et al. [13] used CBR for designing azeotropic distillation systems by using residue curve approach. However the design domain was very limited. Pajula et al. [14,15] presented a general approach for using CBR for separation process synthesis.

A polymerization reaction system case study is given here to demonstrate, how the CBR method is used to improve the inherent safety of the process concept in an evolutionary manner by reasoning on several levels of detail. First the reasoning is made on a process level to find safe general concepts for the process. Then the different systems are studied one by one. If safer alternatives to existing design are found in database, they are substituted to the design. The evaluation can be based on users engineering judgment or safety indices such as the Inherent Safety Index [16]. The value of the index can be included into the cases of database.

The process of case study is an emulsion polymerization, in which unsaturated monomers or their solutions are dispersed in a continuous phase with the aid of an emulsifier [17]. The product is a dispersion of polymers, latex. The raw materials are highly flammable unsaturated hydrocarbons and the reaction is exothermic.

A case base was formed using information based on the safety properties, accidents, design recommendations and existing designs of polymerization processes. The information includes also general design recommendations for reactor systems. The main variables in the emulsion polymerization process are [17]; 1) premixing, 2) preheating, 3) reactor type and mode of operation, 4) number of reactors, 5) reactor construction material, 6) reactor mixing, 7) baffles in reactor, 8) reactor heat transfer system, 9) method of liquid transfers, 10) relief system location, 11) relief equipment type, 12) reaction stopping method, 13) relief recovery system, 14) vent treatment equipment.

The process can be studied in various levels to find out which kinds of design cases (recommendations on good designs or warnings on bad case; e.g. accidents) are available to improve the design. First the study is made in an upper (process) level and then in the more detailed levels. The user interface has windows for both reactor and reaction data (Fig. 5). By altering which parameters in use and how they are weighted, the user can make searches in various levels.

The query results are shown in a separate window (Fig. 6). In this query cases containing recommendations in process level are found. According to the found case the application of a semibatch reactor process is advisable to minimize a runaway hazard apparent in this case (Fig. 7). In the system level recommendations for the reactor + cooling system concept can be searched for exothermic reactions. The found cases can be adapted for reactor size, heat of reaction, heat capacity and heat transfer area to correspond the existing case. In equipment level, the possible relief equipment can be studied using queries in the case-base.

In every level of reasoning the found potentially safer solutions are used to substitute the features in existing design. In this way the design is improved gradually in an evolutionary way. The assessment which design is better to another can be based for instance to safety indices [16] or users own judgment. Also the textual case descriptions include qualitative evaluations on the safety features of designs found in the database.

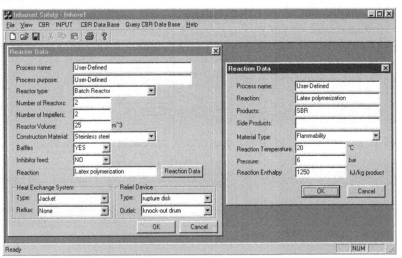

Fig. 5. User input data.

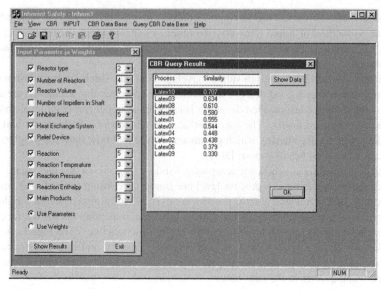

Fig. 6. Input parameters and weight factors for the query, and query result window.

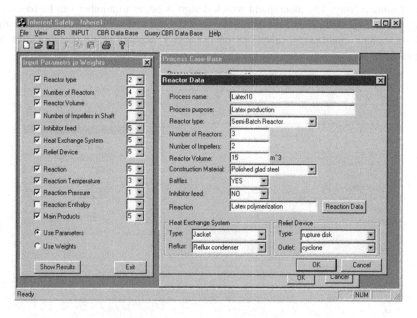

Fig. 7. The best retrieved process.

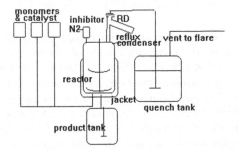

Fig. 8. The improved emulsion polymerisation system.

The final process designed has a semibatch (instead of batch) reactor, which results to a low monomer inventory in the reactor (Fig. 8). In this configuration, the reaction starts immediately when the first monomers are fed to the reactor. There is neither premixing tank for the monomers, which would increase the inventory. Only one large reactor is used instead of several smaller ones to make the system simpler. Two impellers at one shaft are installed to increase the mixing efficiency when the liquid level in tank is changing. Baffles are used for increasing the mixing efficiency. Both a jacket and a reflux condenser accomplish cooling. The reactor construction material is polished glad steel that has better heat transfer properties compared to a glass-lined vessel. Liquid transfers to and from the reactor are accomplished using elevation to reduce number of pumps. The relief system of the reactor includes a rupture disk, which is safer than a relief valve alone in the fouling conditions. The relief is led to a quench tank, which contains quench liquid to stop the reaction and to separate the liquid phase from the relief. This is safer than an ordinary knock-out drum or cyclone. The vent is led to flare system after the quench tank. Ordinary flare is used, since it has a larger capacity than a controlled collection system or a scrubber. An inhibitor addition to reactor is also included to stop the reaction chemically.

A quantitative verification that the improved process presented in Fig. 8 is better than the conventional batch process described in literature [17] can be based on the calculation of Inherent Safety Index [16] values of both processes. The conventional process has an index value of about 28-30 compared to the index value 16 of the improved process shown in Fig. 8.

4. Conclusions

Two prototype applications have been developed to illustrate the use of CBR and object database techniques in process equipment design and inherently safer process design. Main advantages of CBR approach are the directing of user to a systematic documentation practice, and utilization of documentation. The time consumed for routine design can be reduced as a consequence of efficient reuse of existing knowledge. It is obvious that case-based reasoning is a narrow field of application, because configuration and structure of equipment or processes should be somewhat similar to each other.

In the heat exchanger application, the design quality is included. In this case, design quality is one evaluation parameter in the calculation of case similarity. In fact, design quality should be a combination of several parameters such as equipment safety, operational reliability, and economy. Quality parameters are also time dependent, which leads to following the lifetime of equipment in order to get a good case base.

The benefits of the CBR approach presented in the inherent safety application are the following: Inherent safety is difficult to implement without concrete design examples since the principles are very general. The system presented provides real design cases that can be applied to substitute the current designs in the problem under study. The cases represent both good design practices and known accident cases, which have lead to process improvements. If the processes under design and operation are systematically studied in various levels as presented, the reuse of existing design and safety knowledge is greatly enhanced, less design mistakes are made and consequently conceptually safer processes are created.

Object-oriented approach and object database techniques allow more flexible application developing especially in complex process design cases. Object database combines the semantic of object-oriented approach with data management and query facilities of a database system.

References

1. Kolodner, J., Case-based Reasoning, Morgan Kaufman Publishers Inc., San Mateo, California (1993).
2. Loomis, M., Object Databases: The Essentials, Addison-Wesley Publishing Company, Menlo Park, California (1995).
3. Koiranen, T., Hurme, M., Case-based Reasoning Applications in Process Equipment Selection and Design, Scandinavian Conference of Artificial Intelligence SCAI'97, University of Helsinki, Finland (1997).
4. Booch, G., Object Oriented Design with Applications, The Benjamin/Cummings Publishing Company Inc, California (1991).
5. Douglas, J.M., *Conceptual Design of Chemical Processes*, McGraw-Hill, New York 1988.
6. Grossmann, I.E., Kravanja, Z., Mixed-Integer Nonlinear Programming Techniques for Process Systems Engineering Comp. Chem. Eng. 19 (1995) Suppl., S189-S204
7. Khalil, M.S., Evolutionary Methods in Chemical Engineering, Plant Design Report Series No. 64, Helsinki Univesrity of Technology, Espoo (2000), 143 pp.
8. Pajula, E., Koiranen, T., Seuranen, T., Hurme, M., Computer Aided Process Equipment Design from Equipment Parts, Comp. Chem. Eng. 23 (1999) Suppl., S683-S686.
9. Kraslawski, A., Koiranen, T., Nyström, L., Case-Based Reasoning System for Mixing Equipment Selection, Comp. Chem. Eng. 19 (1995) Suppl., S821-S826.
10. Virkki-Hatakka, T., Kraslawski, A., Koiranen, T., Nyström, L., Adaptation Phase in Case-Based Reasoning System for Process Equipment Selection, Comp. Chem. Eng. 21 (1997) Suppl., S643-S648.

11. Surma, J., Braunschweig, B., Case-Base Retrieval in Process Engineering: Supporting Design by Reusing Flowsheets, Engineering Applications of Artificial Intelligence 9 (1996) 385-391.
12. Heikkilä, A.-M., Koiranen, T., Hurme, M., Application of case-based reasoning to safety evaluation of process configuration, HAZARDS XIV, Institution of Chemical Engineers Symposium Series No. 144, IChemE, Rugby (1998), 461-473.
13. King, J.M.P, Bañares-Alcántara, R., Zainuddin, A.M, Minimising environmental impact using CBR: An azeotropic distillation case study, Environmental Modelling & Software 14 (1999) 395-366
14. Pajula, E., Seuranen, T., Hurme, M. Synthesis of separation sequences by case-based reasoning, Comp. Chem. Eng. vol 11, Elsevier 2001, to appear.
15. Pajula, E., Seuranen, T., Koiranen, T., Hurme, M. Synthesis of separation processes by using case-based reasoning, Comp. Chem. Eng. 25 (2001) 775-782.
16. Heikkilä, A.-M., Hurme, M., Järveläinen, M., Safety Considerations in Process Synthesis, Comp. Chem. Eng. 20 (1996) Suppl. S115-S120
17. Kroschwitz, J.I. (Ed.), Encyclopedia of polymer science and engineering, Vol 6, Wiley, New York (1986).

Mining High-Quality Cases for Hypertext Prediction and Prefetching

Qiang Yang, Ian Tian-Yi Li, and Henry Haining Zhang

School of Computing Science
Simon Fraser University
Burnaby, BC, Canada V5A 1S6
(qyang,tlie,hzhangb)@cs.sfu.ca

Abstract. Case-based reasoning aims to use past experience to solve new problems. A strong requirement for its application is that extensive experience base exists that provides statistically significant justification for new applications. Such extensive experience base has been rare, limiting most CBR applications to be confined to small-scale problems involving single or few users, or even toy problems. In this work, we present an application of CBR in the domain of web document prediction and retrieval, whereby a server-side application can decide, with high accuracy and coverage, a user's next request for hypertext documents based on past requests. An application program can then use the prediction knowledge to prefetch or presend web objects to reduce latency and network load. Through this application, we demonstrate the feasibility of CBR application in the web-document retrieval context, exposing the vast possibility of using web-log files that contain document retrieval experiences from millions of users. In this framework, a CBR system is embedded within an overall web-server application. A novelty of the work is that data mining and case-based reasoning are combined in a seamless manner, allowing cases to be mined efficiently. In addition we developed techniques to allow different case bases to be combined in order to yield a overall case base with higher quality than each individual ones. We validate our work through experiments using realistic, large-scale web logs.

1 Introduction

Case-based reasoning (CBR) is a problem-solving framework that focuses on using past experiences to solve new problems [12]. Cognitive evidence points to the approach as a natural explanation for human problem solving. Much work has been done to exploit CBR as a general problem-solving framework, including retrieval [19], conversational CBR [1], case base maintenance [16], and various innovative applications [18].

A prerequisite for successful CBR application is that extensive experience base exists. Such experience base can record users' or systems' behavior in problem solving, in solving traces, consequences, feature selection, and relevance feedback. A alternative to such an experience base is the reliance on individual experts who can articulate their past experiences. However, much empirical work has pointed to the infeasibility of this latter approach, because experts are expensive, subjective and static. In con-

D.W. Aha and I. Watson (Eds.): ICCBR 2001, LNAI 2080, pp. 744-755, 2001.
© Springer-Verlag Berlin Heidelberg 2001

trast, having an accumulated, extensive experience base enables the design of data mining and knowledge discovery systems that can extract cases from a data set. This conversion, if done successfully and repeatedly, can result in a succinct, highly compact set of problem description and solution pairs that give rise to up-to-date case bases. Therefore, having the data itself is often a point of make-or-break for CBR applications.

Unfortunately, extensive experience base has been rare in practice. Much CBR research still relies on small scale, toy-like problems for empirical tests. This situation is dramatically alleviated, however, with the arrival of the World Wide Web (or the Web in short). Much recent work in Computer Science, and indeed AI itself, has been motivated by this sudden availability of data. On the Web, millions of users visit thousands of servers, leaving rich traces of document retrieval, problem solving and data access.

In this paper, we expose the hypertext retrieval on the Web as a potential experience base that is readily available to CBR researchers. Based on vast Web Server logs, we apply CBR in the domain of Web document prediction and retrieval, whereby a server-side application can decide, with high accuracy and coverage, a user's next request for hypertext documents based on past requests. An application program can then use the prediction knowledge to prefetch or presend web objects to reduce latency and network load. Likewise, with highly accurate prediction of users' next possible request, web servers can adapt their user interfaces according to user's interests. Through this application, we demonstrate the feasibility of CBR application in the web-document retrieval context, exposing the vast possibility of using web-log files that contain document retrieval experiences from millions of users. Such web-log files are extensive and up to date (for example, see http://www.web-caching.com for many realistic web logs)

In this framework, a CBR system is embedded within an overall web-server application. A novelty of the work is that data mining and case-based reasoning are combined in a seamless manner, allowing cases to be mined efficiently. In addition, different kinds of data-mined case knowledge from the same data source result in CBR systems with different qualities. Thus, when more than one case base exists, we developed techniques to allow different case bases to be combined in order to yield an integrated case base with higher quality than each individual ones. The integrated case base reasoning system introduces more flexibility and higher quality for CBR application. We validate our work through a series of experiments using realistic, large-scale web logs.

The organization of the paper is as follows. In Section 2 we discuss the web-document retrieval domain, web server logs and case-base representation for the application. In Section 3, we discuss case-knowledge discovery with data mining algorithms. In Section 4, we discuss how different case bases can be combined to give an integrated case base that provides higher quality solutions than individual case bases. In Section 5 we discuss an application of our prediction system in web-document prefetching applications. In Section 6 we conclude the article with a discussion of future work.

2   Web-Document Retrieval and Case Representation

The Web is a globally distributed, dynamic information repository that contains vast amount of digitized information. Every day, more and more information becomes available in multimedia forms. The fundamental framework in which such information is made available to the users is through the well-known client-server models. To retrieve information, a client issues a request that is answered by a server using the HTTP protocol. A by-product of such information exchange is that vast logs are recorded on the server side, indicating the source, destination, file type, time, and size of information transmission. Given a web-server browsing log L, it is possible break down a long access trace into sessions, where each session records a single source request in a consecutive sequence of accesses to the same server. These are called user sessions. These user sessions are indexed on the source of requests, and can be discovered by finding out the boundary between short and long requests. An example data log from a NASA web site is shown in Figure 1.

```
...
uplherc.upl.com--[01/Aug/1995:00:08:52-0400] "GET
/shuttle/resources/orbiters/endeavour-logo.gif HTTP/1.0"  200 5052

pm9.j51.com--[01/Aug/1995:00:08:52-0400] "GET/images/xyz.html HTTP/1.0"  200
669

139.230.35.135--[01/Aug/1995:00:08:52-0400] "GET/images/NASA-logosmall.gif
HTTP/1.0"  200 786
...
```

Fig. 1. An example web log file

The availability of the web server information allows machine-learning researchers to predict users' future requests and provide better information services according to such prediction. The availability of the web related information has inspired an increasing amount of work in user action prediction. Much work has been done in recommendation systems, which provide suggestions for user's future visits on the web based on machine learning or data mining algorithms. An example is the WebWatcher system [10], which makes recommendations on the future hyperlinks that the user might like to visit, based on a model obtained through reinforcement learning. Albrecht et al. [7] presented a Markov model based approach for prediction using a web-server log based on both time interval information and document sequence information. The predicted documents are then sent to a cache on the client side ahead of time. Based on Web server logs, [11, 15] provided detailed statistical analyses of web log data, pointing out the distribution of access patterns in web accesses and using them for prediction. [17] compared n-gram prediction models for different sized n, and discuss how the predictions might be used for prefetching for multimedia files, benefiting the network performance. However, none of the above-mentioned work considered integrating the prediction systems with caching and prefetching systems.

The web-document request problem can be stated as the following: given a training web log, construct a predictive model that suggests future web-document accesses based on past accesses. We consider the web-document request prediction problem as a CBR application. In a case base, the most basic representation is that of a case, consisting of a problem description and a solution component. For example, in a Cable-TV help-desk application, a problem description is "VCR not taping correct channels", and a solution may be "Switch the TV/VCR toggle to VCR, switch to correct channel, and then press Record." In a structured case, the problem description part of a case is structured into a set of discrete features, with feature-value pairs {<F_i, V_i>, i=1, 2 ... n} representing the pattern to be matched against a problem.

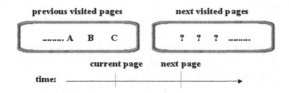

Fig. 2. Moving window algorithm

For the Web-document retrieval problem, our objective is to predict the next document that is going to be retrieved based on users' previous requests. As shown in Figure 2, our goal is to predict what web pages will most likely be accessed next by a user based on all user's previous accesses for pages A, B, and C. In the structured case representation, if we want the prediction to be a URL "D", then we can make "D" to be the solution part of the case, and A, B and C the individual feature-values of the case, as shown in Table 1, Case (a). In this case representation, feature "First" means the first observed request on a page "A". Likewise, "Second" and "Third" features record the second and third observations before making a prediction. In our representation, it is required that "ABC" is a sub-string ending at the cursor rather than a subsequence, where in the former no other symbols occurs in within the sub string while in the latter, there can be gaps in between. When this case is applied to the problem in Figure 2, the answer for the next visited pages within a given prediction window will be "D", regardless of where "D" occurs in that window.

This case representation can be generalized so that the number of features can be anywhere from zero to n, an integer. If it is required that the observed pages occur next to each other with no "gaps" in between, then the problem-description part is also called an n-gram (3-gram in this example).

This case representation can be generalized such that the *Solution* part of a case includes more than one predicted page. The reason is that when observing a number of URL requests, it is possible to guess at several next pages. Furthermore, these predicted pages do not have to occur in the next instant in time. Instead, they can occur within a given time window from the current time. The time window W_2 can either measure the number of document requests in the near future in which we expect the predicted documents to occur, or a real time in the number of seconds. We call W_2 the *prediction window*, and the window W_1 in which the observation is made that matches that problem description part of the case the *observation window*. Applying this generalization, the case representation is shown in Table 1, under Case (b).

Table 1. A case representation for web-document prediction

Problem Description				Solution
Features	First	Second	Third	**Next Page(s)**
Case (a)	"A"	"B"	"C"	"D"
Case (b)	"A"	"B"	"C"	{"D", "E", "F"}

Given a test sequence of web objects with a certain time cursor representing the current time instant, a case can be used on the sequence for making a prediction if the problem description part of the case matches the observations in the observation window W_1 before the time instance. A prediction can then be made on the next occurrence of web objects within the prediction window W_2. In this generalization, the case *successfully applies* to an instance if, when the problem description matches the observed sequence in W_1, *one* of the web objects "D", "E" or "F" occurs in the prediction window W_2. In this work, we restrict the Solution part of cases to contain only one web document.

We will discuss how to obtain cases from a training web log in the next section. A user session can be considered as a sequence of web object accesses. A testing web log consists of many such sessions. Within each session, we can uncover many cases by moving a "cursor" through the sequence of pages requested; the cursor defines a window pair $<W_1, W_2>$. One consequence of this design is that there will be many different cases, each with different quality. We measure the quality of cases in the same way as that for association rules in data-mining literature [2]: we adopt the concepts of *support* and *confidence* for cases. *Support* for a case is defined as the percentage of strings in the web logs in which the case successfully applies. *Confidence* is defined as the conditional probability that the Solution part of the case falls in window W_2, given that the problem description part of the case fall match the sub-string at the time cursor.

To ensure the quality of a case base, we require that the support for all cases be above a certain user-specified threshold θ, and that the confidence for each case be above a threshold σ. However, finding proper thresholds is difficult in practice, an issue we will address in this work.

We now consider quality measure for a case base. A case base consists of a set of cases. For any given observation sequence within a window size W_1, the *application of the case base onto* W_1 takes all applicable cases in the case base -- cases whose Problem-Description part matches the pages in W_1 ending at the cursor -- and outputs a set of predicted pages based on the solutions of these cases. When there is more than one cases to apply, the decision of how to choose cases among the applicable cases to base predictions on is called the *application policy* of the case base reasoner. Some application policies may opt to output the union of all applicable cases while others may select the most confident case to output. Together, the case base composition and application policy determines the overall quality of a case-base reasoner: the *precision of a case base reasoner is* defined as the conditional probability that the case-base reasoner makes successful predictions for all window pairs $<W_1, W_2>$ in the log. The *coverage* of a case base reasoner, a second quality metric, is the percentage of the testing web log on which the case base reasoner can make predictions.

There are other types of case representations to consider. When the problem-description part of a case base consists of sets of pages rather than the last string of length n in observation window W_1, we have the set-representation of a case. In this representation, <{"A", "B"}, "D"> means that if "A" and "B" are observed in W_1, *regardless* of their relative locations in the window, then "D" is predicted in W_2. In our experiments we have found that this representation has much worse performance than the string-based representation. Likewise, we can include other features such as time interval information and page type information as problem features. For lack of space we do not consider these results and extensions here.

3 Mining Web Logs for Case Bases

Given a web server log file, we first preprocess it by removing all extremely long user sessions that are generated by search engines and crawlers. These do not represent typical user profiles. We also remove objects that are accessed less frequently than the minimum support θ. This is because for any given case in a case base, any individual web object appearing in the case must have support no less than that of the case. This is also the rule used by the well-known Apriori algorithm [2] in association rule mining. In fact, in our experience with very large web server logs, after applying this pre-processing rule with a minimum support of 2%, the total size of the web log is reduced by 50%!

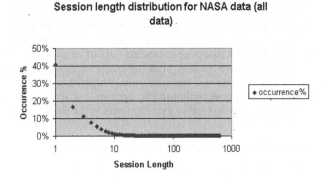

Fig. 3. Session length distribution of a web server log.

We next mine the individual cases, using a *moving-window algorithm*. Briefly, this algorithm scans through an entire user session. For any cursor location in the session, for every string S ending at the cursor in the observation window W_1 and a web object P in the prediction window W_2, there is a potential case <S, P>. For this case, a hash table entry is generated and count updated. When the scan is finished, these counts are used to compute support and confidence for the case. Only cases that satisfy the minimum support and confidence requirements are retained in the hash table T; T is the source knowledge that will be used to generate the final case bases.

Among all potential cases in table T, we also generate a special case D with empty problem description part and with maximal support. Such a default case is in fact the most frequent URL in the training web-server log. This case will be used to *catch* the situations when no other cases make a prediction. If we choose to use the default case, then the coverage of the resulting case base will be *100%*.

Through empirical study, we have found that with web-server logs, the number of sessions decreases exponentially with the length of sessions. Figure 3 shows this fact for a NASA web log. From this fact we can be assured that case-based mining using the moving-window algorithm operates in linear time for constant window sizes, in the size of the logs.

To evaluate the predictive power of the case-based reasoning system, we have utilized a realistic web data log, the NASA data (this and many other logs are available at http://www.web-caching.com/). The NASA data set contains one month worth of all HTTP requests to the NASA Kennedy Space Center WWW server in Florida. The log was collected from 00:00:00 August 1, 1995 through 23:59:59 August 31, 1995. In this period there were totally 1,569,898 requests. After filtering, we reduced the request size down to 479,050 requests. In the web data log, timestamps have 1-second resolution. There are a total of 72,151 unique IP addresses requesting web pages, having a total of 119,838 sessions. A total of 2,926 unique pages are requested. In the following discussions, we will mainly use this log; the observations can be generalized to other logs that we have tested, including an EPA web server log and a university web-server log.

We then apply the moving-window algorithm to get different case bases. In all case bases, we mined the default case D to catch the situations where no other cases can be applied for prediction. We partitioned the case base into different size-n case bases for $n=1, 2, 3, 4$ and 5, where n is the number of pages in the problem description part of a case. We denote a case base consisting only of cases whose problem description parts have n consecutive features, with the exception of the default case, a length-n case base, or $CB(n)$. Note that our case-mining algorithm is significantly different from the sequential mining algorithm in [5], because our moving window algorithm captures high-frequency strings rather than item-sets in the transaction model.

4   From Case Bases to Case-Based Reasoning

Our task is to predict the future web document accesses based on past cases. Thus, having obtained the case bases is only the first step in constructing a case-based reasoner. A second step is to determine, for a given observation, which case among a set of applicable cases to apply in order to make the prediction. Therefore, the case-based reasoner is a pair, consisting of a case base and a case selection strategy.

Our method of constructing a case-based reasoner is analogous to methods for converting association rules to classifiers in data mining literature [13]. We experimented with two strategies. One strategy selects cases based on confidence, and the other on the length of matching features. To measure the system performance, we use the standard precision measurement, defined as the percentage of correct predictions over all predictions in the testing data set.

Figure 4 shows our precision-comparison on different case bases using the NASA data set. We set a minimum support to be ten occurrences and minimum confidence to be 10%. We set the window size for the prediction window to be one. We took the first 100,000 requests in the NASA log file as training data set and the next 25,000 requests as the testing data set.

In Figure 4, we plot the precision results of all five case bases CB(i) with i ranges from one to five. As can be seen, the precision of case bases first increases up to i=2 and then decreases after i=3. We attribute this observation to the fact that when i=1 and increases to 2, there are increasingly more high-confidence cases that cover the testing data. However, the situation is not sustained after i=3 because when i is large, the number of cases increases, causing the number of high-confidence cases for CB(i) to decrease rapidly. This has prompted us to study how to integrate the different case bases CB(i) in order to obtain a high-quality overall case base reasoning system. We discuss this novel extension in the next section.

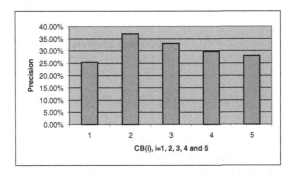

Fig. 4. Precision of case bases with different problem description lengths

5 Integrating Different Case Bases

We wish to combine the power of individual CBR systems in prediction. To do this, we adopt a integrated CBR approach in which we pool the result of each individual CBR for any given observations and then use the integrated case base to select or integrate among the different CBR solutions.

We first study a case-selection method by selecting the most confident case solution for prediction. For any given observation, all CBR systems CB(i), i=1, ... 5, operate to make predictions. The case with the highest confidence is selected by the integrated CBR as the overall system prediction. This method is called Most-Confident CBR. A second integrated CBR method will bias toward CBR systems that make longer observations. For this strategy, a case chosen by a highest i for whom the solution from CB(i) is not the default case is always selected by the CBR. This method prefers longer-length n-grams and is called the longest-match CBR.

Figure 5 shows the result of the CBR in prediction as compared to individual case bases CB(i) for a given problem-description length i, where LongMatch is the longest-match CBR and MostConf is the most-confident CBR. As can be seen, the selection strategy that chooses the most confident cases for prediction gives the highest precision level compared to the other methods. The longest-match CBR performed a close second in comparison.

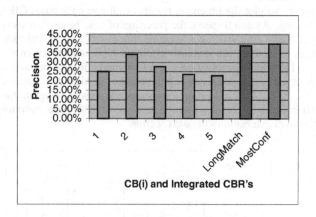

Fig. 5. Comparing CB(i) and Integrated CBR

Both the longest-match and most-confident case-selection strategies for CBR can suggest a single web object as the next URL to be accessed. They are also useful in user-interface agents that help recommend potential hyperlinks for a user. To apply CBR methods in prefetching web objects for enhancing web-access to the problem of caching and prefetching, however, we need an CBR method that recommends more than one web object in the prediction window. In the next section, we highlight this integrated CBR method in the application domain of web-document prefetching and caching.

6   Embedded CBR for Document Prefetching

One way to apply CBR is to embed a CBR application in an integrated system. In this work we are interested in using embedded CBR web-access prediction for Internet caching and prefetching. As the World Wide Web is growing at a very rapid rate, researchers have designed effective caching algorithms to reduce network traffic. The idea behind web caching and prefetching is to maintain a highly efficient but small set of retrieved results in a proxy-server cache, and to prefetch web objects into this cache. An important aspect of proxy-server caching and prefetching is to build an accurate prediction model for each server connected to the proxy server and cache and predict user's requests based on the model.

Lying in the heart of caching algorithms is the so-called ``page replacement policy", which specifies conditions under which a new page will replace an existing one. In proxy-caching, the state of the art techniques are the GD-size policy [8] which considers access costs and varying page sizes, and an enhancement of the GD-size algorithm known as GDSF [3] which incorporates the frequency information. Caching can be further enhanced by prefetching popular documents in order to improve system performance [9]. Our embedded technique will combine the predictions made by different models and give an overall "weight" for each candidate web object, and use the weights to update decisions.

Consider a frequency factor F_i which counts of number of references. With this new factor, the key value can be computed as $K_i = L + F_i * C_i / S_i$ In this formula, K_i is the priority of object i, C_i is the transmission cost of object i, S_i is the size of object i and L is an aging factor such that newer objects receive higher L values. Let $A[i]$ be a sequence of accesses such that $A[1]$ is the most recent access and $A[N]$ the Nth past access. Let K be the set of all cases that can be applied to the observations $A[1..N]$ where these cases are suggested by all CB(i) models. The confidence of each case from a case base CB(j) in K with a predicted document D_i is denoted as $P_{i,j}$. The weight W_i for D_i is then sum of all $P_{i,j}$ over all case bases CB(j). We can then update the caching algorithm by a predictive component – by including the predictive weight in the ranking functions for objects in the cache: $K_i = L + (F_i + W_i) * C_i / S_i$

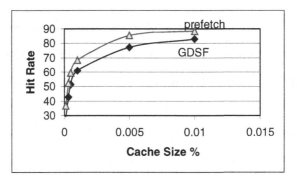

Fig. 6. Comparing prediction-based caching/prefetching, and GDSF caching policy for NASA data.

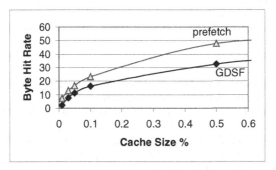

Fig. 7. Comparing prediction-based caching/prefetching, and GDSF caching policy for NASA data on byte hit rate

We follow the same idea with prefetching, by combining the predictions made by all case bases CB(i). The top-N high-probability objects are prefetched and put in a *prefetching buffer.* The buffer serves the same purpose as the cache; when a request arrives, we first check if the object is already in the cache. If not, then we check if the object is in the buffer. If so, then the object returned to the user as a response to the request, and moved into the cache for reuse.

We again used NASA data for experiments; our other experiments including the EPA web logs are not shown here due to space limit. In the experiments, we tested the system performance against two metrics used in network area: hit rate and byte hit rate. The hit rate records the percentage of user requests that can be answered by cache and prefetch buffer, and the byte hit rate measures the percent of bytes that are answered by cache and the prefetch buffer. The results are shown in Figure 6 and 7, where the horizontal axis (Cache Size %) is the size of the cache relative to the size of all objects in testing web logs. As can be seen, using prediction for caching and prefetching makes significant improvement to caching performance.

7   Conclusions

In this paper, we have shown how to data-mine web-server logs to get high quality cases. Our approach is to use a simple case representation and to extract only high-confident cases for prediction. Our result shows that using an integrated CBR system with carefully designed selection criteria can provide significant improvements. We also highlighted an application in network caching and prefetching using embedded CBR.

References

[1] D.W.Aha and L.A.Breslow. Refining conversational case libraries. In Proceedings of the Second International Conference on Case-based Reasoning (ICCBR-97), Providence, RI, July 1997.
[2] R. Agrawal, T. Imielinski, and A. Swami. Mining association rules between sets of items in large databases. In Proc. of the ACM SIGMOD Int'l Conf. on Management of Data (ACM SIGMOD '93), Washington, USA, May 1993.
[3] M. Arlitt, R. Friedrich L. Cherkasova, J. Dilley, and T. Jin. Evaluating content management techniques for web proxy caches. In *HP Technical report*, Palo Alto, Apr. 1999.
[4] D. Aha and H. Munoz-Avila. Applied Intelligence Journal, Special Issue on Interactive CBR. Kluwer 2001.
[5] R. Agrawal and R. Srikant. *Mining sequential patterns.* In Proc. of the Int'l Conf. on Data Engineering (ICDE), Taipei, Taiwan, March 1995.
[6] C. Aggarwal, J. L. Wolf, and P. S. Yu. Caching on the World Wide Web. In *IEEE Transactions on Knowledge and Data Engineering*, volume 11, pages 94--107, 1999.
[7] Albrecht, D. W., Zukerman, I., and Nicholson, A. E. 1999. Pre-sending documents on the WWW: A comparative study. *IJCAI99 – Proceedings of the Sixteenth International Joint Conference on Artificial Intelligence.*
[8] P. Cao and S. Irani. Cost-aware www proxy caching algorithms. In *USENIX Symposium on Internet Technologies and Systems*, Monterey, CA, Dec. 1997.

[9]   E. Markatos and C. Chironaki. A Top Ten Approach for Prefetching the Web. In *Proceedings of the INET'98 Internet Global Summit*. July 1998

[10] Joachims, T., Freitag, D., and Mitchell, T. 1997 WebWatcher: A tour guild for the World Wide Web. *IJCAI 97 – Proceedings of the Fifteenth International Joint Conference on Artificial Intelligence*, 770-775.

[11] T. M. Kroeger and D. D. E. Long. Predicting future file-system actions from prior events. In *USENIX 96*, San Diego, Calif., Jan. 1996.

[12] D. Leake Case-Based Reasoning: Experiences, Lessons, and Future Directions. Menlo Park, CA, AAAI Press. 1996.

[13] B. Liu, W. Hsu, and Y. Ma: "Integrating Classification and Association Rule Mining", Proc. Fourth Int'l Conf. on Knowledge Discovery and Data Mining (KDD), pp. 80-86, AAAI Press, Menlo Park, Calif., 1998.

[14] K. Chinen and S. Yamaguchi. An Interactive Prefetching Proxy Server for Improvement of WWW Latency. In *Proceedings of the Seventh Annual Conference of the Internet Society (INEt'97)*, Kuala Lumpur, June 1997.

[15] Pitkow J. and Pirolli P. Mining longest repeating subsequences to predict www surfing. In *Proceedings of the 1999 USENIX Annual Technical Conference*, 1999.

[16] Smyth, B. and Keane, M.T. 1995. Remembering to Forget: A Competence-Preserving Case Deletion Policy for Case-based Reasoning systems. In Proceedings of the 14th International Joint Conference on Artificial Intelligence, IJCAI-95, pp. 377-382.

[17] Z. Su, Q. Yang, and H. Zhang. A prediction system for multimedia pre-fetching on the Internet. In *Proceedings of the ACM Multimedia Conference 2000*. ACM, October 2000.

[18] Watson (1997). Applying Case-Based Reasoning: techniques for enterprise systems. Morgan Kaufmann Publishers Inc., San Francisco, USA.

[19] D. Wettscherck, and D.W. Aha 1995. Weighting Features. In Proceedings of the 1st International Conference of Case-Base Reasoning, ICCBR-95, pp. 347-358.

Author Index

Lecture Notes in Artificial Intelligence (LNAI)

Lecture Notes in Computer Science